D0085585

The Blue Note Label

Recent Titles in
Discographies

Bobby Hackett: A Bio-Discography
Harold Jones

The Columbia Master Book Discography, Volume I: U.S. Matrix Series 1 through 4999, 1901–1910 with a History of the Columbia Phonograph Company to 1934
Tim Brooks

The Columbia Master Book Discography, Volume II: Principal U.S. Matrix Series 1910–1924
Brian Rust, compiler

The Columbia Master Book Discography, Volume III: Principal U.S. Matrix Series, 1924–1934
Brian Rust, compiler

The Columbia Master Book Discography, Volume IV: U.S. Twelve-Inch Matrix Series, 1906–1931
Brian Rust and Tim Brooks

The Directory of the Armed Forces Radio Service Series
Harry Mackenzie, compiler

Put Your Dreams Away: A Frank Sinatra Discography
Luiz Carlos do Nascimento Silva

Dis Here: A Bio-Discography of Julian "Cannonball" Adderley
Chris Sheridan, compiler

Tristan und Isolde on Record: A Comprehensive Discography of Wagner's Music Drama with a Critical Introduction to the Recordings
Jonathan Brown

From Brass to Gold, Volume I: Discography of A&M Records and Affiliates in the United States
Leslie J. Pfenninger

From Brass to Gold, Volume II: Discography of A&M Records and Affiliates Around the World
Leslie J. Pfenninger

Brunswick Records: A Discography of Recordings, 1916–1931 (4 volumes)
Ross Laird

The Blue Note Label

A Discography, Revised and Expanded

Compiled by
Michael Cuscuna and Michel Ruppli

Discographies, Number 88
Michael Gray, Series Editor

GREENWOOD PRESS
Westport, Connecticut • London

Library of Congress Cataloging-in-Publication Data

Cuscuna, Michael.
The Blue Note label : a discography / compiled by Michael Cuscuna and Michel Ruppli—Rev. and expanded.
p. cm.—(Discographies, ISSN 0192–334X ; no. 88)
Includes index.
ISBN 0–313–31826–3 (alk. paper)
1. Jazz—Discography. 2. Blue Note (Firm)—Discography. 3. Sound recordings—United States—Catalogs. I. Ruppli, Michel. II. Series.
ML156.4.J3C87 2001
016.78165′0266—dc21 00–052112

British Library Cataloguing in Publication Data is available.

Library of Congress Catalog Card Number: 00–052112
ISBN: 0–313–31826–3
ISSN: 0192–334X

First published in 2001

Greenwood Press, 88 Post Road West, Westport, CT 06881
An imprint of Greenwood Publishing Group, Inc.
www.greenwood.com

Printed in the United States of America

The paper used in this book complies with the Permanent Paper Standard issued by the National Information Standards Organization (Z39.48–1984).

10 9 8 7 6 5 4 3 2

Contents

Preface

This book is a discographical listing of all recordings made or issued on the Blue Note label. Only commercially issued recordings are included. Albums or Compact Discs created as premiums or promotional samplers are not covered in the scope of this work.

Part 1 details all sessions made by founders Alfred Lion and Francis Wolff from inception of the label in 1939 up to mid-1967 when Alfred Lion ceased producing sessions for the label (after takeover of Blue Note by Liberty label in May 1966). Almost all sessions in this part were supervised by Alfred Lion. There are some exceptions, and appropriate producers are mentioned. In early sessions, a matrix number was used for the first take, and -1 was added for the second take. For clarification, we have added -0 to first takes. Then a matrix number without a hyphenated take number imply that the take number is not known. In addition, Blue Note generally used a take numbering system, made of a numerical sequence for all takes recorded during one session, regardless of titles. This sequence included all rejected takes and false starts. Original issued take was named the master take, all others being referenced as alternates. The only takes listed in this book are the existing ones.

Part 2 is a listing of Blue Note sessions made between 1967 and 1979, while Blue Note was a part of Liberty label. In 1969, Liberty was purchased by the United Artists group, which was later on absorbed in the Electrical and Musical Industries (EMI) conglomerate.

Part 3 details Blue Note sessions made or issued in a new Blue Note series which started with Blue Note revival in 1985 and includes all recordings made up to the end of 1999. This section also includes sessions made by various EMI companies around the world, but which were initially released on the Blue Note label. These sessions are identified by the prefix EMI followed by the country name which appears before the recording location and date.

Part 4 lists Blue Note reissues of sessions purchased from other labels.

Part 5 lists reissues on Blue Note label of material coming from various EMI labels.

Part 6 lists Blue Note reissues made of sessions leased from other labels.

In parts 1 to 6, all sessions are listed with available details on personnel and recording locations and dates as well as on master numbers and issue numbers. Foreign known issues have also been included when they are not straight reissues of Blue Note issues,or when they were released prior to US equivalent. Most sessions of part 1 and some of parts 2 and 3 have been recorded by famous engineer Rudy Van Gelder (see Blue Note Story on page xi), in his Hackensack, and later Englewood Cliffs, New Jersey recording studio. When these locations are listed, studio name has not been repeated.

Part 7 lists single series used, each issue being listed with reference to pages where titles are detailed.

Part 8 lists album series (45 rm Extended Plays, 33 rpm 10 in. & 12 in.LPs). For each album, numbers in parentheses refer to the pages where involved sessions are described.

In each category of parts 7 and 8, comprehensive lists of foreign issues have been included, along with a table of equivalent singles in part 7. Original Blue Note BLP albums have been repressed in various countries using US number. These reissues have not been mentioned, as they are all identical to original US albums.

Part 9 is a listing of Compact Disc issues,with mention of country of origin, and equivalent LP issue, with number of additional tracks included when applicable.

Following part 9 is an artist index, including all names appearing in the session listings, and referring the user to the pages involved. Pages are listed in parentheses when artists appear as sidemen.

Acknowledgements

This book results from a long and very close collaboration with Michael Cuscuna, who devoted years of his life to researching through Blue Note files, unearthing many unknown sessions and allowing to get a complete listing of all existing material as well as issue of tens of newly discovered albums on Blue Note and Mosaic labels. A first version of this discography (The Blue Note Label) was published in 1988 in the Discography Series; the present book includes all material produced on the Blue Note label up to the end of 1999, a large part of which having been produced by Michael. This book is actually the result of his research rather than mine, which was mainly compiling all data he forwarded to me. The whole jazz community is indebted to Michael for his work, which allows to have a complete view of the most famous jazz label over sixty years. My deepest thanks go to him for his continued support in order to reach a publication as complete as possible.

Many people helped to add full information on all Blue Note releases, namely: Bob Belden, Larry Cohn, Bertrand Uberall, Stephen Platt, Russ Wapensky, Dan Morganstern, the Institute Of Jazz Studies and from EMI around the world: Eli Wolf, Felix Cromey, Tom Evered, Jonna Terrassi, Jim Schumacher, Amalia Moreno, Pierce Melton, Wendy Furness Day, Emma Harper, Tony Wadsworth, Stephen Woof, Yoshiko Tsuge, Hitoshi Namekata, Nicolas Pflug, Diego Brava and Jean-Michel Proust.

A great assistance has also been received during years from Brian Davis, Daniel Richard, Claude Schlouch and Keizo Takada, who helped to trace details on all new issues and reissues and sort out all Japanese albums. My deep thanks go to these friends for all time they spent on this research.

I thank also Bob Rhodes, whose collaboration originally led me to idea of this book when my research was in its early stage.

Helpful details also came from Jack Bratel, Charles Collett, Reg Cooper, Gilles Gautherin, Karl Emil Knudsen, Steve La Vere, Eddie Lambert, Hitoshi Namekata ,Jean Noel Ogouz, Bob Porter, François Postif, Erik Raben, Chris Sheridan, Don Tarrant, Ebbe Traberg, Richard Weize (Bear Family Records). Thanks to all of them.

I made large use of the following publications:

Sidney Bechet Discography, by Hans J. Mauerer (K.E. Knudsen, Copenhagen, 1969)

Ornette Coleman 1958-1979: A Discography,by David Wild & Michael Cuscuna

John Coltrane Discography, by Brian Davis

The Recordings of John Coltrane: A Discography, by David Wild

Erroll Garner: The Most Happy Piano, by Jim Doran (Scarecrow Press, Metuchen, NJ, 1985)

Jazz Directory, by Albert McCarthy (Cassell, London, 1955-1957)

Jazz Records 1897-1942,by Brian Rust (Storyville Publisations, London, 1970)

Jazz Records 1942-1968, by J.G. Jepsen (K.E. Knudsen, Copenhagen, 1962-1969)

Music Masters Record Catalogues (LPs & CDs) (London - 1991-1997)

The Music of Billy May: A Discography, by Jack Mirtle (Greenwood Press, Westport, 1998)

60 Years of Recorded Jazz, by Walter Bruyninckx (Bruyninckx, Mechelen, Belgium, 1990-1999),

Stak-O-Wax by Ken G.Clee (Clee, Philadelphia, 1984),

and the following magazines and periodicals: Bielefelder catalogues, Collectors' Items, Discographical Forum, Down Beat, Jazz Catalogues, Jazz Hot, Jazz Journal International, Jazz Monthly, Jazz Times, Matrix, Micrography, The Gramophone and La Discographie de la France.

Finally, this book is a tribute to Alfred Lion and Frank Wolff, who founded the Blue Note label, thus creating the most original independent jazz recording label.

Michel Ruppli

December 2000

The Blue Note Story

In 1925, 16-year old Alfred Lion noticed a concert poster for Sam Wooding's orchestra near his favorite ice-skating arena in his native Berlin. He'd heard many of his mother's jazz or jazz-influenced records and began to take an interest in the music, especially the rhythm. But that night his life was changed. The impact of what he heard live touched a deep passion within him.

He began to scour Berlin, with little success, for recordings of this unique American black music. There were few records and no sources of information about this phenomenon. His thirst for the music brought him to New York in 1928 where he worked on the docks and slept in Central Park to get closer to the music. An attack by dock workers, who frowned on immigrants taking American jobs, sent him to the hospital and eventually home to Berlin.

In 1931, before Hitler's ascent to power, Lion and his mother migrated to South America where he worked odd jobs. Ultimately, under the employ of an import-export firm, he moved to the United States in the mid '30s.

By 1938, serious appreciation of jazz began to crystalize and grow. Milt Gabler's Commodore Records and Steve Smith's HRS label were launched in reaction to the slick commercial brand of swing that the major labels were issuing. Alfred and writer Max Margulis would create the third important independent label the next year.

On December 23, Alfred Lion attended the celebrated Spirituals to Swing concert at Carnegie Hall. The power, soul and beauty with which boogie woogie piano masters Albert Ammons and Meade Lux Lewis rocked the stage took hold of Alfred. Exactly two weeks later,on January 6 at 2:00 in the afternoon, he brought them into a New York studio to make some recordings. Instinctively, he provided their favorite beverages and food and created an atmosphere of respect, appreciation and warmth that brought out the best in them. They took turns at the one piano, recording four solos each before relinquishing the bench to the other man. The long session ended with two stunning duets. With Max Margulis's financing, Blue Note Records was finally a reality.

Lion pressed up some 50 copies of 78s by each of them. Either out of innovation or naivete, Lion let them play each number so long that the records had to be pressed on 12" discs, a format reserved primarily for classical music at the time. Those first records carried the same label design that Blue Note would use for the next thirty years, but the colors were black and deep pink instead of blue and white. A few small orders began to trickle in as these first records received glowing reviews. Alfred didn't exactly run out and quit his day job, but at least Blue Note was in business.

The label's first brochure in May of '39 carried a statement of purpose written by Margulis that Lion rarely strayed from, throughout the many styles and years during which he built one of the greatest jazz record companies in the world. It read: "Blue Note records are designed simply to serve the uncompromising expressions of hot jazz or swing, in general. Any particular style of playing which represents an authentic way of musical feeling is genuine expression. By virtue of its significance in place, time and circumstance, it possesses its own tradition,artistic standards and audience that keeps it alive. Hot jazz, therefore, is expression and communication, a musical and social manifestation, and Blue Note records are concerned with identifying its impulse, not its sensational and commercial adornments."

Alfred's next session was an all-star quintet under the banner Port of Harlem Jazzmen on April 7,'39. In order to capture the intimacy and vitality of the music, he called the session for 4:30 in the morning, when the artists had finished their club dates. Night sessions were almost unheard of at this time.Two months later, he did another Port of Harlem date, adding Sidney Bechet, who would have a major role in the growth of Blue Note during the next 14 years. Out of that memorable session came his superb soprano saxophone reading of "Summertime", Blue Note's first hit of sorts. Thereafter, this song would belong to Bechet as "Body and Soul" belonged to Coleman Hawkins.

At the end of 1939, Alfred's childhood friend Francis Wolff had caught the last boat out of Nazi-controlled Germany bound for America. He found employment at a photographic studio and joined forces with Lion at night to continue Blue Note. They recorded a handful of sessions before America's entry into World War Two. Each date was astonishingly innovative.Most notable were two stream-of-consciousness piano solos by Earl Hines and four tunes by the Edmond Hall Celeste Quartet, a chamber group of Hall on clarinet, Charlie Christian on acoustic guitar, Meade Lux Lewis on celeste and Israel Crosby on bass.

Looking back in 1969, Frank Wolff wrote, "By 1939,jazz had gathered enough momentum so that an experiment like Blue Note could be tried. We could not round up more that a handful of customers for a while, but we garnered a good deal of favorable publicity through our uncommercial approach and unusual sessions like the Port of Harlem Jazzmen and the Edmond Hall Celeste Quartet. Somehow we set a style, but I would have difficulty to define same. I remember though that people used to say, 'Alfred and Frank record only what they like.' That was true. If I may add three words,we tried to record jazz 'with a feeling'."

When Lion was drafted into the service in mid 1942, he and Wolff decided to suspend operations for the duration of the war. They gave up their one-room office on West 47th Street and sent out notice to their accounts. Although they did stop all recording until Alfred's return, a lucky twist of fate kept Blue Note alive. Milt Gabler, who operated his own label from his Commodore Record Shop, started a wholesale division to distribute his label. Frank went to work for Commodore, which would also distribute Blue Note. Wolff once told Ira Gitler, "With the war, the record business immediately picked up. The soldiers wanted them--the Army wanted them. Records became hot, and Commodore sold a lot of them, mail and wholesale. Shellac was scarce, and only people who had been in business before the war could get a priority.

With the revenues that built up during this time, Lion and Wolff resumed recording in November, 1943.

They set up Blue Note in a large space at 767 Lexington Avenue, which remained the label's home until 1957.

As big bands died an economic death, many fine swing soloists began to organize swingtets (usually three horns and four rhythm), which were affordable formats for small clubs and independent jazz labels like Keynote, HRS and Blue Note. One of the first such Blue Note sessions in 1944 was by the magnificent, underrated tenor saxophonist Ike Quebec,and it bore another jazz classic, "Blue Harlem." After four more exceptional dates with Quebec as well as others by Tiny Grimes, John Hardee, Jimmy Hamilton and Benny Morton, Blue Note halted new recordings in September of 1946.

Except for two sessions with Babs Gonzales in the Spring of '47, the recording hiatus lasted 12 months.Jazz was changing again, and Lion and Wolff could no longer resist the be-bop movement. Ike Quebec had become a close friend and advisor to both of them. Just as he had ushered in their swingtet phase, he would also bring them into modern jazz, introducing them to many of the new music's innovators and encouraging them to document it. This move into be-bop prompted Max Margulis to sell his share of the label to Alfred.

Soon they were recording Fats Navarro and Bud Powell and giving Tadd Dameron, Thelonious Monk, Art Blakey, James Moody, among others, their first dates as leaders. Blue Note made the transition easily, maintaining its identity and standard of excellence. Lion and Wolff became especially fascinated with Monk and helped his career in every conceivable way. Despite critical resistance and poor sales, they recorded him frequently until 1952.

Monk's case was the first major example of what Horace Silver described to me in a 1980 interview, "Alfred Lion and Frank Wolff were men of integrity and real jazz fans. Blue Note was a great label to record for. They gave a first break to a lot of great artists who are still out there doing it today. They gave me my first break. They gave a lot of musicians a chance to record when all the other companies weren't interested. And they would stick with an artist, even if he wasn't selling. Of course, if every record a guy made didn't sell at all, they couldn't stay with him forever. But if a guy was a great player who didn't sell well--and there were many--and if Alfred and Frank believed in him, they would stay with him. You don't find that anymore."

Because of the financial burden of creating artwork, Blue Note was slow and cautious moving from 78s into the 10" lp format. They did not begin issuing lps until late 1951. Likewise, they did not move from 10" to 12" until the end of 1955, well after most labels. But on other levels, the label was far ahead of everyone else. Album covers became a distinctive component in the Blue Note mix. Frank Wolff's extraordinarily sensitive and atmospheric candid photos and the advanced designs of Paul Bacon, Gil Melle and John Hermansader gave Blue Note a look as distinctive as its beautiful Bauhaus record ads of the '40s.

Meanwhile, Lion was making first albums by the likes of Horace Silver, Lou Donaldson, Clifford Brown, Wynton Kelly, Elmo Hope, Kenny Drew, Tal Farlow and Kenny Burrell. He was also making significant sessions with established modern talents like Kenny Dorham, George Wallington, Milt Jackson, Miles Davis, Thad Jones, Sonny Rollins and Herbie Nichols.

In 1952, Alfred became intrigued with "The Gears", a 78 by saxophonist-composer Gil Melle on the Triumph label. He was equally intrigued by the sound of the recording which Gil had done at Rudy Van Gelder's parents' home in Hackensack, New Jersey where Van Gelder had a recording set-up in the living room. Alfred purchased the Triumph sides and recorded four more tracks at Rudy's with Melle the next January to complete a 10" lp. Blue Note had always been known for its superior sound and balance. In Rudy, Alfred found an intelligent, kindred soul from whom he could extract an ideal sound. Van Gelder engineered most of the major jazz recordings of the '50s and '60s for many labels. He told me, "Alfred knew exactly what he wanted to hear. He communicated it to me and I got it for him technically. He was amazing in what he heard and how he would patiently draw it out of me. He gave me confidence and support in any situation.I remember when we first started recording Jimmy Smith.He knew the sound he wanted. I worked at it time and time again. He just kept assuring me that I could do it, I could get what he wanted."

By 1954, Blue Note naturally gravitated toward a system that was much akin to repertory theatre company. They began to use a revolving cast of sidemen and leaders who would assure them the creativity, compatibility and dependability that Blue Note sought. Leaders would appear on each other's projects; recurring sidemen would be groomed to grow into leaders. Sometimes such instances could be purely serendipitous. Horace Silver's first session was to have been a Lou Donaldson quartet date that Lou had to cancel at the last minute to go out of town. Alfred thought it was time for Silver to make his debut anyway and offered him the same date as his own trio session.

And while we are on the subject of Horace Silver, Lion felt in late 1954 that Horace should do a record with horns. He and the pianist arrived at the ideal personnel: Kenny Dorham, Hank Mobley, Doug Watkins and Art Blakey. The date went so well that these five men decided on a common purpose and formed a cooperative band called The Jazz Messengers. The group's idea was to present soulful modern jazz that incorporated the language of be-bop without the virtuosic cliches of its second generation followers and the soulful, warm roots of blues and gospel music. It worked! And it became, with Rudy's engineering, the Blue Note sound.

Art Blakey told me, "At that time,a guy would call the musicians and say,'hey,I got a gig tonight.' They'd come out and play the standard be-bop tunes,just stand there and jam. The people got tired of that. Everybody was just copying. There was no innovating going on. So we decided to put something together and make a presentation for the people. We stayed basically around New York, but made some gigs in other cities. This helped the clubs and the whole scene because other guys would form real bands and start working."

A year later, Blue Note would set in motion another trend in jazz. On the advice of Babs Gonzales and other musicians, Lion and Wolff ventured out to hear a Philadelphia pianist who had abandoned his original instrument and woodshedded intently for more than a year on a rented Hammond organ in the corner of a warehouse. As Frank Wolff told it in 1969, "I first heard Jimmy Smith at Small's Paradise in January of 1956. It was his first gig in New York-one week. He was a stunning sight. A man in convulsions, face contorted, crouched over in apparent agony, his fingers flying, his feet dancing over the pedals. The air was filled with waves of sound I had never heard before. The noise was shattering. A few people sat around, puzzled, but impressed. He came off the stand,smiling, the sweat dripping all over him. 'So what do you think?' 'Yeah,' I said. That's all I could say. Alfred Lion had already made up his mind."

Around the same time, Wolff met Reid Miles, a commercial artist who was a devout classical music fan. They struck up a rapport. Beginning with Blue Note's ninth 12" album, Reid Miles became the designer for the label for the next 11 years. He relied on Alfred to describe the mood and intent of each album and then created wonderful graphic covers that were different from each other, but still maintained an indefinable Blue Note look.

It was 1956, and the cast that gave the label its sound and identity--Lion, Wolff, Van Gelder, Reid, Miles, Blakey, Silver, and Smith--was complete. And for the next decade or so Blue Note dominated the artistic and commercial courses of the music. As Wolff once said, "We established a style, including recording, pressing and covers. The details made the difference."

Unlike the many independent jazz labels that sprang up in the '50s, this label put quality above cost-accounting. If a session was unsuccessful, it was shelved. And each record date was preceded by planning sessions and two or three days of paid rehearsals. This was reflected not only in the perfect execution of the musical ensembles, but also in the varied and ambitious compositions that the musicians were able to tackle. Lion knew that proper preparation before the studio date allowed the musicians to be spontaneous and creative with challenging material when the tapes finally rolled.

Blue Note's closest competitor was Prestige, owned and operated by Bob Weinstock. Bob freely admits that he looked up to Lion and followed his leads closely. Yet he had neither the patience nor inclination to plan and rehearse record dates. As former Prestige producer Bob Porter once put it, "The difference between Blue Note and Prestige is two days of rehearsal."

Throughout the late '50s and '60s, Blue Note continued to discover and launch impressive talents and to take artists from other labels to a new level. The Blue Note magic is most evident in comparisons. Compare John Coltrane's "Blue Train" to any of his many Prestige albums or Jackie McLean's pre-1959 output with his Blue Note albums. The difference is so apparent that one wonders if the history of this music could have been accurately documented without Blue Note. I think not.

During the '50s, Rudy Van Gelder ran his optometry practice in Teaneck by day and recorded jazz dates at his home at night and on weekends. Each label would have a regular day and time that they would use without fail each week for recording or editing and album assembly. By 1959, Rudy must have felt that he needed more than two hours sleep a night. He closed his optometry practice and moved to Englewood Cliffs, where he designed a home and studio to meet his particular needs. After some experimentation, his large-as-life horn sounds, his perfect blend and placement of each instrument, his rich, yet sparkling drum and piano sounds and his echo/room sound mixture sounded better than ever.

Fittingly, Blue Note's last date in Hackensack (July 1,1959) and first in Englewood Cliffs (July 20,1959) were Ike Quebec sessions. After several years on the road and battling some personal problems, Ike returned to the label as a recording artist, musical director and A&R man in 1959. He not only sought out new talent, but urged Lion to sign older musicians like Leo Parker and Dexter Gordon. As a musical director, he would attend most sessions and assist Alfred in producing the albums. He also recorded prolifically as a leader, and his playing was more beautiful, passionate and virile than ever.

Ike died of lung cancer on January 16, 1963 after several months of extreme pain. In 1980, Rudy Van Gelder and I were riding in my car. I put in a tape of Quebec. Rudy asked who it was When I told him, he looked out the window for a few moments and then said quietly, "Ike always played beautifully, even at the end, when he was dying...I mean,literally dying. And he knew it. After Ike's death, Alfred was never the same. They were very close,and that affected him deeply."

Duke Pearson, already a Blue Note recording artist, then took over Ike's duties and remained in that capacity until Frank Wolff's death in 1971.

The early '60s saw Blue Note move to a higher plateau in the record industry. While they had always had strong sales with Jimmy Smith, Horace Silver and others, Donald Byrd's "A New Perspective", a unique 1963 album for jazz group and wordless choir, began crossing over to more general audiences. The next year, the company released two albums that were unsuspecting blockbusters, which had lengthy stays on the pop charts: Lee Morgan's "The Sidewinder" and Horace Silver's "Song For My Father".

Lion, by sticking to the axiom that the music must have soul and feeling, inadvertantly proved that you do not have to drown jazz in gimmicks and sweetening to sell records. But the good fortunes created by "The Sidewinder" also brought pressure from distributors to keep coming up with more records like it. So many great albums would thereafter lead off an obligatory funk tune. Artists like Stanley Turrentine, Grant Green and Herbie Hancock were growing into consistent best sellers at this time.

In addition to continuing its hard bop tradition with Morgan, Mobley, Silver, Blakey and younger men like Hancock, Green, Wayne Shorter, Bobby Hutcherson, Freddie Hubbard and Joe Henderson, the label also moved cautiously into the avant garde. Although a lot of chaotic and inferior music was passing for art in that movement, Lion and Wolff typically found the best and most substantial artists of the genre to record.

Their first project was Jackie McLean's 1963 group with Grachan Moncur, Bobby Hutcherson and Tony Williams, all of whom would soon be recording their own albums as well. Tony's albums led to an association with Sam Rivers. There were also impressive works by Larry Young and Andrew Hill as well as the grand old masters of the avant garde: Cecil Taylor, Eric Dolphy and Ornette Coleman.

Bobby Hutcherson once told me, "Alfred and Frank were more like jazz musicians than record executives. They loved to hang out and have a great time. They loved the music and had a real feel for it." Operating an independent label is a 24-hour-a-day prospect. The kind of men that made Blue Note were not prone to giving up and delegating responsability. Their care and attention to detail were essential. They would most often work days and nights and through the weekend. Spare time was given to scouting music at clubs and hanging out with musician friends. That kind of life takes its toll.

When Al Bennett at Liberty Records made them an offer to sell out of Blue Note in 1965, they took it. Alfred stayed on until mid-1967, when health problems forced him to retire.

Frank Wolff and Duke Pearson divided the producing chores. The roster still maintained many fine straight ahead artists,but the Blue Note magic was on the decline. The absence of Lion and the new cover designs from Liberty's art department had an affect. But there were larger reasons.Jazz was moving into another cycle of hard times, economically and artistically. There was division among stylistic camps; confusion reigned (and led to fusion). There were few working groups and few decent, good-paying clubs. The scene did not provide an environment in which it could nurture young talent and perpetuate itself.

Frank Wolff slaved away at Blue Note until his death in 1971. Leonard Feather wrote, "When Frank came to California on a short visit late in 1970 and stopped over for dinner, I noticed that the perennial enthusiasm had started to fade. He seemed tired and drawn; but he knew of only one life and would continue to live it. He lived it right to the end. From his hospital bed, he remained on the telephone, taking care of details so meaningful to him that he could not bear the thought of delegating the responsability to others."

With Wolff's death and the lessening involvement of Duke Pearson, the label's emphasis shifted more toward fusion. Donald Byrd discovered Larry Mizell and asked him to produce "Black Byrd", a huge hit. Mizell later produced Bobbi Humphrey who was brought to the label by Lee Morgan. Other hits came from Wayne Henderson's production for Ronnie Laws and Dave Grusin-Larry Rosen productions for Earl Klugh and Noel Pointer.

The old Blue Note managed to survive through a program of reissues and previously unreleased material that Blue Note executive Charlie Lourie and I started to release in 1975. That program survived sporadically until 1981; the last active Blue Note artist was Horace Silver, who recorded for the label from 1952 until 1980. Reissues by King Records in Japan and Pathe-Marconi in France became the only signs of life from the once vital label.

In 1982, Charlie and I started Mosaic Records as a by-product of trying to convince current owner Capitol Records to restart Blue Note. Our first releases were complete Blue Note collections by Thelonious Monk and Albert Ammons-Meade Lux Lewis. The next year, the Blue Note catalog in Japan shifted to Toshiba-EMI where Hitoshi Namekata began an agressive program of reissues and previously unissued material to rebuild the label's identity there.

In mid 1984, EMI hired Bruce Lundvall to resurrect the label in earnest in the United States. The label was relaunched the following February with the "One Night With Blue Note" concert of all-star bands of new and old Blue Note artists at New York's Town Hall and the release of 20 reissues. New recordings and more vault discoveries soon followed.

Lundvall felt a responsibility to preserve the spirit and standards of Alfred Lion's creation. Returning artists from the glory days like Kenny Burrell, Tony Williams, Stanley Turrentine, Freddie Hubbard, Jimmy Smith, Andrew Hill, McCoy Tyner and Bobby Hutcherson have always been an important component of the revived label, but equally important has been the documentation of important contemporary voices like Don Pullen, Joe Lovano, Greg Osby, Tim Hagans, Gonzalo Rubalcaba and so many more. Bob Belden became our unofficial Duke Pearson along the way, making his own albums and producing or arranging albums for others.

Crossover success is essential to any jazz label functioning within a large corporation. Rather than chasing the charts with formulaic productions devoid of identity, Bruce has chosen to focus on singular artists with an appeal that can reach beyond the traditional jazz audience. Guitarists Stanley Jordan, John Scofield and Charlie Hunter and vocalists Bobby McFerrin, Dianne Reeves and Cassandra Wilson are a few examples.

"One Night With Blue Note" inspired a "one-time-only" Blue Note Jazz Festival in Mt. Fuji that lasted ten years. These annual get-togethers enabled several generations of Blue Note artists to get to know each other and play together. The event enabled us to bring to life some classic recording ensembles that had never performed live like the the amazing sextet of Bobby Hutcherson, James Spaulding, Freddie Hubbard, Ron Carter and Joe Chambers which had first come together 25 years earlier for Hutcherson's "Components".

The reception of the Mt. Fuji audiences inspired Hitoshi Namekata to launch a sister label Somethin' Else, which has augmented Blue Note, recording Jackie McLean, Ron Carter, Gonzalo Rubalcaba, Ralph Peterson and others (see part 5).

The advent of the Compact Disc enabled Blue Note to make an extraordinary percentage of its catalog available again. But the biggest surprise for the new Blue Note came from a very unexpected area. My first inkling came in the mid '80s when writer-producer-deejay Gilles Peterson took me to a London club where 18-years-olds were dancing to deejays spinning Lee Morgan's "The Sidewinder" and Ronnie Laws' "Always There". Hip hop artists in America and Europe were sampling the rhythms and riffs of dozens of '60s and '70s Blue Note Records by Lou Donaldson, Grant Green, John Patton and Lee Morgan.

Then in 1992, David Field from EMI Records in England called Blue Note with news of unique British hip hop group that was sampling heavily from Blue Note's straight ahead and funk recordings. The group was Us3, named after a Horace Parlan album. "Cantaloop", their reworking of Herbie Hancock's "Cantaloupe Island", became Blue Note's first pop hit in its history. For better and for worse, the remix world was at jazz's door. While manipulating and altering classic jazz performances and inserting them in a new context may rankle our purist instincts, this phenomenon found a new and youthful audience for a music that needed one.

1999 was the label's 60th anniversary and it seemed a perfect time to amend and update the output of this amazing label and organize the plethora of reissues and new sessions that have taken place since our first edition in 1988. I deeply appreciate Michel Ruppli's willingness to deal with my compulsive drive to make this discography as thorough and complete as possible.

My 25-year association with the label has been a constant adventure, with its share of frustrations and wonderful surprises. It has also been filled with great music, lots of laughter and some powerful friendships. For someone who caught the Blue Note bug at the age of 12, I've been a fortunate man.

MICHAEL CUSCUNA

List of Abbreviations Used

Instruments:

ac g	acoustic g
acc	accordion
arr	arranger/arranged
as	alto saxophone
b	bass
bgo	bongos
bjo	banjo
bs	baritone saxophone
c	cornet
cga	congas
cl	clarinet
comp	composer
cond	conductor
dir	director
dm	drums
el b	electric bass
el g	electric guitar
el p	electric piano
Eng h	English horn
euph	euphonium
fl	flute
flh	fluegel horn
frh	French horn
g	guitar
h	horn
hca	harmonica
keyb	keyboards
mand	mandolin
mell	mellophone
orch.	orchestra
org	organ
p	piano
perc	percussion
picc	piccolo flute
ss	soprano saxophone
synth	synthetizer
tamb	tambourine
tb	trombone
ts	tenor saxophone
tu	tuba
v	violin
vb	vibraphone
vo	vocal
vtb	valve trombone
wbd	washboard
xyl	xylophone

Countries:

(Au)	Australia
(Br)	Brazil
(C)	Canada
(Du)	Dutch (The Netherlands)
(E)	England/United Kingdom
(Eu)	Continental Europe
(F)	France
(G)	Germany
(I)	Italy
(In)	India
(J)	Japan
(P)	Portugal
(SA)	South Africa
(Sp)	Spain
(Sw)	Sweden

<u>Labels</u>:

BN	Blue Note
Cap	Capitol
JS	Jazz Selection
Lib.	Liberty
UA	United Artists
Vog	Vogue

<u>Locations</u>:

LA	Los Angeles
NO	New Orleans
NYC	New York City
SF	San Francisco

<u>Studios</u>

Hackensack,NJ : Rudy Van Gelder studio
(up to July 1,1959)

Englewood Cliffs,NJ: Rudy Van Gelder studio
(starting July 20,1959)

Capitol Studios:

Melrose Avenue,LA
(from 1949 until March 1956)

Capitol Tower, Vine Street, Hollywood
(from March 1956 to the present)

Pacific Jazz /Liberty /United Artists Studios:

Same facility on W. Third Street in West Hollywood

<u>Miscellaneous</u>:

aka	also known as
alt.	alternate take
CD	Compact Disc
ed.	edited version
incl.	including
instr.	instrumental
m.c.	master of ceremonies
mono	monophonic recording
narr.	narration
poss.	possibly
prob.	probably
prod.	produced
stereo	stereophonic recording
tk.	take number

Part 1

The Original Blue Note Sessions (1939–1967)

ALBERT AMMONS & MEADE LUX LEWIS:
Meade Lux Lewis(p).
(prob. WMGM Studio) NYC,January 6,1939

tk.1 (486A-1)	The blues,pt.1	BN 8;CD BN 7-99099-2,(J)TOCJ-5231/38
tk.2 (486A-2)	The blues,pt.2	-
tk.3 (486A-3)	The blues,pt.3	BN 9
tk.4 (486A-4)	The blues,pt.4	-

All parts also issued on Mosaic MR3-103,CD BN 7-98450-2,Mosaic MD2-103,Classics(F)722.

Albert Ammons(p).(prob. WMGM Studio) Same date.

tk.5 (441-5)	Boogie woogie stomp	BN 2,BLP7017,BST89902,BN-LA158-G2 BN(J)K23P-9281 Lib(F)LBS82442/43,(J)K22P-6092/93 CD BN 7-96580-2,4-95698-2,(J)CP32-5448, TOCJ-5716/17
tk.6 (GM535-6)	Chicago in mind	BN 4,BLP7017,(J)K23P-9281 Electrola(G)F667787(BOX 1);Vogue(F)LD066
tk.7 (1007)	Suitcase blues	BN 21,BLP7017;Vogue(F)LD066
tk.8 (442-8)	Boogie woogie blues	BN 2,BLP7017,(J)K23P-9281

All titles also issued on BN(F)BLP1209,Vogue(E)EPV1071,Oldie Blues OL 2807,Mosaic MR3-103,CD BN 7-98450-2,Mosaic MD2-103,Classics(F)715.
All titles,except tk.7,also issued on Blues Classics BC27,CD BN 7-99099-2,(J)TOCJ-5231/38, TOCJ-66006.

Meade Lux Lewis(p).(prob. WMGM Studio) Same date.

tk.9	The blues,pt.5	CD BN 7-98450-2,Classics(F)722
tk.10	Untitled Lewis original	CD Classics(F)743
tk.11 (444-11)	Melancholy	BN 1;CD BN 7-98450-2,(J)TOCJ-5231/38, TOCJ-66006,Classics(F)722
tk.12 (443-12)	Solitude	BN 1;CD BN 7-98450-2,(J)TOCJ-5231/38, TOCJ-66006,Classics(F)722

All titles issued on Mosaic MR3-103,CD MD2-103.

Albert Ammons(p).(prob. WMGM Studio) Same date.

tk.13	Untitled Ammons original	
tk.14 (1014)	Bass goin' crazy	BN 21,BLP7017,(F)BLP1209;Vogue(F)LD066 Blues Classics BC27 Oldie Blues(Du)OL 2807 CD BN 7-99099-2,(J)TOCJ-5231/38
tk.15	Backwater blues	
tk.16	Changes in boogie woogie	

All titles issued on Mosaic MR3-103,CD BN 7-98450-2,Mosaic MD2-103,Classics(F)715.

ALBERT AMMONS & MEADE LUX LEWIS:
Albert Ammons,Meade Lux Lewis(p).(prob. WMGM Studio) Same date.

tk.17 (GM537-17) Twos and fews — BN 4,BLP7017,BST2-92465,B1-92812,(E)BNX2,(F)BLP1209,(J)K23P-6725,K23P-9281 Electrola(G)F667787(BOX 1) Oldie Blues(Du)OL 2805 CD BN 7-92465-2,7-92812-2,7-99099-2,(J)CJ25-5181/84,TOCJ-5231/38,TOCJ-66006

tk.18 Nagasaki

Both titles issued on Mosaic MR3-103,CD BN 7-98450-2,Mosaic MD2-103,Classics(F)743.
Note: Last title was listed as "The Sheik Of Araby" on Mosaic issues.

Albert Ammons(p).(prob. WMGM Studio) Same date.

tk.19 Easy rider blues — Mosaic MR3-103 CD BN 7-98450-2,Mosaic MD2-103,Classics(F)715

THE PORT OF HARLEM JAZZMEN:
FRANK NEWTON QUINTET:Frank Newton(tp) Albert Ammons(p) Teddy Bunn(g) Johnny Williams(b) Sidney Catlett(dm). (prob. WMGM Studio) NYC,April 7,1939

GM 512A-6 Daybreak blues — BN 501;Electrola(G)F667786(BOX 1) King(J)DY5806-02;Mosaic MR1-108 CD BN 8-28892-2,(J)TOCJ-5231/38,TOCJ-66007,Classics(F)643

J.C.HIGGINBOTHAM QUINTET:J.C.Higginbotham(tb) Albert Ammons(p) Teddy Bunn(g) Johnny Williams(b) Sidney Catlett(dm).(prob. WMGM Studio) NYC,April 7,1939

GM 513A-5 Weary land blues — BN 501;King(J)DY5806-02;Mosaic MR1-108 CD BN 8-28892-2,(J)TOCJ-5231/38,TOCJ-66007,Classics(F)715

PORT OF HARLEM JAZZMEN:Frank Newton(tp) J.C.Higginbotham(tb) Albert Ammons(p) Teddy Bunn (g) Johnny Williams(b) Sidney Catlett(dm).
(prob. WMGM Studio) NYC,April 7,1939

GM 515-A5 Port of Harlem blues — BN 14,BST89902,BN-LA158-G2
GM 516-2 Mighty blues — BN 3,BLP7022,B6509;Oldie Blues(Du)OL 2822
GM 517-1 Rocking the blues — - - - -

All titles also issued on Electrola(G)F667786(BOX 1),King(J)DY5806-02,Mosaic MR1-108,CD BN 8-28892-2,(J)TOCJ-5231/38,TOCJ-66007,Classics(F)715.

FRANK NEWTON QUINTET:Frank Newton(tp) Meade Lux Lewis(p) Teddy Bunn(g) Johnny Williams(b) Sidney Catlett(dm). (prob. WMGM Studio) NYC,June 8,1939

GM 531 After hours blues — BN 14;Mosaic MR1-108 CD BN 8-28892-2,(J)TOCJ-5231/38,TOCJ-66007,Classics(F)643

J.C.HIGGINBOTHAM QUINTET:J.C.Higginbotham(tb) Meade Lux Lewis(p) Teddy Bunn(g) Johnny Williams(b) Sidney Catlett(dm).(prob. WMGM Studio) NYC,June 8,1939

GM 532B-15 Basin Street blues — BN 7;King(J)DY5806-02;Mosaic MR1-108 CD BN 8-28892-2,(J)TOCJ-5231/38,TOCJ-66007,Classics(F)743

PORT OF HARLEM SEVEN:Frank Newton(tp) J.C.Higginbotham(tb) Sidney Bechet(ss) Meade Lux Lewis (p) Teddy Bunn(g) Johnny Williams(b) Sidney Catlett(dm).
(prob. WMGM Studio) NYC,June 8,1939

GM 532X-12 Blues for Tommy — BN 7,BLP7003,BLP1202;King(J)DY5806-02
JS(F)545;Electrola(G)F667786(BOX 1)
Mosaic MR1-108,MR6-110
CD BN 8-28892-2,(Eu)7-89385-2,
(J)TOCJ-5231/38,TOCJ-66007,
Mosaic MD4-110,Classics(F)608

SIDNEY BECHET QUINTET:Sidney Bechet(ss) Meade Lux Lewis(p) Teddy Bunn(g) Johnny Williams(b) Sidney Catlett(dm).
(prob. WMGM Studio) NYC,June 8,1939

GM 533-14 Summertime — BN 6,BLP7002,BLP1201,BST89902,BST2-92465,
BN-LA158-G2;BN(E)UP36535,UALP 19
Mosaic MR1-108,MR6-110
Sunset(F)SLS50228;King(J)DY5806-02
Electrola(G)F667786(BOX 1);JS(F)545
CD BN 7-92465-2,7-99099-2,8-28891-2,
8-28892-2,4-95698-2,(C)8-56508-2,
(Eu)7-89384-2,(J)CJ25-5181/84,CJ28-5161,
TOCJ-5231/38,CP32-5448,TOCJ-5716/17,
TOCJ-66007,TOCJ-66040,Mosaic MD4-110,
Classics(F)608,EMI(E)5-20535-2

PORT OF HARLEM SEVEN:Frank Newton(tp) J.C .Higginbotham(tb) Sidney Bechet(cl) Meade Lux Lewis (p) Teddy Bunn(g) Johnny Williams(b) Sidney Catlett(dm).
(prob. WMGM Studio) NYC,June 8,1939

GM 536-11 Pounding heart blues — BN 6,BLP7003,BLP1202;King(J)DY5806-02
Electrola(G)F667786(BOX 1)
Mosaic MR1-108,MR6-110
CD BN 8-28892-2,(Eu)7-89385-2,
(J)TOCJ-5231/38,TOCJ-5716/17,TOCJ-66007,
Mosaic MD4-110,Classics(F)608

<u>EARL HINES</u>:
Earl Hines(p).
(poss. WMGM Studio) NYC,July 29,1939

GM 301x-3 The Father's getaway — BN 5,BST89902,BN-LA158-G2
Lib(J)K22P-6092/93
CD BN 7-99099-2
GM 302x-2 Reminiscing at Blue Note — BN 5,CD 7-96580-2,4-95698-2;BN(J)K23P-6725

Both titles also issued on BN(J)K23P-9281,Electrola(G)F667789(BOX 1),Mosaic MR1-119,CD BN 8-28893-2,(J)TOCJ-5231/38,TOCJ-5716/17,TOCJ-66006,Classics(F)538.

<u>PETE JOHNSON BLUES TRIO</u>:
Pete Johnson(p) Ulysses Livingston(g) Abe Bolar(b).
(Reeves Sound Studio) NYC,December 19,1939

RS 653-1	Vine Street bustle	BN 11;CD BN 7-99099-2,(J)TOCJ-5231/38, TOCJ-66006,Classics(F)656
RS 654-2		
RS 655-3	Some day blues	BN 11;CD Classics(F)656
RS 656-4		
RS 657-5		
RS 658-6	Holler stomp (p solo)	BN 12;Electrola(G)F667787(BOX 1) CD BN 7-96580-2,Classics(F)665
RS 659-7	Barrelhouse breakdown	BN 10;CD BN 7-99099-2,(J)TOCJ-5231/38, TOCJ-66006,Classics(F)665
RS 660-8	Kansas City farewell	BN 10;CD Classics(F)665
RS 661-9		
RS 662-10	You don't know my mind (p solo)	BN 12;CD Classics(F)665

All titles issued on BN BLP7019,(F)BLP1209,Mosaic MR1-119,CD BN 8-28893-2.
Note:Blank numbers are rejected takes of same titles.

<u>JOSH WHITE TRIO</u>:
Sidney Bechet(cl) Josh White(g,vo) Wilson Ernest Myers(b).
(Reeves Sound Studio) NYC,March 7,1940

RS 671 A	Careless love (blues)	BN 23,CD 8-35811-2
RS 672	Milk cow blues	- BST89902,BN-LA158-G2,(J)K23P-9283

Both titles also issued on Mosaic MR6-110,CD BN(J)TOCJ-5231/38,TOCJ-66007,Mosaic MD4-110, Classics(F)619.

<u>SIDNEY BECHET BLUE NOTE QUARTET</u>:
Sidney Bechet(cl-1,ss-2) Teddy Bunn(g) George "Pops"Foster(b) Sidney Catlett(dm).
(Reeves Sound Studio) NYC,March 27,1940

RS 709 B	Lonesome blues -1	BN 13,BLP7022;CD BN(J)CJ28-5161
RS 710 A	Dear old Southland -2	BN 13,BLP7002,BLP1201 Electrola(G)F667786(BOX 1) CD BN(Eu)7-89384-2,(J)CJ28-5161, TOCJ-5716/17,TOCJ-66040
RS 711 A	Bechet's steady rider -1	BN 502,BLP7022:Electrola(G)F667786(BOX 1)
RS 712 A	Saturday night blues -1	- -

All titles also issued on BN(J)K23P-9283,Mosaic MR6-110,CD BN 8-28892-2,(J) TOCJ-5231/38, TOCJ-66007,Mosaic MD4-110,Classics(F)619.

<u>TEDDY BUNN</u>:
Teddy Bunn(g,vo).
(Reeves Sound Studio) NYC,March 28,1940

RS 713 A	King Porter stomp	BN 503;CD BN(J)TOCJ-5231/38
RS 714 A	Bachelor blues (voTB)	- -
RS 715 A (RXBN 715*)	Blues without words (alt.) (voTB)	Electrola(G)F667789(BOX 1)* CD BN(J)TOCJ-5716/17
RS 715 B	Blues without words (voTB)	BN 504;CD BN(J)TOCJ-5231/38
RS 716 A	Guitar in high	- -

All titles also issued on Mosaic MR1-119,CD BN 8-28892-2.

5

MEADE LUX LEWIS:
Meade Lux Lewis(p).

	(Reeves Sound Studio)	NYC,September 2 (or 3,or 4 or 5),1940
RS 791 B	Honky tonk train blues	BN 15,BLP7018,BST89902,BN-LA158-G2 BN(J)K23P-9281;Lib(J)K22P6092/93 CD BN 7-99099-2,(J)TOCJ-5231/38
RS 792 C	Bass on top	BN 16,BLP7018;Vogue(E)EPV1065 CD BN 7-99099-2
RS 793 A	Six wheel chaser	BN 16,BLP7018
RS 794 A	Tell your story	BN 15 - (J)K23P-9281 Oldie Blues(Du)OL 2805 Vogue(E)EPV1065,(F)LD066
RS 794 B	Tell your story No.2	BN 22

All 5 titles also issued on Mosaic MR3-103,CD Mosaic MD2-103,Classics(F)743.
Note: Exact date has not been ascertained,but is definiitely earlier than October 4 which was quoted previously.

EDMOND HALL CELESTE QUARTET:
Edmond Hall(cl) Meade Lux Lewis(celeste) Charlie Christian(ac g) Israel Crosby(b).

	(Reeves Sound Studio)	NYC,February 5,1941
R 3459A	Jammin' in four	BN 18,BLP5026 CD BN 7-96581-2,8-35811-2,HMV Jazz(E) 5-20884-2
R 3460	Edmond Hall blues	BN 18,BLP5026
R 3461	Profoundly blue	BN 17,45-1634,BLP5001,BST89902, BN-LA158-G2,BST2-92465 Lib(F)LBS83442/43,(J)K22P-6094/95 Electrola(G)F667789(BOX 1) CD BN 7-92465-2,4-95698-2,(J)CJ25-5181/84, CP32-5448
R 3461-2	Profoundly blue #2	BN BLP5026,CD 8-35811-2
R 3462A-2	Celestial express	BN 17,BLP5026

All titles also issued on BN B6505,Mosaic MR6-109,CD BN 8-21260-2,(J)TOCJ-5231/38,TOCJ-5716/17, Mosaic MD4-109.
All titles,except R 3461-2,also issued on CD Classics(F)830.

MEADE LUX LEWIS:
Meade Lux Lewis(harpsichord).

	(Reeves Sound Studio)	NYC,April 9,1941
	Variations on a theme:	
RS 934 B	Pt.1: 19 ways of playing achorus	BN 19;CD BN 7-99099-2,Classics(F)743
RS 935 B	Pt.3: School of rhythm	BN 20:CD Classics(F)743
RS 937 A	Pt.2: Self portrait	BN 19;CD Classics(F)841
RS 938 A	Pt.4: Feeling tomorrow like I feel today	BN 20 -

All titles also issued on Mosaic MR3-103,CD MD2-103.

Meade Lux Lewis(p). Same date.

BN 639	Rising tide blues	BN 22;Mosaic MR3-103 Vogue(F)LD066;Oldie Blues(Du)OL 2805 CD Mosaic MD2-103,Classics(F)743

JAMES P.JOHNSON:
James P.Johnson(p).

	(WOR Studios)	NYC,November 17,1943
BN 777	J.P.Boogie	BN 24,(J)K23P-6725,K23P-9281 Electrola(G)F667787(BOX 1)
BN 778	Backwater blues	BN 25,BLP7011,(J)K23P-9281 CD BN(J)TOCJ-5231/38,TOCJ-5716/17
BN 779	Carolina Balmoral	BN 25,BLP7011;Time-Life STL-J18 CD BN(J)TOCJ-5231/38,TOCJ-5716/17
BN 780	Gut stomp	BN 24,BLP7011

All titles also issued on Mosaic MR6-109,CD BN 8-28893-2,(J)TOCJ-66006,Mosaic MD4-109, Classics(F)824.

EDMOND HALL'S BLUE NOTE JAZZMEN:
Sidney De Paris(tp) Vic Dickenson(tb) Edmond Hall(cl) James P.Johnson(p) Jimmy Shirley(g) Israel Crosby(b) Sidney Catlett(dm).

	(WOR Studios)	NYC,November 29,1943
BN 901-1	High society (alt.1)	
BN 901-2	High society (alt.2)	BN B6504
BN 901-3	High society -1	BN 28,BLP7007,B6504,B6509 BN(J)NR8102,K23P-9287,CD TOCJ-5716/17
BN 903-1	Blues at Blue Note (alt.)	CD BN 8-35811-2
BN 903-2	Blues at Blue Note	BN 28,BLP7007,B6504,(J)NR8102,K23P-9287
BN 905-1	Night shift blues (alt.)	CD BN 8-35811-2
BN 905-2	Night shift blues -2	BN 29,BLP7007,B6504,B6509 BN(J)NR8102,K23P-9287;Vogue(E)EPV1164
BN 907-1	Royal garden blues (alt.)	BN B6504,(J)NR8102
BN 907-2	Royal garden blues	BN 29,BLP7007,(J)K23P-9287 Vogue(E)EPV1164 CD BN 8-35811-2,(J)TOCJ-5716/17
	Blue Note boogie	Electrola(G)F667787(BOX 1) CD BN 7-99099-2

-1: incorrectly listed as alt.take on B6509.
-2: incorrectly listed as alt.take on B6504.
All 10 titles issued on Mosaic MR6-109,CD BN 8-21262-2,Mosaic MD4-109.
All titles,except alternates,also issued on CD BN(J)TOCJ-5131/38,TOCJ-66011,Classics (F)830.

JAMES P.JOHNSON:
James P.Johnson(p).

	(WOR Studios)	NYC,December 15,1943
BN 781	Mule walk (stomp)	BN 27,BLP7011,BST89902,BN-LA158-G2 BN(J)K23P-9281;Time-Life STL-J18 Lib(J)K22P-6092/93 Electrola(G)F667787(BOX 1) CD BN 7-96580-2,7-99099-2,(J)TOCJ-5231/38
BN 782	Arkansas blues	BN 27,BLP7011,(J)K23P-9281 Time-Life STL-J18 CD BN(J)TOCJ-5231/38
BN 783	Caprice rag	BN 26,BLP7011
BN 784	Improvisations on Pinetop's boogie	-

All titles also issued on Mosaic MR6-109,CD BN 8-28893-2,(J)TOCJ-66006,Mosaic MD4-109,Classics(F) 824.

7

EDMOND HALL'S ALL STAR QUINTET:
Edmond Hall(cl) Red Norvo(vb) Teddy Wilson(p) Carl Kress(g) Johnny Williams(b).
(WOR Studios) NYC,January 25,1944

BN 908-1	Rompin' in '44 (alt.)	
BN 908-2	Rompin' in '44	BN 30,B6505
BN 909	Blue interval	BN 31,BLP5026,B6505 CD BN(J)TOCJ-5716/17
BN 910-1	Smooth sailing (alt.)	
BN 910-2	Smooth sailing	BN 30,B6505
BN 911	Seein' Red	BN 31,BLP5026,B6505,BST89902,BN-LA158-G2

All 6 titles issued on Mosaic MR6-109,CD BN 8-21260-2,Mosaic MD4-109.
All titles,except alternates,also issued on CD BN(J)TOCJ-5231/38,Classics(F)830.

JAMES P.JOHNSON'S BLUE NOTE JAZZMEN:
Sidney De Paris(tp) Vic Dickenson(tb) Ben Webster(ts) James P.Johnson(p) Jimmy Shirley(g) John Simmons(b) Sidney Catlett(dm).
(WOR Studios) NYC,March 4,1944

BN 950-1	Blue Mizz	BN 32,B6506,(J)NR8104,K23P-9286
BN 950-2	Blue Mizz (alt.)	
BN 951-2	Victory stride (alt.)	
BN 951-3	Victory stride	BN 32,B6506,(J)NR8104,K23P-9286
BN 952-2	Joy mentin'	BN 33,B6506,(J)NR8104,K23P-9286
BN 953-2	After you've gone	BN 33,BLP7012,B6506,BST89902, BN-LA158-G2,(J)K23P-9286 King(J)DY5806-02;Time-Life STL-J18 CD BN 4-95698-2

All 6 titles issued on Mosaic MR6-109,CD BN 8-21262-2,Mosaic MD4-109.
All titles,except alternates,also issued on CD BN(J)TOCJ-5231/38,TOCJ-5716/17,TOCJ-66014,Classics(F) 824.

BN 954/959: not used.

ART HODES AND HIS CHICAGOANS:
Max Kaminsky(tp) Ray Conniff(tb) Rod Cless(cl) Art Hodes(p) Jack Bland(g) Bob Haggart(b) Danny Alvin (dm).
NYC,March 18,1944

BN 960-0	Maple leaf rag	BN 505,BEP403,BLP7004,B6509,BST 89902, BN-LA158-G2 CD Dormouse(E)DMI CDX04
BN 960-1	Maple leaf rag (alt.)	BN B6508
BN 961-1	She's crying for me	BN 506,BEP403,BLP7004,B6508
BN 962-0	Yellow dog blues	BN 505 - - - CD BN 8-35811-2,Dormouse(E)DMI CDX04
BN 963-1	Slow 'em down blues (alt.)	BN B6508,CD 8-35811-2
BN 963-2	Slow 'em down blues	BN 506,BEP403,BLP7004,B6502 CD Dormouse(E)DMI CDX04

All 6 titles issued on Mosaic MR5-114,MD4-114.

ART HODES AND HIS CHICAGOANS:
Max Kaminsky(tp) Ray Conniff(tb) Rod Cless(cl) Art Hodes(p) Sid Jacobs(b) Danny Alvin(dm).
NYC,March 22,1944

BN 964-1	Doctor Jazz (alt.)	BN B6508
BN 964-2	Doctor Jazz	BN 507,BLP7004,B6502 CD BN 8-35811-2,Dormouse(E)DMI CDX04
BN 965-0	Shoe shiner's drag	BN 507,BLP7004,B6508 CD BN 8-35811-2,(J)TOCJ-5716/17, Dormouse(E)DMI CDX04
BN 966-1	There'll be some changes made (alt.)	
BN 966-4	There'll be some changes made	BN 508,BLP7004,B6508 CD Dormouse(E)DMI CDX04
BN 967-0	Clark and Randolph	BN 508,BLP7004,B6508 CD BN 8-35811-2,(J)TOCJ-5716/17

All titles,except BN 964-1,issued on Mosaic MR5-114.
All titles issued on CD Mosaic MD4-114.

ART HODES' BACK ROOM BOYS:
Max Kaminsky(tp) Sandy Williams(tb) Art Hodes(p) Jimmy Shirley(g) Israel Crosby(b).
NYC,April 21,1944

BN 968-0	M.K.Blues (tb out)	BN 527,B6502(J)K23P-9288
BN 968-1	M.K.Blues (alt.) (tb out)	BN B6508
BN 969-0	Low down blues (tp out)-1	BN 526,BLP7021,B6508,(J)K23P-9288 CD BN 8-35811-2
BN 970-0	Jug head boogie (alt.1)	BN B6508
BN 970-1	Jug head boogie	BN 527,BLP7021,B6502,(J)K23P-9288 CD BN 7-99099-2,Dormouse(E)DMI CDX04
BN 970-2	Jug head boogie (alt.2)	CD BN 8-35211-2
BN 971-0	S.C.H. Blues (tp,tb out)	CD BN 8-35811-2
BN 972-0	Back room blues (tp,tb out)	BN 526 CD BN 7-96580-2,Dormouse(E)DMI CDX04

-1: incorrectly listed as BN 967-1 on BN 526.Title was shown as "Low down bama blues" on B6508,(J) K23P-9288.
All 8 titles issued on Mosaic MR5-114,CD MD4-114.
All titles,except alternates,also issued on CD BN(J)TOCJ-5231/38,TOCJ-66012.

EDMOND HALL SWINGTET:
Benny Morton(tb) Edmond Hall(cl) Harry Carney(bs) Don Frye(p) Everett Barksdale(g) Alvin Raglin(b) Sidney Catlett(dm).
(WOR Studios) NYC,May 5,1944

BN 973-1	It's been so long (alt.)	
BN 973-3	It's been so long	BN 511,(J)NR8104,K23P-9286
BN 974-0	I can't believe that you're in love with me (alt.)	BN(J)NR8104
BN 974-1	I can't believe that you're in love with me	BN 511,(J)K23P-9286
BN 975-0	Big city blues	BN 36,(J)NR8104,K23P-9286 CD BN(J)TOCJ-5716/17
BN 976-1	Steamin' and beamin'	BN 36,(J)NR8104,K23P-9286

All 6 titles issued on Mosaic MR6-109,CD BN 8-21260-2,(J)TOCJ-5231/38,Mosaic MD4-109.
All titles,except alternates,also issued on Electrola(G)F667788(BOX 1),CD Classics(F)872.

9

ART HODES' BLUE NOTE JAZZMEN:
Max Kaminsky(tp) Vic Dickenson(tb) Edmond Hall(cl) Art Hodes(p) Jimmy Shirley(g) Sid Weiss(b) Danny Alvin(dm).

	(WOR Studios)	NYC,June 1,1944
BN 977-0	Sweet Georgia Brown	BN 34,BLP7006,B6504 CD BN 8-35211-2,Dormouse(E)DMI CDX04
BN 978-0	Squeeze me	BN 35,BLP7006,B6509 CD Dormouse(E)DMI CDX04
BN 978-1	Squeeze me (alt.)	BN B6504,CD 8-35211-2
BN 979-0	Sugar foot stomp (alt.)	-
BN 979-1	Sugar foot stomp	BN 34,BLP7006,B6502,CD 8-35211-2
BN 980-0	Bugle call rag (alt.1)	BN B6504
BN 980-1	Bugle call rag	BN 35,BLP7006,B6509 CD Dormouse(E)DMI CDX04
BN 980-2	Bugle call rag (alt.2)	BN B6504,CD 8-35211-2

All 8 titles issued on Mosaic MR5-114,CD MD4-114.

SIDNEY DE PARIS' BLUE NOTE JAZZMEN:
Sidney De Paris(tp) Vic Dickenson(tb) Edmond Hall(cl) James P.Johnson(p) Jimmy Shirley(g) John Simmons(b) Sidney Catlett(dm).

	(WOR Studios)	NYC,June 21,1944
BN 981-0	Everybody loves my baby	BN 40,BLP7012,B6501,B6506,(J)K23P-9287 CD BN(J)TOCJ-5231/38
BN 981-1	Everybody loves my baby (alt.)	BN B6506,(J)NR8102,K23P-9287 CD BN 8-35211-2
BN 982-0	Ballin' the jack	BN 41,BLP7007,B6506,(J)NR8102,K23P-9287 Vogue(E)EPV1164 CD BN 8-35211-2,(J)TOCJ-5231/38, TOCJ-5716/17
BN 983-0	Who's sorry now (alt.)	CD BN 8-35211-2,(J)TOCJ-5231/38
BN 983-1	Who's sorry now -1	BN 41,BLP7007,B6501,B6506 BN(J)NR8102,K23P-9287;Vogue(E)EPV1164 CD BN(J)TOCJ-5231/38,TOCJ-5716/17
BN 984-0	The call of the blues	BN 40,BLP7012,B6506,BST89902, BN-LA158-G2,(J)NR8102,K23P-9287 CD BN 7-99099-2,8-35211-2,(J)TOCJ-5231/38

-1: incorrectly listed as an alt. take on B6506.
All 6 titles issued on Mosaic MR6-109,CD BN 8-21262-2,Mosaic MD4-109.
All titles,except alternates,also issued on CD BN(J)TOCJ-66011,Classics(F)835.

10

IKE QUEBEC QUINTET:
Ike Quebec(ts) Roger "Ram" Ramirez(p) Tiny Grimes(g) Milt Hinton(b) J.C.Heard(dm).
(WOR Studios) NYC,July 18,1944

BN 985-1	Tiny's exercise	BN 37;CD BN 4-95697-2,(J)TOCJ-5231/38
BN 985-2	Tiny's exercise (alt.)	BN B6507
BN 986-0	She's funny that way	BN 38,BLP5001,(J)K23P-9292 CD BN(J)TOCJ-5231/38
BN 987-0	Indiana (alt.)-1	BN B6507
BN 988-0	Blue Harlem (alt.)-2	BN 544;Electrola(G)F667789(BOX 1) CD BN(J)TOCJ-5231/38
BN 988-1	Blue Harlem	BN 37,45-1634,BLP5001,B6507,BST2-84433, BST2-92465,(J)K23P-9292 CD BN 7-92465-2,8-54363-2,4-95697-2, 4-95698-2,(J)CJ25-5181/84,CP32-5448, TOCJ-5231/38,TOCJ-5716/17
BN 987-2	Indiana	BN 38

-1: incorrectly listed as master take on BN B6507.
-2: issued on BN 544 in two parts with new master numbers (BN 1206 & BN 1207).
All 7 titles issued on Mosaic MR4-107,CD BN(J)TOCJ-66015,Mosaic MD3-107.
All titles,except alternates,also issued on CD Classics(F)957.

MEADE LUX LEWIS:
Meade Lux Lewis(p,whistling-1).
(WOR Studios) NYC,August 22,1944

BN 1201	Yancey special	BN BLP7018,(J)K23P-9281
BN 1202	Chicago flyer	BN 39,BLP7018;Vogue(E)EPV1065 CD BN 7-96580-2,4-95698-2
BN 1203	Blues whistle (Whistlin' blues)-1	BN 39;Vogue(E)EPV1065 CD BN 8-35211-2
BN 1204	Meade's blues	

First three titles also issued on Oldie Blues(Du)OL 2805.
All titles issued on Electrola(G)F667787(BOX 1),Mosaic MR3-103,CD Mosaic MD2-103,Classics(F)841.

IKE QUEBEC SWINGTET:
Jonah Jones(tp) Tyree Glenn(tb) Ike Quebec(ts) Roger Ramirez(p) Tiny Grimes(g) Oscar Pettiford(b) J.C.Heard(dm).
(WOR Studios) NYC,September 25,1944

BN 989-0	Hard tack	BN 510
BN 989-1	Hard tack (alt.)	
BN 990-1	If I had you	BN 510,BLP5001,B6507,BST89002, BN LA-158-G2,(J)K23P-9292 CD BN 4-95697-2,(J)TOCJ-5231/38
BN 991-0	Mad about you	BN 42,B6507 CD BN(J)TOCJ-5231/38
BN 992-0	Facin' the face (alt.)	
BN 992-1	Facin' the face	BN 42

All 6 titles issued on Mosaic MR4-107,CD BN(J)TOCJ-66015,Mosaic MD3-107.
All titles,except alternates,also issued on CD Classics(F)957.

JAMES P.JOHNSON'S BLUE NOTE JAZZMEN:
Sidney De Paris(tp) Vic Dickenson(tb) Edmond Hall(cl) James P.Johnson(p) Jimmy Shirley(g) Al Lucas(b) Arthur Trappier(dm).
(WOR Studios) NYC,October 26,1944

BN 993-0	Tishomingo blues (alt.)	CD BN(J)TOCJ-5231/38
BN 993-2	Tishomingo blues	BN BLP7012,B6506,(J)NR8102,K23P-9287 CD BN 8-35211-2,(J)TOCJ-5231/38
BN 994-0	Walkin' the dog (alt.)	
BN 994-1	Walkin' the dog	BN BLP7012 BN(J)NR8102,K23P-9287;Queen Disc(I)Q-020 Electrola(G)F667787(BOX 1) CD BN 8-35211-2,(J)TOCJ-5231/38
BN 995-0	Easy rider	BN(J)K23P-9287;Electrola(G)F667787(BOX 1) CD BN 8-35811-2,TOCJ-5231/38
BN 996-0	At the ball (alt.)	CD BN 8-35211-2
BN 996-3	At the ball	BN BLP7012;Time-Life STL-J18 BN(J)NR8102,K23P-9287;Queen Disc(I)Q-020 CD BN 8-35211-2,(J)TOCJ-5231/38

All 7 titles issued on Mosaic MR6-109,CD BN 8-21262-2,Mosaic MD4-109.
All titles,except alternates,also issued on CD BN(J)TOCJ-66011,Classics(F)1027.

JIMMY SHIRLEY:
Jimmy Shirley(g,scat vo-1).(WOR Studios) NYC,November 28,1944

BN 997	Stardust	rejected
BN 998	Git wittit-1	-
BN 999-1	Blues on the loose	unissued
BN 999-2	Blues on the loose	-
BN 1000	Git wittit	-
BN 1001	These foolish things	-
BN 1002	These foolish things	-
BN 1003-1	Stardust	-
BN 1003-2	Stardust	-
BN 1004	I ain't got nobody	rejected
BN 1005	I ain't got nobody	unissued

Note: All unisssued titles from this session could have been rejected.

ART HODES' BLUE FIVE:
Max Kaminsky(tp) Mezz Mezzrow(cl) Art Hodes(p) George "Pops" Foster(b) Danny Alvin(dm).
(WOR Studios) NYC,December 11,1944

BN 200-0	Gut bucket blues	BN 528,BLP7023,(J)K23P-9288 Electrola(G)F667786(BOX 1) CD Dormouse(E)DMI CDX04
BN 201-1	Apex blues	BN 45,BLP7006,B6508,(J)K23P-9288 CD BN 8-35811-1
BN 202-0	Shake that thing (alt.)-1	BN B6502,B6508,(J)K23P-9288
BN 202-1	Shake that thing	BN 45,BLP7006 CD Dormouse(E)DMI CDX04
BN 203-0	(Back home again in) Indiana	BN(J)K23P-9288 Electrola(G)F667786(BOX 1)
BN 204-0	Nobody's sweetheart	BN 528,BLP7023
BN 204-1	Nobody's sweetheart (alt.)	BN(J)K23P-9288;Electrola(G)F667786(BOX 1) CD BN 8-35811-2

-1: mistakenly listed as the master take on B6502 & K23P-9288.
All 7 titles issued on Mosaic MR5-114,CD MD4-114.
All titles,except alternates,also issued on CD BN(J)TOCJ-5231/38,TOCJ-66012.

SIDNEY BECHET BLUE NOTE JAZZMEN:
Sidney De Paris(tp) Vic Dickenson(tb) Sidney Bechet(cl-1,ss-2) Art Hodes(p) George "Pops" Foster(b) Mainzie Johnson(dm).
(WOR Studios) NYC,December 20,1944

BN 205-1	Muskrat ramble	rejected
BN 206-1	Saint Louis blues -1	BN 44,BLP7003,BLP1202,K23P-9284 Sunset(F)SLS50228 CD BN 8-28891-2,8-35811-2,(Eu)7-89385-2, (J)CJ28-5161,CP32-5448,TOCJ-66040, HMV Jazz(E)5-20883-2
BN 207-0	Jazz me blues (alt.)-1	
BN 207-3	Jazz me blues -1	BN 44,BLP7003,BLP1202,(J)K23P-9284 CD BN 8-35811-2,(Eu)7-89385-2
BN 208-0	Blue horizon -1	BN 43,BLP7002,BLP1201,BST89902, BN-LA158-G2,(J)K23P-9284 Smithsonian P6-11891;Lib(F)LBS83442/43 CD BN 8-28891-2,8-35811-2,(Eu)7-89384-2, (J)CJ28-5161,TOCJ-5716/17,TOCJ-66040
BN 209-0	Muskrat ramble -2	BN 43,BLP7002,BLP1201 BN(E)UP36535,(J)K23P-9284 Sunset(F)SLS50228 CD BN 8-28891-2,8-35811-2,(Eu)7-89384-2

All titles,except BN 205-1,issued on Mosaic MR6-110,CD BN(J)TOCJ-66008,Mosaic MD4-110.
All titles,except BN 205-1 & BN 207-0,also issued on CD Classics(F)860.

JIMMY SHIRLEY:
Jimmy Shirley(g) Oscar Smith(b).
(WOR Studios) NYC,January 23,1945

BN 210-0	These foolish things	unissued
BN 211-2	Stardust	Electrola(G)F667789(BOX 1);Lib(J)K22P-6094/95 CD BN(J)TOCJ-5231/38
BN 212-1	Blues on the loose	unissued
BN 213-0	I may be wrong	-
BN 214-0	Jimmy's blues	BN 530 CD BN 7-96581-2(J)TOCJ-5231/38

SIDNEY BECHET BLUE NOTE JAZZMEN:
Max Kaminsky(tp) George Lugg(tb) Sidney Bechet(cl-1,ss-2) Art Hodes(p) George "Pops" Foster(b) Fred Moore(dm,vo).
(WOR Studios) NYC,January 29,1945

BN 215-1	High society -1	BN 50,BLP7003,BLP1202 BN(J)K23P-9284;Sunset(F)SLS50228 CD BN 8-35811-2,(Eu)7-89385-2,(J)CJ28-5161, TOCJ-66040
BN 216-2	Salty dog (voFM)-1	BN 49,BLP7002,BLP1201,(J)K23P-9284 CD BN(Eu)7-89384-2
BN 217-1	Weary blues -2	BN 49,BLP7002,BLP1201,(J)K23P-9284 CD BN 8-35811-2,(Eu)7-89384-2
BN 218-1	Jackass blues (alt.)-2	
BN 218-2	Jackass blues -2	BN 50,BLP7003,BLP1202,(J)K23P-9284 CD BN 8-35811-2,(Eu)7-89385-2

All 5 titles issued on Mosaic MR6-110,CD BN(J)TOCJ-66008,Mosaic MD4-110.
All titles,except BN 218-1,also issued on CD BN(J)TOCJ-5231/38,Classics(F)954.

BENNY MORTON'S ALL STARS:
Benny Morton(tb) Barney Bigard(cl) Ben Webster(ts) Sammy Benskin(p) IsraelCrosby(b) Eddie Dougherty (dm).

	(WOR Studios)	NYC,January 31,1945
BN 219-0	My old flame	BN 47,BLP5001;Electrola(G)F667788(BOX 1)
BN 220-0	Conversing in blue	BN 46,BLP5027 -
		CD BN 4-95697-2
BN 221-0	The sheik of Araby	BN 46 -
BN 221-2	The sheik of Araby (alt.)	Electrola(G)F667788(BOX 1)
BN 222-0	Limehouse blues	BN 47,BLP5027,B6507,BST89902,
		BN-LA158-G2;Electrola(G)F667788(BOX 1)

All 5 titles also issued on Mosaic MR1-115,CD BN(J)TOCJ-66014.
All titles,except BN 221-0,also issued on BN(J)NR-8104,K23P-9286.
All titles,except BN 221-2,also issued on CD BN(J)TOCJ-5231/38,TOCJ-5716/17,Classics(F)906.

BUNK JOHNSON & SIDNEY BECHET:
Bunk Johnson(tp) Sandy Williams(tb) Sidney Bechet(cl) Cliff Jackson(p) George "Pops" Foster(b) Mainzie Johnson(dm).

	(WOR Studios)	NYC,March 10,1945
BN 223-1	Milenberg joys	BN 564,BLP7008,BLP1201,BST89902,
		BN-LA158-G2,(J)K23P-9284
		CD BN(Eu)7-89384-2
BN 224	Basin Street blues	rejected
BN 225-0	Lord,let me in the life boat	BN 565,BLP7008,BLP1202,(J)K23P-9284
		CD BN(Eu)7-89385-2
BN 226-0	Days beyond recall	BN 564,BLP7008,BLP1201,(J)K23P-9284
		CD BN 8-35811-2,(Eu)7-89384-2,
		(J)TOCJ-5716/17,TOCJ-66040
BN 227-0	Porto Rico	CD BN 8-28891-2
BN 228-1	Up in Sidney's flat	BN 565,BLP7008,BLP1202,(J)K23P-9284
		CD BN(Eu)7-89385-2

All titles,except BN 224,issued on Mosaic MR6-110,CD Mosaic MD4-110,Classics(F)954.

ORIGINAL ART HODES' TRIO:
Max Kaminsky(tp) Art Hodes(p) Fred Moore(dm,vo).

	(WOR Studios)	NYC,April 6,1945
BN 230-0	K.M.H. Drag (Draggin' the blues)	BN 51,BLP7021,B6502*,CD 8-35811-2
	(KMH blues*)	BN(J)K23P-9288;Vogue(E)V2363
		CD Dormouse(E)DMI CDX 04
BN 231-1	Funny feathers	BN 51;CD BN 7-99099-2
BN 232-0	Blues 'n booze (voFM)	BN 512,BLP7021
	(Blues 'n blues*)	BN(J)K23P-9288*;Vogue(E)V2363
		CD Dormouse(E)DMI CDX 04
BN 229-3	That eccentric rag (alt.)	BN B6508
BN 229-4	That eccentric rag	BN 512,B6502;(J)K23P-9288*
	(Eccentric*)	CD BN 8-35811-2,Dormouse(E)DMI CDX 04

All 5 titles issued on Mosaic MR5-114,CD MD4-114.
All titles,except BN 229-3,also issued on CD BN(J)TOCJ-5231/38,TOCJ-66012.
Note: BN 229-1 and -2 were rejected.BN 229-3 and -4 were recorded at end of the session.

IKE QUEBEC QUINTET:
Ike Quebec(ts) Dave Rivera(p) Napoleon Allen(g) Milt Hinton(b) J.C.Heard(dm).
(WOR Studios) NYC,April 10,1945

BN 233-0	Blue turning grey over you (alt.)	BN(J)K232P-9292 Electrola(G)F667789(BOX 1)
BN 233-1	Blue turning grey over you	CD BN(J)TOCJ-5231/38
BN 234-1	Dolores	BN 516,(J)K23P-9292 Electrola(G)F667789(BOX 1) CD BN(J)TOCJ-5231/38
BN 235-3	The day you came along	
BN 236-1	Sweethearts on parade (alt.)	
BN 236-3	Sweethearts on parade -1	BN 516,(J)K23P-9292 Electrola(G)F667789(BOX 1) CD BN 4-95697-2,(J)TOCJ-5231/38

-1: incorrectly listed as BN 235-3 on BN 516.
All 6 titles issued on Mosaic MR4-107,CD BN(J)TOCJ-66015,Mosaic MD3-107.
All titles,except alternates,also issued on CD Classics(F)957.

ART HODES' HOT SEVEN:
Max Kaminsky(tp) George Lugg(tb) Leonard Bujie Centobie(cl) Art Hodes(p) Chick Robertson (g) Jack Lesberg(b) Danny Alvin(dm).
(WOR Studios) NYC,May 17,1945

BN 237-1	Chacgo gal	BN 552,BLP7015,B6502
BN 238-3	I never knew what a gal could do	BN 551,BLP7015,B6509
BN 239-1	Mr.Jelly Lord	- - CD BN 8-35811-2,4-95981-2, Dormouse(E)DMI CDX 04
BN 240-3	At the jazz band ball	

All titles issued on Mosaic MR5-114,CD BN(J)TOCJ-66013,Mosaic MD4-114.

ART HODES' HOT SEVEN:
Max Kaminsky(tp) George Lugg(tb) Leonard Bujie Centobie(cl) Art Hodes(p) Chick Robertson(g) Jack Lesberg(b) Danny Alvin(dm).
(WOR Studios) NYC,May 23,1945

BN 241-0	Wolverine blues	BN 550,BLP7015,CD 8-35811-2
BN 242-4	Milenberg joys	-
BN 243-0	Walk on down	-
BN 244-2	Willie the weeper	BN 552 - B6502 CD Dormouse(E)DMI CDX 04
BN 244-3	Willie the weeper (alt.)	BN B6509
BN 245-0	Bujie (tp,tb out)	BN 550,BLP7015

All 6 titles issued on Mosaic MR5-114,CD BN(J)TOCJ-66013,Mosaic MD4-114.

IKE QUEBEC SWING SEVEN:
Buck Clayton(tp) Keg Johnson(tb)Ike Quebec(ts) Roger Ramirez(p) Tiny Grimes(g) Grachan Moncur(b) J.C.Heard(dm).
(WOR Studios) NYC,July 17,1945

BN 246-0	I found a new baby (alt.)	
BN 246-1	I found a new baby-1	BN BLP5027,B6507
BN 247-0	I surrender dear	BN BLP5001,(J)K23P-9292;CD BN 4-95697-2
BN 247-1	I surrender dear (alt.)	
BN 248-1	Topsy	BN 515,CD 4-95697-2,4-95698-2;IAJRC 15
BN 249-0	Cup-mute Clayton	- -

-1: incorrectly listed as BN 246-2 on B6507.
All 6 titles issued on Mosaic MR4-107,CD BN(J)TOCJ-66016,Mosaic MD3-107.
All titles,except alternates,also issued on CD BN(J)TOCJ-5231/38,Classics(F)957.

SAMMY BENSKIN TRIO:
Sammy Benskin(p) Billy Taylor(b) Specs Powell(dm).
(WOR Studios) NYC,July 27,1945

BN 250-2	Cherry	BN 522;CD BN(J)TOCJ-5231/38
BN 251-0	Rosetta	
BN 252-0	The world is waiting for the sunrise	BN 522;CD BN 7-99099-2,(J)TOCJ-5231/38
BN 253-0	Wiliphant Winnie	

All titles issued on Mosaic MR1-115,CD BN(J)TOCJ-66014.

ALAMO "PIGMEAT" MARKHAM:
Alamo "Pigmeat" Markham(vo) with Oliver "Rev" Mesheux's Blue Six: Oliver Mesheux (Mustapha Daleel) (tp) Sandy Williams(tb) Vivian Smith(p) Jimmy Shirley(g) Israel Crosby(b) Tommy Benford(dm).
(WOR Studios) NYC,August 31,1945

BN 254-2	Blues before sunrise	BN 48
BN 255-1	You've been a good ol' wagon	BN 509
BN 256-0	How long,how long blues	BN 48
BN 257-1	See see rider	BN 509,CD 8-54364-2

All titles also issued on CD BN(J)TOCJ-5231/38.

ART HODES' BACKROOM BOYS:
Oliver "Rev" Mesheux(tp) Omer Simeon(cl) Art Hodes(p) Al Lucas(b) Fred Moore(dm).
(WOR Studios) NYC,September 14,1945

BN 258-2	None of my jelly roll (alt.)	
BN 259-0	Blues for Jelly (alt.1)	BN B6509
BN 259-1	Blues for Jelly (alt.2)	BN B6502
BN 259-2	Blues for Jelly	BN BLP7021,(J)K23P-9288
BN 260-2	Beale Street blues	
BN 261-0	Jack daily blues	BN BLP7021,(J)K23P-9288
		CD Dormouse(E)DMI CDX 04
BN 258-4	None of my jelly roll	

All 7 titles issued on Mosaic MR5-114,CD MD4-114.
All titles,except alternates,also issued on CD BN(J)TOCJ-5231/38,TOCJ-66012.

ART HODES' HOT FIVE:
Wild Bill Davison(c) Sidney Bechet(cl-1,ss-2) Art Hodes(p) George "Pops" Foster(b) Fred Moore(dm,vo).
(WOR Studios) NYC,October 12,1945

BN 262-1	Save it pretty Mama -1	BN 531,BLP 7005,BLP1203 Vogue(E)EPV1087 CD BN 8-35811-2,(J)TOCJ-66040
BN 263-1	Way down yonder in New Orleans -1	BN 533,BLP7005,BLP1203 Sunset(F)SLS50228 CD BN 8-28891-2
BN 264-1	Memphis blues -2	BN 532,BLP7005,BLP1203 Vogue(E)EPV1087 CD BN 8-35811-2,4-95981-2
BN 265-0	Shine -2	BN 532,BLP7005,BLP1203 Vogue(E)EPV1087 CD BN 8-35811-2
BN 266-1	St.James infirmary (voFM)-2	BN 533,BLP7005,BLP1203 CD BN(J)TOCJ-66040
BN 267-0	Darktown strutter's ball -2	BN 531,BLP7005,BLP1203 Vogue(E)EPV1087,Sunset(F)SLS50228 The Jazz Club(F)2M056-64846
BN 267-2	Darktown strutter's ball (alt.)-1	CD BN 8-35811-2

All 7 titles issued on Mosaic MR6-110,MR5-114,CD BN(J)TOCJ-66013,Mosaic MD4-110,MD4-114.

JIMMY HAMILTON AND THE DUKE'S MEN:
Ray Nance(tp) Henderson Chambers(tb) Jimmy Hamilton(cl) Otto Hardwick(cl-1,as) Harry Carney(bs,cl-1) Jimmy Jones(p) Oscar Pettiford(b) Sidney Catlett(dm).
(WOR Studios) NYC,November 21,1945

BN 268-1	Old Uncle Bud	JS(F)580
BN 269-4	Blues for clarinets -1	BN BLP5027,CD 4-95698-2
BN 270-0	Slapstick	- B6507
BN 271-1	Blues in my music room	- - JS(F)580

All titles also issued on Electrola(G)F667788(BOX 1),Mosaic MR1-115,BN(J)K23P-9292,CD TOCJ-5231/38,TOCJ-66014.
Last three titles also issued on CD BN 4-95697-2.

BABY DODDS' JAZZ FOUR:
Albert Nicholas(cl) Art Hodes(p) Wellman Braud(b) Baby Dodds(dm).
(WOR Studios) NYC,December 26,1945

BN 272-2	Feelin' at ease	BN 519,BLP7021,B6509,(J)K23P-9288 CD BN 8-35811-2
BN 273-2	Careless love	BN 518
BN 274-0	High society (alt.)	
BN 274-2	High society	BN 519
BN 275-0	Winin' boy blues	BN 518,BLP7013,(J)K23P-9288 CD BN 8-35811-2
BN 273-4	Careless love (alt.)	
BN 273-5	Careless love (alt.)	BN BLP7021,B6509,(J)K23P-9288 CD BN 8-35811-2

All 7 titles issued on Mosaic MR5-114,CD MD4-114.
All titles,except alternates,also issued on CD BN(J)TOCJ-5231/38,TOCJ-66012.

17

BECHET-NICHOLAS BLUE FIVE:
Sidney Bechet(cl-1,ss-2) Albert Nicholas(cl) Art Hodes(p) George "Pops" Foster(b) Danny Alvin(dm).
(WOR Studios) NYC,February 12,1946

BN 276-0	Blame it on the blues (alt.)-2	CD BN 8-28891-2
BN 276-1	Blame it on the blues -2,3	BN 517,BLP7008,BLP1201,(J)K23P-9283 Electrola(G)F667786(BOX 1) CD BN 8-35811-2,(Eu)7-89384-2,(J)CJ28-5161, TOCJ-5231/38,TOCJ-66040
BN 277-1	Old stack o'Lee blues -1	BN 54,BLP7022,BLP1202,(J)K23P-9283 Vogue(E)LDE025,(F)LD091 CD BN 8-28891-2,4-95698-2,(Eu)7-89385-2, (J)TOCJ-5231/38,TOCJ-5716/17
BN 278-3	Bechet's fantasy -2	BN 54,BLP7022,BLP1202,(J)K23P-9283 Vogue(E)LDE025,(F)LD091 CD BN 8-28891-2,(Eu)7-89385-2,(J)TOCJ-5231/38 TOCJ-66040
BN 279-0	Weary way blues (alt.)-1	BN BLP7008
BN 279-2	Weary way blues -1	BN 517,BLP1201(J)K23P-9283 CD BN 8-28891-2,8-35811-2,(Eu)7-89384-2, (J)TOCJ-5231/38,TOCJ-5716/17

-3:issued as "Quincy Street stomp" on BN 517.
All 6 titles issued on Mosaic MR6-110,CD BN(J)TOCJ-66008,Mosaic MD4-110.
All titles,except alternates,also issued on CD Classics(F)954.

JOHN HARDEE'S SWINGTET:
John Hardee(ts) Sammy Benskin(p) Tiny Grimes(g) John Simmons(b) Sidney Catlett(dm).
(WOR Studios) NYC,February 28,1946

BN 280-0	Tired	BN 513,(J)K23P-9292 Electrola(G)F667789(BOX 1) CD BN(J)TOCJ-5231/38
BN 281-0	Blue skies	BN 513 -
BN 282-0	Hardee's party	BN 514,CD 4-95697-2
BN 282-1	Hardee's party (alt.)	
BN 283-0	Idaho (alt.)	
BN 283-5	Idaho	BN 514,CD 4-95697-2

All 6 titles issued on Mosaic MR4-107,CD BN(J)TOCJ-66017,Mosaic MD3-107.
All titles,except alternates,also issued on CD Classics(F)1136.

JOHN HARDEE SEXTET:
John Hardee(ts) William Bivens(vb) Sammy Benskin(p) Jimmy Shirley(g) Gene Ramey(b) Sidney Catlett (dm).
(WOR Studios) NYC,May 31,1946

BN 284-1	What is this thing called love	BN 520;CD BN(J)TOCJ-5231/38
BN 285-1	Nervous from the service	-
BN 286-4	River edge rock	BN 521;CD BN 4-95697-2,(J)TOCJ-5231/38
BN 287-0	Sweet and lovely	BN 521,BLP5001,(J)K23P-9292 CD BN(J)TOCJ-5231/38
BN 286-5	River edge rock (alt.)	BN B6507

All titles also issued on Mosaic MR4-107,CD BN(J)TOCJ-66017,Mosaic MD3-107.
All titles,except alternate,also issued on CD Classics(F)1136.

TINY GRIMES SWINGTET:
Trummy Young(tb) John Hardee(ts) Marlowe Morris(p) Tiny Grimes(g) Jimmy Butts(b) Eddie Nicholson (dm).

	(WOR Studios)	NYC,August 14,1946
BN 288-3	C jam blues	BN 525,CD 4-95697-2;BN(J)K23P-9292 Electrola(G)F667789(BOX 1)
BN 289-1	Flying home,pt.1	BN 524 -
BN 290-1	Flying home,pt.2	- -
BN 291-1	Tiny's boogie woogie (alt.)	
BN 291-2	Tiny's boogie woogie	BN 525,CD 7-96581-2,4-95697-2,4-95698-2 Electrola(G)F667789(BOX 1) Lib(J)K22P-6094/95

All 5 titles issued on Mosaic MR4-107,CD BN(J)TOCJ-66017,Mosaic MD3-107.

IKE QUEBEC SWING SEVEN:
Lester "Shad" Collins(tp) Keg Johnson(tb) Ike Quebec(ts) Roger Ramirez(p) John Collins(g) Milt Hinton(b) J.C. Heard(dm).

	(WOR Studios)	NYC,September 23,1946
BN 292-1	The masquerade is over (alt.)	
BN 292-4	The masquerade is over	BN 539
BN 292-5	The masquerade is over (alt.)	
BN 293-2	Basically blue	BN 539,BLP5027,CD 4-95697-2
BN 294-1	Someone to watch over me -1	BN 538
BN 294-2	Someone to watch over me (alt.)-1	
BN 295-2	Zig billion (alt.)	
BN 295-4	Zig billion	BN 538,CD 4-95697-2

-1: Some sources report that BN 294-1 was issued as BN 294-2 on BN 538.
All 8 titles issued on Mosaic MR4-107,CD BN(J)TOCJ-66016,Mosaic MD3-107.
All titles,except alternates,also issued on CD BN(J)TOCJ-5231/38.

BABS GONZALES - BABS' THREE BIPS AND A BOP:
Rudy Williams(as) Tadd Dameron(p,arr,vo) Pee Wee Tinney(g,vo) Art Phipps(b) Charles Simon(dm) Babs Gonzales(vo).

	(WOR Studios)	NYC,February 24,1947
BN 296-1	Lop-pow	BN 535,(Du)1A158-83385/8 CD BN 4-95698-2,(J)TOCJ-5231/38,TOCJ-6147
BN 297-1	Oop-pop-a-da	BN 534;,(Du)1A158-83385/8 CD BN 4-95698-2,Cap.8-52051-2, BN(J)TOCJ-5231/38
BN 298-3	Stomping at the Savoy	BN 534 CD BN(J)TOCJ-5231/38
BN 299-2	Pay dem dues	BN 535

All titles also issued on CD BN 7-84464-2,Classics(F)1124.

BABS GONZALES - BABS' THREE BIPS AND A BOP:
Tadd Dameron(p,vo,arr) Pee Wee Tinney(g,vo) Art Phipps(b) Babs Gonzales(vo).

	(WOR Studios)	NYC,May 7,1947	
BN 300-3	Runnin' around (g out) -1	BN 537	
BN 301-5	Babs' dream	-	CD BN(J)TOCJ-5231/38
BN 302-3	Dob bla bli	BN 536	-
BN 303-1	Weird lullaby -1	-	

-1: Vocal by Babs Gonzales only.
All titles also issued on CD BN 7-84464-2,Classics(F)1124.

TADD DAMERON SEXTET:
Fats Navarro(tp) Ernie Henry(as) Charlie Rouse(ts) Tadd Dameron(p,arr) Nelson Boyd(b) Shadow Wilson (dm).

(WOR Studios) NYC,September 26,1947

BN 304-0	The chase (alt.)	
BN 304-2	The chase	BN 541,BLP5004,(J)W-5501
BN 305-0	The squirrel (alt.)	BN 1597
BN 305-1	The squirrel	BN 540,BLP5004;Vogue(E)EPV1105 CD BN(E)8-57742-2
BN 306-0	Our delight (alt.)	
BN 306-5	Our delight	BN 540,BLP5004,BST2-84433 BN(J)K18P-9124,(J)W-5501 Vogue(E)EPV1105 CD BN 4-95698-2,(J)TOCJ-6147
BN 307-0	Dameronia (alt.)	
BN 307-2	Dameronia	BN 541,BLP5004,BLP1001,BLP2001, BST89902,BN-LA158-G2 BN(Du)1A158-83385/8

All 8 titles issued on BN BLP1531,BN-LA507-H2,(J)LNJ70071,CD BN 7-81531-2,8-33373-2,(J) CJ28-5120,TOCJ-1531.

THELONIOUS MONK SEXTET:
Idrees Sulieman(tp) Danny Quebec West(as) Billy Smith(ts) Thelonious Monk(p) Gene Ramey(b) Art Blakey (dm).

(WOR Studios) NYC,October 15,1947

BN 308-2	Humph	BN 560,BLP5009,BLP1510 Vog(E)EPV1048,(F)EPL7183,LD503-30 CD BN 8-23518-2,(J)TOCJ-1510
BN 309-1	Evonce (alt.)	BN(J)BNJ61011,CD TOCJ-1604
BN 309-4	Evonce	BN 547,BLP1511 CD BN(J)TOCJ-1511
BN 310-1	Suburban eyes	BN 542,BLP5009,BLP1511 CD BN(J)TOCJ-1511
BN 310-2	Suburban eyes (alt.)	BN(J)BNJ61011,CD TOCJ-1604
BN 311-0	Thelonious	BN 542,BLP5002,BLP1510 Lib(J)K22P-6092/93 CD BN 7-95636-2,4-95981-2,(J)CJ28-5162, TOCJ-1510,TOCJ-5824,TOCJ-6147,TOCJ-66032

All 6 titles issued on Mosaic MR4-101,CD BN 7-81510-2,8-30363-2,(J)CJ28-5114.
All titles,except alternates,also issued on BN BN-LA579-H2,CD Classics(F)1118.

<u>THELONIOUS MONK TRIO</u>:
Thelonious Monk(p) Gene Ramey(b) Art Blakey(dm).
(WOR Studios) NYC,October 24,1947

BN 312-0	Nice work if you can get it (alt.)	BN(J)BNJ61011,CD TOCJ-1604
BN 312-1	Nice work if you can get it	BN 1575,BLP5009,BLP1511 CD BN7-99427-2,7-80706-2,(J)TOCJ-1511, TOCJ-5634,TOCJ-6106,TOCJ-66032
BN 313-0	Ruby my dear (alt.)	BN(J)BNJ61011,CD TOCJ-1604
BN 313-1	Ruby my dear	BN 549,BLP5002,BLP1510 BN(J)K23P-6722 CD BN 7-95636-2,8-23518-2,(J)CJ28-5162, TOCJ-1510,TOCJ-5634,TOCJ-5824,TOCJ-5873, TOCJ-6106,TOCJ-66032,Cema S21-57588, EMI-Jazz(E)8-55720-2
BN 314-0	Well you needn't	BN 543,BLP5002,BLP1510 BN(J)K23P-6722;Lib(J)K22P-6092/93 Vogue(E)V2336,EPV1048,(F)EPL7183 CD BN 7-95636-2,8-23518-2,4-95698-2, (J)CJ25-5181/84,CJ28-5162,TOCJ-1510, TOCJ-5187/88,TOCJ-5634,TOCJ-5824, TOCJ-6106,TOCJ-6132,TOCJ-66032, (Sp)5-21755-2,Cema S21-57588, EMI-Jazz(E)8-55720-2
BN 314-1	Well you needn't (alt.)	BN(J)BNJ61011,CD TOCJ-1604
BN 315-0	April in Paris (alt.)	- -
BN 315-1	April in Paris	BN 1575,BLP1510,(J)W-5509 CD BN 7-95636-2,7-96580-2,8-23518-2, (J)CJ28-5162,TOCJ-1510,TOCJ-5634, TOCJ-5824,TOCJ-6106,TOCJ-66032, Cema S21-57588,EMI-Jazz(E)8-55720-2
BN 317-1	Off minor	BN 547,BLP5002,BLP1510 BN(E)UALP 19,(J)K23P-6722,K23P-6725,W-5509 Vogue(E)V2336 CD BN 8-23518-2,(J)CJ28-5162,TOCJ-1510, TOCJ-5634,TOCJ-5824,TOCJ-6106,TOCJ-6147, TOCJ-66032
BN 316-3	Introspection -1	BN BLP1510 CD BN(J)TOCJ-1510

-1: Although this title has an earlier matrix number than "Off minor",the issued take was recorded at the end of the session.
All 10 takes issued on Mosaic MR4-101,CD BN 7-81510-2,8-30363-2,(J)CJ28-5114.
All titles,except alternates,also issued on BN BN-LA579-H2,CD Classics(F)1118.

21

THELONIOUS MONK QUINTET:
George Taitt(tp) Sahib Shihab(as) Thelonious Monk(p) Bob Paige(b) Art Blakey(dm).
(WOR Studios) NYC,November 21,1947

BN 318-3	In walked Bud	BN 548,45-1664,BLP5009,BLP1510 BN(Du)1A158-83385/8,(J)W-5501 Vogue(F)LD503-30 CD BN 7-95636-2,8-23518-2,(J)CJ28-5162, TOCJ-1510,TOCJ-5634,TOCJ-5824,TOCJ-66032, Cema S21-57588,EMI-Jazz(E)8-55720-2
BN 319-0	Monk's mood	BN 1565,BLP1511,(J)K23P-6722 CD BN 7-95636-2,8-23518-2,(J)CJ28-5162, TOCJ-1511,TOCJ-5634,TOCJ-5824,TOCJ-66032, Cema S21-57588,EMI-Jazz(E)8-55720-2
BN 320-0	Who knows?	BN 1565,BLP5009,BLP1511 CD BN(J)CJ28-5162,TOCJ-1511,TOCJ-5824, TOCJ-66032
BN 321-1	'Round midnight (Round about midnight)	BN 543,45-1664,BLP5002,BLP1001,BLP1510, BLP2001,BST89902,BN-LA158-G2, BST2-84433,BST2-92465 BN(Du)1A158-83385/8,(J)K16P-9031/32, K22P-6096/97,K23P-6722,K18P-9124,W-5501 Vogue(E)EPV1048,(F)EPL7183 Lib(F)LBS83442/43 CD BN 7-92465-2,7-95636-2,8-23518-2, 4-95698-2,(C)8-33908-2,8-56508-2, (E)8-53228-2,(J)CJ28-5022,CJ28-5162, CP32-5448,TOCJ-1510,TOCJ-5634,TOCJ-5824, TOCJ-5934,TOCJ-6147,TOCJ-66032,TOCJ-66053, TOCP-7455/56,TOCP-8963,TOCP-50230, Cap(J)CP28-5864,Cema S21-57588,GSC Music 15131,EMI-Jazz(E)8-55720-2,8-55725-2, EMI(E)5-20535-2
BN 320-7	Who knows? (alt.)-1	BN(Du)1A158-83385/8,(J)BNJ61011 CD BN(J)TOCJ-1604

-1: The last take of "Who knows" was recorded at the end of the session.
All 5 takes issued on Mosaic MR4-101,CD BN 7-81510-2,8-30363-2,(J)CJ28-5115.
All titles,except BN 320-7,also issued on BN BN-LA579-H2,CD BN(J)TOCJ-6106,Classics(F)1118.

ART BLAKEY'S MESSENGERS:
Kenny Dorham (as "McKinley Durham")(tp) Howard Bowe(tb) Sahib Shihab(as) Musa Kaleem (Orlando Wright) (ts) Ernie Thompson(bs) Walter Bishop(p) LaVerne Barker(b) Art Blakey(dm).
(WOR Studios) NYC,December 22,1947

BN 322-3	The thin man	BN 545,BLP5010 CD BN 7-97190-2,8-36736-2,(J)TOCJ-5274/76, TOCJ-6147
BN 323-1	Bop alley	BN 546,BLP5010 CD BN(E)8-57742-2
BN 323-2	Bop alley (alt.)	BN(Du)1A158-83385/8
BN 324-2	Groove Street	BN 546
BN 325-1	Musa's vision	BN 545

All 5 takes shown also issued on CD BN 7-84436-2,(J)CJ28-5121.

22

THELONIOUS MONK QUARTET:
Milt Jackson(vb) Thelonious Monk(p) John Simmons(b) Shadow Wilson(dm) Kenny Hagood(vo).
(Apex Studios) NYC,July 2,1948

BN 326-3	All the things you are(voKH)	BN 1201,BN-LA579-H2,(J)K23P-6722,BNJ61012 CD BN(J)TOCJ-1604
BN 327-1	I should care (alt.) (voKH)	BN BN-LA579-H2,(J)K23P-6722,BNJ61012 CD BN(J)TOCJ-1604
BN 327-2	I should care(voKH)	BN 1201,(J)BNJ61012;CD BN(J)TOCJ-1604
BN 328-0	Evidence	BN 549,BLP1509,BN-LA579-H2 Smithsonian P6-11891 CD BN 7-81509-2,7-95636-2,(J)TOCJ-1509, TOCJ-5634,TOCJ-6106,TOCJ-66032, Cema S21-57588,EMI-Jazz(E)8-55720-2
BN 329-0	Misterioso	BN 560,BLP5002,BLP1510,BN-LA579-H2 BN(J)K23P-6722;New World 271 Smithsonian P6-11891 Vog.(E)EPV1048,(F)EPL7183,LD503-30 CD BN 7-95636-2,(J)TOCJ-1510, Cema S21-57588,EMI-Jazz(E)8-55720-2
BN 329-1	Misterioso (alt.)	BN BLP1509,BN-LA579-H2 CD BN 7-81509-2,(J)TOCJ-1509,TOCJ-5824, TOCJ-6106
BN 330-0	Epistrophy	BN 548,BLP5002,BLP1510,BST89902, BN-LA158-G2,BN-LA579-H2 BN(J)K23P-6722;Vogue(F)LD503-30 CD BN 7-95636-2,(E)8-57742-2, (J)CJ28-5162,TOCJ-1510,TOCJ-5634,TOCJ-5824, TOCJ-6106,TOCJ-6271/74,TOCJ-66032, Cema S21-57588,EMI-Jazz(E)8-55720-2
BN 331-1	I mean you	BN 1564,BLP5002,BLP1510,BN-LA579-H2 CD BN 7-95636-2,(J)CJ28-5162,TOCJ-1510, TOCJ-5634,TOCJ-5824,TOCJ-6106,TOCJ-66032

All 8 titles issued on Mosaic MR4-101,CD BN 7-81509-2,8-30363-2,(J)CJ28-5115.
All titles,except alternates,also issued on CD Classics(F)1118.

TADD DAMERON SEPTET:
Fats Navarro(tp) Allen Eager,Wardell Gray(ts) Tadd Dameron(p) Curly Russell(b) Kenny Clarke(dm) Chano Pozo(bgo-1) Kenny Hagood(vo).
(Apex Studios) NYC,September 13,1948

BN 332-0	Jahbero (alt.)-1	BN BLP1532,BN-LA507-H2
BN 332-1	Jahbero-1	BN 559,BLP1532,BN-LA507-H2 BN(Du)1A158-83385/8;New World 271
BN 333-0	Lady Bird	BN 559,BLP5004,BLP1532,BN-LA507-H2, BST2-92465,(Du)1A158-83385/8,(J)W-5501 Smithsonian P6-11891 CD BN 7-92465-2,4-95698-2,(E)8-53230-2, CJ25-5181/84
BN 333-1	Lady Bird (alt.)	BN BLP1532,BN-LA507-H2
BN 334-1	Symphonette	BN 1564,BLP1532,BN-LA507-H2 BN(Du)1A158-83385/8
BN 334-2	Symphonette (alt.)	BN BLP1532,BN-LA507-H2
BN 335-1	I think I'll go away (voKH)	BN(Du)1A158-83385/8 BN(J)BNJ61008(alb.61008/61010)

All 7 titles also issued on CD BN 7-81532-2,8-33373-2,(J)CJ28-5120.
All titles from BLP1532 also issued on CD BN(J)TOCJ-1532.

23

McGHEE-NAVARRO BOPTET:
Howard McGhee(tp,p-1) Fats Navarro(tp) Ernie Henry(as) Milt Jackson(vb-2,p-3) Curly Russell(b) Kenny Clarke(dm).
(Apex Studios) NYC,October 11,1948

BN 336-0	The skunk -3	rejected
BN 336-1	The skunk (alt.)-3	BN BLP1532,BN-LA507-H2
		CD 7-81532-2,(J)TOCJ-1532
BN 337	Boperation -1,2,3	rejected
BN 337-0	Boperation -1,2,3	-
BN 337-1	Boperation -1,2,3	BN 558,BLP5012,BLP1532,BN-LA507-H2
		BN(J)K18P-9274
		CD BN 7-81532-2,8-56399-2,4-95698-2,
		(E)8-57742-2,(J)TOCJ-1532,TOCJ-6271/74,
		TOCJ-66063
BN 337-2	Boperation (alt.)-1,2,3	
BN 336-2	The skunk -3	rejected
BN 336-3	The skunk -3	BN 558,BLP5012,CD BN 7-81532-2
		BN(Du)1A158-83385/8,(J)K18P-9274,
		BNJ61008(alb.61008/61010)
BN 338-0	Double talk,pts.1 & 2 -3	BN 557,BLP5004,BLP1531,BN-LA507-H2
		Vogue(E)EPV1105
		CD BN 7-81532-2,(J)TOCJ-1531
BN 339-0	Double talk,pts.1 & 2(alt.)-3	BN BLP1532,BN-LA507-H2
		CD BN 7-81532-2,(J)TOCJ-1532
BN 336-4	The skunk -3	rejected

All titles,except rejected takes,issued on CD BN 8-33373-2.

JAMES MOODY AND HIS BOP MEN:
Dave Burns,Elmon Wright(tp) Ernie Henry(as) James Moody(ts) Cecil Payne(bs) James "Hen Gates" Foreman (p) Nelson Boyd(b) Teddy Stewart(dm) Gil Fuller(arr).
(Apex Studios) NYC,October 19,1948

BN 340-0	The Fuller bop man (alt.)	
BN 340-4	The Fuller bop man	BN 553,B6503;CD BN(E)8-57742-2
BN 341-0	Workshop	BN 556
BN 342-2	Oh,Henry	BN 555,B6503
BN 343-2	Moodamorphosis	BN 554 -

All 5 takes shown issued on CD BN 7-84436-2.
All titles,except BN 340-0,also issued on Blue Note BLP5006,CD Classics(F)1116.

JAMES MOODY AND HIS BOP MEN:
Dave Burns,Elmon Wright(tp)Ernie Henry(as) James Moody(ts) Cecil Payne(bs) James "Hen Gates" Foreman (p) Nelson Boyd(b) Art Blakey(dm) Chano Pozo(cga,vo) Gil Fuller(arr).
(Apex Studios) NYC,October 25,1948

BN 344-0	Tropicana	BN 553,B6503,(Du)1A158-83385/8
BN 345-1	Cu-ba	BN 554 - -
BN 346-0	Moody's all frantic	BN 556,B6503,CD 4-95698-2
BN 347-0	Tin tin deo (voCP)	BN 555,BLP1001,BLP2001,BST89902,
		BN-LA158-G2,BST2-84429,BST2-92465,
		B1-80701,(Du)1A158-83385/8
		CD BN 7-92465-2,7-80701-2,4-95698-2,
		(J)CJ25-5181/84,CP32-5056,CP32-5448,
		TOCJ-6271/74

All titles also issued on BN BLP5006,CD BN7-84436-2,Classics(F)1116.

24

SIDNEY BECHET'S BLUE NOTE JAZZMEN:
Wild Bill Davison(c) Sidney Bechet(ss) Art Hodes(p) Walter Page(b) Fred Moore(dm).
(WOR Studios) NYC,January 21,1949

BN 348-2 Sister Kate BN 573,BLP7001,BLP1203
CD BN 8-28891-2,Classics(F)1112
BN 349-2 Tiger rag BN 562,BLP7009,BLP1204
Sunset(F)SLS50228;Vogue(F)LD483-30
CD BN 8-35811-2,Classics(F)1112
BN 350-0 Tin roof blues BN 561,BEP401,BLP7009,BLP1204
CD BN 8-35811-2,Classics(F)1112,1140
BN 351-0 I've found a new baby BN BEP401,BLP7014,BLP1204
Vogue(E)V2265,LDE025,(F)LD091;JS(F)818
CD BN(J)TOCJ-66040,Classics(F)1112,1140
BN 352-1 Nobody knows you when you're down and out
BN 571,BLP7001,BLP1203,(J)K23P-9283
CD BN 8-35811-2,(J)CJ28-5161,TOCJ-66040,
Classics(F)1140
BN 353-1 When the Saints go marching in BN 563,BEP401,BLP7009,BLP1204
Sunset(F)SLS50228
CD BN 8-28891-2,(J)TOCJ-66040,Classics(F)1140

All titles also issued on Mosaic MR6-110,CD BN 8-21259-2,(J)TOCJ-66009,Mosaic MD4-110.
Note: Mosaic issues wrongly credit Pops Foster as bassist.

SIDNEY BECHET & HIS BLUE NOTE JAZZMEN:
Wild Bill Davison(c) Ray Diehl(tb) Sidney Bechet(ss) Art Hodes(p) Walter Page(b) Slick Jones(dm).
(WOR Studios) NYC,March 23,1949

BN 354-0 Basin Street blues BN 563,BLP7009,BLP1204,(J)K23P-9283
Sunset(F)SLS50228
CD BN 8-28891-2,(J)CJ28-5161,TOCJ-66040

BN 355-0 Cake walking babies from home (alt)*
BN 355-1 Cake walking babies from home BN 562,BLP7009,BLP1204
CD BN 8-35811-2
BN 356-1 Tailgate ramble BN BLP7014,BLP1204
Vogue(E)V2246,LDE025,(F)LD091;JS(F)819
BN 357-2 At the jazz band ball BN 561,BLP7009,BLP1204
Sunset(F)SLS50228
CD BN 8-35811-2,(J)TOCJ-66040
BN 358-0 Joshua fit the battle of Jericho BN BLP7014,BLP1204
Vogue(E)V2246,LDE025,(F)LD091;JS(F)819
CD BN(J)TOCJ-66040
BN 359-0 Fidgety feet BN 571,BLP7001,BLP1203
CD BN 8-35811-2

* misidentified as the master take on CD 8-21259-2.

All titles,except BN 355-0,also issued on Mosaic MR6-110,CD BN(J)TOCJ-66009,Mosaic MD4-110,
Classics(F)1140.
All titles,except BN 355-1,also issued on BN CD 8-21259-2

BUD POWELL'S MODERNISTS:
Fats Navarro(tp) Sonny Rollins(ts) Bud Powell(p) Tommy Potter(b) Roy Haynes(dm).
(WOR Studios) NYC,August 9,1949

BN 360-0	Bouncing with Bud (alt.1)	BN BLP1532,BST84430 CD BN 7-81532-2,(J)TOCJ-1532
BN 360-1	Bouncing with Bud (alt.2)	BN BLP1531,BST84430 CD BN(J)7-81531-2,TOCJ-1531
BN 360-2	Bouncing with Bud	BN 1567,BLP5003,BLP1503,B1-93204 BN(Du)1A158-83385/8,(J)W-5501 Vogue(E)EPV1033,(F)EPL7181 CD BN 7-93204-2,4-95698-2,(J)CJ25-5181/84, TOCJ-1503,TOCJ-5640,TOCJ-5822, TOCJ-6271/74,TOCJ-66033
BN 361-0	Wail (alt.)	BN BLP1531,BST84430 CD BN 7-81531-2,(J)TOCJ-1531
BN 361-3	Wail	BN 1567,BLP5003,BLP1503 Vogue(E)EPV1033,(F)EPL7181 CD BN 8-54906-2,(E)8-53230-2,(J)TOCJ-1503, TOCJ-5822
BN 362-0	Dance of the infidels (alt.)	BN BLP1532,BST84430 CD BN 7-81532-2,(J)TOCJ-1532
BN 362-1	Dance of the infidels	BN 1568,BLP1503,(J)FCPA 6203,W-5501 Vogue(E)EPV1033,(F)EPL7181 CD BN 7-93204-2*, 8-54906-2,4-95981-2, (J)CJ28-5030,TOCJ-1503,TOCJ-5640,TOCJ-66033
BN 363-1	52nd Street theme	BN 1568,BLP5004,BLP1503,(J)W-5501 Vogue(E)EPV1033,(F)EPL7181 CD BN 8-54363-2,(J)CJ28-5032, TOCJ-1503,TOCJ-5640,TOCJ-5822,TOCJ-66033

All 8 titles also issued on BN-LA507-H2,Mosaic MR5-116,CD BN 7-81503-2,8-30083-2,8-33373-2,(J)CP32-5241.
Note*: On most issues of CD 7-93204-2,BN 362-1 was wrongly used in place of "52nd Street theme".

BUD POWELL TRIO:
Bud Powell(p) Tommy Potter(b) Roy Haynes(dm).Same session.

BN 364-0	You go to my head	BN 1566,BLP5003,BLP1504 BN(E)UALP 19,(J)FCPA 6203 CD BN(J)TOCJ-1504,TOCJ-5822,TOCJ-66033
BN 365-0	Ornithology	BN 1566,BLP5003,BLP1503 CD BN(J)TOCJ-1503,TOCJ-5640,TOCJ-5822, EMI(E)5-21426-2
BN 365-1	Ornithology (alt.)	BN BLP1504;CD BN(J)TOCJ-1504

All titles also issued on Mosaic MR5-116,CD BN CD 7-81503-2,8-30083-2,(J)CP32-5241.

CLYDE BERNHARDT AND HIS KANSAS CITY BUDDIES:
Clyde Bernhardt(tb-1,vo) Sam Taylor(ts) Dave Small(bs) Earl Knight(p) Rene Hall(g) Gene Ramey(b) Gus Johnson(dm).
(Carnegie Hall Studio) NYC,October 6,1949

BN 366 (tk.4) Cracklin' bread	BN 1202,CD Aladdin 4-97870-2
BN 368 (tk.3) Don't tell it	BN 1203
BN 369 (tk.3) Chattanooga -1	-
BN 367 (tk.2) Meet me on the corner -1	BN 1202

All titles also issued on CD BN(J)TOCJ-5231/38.
Note: Above titles are listed in order of recording.The recording studio was in the same building as Carnegie Hall,but not part of the concert hall.

26

HOWARD McGHEE ALL STARS:
Howard McGhee(tp) J.J.Johnson(tb Brew Moore(ts) Kenny Drew(p) Curly Russell(b) Max Roach (dm).
(WOR Studios) NYC,January 23,1950

BN 370-1	Lo-flame (alt.)	BN(Du)1A158-83385/8
BN 370-2	Lo-flame	BN 1574
BN 371-1	Fuguetta	BN 1572
BN 372-0	Fluid drive	BN 1573
BN 373-0	Meciendo	BN 1574
BN 374-0	Donellon square	BN 1573
BN 375-1	I'll remember April	BN 1572

All titles issued on CD BN 4-95747-2.
All titles,except BN 370-1,issued on BN BLP5012,(J)K18P-9274.

SIDNEY BECHET BLUE NOTE JAZZMEN:
Wild Bill Davison(c) Jimmy Archey(tb) Sidney Bechet(ss) Joe Sullivan(p) George "Pops" Foster(b) Slick Jones (dm).
(WOR Studios) NYC,April 19,1950

BN 376-4	Copenhagen	BN 572,BLP7001,BLP1203 CD BN 8-28891-2
BN 377-1	China boy	BN 573,BLP7001,BLP1203 Sunset(F)SLS50228 CD BN 8-35811-2
BN 378-0	Runnin' wild (alt.)	
BN 378-1	Runnin' wild	BN BLP7014,BLP1204 JS(F)820;Vogue(E)LDE025,(F)LD091 CD BN 8-35811-2,(J)TOCJ-66040
BN 379-0	Ain't gonna give nobody none of my jelly roll (alt.)	
BN 379-2	Ain't gonna give nobody none of my jelly roll	BN BLP7014,BLP1204 JS(F)818;Vogue(E)V2265,LDE025,LD091 CD BN 8-28891-2
BN 380-2	Mandy,make up your mind	BN BLP7014,BLP1204 JS(F)820;Vogue(E)LDE025,(F)LD091 CD BN 8-35811-2
BN 381-2	Shim-me-sha-wabble	BN 572,BLP7001,BLP1203 CD BN 8-35811-2

All 8 titles issued on Mosaic MR6-110,CD BN 8-21259-2,(J)TOCJ-66009,Mosaic MD4-110.

BUD POWELL TRIO:
Bud Powell(p) Curly Russell(b) Max Roach(dm).
(WOR Studios) NYC,May 1,1951

BN 382-1	Un poco loco (alt.1)	BN BLP1503,(J)K23P-6723
BN 382-2	Un poco loco (alt.2)	-
BN 382-4	Un poco loco	BN 1577,BLP5003,BLP1503,BST2-84429, ÒBST2-92465,B1-93204,(Du)1A158-83385/8, (In)JAZ 2,(J)K18P-9124,K23P-6725, FCPA 6203,W-5509,New World 271 CD BN 7-92465-2,7-93204-2,8-56399-2, (C)8-56508-2,(E)8-53228-2,(Eu)8-29964-2, CJ25-5181/84,CJ28-5032,CP32-5056,TOCJ-5640, TOCJ-5822,TOCJ-5858,TOCJ-6105,TOCJ-66033, TOCJ-66051
BN 383-0	Over the rainbow (solo p)	BN 1576,BLP5003,BLP1504 BN(J)K23P-6723;Lib(J)K22P-6092/93 CD BN(J)CJ28-5032,CJ28-5178,TOCJ-5640, TOCJ-5822,TOCJ-66033,TOCP-50060
BN 384-0	A night in Tunisia	BN 1576,BLP5003,BLP1503,BLP1001, BLP2001,BST89903,BN-LA159-G2,B1-80701 Lib(J)K22P-6092/93 CD BN 8-54906-2,4-95698-2,(J)CJ28-5032, CP32-5448,TOCJ-5187/88,TOCJ-5640, TOCJ-5822,TOCJ-6105,TOCJ-66033, (Sp)8-34712-2,8-53016-2
BN 384-1	A night in Tunisia (alt.)	BN BLP1503,(J)K23P-6723,FCPA 6203
BN 385-0	It could happen to you (alt.) (solo p)	BN BLP1503;CD BN(J)TOCJ-6105
BN 385-1	It could happen to you (solo p)	BN 1577,BLP5003,BLP1504 CD BN(J)CJ28-5032,TOCJ-5640,TOCJ-5822, TOCJ-66033
	Parisian thoroughfare	BN BLP1503,B1-93204 BN(Du)1A158-83385/8,(J)K23P-6723 CD BN 7-93204-2,7-96580-2,7-99100-2, (J)TOCJ-5640,Cap(J)TOCJ-5191/92, Cema GSC Music 15131

All titles issued on Mosaic MR5-116,CD BN 8-30083-2,(J)CP32-5241.
First four takes shown also issued on CD BN 7-81503-2,last five on CD BN 7-81504-2.
All titles from BLP1503/04 also issued on CD BN(J)TOCJ-1503/04.

SIDNEY DE PARIS BLUE NOTE STOMPERS:
Sidney De Paris(tp) Jimmy Archey(tb) Omer Simeon(cl) Bob Green(p) George "Pops" Foster(b) Joseph (Joe) Smith (dm).
(WOR Studios) NYC,June 14,1951

BN 386-0	When you wore a tulip (alt.)		
BN 386-1	When you wore a tulip	BN BLP7016	
BN 387-2	Weary blues	-	
BN 388-0	Moose march	-	CD 8-35811-2
BN 389-1	Panama	-	
BN 390-0	Please don't talk about me when I'm gone	-	CD 8-35811-2
BN 391-1	A good man is hard to find	-	

All 7 titles issued on BN B6501,Mosaic MR6-109,CD MD4-109.

THELONIOUS MONK QUINTET:
Sahib Shihab(as) Milt Jackson(vb) Thelonious Monk(p) Al McKibbon(b) Art Blakey(dm).
(WOR Studios) NYC,July 23,1951

BN 392-1	Four in one	BN 1589,BLP5009,BLP1511,BN-LA579-H2 CD BN 7-95636-2,(J)CJ28-5162,TOCJ-1511, TOCJ-5634,TOCJ-5824,TOCJ-6106,TOCJ-66032
BN 392-2	Four in one (alt.)	BN BLP1509,BN-LA579-H2 CD BN 7-81509-2,(J)TOCJ-1509
BN 393-0	Criss cross	BN 1590,BLP5011,BLP1509,BST89903, BST2-84429,BN-LA159-G2,BN-LA579-H2, BST2-92465 Smithsonian P6-11891 Swing(F)SW408;Vogue(E)V2161 CD BN 7-92465-2,7-95636-2,8-23518-2, 4-95698-2,(E)8-57742-2,(Eu)8-29964-2, (J)CJ25-5181/84,CJ28-5162,CP32-5056, TOCJ-1509,TOCJ-5824,TOCJ-6106,TOCJ-66032
BN 393-1	Criss cross (alt.)	BN(J)BNJ61012,CD TOCJ-1604
BN 394-0	Eronel	BN 1590,BLP5011,BLP1509,BN-LA579-H2 Swing(F)SW427;Vogue(E)V2303 CD BN(J)TOCJ-1509,TOCJ-5824
BN 395-1	Straight no chaser	BN 1589,BLP5009,BLP1511,BN-LA579-H2, B1-28263 BN(J)K23P-6722,W-5504 CD BN 7-95636-2,8-23518-2,8-28263-2, (C)8-56508-2,(E)8-53230-2,(J)CJ28-5030, CJ28-5162,TOCJ-1511,TOCJ-5634,TOCJ-5824, TOCJ-6106,TOCJ-66032,(Sp)8-34712-2, 8-53016-2,Cema S21-57588,EMI-Jazz(E)8-55720-2
BN 396-0	Ask me now (alt.)-1	BN(J)BNJ61012,CD TOCJ-1604
BN 396-1	Ask me now -1	BN 1591,BLP5009,BLP1511,BN-LA579-H2 CD BN 7-95636-2,8-21381-2,8-23518-2, (J)CJ28-5162,TOCJ-1511,TOCJ-5634,TOCJ-5824, TOCJ-6106,TOCJ-66032
BN 397-2	Willow weep for me -2	BN 1591,45-1646,BLP5011,BLP1509, BN-LA579-H2 Swing(F)SW408;Vogue(E)V2161 CD BN(J)CJ28-5162,TOCJ-1509,TOCJ-5634, TOCJ-6106,TOCJ-66032

-1: as,vb out.
-2: as out.
All 9 titles issued on Mosaic MR4-101,CD BN 7-81511-2,8-30363-2.

29

WYNTON KELLY TRIO:
Wynton Kelly(p) Oscar Pettiford(b) Lee Abrams(dm).
(WOR Studios) NYC,July 25,1951

BN 398	I found a new baby	rejected
BN 399-1	Blue moon	BN 1581,BLP5025,(J)GXF-3151 CD BN(Eu)7-89910-2,(J)TOCJ-5187/88, TOCJ-6271/74,Cap(J)TOCJ-5229
BN 400-2	Fine and dandy -1	BN(J)LNJ70079
BN 401-0	I found a new baby -1	BN BLP5025,(J)GXF-3151
BN 402-1	Cherokee -1	BN 1579,BLP5025,(J)GXF-3151,W-5509 Lib(J)K22P6092/93
BN 403-1	Born to be blue	BN 1578,BLP5025,(J)GXF-3151 CD BN 7-96580-2,4-95698-2
BN 404-0	Where or when -3	BN 1578,(J)LNJ70079
BN 405-0	Moonglow	BN 1579 -
BN 405-1	Moonglow (alt.)	-
BN 406-0	If I should lose you	-
BN 407-0	Born to be blue(alt.)-2,3	-

-1: Franklin Skeete(b) replaces Pettiford.
-2: mislabeled "Foolin' myself" on BN(J)LNJ70079.
-3: recorded at a faster,inaccurate speed on BN(J)LNJ70079.
All titles,except BN 398,issued on BN(J)BNJ71001,CD BN 7-84456-2.
All titles from BLP5025 also issued on CD BN(J)TOCJ-9222.

WYNTON KELLY TRIO:
Wynton Kelly(p) Franklin Skeete(b) Lee Abrams(dm,cga-1).
(WOR Studios) NYC,August 1,1951

BN 408-0	Goodbye	BN 1581
BN 408-1	Goodbye	BN BLP5025,(J)GXF-3151,W-5509
BN 409-2	Foolin' myself	
BN 410-0	There will never be another you	BN BLP5025,(J)GXF-3151;CD BN(J)TOCJ-5873
BN 411-3	Do nothing till you hear from me	BN(J)LNJ70079
BN 412-1	Summertime -1	BN 1580,(J)LNJ70079
BN 413-0	Moonlight in Vermont -2	BN BLP5025,(J)GXF-3151 CD BN(Eu)5-23444-2,(J)CJ28-5178
BN 414-1	Crazy he calls me	BN 1580,BLP5025,(J)GXF-3151
BN 415-2	Opus caprice	BN(Du)1A158-83385/8

-2: Kelly plays celeste on the introduction.
All titles issued on BN(J)BNJ71001,CD BN 7-84456-2.
All titles from BLP5025 also issued on CD BN(J)TOCJ-9222.

SIDNEY BECHET & HIS HOT SIX:
Sidney De Paris(tp) Jimmy Archey(tb) Sidney Bechet(ss) Don Kirkpatrick(p) George "Pops" Foster(b) Mainzie Johnson(dm).
(WOR Studios) NYC,November 5,1951

BN 416-3 tk.3 Original Dixieland one-step BN BLP7020,BLP1207,(J)K23P-9285
Sunset(F)SLS50228
CD BN 8-35811-2,(J)CJ28-5161
BN 417-0 tk.4 Avalon BN BLP7020,BLP1207,(J)K23P-9285
CD BN 8-35811-2,(J)CJ28-5161
BN 418-1 tk.6 That's a plenty BN BLP7020,BLP1207,(J)K23P-9285
CD BN 8-35811-2
BN 419-0 tk.7 Blues my naughty sweetie gives to me
BN BEP401,BLP7020,BLP1207,(J)K23P-9285
CD BN 8-35811-2,(J)CJ28-5161,TOCJ-66040
BN 419-1 tk.9 Blues my naughty sweetie gives to me (alt.)
BN 420-0 tk.13 Ballin' the jack (alt.)
BN 420-1 tk.16 Ballin' the jack BN BLP7020,BLP1207,(J)K23P-9285
BN 421-0 tk.17 There'll be some changes made (alt.) CD BN 8-35811-2
BN 421-1 tk.19 There'll be some changes made BN BLP7020,BLP1202,(J)K23P-9285
CD BN(Eu)7-89385-2,(J)CJ28-5161

All 9 titles issued on Mosaic MR6-110,CD BN 5-30607-2,Mosaic MD4-110.
Note: This session was the first one recorded by Blue Note on tape.

MILT JACKSON QUINTET:
Lou Donaldson(as-1) Milt Jackson(vb) John Lewis(p) Percy Heath(b) Kenny Clarke(dm).
(WOR Studios) NYC,April 7,1952

BN 422-0 tk.1 Tahiti -1 BN 1592,BLP5011,BLP1509
Swing(F)SW407;Vogue(E)EPV1058
BN 423-1 tk.4 Lillie BN 1593,45-1646,BLP5011,BLP1509
Vogue(E)V2303,EPV1058;Swing(F)SW407
BN 423-2 tk.5 Lillie (alt.) BN BLP1509
BN 424-2 tk.8 Bags' groove -1 BN 1593,45-1645,BLP5011,BLP1001,
BLP1509,BLP2001,BST89903,BN-LA159-G2,
BST2-84429,BST2-92465
BN(Du)1A158-83385/8,(J)K18P-9124
Lib(F)LBS83442/3
Swing(F)SW427;Vogue(E)EPV1058
CD BN 7-92465-2,4-95698-2,(E)8-53230-2,
(J)CJ25-5181/84,CJ28-5030,CP32-5056,
TOCJ-5937
BN 425-2 tk.11 What's new? (alt.) BN(J)BNJ61012
BN 425-3 tk.12 What's new? BN 1592,45-1645,BLP5011,BLP1509
Swing(F)SW409;Vogue(E)EPV1058
BN 426-0 tk.14 Don't get around much anymore -1 BN 1594,(J)BNJ61012
BN 426-1 tk.15 Don't get around much anymore (alt.)-1
BN(J)BNJ61012
BN 427-0 tk.16 On the scene -1 BN 1594,BLP5011,BLP1509
Swing(F)SW409

All 9 titles issued on BN-LA590-H2,CD 7-81509-2.
All titles from BLP1509 also issued on CD BN(J)TOCJ-1509.
Note: BN 1594 was issued as by LOU DONALDSON QUINTET.

MILES DAVIS ALL STARS:
Miles Davis(tp) J.J.Johnson(tb) Jackie McLean(as) Gil Coggins(p) Oscar Pettiford(b) Kenny Clarke(dm).
(WOR Studios) NYC,May 9,1952

BN 428-1	tk.2	Dear old Stockholm	BN 1595,BEP204,BLP5013,BLP1501 BN(J)K18P-9124,K22P-6096/97,K16P-9031/32, W-5502;Lib(J)K22P-6074/75 Vogue(E)V2202;Swing(F)SW403 CD BN 7-98287-2,8-23515-2,(J)CJ25-5181/84, CJ28-5023,CJ28-5166,CJ28-5172,TOCJ-5632, TOCJ-5657,TOCJ-5658,TOCJ-5821,TOCJ-6102, TOCJ-6133,TOCJ-6271/74,TOCJ-66035, TOCP-7455/56,Cap(J)TOCJ-5191/92, Toshiba-EMI(J)TOCP-8581,Cema S21-57610, EMI-Jazz(E)4-99158-2
BN 429-2	tk.5	Chance it (alt.)	CD BN(J)TOCJ-5821
BN 429-3	tk.6	Chance it	BN 1596,BLP5013,BLP1501,CD 8-23515-2 Vog(E)EPV1075
BN 430-0	tk.7	Donna (alt.)	BN 45-1633,BLP1501 CD BN(J)TOCJ-5821
BN 430-1	tk.8	Donna	BN 1597,BLP5013,BLP1502,B1-92812,(E)BNX2 Vog(E)V2222,EPV1075;Swing(F)SW404 CD BN 7-92812-2,7-98287-2, EMI-Jazz(E)4-99158-2
BN 431-2	tk.12	Would'n you (alt.)	BN BLP1501;CD BN(J)TOCJ-5821
BN 431-3	tk.13	Would'n you	BN 1595,BEP204,BLP5013,BLP1502 Vog(E)V2222,EPV1075;Swing(F)SW404 CD BN 8-23515-2,(J)TOCJ-66035
BN 432-0	tk.14	Yesterdays (tb,as out)	BN 1596,BEP204,BLP5013,BLP1501,(J)W-5502 Vog(E)EPV1075 CD BN 7-98287-2,8-36633-2,(J)CJ28-5166, TOCJ-5300,TOCJ-5632,TOCJ-5658,TOCJ-6102, TOCJ-66035,(Sp)8-53016-2,Cema S21-57610, EMI Gold(E)5-21427-2,Toshiba-EMI(J)TOCJ-6228
BN 433-0	tk.15	How deep is the ocean (tb,as out)	BN BLP5013,BLP1501 Vogue(E)V2202;Swing(F)SW403 CD BN 7-99095-2,8-23515-2,8-36633-2, (J)CJ28-5166,TOCJ-5632,TOCJ-5658,TOCJ-6102, TOCJ-66035,Cema S21-57610, EMI-Jazz(E)4-99158-2

All titles issued on CD BN 7-81501-2,(J)TOCJ-5659/60.
All titles,except BN 429-2,also issued on United Artists UAS9952.
All titles from BLP1501/02 also issued on CD BN(J)CP32-5221/22.

THELONIOUS MONK SEXTET:
Kenny Dorham(tp) Lou Donaldson(as) Lucky Thompson(ts) Thelonious Monk(p) Nelson Boyd(b) Max Roach(dm).

(WOR Studios)		NYC,May 30,1952
BN 434-1 tk.2	Skippy	BN 1602,BLP1511,BN-LA579-H2 CD BN 7-95636-2,8-56399-2,(J)CJ28-5162, TOCJ-1511,TOCJ-5634,TOCJ-5824,TOCJ-6106, TOCJ-66032
BN 434-2 tk.3	Skippy(alt.)	BN(J)BNJ61011,CD TOCJ-1604
BN 435-1 tk.5	Hornin' in (alt.)	- -
BN 435-3 tk.7	Hornin' in	BN 1603,BLP1511,BN-LA579-H2 CD BN(J)CJ28-5162,TOCJ-1511,TOCJ-5634, TOCJ-5824,TOCJ-6106,TOCJ-66032
BN 436-0 tk.8	Sixteen	BN(J)BNJ61011,CD TOCJ-1604,TOCJ-5824
BN 436-1 tk.9	Sixteen	- CD BN 8-36736-2,TOCJ-1604
BN 437-0 tk.10	Carolina moon	BN 1603,BLP1511,BN-LA579-H2,(J)W-5504 CD BN 8-23518-2,(Eu)5-23444-2,(J)TOCJ-1511
BN 438-0 tk.11	Let's cool one	BN 1602,BLP1511,BN-LA579-H2,(J)W-5504 CD BN 8-23518-2,(J)TOCJ-1511,TOCJ-5634, TOCJ-66032
BN 439-0 tk.12	I'll follow you (tp,as,ts out)	BN(Du)1A158-83385/8,(J)BNJ61011 CD BN(J)TOCJ-1604

All titles also issued on Mosaic MR4-101,CD BN 7-81511-2,8-30363-2.

LOU DONALDSON QUARTET:
Lou Donaldson(as) Horace Silver(p) Gene Ramey(b) Art Taylor(dm).

(WOR Studios)		NYC,June 20,1952
BN 440-0 tk.1	Roccus (alt.)	
BN 440-1 tk.2	Roccus	BN 1598,BLP5021,BLP1537
BN 442-2 tk.7	Cheek to cheek (alt.)	
BN 443-0 tk.8	Lou's blues (alt.)	
BN 443-1 tk.9	Lou's blues	BN 1599,BLP5021,BLP1537 BN(J)K18P-9124;Lib(J)K22P-6131/32
BN 442-4 tk.11	Cheek to cheek	BN 1598,BLP5021,BLP1537 CD BN 7-99095-2,(Eu)7-89914-2,(J)TOCJ-5857
BN 441-2 tk.12	The things we did last Summer	BN 1599,BLP5021,(Du)1A158-83385/8 BN(J)BNJ61008(alb.BNJ61008/61010)

All 7 titles issued on CD BN 7-81537-2.
All titles from BLP1537 also issued on CD BN(J)TOCJ-1537.

VIC DICKENSON QUARTET:
Vic Dickenson(tb) Bill Doggett(org) John Collins(g) Jo Jones(dm).

(WOR Studios)		NYC,June 24,1952
BN 444-2 tk.3	Tenderly	BN 1600;CD BN(J)TOCJ-5716/17
BN 445-1 tk.5	I'm gettin' sentimental over you	BN 1601;CD Premier(E)CDJA 3
BN 446-2 tk.8	Lion's den (alt.)	
BN 446-3 tk.9	Lion's den	BN 1600
BN 447-2 tk.14	In a mellotone	BN 1601

All 5 titles were scheduled on BN LT-1055,which was not released,and then issued on Mosaic MR6-109, CD MD4-109.
All titles,except BN 446-2,also issued on CD BN(J)TOCJ-5231/38.
Note: On the original 78 rpm issues,master numbers were shown as BN 434 to 437 instead of 444-447.BN 447-2 was incorrectly listed as -3,which does not exist.

33

HORACE SILVER TRIO:
Horace Silver(p) Gene Ramey(b) Art Blakey(dm).
(WOR Studios) NYC,October 9,1952

BN 448	tk.1	Horace-scope	BN BLP5018,BLP1520/BST81520,BN-LA474-H2 BN(J)LNJ70108,CD TOCJ-1520
BN 449-1	tk.5	Safari	BN 1608,BLP5018,BLP1001,BLP1520/BST81520, BLP2001,BN-LA474-H2,(J)LNJ70108 Liberty(J)K22P-6092/93;Vogue(E)V2307 CD BN 4-95576-2,4-95698-2,(J)TOCJ-1520
BN 450-6	tk.15	Thou swell	BN 1608,BLP5018,BN-LA474-H2 BN(J)LNJ70108,BNJ61005
BN 451		Yeah	rejected

First three titles also issued on CD BN 7-81520-2.
Note: Safari was erroneously listed on jacket of CDs BN 8-33208-2/HMV Jazz 5-20878-2,which actually used the quintet version of Jan. 13,1958 (see page 76).

Horace Silver(p) Curly Russell(b) Art Blakey(dm).
(WOR Studios) NYC,October 20,1952

BN 452-1	tk.2	Quicksilver	BN BLP1520/BST81520,(J)BNJ61005
BN 453-2	tk.6	Ecaroh	- (J)NP-2017,W-5509 Vogue(E)V2307
BN 454-0	tk.7	Yeah	BN BLP1520/BST81520 CD BN 4-95576-2
BN 455-3	tk.11	Knowledge box	BN(J)BNJ61005
BN 456-3	tk.15	Prelude to a kiss	BN BLP1520/BST81520,CD 5-20809-2

All titles also issued on BN BLP5018,BN-LA474-H2,(J)LNJ70108,CD BN 7-81520-2.
All titles from BLP1520 also issued on CD BN(J)TOCJ-1520.

LOU DONALDSON QUINTET:
Blue Mitchell(tp) Lou Donaldson(as) Horace Silver(p) Percy Heath(b) Art Blakey(dm).
(WOR Studios) NYC,November 19,1952

BN 457-0	tk.1	Sweet juice (tp out)	BN 1609
BN 459-1	tk.8	Down home	BN 1610
BN 460-1	tk.10	The best things in life	BN 1609
BN 458-5	tk.12	If I love again	BN 1610

All titles also issued on BN BLP5021,BLP1537,CD 7-81537-2,(J)TOCJ-1537.

Note:Master numbers 461-464 were used for a purchased session (see details in part 4).

GIL MELLE QUINTET:
Eddie Bert(tb) Gil Melle(ts) Tal Farlow(g) Clyde Lombardi(b) Joe Morello(dm).
Hackensack,N.J.,January 31,1953

BN 465-4	tk.5	Cyclotron
BN 466-2	tk.8	October
BN 467-0	tk.10	Under Capricorn
BN 468-0	tk.13	Venus

All titles issued on BN BEP203,BLP5020,(J)K18P-9275,CD BN 4-95718-2.

34

KENNY DREW TRIO:
Kenny Drew(p) Curly Russell(b) Art Blakey(dm).
Hackensack,N.J.,April 16,1953

BN 469-3 tk.4	Lover come back to me	BN BLP5023,(J)GXF-3151 Lib(J)K22P-6092/93
BN 470-1 tk.6	Yesterdays (alt.)	
BN 470-2 tk.7	Yesterdays	BN BLP5023,(J)GXF-3151,W-5509 CD BN(J)TOCJ-5873
BN 471-0 tk.8	Everything happens to me	BN BLP5023,(J)GXF-3151 CD BN(J)TOCJ-5300,TOCJ-6271/74
BN 472-1 tk.11	It might as well be Spring	BN BLP5023,(J)GXF-3151 CD BN(J)TOCJ-5187/88
BN 473-2 tk.14	Be my love	BN BLP5023,(J)GXF-3151;CD Cap(J)TOCJ-5259
BN 474-1 tk.16	Drew's blues	- -
BN 475-0 tk.17	Gloria	- -
BN 476-1 tk.19	Stella by starlight	- - CD BN(J)CJ28-5178,Cap(J)CP28-5864, TOCJ-5674/75
BN 471-2 tk.20	Everything happens to me (alt.)	

All 10 titles issued on BN(J)BNJ71002,CD BN 4-95747-2,(J)CJ28-5124,TOCJ-9221.
Note: Takes 6 & 20 were selected for 10" 78 rpm release,but never issued as such.

MILES DAVIS ALL STARS:
Miles Davis(tp) J.J.Johnson(tb) Jimmy Heath(ts) Gil Coggins(p) Percy Heath(b) Art Blakey(dm).
(WOR Studios) NYC,April 20,1953

BN 477-1 tk.2	Kelo (alt.)	CD BN(J)TOCJ-5821
BN 477-2 tk.3	Kelo	BN 1620,BLP5022,BLP1501 CD BN 8-23515-2,(J)CJ28-5166,TOCJ-5632, TOCJ-6102,TOCJ-66035
BN 478-1 tk.5	Enigma (alt.)	CD BN(J)TOCJ-5821
BN 478-2 tk.6	Enigma	BN 1618,BLP5022,BLP1501 CD BN 7-98287-2,8-36633-2,(J)CJ28-5166, TOCJ-5632,TOCJ-5658,TOCJ-6102,TOCJ-66035
BN 479-0 tk.7	Ray's idea (alt.)	BN BLP1502;CD BN(J)TOCJ-5821
BN 479-2 tk.9	Ray's idea	BN 1619,BLP5022,BLP1501 CD BN 8-23515-2
BN 480-0 tk.10	Tempus fugit	BN 1618,45-1649,BLP5022,BLP1001,BLP1501, BLP2001,BST2-84429,BST2-92465 BN(Du)1A158-83385/8,(In)JAZ 2,(J)W-5504 Lib.(J)K22P-6074/75 CD BN 7-92465-2,7-98287-2,4-95698-2, (E)8-57742-2,(J)CP32-5448,CJ28-5166, CP32-5056,TOCJ-5632,TOCJ-5657,TOCJ-66035
BN 480-1 tk.11	Tempus fugit (alt.)	BN BLP1502;CD BN(J)TOCJ-5821
BN 481-2 tk.14	C.T.A.(alt.)	BN BLP1501 -
BN 481-3 tk.15	C.T.A.	BN 1620,BLP5022,BLP1501,(Du)1A158-83385/8 CD BN 7-98287-2,(C)8-56508-2,(E)8-53230-2, (J)TOCJ-5632,TOCJ-6102,TOCJ-66035
BN 482-0 tk.16	I waited for you (tb,ts out)	BN 1619,BLP5022,BLP1502 CD BN 7-89032-2,8-36633-2,(J)CJ28-5166, TOCJ-5632,TOCJ-5658,TOCJ-5935,TOCJ-6102, TOCJ-6187,TOCJ-66035,TOCJ-66054, Cema S21-57610,EMI-Jazz(E)4-99158-2

All titles and takes shown issued on CD BN 7-81502-2,(J)TOCJ-5659/60.
All titles,except BN 477-1 & BN 478-1,also issued on United Artists UAS9952.
All titles from BLP1501/02 also issued on CD BN(J)CP32-5221/22.

35

JOHN COLLINS:
John Collins(g) Milt Hinton(b) Kenny Clarke(dm).

Hackensack,N.J.,May 9,1953

tk.3	T'ain't nobody's business	unissued
tk.9	Lover man	-
tk.12	untitled Collins original	-
tk.14	You don't know what love is	-
tk.18	Midnight	-
tk.21	My funny Valentine	-
tk.23	Lover come back to me	-
tk.24	Out of nowhere	-

Note: No tape of this session has survived.

HOWARD McGHEE SEXTET:
Howard McGhee(tp) Gigi Gryce(as,fl-1) Horace Silver(p) Tal Farlow(g) Percy Heath(b) Walter Bolden(dm).
(WOR Studios) NYC,May 20,1953

BN 483-2	tk.3	Shabozz	BN BLP5024
BN 484-2	tk.6	Tranquility	-
BN 485-1	tk.8	Futurity	-
BN 486-0	tk.9	Jarm (fast version)-1	
BN 486-1	tk.10	Jarm -1	BN BLP5024
BN 487-1	tk.12	Ittapanna	-
BN 488-2	tk.15	Goodbye (Gryce out)	-

All titles from BLP5024 also issued on BN(F)BNP25104,(J)K18P-9274.
All titles issued on CD BN 4-95748-2.

LOU DONALDSON-CLIFFORD BROWN QUINTET:
Clifford Brown(tp) Lou Donaldson(as) Elmo Hope(p) Percy Heath(b) Philly Joe Jones(dm).
(WOR Studios) NYC,June 9,1953

BN 489-1	tk.2	Bellarosa	BN 1623,BLP5030,BN-LA267-G,BST84428 CD BN(J)CP32-5244,TOCJ-1605
BN 490-1	tk.4	Carving the rock (alt.1)	BN BST84428;CD BN(J)TOCJ-1605
BN 490-3	tk.6	Carvin' the rock	BN 1624,BLP5030,BLP1526 BN(Du)1A158-83385/8 CD BN 4-95698-2,(J)CP32-5244
BN 491-0	tk.7	Cookin' (alt.)	BN BST84428,CD BN(J)TOCJ-1605
BN 491-1	tk.8	Cookin'	BN 1623,BLP5030,BLP1526,(Du)1A158-83385/8 CD BN(J)CP32-5244
BN 492-0	tk.9	Brownie speaks	BN 1622,45-1647,BLP5030,BLP1526, BN-LA267-G,BST2-84433, BN(J)W-5504 CD BN 8-23373-2,(J)CP32-5244
BN 493-0	tk.10	De-dah	BN 1624,BLP5030,BLP1526,BN-LA267-G BN(J)W-5504,CD CP32-5244
BN 494-0	tk.11	You go to my head	BN 1622,45-1647,BLP5030,BLP1526 CD BN 8-23373-2,(J)CP32-5244
BN 490-5	tk.14	Carving the rock (alt.2)	BN BST84428;CD BN(J)TOCJ-1605

All titles also issued on Mosaic MR5-104,CD BN 7-81526-2,8-34195-2.
All titles from BLP1526 also issued on CD BN(J)TOCJ-1526.

36

ELMO HOPE TRIO:
Elmo Hope(p) Percy Heath(b) Philly Joe Jones(dm).

Hackensack,N.J.,June 18,1953

BN 495-1	tk.2	Happy hour	BN BLP5029
BN 496-2	tk.5	Freffie	- (Du)1A158-83385/8
BN 497-2	tk.8	Carvin' the rock	-
BN 498-0	tk.9	Hot sauce	- CD BN(J)TOCJ-5187/88,
BN 499-0	tk.10	Mo is on	- CD 8-57742-2
BN 499-1	tk.11	Mo is on(alt.)	
BN 500-1	tk.13	Stars over Marrakesh	BN BLP5029
BN 501-1	tk.19	I remember you	- (J)W-5509
	tk.20	It's a lovely day today	BN(Du)1A158-83385/8 CD BN 7-99095-2,(J)TOCJ-5855
BN 502-2	tk.23	Sweet and lovely	BN BLP5029

All titles from BLP5029 also issued on BN(J)K18P-9271,CD TOCJ-9223.
All titles and takes shown issued on CD BN 7-84438-2.

J.J.JOHNSON SEXTET:
Clifford Brown(tp) J.J.Johnson(tb)Jimmy Heath(ts-1,bs-2) John Lewis(p) Percy Heath(b) Kenny Clarke (dm).

(WOR Studios) NYC,June 22,1953

BN 503-2	tk.3	Capri (alt.)-1	BN BLP1506
BN 503-3	tk.4	Capri -1,3	BN 1621,BLP5028,BLP1505
BN 504-0	tk.5	Lover man -1	BN BLP5028,BLP1505 CD BN 4-97154-2,(C)8-56508-2
BN 505-0	tk.6	Turnpike -1,2	BN 1621,BLP5028,BLP1505
BN 505-2	tk.8	Turnpike (alt.)-1,2	BN BLP1506
BN 506-2	tk.11	Sketch one -2	BN BLP5028,BLP1505
BN 507-0	tk.12	It could happen to you (tp,sax out)	- BLP1506
BN 508-0	tk.14	Get happy -1	BN BLP5028,BLP1001,BLP1505,BLP2001, BST89903,BN-LA159-G2 CD BN 8-23373-2,4-95698-2,(J)TOCJ-6271/74, Cema GSC Music 15131
BN 508-1	tk.15)	Get happy (alt.)-1	BN-LA267-G,BST84428,(Du)1A158-83385/8 CD BN(J)TOCJ-1605

-3: Master number was incorrectly listed as BN 503-0 on BN 1621.
All titles and takes shown issued on Mosaic MR5-104,CD BN 7-81505-2,8-34195-2.
All titles from BLP1505/06 also issued on CD BN(J)TOCJ-1505/06.

37

BUD POWELL TRIO:
Bud Powell(p) George Duvivier(b) Art Taylor(dm).
(WOR Studios) NYC,August 14,1953

BN 510-6 tk.8 Autumn in New York BN BLP5041,BLP1504,(J)K23P-6723
CD BN 8-54906-2,(J)CJ28-5032,TOCJ-5640,
TOCJ-5822,TOCJ-6105,TOCJ-66033,TOCP-50060,
Cap(J)CP28-5864
BN 509-1 tk.9 Reets and I BN BLP5041,BLP1504
CD BN 7-81203-2,7-93204-2,(J)CJ28-5032,
TOCJ-5640,TOCJ-5822,TOCJ-66033
BN 509-2 tk.10 Reets and I (alt.) BN BST84430,(J)BNJ61008(alb.61008/10)
BN 511-2 tk.17 Sure thing BN 1629,BLP5041,BLP1504
BN 512-0 tk.18 Collard greens and black-eyed peas (alt.)
BN BST84430,(J)BNJ61008(alb.61008/10)
BN 512-2 tk.20 Collard greens and black-eyed peas
BN 1629,BLP5041,BLP1504,BST2-84433,
B1-93204
CD BN 7-81203-2,7-93204-2,8-54906-2,
(C)8-56508-2,(Eu)7-89915-2,(J)TOCJ-5822
BN 513-0 tk.21 Polka dots and moonbeams BN BLP5041,BLP1504
CD BN(J)TOCP-50060
BN 514-1 tk.23 I want to be happy BN 1628,BLP5041,BLP1504,(J)FCPA 6203
CD BN 8-54906-2,(J)TOCP-50060
BN 515-1 tk.25 Audrey BN BLP5041,BLP1504
CD BN(J)TOCJ-5822,TOCJ-66033
BN 516-0 tk.27 The glass enclosure BN 1628,BLP5041,BLP1504,BST2-92465,
B1-92812,B1-93204,(E)BNX2
CD BN 7-81203-2,7-92465-2,7-92812-2,
7-93204-2,4-95698-2,(J)CJ28-5032,TOCJ-5640,
TOCJ-5822,TOCJ-66033
BN 517-0 I've got you under my skin rejected

All titles,except BN 517-0,issued on Mosaic MR5-116,CD BN CD 7-81504-2,8-30083-2.
All titles from BLP1504 also issued on CD BN(J)TOCJ-1504.

SIDNEY BECHET BLUE NOTE JAZZMEN:
Jonah Jones(tp) Jimmy Archey(tb) Sidney Bechet(ss) Buddy Weed(p) Walter Page(b) Johnny Blowers(dm).
(Audio Video Studios) NYC,August 25,1953

BN 518-3 tk.4 All of me BN BLP7026,BLP1207,(J)K23P-9285
CD BN 8-28891-2,(J)CJ28-5161,TOCJ-66040
BN 519-1 tk.6 I'm a ding dong Daddy (from Dumas)
(see note) BN BLP7026,BLP1207,(J)K23P-9285
BN 520-0 tk.7 Black and blue (alt.)
BN 520-1 tk.8 Black and blue BN BLP7026,BLP1207,(J)K23P-9285
CD BN 8-28891-2,(J)CJ28-5161,TOCJ-66040
BN 521-1 tk.13 Shine BN BLP7026,(J)K23P-9285
BN 522-0 tk.17 Rose of the Rio Grande (alt.) CD BN 8-28891-2
BN 522-2 tk.19 Rose of the Rio Grande BN BLP7026,BLP1207,(J)K23P-9285
CD BN(J)CJ28-5161
BN 523-0 tk.20 Sweet Georgia Brown BN BLP7026,BLP1207,(J)K23P-9285
CD BN(J)CJ28-5161

All 8 titles issued on Mosaic MR6-110,CD BN 5-30607-2,Mosaic MD4-110.
Note: BN 519 title is listed as shown in Blue Note files,and as used on CD 5-30607-2. All other issues used abridged title "Ding dong Daddy".

38

CLIFFORD BROWN SEXTET:
Clifford Brown(tp) Gigi Gryce(fl-1,as) Charlie Rouse(ts) John Lewis(p) Percy Heath(b) Art Blakey(dm).
(Audio Video Studios) NYC,August 28,1953

BN 524-0	tk.1	Wail bait (alt.)	BN BST84428;CD BN(J)TOCJ-1605
BN 524-2	tk.3	Wail bait	BN BLP5032,BLP1526,BN-LA267-G BN(Du)1A158-83385/8 CD BN(J)CP32-5244
BN 525-1	tk.9	Hymn of the Orient	BN 45-1648,BLP5032,BLP1526,BN-LA267-G BN(Du)1A158-83385/8 CD BN 8-23373-2,(F)8-54185-2,(J)CP32-5244, TOCJ-5750,TOCJ-6133,TOCJ-6271/74
BN 526-1	tk.13	Brownie eyes -1	BN BLP5032,BN-LA267-G,BST84428 CD BN 8-23373-2,(J)CP32-5244
BN 527-0	tk.18	Cherokee (alt.)	BN BST84428;CD BN(J)TOCJ-1605
BN 527-1	tk.21	Cherokee	BN BLP5032,BLP1526,BST89903,BN-LA159-G2, BN-LA267-G,BST2-84429 BN(Du)1A158-83385/8,(J)K18P-9124, K16P-9031/32,K22P-6096/97,W-5504 CD BN 8-23373-2,(E)8-57742-2, (J)CJ25-5181/84,CP32-5056,CP32-5244
BN 528-0	tk.23	Easy living -1	BN 45-1648,BLP5032,BLP1001,BLP1526, BLP2001,BN-LA267-G,BST2-92465,(J)W-5504 CD BN 7-92465-2,7-96098-2,8-23373-2, 4-95698-2,(J)CJ28-5179,CP32-5244,TOCJ-5935, TOCJ-66054,TOCP-7455/56
BN 529-0	tk.24	Minor mood	BN BLP5032,BLP1526,CD BN(J)CP32-5244
BN 525-3	tk.26	Hymn of the Orient (alt.)	BN BST84428;CD BN(J)TOCJ-1605

All 9 titles also issued on Mosaic MR5-104,CD BN 7-81526-2,8-34195-2.
All titles from BLP1526 also issued on CD BN(J)TOCJ-1526.

GIL MELLE QUINTET:
Urbie Green(tb) Gil Melle(ts-1,bs-2) Tal Farlow(g) Clyde Lombardi(b) Joe Morello(dm).
Hackensack,N.J.,October 25,1953

BN 526-2	tk.3	Lover man -1	Vogue(E)EPV1116
BN 528-2	tk.11	Spellbound -1	Vogue(E)V2347
BN 529-1	tk.14	Transition -1	
BN 530-1	tk.16	A lion lives here -2	
BN 531-2	tk.19	Timepiece -2	Vogue(E)EPV1116 CD BN 4-95698-2
BN 527-5	tk.23	Gingersnaps -1	Vogue(E)V2347,EPV1116
BN 532-0	tk.27	The nearness of you (tb out) -2	

All titles,except last,issued on BN BLP5033,(J)K18P-9275.
All titles issued on CD BN 4-95718-2.

39

HORACE SILVER TRIO/ART BLAKEY-SABU:
Horace Silver(p) Percy Heath(b) Art Blakey(dm) Sabu Martinez-1(bgo,cga).
(WOR Studios) NYC,November 23,1953

BN 533-0	tk.1	Message from Kenya (p,b out)-1	BN 1626,45-1626,BLP1001,BLP2001,B1-80701 CD BN 4-94031-2,4-95698-2,(J)TOCJ-5274/76
BN 534-2	tk.6	Opus de funk	BN 1625,BN-LA402-H2,BN-LA474-H2,B1-91143 BN(J)NP2017,K18P-9124,W-5509 Lib(J)K22P6092/93 CD BN 7-91143-2,7-96580-2,4-95576-2, (J)CJ25-5181/84,CJ28-5030,CJ28-5033, TOCJ-5187/88,TOCJ-5274/76,TOCJ-5827, TOCJ-5873,TOCJ-66034,Cema GSC Music 15131
BN 535-1	tk.9	Day in,day out	BN 1625,BN-LA474-H2
BN 536-0	tk.11	Nothing but the soul (p,b out)	BN 1626,45-1626
BN 537-1	tk.14	I remember you	BN BN-LA474-H2
BN 538-0	tk.15	Silverware	-
BN 539-0	tk.18	How about you	-
BN 540-0	tk.21	Buhaina	- (J)BNJ61005

All titles,except last,issued on BN BLP1520/BST81520,CD BN(J)TOCJ-1520.
All titles also issued on BN BLP5034,(J)LNJ70108,CD BN 7-81520-2.

SAL SALVADOR QUINTET:
Frank Socolow(ts) John Williams(p) Sal Salvador(g) Kenny O'Brien(b) Jimmy Campbell(dm).
Hackensack,N.J.,December 24,1953

BN 536-2	(tk.3)	Gone with the wind	BN(J)W-5511;Lib(J)K22P-6094/95
BN 537-2	(tk.3)	Too marvelous for words	
BN 538-0	(tk.1)	This can't be love	
BN 539-1	(tk.2)	After you've gone	
BN 540-1	(tk.2)	My old flame (ts out)	
BN 541-3	(tk.4)	Get happy (ts out)	

All titles issued on BN BLP5035,(J)GXF-3171,CD BN 4-96548-2,(J)CJ28-5127,TOCJ-9224.
Note: On this session,take numbers shown in parentheses do not use the BN system and one sequence was used for each title.

URBIE GREEN SEPTET:
Doug Mettome(tp,bar horn) Urbie Green(tb) John Murtaugh(ts) Sam Staff(bs) Jimmy Lyon(p) Danny Martucci(b) Jimmy Campbell(dm).
Hackensack,N.J.,December 27,1953

BN 542-2	(tk.3)	Johnbo mambo	
BN 543-0	(tk.1)	Skylark	BN 1627
BN 544-2	(tk.3)	Incubator	
BN 545-2	(tk.3)	Dansero	BN 1627
BN 546-2	(tk.6)	Stairway to the stars	
BN 547-2	(tk.3)	La salle	

All titles issued on BN BLP5036.
Note: On this session,a take sequence was used for each title.

40

ART BLAKEY QUINTET-A NIGHT AT BIRDLAND:
Clifford Brown(tp) Lou Donaldson(as) Horace Silver(p) Curly Russell(b) Art Blakey(dm) Pee Wee Marquette (m.c.).

	(Birdland Club)	NYC,February 21,1954
Set #1:		
	Pee Wee Marquette's intro	BN BLP1521,B1-28263,CD 7-28263-2
tk.1	Wee dot (alt.)	BN-LA473-J2,(J)BNJ61002;Mosaic MR5-104 CD BN 7-46519-2,8-34195-2,(J)TOCJ-1602
tk.2	Now's the time	BN 45-1678,BLP5039,BLP1522,(In)JAZ 1, (J)NR8839;Mosaic MR5-104 CD BN 7-46520-2,8-34195-2
tk.3	Quicksilver	rejected
Set #2:		
tk.4	Confirmation	BN BLP5039,BLP1522,(J)NR8839,K23P-6724 CD BN 7-46520-2
tk.5	Once in a while (as out)	BN 45-1656,BLP5037,BLP1521,(J)NR8838 CD BN 7-46519-2,8-23373-2
tk.6	Mayreh	BN BLP5038,BLP1521,(J)NR8838 CD BN 7-46519-2

All titles also issued on Mosaic MR5-104,CD BN 8-34195-2.
BLP1521/22 were reissued as BST81521/22,and also issued as CD BN(J)TOCJ-1521/22.

Set #3:		
tk.7	Our delight	rejected
tk.8	If I had you (tp out)	BN 45-1657,BLP5039,BLP1522,(J)NR8839, K18P-9124;Mosaic MR5-104 CD BN 7-46520-2,8-34195-2
tk.9	Split kick	BN BLP5037,BLP1521,(J)NR8838,W-5505 Mosaic MR5-104 CD BN 7-46519-2,8-34195-2,(J)TOCJ-5274/76, TOCJ-5823,TOCJ-66031
tk.10	Lou's blues	BN(J)BNJ61002;Mosaic MR5-104 CD BN 7-46520-2,8-34195-2,(J)TOCJ-1602

BLP1521/22 were reissued as BST81521/22,and also issued as CD BN(J)TOCJ-1521/22.

Set #4:		
tk.11	Wee dot	rejected
tk.12	A night in Tunisia	BN BLP5038,BLP1521,(J)NR8838,W-5505, BNJ71106;Mosaic MR5-104 CD BN 7-46519-2,7-89032-2,8-23373-2, 8-34195-2,(J)CJ25-5181/84,TOCJ-5750, TOCJ-5758,Toshiba-EMI(J)TOCJ-6098/99
tk.13	Quicksilver (alt.)	BN BLP1522,(J)NR8839;Mosaic MR5-104 CD BN 7-46520-2,8-34195-2
tk.14	Confirmation	rejected

BLP1521/22 were reissued as BST81521/22,and also issued as CD BN(J)TOCJ-1521/22.

41

ART BLAKEY QUINTET-A NIGHT AT BIRDLAND:
Clifford Brown(tp) Lou Donaldson(as) Horace Silver(p) Curly Russell(b) Art Blakey(dm) Pee Wee Marquette (m.c.).

	(Birdland Club)	NYC,February 21,1954
Set #5:		
tk.15	Blues (Improvisation)	BN-LA473-J2,(J)NR8838,BNJ61002 CD BN 7-46519-2,(J)TOCJ-1602
tk.16	The way you look tonight	BN-LA473-J2,(J)NR8839,BNJ61002 CD BN 7-46520-2,(J)TOCJ-1602
tk.17	Wee dot	BN 45-1657,BLP5038,BLP1522,(J)NR8839 CD BN 7-46520-2,7-97190-2,8-23373-2, 8-54899-2,(J)TOCJ-5274/76
tk.18	Quicksilver	BN 45-1656,BLP5037,BLP1521,(J)NR8838 CD BN 7-46519-2,7-97190-2,4-95698-2, Cap(J)TOCJ-5191/92
	Lullaby of Birdland (Finale)	BN BLP5039,BLP1522,(J)NR8839 CD BN 7-46520-2

All titles also issued on Mosaic MR5-104,CD BN 8-34195-2.
BLP1521/22 were reissued as BST81521/22,and also issued as CD BN(J)TOCJ-1521/22.

MILES DAVIS QUARTET:
Miles Davis(tp) Horace Silver(p) Percy Heath(b) Art Blakey(dm).
Hackensack,N.J.,March 6,1954

BN 548-3	tk.4	Take off	CD BN(J)TOCJ-6102
BN 549-0	tk.6	Lazy Susan	BN 45-1649,(J)W-5504
BN 550-0	tk.8	The leap	BN 45-1650;CD BN(J)TOCJ-6102
BN 551-0	tk.9	Well you needn't	BN 45-1633,(J)W-5504 CD BN 7-98287-2,8-23515-2,(J)CJ28-5166, TOCJ-6102,TOCJ-66035
BN 552-0	tk.10	Weirdo	BN 45-1650,(Du)1A158-83385/8,(J)W-5504 CD BN 7-98287-2,8-36633-2,8-56399-2, (J)TOCJ-5658,TOCJ-6102,TOCJ-66035, TOCJ-66063
BN 553-1	tk.12	It never entered my mind	BN BST89903,BN-LA159-G2 Lib(J)K22P-6074/75 CD BN 7-98287-2,8-35282-2,8-36633-2,5-24271-2 BN(C)8-56508-2,(E)8-53229-2,(J)CJ28-5166, CJ28-5179,TOCJ-5658,TOCJ-5821,TOCJ-6102, TOCJ-66035,Cema S21-57610, EMI-Jazz(E)4-99158-2

All titles issued on BN BLP5040,BLP1502,United Artists UAS9952,CD BN 7-81501-2, (J)CP32-5222, TOCJ-5659/60.
All titles,except BN 549-0,also issued on CD BN(J)TOCJ-5632.

TAL FARLOW QUARTET:
Tal Farlow,Don Arnone(g) Clyde Lombardi(b) Joe Morello(dm).
Hackensack,N.J.,April 11,1954

BN 554-3	tk.4	Tina	
BN 555-1	tk.6	Splash	
BN 556-1	tk.8	Rock' n' rye	
BN 557-2	tk.12	Lover	CD BN 7-96581-2,(J)TOCJ-6271/74, HMV Jazz(E)5-20884-2,Toshiba-EMI(J)TOCJ-6228
BN 558-2	tk.15	All through the night	BN(J)W-5511
BN 559-1	tk.17	Flamingo	Lib(J)K22P-6094/95

All titles issued on BN BLP5042,(F)BNP25104,(J)GXF-3171,CD BN 4-95748-2,(J)CJ28-5127, TOCJ-9225.

42

FRANK FOSTER - HERE COMES FRANK FOSTER:
Benny Powell(tb) Frank Foster(ts) Gildo Mahones(p) Percy Heath(b) Kenny Clarke(dm).
Hackensack,N.J.,May 5,1954

BN 560-2	tk.3	Little Red	BN BLP5043
BN 561-4	tk.8	Gracias	-
BN 562-0	tk.9	How I spent the night	-
BN 562-1	tk.10	How I spent the night (alt.)	
BN 563-1	tk.12	Blues for Benny	BN BLP5043
BN 564-0	tk.13	The heat's on	-
BN 565-0	tk.14	Out of nowhere	-

All titles issued on CD BN 4-95750-2.

ELMO HOPE QUINTET:
Freeman Lee(tp) Frank Foster(ts) Elmo Hope(p) Percy Heath(b) Art Blakey(dm).
Hackensack,N.J.,May 9,1954

BN 566-2	tk.3	Crazy	BN BLP5044;CD BN(J)TOCJ-5710,TOCJ-5857
BN 566-3	tk.4	Crazy (alt.)	BN(Du)1A158-83385/8;CD BN 8-56399-2
BN 567-3	tk.8	Later for you	BN BLP5044
BN 568-1	tk.10	Abdullah	-
BN 569-1	tk.12	Chips	-
BN 570-2	tk.15	Maybe so	-
BN 571-2	tk.18	Low tide	-

All titles from BLP5044 also issued on BN(J)K18P-9271,TOCJ-9226.
All 7 titles issued on CD BN 7-84438-2,(J)CJ28-5125.

GEORGE WALLINGTON AND HIS BAND - SHOWCASE:
Dave Burns(tp) Jimmy Cleveland(tb) Frank Foster(ts) Danny Bank(bs,fl) George Wallington(p) Oscar Pettiford(b) Kenny Clarke(dm) Quincy Jones(arr).
(Audio Video Studios) NYC,May 12,1954

BN 572-3	tk.4	Summertime	BN BLP5045,(J)K18P-9276
BN 572-4	tk.5	Summertime (alt.)	
BN 573-2	tk.8	Festival	BN BLP5045,(J)K18P-9276
BN 573-3	tk.9	Festival(alt.)	BN B6503
BN 574-2	tk.12	Christina	BN BLP5045,(J)K18P-9276
BN 575-0	tk.13	Frankie and Johnnie	- B6503,(J)K18P-9276
BN 575-1	tk.14	Frankie and Johnnie (alt.)	
BN 576-1	tk.16	Baby Grand	BN BLP5045,B6503,(J)K18P-9276
BN 577-0	tk.19	Bumpkins	BN BLP5045,(J)K18P-9276
BN 577-1	tk.20	Bumpkins (alt.)	BN B6503

All titles issued on BN(J)BNJ71003,CD BN 4-95750-2,(J)CJ28-5126.

Note: BN 577 was the last number used in this master series.

43

JULIUS WATKINS SEXTET:
Julius Watkins(frh) Frank Foster(ts) George Butcher(p) Perry Lopez(g) Oscar Pettiford(b) Kenny Clarke (dm).

Hackensack,N.J.,August 8,1954

tk.3	Linda Delia	BN 45-1658
tk.6	Perpetuation	
tk.7	I have known (p out)	BN 45-1658
tk.8	Leete	

All titles issued on BN BLP5053,(J)K18P-9273,CD BN 4-95749-2.

LOU DONALDSON SEXTET:
Kenny Dorham(tp) Matthew Gee(tb) Lou Donaldson(as) Elmo Hope(p) Percy Heath(b) Art Blakey(dm).

Hackensack,N.J.,August 22,1954

tk.3	Caracas	BN BLP1537;CD BN(J)TOCJ-5964
tk.4	The stroller	-
tk.6	Mo's bluff	-
tk.10	After you've gone	BN(J)BNJ61008(alb.BNJ61008/010)

All titles also issued on BN BLP5055,CD 7-81537-2.
First three titles also issued on CD BN(J)TOCJ-1537.

GIL MELLE QUARTET:
Gil Melle(bs) Lou Mecca(g) Bill Phillips(b) Vinnie Thomas(dm).

Hackensack,N.J.,September 5,1954

tk.4	Lullaby of Birdland	
tk.8	Ballad for guitar	
tk.10	Metropolitan-1	
tk.18	Newport news	CD BN(Eu)5-23444-2
tk.19	Quadrille for moderns	
tk.20	Summertime	

-1:recorded as "South of Heidelberg".
All titles issued on BN BLP5054,CD 4-95718-2.

J.J.JOHNSON QUINTET - THE EMINENT JAY JAY JOHNSON:
J.J.Johnson(tb) Wynton Kelly(p) Charlie Mingus(b) Kenny Clarke(dm) Sabu Martinez(cga).

Hackensack,N.J.,September 24,1954

tk.2	Too marvelous for words	BN BLP1505
tk.4	Jay	BN 45-1651,BLP1505
tk.5	Old devil moon	- - CD 4-97156-2
		BN(E)BNSLP-4,(J)K18P-9124
tk.7	It's you or no one (cga out)	BN BLP1505
tk.10	Time after time (cga out)	BN BLP1506;CD BN(J)TOCJ-1506
tk.11	Coffee pot	BN BLP1505,(J)W-5504

All titles also issued on BN BLP5057,CD 7-81506-2.
All titles,except tk.10,also issued on CD BN(J)TOCJ-1505.
Note: On initial pressings of 7-81506-2,these titles appeared in the sequence of the original LP rather than in recording order as stated on the CD credits.

HORACE SILVER QUINTET:
Kenny Dorham(tp) Hank Mobley(ts) Horace Silver(p) Doug Watkins(b) Art Blakey(dm).
Hackensack,N.J.,November 13,1954

tk.3	Room 608	BN 45-1631,CD 7-91143-2,(J)CJ25-5181/84
tk.6	Creepin' in	-
tk.8	Doodlin'	BN 45-1630,BST84325,B1-91143 CD BN 7-91143-2,7-97190-2,4-95576-2, (J)TOCJ-5274/76,TOCJ-5827,TOCJ-6271/74, Cema S21-57589,EMI-Jazz(E)4-93466-2, EMI(E)5-21426-2
tk.10	Stop time	BN(Du)1A158-83385/8,(J)FCPA 6206 New World 271 CD BN 4-95981-2

All titles issued on BN BLP5058,BLP1518/BST81518,CD 7-46140-2.

LEONARD FEATHER PRESENTS:BEST OF THE WEST:
Harry Edison(tp) Bob Enevoldsen(vtb-1,ts-2) Herb Geller(as) Lorraine Geller(p) Joe Mondragon(b) Larry Bunker(dm).
(produced by Leonard Feather) LA,December 31,1954

tk.1	Arcadia-1	BN BLP5060
tk.2	Santa Anita-1	BN BLP5059
tk.5	Hooray for Hollywood-1	- CD BN(Eu)5-23444-2
tk.7	Blindfold test No.3-1,2	BN BLP5060

Conte Candoli(tp) John Graas(frh) Charlie Mariano(as) Marty Paich(p) Monty Budwig(b) Stan Levey(dm).
(produced by Leonard Feather) Same date.

tk.10	Van Nuys indeed	BN BLP5060
tk.12	Burbank bounce	-
tk.17	Culver City	BN BLP5059
tk.18	Blindfold test No.1	-

Conte Candoli(tp) Buddy Collette(fl-1,as-2) Jimmy Giuffre(ts-3,cl-4,bs-5) Gerald Wiggins(p) Howard Roberts(g) Curtis Counce(b) Stan Levey(dm).
(produced by Leonard Feather) Same date.

tk.23	Here's Pete-1,3,5	BN BLP5060
tk.25	Blindfold test No.2 -1,2,4	BN BLP5059
tk.30	Santa Monica-2,3,5	-
tk.32	No love,no nothing-2,4,5	BN BLP5060

Note: Most of the selections on above three sessions were arranged by Shorty Rogers.
All 12 titles from this date have also been issued in 12 in.LP form as BN(Sp)BLP5059/5060 (produced by Fresh Sound Records).

45

KENNY DORHAM SEXTET:
Kenny Dorham(tp) Hank Mobley(ts) Cecil Payne(bs) Horace Silver(p) Percy Heath(b) Art Blakey(dm).
Hackensack,N.J.,January 30,1955

tk.2	Venetia's dance	BN BLP1535
tk.6	K.D.'s motion	-
tk.9	K.D.'s cab ride (Echo of Spring)	BN(Du)1A158-83385/8 BN(J)BNJ61008(alb.61008/010),CD TOCJ-1601
tk.12	The villa	BN BLP1535

All titles issued on CD BN 7-46815-2.
All titles,except tk.9,also issued on CD BN(J)TOCJ-1535.
Note: The correct title of the Dorham composition "Echo of Spring" was not known at time of release and take 9 was called "K.D.'s cab ride".

HORACE SILVER QUINTET:
Kenny Dorham(tp) Hank Mobley(ts) Horace Silver(p) Doug Watkins(b) Art Blakey(dm).
Hackensack,N.J.,February 6,1955

tk.3	Hippy	
tk.5	To whom it may concern	
tk.9	Hankerin'	
tk.13	The preacher	BN 45-1630,BST84325,B1-91143,BST2-92465 BN(J)K18P-9124,FCPA 6206,W-5506 CD BN 7-91143-2,7-92465-2,4-95576-2, (Eu)7-80703-2,(F)8-54185-2,(J)CJ28-5033, CP32-5448,TOCJ-5827,TOCJ-5964,TOCJ-66034, Cema S21-57589,EMI-Jazz(E)4-93466-2, Premier(E)CDJA 2

All titles issued on BN BLP5062,BLP1518/BST81518,CD 7-46140-2.

GIL MELLE QUINTET:
Gil Melle(bs) Don Butterfield(tu) Lou Mecca(g) Bill Phillips(b) Vinnie Thomas(dm).
Hackensack,N.J.,February 27,1955

tk.1	Five impressions of color: (Spectrum violet/Sea green/Royal blue/Ebony/Spectrum red)
tk.5	Life begins at midnight
tk.7	Threadneedle Street
tk.9	Night train to Wildwood

All titles issued on BN BLP5063,CD 4-95718-2.

JULIUS WATKINS SEXTET:
Julius Watkins(frh) Hank Mobley(ts) Duke Jordan(p) Perry Lopez(g) Oscar Pettiford(b) Art Blakey(dm).
Hackensack,N.J.,March 20,1955

tk.4	B and B (g out)
tk.6	Garden delights
tk.11	Jordu (as "Jor-du") (g out)
tk.13	Julie Ann (ts out)
tk.15	Sparkling Burgundy

All titles issued on BN BLP5064,(J)K18P-9273,CD BN 4-95749-2.

 46

LOU MECCA QUARTET:
Jack Hitchcock(vb) Lou Mecca(g) Vinnie Burke(b) Jimmy Campbell(dm).
Hackensack,N.J.,March 25,1955

tk.2	You go to my head	
tk.4	Bernie's tune	
tk.6	Stan's invention	
tk.8	All the things you are	
tk.10	Just one of those things	
tk.11	The song is you	

All titles issued on BN BLP5067,CD BN(J)CJ28-5127,TOCJ-9228.

HANK MOBLEY QUARTET:
Hank Mobley(ts) Horace Silver(p) Doug Watkins(b) Art Blakey(dm).
Hackensack,N.J.,March 27,1955

tk.2	Walking the fence (alt.)	
tk.3	Walking the fence	BN BLP5066,(J)K18P-9276
tk.5	Avila and Tequila	- -
		CD BN 8-37052-2,(C)8-56508-2,(J)CJ28-5035, TOCJ-5296,TOCJ-6271/74,TOCJ-66043
tk.6	Hank's pranks (alt.)	
tk.8	Hank's pranks	BN BLP5066,(J)K18P-9276
tk.10	Just coolin'	- -
tk.12	My sin	- -
tk.14	Love for sale	- -

All titles issued on Mosaic MQ 10-181,CD BN(J)CJ28-5128,Mosaic MD6-181.
All titles from BLP5066 also issued on CD BN(J)TOCJ-9201.

KENNY DORHAM OCTET:
Kenny Dorham(tp) J.J.Johnson(tb) Hank Mobley(ts) Cecil Payne(bs) Horace Silver(p) Oscar Pettiford(b) Art Blakey(dm) Carlos "Patato" Valdes(cga) Richie Goldberg(cowbell-1).
Hackensack,N.J.,March 29,1955

tk.2	Minor's holiday (alt.)-1	
tk.3	Minor's holiday -1	CD BN 8-53648-2,(J)CJ25-5181/84,CJ28-5031, TOCJ-5274/76,TOCJ-6271/74, Cap(J)TOCJ-5191/92
tk.5	Basheer's dream	BN(Du)1A158-83385/8
tk.7	Afrodisia-1	BN(Du)1A158-83385/8,(E)BNSLP-1 BN(J)BNJ71106 CD BN 7-95590-2,5-21688-2,(J)CP32-5448, TOCJ-5758,TOCJ-5936,TOCJ-5778,TOCJ-5964, TOCJ-6133,TOCJ-6191,TOCJ-66055, HMV Jazz(E)5-20885-2,Toshiba-EMI(J) TOCP-50370
tk.8	Lotus flower	CD BN 8-53648-2

All titles,except take 2,issued on BN BLP5065,BLP1535,CD BN(J)TOCJ-1535.
All titles issued on CD BN 7-46815-2.

47

GEORGE LEWIS AND HIS NEW ORLEANS BAND:
Avery "Kid" Howard(tp,vo) Jim Robinson(tb) George Lewis(cl) Alton Purnell(p,vo) George Guesnon(bjo) Alcide "Slow Drag" Pavageau(b) Joe Watkins(dm,vo).

Hackensack,N.J.,April 8,1955

tk.3	When you wore a tulip (alt.)	
tk.5	Gettysburg march (alt.)	
tk.8	Walking with the King (voKH)	BN BLP7027,BLP1205,(J)K23P-9291
tk.9	Gettysburg march	- - -
tk.12	Savoy blues	BN BLP7028,BLP1205,(J)K23P-9291
tk.14	Nobody knows the way I feel this morning	- -
tk.16	My bucket got a hole in it (voJW)	BN BLP7027,BLP1205 -

All titles issued on Mosaic MR5-132,CD BN 8-21261-2,Mosaic MD3-132.

GEORGE LEWIS AND HIS NEW ORLEANS BAND:
Avery "Kid" Howard(tp,vo) Jim Robinson(tb) George Lewis(cl) Alton Purnell(p,vo) George Guesnon(bjo) Alcide "Slow Drag" Pavageau(b) Joe Watkins(dm,vo).

Hackensack,N.J.,April 11,1955

tk.19	I can't escape from you	BN BLP7028,(J)K23P-9291
tk.20	Mahogany Hall stomp	BN BLP7027,BLP1205,(J)K23P-9291 CD BN 4-95981-2
tk.23	Move the body over (voJW)	
tk.26	Lord,Lord you sure been good to me (voKH)	BN BLP7028,BLP1205,(J)K23P-9291
tk.27	Gettysburg march (alt.)	CD BN 8-35811-2
tk.29	High society	BN BLP7028,BLP1205,(J)K23P-9291
tk.30	See see rider blues (voAP)	BN BLP7027 - -
tk.31	Heebie jeebies (voAP)	BN BLP7028 - -
tk.33	When you wore a tulip	BN BLP7027 - - CD BN 8-35811-2

All titles issued on Mosaic MR5-132,CD BN 8-21261-2,Mosaic MD3-132.

HERBIE NICHOLS TRIO:
Herbie Nichols(p) Al McKibbon(b) Art Blakey(dm).

Hackensack,N.J.,May 6,1955

tk.1	The third world	BN BLP5068,CD 7-99176-2
tk.2	The third world (alt.)	
tk.3	Step tempest	BN BLP5068,CD 7-99176-2
tk.4	Dance line	-
tk.6	Blue chopsticks	- CD 7-99176-2
tk.8	Double exposure (alt.)	
tk.9	Double exposure	BN BLP5068
tk.10	Cro-Magnon nights	CD BN 7-99176-2
tk.11	Cro-Magnon nights (alt)	

All titles issued on Mosaic MR5-118,CD BN 8-59352-2,Mosaic MD3-118.
All titles from BN BLP5068 also issued on BN BN-LA485-H2,(J)K18P-9272,CD TOCJ-9229.

 48

<u>HERBIE NICHOLS TRIO</u>:
Herbie Nichols(p) Al McKibbon(b) Art Blakey(dm).
Hackensack,N.J.,May 13,1955

tk.14	It didn't happen (alt.)	
tk.16	Amoeba's dance	BN BLP5069
tk.17	Brass rings (alt.)	
tk.18	Brass rings	BN BLP5069
tk.19	2300 Skiddoo (alt.)	
tk.20	2300 Skiddoo	BN BLP5069,CD 7-99176-2
tk.21	Shuffle Montgomery (alt.)	
tk.22	It didn't happen	BN BLP5069
tk.23	Crisp day	-
tk.24	Shuffle Montgomery	- CD 7-99176-2

All titles issued on Mosaic MR5-118,CD BN 8-59352-2,Mosaic MD3-118.
All titles from BN BLP5069 also issued on BN BN-LA485-H2,(J)K18P-9272,CD TOCJ-9230.

<u>JAY JAY JOHNSON QUINTET</u>:
J.J.Johnson(tb) Hank Mobley(ts) Horace Silver(p) Paul Chambers(b) Kenny Clarke(dm).
Hackensack,N.J.,June 6,1955

tk.2	Pennies from heaven (alt.)	
tk.3	Pennies from heaven	BN 45-1632,BLP5070,BLP1506/BST81506
tk.6	Viscosity	- -
tk.7	Viscosity (alt.)	CD BN(C)8-56508-2
tk.9	You're mine you	BN BLP5070,BLP1506/BST81506
tk.11	Daylie double	- -
tk.15	Groovin'	BN 45-1632,BLP5070,BLP1506/BST81506, (J)W-5504
tk.16	Portrait of Jennie	BN BLP5070,BLP1506/BST81506
tk.18	Daylie double (alt.)	

All titles issued on CD BN 7-81506-2.
All titles from BST81506 also issued on CD BN(J)TOCJ-1506.

<u>HERBIE NICHOLS TRIO</u>:
Herbie Nichols(p) Al McKibbon(b) Max Roach(dm).
Hackensack,N.J.,August 1,1955

tk.4	The gig	BN BLP1519,BN-LA485-H2,(Du)1A158-83385/8 CD BN 7-99176-2,4-95698-2,(J)TOCJ-6132, TOCJ-6271/74
tk.5	Applejackin' (alt.)	
tk.6	Hangover triangle	BN BLP1519,BN-LA485-H2,CD 7-99176-2
tk.8	Lady sings the blues	- - BN(Du)1A158-83385/8,(J)W-5509 CD BN 7-96904-2,7-99176-2,4-95698-2, 4-97154-2,(J)TOCJ-5187/88,TOCJ-5964
tk.10	Chit-chatting	BN BLP1519,BN-LA485-H2
tk.11	House party starting	- - CD 7-99176-2
tk.12	The gig (alt.)	CD BN(J)TOCJ-1608

All titles issued on Mosaic MR5-118,CD BN 8-59352-2,Mosaic MD3-118.
All titles from BLP1519 also issued on CD BN(J)TOCJ-1519.

49

HERBIE NICHOLS TRIO:
Herbie Nichols(p) Al McKibbon(b) Max Roach(dm).

Hackensack,N.J.,August 7,1955

tk.2	Furthermore (alt. #1)	
tk.3	Furthermore	CD BN(J)TOCJ-1608
tk.5	117th Street (alt.)	
tk.6	117th Street	CD BN(J)TOCJ-1608
tk.7	Sunday stroll	CD BN 7-99176-2,(J)TOCJ-1608
tk.10	Nick at T's	-
tk.11	Furthermore (alt. #2)	
tk.12	Terpsichore	BN BLP1519,BN-LA485-H2 CD BN 7-99176-2,(J)TOCJ-1519
tk.13	'Orse at safari	CD BN(J)TOCJ-1608
tk.14	Applejackin' (alt.)	
tk.15	Applejackin'	CD BN(J)TOCJ-1608

All titles issued on Mosaic MR5-118,CD BN 8-59352-2,Mosaic MD3-118.

THE JAZZ MESSENGERS AT THE CAFE BOHEMIA:
Kenny Dorham(tp) Hank Mobley(ts) Horace Silver(p) Doug Watkins(b) Art Blakey(dm).
(Cafe Bohemia) NYC,November 23,1955

Set #1:

tk.1	Blues	rejected
tk.2	Like someone in love	BN BLP1508,(J)FCPA 6204 CD BN 7-46522-2
tk.3	Deciphering the message	rejected
tk.4	I waited for you	BN BLP1508,(J)K18P-9124 CD BN 7-46522-2
tk.5	Minor's holiday	BN BLP1507,(E)BNX 1,(J)FCPA 6204 CD BN 7-46521-2,7-48337-2,7-97190-2, (F)8-54185-2,(J)CJ28-5031,TOCJ-5274/76, TOCJ-5823,TOCJ-66031

Set #2:

tk.6	Soft winds	BN 45-1693,BLP1507,(J)FCPA 6204 CD BN 7-46521-2
tk.7	Avila and Tequila -1	BN 45-1695,BLP1508,BST2-92465 CD 7-46522-2,7-92465-2,7-97190-2, (J)TOCJ-5274/76
tk.8	Yesterdays (ts out)	BN BLP1508,(J)FCPA 6204 CD BN 7-46522-2
tk.9	What's new (tp,ts out)	BN(J)DY5805-01;CD BN 7-46521-2
tk.10	Alone together (tp out)	BN BLP1507,(J)K23P-6724 CD BN 7-46521-2,Cema GSC Music 15131
tk.11	Decipherin' the message/The theme	BN(J)DY5805-01;CD BN 7-46521-2

-1: Band plays various perc. instruments.

Set #3:

tk.12	Prince Albert	BN BLP1507,CD 7-46521-2,(J)TOCJ-5274/76
tk.13	Just one of those things	BN(J)DY5805-01;CD BN 7-46522-2
tk.14	Gone with the wind	- -

All titles from DY5805-1 were initially scheduled for release on BN(J)GXF-3074,which was not issued,and later reissued on BN(J)BNJ61007,CD TOCJ-1603.
BLP1507/08 were reissued as BST81507/08,and also as CD BN(J)TOCJ-1507/08.

50

THE JAZZ MESSENGERS AT THE CAFE BOHEMIA:
Kenny Dorham(tp) Hank Mobley(ts) Horace Silver(p) Doug Watkins(b) Art Blakey(dm).
(Cafe Bohemia) NYC,November 23,1955

Set #4:

tk.15	Sportin' crowd	BN BLP1508,(Du)1A158-83385/8,(J)FCPA 6204 CD BN 7-46522-2
tk.16	Prince Albert	rejected
tk.17	Hank's symphony	BN(J)DY5805-01;CD BN 7-46522-2
tk.18	Lady Bird	BN(J)DY5805-01;CD BN 7-46521-2
tk.19	The theme	BN BLP1507,(J)FCPA 6204 CD BN 7-46521-2
	The theme (incomplete)	BN BLP1508,CD 7-46522-2

All titles from DY5805-1 were initially scheduled for release on BN(J)GXF-3074,which was not issued,and later reissued on BN(J)BNJ61007,CD TOCJ-1603.
BLP1507/08 were reissued as BST81507/08,and also as CD BN(J)TOCJ-1507/08.

JIMMY SMITH AT THE ORGAN:
Jimmy Smith(org) Thornel Schwartz(g) Bazeley "Bey" Perry(dm).
Hackensack,N.J.,February 18,1956

tk.2	You get 'cha	BN 45-1635,CD 8-33206-2
	The champ	rejected
tk.6	Lady be good	Sunset SUM1175,SUS5175
tk.7	The preacher	BN 45-1636,BN-LA400-H2 CD BN(J)TOCJ-5825,TOCJ-5925,TOCJ-6271/74
tk.8	But not for me	Sunset SUM1175,SUS5175
tk.12	The way you look tonight	- - BN(J)K18P-9124,CD CJ28-5034,CP32-5448, TOCJ-5645/46,TOCJ-66037
tk.13	The high and the mighty	BN 45-1635
tk.15	Tenderly	BN 45-1637;Sunset SUM1175,SUS5175
tk.16	Joy	BN 45-1637
tk.18	Midnight sun	BN 45-1636

All titles,except the rejected one,issued on BN BLP1512,CD 8-57191-2,(J)TOCJ-1512.

THAD JONES:
Thad Jones(tp) Tommy Flanagan(p) Kenny Burrell(g) Oscar Pettiford(b) Shadow Wilson(dm).
(Audio-Video Studios) NYC,March 12,1956

	Scratch	rejected

KENNY BURRELL:
Frank Foster(ts) Tommy Flanagan(p) Kenny Burrell(g) Oscar Pettiford(b) Shadow Wilson(dm).
(Audio-Video Studios) NYC,March 12,1956

tk.10	Phinupi	BN BLP1543 CD BN(J)TOCJ-6035,Cema GSC Music 15131
tk.13	Now see how you are	BN BLP1543;CD BN 8-30493-2
tk.27	How about you	-
tk.42	My heart stood still	BN(J)GXF-3070,BNJ61008(alb.61008/010) CD BN(J)TOCJ-1609
tk.43	Cheetah (ts out)	BN BLP1543,CD 7-96581-2,8-30493-2
tk.64	Moten swing (ts out)	- CD BN(J)TOCJ-66042
	All the things you are	rejected

All titles,except rejected one,also issued on CD BN 5-24561-2.
All titles from BLP1543 also issued on CD BN(J)TOCJ-1543.

51

<u>THAD JONES</u> - <u>DETROIT-NEW YORK JUNCTION</u>:
Thad Jones(tp) Billy Mitchell(ts) Tommy Flanagan(p) Kenny Burrell(g) Oscar Pettiford(b) Shadow Wilson (dm).
(Audio-Video Studios) NYC,March 13,1956

tk.3	Tariff	
tk.14	Blue room	
tk.19	Little girl blue (ts,p,dm out)	BN(J)K18P-9124
tk.28	Scratch	
tk.30	Zec	

All titles issued on BN BLP1513,Mosaic MQ5-172,CD BN(J)TOCJ-1513,Mosaic MD3-172.

<u>JIMMY SMITH AT THE ORGAN,Vol.2</u>:
Jimmy Smith(org) Thornel Schwartz(g) Donald Bailey(dm).
Hackensack,N.J.,March 27,1956

tk.2	Turquoise	
tk.3	Moonlight in Vermont	Sunset SUM1175/SUS5175 BN(J)K16P-9031/32,K22P-6096/97
tk.7	Ready 'n 'able	
tk.8	Deep purple	Sunset SUM1175/SUS5175
tk.10	Gone with the wind	
tk.12	The champ	BN 45-1641,BST89901,BN-LA400-H2, BST2-92465 BN(F)LBS83442/3,(Du)1A158-83391/4 BN(J)LNP-88046,W-5507 CD BN 7-91140-2,7-92465-2,7,(I)7-89032-2, (J)CJ25-5181/84,TOCJ-5645/46,TOCJ-5825
tk.13	Bayou	BN 45-1642
tk.16	Bubbis	-

All titles,except tk.10,issued on BN BLP1514,CD BN(J)TOCJ-1514.
All titles issued on CD BN 8-57191-2.

<u>BABS GONZALES WITH JIMMY SMITH TRIO</u>:
Babs Gonzales(vo) Jimmy Smith(org) Thornel Schwartz(g) Donald Bailey(dm).
Hackensack,N.J.,March 27,1956

tk.1	You need connections	
tk.2	'Round midnight	CD BN 8-35471-2,5-21153-2

Both titles issued on BN 45-1638,(J)K18P-9280,CD BN 7-84464-2.
Note:CD BN issue mistates recording date as June 18,1956.

<u>GIL MELLE</u> - <u>PATTERNS IN JAZZ</u>:
Eddie Bert(tb) Gil Melle(bs) Joe Cinderella(g) Oscar Pettiford(b) Ed Thigpen(dm).
Hackensack,N.J.,April 1,1956

tk.5	Weird valley	
tk.10	The set break	CD BN(J)TOCJ-6271/74
tk.11	Moonlight in Vermont	
tk.12	Long ago and far away	CD BN(J)TOCJ-5964
tk.13	The Arab barber blues (tb out)	
tk.14	Nice question (tb out)	

All titles issued on BN BLP1517,CD 4-95718-2,(J)TOCJ-1517.

52

JUTTA HIPP AT THE HICKORY HOUSE:
Jutta Hipp(p) Peter Ind(b) Ed Thigpen(dm).
(The Hickory House) NYC,April 5,1956

Take me in your arms	BN BLP1515 CD BN(J)TOCJ-6271/74,TOCJ-66053	
Dear old Stockholm	BN BLP1515	
Billie's bounce	-	
I'll remember April	-	
Lady Bird	-	
Mad about the boy	-	CD BN(J)TOCJ-5964
Ain't misbehavin'	-	
These foolish things	-	
Jeepers creepers	-	
The moon was yellow	-	
Gone with the wind	BN BLP1516	
After hours	-	
The squirrel	-	
We'll be together again	-	
Horatio	-	
I married an angel	-	
Moonlight in Vermont	-	
Star eyes	-	
If I had you	-	
My heart stood still	-	

All titles from BLP1515/16 were also issued on CD BN(J)TOCJ-1515/16.

INTRODUCING JOHNNY GRIFFIN:
Johnny Griffin(ts) Wynton Kelly(p) Curly Russell(b) Max Roach(dm).
Hackensack,N.J.,April 17,1956

tk.2	Chicago calling	BN 45-1639,BLP1533
tk.3	Mil dew	- - (J)K18P-9125 CD BN(F)8-54185-2
tk.6	The boy next door	BN 45-1640,BLP1533
tk.8	It's all right with me	BN BLP1533,(J)K18P-9125 CD BN 7-95591-2,(J)CJ25-5181/84,TOCJ-5964, TOCJ-6271/74 Lib(J)K22P-6131/32
tk.10	Nice and easy	BN 45-1640,BLP1533
tk.12	The way you look tonight	BN(Du)1A158-83385/8 BN(J)BNJ61008(alb.61008/010),CD TOCJ-1601
tk.13	Lover man	BN BLP1533
tk.14	These foolish things	-
tk.16	Cherokee	BN(J)BNJ61008(alb.61008/010),CD TOCJ-1601

All titles issued on BN 7-46536-2.
All titles from BLP 1533 also issued on CD BN(J)TOCJ-1533.

53

<u>HERBIE NICHOLS TRIO</u>:
Herbie Nichols(p) Teddy Kotick(b) Max Roach(dm).

Hackensack,N.J.,April 19,1956

tk.1	Wildflower	BN BLP1519,BN-LA485-H2
tk.3	Mine (alt.)	CD BN(J)TOCJ-1608
tk.4	Mine	BN BLP1519,BN-LA485-H2 CD BN 7-99427-2,5-20808-2
tk.8	Trio (Argumentative variation*)	BN(J)BNJ61009(alb.61008/010)*,CD TOCJ-1608
tk.10	Trio (alt.)	
tk.11	Spinning song (alt.)	CD BN(J)TOCJ-1608
tk.12	Spinning song	BN BLP1519,BN-LA485-H2,CD 7-99176-2
tk.13	Riff primatif	BN(J)BNJ61009(alb.61008/010) CD BN 7-99176-2,(J)TOCJ-1608
tk.14	Riff primatif (alt.)	
tk.15	Query (alt.)	CD BN(J)TOCJ-1608
tk.16	Query	BN BLP1519,BN-LA485-H2

All titles issued on Mosaic MR5-118,CD BN 8-59352-2,Mosaic MD3-118.
All titles from BLP1519 also issued on CD BN(J)TOCJ-1519.

<u>INTRODUCING KENNY BURRELL</u>:
Tommy Flanagan(p) Kenny Burrell(g) Paul Chambers(b) Kenny Clarke(dm) Candido Camero(cga).

Hackensack,N.J.,May 29,1956

tk.2	Fugue 'n 'blues (cga out)	BN BLP1523
tk.3	Takeela	- Lib(J)K22P-6094/95
tk.6	Delilah	BN 45-1653,BLP1523 CD BN(J)TOCJ-5964,TOCJ-66042
tk.7	Get happy	BN BLP1543;CD BN(J)TOCJ-1543,TOCJ-66042
	But not for me (g solo)	rejected

All titles,except rejected one,also issued on CD BN 5-24561-2,(J)CJ28-5144.
First three titles also issued on CD BN(J)TOCJ-1523.

Same.

Hackensack,N.J.,May 30,1956

tk.11	Blues for Skeeter	BN BLP1523
tk.13	This time the dream's on me	BN 45-1653,BLP1523;CD BN(J)TOCJ-66042
tk.16	Weaver of dreams (cga out)	BN BLP1523,K18P-9124
tk.17	Rhythmorama -1	-
tk.18	But not for me (g solo)	BN BLP1543 CD BN(J)TOCJ-1543,TOCJ-66042, Cap(J)TOCJ-5195

-1: Clarke & Candido only.
All titles also issued on CD BN 5-24561-2,(J)CJ28-5144.
First four titles also issued on CD BN(J)TOCJ-1523.

54

KENNY DORHAM - ROUND ABOUT MIDNIGHT AT THE CAFE BOHEMIA:
Kenny Dorham(tp) Frank J.R.Monterose(ts) Bobby Timmons(p) Sam Jones(b) Arthur Edgehill(dm).
(Cafe Bohemia) NYC,May 31,1956

Set #1:		
tk.1	Hill's edge	rejected
tk.2	K.D.'s blues (alt.)	BN(J)BNJ61004;CD BN 7-46542-2,(J)TOCJ-1607
tk.3	My heart stood still	rejected
tk.4	Mexico City	-
tk.5	Autumn in New York (ts out)	BN BLP1524,(J)K18P-9124 CD BN 7-46541-2,(J)TOCJ-1524,Cema GSC Music 15131
tk.6	Monaco (alt.)	BN(J)BNJ61004;CD BN 7-46542-2(J)TOCJ-1607
tk.7	N.Y. Theme	- - -
Set #2: Kenny Burrell(g) added.		
tk.8	K.D.'s blues	BN(J)BNJ61003;CD BN 7-46541-2,(J)TOCJ-1606
tk.9	Hill's edge	BN BLP1524 CD BN 7-46541-2,(J)TOCJ-1524
tk.10	My heart stood still	rejected
	A night in Tunisia	BN BLP1524 CD BN 7-46541-2,(J)TOCJ-1524
tk.11	Who cares? (alt.) (ts,g out)	BN(J)BNJ61004;CD BN 7-46542-2,(J)TOCJ-1607
tk.12	Royal Roost	BN(J)BNJ61003;CD BN 7-46542-2,(J)TOCJ-1606
tk.13	The theme	rejected
Set #3: Same.		
tk.14	Mexico City	BN BLP1524,CD 7-46541-2,8-53648-2
tk.15	'Round about midnight (g out)	- (J)W-5505;CD BN 7-46541-2
tk.16	Monaco	- CD 7-46541-2
tk.17	Who cares? (ts out)	BN(J)BNJ61003;CD BN 7-46541-2,(J)TOCJ-1606
tk.18	My heart stood still	- CD BN 7-46542-2 -
tk.19	The theme	rejected

First three titles also issued on CD BN TOCJ-1524.

Set #4: Same.		
tk.20	Riffin'	BN(J)BNJ61004;CD BN 7-46542-2,TOCJ-1607
tk.21	Mexico City (alt.)	BN BLP1543,(J)BNJ61003 CD BN 7-46541-2,(J)TOCJ-1543,TOCJ-1606
tk.22	The prophet	BN(J)BNJ61003;CD BN 7-46542-2 -

Note: Titles on BN(J)BNJ61003 were initially scheduled for issue on BN(J)GXF3077,which was not released.BLP1543 was issued as by Kenny Burrell.
All titles from 7-46541-2 & 7-46542-2 were reissued in CD set BN 8-32576-2.

THE INCREDIBLE JIMMY SMITH:
Jimmy Smith(org) Thornel Schwartz(g) Donald Bailey(dm).
Hackensack,N.J.,June 17,1956

tk.2	Willow weep for me	BN 45-1644,BLP1525;CD BN(J)TOCJ-1525
	All the things you are	rejected
tk.11	Jamey	
tk.13	My funny Valentine	
tk.14	Autumn leaves	BN 45-1643,BLP1525,(J)K22P-6125/26 CD BN(J)CJ28-5034,TOCJ-1525,TOCJ-5645/46, TOCJ-66037

All titles,except rejected one,issued on CD CD 8-57191-2.

55

THE INCREDIBLE JIMMY SMITH:
Jimmy Smith(org) Thornel Schwartz(g) Donald Bailey(dm).
Hackensack,N.J.,June 18,1956

tk.16	Fiddlin' the minors	BN 45-1644,BLP1525
tk.18	Lover come back to me	-
		CD BN(J)CJ28-5034,TOCJ-5825,TOCJ-66037
tk.19	Well you needn't	BN BLP1525
tk.20	I cover the waterfront	BN 45-1652,45-1925,BLP1525
		Sunset SUM1175,SUS5175
tk.21	I can't give you anything but love	
		BN 45-1652,45-1925,(J)K18P-9280
tk.24	Judo mambo	BN 45-1643,BLP1525;CD BN(J)TOCJ-5964
tk.25	Slightly Monkish	

All titles issued on CD BN 8-57191-2.
All titles from BLP1525 also issued on CD BN(J)TOCJ-1525.

THAD JONES - THE MAGNIFICENT THAD JONES:
Thad Jones(tp) Billy Mitchell(ts) Tommy Flanagan(p) Kenny Burrell(g) Eddie Jones(b) Elvin Jones (dm).
Hackensack,N.J.,July 9,1956

	Billie Doo	rejected
	Let's	-
	In a mellow tone	-
tk.8	Something to remember you by (tp,g only)	
		BN(J)BNJ61009(alb.61008/10)
		Mosaic MQ5-172
		CD BN 7-46814-2,Mosaic MD3-172
	Thedia (incomplete)	rejected

Thad Jones(tp) Billy Mitchell(ts) Barry Harris(p) Percy Heath(b) Max Roach(dm).
Hackensack,N.J.,July 14,1956

tk.2	Thedia	BN BLP1527
tk.6	April in Paris	BN 45-1659,BLP1527,(J)W-5508
		CD BN 7-99100-2,(J)CJ28-5172,TOCJ-6133, TOCJ-6271/74,TOCJ-66052,TOCP-7455/56, Cap(J)TOCJ-5618/19
tk.7	I've got a crush on you (ts out)	BN BLP1546
		CD BN 7-99427-2,(J)TOCJ-1546
tk.10	Billie-Doo	BN BLP1527
tk.11	If I love again	-
tk.12	If someone had told me (ts out)	BN 45-1659,BLP1527

All titles also issued on Mosaic MQ5-172,CD BN 7-46814-2,Mosaic MD3-172
All titles from BLP1527 also issued on CD BN(J)TOCJ-1527.

JUTTA HIPP QUINTET:
Jerry Lloyd(tp) Zoot Sims(ts) Jutta Hipp(p) Ahmed Abdul-Malik(b) Ed Thigpen(dm).
Hackensack,N.J.,July 28,1956

tk.4	Violets for your furs	BN BLP1530 CD BN(J)TOCJ-66054,Premier(E)CDJA 1
tk.5	These foolish things	BN(Du)1A158-83385/8 BN(J)BNJ61009(alb.61008/10)
tk.6	Down home	BN BLP1530
tk.7	Wee dot	-
tk.9	Too close for comfort	-
tk.10	'S wonderful	BN(J)BNJ61009(alb.61008/010)
tk.14	Almost like being in love	BN BLP1530,CD 8-29095-2
tk.15	Just blues	-

All titles also issued on CD BN 8-52439-2.
All titles from BLP1530 also issued on CD BN(J)TOCJ-1530.

THE INCREDIBLE JIMMY SMITH AT CLUB 'BABY GRAND':
Jimmy Smith(org) Thornel Schwartz(g) Donald Bailey(dm) Mitch Thomas(m.c.).
(Club 'Baby Grand') Wilmington,Delaware,August 4,1956

Set #1 (Afternoon):

tk.1	Blues	rejected
tk.2	Indiana	-
tk.3	My old flame	-
tk.4	This can't be love	-
tk.5	Where or when	-

Set #2 (Afternoon):

	Introduction by Mitch Thomas	BN BLP1528;CD BN(J)TOCJ-1528
tk.6	It's all right with me	BN BLP1529;CD BN(J)TOCJ-1529
tk.7	I'll remember April	rejected
tk.8	Joy Spring	-
tk.9	Caravan	BN BLP1529,(J)K22P-6125/26 CD BN(J)TOCJ-1529
tk.10	Love is a many splendored thing	BN 45-1666,BLP1529;CD BN(J)TOCJ-1529

Set #1 (Night):

tk.11	Lady Bird	rejected
tk.12	Where or when	BN 45-1665,BLP1528;CD BN(J)TOCJ-1528
tk.13	Stella by starlight	rejected
tk.14	Red sails in the sunset	-
tk.15	Blues	-

Set #2 (Night):

tk.16	Red sails in the sunset	rejected
tk.17	Someone to watch over me	-
tk.18	A night in Tunisia	-
tk.19	The nearness of you	-
tk.20	The preacher -1	BN 45-1660,BLP1528;CD BN(J)TOCJ-1528

-1: as "The new preacher" on BN 45-1660.

Set #3 (Night):

tk.21	Mitch's movement	rejected
tk.22	Jean Elaine	-
tk.23	Rosetta	BN BLP1529;CD BN(J)TOCJ-1529
tk.24	Get happy	- CD 8-33206-2,(J)TOCJ-1529
tk.25	Sweet Georgia Brown	BN BLP1528;CD BN(J)TOCJ-1528

PAUL CHAMBERS SEXTET - WHIMS OF CHAMBERS:
Donald Byrd(tp) John Coltrane(ts) Horace Silver(p) Kenny Burrell(g) Paul Chambers(b) Philly Joe Jones (dm).
Hackensack,N.J.,September 21,1956

tk.3	We six	BN BN-LA451-H2;CD BN(J)TOCJ-66041	
tk.5	Omicron	-	
tk.6	Tale of the finges (tp,ts,g out)		
tk.8	Whims of Chambers (tp,ts out)	BN(J)K18P-9125	
tk.9	Nita	BN BN-LA451-H2,CD 7-99175-2	
tk.11	Just for the love	- -	4-98240-2
tk.13	Dear Ann (ts out)		

All titles issued on BN BLP1534,CD 8-37647-2,(I)7-89872-2.

J.R.MONTEROSE:
Ira Sullivan(tp) Frank "J.R." Monterose(ts) Horace Silver(p) Wilbur Ware(b) Philly Joe Jones(dm).
Hackensack,N.J.,October 21,1956

tk.2	Wee jay (alt.)	CD BN(J)TOCJ-1601
tk.3	Wee jay	BN BLP1536;CD BN(J)TOCJ-5964,TOCJ-6271/74
tk.7	Mark V	-
tk.9	The third	-
tk.10	Bobbie pin	-
tk.12	Ka-link	-
tk.15	Beauteous	- (J)K18P-9125

All titles issued on CD BN 8-29102-2.
All titles from BLP1536 also issued on BN B1-29102,CD BN(J)TOCJ-1536.

LEE MORGAN INDEED!:
Lee Morgan(tp) Clarence Sharpe(as) Horace Silver(p) Wilbur Ware(b) Philly Joe Jones(dm).
Hackensack,N.J.,November 4,1956

tk.3	Gaza strip	BN 45-1661,BLP1538,(J)K18P-9125
tk.4	Reggie of Chester	- - (Du)1A158-83385/8
tk.6	Little T	-
tk.7	Little T (alt.)	
tk.9	Stand by	BN BLP1538
tk.11	Roccus	-
tk.14	The lady	-

All titles issued on Mosaic MQ6-162,CD Mosaic MD4-162.
All titles from BLP1538 also issued on CD BN(J)TOCJ-1538.

58

HORACE SILVER QUINTET - 6 PIECES OF SILVER:
Donald Byrd(tp) Hank Mobley(ts) Horace Silver(p) Doug Watkins(b) Louis Hayes(dm).
Hackensack,N.J.,November 10,1956

tk.3	Enchantment	BN 45-1654,BLP1539,CD 8-33208-2
tk.7	Virgo	-
tk.10	Shirl (tp,ts out)	- BN-LA474-H2
tk.11	Senor blues (alt.)-1	BN 45-1655,BN-LA945-H
		BN(Du)1A158-83385/8,(J)BNJ61005
		CD BN (J)TOCJ-1601
tk.12	Senor blues	BN BLP1539,BST84325,BST2-84433,BST89903,
		BN-LA159-G2,BST2-92471,B1-80679,B1-91143
		BN(J)NP-2006,FCPA 6206,W-5506
		CD BN 7-91143-2,7-92471-2,7-97960-2,
		4-95576-2,(C)8-56508-2,(F)8-54185-2,8-54197-2,
		(J)CJ25-5181/84,CJ28-5033,CJ28-5177,
		TOCJ-5827,TOCJ-5937,TOCJ-6132,TOCJ-66034,
		TOCJ-66053,Toshiba-EMI(J)TOCP-50370,
		Cema S21-57589,EMI-Music 4-98899-2,
		EMI-Jazz(E)4-93466-2
tk.14	Camouflage	BN 45-1654,BLP1539
tk.15	Cool eyes	BN 45-1655,BLP1539,CD 7-91143-2,4-95576-2
tk.18	For heaven's sake (tp,ts out)	- BN-LA474-H2

-1: First five notes are missing on BNJ61005.
All titles also issued on CD BN 7-81539-2,5-25648-2.
All titles from BLP1539 also issued on CD BN(J)TOCJ-1539.

HANK MOBLEY SEXTET:
Donald Byrd,Lee Morgan(tp) Hank Mobley(ts) Horace Silver(p) Paul Chambers(b) Charlie Persip(dm).
Hackensack,N.J.,November 25,1956

tk.2	Double whammy	BN BLP1540
tk.3	Barrel of funk	-
tk.4	Barrel of funk (alt.)	
tk.6	Mobleymania (*aka*: B for BB)	BN BLP1540
tk.7	Touch and go	-

All titles issued on Mosaic MQ10-181,CD MD6-181.
All titles from BLP1540 also issued on CD BN(J)TOCJ-1540.

LEE MORGAN:
Lee Morgan(tp) Kenny Rogers(as) Hank Mobley(ts) Horace Silver(p) Paul Chambers(b) Charlie Persip(dm).
(Arrangements by Benny Golson-1,Owen Marshall-2).
Hackensack,N.J.,December 2,1956

tk.2	Latin hangover -1	
tk.5	Whisper not -1	BN(J)W-5507
		CD BN 5-21052-2,(J)CJ28-5024,CJ28-5037,
		TOCJ-5964,TOCJ-66039
tk.8	His sister -2	
tk.9	D's fink -2	
tk.11	Slightly hep -1	
tk.13	Where am I? -1	

All titles issued on BN BLP1541/BST81541,Mosaic MQ6-162,CD BN(J)CJ28-5145,Mosaic MD4-162.

SONNY ROLLINS:
Donald Byrd(tp) Sonny Rollins(ts) Wynton Kelly(p) Gene Ramey(b) Max Roach(dm).
Hackensack,N.J.,December 16,1956

tk.1	Decision	BN 45-1669,BN-LA401-H2,BST2-84433, BST2-92465,B1-93203 CD BN 7-92465-2,7-93203-2,7-97960-2, (C)8-56508-2,(F)8-54185-2,8-54197-2, (J)CJ28-5167,TOCJ-5826,TOCJ-66036
tk.3	Plain Jane	BN 45-1670,BN-LA401-H2,CD 8-23516-2
tk.5	Sonnysphere	
tk.6	How are things in Glocca Morra	BN BN-LA401-H2,B1-93203,(J)K18P-9125 CD BN 7-93203-2,(E)8-53223-2,(J)CJ28-5167, TOCJ-5639,TOCJ-6103,TOCJ-66036
tk.8	Blues note	BN BN-LA401-H2,(J)W-5507 CD BN(J)CJ28-5030

All titles issued on BN BLP1542,CD 7-81542-2,8-21371-2.

HANK MOBLEY AND HIS ALL STARS:
Hank Mobley(ts) Milt Jackson(vb) Horace Silver(p) Doug Watkins(b) Art Blakey(dm).
Hackensack,N.J.,January 13,1957

tk.2	Reunion	BN 45-1671,(J)W-5508
tk.3	Lower stratosphere	-
tk.4	Don't walk	
tk.6	Ultramarine	
tk.7	Mobley's musings	

All titles issued on BN BLP1544,BN-LA590-H2,Mosaic MQ10-181,CD BN 8-37668-2,(J)TOCJ-1544, Mosaic MD6-181.

LOU DONALDSON QUINTET - WAILIN' WITH LOU:
Donald Byrd(tp) Lou Donaldson(as) Herman Foster(p) Peck Morrison(b) Art Taylor(dm).
Hackensack,N.J.,January 27,1957

tk.3	Stella by starlight	unissued
tk.4	That good old feeling	BN 45-1663
tk.6	Caravan	BN 45-1662,(J)K22P-6096/97
tk.7	L.D.Blues	BN 45-1663
tk.9	Old folks	BN 45-1662
tk.10	There is no greater love	CD BN(J)TOCJ-66044,TOCJ-66054
tk.12	Move it	

All titles,except tk.3,issued on BN BLP1545,CD BN(J)TOCJ-1545.

THE MAGNIFICENT THAD JONES:
Thad Jones(tp) Benny Powell(tb) Gigi Gryce(as) Tommy Flanagan(p) George Duvivier(b) Art Taylor(dm).
Hackensack,N.J.,February 2,1957

tk.5	Slipped around	BN BLP1546
tk.6	Going off stage	
tk.9	Let's	BN BLP1546
tk.10	Ill wind	-
tk.14	Thadrack	-

All titles on Mosaic MQ5-172,CD MD3-172.
All titles from BLP1546 also issued on CD BN(J)TOCJ-1546.

KENNY BURRELL - K.B.BLUES:
Hank Mobley(ts) Horace Silver(p) Kenny Burrell(g) Doug Watkins(b) Louis Hayes(dm).
Hackensack,N.J.,February 10,1957

	Felicity	rejected
tk.3	Nica's dream	
tk.6	D.B. Blues	BN 45-1674 CD BN 8-30493-2,(J)TOCJ-1609
tk.7	K.B. Blues (alt.)	
tk.8	K.B. Blues	BN 45-1674;CD BN(J)TOCJ-1609
tk.9	Out for blood	

All titles,except rejected one,issued on BN(J)GXF-3052,CD BN 5-24561-2.

JIMMY SMITH - A DATE WITH JIMMY SMITH:
Donald Byrd(tp) Lou Donaldson(as) Hank Mobley(ts) Jimmy Smith(org) Eddie McFadden(g) Art Blakey (dm).
(Manhattan Towers) NYC,February 11,1957

tk.3	Falling in love with love	BN BLP1547
tk.4	First night blues (horns out)	
tk.5	Funk's oats	BN 45-1677,BLP1547
tk.6	Zing! Went the strings of my heart (horns out)	BN BLP1556,TOCJ-1556
tk.8	Groovy date	BN BLP1548
tk.9	I let a song go out of my heart	-

All titles issued on Mosaic MQ5-154,CD MD3-154.
All titles from BLP1547/48 also issued on CD BN(J)TOCJ-1547/48.

JIMMY SMITH:
Lou Donaldson(as) Jimmy Smith(org).
(Manhattan Towers) NYC,February 12,1957

tk.1	I'm getting sentimental over you	BN 45-1668,BLP1548;CD BN(J)TOCJ-1548
tk.2	Summertime	BN 45-1667,BLP1551 CD BN 8-33206-2,(J)CJ28-5034,TOCJ-1551, TOCJ-5260,TOCJ-5825,TOCJ-66037

Both titles also issued on Mosaic MQ5-154,CD MD3-154.

Lou Donaldson(as) Jimmy Smith(org) Eddie McFadden(g) Donald Bailey(dm).
Same session.

tk.4	Somebody loves me (as out)	BN BLP1556,(J)K22P-6125/26 CD BN(J)TOCJ-1556
tk.5	Plum Nellie	BN BLP1552;CD BN(J)TOCJ-1552
tk.6	Plum Nellie (alt.)	BN 45-1668,(J)K18P-9280

All titles issued on Mosaic MQ5-154,CD MD3-154.

Note: 45-1668 was not released.

JIMMY SMITH:
Lou Donaldson(as) Jimmy Smith(org) Kenny Burrell(g) Art Blakey(dm).
Same session.

tk.8	Billie's bounce	BN BLP1552
tk.10	Yardbird suite	BN BLP1551,BST89903,BN-LA159-G2
tk.11	There's a small hotel (as out)	-
tk.12	All day long	BN 45-1676,BLP1551,BST89901
		CD BN 7-91140-2

All titles issued on Mosaic MQ5-154,CD MD3-154.
All titles from BLP1551/52 also issued on CD BN(J)TOCJ-1551/52.

JIMMY SMITH:
Jimmy Smith(org) Eddie McFadden(g) Donald Bailey(dm).
(Manhattan Towers) NYC,February 13,1957

tk.3	The third day	
tk.4	All the things you are -1	BN BLP1556
tk.6	The fight-1	-
tk.7	There'll never be another you	BN 45-1686,BLP1556
tk.8	How high the moon	BN 45-1667,BLP1547
		CD BN(J)TOCJ-1547,TOCJ-66037
tk.9	Buns a plenty	BN BLP1552
tk.10	The duel -2	-
tk.12	Blue moon	BN 45-1685,BLP1556,BN-LA400-H2
tk.13	Cherokee	

-1: organ solo.
-2: Jimmy Smith(org) Art Blakey(dm).
All titles issued on Mosaic MQ5-154,CD MD3-154.
All titles from BLP1552/56 also issued on CD BN(J)TOCJ-1552/56.

CLIFFORD JORDAN/JOHN GILMORE - BLOWING IN FROM CHICAGO:
Clifford Jordan,John Gilmore(ts) Horace Silver(p) Curly Russell(b) Art Blakey(dm).
Hackensack,N.J.,March 3,1957

tk.2	Evil eye	BN BLP1549
tk.3	Status quo	- CD BN(J)TOCJ-5964
tk.5	Let it stand	
tk.7	Bo-till	BN BLP1549
tk.9	Everywhere	-
tk.12	Blue lights	-
tk.13	Billie's bounce	-

All titles issued on CD BN 8-28977-2.
All titles from BLP1549 also issued on BN BN-LA521-H2,B1-28977,CD BN(J)TOCJ-1549.

ART BLAKEY - ORGY IN RHYTHM:
Herbie Mann(fl) Ray Bryant(p) Wendell Marshall(b) Art Blakey(dm,vo) Jo Jones,Art Taylor,Charles "Specs" Wright(dm) Sabu Martinez(bgo,timbales,vo) Carlos "Patato" Valdes,Jose Valiente(cga) Umbaldo Nieto (timbales) Evilio Quintero(concerro,maracas,tree log).

	(Manhattan Towers)	NYC,March 7,1957
tk.1	Toffi (voAB)	BN BLP1554
tk.4	Split skins -1	-
tk.5	Elephant walk (voSM)	BN 45-1696,BLP1555
tk.6	Ya ya	BN 45-1679,BLP1554
tk.9	Abdallah's delight	BN 45-1696,BLP1555
tk.11	Buhaina chant (voSM)	BN BLP1554
tk.12	Come out and meet me tonight (voSM)	BN 45-1679,BLP1555
tk.13	Amuck	- CD BN(J)TOCJ-5274/76

-1: Blakey,Taylor & Jones only.All others out.

All titles issued on CD BN 8-56586-2.
Note: This was the first session by Blue Note to be recorded in both mono and stereo.
All titles from BLP1554 were also issued on BN BST81554,CD BN(F)7-89390-2,(J)TOCJ-1554/55.
All titles from BLP1555 were also issued on BN BST81555,CD BN(J)TOCJ-1554/55.

HANK MOBLEY QUINTET:
Art Farmer(tp) Hank Mobley(ts) Horace Silver(p) Doug Watkins(b) Art Blakey(dm).
Hackensack,N.J.,March 8,1957

tk.1	Wham and they're off	BN BLP1550
tk.4	Wham and they're off (alt.)	BN(Du)1A158-83385/8,(J)BNJ61005
tk.5	Funk in deep freeze (alt.)	
tk.6	Funk in deep freeze	BN 45-1675,BLP1550 CD BN 8-37052-2,(F)54185-2,8-54197-2
tk.7	Starting from scratch	BN BLP1550
tk.8	Stellawise	BN 45-1684,BLP1550
tk.9	Bass on balls	- -
tk.10	Fin de l'affaire -1	BN 45-1675,BLP1550,CD 8-37052-2

-1: as "End of the affair" on BN 45-1675.
All titles issued on Mosaic MQ10-181,CD BN 7-46816-2,Mosaic MD6-181.
All titles from BLP1550 also issued on CD BN(J)TOCJ-1550.

LEE MORGAN:
Lee Morgan(tp) Gigi Gryce(as,fl-1) Benny Golson(ts,arr) Wynton Kelly(p) Paul Chambers(b) Charlie Persip (dm).
Hackensack,N.J.,March 24,1957

tk.3	Hasaan's dream -1	BN BLP1557
tk.5	I remember Clifford	- (J)K22P-6096/97;K16P-9031/32 CD BN 7-91138-2,(F)8-54185-2, (J)CJ28-5037,CJ28-5179,CP32-5448,TOCJ-5828, TOCJ-6133,TOCJ-66039,TOCJ-66054, Toshiba-EMI(J)TOCP-50370,TOCP-65352
tk.7	Mesabi chant	BN BLP1557
tk.10	Tip-toeing (alt.)	
tk.11	Tip-toeing	BN BLP1557
tk.13	Domingo	-

All titles issued on Mosaic MQ6-162,CD BN 7-46817-2,Mosaic MD4-162.
All titles from BLP1557 also issued on CD BN(J)TOCJ-1557.

JOHNNY GRIFFIN - A BLOWING SESSION:
Lee Morgan(tp) Hank Mobley,John Coltrane,Johnny Griffin(ts) Wynton Kelly(p) Paul Chambers(b) Art Blakey (dm).
Hackensack,N.J.,April 6,1957

tk.1	Smokestack (alt.)	
tk.2	Smokestack	CD BN 4-98240-2,(J)TOCJ-66041
tk.3	The way you look tonight	BN(Du)1A158-83391/4
tk.4	Ball bearings	
tk.5	All the things you are	BN(J)FCPA 6211,W-5508

All titles,except tk.1,issued on BN BLP1559,BN-LA521-H2,CD 7-81559-2.
All titles issued on CD BN 4-99009-2.

SONNY ROLLINS:
J.J.Johnson(tb) Sonny Rollins(ts) Horace Silver(p) Paul Chambers(b) Art Blakey(dm).
Hackensack,N.J.,April 14,1957

tk.1	Why don't I?	BN 45-1687,BN-LA401-H2,(J)K18P-9125 CD BN 7-93203-2,(J)CJ28-5167,TOCJ-5639, TOCJ-5826,TOCJ-6103,TOCJ-6131,TOCJ-66036
tk.4	Wail march	CD BN(J)TOCJ-6035
tk.6	Reflections -1	BN BN-LA401-H2;Mosaic MR4-101 Lib(J)K22P-6074/75 CD BN 8-23516-2,8-30363-2,(E)8-53223-2, (J)TOCJ-5826,HMV Jazz(E)5-20882-2
tk.7	Poor butterfly	BN BN-LA401-H2,B1-93203,CD BN 7-93203-2
tk.11	You stepped out of a dream	BN 45-1687,BN-LA401-H2 CD BN 8-21381-2,8-23516-2,(J)TOCJ-66036
tk.12	Misterioso -2	BN BN-LA401-H2,B1-93203;Mosaic MR4-101 BN(Du)1A158-83391/4 CD BN 7-93203-2,8-30363-2, (J)CJ28-5162,TOCJ-5639,TOCJ-5826,TOCJ-6103, TOCJ-66032

-1: Johnson out.Thelonious Monk(p) replaces Silver.
-2: Thelonious Monk(p) added.
All titles issued on BLP1558,CD 7-46818-2,7-81558-2,8-21371-2,4-97809-2.

HANK MOBLEY SEXTET - HANK:
Donald Byrd(tp) John Jenkins(as) Hank Mobley(ts) Bobby Timmons(p) Wilbur Ware(b) Philly Joe Jones (dm).
Hackensack,N.J.,April 21,1957

tk.2	Easy to love	BN 45-1688 CD BN 7-95591-2,(J)CJ28-5035,TOCJ-66043
tk.3	Fit for a hanker	
tk.4	Hi groove,low feedback	
tk.7	Time after time	BN 45-1688
tk.9	Dance of the infidels	

All titles issued on BN BLP1560,Mosaic MQ10-181,CD BN(J)TOCJ-1560,Mosaic MD6-181.

Note:45-1688 was possibly not released.

64

SABU - PALO CONGO:
Sabu Martinez(cga,bgo,vo) Evaristo Baso(b) Arsenio Rodriguez(cga,g,vo) Raul "Caesar" Travieso(cga,vo) Israel Moises "Quique" Travieso,Ray "Mosquito" Romero(cga) Willie Capo,Sarah Bavo(vo).
(Manhattan Towers) NYC,April 28,1957

tk.1	Aggo elegua (voWC & band)	
tk.4	Billumba-Palo congo (voWC & band)	
tk.7	Choferito-Plena (voSB,WC)	
tk.8	El cumbanchero (voWC & band)	
tk.11	Tribilin cantore (voWC & band)	
tk.13	Asabache (Baso & Romero out)	
tk.14	Simba (voWC)	
tk.15	Rhapsodia del maravilloso	BN B1-80701,CD 7-80701-2

All titles issued on BN BLP1561 (mono),CD BN 5-22665-2,(J)TOCJ-1561 (stereo).
Note: This session was the second one recorded by Blue Note in both mono and stereo.
All studio sessions would be recorded in both formats hereafter.

HORACE SILVER QUINTET - THE STYLINGS OF SILVER:
Art Farmer(tp) Hank Mobley(ts) Horace Silver(p) Teddy Kotick(b) Louis Hayes(dm).
Hackensack,N.J.,May 8,1957

tk.2	Metamorphosis	
tk.4	No smoking	BN 45-1673;CD BN(J)TOCJ-5827
tk.7	The back beat	BN 45-1672
tk.10	Soulville	BN 45-1673,CD 7-91143-2,4-95576-2
tk.14	My one and only love	BN(J)K18P-9125
tk.17	Home cookin'	BN 45-1672,BN-LA402-H2,B1-91143 CD BN 7-91143-2,4-95576-2,(J)CJ28-5033

All titles issued on BN BLP1562/BST81562,CD BN(J)TOCJ-1562.

JIMMY SMITH - JIMMY SMITH PLAYS PRETTY JUST FOR YOU:
Jimmy Smith(org) Eddie McFadden(g) Donald Bailey(dm).
(Manhattan Towers) NYC,May 8,1957

tk.3	I can't get started	BN 45-1682,BLP1563 CD BN(J)CJ28-5034,CJ28-5179,TOCJ-5935, TOCJ-66037		
tk.5	The very thought of you	BN 45-1683,BLP1563		
tk.6	Autumn in New York		-	
tk.10	Somebody loves me	CD BN(J)TOCJ-1612		
tk.12	Old devil moon	BN	BLP1563;CD BN(J)TOCJ-5858	
tk.16	East of the sun	BN 45-1683	-	
tk.17	Penthouse serenade	BN 45-1682	-	
tk.18	Jitterbug waltz	BN 45-1686	-	
tk.20	The nearness of you		-	CD BN(J)TOCJ-66054

Note: Japanese issue of BLP1563 was in stereo.
All titles from BLP1563 were also issued on CD BN(J)TOCJ-1563.

PAUL CHAMBERS QUINTET:
Donald Byrd(tp) Clifford Jordan(ts) Tommy Flanagan(p) Paul Chambers(b) Elvin Jones(dm).
Hackensack,N.J.,May 19,1957

tk.3	Four strings	BN BLP1564
tk.4	Four strings (alt.)	
tk.8	Minor run-down	BN BLP1564
tk.9	Beauteous	-
tk.12	What's new?	-
tk.15	The hand of love	-
tk.16	Softly as in a morning sunrise (tp,ts out)	-

All titles issued on CD BN 8-52441-2,which is the first stereo issue of this session.
All titles from BLP1564 also issued on CD BN(J)TOCJ-1564.

CLIFF JORDAN:
Lee Morgan(tp) Curtis Fuller(tb)John Jenkins(as) Clifford Jordan(ts) Ray Bryant(p) Paul Chambers(b) Art Taylor(dm).
Hackensack,N.J.,June 2,1957

tk.4	St. John	
tk.5	Not guilty (tp out)	
tk.6	Blue shoes (tp out)	
tk.8	Beyond the blue horizon	CD BN(J)TOCJ-6035
tk.9	Ju-ba (tb out)	

All titles issued on BN BLP1565,CD BN(J)TOCJ-1565 (mono),CD BN(J)TOCJ-9177 (stereo).
Note: The stereo master of "Blue shoes" has been lost and all issues of tk. 6 are in mono.

LOU DONALDSON - SWING AND SOUL:
Lou Donaldson(as) Herman Foster(p) Peck Morrison(b) Dave Bailey(dm) Ray Barretto(cga).
Hackensack,N.J.,June 9,1957

tk.1	Herman's mambo	BN 45-1681,BLP1566,BST81566
tk.4	Peck time	BN 45-1680 - -
tk.6	There'll never be another you	BN BLP1566,(Du)1A158-83391/4 BN(J)BNJ61009(alb.61008/010)
tk.7	There'll never be another you	BN BST81566
tk.8	Groove junction	BN BLP1566/BST81566
tk.10	Dorothy	BN 45-1680 -
tk.11	Grits and gravy	BN 45-1681 - CD BN 8-27298-2,(Eu)7-89915-2
tk.12	I won't cry anymore	BN BLP1566/BST81566

Note: tk.6 was recorded in mono only.
All titles from BST81566 were also issued on CD BN(J)TOCJ-1566.

 66

CURTIS FULLER - THE OPENER:
Curtis Fuller(tb) Hank Mobley(ts) Bobby Timmons(p) Paul Chambers(b) Art Taylor(dm).
Hackensack,N.J.,June 16,1957

tk.3	Dizzy's bounce	
tk.6	Soon	CD BN 7-99427-2
tk.8	A lovely day to spend an evening (ts out)	
tk.10	Here's to my lady (ts out)	
tk.12	Oscalypso	BN 45-1690
tk.14	Hugore	-

All titles issued on BN BLP1567,Mosaic MQ5-166,CD BN(J)TOCJ-1567,Mosaic MD3-166.
Note: The Mosaic issue was the first stereo issue.

HANK MOBLEY:
Bill Hardman(tp) Curtis Porter(Shafi Hadi)(as-1,ts-2) Hank Mobley(ts) Sonny Clark(p) Paul Chambers(b) Art Taylor(dm).
Hackensack,N.J.,June 23,1957

tk.2	Mighty Moe and Joe-1	BN(Du)1A158-83391/4 CD BN(J)TOCJ-1568
tk.2/3	Mighty Moe And Joe-1	BN BLP1568;CD BN 5-21052-2,(J)TOCJ-6035
tk.5	News-2	- CD BN(J)TOCJ-1568
tk.6	Bags' groove-2	- - TOCJ-66043
tk.8	Double exposure-2	- -
tk.10	Falling in love with love-1	- CD BN 7-81331-2,(J)TOCJ-1568,TOCJ-5299

All titles,except the first,issued on BN BLP1568,CD BN(J)CJ28-5146.
All titles issued in stereo on Mosaic MQ10-181,CD MD6-181.
Note: The first stereo issue of this session,(J)TOCJ-1568,use the unedited tk.2 for the first tune and is missing the insert ending of tk.8.

JIMMY SMITH - CHEROKEE:
Jimmy Smith(org,p-1) Eddie McFadden(g,except -1) Donald Bailey(dm).
(Manhattan Towers) NYC,July 3,1957

	They can't take that away from me	rejected
tk.3	What is this thing called love	CD BN(J)TOCJ-1612
	Perdido-1	rejected
tk.5	You dig it-1	-
tk.6	On the sunny side of the street	CD BN(J)TOCJ-1612
tk.8	Laura	-
tk.14	I'm in the mood for love	-
tk.15	Things ain't what they used to be	-
tk.16	Cherokee	-
tk.17	Eekin'-1	rejected

Note: Bass on -1 is probably played by Eddie McFadden.

JIMMY SMITH TRIO + L.D.:
Lou Donaldson(as) Jimmy Smith(org) Eddie McFadden(g) Donald Bailey(dm).
(Manhattan Towers) NYC,July 4,1957

tk.4	Cha cha J	BN 45-1711 BN(J)K18P-9280,BNJ61013,CD TOCJ-1610		
tk.5	'Round midnight (as out)		-	-
tk.6	Street of dreams		-	-
tk.7	Star eyes		-	-
tk.8	Darn that dream		-	-
tk.9	Soft winds		-	-
tk.12	Doodlin' (as out)	rejected		
tk.14	Hollerin' and screamin'	BN(J)BNJ61013,CD TOCJ-1610		

PAUL CHAMBERS - BASS ON TOP:
Hank Jones(p) Kenny Burrell(g) Paul Chambers(b) Art Taylor(dm).
Hackensack,N.J.,July 14,1957

tk.3	Dear old Stockholm	BN BLP1569/BST81569
tk.5	Chasin' the Bird	-
tk.6	I'm confessin'	-
tk.8	The theme	-
tk.9	Yesterdays	- (J)NP9021,K18P-9125, CD BN(J)CJ28-5172,TOCJ-6271/74, TOCP-7455/56
tk.10	You'd be so nice to come home to	BN BLP1569/BST81569,CD 7-95591-2
tk.12	Chamber mates	BN(J)BNJ61009(alb.61008/010)

All titles issued on CD BN 7-46533-2.
All titles from BLP1569/BST81569 also issued on CD BN(J)TOCJ-1569.

SONNY CLARK - DIAL S FOR SONNY:
Art Farmer(tp) Curtis Fuller(tb) Hank Mobley(ts) Sonny Clark(p) Wilbur Ware(b) Louis Hayes(dm).
Hackensack,N.J.,July 21,1957

tk.2	Sonny's mood	BN BLP1570	
tk.5	Bootin' it		
tk.5/ins*	Bootin' it	BN BLP1570	
tk.8	Dial S for Sonny	-	CD BN(J)CJ28-5036,TOCJ-66038
tk.11	It could happen to you	-	CD BN(J)TOCJ-5829
tk.13	Shoutin' on a riff	-	CD BN(J)TOCJ-6035
tk.15	Love walked in (tp,tb,ts out)	-	CD BN 7-99427-2,5-20808-2

All titles issued on CD BN 8-56585-2.
All titles from BLP1570 also issued on CD BN(J)CJ28-5147.
Note: CD 8-56585-2 includes all takes in stereo.The insert* ending used to the mono master of tk.5 could not be found in stereo.The edited mono master and tk.5 in stereo both appear on the CD.

BUD! - THE AMAZING BUD POWELL:
Bud Powell(p) Paul Chambers(b) Art Taylor(dm).

Hackensack,N.J.,August 3,1957

tk.1	Blue pearl	BN BLP1571/BST81571,B1-93204,(J)BNJ27002, FCPA 6203,K23P-6723,K18P-9125 Lib(J)K22P-6092/93 CD BN 7-93204-2,(J)CJ28-5032,TOCJ-6035, TOCJ-6105,TOCJ-66033,TOCP-50060
tk.2	Blue pearl (alt.)	BN BST84430,(Du)1A158-83391/4,(J)BNJ27002, BNJ61009(alb.61008/010) CD BN(J)TOCJ-1601
tk.4	Keepin' in the groove	BN BLP1571/BST81571
tk.5	Some soul	-
tk.6	Frantic fancies	- CD BN(J)TOCJ-5822,TOCJ-66033
tk.7	Bud on Bach (solo p)	BN BLP1571/BST81571,B1-93204,(J)K23P-6723; FCPA 6203 CD BN 7-93204-2,8-54906-2,(J)TOCJ-5822

All titles also issued on Mosaic MR5-116,CD BN 7-81571-2,8-30083-2.
All titles from BLP1571 also issued on CD BN(J)TOCJ-1571.

Curtis Fuller(tb) added.Same session.

tk.9	Idaho	
tk.11	Don't blame me	
tk.18	Moose the mooche	CD BN(J)CJ28-5032

All titles issued on BN BLP1571/BST81571,Mosaic MR5-116,CD BN 7-81571-2,8-30083-2,(J) TOCJ-1571.

CURTIS FULLER - BONE & BARI:
Curtis Fuller(tb) Tate Houston(bs) Sonny Clark(p) Paul Chambers(b) Art Taylor(dm).

Hackensack,N.J.,August 4,1957

tk.2	Algonquin	BN 45-1689
tk.5	Bone and bari	
tk.7	Nita's waltz	
tk.8	Again (tb out)	
tk.10	Heart and soul (bs out)	
tk.13	Pick up	BN 45-1689

All titles issued on BN BLP1572,Mosaic MQ5-166,CD BN(J)TOCJ-1572,Mosaic MD3-166.
BN 45-1689 was possibly not released.
Note: The Mosaic LP & the CD issues are stereo.

JOHN JENKINS WITH KENNY BURRELL:
John Jenkins(as) Sonny Clark(p) Kenny Burrell(g) Paul Chambers(b) Dannie Richmond(dm).
Hackensack,N.J.,August 11,1957

tk.2	Chalumeau (alt.)	
tk.2/1	Chalumeau	BN BLP1573
tk.3	From this moment on	-
tk.4	Motif	-
tk.5	Everything I have is yours	-
tk.7	Sharon (alt.)	
tk.7/6	Sharon	BN BLP1573
tk.9	Blues for two	-

All titles issued on CD BN 8-52437-2.
Note: Because the stereo session tapes did not survive in full,the edited mono masters of tk.2/1 and tk.6/7 could not be duplicated.The stereo CD version carries the edited mono masters and the stereo basic takes that they were made from.
All titles from BLP1573 also issued on CD BN(J)TOCJ-1573.

HANK MOBLEY QUINTET - CURTAIN CALL:
Kenny Dorham(tp) Hank Mobley(ts) Sonny Clark(p) Jimmy Rowser(b) Art Taylor(dm).
Hackensack,N.J.,August 18,1957

tk.3	My reverie
tk.6	Curtain call
tk.9	On the bright side
tk.10	The Mobe
tk.11	Don't get too hip
tk.12	Deep in a dream (tp out)

All titles issued on BN(J)BNJ61006,Mosaic MQ10-181,CD BN(J)TOCJ-1611,Mosaic MD6-181.
Note: Bass player was mistakenly listed as George Joyner on BNJ61006.

LEE MORGAN - CITY LIGHTS:
Lee Morgan(tp) Curtis Fuller(tb) George Coleman(as-1,ts-2) Ray Bryant(p) Paul Chambers(b) Art Taylor (dm).
Hackensack,N.J.,August 25,1957

tk.1	Just by myself -2	
tk.4	City lights -2	CD BN 8-54363-2
tk.6	Tempo de waltz -1	
tk.9	You're mine you -2	
tk.10	Kin folks -1	

All titles issued on BN BLP1575/BST81575,Mosaic MQ6-162,CD BN(J)TOCJ-1575,Mosaic MD4-162.

Note: This was an afternoon session.The Jimmy Smith session that follows the same day took place at Manhattan Towers at night.

<u>JIMMY SMITH</u> - <u>HOUSE PARTY/THE SERMON</u>:
Lee Morgan(tp) Curtis Fuller(tb) George Coleman(as) Jimmy Smith(org) Eddie McFadden-1 or Kenny Burrell-2 (g) Donald Bailey(dm).
(Manhattan Towers) NYC,August 25,1957

tk.2	J.O.S. (tb out) -1	BN BLP4011/BST84011 CD BN 7-46546-2,5-24541-2,(J)TOCJ-4011
tk.3	What is this thing called love -1	BN LT-992,(E)UALP21 CD BN 7-46546-2,(J)TOCJ-5825
tk.4	Just friends -1	BN BLP4002/BST84002,CD 7-46546-2,5-24542-2
tk.5	Cherokee -2	BN LT-992 CD BN 7-46546-2,(J)TOCJ-4002,TOCJ-5645/46
tk.6	Litle girl blue (tp,tb,as out) -2	BN LT-1092,CD 8-21282-2,(J)TOCJ-5941/44
tk.8	'S wonderful (tb,as out) -1	BN(J)BNJ50101 CD BN 7-46097-2,7-80706-2,(J)CJ28-5034, TOCJ-5296,TOCJ-5941/44,TOCJ-66037
tk.9	Blue room (tp,as,g out)	BN(J)BNJ50101;CD BN 7-46097-2
tk.11	Blues after all -2	BN BLP4002/BST84002 CD BN 7-46546-2,8-33206-2,5-24542-2 (J)TOCJ-4002,Toshiba-EMI(J)TOCJ-6098/99

Note: On LT-992,Art Blakey is incorrectly credited as the drummer.

<u>SONNY CLARK</u> - <u>SONNY'S CRIB</u>:
Donald Byrd(tp) Curtis Fuller(tb) John Coltrane(ts) Sonny Clark(p) Paul Chambers(b) Art Taylor(dm).
Hackensack,N.J.,September 1,1957

tk.2	News for Lulu	BN BLP1576/BST81576
tk.3	Sonny's crib	BN 45-1697,BLP1576/BST81576 CD BN 4-98240-2,(J)CJ28-5036,TOCJ-66041
tk.4	Sonny's crib (alt.)	
tk.6	Speak low (alt.) (see note)	
tk.7/6	Speak low	BN 45-1719,BLP1576/BST81576,BST89903, BN-LA159-G2;CD BN 7-99175-2,(J)TOCJ-66041
tk.9	With a song in my heart (alt.) (see note)	
tk.10/9	With a song in my heart	BN BLP1576/BST81576 CD BN(J)TOCJ-5829,TOCJ-66038
tk.12	Come rain or come shine	BN BLP1576/BST81576

All titles and takes shown issued on CD BN 7-46819-2,4-97367-2.
Note: BLP1576 & BST81576 used tk.7 with tp & p solos from tk.6 and tk.10 with p solo from tk.9.The first CD issue (7-46819-2) used tks. 6 & 9 with the edited solos missing.The second CD issue (4-97367-2) has the takes restored to full performance.
All titles from BST81576 also issued on CD BN(J)TOCJ-1576.

71

JOHN COLTRANE - BLUE TRAIN:
Lee Morgan(tp) Curtis Fuller(tb) John Coltrane(ts) Kenny Drew(p) Paul Chambers(b) Philly Joe Jones(dm).
Hackensack,N.J.,September 15,1957

tk.2	Lazy bird (alt.)	
tk.3	Lazy bird	
tk.6	Moment's notice	BN 45-1718,(Du)1A158-83391/4,(J)FCPA 6202 CD BN 7-99175-2,(J)CJ25-5181/84,TOCJ-5630, TOCJ-6104,TOCJ-6131,TOCJ-66041
tk.8	Blue train (alt.)	CD BN(J)TOCJ-1601,TOCJ-66041
tk.9/8	Blue train	BN 45-1691,BST89903,BN-LA159-G2, BST2-84429,BST2-92468 BN(J)FCPA 6202,W-5512,NP9022,LNS90031, LNP95060,K16P-9031/32,K22P-6096/97 UA UA-XW134,(G)UAS29816;Lib(F)LBS83442/3 CD BN 7-92468-2,7-96110-2,7-99175-2, 8-56399-2,4-97154-2,4-98240-2,5-20070-2, (C)8-56508-2,(E)8-53223-2,(Eu)8-29964-2, (F)8-54185-2,8-54197-2,(J)CJ28-5171,CJ28-5176, CP32-5056,TOCJ-5630,TOCJ-5933,TOCJ-6104, TOCJ-66041,TOCJ-66051,TOCJ-66060, TOCJ-66063,TOCP-7455/56,TOCP-8963, TOCP-50230,(Sp)8-34712-2,8-53016-2,5-21755-2, EMI-Music 4-98899-2,EMI(E)5-21426-2
tk.11	Locomotion	BN(J)K18P-9125,FCPA 6202;Sunset(E)SLS50229 CD BN 4-98240-2,(J)TOCJ-6035
tk.12	I'm old fashioned	BN(E)UALP 17 CD BN 7-96098-2,5-24271-2,(J)CJ28-5023, CJ28-5172,TOCJ-5630,TOCJ-6104,TOCJ-6271/74, TOCJ-66041,EMI Gold(E)5-21427-2, HMV Jazz(E)5-20882-2

All titles issued on CD BN 8-53428-2.
All titles,except alternates,issued on BN BLP1577/BST81577,CD 7-46095-2,(J)TOCJ-1577,DVD-CD Classic DAD-101028.
Note: The piano solo on tk.9 was edited in from tk.8.

SONNY ROLLINS - NEWK'S TIME:
Sonny Rollins(ts) Wynton Kelly(p) Doug Watkins(b) Philly Joe Jones(dm).
Hackensack,N.J.,September 22,1957

tk.5	Tune up	BN BST89903,BN-LA159-G2,BN-LA401-H2, B1-93203,(J)K18P-9126 CD BN 7-93203-2,(Eu)8-29964-2,(J)CJ28-5167, TOCJ-5639,TOCJ-5826,TOCJ-6103, TOCJ-6271/74,TOCJ-66036,TOCP-7455/56, TOCP-50230,Cap(J)TOCJ-5191/92, (Sp)8-34712-2,8-53016-2
tk.9	Asiatic raes	BN(In)JAZ 1 CD BN(J)TOCJ-5639,TOCJ-5755/56,TOCJ-6103, TOCJ-66036
tk.13	The surrey with the fringe on top (p,b out)	BN BN-LA401-H2;Lib(J)K22P-6074/75 CD BN(J)CJ28-5167,TOCJ-5639,TOCJ-5934, TOCJ-6103,TOCJ-66036
tk.15	Wonderful,wonderful	BN(E)UALP 19
tk.17	Namely you	BN BN-LA401-H2,CD 8-34873-2,(J)TOCJ-5260
tk.19	Blues for Philly Joe	CD BN 8-23516-2

All titles issued on BN BLP4001/BST84001,CD 7-84001-2,8-21371-2.

 72

LEE MORGAN - THE COOKER:
Lee Morgan(tp) Pepper Adams(bs) Bobby Timmons(p) Paul Chambers(b) Philly Joe Jones(dm).
Hackensack,N.J.,September 29,1957

tk.3	Just one of those things (alt.)	CD BN(J)TOCJ-1601
tk.4	Just one of those things	BN BLP1578/BST84178,BN-LA224-G CD BN 7-95591-2,(J)CJ28-5037
tk.6	Heavy dipper	BN BLP1578/BST84178,BN-LA224-G
tk.7	A night in Tunisia	BN 45-1692,BLP1578/BST84178,B1-91138, CD 7-91138-2
tk.9	Lover man	BN BLP1578/BST84178;CD BN(J)TOCJ-5828
tk.10	New-Ma	- -

All titles issued on Mosaic MQ6-162,CD Mosaic MD4-162.
All titles from BST81578 also issued on CD BN(J)TOCJ-1578.
Note: The stereo take 7 has a different insert ending on all issues until the Mosaic release which matches the mono

SONNY CLARK TRIO:
Sonny Clark(p) Paul Chambers(b) Philly Joe Jones(dm).
Hackensack,N.J.,October 13,1957

tk.2	I didn't know what time it was (alt.)	BN(J)GXF-3069,BNJ61017,CD TOCJ-1617
tk.3	I didn't know what time it was	BN BLP1579/BST84179;CD BN(Sp)5-21755-2
tk.5	Two bass hit	- CD BN 7-96904-2,(J)CJ28-5030
tk.7	Two bass hit (alt.)	BN(J)GXF-3069,BNJ61017,CD TOCJ-1617
tk.8	Be-bop	BN BLP1579/BST84179,(J)FCPA 6207 CD BN 7-89032-2
tk.9	Tadd's delight (alt.)	BN(J)GXF-3069,BNJ61017,CD TOCJ-1617
tk.10	Tadd's delight	BN BLP1579/BST84179
tk.11	Softly as in a morning sunrise	BN 45-1719,BLP1579/BST84179, (J)K16P-9031/32,K18P-9126,K22P-6096/97, K23P-6726,FCPA6207,W-5509 CD BN(J)CJ28-5021,CJ28-5036,CJ28-5172, CP32-5448,TOCJ-5187/88,TOCJ-5829, TOCJ-5934,TOCJ-66038,TOCJ-66053, TOCP-50230,Cap(J)TOCJ-5714
tk.12	I'll remember April (p solo)	BN BLP1579,K23P-6726,FCPA 6207,W-5509 CD BN(J)CJ28-5022,TOCJ-5829,TOCJ-5851, TOCJ-5873,TOCJ-66038

All titles and takes shown issued on CD BN 7-46547-2.
All titles from BST81579 also issued on CD BN(J)TOCJ-1579.
Note: CD incorrectly states the recording date as November 13,1957.

HANK MOBLEY - POPPIN':
Art Farmer(tp) Hank Mobley(ts) Pepper Adams(bs) Sonny Clark(p) Paul Chambers(b) Philly Joe Jones(dm).
Hackensack,N.J.,October 20,1957

tk.3	Gettin' into something	
tk.6	Poppin'	
tk.8	East of Brooklyn (*aka* Night watch)	CD BN(Eu)5-23444-2
tk.9	Tune up	
tk.12	Darn that dream	

All titles issued on BN(J)GXF-3066,Mosaic MQ10-181,CD BN(J)TOCJ-1620,Mosaic MD6-181.

JOHNNY GRIFFIN - THE CONGREGATION:
Johnny Griffin(ts) Sonny Clark(p) Paul Chambers(b) Kenny Dennis(dm).
Hackensack,N.J.,October 23,1957

tk.4	It's you or no one	BN BLP1580,(J)K18P-9126
tk.6	I'm glad there is you	- CD BN(Au)8-57460-2
tk.10	Latin Quarter	-
tk.11	Main Spring	-
tk.12	I remember you	BN(J)BNJ61009(alb.61008/010),CD TOCJ-1601
tk.14	The congregation	BN BLP1580;CD BN(Eu)7-80703-2

All titles from BLP1580 (mono) also issued on BN B1-89383,CD BN(J)TOCJ-1580 (stereo).
All titles also issued on CD BN 7-89383-2.

SONNY ROLLINS - A NIGHT AT THE VILLAGE VANGUARD:
Sonny Rollins(ts) Don Bailey(b) Pete La Roca(dm).
(Village Vanguard) NYC,November 3,1957 (afternoon)

tk.1	Woody'n you	rejected
tk.2	A night in Tunisia	BN BLP1581 Lib(J)K22P-6131/32 CD BN 7-46517-2,8-21371-2,4-99795-2, (J)CJ28-5167,TOCJ-1581,TOCJ-5639,TOCJ-6103, TOCJ-66036
tk.3	I've got you under my skin	BN BN-LA475-H2,(J)K18P-9277,BNJ61014 CD BN 7-46517-2,8-21371-2,8-35282-2, 4-99795-2,(J)TOCJ-1613
tk.4	What is this thing called love	rejected
tk.5	Old devil moon	-

Sonny Rollins(ts) Wilbur Ware(b) Elvin Jones(dm).
(Village Vanguard) NYC,November 3,1957 (evening)

tk.6	A night in Tunisia	BN BN-LA475-H2,(J)K18P-9277,BNJ61014 CD BN 7-46517-2,7-89032-2,(J)TOCJ-1613
tk.7	Softly as in a morning sunrise (alt.)	BN BN-LA475-H2,(J)K18P-9277,BNJ61014 CD BN 7-46517-2,(J)TOCJ-1613
tk.8	Four	BN BN-LA475-H2,(J)K18P-9278,BNJ61015 CD BN 7-46517-2,8-23516-2,(J)TOCJ-1614
tk.9	Woody'n you	BN BN-LA475-H2,(J)K18P-9278,BNJ61015 CD BN 7-46517-2,(J)TOCJ-1614
tk.10	That old devil moon	BN BLP1581,(J)K22P-6096/97 CD BN 7-46517-2,(J)CJ25-5181/84,TOCJ-5826, TOCJ-66036
tk.11	What is this thing called love	BN BN-LA475-H2,(J)K18P-9277,BNJ61014 CD BN 7-46518-2,(J)TOCJ-1613
tk.12	Softly as in a morning sunrise	BN BLP1581,(J)K18P-9277 Lib(J)K22P-6074/75 CD BN 7-46518-2,7-93203-2,(J)CJ28-5167, TOCJ-5639,TOCJ-5826,TOCJ-6103,TOCJ-66036
tk.13	Sonnymoon for two	BN 45-1698,BLP1581,B1-93203,(J)K18P-9126, W-5505 CD BN 7-46518-2,7-93203-2,8-23516-2, (J)TOCJ-5826
tk.14	I can't get started	BN BLP1581 CD BN 7-46518-2,4-95981-2,(Eu)7-89914-2, (J)CJ28-5167,TOCJ-5826,TOCJ-66036
tk.15	I'll remember April	BN BN-LA475-H2,(J)K18P-9278,BNJ61015 CD BN 7-46518-2,(J)CJ28-5167,TOCJ-1614

(session continued on next page)

tk.16	Get happy (long version)	BN BN-LA475-H2,(J)K18P-9278,BNJ61015 CD BN 7-46518-2,(J)TOCJ-1614
tk.17	Striver's row	BN BLP1581,BN-LA401-H2, CD BN 7-46518-2,7-93203,(Sp)5-21755-2
tk.18	All the things you are	BN BN-LA475-H2,(J)K18P-9278,BNJ61015 CD BN 7-46518-2,8-23516-2,(J)CJ28-5167, TOCJ-1614
tk.19	Get happy (short version)	BN BN-LA475-H2,(J)K18P-9278,BNJ61015 CD BN 7-46518-2,(J)TOCJ-1614
tk.20	Striver's row	rejected

All titles,except last,issued on CD BN 8-21371-2,4-99795-2.
All titles from BLP 1581 (mono) also issued on BN BST81581,CD BN(J)TOCJ-1581 (stereo).
Note: CD 4-99795-2 also includes introduction by Rollins before takes 2,9 and 10.

CLIFF JORDAN - CLIFF CRAFT:
Art Farmer(tp) Clifford Jordan(ts) Sonny Clark(p) George Tucker(b) Louis Hayes(dm).
Hackensack,N.J.,November 10,1957

tk.1	Confirmation	BN(J)FCPA 6211
tk.4	Anthropology	CD BN 7-89032-2
tk.7	Soul-lo blues	BN 45-1699 (poss. not released)
tk.9	Laconia	
tk.11	Cliff craft	
tk.13	Sophisticated lady (tp out)	CD BN 4-94035-2,5-20809-2

All titles issued on BN BLP1582(mono),CD 8-56584-2,(J)TOCJ-1582(stereo).

JIMMY SMITH - GROOVIN' AT SMALL'S PARADISE:
Jimmy Smith(org) Eddie McFadden(g) Donald Bailey(dm).
(Small's Paradise) NYC,November 15,1957

tk.1	Imagination	BN BLP1586
tk.2	Walkin'	
tk.3	My funny Valentine	BN BLP1585 CD BN(J)CJ28-5034,TOCJ-66037
tk.4	It's only a paper moon	
tk.5	I can't give you nothing	
tk.6	Laura	BN BLP1585
tk.7	Indiana	BN BLP1586
tk.8	Body and soul	-
tk.9	The champ	
tk.10	Lover man	BN 45-1704,BLP1586
tk.11	Slightly Monkish	BN BLP1585
tk.12	Lover man	rejected
tk.13	After hours	BN 45-1703,BLP1585
tk.14	Just friends	BN 45-1704,BLP1586 BN(J)K22P-6125/26
tk.15	Rhapsody in blue (org solo)	rejected
tk.16	Indiana	-

All titles,except tk.12,15 & 16,issued on CD BN 4-99777-2.
All titles from BLP1585/86 also issued on CD BN(J)TOCJ-1585/86.

75

LEE MORGAN - CANDY:
Lee Morgan(tp) Sonny Clark(p) Doug Watkins(b) Art Taylor(dm).
Hackensack,N.J.,November 18,1957

tk.4	Since I fell for you	BN BLP1590,B1-91138;Sunset SUS 5263 CD BN 7-91138-2,7-96098-2
tk.7	Personality	BN BLP1590;Sunset SUS 5263
tk.14	All at once you love her (as "Untitled (Morgan tune)" on *)	BN(J)BNJ61010(alb.61008/010)*,CD TOCJ-5856
	Who do you love I hope	rejected

First three titles also issued on Mosaic MQ6-162,CD BN 7-46508-2,Mosaic MD4-162.
First two titles also issued on CD BN(J)TOCJ-1590.
Note: The Sunset LP was the first stereo issue of tk.4 & tk.7.

JIMMY SMITH - LONESOME ROAD:
Jimmy Smith(org) Eddie McFadden(g) Donald Bailey(dm).
(Manhattan Towers) NYC,November 20,1957

tk.2	Our love is here to stay
tk.4	Lonesome road
tk.5	Margie
tk.9	Diane
tk.10	Blue Lou
tk.11	Taking a chance on love
tk.12	Danny boy
tk.13	I want a little girl

All titles were scheduled on BN(J)GXF-3078,which was not released,and finally issued on CD BN(J) TOCJ-1615.

CURTIS FULLER-ART FARMER:
Art Farmer(tp) Curtis Fuller(tb) Sonny Clark(p) George Tucker(b) Louis Hayes(dm).
Hackensack,N.J.,December 1,1957

tk.3	Quantrale	BN 45-1702
tk.4	Two quarters of a mile	-
tk.6	Little messenger	CD BN(J)CJ25-5181/84,TOCJ-6035,TOCJ-6271/74
tk.8	It's too late now	
tk.9	Jeanie	
tk.12	Carvon	

All titles issued on BN BLP1583,CD BN(J)CJ28-5148 (mono),Mosaic MQ5-166,CD BN(J)TOCJ-1583, Mosaic MD3-166 (stereo).
Note: BN 45-1702 was possibly not released.

SONNY CLARK QUINTET:
Clifford Jordan(ts) Sonny Clark(p) Kenny Burrell(g) Paul Chambers(b) Pete La Roca(dm).
Hackensack,N.J.,December 8,1957

tk.4	Minor meeting	CD BN(J)CJ28-5036,TOCJ-5829,TOCJ-6271/74 , TOCJ-66038
tk.6	Eastern incident	
tk.10	Little Sonny	

All titles scheduled for issue on BN BLP1592 (not released) and later issued on BN(J) LNJ70093, K18P-9279,BNJ61016,CD BN 5-22674-2,(J)TOCJ-1592.

76

LOU DONALDSON - LOU TAKES OFF:
Donald Byrd(tp) Curtis Fuller(tb) Lou Donaldson(as) Sonny Clark(p) Jamil Nasser (George Joyner)(b) Art Taylor(dm).

Hackensack,N.J.,December 15,1957

tk.4	Groovin' high	CD BN 8-27298-2,(J)TOCJ-66044
tk.5	Strollin' in	
tk.6	Sputnik	BN 45-1713
tk.8	Dewey Square	

All titles issued on BN BLP1591,CD BN(J)CJ28-5149,DVD-CD Classic DAD-1026.

SONNY CLARK - COOL STRUTTIN':
Art Farmer(tp) Jackie McLean(as) Sonny Clark(p) Paul Chambers(b) Philly Joe Jones(dm).

Hackensack,N.J.,January 5,1958

tk.1	Blue minor	BN BLP1588/BST81588,(J)NP-2008,NP9021, K16P-9031/32,K18P-9126,K22P-6096/97, FCPA 6207,W-5508 CD BN(J)CJ28-5036
tk.2	Cool struttin'	BN 45-1714,BLP1588/BST81588 BN(J)NP9022,LNS90031,LNP95060,FCPA 6207 CD BN(F)8-54185-2,(J)CJ25-5181/84,CJ28-5036, CJ28-5171,CJ28-5176,TOCJ-5829,TOCJ-5851, TOCJ-5925,TOCJ-5933,TOCJ-6132,TOCJ-66038, TOCJ-66051,TOCP-7455/56,TOCP-8963, Toshiba-EMI(J)TOCP-8751,Victor(J)VICJ-5154
tk.4	Royal flush	BN BLP1592 BN(J)LNJ70093,K18P-9279,BNJ61016, CD TOCJ-1592
tk.5	Sipping at Bell's	BN BLP1588/BST81588
tk.6	Deep night	- CD BN(J)CJ28-5024,TOCJ-5829,TOCJ-66038
tk.7	Lover	BN BLP1592,CD 7-81331-2 BN(J)LNJ70093,K18P-9279,BNJ61016 CD BN(J)TOCJ-1592

All titles issued on CD BN 7-46513-2,4-95327-2.
All titles from BLP1588 also issued on CD BN(J)CP35-3089.
All titles from BST81588 also issued on CD BN(J)TOCJ-1588.
Note: BN BLP1592 was not released.

HORACE SILVER - FURTHER EXPLORATIONS BY THE HORACE SILVER QUINTET:
Art Farmer(tp) Clifford Jordan(ts) Horace Silver(p) Teddy Kotick(b) Louis Hayes(dm).

Hackensack,N.J.,January 13,1958

tk.3	The outlaw	BN 45-1705,CD 4-95576-2
tk.9	Melancholy mood (tp,ts out)	BN BN-LA474-H2
tk.10	Moonrays	
tk.12	Ill wind	BN(J)K18P-9126
tk.16	Pyramid	CD BN 8-33208-2
tk.21	Safari	BN 45-1705 CD BN 8-33208-2,(J)TOCJ-6035,TOCJ-66034

All titles issued on BN BLP1589/BST81589,CD 8-56583-2.
Note: CDs 8-33208-2 and equivalent HMV Jazz(E) 5-20878-2 mentioned "Safari" as from October 9,1952 session,but actually used above version.

<u>CURTIS FULLER</u> - <u>TWO BONES</u>:
Curtis Fuller,Slide Hampton(tb) Sonny Clark(p) George Tucker(b) Charlie Persip(dm).
Hackensack,N.J.,January 22,1958

tk.2	Pajama tops	
tk.3	Slide's ride	
tk.6	Loquacious lady	
tk.10	Mean Jean	
tk.14	Fuss budget	
tk.15	Oatmeal cookie	
tk.17	Da-baby	

All titles issued on BN(J)GXF-3064,Mosaic MQ5-166,CD Mosaic MD3-166.
Note: Drummer was mistakenly identified as Al Harewood on GXF-3064.

<u>LEE MORGAN</u> - <u>CANDY</u>:
Lee Morgan(tp) Sonny Clark(p) Doug Watkins(b) Art Taylor(dm).
Hackensack,N.J.,February 2,1958

tk.5	Who do you love,I hope?	CD BN 7-99095-2,8-29095-2
tk.9	Candy	BN(J)NP9020C,FCPA 6213,CD CJ28-5037, CJ28-5172,CJ28-5177,TOCJ-5828,TOCJ-6271/74, TOCJ-66039
tk.12	C.T.A.	CD BN 8-54901-2,(J)TOCJ-5260,TOCJ-6035
tk.14	All the way	

All titles issued on BN BLP1590,Sunset SUS5263,Mosaic MQ6-162,CD BN 7-46508-2,(J)TOCJ-1590, Mosaic MD4-162.
Note: The Sunset LP was the first stereo issue of this session.Ending of take 9 is not identical to the mono take.This difference was repaired for all subsequent issues.

<u>HANK MOBLEY</u> - <u>PECKIN' TIME</u>:
Lee Morgan(tp) Hank Mobley(ts) Wynton Kelly(p) Paul Chambers(b) Charlie Persip(dm).
Hackensack,N.J.,February 9,1958

tk.2	High and flighty (alt.)		
tk.3	High and flighty	BN BLP1574;CD BN(J)CJ25-5181/84	
tk.4	Stretchin' out (alt.)		
tk.5	Stretchin' out	BN BLP1574	
tk.6	Peckin' time	-	
tk.10	Git-go blues	-	
tk.11	Speak low	-	CD BN(J)CJ28-5035,TOCJ-66043
tk.12	Speak low (alt.)		

All titles issued on Mosaic MQ10-181,CD BN 7-81574-2,(J)CJ28-5081,Mosaic MD6-181.
All titles from BLP1574 were also issued on CD BN(J)TOCJ-1574.

<u>JIMMY SMITH</u> - <u>HOUSE PARTY</u>:
Lou Donaldson(as) Jimmy Smith(org) Eddie McFadden(g) Donald Bailey(dm).
(Manhattan Towers) NYC,February 25,1958

	No way out (as out)	rejected
	unknown title (as out)	-
tk.5	Lover man	BN BLP4002/BST84002,BN-LA400-H2 CD BN 7-46097-2,5-24542-2,(J)TOCJ-4002, TOCJ-5300,TOCJ-5856
	Strike up the band	rejected

JIMMY SMITH - HOUSE PARTY/THE SERMON:
Lee Morgan(tp) Lou Donaldson(as) Tina Brooks(ts) Jimmy Smith(org) Kenny Burrell(g) Art Blakey(dm).
Same session.

tk.12	Confirmation	BN LT-992,CD 5-24542-2
tk.13	Au privave	BN BLP4002/BST84002 CD BN 5-24542-2,(J)TOCJ-4002
tk.14	Flamingo (as,ts out)	BN BLP4011/BST84011,BST89901 CD BN 5-24541-2,(J)TOCJ-4011,TOCJ-5645/46
tk.15	The sermon	BN 45-1879,L4011,BLP4011/BST84011, BST89901,BN-LA400-H2,B1-91140 BN(F)45-001(E)BNX 1,(J)NP9021,LNP-88046 CD BN 7-48337-2,7-91140-2,5-24541-2, (F)8-54188-2,(J)TOCJ-4011,TOCJ-5645/46

All titles also issued on BN 7-46097-2.

JIMMY SMITH - SOFTLY AS A SUMMER BREEZE:
Jimmy Smith(org) Eddie McFadden(g) Donald Bailey(dm).
(Manhattan Towers) NYC,February 26,1958

tk.3	Fugueing the blues	rejected
tk.4	Ham and eggs	-

Jimmy Smith(org) Kenny Burrell(g) Philly Joe Jones(dm).
Same session.

tk.5	It could happen to you	
tk.6	Hackensack	BN(E)BST83367/8 CD BN 8-33206-2,8-54363-2,(Eu)5-23444-2
tk.7	These foolish things	
tk.8	Sometimes I'm happy	

All titles issued on BN BLP4200/BST84200,CD 4-97505-2,(J)TOCJ-4200.

Jimmy Smith(org) Eddie McFadden(g) Donald Bailey(dm).
Same session.

tk.10	Someone to watch over me	BN BLP4200/BST84200.
tk.12	Ode to Philly Joe -1	- (E)BST83367/8
tk.14	September song	rejected
tk.16	Ham and eggs	-
tk.18	Fugueing the blues	-

-1: originally titled "Home cookin'" and issued as such on BN(E)BST83367/8.
First two titles also issued on CD BN 4-97505-2,(J)TOCJ-4200.

CANNONBALL ADDERLEY - SOMETHIN' ELSE!!!:
Miles Davis(tp) Julian "Cannonball" Adderley(as) Hank Jones(p) Sam Jones(b) Art Blakey(dm).
Hackensack,N.J.,March 9,1958

tk.2	Autumn leaves	BN 45-1737,L1595,BLP1595,BN-LA169-F, BST2-92468;Classic BST81595-45 BN(J)BNJ27001,NP9021,LNS90031,LNP95059B, K16P-9031/32,K18P-9126,K22P-6096/7, FCPA 6202,W-5512 Lib(F)LBS83442/3,(J)K22P-6074/75 CD BN 7-92468-2,7-96098-2,7-98287-2, 8-36633-2,5-20070-2,(F)8-54185-2,8-54197-2, (J)CJ25-5181/84,CJ28-5024,CJ28-5166, CJ28-5172,TOCJ-5638,TOCJ-5657,TOCJ-5658, TOCJ-5821,TOCJ-5934,TOCJ-66035,TOCJ-66052, TOCP-7455/56,TOCP-8963,Cap(J)TOCJ-5713, Toshiba-EMI(J)TOCP-8751,TOCP-65352,Victor(J) VICJ-5154,EMI-Music 4-98900-2,Cema S21-57610
tk.3	Love for sale	BN BLP1595,BN-LA169-F,(Du)BST83249, (E)BNX 1,(J)FCPA 6202;Lib(E)LBS83249 CD BN 7-48337-2,7-95591-2,8-23515-2, (J)CJ28-5166,TOCJ-5299,TOCJ-5638, TOCJ-5657,TOCJ-5750,TOCJ-66035,TOCJ-66071
tk.4	Somethin' else	BN 45-1738,BLP1595,BN-LA169-F,BST2-84433 BN(E)UALP 19,(J)NP9020C,LNP95060, FCPA 6202,W-5512 CD BN 7-97960-2,7-98287-2,8-23515-2, (E)8-53225-2,(J)CJ28-5166,TOCJ-5821, TOCJ-66035,Cap(J)TOCJ-5191/92, Toshiba-EMI(J)TOCJ-6098/99,HMV Jazz(E) 5-20882-2
tk.6	One for Daddy-O	BN 45-1739,L1595,BLP1595,BN-LA169-F CD BN 8-36633-2,8-54898-2,(J)TOCJ-5658, (Sp)5-21755-2
tk.7	Bangoon (Alison's uncle)	BN(Du)1A158-83391/4 BN(J)BNJ61010(alb.61008/010),BNJ27001 Classic BST81595-45 CD BN(J)TOCJ-1601
tk.11	Dancing in the dark (tp out)	BN BLP1595,BN-LA169-F;Lib(J)K22P-6131/32 CD BN 8-35282-2,(J)TOCJ-5857,TOCJ-6131

Note: Singles were issued as by "Cannonball Adderley's Five Stars".
The tune issued as "Alison's Uncle" by Nat Adderley is actually "Bangoon" by Hank Jones and appears as such on CD 4-95329-2.
All titles issued on CD BN 7-46338-2,4-95329-2.
All titles from BLP1595 (mono) were also issued on CD BN(J)CP35-3070 (mono),BN BST81595,CD BN(J)TOCJ-1595,Mobile Fidelity UDCD 563 (stereo),DVD-CD Classic DAD-1022.

TINA BROOKS - MINOR MOVE:
Lee Morgan(tp) Tina Brooks(ts) Sonny Clark(p) Doug Watkins(b) Art Blakey(dm).
Hackensack,N.J.,March 16,1958

tk.3	Minor move (alt.)	CD BN(J)TOCJ-1601
tk.7	The way you look tonight	
tk.9	Nutville	
tk.10	Star eyes	
tk.11	Everything happens to me	
tk.15	Minor move	

All titles issued on CD BN 5-22671-2.
All titles,except tk.3,issued on BN(J)GXF-3072,Mosaic MR4-106,CD BN(J)TOCJ-1616.

80

BENNIE GREEN -BACK ON THE SCENE:
Bennie Green(tb) Charlie Rouse(ts) Joe Knight(p) George Tucker(b) Louis Hayes(dm).
Hackensack,N.J,March 23,1958

tk.2	I love you	BN 45-1706
tk.4	Melba's mood	BN 45-1707
tk.8	Just friends	-
tk.12	Green Street	
tk.13	Bennie blows the blues	
tk.15	You're mine you	BN 45-1706

All titles issued on BN BLP1587/BST81587,CD BN(J)TOCJ-1587.

LOUIS SMITH - SMITHVILLE:
Louis Smith(tp) Charlie Rouse(ts) Sonny Clark(p) Paul Chambers(b) Art Taylor(dm).
Hackensack,N.J.,March 30,1958

tk.1	Tunesmith (Bakin')	BN(J)BNJ61010(alb.61008/61010)	
tk.8	There'll never be another you	BN BLP1594;CD BN(J)TOCJ-6035	
tk.11	Au privave	BN(Du)1A158-83391/4 BN(J)BNJ61010(alb.61008/010)	
tk.13	Smithville	BN 45-1715,BLP1594	
tk.16	Embraceable you	-	CD BN(J)TOCJ-6271/74
tk.17	Later	-	
tk.18	Wetu	-	

All titles from BLP1594 also issued on CD BN(J)TOCJ-1594.
Note: Takes 1 & 11 have survived only in stereo. All other titles have survived only in mono.

JIMMY SMITH:
Lou Donaldson(as-1) Tina Brooks(ts-2)Jimmy Smith(org) Eddie McFadden(g) Donald Bailey(dm).
(Live,Small's Paradise) NYC,April 7,1958

Set #1:

tk.1	Small's minor	rejected
tk.2	What's new?-1	CD BN 7-84441-2
tk.3	Fugueing the blues-1	rejected
tk.4	Red sails in the sunset-1	-
tk.5	Cool blues-1,2	BN LT-1054,CD 7-84441-2

Set #2: Same.

tk.6	September song	rejected
tk.7	Yesterdays	-
tk.8	Small's minor	CD BN 7-84441-2
tk.9	Once in a while-1	-
tk.10	Bye bye blackbird-1	rejected

Lou Donaldson(as) Tina Brooks(ts) Jimmy Smith(org) Eddie McFadden(g) Art Blakey(dm).
(Live,Small's Paradise) NYC,April 7,1958

Set #3:

tk.11	A night in Tunisia	BN LT-1054
tk.12	Dark eyes	-
tk.13	Groovin' at Small's	-

All titles also issued on CD BN 7-84441-2

Lou Donaldson(as) Jimmy Smith(org) Eddie McFadden(g) Donald Bailey(dm).Same session.

tk.14	Mary Ann	rejected

BENNIE GREEN - SOUL STIRRIN':
Bennie Green(tb,vo) Billy Root,Gene Ammons(as "Jug")(ts) Sonny Clark(p) Ike Isaacs(b) Elvin Jones(dm) Babs Gonzales(vo).

Hackensack,N.J.,April 28,1958

tk.2	Lullaby of the doomed	BN 45-1709,BLP1599,BST81599
tk.5	We wanna cook -1	- - -
tk.9	That's all	BN 45-1708 - -
tk.12	Soul stirrin' (voBGr,BGo)	BN BST81599
tk.12/13	Soul stirrin' (voBGr,BGo)(see note)	BN 45-1708,BLP1599 BN(J)BNJ61010(alb.61008/010)
tk.15	B.G. Mambo	BN BLP1599,BST81599
tk.19	Black pearl	- -

-1: Band vocal on this title.
Note: Mono album BLP1599 used a spliced master (tk.12 up to p solo and tk.13 for p solo and ensemble),in place of the stereo take 12 used in BST81599.
All titles issued on CD BN 8-59381-2.
All titles from BST81599 also issued on CD BN(J)TOCJ-1599.

KENNY BURRELL - BLUE LIGHTS:
Louis Smith(tp) Junior Cook-1,Tina Brooks-2(ts) Duke Jordan(p) Kenny Burrell(g) Sam Jones(b) Art Blakey (dm).

(Manhattan Towers) NYC,May 14,1958

tk.1	I never knew -1,2	BN(J)GXF-3070,BNJ61010(alb.61008/010) CD BN(J)TOCJ-1609
tk.2	Scotch blues -1,2	BN BLP1596/BST81596;Lib(J)K22P-6094/95
tk.4	The man I love	BN BLP1597/BST81597,CD 7-80706-2
tk.8	Yes baby -1,2	BN 45-1716,BLP1596/BST81596
tk.9	Phinupi -1	BN BLP1597/BST81597,CD 8-30493-2

All titles also issued on CD BN 7-81596-2 in mono,8-57184-2 in stereo
All titles from BST81596/97 also issued on CD BN(J)TOCJ-1596/97.

Bobby Timmons(p) replaces Jordan.Same session.

tk.10	Chuckin'-1,2	BN BLP1597/BST81597
tk.11	Autumn in New York (tp out)	BN BLP1596/BST81596,(J)W-5511 CD BN(J)TOCJ-66042
tk.12	Rock salt -1,2	BN 45-1717,BLP1597/BST81597
tk.14	Caravan -1,2	BN BLP1596/BST81596 CD BN 4-94035-2,(J)TOCJ-66042

All titles also issued on CD BN 7-81597-2 in mono,8-57184-2 in stereo.
All titles from BST81596/97 also issued on CD BN(J)TOCJ-1596/97.

 82

<u>THE AMAZING BUD POWELL</u> - <u>TIME WAITS</u>:
Bud Powell(p) Sam Jones(b) Philly Joe Jones(dm).
Hackensack,N.J.,May 24,1958

tk.4	John's abbey (alt.)	BN BST84430,(J)BNJ61010(alb.61008/010) CD BN(J)TOCP-50060
tk.5	Sub city (alt.)	BN BLP1598
tk.8	Sub city	- Lib(J)K22P-6092/93
tk.9	John's abbey	BN BLP1598,B1-93204 CD BN 7-93204-2,(F)8-54185-2,8-54197-2, (J)CJ28-5032,TOCJ-5822,TOCJ-6105,TOCJ-66033
tk.10	Buster rides again	BN 45-1712,BLP1598 CD BN 7-93204-2,(J)CJ28-5032,TOCJ-66033
tk.11	Dry soul	BN 45-1712,BLP1598
tk.12	Marmalade	-
tk.14	Monopoly	BN BLP1598,B1-93204,(J)K23P-6723,FCPA 6203 CD BN 7-93204-2,(J)CJ28-5032
tk.16	Time waits	BN BLP1598,(J)K23P-6723,FCPA 6203 CD BN 8-54906-2

All titles also issued on Mosaic MR5-116,CD BN 7-46820-2,8-30083-2,5-21227-2.
All titles from BLP1598 (mono) also issued on BN BST81598,CD BN(J)TOCJ-1598 (stereo).

<u>BILL HENDERSON & THE HORACE SILVER QUINTET</u>:
Donald Byrd(tp) Junior Cook(ts) Horace Silver(p) Gene Taylor(b) Louis Hayes(dm) Bill Henderson(vo).
Hackensack,N.J.,June 15,1958

tk.9	Tippin'	BN 45-1710
tk.11	Senor blues (voBH)	- CD 4-95576-2,5-21153-2,(J)TOCJ-5298

Both titles also issued on BN BN-LA945-H,(J)BNJ61005,CD BN 7-81539-2,5-25648-2.

<u>JIMMY SMITH</u>:
Jimmy Smith(org) Kenny Burrell(g) Donald Bailey(dm).
Hackensack,N.J.,July 15,1958

tk.2	Bye bye blackbird	BN LT-1092,CD 8-21282-2
tk.3	September song	- -
tk.7	Since I fell for you	BN 45-1769 ,LT-1092,CD 8-53360-2
tk.9	Since I fell for you (alt.)	CD BN 8-53360-2
tk.10	Just a lucky so and so	BN LT-1092,CD 8-21282-2
tk.11	Motoring along	BN 45-1769,BLP4050/BST84050 CD BN 8-53360-2,(J)TOCJ-4050
tk.14	Ruby	BN LT-1092,CD 8-21282-2
tk.15	Motoring along (alt.)	CD BN 8-53360-2

<u>JIMMY SMITH</u> - <u>SIX VIEWS OF THE BLUES</u>:
Cecil Payne(bs) Jimmy Smith(org) Kenny Burrell(g) Don Bailey(b) Art Blakey-1 or Donald Bailey-2 (dm).
Hackensack,N.J.,July 16,1958

tk.3	St. Louis blues -1	
tk.8	The swingin' shepherd blues -1	BN 45-1711,(J)K18P-9280
tk.9	Blues #1 -1	
tk.10	Blues #2 -2	
tk.14	Blues #3 -2	
tk.16	Blues #4 -2	

All titles issued on CD BN 5-21435-2.

LOU DONALDSON - BLUES WALK:
Lou Donaldson(as) Herman Foster(p) Peck Morrison(b) Dave Bailey(dm) Ray Barretto(cga).
Hackensack,N.J.,July 28,1958

tk.2	Play,Ray	BN 45-1721
tk.5	The masquerade is over	BN 45-1720,L1593
tk.10	Autumn nocturne	BN 45-1721;CD Cap(J)TOCJ-5861
tk.11	Calling all cats	BN(E)BNX 1;CD BN 7-48337-2
tk.13	Move	
tk.15	Blues walk	BN 45-1720,L1593,BST89903,BN-LA159-G2, BST2-84429,(In)JAZ 2,(J)W-5507 CD BN 7-96110-2,8-27298-2,5-20070-2, (Au)8-14808-2,(C)8-56508-2,(F)8-54185-2, 8-54197-2,(J)CP32-5057,TOCJ-5298,TOCJ-5937, TOCJ-6035,TOCJ-66044,EMI Gold(E)5-21427-2

All titles issued on BN BLP1593/BST81593,CD 7-46525-2.

DIZZY REECE - BLUES IN TRINITY:
Dizzy Reece,Donald Byrd(tp) Tubby Hayes(ts) Terry Shannon(p) Lloyd Thompson(b) Art Taylor(dm).
(Produced by Tony Hall) (Decca Studios) London,August 24,1958

1001	Blues in Trinity -1	BN BLP4006
1002	Colour blind -1	-
1003	Just a penny	CD BN(J)TOCJ-5941/44
1004	Round about midnight -1,2	BN BLP4006
1005	I had the craziest dream (ts out) -1	
1006	Eboo	CD BN(J)TOCJ-5941/44
1007	Close up	BN BLP4006
1008	Shepherd's serenade	-

-1: Byrd out.
-2: Reece out.
All titles issued on CD BN 8-32093-2.
All titles from BLP 4006 (mono) also issued on BN B1-32093,CD BN(J)TOCJ-4006 (stereo).
Note: Because of restrictive British musicians' union regulations,the credits to this album listed the recording location as Paris.

INTRODUCING THE THREE SOUNDS:
Gene Harris(p) Andrew Simpkins(b) Bill Dowdy(dm).
Hackensack,N.J.,September 16,1958

tk.5	Willow weep for me	BN 45-1722,BLP1600/BST81600,(J)K23P-6726, W-5510 CD BN 7-46531-2,8-27323-2,(J)CJ28-5168, TOCJ-5300
tk.6	Both sides	BN 45-1723,BLP1600/BST81600,CD 7-46531-2
tk.8	Bobby	BN(J)BNJ61019 CD BN 7-46531-2,8-27323-2
tk.9	Mo-Ge	BN 45-1723,CD 7-46531-2 BN(Du)1A158-83391/4,(J)BNJ61019
tk.10	Angel eyes	BN 45-1724,BLP4014/BST84014 CD BN(J)CJ28-5077,CJ28-5168,TOCJ-4014
tk.12	Tenderly	BN 45-1722,BLP1600/BST81600 CD BN 7-46531-2,(J)CJ28-5168,Toshiba-EMI(J) TOCJ-6098/99,TOCJ-66048
tk.15	Soft touch	BN(J)BNJ61019;CD BN 7-46531-2
tk.17	It's nice	BN 45-1724,BLP1600/BST81600,CD 7-46531-2
tk.18	Falling in love with love	BN BLP4014/BST84014;CD BN(J)CJ28-5077, TOCJ-4014

All titles from BST81600 also issued on CD BN(J)TOCJ-1600.

84

INTRODUCING THE THREE SOUNDS:
Gene Harris(p,celeste-1) Andrew Simpkins(b) Bill Dowdy(dm).
Hackensack,N.J.,September 28,1958

tk.2	Don't get around much anymore	BN(J)BNJ61019
tk.4	O sole mio	BN 45-1725,BLP1600/BST81600
tk.7	Blue bells -1	- -
tk.11	Time after time	BN 45-1726,BLP4014/BST84014 CD BN(J)CJ28-5077,TOCJ-4014
tk.12	Would 'n you	BN BLP1600/BST81600,(Du)1A158-83391/4 CD BN 8-27323-2
tk.14	It might as well be Spring	BN(J)BNJ61019
tk.16	Goin' home (alt.)	-
tk.18	Goin' home	BN 45-1726,BLP1600/BST81600

All titles,except tk.11,also issued on CD BN 7-46531-2.
All titles from BST81600 also issued on CD BN(J)TOCJ-1600.

BILL HENDERSON WITH JIMMY SMITH TRIO:
Bill Henderson(vo) Jimmy Smith(org) Ray Crawford(g) Donald Bailey(dm).
Hackensack,N.J.,October 14,1958

tk.13	Willow weep for me	BN 45-1728
tk.19	Ain't no use	BN 45-1727,CD 7-96582-2
tk.23	Angel eyes	-
tk.26	Ain't that love	BN 45-1728

All titles also issued on BN(J)K18P-9280,CD BN 4-97505-2.

ART BLAKEY AND THE JAZZ MESSENGERS - MOANIN':
Lee Morgan(tp) Benny Golson(ts) Bobby Timmons(p) Jymie Merritt(b) Art Blakey(dm).
Hackensack,N.J.,October 30,1958

tk.1 Are you real? CD BN(J)TOCJ-5857
tk.3 Moanin' (alt.) CD BN(J)CP32-5448,TOCJ-5941/44
tk.4 Moanin' BN 45-1735,L4003,BST89903,BST2-84429, BN-LA159-G2,BST2-92471,B1-93205, (F)45-002,BST84383,(Du)BST83249,(E)UALP 19, (J)NP9020C,LBN80259,LNS90031,LNP95059B, K23P-6724,FCPA 6205,W-5506;Lib(E)LBS83249
CD BN 7-92471-2,7-93205-2,7-96110-2, 7-97190-2,8-34957-2,8-54899-2,5-20070-2, (E)8-53225-2,(Eu)8-29964-2,(F)8-54185-2, 8-54197-2,(J)CJ25-5181/84,CJ28-5031,CJ28-5171, CP32-5057,TOCJ-5203,TOCJ-5269,TOCJ-5274/76 TOCJ-5823,TOCJ-5925,TOCJ-5933,TOCJ-66031, TOCJ-66051,TOCJ-66060,TOCJ-66071, TOCP-7455/56,TOCP-8963,Cap(J)TOCJ-66005, Toshiba-EMI(J)TOCP-8581,32 Jazz 32025-2, The Right Stuff 8-57072-2,Cema S21-56914, S21-57592,EMI-Jazz(E)4-93467-2,4-93469-2, EMI-Music 4-98900-2,EMI(E)5-21426-2

tk.7/9/12/14 The drum miniature suite:
Drum thunder/
Cry a blue tear/
Harlem's disciples CD BN(J)TOCJ-5755/56
tk.16 Along came Betty BN 45-1736,CD 8-54899-2
tk.19 Blues march - L4003,BST2-84433,B1-93205 BN(F)45-002,BST84383,(Du)1A158-83391/4, BN(J)NP9021,LBN80259,LNP95059B, K18P-9126,K22P-6096/97,K23P-6724, FCPA 6205,W-5506:Lib(F)LBS83442/3
CD BN 7-93205-2,7-97190-2,7-97960-2, (J)CJ28-5030,CJ28-5031,TOCJ-5269, TOCJ-5274/76,TOCJ-5823,TOCJ-5963, TOCJ-66031,(Sp)8-34712-2,8-53016-2 Toshiba-EMI(J)TOCP-50370, Cema S21-56914,EMI-Jazz(E)4-93467-2
tk.21 Come rain or come shine CD BN 8-35282-2,(J)TOCJ-5853,TOCJ-5934

All titles,except take 3,issued on BN BLP4003/BST84003,CD BN(J)CP35-3090.
All takes shown issued on CD BN 7-46516-2,4-95324-2.
Note: An additional warm up and dialogue between Lee Morgan & Rudy Van Gelder,recorded before take 4, was included in CD BN 4-95324-2,(J)TOCJ-66060.

ART BLAKEY - DRUMS AROUND THE CORNER:
Lee Morgan(tp) Bobby Timmons(p) Jymie Merritt(b) Art Blakey,Philly Joe Jones(dm,tympani) Roy Haynes (dm)Ray Barretto(cga).
(Manhattan Towers) NYC,November 2,1958

tk.4 Let's take 16 bars
tk.6 Moose the mooche
tk.7 Drums in the rain
tk. 11 Lee's tune
tk.13 Blakey's blues
tk.15 Lover

Al titles issued on CD BN 5-21455-2.
Note: This is the first session where Rudy Van Gelder used the same master tape for both mono and stereo. Hereafter,there would be no more mono/stereo variances.

 86

ART BLAKEY - A MESSAGE FROM BLAKEY - HOLIDAY FOR SKINS:
Donald Byrd(tp) Ray Bryant(p) Wendell Marshall(b) Art Blakey,Art Taylor,Philly Joe Jones(dm) Sabu Martinez,Ray Barretto,Chonguito Vincente,Victor Gonzales,Julio Martinez(bgo,cga) Andy Delannoy (maracas) Fred Pagani(timbales) & chants by Blakey,Jones, Austin Cromer,Hal Rasheed.
(Manhattan Towers) NYC,November 9,1958

tk.2	Aghano (instr.) (tp,g out)	BN BLP4004
tk.3	The feast (voPJJ)	- B1-80701
		CD BN 7-80701-2,(J)TOCJ-5733
tk.4	Reflection (instr.)	BN BLP4005
tk.7	Mirage	BN BLP4004;CD BN(J)TOCJ-5274/76
tk.8	Swingin' kilts	BN BLP4005
tk.9	Dinga (tp,p out)	-
tk.12	O'Tinde (tp,p,b out)	- B1-80701,CD 7-80701-2
tk.13	Lamento Africano (tp out)	BN BLP4004

All titles from BLP4004/05 (mono) also issued on BN BST84004/05,CD BN(J)TOCJ-4004/05 (stereo).

SONNY CLARK TRIO:
Sonny Clark(p) Jymie Merritt(b) Wesley Landers(dm).
Hackensack,N.J.,November 16,1958

tk.3	Black velvet	BN 45-1731,(J)LNJ70079,GXF-3069
tk.4	I'm just a lucky so and so	BN 45-1730 - -
		CD BN 5-20809-2
tk.5	Gee baby,ain't I good to you	BN 45-1731,(J)GXF-3069
tk.6	Gee baby,ain't I good to you (alt.)	
		BN(J)LNJ70079,GXF-3051
tk.8	Ain't no use	BN 45-1730,(J)LNJ70079,GXF-3069
tk.9	The breeze and I	BN 45-1729 - -
		CD BN(J)CJ28-5036,TOCJ-5299,TOCJ-66038
tk.13	I can't give you anything but love	BN 45-1729,(J)LNJ70079,GXF-3069
		CD Cap(J)TOCJ-5195

All titles issued on BN(J)BNJ61017,CD BN 8-21283-2,(J)TOCJ-1617.
Note: Date was erroneously shown as October 16 on BN(J)GXF-3069.

BENNIE GREEN QUINTET:
Bennie Green(tb) Eddy Williams(ts) Sonny Clark(p) Paul Chambers(b) Jerry Segal(dm) Babs Gonzales(vo).
Hackensack,N.J.,November 23,1958

tk.6	On the street where you live	BN 45-1732,(J)GXF-3063;CD BN 8-29095-2
tk.9	Can't we be friends	BN 45-1734 -
tk.13	Minor revelation	- -
tk.14	Why do I love you?	-
tk.15	Encore (voBG)(45 take)	BN 45-1733,(Du)1A158-83391/4
		CD BN 7-84464-2
tk.16	Encore (voBG)(LP take) (alt.)	BN(J)GXF-3063;CD BN 7-84464-2
tk.19	Bye bye blackbird	BN 45-1732,(J)GXF-3063
tk.21	It's groovy	-
tk.22	Ain't nothin' but the blues	BN 45-1733 -

All titles issued on BN(J)BNJ61020,CD TOCJ-1619.

<u>SONNY CLARK</u> - <u>BLUES IN THE NIGHT</u>:
Sonny Clark(p) Paul Chambers(b) Wesley Landers(dm).
Hackensack,N.J.,December 7,1958

tk.3	Can't we be friends?	
tk.4	I cover the waterfront	
tk.8	Somebody loves me	
tk.9	Blues in the night (short version)	
		CD BN(J)CJ28-5036,CJ28-5178,TOCJ-5750, TOCJ-5937,TOCJ-66038,Cap(J)TOCJ-5229
tk.10	Blues in the night (long version)(alt.)	
tk.12	All of you	Lib(J)K22P-6092/93
tk.14	Dancing in the dark	CD BN(Eu)7-89914-2

All titles issued on BN(J)GXF-3051,BNJ61018,CD 8-21283-2,(J)TOCJ-1618.

<u>LOU DONALDSON</u> - <u>LIGHT FOOT</u>:
Lou Donaldson(as) Herman Foster(p) Peck Morrison(b) Jimmy Wormsworth(dm) Ray Barretto(cga).
Hackensack,N.J.,December 14,1958

tk.1	Walkin' by the river	BN BLP4053
tk.6	Green eyes	-
tk.7	Light foot	- CD 8-27298-2
tk.9	Hog maw	BN 45-1806,BLP4053,CD BN(F)54188-2
tk.11	Jump up	unissued
tk.12	Mary Ann	BN BLP4053
tk.13	Day dreams	BN 45-1806,BLP4053,CD BN(J)TOCJ-5855
tk.14	Stella by starlight	- CD BN(J)TOCJ-5260
tk.17	Stella by starlight (alt.)	CD BN(J)TOCJ-5941/44

All titles from BLP4053 (mono) also issued in stereo on BN BST84053,CD BN(J)TOCJ-4053.

<u>DONALD BYRD</u> - <u>OFF TO THE RACES</u>:
Donald Byrd(tp) Jackie McLean(as Pepper Adams(bs) Wynton Kelly(p) Sam Jones(b) Art Taylor(dm).
Hackensack,N.J.,December 21,1958

tk.3	Sudwest funk	
tk.4	Lover come back to me	CD BN(J)TOCJ-5934
tk.6	When your love has gone (as,bs out)	
tk.8	Off to the races	
	(*aka* The long Two/Four)	BN B2S-5256
tk.10	Paul's pal	
tk.12	Down tempo	

All titles issued on BN BLP4007/BST84007,CD BN(J)TOCJ-4007,Mosaic MD4-194.

THE AMAZING BUD POWELL - THE SCENE CHANGES:
Bud Powell(p) Paul Chambers(b) Art Taylor(dm).
Hackensack,N.J.,December 29,1958

tk.1	The scene changes	BN BLP4009,B1-93204,(J)NP-2009 CD BN 7-93204-2,(J)CJ28-5032,TOCJ-66033
tk.3	Down with it	BN BLP4009
tk.4	Comin' up (alt.)	BN BST84430;CD BN(J)TOCJ-5941/44,
tk.6	Comin' up	BN BLP4009;CD BN 8-54906-2,(J)TOCJ-5260
tk.9	Duid deed	-
tk.10	Cleopatra's dream	- B1-93204,(J)NP-2009,BNJ27002, W-5509,NP9020C,LNP95060,LNS90031, K18P-9127,K22P-6096/97,K23P-6723;FCPA 6203 CD BN 7-93204-2,(J)CJ25-5181/84,CJ28-5022, CJ28-5032,CJ28-5171,TOCJ-5203,TOCJ-5640, TOCJ-5822,TOCJ-5933,TOCJ-6105,TOCJ-6132, TOCJ-6152,TOCJ-66033,TOCJ-66053, TOCP-7455/56,TOCP-8963,TOCP-50060, Cap(J)TOCJ-6182,TOCJ-66005, Toshiba-EMI(J)TOCP-8581,Victor(J)VICJ-5154
tk.12	Gettin' there	BN BLP4009
tk.14	Crossin' the channel	- Lib(J)K22P-6092/93
tk.16	Danceland	BN BLP4009 BN(J)K23P-6723,(J)FCPA 6203 CD BN(J)TOCP-50060
tk.17	Borderick	BN BLP4009,(J)K23P-6723,FCPA 6203 CD BN(J)TOCP-50060

All takes shown issued on Mosaic MR5-116,CD BN 7-46529-2,8-30083-2.
All titles from BLP4009 (mono) also issued in stereo on BN BST84009,CD BN(J)TOCJ-4009.

JACKIE McLEAN - JACKIE'S BAG:
Donald Byrd(tp) Jackie McLean(as) Sonny Clark(p) Paul Chambers(b) Philly Joe Jones(dm).
Hackensack,N.J.,January 18,1959

tk.3	Quadrangle (p out)	BN BLP4051/BST84051,CD 7-46142-2
tk.8	Blues inn	- - BN(J)FCPA 6213
tk.10	Fidel	BN BLP4051/BST84051,CD 7-46142-2
tk.12	Unknown title	rejected
tk.13	Untitled blues	-

All titles from BST84051 also issued on CD BN(J)TOCJ-4051.

BENNIE GREEN - WALKIN' AND TALKIN':
Bennie Green(tb) Eddy Williams(ts) Gildo Mahones(p) George Tucker(b) Al Dreares(dm).
Hackensack,N.J.,January 25,1959

tk.2	All I do is dream of you	
tk.11	This love of mine	CD BN 8-35282-2
tk.17	Hoppin' Johns	
tk.21	Green leaves	
tk.22	Walkin' and talkin'	
tk.25	The shouter	

All titles issued on BN BLP4010/BST84010,CD BN(J)TOCJ-4010.

FINGER POPPIN' WITH THE HORACE SILVER QUINTET:
Blue Mitchell(tp) Junior Cook(ts) Horace Silver(p) Gene Taylor(b) Louis Hayes(dm).
Hackensack,N.J.,January 31,1959

tk.11	Cookin' at the Continental	BN 45-1741,BN-LA402-H2,B1-91143 BN(Du)1A158-83391/4;CD BN 7-91143-2, 4-95576-2,(J)CJ28-5033,TOCJ-66034
tk.24	Mellow D	BN 45-1742
tk.29	You happened my way (tp,ts out)	
tk.30	Swinging the samba	BN 45-1742 CD BN 4-95576-2,4-97222-2,(J)TOCJ-5827
tk.32	Finger poppin'	BN 45-1740 CD BN 8-33208-2,(J)TOCJ-5755/56
tk.34	Sweet stuff (tp,ts out)	BN BN-LA474-H2
tk.37	Come on home	BN 45-1740
tk.39	Juicy Lucy	BN 45-1741,CD 4-95576-2

All titles issued on BN BLP4008/BST84008,CD 7-84008-2.

THE THREE SOUNDS - BOTTOMS UP:
Gene Harris(p,celeste) Andrew Simpkins(b) Bill Dowdy(dm).
Hackensack,N.J.,February 11,1959

tk.3	Soft winds	rejected
tk.5	Nothing ever changes my love for you	BN 45-1744,BLP4014
tk.10	Let's love	unissued
tk.12	Besame mucho	BN 45-1743,BLP4014 CD BN(J)CJ28-5021,CJ28-5168,TOCJ-5755/56, TOCJ-66048
tk.13	Jenny Lou	BN 45-1743,BLP4014
tk.16	It could happen to you	unissued
tk.17	I could write a book	BN 45-1744,BLP4014
tk.21	Love walked in	-

All titles from BLP4014 (mono) also issued in stereo on BN BST84014,CD BN(J)CJ28-5077,TOCJ-4014.

LOU DONALDSON WITH THE THREE SOUNDS - LD + 3:
Lou Donaldson(as) Gene Harris(p) Andrew Simpkins(b) Bill Dowdy(dm).
Hackensack,N.J.,February 18,1959

tk.3	Just friends	
tk.4	Don't take your love from me	
tk.6	Confirmation	
tk.7	Jump up	
tk.8	Smooth groove	BN 45-1772
tk.10	Three little words	
tk.11	Blue moon	BN 45-1772;CD BN(J)CJ25-5181/84,TOCJ-66044

All titles issued on BN BLP4012/BST84012,CD BN(J)TOCJ-4012.

ART BLAKEY'S JAZZ MESSENGERS:
Lee Morgan(tp) Hank Mobley(ts) Bobby Timmons(p) Jymie Merritt(b) Art Blakey(dm).
Hackensack,N.J.,March 8,1959

tk.5	Jimerick	rejected
tk.10	Quick trick	-
tk.14	Hipsippy blues	-
tk.15	M and M	-
tk.19	Close your eyes	-
tk.21	Just coolin'	-

90

Note: A Tommy Flanagan session from March 10,1959 issued in Japan was actually recorded for United Artists label and is listed in part 5 (see page 622).

<u>ART BLAKEY - PAUL CHAMBERS</u>:
Paul Chambers(b) Art Blakey(dm).
Hackensack,N.J.,March 29,1959

tk.1	I've got my love to keep me warm	CD BN 7-99095-2
tk.2	What is this thing called love	

Both titles issued on CD BN 5-21455-2.

<u>SONNY CLARK</u> - <u>MY CONCEPTION</u>:
Donald Byrd(tp) Hank Mobley(ts) Sonny Clark(p) Paul Chambers(b) Art Blakey(dm).
Same session.

tk.4	Blues blue
tk.7	Royal flush
tk.9	Junka
tk.11	Minor meeting
tk.12	My conception
tk.16	Some Clark bars

All titles issued on BN(J)GXF-3056,CD BN 5-22674-2,(J)TOCJ-66079.

<u>KENNY BURRELL</u>:
Tommy Flanagan(p) Kenny Burrell(g) George Duvivier(b) Elvin Jones(dm).
Hackensack,N.J.,April 12,1959

tk.3	Sugar hill	rejected
tk.11	Squeeze me	-
tk.17	Soft winds	-

<u>ART BLAKEY AND THE JAZZ MESSENGERS AT THE JAZZ CORNER OF THE WORLD</u>:
Lee Morgan(tp) Hank Mobley(ts) Bobby Timmons(p) Jymie Merritt(b) Art Blakey(dm,m.c.-1) Pee Wee Marquette(m.c.-2).
(Birdland Club) NYC,April 15,1959

Pee Wee Marquette's intro	BN BLP4015,CD BN(F)8-54197-2
Just coolin'-1	-
The theme (short version)-2	- B1-28263
	CD BN 8-28263-2,(F)8-54197-2
Close your eyes-1	BN 45-1787,BLP4015
M and M	BN BLP4016
Hipsippy blues-2	BN 45-1786,BLP4015
	CD BN(J)TOCJ-5823,TOCJ-66031
Chicken an' dumplins-1	BN 45-1788,BLP4016
	CD BN(Eu)7-89915-2,(J)TOCJ-5274/76
Hi-fly	BN 45-1788,BLP4016
Art's revelation	-
Justice (*aka*: Evidence)	BN BLP4015,(J)K23P-6724
	CD BN 7-97190-2
The theme (long version)-2	BN BLP4016

BLP4015/16 (mono) were also issued as BN BST84015/16,CD BN(J)TOCJ-4015/16 (stereo).
All titles also issued on CD BN 8-28888-2.
Note: Above titles are listed in order of performance.

JACKIE McLEAN - NEW SOIL:
Donald Byrd(tp) Jackie McLean(as) Walter Davis(p) Paul Chambers(b) Pete La Roca(dm).
Hackensack,N.J.,May 2,1959

tk.5	Formidable	BN LT-1085;CD BN(J)TOCJ-5941/44
tk.6	Greasy	BN 45-1776,BLP4013,B1-57745,(J)FCPA 6213 CD BN 8-57745-2,4-97222-2
tk.8	Sweet cakes	BN BLP4013;CD BN(J)TOCJ-5740
tk.10	Davis cup	-
tk.13	Minor apprehension	- CD BN(J)CJ28-5163
tk.14	Hip strut	-

All titles from BLP4013 (mono) also issued on BN BST84013,CD BN(J)TOCJ-4013 (stereo).
All titles also issued on CD BN 7-84013-2.

LEON EASON:
Leon Eason(tp,vo) Dottie Dudley(org) John Simmons(b) Ronnie Cole(dm).
Hackensack,N.J.,May 17,1959

tk.1	I'm in the mood for love	BN 45-1745
tk.3	I'm in the mood for love (LP version)	CD BN 5-21153-2
tk.7	Because of you (alt.)	unissued
tk.8	Because of you	BN 45-1746 (poss. not released)
tk.13	Song of the islands	-
tk.14	That's my home	BN 45-1747 (poss. not released)
tk.18	I'm just a gigolo	-
tk.20	All of me	unissued
tk.23	Blueberry hill	-
tk.24	Cape Cod	-
tk.31	Lazy river	BN 45-1745
tk.35	I'll never smile again	unissued
tk.37	Sweethearts on parade	-

Note: Take 1 was recorded in mono only.It was mistakenly listed as being on CD 5-21153-2,which actually used take 3.

THE THREE SOUNDS - GOOD DEAL:
Gene Harris(p) Andrew Simpkins(b) Bill Dowdy(dm).
Hackensack,N.J.,May 20,1959

tk.4	Tracy's blue	BN 45-1756,BLP4020,B2S 5256
tk.5	It's only a paper moon	CD BN(J)TOCJ-5941/44
tk.6	That's all	BN 45-1758,BLP4020
tk.7	There is no greater love	CD BN(J)TOCJ-5941/44
tk.8	Satin doll	BN BLP4020,(J)K23P-6726 CD BN(J)CJ28-5168,CJ28-5178,TOCJ-6132, TOCJ-6271/74,TOCJ-66048,TOCJ-66053, Cap(J)TOCJ-5674/75,TOCJ-5714
tk.10	Soft winds	BN BLP4020
tk.12	St. Thomas	BN 45-1758,BLP4020 CD BN(J)CJ28-5168,TOCJ-66048
tk.13	Robbins' nest	BN 45-1757,BLP4020
tk.14	Don't blame me	BN 45-1756 -
tk.15	Down the track	BN 45-1757 - CD 8-27323-2

All titles from BLP4020 (mono) also issued on BN BST84020,CD BN(J)TOCJ-4020 (stereo).

JIMMY SMITH - HOME COOKIN'/STANDARDS:
Jimmy Smith(org) Kenny Burrell(g) Donald Bailey(dm).
Hackensack,N.J.,May 24,1959

tk.1	It might as well be Spring	CD BN 8-21282-2
tk.2	Mood indigo	-
tk.4	While we're young	-
tk.6	I didn't know what time it was	-
tk.9	But beautiful	-
tk.10	The last dance	unissued
tk.12	Groanin'	CD BN 8-53360-2
tk.13	Memories of you	CD BN 8-21282-2
tk.14	I got a woman	BN 45-1767,BLP4050/BST84050,(J)LNP-88046 CD BN 8-53360-2,(J)TOCJ-4050

DONALD BYRD - BYRD IN HAND:
Donald Byrd(tp) Charlie Rouse(ts) Pepper Adams(bs) Walter Davis(p) Sam Jones(b) Art Taylor (dm).
Hackensack,N.J.,May 31,1959

tk.1	Here am I	BN 45-1763
tk.2	Witchcraft	
tk.3	The Injuns	
tk.7	Devil whip	BN(Du)1A158-83391/4
tk.10	Bronze dance	
tk.16	Clarion calls	

All titles issued on BN BLP4019/BST84019,CD BN 7-84019-2,Mosaic MD4-194.
Note: The CD BN reissue mistates the recording year as 1969.

JIMMY SMITH - HOME COOKIN':
Percy France(ts) Jimmy Smith(org) Kenny Burrell(g) Donald Bailey(dm).
Hackensack,N.J.,June 16,1959

tk.4	Messin' around	BN BLP4050/BST84050
tk.8	Sugar hill (ts out)	- CD BN(Sp)5-21755-2
tk.10	Gracie	-
tk.14	Come on baby	BN 45-1768,BLP4050/BST84050
tk.15	One o'clock jump	rejected
tk.18	Apostrophe	BN LT-1092;CD BN(J)TOCJ-5941/44
tk.19	See see rider	BN 45-1768,BLP4050/BST84050,(J)LNP-88046

All titles,except tk.15,issued on CD 8-53360-2.
All titles from BST84050 also issued on CD BN(J)TOCJ-4050.

IKE QUEBEC:
Ike Quebec(ts) Edwin Swanston(org) Clifton "Skeeter" Best(g) Charles "Sonny" Wellesley(b) Les Jenkins (dm).
Hackensack,N.J.,July 1,1959

tk.1	A light reprieve	
tk.6	Blue Friday	BN 45-1749
tk.10	Zonky	
tk.11	Blue Monday	BN 45-1748
tk.14	Buzzard lope	BN 45-1749
tk.16	Later for the rock	
tk.22	Sweet and lovely	
tk.23	Dear John	BN 45-1748

All titles issued on Mosaic MR3-121,CD BN(J)TOCJ-66083,Mosaic MD2-121.

IKE QUEBEC:
Ike Quebec(ts) Edwin Swanston(org) Clifton "Skeeter" Best(g) Charles "Sonny" Wellesley(b) Les Jenkins (dm).

Englewood Cliffs,N.J.,July 20,1959

tk.8	Uptight	CD BN(J)TOCJ-66083
tk.12	Cry me a river	-
	Latin strain (incomplete)	rejected

WALTER DAVIS Jr. - DAVIS CUP:
Donald Byrd(tp) Jackie McLean(as) Walter Davis Jr.(p) Sam Jones(b) Art Taylor(dm).
Englewood Cliffs,N.J.,August 2,1959

tk.6	Minor mind	CD BN(J)TOCJ-5755/56
tk.14	'S make it	
tk.17	Loodle-lot	
tk.21	Millie's delight	
tk.23	Rhumba numba	
tk.24	Sweetness	

All titles issued on BN BLP4018/BST84018,B1-32098,CD 8-32098-2.

KENNY BURRELL ON VIEW AT THE FIVE SPOT CAFE:
Roland Hanna(p) Kenny Burrell(g) Ben Tucker(b) Art Blakey(dm).
(Five Spot Cafe) NYC,August 25,1959 (Set One)

tk.1	Tricotism	rejected
tk.2	The next time you see me,things won't be the same	unissued
tk.3	If you could see me now	BN(J)GXF-3070;CD BN 7-46538-2,(J)TOCJ-1609
tk.4	Hallelujah	rejected
tk.5	Beef stew blues	-
tk.6	The take off/36-23-36	-

Tina Brooks(ts-1) Bobby Timmons(p) Kenny Burrell(g) Ben Tucker(b) Art Blakey(dm).
(Five Spot Cafe) NYC,August 25,1959 (Set Two)

tk.7	Love walked in	rejected
tk.8	Swingin'-1	BN(J)GXF-3070 CD BN 7-46538-2,(J)TOCJ-1609,TOCJ-5941/44
tk.9	Lover man-1	rejected
tk.10	Birks' works-1	BN BLP4021/BST84021,(J)K18P-9127 CD BN 7-46538-2,7-89032-2,(J)TOCJ-4021, TOCJ-66042
tk.11	Lady be good-1,2	BN BLP4021/BST84021 CD BN 7-46538-2,(J)TOCJ-4021
tk.12	The next time you see me,things won't be the same	rejected

-2: see note on next page.

Roland Hanna(p) Kenny Burrell(g) Ben Tucker(b) Art Blakey(dm).
(Five Spot Cafe) NYC,August 25,1959 (Set Three)

tk.13	If you could see me now	rejected
tk.14	Beef stew blues	BN(J)GXF-3070 CD BN 7-46538-2,(J)CJ28-5030,TOCJ-1609
tk.15	Hallelujah	BN BLP4021/BST84021 CD BN 7-46538-2,(J)TOCJ-4021
tk.16	The take off	unissued

<u>KENNY BURRELL ON VIEW AT THE FIVE SPOT CAFE</u>:
Roland Hanna(p) Kenny Burrell(g) Ben Tucker(b) Art Blakey(dm).
(Five Spot Cafe) NYC,August 25,1959 (Set Four)

tk.17	Our delight	unissued
tk.18	The next time you see me, things won't be the same	-
tk.19	36-23-36	BN BLP4021/BST84021 CD BN 7-46538-2,(J)TOCJ-4021

Tina Brooks(ts-1) Bobby Timmons(p) Kenny Burrell(g) Ben Tucker(b) Art Blakey(dm).
(Five Spot Cafe) NYC,August 25,1959 (Set Five)

tk.20	Love walked in	rejected
tk.21	Swingin'-1	-
tk.22	Lover man	BN BLP4021/BST84021 CD BN 7-46538-2,(J)TOCJ-4021,TOCJ-6134, TOCJ-66042
tk.23	Birks' works-1	rejected
tk.24	Lady be good-1	-
tk.25	36-23-36/Theme-1	-

Note: Takes 11 & 24 use the melody of Thelonious Monk's "Hackensack" composition.

<u>HORACE SILVER</u> - <u>BLOWIN' THE BLUES AWAY</u>:
Blue Mitchell(tp) Junior Cook(ts) Horace Silver(p) Gene Taylor(b) Louis Hayes(dm).
Englewood Cliffs,N.J.,August 29,1959

tk.3	Blowin' the blues away	BN 45-1751,BLP4017/BST84017 BN(E)BNX 1,(J)NP-2006,NP9020C,LNP95060, K18P-9127,FCPA 6206 CD BN 7-46526-2,7-48337-2,7-91143-2, 4-95342-2,4-95576-2,(J)CJ28-5033,TOCJ-4017, TOCJ-66034,TOCJ-66051,TOCP-7455/56
	Break city	rejected
	Peace	-
tk.18	Baghdad blues	BN 45-1751,BLP4017/BST84017 CD BN 7-46526-2.4-95342-2,(J)TOCJ-4017
	Sister Sadie	rejected

-1:Mitchell & Cook out.

Same.
Englewood Cliffs,N.J.,August 30,1959

tk.2	Sister Sadie	BN 45-1750,BLP4017/BST84017,BST84325, B1-91143 BN(J)NP9021,LNP95059B,FCPA 6206,W-5506 CD BN 7-91143-2,4-95576-2,(J)TOCJ-4017, TOCJ-5827,TOCJ-66034,Cema S21-57589, EMI-Jazz(E)4-93466-2,Premier(E)CDJA 1
	Repetition	rejected
tk.8	Peace	BN BLP4017/BST84017,BN-LA402-H2,B1-91143 CD BN 7-91143-2,4-95576-2,(J)CJ28-5033, TOCJ-4017
tk.11	How did it happen	BN BN-LA945-H;CD BN(J)TOCJ-5941/44
tk.14	Break city	BN 45-1750,BLP4017/BST84017 CD BN(J)TOCJ-4017

All issued titles also issued on CD BN 7-46526-2,4-95342-2.

<u>HORACE SILVER</u> - <u>BLOWIN' THE BLUES AWAY</u>:
Horace Silver(p) Gene Taylor(b) Louis Hayes(dm).

Englewood Cliffs,N.J.,September 13,1959

tk.7	Melancholy mood	
tk.8	The St. Vitus dance	BN(J)K23P-6725

Both titles issued on BN BLP4017/BST84017,BN-LA474-H2,CD 7-46526-2,4-95342-2,(J)TOCJ-4017.

<u>DONALD BYRD</u> - <u>FUEGO</u>:
Donald Byrd(pocket tp) Jackie McLean(as) Duke Pearson(p) Doug Watkins(b) Lex Humphries(dm).

Englewood Cliffs,N.J.,October 4,1959

tk.3	Lament	BN(J)FCPA 6210
tk.8	Amen	BN 45-1764;CD BN(Eu)7-80703-2,5-20070-2, (J)CJ25-5181/84,TOCJ-6271/74
tk.14	Fuego	BN 45-1764 BN(J)NP9022,LNP95060,K18P-9127,FCPA 6210, W-5507,CD TOCJ-6133
tk.15	Low life	BN(J)FCPA 6210,CD TOCJ-5296
tk.17	Bup a loup	
tk.18	Funky Mama	

All titles issued on BN BLP4026/BST84026,CD 7-46534-2.

<u>THE THREE SOUNDS</u>:
Gene Harris(p) Andrew Simpkins(b) Bill Dowdy(dm).

Englewood Cliffs,N.J.,October 8,1959

	Love for sale	rejected
	Blue'n boogie	-
tk.5	Wrap your troubles in dreams	unissued
tk.6	Stars fell on Alabama	-
	Star eyes	rejected
tk.10	Alone together	CD BN 8-21281-2
tk.11	My funny Valentine	unissued
	Will you still be mine	rejected
	Blues	-
tk.18	Takin' a chance on love	unissued
tk.20	Blue'n boogie	rejected
tk.25	Thinking of you	CD BN 8-21281-2
tk.26	Good night ladies	-
	Body and soul	rejected
tk.29	If I should lose you	unissued
tk.30	Everything happens to me	-
tk.31	But not for me	-
	Bags' groove	rejected
	My little suede shoes	-
tk.34	C jam blues	unissued
	Out of the past	rejected
tk.36	Moonlight in Vermont	unissued
	Babe's blues	rejected
	They can't take that away from me	-
tk.40	Lover man	unissued
tk.42	Sweet and lovely	-
tk.43	Lights out	CD BN 8-21281-2
	This can't be love	rejected
tk.48	Autumn leaves	unissued

96

JACKIE McLEAN - SWING,SWANG,SWINGIN'!:
Jackie McLean(as) Walter Bishop(p) Jimmy Garrison(b) Art Taylor(dm).
Englewood Cliffs,N.J.,October 20,1959

tk.5	Let's face the music and dance	BN BLP4024,(J)W-5513 CD BN 7-99095-2,(J)TOCJ-5934,TOCJ-66046
tk.10	I remember you	BN BLP4024
	Tune up	rejected
tk.12	Stablemates	BN BLP4024
tk.17	I love you	- (J)K18P-9127 Lib(J)K22P-6131/32 CD BN 7-95591-2
tk.20	What's new	BN 45-1760,BLP4024,(J)FCPA 6213 CD BN(J)CJ28-5163,CJ28-5172,TOCJ-66052, TOCP-7455/56
tk.23	I'll take romance	BN BLP4024
tk.24	116th and Lenox	BN 45-1760,BLP4024,CD 8-54363-2

All titles from BLP4024 (mono) also issued in stereo on BN BST84024,CD 8-56582-2.

DUKE PEARSON - PROFILE:
Duke Pearson(p) Gene Taylor(b) Lex Humphries(dm).
Englewood Cliffs,N.J.,October 25,1959

tk.9	Witchcraft	CD BN(Eu)7-89914-2
tk.14	Two mile run	
tk.18	Gate City blues	BN 45-1754,B2S-5256
tk.19	Taboo	BN 45-1755
tk.27	Black coffee	BN 45-1754,(J)K23P-6726 CD BN(J)TOCJ-5296,Cap(J)CP28-5864
tk.28	I'm glad there is you	CD BN(J)TOCJ-6190,TOCJ-66054, Cap(J)TOCJ-5195
tk.30	Like someone in love	BN 45-1755,(J)W-5510 CD BN 7-81331-2,(J)TOCJ-5299

All titles issued on BN BLP4022/BST84022,CD BN(J)CJ28-5092,TOCJ-4022.

LOU DONALDSON - THE TIME IS RIGHT:
Blue Mitchell(tp) Lou Donaldson(as) Horace Parlan(p) Laymon Jackson(b) Dave Bailey(dm) Ray Barretto (cga).
Englewood Cliffs,N.J.,October 31,1959

tk.4	Mack the knife	BN 45-1752 CD BN 8-27298-2,Cap(J)TOCJ-5202
tk.6	Be my love (tp out)	BN 45-1753;CD BN(J)TOCJ-5740,TOCJ-66044
tk.8	Crosstown shuffle	BN B1-30721
tk.12	Tangerine	
tk.13	Lou's blues	BN 45-1753,BST2-84433 CD BN(Sp)8-34712-2,Cema GSC Music 15131
	Time on my hands	rejected
tk.19	The nearness of you	BN 45-1752
	It's only a paper moon	rejected

All titles issued on BN BLP4025/BST84025,CD BN(J)TOCJ-4025.

ART BLAKEY'S JAZZ MESSENGERS - AFRICAINE:
Lee Morgan(tp) Wayne Shorter(ts) Walter Davis(p) Jymie Merritt(b) Art Blakey(dm)Dizzy Reece(cga-1).
Englewood Cliffs,N.J.,November 10,1959

tk.3	The midget	BN LT-1088,CD 4-97507-2	
tk.4	Lester left town	-	-
tk.8	Celine	-	-
tk.10	Splendid	-	-
tk.12	Haina -1	-	-
tk.14	Africaine -1	-	-
	It's only a paper moon	rejected	

DIZZY REECE:
Dizzy Reece(tp) Hank Mobley(ts) Wynton Kelly(p) Paul Chambers(b) Art Taylor(dm).
Englewood Cliffs,N.J.,November 14,1959

The rebound	rejected
Variations on Monk	-
I'll close my eyes	-
The rake	-

DIZZY REECE - STAR BRIGHT:
Dizzy Reece(tp) Hank Mobley(ts) Wynton Kelly(p) Paul Chambers(b) Art Taylor(dm).
Englewood Cliffs,N.J.,November 19,1959

tk.3	The rebound	BN 45-1759
tk.7	A variation on Monk	
tk.11	I wished on the moon	CD BN(Eu)7-89910-2
tk.15	The rake	BN 45-1759
tk.19	I'll close my eyes	CD BN(J)TOCJ-6133
tk.22	Groovesville	

All titles issued on BN BLP4023/BST84023,CD BN(J)TOCJ-4023.

LOU DONALDSON - THE TIME IS RIGHT:
Blue Mitchell(tp) Lou Donaldson(as) Horace Parlan(p) Sam Jones(b) Al Harewood(dm).
Englewood Cliffs,N.J.,November 28,1959

tk.3	Idaho	BN BLP4025/BST84025;CD BN(J)TOCJ-4025
	Untitled Donaldson blues	rejected
	But not for me	-

SONNY RED - OUT OF THE BLUE:
Sonny Red(as) Wynton Kelly(p) Sam Jones(b) Roy Brooks(dm).
Englewood Cliffs,N.J.,December 5,1959

tk.3	Bluesville	BN 45-1761,BLP4032	
tk.5	Stay as sweet as you are	-	-
tk.10	I've never been in love before		-
tk.12	Blues in the pocket	BN 45-1762	-
tk.13	Alone too long		-
tk.14	Alone too long	BN 45-1762	
tk.19	Nadia	BN BLP4032	
	All the things you are	rejected	

All titles from BLP4032 (mono) also issued on BN BST84032,CD 8-52440-2,(J)TOCJ-4032 (stereo).

DUKE PEARSON - TENDER FEELIN'S:
Duke Pearson(p) Gene Taylor(b) Lex Humphries(dm).
Englewood Cliffs,N.J.,December 16,1959

	The golden striker	rejected
	Bluebird of happiness	-
	Something gotta give	-
tk.10	On Green Dolphin Street	BN BLP4035/BST84035;CD BN(J)TOCJ-4035
tk.16	When sunny gets blue	- -
	I'm a fool to want you	rejected
	One for my baby	-
	I love you	-

Same. Englewood Cliffs,N.J.,December 19,1959

	One for my baby	rejected
tk.36	The golden striker	BN BLP4035
tk.38	I love you	- (J)K23P-6726,CD CJ28-5023
tk.46	I'm a fool to want you	-
		CD BN(J)CJ28-5178,TOCJ-5260,TOCJ-5935, TOCJ-6132
tk.47	Bluebird of happiness	BN BLP4035
		CD BN(J)TOCJ-5187/88,TOCJ-5755/56
tk.56	Three a.m.	BN BLP4035

All titles from BLP4035 also issued on BN BST84035,CD BN(J)CP32-9515.

JIMMY SMITH - CRAZY BABY:
Jimmy Smith(org) Quentin Warren(g) Donald Bailey(dm).
Englewood Cliffs,N.J.,January 4,1960

tk.1	Alfredo	BN 45-1767,BLP4030		
tk.2	Mack the knife	BN 45-1766	-	BN-LA400-H2
tk.4	Makin' whoopee	BN 45-1765	-	CD Premier(E)CDJA 1
tk.7	What's new	-	-	CD Cap(J)TOCJ-6182
tk.8	Sonnymoon for two		-	
tk.9	If I should lose you			
tk.10	When Johnny comes marching home	BN 45-1766,BLP4030,BST89901,B1-91140 BN(J)LNP-88046 CD BN 7-91140-2,(J)CJ25-5181/84, CJ28-5034,TOCJ-5645/46,TOCJ-5825, TOCJ-66037,TOCP-7455/56		
tk.11	When lights are low	CD BN(J)TOCJ-5857		
tk.12	A night in Tunisia	BN BLP4030,(E)BST83367/8		

All titles from BLP4030 (mono) also issued on BN BST84030,CD BN(J)TOCJ-4030 (stereo).
All titles issued on CD BN 7-84030-2.

DONALD BYRD - BYRD IN FLIGHT:
Donald Byrd(tp) Hank Mobley(ts) Duke Pearson(p) Doug Watkins(b) Lex Humphries(dm).
Englewood Cliffs,N.J.,January 17,1960

	That's all	rejected
tk.6	Soulful Kiddy	CD BN 8-52435-2
tk.8	Gate City	BN 45-1798,BLP4048/BST84048,CD 8-52435-2 Lib.LN-10200
	Carol	rejected

SONNY RED - OUT OF THE BLUE:
Sonny Red(as) Wynton Kelly(p) Paul Chambers(b) Jimmy Cobb(dm).
Englewood Cliffs,N.J.,January 23,1960

tk.3	Blues for Kokee	CD BN(J)TOCJ-5941/44
tk.7	You're driving me crazy	-
tk.8	Stairway to the stars	BN BLP4032;CD BN(J)TOCJ-4032
tk.10	Crystal	
tk.13	The lope	BN BLP4032;CD BN(J)TOCJ-4032
tk.15	Lost April	
tk.17	You're sensational	

All titles issued on CD BN 8-52440-2.

DONALD BYRD - BYRD IN FLIGHT:
Donald Byrd(tp) Hank Mobley(ts) Duke Pearson(p) Doug Watkins(b) Lex Humphries(dm).
Englewood Cliffs,N.J.,January 25,1960

tk.14	Child play	
tk.17	Ghana	BN 45-1799,BLP4048/BST84048,(E)BNSLP-4 Lib.LN-10200 CD BN 7-95590-2,(J)TOCJ-4048
tk.18	Lex	BN BLP4048/BST84048;CD BN(J)TOCJ-4048
tk.21	Carol	

All titles issued on CD BN 8-52435-2.

LOU DONALDSON - SUNNY SIDE UP:
Bill Hardman(tp) Lou Donaldson(as) Horace Parlan(p) Sam Jones(b) Al Harewood(dm).
Englewood Cliffs,N.J.,February 5,1960

	Blues for J.P.	rejected
tk.9	Politely	BN 45-1774,BLP4036/BST84036,B1-32095 CD BN 8-32095-2,(J)TOCJ-4036
tk.11	(Way down upon the) Swanee River	CD BN 8-32095-2,(J)TOCJ-5941/44
tk.13	Softly as in a morning sunrise	BN BLP4036/BST84036,B1-32095 CD BN 8-32095-2,(J)TOCJ-4036
	The man I love	rejected
tk.18	Goose grease	BN 45-1773,BLP4036/BST84036,B1-32095 CD BN 8-32095-2,(J)TOCJ-4036
	The truth	rejected

HANK MOBLEY - SOUL STATION:
Hank Mobley(ts) Wynton Kelly(p) Paul Chambers(b) Art Blakey (dm).
Englewood Cliffs,N.J.,February 7,1960

tk.3	Remember	BN 45-1797 CD BN 7-99095-2,(J)CJ25-5181/84,CJ28-5035, CJ28-5177,TOCJ-6131,TOCJ-66043,TOCJ-66060 Cap(J)TOCJ-5191/92
tk.4	Split feelin's	BN(Du)1A158-83391/4
tk.12	Dig dis	BN 45-1797,(E)BNX 1;CD BN 7-48337-2
tk.18	This I dig of you	CD BN 8-37052-2,(E)8-53225-2,(Sp)5-21755-2, HMV Jazz(E)5-20882-2
tk.20	Soul station	
tk.25	If I should lose you	

All titles issued on BN BLP4031/BST84031,CD 7-46528-2,4-95343-2.

100

FREDDIE REDD QUARTET - THE MUSIC FROM 'THE CONNECTION':
Jackie McLean(as) Freddie Redd(p) Mike Mattos(b) Larry Ritchie(dm).
Englewood Cliffs,N.J.,February 15,1960

tk.2	Time to smile	
tk.4	Jim Dunn's dilemma	
tk.10	Wigglin'	
tk.14	Music forever	
tk.16	Theme for Sister Salvation	CD BN(J)TOCJ-5755/56,TOCJ-6271/74
tk.17	Who killed Cock Robin?	
tk.21	O.D.	

All titles issued on BN BLP4027/BST84027,B1-89392,Mosaic MR3-124,CD BN 7-89392-2,Mosaic MD2-124.

LOU DONALDSON - SUNNY SIDE UP:
Bill Hardman(tp) Lou Donaldson(as) Horace Parlan(p) Laymon Jackson(b) Al Harewood(dm).
Englewood Cliffs,N.J.,February 28,1960

tk.21	The man I love	CD BN 7-99427-2,5-20808-2,(J)TOCJ-66044
tk.25	Blues for J.P.	BN 45-1774
tk.26	The truth (tp out)	BN 45-1773,B2S-5256 CD BN(J)TOCJ-5755/56
tk.28	It's you or no one	

All titles issued on BN BLP4036/BST84036,B1-32095,CD 8-32095-2,(J)TOCJ-4036.

HORACE PARLAN - MOVIN' AND GROOVIN':
Horace Parlan(p) Sam Jones(b) Al Harewood(dm).
Englewood Cliffs,N.J.,February 29,1960

tk.2	Bags' groove	BN 45-1771
tk.3	Stella by starlight	
tk.5	There is no greater love	BN 45-1771;CD BN(J)CJ28-5178
tk.7	On Green Dolphin Street	
tk.8	C jam blues	BN 45-1770 CD BN 5-20809-2,(J)TOCJ-5298, Premier(E)CDJA 1
tk.10	Up in Cynthia's room	BN 45-1770
tk.11	Lady Bird	
tk.13	It could happen to you	Lib(J)K22P-6092/93

All titles issued on BN BLP4028/BST84028,Mosaic MQ8-197,CD BN(J)CJ28-5068,Mosaic MD5-197.

101

ART BLAKEY AND THE JAZZ MESSENGERS - THE BIG BEAT:
Lee Morgan(tp) Wayne Shorter(ts) Bobby Timmons(p) Jymie Merritt(b) Art Blakey(dm).
Englewood Cliffs,N.J.,March 6,1960

tk.1	It's only a paper moon (alt.)	CD BN(J)TOCJ-5941/44
tk.3	It's only a paper moon	BN 45-1789,(F)BST84383;CD BN(Eu)4-93072-2
tk.7	Dat dere -1	BN 45-1790,B1-93205,(F)BST84383 CD BN 7-93205-2,7-97190-2,8-56508-2, (Eu)4-93072-2,(J)CJ28-5031,TOCJ-5269, TOCJ-5274/76,TOCJ-6271/74,TOCJ-66031, Cema S21-56914,EMI-Jazz(E)4-93467-2, EMI-Music 4-98899-2
tk.10	The chess players	BN 45-1775
tk.13	Lester left town	BN 45-1789,B1-93205 CD BN 7-93205-2,7-97190-2,Cema S21-56914, EMI-Jazz(E)4-93467-2
tk.17	Sakeena's vision	
tk.22	Politely	

-1: shown as pts. 1 & 2 on sides of 45-1790.Pt. 1 was reissued on CD BN 4-94030-2.
All 7 titles issued on Mosaic MR10-141,CD BN 7-46400-2,Mosaic MD6-141.
All titles,except tk.1,issued on BN BLP4029/BST84029,CD BN(J)TOCJ-4029.

SONNY RED:
Sonny Red(as) Hank Jones(p) Paul Chambers(b) Art Taylor(dm).
Englewood Cliffs,N.J.,March 10,1960

tk.5	The lamp is low	rejected
tk.10	How about you	-
tk.12	Invitation	-
tk.17	That old black magic	-

JIMMY SMITH - OPEN HOUSE (BST84269)/PLAIN TALK (BST84296):
Blue Mitchell(tp) Jackie McLean(as) Ike Quebec(ts) Jimmy Smith(org) Quentin Warren(g) Donald Bailey(dm).
Englewood Cliffs,N.J.,March 22,1960

tk.2	Plain talk	BN BST84296 BN(Du)1A158-83391/4
tk.3	Sister Rebecca	BN BST84269,CD 8-33206-2
tk.4	Embraceable you (tp,ts out)	- CD 7-99427-2,5-20808-2
tk.6	Old folks (tp,as out)	- CD BN(J)TOCJ-5645/46
tk.7	Open house	- -
tk.8	My one and only love (as,ts out)	BN BST84296 BN(J)K22P-6125/26
tk.10	Big fat mama (as out)	BN BST84296,(E)BST83367/8
tk.12	Time after time (tp,as out)	-

All titles also issued on CD BN 7-84269-2.

DIZZY REECE - COMIN' ON:
Dizzy Reece(tp) Stanley Turrentine(ts) Bobby Timmons(p) Jymie Merritt(b) Art Blakey(dm).
Englewood Cliffs,N.J.,April 3,1960

tk.2 The case of the frightened lover
tk.11 The story of love
tk.18 Ye olde blues
tk.22 Tenderly
tk.25/28 Achmet -1

-1: Dizzy Reece also plays congas.
All titles issued on CD BN 5-22019-2.

JACKIE McLEAN - CAPUCHIN SWING:
Blue Mitchell(tp) Jackie McLean(as) Walter Bishop(p) Paul Chambers(b) Art Taylor(dm).
Englewood Cliffs,N.J.,April 17,1960

tk.2 Francisco CD BN(J)TOCJ-66046
tk.7 Just for now
tk.8 Condition blue
tk.14 Capuchin swing
tk.15 Don't blame me (tp,as out)
tk.19 On the Lion

All titles issued on BN BLP4038/BST84038,CD BN(J)TOCJ-4038.

HORACE PARLAN - US THREE:
Horace Parlan(p) George Tucker(b) Al Harewood(dm).
Englewood Cliffs,N.J.,April 20,1960

tk.2 Come rain or come shine
tk.3 I want to be loved
tk.6 Return engagement
tk.7 Us three BN(J)W-5510
CD BN(J)TOCJ-5187/88,TOCJ-5755/56,
TOCJ-6132,TOCJ-6271/74,TOCJ-66053,
Cap(J)TOCJ-5191/92
tk.11 The lady is a tramp
tk.12 Wadin' CD BN(J)TOCJ-5740
tk.13 Walkin' CD BN(J)TOCJ-5937

All titles issued on BN BLP4037/BST84037,Mosaic MQ8-197,CD BN 8-56581-2,Mosaic MD5-197.

JIMMY SMITH - MIDNIGHT SPECIAL (BLP4078)/BACK AT THE CHICKEN SHACK (BLP4117):
Stanley Turrentine(ts) Jimmy Smith(org) Donald Bailey(dm).
Englewood Cliffs,N.J.,April 25,1960

tk.2 A subtle one BN BLP4078/BST84078,CD 7-84078-2
tk.3 When I grow too old to dream BN BLP4117/BST84117
CD BN 7-46402-2,(J)TOCJ-4117
tk.5 Why was I born BN BLP4078/BST84078,CD 7-84078-2
tk.5A Minor chant BN 45-1878,BLP4117/BST84117
CD BN 7-46402-2,8-33206-2,(J)TOCJ-4117,
TOCJ-5825

<u>JIMMY SMITH</u> - <u>MIDNIGHT SPECIAL</u> (BLP4078)/<u>BACK AT THE CHICKEN SHACK</u> (BLP4117):
Kenny Burrell(g) added.Same session.

tk.7	Messy Bessie	BN BLP4117/BST84117 CD BN 7-46402-2,(J)TOCJ-4117
tk.10	On the sunny side of the street	BN LT-1092 CD BN 7-46402-2,(J)TOCJ-5941/44
tk.12	Midnight special	BN 45-1819,L4078,BLP4078/BST84078, BST89901,BN-LA400-H2,(J)LNP-88046 CD BN 7-84078-2,(Au)8-57460-2, (J)TOCJ-5645/46
tk.16	Back at the chicken shack (Back to the chicken shack*)	BN 45-1877,BLP4117/BST84117,BST2-84429*, BST89904,BN-LA160-H2,BN-LA400-H2, B1-91140,BST2-92471,(E)BST83367/8, (In)JAZ 2* CD BN 7-46402-2,7-91140-2,7-92471-2, 7-96110-2,8-34957-2,5-20070-2,(C)8-56508-2, (E)8-53234-2,(F)8-54197-2,(J)CJ28-5034, CP32-5057,TOCJ-4117,TOCJ-5645/46, TOCJ-66037
tk.17	One o'clock jump	BN 45-1820,L4078,BLP4078/BST84078,(J) K22P-6125/6;CD BN 7-84078-2,(J)TOCJ-5645/46
tk.19	The jumpin' blues (Jumping the blues*)	BN 45-1820*,BLP4078*/BST84078*,B1-91140 BN(Du)1A158-83391/4,(J)BNJ71106* CD BN 7-84078-2,7-91140-2,(J)CJ28-5034, TOCJ-5298,TOCJ-5755/56,TOCJ-5758, TOCJ-66037

<u>LEE MORGAN</u> - <u>LEEWAY</u>:
Lee Morgan(tp) Jackie McLean(as) Bobby Timmons(p) Paul Chambers(b) Art Blakey(dm).
Englewood Cliffs,N.J.,April 28,1960

tk.6	Nakatini suite	
tk.13	There are soulful days	BN(J)FCPA 6213
tk.17	The Lion and the Wolff	
tk.18	Midtown blues	

All titles issued on BN BLP4034/BST84034,B1-32089,CD 8-32089-2.

<u>DIZZY REECE</u> - <u>SOUNDIN' OFF</u>:
Dizzy Reece(tp) Walter Bishop(p) Doug Watkins(b) Art Taylor(dm).
Englewood Cliffs,N.J.,May 12,1960

	It's you or no one	rejected	
tk.6	Yesterdays	BN	BLP4033
tk.7	Our love is here to stay		-
tk.9	Once in a while		-
tk.10	Ghost of a chance	BN 45-1777	-
tk.15	Blue streak	-	-
tk.16	Eb pob		-

All titles from BLP4033 also issued on CD BN(J)TOCJ-4033.

<u>JIMMY SMITH</u>:
Stanley Turrentine(ts) Jimmy Smith(org) Quentin Warren(g) Sam Jones(b) Donald Bailey(dm).
Englewood Cliffs,N.J.,June 13,1960

tk.2	Smith walk	BN(J)BNJ50101;	CD BN 7-84164-2
tk.3	Lonesome road	-	-
	Organic greenery (b out)	rejected	

104

STANLEY TURRENTINE - LOOK OUT!:
Stanley Turrentine(ts) Horace Parlan(p) George Tucker(b) Al Harewood(dm).
Englewood Cliffs,N.J.,June 18,1960

tk.4	Return engagement	BN BLP4039/BST84039;CD BN(J)TOCJ-5740
tk.5	Little Sheri	- B1-93201
		CD BN 7-93201-2,(F)8-54185-2
tk.6	Little Sheri (alt.)	BN 45-1781,(Du)1A158-83391/4
tk.7	Look out	BN 45-1780,BLP4039/BST84039
		CD BN(J)CJ25-5181/84
tk.11	Journey into melody	BN 45-1780,BLP4039/BST84039
tk.15	Minor chant	BN 45-1781 -
tk.18	Tin tin deo	CD BN(J)TOCJ-5941/44
tk.20	Yesterdays	
tk.22	Tiny capers	BN BLP4039/BST84039

All titles issued on CD BN 7-46543-2.
All titles from BST84039 also issued on Sunset SUS5255,CD BN(J)TOCJ-4039.

FREDDIE HUBBARD - OPEN SESAME:
Freddie Hubbard(tp) Tina Brooks(ts) McCoy Tyner(p) Sam Jones(b) Clifford Jarvis (dm).
Englewood Cliffs,N.J.,June 19,1960

tk.3	Hub's nub	BN BLP4040/BST84040
tk.5	Gypsy blue (alt.)	
tk.6	Gypsy blue	BN 45-1779,BLP4040/BST84040
		CD BN(J)TOCJ-5755/56
tk.8	Open sesame (alt.)	CD BN(J)TOCJ-5941/44
tk.9	Open sesame	BN BLP4040/BST84040,B1-93202,(J)W-5513
		CD BN 7-93202-2,(C)8-56508-2,(F)8-54185-2,
		8-54197-2,(J)CJ28-5164,CJ32-5016,TOCJ-6133,
		TOCJ-6271/74,TOCJ-66051
tk.11	One mint julep	BN 45-1779,BLP4040/BST84040,BN-LA356-H2
		CD BN(Eu)7-89915-2
tk.17	But beautiful	BN BLP4040/BST84040
		CD BN 8-56691-2,(J)TOCJ-5935,TOCJ-6187
tk.22	All or nothing at all	BN BLP4040/BST84040,BN-LA356-H2
		CD BN 8-35282-2,8-59071-2

All titles issued on CD BN 7-84040-2.
All titles from BST84040 also issued on CD BN(J)TOCJ-4040,DVD-CD Classic DAD-1019.

105

TINA BROOKS - TRUE BLUE:
Freddie Hubbard(tp) Tina Brooks(ts) Duke Jordan(p) Sam Jones(b) Art Taylor(dm).
Englewood Cliffs,N.J.,June 25,1960

tk.5	Miss Hazel	
tk.7	Good old soul	BN 45-1782
	Good old soul (alt.)	CD BN(J)TOCJ-5941/44
tk.8	Nothing ever changes my love for you	
tk.14	True blue	BN 45-1783,B1-80679,(E)BNSLP-2
		CD BN 7-80679-2,(J)TOCJ-5755/56,TOCJ-5779,
		TOCJ-5937,TOCJ-6131,TOCJ-6191
	True blue (alt.)	CD BN(J)TOCJ-5941/44
tk.18	Up tight's creek	
tk.22	Theme for Doris	BN 45-1783

All titles,except alternates,issued on BN BLP4041,B1-28975,Mosaic MR4-106,CD BN(J) TOCJ-4041.
All titles and takes shown issued on CD BN 8-28975-2.
Note: BN 45-1783 was possibly not issued.

DUKE PEARSON:
Ike Quebec(ts-1) Duke Pearson(p) Israel Crosby(b) Vernel Fournier(dm).
Englewood Cliffs,N.J.,June 26,1960

tk.2	For all we know-1	CD BN 5-21484-2
tk.6	I'll remember April	unissued
tk.9	I see your face before me	CD BN 5-21484-2
tk.12	Sweet slumber-1	-
tk.13	Midnight sun	unissued

THE THREE SOUNDS - MOODS (BLP4044)/FEELIN' GOOD (BLP4072):
Gene Harris(p,celeste) Andrew Simpkins(b) Bill Dowdy(dm).
Englewood Cliffs,N.J.,June 28,1960

tk.3	I let a song go out of my heart	BN BLP4072
tk.5	Loose walk	BN 45-1791,BLP4044
tk.6	Things ain't what they used to be	BN 45-1794 -
		CD BN(J)TOCJ-5937
tk.7	Love for sale	BN 45-1793,L4044,BLP4044
		CD BN(J)CJ28-5168,TOCJ-66048
tk.9	Li'l darlin'	BN 45-1791,BLP4044
tk.10	I'm beginning to see the light	BN 45-1792 -
tk.11	Tammy's breeze	- -
tk.12	Two bass hit	BN BLP4072
tk.15	On Green Dolphin Street	BN 45-1793,L4044,BLP4044
		CD 8-27323-2,(J)CJ28-5168,TOCJ-5187/88,
		TOCJ-66048,TOCJ-66052
tk.16	It could happen to you	BN BLP4072;CD BN(J)CJ28-5168,TOCJ-66048
tk.17	Straight no chaser	- CD 8-35471-2
tk.18	Blues after dark	-
tk.20	Parker's pad	BN 45-1824,BLP4072
tk.21	When I fall in love	- -
		CD BN 8-27323-2,(J)CJ28-5168,TOCJ-5873
tk.22	I got it bad and that ain't good	BN BLP4072
tk.23	Sandu	BN BLP4044

All titles from BLP4044 (mono) also issued on BN BST 84044,CD BN(J)CP32-9518 (stereo).
All titles from BLP4072 also issued on BN BST84072,CD BN(J)TOCJ-4072 stereo).

STANLEY TURRENTINE & THE THREE SOUNDS:
Stanley Turrentine(ts) Gene Harris(p) Andrew Simpkins(b) Bill Dowdy(dm).
Englewood Cliffs,N.J.,June 29,1960

tk.3	Alone together	
tk.7	Strike up the band	
tk.10	There is no greater love	
tk.11	Blue hour	
tk.14	Where or when	

All titles issued on CD BN 5-24586-2,(J)TOCJ-66082.

HORACE SILVER - HORACE-SCOPE:
Blue Mitchell(tp) Junior Cook(ts) Horace Silver(p) Gene Taylor(b) Roy Brooks(dm).
Englewood Cliffs,N.J.,July 8,1960

	Me and my baby	rejected
tk.10	Where you at?	BN 45-1785,BLP4042/BST84042 CD BN 7-84042-2,BN 8-33208-2
tk.14	Strollin'	BN 45-1784,BLP4042/BST84042,BN-LA402-H2 CD BN 7-84042-2,4-95576-2
	Nica's dream	rejected
tk.22	Without you	BN BLP4042/BST84042,CD 7-84042-2

HORACE SILVER - HORACE-SCOPE:
Blue Mitchell(tp) Junior Cook(ts) Horace Silver(p) Gene Taylor(b) Roy Brooks(dm).
Englewood Cliffs,N.J.,July 9,1960

tk.23	Nica's dream	BN 45-1784,BN-LA402-H2,(E)BNSLP-2 CD BN 4-95576-2,(J)CJ25-5181/84,CJ28-5033, TOCJ-5779,TOCJ-5793,TOCJ-5827,TOCJ-66034
tk.31	Horace-scope	CD BN(J)TOCJ-5740
tk.34	Yeah!	
tk.38	Me and my baby	BN 45-1785

All titles issued on BN BLP4042/BST84042,CD 7-84042-2.

DONALD BYRD - BYRD IN FLIGHT:
Donald Byrd(tp) Jackie McLean(as) Duke Pearson(p) Reggie Workman(b) Lex Humphries(dm).
Englewood Cliffs,N.J.,July 10,1960

	Kimyas	rejected
	Cecile	-
tk.6	Little boy blue (as out)	BN 45-1798,BLP4048/BST84048 CD BN 8-52435-2,(J)TOCJ-4048
	Between the devil and the deep blue sea	rejected
tk.14	Bo	BN BN 8-52435-2,(J)TOCJ-4048
tk.16	My girl Shirl	BN BLP4048/BST84048 CD BN 8-52435-2,(J)TOCJ-4048,TOCJ-5755/56

107

HORACE PARLAN QUINTET - SPEAKIN' MY PIECE:
Tommy Turrentine(tp) Stanley Turrentine(ts) Horace Parlan(p) George Tucker(b) Al Harewood(dm).
Englewood Cliffs,N.J.,July 14,1960

tk.4	Rastus	BN BLP4043/BST84043
tk.7	Rastus (alt.)	CD BN(J)TOCJ-5941/44
tk.10	Borderline	BN 45-1778,BLP4043/BST84043
tk.16	Speakin' my piece	-
tk.19	Oh so blue	-
tk.20	Oh so blue (alt.)	
tk.24	Up in Cynthia's room	BN BLP4043/BST84043
tk.26	Wadin'	BN 45-1778,BLP4043/BST84043,BST2-84433 CD BN 7-97960-2 BN(Du)1A158-83391/4

All titles issued on Mosaic MQ8-197,CD MD5-197
All titles from BST84043 also issued on CD BN(J)TOCJ-4043.

DIZZY REECE - COMIN' ON:
Dizzy Reece(tp) Stanley Turrentine,Musa Kaleem(ts) Duke Jordan(p) Sam Jones(b) Al Harewood(dm).
Englewood Cliffs,N.J.,July 17,1960

tk.4	Goose dance -1	CD BN 5-22019-2
tk.6/7	Sands	-
tk.11	Comin' on	-
tk.12	Achmet -1,2	rejected
tk.14	The case of the frightened lover	-
tk.17	The things we did last Summer -3	CD BN 5-22019-2

-1: Musa Kaleem also plays fl on the melody.
-2: Dizzy Reece also plays congas.
-3: Turrentine & Kaleem out.

LOU DONALDSON - MIDNIGHT SUN:
Lou Donaldson(as) Horace Parlan(p) George Tucker(b) Al Harewood(dm) Ray Barretto(cga).
Englewood Cliffs,N.J.,July 22,1960

tk.2	The squirrel
tk.5	Si si Safronia
tk.6	Dog walk
tk.7	Exactly like you
tk.10	Avalon
tk.12	Midnight sun (cga out)
tk.13	Candy

All titles issued on BN LT-1028.
Note: On BN LT-1028,the bass player was erroneously listed as Ben Tucker.

HAROLD LAND - TAKE AIM:
Martin Banks(tp) Harold Land(ts) Amos Trice(p) Clarence Jones(b) Leon Pettis(dm).
(prod. by Leonard Feather)(Radio Recorders) LA,July 25,1960

You're my thrill
Reflections
Land of peace
Blue Nellie
Take aim
As you like it

All titles issued on BN LT-1057.

<u>DUKE JORDAN</u> - <u>FLIGHT TO JORDAN</u>:
Dizzy Reece(tp) Stanley Turrentine(ts)Duke Jordan(p) Reggie Workman(b) Art Taylor(dm).
Englewood Cliffs,N.J.,August 4,1960

tk.4	Flight to Jordan	BN 45-1801,BLP4046 BN(J)FCPA 6208,W-5508 CD BN(J)CJ28-5171,CJ28-5176
tk.8	Si-joya	BN BLP4046,(J)FCPA 6208 CD BN(J)TOCJ-5875,TOCJ-6132,TOCJ-6271/74, TOCJ-66053,Cap(J)TOCJ-5204,TOCJ-5618/19
tk.18	Split quick	BN BLP4046,(J)FCPA 6208
tk.19	Squawkin'	-
tk.25	Diamond stud	CD BN(J)TOCJ-5941/44
tk.27	Starbrite	BN 45-1801,BLP4046,(J)FCPA 6208 CD BN(J)TOCJ-5854
tk.29	Deacon Joe	BN BLP4046
tk.31	I should care (tp,ts out)	CD BN(J)CJ28-5022,TOCJ-5187/88,TOCJ-5873

All titles issued on CD BN 7-46824-2.
All titles from BLP4046 (mono) also issued on BN BST84046,CD BN(J)TOCJ-4046 (stereo).
Note: 45-1801 was possibly not released.

<u>ART TAYLOR</u> - <u>A.T.'S DELIGHT</u>:
Dave Burns(tp) Stanley Turrentine(ts) Wynton Kelly(p) Paul Chambers(b) Art Taylor(dm) Carlos "Patato" Valdes(cga-1).
Englewood Cliffs,N.J.,August 6,1960

tk.3	Syeeda's song flute	CD BN(J)TOCJ-5755/56
tk.9	High seas	
tk.11	Move-1	
tk.21	Epistrophy-1	BN 45-1800,CD 8-35471-2
tk.24	Blue interlude	
tk.26	Cookoo and fungi (tp,p out)-1	BN 45-1800

All titles issued on BN BLP4047/BST84047,CD 7-84047-2.

<u>ART BLAKEY AND THE JAZZ MESSENGERS</u>:
Lee Morgan(tp) Wayne Shorter(ts) Bobby Timmons(p) Jymie Merritt(b) Art Blakey(dm).
Englewood Cliffs,N.J.,August 7,1960

tk.3	When your lover has gone	CD BN 7-84049-2,(J)TOCJ-5941/44
tk.7	Noise in the attic	BN BLP4245/BST84245,CD 7-84245-2
tk.9	Sleeping dancer sleep on (alt.)	CD BN 7-84245-2
tk.10	Sleeping dancer sleep on	BN BLP4245/BST84245,CD 7-84245-2
tk.11	Sincerely Diana	BN BLP4049/BST84049;Sunset(E)SLS50190 CD BN 7-46532-2,7-84049-2
tk.15	Sincerely Diana (alt.)	CD BN 7-84049-2
	Kozo's waltz	rejected
tk.27	Yama	BN 45-1795,BLP4049/BST84049 CD BN 7-46532-2,7-84049-2

All titles,except "Kozo's waltz",also issued on Mosaic MR10-141,CD MD6-141.

109

FREDDIE REDD QUINTET - SHADES OF REDD:
Jackie McLean(as) Tina Brooks(ts) Freddie Redd(p) Paul Chambers(b) Louis Hayes(dm).
Englewood Cliffs,N.J.,August 13,1960

tk.1	Thespian	BN BLP4045/BST84045
tk.4	Blues-blues-blues	-
tk.5	Shadows	-
tk.6	Swift	-
tk.7	Ole! (alt.)	
tk.9	Ole!	BN BLP4045/BST84045
tk.11	Just a ballad for my baby	-
tk.16	Melanie	-
tk.17	Melanie (alt.)	CD BN(J)TOCJ-5941/44

All titles issued on Mosaic MR3-124,CD BN 8-21738-2,Mosaic MD2-124.
All titles from BST84045 also issued on CD BN(J)TOCJ-4045.

ART BLAKEY AND THE JAZZ MESSENGERS:
Lee Morgan(tp) Wayne Shorter(ts) Bobby Timmons(p) Jymie Merritt(b) Art Blakey(dm).
Englewood Cliffs,N.J.,August 14,1960

	Yama	rejected
tk.31	Kozo's waltz	BN BLP4049/BST84049;Sunset(E)SLS50190 CD BN 7-46532-2,7-84049-2
tk.34	Giantis	BN BLP4245/BST84245 CD BN 7-84245-2,(Eu)4-93072-2, (J)TOCJ-5274/76
tk.42	Johnny's blue	BN BLP4245/BST84245,CD 7-84245-2
tk.46	So tired	BN 45-1795,BLP4049/BST84049,(E)BNSLP-2 CD BN 7-46532-2,7-84049-2,(Eu)4-93072-2, (J)TOCJ-5779
tk.48	Like someone in love	BN BLP4245/BST84245,CD 7-84245-2
tk.54	A night in Tunisia	BN 45-1796,BLP4049/BST84049,B1-93205 BN(F)BST84383,(J)NP9020C,LBN80259, LNP95059B,K18P-9127,K23P-6724,FCPA 6205, W-5506 CD BN 7-46532-2,7-84049-2,7-93205-2, 7-97190-2,7-89032-2,(Eu)4-93072-2, (J)CJ28-5031,TOCJ-5269,TOCJ-5274/76, TOCJ-5823,TOCJ-66031,Cema S21-56914, EMI-Jazz(E)4-93467-2

All titles,except first,also issued on Mosaic MR10-141,CD MD6-141.

110

<u>JACKIE McLEAN</u> - <u>JACKIE'S BAG</u> (BLP4051)/<u>STREET SINGER</u> (GXF-3067):
Blue Mitchell(tp) Jackie McLean(as) Tina Brooks(ts) Kenny Drew(p) Paul Chambers(b) Art Taylor(dm).
Englewood Cliffs,N.J.,September 1,1960

tk.3	Melonae's dance	
tk.5	Appointment in Ghana	BN BLP4051/BST84051,BST2-92468,B1-80701 BN(Du)1A158-83391/4,(J)FCPA 6213 CD BN 7-92468-2,7-80701-2,(F)8-54185-2, (J)CJ28-5163,TOCJ-6131,TOCJ-66046
tk.6	Medina	
tk.11	Isle of Java	BN BLP4051/BST84051
tk.12	Street singer	BN BLP4052;Mosaic MR4-106 CD BN 8-21737-2
tk.15	Ballad for Doll	BN BLP4051/BST84051

All titles issued on BN(J)GXF-3067,CD BN 7-46142-2,(J)TOCJ-66080.
All titles from BST84051 also issued on CD BN(J)TOCJ-4051.
Note: BLP4052 was not released.

<u>ART BLAKEY AND THE JAZZ MESSENGERS MEET YOU AT THE JAZZ CORNER OF THE WORLD</u>:
Lee Morgan(tp) Wayne Shorter(ts) Bobby Timmons(p) Jymie Merritt(b) Art Blakey(dm).
(Birdland Club) NYC,September 14,1960

Set #1:

tk.1	The breeze and I	rejected
tk.2	These are the things I love	-

Set #2:

tk.3	The summit	BN BLP4055/BST84055
tk.4	High modes	-
tk.5	The theme	-

All titles also issued on Mosaic MR10-141,CD BN(J)TOCJ-4055,Mosaic MD6-141.

Set #3:

tk.6	The opener	rejected
tk.7	What,know (Goldie)	BN 45-1821,BLP4054/BST84054
tk.8	The theme	-

Last two titles also issued on Mosaic MR10-141,CD BN(J)TOCJ-4054,Mosaic MD6-141.

Set #4:

tk.9	The breeze and I	BN BLP4054/BST84054,(J)K23P-6724
tk.10	The opener	-
tk.11	These are the things I love	BN BLP4055/BST84055
tk.12	Round about midnight	BN BLP4054/BST84054;CD BN(J)TOCJ-5274/76
tk.13	Night watch (*aka* East of Brooklyn)	rejected

All titles,except last,also issued on Mosaic MR10-141,CD MD6-141.
All titles from BST84054/55 also issued on CD BN(J)TOCJ-4054/55.

Set #5:

tk.14	The opener	rejected
tk.15	Night watch (*aka* East of Brooklyn)	BN BLP4055/BST84055 Mosaic MR10-141, CD BN(J)TOCJ-4055,Mosaic MD6-141
tk.16	The breeze and I	rejected
tk.17	These are the things I love	-

111

IKE QUEBEC QUARTET:
Ike Quebec(ts) Sir Charles Thompson (as "Lord Bentley")(org) Milt Hinton(b) J.C.Heard(dm).
Englewood Cliffs,N.J.,September 25,1960

tk.6	If I could be with you (one hour tonight)	BN 45-1803,CD 8-56690-2
tk.9	Mardi Gras	BN 45-1804
tk.12	What a difference a day makes	BN 45-1802
tk.14	For all we know	BN 45-1805
tk.18	Ill wind	- CD 8-54365-2,(J)TOCJ-5854
tk.19	I've got the world on a string	BN 45-1802
tk.21	Me' n Mabe	BN 45-1803
tk.24	Everything happens to me (short version)	BN 45-1804,CD 8-56690-2
tk.25	Everything happens to me (long version)	

All titles issued on Mosaic MR3-121,CD MD2-121.
Note: BN 45-1805 was possibly not released.

TINA BROOKS - BACK TO THE TRACKS:
Blue Mitchell(tp) Tina Brooks(ts) Kenny Drew(p) Paul Chambers(b) Art Taylor (dm).
Englewood Cliffs,N.J.,October 20,1960

tk.3	Back to the tracks	BN BLP4052,CD 8-21737-2;Mosaic MR4-106
tk.7	The ruby and the pearl	- - -
tk.11	For heaven's sake	- - -
tk.13	The blues and I	- - -
	David the king	rejected

Note: BLP4052 was not released.

FREDDIE HUBBARD - GOIN' UP:
Freddie Hubbard(tp) Hank Mobley(ts) McCoy Tyner(p) Paul Chambers(b) Philly Joe Jones(dm).
Englewood Cliffs,N.J.,November 6,1960

tk.2	Blues for Brenda	BN BN-LA356-H2
tk.9	Karioka	CD BN 8-59071-2
tk.17	Asiatic raes (*aka* Lotus blossom)	CD BN(J)CJ28-5164
tk.19	A peck a sec (*aka* The latest)	
tk.21	The changing scene	BN 45-1809
tk.24	I wished I knew	BN 45-1809,BN-LA356-H2,CD 8-56691-2

All titles issued on BN BLP4056/BST84056,CD 8-59380-2.

 112

<u>DONALD BYRD AT THE HALF NOTE CAFE</u> - <u>JAZZ AT THE WATERFRONT</u>:
Donald Byrd(tp) Pepper Adams(bs) Duke Pearson(p) Laymon Jackson(b) Lex Humphries(dm).
(Half Note Cafe) NYC,November 11,1960

Set #1:		
tk.1	Theme from Mr. Lucky	CD BN 7-46540-2
tk.2	Kimyas	rejected
tk.3	A portrait of Jennie (bs out)	-
tk.4	One more for the road	-
tk.5	Jeannine	BN BLP4061,B1-80679,B1-28263,(E)BNSLP-2 CD BN 7-46540-2,7-80679-2,8-28263-2, (J)TOCJ-5779
tk.6	Pure D.funk	BN BLP4061,(J)W-5505 CD BN 7-46540-2
Set #2:		
tk.7	My girl Shirl	BN BLP4060,CD 7-46539-2
tk.8	Soulful kiddy	- -
tk.9	A portrait of Jennie (bs out)	- -
tk.10	Chant	-
tk.11	The theme	rejected
Set #3:		
tk.12	Theme from Mr. Lucky	rejected
tk.13	That's all	-
tk.14	Kimyas	BN BLP4061,CD 7-46540-2
tk.15	Cecile	BN BLP4060,CD 7-46539-2
tk.16	The theme:Pure D. funk	-
Set #4:		
tk.17	When sunny gets blue	BN BLP4061,(J)K18P-9127 CD BN 7-46540-2
tk.18	Between the devil and the deep blue sea	CD BN 7-46540-2
tk.19	Child's play	CD BN 7-46539-2
Set #5:		
tk.20	Theme from Mr. Lucky	rejected
tk.21	The theme	-
Set #6:		
tk.22	A portrait of Jennie	rejected
tk;23	Pure D. funk	-

All titles from BLP4060/61 (mono) also issued on BN BST84060/61,CD BN(J)TOCJ-4060/61 (stereo).
All released titles from above sets also issued on CD BN 8-57187-2.

<u>HANK MOBLEY</u> - <u>ROLL CALL</u>:
Freddie Hubbard(tp) Hank Mobley(ts) Wynton Kelly(p) Paul Chambers(b) Art Blakey(dm).
Englewood Cliffs,N.J.,November 13,1960

tk.7	Take your pick	BN BLP4058/BST84058,CD 8-37052-2
tk.18	The breakdown	-
tk.20	My groove,your move	- (E)UALP 17
tk.29	A Baptist beat	- CD BN(Eu)7-80703-2 BN(E)BNSLP-3;CD BN(J)TOCJ-5780
tk.31	A Baptist beat (alt.)	
tk.34	Roll call	BN BLP4058/BST84058 CD BN(J)CJ28-5035,TOCJ-66043
tk.35	The more I see you	BN BLP4058/BST84058

All titles issued on CD BN 7-46823-2.
All titles from BST84058 also issued on CD BN(J)TOCJ-4058,DVD-CD Classic DAD-1016.

<u>GRANT GREEN</u> - <u>FIRST SESSION</u>:
Wynton Kelly(p) Grant Green(g) Paul Chambers(b) Philly Joe Jones(dm).
Englewood Cliffs,N.J.,November 26,1960

tk.2	Just friends	CD BN 5-27548-2
tk.4	Sonnymoon for two	-
tk.7	He's a real gone guy	-
	A night in Tunisia	rejected
tk.11	Seepin'	CD BN 5-27548-2
tk.12	Grant's first stand	-
	Jordu	rejected

<u>HORACE PARLAN</u> - <u>HEADIN' SOUTH</u>:
Horace Parlan(p) George Tucker(b) Al Harewood(dm) Ray Barretto(cga).
Englewood Cliffs,N.J.,December 6,1960

tk.2	Jim loves Sue	
tk.7	Headin' South	CD BN 4-97156-2
tk.8	Congalegre	BN B1-57745,(E)BNSLP-1,(J)TOJJ-5849 CD BN 7-95590-2,(J)TOCJ-5778,TOCJ-5849
tk.9	Prelude to a kiss (cga out)	
tk.10	Summertime (cga out)	CD BN 8-29095-2
tk.12	The song is ended	CD BN 7-99095-2
tk.16	My mother's eyes	
tk.17	Low down (cga out)	

All titles issued on BN BLP4062/BST84062,Mosaic MQ8-197,CD BN(J)TOCJ-4062,Mosaic MD5-197.

<u>KENNY DREW</u> - <u>UNDERCURRENT</u>:
Freddie Hubbard(tp) Hank Mobley(ts) Kenny Drew(p) Sam Jones(b) Louis Hayes(dm)
Englewood Cliffs,N.J.,December 11,1960

tk.3	The pot's on	
tk.7	Lion's den	BN(J)FCPA 6208
tk.11	Groovin' the blues	CD BN(J)TOCJ-5937
tk.16	Ballade	BN(J)FCPA 6208,CD CJ28-5022,TOCJ-6132
tk.19	Undercurrent	- W-5508
tk.22	Funk-cosity	-

All titles issued on BN BLP4059/BST84059,CD 7-84059-2,DVD-CD Classic DAD-1024.

 114

THE THREE SOUNDS - HERE WE COME (BLP4088)/IT JUST GOT TO BE (BLP4120):
Gene Harris(p) Andrew Simpkins(b) Bill Dowdy(dm). Englewood Cliffs,N.J.,December 13,1960

tk.1	If I were a bell	BN BLP4120,CD 8-27323-2,8-29095-2
tk.4	Summertime	BN 45-1827,BLP4088,CD 8-27323-2, (J)CJ28-5168,TOCJ-66048
tk.5	Here we come	BN 45-1825,BLP4088
tk.7	It just got to be me	BN BLP4120
	Bye bye blackbird	rejected
tk.11	Poinciana	BN BLP4088,CD 8-27323-2
tk.14	The girl next door	unissued
tk.15	South of the border	BN BLP4120
tk.17	Sonnymoon for two	BN BLP4088
tk.18	This is the way 'tis	unissued

Same. Englewood Cliffs,N.J.,December 14,1960

tk.19	Blue 'n' boogie	BN BLP4120
tk.20	The nearness of you	BN 45-1898 -
tk.23	Just squeeze me	BN 45-1826,BLP4088
tk.25	Broadway	BN 45-1827 - CD Cap(J)CP28-5864
tk.26	Now's the time	BN 45-1826 - CD BN(J)CJ28-5168,TOCJ-66048
	Lover come back to me	rejected
tk.30	One for Renee	BN 45-1898,BLP4120,CD 8-27323-2
tk.31	Stella by starlight	- CD BN(J)TOCJ-66048
tk.32	Real Gene	-
tk.33	Our love is here to stay	BN 45-1825,BLP4088

All titles from BLP4088/4120 (mono) also issued on BN BST84088/84120,CD BN(J)TOCJ-4088/4120 (stereo).

STANLEY TURRENTINE WITH THE THREE SOUNDS - BLUE HOUR:
Stanley Turrentine(ts) Gene Harris(p) Andrew Simpkins(b) Bill Dowdy(dm).
Englewood Cliffs,N.J.,December 16,1960

	Between the devil and the deep blue sea	rejected
tk.7	I want a little girl	BN BLP4057;CD(Au)8-14808-2
tk.8	Blue riff	BN 45-1813 - (E)BNX 1 CD BN 7-48337-2
tk.13	Gee baby,ain't I good to you	BN 45-1813,BLP4057
tk.15	Gee baby,ain't I good to you (alt.)	CD BN(J)TOCJ-66082
tk.17	Since I fell for you	BN BLP4057,B1-93201 CD BN 7-93201-2,7-95281-2,Cema S21-57590
tk.19	Willow weep for me	BN BLP4057;CD BN 7-95281-2,8-54365-2 (J)CJ28-5170,EMI Gold(E)5-21427-2
tk.24	Just in time	CD BN(J)TOCJ-66082
tk.28	Blues in the closet	CD BN(J)TOCJ-5941/44,TOCJ-66082

All titles,except rejected one,also issued on CD BN 5-24586-2.
All titles from BLP4057 (mono) also issued in stereo on BN BST84057,CD 7-84057-2.

STANLEY TURRENTINE:
Tommy Turrentine(tp) Stanley Turrentine(ts) Horace Parlan(p) George Tucker(b) Al Harewood(dm).
Englewood Cliffs,N.J.,December 18,1960

Fine lil' lass	rejected
Thomasville	-
Then I'll be tired of you	-
My girl is just enough woman for me	-
Stolen sweets	-

 115

<u>JACKIE McLEAN</u> - <u>BLUESNIK</u>:
Freddie Hubbard(tp) Jackie McLean(as) Kenny Drew(p) Doug Watkins(b) Pete La Roca(dm).
Englewood Cliffs,N.J.,January 8,1961

tk.5	Blues function	BN BLP4067
tk.7	Cool green	-
tk.8	Goin' 'way blues	-
tk.11	Goin' 'way blues (alt.)	
tk.13	Torchin' (alt.)	
tk.15	Torchin'	BN BLP4067
tk.20	Drew's blues	- CD BN(J)TOCJ-5260
tk.20A	Bluesnik	- (J)BNJ71106
		CD BN(J)TOCJ-5758,TOCJ-66046

All titles issued on CD BN 7-84067-2
All titles from BLP4067 (mono) also issued on BN BST84067,CD BN(J)TOCJ-4067 (stereo).

<u>KENNY DORHAM</u> - <u>WHISTLE STOP</u>:
Kenny Dorham(tp) Hank Mobley(ts) Kenny Drew(p) Paul Chambers(b) Philly Joe Jones(dm).
Englewood Cliffs,N.J.,January 15,1961

tk.2	"Philly" twist	CD BN 8-53648-2,(Eu)5-23444-2,(Sp)5-21755-2
tk.11	Whistle stop	
tk.19	Windmill	
tk.20	Sunset	
tk.25	Sunrise in Mexico	
tk.31	Dorham's epitaph	
tk.34	Buffalo	

All titles issued on BN BLP4063/BST84063,B1-28978,CD 8-28978-2,5-25646-2.

<u>FREDDIE REDD</u> - <u>REDD'S BLUES</u>:
Benny Bailey(tp) Jackie McLean(as) Tina Brooks(ts) Freddie Redd(p) Paul Chambers(b) Sir John Godfrey (dm).
Englewood Cliffs,N.J.,January 17,1961

tk.2	Love lost
tk.6	Somewhere
tk.7	Old spice
tk.11	Blues for Betsy
tk.18	Now
tk.20	Cute doot

All titles issued on Mosaic MR3-124,CD BN(J)TOCJ-66076,Mosaic MD2-124.

STANLEY TURRENTINE - COMIN' YOUR WAY:
Tommy Turrentine(tp) Stanley Turrentine(ts) Horace Parlan(p) George Tucker(b) Al Harewood (dm).
Englewood Cliffs,N.J.,January 20,1961

tk.1	Then I'll be tired of you	BN BN-LA883-J2,CD 7-95281-2
tk.9	My girl is just enough woman for me	-
tk.15	Stolen sweets	-
tk.21	Fine Li'l lass(alt.)	
tk.22	Fine Li'l lass	BN BN-LA883-J2
tk.26	Thomasville	-
tk.41	Just in time	
tk.43	Someone to watch over me	BN BN-LA883-J2 CD BN 7-95281-2,(J)CJ28-5170,TOCJ-5750, TOCJ-5935

All titles,except tk.21 & tk.41,were first scheduled on BN BLP4065,which was not released,and finally issued on BN BLJ-84065 in 1987,and later reissued as CD BN(J)TOCJ-4065.
All titles and takes shown issued on CD BN 7-84065-2.

LOU DONALDSON - HERE'TIS:
Lou Donaldson(as) Baby Face Willette(org) Grant Green(g) Dave Bailey(dm).
Englewood Cliffs,N.J.,January 23,1961

tk.1	Watusi jump	BN 45-1808,BLP4066
tk.4	Here 'tis	BN 45-1807 - CD 8-27298-2
tk.12	Cool blues	- B1-28263 CD BN 8-28263-2,(J)TOCJ-5239,TOCJ-5936, TOCJ-6131,TOCJ-6271/74,TOCJ-66044
tk.13	Walk wid me	BN BLP4066
tk.16	A foggy day	-
tk.17	Untitled Donaldson blues	rejected

All titles from BLP4066 (mono) also issued on BN BST84066,CD BN(J)TOCJ-4066 (stereo).

GRANT GREEN - GRANT'S FIRST STAND:
Grant Green(g) Baby Face Willette(org) Ben Dixon(dm).
Englewood Cliffs,N.J.,January 28,1961

tk.8	A wee bit o' Green	BN 45-1812
tk.9	Miss Ann's tempo	BN 45-1811,CD 8-27312-2,8-34957-2
tk.12	T'ain't nobody's business if I do	-
tk.14	Baby's minor lope	CD BN 8-33205-2
tk.18	Lullaby of the leaves	Lib(J)K22P-6094/95 CD BN(J)CJ28-5169,TOCJ-5299,TOCJ-66045, TOCJ-66052
tk.21	Blues for Willarene	

All titles issued on BN BLP4064/BST84064,CD BN 5-21959-2,(J)TOCJ-4064.

BABY FACE WILLETTE - FACE TO FACE:
Fred Jackson(ts) Baby Face Willette(org) Grant Green(g) Ben Dixon(dm).
Englewood Cliffs,N.J.,January 30,1961

tk.7	Face to face	BN B1-96563,CD 7-96563-2
tk.8	Face to face (alt.)	CD BN(J)TOCJ-5941/44
tk.11	Something strange	BN 45-1815,B1-29092 CD BN 8-29092-2,(F)8-54188-2,(J)TOCJ-5644, TOCJ-5755/56
tk.12	Something strange (alt.)	
tk.17	Whatever Lola wants	
tk.18	Goin' down	BN 45-1816
tk.19	Swingin' at Sugar Ray's	BN 45-1815;CD BN(J)TOCJ-6067,TOCJ-6271/74
tk.24	High 'n' low	

All titles, except tk.8 & tk.12,issued on BN BLP4068 (mono),BST84068,CD BN(J)TOCJ-4068 (stereo).
All titles issued on CD BN 8-59382-2

ART BLAKEY'S JAZZ MESSENGERS:
Lee Morgan(tp) Wayne Shorter(ts) Bobby Timmons(p) Jymie Merritt(b) Art Blakey(dm).
Englewood Cliffs,N.J.,February 12,1961

	Look at the birdie	rejected
tk.8	United	BN(J)GXF-3060 CD BN 5-21956-2
tk.15	Ping pong	BN(J)GXF-3060 CD BN 5-21956-2
	Mastermind	rejected
	Petty Larceny	-
tk.27	Blue Ching	BN(J)GXF-3060 CD BN 8-21287-2
tk.28	Pisces	BN(J)GXF-3060 CD BN 8-21287-2

All titles,excepted rejected ones,also issued on Mosaic MR10-141,CD MD6-141.

ART BLAKEY'S JAZZ MESSENGERS:
Lee Morgan(tp) Wayne Shorter(ts) Bobby Timmons(p) Jymie Merritt(b) Art Blakey(dm).
Englewood Cliffs,N.J.,February 18,1961

tk.2	Look at the birdie	BN BST84347;CD 5-21956-2
tk.4	Mastermind	- -
tk.10	Ping pong	- B1-80679 - CD BN 7-97190-2,7-80679-2,(Eu)4-93072-2
tk.12	Petty larceny	BN BLP4156/BST84156;Sunset(E)SLS50190 CD BN 8-21287-2,(J)TOCJ-4156
	Roots and herbs	rejected

First four titles also issued on Mosaic MR10-141,CD MD6-141.

Walter Davis Jr.(p) replaces Timmons.Same date.

tk.18	Roots and herbs	BN BST84347
tk.26	United	- (E)UALP 17 CD BN(J)TOCJ-5274/76

Both titles also issued on Mosaic MR10-141,CD BN 5-21956-2,Mosaic MD6-141.

STANLEY TURRENTINE - UP AT MINTON'S:
Stanley Turrentine(ts) Horace Parlan(p) Grant Green(g) George Tucker(b) Al Harewood(dm).
(Play Room,Minton's Club) NYC,February 23,1961

Set #1:

tk.1	The serpent's tooth	unissued
tk.2	By myself	-
tk.3	Blues-1	-

Set #2:

tk.4	Love for sale	BN BLP4070/BST84070,CD 8-28885-2
tk.5	In your own sweet way	unissued
tk.6	Come rain or come shine	BN BLP4070/BST84070,CD 8-28885-2
tk.7	But not for me	BN BLP4069/BST84069 -

Set #3:

tk.8	Stanley's time	BN BLP4069/BST84069,CD 8-28885-2
tk.9	Broadway	- -
tk.10	Later at Minton's	BN BLP4070/BST84070,CD 8-28885-2
tk.11	Yesterdays	BN BLP4069/BST84069 -
tk.12	Squeeze me	unissued

All titles from BST84069/70 also issued on CD BN(J)TOCJ-4069/70.

Set #4:

tk.13	Blues -1	unissued
tk.14	Just in time	-
tk.15	Summertime	BN BLP4070/BST84070,(Du)1A158-83391/4 CD BN 8-28885-2,(J)TOCJ-4070
tk.16	This can't be love	unissued
tk.17	Softly as in a morning sunrise (ts,g out)	-
tk.18	I'll remember April	-

-1:possibly same tune as "Stanley's time".

TINA BROOKS - THE WAITING GAME:
Johnny Coles(tp) Tina Brooks(ts) Kenny Drew(p) Wilbur Ware(b) Philly Joe Jones(dm).
Englewood Cliffs,N.J.,March 2,1961

tk.1	Dhyana
tk.6	The waiting game
tk.7	Talkin' about
tk.19	David the King
tk.21	One for Myrtle
tk.22	Stranger in paradise

All titles issued on Mosaic MR4-106,CD BN(J)TOCJ-66075.

ART BLAKEY'S JAZZ MESSENGERS - THE WITCH DOCTOR:
Lee Morgan(p) Wayne Shorter(ts) Bobby Timmons(p) Jymie Merritt(b) Art Blakey(dm).
Englewood Cliffs,N.J.,March 14,1961

tk.6	The witch doctor (alt.)	
tk.14	Those who sit and wait	BN BST84258
tk.21	A little busy	- B1-57745 CD BN 8-57745-2,(Eu)4-93072-2
tk.23	Joelle	BN BST84258
tk.28	Afrique	- CD BN(Eu)4-93072-2,(J)TOCJ-5274/76
tk.29	Lost and found	BN BST84258
tk.30	The witch doctor	- CD BN(Eu)4-93072-2

All titles issued on Mosaic MR10-141,CD BN 5-21957-2,Mosaic MD6-141.

HORACE PARLAN - ON THE SPUR OF THE MOMENT:
Tommy Turrentine(tp) Stanley Turrentine(ts) Horace Parlan(p) George Tucker(b) Al Harewood (dm).
Englewood Cliffs,N.J.,March 18,1961

tk.1	Ray C.	BN 45-1835,BLP4074/BST84074
tk.2	On the spur of the moment (alt.)	
tk.3	On the spur of the moment	BN 45-1835,BLP4074/BST84074
tk.7	And that I am so in love	-
tk.11	Pyramid (alt.)	CD BN(J)TOCJ-5941/44
tk.17	Skoo Chee	BN BLP4074/BST84074
tk.18	Al's tune	-
tk.28	Pyramid	-

All titles issued on Mosaic MQ8-197,CD BN 8-21735-2,Mosaic MD5-197.
All titles from BST84074 also issued on CD BN(J)TOCJ-4074.

KENNY DORHAM SEXTET:
Kenny Dorham(tp) Charles Davis(bs) Kenny Drew(p) Grant Green(g) Wilbur Ware(b) Kal ? (dm).
Englewood Cliffs,N.J.,March 19,1961

tk.9	Mason Dixon line	rejected
tk.20	Blues lament	-
tk.24	Cross 'D' track	-
tk.26	Blue Ching	-
tk.27	Spadesville	-
tk.31	9 1/2 Street	-

HANK MOBLEY - WORKOUT:
Hank Mobley(ts) Wynton Kelly(p) Grant Green(g) Paul Chambers(b) Philly Joe Jones(dm).
Englewood Cliffs,N.J.,March 26,1961

tk.3	Smokin'	BN BLP4080,CD 8-37052-2 Lib(J)K22P-6131/32
tk.4	Uh huh	BN BLP4080,CD 8-56399-2
tk.8	The best things in life are free	-
tk.11	Workout	- (J)FCPA 6211,W-5507 CD BN(J)CJ28-5035,TOCJ-66043
tk.15	Greasin' easy	BN BLP4080
tk.21	Three coins in the fountain (g out)	BN BST84431 CD BN 7-84431-2,(Eu)7-89914-2, (J)TOCJ-5941/44

All titles also issued on CD BN 7-84080-2.
All titles from BLP4080 (mono) also issued on BN BST84080,CD BN(J)CP32-9522 (stereo).

 120

GRANT GREEN - GREEN STREET:
Grant Green(g) Ben Tucker(b) Dave Bailey(dm).
Englewood Cliffs,N.J.,April 1,1961

tk.2	Green with envy	BN BLP4071/BST84071,B1-32088
tk.3	Green with envy (alt.)	
tk.7	Grant's dimensions	BN BLP4071/BST84071,B1-32088
tk.9	Alone together (alt.)	CD BN(J)TOCJ-5941/44
tk.10	Alone together	BN BLP4071/BST84071,B1-32088 CD BN(J)CD CJ28-5169,TOCJ-66045
tk.16	'Round about midnight	BN BLP4071/BST84071,B1-32088,CD 8-27312-2
tk.24	No.1 Green Street	- -

All titles issued on CD BN 8-32088-2.
All titles from BST84071 also issued on CD BN(J)TOCJ-4071.

FREDDIE HUBBARD - HUB CAP:
Freddie Hubbard(tp) Julian Priester(tb) Jimmy Heath(ts) Cedar Walton(p) Larry Ridley(b) Philly Joe Jones (dm).
Englewood Cliffs,N.J.,April 9,1961

tk.3	Earmon Jr.	
tk.6	Hub cap	BN BN-LA356-H2,(J)K18P-9127 CD BN(J)CJ25-5181/84,CJ28-5164, (Sp)5-21755-2
tk.11	Cry me not	BN 45-1810,BN-LA356-H2,B1-93202 CD BN 7-93202-2,7-96098-2,8-56691-2 BN(Du)1A158-83391/4,(In)JAZ 2
tk.14	Plexus (alt.)	
tk.15	Plexus	CD BN 8-32993-2
tk.18	Luana	BN BN-LA356-H2
tk.21	Osie Mae	BN 45-1810,CD 8-59071-2

All titles,except tk.14,issued on BN BLP4073/BST84073,BN-LA496-H2,CD BN(J)TOCJ-4073.
All titles issued on CD BN 7-84073-2.

DONALD BYRD - CHANT:
Donald Byrd(tp) Pepper Adams(bs) Herbie Hancock(p) Doug Watkins(b) Teddy Robinson(dm).
Englewood Cliffs,N.J.,April 17,1961

tk.3	I'm an old cowhand	BN LT-991
tk.6	You're next	-
tk.10	Great God	- (E)UALP21
tk.13	Chant	-
tk.15	Sophisticated lady (tp out)	-
tk.19	Cute	rejected
tk.20	That's all	BN LT-991

All titles from LT-991 also issued on CD Mosaic MD4-194.
Note: Drummer was erroneously listed as Eddy Robinson on BN LT-991.

121

LOU DONALDSON - GRAVY TRAIN:
Lou Donaldson(as) Herman Foster(p) Ben Tucker(b) Dave Bailey(dm) Alec Dorsey(cga).
Englewood Cliffs,N.J.,April 27,1961

tk.1	Glory of love	BN-45-1832,BLP4079
tk.3	Glory of love (alt.)	
tk.7	Gravy train	BN 45-1830,BLP4079,B1-30721
tk.9	Gravy train (alt.)	CD BN(J)TOCJ-5941/44
tk.11	Polka dots and moonbeams (cga out)	BN 45-1831,BLP4079 CD BN(Eu)7-89910-2,(J)TOCJ-5935,TOCJ-66044
tk.12	Candy	BN BLP4079
tk.14	South of the border	BN 45-1831,BLP4079,E)BNSLP-4 CD BN 7-95590-2
tk.15	Twist time	BN BLP4079
tk.19	Avalon	BN 45-1832,BLP4079

All titles from BLP4079 (mono) also issued on BN BST84079,CD BN(J)TOCJ-4079 (stereo).
All titles issued on CD BN 8-53357-2.

DONALD BYRD - THE CAT WALK:
Donald Byrd(tp) Pepper Adams(bs) Duke Pearson(p) Laymon Jackson(b) Philly Joe Jones(dm).
Englewood Cliffs,N.J.,May 2,1961

tk.2	Say you're mine
tk.5	Hello bright sunflower
tk.8	Each time I think of you
tk.10	Duke's mixture
tk.14	The cat walk
tk.15	Cute

All titles issued on BN BLP4075/BST84075,CD BN(J)TOCJ-4075,Mosaic MD4-194.

DEXTER GORDON- - DOIN' ALLRIGHT:
Freddie Hubbard(tp) Dexter Gordon(ts) Horace Parlan(p) George Tucker(b) Al Harewood(dm).
Englewood Cliffs,N.J.,May 6,1961

tk.5	I was doing all right	BN BLP4077,CD 8-23514-2
tk.10	I want more	CD BN(J)TOCJ-5941/44
tk.12	You've changed	BN BLP4077,BN-LA393-H2 CD BN 7-96579-2,(J)TOCJ-66047,TOCJ-66054, EMI-Jazz(E)4-99159-2
tk.13	Society red	BN BLP4077,B1-91139 CD BN 7-91139-2,(F)8-54185-2,(J)CJ28-5038
tk.20	It's you or no one	BN BLP4077,BN-LA393-H2,B1-91139 CD BN 7-91139-2,(E)8-53223-2,(J)CJ28-5038
tk.18	For regulars only (alt.)	
tk.21	For regulars only	BN BLP4077,(Du)1A158-83391/4

All titles from BLP4077 (mono) also issued on BN BST84077,CD BN(J)TOCJ-4077 (stereo).
All titles issued on CD BN 7-84077-2,8-34200-2.

122

DEXTER GORDON - DEXTER CALLING:
Dexter Gordon(ts) Kenny Drew(p) Paul Chambers(b) Philly Joe Jones(dm).
Englewood Cliffs,N.J.,May 9,1961

tk.4	Landslide	BN LT-1051;CD BN(J)TOCJ-5941/44
tk.8	Modal mood	BN 45-1829,BN-LA393-H2;Up Front UPF-188 CD BN(Sp)5-21755-2
tk.13	Clear the Dex	BN BN-LA393-H2;Up Front UPF-188 CD BN 8-32993-2
tk.20	Soul sister	BN 45-1828;Up Front UPF-188
tk.26	Smile	CD BN B1-91139 - CD BN 7-91139-2,(J)CJ28-5038,CJ32-5016, TOCJ-5299,TOCJ-66047,TOCJ-66052, (Sp)8-53016-2
tk.28	Ernie's tune	BN 45-1829,BN-LA393-H2;Up Front UPF-188 CD BN 7-96579-2,8-23514-2
tk.32	I want more	
tk.34	The end of a love affair	BN BN-LA393-H2

All titles,except first,issued on BN BLP4083 (mono),BST84083,CD BN(J)TOCJ-4083 (stereo).
All titles issued on CD BN 7-46544-2,8-34200-2.

THE HORACE SILVER QUINTET AT THE VILLAGE GATE - DOIN' THE THING:
Blue Mitchell(tp) Junior Cook(ts) Horace Silver(p) Gene Taylor(b) Roy Brooks(dm).
(Village Gate Club) NYC,May 19,1961

tk.1	The gringo	rejected
tk.2	Kiss me right	-
tk.3	Doin' the thing	BN 45-1818,BLP4076/BST84076,(J)W-5505 CD BN 7-84076-2,(J)TOCJ-4076
tk.4	Filthy McNasty	BN 45-1817,BLP4076/BST84076,BST84325, B1-28263 CD BN 7-84076-2,8-28263-2,4-95576-2, (E)8-53233-2,(J)CJ28-5033,TOCJ-4076, TOCJ-6191,TOCJ-66034
	The theme (Cool eyes)	BN BLP4076/BST84076 CD BN 7-84076-2,(J)TOCJ-4076
tk.5	Senor blues	rejected
tk.6	It ain't s'posed to be like that	BN BN-LA945-H CD BN 7-84076-2,(J)TOCJ-5941/44
tk.7	The gringo	rejected
tk.8	Kiss me right	-
tk.9	Filthy McNasty	-
tk.10	Doin' the thing	-
	The theme (Cool eyes)	-
tk.11	It ain't s'posed to be like that	-
tk.12	The gringo	-
tk.13	Kiss me right	-
tk.14	It ain't s'posed to be like that	-
tk.15	Filthy McNasty	-
	The theme (Cool eyes)	-

 123

<u>THE HORACE SILVER QUINTET AT THE VILLAGE GATE</u> - <u>DOIN' THE THING</u>:
Blue Mitchell(tp) Junior Cook(ts) Horace Silver(p) Gene Taylor(b) Roy Brooks(dm).
(Village Gate Club) NYC,May 20,1961

	Cool eyes (alt. full version))	BN BN-LA945-H,CD 7-84076-2
tk.16	It ain't s'posed to be like that	rejected
tk.17	The gringo	BN BLP4076/BST84076 CD BN 7-84076-2,(J)TOCJ-4076
tk.18	Filthy McNasty	rejected
tk.19	It ain't s'posed to be like that	-
tk.20	Doin' the thing	-
tk.21	Kiss me right	BN BLP4076/BST84076 CD BN 7-84076-2,TOCJ-4076
tk.22	The gringo	rejected
tk.23	Filthy McNasty	-
tk.24	Doin' the thing	-
tk.25	It ain't s'posed to be like that	-
tk.26	The gringo	-
tk.27	Filthy McNasty	-
	The theme (Cool eyes)	-

<u>BABY FACE WILLETTE</u> - <u>STOP AND LISTEN</u>:
Baby Face Willette(org) Grant Green(g) Ben Dixon(dm).
Englewood Cliffs,N.J.,May 22,1961

tk.4	Jumpin' Jupiter	BN BLP4084
tk.7	Work song	- (E)8-53234-2,(J)K22P-6125/26
tk.8	Stop and listen	-
tk.11	Chances are few	-
tk.12	Soul walk	-
tk.15	At last	- (J)K22P-6125/26
tk.16	They can't take that away from me	CD BN(J)TOCJ-5941/44
tk.18	Willow weep for me	BN BLP4084;CD BN(J)TOCJ-5239

All titles issued on CD BN 8-28998-2.
All titles from BLP4084 (mono) also issued on BN BST84084,B1-28998,CD BN(J)TOCJ-4084 (stereo).

<u>ART BLAKEY AND THE JAZZ MESSENGERS</u> - <u>THE FREEDOM RIDER</u>:
Lee Morgan(tp) Wayne Shorter(ts) Bobby Timmons(p) Jymie Merritt(b) Art Blakey(dm).
Englewood Cliffs,N.J.,May 27,1961

tk.2	The back sliders (alt.)	CD BN 5-21956-2
tk.4	The back sliders	BN BST84347,CD 5-21956-2
tk.6	The freedom rider (dm solo)	BN BLP4156/BST84156 CD BN(Eu)4-93072-2,(J)TOCJ-5274/76
tk.7	Tell it like it is	BN BLP4156/BST84156
tk.13	El toro	- Sunset(E)SLS50190
tk.19	Blue lace	- -
tk.25	Uptight	BN(J)GXF-3060

All titles issued on Mosaic MR10-141,CD MD6-141.
Last five titles also issued on CD BN 8-21287-2.
All titles from BST84156 also issued on CD BN(J)TOCJ-4156.

124

GRANT GREEN - SUNDAY MORNIN':
Kenny Drew(p) Grant Green(g) Ben Tucker(b) Ben Dixon(dm).
Englewood Cliffs,N.J.,June 4,1961

tk.3	Come sunrise	BN BLP4099,(J)FCPA 6209
		CD BN 7-96581-2,HMV Jazz(E)5-20884-2
tk.11	Freedom march	BN BLP4099,(J)FCPA 6209
tk.17	Sunday morning-1	-
		CD BN(J)CJ25-5181/84,CJ28-5169, TOCJ-5755/56,TOCJ-6271/74
tk.19	Exodus	BN BLP4099
		CD BN(J)TOCJ-5875,Cap(J)TOCJ-5204
tk.21	Tracin' Tracy	CD BN(J)TOCJ-5941/44
tk.23	God bless the child	BN BLP4099;CD BN(J)TOCJ-66045
tk.26	So what	- (J)FCPA 6209,W-5511
		CD BN(J)CJ28-5176,TOCJ-5937

-1 as Sunday mornin' on CD 8-52434-2.
All titles issued on CD BN 8-52434-2.
All titles from BLP4099 (mono) also issued on BN BST84099,CD BN(J)TOCJ-4099 (stereo).

STANLEY TURRENTINE - DEARLY BELOVED:
Stanley Turrentine(ts) Shirley Scott(as "Little Miss Cott")(org) Roy Brooks Jr.(dm).
Englewood Cliffs,N.J.,June 8,1961

tk.2	Yesterdays	CD BN(J)CJ28-5170
tk.4	My shining hour	
tk.5	Troubles of the world	
tk.12	Wee hour theme	BN 45-1814,B2S-5256
tk.14	Nothing ever changes my love for you	
tk.15	Dearly beloved	
tk.17	Baia	BN 45-1814

All titles issued on BN BLP4081/BST84081,CD BN(J)TOCJ-4081.

HORACE PARLAN - UP AND DOWN:
Booker Ervin(ts) Horace Parlan(p) Grant Green(g) George Tucker(b) Al Harewood(dm).
Englewood Cliffs,N.J.,June 18,1961

tk.4	Light blue	BN BLP4082/BST84082
tk.8	Up and down	-
tk.10	The Book's beat	-
tk.14	Fugee (alt.)	
tk.15	Fugee	BN BLP4082/BST84082
tk.16	Lonely one	-
tk.18	The other part of town	-

All titles issued on Mosaic MQ8-197,CD MD5-197
All titles from BST84082 also issued on CD BN(J)TOCJ-4082.

125

JIMMY SMITH:
Jimmy Smith(org) Quentin Warren(g) Donald Bailey(dm).

Englewood Cliffs,N.J.,June 22,1961

tk.3	Here's to my lady	unissued
tk.7	Straight life	-
tk.9	Stompy	-
tk.10	Minor fare (alt.)	-
tk.12	Minor fare	-
tk.14	Stardust	-
tk.15	Jimmy's blues	-
tk.16	Swanee	-
tk.17	Sweet Sue	-
tk.18	Yes Sir,that's my baby	-

GRANT GREEN - GRANTSTAND:
Yusef Lateef(ts-1,fl-2) Jack McDuff(org) Grant Green(g) Al Harewood(dm).

Englewood Cliffs,N.J.,August 1,1961

tk.3	Green's greenery -1	CD BN(J)TOCJ-5941/44
tk.8	Blues in Maude's flat -1	BN BLP4086/BST84086
		CD BN 8-27312-2,(F)8-54188-2
tk.11	My funny Valentine -2	BN BLP4086/BST84086
		CD BN(J)TOCJ-5935,TOCJ-66054
tk.12	Grantstand -1	BN BLP4086/BST84086,B1-89622,CD 7-89622-2
tk.15	Old folks	-
	Blue and Green -1	rejected

All titles,except last,issued on CD BN 7-46430-2.
All titles from BST84086 also issued on CD BN(J)TOCJ-4086.

THE THREE SOUNDS - HEY THERE!:
Gene Harris(p) Andrew Simpkins(b) Bill Dowdy(dm).

Englewood Cliffs,N.J.,August 13,1961

tk.1	Shiny stockings	BN BST84434;CD BN(J)TOCJ-5857
tk.4	Sermonette	BN 45-1856,BLP4102
tk.9	Work song	BN BST84434,CD 7-84434-2
tk.14	Between the devil and the deep blue sea	- -
tk.15	You are my sunshine	BN 45-1855,BLP4102
		CD BN(J)CJ28-5168,TOCJ-5296,TOCJ-66048
tk.16	Nothin' but the blues	BN 45-1855,BLP4102;CD BN(J)TOCJ-5298
tk.17	Dap's groove	BN 45-1856 -
tk.18	The masquerade is over	-
tk.19	Hey there	- CD BN(J)CJ28-5168
tk.21	Walking the floor over you	BN BST84434,CD 7-84434-2
tk.22	Sweet and lovely	- -
tk.23	Stompin' at the Savoy	BN BLP4102,CD 8-27323-2,(C)8-56508-2
tk.24	Little girl blue	-
	In a mellow tone	rejected
tk.26	Blue Daniel	BN BST84434,CD 7-84434-2
tk.27	Street of dreams	BN BLP4102
tk.29	Wait a minute	BN BST84434,CD 7-84434-2
tk.30	Stairway to the stars	- CD BN(J)TOCJ-5858
tk.32	Billy boy	unissued
tk.33	Lazy cat	BN BST84434,CD 7-84434-2
	Here we come	rejected

All titles from BLP4102 (mono) also issued on BN BST84102,CD BN(J)TOCJ-4102 (stereo).
Note: The CD 7-84434-2 incorrectly states the recording date as August 31,1961.

126

ART BLAKEY'S JAZZ MESSENGERS:
Freddie Hubbard(tp) Curtis Fuller(tb) Wayne Shorter(ts) Cedar Walton(p) Jymie Merritt(b) Art Blakey(dm).
(Village Gate) NYC,August 17,1961

	Arabia	BN BN-LA473-J2,CD 7-84452-2
	The promised land	- -
	Down under	rejected
	Children of the night	-
	Mosaic	-

FREDDIE HUBBARD- READY FOR FREDDIE:
Freddie Hubbard(tp) Bernard McKinney(euph) Wayne Shorter(ts) McCoy Tyner(p) Art Davis(b) Elvin Jones (dm). Englewood Cliffs,N.J.,August 21,1961

tk.5	Arietis	BN BLP4085;CD BN 8-59071-2,(J)CJ28-5164
tk.6	Arietis (alt.)	CD BN(J)TOCJ-5941/44
tk.7	Marie Antoinette	BN BLP4085
tk.10	Marie Antoinette (alt.)	CD BN(J)TOCJ-5941/44
tk.12	Crisis	BN BLP4085,BN-LA356-H2
tk.13	Weaver of dreams -1	- -
		CD BN 8-56691-2,(J)CJ28-5164
tk.16	Birdlike	BN BLP4085,B1-93202,CD 7-93202-2

-1: McKinney & Shorter present in intro only.
All titles issued on CD BN 8-32094-2.
All titles from BLP4085 (mono) also issued on BN BST84085,B1-32094,CD BN(J)TOCJ-4085 (stereo).

GRANT GREEN - REMEMBERING (GXF-3071)/STANDARDS(8-21284-2):
Horace Parlan(p-1) Grant Green(g) Wilbur Ware(b) Al Harewood(dm).
Englewood Cliffs,N.J.,August 29,1961

	Love walked in-1	rejected
tk.5	I'll remember April	BN(J)GXF-3071
tk.6	You and the night and the music	-
tk.9	All the things you are	-
tk.13	If I had you (alt.)	
tk.14	If I had you	BN(J)GXF-3071
tk.15	I remember you	-
tk.17	You stepped out of a dream	
tk.18	Love walked in	BN(J)GXF-3071

All titles,except the first one,issued on CD BN 8-21284-2.

LEO PARKER - LET ME TELL YOU 'BOUT IT:
John Burks(tp) Bill Swindell(ts) Leo Parker(bs) Yusef Salim(p) Stan Conover(b) Purnell Rice(dm).
Englewood Cliffs,N.J.,September 9,1961

tk.4	Glad lad	BN(Du)1A158-83391/4
tk.5	Low Brown (alt.)	
tk.6	Low Brown	BN 45-1823,BLP4087/BST84087
tk.9	Parker's pals	- -
tk.11	TCTB	-
tk.18	The Lion's roar	CD BN(J)TOCJ-5941/44
tk.25	Vi	BN BLP4087/BST84087
tk.28	Let me tell you 'bout it	BN 45-1822 -
tk.31	Blue Leo (tp,ts out)	- -

All titles issued on CD BN 7-84087-2.
All titles from BST84087 also issued on CD BN(J)TOCJ-4087.

127

STANLEY TURRENTINE - Z.T.'S BLUES:
Stanley Turrentine(ts) Tommy Flanagan(p) Grant Green(g) Paul Chambers(b) Art Taylor(dm).
Englewood Cliffs,N.J.,September 13,1961

tk.1	For heaven's sake	
tk.4	The lamp is low	
tk.6	More than you know	CD BN 7-95281-2,(J)CJ28-5170,CJ28-5179
tk.7	I wish I knew	
tk.10	Z.T.'s blues	
tk.13	Be my love	CD BN(J)TOCJ-5856
tk.15	The way you look tonight	CD BN(J)CJ28-5170

All titles issued on BN BST84424,CD 7-84424-2.

DONALD BYRD - ROYAL FLUSH:
Donald Byrd(tp) Pepper Adams(bs) Herbie Hancock(p) Butch Warren(b) Billy Higgins(dm).
Englewood Cliffs,N.J.,September 21,1961

tk.1	Jorgie's	BN 45-1854,BLP4101		
tk.6	Shangri-la		-	CD BN(F)4-97517-2
tk.10	Hush	BN 45-1853	-	CD BN(J)TOCJ-66060
tk.16	6 m's	-	-	
tk.19	Requiem		-	
	Child's play	rejected		
tk.26	I'm a fool to want you	BN BLP4101 CD BN(J)TOCJ-66054		

All titles from BLP4101 (mono) also issued on BN BST84101,CD BN(J)TOCJ-4101,Mosaic MD4-194 (stereo).
Note: 45-1854 was possibly not released.

LOU DONALDSON - MAN WITH A HORN:
Lou Donaldson(as) Jack McDuff(org) Grant Green(g) Joe Dukes(dm).
Englewood Cliffs,N.J.,September 25,1961

tk.2	Please	CD BN 5-21436-2
tk.9	People will say we're in love	rejected
tk.11	Prisoner of love	CD BN 5-21436-2
tk.12	Man with a horn	-
	Trees	rejected
tk.19	Stardust	CD BN 5-21436-2
tk.21	Misty	-

ART BLAKEY AND THE JAZZ MESSENGERS - MOSAIC:
Freddie Hubbard(tp) Curtis Fuller(tb) Wayne Shorter(ts) Cedar Walton(p) Jymie Merritt(b) Art Blakey(dm).
Englewood Cliffs,N.J.,October 2,1961

tk.4	Children of the night	BN(J)LBN80259
tk.6	Mosaic	BN BST2-92468 CD BN 7-92468-2,7-93205-2,7-97190-2, 8-56399-2,(F)8-54191-2,(J)CJ28-5031, CJ32-5016,TOCJ-5269,TOCJ-5274/76,TOCJ-5823 TOCJ-66031,TOCJ-66063
tk.14	Down under	CD BN 8-54899-2,(Sp)5-21755-2
tk.19	Crisis	BN B1-28263,CD 8-28263-2
tk.22	Arabia	CD BN 7-97190-2

All titles issued on BN BLP4090/BST84090,CD 7-46523-2.

128

<u>LEO PARKER</u> - <u>ROLLIN' WITH LEO</u>:
Dave Burns(tp) Bill Swindell(ts Leo Parker(bs) Johnny Acea(p) Stan Conover(b) Purnell Rice(dm).
Englewood Cliffs,N.J.,October 12,1961

tk.1	Rollin' with Leo	BN 45-1834,BST84095,LT-1076,CD 7-84095-2
tk.8	Music hall beat	- - -
	Bad girl	rejected
	Jumpin' Leo	-
	Stuffy	-
	Mad lad returns	-

Note: BST84095 was released in 1986.Mono version (BLP4095) was not released.

<u>LEO PARKER</u> - <u>ROLLIN' WITH LEO</u>:
Dave Burns(tp) Bill Swindell(ts) Leo Parker(bs) Johnny Acea(p) Al Lucas(b) Wilbert Hogan(dm).
Englewood Cliffs,N.J.,October 20,1961

	Rollin' with Leo	rejected
	Music hall beat	-
tk.22	Bad girl	BN 45-1833,BST84095
tk.27	Mad lad returns	-
tk.30	Stuffy	-
tk.32	Jumpin' Leo	-
tk.37	Talkin' the blues	BN 45-1834 -
tk.38	The Lion's roar	BN 45-1833 -

All titles from BST84095 also issued on BN LT-1076,CD 7-84095-2.
Note: BST 84095 was released in 1986.Mono version (BLP4095) was not released. 45-1833 & 45-1834 were possibly not released.

<u>JACKIE McLEAN</u> - <u>A FICKLE SONANCE</u>:
Tommy Turrentine(tp) Jackie McLean(as) Sonny Clark(p) Butch Warren(b) Billy Higgins(dm).
Englewood Cliffs,N.J.,October 26,1961

tk.1	Enitnerrut
tk.8	Five will get you ten
tk.9	Subdued
tk.11	A fickle sonance
tk.13	Lost
tk.18	Sundu

All titles issued on BN BLP4089/BST84089,CD BN 5-24544-2,(J)TOCJ-4089.

<u>GRANT GREEN</u> - <u>FIRST SESSION</u>:
Sonny Clark(p) Grant Green(g) Butch Warren(b) Billy Higgins(dm).
Englewood Cliffs,N.J.,October 27,1961

tk.4	Woody 'n you	CD BN 5-27548-2
tk.7	Woody 'n you	-
	Lady Bird (incomplete)	rejected

129

SONNY CLARK - LEAPIN' AND LOPIN':

Tommy Turrentine(tp) Charlie Rouse(ts) Sonny Clark(p) Butch Warren(b) Billy Higgins(dm).
Englewood Cliffs,N.J.,November 13,1961

tk.5	Melody in C (alt.)	CD BN(J)TOCJ-5941/44
tk.7	Voodoo	BN BLP4091/BST84091
tk.11	Zellmar's delight	
tk.12	Somethin' special	BN BLP4091/BST84091 CD BN(J)CJ28-5036,TOCJ-5829,TOCJ-66038
tk.17	Midnight mambo	BN BLP4091/BST84091
tk.18	Melody in C	-
tk.21	Eric walks	-

All titles issued on CD BN 7-84091-2.
All titles from BST84091 also issued on CD BNJ)TOCJ-4091.

Ike Quebec(ts) Sonny Clark(p) Butch Warren(b) Billy Higgins(dm).
Same session.

tk.24	Deep in a dream	BN BLP4091/BST84091,(Du)1A158-83391/4 CD BN 7-84091-2,7-99178-2,(J)CJ28-5179, TOCJ-5829,TOJ-66038

IKE QUEBEC - HEAVY SOUL:

Ike Quebec(ts) Freddie Roach(org) Milt Hinton(b) Al Harewood(dm).
Englewood Cliffs,N.J.,November 26,1961

tk.4	Acquitted	BN 45-1836,BLP4093,CD 7-99178-2		
tk.13	Heavy soul	BN 45-1837	-	
tk.14	Just one more chance	BN 45-1836	-	CD BN(J)TOCJ-66060
tk.20	Que's dilemma	BN 45-1839	-	CD 7-99178-2
tk.24	I want a little girl	-	-	
tk.29	Blues for Ike	CD BN(J)TOCJ-5941/44		
tk.30	Brother can you spare a dime	BN 45-1838,BLP4093		
tk.32	The man I love	BN 45-1837	-	CD 8-29095-2,8-56690-2
tk.34	Nature boy (org,dm out)	BN 45-1838 CD BN 7-96098-2,7-99178-2,8-34873-2 BN(Du)1A158-83391/4	-	

Note: BN 45-1836 & 45-1839 were possibly not released.
All titles issued on CD BN 8-32090-2.
All titles from BLP4093 (mono) also issued on BN BST84093,B1-32090,CD BN(J)TOCJ-4093 (stereo).

<u>ART BLAKEY AND THE JAZZ MESSENGERS</u> - <u>BUHAINA'S DELIGHT</u>:
Freddie Hubbard(tp) Curtis Fuller(tb) Wayne Shorter(ts) Cedar Walton(p) Jymie Merritt(b) Art Blakey(dm).
Englewood Cliffs,N.J.,November 28,1961

tk.4	Moon river (alt.)	CD BN 7-84104-2
tk.6	Moon river	BN BLP4104/BST84104 BN(Du)1A158-83391/4,(J)LBN80259 CD BN 7-84104-2,(J)CJ25-5181/84,CJ28-5031, TOCJ-4104,TOCJ-5274/76,TOCJ-5674/75, TOCJ-5858,TOCJ-66031,Cap(J)TOCJ-5204, TOCJ-5229
tk.8	Contemplation	BN 45-1850,BLP4104/BST84104 CD BN 7-84104-2,(J)TOCJ-4104
tk.15	Backstage Sally	CD BN 7-84104-2
	Reincarnation blues	rejected
	Shaky Jake	-
	Bu's delight	-
	Shaky Jake	-
tk.36	Reincarnation blues (alt. version)	CD BN 7-84104-2
tk.37	Bu's delight (alt. version)	- (J)TOCJ-5274/76

<u>HANK MOBLEY</u> - <u>ANOTHER WORKOUT</u>:
Hank Mobley(ts) Wynton Kelly(p) Paul Chambers(b) Philly Joe Jones(dm).
Englewood Cliffs,N.J.,December 5,1961

tk.2	Gettin' and jettin'	
tk.8	Out of Joe's bag	
tk.9	Hank's other soul	
tk.15	I should care	CD BN(J)CJ28-5035,TOCJ-5935
tk.16	Hello young lovers	-

All titles were first scheduled on BN(J)GXF-3079 (not released) and later issued on BN BST84431,CD 7-84431-2.

<u>IKE QUEBEC</u> - <u>IT MIGHT AS WELL BE SPRING</u>:
Ike Quebec(ts) Freddie Roach(org) Milt Hinton(b) Al Harewood(dm).
Englewood Cliffs,N.J.,December 9,1961

tk.2	A light reprieve	BN 45-1866,BLP4105
tk.5	It might as well be Spring	BN 45-1867 - CD BN 7-99178-2,(J)TOCJ-5260
tk.7	Lover man	BN 45-1866,BLP4105,CD 8-56690-2
	M.D. Bounce	rejected
tk.15	Ol' man river	BN BLP4105
tk.21	Willow weep for me	- CD 8-56690-2
tk.26	Easy don't hurt	BN 45-1867,BLP4105 CD BN 7-99178-2,4-95317-2,(F)8-54188-2

All titles from BLP4105 (mono) also issued on BN BST84105,CD 8-21736-2 (stereo).
Note: BN 45-1866 & 45-1867 were possibly not released.

131

DONALD BYRD - FREE FORM:
Donald Byrd(tp) Wayne Shorter(ts) Herbie Hancock(p) Butch Warren(b) Billy Higgins(dm).
Englewood Cliffs,N.J.,December 11,1961

tk.2	Nai Nai	BN L4118,BLP4118	
tk.9	French spice	-	CD BN(J)TOCJ-1621
tk.15	Night flower	-	
tk.20	Three wishes	CD BN 4-95569-2	
tk.23	Pentecostal feeling	BN L4118,BLP4118;CD BN(Eu)7-80703-2	
tk.24	Free form	-	

All titles issued on CD BN 7-84118-2.
All titles from BLP4118 (mono) also issued on BN BST84118,CD BN(J)TOCJ-4118 (stereo).

TADD DAMERON:
Donald Byrd(tp) Curtis Fuller(tb) Julius Watkins(frh) Sam Rivers(ts) Cecil Payne(bs) Tadd Dameron(p,arr) Paul Chambers(b) Philly Joe Jones(dm).
Englewood Cliffs,N.J.,December 14,1961

tk.7	The elder speaks
tk.19	Bevan beeps
tk.22	Lament for the living
tk.31	Aloof spoof

All titlees issued on CD BN 5-21484-2.

IKE QUEBEC - BLUE AND SENTIMENTAL:
Ike Quebec(ts,p-1) Grant Green(g) Paul Chambers(b) Philly Joe Jones(dm).
Englewood Cliffs,N.J.,December 16,1961

tk.3	Like	BN BLP4098	
tk.4	Don't take your love from me	-	
tk.15	Minor impulse-1	-	CD BN(J)TOCJ-5755/56
tk.17	Blues for Charlie-1	-	
tk.22	That old black magic	CD BN(Eu)7-89914-2	
tk.26	It's alright with me	CD BN 7-95591-2 ,(J)TOCJ-5941/44	
tk.28	Blue and sentimental	BN BLP4098,BST89904,BN-LA160-G2 CD BN 7-99178-2,(E)8-53229-2,(J)TOCJ-5935, HMV Jazz(E)5-20882-2	

All titles issued on CD BN 7-84098-2.
All titles from BLP4098 (mono) also issued on BN BST84098,CD BN(J)TOCJ-4098 (stereo).

ART BLAKEY AND THE JAZZ MESSENGERS - BUHAINA'S DELIGHT:
Freddie Hubbard (tp) Curtis Fuller(tb) Wayne Shorter(ts) Cedar Walton(p) Jymie Merritt(b) Art Blakey(dm).
Englewood Cliffs,N.J.,December 18,1961

tk.1	Reincarnation blues	
tk.7	Backstage Sally	BN 45-1850
tk.10	Bu's delight	CD BN(J)TOCJ-5260
tk.12	Shaky Jake	

All titles issued on BN BLP4104/BST84104,CD 7-84104-2,(J)TOCJ-4104.

GRANT GREEN - GOODEN'S CORNER:
Sonny Clark(p) Grant Green(g) Sam Jones(b) Louis Hayes(dm).
Englewood Cliffs,N.J.,December 23,1961

tk.3	Moon river	BN(J)GXF-3058;Lib(J)K22P-6094/95 CD BN(Eu)7-89910-2,(J)TOCJ-6149
tk.8	On Green Dolphin Street	BN(J)GXF-3058,CD TOCJ-6148
tk.17	What is this thing called love	- -
tk.24	Count every star -1	BN BLP4098/BST84098,BST84432 CD BN 7-84098-2,7-84432-2,(J)TOCJ-5858, TOCJ-6067
tk.25	Shadrack	BN(J)GXF-3058,CD TOCJ-6148
tk.26	Gooden's corner	- CD TOCJ-6149
tk.27	Two for one	- -

-1: Ike Quebec(ts) added.This title was scheduled on BN(J)GXF-3075,which was not released.
All titles issued on Mosaic MR6-133,CD CD BN 8-57194-2,Mosaic MD4-133.

STANLEY TURRENTINE - THAT'S WHERE IT'S AT:
Stanley Turrentine(ts) Les McCann(p) Herbie Lewis(b) Otis Finch(dm).
Englewood Cliffs,N.J.,January 2,1962

tk.1	Soft pedal blues	BN 45-1846,BLP4096/BST84096
tk.6	We'll see yaw'll after while,ya heah	BN 45-1848 -
tk.7	Light blue	BN BLP4096/BST84096;CD BN(J)TOCJ-5755/56
tk.9	Light blue (alt.)	CD BN(J)TOCJ-5941/44
tk.11	Dorene don't cry,I	BN 45-1847,BLP4096/BST84096
tk.14	Smile,Stacey	BN 45-1845 - B1-93201 CD BN 7-93201-2
tk.23	Pia	BN 45-1847,BLP4096/BST84096

All titles issued on CD BN 7-84096-2.
All titles from BST84096 also issued on CD BN(J)TOCJ-4096.
Note: 45-1847 was possibly not released.

GRANT GREEN - NIGERIA:
Sonny Clark(p) Grant Green(g) Sam Jones(b) Art Blakey(dm).
Englewood Cliffs,N.J.,January 13,1962

tk.4	Airegin (alt.)	
tk.5	Airegin	BN LT-1032 CD BN(J)CJ28-5169
tk.7	Nancy (with the laughing face)	CD BN 8-54365-2
tk.8	I concentrate on you	BN LT-1032
tk.12	The things we did last Summer	-
tk.21	The song is you	-
tk.24	It ain't necessarily so	-

All titles issued on Mosaic MR6-133,CD BN 8-57194-2,(J)TOCJ-6148,Mosaic MD4-133.

133

IKE QUEBEC - EASY LIVING (BST84103)/CONGO LAMENT (LT-1089):
Bennie Green(tb) Ike Quebec,Stanley Turrentine(ts) Sonny Clark(p) Milt Hinton(b) Art Blakey (dm).
Englewood Cliffs,N.J.,January 20,1962

tk.4	Congo lament	BN BST84103
tk.12	Que's pill	-
tk.15	See see rider	- CD 7-99178-2
tk.22	B.G.'s groove two	
tk.27	I.Q. Shuffle	

All titles issued on BN LT-1089,CD 7-46846-2.

Green & Turrentine out.Same session.

tk.29	I've got a crush on you	CD BN 7-99178-2,5-20808-2,(J)TOCJ-66054
tk.33	Easy living	
tk.35	Nancy (with the laughing face)	CD BN 8-35282-2,8-56690-2,(J)TOCJ-5300

All titles issued on BN BST84103,CD 7-46846-2.
Note: BST84103 was released in 1987 and reissued as CD BN(J)TOCJ-4103.The mono version (BLP4103) was never issued.

JIMMY SMITH PLAYS FATS WALLER:
Jimmy Smith(org) Quentin Warren(g) Donald Bailey(dm).
Englewood Cliffs,N.J.,January 23,1962

tk.1	Everybody loves my baby	BN 45-1851,BLP4100
tk.2	Ain't she sweet	- -
tk.4	Ain't misbehavin'	- (J)K22P-6125/26 CD BN(J)CJ28-5034,TOCJ-66037,TOCJ-66052
tk.7	T'ain't nobody's business if I do	rejected
tk.8	I've found a new baby	BN BLP4100
tk.11	Honeysuckle rose	BN 45-1852,BLP4100
tk.12	Bess you is my woman (org solo)	rejected
tk.14	Squeeze me	BN BLP4100
tk.16	Lulu's back in town	BN 45-1852,BLP4100

All titles from BLP4100 (mono) also issued on BN BST84100,CD BN(J)TOCJ-4100 (stereo).

ART BLAKEY AND THE AFRO-DRUM ENSEMBLE - THE AFRICAN BEAT:
Yusef Lateef(fl,oboe,ts,cowbell,thumb p) Solomon Ilori(vo,pennywhistle,talking dm) Ahmed Abdul-Malik (b) Art Blakey(dm,tympani,gong,telegraph dm) Curtis Fuller(tympani) Chief Bey(cga,telegraph dm,double gong) Montego Joe(Bambara dm,double gong,corboro dm,log dm) Garvin Masseaux(chekere,African maracas,cga) James Ola Folami(cga) Robert Crowder(bata dm,cga)
Englewood Cliffs,N.J.,January 24,1962

tk.1	Prayer by Solomon G. Ilori	
tk.2/4	Ife l'ayo (There is happiness in love)	BN 45-1849;CD BN(J)TOCJ-5274/76
tk.10	Ero ti nr'ojeje	
tk.16	The mystery of love	BN B1-80701,7-80701-2
tk.17	Ayiko Ayiko (Welcome,welcome my darling)	
tk.25	Obirin African (Woman of Africa)	BN 45-1849,CD 4-94031-2
tk.26	Tobi Ilu	

All titles issued on BN BLP4097/BST84097,CD BN 5-22666-2,(J)TOCJ-4097.

134

GRANT GREEN - OLEO:
Sonny Clark(p) Grant Green(g) Sam Jones(b) Louis Hayes(dm).
Englewood Cliffs,N.J.,January 31,1962

tk.4	My favorite things	BN(J)GXF-3065;CD HMV Jazz(E)5-20882-2
tk.5	Hip funk	-
tk.6	Oleo	-
tk.8	Oleo (alt.)	
tk.11	Little girl blue	BN(J)GXF-3065
tk.15	Tune up	-
	Lament	rejected

All titles,except last,issued on Mosaic MR6-133,CD BN 8-57194-2,(J)TOCJ-6149,Mosaic MD4-133.

THE THREE SOUNDS - OUT OF THIS WORLD:
Gene Harris(p,org-1) Andrew Simpkins(b) Bill Dowdy(dm).
Englewood Cliffs,N.J.,February 4,1962

tk.2	Sometimes I'm happy	CD BN 8-21281-2
tk.4	Easy does it	unissued
tk.6	Azule scrape	CD BN 8-21289-2
tk.7	Out of this world	BN BLP4197
tk.9	Girl of my dreams	-
tk.10	The old lamplighter	unissued
tk.11	Just in time	BN BLP4197;CD BN(J)TOCJ-66048
tk.14	I thought about you	unissued
tk.18	Blues on trial-1	CD BN 5-21484-2
tk.20	Softly as in a morning sunrise	unissued
tk.22	Makin' whoopee	CD BN 8-21281-2,(J)TOCJ-66048
tk.23	For dancers only	CD BN 8-21289-2
tk.24	Nature boy	-
tk.25	Remember	unissued
tk.26	Wadin'	-
tk.27	Mountain greenery	-
tk.29	What a difference a day makes	-
tk.30	Tadd's delight	CD BN 8-21289-2

-1: Ike Quebec(ts) added.This title was issued as by Ike Quebec & The 3 Sounds.
All titles from BLP4197 (mono) also issued on BN BST84197,CD BN(J)TOCJ-4197 (stereo).

FRED JACKSON - HOOTIN' AND TOOTIN':
Fred Jackson(ts) Earl Vandyke(org) Willie Jones(g) Wilbert Hogan(dm).
Englewood Cliffs,N.J.,February 5,1962

tk.4	Dippin' in the bag	BN 45-1842
tk.11	That's where it's at	
tk.12	Easing on down	BN 45-1843
tk.13	Southern exposure	BN 45-1844;CD BN(F)8-54188-2
tk.20	Preach brother	BN 45-1843,B1-29092 CD BN(Eu)7-80703-2,(J)TOCJ-5644, TOCJ-5755/56
tk.22	Hootin' n' tootin'	BN 45-1842,B1-96563,CD 7-96563-2
tk.24	Way down home	

All titles issued on BN BLP4094/BST84094,CD 8-21819-2,(J)TOCJ-4094.
Note: 45-1844 was possibly not released.

135

IKE QUEBEC - WITH A SONG IN MY HEART:
Ike Quebec(ts) Earl Vandyke(org) Willie Jones(g) Wilbert Hogan(dm).
Same session.

tk.28	Intermezzo	BN 45-1840
tk.32	But not for me	BN 45-1841,CD 7-99427-2
tk.34	All the way	-
tk.37	All of me	BN 45-1840,CD 4-97154-2

Note: BN 45-1841 was possibly not released.
All titles issued on BN LT-1052,Mosaic MR3-121,CD MD2-121.

IKE QUEBEC - WITH A SONG IN MY HEART:
Ike Quebec(ts) Earl Vandyke(org) Willie Jones(g) Sam Jones(b) Wilbert Hogan (dm).
Englewood Cliffs,N.J.,February 13,1962

tk.3	How long has this been going on?	BN LT-1052,CD 7-80706-2
tk.6	What is there to say	- CD 7-99178-2
	Gone with the wind	rejected
tk.15	Imagination	BN LT-1052,CD 8-56690-2
tk.24	With a song in my heart	-
tk.27	There is no greater love	- CD 8-56690-2
	Be my love	rejected

All titles,except the rejected ones,issued on Mosaic MR3-121,CD MD2-121.

GRANT GREEN - BORN TO BE BLUE:
Ike Quebec(ts) Sonny Clark(p) Grant Green(g) Sam Jones(b) Louis Hayes(dm).
Englewood Cliffs,N.J.,March 1,1962

tk.4	Someday my prince will come	BN BST84432
tk.11	If I should lose you	-
tk.15	My one and only love	-
tk.20	Back in your own backyard	-
tk.23	Born to be blue	- CD 8-56690-2,5-20070-2
tk.24	Born to be blue (alt.)	
tk.29	Cool blues	
tk.31	Outer space	

Note: First five titles were first scheduled on BN(J)GXF-3075,which was not released.
All titles issued on Mosaic MR6-133,CD BN 7-84432-2,Mosaic MD4-133.

THE THREE SOUNDS - BLACK ORCHID (BLP4155)/OUT OF THIS WORLD (BLP4197):
Gene Harris(p) Andrew Simpkins(b) Bill Dowdy(dm).
Englewood Cliffs,N.J.,March 7,1962

tk.1	You make me feel so young	BN BLP4197;CD BN(Eu)7-89914-2
tk.2	I'll be around (long version)	unissued
tk.3	I'll be around	BN BLP4197
tk.4	Secret love	BN BLP4155,CD 8-21289-2
tk.5	Over the rainbow	unissued
tk.6	Oh well,oh well	BN BLP4155,CD 8-21289-2
tk.7	Black orchid	- -
tk.8	A foggy day	- -
tk.10	For all we know	- - (J)TOCJ-66048

All titles from BLP4155/4197 (mono) also issued on BN BST84155/84197,CD BN(J)TOCJ-4155/4197 (stereo).

<u>THE THREE SOUNDS</u> - <u>BLACK ORCHID</u> (BLP4155)/<u>OUT OF THIS WORLD</u> (BLP4197):
Gene Harris(p) Andrew Simpkins(b) Bill Dowdy(dm).
Englewood Cliffs,N.J.,March 8,1962

	Crazy rhythm	rejected
tk.12	My silent love	BN BLP4197
	It's a wonderful world	rejected
tk.16	Babe's blues	BN BST84434,CD 7-84434-2
tk.17	Sanctified Sue	BN BLP4197
tk.18	Saucer eyes	BN BLP4155,CD 8-21289-2,8-27323-2
tk.19	Don't go,don't go	- -
tk.20	Out of the past	BN BLP4197
tk.21	At last	BN BLP4155,CD 8-21289-2,8-27323-2

All titles from BLP4155/4197 (mono) also issued on BN BST84155/84197,CD BN(J)TOCJ-4155/4197 (stereo).

<u>JACKIE McLEAN</u> - <u>LET FREEDOM RING</u>:
Jackie McLean(as) Walter Davis(p) Herbie Lewis(b) Billy Higgins(dm).
Englewood Cliffs,N.J.,March 19,1962

tk.6	Melody for Melonae	CD BN(J)TOCJ-66046
tk.8	I'll keep loving you	CD BN(J)CJ28-5163
tk.12	Rene	
tk.13	Omega	

All titles issued on BN BLP4106/BST84106,CD 7-46527-2.

<u>DODO GREENE</u> - <u>MY HOUR OF NEED</u>:
Dodo Greene(vo) with Ike Quebec(ts) Sir Charles Thompson(org) Grant Green(g) Milt Hinton(b) Al Harewood(dm).
Englewood Cliffs,N.J.,April 2,1962

tk.5	Little things mean a lot	BN 45-1859
tk.14	Down by the riverside	BN 45-1861,CD 5-21151-2,(Eu)7-80703-2
tk.18	Trouble in mind	BN 45-1858
tk.19	Let there be love	-

All titles issued on BN BLP9001/BST89001,CD 8-52442-2.
Note: 45-1858 & 45-1861 were possibly not released.

<u>FRED JACKSON</u>:
Fred Jackson(ts) Earl Vandyke(org) Willie Jones(g) Sam Jones(b) Wilbert Hogan(dm).
Englewood Cliffs,N.J.,April 9,1962

tk.9	Minor exposure -1
tk.18	Little Freddie -1
tk.19	Teena
tk.23	Mr. B.J.
tk.30	Stretchin' out
tk.33	Egypt land
tk.35	On the spot -1

-1: add unknown (cga,shaker).
All titles issued on CD BN 8-21819-2.

DODO GREENE - MY HOUR OF NEED:
Dodo Greene(vo) with Ike Quebec(ts) Sir Charles Thompson(org) Grant Green(g) Herbie Lewis (b) Billy Higgins(dm).
Englewood Cliffs,N.J.,April 17,1962

tk.5	I won't cry anymore	BN 45-1857
tk.7	Lonesome road	BN 45-1860
tk.14	There must be a way	-
tk.20	You are my sunshine	BN 45-1859
tk.30	My hour of need	BN 45-1857
tk.32	I'll never stop loving you	BN 45-1861

All titles issued on BN BLP9001/BST89001,CD 8-52442-2.
Note: 45-1861 was possibly not released.

GRANT GREEN - THE LATIN BIT:
Johnny Acea(p) Grant Green(g) Wendell Marshall(b) Willie Bobo(dm) Carlos "Patato" Valdes(cga) Garvin Masseaux(chekere).
Englewood Cliffs,N.J.,April 26,1962

tk.2	Mambo inn	BN 45-1870,BLP4111,(E)BNSLP-1 CD BN 7-95590-2,(J)TOCJ-5778,HMV Jazz(E) 5-20885-2,EMI(E)5-21426-2
tk.4	My little suede shoes	BN BLP4111,CD 8-33205-2
tk.7	Brazil	- (E)BNSLP-4
tk.11	Besame mucho	BN 45-1870,BLP4111
tk.14	Blues for Juanita (cga,chekere out)	
tk.15	Tico tico	BN BLP4111 CD BN(J)CJ28-5169,CJ28-5177,TOCJ-66045
tk.16	Mama Inez	BN BLP4111,CD 4-97156-2

All titles issued on CD BN 8-37645-2.
All titles from BLP4111 (mono) also issued on BN BST84111,CD BN(J)TOCJ-4111 (stereo).
Note: 45-1870 was possibly not released.

DON WILKERSON - ELDER DON:
Don Wilkerson(ts) John Acea(p) Grant Green(g) Lloyd Trotman(b) Willie Bobo(dm).
Englewood Cliffs,N.J.,May 3,1962

tk.5	Drawin' a tip	BN BLP4121
tk.6	Senorita Eula	- B1-57745,CD 8-57745-2
tk.9	Poor butterfly	-
tk.13	Scrappy	-
tk.15	San Antonio rose	- CD BN(Eu)5-23444-2
tk.17	Naughty Neenie	rejected
tk.22	Lone star shuffle	BN BLP4121;CD BN(J)TOCJ-6067

All titles from BLP4121 (mono) also issued in stereo on BN BST84121,CD BN 5-24555-2,(J)TOCJ-4121.

DEXTER GORDON - LANDSLIDE:
Tommy Turrentine(tp) Dexter Gordon(ts) Sir Charles Thompson(p) Al Lucas(b) Willie Bobo(dm).
Englewood Cliffs,N.J.,May 5,1962

tk.11	Serenade in blue	BN LT-1051,CD 8-34200-2
tk.12	You said it	- -
tk.19	Love locked out	- -
	Six bits Jones	rejected
	McSplivens	-
	How now	-

LOU DONALDSON - THE NATURAL SOUL:
Tommy Turrentine(tp) Lou Donaldson(as) John Patton(org) Grant Green(g) Ben Dixon(dm).
Englewood Cliffs,N.J.,May 9,1962

tk.4	Spaceman twist	BN 45-1895,BLP4108		
tk.8	People will say we're in love			
tk.13	That's all	BN 45-1869,BLP4108		
tk.15	Funky Mama -1	BN 45-1868	-	
tk.19	Love walked in		-	
tk.20	Sow belly blues		-	CD 8-27298-2
tk.23	Nice 'n' greasy		-	

-1: shown as pts. 1 & 2 on sides of 45-1868.Pt.1 was reissued on CD BN 4-94030-2.
All titles issued on CD BN 7-84108-2.
All titles from BLP4108 (mono) also issued on BN BST84108,CD BN(J)TOCJ-4108 (stereo).
Note: 45-1869 was possibly not released.

SONNY STITT:
Sonny Stitt(as,ts-1) Dexter Gordon(ts-1) Don Patterson(org) Paul Weedon(g) Billy James(dm).
Englewood Cliffs,N.J.,May 14,1962

tk.4	Lady be good-1	CD BN 8-34200-2,5-21484-2
tk.6 or 7	Unknown title No.1	rejected
tk.10	There will never be another you	-
tk.11	Unknown title No.1 -1	-
tk.12 or 13	Unknown title No.2 (Charleston)-1	-
tk.14	Bye bye blackbird	-

IKE QUEBEC:
Ike Quebec(ts) Freddie Roach(org) Grant Green(g) Butch Warren(b) Wilbert Hogan(dm).
Englewood Cliffs,N.J.,May 25,1962

Sonny boy	rejected
Take your shoes off	-
Cop 'n blo	-
Early morning shuffle	-
Travelin'	-
Born to be blue	-
Throwing a brick	-

139

HERBIE HANCOCK - TAKIN' OFF:
Freddie Hubbard(tp,flh-1) Dexter Gordon(ts) Herbie Hancock(p) Butch Warren(b)Billy Higgins(dm).
Englewood Cliffs,N.J.,May 28,1962

tk.1	Empty pockets	BN BN-LA399-H2,CD 8-54904-2
tk.3	Empty pockets (alt.)	
tk.4	Three bags full -1	BN 45-1862,BN-LA399-H2
tk.5	Three bags full (alt.)-1	
tk.6	Watermelon man	BN 45-1862,BST89907,BST2-84433,B1-91142 BN(Du)BST83249,(G)F671097,(J)NP-2012, NP9022,LNS90031,LNP95059B,K18P-9127, K22P-6096/97,K16P-9031/32,FCPA 6214, W-5512 CD BN 7-91142-2,7-97960-2,8-29331-2, (E)8-53228-2,(F)4-97517-2,(J)CJ28-5040, CJ28-5177,TOCJ-5203,TOCJ-5637,TOCJ-5830, TOCJ-5966,TOCJ-6110,TOCJ-66050, (Sp)8-53016-2,Cap(J)TOCJ-6060, Toshiba-EMI(J)TOCP-50370, EMI-Music 4-98900-2
tk.7	Watermelon man (alt.)	
tk.10	The maze	
tk.13	Driftin'-1	BN 45-1863,BN-LA399-H2,(G)F671097 CD BN 7-91142-2,8-29331-2,(J)TOCJ-5740
tk.20	Alone and I	BN 45-1863;CD Toshiba-EMI(J)TOCP-6228

All titles issued on CD BN 8-37643-2,4-95569-2.
All titles,except alternates,issued on BN BLP4109/BST84109,CD 7-46506-2.

IKE QUEBEC:
Ike Quebec(ts) Freddie Roach(org) Grant Green(g) Butch Warren(b) Wilbert Hogan(dm).
Englewood Cliffs,N.J.,June 1,1962

tk.8	Take your shoes off	rejected
tk.13	Cop 'n blo	-
tk.20	Sonny boy	-
tk.32	Throwing a brick	-
tk.40	Early morning shuffle	-
tk.44	Travelin'	-

JACKIE McLEAN QUINTET:
Kenny Dorham(tp) Jackie McLean(as) Sonny Clark(p) Butch Warren(b) Billy Higgins(dm).
Englewood Cliffs,N.J.,June 14,1962

tk.1	Three minors	CD BN(J)CJ28-5163
tk.6	Iddy bitty	
tk.10	The way I feel	
tk.13	Marilyn's dilemma	
tk.14	Blues in a jiff	
tk.15	Blues for Jackie	

All titles first scheduled on BN BLP4116/BST84116 (not released),and later issued on BN BN-LA483-J2, (J)LNJ80118,CD BN 5-22669-2,(J)TOCJ-4116.

DON WILKERSON - PREACH BROTHER!:
Don Wilkerson(ts,tamb-1) Sonny Clark(p) Grant Green(g) Butch Warren(b) Billy Higgins(dm) Jual Curtis (tamb-2).
Englewood Cliffs,N.J.,June 18,1962

tk.3	Jeanie-Weenie	BN 45-1865
tk.4	Pigeon peas	
tk.6	Eldorado shuffle	
tk.8	Homesick blues	BN 45-1864
tk.9	Camp meetin'-2	- CD 4-94030-2
tk.13	Dem tambourines -1,2	BN 45-1865,B1-80679,(E)BNSLP-2,(J)BNJ71106 CD BN 7-80679-2,(J)TOCJ-5758,TOCJ-5779, TOCJ-5882,TOCJ-5936,TOCJ-6191,TOCJ-66055

All titles issued on BN BLP4107/BST84107,CD BN 5-24555-2,(J)TOCJ-4107.
Note: 45-1865 was possibly not released.

FRED JACKSON:
Fred Jackson(ts,cowbell-1) John Patton(p) Grant Green(g) Herbie Lewis(b) Ben Dixon(dm).
Englewood Cliffs,N.J.,June 21,1962

tk.5	T'ain't no big thing	rejected
	Peace pipe	-
tk.14	Cowbell boogie -1	CD BN 5-21484-2
	Jacksonville	rejected

DEXTER GORDON - LANDSLIDE:
Dave Burns(tp) Dexter Gordon(ts) Sonny Clark(p) Ron Carter(b) Philly Joe Jones(dm).
Englewood Cliffs,N.J.,June 25,1962

tk.6	Blue gardenia	BN LT-1051,CD8-34200-2
tk.12	Second balcony jump	- -
tk.21	Six bits Jones	- -
	Three o'clock in the morning	rejected
	McSplivens	-
	My heart stood still	-

THE THREE SOUNDS:
Gene Harris(p) Andrew Simpkins(b) Bill Dowdy(dm).
Englewood Cliffs,N.J.,June 27,1962

tk.4	My romance	unissued
tk.6	El dormido	-
tk.7	June night	-
tk.8	But beautiful	-
tk.11	There they go	-
tk.12	The best things in life are free	CD BN 8-21281-2
tk.13	Cry me a river	-
tk.14	Back home	CD BN 8-21289-2
tk.18	You dig it	-
tk.21	Moon river	unissued
tk.22	In a little Spanish town	-
tk.24	Again	CD BN 8-21281-2
tk.25	Theme for M Squad	CD BN 8-21289-2

141

THE THREE SOUNDS:
Gene Harris(p) Andrew Simpkins(b) Bill Dowdy(dm).
Englewood Cliffs,N.J.,June 28,1962

tk.30	Witchcraft	CD BN 8-21281-2,8-35282-2
tk.31A	Blues for Beth	unissued
tk.32	Stay as sweet as you are	CD BN 8-21281-2
	Drivin' Home	rejected
tk.36	For me and my gal	unissued
tk.39	Red sails in the sunset	CD BN 8-21281-2

HORACE SILVER - THE TOKYO BLUES:
Blue Mitchell(tp) Junior Cook(ts) Horace Silver(p) Gene Taylor(b) John Harris Jr.(dm).
Englewood Cliffs,N.J.,July 13,1962

tk.3	The Tokyo blues	BN 45-1871,BLP4110,BST84325 BN(J)FCPA 6206,BNJ71106 CD BN 4-95576-2,(J)CJ28-5033,TOCJ-5758, TOCJ-66034
	Ah! So	rejected
tk.9	Sayonara blues	BN 45-1872,BLP4110,CD 4-95576-2
	Too much saki	rejected

All titles from BLP4110 (mono) also issued on BN BST84110,CD 8-53355-2 (stereo).

HORACE SILVER - THE TOKYO BLUES:
Blue Mitchell(tp) Junior Cook(ts) Horace Silver(p) Gene Taylor(b) John Harris Jr.(dm).
Englewood Cliffs,N.J.,July 14,1962

tk.20	Ah! So	
tk.21	Cherry blossom (tp,ts out)	BN BN-LA474-H2
tk.24	Too much saki	BN 45-1873

All titles issued on BN BLP4110/BST84110,CD 8-53355-2.

STANLEY TURRENTINE:
Tommy Turrentine(tp) Stanley Turrentine(ts) Herbie Hancock(p) Kenny Burrell(g) Butch Warren(b) Roger Humphries(dm).
Englewood Cliffs,N.J.,August 3,1962

You said it	rejected
Jubilee shout	-
Brother Tom	-

FREDDIE ROACH - DOWN TO EARTH:
Percy France(ts) Freddie Roach(org) Kenny Burrell(g) Clarence Johnston(dm).
Englewood Cliffs,N.J.,August 23,1962

tk.3	Lion down	BN 45-1880
tk.10	Ahm Miz	
tk.17	Lujon	
tk.18	De bug	BN 45-1880
tk.19	Althea soon	
tk.23	More mileage	

All titles issued on BN BLP4113/BST84113,CD BN(J)TOCJ-4113.
Note: 45-1880 was possibly not released.

DEXTER GORDON - GO!:
Dexter Gordon(ts) Sonny Clark(p) Butch Warren(b) Billy Higgins(dm).
Englewood Cliffs,N.J.,August 27,1962

tk.3	Three o'clock in the morning	BN BST2-84433,B1-91139;CD BN 7-91139-2, 7-97960-2,8-56508-2,(J)CJ28-5038,TOCJ-5857
tk.4	Second balcony jump	CD BN 8-23514-2
tk.6	Where are you?	
tk.8	Cheese cake	BN BST2-92468,B1-91139 CD BN 7-91139-2,7-92468-2,(F)8-54191-2, 8-54197-2,(J)CJ25-5181/84,CJ28-5038, TOCJ-5882,TOCJ-6131,TOCJ-6271/74, TOCJ-66047,TOCJ-66060
tk.12	I guess I'll hang my tears out to dry	BN(E)BNX 1,UALP 19;CD BN 7-48337-2, 7-96098-2,7-96579-2,8-21381-2,8-23514-2, 8-35282-2,(E)8-53223-2,(Eu)8-29964-2, (J)TOCJ-5935,HMV Jazz(E)5-20882-2
tk.13	Love for sale	CD BN 7-95591-2,4-95981-2,4-97156-2, (J)TOCJ-66047

All titles issued on BN BLP4112/BST84112,CD 7-46094-2,8-34200-2,4-98794-2.

DEXTER GORDON - A SWINGIN' AFFAIR:
Same.
Englewood Cliffs,N.J.,August 29,1962

tk.3	McSplivens	CD BN 8-23514-2
tk.6	The backbone	
tk.15	Soy califa	BN BN-LA393-H2,B1-91139;CD BN 7-91139-2, 5-20070-2,8-34957-2,(J)TOCJ-5849,TOCJ-66047
tk.21	You stepped out of a dream	
tk.20	Until the real thing comes along	CD BN 8-54365-2,EMI Gold(E)5-21427-2
tk.22	Don't explain	BN BN-LA393-H2,B1-91139 CD BN 7-91139-2,7-96579-2,8-34873-2, 5-24271-2,(C)8-33908-2,8-56508-2,(J)CJ28-5038, TOCJ-5300,TOCJ-66047,EMI-Jazz(E)4-99159-2

All titles issued on BN BLP4133/BST84133,CD 7-84133-2,8-34200-2.

GRANT GREEN:
Ike Quebec(ts) Sonny Clark(p) Grant Green(g) Wendell Marshall(b) Willie Bobo(dm) Carlos "Patato" Valdes (cga).
Englewood Cliffs,N.J.,September 7,1962

tk.5	Grenada
tk.12	Hey there

Both titles issued on Mosaic MR6-133,CD BN 8-37645-2,Mosaic MD4-133.
Note: Sonny Clark's name was inadvertantly left off of the Blue Note CD reissue.

SHEILA JORDAN - A PORTRAIT OF SHEILA:
Sheila Jordan(vo) with Barry Galbraith(g) Steve Swallow(b) Denzil Best(dm).
Englewood Cliffs,N.J.,September 19,1962

tk.8	Falling in love with love	
tk.13	Am I blue	
tk.19	Dat dere (g,dm out)	CD BN 5-21151-2,(C)4-94888-2
tk.22	If you could see me now	CD BN(J)TOCJ-6135
tk.27	Baltimore oriole (g out)	CD BN 7-96583-2,(C)4-94888-2,(Eu)5-23444-2, Cap.5-23566-2
tk.31	When the world was young	

All titles issued on BN BLP9002/BST89002,CD 7-89002-2.

143

DODO GREENE:
Dodo Greene(vo) with Ike Quebec,Eddie Chamblee(ts) Edwin Swanston(org) Grant Green(g) Wendell Marshall(b) Jual Curtis(dm) Dionne Warwick,unknown(tamb).
Englewood Cliffs,N.J.,September 24,1962

tk.6	You don't know me	CD BN 8-52442-2,(Sp)8-56842-2
	Nothing Like True Love	rejected
	Jazz In My Soul	-
tk.26	Not one tear	CD BN 8-52442-2
tk.28	I hear	-
tk.38	Time after time	-

JACKIE McLEAN - TIPPIN' THE SCALES:
Jackie McLean(as) Sonny Clark(p) Butch Warren(b) Art Taylor(dm).
Englewood Cliffs,N.J.,September 28,1962

tk.5	Nursery blues	BN BST84427,(J)GXF-3062
tk.8	Two for one (alt.)	
tk.9	Two for one (alt.)	
tk.11	Rainy blues	BN BST84427,(J)GXF-3062
tk.15	Tippin' the scales (alt.)	
tk.16	Tippin' the scales	BN BST84427,(J)GXF-3062
tk.17	Nicely	- - CD CJ28-5163
tk.20	Cabin in the sky	- - - Lib(J)K22P-6131/32
tk.21	Two for one	BN BST84427,(J)GXF-3062

Note: This session was first issued in Japan on BN(J)GXF-3062.
All titles issued on CD BN 7-84427-2.

IKE QUEBEC - BOSSA NOVA SOUL SAMBA:
Ike Quebec(ts) Kenny Burrell(g) Wendell Marshall(el b) Willie Bobo(dm) Garvin Masseaux(chekere).
Englewood Cliffs,N.J.,October 5,1962

tk.2	Loie (alt.)	
tk.3	Loie	BN 45-1874,BLP4114/BST84114 CD BN 7-95590-2,(J)CJ28-5024,TOCJ-5852, TOCJ-5882,TOCJ-6131,TOCJ-6271/74
tk.7	Liebestraum	BN 45-1875,BLP4114/BST84114 CD BN(J)CJ28-5023,Cap(J)TOCJ-5202
tk.8	Lloro tu despedida	BN 45-1874,BLP4114/BST84114,CD 4-97156-2
tk.10	Shu shu (alt.)	
tk.13	Shu shu	BN 45-1875,BLP4114/BST84114,B1-99106
tk.18	Favela (alt.)	
tk.19	Favela	BN BLP4114/BST84114,CD 7-99178-2
tk.24	Linda flor	-
tk.27	Me 'n you	-
tk.35	Goin' home	-
tk.38	Blue samba	BN 45-1876 -

All titles issued on CD BN 8-52443-2.
All titles from BST84114 also issued on CD BN(J)TOCJ-4114.

 144

FREDDIE HUBBARD - HUB-TONES:
Freddie Hubbard(tp) James Spaulding(fl-1,as) Herbie Hancock(p) Reggie Workman(b) Clifford Jarvis(dm).
Englewood Cliffs,N.J.,October 10,1962

tk.3	You're my everything	BN BLP4115/BST84115 CD BN 8-59071-2,(J)CJ28-5164
tk.4	You're my everything (alt.)	
tk.5	Lament for Booker -1	BN BLP4115/BST84115,CD 8-56691-2
tk.7	For Spee's sake	-
tk.8	For Spee's sake (alt.)	
tk.14	Prophet Jennings -1	BN BLP4115/BST84115
tk.19	Hub-tones (alt.)	
tk.20	Hub-tones	BN BLP4115/BST84115,B1-93202 CD BN 7-93202-2,(F)8-54191-2,(J)CJ28-5164

All titles issued on CD BN 7-84115-2,4-99008-2.
All titles from BST84115 also issued on CD BN 7-46507-2,(J)TOCJ-4115.

SHEILA JORDAN - A PORTRAIT OF SHEILA:
Sheila Jordan(vo) with Barry Galbraith(g) Steve Swallow(b) Denzil Best(dm).
Englewood Cliffs,N.J.,October 12,1962

	Laugh,clown,laugh	rejected	
tk.43	I'm a fool to want you	BN BLP9002/BST89002	
tk.46	Hum drum blues (g out)	-	
tk.59	Willow weep for me	-	
tk.61	Let's face the music and dance	-	CD 7-99095-2
tk.65	Who can I turn to now (b,dm out)	-	
tk.66	Laugh,clown,laugh	-	

All titles,except first,also issued on CD BN 7-89002-2.

GENE HARRIS:
Gene Harris(org) Grant Green(g) Al Harewood(dm).
Englewood Cliffs,N.J.,October 15,1962

tk.4	untitled blues	rejected
tk.5	untitled fast blues	-
tk.6	Georgia on my mind	-
tk.10	Playmates	-
tk.11	Please send me someone to love	-
tk.15	Sack o'woe	-

145

STANLEY TURRENTINE - JUBILEE SHOUT:
Tommy Turrentine(tp) Stanley Turrentine(ts) Sonny Clark(p) Kenny Burrell(g) Butch Warren(b) Al Harewood(dm).

Englewood Cliffs,N.J.,October 18,1962

tk.9	You said it	BN BN-LA883-J2,(J)GXF-3025
tk.14	Cotton walk	- -
tk.19	Little girl blue -1	
tk.21	Brother Tom	BN BN-LA883-J2,(J)GXF-3025
tk.26	My ship	- -
tk.29	Jubilee shout	- -

-1: erroneously listed as "You better go now" on BN BST84122.
All titles issued on BN BST84122,CD 7-84122-2.
Note: Mono version (BLP 4122) of BST84122 was not released.

DODO GREENE:
Dodo Greene(vo) with Ike Quebec(ts) Johnny Acea(p) Grant Green(g) Wendell Marshall(b) Jual Curtis(dm).

Englewood Cliffs,N.J.,November 2,1962

	A little help from above	rejected
tk.8	Everybody's happy but me	CD BN 8-52442-2
tk.11	Jazz in my soul	-
	Go down	rejected
	Bye bye blackbird	-

CHARLIE ROUSE:
Charlie Rouse(ts) Kenny Burrell,Chauncey "Lord" Westbrook(g) Edwyn Payne(b) Willie Bobo(dm) Carlos "Patato" Valdes(cga) Garvin Masseaux(chekere).

Englewood Cliffs,N.J.,November 12,1962

	Samba de Orfeu	rejected
	Back down to the tropics	-
	Velhos tempos	-

CHARLIE ROUSE - BOSSA NOVA BACCHANAL:
Charlie Rouse(ts) Kenny Burrell,Chauncey "Lord" Westbrook(g) Larry Gales(b) Willie Bobo(dm) Carlos "Patato" Valdes(cga) Garvin Masseaux(chekere).

Englewood Cliffs,N.J.,November 26,1962

tk.4	Back to the Tropics (Back down to the tropics*)	BN 45-1881,CD 7-95590-2* BN(E)BNSLP-1* CD BN(J)TOCJ-5778,TOCJ-5852,HMV Jazz(E) 5-20885-2*
tk.11	Meci Bon Dieu	BN(J)TOJJ-5849,CD TOCJ-5849
tk.16	Samba de Orfeu	BN(E)BNSLP-4;CD BN 4-97156-2
tk.25	Velhos tempos	BN 45-1881
tk.31	Un dia	BN 45-1883
tk.32	In Martinique	BN 45-1882
tk.38	Aconteceu	-

All titles issued on BN BLP4119/BST84119,CD BN(J)TOCJ-4119.
Note: 45-1883 was possibly not released.

<u>GRANT GREEN</u> - <u>GOIN' WEST</u>:
Herbie Hancock(p) Grant Green(g) Reggie Workman(b) Billy Higgins(dm).
Englewood Cliffs,N.J.,November 30,1962

tk.4	Wagon wheels	BN BST84310	
tk.6	Tumbling tumbleweeds	-	
tk.9	Red River Valley	-	CD BN(J)CJ28-5169
tk.13	On top of Old Smokey	-	
	Home on the range	rejected	
	I'm an old cowhand	-	
tk.20	I can't stop loving you	BN BST84310	

<u>FREDDIE ROACH</u>:
Freddie Roach(org) Kenny Burrell(g) Ronnie Cole(dm).
Englewood Cliffs,N.J.,December 4,1962

Is you or is you ain't my baby	rejected
Googa Mooga	-
Blues in the front room	-

<u>GRANT GREEN</u> - <u>FEELIN' THE SPIRIT</u>:
Herbie Hancock(p) Grant Green(g) Butch Warren(b) Billy Higgins(dm) Garvin Masseaux(tamb).
Englewood Cliffs,N.J.,December 21,1962

tk.2	Go down Moses	BN BLP4132,CD 8-33205-2,(Eu)7-80703-2
tk.3	Just a closer walk with Thee	-
tk.5	Joshua fit de battle of Jericho	- (J)K22P-6096/97,K16P-9031/32 CD BN(J)CJ28-5169,TOCJ-5925,TOCJ-66045
tk.6	Sometimes I feel like a motherless child (tamb out)	BN BLP4132
tk.7	Nobody knows the trouble I've seen	-
tk.8	Deep river (tamb out)	

All titles issued on CD BN 7-46822-2.
All titles from BLP4132 (mono) also issued on BN BST84132,CD BN(J)TOCJ-4132 (stereo).

<u>FREDDIE HUBBARD</u> - <u>HERE TO STAY</u>:
Freddie Hubbard(tp) Wayne Shorter(ts) Cedar Walton(p) Reggie Workman(b) Philly Joe Jones(dm).
Englewood Cliffs,N.J.,December 27,1962

tk.4	Full moon and empty arms	CD BN(J)CJ28-5164,TOCJ-5858
tk.9	Assunta	
tk.18	Father and son	CD BN(J)TOCJ-5882
tk.20	Nostrand and Fulton	
tk.23	Body and soul	CD BN 8-56691-2
tk.25	Philly mignon	

All titles were initially scheduled on BN BLP4135 (not released) and later issued on BN BN-LA496-H2 and,in 1986,on BN BST84135.
All titles also issued on CD BN 7-84135-2.

147

KENNY BURRELL - MIDNIGHT BLUE:
Stanley Turrentine(ts) Kenny Burrell(g) Major Holley(b) Bill English(dm) Ray Barretto(cga).
Englewood Cliffs,N.J.,January 8,1963

tk.10	Kenny's sound	
tk.14	Saturday night blues	BN BLP4123/BST84123 BN(E)UALP 19,(J)FCPA 6209,W-5511
tk.16	Wavy gravy -1	BN 45-1886,BLP4123/BST84123,(J)FCPA 6209
tk.23	Chitlins con carne	BN 45-1885,BLP4123/BST84123,BST89904, BST2-84429,BN-LA160-G2,(Du)1A158-83395/8 CD BN 7-96110-2,8-30493-2,(Au)8-14808-2, (Eu)7-89915-2,(J)CP32-5057,TOCJ-5298, TOCJ-5937,TOCJ-6271/74,TOCJ-66042, EMI-Music 4-98900-2,HMV Jazz(E)5-20884-2, EMI(E)5-21426-2
tk.28	Mule (cga out)	BN BLP4123/BST84123 CD HMV Jazz(E)5-20882-2
tk.31	Midnight blue (ts out)	BN BLP4123/BST84123,(E)BNX 1, (J)K22P-6096/97,K16P-9031/32,FCPA 6209 Lib(F)LBS83442/43 CD BN 7-48337-2,8-30493-2,5-20070-2, (Eu)8-29964-2,(F)8-54188-2,8-54197-2, (J)TOCJ-5755/56,TOCJ-66042,TOCJ-66060, (Sp)5-21755-2,Premier(E)CDPR 127
tk.35	K twist (ts out)	
tk.44	Gee baby ain't I good to you (ts,cga out)	BN BLP4123/BST84123,(J)FCPA 6209 CD BN 8-56399-2
tk.49	Soul lament (g solo)	BN BLP4123/BST84123,(J)FCPA 6209

-1: shown as pts. 1 & 2 on sides of 45-1886.Pt.1 was reissued on CD BN 4-94030-2.
All titles issued on BN CD 7-46399-2,4-95338-2.
All titles from BST84123 also issued on CD BN(J)TOCJ-4123.
Note: On CD 4-95338-2,the recording date is incorrectly listed as April 21,1967.

DONALD BYRD - A NEW PERSPECTIVE:
Donald Byrd(tp) Hank Mobley(ts) Donald Best(vb) Herbie Hancock(p) Kenny Burrell(g) Butch Warren(b) Lex Humphries(dm) & vocal choir dir. by Coleridge Perkinson,Duke Pearson(arr).
Englewood Cliffs,N.J.,January 12,1963

tk.5 (14283-E*)	Cristo redentor	BN 45-1907,L4124,BST89904,BST2-84429, BN-LA160-G2,BST2-92471 BN(Du)1A158-83395/8 Lib.LN-10200;UA UA-XW510-X* CD BN 7-92471-2,7-96110-2,(F)8-54188-2, (J)CJ25-5181/84,CP32-5056,Cema S21-57592, EMI-Jazz(E)4-93469-2,EMI-Music 4-98899-2
tk.8	Chant	
tk.11	Elijah	BN 45-1907,L4124
tk.17	The black disciple	
tk.19	Beast of burden	

All titles issued on BN BLP4124/BST84124,CD 7-84124-2,4-99006-2.
Note: On CD 7-84124-2.the recording date is incorrectly listed as November 12,1963.

STANLEY TURRENTINE - NEVER LET ME GO:
Stanley Turrentine(ts) Shirley Scott(org) Sam Jones(b) Clarence Johnston(dm).
Englewood Cliffs,N.J.,January 18,1963

	Without a song	rejected
tk.12	Never let me go	BN 45-1894,BLP4129/BST84129 CD BN 7-84129-2,(J)TOCJ-4129
	Major's minor	rejected
tk.19	They can't take that away from me	CD BN 7-84129-2,7-99427-2,5-20808-2

FREDDIE ROACH - MO' GREENS PLEASE:
Freddie Roach(org) Kenny Burrell(g) Clarence Johnston(dm).
Englewood Cliffs,N.J.,January 21,1963

tk.1	Blues in the front room	BN 45-1891,BLP4128;CD BN(J)TOCJ-5239
tk.8	I know	BN 45-1890 - CD 4-94030-2
tk.11	Is you or is you ain't my baby	-
tk.21	Party time	BN 45-1892 - (E)BNSLP-3 CD BN(J)TOCJ-5780
tk.23	Baby don't you cry	BN BLP4128
	Bird call	rejected

All titles from BLP4128 (mono) also issued on BN BST84128,CD BN(J)TOCJ-4128 (stereo).

LOU DONALDSON - GOOD GRACIOUS:
Lou Donaldson(as) John Patton(org) Grant Green(g) Ben Dixon(dm).
Englewood Cliffs,N.J.,January 24,1963

tk.2	The Holy ghost	
tk.4	Good gracious	BN 45-1896,(E)BNSLP-3
tk.5	Caracas	BN B1-94709,CD 4-94709-2,(J)TOCJ-5780
tk.10	Cherry	
tk.15	Bad John	
tk.16	Don't worry about me	

All titles issued on BN BLP4125 (mono),BST84125,B1-54325,CD 8-54325-2 stereo).
Note: 45-1896 was possibly not released.

JIMMY SMITH - I'M MOVIN' ON:
Jimmy Smith(org) Grant Green(g) Donald Bailey(dm).
Englewood Cliffs,N.J.,January 31,1963

tk.2	Hotel happiness	BN BLP4255/BST84255
tk.7	Organic greenery (*aka* Blues for Little Jim)	BN(J)BNJ50101
tk.11	Cherry	BN BLP4255/BST84255,8-33206-2
tk.13	T'ain't no use	-
tk.15	I'm movin' on	- B1-96563,(E)BST83367/8, (J)LNP-88046 CD BN 7-96563-2,Cema GSC Music 15131
tk.16	Back talk	BN BLP4255/BST84255;CD BN(J)TOCJ-5644
tk.17	Day in,day out	BN(J)BNJ50101
tk.20	What kind of fool am I	BN BLP4255/BST84255

All titles issued on CD 8-32750-2.

149

JIMMY SMITH - BUCKET!:
Jimmy Smith(org) Quentin Warren(g) Donald Bailey(dm).
Englewood Cliffs,N.J.,February 1,1963

tk.25	Careless love	BN BLP4235/BST84235
tk.28	Sassy Mae	BN 45-1927,L4235,BLP4235/BST84235 BN(E)BST83367/8
tk.29	Sassy Mae (alt.)	
tk.30	John Brown's body	BN L4235,BLP4235/BST84235
tk.33	Come rain or come shine	BN BLP4235/BST84235,B2S-5256
tk.34	Trouble in mind	
tk.37	Three for four	BN BLP4235/BST84235,(E)BST83367/8
tk.38	Bucket	BN 45-1927,L4235,BLP4235/BST84235 BN-LA400-H2,(E)BST83367/8 CD BN 4-94030-2
tk.43	Just squeeze me	BN BLP4235/BST84235

All titles issued on CD BN 5-24550-2.

JIMMY SMITH - ROCKIN' THE BOAT:
Lou Donaldson(as) Jimmy Smith(org) Quentin Warren(g) Donald Bailey(dm) John Patton(tamb-1).
Englewood Cliffs,N.J.,February 7,1963

tk.2	Matilda,Matilda -1	BN 45-1905,(J)LNP-88046
tk.6	Pork chop -1	BN 45-1906,BN-LA400-H2
tk.7	When my dreamboat comes home	BN 45-1904,(E)BST83367/8
tk.8	Please send me someone to love	BN(Du)1A158-83395/8 CD BN 8-54365-2,(J)TOCJ-5239
tk.11A	Just a closer walk with Thee -1	BN(E)BST83367/8
tk.15	Can heat	BN 45-1905,BST89901,B1-29092,CD 8-29092-2
tk.17	Trust in me	

All titles issued on BN BLP4141/BST84141,CD BN(J)TOCJ-4141.

JIMMY SMITH - PRAYER MEETIN':
Stanley Turrentine(ts) Jimmy Smith(org) Quentin Warren(g) Donald Bailey(dm).
Englewood Cliffs,N.J.,February 8,1963

tk.4	Stone cold dead in the market	BN(E)BST83367/8
tk.7	Picnickin'	
tk.8	Prayer meetin'	BN 45-1909,BN-EP-45-8001,BST89901
tk.10	I almost lost my mind	CD BN(J)TOCJ-5825
tk.11	When the Saints go marching in	BN BN-EP-45-8001,(E)BST83367/8 BN(J)K22P-6125/26
tk.13	Red top	BN 45-1910

All titles issued on BN BLP4164/BST84164,CD 7-84164-2,(J)TOCJ-4164.

JACKIE McLEAN - VERTIGO:
Donald Byrd(tp) Jackie McLean(as) Herbie Hancock(p) Butch Warren(b) Tony Williams(dm).
Englewood Cliffs,N.J.,February 11,1963

tk.2	Vertigo	
tk.6	Dusty foot (*aka* Soul time)	
tk.9	Marney	
tk.14	Yams	CD BN 8-54904-2,4-95569-2
tk.17	Cheers	

All titles issued on BN LT-1085,CD 5-22669-2.

150

STANLEY TURRENTINE - NEVER LET ME GO:
Stanley Turrentine(ts) Shirley Scott(org) Major Holley(b) Al Harewood(dm) Ray Barretto (cga,tamb-1).
Englewood Cliffs,N.J.,February 13,1963

tk.6	Trouble -1,2 (see note)	BN 45-1893
tk.16	Major's minor	BN 45-1894
tk.19	Without a song	
tk.22	God bless the child (Barretto out)	BN B1-93201 CD BN 7-93201-2,7-95281-2,8-34873-2,5-24271-2 BN(C)8-56508-2,(E)8-53229-2,(J)CJ28-5170, TOCJ-5239,TOCJ-6131,TOCJ-6271/74, TOCJ-66052,Cema S21-57590,GSC Music 15131, HMV Jazz(E)5-20882-2
tk.24	You'll never get away from me	
tk.28	Sara's dance	BN(E)BNSLP-3 CD BN(J)TOCJ-5780,TOCJ-5882,TOCJ-5936

-2: shown as pts. 1 & 2 on sides of 45-1893.Pt.1 was reissued on CD BN 4-94030-2.
Note: A second version of 45-1893 has been released using a later recording of this title (see page 162).
All titles issued on BN BLP4129/BST84129,CD 7-84129-2,(J)TOCJ-4129.

THE HORACE PARLAN SEXTET - HAPPY FRAME OF MIND:
Johnny Coles(tp) Booker Ervin(ts) Horace Parlan(p) Grant Green(g) Butch Warren(b) Billy Higgins(dm).
Englewood Cliffs,N.J.,February 15,1963

tk.6	Happy frame of mind	
tk.7	A tune for Richard	
tk.10	Home is Africa	BN B1-80701,CD 7-80701-2
tk.15	Dexi	
tk.18	Back from the gig	
tk.21	Kucheza blues (g out)	

All titles first scheduled on BN BLP4134 (not released) and later issued on BN BN-LA488-H2 as by Booker Ervin.They have finally been issued on BN BST84134 in 1986,and reissued on Mosaic MQ8-197,CD BN 7-84134-2,Mosaic MD5-197.

GRANT GREEN - BLUES FOR LOU:
John Patton(org) Grant Green(g) Ben Dixon(dm).
Englewood Cliffs,N.J.,February 20,1963

tk.6	Look at that girl	CD BN 5-21438-2
tk.10	Personality	-
tk.11	The surrey with the fringe on top	-
tk.15	This little girl of mine	-
	I'm just a lucky so and so	rejected
tk.24	Have you ever had the blues	CD BN 5-21438-2
tk.28	Don't let the sun catch you crying	-
tk.31	Big John	-

151

HANK MOBLEY - NO ROOM FOR SQUARES(4149)/THE TURNAROUND (4186):
Donald Byrd(tp) Hank Mobley(ts) Herbie Hancock(p) Butch Warren(b) Philly Joe Jones(dm).
Englewood Cliffs,N.J.,March 7,1963

tk.4	Old world,new imports	BN BLP4149/BST84149 CD BN 5-24539-2,(J)TOCJ-4149
tk.7	Up a step	BN BLP4149/BST84149 CD BN 5-24539-2,(J)TOCJ-4149
tk.17	The feelin's good	BN BST84435,CD 5-27549-2
tk.21	East of the village	BN BLP4186/BST84186 CD BN 5-24540-2,(J)TOCJ-4186
tk.26	Yes indeed	CD BN 5-27549-2
tk.29	The good life	BN BLP4186/BST84186 CD BN 8-34873-2,5-24540-2,(J)TOCJ-4186

All titles issued on CD BN 7-84435-2.

FREDDIE ROACH - MO' GREENS PLEASE:
Conrad Lester(ts) Freddie Roach(org) Eddie Wright(g) Clarence Johnston(dm).
Englewood Cliffs,N.J.,March 11,1963

tk.7	Googa mooga	BN 45-1890
tk.10	Two different worlds	
tk.17	Mo' greens please	BN 45-1891,CD(Eu)7-89915-2
tk.27	Nada bossa	BN 45-1892
tk.30	Unchained melody	BN(J)K22P-6125/26,CD TOCJ-5755/56, TOCJ-5875

All titles issued on BN BLP4128/BST84128,CD BN(J)TOCJ-4128.

HERBIE HANCOCK - MY POINT OF VIEW:
Donald Byrd(tp) Grachan Moncur III(tb) Hank Mobley(ts) Herbie Hancock(p) Grant Green(g) Chuck Israels(b) Anthony Williams(dm).
Englewood Cliffs,N.J.,March 19,1963

tk.2	A tribute to someone (tb,g out)	
tk.8	King Cobra (g out)	BN BST89907,CD 7-91142-2
tk.10	Blind man,blind man -1	BN 45-1887,BST89907,BN-LA399-H2,B1-28263, (G)F671097 CD BN 8-28263-2,8-29331-2,(J)CJ28-5040, TOCJ-5830,TOCJ-5966,TOCJ-6067,TOCJ-6110, TOCJ-6141,TOCJ-6191,TOCJ-66050
tk.11	Blind man,blind man (alt.)	CD BN(J)TOCJ-66021
tk.17	The pleasure is mine (g out)	
tk.20	And what if I don't	BN-LA399-H2,(G)F671097 CD BN 8-29331-2,(F)4-97517-2

-1: shown as pts. 1 & 2 on sides of 45-1887.Pt.1 was reissued on CD BN 4-94030-2.
All titles, except tk.11,issued on BN BLP4126/BST84126,CD 7-84126-2.
All titles issued on CD BN 4-95569-2,5-21226-2.

KENNY BURRELL:
Seldon Powell(fl-1,bs-2) Hank Jones(p-3,org-4) Kenny Burrell(g) Milt Hinton(b) Osie Johnson(dm).
Englewood Cliffs,N.J.,March 27,1963

tk.13	The good life -4	BN 45-1884
tk.21	Stairway to the stars -2,3	
tk.27	Loie -1,3	BN 45-1884 CD BN 8-30493-2,8-34957-2,(J)TOCJ-66042

All titles issued on BN(J)GXF-3057,GXK-8170.

KENNY DORHAM - UNA MAS:
Kenny Dorham(tp) Joe Henderson(ts) Herbie Hancock(p) Butch Warren(b) Anthony Williams(dm).
Englewood Cliffs,N.J.,April 1,1963

tk.6	Sao Paulo	BN BLP4127,CD 7-89287-2
tk.9	Straight ahead	- CD BN(J)TOCJ-6141
tk.13	Una mas (One more time)	-
		CDBN 8-53648-2,(C)8-56508-2,(F)8-54191-2
tk.16	If ever I would leave you	

All titles issued on CD BN 7-46515-2,5-21228-2.
All titles from BLP4127 (mono) also issued on BN BST84127,CD BN(J)TOCJ-4127 (stereo).

KENNY BURRELL:
Seldon Powell(ts) Hank Jones(p) Kenny Burrell(g) Milt Hinton(b) Osie Johnson(dm).
Englewood Cliffs,N.J.,April 2,1963

tk.35	I hadn't anyone 'til you	BN(J)GXF-3057,GXK-8170

BIG JOHN PATTON - ALONG CAME JOHN:
Fred Jackson,Harold Vick(ts) John Patton(org) Grant Green(g) Ben Dixon(dm).
Englewood Cliffs,N.J.,April 5,1963

tk.2	The silver meter	BN 45-1888,B1-96563,B1-30728 CD BN 7-96563-2,8-30728-2
tk.3	Spiffy diffy	
tk.12	Gee gee	
tk.14	Along came John	BN 45-1889,B1-30728,CD 8-30728-2
tk.20	Pig foot	CD BN(Eu)7-89915-2
tk.21	I'll never be free	BN 45-1889

All titles issued on BN BLP4130/BST84130,CD BN 8-31915-2,(J)TOCJ-4130,(SA)8-31915-2.

HORACE SILVER:
Blue Mitchell,Kenny Dorham(tp) Grachan Moncur III(tb) Julius Watkins(frh) Junior Cook,Jimmy Heath(ts) Charles Davis(bs) Horace Silver(p)Gene Taylor(b) Roy Brooks(dm).
Englewood Cliffs,N.J.,April 11,1963

	Silver's serenade	rejected
	Sweet sweetie dee	-
	Nineteen bars	-
	Next time I fall in love	-

Same. Englewood Cliffs,N.J.,April 12,1963

	The dragon lady	rejected
	Let's go to the nitty gritty	-
	Nineteen bars	-

CHARLIE ROUSE:
Charlie Rouse(ts) Joe Zawinul(p) Grant Green(g) Sam Jones(b) Frankie Dunlop(dm).
Englewood Cliffs,N.J.,April 17,1963

tk.4	Clo-E	rejected
tk.13	Little Sherri	-
tk.17	What kind of fool am I	-
tk.24	I left my heart in San Francisco	-

153

SOLOMON ILORI AND HIS AFRO-DRUM ENSEMBLE - AFRICAN HIGH LIFE:
Solomon Ilori(vo,pennywhistle,talking dm,g) with Hosea Taylor(as) Jay Berliner(g) Ahmed Abdul-Malik(b) Chief Bey,Montego Joe(cga) Josiah Ilori(sakara dm,cowbell) Robert Crowder(cga,chekere,cowbell) Garvin Masseaux(cga,xyl,cowbell) Coleridge Perkinson(dir).

Englewood Cliffs,N.J.,April 25,1963

tk.8	Yaba E (Farewell)	BN 45-1899,CD 4-94031-2
tk.15	Ise Oluwa (God's work is indestructible)	
tk.17	Jojolo (Look at this beautiful girl)	BN 45-1900
tk.25	Follow me to Africa	- CD 4-94031-2
tk.32	Aiye le(The troubled world)	
tk.43	Tolani(African love song)	

All titles issued on BN BLP4136/BST84136,CD BN(J)TOCJ-4136.

JACKIE McLEAN - ONE STEP BEYOND:
Grachan Moncur III(tb) Jackie Mclean(as) Bobby Hutcherson(vb) Eddie Khan(b) Anthony Williams(dm).

Englewood Cliffs,N.J.,April 30,1963

tk.3	Frankenstein	BN BLP4137;CD BN(F)8-54194-2
tk.5	Saturday and Sunday	-
tk.9	Saturday and Sunday(alt.)	
tk.14	Blue rondo	BN BLP4137,(J)K18P-9128 CD BN 8-32993-2,(J)CJ28-5163,CJ32-5016, TOCJ-5755/56,TOCJ-6271/74,TOCJ-66046
tk.16	Ghost town	

All titles issued on CD BN 7-46821-2.
All titles from BLP4137 (mono) also issued on BN BST84137,CD BN(J)TOCJ-4137 (stereo).
Note: The CD issue incorrectly lists the recording date as March 1,1963.

HORACE SILVER - SILVER'S SERENADE:
Blue Mitchell(tp) Junior Cook(ts) Horace Silver(p) Gene Taylor(b) Roy Brooks(dm).

Englewood Cliffs,N.J.,May 7,1963

	Sweet sweetie dee	rejected
tk.7	Silver's serenade	BN 45-1902,BN-LA402-H2,CD 4-95576-2
tk.10	Nineteen bars	

Last two titles issued on BN BLP4131/BST84131,CD 8-21288-2

Same — Englewood Cliffs,N.J.,May 8,1963

tk.16	Let's go to the nitty gritty	BN 45-1902
tk.21	The dragon lady	BN 45-1903
tk.25	Sweet sweetie dee	-

All titles issued on BN BLP4131/BST84131,CD 8-21288-2

154

GRANT GREEN - AM I BLUE:
Johnny Coles(tp) Joe Henderson(ts) John Patton(org) Grant Green(g) Ben Dixon(dm).
Englewood Cliffs,N.J.,May 16,1963

tk.3	Am I blue	BN BLP4139/BST84139
tk.5	Take these chains from my heart	-
tk.10	Sweet slumber	-
	Gee baby,ain't I good to you (incomplete)	rejected
tk.23	I wanna be loved	BN BLP4139/BST84139
tk.25	For all we know	-

All titles from BST84139 also issued on CD BN(J)TOCJ-4139.

DONALD BYRD:
Donald Byrd(tp) Sonny Red(as) Jimmy Heath(ts) Herbie Hancock(p) Eddie Khan(b) Albert Heath(dm).
Englewood Cliffs,N.J.,May 20,1963

tk.5	All numbers	CD BN 8-21286-2
	On the trail	rejected

DEXTER GORDON - OUR MAN IN PARIS:
Dexter Gordon(ts) Bud Powell(p) Pierre Michelot(b) Kenny Clarke(dm).
(prod. by Francis Wolff)(CBS Studios) Paris,May 23,1963

(tk.3)	Our love is here to stay	BN BST84430,CD 7-99427-2,5-20808-2, EMI-Jazz(E)4-99159-2
(tk.4)	Broadway	BN BLP4146/BST84146 CD BN 8-23514-2,(J)CJ28-5038,TOCJ-66047, Toshiba-EMI(J)TOCJ-6098/99, EMI-Jazz(E)4-99159-2
(tk.5)	Stairway to the stars	BN BLP4146/BST84146 CD BN(J)CJ28-5179,EMI-Jazz(E)4-99159-2
(tk.1)	A night in Tunisia	BN BLP4146/BST84146
(tk.8)	Willow weep for me	- CD BN 7-96579-2,(E)8-53225-2,(J)TOCJ-66047
(tk.3)	Scrapple from the apple	BN BLP4146/BST84146(J)FCPA 6211,W-5508 CD BN(J)CJ28-5038
(tk.2)	Like someone in love (ts out)	BN BST84430,(J)K18P-9128;Lib(J)K22P-6131/32 CD BN 7-93204-2,8-30083-2,(J)CJ28-5032, TOCJ-66033,TOCP-50060

Notes: On this session,a take sequence was used for each title.
All titles issued on CD BN 7-46394-2,8-34200-2.
All titles from BST84146 also issued on CD BN(J)TOCJ-4146.BST84430 was issued as by Bud Powell.

HAROLD VICK - STEPPIN' OUT:
Blue Mitchell(tp) Harold Vick(ts) John Patton(org) Grant Green(g) Ben Dixon(dm).
Englewood Cliffs,N.J.,May 27,1963

tk.5	Trimmed in blue	
tk.7	Vicksville	BN 45-1897
tk.12	Steppin' out	CD BN(J)TOCJ-5882
tk.14	Our Miss Brooks	
tk.15	Our Miss Brooks -1	BN 45-1897
tk.16	Dotty's dream	
tk.17	Laura	

-1: short version (mono only).
All titles,except tk.15,issued on BN BLP4138/BST84138,CD 8-52433-2.

155

JOE HENDERSON - PAGE ONE:
Kenny Dorham(tp) Joe Henderson(ts) McCoy Tyner(p) Butch Warren(b) Pete La Roca(dm).
Englewood Cliffs,N.J.,June 3,1963

tk.6	Recorda me	BN 45-1901,CD 7-95627-2,7-89287-2,(J)TOCJ-5755/56,TOCJ-6271/74
tk.12	Jinrikisha	
tk.14	Blue bossa	BN 45-1901,BST2-84433,BST2-92471 BN(Du)1A158-83395/8,(J)K18P-9128, K22P-6096/97,FCPA 6211,W-5513 CD BN 7-92471-2,7-95627-2,7-97960-2, 7-89287-2,8-32993-2,8-53648-2,4-94030-2, 4-97156-2,(C)8-56508-2,(F)8-54191-2, (J)CJ28-5024,CJ28-5171,TOCJ-66051, TOCP-50230,HMV Jazz(E)5-20885-2
tk.18	La mesha	CD BN 8-56399-2,8-56692-2
tk.20	Out of the night	CD BN 8-56692-2
tk.25	Home stretch	

All titles issued on BN BLP4140/BST84140,CD 7-84140-2,4-98795-2.

LOU DONALDSON - MAN WITH A HORN:
Irvin Stokes(tp) Lou Donaldson(as) John Patton(org) Grant Green(g) Ben Dixon(dm).
Englewood Cliffs,N.J.,June 7,1963

tk.3	Cherry pink and apple blossom white	CD BN 5-21436-2,(J)TOCJ-5851
tk.9	Soul meetin'	-
tk.10	Hipty hop	-
tk.20	My melancholy baby	-
tk.22	When I fall in love (tp out)	rejected
tk.24	People will say we're in love	-

GRANT GREEN - BLUES FOR LOU:
John Patton(org) Grant Green(g) Ben Dixon(dm).
Same session.

tk.26	Blues for Lou	CD BN 5-21438-2

JOHN PATTON - BLUE JOHN:
Tommy Turrentine(tp-1) George Braith(ss,strich) John Patton(org) Grant Green(g) Ben Dixon(dm).
Englewood Cliffs,N.J.,July 11,1963

tk.3	Blue John	BN BST84143,CD 7-84143-2
tk.14	Nicety -1	- -
tk.15	Jean De Fleur -1	rejected
tk.27	Extension-1	-
tk.32	I need you so -2	-

-2: Braith out.
Note: First two titles were initially scheduled on BN BLP4143,which was not released.BST84143 was released in 1986 and reissued on CD BN 7-84143-2.

<u>JOHNNY COLES</u> - <u>LITTLE JOHNNY C</u>:
Johnny Coles(tp) Leo Wright(as) Joe Henderson(ts) Duke Pearson(p) Bob Cranshaw(b) Walter Perkins(dm).
Englewood Cliffs,N.J.,July 18,1963

tk.8	Little Johnny C	BN BLP4144/BST84144 CD Cap(J)TOCJ-5191/92
tk.12	Hobo Joe	BN BLP4144/BST84144
tk.21	Jano	-
	So sweet my little girl	rejected

First three titles also issued on CD BN 8-32129-2.

<u>DON WILKERSON</u> - <u>SHOUTIN'</u>:
Don Wilkerson(ts) John Patton(org) Grant Green(g) Ben Dixon(dm).
Englewood Cliffs,N.J.,July 29,1963

tk.4	Sweet cake	CD BN(F)8-54188-2
tk.8	Cookin' with Clarence	
tk.12	Movin' out	
tk.13	Happy Johnny	BN(E)BNSLP-2;CD BN(J)TOCJ-5779
tk.17	Easy living	
tk.21	Blues for J	

All titles issued on BN BLP4145/BST84145,CD BN 5-24555-2,(J)TOCJ-4145.

<u>JOHN PATTON</u> - <u>BLUE JOHN</u>:
George Braith(ss) John Patton(org) Grant Green(g) Ben Dixon(dm).
Englewood Cliffs,N.J.,August 2,1963

tk.16	Hot sauce	BN BST84143,B1-30728 CD BN 7-84143-2,8-30728-2
tk.20	Bermuda Clay house	BN BST841343,B1-30728 CD BN 7-84143-2,8-30728-2
tk.26	Chunky chicks	rejected
tk.34	Dem dirty blues	BN BST84143,CD 7-84143-2
tk.36	Country girl	- -
tk.45	Untitled Patton tune	rejected
tk.49	Davene	-
tk.62	Kinda slick	-

Note:BST84143 was released in 1986 and reissued on CD BN 7-84143-2.Mono version (BLP4143) was not released.

<u>JOHNNY COLES</u> - <u>LITTLE JOHNNY C</u>:
Johnny Coles(tp) Leo Wright(as-1,fl-2) Joe Henderson(ts) Duke Pearson(p) Bob Cranshaw(b) Pete La Roca (dm).
Englewood Cliffs,N.J.,August 9,1963

tk.4	Heavy legs -1
tk.18	My secret passion -2,3
tk.22	So sweet my little girl -1

-3: mistitled "My sweet passion" on CD 8-32129-2.
All titles issued on BN BLP4144/BST84144,CD 8-32129-2.

BLUE MITCHELL - STEP LIGHTLY:
Blue Mitchell(tp) Leo Wright(as) Joe Henderson(ts) Herbie Hancock(p) Gene Taylor(b) Roy Brooks(dm).
Englewood Cliffs,N.J.,August 13,1963

tk.4	Little stupid	
tk.11	Cry me a river	CD BN(J)TOCJ-66052
tk.14	Mamacita	BN B1-57745,CD 8-57745-2
tk.15	Sweet and lovely	CD BN 7-89287-2
tk.22	Step lightly	
tk.24	Bluesville	

All titles initially scheduled on BN BLP4142 (not released) and later issued on BN LT-1082,Mosaic MQ6-178,CD BN(J)TOCJ-4142,Mosaic MD4-178.

HERBIE HANCOCK - INVENTIONS AND DIMENSIONS:
Herbie Hancock(p) Paul Chambers(b) Willie Bobo(dm,timbales-1) Osvaldo "Chihuahua" Martinez (cga-2, bgo,finger cymbals-3,guiro-4).
Englewood Cliffs,N.J.,August 30,1963

tk.1	(12567)	Succotash -4	BN BST89907 CD BN(F)4-97517-2,(J)CJ28-5040,TOCJ-66050
tk.2	(12568)	Triangle -2	BN BN-LA399-H2
tk.4		Mimosa (alt.)-3	CD BN(J)TOCJ-66021
tk.5	(12565)	Mimosa -3	
tk.9	(12566)	A jump ahead	
tk.13	(12564)	Jack Rabbit -1,2	CD BN 8-54904-2,(J)TOCJ-5882,TOCJ-6110

All titles, except tk.4, issued on BN BLP4147/BST84147,BN-LA152-F,CD 7-84147-2.
All titles issued on CD BN 4-95569-2.
Note: Master numbers shown in parenthesis were assigned by United Artists for issue on BN BN-LA152-F.

GEORGE BRAITH - TWO SOULS IN ONE:
George Braith(ss,strich) Billy Gardner(org) Grant Green(g) Donald Bailey(dm).
Englewood Cliffs,N.J.,September 4,1963

tk.8	Mary had a little lamb	BN B1-29092,CD 8-29092-2
tk.17	Poinciana	
tk.26	Mary Ann	
tk.27	Home street	
tk.33	Braith-a-way	

All titles issued on BN BLP4148/BST84148,CD BN 5-24558-2,(J)TOCJ-4148.

JOE HENDERSON - OUR THING:
Kenny Dorham(tp) Joe Henderson(ts) Andrew Hill(p) Eddie Khan(b) Pete La Roca(dm).
Englewood Cliffs,N.J.,September 9,1963

tk.10	Teeter totter (alt.)	
tk.14	Our thing	BN BLP4152/BST84152,B2S-5256 CD BN 7-89287-2,7-95627-2,(Sp)5-21755-2
tk.17	Escapade	BN BLP4152/BST84152
tk.23	Back road	-
tk.27	Pedro's time	-
tk.28	Teeter totter	-

All titles issued on CD BN 7-84152-2,5-25647-2.
All titles from BST84152 also issued on CD BN(JTOCJ-4152.

158

JACKIE McLEAN - DESTINATION...OUT!:
Grachan Moncur III(tb) Jackie McLean(as) Bobby Hutcherson(vb) Larry Ridley(b) Roy Haynes (dm).
Englewood Cliffs,N.J.,September 20,1963

tk.4	Esoteric	BN BLP4165
tk.7	Love and hate	-
	Secret love (incomplete)	rejected
tk.19	Kahlil the prophet	BN BLP4165;CD BN(F)8-54194-2
tk.24	Riff raff	- (Du)1A158-83395/8

BLP4165 (mono) = BN BST84165,B1-32087,CD 8-32087-2 (stereo)

HANK MOBLEY - NO ROOM FOR SQUARES:
Lee Morgan(tp) Hank Mobley(ts) Andrew Hill(p) John Ore(b) Philly Joe Jones(dm)
Englewood Cliffs,N.J.,October 2,1963

tk.2	No room for squares	BN BLP4149/BST84149 CD BN 8-37052-2,5-24539-2,(F)8-54191-2, (J)TOCJ-5755/56,TOCJ-66043
tk.3	No room for squares (alt.)	CD BN 5-24539-2
tk.8	Three way split	BN BLP4149/BST84149;CD BN 5-24539-2
tk.13	Comin' back	CD BN 5-27549-2
tk.17	Me 'n ' you	BN BLP4149/BST84149;CD BN 5-24539-2
tk.19	Carolyn (alt.)	CD BN 5-24539-2
tk.22	Carolyn	BN BLP4149/BST84149;CD BN 5-24539-2
tk.29	Syrup and biscuits	CD BN 5-27549-2

All titles issued on CD BN 7-84149-2.
All titles from BST84149 also issued on CD BN(J)TOCJ-4149.

STANLEY TURRENTINE:
Blue Mitchell(tp) Tom McIntosh(tb) Stanley Turrentine(ts) Charles Davis(bs) Shirley Scott (org) Earl May(b) Ben Dixon(dm).
Englewood Cliffs,N.J.,October 14,1963

	Cherry point	rejected
	One o'clock jump	-
	Midnight blue	-

STANLEY TURRENTINE - A CHIP OFF THE OLD BLOCK:
Blue Mitchell(tp) Stanley Turrentine(ts) Shirley Scott(org) Earl May(b) Al Harewood(dm).
Englewood Cliffs,N.J.,October 21,1963

tk.9	Cherry point	BN BN-LA394-H2
tk.17	Blues in hoss' flat	
tk.20	Midnight blue	
tk.25	One o'clock jump	BN BN-LA394-H2;CD BN(J)CJ28-5170
tk.30	Spring can really hang you up the most	

All titles issued on BN BLP4150/BST84150,CD BN(J)TOCJ-4150.

 159

<u>HORACE SILVER QUINTET</u>:
Blue Mitchell(tp) Junior Cook(ts) Horace Silver(p) Gene Taylor(b) Roy Brooks(dm).
Englewood Cliffs,N.J.,October 31,1963

tk.1	Calcutta cutie	BN BLP4185/BST84185,CD BN(J)TOCJ-4185
tk.5	Lonely woman (tp,ts out)	- BN-LA474-H2
		CD BN(J)TOCJ-4185
tk.14	Sanctimonious Sam	BN BN-LA945-H
tk.17	Que pasa (tp,ts out)	- CD BN(Eu)8-29964-2

All titles issued on CD BN 7-84185-2,4-99002-2.

<u>GRANT GREEN</u> - <u>IDLE MOMENTS</u>:
Joe Henderson(ts) Bobby Hutcherson(vb) Duke Pearson(p) Grant Green(g) Bob Cranshaw(b) Al Harewood (dm).
Englewood Cliffs,N.J.,November 4,1963

tk.11	Jean De Fleur (alt.)	
tk.14	Idle moments	BN BLP4154/BST84154
		CD BN 7-89287-2,8-27312-2,(Au)8-14808-2,
		(J)TOCJ-4154
tk.28	Nomad	BN BLP4154/BST84154:CD BN,(J)TOCJ-4154
tk.32	Django (alt.)	

All titles issued on CD BN 7-84154-2,4-99003-2.

<u>ANDREW HILL</u> - <u>BLACK FIRE</u>:
Joe Henderson(ts) Andrew Hill(p) Richard Davis(b) Roy Haynes(dm).
Englewood Cliffs,N.J.,November 8,1963

tk.3	Land of Nod	BN BLP4151
tk.7	Black fire (alt.)	
tk.9	Cantarnos	BN BLP4151
tk.15	McNeil Island (dm out)	- CD 7-89287-2
tk.17	Tired trade (ts out)	- Lib(J)K22P-6092/93
		CD BN 7-89287-2,(J)TOCJ-5187/88
tk.20	Pumpkin	BN BLP4151,CD 5-21052-2
tk.22	Pumpkin (alt.)	
tk.23	Subterfuge (ts out)	BN BLP4151
tk.27	Black fire	- BST2-92474
		BN(Du)1A158-83395/8,(J)K18P-9128
		CD BN 7-92474-2,(F)8-54194-2,
		(J)TOCJ-6271/74

All titles issued on Mosaic MQ10-161,CD BN 7-84151-2,Mosaic MD7-161.
All titles from BLP4151 (mono) also issued on BN BST84151,CD BN(J)TOCJ-4151 (stereo).

<u>GRANT GREEN</u> - <u>IDLE MOMENTS</u>:
Joe Henderson(ts) Bobby Hutcherson(vb) Duke Pearson(p) Grant Green(g) Bob Cranshaw(b) Al Harewood (dm).
Englewood Cliffs,N.J.,November 15,1963

tk.36	Django	Lib(J)K22P-6094/95
		CD BN(E)8-53225-2,(J)CJ28-5169,TOCJ-66045
tk.39	Jean De Fleur	BN B1-89622

Both titles issued on BN BLP4154/BST84154,CD 7-84154-2,4-99003-2,(J)TOCJ-4154.

160

GRACHAN MONCUR III - EVOLUTION:
Lee Morgan(tp) Grachan Moncur III(tb) Jackie McLean(as) Bobby Hutcherson(vb) Bob Cranshaw(b) Anthony Williams(dm).
Englewood Cliffs,N.J.,November 21,1963

tk.11	Monk in Wonderland	CD BN 8-35471-2,(F)8-54194-2
tk.12	The coaster	
tk.14	Evolution	CD BN 8-56399-2
tk.17	Air raid	

All titles issued on BN BLP4153/BST84153,CD 7-84153-2.

FREDDIE ROACH - GOOD MOVE:
Freddie Roach(org) Eddie Wright(g) Clarence Johnston(dm).
Englewood Cliffs,N.J.,November 29,1963

tk.3	T'ain't what you do	BN BLP4158/BST84158
tk.13	It ain't necessarily so	-
tk.22	Pastel	-
tk.32	I'm just a lucky so and so	rejected
tk.34	I.Q. Blues	BN BLP4158/BST84158 CD BN(F)8-54188-2
tk.43	What a difference a day makes	rejected
tk.44	Blues X	-
tk.46	The bees	-

All titles from BST84158 also issued on CD BN 5-24551-2,(J)TOCJ-4158.

Blue Mitchell(tp) Hank Mobley(ts) added.
Englewood Cliffs,N.J.,December 9,1963

tk.53	When Malindy sings	BN B1-29092,(Du)1A158-83395/8 CD BN 8-29092-2
tk.55	Wine,wine,wine	BN B1-96563
tk.62	On our way up	CD BN(J)TOCJ-5644,TOCJ-5882
tk.65	Lots of lovely love	

All titles issued on BN BLP4158/BST84158,CD BN 5-24551-2,(J)TOCJ-4158.

ANDREW HILL - SMOKESTACK:
Andrew Hill(p) Richard Davis,Eddie Khan(b) Roy Haynes(dm).
Englewood Cliffs,N.J.,December 13,1963

tk.4	Smokestack (alt.)	
tk.6	Smokestack	BN BLP4160/BST84160,B1-32097
tk.9	Wailing wall	- -
tk.11	Ode to Von	- -
tk.15	Ode to Von (alt.)	
tk.16	The day after	BN BLP4160/BST84160,B1-32097
tk.17	The day after (alt.)	
tk.21	Verne (Khan out)	BN BLP4160/BST84160,B1-32097
tk.22	Not so (alt.)	
tk.23	Not so	BN BLP4160/BST84160,B1-32097
tk.24	30 Pier Avenue	- -

Note: All bass solos are by Davis except last title solo by Eddie Khan.
All titles issued on Mosaic MQ10-161,CD BN 8-32097-2,Mosaic MD7-161.
All titles from BST84160 also issued on CD BN(J)TOCJ-4160.

<u>GEORGE BRAITH</u> - <u>SOUL STREAM</u>:
George Braith(ss,ts,strich) Billy Gardner(org) Grant Green(g) Hugh Walker(dm).
Englewood Cliffs,N.J.,December 16,1963

tk.10	The man I love	
tk.15	Boop bop bing bash	BN B1-96563 CD BN 7-96563-2,(J)TOCJ-5882,TOCJ-6067
tk.19	Billy told	
tk.23	Outside around the corner	
tk.26	Soul stream	
tk.39	Jo Anne	

All titles issued on BN BLP4161/BST84161,CD BN 5-24558-2,(J)TOCJ-4161.

<u>LEE MORGAN</u> - <u>THE SIDEWINDER</u>:
Lee Morgan(tp) Joe Henderson(ts) Barry Harris(p) Bob Cranshaw(b) Billy Higgins(dm).
Englewood Cliffs,N.J.,December 21,1963

tk.2	Totem pole (alt.)	
tk.4	Totem pole	
tk.11	Boy,what a night	
tk.19	Hocus pocus	BN-LA224-G
tk.25	The sidewinder	BN 45-1911,L4157,BST 89904,BN-LA160-G2, BN-LA224-G,BST2-84429,B1-91138,B1-94704, BST2-92471,B1-80679 BN(Du)BST83249,1A158-83395/8,(E)BNX 1, (In)JAZ 2,(J)NP9020C,LNP95059B,LNS90031, FCPA 6213,W-5513 UA XW-136;Lib(F)LBS83442/3 CD BN 7-48337-2,7-91138-2,7-92471-2, 7-80679-2,7-96110-2,8-32993-2,8-54901-2, 8-56399-2,8-56508-2,4-94704-2,5-20070-2, (E)8-53233-2,(F)8-54188-2,8-54197-2, (J)CJ25-5181/84,CJ28-5021,CJ28-5037, CJ28-5064,CJ28-5171,CP32-5057,TOCJ-5203, TOCJ-5828,TOCJ-5925,TOCJ-5933,TOCJ-6153, TOCJ-66039,TOCJ-66055,TOCJ-66060, TOCJ-66063,TOCP-7455/56,TOCP-8963, TOCP-50230,32 Jazz 32025-2, The Right Stuff 8-57071-2,Cema S21-57592, EMI-Jazz(E)4-93469-2,EMI-Music 4-98900-2, Premier(E)CDPR 127
tk.27	Gary's notebook	BN L4157,CD 7-89287-2

All titles,except tk.2,issued on BN BLP4157/BST84157,CD 7-46137-2
All titles issued on CD BN 7-84157-2,4-95332-2.

<u>BOBBY HUTCHERSON</u> - <u>THE KICKER</u>:
Joe Henderson(ts) Bobby Hutcherson(vb) Duke Pearson(p) Grant Green(g) Bob Cranshaw(b) Al Harewood (dm).
Englewood Cliffs,N.J.,December 29,1963

tk.8	The kicker
tk.11	Bedouin
tk.23	For Duke P. (g out)
tk.24	Step lightly
tk.35	Mirrors (g out)
tk.36	If ever I would leave you (g out)

All titles issued on CD BN 5-21437-2.

 162

ANDREW HILL - JUDGMENT!:
Bobby Hutcherson(vb) Andrew Hill(p) Richard Davis(b) Elvin Jones(dm).
Englewood Cliffs,N.J.,January 8,1964

1280	tk.3	Judgment	BN BLP4159/BST84159
1281	tk.8	Flea flop	-
1282	tk.13	Siete ocho	- CD BN(F)8-54194-2
1283	tk.15	Alfred	-
	tk.20	Yokada,yokada (alt.)	
1284	tk.21	Yokada,yokada	BN BLP4159/BST84159
1285	tk.26	Reconciliation	-

All titles issued on Mosaic MQ10-161,CD BN 8-28981-2,MD7-161.
All titles from BST84159 also issued on BN B1-28981,CD BN(J)TOCJ-4159.

STANLEY TURRENTINE - HUSTLIN':
Stanley Turrentine(ts) Shirley Scott(org) Kenny Burrell(g) Bob Cranshaw(b) Otis Finch(dm).
Englewood Cliffs,N.J.,January 24,1964

1286	tk.3	Something happens to me	
1287	tk.8	The hustler	CD BN 8-32993-2
1288	tk.9	Love letters	
1289	tk.24	Goin' home	
1290	tk.26	Lady fingers	
1291	tk.28	Trouble No.2 (see note)	BN 45-1893,BN-LA394-H2,(E)UALP 19 CD BN(J)TOCJ-5733

All titles issued on BN BLP4162/BST84162,CD BN(J)TOCJ-4162.
Note: Last title was released on a second version of 45-1893 (see page 150 for details of first version)

HORACE SILVER:
Blue Mitchell(tp) Junior Cook(ts) Horace Silver(p) Gene Taylor(b) Roy Brooks(dm).
Englewood Cliffs,N.J.,January 28,1964

1292		Revlis	rejected
1293	tk.11	Sighin' and cryin'	BN BN-LA945-H
1294	tk.14	Silver threads among the soul	BN(Du)1A158-83391/4

Last two titles also issued on CD BN 7-84185-2,4-99002-2.

ART BLAKEY AND THE JAZZ MESSENGERS - FREE FOR ALL:
Freddie Hubbard(tp) Curtis Fuller(tb) Wayne Shorter(ts) Cedar Walton(p) Reggie Workman(b) Art Blakey (dm) Wellington Blakey(vo).
Englewood Cliffs,N.J.,February 10,1964

1296	tk.3	The core	BN BLP4170;CD BN(J)TOCJ-5274/76
1295	tk.5	Hammer head	- CD 8-32993-2,8-59071-2
	tk.6	My funny Valentine (voWB)	rejected
	tk.10	Eva	-
1298	tk.15	Pensativa	BN BLP4170
1297	tk.16	Free for all	- (J)LBN80259 CD BN 7-93205-2,7-97190-2
		Soul girl (voWB)	rejected

All titles from BLP4170 (mono) also issued on BN BST84170,CD 7-84170-2 (stereo).

 163

GRANT GREEN:
John Gilmore(ts) Bobby Hutcherson(vb) Duke Pearson(p) Grant Green(g) Butch Warren(b) Billy Higgins (dm).

Englewood Cliffs,N.J.,February 12,1964

1299	Untitled Grant Green tune No.3	rejected
1300	Minor league	-
1301	Grant's tune	-
1302	Un poco loco	-
1303	Ezz-thetic	-

LEE MORGAN - SEARCH FOR THE NEW LAND:
Lee Morgan(tp)Wayne Shorter(ts) Herbie Hancock(p) Grant Green(g) Reggie Workman(b) Billy Higgins (dm).

Englewood Cliffs,N.J.,February 15,1964

1304 tk.3	Mr. Kenyatta	BN L4169,B1-80701,CD 7-91138-2,7-80701-2
1305 tk.5	Search for the new land	CD BN 8-56399-2
1306 tk.10	The joker	BN L4169
1307 tk.14	Morgan the pirate	BN(Du)1A158-83395/8
1308 tk.16	Melancholee	

All titles issued on BN BLP4169/BST84169,CD 7-84169-2.

ERIC DOLPHY - OUT TO LUNCH:
Freddie Hubbard(tp) Eric Dolphy(fl-1,as-2,bass cl-3) Bobby Hutcherson(vb) Richard Davis(b) Anthony Williams(dm).

Englewood Cliffs,N.J.,February 25,1964

1309 tk.4	Gazzelloni -1	CD BN 8-35414-2
1310 tk.10	Hat and beard -3	BN(Du)1A158-83395/8 CD BN 8-35471-2,(F)8-54194-2,8-54197-2, (J)CJ25-5181/84,TOCJ-6271/74
1311 tk.12	Something sweet,something tender -3	BN(J)K18P-9128
1312 tk.17	Out to lunch -2	BN BST89904,BN-LA160-G2,BST2-92474 BN(J)NP9022,LNP95060 CD BN 7-92474-2,(F)8-54194-2,Knitting Factory CD 249
1313 tk.21	Straight up and down -2	

All titles issued on BN BLP4163/BST84163,B1-46524,CD 7-46524-2,4-98793-2.

FREDDIE ROACH:
Joe Henderson(ts) Freddie Roach(org) Eddie Wright(g) Clarence Johnston(dm).

Englewood Cliffs,N.J.,March 18,1964

	Next time you see me	rejected
	The right time	-
	I'll get along somehow	-

164

FREDDIE ROACH - BROWN SUGAR:
Joe Henderson(ts) Freddie Roach(org) Eddie Wright(g) Clarence Johnston(dm).
Englewood Cliffs,N.J.,March 19,1964

1314	tk.4	Next time you see me	BN 45-1914
1315	tk.8	Brown sugar	- B1-96563,CD 7-96563-2,4-94030-2
1316	tk.19	Have you ever had the blues	
1317	tk.22	All night long	
1318	tk.27	The midnight sun will never set	
1319	tk.28	The right time	CD BN 7-89287-2

All titles issued on BN BLP4168/BST84168,CD BN(J)TOCJ-4168.

ANDREW HILL - POINT OF DEPARTURE:
Kenny Dorham(tp) Eric Dolphy(fl-1,as-2,bass cl-3) Joe Henderson(ts) Andrew Hill(p) Richard Davis(b) Anthony Williams(dm).
Englewood Cliffs,N.J.,March 21,1964

1321	tk.6	Refuge -2	BN BLP4167,CD 7-89287-2
	tk.7	Dedication (alt.)-1	
1322	tk.8	Dedication -1	BN BLP4167
1323	tk.10	New monastery -2	- CD BN(F)8-54194-2
	tk.13	New monastery (alt.)-2	
	tk.18	Flight 19 (alt.)-1	
1324	tk.19	Flight 19 -1	BN BLP4167,(Du)1A158-83395/8
1320	tk.24	Spectrum -1,2,3	-

All titles,except tk.13,also issued on CD BN 7-84167-2.
All titles issued on Mosaic MQ10-161,CD BN 4-99007-2,Mosaic MD7-161 .
All titles from BLP4167 (mono) also issued on BN BST84167,CD BN(J)TOCJ-4167 (stereo).

GEORGE BRAITH:
George Braith(ss,as,ts) Billy Gardner(org) Grant Green(g) Hugh Walker(dm).
Englewood Cliffs,N.J.,March 24,1964

Nut city	rejected
Sweetville	-
Ethlyn's love	-

GEORGE BRAITH - EXTENSION:
George Braith(ss,as,ts) Billy Gardner(org) Grant Green(g) Clarence Johnston(dm).
Englewood Cliffs,N.J.,March 27,1964

1325	tk.5	Nut city	
1326	tk.10	Sweetville	BN L4171
1327	tk.14	Ethlyn's love	
1328	tk.15	Out here	
1329	tk.31	Extension	
1330	tk.33	Ev'rytime we say goodbye	BN L4171

All titles issued on BN BLP4171/BST84171,CD BN 5-24558-2,(J)TOCJ-4171.

JOE HENDERSON:
Kenny Dorham(tp) Joe Henderson(ts) Andrew Hill(p) Eddie Khan(b) Elvin Jones(dm).
Englewood Cliffs,N.J.,April 7,1964

1331	Short story	rejected

165

JOE HENDERSON - IN 'N ' OUT:
Kenny Dorham(tp) Joe Henderson(ts) McCoy Tyner(p) Richard Davis(b) Elvin Jones(dm).
Englewood Cliffs,N.J.,April 10,1964

1332 tk.6 Punjab CD BN 7-95627-2
tk.7 In' 'n out (alt.)
1333 tk.9 In' 'n out CD BN 7-89287-2
1334 tk.11 Short story CD BN 8-53648-2
1335 tk.14 Brown's town
1336 tk.19 Serenity CD BN 7-95627-2,(J)TOCJ-6131

All titles issued on CD BN 8-29156-2.
All titles,except tk.7,issued on BN BLP4166/BST84166,CD 7-46510-2.

ART BLAKEY AND THE JAZZ MESSENGERS - INDESTRUCTIBLE:
Lee Morgan(tp) Curtis Fuller(tb) Wayne Shorter(ts) Cedar Walton(p) Reggie Workman(b) Art Blakey(dm).
Englewood Cliffs,N.J.,April 15,1964

tk.7 It's a long way down CD BN 7-46429-2;BN(J)GXF-3060
Mr. Jin rejected
When love is new -

ART BLAKEY AND THE JAZZ MESSENGERS - INDESTRUCTIBLE:
Same.
Englewood Cliffs,N.J.,April 16,1964

1337 The Egyptian rejected
Calling Miss Khadija -
1338 When love is new -
Sortie -

ART BLAKEY AND THE JAZZ MESSENGERS - INDESTRUCTIBLE:
Same. Englewood Cliffs,N.J.,April 24,1964

tk.3 When love is new BN L4193,BLP4193/BST84193
CD BN 7-46429-2,7-97190-2,(J)TOCJ-4193,
TOCJ-5274/76
The Egyptian rejected
It's a long way down -

WAYNE SHORTER - NIGHT DREAMER:
Lee Morgan(tp)Wayne Shorter(ts)McCoy Tyner(p)Reggie Workman(b)Elvin Jones(dm).
Englewood Cliffs,N.J.,April 29,1964

1339 tk.3 Night dreamer BN BLP4173
CD BN(J)CJ28-5039,TOCJ-6131,TOCJ-66049
1340 tk.5 Armageddon BN BLP4173
1341 tk.9 Oriental folk song -
1342 tk.12 Virgo (tp out) - CD 7-91141-2
tk.14 Virgo (alt.) (tp out)
1343 tk.27 Black Nile BN BLP4173
BN(J)K18P-9128,FCPA 6211,W-5513
CD BN 8-59072-2,4-94031-2,(J)TOCJ-5882
1344 tk.35 Charcoal blues (tp out) BN BLP4173,(In)JAZ 1

All titles issued on CD BN 7-84173-2.
All titles from BLP4173 (mono) also issued on BN BST84173,CD BN(J)TOCJ-4173 (stereo).

166

FREDDIE HUBBARD - BREAKING POINT:
Freddie Hubbard(tp) James Spaulding(fl-1,as) Ronnie Mathews(p) Eddie Khan(b) Joe Chambers(dm).
Englewood Cliffs,N.J.,May 7,1964

1345 tk.3	D minor mint	BN BLP4172,B1-93202
		CD BN 7-93202-2,(J)CJ28-5164
1346 tk.10	Far away -1	BN BLP4172
1347 tk.11	Breaking point	- BN-LA356-H2
1348 tk.14	Blue frenzy	- -
		BN(J)K18P-9128
		CD BN 8-59071-2,(Au)8-57460-2
tk.15	Blue frenzy	BN 45-1908
1349 tk.23	Mirrors -1	BN BLP 4172,BN-LA356-H2,B1-93202
		CD BN 7-93202-2,8-56691-2
tk.24	Mirrors -1	BN 45-1908

All titles issued on CD BN 7-84172-2.
All titles from BLP4172 (mono) also issued on BN BST84172,CD BN(J)TOCJ-4172 (stereo).

ART BLAKEY AND THE JAZZ MESSENGERS - INDESTRUCTIBLE:
Lee Morgan(tp) Curtis Fuller(tb) Wayne Shorter(ts) Cedar Walton(p) Reggie Workman(b) Art Blakey(dm).
Englewood Cliffs,N.J.,May 15,1964

1350 tk.3	Sortie	BN BLP4193
1351 tk.8	It's a long way down	rejected
1352 tk.19	Mr. Jin	BN BLP4193
1353 tk.27	Calling Miss Khadija	BN L4193,BLP4193
		CD BN(J)CJ28-5031,TOCJ-5274/76
1354 tk.33	The Egyptian	BN BLP4193,CD 7-97190-2

All titles from BLP4193 (mono) also issued on BN BST84193,CD BN(J)TOCJ-4193 (stereo).
All titles,except 1351,issued on CD BN 7-46429-2.

GRANT GREEN - MATADOR:
McCoy Tyner(p) Grant Green(g) Bob Cranshaw(b) Elvin Jones(dm).
Englewood Cliffs,N.J.,May 20,1964

1355 tk.2	Matador	
1356 tk.4	Green jeans	
1357 tk.17	My favorite things	BN B1-80679-1,B1-89622
		CD BN 8-33205-2,4-97154-2,(J)TOCJ-5733
1358 tk.29	Bedouin	

All titles issued on BN(J)GXF-3053,CD BN 7-84442-2.
Note:The CD reissue incorrectly lists the recording date as May 20, 1965.

HAROLD VICK:
Harold Vick(ts) George Coleman(as-1,ts-2) John Patton(org) Grant Green(g) Ben Dixon(dm).
Englewood Cliffs,N.J.,May 27,1964

1359	Soul call -2	rejected
1360	Like Alice -1	-

DEXTER GORDON - ONE FLIGHT UP:
Donald Byrd(tp-1) Dexter Gordon(ts) Kenny Drew(p) Niels-Henning Orsted Pedersen(b) Art Taylor(dm).
(Prod. by Frank Wolff)(Barclay Studios) Paris,June 2,1964

1387	tk.13	Coppin' the haven -1	BN BLP4176
1386	tk.17	Tanya -1	- BN-LA393-H2,CD 7-91139-2
1389	tk.20	Kong Neptune (*aka* King Neptune)	
1388	tk.23	Darn that dream	BN BLP4176;Hip-O HIPD-64557
			CD BN 7-96579-2,(J)TOCJ-5858,TOCJ-66047

All titles issued on CD BN 7-84176-2,8-34200-2.
All titles from BLP4176 (mono) also issued on BN BST84176,CD BN(J)TOCJ-4176 (stereo).

STANLEY TURRENTINE - IN MEMORY OF:
Blue Mitchell(tp) Curtis Fuller(tb) Stanley Turrentine(ts) Herbie Hancock(p,perc-1) Bob Cranshaw(b,perc-1) Otis Finch(dm).
Englewood Cliffs,N.J.,June 3,1964

1361	tk.2	Fried pies -2	
1362	tk.5	In memory of -2	CD BN 7-93201-2
1363	tk.13	Sunday in New York	
1365	tk.30	Make someone happy	
1364	tk.35	Jodie's cha cha	
1366	tk.38	Niger mambo -1	CD BN 4-94031-2,4-97222-2

-2: Mickey Roker(cga) added.
All titles issued on BN LT-1037.
Note: Takes 2,5 & 30 were first scheduled on BN BLP4234/BST84234,which were never released.

GRANT GREEN - SOLID:
James Spaulding(as) Joe Henderson(ts) McCoy Tyner(p) Grant Green(g) Bob Cranshaw(b) Elvin Jones(dm).
Englewood Cliffs,N.J.,June 12,1964

tk.3	Grant's tune	BN LT-990,B1-33580,(E)UALP21
tk.14	Minor league	- -
tk.25	Wives and lovers (as,ts out)	BN B1-89622,CD 7-84442-2,8-57749-2
tk.28	The kicker	BN LT-990,B1-33580
	Spanish dancer -1	rejected
tk.35	Ezz-thetic	BN LT-990,B1-33580,CD 8-27312-2
tk.37	Solid	-

-1: Duke Pearson(tp) added.
All titles,except the rejected one,issued on CD BN 8-33580-2.

HERBIE HANCOCK - EMPYREAN ISLES:
Freddie Hubbard(c) Herbie Hancock(p) Ron Carter(b) Anthony Williams(dm).
Englewood Cliffs,N.J.,June 17,1964

	tk.3	Oliloqui Valley (alt.)	
1372	tk.5	One finger snap	BN BLP4175,B1-91142 CD 7-91142-2,(J)CJ28-5040,TOCJ-5637, TOCJ-5830,TOCJ-5966,TOCJ-66050
1373	tk.14	Cantaloupe island	BN BLP4175,BN-LA399-H2,B1-91142,B1-80679, B1-28263;Hip-O HIPD-64557 BN(Du)1A158-83395/8,(G)F671097,(J)K18P-9128 CD BN 7-91142-2,7-80679-2,8-28263-2, 8-29331-2,8-32993-2,8-54904-2,(C)8-56508-2, (E)8-53233-2,(F)8-54191-2,8-54197-2,4-97517-2, (J)CJ25-5181/84,CJ28-5040,TOCJ-5298, TOCJ-5637,TOCJ-5830,TOCJ-5925,TOCJ-5936, TOCJ-5966,TOCJ-6110,TOCJ-6132,TOCJ-6141, TOCJ-6271/74,TOCJ-66050,TOCJ-66055, (Sp)5-21755-2,Toshiba-EMI(J)TOCP-8751, The Right Stuff 8-57072-2,EMI-Music 4-98899-2, EMI(E)5-21426-2
1374	tk.17	The egg	BN BLP4175
	tk.19	One finger snap (alt.)	
1375	tk.24	Oliloqui valley	BN BLP 4175,BST89907,B1-99106 CD BN 7-99106-2

All titles issued on CD CD BN 7-84175-2,4-95569-2,4-98796-2.
All titles from BLP4175 (mono) also issued on BN BST84175,CD BN(J)TOCJ-4175 (stereo).

BIG JOHN PATTON - THE WAY I FEEL:
Richard Williams(tp) Fred Jackson(ts,bs-1) John Patton(org) Grant Green(g) Ben Dixon(dm).
Englewood Cliffs,N.J.,June 19,1964

1376	tk.9	Jerry	BN B2S-5256,CD 8-30728-2
1377	tk.17	The rock	
1378	tk.20	The way I feel -1	
1379	tk.22	Just 3/4	
1380	tk.28	Davene (tp,ts out)	

All titles issued on BN BLP4174/BST84174,CD BN(J)TOCJ-4174,(SA)8-31916-2.

ANDREW HILL - ANDREW!!!:
John Gilmore(ts) Bobby Hutcherson(vb) Andrew Hill(p) Richard Davis(b) Joe Chambers(dm).
Englewood Cliffs,N.J.,June 25,1964

1382	tk.6	Black Monday	BN BLP4203/BST84203
1383	tk.12	Symmetry	-
	tk.14	Symmetry (alt.)	
1384	tk.17	The griots (ts out)	BN BLP4203/BST84203
	tk.18	The griots (alt.) (ts out)	
1385	tk.20	Duplicity	BN BLP4203/BST84203
1386	tk.31	Le serpent qui danse	-
1381	tk.33	No doubt	-

All titles also issued on Mosaic MQ10-161,CD MD7-161.

169

GRACHAN MONCUR III - SOME OTHER STUFF:
Grachan Moncur III(tb) Wayne Shorter(ts) Herbie Hancock(p) Cecil McBee(b) Anthony Williams(dm).
Englewood Cliffs,N.J.,July 6,1964

1382	tk.1	The twins	
1383	tk.6	Gnostic	
1384	tk.14	Thandiwa	CD BN(F)8-54194-2
1385	tk.19	Nomadic	

All titles issued on BN BLP4177/BST84177,B1-32092,CD 8-32092-2.

1386/89: see June 2,1964 session.

BLUE MITCHELL - THE THING TO DO:
Blue Mitchell(tp) Junior Cook(ts) Chick Corea(p) Gene Taylor(b) Aloysius Foster(dm).
Englewood Cliffs,N.J.,July 30,1964

1391	tk.5	Fungii Mama -1	BN 45-1921,BST2-92471 CD BN 7-92471-2,(F)8-54191-2,(J)TOCJ-6133
1392	tk.14	Step lightly	
1393	tk.15	The thing to do	
1394	tk.17	Chick's tune	CD GRP GRD5-9819
1395	tk.19	Mona's mood	

-1 shown as pts. 1 & 2 on sides of 45-1921.Pt.1 was reissued on CD BN 4-94030-2.
All titles issued on BN BLP4178/BST84178,Mosaic MQ6-178;CD BN 7-84178-2,Mosaic MD4-178.

WAYNE SHORTER - JUJU:
Wayne Shorter(ts) McCoy Tyner(p) Reggie Workman(b) Elvin Jones(dm).
Englewood Cliffs,N.J.,August 3,1964

1396	tk.10	Yes or no	CD BN(J)CJ25-5181/84,CJ28-5039,TOCJ-6271/74, TOCJ-66049
1397	tk.12	Mahjong	CD BN 8-59072-2
1398	tk.15	House of jade	
	tk.16	House of jade (alt.)	
	tk.18	Juju (alt.)	
1399	tk.19	Juju	CD BN 7-91141-2,(J)CJ28-5039
1400	tk.27	Deluge	
1401	tk.29	Twelve more bars to go	

All titles,except tks.16 & 18,issued on BN BLP4182/BST84182,CD 7-46514-2
All titles issued on CD BN 8-37644-2,4-99005-2.

JACKIE McLEAN - IT'S TIME:
Charles Tolliver(tp) Jackie McLean(as) Herbie Hancock(p) Cecil McBee(b) Roy Haynes(dm).
Englewood Cliffs,N.J.,August 5,1964

1402	tk.5	Truth	
1403	tk.17	Snuff	
1404	tk.18	Das dat	CD BN(J)CJ28-5163
1405	tk.24	Revillot	
1406	tk.31	Cancellation	
1407	tk.33	It's time	CD BN(J)CJ25-5181/84,TOCJ-66046

All titles issued on BN BLP4179/BST84179,Mosaic MQ6-150,CD BN(J)TOCJ-4179,Mosaic MD4-150.

 170

<u>LEE MORGAN</u> - <u>TOM CAT</u>:
Lee Morgan(tp) Curtis Fuller(tb) Jackie McLean(as) McCoy Tyner(p) Bob Cranshaw(b) Art Blakey(dm).
Englewood Cliffs,N.J.,August 11,1964

1408 tk.7 Exotique
1409 tk.8 Tom Cat
1410 tk.14 Twice around
1411 tk.29 Rigormortis (*aka* Riggormortes)
1412 tk.35 Twilight mist CD BN 8-54901-2

All titles issued on BN LT-1058,CD 7-84446-2.

<u>HORACE SILVER QUINTET</u>:
Carmell Jones(tp) Joe Henderson(ts) Horace Silver(p) Teddy Smith(b) Roger Humphries(dm).
(Live at Pep's) Philadelphia,Pa.,August 15,1964

tk.1 I'll remember April rejected
tk.2 The kicker -
tk.3 Pretty eyes -
tk.4 Que pasa -
tk.5 Skinny Minnie -
tk.6 Mexican hip dance -
tk.7 The natives are restless tonight -
tk.8 Que pasa -
tk.9 The kicker -
tk.10 Mexican hip dance -
tk.11 The natives are restless tonight -
tk.12 Skinny Minnie -
tk.13 Pretty eyes -
tk.14 Que pasa -
tk.15 Mexican hip dance -
tk.16 The kicker -
tk.17 Pretty eyes -
tk.18 The natives are restless tonight -
tk.19 Que pasa -
tk.20 The kicker -
tk.21 The natives are restless tonight -
tk.22 Que pasa -
tk.23 The kicker -

Note: Above titles were recorded during afternoon and night sets.Further titles from these sessions were not recorded.Four master numbers were arbitrarily assigned:

1413 The natives are restless tonight
1414 Que pasa
1415 Pretty eyes
1416 The kicker

171

ANTHONY WILLIAMS - LIFE TIME:
Sam Rivers(ts) Richard Davis,Gary Peacock(b) Anthony Williams(dm).
Englewood Cliffs,N.J.,August 21,1964

	Two pieces of one:	
1417 tk.5	Green	
1418 tk.7	Red	
1419 tk.9	Tomorrow afternoon (Davis out)	BN(J)W-5513 CD BN(F)8-54194-2,(J)CJ25-5181/84

All titles issued on BN BLP4180/BST84180,CD 7-84180-2 4-99004-2.
Note: Bass credits were incorrectly listed on CD 7-84180-2.

Herbie Hancock(p) Ron Carter(b).
Englewood Cliffs,N.J.,August 24,1964

1420 tk.12	Barb's song to the wizard	BN BLP4180/BST84180 CD BN 7-84180-2,4-99004-2

Bobby Hutcherson(vb,marimba) Herbie Hancock(p) Anthony Williams(dm,tympani,woodblocks,maracas, triangle).
Englewood Cliffs,N.J.,August 24,1964

1421 tk.17	Memory	BN BLP4180/BST84180 CD BN 7-84180-2,4-99004-2

STANLEY TURRENTINE - Mr. NATURAL:
Lee Morgan(tp) Stanley Turrentine(ts) McCoy Tyner(p) Bob Cranshaw(b) Elvin Jones(dm) Ray Barretto (cga).
Englewood Cliffs,N.J.,September 4,1964

1422 tk.1	Shirley	
1423 tk.11	Stanley's blues (*aka* Wahoo)	
1424 tk.14	Tacos	CD BN(Eu)7-89915-2
1425 tk.22	Can't buy me love (cga out)	CD BN 7-94861-2,(Eu)4-93991-2,(J)CJ28-5170, TOCJ-5296
1426 tk.23	My girl (tp,cga out)	

Note: Takes 1 & 14 were first scheduled on BN BLP4234/BST84234,which were never released.
All titles issued on BN LT-1075.

JACKIE McLEAN:
Charles Tolliver(tp) Jackie McLean(as) Bobby Hutcherson(vb) Cecil McBee(b) Steve Ellington(dm).
Englewood Cliffs,N.J.,September 9,1964

1427	Plight	rejected
1428	Wrong handle	-

<u>GRANT GREEN</u> - <u>TALKIN' ABOUT</u>:
Larry Young(org) Grant Green(g) Elvin Jones(dm).
Englewood Cliffs,N.J.,September 11,1964

1429 tk.3	Talkin' about J.C.	BN B1-89622,(J)TOJJ-5849 CD BN 7-99177-2,7-89622-2,8-33205-2, (J)TOCJ-5644,TOCJ-5849,TOCJ-66045
1430 tk.8	People	
1431 tk.12	Luny tune	
1432 tk.14	I'm an old cowhand	CD BN(J)TOCJ-5740
1433 tk.17	You don't know what love is	

All titles issued on BN BLP4183/BST84183,Mosaic MR9-137,CD BN 5-21958-2,(J)TOCJ-4183,Mosaic MD6-137.

<u>KENNY DORHAM</u> - <u>TROMPETA TOCCATA</u>:
Kenny Dorham(tp) Joe Henderson(ts) Tommy Flanagan(p) Richard Davis(b) Albert Heath(dm).
Englewood Cliffs,N.J.,September 14,1964

1434 tk.4	The fox	CD BN 8-53648-2
1435 tk.6	Night watch	
1436 tk.10	Trompeta toccata	
1437 tk.11	Mamacita	BN 45-1922,CD 7-89287-2

All titles issued on BN BLP4181/BST84181,CD 7-84181-2.
Note: The CD reissue incorrectly lists the recording date as September 4,1964.

<u>JACKIE McLEAN</u> - <u>ACTION</u>:
Charles Tolliver(tp) Jackie McLean(as) Bobby Hutcherson(vb) Cecil McBee(b) Billy Higgins (dm).
Englewood Cliffs,N.J.,September 16,1964

1438 tk.1	Action	
1439 tk.3	Wrong handle	
1440 tk.15	I hear a rhapsody	CD BN(J)TOCJ-66046,Cema GSC Music 15131
1441 tk.19	Plight	
1442 tk.20	Hootnan -1	

-1: as "Hootman" on Mosaic issues.
All titles issued on BN BLP4218/BST84218,Mosaic MQ6-150,CD BN(J)TOCJ-4218,Mosaic MD4-150.

<u>FREDDIE ROACH</u> - <u>ALL THAT'S GOOD</u>:
Conrad Lester(ts) Freddie Roach(org) Calvin Newborn(g) Clarence Johnston(dm) Phyllis Smith,Willie Tate, Marvin Robinson(vo).
Englewood Cliffs,N.J.,October 16,1964

1444 tk.8	Blues for 007
1445 tk.15	Busted
1446 tk.22	Loie
1447 tk.32	Cloud 788
1448 tk.33	All that's good
1443 tk.45	Journeyman

All titles issued on BN BLP4190/BST84190,CD BN(J)TOCJ-4190.

173

KENNY BURRELL - FREEDOM:
Stanley Turrentine(ts) Herbie Hancock(p) Kenny Burrell(g) Ben Tucker(b) Bill English(dm) Ray Barretto (cga).
Englewood Cliffs,N.J.,October 22,1964

1449 tk.2 Love,your magic spell is everywhere (ts out)
Lib(J)K22P-6094/95
CD BN 8-30493-2

1450 tk.20 Freedom
1451 tk.25 Lonesome road
1452 tk.31 G minor bash
1453 tk.42 K twist

All titles issued on BN(J)GXF-3057.

HORACE SILVER - SONG FOR MY FATHER:
Carmell Jones(tp) Joe Henderson(ts) Horace Silver(p) Teddy Smith(b) Roger Humphries(dm).
Englewood Cliffs,N.J.,October 26,1964

1454 tk.4 The kicker — BN B2S-5256,CD 7-89287-2,(J)TOCJ-5260, TOCJ-5750

1455 tk.9 Que pasa — BN 45-1913,L4185,B1-93206
CD BN 7-93206-2,7-89287-2,4-95576-2

1456 tk.16 The natives are restless tonight
1457 tk.26 Song for my father — BN 45-1912,L4185,BST89904,BN-LA160-G2, BN-LA402-H2,BST2-84429,BST2-92471, B1-92812,B1-93206,B1-28263
BN(Du)1A158-83395/8,(E)BNX2,(In)JAZ 2
BN(J)NP9020C,LNP95059B,K22P-6096/97, K16P-9031/32,FCPA 6206,W-5506
CD BN 7-92471-2,7-92812-2,7-93206-2, 7-96110-2,8-28263-2,8-33208-2,4-95576-2, 5-20070-2,(C)8-56508-2,(E)8-53228-2, (F)8-54191-2,(J)CJ28-5033, CJ28-5171, CP32-5057,TOCJ-5296,TOCJ-5793,TOCJ-5827, TOCJ-5925,TOCJ-5933,TOCJ-5963,TOCJ-66034, TOCP-50230,(Sp)8-34712-2,8-53016-2,
32 Jazz 32025-2,The Right Stuff 8-57071-2,
Cema S21-57589,S21-57592,
EMI-Jazz(E)4-93466-2,4-93469-2,
EMI-Music 4-98900-2

All titles issued on BN BLP4185/BST84185,CD 7-84185-2,4-99002-2,(J)TOCJ-4185.

SOLOMON ILORI:
Solomon Ilori(vo) with Donald Byrd(tp) Hubert Laws(fl-1,ts-2) Bob Cranshaw(b) Elvin Jones(dm) Chief Bey,Roger Sanders,Ladji Camara,Sunny Morgan(perc,vo) Coleridge Perkinson (musical director).
Englewood Cliffs,N.J.,October 30,1964

1458 tk.4 Bamu bamu l'ayo (I have the strength to sing)-1,3 — unissued
1459 tk.11 Toni omo re (Loving your child)-1,4 — -
1460 tk.17 Agbamurero (Rhino)-1,3 — -
1461 tk.25 Gbogbo omo ibile(Going home)-2 — -
1462 tk.33 Igbesi aiye (Song of praise to God)(instr.)-2 — -

-3: lead vocal with group vocal on these titles.
-4: lead vocal only on this title.

174

WAYNE SHORTER:
Freddie Hubbard(tp) Wayne Shorter(ts) Herbie Hancock(p) Ron Carter(b) Billy Higgins(dm).
Englewood Cliffs,N.J.,November 2,1964

1462?		Witch hunt	rejected
		Dance cadaverous	-
		Speak no evil	-

DUKE PEARSON:
Donald Byrd(tp) James Spaulding(as) Joe Henderson(ts) Duke Pearson(p) Bob Cranshaw(b) Otis Finch (dm).
Englewood Cliffs,N.J.,November 6,1964

1463		Amanda	rejected
		E.S.P.	-
		Fly,little bird,fly	-

LARRY YOUNG - INTO SOMETHIN':
Sam Rivers(ts) Larry Young(org) Grant Green(g) Elvin Jones(dm).
Englewood Cliffs,N.J.,November 12,1964

1464	tk.3	Plaza de toros	BN B1-96563 CD BN 7-96563-2,(E)8-53234-2,(J)TOCJ-5733
1465	tk.5	Tyrone	CD BN 7-99177-2
1466	tk.9	Back up	CD BN(J)TOCJ-6067
1467	tk.10	Paris eyes	CD BN 7-99100-2
	tk.22	Ritha (quartet version)	
1468	tk.23	Ritha -1	

-1: Rivers out.
All titles,except tk.22,issued on BN BLP4187/BST84187,CD BN(J)TOCJ-4187.
All titles issued on Mosaic MR9-137,CD BN 8-21734-2,Mosaic MD6-137.

GRANT GREEN - STREET OF DREAMS:
Bobby Hutcherson(vb) Larry Young(org) Grant Green(g) Elvin Jones(dm).
Englewood Cliffs,N.J.,November 16,1964

1469	tk.5	Lazy afternoon	BN BLP4253/BST84253,B1-89622,CD 7-89622-2
1470	tk.8	I wish you love	-
1471	tk.12	Somewhere in the night	- CD 8-33205-2
1472		This is all I ask	rejected
1473	tk.26	Street of dreams	BN BLP4253/BST84253

All titles from BST84253 also issued on Mosaic MR9-137,CD BN 8-21290-2,Mosaic MD6-137.

DONALD BYRD:
Donald Byrd(tp) Jimmy Heath(ts) McCoy Tyner(p) Walter Booker(b) Joe Chambers(dm).
Englewood Cliffs,N.J.,November 18,1964

1474	tk.6	I am so excited by you	CD BN 8-59963-2
	tk.9	Gingerbread boy	-

 175

<u>DUKE PEARSON</u> - <u>WAHOO!</u>:
Donald Byrd(tp) James Spaulding(fl-1,as) Joe Henderson(ts) Duke Pearson(p) Bob Cranshaw(b) Mickey Roker(dm).

Englewood Cliffs,N.J.,November 21,1964

1475	tk.3	Amanda	CD BN 7-89287-2,5-21152-2
1476	tk.6	E.S.P. (Extra sensory preception)	CD BN(J)TOCJ-5882
1477	tk.12	Bedouin -1	
1478	tk.15	Wahoo -1	BN B1-57745,CD 8-57745-2,(J)TOCJ-6271/74
1479	tk.22	Fly,little bird,fly	
1480	tk.28	Farewell Machelle (horns out)	

All titles issued on BN BLP4191/BST84191,CD 7-84191-2.

<u>JOE HENDERSON</u> - <u>INNER URGE</u>:
Joe Henderson(ts) McCoy Tyner(p) Bob Cranshaw(b) Elvin Jones(dm).

Englewood Cliffs,N.J.,November 30,1964

1481	tk.2	Inner urge	
1482	tk.10	You know I care	CD BN 8-56692-2
1483	tk.15	Isotope	CD BN 7-89287-2
1484	tk.21	Night and day	Lib(J)K22P-6131/32 CD BN 7-95591-2
1485	tk.23	El barrio	CD BN 7-95627-2,7-89287-2

All titles issued on BN BLP4189/BST84189,CD 7-84189-2.

<u>SAM RIVERS</u> - <u>FUCHSIA SWING SONG</u>:
Sam Rivers(ts) Jaki Byard(p) Ron Carter(b) Anthony Williams(dm).

Englewood Cliffs,N.J.,December 11,1964

1487	tk.3	Fuchsia swing song	
1488	tk.6	Cyclic episode	
1489	tk.10	Luminous monolith	BN(Du)1A158-83395/8 CD BN(F)8-54194-2
	tk.12	Luminous monolith (alt.)	
1490	tk.15	Ellipsis	
	tk.17	Downstairs blues upstairs (alt.1)	
	tk.18	Downstairs blues upstairs (alt.2)	
	tk.19	Downstairs blues upstairs (alt.3)	
1491	tk.20	Downstairs blues upstairs	
1492	tk.23	Beatrice	

All titles issued on Mosaic MQ5-167,CD MD3-167.
All titles,except tks.12,17,18 & 19,issued on BN BLP4184/BST84184,CD BN(J)TOCJ-4184.

<u>DONALD BYRD</u> - <u>I'M TRYIN' TO GET HOME</u>:
Ernie Royal,Snooky Young,Jimmy Owens,Clark Terry(tp) Donald Byrd(tp,flh) J.J. Johnson,Jimmy Cleveland,Henry Coker,Benny Powell(tb) Jim Buffington,Bob Northern(frh) Don Butterfield(tu) Stanley Turrentine(ts) Freddie Roach(org) Herbie Hancock(p) Grant Green(g) Bob Cranshaw(b) Grady Tate(dm) & vocal choir (8 voices) dir.& cond. by Coleridge Perkinson,Duke Pearson(arr).

Englewood Cliffs,N.J.,December 17,1964

1493	tk.3	I'm tryin' to get home	
1494	tk.5	March children	
1495	tk.11	Brother Isaac	BN 45-1916,CD 4-94030-2

All titles issued on BN BLP4188/BST84188,CD 7-84188-2.

176

DONALD BYRD - I'M TRYIN' TO GET HOME:
Ernie Royal,Snooky Young,Jimmy Owens,Joe Ferrante(tp)Donald Byrd(tp,flh) J.J. Johnson,Jimmy Cleveland, Henry Coker,Benny Powell(tb) Jim Buffington,Bob Northern(frh) Don Butterfield(tu) Stanley Turrentine(ts) Herbie Hancock(p) Bob Cranshaw(b) Grady Tate(dm) unknown(chimes-1,perc,tamb) & vocal choir (8 voices) dir.& cond. by Coleridge Perkinson,Duke Pearson(arr).
Englewood Cliffs,N.J.,December 18,1964

1496 tk.17 I've longed and searched for my mother -1
BN 45-1916

1497 tk.20 Noah
1498 tk.26 Pearly gates

All titles issued on BN BLP4188/BST84188,CD 7-84188-2.

WAYNE SHORTER - SPEAK NO EVIL:
Freddie Hubbard(tp) Wayne Shorter(ts) Herbie Hancock(p) Ron Carter(b) Elvin Jones(dm).
Englewood Cliffs,N.J.,December 24,1964

1499	tk.6	Witch hunt	CD BN 8-59072-2,(J)CJ28-5039,TOCJ-66049
1500	tk.12	Wild flower	
1501	tk.14	Speak no evil	BN B1-91141,BST2-92468,BST2-92468 BN(Du)1A158-83395/8 CD BN 7-91141-2,7-92468-2,(C)8-56508-2, (F)8-54191-2,J)CJ28-5039,TOCJ-66049
1502	tk.17	Infant eyes (tp out)	BN B1-91141,CD 7-91141-2,8-34873-2
1503	tk.25	Fee-fi-fo-fum	CD BN 8-59072-2
1504	tk.27	Dance cadaverous	
	tk.30	Dance cadaverous (alt)	

All titles issued on CD BN 4-99001-2.
All titles,except tk.30,issued on BN BLP4194/BST84194,B1-46509,CD 7-46509-2.

CHARLIE ROUSE:
Freddie Hubbard(tp) Charlie Rouse(ts) McCoy Tyner(p) Bob Cranshaw(b) Billy Higgins(dm).
Englewood Cliffs,N.J.,January 22,1965

1505	tk.1	One for five	CD BN 5-21484-2
1506	tk.9	Little Sherri	rejected
		untitled original	-
		untitled minor blues	-
1507		I'm glad there is you	-

JACKIE McLEAN - RIGHT NOW:
Jackie McLean(as) Larry Willis(p) Bob Cranshaw(b) Clifford Jarvis(dm).
Englewood Cliffs,N.J.,January 29,1965

1508	tk.2	Right now	BN BLP4215/BST84215
	tk.3	Right now (alt.)	
1509	tk.10	Poor Eric	BN BLP4215/BST84215
1510	tk.15	Christel's time	-
1511	tk.22	Eco	-

All titles issued on CD BN 7-84215-2,Mosaic MQ6-150,CD Mosaic MD4-150.
All titles from BST842Ò15 also issued on CD BN(J)TOCJ-4215.

177

HANK MOBLEY - THE TURNAROUND!:
Freddie Hubbard(tp) Hank Mobley(ts) Barry Harris(p) Paul Chambers(b) Billy Higgins(dm).
Englewood Cliffs,N.J.,February 5,1965

1512 tk.7	Pat' n' chat	BN BLP4186/BST84186
1513 tk.9	Third time around	BN BST84435,CD 5-27549-2
1514 tk.15	Hank's waltz	- -
1515 tk.19	The turnaround -1	BN 45-1915,BLP4186/BST84186 CD BN 8-37052-2,4-94030-2,(F)8-54188-2
1516 tk.23	Straight ahead (*aka* Kismet)	BN BLP4186/BST84186
1517 tk.25	My sin	-

-1: shown as pts. 1 & 2 on sides of 45-1915.Pt.1 was reissued on CD BN 4-94030-2.
All titles issued on CD BN 7-84186-2.
All titles from BST84186 also issued on CD BN 5-24540-2,(J)TOCJ-4186.

ANDREW HILL:
Freddie Hubbard(c) Joe Henderson(ts) Andrew Hill(p) Richard Davis(b) Joe Chambers(dm).
Englewood Cliffs,N.J.,February 10,1965

1518 tk.2	Euterpe (Intuition)	BN BN-LA459-H2	
tk.4	Euterpe (Intuition) (alt.)		
1519 tk.6	Calliope (Deception)	BN BN-LA459-H2	
1520 tk.7	Pax (Image of time)	-	CD 7-89287-2
1521 tk.8	Eris (Heritage)	-	
1522 tk.10	Erato (Moon chile) (c,ts out)	BN BN-LA459-H2	
1523 tk.11	Roots 'n herbs (c,ts out)		

All titles issued on Mosaic MQ10-161,CD MD7-161.

FREDDIE HUBBARD - BLUE SPIRITS:
Freddie Hubbard(tp) Bernard McKinney (Kiane Zawadi)(euph) James Spaulding(fl-1,as-2) Joe Henderson (ts) Harold Mabern(p) Larry Ridley(b) Clifford Jarvis(dm) Big Black(cga).
Englewood Cliffs,N.J.,February 19,1965

1524	Outer forces -2	rejected
1525 tk.24	Soul surge -2	BN BLP4196,CD 7-46545-2
1526 tk.26	Cunga black -1,2	- -

All titles from BLP4196 (mono) also issued on BN BST84196,CD BN(J)TOCJ-4196 (stereo).

Freddie Hubbard(tp) Bernard McKinney (Kiane Zawadi)(euph) James Spaulding(fl-1,as-2) Hank Mobley(ts) McCoy Tyner(p) Bob Cranshaw(b) Pete La Roca(dm).
Englewood Cliffs,N.J.,February 26,1965

1527 tk.3	Jodo -2	BN BN-LA356-H2 CD BN 8-59071-2,(J)CJ28-5164,TOCJ-1621
1528 tk.11	Blue spirits -1,2	
1529 tk.15	Outer forces -2	BN B1-93202,CD 7-93202-2

All titles issued on BN BLP4196/BST84196,CD 7-46545-2,(J)TOCJ-4196.

178

WAYNE SHORTER - THE SOOTHSAYER:
Freddie Hubbard(tp) James Spaulding(as) Wayne Shorter(ts) McCoy Tyner(p) Reggie Workman(b) Tony Williams(dm).

Englewood Cliffs,N.J.,March 4,1965

	tk.7	Angola (alt.)	CD BN(J)TOCJ-6141	
1531	tk.11	Lost	BN LT-988,B1-91141,CD 7-91141-2	
1532	tk.12	Valse triste	-	
1533	tk.14	The big push	-	
1534	tk.17	The soothsayer	-	
1535	tk.20	Lady Day	-	(E)UALP21;CD BN 4-97154-2
1530	tk.22	Angola	-	CD BN(J)TOCJ-66049

All titles issued on CD BN 7-84443-2.

BIG JOHN PATTON - OH BABY!:
Blue Mitchell(tp) Harold Vick(ts) John Patton(org) Grant Green(g) Ben Dixon(dm).

Englewood Cliffs,N.J.,March 8,1965

1536	tk.7	One to twelve	
1537	tk.10	Night flight	BN(Du)1A158-83395/8
1538	tk.21	Oh baby	
1539	tk.27	Each time	CD BN(J)TOCJ-5882
1540	tk.29	Good juice	CD BN(J)TOCJ-5644
1541	tk.33	Fat Judy	BN 45-1920,B1-96563,B1-30728 CD BN 7-96563-2,8-30728-2

-1: shown as pts. 1 & 2 on sides of 45-1920.Pt.1 was reissued on CD BN 4-94030-2,4-97222-2.
All titles issued on BN BLP4192/BST84192,CD BN(J)TOCJ-4192.

HERBIE HANCOCK:
Freddie Hubbard(tp) George Coleman(ts) Herbie Hancock(p) Ron Carter(b) Stu Martin(dm).

Englewood Cliffs,N.J.,March 11,1965

1542	Maiden voyage	rejected
1543	Dolphin dance	-
1544	Little one	-

HERBIE HANCOCK - MAIDEN VOYAGE:
Freddie Hubbard(tp) George Coleman(ts) Herbie Hancock(p) Ron Carter(b) Anthony Williams(dm).
Englewood Cliffs,N.J.,March 17,1965

1545 tk.2	Maiden voyage	BN BST89907,BN-LA399-H2,BST2-84429, B1-91142,BST2-92468 BN(Du)1A158-83395/8,(G)F671097, (J)NP9022,FCPA 6214,W-5513 CD BN 7-91142-2,7-92468-2,7-96110-2, 8-29331-2,(C)8-33908-2,8-56508-2,(Eu)8-29964-2, (F)8-54191-2,4-97517-2,(J)CJ28-5040,CJ28-5171, CP32-5056,TOCJ-5637,TOCJ-5830,TOCJ-5933, TOCJ-5966,TOCJ-6110,TOCJ-6141,TOCJ-6188, TOCJ-66050,TOCJ-66051,TOCP-8963, TOCP-7455/56,(Sp)8-34712-2, Toshiba-EMI(J)TOCJ-6098/99,TOCP-8581, The Right Stuff 8-57071-2
1546 tk.4	The eye of the hurricane	BN(E)BNX 1,UALP 17 CD BN 7-48337-2,8-54904-2,(J)CJ28-5030, CJ28-5040,TOCJ-5637,TOCJ-5830,TOCJ-5966, TOCJ-6110,TOCJ-66050
1547 tk.6	Dolphin dance	BN B1-91142,CD 7-91142-2,(J)TOCJ-5966
1548 tk.9	Survival of the fittest	
1549 tk.10	Little one	

All titles issued on BN BLP4195/BST84195,CD 7-46339-2,4-95331-2,4-95569-2.

GRANT GREEN - I WANT TO HOLD YOUR HAND:
Hank Mobley(ts) Larry Young(org) Grant Green(g) Elvin Jones(dm).
Englewood Cliffs,N.J.,March 31,1965

1550 tk.2	Corcovado (Quiet nights)	BN 45-1919,L4202 CD BN 8-35283-2,Cap(J)TOCJ-5229
1551 tk.4	At long last love	CD BN 7-95591-2
1552 tk.10	Speak low	CD BN 7-27312-2,(C)8-56508-2
1553 tk.11	This could be the start of something big (ts out)	
1554 tk.16	I want to hold your hand	BN 45-1919,L4202 CD BN 7-94861-2,(J)CJ28-5169,TOCJ-5874, TOCJ-6134,TOCJ-6188,TOCJ-66045, Cap(J)TOCJ-5201
1555 tk.21	Stella by starlight	

All titles issued on BN BLP4202/BST84202,Mosaic MR9-137,CD Mosaic MD6-137,BN 8-59962-2.

BOBBY HUTCHERSON - DIALOGUE:
Freddie Hubbard(tp) Sam Rivers(fl-1,ss-2,ts-3,bass cl-4) Bobby Hutcherson(vb,marimba-5) Andrew Hill(p) Richard Davis(b) Joe Chambers(dm).
Englewood Cliffs,N.J.,April 3,1965

1556 tk.3	Catta -3	BN BLP4198;CD BN(J)CJ25-5181/84
1557 tk.11	Jasper -3,4	BN LT-996,(E)UALP21
1558 tk.18	Idle while -1	BN BLP4198
1559 tk.24	Ghetto lights -2,4	-
1560 tk.29	Les noirs marchent -1	-
1561 tk.30	Dialogue -4,5	-

All titles from BLP4198 (mono) also issued on BN BST84198,CD BN(J)TOCJ-4198.
All titles also issued on CD BN 7-46537-2.

LEE MORGAN:
Lee Morgan(tp) Joe Henderson(ts) Ronnie Mathews(p) Victor Sproles(b) Billy Higgins(dm).
Englewood Cliffs,N.J.,April 9,1965

1562 tk.2/4	Venus di mildew	CD BN 7-46428-2,5-21229-2
	Desert moonlight	rejected

Note: The CD incorrectly lists the recording date as April 19, 1965.

FREDDIE HUBBARD - LIVE AT CLUB LA MARCHAL/THE NIGHT OF THE COOKERS:
Freddie Hubbard,Lee Morgan(tp)James Spaulding(as)Harold Mabern(p)Larry Ridley(b)Pete La Roca(dm)Big Black(cga).
(Club La Marchal,Brooklyn) NYC,April 9,1965

1601	Jodo (Morgan out)
1598	Breaking point

Both titles issued on BN BLP4208/BST84208,CD 8-28882-2,(J)TOCJ-4208.

Same with James Spaulding(fl-1,as).
(Club La Marchal,Brooklyn) NYC,April 10,1965

1599	Pensativa -1
1600	Walkin' (Hubbard out)

Both titles issued on BN BLP4207/BST84207,CD 8-28882-2,(J)TOCJ-4207.

STANLEY TURRENTINE:
Ernie Royal,Snooky Young(tp) Clark Terry(tp,flh) Henry Coker,Jimmy Cleveland,Tony Studd(tb) Phil Woods(cl,as) Jerry Dodgion(fl,alto fl,picc,cl,as) Budd Johnson(cl,ss,ts,bass cl) Bob Ashton(cl,ts) Danny Bank(fl,alto fl,cl,bass cl,bs) Stanley Turrentine(ts) Roger Kellaway(p) Kenny Burrell(g) Bob Cranshaw(b) Grady Tate(dm) Oliver Nelson(arr,cond).
Englewood Cliffs,N.J.,April 13,1965

	A kettle of fish	rejected
1563	Bayou	-
1564	Mattie J	-

STANLEY TURRENTINE - JOYRIDE:
Ernie Royal,Snooky Young(tp) Clark Terry(tp,flh) J.J.Johnson,Jimmy Cleveland,Tony Studd(tb) Phil Woods(cl,as) Jerry Dodgion(fl,alto fl,picc,cl,as) Budd Johnson(cl,ss,ts,bass cl) Bob Ashton(cl,ts) Danny Bank(fl,alto fl,cl,bass cl,bs) Stanley Turrentine(ts) Herbie Hancock(p) Kenny Burrell(g) Bob Cranshaw(b) Grady Tate(dm) Oliver Nelson(arr,cond).

Englewood Cliffs,N.J.,April 14,1965

1563 tk.2	Bayou	BN BLP4201
1570 tk.10	Gravy train	
1567 tk.16	I wonder where our love has gone	BN BLP4201
1566 tk.23	Little Sheri	-
1565 tk.28	A taste of honey	- CD BN(J)CJ28-5170
1569 tk.30	River's invitation	BN 45-1917,L4201,BLP4201,BST89904, BN-LA160-G2,B1-93201 BN(Du)1A158-83395/8,(J)BNJ71106 CD BN 7-93201-2,4-97155-2,(F)8-54188-2, (J)TOCJ-5758,Cema S21-57590,HMV Jazz(E) 5-20883-2
1568 tk.33	A kettle of fish	
1564 tk.34	Mattie T	BN L4201,BLP4201

All titles issued on CD BN 7-46100-2.
All titles from BLP4201 (mono) also issued on BN BST84201,CD BN(J)TOCJ-4201 (stereo).

LEE MORGAN - THE RUMPROLLER:
Lee Morgan(tp) Joe Henderson(ts) Ronnie Mathews(p) Victor Sproles(b) Billy Higgins(dm).

Englewood Cliffs,N.J.,April 21,1965

1571 tk.2	The rumproller -1	BN 45-1918,BST2-84433,B1-91138 CD BN 7-91138-2,7-97960-2
1572 tk.3	Desert moonlight	CD BN(J)CJ28-5037,TOCJ-5828,TOCJ-66039
1573 tk.5	Edda	
1574 tk.7	Eclipso	CD BN 4-97156-2
1575 tk.9	The lady	

-1: shown as pts. 1 & 2 on sides of 45-1918.Pt.1 was reissued on CD BN 4-94030-2.
All titles issued on BN BLP4199/BST84199,CD 7-46428-2,5-21229-2,(J)TOCJ-4199.

PETE LA ROCA - BASRA:
Joe Henderson(ts) Steve Kuhn(p) Steve Swallow(b) Pete La Roca(dm).

Englewood Cliffs,N.J.,May 19,1965

1576 tk.8	Candu	
1577 tk.15	Malaguena	CD BN 7-89287-2
1578 tk.16	Basra	
1579 tk.18	Lazy afternoon	CD BN 7-89287-2,7-96098-2,8-56692-2, (F)8-54191-2
1580 tk.19	Eiderdown	CD BN(J)TOCJ-5740
1581 tk.20	Tears come from heaven	

All titles issued on BN BLP4205/BST84205,B1-32091,CD 8-32091-2.

182

SAM RIVERS - CONTOURS:
Freddie Hubbard(tp Sam Rivers(fl-1,ss-2,ts-3) Herbie Hancock(p) Ron Carter(b) Joe Chambers(dm).
Englewood Cliffs,N.J.,May 21,1965

1582	tk.6	Point of many returns -2	CD BN 8-35414-2
1583	tk.10	Dance of the tripedal -3	
1584	tk.12	Mellifluous cacophony -3	
1585	tk.18	Euterpe -1	
	tk.25	Mellifluous cacophony (alt.)-3	

All titles,except alt.,issued on BN BLP4206/BST84206.
All titles issued on Mosaic MQ5-167,CD MD3-167.

DEXTER GORDON - CLUBHOUSE:
Freddie Hubbard(tp) Dexter Gordon(ts) Barry Harris(p) Bob Cranshaw(b) Billy Higgins(dm).
Englewood Cliffs,N.J.,May 27,1965

1586	tk.3	Hanky panky	BN(E)UALP21
1587	tk.5	Devilette-1	
1588	tk.7	Clubhouse	
1589	tk.14	Jodi (tp out)	
1590	tk.17	I'm a fool to want you	CD BN 7-96579-2,(J)TOCJ-6187,TOCJ-66047, (Sp)5-21755-2,EMI-Jazz(E)4-99159-2, Toshiba-EMI(J)TOCP-65352
1591	tk.22	Lady Iris B	

-1: Ben Tucker(b) replaces Cranshaw.
All titles issued on BN LT-989,CD 7-84445-2,8-34200-2.

DEXTER GORDON - GETTIN' AROUND:
Dexter Gordon(ts) Bobby Hutcherson(vb) Barry Harris(p) Bob Cranshaw(b) Billy Higgins(dm).
Englewood Cliffs,N.J.,May 28,1965

1592	tk.4	Le coiffeur	BN BLP4204 CD BN 7-99100-2,Toshiba-EMI(J)TOCJ-6228
1593	tk.11	Manha de carnaval	BN BLP4204 Lib(J)K22P-6131/32 CD BN(J)CJ28-5024,CJ28-5038,CJ28-5172, TOCJ-5260,TOCJ-5934,TOCJ-66047, TOCP-50230,Cap(J)TOCJ-5204
		Very saxily yours	rejected
	tk.23	Flick of a trick	
1594	tk.28	Everybody's somebody's fool	BN BLP4204

All titles,excepted the rejected one,issued on CD BN 7-46681-2,8-34200-2.
All titles from BLP4204 (mono) also issued on BN BST84204,CD BN(J)TOCJ-4204 (stereo).

Same.
Englewood Cliffs,N.J.,May 29,1965

	tk.6	Very saxily yours	
1595	tk.10	Shiny stockings	BN BLP4204,BN-LA393-H2
1596	tk.15	Who can I turn to	-
1597	tk.17	Heartaches	- CD 8-23514-2

All titles issued on CD BN 7-46681-2,8-34200-2.
All titles from BLP4204 (mono) also issued on BN BST84204,CD BN(J)TOCJ-4204 (stereo).

1598/1601: see page 180 (April 9/10,1965 sessions).

<u>BOBBY HUTCHERSON</u> - <u>COMPONENTS</u>:
Freddie Hubbard(tp) James Spaulding(fl-1,as) Bobby Hutcherson(vb & marimba-2) Herbie Hancock(p & org-3) Ron Carter(b) Joe Chambers(dm).
Englewood Cliffs,N.J.,June 10,1965

1602	tk.2	Components	
1603	tk.17	Tranquility	
1604	tk.26	Little B's poem -1	BN BST2-92468,(Du)1A158-83395/8,(J)TOJJ-5849 CD BN 7-92468-2,(J)TOCJ-5849,HMV Jazz(E) 5-20868-2
1605	tk.28	Juba dance -1,2	
1606	tk.37	Movement -1,2	
1607	tk.41	Air -2,3	
1608	tk.50	Pastoral	
	tk.51	West 22nd Street theme	CD BN(F)8-54191-2

All titles issued on BN BLP4213/BST84213,B1-29027,CD 8-29027-2.
Note: 29027 issues incorrectly state recording date as June 14.

<u>WAYNE SHORTER</u> - <u>ET CETERA</u>:
Wayne Shorter(ts) Herbie Hancock(p) Cecil McBee(b) Joe Chambers(dm).
Englewood Cliffs,N.J.,June 14,1965

1609	tk.3	Barracudas -1	BN(J)GXF-3059
1610	tk.7	Indian song (Shairkhan the tiger)	- TOJJ-5849,CD TOCJ-5849
1611	tk.16	Toy tune	
1612	tk.20	Penelope	BN(J)GXF-3059
1613	tk.22	Etcetera	- CD TOCJ-66049

-1: *aka* "Time of the barracudas" and "General assembly".
All titles issued on BN LT-1056,B1-33581,CD 8-33581-2.

<u>HANK MOBLEY</u> - <u>DIPPIN'</u>:
Lee Morgan(tp) Hank Mobley(ts) Harold Mabern(p) Larry Ridley(b) Billy Higgins(dm).
Englewood Cliffs,N.J.,June 18,1965

1615	tk.10	Recado bossa nova	BN(E)BNSLP-4 CD BN 7-95590-2,8-37052-2,(J)CJ28-5021, CJ28-5035,CJ28-5172,CJ32-5016,TOCJ-5203, TOCJ-5852,TOCJ-5925,TOCJ-5933,TOCJ-66043, TOCJ-66052,TOCP-7455/56,TOCP-50230
1616	tk.22	Ballin'	
1617	tk.27	The vamp	
1618	tk.31	The dip	
1619	tk.36	I see your face before me	
1614	tk.37	The breakthrough	

All titles issued on BN BLP4209/BST84209,CD 7-46511-2.

<u>LEE MORGAN</u> - <u>THE GIGOLO</u>:
Lee Morgan(tp) Wayne Shorter(ts) Harold Mabern(p) Bob Cranshaw(b) Billy Higgins(dm).
Englewood Cliffs,N.J.,June 25,1965

1620	tk.3	Trapped	BN BLP4212/BST84212 CD BN 7-84212-2,8-54901-2,(J)TOCJ-4212, (Sp)5-21755-2
1621		The gigolo	rejected
		A stitch in time	-
		Yes I can,no you can't	-

1622-1630: not used.

LEE MORGAN - THE GIGOLO:
Lee Morgan(tp) Wayne Shorter(ts) Harold Mabern(p) Bob Cranshaw(b) Billy Higgins(dm).
Englewood Cliffs,N.J.,July 1,1965

1631 tk.1	The gigolo (alt.)	
1631 tk.3	The gigolo	
1632 tk.11	You go to my head	BN BN-LA224-G
1633 tk.17	Yes I can,no you can't	
1634 tk.32	Speedball	BN BN-LA224-G,B1-91138 CD BN 7-91138-2,(F)8-54191-2,(J)CJ28-5037, TOCJ-6100,TOCJ-66039

All titles issued on CD BN 7-84212-2.
Last four titles issued on BN BLP4212/BST84212,CD BN(J)TOCJ-4212.

BLUE MITCHELL - DOWN WITH IT:
Blue Mitchell(tp) Junior Cook(ts) Chick Corea(p) Gene Taylor(b) Aloysius Foster(dm).
Englewood Cliffs,N.J.,July 14,1965

1635 tk.2	Samba de Stacy	
1636 tk.5	Hi-heel sneakers	BN B1-80679,(J)W-5513 CD BN 7-99105-2,(J)TOCJ-66055
1637 tk.7	Alone,alone and alone	
1638 tk.9	Perception	
1640 tk.25	March on Selma	
1639 tk.32	One shirt	

All titles issued on BN BLP4214/BST84214,B1-54327,Mosaic MQ6-178,CD BN 8-54327-2,Mosaic MD4-178.

JACKIE McLEAN:
Charles Tolliver(tp) Jackie McLean(as) Bobby Hutcherson(vb) Larry Ridley(b) Jack DeJohnette(dm).
Englewood Cliffs,N.J.,July 30,1965

	Climax	rejected
1641	On the Nile	-

ANTHONY WILLIAMS - SPRING:
Wayne Shorter,Sam Rivers(ts) Herbie Hancock(p) Gary Peacock(b) Anthony Williams(dm).
Englewood Cliffs,N.J.,August 12,1965

1642 tk.2	Extras (p out)	
1643 tk.4	Tee	
1644 tk.6	From before	BN(J)K18P-9128
1645 tk.18	Love song (Shorter out)	CD Toshiba-EMI(J)TOCJ-6098/99
1646 tk.19	Echo (dm solo)	

All titles issued on BN BLP4216/BST84216,CD 7-46135-2.

185

<u>FREDDIE ROACH</u>:
Freddie Roach(org) Kahlil Rahman(vb) Eddie Wright(g) Clarence Johnston(dm).
Englewood Cliffs,N.J.,September 16,1965

Matrix	Take	Title	Issue
	tk.4	Bread and butter	rejected
1647	tk.5	Hi heel sneakers	-
1648	tk.6	Avatar blues	-
	tk.10	Spring is here	-
	tk.14	St. Thomas	-
1649	tk.18	King of the road	-

<u>LEE MORGAN</u>:
Lee Morgan(tp) Jackie McLean(as) Hank Mobley(ts) Herbie Hancock(p) Larry Ridley(b) Billy Higgins(dm).
Englewood Cliffs,N.J.,September 17,1965

Matrix	Take	Title	Issue
1650		Most like Lee	rejected
		Ceora (as out)	-
		Our man Higgins	-

<u>LEE MORGAN</u> - <u>CORNBREAD</u>:
Lee Morgan(tp) Jackie McLean(as) Hank Mobley(ts) Herbie Hancock(p) Larry Ridley(b) Billy Higgins(dm).
Englewood Cliffs,N.J.,September 18,1965

Matrix	Take	Title	Issue
1651	tk.1	Ceora (as out)	BN BN-LA224-G,B1-91138 CD BN 7-91138-2,(F)4-97517-2,(J)TOCJ-5828
1652	tk.2	Our man Higgins	CD BN 8-54901-2
1653	tk.6	Most like Lee	BN L4222
1654	tk.12	Cornbread	BN 45-1930,L4222,B1-94704,CD 7-91138-2, 4-94704-2,(Eu)7-89915-2,(J)CJ28-5037, TOCJ-5828,TOCJ-66039
1655	tk.15	Ill wind (as out)	

All titles issued on BN BLP4222/BST84222 CD 7-84222-2.

<u>JACKIE McLEAN</u> - <u>JACKNIFE</u>:
Lee Morgan-1,Charles Tolliver-2 (tp) Jackie McLean(as) Larry Willis(p) Larry Ridley(b) Jack DeJohnette (dm).
Englewood Cliffs,N.J.,September 24,1965

Matrix	Take	Title
1656	tk.4	Soft blue -1,2
1657	tk.7	Climax -1
1658	tk.9	On the Nile -2
1659	tk.11	Jacknife -2
1660	tk.16	Blue fable -1

All titles scheduled on BN BLP4223/BST84223 (not released) and later issued on BN BN-LA457-H2,Mosaic MQ6-150,CD Mosaic MD4-150.

<u>THE HORACE SILVER QUINTET</u> - <u>THE CAPE VERDEAN BLUES</u>:
Woody Shaw(tp) Joe Henderson(ts) Horace Silver(p) Bob Cranshaw(b) Roger Humphries(dm).
Englewood Cliffs,N.J.,October 1,1965

Matrix	Take	Title	Issue
1661	tk.4	Pretty eyes	BN 45-1923,B1-93206,CD 7-93206-2
1662	tk.6	The African queen	BN 45-1924
1663	tk.16	The Cape Verdean blues	BN 45-1923,BN-LA402-H2,B1-93206,(E)BNSLP1 CD BN 7-93206-2,7-95590-2,4-95576-2,(J) TOCJ-5778,TOCJ-5827,TOCJ-5936,TOCJ-66034, Cema S21-57589,EMI-Jazz(E)4-93466-2, HMV Jazz(E)5-20885-2,Premier(E)CDJA 2

All titles issued on BN BLP4220/BST84220,CD 7-84220-2.

 186

<u>ANDREW HILL</u> - <u>COMPULSION!!!</u>:
Freddie Hubbard(tp,flh) John Gilmore(ts,bass cl) Andrew Hill(p) Cecil McBee(b) Joe Chambers (dm) Nadi Qumar(African dm,African thumb p) Renaud Simmons(cga).

Englewood Cliffs,N.J.,October 8,1965

1664 tk.3	Compulsion	
1665 tk.6	Limbo	
1666 tk.10	Legacy -1	
1667 tk.14	Premonition -2	

-1: Hubbard & Gilmore out.
-2: Richard Davis(bowed b) added.
All titles issued on BN BLP4217/BST84217,Mosaic MQ10-161,CD MD7-161.

<u>WAYNE SHORTER</u> - <u>THE ALL SEEING EYE</u>:
Freddie Hubbard(tp,flh) Alan Shorter(flh-1) Grachan Moncur III(tb) James Spaulding(as) Wayne Shorter(ts) Herbie Hancock(p) Ron Carter(b) Joe Chambers (dm).

Englewood Cliffs,N.J.,October 15,1965

1668 tk.2	The all seeing eye	CD BN(J)CJ28-5039,TOCJ-66049
1669 tk.3	Genesis	
1670 tk.8	Chaos	CD BN 8-59072-2
1671 tk.20	Face of the deep	
1672 tk.24	Mephistopheles -1	

All titles issued on BN BLP4219/BST84219,B1-29100,CD 8-29100-2,5-24543-2.

<u>THE HORACE SILVER QUINTET</u> - <u>THE CAPE VERDEAN BLUES</u>:
Woody Shaw(tp) J.J.Johnson(tb) Joe Henderson(ts) Horace Silver(p) Bob Cranshaw(b) Roger Humphries (dm).

Englewood Cliffs,N.J.,October 22,1965

1673 tk.7	Nutville	BN BN-LA402-H2 CD BN 7-93206-2,7-89287-2,4-95576-2, 32 Jazz 32039-2
1674 tk.15	Bonita	
1675 tk.22	Mo' Joe	

All titles issued on BN BLP4220/BST84220,CD 7-84220-2.

<u>LARRY YOUNG</u> - <u>UNITY</u>:
Woody Shaw(tp) Joe Henderson(ts) Larry Young(org) Elvin Jones(dm).

Englewood Cliffs,N.J.,November 10,1965

1676 tk.5	If	CD BN 7-89287-2,(J)CJ25-5181/84
1677 tk.17	Beyond all limits	
1678 tk.18	Monk's dream (tp,ts out)	CD BN 7-99177-2,8-35471-2,(J)TOCJ-5239
1679 tk.21	The Moontrane	BN BST2-92468,(Du)1A158-83395/8 CD BN 7-92468-2,7-99177-2,8-32993-2, 4-97154-2,(F)8-54194-2,32 Jazz 32039-2
1680 tk.22	Zoltan	
1681 tk.25	Softly as in a morning sunrise	CD BN 7-89287-2,(J)CJ32-5016,TOCJ-6271/74

All titles issued on BN BLP4221/BST84221,Mosaic MR9-137,CD BN 7-84221-2,4-97808-2,Mosaic MD6-137.

LEE MORGAN - INFINITY:
Lee Morgan(tp) Jackie McLean(as) Larry Willis(p) Reggie Workman(b) Billy Higgins(dm).
Englewood Cliffs,N.J.,November 16,1965

1682	tk.1	Infinity	
1683	tk.5	Growing pains	
1684	tk.17	Miss Nettie B	
1685	tk.25	Portrait of doll (*aka* My lady)	
1686	tk.26	Zip code	

All titles issued on BN LT-1091,CD 4-97504-2,(J)TOCJ-1627.

JACKIE McLEAN - CONSEQUENCE:
Lee Morgan(tp) Jackie McLean(as) Harold Mabern(p) Herbie Lewis(b) Billy Higgins(dm).
Englewood Cliffs,N.J.,December 3,1965

1687	tk.3	Consequence	
1688	tk.4	Bluesanova	
1689	tk.10	Tolypso	
1690	tk.11	Slumber (*aka* Soft touch)	
1691	tk.12	Vernestune (*aka* The three minors)	
1692	tk.16	My old flame	BN(E)UALP21 CD BN(J)CJ28-5163,TOCJ-66046

All titles issued on BN LT-994,Mosaic MQ6-150,CD MD4-150.

THE ORNETTE COLEMAN TRIO AT THE 'GOLDEN CIRCLE',STOCKHOLM:
Ornette Coleman(as) Dave Izenzon(b) Charles Moffett(dm,glockenspiel).
(prod. by Frank Wolff)(Gyllene Cirkeln) Stockholm,Sweden,December 3,1965

	tk.1	The blessing	rejected
	tk.2	Dee Dee	-
	tk.3	Faces and places	unissued
1691	tk.4	Antiques	BN BLP4225,(J)FCPA 6215
	tk.5	Dawn	rejected
	tk.6	European echoes	-
	tk.7	The riddle	unissued
1692	tk.8	Morning song	BN BLP4225,(J)FCPA 6215
	tk.9	Snowflakes and sunshine-1	rejected
	tk.10	Dee Dee	-
1693	tk.11	Dawn	BN BLP4224 CD BN 8-23372-2,(F)8-54194-2

-1:Ornette Coleman plays tp & v on this title.

Same.
(prod. by Frank Wolff)(Gyllene Cirkeln) Stockholm,December 4,1965 (afternoon)

	tk.12	Dee Dee	rejected
	tk.13	Faces and places	-
1694	tk.14	European echoes	BN BLP4224,BST89904,BN-LA160-G2 Lib(F)LBS83442/43 CD BN(J)CJ25-5181/84,TOCJ-6271/74
	tk.15	Dawn	unissued
	tk.16	The riddle	rejected
	tk.17	Snowflakes and sunshine-1	-

-1: Ornette Coleman plays tp & v on this title.
All titles from BLP4224/25 (mono) also issued on BN BST84224/25,CD 7-84224-2/84225-2 (stereo).

188

THE ORNETTE COLEMAN TRIO AT THE 'GOLDEN CIRCLE',STOCKHOLM:
Ornette Coleman(as) Dave Izenzon(b) Charles Moffett(dm,glockenspiel).
(prod. by Frank Wolff)
(Gyllene Cirkeln) Stockholm,December 4,1965 (afternoon)

	tk.18	Morning song	unissued
	tk.19	Antiques	rejected
	tk.20	The clergyman (Clergyman's dream)	-

Same. (Gyllene Cirkeln) Stockholm,December 4,1965 (evening)

	tk.21	Dawn	rejected
	tk.22	Dee Dee	unissued
	tk.23	Faces and places	rejected
	tk.24	European echoes	-
1695	tk.25	The riddle	BN BLP4225
	tk.26	Antiques	unissued
1696	tk.27	Dee Dee	BN BLP4224,(J)FCPA 6215 CD BN 8-23372-2
1697	tk.28	Snowflakes and sunshine -1	BN BLP4225
1698	tk.29	Faces and places	BN BLP4224,(J)FCPA 6215,W-5514
	tk.30	Morning song	unissued
	tk.31	European echoes	-
	tk.32	Dee Dee	-

-1: Ornette Coleman plays tp & v on this title.
All titles from BLP4224/25 (mono) also issued on BN BST84224/25,CD 7-84224-2/84225-2 (stereo).

BIG JOHN PATTON - LET 'EM ROLL:
Bobby Hutcherson(vb) John Patton(org) Grant Green(g) Otis Finch(dm).
Englewood Cliffs,N.J.,December 11,1965

1693	tk.2	The shadow of your smile	
1694	tk.5	The turnaround	BN B1-30728,(E)BNSLP-3 CD BN 8-30728-2,5-20070-2,(E)8-53234-2, (J)TOCJ-5780
1695	tk.14	Latona	BN B1-30728,(E)BNSLP-1 CD BN 7-95590-2,8-30728-2,(J)TOCJ-5778, TOCJ-6100
1696	tk.21	Jakey	
1697	tk.25	Let 'em roll	CD BN(F)8-54188-2,8-54197-2,(J)TOCJ-6067
1698	tk.28	One step ahead	

All titles issued on BN BLP4239/BST84239,CD 7-89795-2.

HANK MOBLEY - A CADDY FOR DADDY:
Lee Morgan(tp) Curtis Fuller(tb) Hank Mobley(ts) McCoy Tyner(p) Bob Cranshaw(b) Billy Higgins(dm).
Englewood Cliffs,N.J.,December 18,1965

1669	tk.7)	Third time around	BN BLP4230,CD 8-37052-2
1670	tk.12	Venus di Mildew (tb out)	-
	tk.19	Untitled Fuller original	rejected
1671	tk.20	Ace,deuce,trey	BN BLP4230
1672	tk.23	The morning after	-
1673	tk.27	A caddy for Daddy	-

All titles from BLP4230 (mono) also issued on BN BST84230,CD 7-84230-2 (stereo).

189

DON CHERRY - COMPLETE COMMUNION:
Don Cherry(c) Leandro "Gato" Barbieri(ts) Henry Grimes(b) Edward Blackwell(dm).
Englewood Cliffs,N.J.,December 24,1965

1675	tk.2	Complete communion:
		Complete communion/
		And now/
		Golden heart/
		Remembrance
1674	tk.3	Elephantasy:
		Elephantasy/
		Our feelings/
		Bishmallah/
		Wind,sand and stars

All titles issued on BN BLP4226/BST84226,Mosaic MQ3-145,CD BN 5-22673-2,Mosaic MD2-145.

BLUE MITCHELL:
Blue Mitchell(tp) Junior Cook(ts) Chick Corea(p) Gene Taylor(b) Joe Chambers(dm).
Englewood Cliffs,N.J.,December 29,1965

1676	Bring it on home to me	rejected
1677	Port Rico rock	-

BLUE MITCHELL - BRING IT HOME TO ME:
Blue Mitchell(tp) Junior Cook(ts) Harold Mabern(p) Gene Taylor(b) Billy Higgins(dm).
Englewood Cliffs,N.J.,January 6,1966

1678	tk.8	Port Rico rock	
1679	tk.14	Portrait of Jenny	
1681	tk.23	Gingerbread boy	BN(Du)1A158-83395/8
1682	tk.24	Bring it home to me	
1680	tk.30	Blues 3 for 1	
1683	tk.31	Blue's theme	

All titles issued on BN BLP4228/BST84228,Mosaic MQ6-178,CD MD4-178.

JOE HENDERSON - MODE FOR JOE:
Lee Morgan(tp) Curtis Fuller(tb) Joe Henderson(ts) Bobby Hutcherson(vb) Cedar Walton(p) Ron Carter(b) Joe Chambers(dm).
Englewood Cliffs,N.J.,January 27,1966

1685	tk.2	A shade of jade	BN BLP4227
1686	tk.8	Caribbean fire dance	- CD 7-89287-2
1687	tk.18	Granted	-
1688	tk.19	Mode for Joe	- (Du)1A158-83395/8 CD BN 7-95627-2,7-89287-2,(F)8-54191-2, 8-54197-2
1689	tk.26	Black	BN BLP4227
	tk.27	Black (alt.)	
1690	tk.31	Free wheelin'	BN BLP4227

All titles from BLP4227 (mono) also issued on BN BST84227,CD BN(J)TOCJ-4227 (stereo).
All titles issued on CD BN 7-84227-2.

190

WAYNE SHORTER - ADAM'S APPLE:
Wayne Shorter(ts) Herbie Hancock(p) Reggie Workman(b) Joe Chambers(dm).
Englewood Cliffs,N.J.,February 3,1966

1699 tk.3	Adam's apple	BN BLP4232,BST84232,B1-91141,(J)BNJ71106 CD BN 7-46403-2,7-91141-2,(F)8-54188-2, (J)CJ28-5039,CJ32-5016,TOCJ-4232,TOCJ-5758, TOCJ-66049
	Teru	rejected
	502 blues (Drinkin' and drivin')	-

BOBBY HUTCHERSON - HAPPENINGS:
Bobby Hutcherson(vb,marimba-1,dm-1) Herbie Hancock(p) Bob Cranshaw(b) Joe Chambers(dm,vb-1).
Englewood Cliffs,N.J.,February 8,1966

1691 tk.2	Aquarian moon	BN(J)NP9022,LNP95060
1692 tk.7	Rojo	
1693 tk.10	Bouquet	CD BN 7-96098-2
1694 tk.12	Head start	
1695 tk.16	When you are near	BN B2S-5256
1696 tk.21	Maiden voyage	CD BN 4-95569-2,(J)CJ28-5021,CJ32-5016, TOCJ-6271/74,HMV Jazz(E)5-20868-2
1697 tk.26	The omen -1	

All titles issued on BN BLP4231/BST84231,CD 7-46530-2.

WAYNE SHORTER - ADAM'S APPLE:
Wayne Shorter(ts) Herbie Hancock(p) Reggie Workman(b) Joe Chambers(dm).
Englewood Cliffs,N.J.,February 24,1966

1700 tk.11	Footprints	BN BLP4232/BST84232,B1-91141 CD BN 7-91141-2,(C)8-56508-2,(F)8-54191-2, 8-54197-2
1701 tk.14	El gaucho	BN BLP4232/BST84232
1702 tk.16	502 blues (Drinkin' and drivin')	-
1703 tk.17	Chief Crazy Horse	- CD 8-59072-2
1704 tk.20	Teru	-
1705 tk.22	The collector (*aka* Teo's bag)	BN(J)GXF-3059;CD BN 4-95569-2

All titles issued on CD BN 7-46403-2.
All titles from BST84232 also isued on CD BN(J)TOCJ-4232.

FREDDIE HUBBARD:
Freddie Hubbard(tp) Joe Henderson(ts) Hosea Taylor(as-1,bassoon-2) Herbie Hancock(p,celeste-2) Reggie Workman(b) Elvin Jones(dm).
Englewood Cliffs,N.J.,March 5,1966

1706 tk.6	The melting pot -1	BN(Du)1A158-83395/8;CD BN 7-46545-2
1707 tk.10	True colors -2	-
	For B.P.	rejected

191

ANDREW HILL QUARTET:
Sam Rivers(ts) Andrew Hill(p) Walter Booker(b) J.C.Moses(dm).
Englewood Cliffs,N.J.,March 7,1966

1708	tk.1	Violence -1	BN BN-LA453-H2
	tk.3	Violence (alt.)-1	
1709	tk.5	Hope -1	BN BN-LA453-H2
1710	tk.7	Illusion	-
1711	tk.10	Pain (ts out)	-
1712	tk.16	Desire	-
	tk.18	Desire (alt.)	
1713	tk.19	Lust (ts out)	BN BN-LA453-H2

-1: Hill plays celeste during bass solos.
All titles issued on Mosaic MQ10-161,CD MD7-161.
Note: All issued titles were initially scheduled on BN BLP4233 (not released).
BN-LA453-H2 was released as by Sam Rivers.

HANK MOBLEY - A SLICE OF THE TOP:
Lee Morgan(tp) Kiane Zawadi(euph) Howard Johnson(tu) James Spaulding(fl-1,as) Hank Mobley(ts,arr) McCoy Tyner(p) Bob Cranshaw(b) Billy Higgins(dm) Duke Pearson(arr).
Englewood Cliffs,N.J.,March 18,1966

1714	tk.1	A touch of blue	
1715	tk.9	A slice of the top	
1716	tk.15	Hank's other bag	
1717	tk.21	There's a lull in my life -1	BN(E)UALP21
1718	tk.25	Cute 'n pretty -1	

All titles issued on BN LT-995,B1-33582,CD 8-33582-2.
Note: Takes 9,15 and 21 were first scheduled on BN BLP4241,which was not released.
The bassist was incorrectly listed as Reggie Workman on LT-995.

LEE MORGAN - DELIGHTFULEE:
Lee Morgan,Ernie Royal(tp) Tom McIntosh(tb) Jim Buffington(frh) Don Butterfield(tu) Phil Woods(fl,as) Wayne Shorter(ts) Danny Bank(fl,bs,bass cl) McCoy Tyner(p) Bob Cranshaw(b) Philly Joe Jones(dm) Oliver Nelson(arr).
Englewood Cliffs,N.J.,April 8,1966

1719	tk.3	Sunrise-sunset	BN BLP4243;CD BN(J)TOCJ-5299,TOCJ-5875, Cap(J)TOCJ-5204
1720	tk.17	The delightful Deggie	
1721	tk.25	Filet of soul (Hoppin' John)	
1722	tk.35	Yesterday	BN BLP4243 CD BN 7-94861-2,(J)CJ28-5023,CJ28-5037, CJ32-5016,TOCJ-5874,TOCJ-66039, Cap(J)TOCJ-5201
1723	tk.36	Zambia	CD BN 4-94031-2
1724	tk.43	Need I?	

All titles from BLP4243 (mono) also issued on BN BST84243,CD BN(J)TOCJ-4243 (stereo).
All titles issued on BN 7-84243-2.

 192

JACKIE McLEAN - HIGH FREQUENCY:
Jackie McLean(as) Larry Willis(p) Don Moore(b) Jack DeJohnette(dm).
Englewood Cliffs,N.J.,April 18,1966

1725 tk.3 High frequency
1726 tk.8 Jossa bossa
1727 tk.15 Combined effort
1728 tk.20 Moonscape
1729 tk.21 The bull frog

All titles scheduled on BN BLP4236/BST84236 (not released) and later issued on BN BN-LA457-H2,Mosaic MQ6-150,CD Mosaic MD4-150.

BIG JOHN PATTON - GOT A GOOD THING GOIN':
John Patton(org) Grant Green(g) Hugh Walker(dm) Richard Landrum(cga).
Englewood Cliffs,N.J.,April 29,1966

1730	tk.7	Soul woman	
1731	tk.28	Amanda	BN 45-1926,B1-30728,CD 8-30728-2
1732	tk.37	The shake	
1733	tk.42	Ain't that peculiar	BN 45-1926,L4229,B1-30728 CD BN 7-99105-2,4-94211-2
1734	tk.45	The yodel	BN L4229;CD BN(J)TOCJ-6067

All titles issued on BN BLP4229/BST84229,CD BN(J)TOCJ-4229.

CECIL TAYLOR - UNIT STRUCTURES:
Eddie Gale(tp) Jimmy Lyons(as) Ken McIntyre(as-1,oboe-2,bass cl-3) Cecil Taylor(p,bells) Henry Grimes, Alan Silva(b) Andrew Cyrille(dm).
Englewood Cliffs,N.J.,May 19,1966

	tk.1	Enter,evening (alt.)-2	
1735	tk.2	Enter,evening (Soft line structure)-2	Smithsonian P-11891
1736	tk.7	Steps-1 (tp out)	CD BN(F)8-54194-2
1737	tk.27/23/24/8/18	Tales (8 whisps)-4	BN(Du)1A158-83395/8;CD BN 4-95981-2
1738	tk.31/41/45/43	Unit structure/As of a now/Section -3	

-4: Taylor,Silva,Cyrille only.
All titles,except take 1,issued on BN BLP4237/BST84237,CD BN(J)TOCJ-4237.
All titles issued on CD BN 7-84237-2.

LEE MORGAN - DELIGHTFULEE:
Lee Morgan(tp) Joe Henderson(ts) McCoy Tyner(p) Bob Cranshaw(b) Billy Higgins(dm).
Englewood Cliffs,N.J.,May 27,1966

1739	tk.4	Nite-flite	BN B1-94704,CD 7-89287-2,4-94704-2
1740	tk.5	Zambia	
1741	tk.20	The delightful Deggie	
1742	tk.21	Ca-Lee-So	BN B2S-5256

All titles issued on BN BLP4243/BST84243,CD 7-84243-2,(J)TOCJ-4243.

 193

<u>HANK MOBLEY</u>:
Lee Morgan(tp) Hank Mobley(ts) McCoy Tyner(p) Bob Cranshaw(b) Billy Higgins(dm).
Englewood Cliffs,N.J.,June 17,1966

1743	tk.3	Straight no filter	
1744	tk.14	Chain reaction	CD BN 5-21152-2
1745	tk.15	Soft impressions	

All titles were first scheduled on BN BLP4241 (not released).They were later issued on BN BST84435 in 1986,and reissued on CD BN 7-84435-2,5-27549-2.

<u>DONALD BYRD</u> - <u>MUSTANG</u>:
Donald Byrd(tp) Sonny Red(as) Hank Mobley(ts) McCoy Tyner(p) Walter Booker(b) Freddie Waits(dm).
Englewood Cliffs,N.J.,June 24,1966

1746	tk.4	On the trail	BN BLP4238	
1747	tk.9	I'm so excited by you	-	
1748	(tk.15	Mustang	-	B1-89606,CD 7-89606-2,(E)8-53233-2
		Dixie Lee	rejected	
1750	tk.24	I got it bad and that ain't good	BN BLP4238	
1751	tk.29	Fly little bird,fly	-	
1749	tk.31	Dixie Lee	-	B1-57745
			CD BN 8-57745-2,(J)TOCJ-6100	

All titles from BLP 4238 (mono) also issued on BN BST84238,CD BN 8-59963-2,(J)TOCJ-4238 (stereo).

<u>STANLEY TURRENTINE</u> - <u>ROUGH 'N ' TUMBLE</u>:
Blue Mitchell(tp) James Spaulding(as) Stanley Turrentine(ts) Pepper Adams(bs) McCoy Tyner(p) Grant Green (g) Bob Cranshaw(b,el b-1) Mickey Roker(dm) Duke Pearson(arr).
Englewood Cliffs,N.J.,July 1,1966

1752	tk.2	What could I do without you?	BN 45-1933
1754	tk.11	The shake	
1755	tk.12	Walk on by	BN 45-1929,L4240
			CD BN 7-99105-2,8-57749-2,Cema S21-57590
1756	tk.15	And satisfy	BN 45-1929,L4240,B1-57745,CD 8-57745-2
1757	tk.22	Baptismal -1	
1753	tk.23	Feeling good	BN 45-1933
			CD BN 7-93201-2,Cema S21-57590

All titles issued on BN BLP4240/BST84240,CD BN 5-24552-2.

<u>STANLEY TURRENTINE</u> - <u>EASY WALKER</u>:
Stanley Turrentine(ts) McCoy Tyner(p) Bob Cranshaw(b) Mickey Roker(dm).
Englewood Cliffs,N.J.,July 8,1966

1758	tk.5	Yours is my heart alone	
1759	tk.8	Meat wave	BN B1-80679,CD 7-80679-2
1760	tk.11	What the world needs now is love	CD BN 8-57749-2,Cema S21-57590
1761	tk.15	Easy walker	
1762	tk.23	They all say I'm the biggest fool	CD BN 7-95281-2
1763	tk.24	Alone together	CD BN(J)CJ28-5170

All titles issued on BN BLP4268/BST84268,B1-29908-2,CD 8-29908-2.

194

BOBBY HUTCHERSON - STICK UP!:
Joe Henderson(ts) Bobby Hutcherson(vb) McCoy Tyner(p) Herbie Lewis(b) Billy Higgins(dm).
Englewood Cliffs,N.J.,July 14,1966

1764 tk.16 Verse
1765 tk.27 8/4 beat — BN B1-80679,CD 7-80679-2,7-89287-2
1766 tk.34 Summer nights (ts out)
1767 tk.36 Una muy bonita — BN B1-57745
CD BN(J)TOCJ-6100,HMV Jazz(E)5-20868-2
1768 tk.40 Black circle — CD BN 7-89287-2
1769 tk.41 Blues mind matter

All titles issued on BN BLP4244/BST84244,CD 8-59378-2.

HERBIE HANCOCK:
Melvin Lastie(c) Julian Priester(tb) Stanley Turrentine(ts) Pepper Adams(bs) Herbie Hancock(p) Eric Gale, Billy Butler(g) Bob Cranshaw(b) Bernard Purdie(dm).
Englewood Cliffs,N.J.,July 19,1966

1770 tk.12 untitled ballad — rejected
1771 tk.14 untitled blues — -
1772 tk.15 Soul villa — -
1773 tk.17 untitled blues No.2 — -
1774 tk.21 Don't even go there — CD BN 4-95569-2,5-21484-2
1775 tk.26 You know what to do — rejected

LARRY YOUNG - OF LOVE AND PEACE:
Eddie Gale(tp) James Spaulding(fl-1,as-2) Herbert Morgan(ts) Larry Young(org) Wilson Moorman III,Jerry Thomas(dm).
Englewood Cliffs,N.J.,July 28,1966

1776 tk.2 Pavanne -2
1777 tk.4 Of love and peace -1
1778 tk.8 Seven steps to heaven -2 — CD BN 7-99177-2
1779 tk.10 Falaq -2

All titles issued on BN BLP4242/BST84242,Mosaic MR9-137,CD MD6-137.

JACK WILSON - SOMETHING PERSONAL:
Roy Ayers(vb) Jack Wilson(p) Ray Brown(b) Varney Barlow(dm).
(Annex Studios) LA,August 9,1966

(tk.3) Serenata — BN BLP4251/BST84251
(tk.4) One and four (Mr. day)
(tk.8) C.F.D. — BN BLP4251/BST84251,B2S-5256

Same. (Annex Studios) LA,August 10,1966 (afternoon)

(tk.3) Harbor Freeway 5 p.m. — BN BLP4251/BST84251
(tk.3) Shosh — -

Roy Ayers(vb) Jack Wilson(p) Ray Brown(cello) Charles "Buster" Williams(b) Varney Barlow(dm).
(Annex Studios) LA,August 10,1966 (night)

(tk.11) The Sphinx — BN BLP4251/BST84251
(tk.4) A most unsoulful woman — -

All titles from these three sessions issued on CD BN 8-52436-2.
All titles from BST84251 also issued on CD BN(J)TOCJ-4251.
Note: These sessions were produced by Jack Tracy.

195

ORNETTE COLEMAN - THE EMPTY FOXHOLE:
Ornette Coleman(tp-1,as-2,v-3) Charlie Haden(b) Ornette Denardo Coleman(dm).
(prod. by Frank Wolff) Englewood Cliffs,N.J.,September 9,1966

1780	tk.1	The empty foxhole -1	
1781	tk.2	Freeway express -1	
1782	tk.5	Zig zag -2	CD BN 8-23372-2
1783	tk.8	Faithful -2	
1784	tk.9	Sound gravitations -3	
1785	tk.12	Good old days-2	CD BN 8-23372-2

All titles issued on BN BLP4246/BST84246,B1-28982,CD 8-28982-2.

DON CHERRY - SYMPHONY FOR IMPROVISERS:
Don Cherry(c) Leandro "Gato" Barbieri(ts) Pharoah Sanders(ts,picc) Karl Berger(p,vb) Henry Grimes, Jean-François Jenny Clark(b) Edward Blackwell(dm).
Englewood Cliffs,N.J.,September 19,1966

1786 tk.2 Symphony for improvisers:
(a-Symphony for improvisers/b-Nu creative love/
c-What's not serious/d-Infant happiness)
1787 tk.5 Manhattan cry:
(a-Manhattan cry/b-Lunatic/c-Sparkle plenty/d-Om nu)

All titles issued on BN BLP4247/BST84247,B1-28976,Mosaic MQ3-145,CD BN 8-28976-2,Mosaic MD2-145.

STANLEY TURRENTINE - THE SPOILER:
Blue Mitchell(tp) Julian Priester(tb) James Spaulding(fl-1,as) Stanley Turrentine(ts) Pepper Adams(bs) McCoy Tyner(p) Bob Cranshaw(b,el b-4) Mickey Roker(dm) Joseph Rivera(shakers-2,tamb-3) Duke Pearson(arr).
Englewood Cliffs,N.J.,September 22,1966

1788	tk.6	La fiesta -2	BN BLP4256/BST84256,CD 4-97156-2
1789	tk.8	Sunny -2,4	- CD BN(Eu)4-93991-2,Cema S21-57590
1790	tk.11	The magilla -3	BN BLP4256/BST84256
1791	tk.16	Theme from "The Oscar" (Maybe September)-1	-
1792	tk.20	When the sun comes out	-
1793	tk.29	Lonesome lover	CD BN 7-93201-2
1794	tk.32	You're gonna hear from me	BN BLP4256/BST84256

All titles issued on CD 8-53359-2.

LEE MORGAN - CHARISMA:
Lee Morgan(tp) Jackie McLean(as) Hank Mobley(ts) Cedar Walton(p) Paul Chambers(b) Billy Higgins(dm).
Englewood Cliffs,N.J.,September 29,1966

1795	tk.4	The double up	
1796	tk.6	Somethin' cute	
1797	tk.15	Sweet honey bee	BN 45-1947 CD BN(J)TOCJ-66039,HMV(E)5-20871-2
1798	tk.17	The Murphy man	
1799	tk.20	Hey Chico	BN 45-1947;CD BN(J)TOCJ-6100
1800	tk.22	Rainy night	

All titles issued on BN BST84312,CD 8-59961-2.

CECIL TAYLOR - CONQUISTADOR:
Bill Dixon(tp) Jimmy Lyons(as) Cecil Taylor(p) Henry Grimes,Alan Silva(b) Andrew Cyrille(dm).
Englewood Cliffs,N.J.,October 6,1966

1781	tk.2	With (Exit)	BN BLP4260/BST84260,CD 7-46535-2
	tk.6	With (Exit) (alt.)	
1782	tk.10	Conquistador	BN BLP4260/BST84260,CD 7-46535-2

All titles issued on CD BN 7-84260-2.

SAM RIVERS - A NEW CONCEPTION:
Sam Rivers(fl-1,ss-2,ts-3) Hal Galper(p) Herbie Lewis(b) Steve Ellington(dm).
Englewood Cliffs,N.J.,October 11,1966

1783	tk.5	I'll never smile again -2,3	BN BLP4249/BST84249
		The touch of your lips -3	rejected
1784	tk.17	That's all -2	BN BLP4249/BST84249
1785	tk.18	When I fall in love -3	-
1786	tk.21	What a difference a day made -2,3	-
1787	tk.23	Detour ahead -1,2,3	-
1788	tk.24	Temptation -1,2,3	-
1789	tk.25	Secret love -1	-

All released titles also issued on Mosaic MQ5-167,CD MD3-167.

THE THREE SOUNDS - VIBRATIONS:
Gene Harris(p) Andy Simpkins(b) Kalil Madi(dm).
Englewood Cliffs,N.J.,October 25,1966

tk.3	Let's go get stoned	BN L4248
tk.5	Fever	BN(J)TOJJ-5849,CD TOCJ-5849
tk.9	The lamp is low	
tk.12	Charade	
	Doodlin'	rejected
tk.18	Yeh yeh	
tk.23	Django	
tk.33	Yours is my heart alone	
tk.35	Something you got-1	BN L4248
tk.40	The frown-1	BN 45-1928,L4248,(J)NP-2019
tk.46	It was a very good year-1	- - CD 8-35282-2, (Eu)7-89914-2

-1: Gene Harris(org) overdubbed on.
All titles,except the rejected one,issued on BN BLP4248/BST84248.

HORACE SILVER - THE JODY GRIND:
Woody Shaw(tp) Tyrone Washington(ts) Horace Silver(p) Larry Ridley(b) Roger Humphries(dm).
Englewood Cliffs,N.J.,November 2,1966

1780	tk.2	Mexican hip dance	BN(Du)1A158-83395/8 CD BN 7-93206-2,4-95576-2,(J)TOCJ-6100
1781	tk.9	The jody grind -1	BN 45-1932,L4250,BN-LA402-H2,B1-93206 UA XW-137 BN(Du)BST83249,(E)BNSLP-3 CD BN 7-93206-2,8-34957-2,4-95576-2, (J)TOCJ-5780,(Sp)5-21755-2,Cema S21-57589, EMI-Jazz(E)4-93466-2
1782	tk.16	Dimples	

-1: shown as pts. 1 & 2 on sides of 45-1932.Pt.1 was reissued on CD BN 4-94030-2.
All titles issued on BN BLP4250/BST84250,CD 7-84250-2.

DON CHERRY - WHERE IS BROOKLYN?:
Don Cherry(c) Pharoah Sanders(ts,picc-1) Henry Grimes(b) Edward Blackwell(dm).
Englewood Cliffs,N.J.,November 11,1966

1783 tk.12 There is the bomb BN(Du)1A158-83395/8
CD BN 8-35472-2,(F)8-54194-2

1784 tk.14 Unite -1
1785 tk.15 The thing
1786 tk.16 Awake Nu
1787 tk.17 Taste maker

All titles issued on BN BST84311,Mosaic MQ3-145,CD MD2-145.
Note: Original album title for above session was "The Art Of Smiling" and was changed before release.

BLUE MITCHELL - BOSS HORN:
Blue Mitchell(tp) Julian Priester(tb) Jerry Dodgion(fl-1,as) Junior Cook(ts) Pepper Adams(bs) Cedar Walton (p) Gene Taylor(b) Mickey Roker(dm) Duke Pearson(arr).
Englewood Cliffs,N.J.,November 17,1966

1788 tk.5 O Mama Enit
1789 tk.15 Rigor Mortez
1790 tk.17 I should care
1791 tk.22 Millie

All titles issued on BN BLP4257/BST84257,Mosaic MQ6-178,CD MD4-178.

Chick Corea(p) replaces Walton.Same session.

1792 tk.31 Straight up and down
1793 tk.42 Tones for Joan's bones -1

Both titles issued on BN BLP4257/BST84257,Mosaic MQ6-178,CD BN 7-89282-2,Mosaic MD4-178.

HORACE SILVER - THE JODY GRIND:
Woody Shaw(tp) James Spaulding(fl-1,as-2) Tyrone Washington(ts) Horace Silver(p) Larry Ridley(b) Roger Humphries(dm).
Englewood Cliffs,N.J.,November 23,1966

1794 tk.25 Mary Lou -1
1795 tk.31 Blue Silver -2 BN L4250,CD 8-33208-2
1796 tk.33 Grease piece -2

All titles issued on BN BLP4250/BST84250,CD 7-84250-2.

LEE MORGAN - THE RAJAH:
Lee Morgan(tp) Hank Mobley(ts) Cedar Walton(p) Paul Chambers(b) Billy Higgins(dm).
Englewood Cliffs,N.J.,November 29,1966

1797 tk.3 Davisamba
1798 tk.15 Once in a lifetime CD BN(E)8-53229-2
1799 tk.21 The rajah
1800 tk.36 Is that so
1801 tk.42 A pilgrim's funny farm
1802 tk.44 What now my love

All titles issued on BN BST84426,CD 7-84426-2.

198

DUKE PEARSON - SWEET HONEY BEE:
Freddie Hubbard(tp) James Spaulding(fl-1,as-2) Joe Henderson(ts) Duke Pearson(p) Ron Carter(b) Mickey Roker(dm).

Englewood Cliffs,N.J.,December 7,1966

1803	tk.1	Gaslight	CD BN 7-89287-2
1804	tk.10	Ready Rudy? -2	BN 45-1931
1805	tk.12	Big Bertha -2	CD BN 7-89287-2
1806	tk.17	After the rain (tp,ts out)-1	CD BN 8-54365-2
1807	tk.27	Sweet honey bee -1	BN 45-1931
			CD BN(J)TOCJ-6100,TOCJ-66053
1808	tk.28	Empathy -1	
1809	tk.32	Sudel -2	

All titles issued on BN BLP4252/BST84252,B1-89792,CD 7-89792-2.

DONALD BYRD - BLACKJACK:
Donald Byrd(tp) Sonny Red(as) Hank Mobley(ts) Cedar Walton(p) Walter Booker(b) Billy Higgins(dm).

Englewood Cliffs,N.J.,January 9,1967

1810	tk.5	Loki	BN BLP4259
1811	tk.9	Eldorado	- Lib.LN-10200
1812	tk.10	West of the Pecos	- B1-89606,CD 7-89606-2
		Blackjack	rejected
1814	tk.28	Beale Street	BN BLP4259,B1-89907
			CD BN 7-89907-2,(Eu)5-23444-2
1813	tk.29	Blackjack	BN BLP4259,B1-89606,B1-99106,B1-35636
			Lib.LN-10200
			CD BN 7-89606-2,7-99106-2,8-35636-2
1815	tk.33	Pentatonic	BN BLP4259

All titles from BLP4259 (mono) also issued on BN BST84259,CD 8-21286-2,(J)TOCJ-4259 (stereo).

LEE MORGAN - STANDARDS:
Lee Morgan(tp) James Spaulding(fl,as) Wayne Shorter(ts) Pepper Adams(bs) Herbie Hancock(p) Ron Carter(b) Mickey Roker(dm) Duke Pearson(arr).

Englewood Cliffs,N.J.,January 13,1967

	tk.2	Blue gardenia (alt.)	
1816	tk.6	Blue gardenia	
1817	tk.20	God bless the child	CD BN 4-97154-2
1818	tk.24	Somewhere	
1819	tk.39	If I were a carpenter	
1820	tk.41	A lot of living to do	
1821	tk.46	This is the life	

All titles issued on CD 8-23213-2.

LOU DONALDSON - LUSH LIFE:
Freddie Hubbard(tp) Garnett Brown(tb) Lou Donaldson(as) Jerry Dodgion(fl,as) Wayne Shorter(ts) Pepper Adams(bs) McCoy Tyner(p) Ron Carter(b) Al Harewood(dm) Duke Pearson(arr).
Englewood Cliffs,N.J.,January 20,1967

1822 tk.4	Sweet and lovely	
1823 tk.6	You've changed	
1824 tk.7	Sweet slumber	CD BN 8-27298-2
1825 tk.9	It might as well be Spring	
1826 tk.11	What will I tell my heart	
1827 tk.14	The good life	
1828 tk.15	Star dust	Lib(J)K22P-6131/32;CD BN(J)TOCJ-5858

All titles first issued on BN(J)GXF-3068 (entitled "Sweet Slumber").They were later issued on BN BST84254 in 1986 and reissued on CD BN 7-84254-2.Mono version (BLP4254) was never issued.

JACKIE McLEAN - HIPNOSIS:
Grachan Moncur III(tb) Jackie McLean(as) Lamont Johnson(p) Scotty Holt(b) Billy Higgins(dm).
Englewood Cliffs,N.J.,February 3,1967

1829 tk.7	Hipnosis
1830 tk.11	Slow poke
1831 tk.21	The breakout
1832 tk.30	Back home
1833 tk.40	The reason why

All titles issued on BN BN-LA483-J2,(J)GXF-3022.

ANDREW HILL:
Robin Kenyatta(as) Sam Rivers(fl-1,ss-2,ts-3) Andrew Hill(p-4,org-5) Cecil McBee(b) Teddy Robinson(dm) Nadi Qumar(thumb p-6,African dm-7,perc-8).
Englewood Cliffs,N.J.,February 10,1967

1834 tk.2	Prevue -2,5,8	unissued
1835 tk.5	Yomo -3,4,5,6,7	-
1836 tk.8	I -1,3,4,7	-
1837 tk.9	Awake -1,3,4	-
1838 tk.11	Now -3,4,8	-

STANLEY TURRENTINE:
Donald Byrd(tp) Julian Priester(tb) Jerry Dodgion(fl,as) Joe Farrell(ts,fl) Stanley Turrentine(ts) Pepper Adams(bs,cl) Kenny Barron(p) Bucky Pizzarelli(g) Ron Carter(b) Mickey Roker(dm) Duke Pearson(arr).
Englewood Cliffs,N.J.,February 17,1967

1839 tk.4	She's a Carioca	BN BN-LA394-H2,CD 8-35283-2
1840 tk.9	Samba do aviao	-
1841 tk.14	Manha de carnaval	BN LT-993;CD BN(J)CJ28-5170
1842 tk.15	What now my love	-
1843 tk.24	Night song	BN BN-LA394-H2
1844 tk.32	Here's that rainy day	BN LT-993
1845 tk.41	Blues for Del	-

<u>HANK MOBLEY</u> - <u>THIRD SEASON</u>:
Lee Morgan(tp) James Spaulding(fl-1,as) Hank Mobley(ts) Cedar Walton(p) Sonny Greenwich(g) Walter Booker(b) Billy Higgins(dm).
Englewood Cliffs,N.J.,February 24,1967

1846 tk.15 Don't cry,just sigh -2
1847 tk.16 Third season
1848 tk.29 Give me that feelin'
1849 tk.30 Boss bossa-1
1850 tk.33 The steppin' stone
1851 tk.36 An aperitif

-2: Spaulding & Greenwich out.
All titles issued on BN LT-1081,CD 4-97506-2.

<u>WAYNE SHORTER</u> - <u>SCHIZOPHRENIA</u>:
Curtis Fuller(tb) James Spaulding(fl-1,as) Wayne Shorter(ts) Herbie Hancock(p) Ron Carter(b) Joe Chambers(dm).
(produced by Frank Wolff) Englewood Cliffs,N.J.,March 10,1967

1852	tk.3	Schizophrenia -1	CD BN 8-59072-2
1853	tk.10	Go -1	
1854	tk.20	Playground	
1855	tk.28	Tom Thumb	BN B1-91141,B1-80679 CD BN 7-91141-2,7-80679-2
1856	tk.32	Miyako	CD BN(J)TOCJ-5740
1857	tk.35	Kryptonite -1	CD BN(J)CJ28-5039,TOCJ-66049

All titles issued on BN BST84297,B1-32096,CD 8-32096-2.

<u>SAM RIVERS</u> - <u>DIMENSIONS & EXTENSIONS</u>:
Donald Byrd(tp) Julian Priester(tb) James Spaulding(fl-1,as) Sam Rivers(fl-1,ss-2,ts-3) Cecil McBee(b) Steve Ellington(dm).
Englewood Cliffs,N.J.,March 17,1967

1858 tk.10 Paean -2
1859 tk.20 Precis -3
1860 tk.25 Helix -3
1861 tk.32 Effusive melange -3
1862 tk.33 Involution (tp,tb out) -1
1863 tk.34 Afflatus (ts,b,dm only) -3

All titles initially scheduled on BN BLP4261 (not released) and later issued on BN BN-LA453-H2.They have finally been issued on BN BST84261 in 1986 and reissued on Mosaic MQ5-167,CD BN 7-84261-2,Mosaic MD3-167.

JACKIE McLEAN - NEW AND OLD GOSPEL:
Ornette Coleman(tp) Jackie McLean(as) Lamont Johnson(p) Scotty Holt(b) Billy Higgins(dm).
Englewood Cliffs,N.J.,March 24,1967

1864 tk.6 Old gospel — CD BN 8-23372-2,8-35414-2
1865 tk.9 Strange as it seems
1866 tk.10 Lifeline:
A - Offspring
B - Midway
C - Vernzone
D - The inevitable end

All titles issued on BN BLP4262/BST84262,CD 8-53356-2.

LOU DONALDSON - ALLIGATOR BOGALOO:
Melvin Lastie(c) Lou Donaldson(as) Lonnie Smith(org) George Benson(g) Leo Morris (Idris Muhammad) (dm).
Englewood Cliffs,N.J.,April 7,1967

1867 tk.4 One cylinder — BN B1-94709,CD 4-94709-2,(J)TOCJ-5864
1868 tk.6 Aw shucks — BN(Du)1A158-83401/4;Trip TLP-5059
1869 tk.8 Alligator bogaloo — BN 45-1934,BST2-92471,B1-92812,B1-30721
BN(Du)BST83249,(E)BNX2;Lib(E)LBS83249
CD BN 7-92471-2,7-92812-2,8-27298-2,
8-30721-2,4-94030-2,(F)8-54188-2,
(J)TOCJ-5864,TOCJ-5925,TOCJ-5933,TOCJ-6153,
TOCJ-6191,TOCJ-66044,TOCJ-66055,
TOCP-8963,TOCP-50230,Cema S21-57592,
EMI-Jazz(E)4-93469-2,EMI(E)5-21426-2
1870 tk.15 Rev. Moses — BN 45-1934,B1-30721,(E)BNSLP-3
CD BN 8-30721-2,4-94030-2,(Eu)7-80703-2,
(J)TOCJ-5780
1871 tk.17 I want a little girl (c out) — Trip TLP-5059
1872 tk.18 The thang

All titles issued on BN BLP4263/BST84263,B1-84263,CD 7-84263-2.

LEE MORGAN - SONIC BOOM:
Lee Morgan(tp) David "Fathead" Newman(ts) Cedar Walton(p) Ron Carter(b) Billy Higgins(dm).
Englewood Cliffs,N.J.,April 14,1967

1878 tk.7 Sonic boom — BN LT-987:CD BN(J)TOCJ-1630

McCOY TYNER - THE REAL McCOY:
Joe Henderson(ts) McCoy Tyner(p) Ron Carter(b) Elvin Jones(dm).
Englewood Cliffs,N.J.,April 21,1967

1873 tk.1 Contemplation
1874 tk.6 Passion dance — BN BST2-92474,(J)FCPA 6214
CD BN 7-92474-2,8-37051-2,(F)8-54191-2,
(J)CJ28-5165,TOCJ-6132,TOCJ-6271/74,
TOCJ-66053
1875 tk.7 Blues on the corner — BN(J)FCPA 6214
CD BN 7-89287-2,(J)CJ28-5030
1876 tk.12 Four by five — CD BN 8-33207-2
1877 tk.18 Search for peace — BN(J)FCPA 6214
CD BN 8-37051-2,(E)8-53229-2,(J)CJ28-5165

All titles issued on BN BLP4264/BST84264,CD 7-46512-2,4-97807-2.

202

LEE MORGAN - SONIC BOOM:
Lee Morgan(tp) David "Fathead" Newman(ts) Cedar Walton(p) Ron Carter(b) Billy Higgins(dm).
Englewood Cliffs,N.J.,April 28,1967

1879 tk.8	Sneaky Pete	
1880 tk.9	The mercenary	
1881 tk.14	Mumbo jumbo	
1882 tk.20	Fathead	BN(E)UALP21
1883 tk.22	I'll never be the same (ts out)	

All titles issued on BN LT-987,CD BN(J)TOCJ-1630.

DONALD BYRD - SLOW DRAG:
Donald Byrd(tp) Sonny Red(as) Cedar Walton(p) Walter Booker(b) Billy Higgins(dm,vo).
Englewood Cliffs,N.J.,May 12,1967

1884 tk.3	Book's bossa	BN B1-89606,CD 7-89606-2,4-97156-2
1885 tk.15	The loner	
1886 tk.18	Jelly roll	BN B1-89606,B1-94708 CD BN 7-89606-2,4-94708-2,(C)8-56508-2
1887 tk.22	Slow drag (voBH)	BN B1-89606,CD 7-89606-2,(F)8-54188-2, 8-54197-2,(J)TOCJ-5733
1888: not used		
1889 tk.29	My ideal	
1890 tk.30	Secret love	

All titles issued on BN BST84292,CD BN(J)TOCJ-4292.

ANDREW HILL - CHAINED:
Andrew Hill(p) Ron Carter(b) Teddy Robinson(dm).
Englewood Cliffs,N.J.,May 17,1967

1891 tk.1	Nine at the bottom -2	unissued
1891 tk.3	Nine at the bottom (alt.) -2	-
1892 tk.4	Six at the top -1	-
1893 tk.7	Chained	-
1894 tk.9	Moma	-
1895 tk.11	Absolution -2	-
1896 tk.14	Interfusion	-

-1: Hill also plays ss.
-2: Hill also plays org.
Note:All titles,except tk.3,were scheduled on BN(J)GXF-3080 (not released).

HANK MOBLEY - FAR AWAY LANDS:
Donald Byrd(tp) Hank Mobley(ts) Cedar Walton(p) Ron Carter(b) Billy Higgins(dm).
Englewood Cliffs,N.J.,May 26,1967

1898 tk.3	No argument	
1899 tk.6	The hippity hop	
1900 tk.9	Bossa for baby	
1901 tk.12	Soul time (*aka* Dusty foot)	BN(J)BNJ71106,CD TOCJ-5758
1902 tk.27	Far away lands	
1903 tk.32	A dab of this and that	

All titles issued on BN BST84425,CD 7-84425-2.

203

STANLEY TURRENTINE:
Blue Mitchell,Tommy Turrentine(tp) Julian Priester(tb) Jerry Dodgion(fl,as) Stanley Turrentine(ts) Al Gibbons(ts,bass cl) Pepper Adams(bs,cl) McCoy Tyner(p) Walter Booker(b) Mickey Roker(dm) Duke Pearson(arr).

Englewood Cliffs,N.J.,June 9,1967

1904 tk.16	With this ring	unissued
1905 tk.15	Silver tears	-
1906 tk.20	A bluish bag	-
1907 tk.26	Come back to me	-
1908 tk.30	Days of wine and roses	-
1909 tk.45	Message to Michael	rejected

THE THREE SOUNDS - LIVE AT THE LIGHTHOUSE:
Gene Harris(p) Andrew Simpkins(b) Donald Bailey(dm).
(prod. by Dick Bock)(Live,Lighthouse Club) Hermosa Beach,Calif.,June 9 & 10,1967

Still I'm sad	BN 45-1935,BLP4265/BST84265, (Du)BST83249,(J)NP-2019
June night	BN BLP4265/BST84265
I thought about you	-
Summertime	-
Makin' bread again	BN 45-1935,BLP4265/BST84265
Here's that rainy day (see note)	BN BLP4265/BST84265
Blues march	-
Never say yes	
River shallow	
Sunny	
Bad bad whiskey	
C jam blues (Set call)	
Sylvie	unissued
Like someone in love	-
Georgia on my mind	-
Goin' out of my head	-
Yesterday	-
The shadow of your smile	-
Stella by starlight	-
Bluesette	-
Makin' whoopee	-
Cute	-
Sherry	-
It was a very good year	-
Li'l darlin'	-

First twelve titles issued on CD BN 5-23995-2.
Note: On "Here's that rainy day",the piano intro is edited on LP,but complete on CD.

Gene Harris(p) Andrew Simpkins(b) Donald Bailey(dm).
(prod. by Dick Bock)(Lighthouse Club) Hermosa Beach,Calif.,June 10,1967 (afternoon)
Gene Harris(org) overdubbed on.

Takin' it easy	
Drown in my own tears	
Why am I treated so bad	
Cryin' time	BN BLP4265/BST84265
I held my head in shame	-

All titles issued on CD BN 5-23995-2.
Note: These 5 titles were not recorded before an audience.

STANLEY TURRENTINE:
Marvin Stamm,Joe Shepley(tp,flh) Julian Priester,Garnett Brown(tb) Al Gibbons(fl,as,bass cl) Joe Farrell (fl,ts) Stanley Turrentine(ts) Mario Rivera(bs) McCoy Tyner(p) Bob Cranshaw(b) Ray Lucas(dm) Duke Pearson (arr).

Englewood Cliffs,N.J.,June 23,1967

1910	tk.4	Better luck next time	BN BN-LA394-H2
1911	tk.11	Bonita	-
1912	tk.14	Return of the prodigal son	BN LT-993,(E)UALP21 CD BN(Eu)4-93991-2
1913	tk.16	Flying jumbo (Prez delight)	BN BN-LA394-H2
1914	tk.27	Ain't no mountain high enough	BN LT-993:CD BN(Eu)4-93991-2
1915	tk.32	New time shuffle	-

LEE MORGAN - THE PROCRASTINATOR:
Lee Morgan(tp) Wayne Shorter(ts) Bobby Hutcherson(vb) Herbie Hancock(p) Ron Carter(b) Billy Higgins (dm).

Englewood Cliffs,N.J.,July 14,1967

1916	tk.2	The procrastinator	CD BN 8-54901-2
1917	tk.9	Stop-start	
1918	tk.19	Rio	
1919	tk.20	Soft touch (*aka* Slumber)	
1920	tk.24	Party time	
1921	tk.25	Dear Sir	

All titles issued on BN BN-LA582-J2,B1-33579,(J)GXF-3023,CD BN 8-33579-2,(J)TOCJ-1629.

BOBBY HUTCHERSON - OBLIQUE:
Bobby Hutcherson(vb,dm-1) Herbie Hancock(p) Albert Stinson(b) Joe Chambers(dm,gong-1,tympani-1).

Englewood Cliffs,N.J.,July 21,1967

1922	tk.2	Subtle Neptune	
1923	tk.7	My joy	
1925	tk.16	Theme from "Blow up"	CD BN 8-57748-2,4-95569-2,(F)4-97517-2, HMV Jazz(E)5-20868-2
1926	tk.20	Oblique	
1927	tk.25	Bi-sectional -1	
1924	tk.28	'Til then	CD HMV Jazz(E)5-20868-2

All titles issued on BN(J)GXF-3061,CD BN 7-84444-2.

STANLEY TURRENTINE:
Blue Mitchell(tp) Garnett Brown(tb) James Spaulding(fl,as) Stanley Turrentine(ts) McCoy Tyner(p) Duke Pearson(org-1,arr) Bob Cranshaw(b) Ray Lucas(dm) Richard Landrum(cga,bgo,tamb).

Englewood Cliffs,N.J.,July 28,1967

1928	tk.3	The look of love	unissued
1929	tk.14	You want me to stop loving you	BN B1-31883,CD 8-31883-2
1930	tk.18	Dr. Feelgood -1	unissued
1930	tk.21	Dr. Feelgood -1	-
1931	tk.34	Up,up and away	-
1932	tk.36	Georgy girl	-
1933	tk.39	A foggy day -2	CD BN 8-29908-2

-2: Turrentine,Tyner,Cranshaw,Lucas only.

Note: This session was the last one supervised by Alfred Lion.

Part 2

The Liberty/United Artists Era (1967–1979)

JACKIE McLEAN - 'BOUT SOUL:
Woody Shaw(tp) Grachan Moncur III(tb) Jackie McLean(as) Lamont Johnson(p) Scotty Holt(b) Rashied Ali (dm) Barbara Simmons(recitation-1)

Englewood Cliffs,N.J.,September 8,1967

1934 tk.2	Big Ben's voice (alt.) (tb out)	
1934 tk.3	Big Ben's voice (tb out)	BN BST84284
1935 tk.4	Conversion point	-
1936 tk.8	Soul -1	- B1-54360,CD BN 8-54360-2 BN(Du)BST83249;Lib(E)LBS83249
1937 tk.14	Dear Nick,dear John (tp,tb out)	BN BST84284
1938 tk.17	Erdu	-

All titles on CD BN 8-59383-2
All titles from BST84284 also issued on CD BN(J)TOCJ-4284.

DUKE PEARSON - THE RIGHT TOUCH:
Freddie Hubbard(tp) Garnett Brown(tb) James Spaulding(as) Jerry Dodgion(fl,as) Stanley Turrentine(ts) Duke Pearson(p) Gene Taylor(b) Grady Tate(dm).

Englewood Cliffs,N.J.,September 13,1967

1939	My love waits	rejected	
1940	Chili peppers	-	
1941 tk.23	Make it good	BST84267,CD 8-28269-2	
1942 tk.25	Los malos hombres	-	-
1942 tk.30	Los malos hombres (alt.)		-
1943 tk.33	Scrap iron	BN BST84267	-
1944 tk.35	Rotary	-	-
1939 tk.37	My love waits	-	-
1940 tk.38	Chili peppers	-	B1-80679, CD 7-80679-2,8-28269-2

All titles from BST84267 also issued on BN B1-28269,CD BN(J)TOCJ-9251.

LARRY YOUNG - CONTRASTS:
Hank White(flh) Tyrone Washington,Herbert Morgan(ts) Larry Young(org) Eddie Wright(g) Eddie Gladden(dm) Stacey Edwards(cga) Althea Young(vo).

Englewood Cliffs,N.J.,September 18,1967

1945 tk.4	Evening (g out)	
1946 tk.6	Majestic soul	CD BN 8-35414-2
1947 tk.7	Means happiness (g out)	
1949 tk.11	Major affair (g,cga out)	BN(Du)BST83249,1A158-83395/8 CD BN 7-99177-2
1948 tk.17	Tender feelings (g,cga out)	
1950 tk.21	Wild is the wind (voAY) (org,g,dm only)	

All titles issued on BN BST84266,Mosaic MR9-137,CD MD6-137.

<u>JACK WILSON</u> - <u>EASTERLY WINDS</u>:
Lee Morgan(tp) Garnett Brown(tb) Jackie McLean(as) Jack Wilson(p) Bob Cranshaw(b) Billy Higgins(dm).
Englewood Cliffs,N.J.,September 22,1967

1951 tk.4	Frank's tune	
1952 tk.11	Easterly winds	
1953 tk.16	Nirvana	
1954 tk.17	On children	BN B1-80679-1,CD 7-80679-2
1955 tk.20	Do it	CD BN(J)TOCJ-6100
1956 tk.23	A time for love (tp,tb,as out)	

All titles issued on BN BST84270,CD BN(J)TOCJ-4270.

<u>DONALD BYRD</u>:
Donald Byrd(tp) Sonny Red(as) Pepper Adams(bs) Chick Corea(p) Miroslav Vitous(b) Joe Chambers(dm).
Englewood Cliffs,N.J.,September 29,1967

1957	The creeper	rejected
1958	Chico San	-

<u>DONALD BYRD</u> - <u>THE CREEPER</u>:
Donald Byrd(tp) Sonny Red(as) Pepper Adams(bs) Chick Corea(p) Miroslav Vitous(b) Mickey Roker(dm).
Englewood Cliffs,N.J.,October 5,1967

1959 tk.4	Blues well done
1960 tk.6	Early Sunday morning
1961 tk.8	I will wait for you (as,bs out)
1962 tk.15	Chico San
1957 tk.18	The creeper
1963 tk.21	Samba Yantra
1964 tk.25	Blues medium rare

All titles issued on BN LT-1096,CD Mosaic MD4-194.

<u>HANK MOBLEY</u> - <u>HI VOLTAGE</u>:
Blue Mitchell(tp) Jackie McLean(as) Hank Mobley(ts) John Hicks(p) Bob Cranshaw(b) Billy Higgins(dm).
Englewood Cliffs,N.J.,October 9,1967

1965 tk.4	Two and one
1966 tk.6	Bossa de luxe
1967 tk.12	Hi voltage
1968 tk.15	Flirty Gerty
1969 tk.16	Advance notice
1970 tk.18	No more goodbyes (tp,as out)

All titles issued on BN BST84273,CD 7-84273-2.

<u>LOU DONALDSON</u> - <u>Mr. SHING-A-LING</u>:
Blue Mitchell(tp) Lou Donaldson(as) Lonnie Smith(org) Jimmy "Fats" Ponder(g) Leo Morris (Idris Muhammad)(dm).
Englewood Cliffs,N.J.,October 27,1967

1971 tk.2	Ode to Billie Joe (tp out)	BN B1-54360,CD 8-54360-2,(J)TOCJ-5864
1972 tk.10	Peepin'	BN 45-1937,BST89904,BN-LA160-G2,B1-30721 CD BN 8-30721-2,8-37745-2,8-29092-2
1973 tk.16	The kid	BN 8-29092-1,CD 8-29092-2
1974 tk.17	The shadow of your smile	CD BN 8-57748-2,(J)TOCJ-66044
1975 tk.18	The humpback	BN 45-1937,(J)NP-2020

All titles issued on BN BST84271,B1-84271,CD 7-84271-2.
<u>ANDREW HILL</u>:

ANDREW HILL:
Woody Shaw(tp) Robin Kenyatta(as) Sam Rivers(ss,ts) Howard Johnson(bs,tu) Andrew Hill(p) Herbie Lewis(b) Teddy Robinson(dm).

Englewood Cliffs,N.J.,October 31,1967

1977 tk.3	Orba	unissued
1978 tk.7	Mother's tale	-
1979 tk.14	Enamorado	-
1980 tk.15	For blue people only	-
1981 tk.20	Requiem for truth	-

LEE MORGAN - THE SIXTH SENSE:
Lee Morgan(tp) Jackie McLean(as) Frank Mitchell(ts) Cedar Walton(p) Victor Sproles(b) Billy Higgins(dm).

Englewood Cliffs,N.J.,November 10,1967

1982 tk.7	Anti climax	CD BN(J)TOCJ-5828,TOCJ-66039
1983 tk.11	Psychedelic	CD BN 8-35472-2,(J)TOCJ-5828
1984 tk.17	Short Count	
1985 tk.20	The sixth sense	
1986 tk.22	Afreaka (*aka* Mission eternal)	BN B1-57745,CD 8-57745-2
1987 tk.24	The cry of my people (as,ts out)	

All titles issued on BN BST84335,CD BN 5-22467-2,(J)TOCJ-5736.
Note: On CD 5-22467-2,last title is mislabelled "The city of my people".

BLUE MITCHELL - HEADS UP!:
Blue Mitchell,Burt Collins(tp) Julian Priester(tb)Jerry Dodgion(fl-1,as) Junior Cook(ts) Pepper Adams(bs) McCoy Tyner(p) Gene Taylor(b) Al Foster(dm).
Arrangements by Melba Liston-2,Jimmy Heath-3,Don Pickett-4,Duke Pearson-5.

Englewood Cliffs,N.J.,November 17,1967

1988 tk.8	Len Sirrah -2	BN BST84272
1989 tk.14	Togetherness -3	-
1989 tk 16	Togetherness (alt.)-3	
1990 tk.18	Heads up,feet down -3	BN BST84272
1991 tk 23	Good humor man (alt.)-4	
1991 tk.24	Good humor man -4	BN BST84272,B1-89907,CD 7-89907-2
1992 tk.32	The folks who live on the hill -5	-
1993 tk.34	The people in Nassau -1,5	-

All titles issued on Mosaic MQ6-178,CD MD4-178.

McCOY TYNER - TENDER MOMENTS:
Lee Morgan(tp)Julian Priester(tb) Bob Northern(frh) Howard Johnson(tu) James Spaulding(fl,as) Bennie Maupin(ts) McCoy Tyner(p) Herbie Lewis(b) Joe Chambers(dm).

Englewood Cliffs,N.J.December 1,1967

1994 tk.3	Mode to John	CD BN 4-97154-2
1995 tk.9	The high priest	CD BN 8-33207-2,(J)CJ28-5165
1996 tk.12	Man from Tanganyika	BN B1-80701,(In)JAZ 1 CD BN 7-80701-2,8-37051-2
1997 tk.18	Utopia	
1998 tk.21	All my yesterdays	
1999 tk.22	Lee plus three (tp,p,b,dm only)	CD BN(J)CJ28-5165

All titles issued on BN BST84275,CD 7-84275-2.

INTRODUCING DUKE PEARSON'S BIG BAND:
Randy Brecker,Burt Collins,Joe Shepley,Marvin Stamm(tp) Garnett Brown,Benny Powell,Julian Priester(tb) Kenny Rupp(bass tb) Jerry Dodgion(fl,picc,as) Al Gibbons(fl,as,bass cl) Frank Foster,Lew Tabackin(ts) Pepper Adams(bs,cl) Duke Pearson(p,arr,dir) Bob Cranshaw (b) Mickey Roker(dm).
Englewood Cliffs,N.J.,December 15,1967

2000 tk.6	Ready when you are C.B.	
2001 tk.11	Ground hog	BN B1-54360,CD 8-54360-2
2002 tk.19	Mississippi dip	CD BN(Eu)5-23444-2
2003 tk.24	A taste of honey	
2005 tk.30	Bedouin	
2004 tk.37	New time shuffle	CD BN 4-97155-2
2006 tk.40	Straight up and down	
2007 tk.47	New girl	
2008 tk.54	Time after time	

All titles issued on BN BST84276,CD 4-94508-2,(J)TOCJ-4276.

JACKIE McLEAN - DEMON'S DANCE:
Woody Shaw(tp,flh) Jackie McLean(as) Lamont Johnson(p) Scotty Holt(b) Jack DeJohnette(dm).
Englewood Cliffs,N.J.,December 22,1967

2009 tk.5	Floogeh	
2010 tk.11	Sweet love of mine	CD BN(J)CJ28-5163,TOCJ-5296,TOCJ-66046, TOCJ-66051,Cap(J)TOCJ-5191/92
2011 tk.13?	Demon's dance	
2012 tk.14?	Toy land	
2013 tk.21?	Message from Trane	CD BN(Sp)5-21755-2
2014 tk.22	Boo Ann's grand	

All titles issued on BN BST84345,CD 7-84345-2.

TYRONE WASHINGTON - NATURAL ESSENCE:
Woody Shaw(tp) James Spaulding(fl-1,as) Tyrone Washington(ts)Kenny Barron(p) Reggie Workman(b) Joe Chambers(dm).
Englewood Cliffs,N.J.,December 29,1967

2015 tk.4	Ethos -1
2016 tk.7	Soul dance
2017 tk.11	Yearning for love
2018 tk.14	Positive path
2019 tk.15	Natural essence
2020 tk.18	Song of peace (ts,b,dm only)

All titles issued on BN BST84274,CD BN(J)TOCJ-4274.

BOOKER ERVIN - THE IN BETWEEN:
Richard Williams(tp) Booker Ervin(fl-1,ts) Bobby Few(p) Cevera Jeffries(b) Lennie McBrowne(dm).
Englewood Cliffs,N.J.,January 12,1968

2021 tk.6	Sweet Pea
2022 tk.8	The in between
2023 tk.12	Mour
2024 tk.19	The muse -1
2025 tk.26	Tyra
2026 tk.28	Largo (tp out)

All titles issued on BN BST84283,CD 8-59379-2.

209

<u>HANK MOBLEY</u> - <u>REACH OUT!</u>:
Woody Shaw(tp,flh-1) Hank Mobley(ts) Lamont Johnson(p) George Benson(g) Bob Cranshaw(b) Billy Higgins(dm).

Englewood Cliffs,N.J.,January 19,1968

2027 tk.6	Up,over and out	BN(Du)1A158-83401/4
2028 tk.8	Lookin' East	
2029 tk.9	Goin' out of my head	BN 45-1938;CD BN(J)TOCJ-66043
2030 tk.12	Beverly	
2031 tk.15	Good pickin's -1	
2032 tk.19	Reach out,I'll be there	BN 45-1938,CD7-99105-2

All titles issued on BN BST84288,CD 8-59964-2

<u>STANLEY TURRENTINE</u>:
Marvin Stamm,Burt Collins(tp,flh) Garnett Brown,Benny Powell(tb) Jerry Dodgion,Al Gibbons,Joe Farrell (reeds) Stanley Turrentine(ts) McCoy Tyner(p) Everett Barksdale(g) Bob Cranshaw(b) Grady Tate(dm).

Englewood Cliffs,N.J.,January 25,1968

2033	Spooky	BN 45-1936,BN1-31883 CDBN 8-31883-2,(Eu)4-93991-2
2034	Elusive butterfly	CD BN(Eu)4-93991-2
2035	Love is blue	BN 45-1936
2036	When I look into your eyes	unissued

<u>LARRY YOUNG</u> - <u>HEAVEN ON EARTH</u>:
Byard Lancaster(fl-1,as-2) Herbert Morgan(ts) Larry Young(org) George Benson(g) Edward Gladden(dm) Althea Young(vo).

Englewood Cliffs,N.J.,February 9,1968

2037 tk.1	Call me	
2038 tk.3	The infant -2	
2039 tk.6	The cradle (org,dm only)	
2040 tk.10	Heaven on earth	BN B1-35636,CD 8-35636-2
2041 tk.11	The hereafter -1	
2042 tk.12	My funny Valentine (voAY) (ts out)	BN(J)K22P-6125/26

All titles issued on BN BST84304,Mosaic MR9-137,CD MD6-137.

<u>LEE MORGAN</u> - <u>TARU</u>:
Lee Morgan(tp) Bennie Maupin(ts) John Hicks(p) George Benson(g) Reggie Workman(b) Billy Higgins (dm).

Englewood Cliffs,N.J.,February 15,1968

2043 tk.6	Haeschen
2044 tk.11	Avoctja one
2045 tk.22	Durem
2046 tk.24	Dee Lawd
2047 tk.28	Taru,what's wrong with you (*aka* What's wrong?)
2048 tk.29	Get yourself together

All titles issued on BN LT-1031,CD BN 5-22670-2,(J)TOCJ-1631.

HORACE SILVER - SERENADE TO A SOUL SISTER:
Charles Tolliver(tp) Stanley Turrentine(ts) Horace Silver(p) Bob Cranshaw(b,el b-1) Mickey Roker(dm).
Englewood Cliffs,N.J.,February 23,1968

2049 tk.5	Serenade to a soul sister	BN 45-1939,BN-LA402-H2,B1-93206 CD BN 7-93206-2,4-95576-2
2050 tk.10	Psychedelic Sally -1	BN 45-1939,BN-LA402-H2 CD 4-94030-2,4-95576-2,(J)TOCJ-6100
2051 tk.20	Rain dance	

All titles issued on BN BLP4277/BST84277,CD 7-84277-2.

HERBIE HANCOCK - SPEAK LIKE A CHILD:
Thad Jones(flh) Peter Phillips(bass tb) Jerry Dodgion(alto fl) Herbie Hancock(p) Ron Carter(b) Mickey Roker (dm).
Englewood Cliffs,N.J.,March 6,1968

2058 tk.4	Riot (alt.1)	CD BN(J)TOCJ-66021
2058 tk.5	Riot (alt.2)	-
2058 tk.6	Riot	BN BST89907,B1-91142,(J)K23P-6725 CD BN 7-91142-2,7-96904-2,(J)CJ32-5016, TOCJ-5637,TOCJ-5830,TOCJ-5966,TOCJ-6110, TOCJ-66050
2059 tk.12	Speak like a child	BN BN-LA399-H2,B1-91142,CD 7-91142-2, (F)4-97517-2,(J)CJ28-5040,TOCJ-5637, TOCJ-6110,TOCJ-66050,TOCJ-66053
2060 tk.19	First trip (p,b,dm only)	

Last three titles issued on BN BLP4279/BST84279,CD 7-46136-2.
All titles issued on CD BN 4-95569-2

JOHN PATTON - THAT CERTAIN FEELING:
Junior Cook(ts) John Patton(org) Jimmy Ponder(g) Clifford Jarvis(dm).
Englewood Cliffs,N.J.,March 8,1968

2052 tk.2	Daddy James	
2053 tk.9	Early A.M.	
2054 tk.14	Minor swing	BN(Du)1A158-83401/4
2055 tk.16	Dirty fingers	BN B1-30728
2056 tk.19	I want to go home (ts out)	BN B1-29092,CD8-29092-2
2057 tk.23	String bean	BN B1-35636,CD 8-35636-2

All titles issued on BN BLP4281/BST84281.

HERBIE HANCOCK - SPEAK LIKE A CHILD:
Thad Jones(flh) Peter Phillips(bass tb) Jerry Dodgion(alto fl) Herbie Hancock(p) Ron Carter(b) Mickey Roker(dm).
Englewood Cliffs,N.J.,March 9,1968

2061 tk.20	Goodbye to childhood (alt.)	CD BN(J)TOCJ-66021
2061 tk.23	Goodbye to childhood	BN BST89907,BN-LA399-H2 BN(In)JAZ 1,(J)FCPA 6214
2062 tk.26	The sorcerer (p,b,dm only)	BN(J)W-5510;Lib(J)K22P-6092/93 CD BN 8-54904-2,(F)4-97517-2,(J)CJ28-5022, TOCJ-5187/88,TOCJ-5830
2063 tk.32	Toys	BN BN-LA399-H2

Last three titles issued on BN BLP4279/BST84279,CD 7-46136-2.
All titles issued on CD BN 4-95569-2.

211

BOBBY HUTCHERSON - PATTERNS:
James Spaulding(fl-1,as) Bobby Hutcherson(vb) Stanley Cowell(p) Reggie Workman(b) Joe Chambers(dm).
Englewood Cliffs,N.J.,March 14,1968

2069 tk.1	Patterns (alt.)			
2069 tk.3	Patterns	BN LT-1044,B1-33583		
2070 tk.8	Effi -1	-	-	CD BN(J)TOCJ-5733
2071 tk.10	Nocturnal -1	-	-	
2072 tk.14	Irina	-	-	
2073 tk.25	Ankara	-	-	
2074 tk.29	A time to go -1	-	-	

All titles issued on CD BN 8-33583-2.
Note: On the CD reissue, the first three and second three tunes are flipped,so that tracks 1-3 match tracks 4-6 in the credits.

LOU DONALDSON - MIDNIGHT CREEPER:
Blue Mitchell(tp) Lou Donaldson(as) Lonnie Smith(org) George Benson(g) Leo Morris (Idris Muhammad) (dm).
Englewood Cliffs,N.J.,March 15,1968

tk.4	Elizabeth (tp out)	
tk.8	Dapper Dan	
tk.11	Love power	BN 45-1941
tk.14	Midnight creeper	- B1-30721,(J)NP-2020 CD BN 8-30721-2,8-37745-2,(E)8-53225-2, (J)TOCJ-5864,TOCJ-66044
tk.17	Bag of jewels	

All titles issued on BN BST84280,CD BN 5-24549-2,(J)TOCJ-4280.

FRANK FOSTER - MANHATTAN FEVER:
Marvin Stamm(tp) Garnett Brown(tb) Frank Foster(ts) Richard Wyands(p) Bob Cranshaw(b,el b) Mickey Roker (dm).
Englewood Cliffs,N.J.,March 21,1968

2075 tk.10	You gotta be kiddin'
2076 tk.17	Stampede
2077 tk.20	Manhattan fever
2078 tk.26	Little Miss No Nose
2079 tk.27	Seventh Avenue bill
2080 tk.29	Loneliness (tp,tb out)

All titles issued on BN BLP4278/BST84278.

HORACE SILVER - SERENADE TO A SOUL SISTER:
Charles Tolliver(tp) Bennie Maupin(ts) Horace Silver(p) John Williams(b) Billy Cobham Jr.(dm).
Englewood Cliffs,N.J.,March 29,1968

2081	Kindred spirits	
2082	Jungle juice	
2083	Next time I fall in love (p,b,dm only)	BN BN-LA474-H2

All titles issued on BN BLP4277/BST84277,CD 7-84277-2.

212

ELVIN JONES - PUTTIN' IT TOGETHER:
Joe Farrell(ts-1,ss-2,alto fl-3,picc-4) Jimmy Garrison(b) Elvin Jones(dm).
Englewood Cliffs,N.J.,April 8,1968

2084 tk.2	Village Greene -1	
2085 tk.3	Sweet little Maia -2	
2086 tk.8	Reza -1	CD BN(J)CJ32-5016
2087 tk.16	For heaven's sake -3	
2088 tk.17	Keiko's birthday march -4	
2089 tk.24	Gingerbread boy -1	
2090 tk.27	Jay-Ree -1	

All titles issued on BN BLP4282/BST84282,CD BN 7-84282-2,Mosaic MD8-195.

THE 3 SOUNDS - COLDWATER FLAT:
Gene Harris(p) Andrew Simpkins(b) Donald Bailey(dm) with Melvin Moore,Buddy Childers,Bobby Bryant,Freddy Hill(tp) Lou Blackburn,Pete Myers,Billy Byers(tb) Ernie Tack(bass tb) Anthony Ortega,Frank Strozier(as) Plas Johnson(ts) Bill Green(bs) Ken Watson(perc) Roger Hutchinson( ) Oliver Nelson(arr).
(Liberty Studios) LA,April 10,1968

The look of love	CD BN 8-57749-2
Georgia on my mind -1	CD BN(Eu)5-23444-2
The grass is greener	
I remember Bird	

-1: listed as "Georgia" on LP
All titles issued on BN BST84285.

Hutchinson out.Jay Migliori(ts) replaces Johnson.Lou Singer(tympani,perc) added.
(Liberty Studios) LA,April 11,1968

My romance
Lonely bottles
Do do do (What now is next)
Coldwater flat
Last train to Clarksville

All titles issued on BN BST84285.

Gene Harris(p) Andrew Simpkins(b) Donald Bailey(dm) with Melvin Moore,Buddy Childers,Conte Candoli, Freddy Hill(tp) Lou Blackburn,Milt Bernhart,Billy Byers(tb) Ernie Tack(bass tb) Anthony Ortega,Frank Strozier(as) Plas Johnson,Tom Scott(ts) Bill Green(bs) Ken Watson(perc) Lou Singer(tympani) Roger Hutchinson( ) Oliver Nelson(arr).
(Liberty Studios) LA,April 12,1968

Star Trek — BN BST84285,CD 8-57748-2,EMI(E)5-20535-2

STANLEY TURRENTINE-THE LOOK OF LOVE:
Snooky Young,Jimmy Nottingham(flh) Jim Buffington(frh) Benny Powell(bass tb) Stanley Turrentine(ts) Hank Jones-1 or Duke Pearson-2 (p) Kenny Burrell(g) George Duvivier(b) Grady Tate(dm) Thad Jones-1, Duke Pearson-2(arr).
Englewood Cliffs,N.J.,April 15,1968
Strings (14 pieces) overdubbed on all titles.Englewood Cliffs,N.J.,May 27,1968

2091 tk.7	Blues for Stan -1	
2092 tk.18	Smile -1	BN BN-LA394-H2
2093 tk.22	The look of love -2	BN 45-1940;Liberty C-0942 CD BN(Eu)4-93991-2

All titles issued on BN BST84286.

213

ANDREW HILL:
Woody Shaw(tp) Frank Mitchell(ts) Andrew Hill(p) Jimmy Ponder(g)Reggie Workman(b) Idris Muhammad (Leo Morris)(dm).
Englewood Cliffs,N.J.,April 19,1968

2094 tk.11	Bayou Red	
2095 tk.21/22	Venture inward (g out)	
2096 tk.27	Soul special	BN B1-35636,CD 8-35636-2
2097 tk.32	MC	
2098 tk.33	Love nocturne (g out)	

All titles issued on CD BN 5-22672-2.

ORNETTE COLEMAN QUARTET - NEW YORK IS NOW/LOVE CALL:
Ornette Coleman(tp-1,as-2,v-3) Dewey Redman(ts) Jimmy Garrison(b) Elvin Jones(dm).
(A & R Studios) NYC,April 29,1968

2099 tk.2	We now interrupt for a commercial -3,4	BN BST84287,CD 7-84287-2,8-35414-2
tk.7	Love call (alt.)-1	CD BN 7-84356-2
3000 tk.8	The garden of souls -2,5	BN BST84287,CD 7-84287-2
3001 tk.12	Open to the public -2	BN BST84356,CD 7-84356-2
3002 tk.14/15	Toy dance -2	BN BST84287,CD 7-84287-2
3003 tk.16	Check-out time (alt.) -2	CD BN 7-84356-2
3004 tk.18	Airborne-2	BN BST84356,CD 7-84356-2
tk.19	Broad way blues (alt.) -2	CD BN 7-84287-2,(F)8-54194-2

-4: On original LP,announcements were overdubbed by Mel Fuhrman.On CD,the announcements are by the group as originally performed.
-5: This master contains opening theme statement from the rejected tk.14 on the May 7,1968 session.

STANLEY TURRENTINE - THE LOOK OF LOVE:
Snooky Young,Jimmy Nottingham(flh) Jim Buffington(frh) Benny Powell(bass tb) Stanley Turrentine(ts) Hank Jones(p) Kenny Burrell(g) George Duvivier(b) Grady Tate(dm).
Englewood Cliffs,N.J.,May 2,1968
Strings (14 pieces) arr. by Duke Pearson,overdubbed on.
Englewood Cliffs,N.J.,May 27,1968

3011 tk.29	A beautiful friendship (g out)	BN BST84286
3012 tk.37	This guy's in love with you	BN 45-1940 - CD BN 8-57749-2,4-97222-2, HMV Jazz(E)5-20881-2
301 tk.42	I'm always drunk in San Francisco	BN BST84286
3014 tk.49	Emily	-
3015	Cabin in the sky	rejected

LEE MORGAN - CARAMBA!:
Lee Morgan(tp) Bennie Maupin(ts) Cedar Walton(p) Reggie Workman(b) Billy Higgins(dm).
Englewood Cliffs,N.J.,May 3,1968

3005 tk.4	Helen's ritual	BN BST84289
3006 tk.6	Suicide City	-
3007 tk.16	Cunning Lee	-
3008 tk.19	Caramba (*aka* Dig dis)	- B1-94704 CD BN 4-94704-2,HMV Jazz(E)5-20885-2
3009 tk.21	Soulita	BN BST84289
3010 tk.23	A baby's smile (ts out)	

All titles issued on CD BN 8-53358-2.

<u>ORNETTE COLEMAN QUARTET</u> - <u>NEW YORK IS NOW/LOVE CALL</u>:
Ornette Coleman(tp-1,as-2) Dewey Redman(ts) Jimmy Garrison(b) Elvin Jones(dm).
(A & R Studios) NYC,May 7,1968

3018 tk.4	Love call -1	BN BST84356,CD 7-84356-2
3019 tk.5	Round trip -2	BN BST84287,CD 7-84287-2,8-23372-2
3017 tk.7	Just for you -1	BN(Du)1A158-83401/4 CD BN 7-84356-2
3016 tk.12/16	Broad way blues -2	BN BST84287,BST2-92474, BN(Du)1A158-83401/4, CD 7-84287-2,7-92474-2,8-23372-2
tk.13	Check out time -2	BN BST84356,CD 7-84356-2
tk.14	The garden of souls -2,3	BN BST84287,CD 7-84287-2

-3: Issued versions of this title uses opening theme of this take spliced onto the April 29,1968 master.
Note: tk.4 (Love call) was edited on LP issue.

<u>STANLEY TURRENTINE</u> - <u>AIN'T NO WAY</u>:
Stanley Turrentine(ts) Shirley Scott(org) Jimmy Ponder(g) Bob Cranshaw(b) Ray Lucas(dm).
Englewood Cliffs,N.J.,May 10,1968

3020	I got the feeling	rejected
3021	She's looking good	-
3022 tk.8	Ain't no way	BN LT-1095,CD 8-54719-2

<u>STANLEY TURRENTINE</u> - <u>THE LOOK OF LOVE</u>:
Snooky Young,Jimmy Nottingham(flh) Jim Buffington(frh) Benny Powell(bass tb) Stanley Turrentine(ts) Roland Hanna(p) Kenny Burrell(g) George Duvivier(b) Mickey Roker(dm).
Englewood Cliffs,N.J.,May 13,1968
Strings (14 pieces) arr by Duke Pearson,overdubbed on all titles,
Englewood Cliffs,N.J.,May 27,1968.

3023 tk.67	Cabin in the sky	
3024 tk.76	Here,there and everywhere	CD BN(J)TOCJ-5874,Cap(J)TOCJ-5201
3025 tk.92	MacArthur Park	CD BN(Eu)4-93991-2

All titles issued on BN BST84286.

<u>McCOY TYNER</u> - <u>TIME FOR TYNER</u>:
Bobby Hutcherson(vb) McCoy Tyner(p) Herbie Lewis(b) Freddie Waits(dm).
Englewood Cliffs,N.J.,May 17,1968

3026 tk.2	Little madimba	
3027 tk.8	May street	
3028 tk.11	I didn't know what time it was	CD BN(J)CJ28-5022,CJ28-5165,TOCJ-5934
3029 tk.18	African village	
3030 tk.20	The surrey with the fringe on top (vb out)	Lib(J)K22P-6092/93 CD BN 8-29095-2,8-33207-2,(J)CJ28-5165, CJ32-5016,TOCJ-5187/88,TOCJ-5873
3031 tk.23	I've grown accustomed to your face (p solo)	

All titles issued on BN BST84307,CD 7-84307-2.

215

BOOKER ERVIN:
Woody Shaw(tp) Booker Ervin(ts) Kenny Barron(p) Jan Arnett(b) Billy Higgins(dm).
Englewood Cliffs,N.J.,May 24,1968

tk.2	In a Capricornian way	BN(Du)1A158-83401/4
tk.7	Den Tex	
tk.9	Lynn's tune	
tk.11	204	
tk.12	Gichi	

All titles first scheduled on BN BST84314 (not released) and later issued on BN BN-LA488-H2.

DUKE PEARSON:
Jerry Dodgion(fl,alto fl) Bobby Hutcherson(vb) Duke Pearson(p) Sam Brown(ac g) Al Gafa(el g) Bob Cranshaw (b) Mickey Roker(dm) Victor Pantoja(cga).
Englewood Cliffs,N.J.,June 24,1968

3048	Los ojos alegres (The happy eyes)	rejected
3049 tk.22	Bunda amerela (Little yellow streetcar)	BN BST84293;CD BN(J)TOCJ-5738
3050	The phantom	rejected
3051	The moana surf	-
3052	Say you're mine (p,b,dm only)	-
3053 tk.30	Rosemary's baby (el g,cga out)	BN B1-35220,CD 8-35220-2

JACKIE McLEAN:
Woody Shaw(tp) Jackie McLean(as) Tyrone Washington(ts) Bobby Hutcherson(vb) Scotty Holt(b) Norman Connors(dm).
(Plaza Sound Studios) NYC,July 5,1968

3054	In case you haven't heard	rejected
3055	Hymn to Rap	-
3056	One for Jeru	-
3057	Kupenda	-
3058	Abrasion	-

BOBBY HUTCHERSON- TOTAL ECLIPSE:
Harold Land(fl-1,ts-2) Bobby Hutcherson(vb) Chick Corea(p) Reggie Johnson(b) Joe Chambers(dm).
(Plaza Sound Studios) NYC,July 12,1968

3059	Herzog -2	CD BN 8-35414-2,(Sp)5-21755-2
3060	Same shame -2	
3062 tk.21	Matrix -2	BN(Du)1A158-83401/4
3063 tk.24	Pompeian -1	
3061 tk.25	Total eclipse -2	

All titles issued on BN BST84291,CD 7-84291-2.

216

<u>LONNIE SMITH</u> - <u>THINK!</u>:
Lee Morgan(tp) David Newman(fl-1,ts-2) Lonnie Smith(org) Herman Henry,Melvin Sparks(g) Marion Booker Jr. (dm) Henry "Pucho" Brown(timbales-3) William Bivens,Norberto Apellaniz(cga-3).
Englewood Cliffs,N.J.,July 23,1968

3064	tk.12	The call of the wild -1,2,3	
3065	tk.24	Slouchin' -2,3	CD BN(J)TOCJ-5239
3066	tk.31	Son of ice bag -2	BN 45-1945
3067	tk.51	Three blind mice -2	
3068	tk.57	Think -2	BN 45-1945 CD BN 7-99105-2,TOCJ-5936,TOCJ-66055

All titles issued on BN BST84290,CD 7-84290-2.

<u>ANDREW HILL</u> - <u>GRASS ROOTS</u>:
Lee Morgan(tp) Booker Ervin(ts) Andrew Hill(p) Ron Carter(b) Freddie Waits(dm)
Englewood Cliffs,N.J.,August 5,1968

3069	tk.10	Grass roots	
3070	tk.20	Venture inward	
3071	tk.23	Bayou red	
3072	tk.36	Soul special	
3073	tk.41	Mira	BN(E)BNSLP-4;CD BN 7-95590-2

All titles issued on BN BST84303,CD 5-22672-2.

<u>BIG JOHN PATTON</u> - <u>BOOGALOO</u>:
Vincent McEwan(tp) Harold Alexander(ts,fl-1) John Patton(org) George Edward Brown(dm) Richard Landrum(cga).
Englewood Cliffs,N.J.,August 9,1968

3074	tk.4	Boogaloo boogie	BN B1-30728
3075	tk.6	Spirit	
3076	tk.7	Barefootin'	BN B1-30728
3077	tk.8	B & J (Two sisters)-1	
3078	tk.10	Milk and honey (cga out)	
3079	tk.11	Shoutin' but no poutin'	

All titles issued on BN B1-31878,CD BN 8-31878-2.

<u>REUBEN WILSON</u>:
Trevor Lawrence(ts) Reuben Wilson(org) Eric Gale(g) Tommy Derrick(dm).
Englewood Cliffs,N.J.,August 16,1968

3080	Knock on wood	unissued
3081	Tom's thumb	-
3082	Ronnie's Bonnie	-
3083	Baby I love you	-
3084	Robbin',mashin' & squeezin'	-

<u>TYRONE WASHINGTON</u>:
Tyrone Washington(ts) Herbie Hancock(p) Herbie Lewis(b) Jack DeJohnette(dm).
Englewood Cliffs,N.J.,August 16,1968

3085	tk.2 or 4	Untitled (medium tempo)	rejected
3086	tk.6 or 8	Untitled (3/4)	-
3087	tk.9 or 10	Rene	-
3088	tk.11 or 12	T	-
3089	tk.14 or 15	Untitled (9/4)	-

McCOY TYNER - EXPANSIONS:
Woody Shaw(tp) Gary Bartz(wooden fl-1,as)Wayne Shorter(cl-1,ts)McCoy Tyner(p) Ron Carter(cello) Herbie Lewis(b) Freddie Waits(dm).

Englewood Cliffs,N.J.,August 23,1968

3090 tk.1	Song of happiness -1	
3091 tk.7	Vision	BN(J)W-5514
3092 tk.12	Peresina	CD BN 8-37051-2
3093 tk.21	Smitty's place	CD BN 8-33207-2
		BN(J)K23P-6725,CD CJ28-5165
3094 tk.27	I thought I'd let you know	-

All titles issued on BN BST84338,CD 7-84338-2.

STANLEY TURRENTINE with SHIRLEY SCOTT - THE COMMON TOUCH:
Stanley Turrentine(ts) Shirley Scott(org) Jimmy Ponder(g) Bob Cranshaw(el b) Leo Morris (Idris Muhammad)(dm).

Englewood Cliffs,N.J.,August 30,1968

3095 tk.2	Blowin' in the wind	CD BN 8-35472-2,(Eu)4-93991-2
3096 tk.8	Boogaloo	BN B1-35636,CD 8-35636-2
3097 tk.10	Common touch	
3098 tk.21	Buster Brown	
3099 tk.24	Living through it all	
3100 tk.28	Lonely Avenue	

All titles issued on BN BST84315,CD 8-54719-2.

ELVIN JONES - THE ULTIMATE:
Joe Farrell(fl-1,ss-2,ts-3) Jimmy Garrison(b) Elvin Jones(dm).

Englewood Cliffs,N.J.,September 6,1968

4001 tk.3	What is this? -2
4002 tk.6	In the truth -3
4003 tk.9	Ascendant -2
4004 tk.23	Sometimes joie -3
4005 tk.25	Yesterdays -3
4006 tk.26	We'll be together again -1

All titles issued on BN BST84305,CD Mosaic MD8-195.

DUKE PEARSON - THE PHANTOM:
Jerry Dodgion(fl,alto fl) Bobby Hutcherson(vb) Duke Pearson(p,arr) Sam Brown(ac g) Al Gafa(el g) Bob Cranshaw(b) Mickey Roker(dm) Carlos "Patato" Valdes(cga,guiro).

Englewood Cliffs,N.J.,September 11,1968

4013 tk.7	Los ojos alegres (The happy eyes)	
4014 tk.8	Blues for Alvina (vb,ac g out)	
4015 tk.11	The phantom	BN B1-89907
4016	Bunda amerela (Little yellow streetcar)	rejected
4017 tk.22	The Moana surf	
4018 tk.24	Say you're mine (p,b,dm only)	

All titles,except 4016,issued on BN BST84293,CD BN(J)TOCJ-5738.

BLUE MITCHELL - COLLISION IN BLACK:
Monk Higgins(p,org,arr) Al Vescovo(g) Bob West(b) Paul Humphrey(dm) Miles Grayson(p,perc) Dee Ervin (org,perc) John Cyr(perc). (RPM Studios) LA,September 9,1968
Blue Mitchell(tp) overdubbed on. (RPM Studios) LA,September 11,1968
Jack Redmond,Dick Hyde(tb) Jim Horn,Ernie Watts(fl) Monk Higgins,Anthony Ortega(ts) overdubbed on. (RPM Studios) LA,September 12,1968

2944	Collision in black	BN 45-1944
2945	Deeper in black	
2946	Jo ju ja	
2947	Blue on black	
2948	Swahili suite	BN 45-1944
2949	Monkin' around	
2950	Keep your nose clean	
2951	I ain't jivin'	
2952	Digging in the dirt	
2953	Who dun it	
2954	Kick it	
2955	Keep your soul	

All titles issued on BN BST84300.

LEE MORGAN:
Lee Morgan(tp) Frank Mitchell(ts) Harold Mabern(p) Mickey Bass(b) Billy Higgins(dm).
Englewood Cliffs,N.J.,September 13,1968

4007 tk.4	Blues for Mr. Tatum	rejected
4008 tk.8	The sleepwalker	-
4009 tk.11	Mickey's tune	CD BN 5-22467-2
4010 tk.16	The chief	rejected
4011 tk.21	Leebop	CD BN 5-22467-2
4012 tk.29	Extemporaneous	-

GENE HARRIS & THE THREE SOUNDS - ELEGANT SOUL:
Gene Harris(p) Andrew Simpkins(b) Carl Burnett(dm) with Jim Horn(fl) Alan Estes(vb) Al Vescovo(g) Paul Humphrey(dm) Miles Grayson,Dee Ervin(perc) Leonard Malarsky,Louis Kievman,Jesse Erlich,William Kurash, Henry Felber,Albert Steinberg(strings) Monk Higgins(arr,cond).
(RPM Studios) LA,September 19,1968

2958	Sittin' duck	BN 45-1950 (ed.),B1-94027,CD 4-94027-2
2959	(Sock it to me) Harper Valley P.T.A.	BN 45-1942
2963	Book of Slim	CD BN 5-21152-2

All titles issued on BN BST84301,CD BN(SA)8-31918-2.

Gene Harris(p) Andrew Simpkins(b) Carl Burnett(dm) with Bob Jung(reeds) Alan Estes(vb,perc) Al Vescovo(g) Paul Humphrey(dm) Miles Grayson,Dee Ervin(perc) Leonard Malarsky,Ralph Schaeffer,Dave Burk,Henry Felber,Ron Fulsom,Tibor Zelig(v) Phil Goldberg,Leonard Selic(viola) Jerry Kessler(cello) Monk Higgins(arr,cond).
(RPM Studios) LA,September 20,1968

2956	Elegant soul	BN 45-1942
2957	Do it right now	
2960	Sugar hill	BN 45-1950,CD 8-54363-2
2962	Black gold	
2961	African sweets	
2964	Walls of respect	

All titles issued on BN BST84301,CD BN(SA)8-31918-2.

219

EDDIE GALE - GHETTO MUSIC:
Eddie Gale(tp,soprano recorder,Jamaican thumb p,steel dm,birdwhistle) Russell Lyle(fl-1,ts) Judah Samuel, James "Tokio" Reid(b) Richard Hackett,Thomas Holman(dm) Elaine Beener (lead singer) JoAnn Gale(vo, g-2) Sylvia Bibbs,Barbara Dove,Evelyn Goodwin,Art Jenkins,Fulumi Prince,Norman Wright,Edward Walrond,Sondra Walston,Mildred Weston(vo).

Englewood Cliffs,N.J.,September 20,1968

4019 tk.3	The coming of Gwilu -1	
4020 tk.6	The rain -2	
4021 tk.9	A walk with Thee	
4022 tk.11	Fulton Street	
4023 tk.15	An understanding	

All titles issued on BN BST84294.

JACK WILSON - SONG FOR MY DAUGHTER:
Stan Levey(vb-1,shaker-2) Jack Wilson(p) John Gray(g) Ray Brown(b) Varney Barlow(dm) with strings arr. & dir. by Billy Byers (7 v,2 violas,3 cellos).

(Liberty Studios) LA,September 28,1968

5537 (tk.3/5)	Imagine -2	
5539 (tk.5)	Changing with the times -1	
5544 (tk.6)	Se todas fossem iguais a voce -2	CD BN 8-35283-2

All titles issued on BN BST84328.

STANLEY TURRENTINE - ALWAYS SOMETHING THERE:
Burt Collins(flh) Jimmy Cleveland(tb) Jim Buffington,Dick Berg(frh) Jerry Dodgion(fl,cl,as) Jerome Richardson(fl,cl,ts) Stanley Turrentine(ts) Hank Jones(p) Barry Galbraith (g) Bob Cranshaw(b,el b) Mel Lewis(dm) & 10 strings overdubbed on, incl. Gene Orloff(v),Thad Jones(arr).

(A & R Studios) NYC,,October 1,1968

4024	Fool on the hill	
4025	Little green apples	BN BN-LA394-H2

Both titles issued on BN BST84298,CD (Eu)4-93991-2.

REUBEN WILSON - ON BROADWAY:
Trevor Lawrence(ts) Reuben Wilson(org) Malcolm Riddick(g) Tommy Derrick(dm).

Englewood Cliffs,N.J.,October 4,1968

3811 tk.2	Baby I love you	
3814 tk.6	Poinciana	
3810 tk.8	On Broadway	BN 8-29092-1,CD 8-54363-2,(J)TOCJ-5239
3812 tk.12	Ain't that peculiar	
3813 tk.16	Ronnie's Bonnie	BN B1-28263,B1-94707,CD 8-28263-2,4-94707-2

All titles issued on BN BST84295.

ANDREW HILL - DANCE WITH DEATH:
Charles Tolliver(tp) Joe Farrell(ss-1,ts) Andrew Hill(p) Victor Sproles(b) Billy Higgins(dm).

Englewood Cliffs,N.J.,October 11,1968

4029 tk.4	Yellow violet-1	BN LT-1030	
4030 tk.8	Partitions	-	
4031 tk.10	Dance with death	unissued	
4031 tk.14	Dance with death	BN LT-1030	
4032 tk.22	Fish 'n rice	-	CD BN(Eu)7-89915-2
4033 tk.27	Love nocturne	-	
4034 tk.29	Black sabbath	-	

STANLEY TURRENTINE - ALWAYS SOMETHING THERE:
Burt Collins(tp,flh) Jimmy Cleveland(tb) Brooks Tillotson,Dick Berg(frh) Jerry Dodgion (fl,cl,as) Jerome Richardson(fl,cl,ts) Stanley Turrentine(ts) Herbie Hancock(p) Kenny Burrell(g) Bob Cranshaw(b,el b) Mel Lewis(dm) & 11 strings overdubbed on, incl. Gene Orloff(v),Thad Jones(arr).
(A & R Studios) NYC,October 14,1968

4026	Hey Jude	CD BN 7-94861-2,(Eu)4-93991-2
4027	Light my fire	-
4028	(There's) Always something there (to remind me)	BN 45-1948,CD 8-57749-2

All titles issued on BN BST84298.

JOHN PATTON - UNDERSTANDING:
Harold Alexander(fl-1,ts) John Patton(org) Hugh Walker(dm).
Englewood Cliffs,N.J.,October 25,1968

4035 tk.1	Alfie's theme	BN B1-28263,(J)K22P-6125/26 CDBN 8-28263-2,8-57748-2,(J)TOCJ-5239, TOCJ-5936
4036 tk.2	Understanding	
4037 tk.5	Chitlins con carne -1	CD BN 8-30728-2
4038 tk.9	Soul man	CD BN 7-99105-2
4039 tk.11	Ding dong	
4040 tk.14	Congo chant	

All titles issued on BN BST84306,B1-31223,CD 8-31223-2.

STANLEY TURRENTINE - ALWAYS SOMETHING THERE:
Thad Jones(tp,arr) Burt Collins(flh) Jimmy Cleveland(tb) Jim Buffington,Dick Berg(frh) Jerry Dodgion (fl,cl,as) Jerome Richardson(fl,cl,ts) Stanley Turrentine(ts) Herbie Hancock(p) Kenny Burrell(g) Bob Cranshaw(b,el b) Mickey Roker(dm) & 12 strings overdubbed on, incl. Gene Orloff(v).
(A & R Studios) NYC,October 28,1968

4041	Home town	
4042	Stoned soul picnic	CD BN(Eu)4-93991-2
4043	When I look into your eyes	BN 45-1948
4044	Those were the days	BN BN-LA394-H2
4045	Song for Bonnie	-

All titles issued on BN BST84298.

LOU DONALDSON - SAY IT LOUD!:
Blue Mitchell(tp) Lou Donaldson(el as) Charles Earland(org) Jimmy Ponder(g) Leo Morris (Idris Muhammad)(dm).
Englewood Cliffs,November 6,1968

tk.1	Brother soul (alt.)	BN B1-31883,CD BN 8-31883-2
tk.2	Brother soul	BN BST84299,B1-94709 CD BN 8-37745-2,4-94709-2
tk.3	Snake bone	BN 45-1943,BST84299,B1-30721,CD 8-30721-2
tk.8	Say it loud,I'm black and I'm proud -1	- - - CD BN 8-30721-2,8-35472-2,(J)TOCJ-5864
tk.10	Caravan	BN BST84299,CD 8-37745-2
tk.12	Summertime	- -
tk.16	Red top	unissued

-1: with band vocal on this title.

221

McCOY TYNER:
McCoy Tyner(p) Herbie Lewis(b) Freddie Waits(dm) Nat Bettis(perc).
Englewood Cliffs,N.J.,November 22,1968

3066 tk.4	untitled long tune	rejected
3067 tk.9	Beautiful Brazil	-
3068 tk.14	Planet X (perc out)	BN BN-LA460-H2,CD 8-33207-2
3069 tk.16	You stepped into some changes	rejected

BOBBY HUTCHERSON - SPIRAL:
Harold Land(ts) Bobby Hutcherson(vb) Stanley Cowell(p) Reggie Johnson(b) Joe Chambers(dm).
Englewood Cliffs,N.J.,November 25,1968

tk.8	Spiral	BN LT-996,CD 4-97508-2
tk.14	Visions	- -
tk.18	Poor people's march	- -
	Procession	rejected
tk.28	Ruth	BN LT-996,CD 4-97508-2
tk.36	The wedding march	- -
	Photon in the paper world	rejected

DUKE PEARSON - NOW HEAR THIS:
Jimmy Bessy,Randy Brecker,Burt Collins,Joe Shepley,Marvin Stamm(tp) Garnett Brown,Jimmy Cleveland, Benny Powell(tb) Kenny Rupp(bass tb) Jerry Dodgion,Al Gibbons(as) Frank Foster(ts,arr-1) Lew Tabackin (ts) Pepper Adams(bs) Duke Pearson(p,arr) Bob Cranshaw(b) Mickey Roker(dm) Andy Bey(vo).
Englewood Cliffs,N.J.,December 2,1968

3056	Days of wine and roses	rejected
3057	Here's that rainy day	-
3058	Minor league	-
3059	I'm tired of cryin' over you	-

Same.
Englewood Cliffs,N.J.,December 3,1968

3061 tk.25	Make it good	CD BN 4-94508-2
3062 tk.35	Amanda	
3063 tk.43	Dad digs Mom	
3060 tk.47	Disapproachment-1	CD BN 4-94508-2
3056 tk.53	Days of wine and roses	-
3057 tk.54	Here's that rainy day	-
3058 tk.55	Minor league	-
3064 tk.60	Tones for Joan's bones	-
3059 tk.62	I'm tired of cryin' over you (voAB)	

All titles issued on BN BST84308.

INTRODUCING KENNY COX AND THE CONTEMPORARY JAZZ QUINTET:
Charles Moore(tp) Leon Henderson(ts) Kenny Cox(p) Ron Brooks(b) Danny Spencer(dm).
(United Sound Systems) Detroit,Michigan,December 9,1968

3050 tk.1	Eclipse	
3048 tk.2	Diahnn	
3047 tk.3	Trance dance	BN(Du)1A158-83401/4
3049 tk.4	Number four	
3046 tk.5	Mystique	
3051 tk.7	You	

All titles issued on BN BST84302.

222

JACK WILSON - SONG FOR MY DAUGHTER:
Victor Feldman(vb-1,tympani-2) Jack Wilson(p) Howard Roberts(g-3) Andy Simpkins(b) Jimmie Smith (dm) & strings arr. & cond. by Billy Byers (8 v,2 violas,2 cellos).
(Liberty Studios) LA,December 16,1968

5543 (tk.8) Eighty-one
5538 (tk.7) Herman's helmet -1,3
5540 (tk.8) Night creature (3rd movement:Dazzling creature)-2

All titles issued on BN BST84328.

LONNIE SMITH - TURNING POINT:
Lee Morgan(tp) Julian Priester(tb) Bennie Maupin(ts) Lonnie Smith(org) Melvin Sparks(g) Leo Morris (Idris Muhammad)(dm).
Englewood Cliffs,N.J.,January 3,1969

3307	tk.7	See saw	CD BN(J)TOCJ-6100
3308	tk.11	Eleanor Rigby	CD BN 7-94861-2 BN(J)K22P-6125/26
3309	tk.15	Turning point	
3310	tk.19	Slow high	
3311	tk.27	People sure act funny (tp,tb,ts out)	BN B1-94027

All titles issued on BN BST84313,CD BN(J)TOCJ-4313.

THE HORACE SILVER QUINTET - YOU GOTTA TAKE A LITTLE LOVE:
Randy Brecker(tp-1,flh-2) Bennie Maupin(fl-3,ts) Horace Silver(p) John Williams(b) Billy Cobham Jr.(dm).
Englewood Cliffs,N.J.,January 10,1969

3393	tk.7	The rising sun -1	BN BST84309
3394	tk.15	You gotta take a little love -1	BN 45-1946,BST84309,BN-LA402-H2
3395		It's time -2	rejected
3396	tk.25	Lovely's daughter -3	BN BST84309

Same.
Englewood Cliffs,N.J.,January 17,1969

3397	tk.29	Brain wave -1	
3398	tk.34	The belly dancer -1	
3399	tk.36	Down and out -1	BN 45-1946
3395	tk.42	It's time -2	CD BN 4-95576-2

All titles issued on BN BST84309.

FRANK FOSTER:
Burt Collins(tp,piccolo tp-1) Jimmy Cleveland(tb) Ed Pazant(fl,as,oboe-1) Frank Foster(alto cl-1,ts) George Cables(p) Buster Williams(b) Mickey Roker(dm).
Englewood Cliffs,N.J.,January 31,1969

3322	tk.1	Slug's bag	unissued
3323	tk.7	Buster Brown	-
3324	tk.15	Fly by night- 1	BN(Du)1A158-83401/4
3325	tk.23	Hip shakin'	unissued
3326	tk.27	What's new from the monster mill	-
3327	tk.31	The house that love built -2	-

-2: Collins,Cleveland & Pazant out.
Note: All titles were scheduled on BN BST84316,which was not released.

223

LARRY YOUNG - MOTHER SHIP:
Lee Morgan(tp) Herbert Morgan(ts) Larry Young(org) Eddie Gladden(dm).
Englewood Cliffs,N.J.,February 7,1969

553	tk.2	Visions	CD BN 7-99177-2
554	tk.6	Love drops	
555	tk.8	Trip merchant	
556	tk.12	Mother ship	
557	tk.13	Street scene	BN 8-29092-1,CD 8-29092-2

All titles issued on BN LT-1038,Mosaic MR9-137,CD MD6-137.

DUKE PEARSON - MERRY OLE SOUL:
Duke Pearson(p,celeste) Bob Cranshaw(b) Mickey Roker(dm).
Englewood Cliffs,N.J.,February 25,1969

3705	tk.4	Sleigh ride	BN BST84323;CD BN(J)28WD-1001
	tk.9	Have yourself a merry Christmas	rejected
	tk.16	Go tell it on the mountain	-
	tk.17	Little drummer boy	-
3709	tk.22	Old fashioned Christmas	unissued
	tk.32	Santa Claus is coming to town	rejected
	tk.34	Silent night	-
	tk.35	Jingle bells	-
	tk.37	Wassail song	-

(see remakes of rejected titles on August 19,1969 session)

REUBEN WILSON:
Richard Williams(tp) Trevor Lawrence(ts) Reuben Wilson(org) Jimmy Ponder(g) George Baker(b) Tommy Derrick(dm).
Englewood Cliffs,N.J.,February 28,1969

3737	Hot rod	rejected
3738	Stormy	-
3739	Cruisin'	-
3740	I'm gonna make you love me	-

STANLEY TURRENTINE - ANOTHER STORY:
Thad Jones(flh) Stanley Turrentine(ts) Cedar Walton(p) Buster Williams(b) Mickey Roker(dm).
Englewood Cliffs,N.J.,March 3,1969

3743	tk.2	The way you look tonight
3744	tk.11	Quittin' time
3745	tk.22	Stella by starlight (flh out)
3746	tk.28	Six and four
3747	tk.31	Get it

All titles issued on BN BST84336.

<u>ELVIN JONES</u>:
Lee Morgan(tp) Joe Farrell(fl-1,alto fl-2,ss-3,ts-4) George Coleman(ts) Wilbur Little(b) Elvin Jones (dm) Candido Camero(cga) Miovelito Valles(perc).
Englewood Cliffs,N.J.,March 14,1969

3852 tk.1	Dido Afrique -1,4	
3853 tk.4	Champagne baby (perc out) -3	
3854 tk.8	Inner space (cga,perc out) -4	BN(Du)1A158-83401/4
3855 tk.14	Raynay -4	
3856 tk.18	Once I loved (O amor em paz) (Coleman out) -2	

All titles issued on BN BN-LA506-H2,CD Mosaic MD8-195.

<u>REUBEN WILSON</u> - <u>LOVE BUG</u>:
Lee Morgan(tp) George Coleman(ts) Reuben Wilson(org) Grant Green(g) Leo Morris (Idris Muhammad) (dm).
Englewood Cliffs,N.J.,March 21,1969

3959 tk.3/4	Love bug	BN B1-94907,CD 4-94707-2,(J)TOCJ-6191
3961 tk.9	Back out	CD BN 8-37741-2
3960 tk.12	Stormy	
3956 tk.15	Hot rod	BN B1-96563,B1-35636,B1-94707 CD BN 8-27533-2,8-35636-2,4-94707-2, (J)TOCJ-5644
3958 tk.16	I say a little prayer	CD BN 8-57749-2
3957 tk.17	I'm gonna make you love me	

All titles issued on BN BST84317,B1-29905,CD 8-29905-2.

<u>McCOY TYNER</u>:
Harold Vick(ss) Al Gibbons(reeds,fl) McCoy Tyner(p) Herbie Lewis(b) Freddie Waits(dm) & string quartet: Julian Barber,Emanuel Green(v) Gene Orloff (viola) Kermit Moore(cello,dir).
Englewood Cliffs,N.J.,April 4,1969

tk.4	Shaken but not forsaken	
tk.10	Cosmos	
tk.15	Song for my lady	CD BN 8-37051-2 BN(Du)1A158-83401/4
tk.19	Vibration blues (p,b,dm only)	

All titles issued on BN BN-LA460-H2.

<u>DUKE PEARSON</u> - <u>HOW INSENSITIVE</u>:
Duke Pearson(flh,p,el p,arr) Al Gafa(el g) Bob Cranshaw(b) Mickey Roker(dm) Airto Moreira(perc) Andy Bey(vo) with New York Group Singers' Big Band: Art Lang,Tony Wells,Charles Magruder,James Ryan, Don Riddell,Christine Spencer,June Magruder,Curley Hale,Joan Wibe, Robin Green,Elise Bretton,Adrienne Abbot,Lillian Clark,Robert Carlson,David Vogel,Helen Mils(voices) Jack Manno(arr,cond).
Englewood Cliffs,N.J.,April 11,1969

4019 tk.3	Cristo redentor	CD BN 7-80703-2,5-21152-2
4018 tk.9	Give me your love (voAB)	
4017 tk.17	Stella by starlight	CD BN(J)TOCJ-5740
4020 tk.21	Little song	

All titles issued on BN BST84344,CD BN(J)TOCJ-4344.

225

DUKE PEARSON - HOW INSENSITIVE:
Duke Pearson(flh-1,p,el p,arr) Al Gafa(el g) Bob Cranshaw(b) Mickey Roker(dm) Airto Moreira(perc) Andy Bey(vo) with New York Group Singers' Big Band: Art Lang,Tony Wells,Charles Magruder,James Ryan, Don Riddell,Christine Spencer,June Magruder,Curley Hale,Joan Wibe,Robin Green,Elise Bretton,Adrienne Abbot,Lillian Clark,Harry Duvall,William Ruthenberg,Camilla Duncan(voices) Jack Manno(arr,cond).
Englewood Cliffs,N.J.,April 14,1969

4021 tk.29	Clara (voAB)-1	BN BST84344;CD BN(J)TOCJ-4344
4022 tk.39	My love waits	- -
4023 tk.43	Old fashioned Christmas	unissued
4024 tk.44	How insensitive (p solo)	BN BST84344;CD BN(J)TOCJ-4344

HERBIE HANCOCK - THE PRISONER:
Johnny Coles(flh) Garnett Brown(tb) Tony Studd(bass tb) Hubert Laws(fl) Joe Henderson(alto fl,ts) Jerome Richardson(bass cl) Herbie Hancock(p) Buster Williams(b) Albert "Tootie" Heath(dm).
Englewood Cliffs,N.J.,April 18,1969

4011 tk.4/5	The prisoner -1 (alt.)	CD BN (J)TOCJ-66021
4011 tk.10	The prisoner -1	BN BST84321,BN-LA399-H2, CD BN 7-46845-2,7-89287-2,(J)TOCJ-4321
4012 tk.31	He who lives in fear -1	BN BST84321,BST89907,CD 7-46845-2

-1: Hancock plays electric piano on the ensemble sections.
All titles issued on CD BN 4-95569-2,5-25649-2.

Same.
Englewood Cliffs,N.J.,April 21,1969

4013 tk.40	I have a dream	BN BST84321,BST89907 CD BN 7-46845-2,8-35472-2,8-54904-2, 4-95569-2,5-25649-2,(J)CJ28-5040,TOCJ-4321, TOCJ-5830,TOCJ-66050

JACK WILSON - SONG FOR MY DAUGHTER:
Jack Wilson(p) + ?
(Liberty Studios) LA,April 21,1969

tk.1	Sunny	unissued

Tommy Vig(vb) Jack Wilson(p) Howard Roberts(g) Ray Brown(b) Donald Bailey(dm).
(Liberty Studios) LA,April 23,1969

	Scarborough fair/Canticle	rejected
5546 tk.6	Soft Summer rain	BN BST84328

HERBIE HANCOCK - THE PRISONER:
Johnny Coles(flh) Garnett Brown(tb) Jack Jeffers(bass tb) Jerome Richardson(fl) Joe Henderson(alto fl,ts) Romeo Penque(bass cl) Herbie Hancock(p) Buster Williams(b) Albert "Tootie" Heath(dm).
Englewood Cliffs,N.J.,April 23,1969

4014 tk.42	Firewater	BN BST84321,CD 7-46845-2,(J)TOCJ-4321 BN(Du)1A158-83401/4
4014 tk.45	Firewater (alt.)	CD BN(J)TOCJ-66021
4015 tk.52	Promise of the sun	BN BST84321,CD 7-46845-2,(F)4-97517-2, (J)TOCJ-4321

All titles issued on CD BN 4-95569-2,5-25649-2.

<u>LOU DONALDSON</u> - <u>HOT DOG</u>:
Ed Williams(tp) Lou Donaldson(el as) Charles Earland(org) Melvin Sparks(g) Leo Morris (Idris Muhammad) (dm).

Englewood Cliffs,N.J.,April 25,1969

tk.1	Turtle walk	BN B1-99106,B1-30721,B1-94709 CD BN 7-99106-2,8-30721-2,8-37745-2, 4-94709-2,(J)TOCJ-5864,TOCJ-6100,TOCJ-66044
tk.4	It's your thing	BN B1-54360,CD 8-54360-2,(J)TOCJ-5644, TOCJ-5864
tk.8	Hot dog	BN 45-1949,CD(Eu) 7-89915-2
tk.11	Who's making love (to your old lady)-1	- B1-99106,B1-30721 CD BN 7-99106-2,8-27533-2,(J)TOCJ-5864
tk.14	Bonnie	

-1: band vocal on this title.
All titles issued on BN BST84318,B1-28267,CD 8-28267-2.

<u>EDDIE GALE</u> - <u>BLACK RHYTHM HAPPENING</u>:
Eddie Gale(tp) Roland Alexander(fl,ss) Jimmy Lyons(as) Russell Lyle(fl,ts) JoAnn Gale Stevens(g-1,vo) Judah Samuel,Henry Pearson(b) Elvin Jones(dm) John Robinson(African dm) Noble Gale Singers (Fulumi Prince,Sylvia Bibbs,Paula Nadine Larkin,Carol Ann Robinson,Sondra Walston,William Norwood,Charles Davis) (vo).

Englewood Cliffs,N.J.,May 2,1969

4219	Ghetto Summertime -3	BN 45-1952
4220	The gleeker -1	
4221	It must be you	
4222	Black rhythm happening -1	BN 45-1952,B1-35636,CD 8-35472-2,8-35636-2
4223	Look at Teyonda -2	
4224	Song of will	
4379	Ghetto love night	
4380	Mexico thing	

-2: recitation by Norwood.
-3: Eddie Gale(tp) Judah Samuel,Henry Pearson(b) Elvin Jones(dm).
All titles issued on BN BST84320.

<u>DUKE PEARSON</u> - <u>HOW INSENSITIVE</u>:
Duke Pearson(p) Dorio Ferreira(g,perc) Bebeto Jose Souza(b) Airto Moreira(dm) Mickey Roker(perc) Flora Purim(vo).

Englewood Cliffs,N.J.,May 5,1969

6181 tk.16	Sandalia dela	BN BST84344,(E)BNSLP-1 CD BN 7-95590-2,(J)TOCJ-5778
6182 tk.24	Tears	BN BST84344
6202 tk.29	Upa neguinho	BN B1-35220, CD 8-35220-2, 4-97156-2
6201 tk.34	Lamento	BN BST84344

All titles from BST84344 also issued on CD BN(J)TOCJ-4344.

227

DONALD BYRD - FANCY FREE:
Donald Byrd(tp) Julian Priester(tb) Lew Tabackin(fl) Frank Foster(ts) Duke Pearson(el p) Jimmy Ponder(g) Roland Wilson(b) Joe Chambers(dm) Nat Bettis,John Robinson(perc).
Englewood Cliffs,N.J.,May 9,1969

4279 tk.2	Weasil	BN 7-99106-1 CD BN 7-89606-2,7-99106-2
4278 tk.8	I love the girl	

Both titles issued on BN BST84319,CD 7-89796-2.

ANDREW HILL - LIFT EVERY VOICE:
Woody Shaw(tp) Carlos Garnett(ts) Andrew Hill(p) Richard Davis(b) Freddie Waits(dm) Lawrence Marshall vocal choir (LaReine LaMer,Gail Nelson,Joan Johnson,Benjamin Franklin Carter,Antenett Goodman Ray, Ron Steward,Lawrence Marshall).
Englewood Cliffs,N.J.,May 16,1969

4363	Ghetto lights	
4361 tk.3	Two lullabies	
4359 tk.15	Hey hey	CD BN 7-80703-2
4362	Love chant	
4360	Lift every voice	

All titles issued on BN BST84330,CD 5-27546-2.

LEE MORGAN:
Lee Morgan,Burt Collins,Joe Shepley(tp,flh) Jean "Toots" Thielemans(hca,g) Duke Pearson(p,arr) Al Gafa, Wally Richardson(g) Ron Carter(b) Mickey Roker(dm) Airto Moreira(perc).
(A & R Studios) NYC,May 22,1969

4377 tk.6	Midnight cowboy	BN 45-1951,CD 8-57748-2,4-97222-2
4378 tk.13	Popi (Morgan out)	-

BLUE MITCHELL - BANTU VILLAGE:
Blue Mitchell,Bobby Bryant(tp) Charlie Loper(tb) Buddy Collette(fl) Bill Green(fl,as) Plas Johnson(ts) Dee Ervin(p,perc) Monk Higgins(p,perc,arr,cond) Al Vescovo,Freddy Robinson(g) Bob West(b) John Guerin (dm) Alan Estes(cga).
(RPM Studios) LA,May 22,1969

5170	Blue Dashiki	CD BN 4-94031-2
5168	Heads down	
5166	Flat backing	BN B1-54360

All titles issued on BN BST84324.

BLUE MITCHELL - BANTU VILLAGE:
Blue Mitchell,Bobby Bryant(tp) Charlie Loper(tb) Buddy Collette(fl) Bill Green(fl,as) Plas Johnson(ts) Dee Ervin(p,perc) Monk Higgins(p,perc,arr,cond) Al Vescovo,Freddy Robinson(g) Wilton Felder(b) Paul Humphrey(dm) King Errison(cga).
(RPM Studios) LA,May 23,1969

4779/80	H.N.I.C.	BN 45-1954
5167	Na ta ka	
5171	Bush girl	
5169	Bantu Village	

All titles issued on BN BST84324.

From May 22 or May 23 session:

	3-6-9	unissued

DONALD BYRD - FANCY FREE:
Donald Byrd(tp) Julian Priester(tb) Jerry Dodgion(fl) Frank Foster(ts) Duke Pearson(el p) Jimmy Ponder(g) Roland Wilson(b) Leo Morris (Idris Muhammad)(dm) Nat Bettis,John Robinson(perc).
Englewood Cliffs,N.J.,June 6,1969

4276 tk.10	Fancy free	BN(Du)1A158-83401/4 CD The Right Stuff 8-57072-2
4277 tk.23	The uptowner	

Both titles issued on BN BST84319,CD 7-89796-2.

JOHN PATTON:
Marvin Cabell(ss,ts) George Coleman(ts) John Patton(org) Leroy Williams(dm).
Englewood Cliffs,N.J.,June 9,1969

tk.5	Buddy boy	CN BN 8-53924-2
tk.16	2 J	-
tk.23	Man from Tanganyika	BN B1-30728,CD BN 8-35221-2
tk.25	Sissy strut	- -
tk.30	Dragon slayer	-
tk.33	Sweet Pea	CD BN 8-53924-2

JACK McDUFF - DOWN HOME STYLE:
Jay Arnold(ts) Jack McDuff(org) Charlie Freeman(g) unknown(el b) Sammy Greason(dm).
Memphis,June 10,1969

4467	The vibrator	BN 45-1957
4468	Down home style -1	BN 45-1953
4469	Memphis in June -1	
4470	Theme from electric surfboard	BN 45-1953
4471	It's all a joke	
4472	Butter (for yo' popcorn)-1	BN B1-96563,CD 7-96563-2
4473	Groovin' (On a Sunday afternoon)	
4474	As she walked away	

-1: unidentified large band added.
All titles issued on BN BST84322,B1-54329,CD 8-54329-2.

ANDREW HILL:
Carlos Garnett(ts) Karl Porter(bassoon) Andrew Hill(p) Richard Davis(b) Freddie Waits(dm) Sanford Allen (v) Selwart Clarke,Booker Rowe(viola) Kermit Moore(cello).
Englewood Cliffs,N.J.,June 13,1969

	Soulmate	rejected
	untitled	-
	untitled	-

JACK WILSON:
Jack Wilson(p) Ike Isaacs(b) Donald Bailey(dm).
(Liberty Studios) LA,June 19,1969

5541 (tk.6)	Scarborough fair/Canticle	BN BST84328
(tk.2)	Soulin'	unissued
(tk.1)	Soft Summer rain	rejected

229

JACK WILSON:
Jack Wilson(p) Ike Isaacs(b) Donald Bailey(dm) .
(Liberty Studios) LA,June 21,1969
Betty Marks,Israel Baker(v) Dave Burk,Myer Bellow(viola) Kurt Reher,Jesse Ehrlich(cello) Billy Byers(arr,cond) overdubbed on.
(Liberty Studios) LA,June 26,1969

5542 (tk.5)	Song for my daughter (b,dm out)	BN BST84328
(tk.1)	Street scene	unissued
5545 (tk.5)	Stormy	BN BST84328
(tk.2)	Non sectarian blues (Presbyterian blues)	unissued

STANLEY TURRENTINE - AIN'T NO WAY:
Stanley Turrentine(ts) McCoy Tyner(p,el p-1) Gene Taylor(b) Billy Cobham(dm).
Englewood Cliffs,N.J.,June 23,1969

tk.4	Intermission walk	BN LT-1095	
tk.7	Stan's shuffle	-	
tk.14	Watch what happens	-	CD 7-95281-2
tk.19	Wave	-	CD 8-35283-2,(Eu)4-93991-2
	Three quarters -1	rejected	

All issued titles also on CD BN 8-29908-2.

DONALD BYRD:
Donald Byrd(tp) Kenny Rupp(frh) Al Gibbons(fl) Gary Campbell(ts) Duke Pearson(el p) Wally Richardson (g) Bob Cranshaw(el b) Freddie Waits(dm) Roland Wilson(cga) & 3 vocalists.
(A & R Studios) NYC,July 7,1969

4612-9	Now wheddy (horns out)	rejected
4613-5	Yano	-
4614-3	Congo (instr.)	-

HANK MOBLEY - THE FLIP:
Dizzy Reece(tp) Slide Hampton(tb) Hank Mobley(ts) Vince Benedetti(p) Alby Cullaz(b) Philly Joe Jones (dm).
(Barclay Studios) Paris,July 12,1969

4804 tk.5	Early morning stroll	
4805 tk.12	18th hole	
4806 tk.18	Feelin' folksy	
4807 tk.24	Snappin' out	
4808 tk.26	The flip	BN 8-57745-1,CD 8-57745-2

All titles issued on BN BST84329.

ANDREW HILL:
Bennie Maupin-1(fl,ts) Andrew Hill(p) Ron Carter(b Mickey Roker(dm) & string quartet: Sanford Allen(v) Al Brown,Selwart Clarke(viola) Kermit Moore(cello,dir).
Englewood Cliffs,N.J.,August 1,1969

tk.5	Poinsettia -1	BN BN-LA459-H2
tk.8	Fragments	-
tk.12	Not so	rejected
tk.15	Illusion -1	BN BN-LA459-H2,CD 5-21152-2
tk.20	Soulmate	rejected

230

LONNIE SMITH - MOVE YOUR HAND:
Rudy Jones(ts) Ronnie Cuber(bs) Lonnie Smith(org,vo) Larry McGee(g) Sylvester Goshay(dm).
(Club Harlem) Atlantic City,August 9,1969

4809 tk.2	Charlie Brown	BN BST84326,B1-31249
4810 tk.4	Satisfaction	rejected
4811 tk.5	Move your hand (voLS)-1	BN 45-1955,BST84326,B1-99106,B1-31249 CD BN 4-94030-2
4812 tk.6	Sunshine superman	BN BST84326,B1-31249 BN(J)K22P-6125/26,CD (J)TOCJ-5644
4813 tk.7	Dancin' In An Easy Groove	BN B1-31883,CD 8-31883-2
4814 tk.8	Layin' in the cut	BN BST84326,B1-31249

-1: shown as pts. 1 & 2 on sides of 45-1955. Pt. 1 was reissued in CD BN 4-94030-2.
All titles,except 4810,issued on CD BN 8-31249-2.

BOBBY HUTCHERSON - MEDINA:
Harold Land(ts,fl-1) Bobby Hutcherson(vb) Stanley Cowell(p) Reggie Johnson(b) Joe Chambers(dm).
Englewood Cliffs,N.J.,August 11,1969

4915 tk.7	Avis
4916 tk.11	Ungano
4917 tk.16	Orientale -1
4918 tk.18	Medina
4919 tk.24	Comes Spring
4920 tk.28	Dave's chant

All titles issued on BN LT-1086,CD 4-97508-2.

JOHN PATTON- ACCENT ON THE BLUES:
Marvin Cabell(fl,saxello,ts) John Patton(org) James Ulmer(g) Leroy Williams(dm).
Englewood Cliffs,N.J.,August 15,1969

4992 tk.10	Lite hit (alt.)	BN B1-31883*,CD 8-31883-2*
4992 tk.11	Lite hit	
4993 tk.21	Freedom jazz dance	CD BN 8-30728-2
4994 tk.23	Captain Nasty	
4995 tk.27	Don't let me lose this dream	
4996 tk.31	Rakin' and scrapin'	
4997 tk.34	Village Lee	

All titles,except tk.10,issued on BN BST84340,B1-53924, CD 8-53924-2.
Note: Lite hit (alt.) was mislabelled Village Lee (alt.) on issues marked *.

DUKE PEARSON- MERRY OLE SOUL:
Duke Pearson(p,celeste) Bob Cranshaw(b) Mickey Roker(dm) Airto Moreira(perc).
(A & R Studios) NYC,August 19,1969

3705	(tk.8)	Sleigh ride	rejected
3712	(tk.4)	Jingle bells	BN BST84323;CD Cap(J)TOCJ-5189
3706	(tk.9)	Have yourself a merry Christmas	- -
3707	(tk.7)	Go tell it on a mountain	-
3708	(tk.2)	Little drummer boy	-
3711	(tk.1)	Silent night	-
3710	(tk.2)	Santa Claus is coming to town	-
3725	(tk;3)	Wassail song	-
	(tk.2)	O little town of Bethlehem (p solo)	-

All titles from BST84323 also issued on CD BN(J)28WD-1001,TOCJ-5648.

LOU DONALDSON - EVERYTHING I PLAY IS FUNKY:
Eddie Williams(tp) Lou Donaldson(as-1,el as-2) Charles Earland(org) Melvin Sparks(g) Jimmy Lewis(el b) Leo Morris (Idris Muhammad)(dm).

Englewood Cliffs,N.J.,August 22,1969

5027 tk.4	Donkey walk -2	BN UAS-2301,BST84337,B1-31248 CD BN 8-31248-2,(J)TOCJ-5864
5028 tk.6	untitled original blues No.1	rejected
5029 tk.8	West Indian Daddy -1	BN UAS-2301,BST84337,B1-31248,CD 8-31248-2
tk.10	untitled original blues No.2	rejected
tk.12	Candy men	-

THE THREE SOUNDS - SOUL SYMPHONY:
Gene Harris(p) Henry Franklin(b) Carl Burnett(dm) with David Duke(frh) Buddy Collette(fl,alto fl) Freddy Robinson(g) Alan Estes(perc) & strings led by Sid Sharp.Monk Higgins (comp,arr,cond).
(Liberty Studios) LA,August 26,1969

5087	Repeat after me	BN BST 84341,B1-94027 CD BN 4-94027-2,(SA)8-31917-2
5088	Upper four hundred	BN BST84341,CD BN(SA)8-31917-2
5089	Popsicle pimp	- -
5090	Black sugar	- -

Duke out.

(Liberty Studios) LA,August 27,1969

Soul symphony (see below)

Same as on Aug. 26,except Art Maebe(frh) added,Jim Getzoff(v) replaces Sid Sharp.
(Liberty Studios) LA,August 28,1969

Soul symphony (see below)

Presumably taken from above two sessions,with Specialties Unlimited (Alex Brown,Clydie King,Mamie Galore)(background vo) overdubbed later on.

5086	Soul symphony	BN BST84341,CD BN(SA) 8-31917-2

WAYNE SHORTER - SUPER NOVA:
Wayne Shorter(ss) John McLaughlin(el g,ac g-1) Sonny Sharrock(el g) Miroslav Vitous(b) Jack DeJohnette (dm,perc-1) Chick Corea(dm,vb-1).
(A & R Studios) NYC,August 29,1969

5052 tk.2	Capricorn	
5053 tk.3	Super nova	BN(J)W-5514 CD BN 8-59072-2,(J)CJ28-5039,TOCJ-66049
5054 tk.9	Water babies	BN(Du)1A158-83401/4;CD BN 7-91141-2
5055 tk.10	Swee-Pea -1	

All titles issued on BN BST84332,CD 7-84332-2.

Wayne Shorter(ss) Sonny Sharrock(el g) Walter Booker(ac g-1) Miroslav Vitous(b) Jack DeJohnette (dm,African thumb p-1) Chick Corea(dm,perc-1) Airto Moreira(perc) Maria Booker(vo).
(A & R Studios) NYC,September 2,1969

5056 tk.4	Dindi (voMB) -1	BN BST84332,CD 7-84332-2
5057 tk.6	More than human	- -

LEE MORGAN:
Lee Morgan(tp) Julian Priester(tb) George Coleman(ts) Harold Mabern(p) Walter Booker(b) Mickey Roker (dm). Englewood Cliffs,N.J.,September 12,1969

5142	Stormy weather	
5143	Mr. Johnson	
5144	Untitled boogaloo	CD BN 5-21152-2

All titles issued on BN BN-LA582-J2,(J)GXF-3024,CD BN(J)TOCJ-1629.

<u>JIMMY McGRIFF</u> - <u>ELECTRIC FUNK</u>:
Jimmy McGriff(org) Horace Ott(el p,arr) & unknown tp,ts,horn section,g,el b,dm.
NYC,September ,1969

	Back on the track	
	Chris cross	CD BN 8-57063-2 BN(E)B1-30724,CD 8-30724-2
	Miss Poopie	
	The bird wave	BN B1-35636,CD 8-35636-2
	Spear for moon dog,pt.1	
	Spear for moon dog,pt.2	
	Tight times	
	Spinning wheel	
	Funky junk	

All titles issued on BN BST84350,CD 7-84350-2.

<u>ELVIN JONES</u> - <u>POLYCURRENTS</u>:
Joe Farrell(English h-1,fl-2,ts-3) George Coleman(ts) Pepper Adams(bs) Wilbur Little(b) Elvin Jones(dm) Candido Camero(cga).
Englewood Cliffs,N.J.,September 26,1969

5210 tk.1	Mr. Jones -3	BN BST84331,BN-LA110-F
5211 tk.3	Yes -4	-
tk.5	unknown title (cga out) -3	rejected
5212 tk.9	Agappe love -2	BN BST84331
5214 tk.12	Whew (bs,cga out)-3	-
5213 tk.14	Agenda-1	-

-4: Fred Tompkins(fl) Joe Farrell(bass fl) Wilbur Little(b) Elvin Jones(dm).
All titles,except tk.5, also issued on CD BN 7-84331-2,Mosaic MD8-195.

<u>DUKE PEARSON</u>:
Burt Collins(tp) Al Gibbons(fl) Jerry Dodgion(as) Frank Foster(ts) Bobby Hutcherson(vb) Duke Pearson (el p-1,p) Al Gafa(g) Bob Cranshaw(b) Mickey Roker(dm) Airto Moreira(perc,vo) Stella Mars(vo).
(A & R Studios) NYC,October 3,1969

5220-5	Once I loved (voAM,SM) (O amor em paz)	CD BN 8-35220-2,8-35283-2,(Au)8-14710-2
5221-5	Xibaba (voAM)-1	BN B1-35220,CD 8-35220-2
5222-2	Is that so?	rejected

<u>BOBBY HUTCHERSON</u> - <u>NOW!</u>:
Harold Land(ts) Bobby Hutcherson(vb) Kenny Barron(p) Wally Richardson(el g) Herbie Lewis(b) Joe Chambers(dm) Candido Camero(cga) Gene McDaniels(vo) Christine Spencer,Hilda Harris,Albertine M. Robinson(background vo).
(A & R Studios) NYC,October 3,1969

5223 tk.3	Herbie's tune (McDaniels out)	unissued
5224	Slow change	rejected
5225 tk.6	Now (g,cga out)	BN BST84333
5226 tk.10	Hello to the wind	-
5227	The creator	rejected
5228	Black heroes	-

GRANT GREEN - CARRYIN' ON:
Claude Bartee(ts) William Bivens(vb) Clarence Palmer(el p) Grant Green(g) Jimmy Lewis(el b) Leo Morris (Idris Muhammad)(dm).
Englewood Cliffs,N.J.,October 3,1969

5251 tk.5	Hurt so bad	BN BST84327
5246 tk.12	I don't want nobody to give me nothing	- B1-89622
		CD BN 7-89622-2,(J)TOCJ-5733
5247 tk.19	Ease back	BN BST84327,B1-94705,CD 4-94705-2
5248 tk.20	Upshot	-
5249 tk.24	Cease the bombing -1	- B1-89622
		CD BN 7-89622-2,8-35472-2,8-37741-2
tk.26 or 27	Wichita lineman	unissued
5250 tk.30	By the time I get to Phoenix	-

-1: Earl Neal Creque(el p) replaces Palmer.
All titles from BST84327 also issued on BN B1-31247,CD 8-31247-2.

LEE MORGAN:
Lee Morgan(tp) Julian Priester(tb) George Coleman(ts) Harold Mabern(p) Walter Booker(b) Mickey Roker (dm).
Englewood Cliffs,N.J.,October 10,1969

5284	Free flow
5285	Uncle Rough
5286	Claw-til-da
5287	The stroker

All titles issued on BN BN-LA582-J2,(J)GXF-3024,CD BN(J)TOCJ-1629.

REUBEN WILSON:
Lee Morgan(tp) George Coleman(ts) Reuben Wilson(org) Grant Green(g) Jimmy Lewis(el b) Leo Morris (Idris Muhammad)(dm) Joe Sircus(cga-1).
Englewood Cliffs,N.J.,October 31,1969

(tk.5)	Hold on,I'm comin'	BN B1-31883
		CD BN 8-29905-2,8-31883-2,(J)TOCJ-6067
	Ma cherie amour -1	rejected

BOBBY HUTCHERSON - NOW!:
Harold Land(ts) Bobby Hutcherson(vb) Stanley Cowell(p-1,el p-2) Wally Richardson(el g) Herbie Lewis(b) Joe Chambers(dm) Candido Camero(bgo,cga) Gene McDaniels(vo) Christine Spencer,Eileen Gilbert, Maeretha Stewart(background vo).
(A & R Studios) NYC,November 5,1969

5498 (tk.5)	Black heroes (cga out) -1	CD BN 8-35472-2
5497 (tk.8/9)	The creators -2	
5496 (tk.2)	Slow change -2	CD BN(J)TOCJ-1621

All titles issued on BN BST84333.

ANDREW HILL:
Woody Shaw,Dizzy Reece(tp) Julian Priester(tb) Bob Northern(frh) Howard Johnson(bass cl, tu) Joe Farrell (alto fl,ss,ts,oboe) Andrew Hill(p) Ron Carter(b) Lenny White(dm).
Englewood Cliffs,N.J.,November 7,1969

5515	Laverne	rejected
	Untitled No.1	-
5516	Passing ships	-

 234

ANDREW HILL:

Woody Shaw,Dizzy Reece(tp) Julian Priester(tb) Bob Northern(frh) Howard Johnson(bass cl, tu) Joe Farrell (alto fl,ss,ts,oboe) Andrew Hill(p) Ron Carter(b) Lenny White(dm).

Englewood Cliffs,N.J.,November 14,1969

	Untitled No.2	rejected
5517	Noon tide	-
5518	Tomorrow	-
5519	Plantation bag	-

DUKE PEARSON:

Burt Collins(tp) Al Gibbons(fl) Jerry Dodgion(as) Lew Tabackin(ts) Bobby Hutcherson(vb) Duke Pearson (el p) Ralph Towner(g) Wally Richardson(el g) Bob Cranshaw(b) Mickey Roker(dm) Airto Moreira(perc).

(A & R Studios) NYC,November 21,1969

5565-7	Come on over,my love	rejected
5566-9	Dialogue	-
5567-1	Captain Bacardis	CD BN 8-35220-2
5568-5	I don't know	BN B1-35220,CD 8-35220-2

KENNY COX AND THE CONTEMPORARY JAZZ QUINTET - MULTIDIRECTION:

Charles Moore(tp) Leon Henderson(ts) Kenny Cox(p) Ron Brooks(b) Danny Spencer(dm).

(G.M. Recording Studios) Detroit,November 26,1969

5587-4	Gravity point
5588-3	What other one
5589-1	Smick in
5590-2	Sojourn
5591-1	Spellbound
5592-1	Multidirection

All titles issued on BN BST84339.

JACK McDUFF - MOON RAPPIN':

Unknown(tp) Bill Phillips(fl,ts) unknown(ts,bs) Jack McDuff(org,arr) Jerry Byrd(g) Richard Davis(el b) Joe Dukes(dm).

(Session #1852)

(Soundview Recording Studio) Kings Park,N.Y.,December 1,1969

5833	Flat backin'	BN BST84334;CD BN(J)TOCJ-4334

Same.Jean DuShon (vo) added.

(Soundview Recording Studio) Kings Park,N.Y.,December 2,1969

5834	Oblighetto (voJDS)	BN 45-1957,BST84334;CD BN(J)TOCJ-4334

Same.DuShon out.

(Soundview Recording Studio) Kings Park,N.Y.,December 3,1969

5835	Moon rappin'	BN BST84334;CD BN(J)TOCJ-1621,TOCJ-4334

Same.Richard Davis out.

(Soundview Recording Studio) Kings Park,N.Y.,December 11,1969

5836	Made in Sweden
5837	Loose foot

Both titles issued on BN BST84334,CD BN(J)TOCJ-4334.

235

REUBEN WILSON - BLUE MODE:
John Manning(ts) Reuben Wilson(org) Melvin Sparks(g) Tommy Derrick(dm).
Englewood Cliffs,N.J.,December 12,1969

tk.5	Bambu	CD BN(J)TOCJ-5849
tk.9	Bus ride	BN B1-35636,B1-94707,CD 8-35636-2,4-94707-2
tk.14	Twenty five miles	
tk.19	Orange peel	BN 45-1961,B1-89907,B1-94707 CD BN 7-89907-2,4-94707-2
tk.23	Blue mode	BN B1-94707,CD 4-94707-2
tk.25	Knock on wood	BN 45-1961;CD HMV Jazz(E)5-20881-2

All titles issued on BN BST84343,B1-29906,CD 8-29906-2.

DONALD BYRD - KOFI:
Donald Byrd(flh) William Campbell(tb-1) Lew Tabackin(fl,ts) Frank Foster(ts) Duke Pearson(el p) Bob Cranshaw(el b-2) Ron Carter(b) Airto Moreira(dm).
(A & R Studios) NYC,December 16,1969

4615-4	Kofi -1
4616-4	Fufu -2

Both titles issued on B1-31875,CD BN 8-31875-2.

LONNIE SMITH:
Dave Hubbard(ts) Ronnie Cuber(bs) Lonnie Smith(org) Larry McGee(g) Marion Booker(dm).
Englewood Cliffs,N.J.,December 19,1969

5713	25 miles	rejected
5714	Seven steps to heaven	-
5715	Psychedelic Pi	-
5716	Original Latin blues	-

JAZZ WAVE LTD. ON TOUR:
THAD JONES-MEL LEWIS ORCHESTRA: Thad Jones(flh) Snooky Young,Al Porcino,Danny Moore, Marvin Stamm(tp) Benny Powell,Jimmy Knepper,Bob Burgess,Julian Priester(tb) Jerome Richardson,Jerry Dodgion,Eddie Daniels,Joe Henderson,Pepper Adams(reeds) Roland Hanna(p) Richard Davis(b) Mel Lewis (dm). (Concerts) Germany,December ,1969

Don't get Sassy	BN BST89905,CD 7-89287-2

Jimmy McGriff(org) with Thad Jones-Mel Lewis Orchestra (same as above).Same date.

Slow but sure	BN BST89905

Freddie Hubbard(tp) Roland Hanna(p) Ron Carter(b) Louis Hayes(dm).
Same date.

Body and soul	BN BST89905
Without a song	unissued
Hubtones	-
Spacetrack	-

Jeremy Steig(fl) Ron Carter(b) Louis Hayes(dm).Same date.

Reza	BN BST89905

Kenny Burrell(g).Same date.

People	BN BST89905

Kenny Burrell(g) Richard Davis(b) Mel Lewis(dm).Same date.

	Greensleeves	BN BST89905

Freddie Hubbard(tp) Jeremy Steig(fl) Jimmy McGriff(org) Kenny Burrell(g) with Thad Jones-Mel Lewis Orchestra (same as above).Same date.

	Finale (Once around)	BN BST89905

LONNIE SMITH - DRIVES:
Dave Hubbard(ts) Ronnie Cuber(bs) Lonnie Smith(org) Larry McGee(g) Joe Dukes(dm).
Englewood Cliffs,N.J.,January 2,1970

5717 tk.30	Twenty five miles	
5718	Who's afraid of Virginia Woolf?	
5719	Spinning wheel	BN B1-89907,CD 5-23559-2
5720	Seven steps to heaven	
5721 tk.34	Psychedelic Pi	CD BN 5-21152-2

All titles issued on BN BST84351,B1-28266,CD 8-28266-2.

LOU DONALDSON - EVERYTHING I PLAY IS FUNKY:
Blue Mitchell(tp) Lou Donaldson(el as,vo-1) Lonnie Smith(org) Melvin Sparks(g) Jimmy Lewis(el b) Idris Muhammad(dm) (with band vocal on -1).
Englewood Cliffs,N.J.,January 9,1970

5760	Tennessee waltz	BN BST84359,B1-89794, CD 7-89794-2
5761 tk.8	Everything I do gonh be funky -1	BN 45-1956,L4337,BST84337,B1-96563, B1-30721;CD BN 7-96563-2,8-30721-2, 8-37745-2,(C)8-56508-2
tk.10	untitled original blues	rejected
5762 tk.12	Over the rainbow	BN BST84337
5764 tk.14	Hamp's hump	BN UAS-2301,BST84337,B1-30721 CD BN 8-30721-2
5763 tk.16	Minor bash	BN 45-1956,UAS-2301,BST84337,B1-94709 CD BN 8-37745-2,4-94709-2

All titles from BST84337 also issued on BN B1-31248,CD 8-31248-2.

ANDREW HILL:
Charles Tolliver(tp,flh) Pat Patrick(fl,as,bs) Bennie Maupin(fl,ts,bass cl) Andrew Hill(p) Ron Carter(b) Paul Motian(dm). Englewood Cliffs,N.J.,January 16,1970

5827 tk.2	One for one	BN BN-LA459-H2	
5828 tk.9	Diddy wah	-	CD 8-35414-2
	untitled	rejected	

Note: Drummer was wrongly listed as Ben Riley on BN BN-LA459-H2.

THAD JONES-MEL LEWIS - CONSUMMATION:
Thad Jones(flh,arr,dir) Snooky Young,Al Porcino,Marvin Stamm,Danny Moore(tp) Eddie Bert,Benny Powell,Jimmy Knepper(tb) Cliff Heather(bass tb) Jim Buffington,Dick Berg,Earl Chapin,Julius Watkins(frh) Howard Johnson(tu) Jerome Richardson(fl,ss,as) Jerry Dodgion (fl,cl,as) Eddie Daniels(fl,cl,ts) Billy Harper (fl,ts) Richie Kamuca(bs,cl) Roland Hanna (p) Richard Davis (b) Mel Lewis(dm,dir).
(A & R Studios) NYC,January 20,1970

5854 tk.8	Dedication
5861 tk.14	Consummation

Both titles issued on BN BST84346,Mosaic MQ7-151,CD Mosaic MD5-151.

237

THAD JONES-MEL LEWIS - CONSUMMATION:
Thad Jones(flh,arr,dir) Snooky Young,Al Porcino,Marvin Stamm,Danny Moore(tp) Eddie Bert,Benny Powell,Jimmy Knepper(tb) Cliff Heather(bass tb Jerome Richardson(fl,ss,as) Jerry Dodgion(fl,cl,as) Eddie Daniels(fl,cl,ts) Billy Harper(fl,ts) Richie Kamuca(bs,cl) Roland Hanna(p) Richard Davis(b) Mel Lewis (dm,dir).

(A & R Studios) NYC,January 21,1970

5855 tk.7	It only happens every time	
5856 tk.11	Tiptoe	BN BN-LA392-H2

Both titles issued on BN BST84346,Mosaic MQ7-151,CD Mosaic MD5-151.

ANDREW HILL:
Charles Tolliver(tp,flh) Pat Patrick(fl,as,bs) Bennie Maupin(fl,ts,bass cl) Andrew Hill(p) Ron Carter(b) Ben Riley(dm).

Englewood Cliffs,N.J.,January 23,1970

5829 tk.27	Satin lady	rejected
5830 tk.35	Without malice	BN BN-LA459-H2
5831 tk.38	Ocho rios	rejected
5832 tk.52	Ode to infinity	-

THAD JONES-MEL LEWIS - CONSUMMATION:
Thad Jones(flh,arr,dir) Snooky Young,Al Porcino,Marvin Stamm,Danny Moore(tp) Eddie Bert,Benny Powell,Jimmy Knepper(tb) Cliff Heather(bass tb) Jerome Richardson(fl,ss,as) Jerry Dodgion(fl,cl,as) Eddie Daniels(fl,cl,ts) Billy Harper(fl,ts) Joe Farrell(bs) Roland Hanna(p) Richard Davis(b) Mel Lewis(dm,dir).

(A & R Studios) NYC,January 28,1970

5860 (tk.8)	Fingers	BN BST84346;Mosaic MQ7-151 CD Mosaic MD5-151
	Ahunk,ahunk	rejected

GRANT GREEN - GREEN IS BEAUTIFUL:
Blue Mitchell(tp) Claude Bartee(ts) Emmanuel Riggins(org) Grant Green(g) Jimmy Lewis(el b) Idris Muhammad(dm) Candido Camero(cga) Richard Landrum(bgo).

Englewood Cliffs,N.J.,January 30,1970

5886	Ain't it funky now	BN 45-1960,B1-89622,B1-89907,B1-96563, B1-94705 CD BN 7-89907-2,7-96563-2,8-37741-2, 4-94705-2
5887	Windjammer -1	BN BST2-92477,B1-89622,B1-94705, (Du)1A158-83401/4 CD BN 7-92477-2,7-89622-2,4-94705-2 ,(J) TOCJ-6100
5888	A day in the life	CD BN(J)TOCJ-5874,Cap(J)TOCJ-5201
5889	Dracula	
5890	I'll never fall in love again	CD BN 8-57749-2

-1: Neal Creque(org) replaces Riggins.

All titles issued on BN BST84342,B1-28265,CD 8-28265-2.

McCOY TYNER - EXTENSIONS:
Wayne Shorter(ss,ts) Gary Bartz(as) McCoy Tyner(p) Alice Coltrane(harp) Ron Carter(b) Elvin Jones(dm).
Englewood Cliffs,N.J.,February 9,1970

tk.3	The wanderer (harp out)	CD BN 8-37051-2,(C)8-56508-2,(J)CJ28-5165
tk.4	Message from the Nile	BN 8-57745-1,8-57745-2
tk.5	His blessings	
tk.6	Survival blues	

All titles were scheduled on BN BST84419 (not released) and issued on BN BN-LA006-F,CD 8-37646-2

JEREMY STEIG - WAYFARING STRANGER/LEGWORK:
Jeremy Steig(fl) Eddie Gomez(b).
(A & R Studios) NYC,February 11, 1970

All is one	BN BST84354
Space	-

Don Alias(dm,perc) added. Same session.

Waves	BN BST84354
In the beginning	-
Mint tea	-
Howlin' for Judy	Solid State SS-18068;BN B1-54360 CD BN 8-54360-2,4-97222-2
Permutations	Solid State SS-18068
Alias	-
Nardis	-

Sam Brown(g) added. Same session.

Wayfaring stranger	BN BST84354
Hot head	Solid State SS-18068
Piece of freedom	-

DUKE PEARSON:
Burt Collins(tp) Kenny Rupp(tb) Jerry Dodgion(as,alto fl-2) Frank Foster(ts,alto cl-3) Lew Tabackin(ts,fl-4) Duke Pearson(p-1,el p) Ron Carter(b) Mickey Roker(dm) Andy Bey(vo).
Englewood Cliffs,N.J.,February 13,1970

5921 tk.2	I don't care who knows it (voAB)	BN B1-35220,CD 8-35220-2
5922 tk.6	Chant Ossanha -2,3	- -
5923 tk.15	A beautiful friendship -1	- -
5924 tk.29	Emily -1,2,4 (Foster out)	BN BN-LA317-G
5925 tk.33	Bloos	BN B1-35220,CD 8-35220-2
5926 tk.36	Horn in	-

Note: On album BN-LA317-G,Bob Cranshaw is incorrectly listed as bassist on 5922.

ANDREW HILL:
Lee Morgan(tp) Bennie Maupin(ts,bass cl-1,fl-2) Andrew Hill(p) Ron Carter(b) Ben Riley(dm) & choir: Lawrence Marshall,Gail Nelson,Lillian Williams,Benjamin Franklin Carter,Hugh Harnell,Joan Johnson,Milt Grayson,LaReine LaMer,Ron Steward (vo).
Englewood Cliffs,N.J.,March 6,1970

6024 tk.3	Blue spark	CD BN 5-27546-2
6025 tk.8	A tender tale -1	-
6026 tk.14	Drew's tune -2	-

GENE HARRIS AND THE THREE SOUNDS - LIVE AT THE "IT" CLUB:
Gene Harris(p) Henry Franklin(b,el b) Carl Burnett(dm).
(Live at the It Club) LA,March 6,1970

Funky Pullett	BN B1-35338,CD 8-35338-2
I'm still sad	- -
Baby man	- -
Love for sale	- -
Sittin' duck	- -
On Green Dolphin Street	- -
Tammy's Breeze	-
John Brown's Body	-

Gene Harris(p) Henry Franklin(b,el b) Carl Burnett(dm).
(Live at the It Club) LA,March 6 & 7,1970

Put on train -1	CD BN 5-23997-2
Virgin pearl	rejected
I'm in love	CD BN 5-23997-2
Down home	-
Girl talk	-
Black fox -1	-
This guy's in love (with announcement)	rejected
Apollo 21 -1	CD BN 5-23997-2
Eleanor Rigby -1	-
Get back -1	CD BN 7-94861-2,5-23997-2
Judy,Judy,Judy	rejected
How insensitive -1	-
Come together -1	CD BN 5-23997-2

-1: Henry Franklin(sand blocks,jaw bone) Carl Burnett(cga,tamb) Monk Higgins(cabasa,claves,jaw bone, vibraslap) overdubbed on in various combinations,but these overdubs were not used on issued masters.

Note: The first seven titles were intended to be issued as "Put On Train".The next six titles were intended to be issued as "Apollo 21".Several tunes have since been rejected because of poor edits in the master tapes.

ANDREW HILL:
Lee Morgan(tp) Bennie Maupin(ts) Andrew Hill(p) Ron Carter(b) Ben Riley(dm) & choir: Lawrence Marshall,Gail Nelson,Lillian Williams,Benjamin Franklin Carter,Hugh Harnell,Joan Johnson,Milt Grayson, LaReine LaMer,Ron Steward (vo). Englewood Cliffs,N.J.,March 13,1970

6060 tk.21	Natural spirit	CD BN 5-27546-2
6061 tk.33	Such it is	-
6062 tk.43	Mother Mercy -1	-

-1: Bennie Maupin plays fl on intro.

JACK McDUFF - TO SEEK A NEW HOME:
Martin Drover,Terry Noonan,Bud Parks(tp) John Bennett,Adrian Drover(tb) David Statham,Willie Watson (frh) Norman Leppard,Dick Morrissey,Jack Whitford,Dave Willis(fl,saxes) Jack McDuff(org,p) J.J.Jackson (p,perc) Typhena Partridge(harp) Terry Smith(g-1) Larry Steele(el b) Trevor Armstrong(dm).
(Island Studios) London,March 23,1970

6151	Come and carry me home -1	BN BST84348

Same.J.J.Jackson plays perc only. London,March 24,1970

6153	Mystic John	BN 45-1958,BST84348

 240

JACK McDUFF - TO SEEK A NEW HOME:
Martin Drover,Terry Noonan,Bud Parks(tp)John Bennett,Adrian Drover(tb) David Statham,Willie Watson (frh) Norman Leppard,Dick Morrissey,Jack Whitford,Dave Willis(fl,saxes) Jack McDuff(org,p) J.J.Jackson (p,perc) Typhena Partridge(harp) Peter Chapman(b) Trevor Armstrong(dm) Jerry Long (vo).
(Island Studios) London,March 25,1970

6154 Seven keys for seven doors BN BST84348

Martin Drover,Bud Parks(tp) John Bennett(tb) Norman Leppard,Dick Morrissey(fl,ts) Jack McDuff(org) J.J. Jackson(p,perc) Terry Smith(g) Larry Steele(el b) Phil Leaford(dm).
(Island Studios) London,March 26,1970

6155 Hunk o' funk BN 45-1958,BST84348,B1-35636
CD 8-35636-2,(E)8-53234-2

Martin Drover,Bud Parks(tp) John Bennett(tb) Norman Leppard,Dick Morrissey(fl,ts) Jack McDuff(org) Chris Parren(el p) Terry Smith(g) Larry Steele(el b) Phil Leaford(dm) J.J.Jackson (arr).Same date.

6152 Yellow Wednesday BN BST84348

WAYNE SHORTER - MOTO GROSSO FEIO:
Wayne Shorter(ss,ts) Chick Corea(marimba,dm,perc) John McLaughlin(12 string g) Dave Holland(g,b) Ron Carter(b,cello) Miroslav Vitous(b) Michelin Prell(dm,perc).
(A & R Studios) NYC,April 3,1970

6122 tk.4 Moto grosso feio
6123 tk.7 Antigua
6124 tk.9 Vera Cruz
6125 tk.12 Iska
6126 tk.14 Montezuma

All titles issued on BN BN-LA014-G.

CHICK COREA - THE SONG OF SINGING:
Chick Corea(p) Dave Holland(b) Barry Altschul(dm).
(A & R Studios) NYC,April 7,1970

6160 (tk.3) Flesh BN BST84353
6157 (tk.2) Toy room - BN-LA395-H2,CD 7-89282-2
6162 (tk.1) Nefertiti - -
CD BN 7-89282-2,(J)TOCJ-5633,TOCJ-6271/74
(tk.2) Blues connotation BN BN-LA472-H2,CD 7-89282-2

All titles also issued on CD BN 7-46401-2,7-84353-2.
All titles from BST84353 also issued on CD BN(J)TOCJ-4353.

Same. (A & R Studios) NYC,April 8,1970

6159 (tk.2) Rhymes BN BST84353,CD 7-46401-2
6158 (tk.1) Ballad I - BN-LA395-H2,CD 7-46401-2
(tk.2) Ballad II
6161 (tk.3) Ballad III BN BST84353,BN-LA395-H2
CD CD BNP7-46401-2,
(tk.1) Drone -1 BN BN-LA882-J2,CD 7-46401-2
BN(F)2S062-61900,(J)GXF-3026

-1: Barry Altschul plays percussion on sections of this piece.
All titles,except last,issued on CD BN 7-84353-2.
All titles from BST84353 also issued on CD BN(J)TOCJ-4353.

HORACE SILVER QUINTET - THAT HEALIN' FEELIN':
Randy Brecker(tp,flh) George Coleman(ts) Horace Silver(p,el p-1) Bob Cranshaw(b) Mickey Roker(dm) Andy Bey(vo).

Englewood Cliffs,N.J.,April 8,1970

	The happy medium (voAB)-1	CD BN 4-95576-2
tk.7	That healin' feelin'	
tk.17	Love vibrations (voAB)	
tk.21	The show has begun (voAB)	BN 45-1964,CD 5-21153-2
	Peace (voAB)	CD BN 4-95576-2

All titles issued on BN BST84352,B1-29907.

DUKE PEARSON - IT COULD ONLY HAPPEN WITH YOU:
Burt Collins,Joe Shepley(tp) Kenny Rupp(tb) Hermeto Pascoal(fl,g-1,b-2) Al Gibbons(alto fl,as) poss. Frank Foster(ts) Duke Pearson(p,el p) Theo(g,b-3) Bob Cranshaw(b,el b) Mickey Roker(dm) Flora Purim (vo).

Englewood Cliffs,N.J.,April 10,1970

6128 tk.5	It could only happen with you (voFP)	CD BN(J)TOCJ-5845
6129 tk.10	Gira,girou (voFP)	
6130 tk.19	Book's bossa	
6131 tk.20	Lost in the stars -2	
6132 tk.22	Stormy (voFP)-1	BN B1-97158,(E)BNSLP-4 CD BN 4-97158-2,(J)TOCJ-5846
6133 tk.27	Hermeto -3	

-2: Theo out.
All titles issued on BN BN-LA317-G.

JOE WILLIAMS - WORTH WAITING FOR...:
Joe Williams(vo) with unidentified orchestra arr. & cond. by Horace Ott.

(United Artists Studios) LA,May 5,1970

Baby	BN 45-1979
Here's that rainy day	
Something	
Bridges	BN 45-1979
I'd be a fool right now	

All titles issued on BN BST84355.

Same.

(United Artists Studios) LA,May 6,1970

I hold no grudge	
Lush life	CD BN 8-21146-2, 4-94035-2
Little girl	
Didn't we	

All titles issued on BN BST84355.

Same.

(United Artists Studios) LA,May 8,1970

Oh darling
Can't take my eyes off you
You send me

All titles issued on BN BST84355.

DONALD BYRD - ELECTRIC BYRD:
Donald Byrd(tp) Bill Campbell(tb) Hermeto Pascoal(fl-1) Jerry Dodgion(fl,ss,as) Frank Foster(alto cl,ts) Lew Tabackin(fl,ts) Pepper Adams(bs,cl) Duke Pearson(el p) Wally Richardson(g) Ron Carter(b) Mickey Roker (dm) Airto Moreira(perc).

Englewood Cliffs,N.J.,May 15,1970

6344 tk.2	Estavanico	
6343 tk.4	Essence	
6341 tk.5	The Dude	BN B1-89606,CD 7-89606-2 Lib.LN-10200
6342 tk.8	Xibaba -1	

All titles issued on BN BST84349,B1-36195,CD BN 8-36195-2.

LONNIE SMITH:
Dave Hubbard(ts) Ronnie Cuber(bs) Lonnie Smith(org,vo) George Benson(g) Joe Dukes(dm) Gary Jones (cga) Clifford Mack(tamb).

(Club Mozambique) Detroit,May 21,1970

tk.1	Love bowl -1	BN B1-31880,CD 8-31880-2	
tk.2	Piece of mind(voLS)	-	-
tk.3	Play it back	rejected	
tk.4	I can't stand it (voLS)	BN B1-97158,B1-31880,CD 8-31880-2	
tk.5	Move your hand (voLS)	rejected	
tk.6	I want to thank you for loving me	-	
tk.7	Scream	BN B1-31880,CD 8-31880-2	
tk.8	Expressions	-	-
tk.9	Play it back	-	-
tk.10	I want to thank you for loving me	-	-
tk.11	Seven steps to heaven	-	-
tk.12	Piece of mind (voLS)	rejected	
tk.13	Come together (voLS)	-	
tk.14	Days of wine and roses -2	-	
tk.15	I'm doing bad,I'm doing fine (voLS)	-	

-1: Jones & Mack out.
-2: Hubbard,Cuber,Jones & Mack out.

THAD JONES-MEL LEWIS - CONSUMMATION:
Thad Jones(flh,arr,dir) Snooky Young,Al Porcino,Marvin Stamm,Danny Moore(tp) Eddie Bert,Benny Powell,Jimmy Knepper(tb) Cliff Heather(bass tb) Howard Johnson(tu) Jerome Richardson(fl,ss,as) Jerry Dodgion(fl,cl,as) Eddie Daniels(fl,cl,ts) Billy Harper(fl,ts) Pepper Adams(bs,cl) Roland Hanna(p,el p-1) David Spinozza(g-1) Richard Davis(b,el b-1) Mel Lewis (dm,dir).

(A & R Studios) NYC,May 25,1970

5858 (tk.18)	Us-1	BN 45-1962
5857 (tk.1)	A child is born	BN BN-LA392-H2 BN(Du)1A158-83401/4,(E)UALP 19
5859 (tk.8)	Ahunk,ahunk (7:54)-1	CD BN 4-97155-2

All titles issued on BN BST84346,Mosaic MQ7-151,CD Mosaic MD5-151.
Note: An edited version (2:46) of 5859 has been issued on BN 45-1962.

243

GRANT GREEN:
Claude Bartee(ts) Emmanuel Riggins(org) Grant Green(g) Herbie Lewis(b) Idris Muhammad (Leo Morris) (dm).

Englewood Cliffs,N.J.,May 29,1970

6478	I can't leave your love alone	unissued
6479	Let yourself go	-
6480	Love on a two-way street	-
6481	Green acid	-
6482	Raindrops keep fallin' on my head	-
6483	Something	-
6484	Let it rain	-

LOU DONALDSON - PRETTY THINGS:
Blue Mitchell(tp) Lou Donaldson(el as) Leon Spencer Jr(org) Ted Dunbar(g) Idris Muhammad(dm).

Englewood Cliffs,N.J.,June 12,1970

6520 (tk.3)	Curtis' song	BN BST84359,B1-89794,CD 7-89794-2
6521 (tk.6)	Love	- - -
6522	Cold duck	rejected
6523 (tk.7)	Sassie Lassie	BN BST84359,B1-89794,CD 7-89794-2
6524	Just for a thrill	- - -
6525	Pot belly	- - B1-89907,B1-94709 CD BN 7-89794-2,8-37745-2,4-94709-2,(J) TOCJ-5864

HORACE SILVER QUINTET - THAT HEALIN' FEELIN':
Randy Brecker(tp) Houston Person(ts) Horace Silver(el p) Jimmy Lewis(el b) Idris Muhammad(dm) Gail Nelson or Jackie Verdell(vo).

Englewood Cliffs,N.J.,June 18,1970

tk.6	Nobody knows (voGN)	
tk.12	Permit me to introduce you to myself (voJV)	
tk.14	Wipe away the devil (voJV)	
tk.21	There's much to be done (voJV)	BN 45-1964

All titles issued on BN BST84352,B1-29907.

REUBEN WILSON:
Harold Ousley,Ramon Morris(ts) Reuben Wilson(org) Ted Dunbar(g) William Curtis(dm).

Englewood Cliffs,N.J.,June 26,1970

Son of man	unissued
Do-Ba-Dat-San!	-
Dance ville	-
What's gonna happen to me	-
Weaver of dreams	-

JACK WILSON:
Jack Wilson(p,el p) Ike Isaacs(b,el b) Donald Bailey(dm).

(Live,Memory Lane) LA,July 8,1970

Set #1:

Tears inside	rejected
Equinox/One and four	-
Street scene	-
Night mist	-
Caravan	-
Soulin'	-

JACK WILSON:
Jack Wilson(p,el p)Ike Isaacs(b,el b) Donald Bailey(dm).

	(Live,Memory Lane)	LA,July 8,1970
Set #2:		
	Ahmad's blues/New rhumba	rejected
	Something/After supper	-
	Ada	-
	Little sunflower/Soulin'	-
Set #3:		
	Ramblin'	rejected
	Squeeze me	-
	Wave	-
	I hear a rhapsody/Soulin'	-

Same.

	(Live,Memory Lane)	LA,July 9,1970
Set #1:		
	Little sunflower	rejected
	Ramblin'	-
	Nightmist	-
	Ada	-
	Soulin'	-
Set #2:		
	Ahmad's blues	rejected
	If it's the last thing I do	-
	Blues/Wine/Soulin'	-
Set #3:		
	untitled (bass feature)	rejected
	Street scene	-
	Medley	-
	Soulin'	-

LEE MORGAN - LIVE AT THE LIGHTHOUSE:
Lee Morgan(tp,flh) Bennie Maupin(fl,ts,bass cl) Harold Mabern(p) Jymie Merritt(el b) Mickey Roker(dm).

	(Lighthouse Club)	Hermosa Beach,Calif.,July 10,1970
Set #1:		
	The beehive	rejected
	Something like this	CD BN 8-35228-2,(J)TOCJ-6039
	Yunjanna/Speedball (theme)	rejected
Set #2:		
	I remember Britt	rejected
	Absolutions/Speedball (theme)	-
Set #3:		
	Neophilia	rejected
	416 East 10th Street	CD BN 8-35228-2
	The sidewinder/Speedball (theme)	- (J)TOCJ-6039
Set #4:		
	Peyote	rejected
	Ceora (incomplete)	-
	Speedball -1	CD BN 8-35228-2,(J)TOCJ-6039

-1: Jack DeJohnette sits in,replacing Mickey Roker(dm).

Same.

	(Lighthouse Club)	Hermosa Beach,Calif.,July 11,1970
Set #1:		
	Aon	CD BN 8-35228-2
	Yunjanna/Speedball (theme)	rejected

245

LEE MORGAN - LIVE AT THE LIGHTHOUSE:

Lee Morgan(tp,flh) Bennie Maupin(fl,ts,bass cl) Harold Mabern(p) Jymie Merritt(el b) Mickey Roker(dm).
(Lighthouse Club) Hermosa Beach,Calif.,July 11,1970

Set #2:

	Something like this	rejected
	I remember Britt	CD BN 8-35228-2
	The beehive/Speedball (theme)	rejected

Set #3:

	Neophilia	rejected
	Nommo	BN BST89906,CD BN 8-35228-2,(J)TOCJ-6039

Set #4:

	Peyote	rejected
	Absolutions	BN BST89906, CD BN 8-35228-2

Same. (Lighthouse Club) Hermosa Beach,Calif.,July 12,1970

Set #1:

	Something like this	rejected
	Yunjanna	CD BN 8-35228-2

Set #2:

	I remember Britt	rejected
	Absolutions	-

Set #3:

	Neophilia	
	The beehive	CD BN (J)TOCJ-6039

Both titles issued on BN BST89906,CD BN 8-35228-2.

Note: On the LP version of "The beehive",a theme statement of "Speedball" taken from one of the set endings from the first two nights is spliced onto the end.On CD,the song ends as it was actually played.

Set #4:

	Peyote	CD BN 8-35228-2
	Nommo	rejected

BOBBY HUTCHERSON - SAN FRANCISCO:

Harold Land(fl-2,ts,oboe-3) Joe Sample(p,el p-4) Bobby Hutcherson(vb,marimba-1,perc) John Williams(b, el b-5) Mickey Roker(dm).
(United Artists Studios) LA,July 15,1970

7187 tk.13	Prints tie -1,4,5	Up Front UPF-193
7186 tk.17	Goin' down South -1,5	BN B1-54360,CD 8-28263-2,(J)TOCJ-5936, HMV Jazz(E)5-20868-2
7190 tk.25	Procession-3	Up Front UPF-193
7189 tk.26	Ummh -4,5	BN 45-1966,B1-89907,CD 7-89907-2 Up Front UPF-193
7188 tk.36	Jazz	
7191 tk.39	A night in Barcelona -2,5	CD BN(J)TOCJ-6285

All titles issued on BN BST84362,B1-28268,CD 8-28268-2.

ELVIN JONES - COALITION:

Frank Foster(ts-1,alto cl-2) George Coleman(ts) Wilbur Little(b) Elvin Jones(dm) Candido Camero(cga-3, tamb-2). Englewood Cliffs,N.J.,July 17,1970

6675	Simone -1,3	
6673	5/4 thing -1,3	BN(J)W-5514
6674	Ural stradania -1,3	
6672	Yesterdays -1	
6671	Shinjitu -2,3	

All titles issued on BN BST84361,CD Mosaic MD8-195.

 246

McCOY TYNER:
Hubert Laws(fl,alto fl) Andrew White(oboe) Gary Bartz(ss,as) McCoy Tyner(p) Herbie Lewis(b) Freddie Waits(dm,tympani,chimes).

Englewood Cliffs,N.J.,July 21,1970

tk.5	Forbidden land	BN BN-LA460-H2,	CD 4-93384-2
tk.7	Hope	-	-
tk.11	Asian lullaby	-	-
	untitled -1	rejected	

-1: Free improvisation in which everyone plays perc.

HANK MOBLEY - THINKING OF HOME:
Woody Shaw(tp) Hank Mobley(ts) Cedar Walton(p) Eddie Diehl(g) Mickey Bass(b) Leroy Williams(dm).

Englewood Cliffs,N.J.,July 31,1970

6734 tk.6 You gotta hit it
6735 tk.8 Justine
6738 tk.10 Gayle's groove
6736 tk.18 Talk about gittin' it
6737 tk.23 Suite:
a) Thinking of home
b) The flight
c) Home at last

All titles were initially scheduled on BN BST84367 & BST84417,which were not released,and later issued on BN LT-1045.

CHICK COREA:
Anthony Braxton(cl-1,contrabass cl-2,sopranino sax-3,perc-3) Chick Corea(p,celeste-3,perc-3) Dave Holland (g-3,b-4,cello-3,perc-3).

(A & R Studios) NYC,August 13,1970

Duet for bass and piano #1 -4
Duet for bass and piano #2 -4
Danse for clarinet and piano #1 -1
Danse for clarinet and piano #2 -1
Chimes I -2,3,4
Chimes II -3,4

All titles issued on BN BN-LA472-H2,CD 7-84465-2.
Note: On all issues,date was erroneously shown as October 13.

GRANT GREEN ALIVE!:
Claude Bartee(ts) William Bivens(vb) Ronnie Foster(org) Grant Green(g) Idris Muhammad(dm) Joseph Armstrong(cga).

(The Cliche Lounge) Newark,N.J.,August 15,1970

6759	Let the music take your mind	BN BST84360,CD 7-89793-2
6761	Sookie sookie	BN 45-1965,BST84360,B1-89622,B1-99106, B1-28263,B1-94705 CD BN 7-89622-2,7-89793-2,7-99106-2, 8-28263-2,8-37741-2,4-94705-2,(C)8-56508-2, (J)TOCJ-5733,TOCJ-5936,TOCJ-6191, TOCJ-66045,TOCJ-66055,EMI Music(C)4-94893-2
	It's your thing	BN B1-31883,CD BN 8-31883-2
	Hey Western Union man	- - (J)TOCJ-6067
	Maiden Voyage	

All titles issued on CD BN 5-25650-2.

GRANT GREEN ALIVE!:
Claude Bartee(ts) William Bivens(vb) Neal Creque(org) Grant Green(g) Idris Muhammad(dm) Joseph Armstrong(cga). Same date.

6760	Time to remember	BN 45-1965
6762	Down here on the ground	BN B1-54360,CD 5-23559-2

Both titles issued on BN BST84360,CD 7-89793-2,5-25650-2.

CHICK COREA:
Anthony Braxton(fl-3,cl-1,sopranino sax-1,as-2,chimes-4) Chick Corea(p-1,2,3,celeste-1,4,vb-4) Dave Holland(g-3,b-1,2,cello-1,perc-4) Barry Altschul(dm-1,2,woodblocks-1,bass marimba-3,4).
(A & R Studios) NYC,August 19,1970

Starp -1	BN BN-LA472-H2;CD GRP GRD5-9819
73° Kelvin -2	-
Ballad -3	-
Percussion piece -4	BN BN-LA882-J2
	BN(F)2S062-61901,(J)GXF-3027

All titles also issued on CD BN 7-84465-2.
Note: On all issues,date was erroneously shown as October 19.

CHICK COREA - CIRCULUS:
Anthony Braxton(sopranino sax,as,cl,contrabass cl) Chick Corea(p,perc,bass marimba) Dave Holland (g,b) Barry Altschul(b,dm,perc,vb,bass marimba).
(A & R Studios) NYC,August 21,1970

tk.1	Quartet piece #1	BN(F)2S062-61900,(J)GXF-3026
tk.2	Quartet piece #2	BN(F)2S062-61901,(J)GXF-3027
tk.3	Quartet piece #3	- -

All titles issued on BN LA882-J2.
Note: On all issues,date was erroneously shown as October 21.

WAYNE SHORTER - ODYSSEY OF ISKA:
Wayne Shorter(ss-1,ts-2) Dave Friedman(vb,marimba) Gene Bertoncini(g) Ron Carter,Cecil McBee(b) Billy Hart & Al Mouzon(dm) Frank Cuomo(dm,perc).
(A & R Studios) NYC,August 26,1970

6781 tk.3	Wind -1	
6782 tk.5	Storm -1	
6783 tk.10	Calm -2	CD BN 8-59072-2
6784 tk.12	De pois do amor,o vazio (After love,emptiness) -1	BN(J)W-5514
6785 tk.18	Joy -2	

All titles issued on BN BST84363,CD 7-84363-2.

McCOY TYNER - ASANTE:
Andrew White(as) McCoy Tyner(p,wooden fl-1) Ted Dunbar(g) Buster Williams(b) Billy Hart(dm,African perc) M'tume(cga,perc)-2 Songai Sandra Smith(vo).
Englewood Cliffs,N.J.,September 10,1970

6796	Malika (voSSM) -1	CD BN 4-94031-2,(J)TOCJ-1621
6797	Asante (voSSM) -2	
6798	Goin' home -2	CD BN 8-33207-2,(J)CJ28-5165
6799	Fulfillment -1	

All titles issued on BN BN-LA223-G, CD 4-93384-2.

REUBEN WILSON - GROOVY SITUATION:
Earl Turbinton(as) Reuben Wilson(org) Eddie Diehl(g) Harold White(dm).
Englewood Cliffs,N.J.,September 18,1970

6821	Signed,sealed,delivered,I'm yours	BN BST84365
	A groovy situation	rejected
	If you let me make love to you then why can't I touch you	-

REUBEN WILSON - GROOVY SITUATION:
Earl Turbinton(as) Reuben Wilson(org) Eddie Diehl(g) Harold White(dm).
Englewood Cliffs,N.J.,September 25,1970

6820	Happy together
6816	While the world lies waiting
6818	If you let me make love to you then why can't I touch you
6819	A groovy situation
6817	Sweet tooth

All titles issued on BN BST84365.

JIMMY McGRIFF - SOMETHING TO LISTEN TO:
Unknown(ts) Jimmy McGriff(org) unknown(g) unknown(dm) & unidentified orchestra added on all titles, except first.
NYC,c.Autumn 1970

Indiana	BN UAS-2300
Malcolm's blues	
Satin doll	BN UAS-2300
Deb sombo	
Something to listen to	BN UAS-2300
Shiny stockings	-

All titles issued on BN BST84364.

BIG JOHN PATTON - MEMPHIS TO NEW YORK SPIRIT:
Marvin Cabell(fl,ts) John Patton(org) James Ulmer(g) Leroy Williams(dm).
Englewood Cliffs,N.J.,October 2,1970

tk.2	Steno	BN B1-35221,CD 8-35221-2
tk.4	The Mandingo	- -
tk.5	Bloodyun	- -
tk.10	Ugetsu	rejected
tk.12	Footprints	BN B1-35221,B1-30728,CD 8-35221-2,8-30728-2
tk.16	Memphis	- -
		CD BN 8-35221-2,(Eu)5-23444-2

Note: Issued titles were originally planned on BN BST84366,which was not used,and later scheduled for issue on BN BST84418,which was not released.

WAYNE SHORTER:
Wayne Shorter(ts) McCoy Tyner(p) Miroslav Vitous(b) Alphonse Mouzon(dm,perc) Barbara Burton (vb,bells,perc).
(A & R Studios) NYC,October 13,1970

tk.3	Pt.1:The creation -1	rejected
tk.4	Pt.2 (B.Because)	-
tk.5	Pt.3 (Cee)	-
tk.7	Pt.4 (Dee) -1	-
tk.8	Pt.5 (Effe)	-

-1: Shorter,Tyner & Vitous play perc on the intro.

CANDIDO - BEAUTIFUL:
Bernie Glow,Pat Russo(tp) Alan Raph(tb,bass tb) Joe Grimm(ss,bs) Frank Anderson(org,p) David Spinozza (g) Gerry Jemmott(el b) Herbie Lovelle(dm) Candido Camero(cga,bgo) Joe Cain(arr).
(A & R Studios) NYC,October 20,1970

6910	I'm on my way
6911	New world in the morning
6912	Tic tac toe
6913	Hey,Western Union man

All titles issued on BN BST84357,CD BN(J)TOCJ-4357.

CANDIDO - BEAUTIFUL:
Bernie Glow,Pat Russo(tp) Alan Raph(tb,bass tb) Joe Grimm(fl,ss,bs) Frank Anderson(org,p) David Spinozza (g) Richard Davis(el b) Herbie Lovelle(dm) Candido Camero(cga,bgo) Joe Cain(arr).
(A & R Studios) NYC,October 27,1970

6914	I shouldn't believe	
6915	Beautiful	
6916	Money man	
6917	Serenade to a savage (omit horns)	BN B1-35636,CD 8-35636-2
6954	Ghana spice,pt.1 -1	CD BN 4-94031-2
6955	Ghana spice,pt.2 -1	

-1: fl,el b,dm only.
All titles issued on BN BST84357,CD BN(J)TOCJ-4357.

LOU DONALDSON - THE SCORPION:
Fred Ballard(tp) Lou Donaldson(el as) Leon Spencer(org) Melvin Sparks(g) Idris Muhammad(dm).
(The Cadillac Club) Newark,N.J.,November 7,1970

Set #1

tk.1	Foot pattin' time	CD BN 8-31876-2
tk.2	The scorpion (alt.)	BN B1-31883,CD 8-31883-2
tk.3	I'll be there	rejected
tk.4	Bye bye blackbird	-
tk.5	Brother soul (theme)	-

Set #2

tk.6	Turn it on (Leon's tune)	rejected
tk.7	untitled bossa nova	-
tk.8	untitled blues (voLD)	-
tk.9	Funky mama	-
tk.10	Laura	BN B1-31876,CD 8-31876-2
tk.11	This is happiness	rejected
tk.12	Brother soul (theme)	-

LOU DONALDSON - THE SCORPION:
Fred Ballard(tp) Lou Donaldson(el as) Leon Spencer(org) Melvin Sparks(g) Idris Muhammad(dm).
(The Cadillac Club) Newark,N.J.,November 7,1970

Set #3		
tk.13	Alligator boogaloo	BN B1-31876,CD 8-31876-2
tk.14	The scorpion	- -
tk.15	I'll be there	rejected
tk.16	Bye bye blackbird	unissued
tk.17	Turn it on	rejected
tk.18	This is happiness	-
tk.19	Peepin'	CD BN 8-31876-2
tk.20	The masquerade is over	BN B1-31876,CD 8-31876-2

HORACE SILVER - THE UNITED STATES OF MIND PHASE 2:TOTAL RESPONSE:
Cecil Bridgewater(tp,flh) Harold Vick(ts) Horace Silver(el p) Richie Resnicoff(g) Bob Cranshaw(el b) Mickey Roker(dm) Salome Bey(vo).
Englewood Cliffs,N.J.,November 15,1970

7381	Big business	
7384	Total response	
8827	What kind of animal am I	
8829	Acid,pot or pills	BN 45-1975,CD 8-35472-2

All titles issued on BN BST84368,CD BN(J)TOCJ-1622.

BROTHER JACK McDUFF - WHO KNOWS WHAT TOMORROW GONNA BRING:
Randy Brecker,Olu Dara(tp) Dick Griffin,John Pierson(tb) Jack McDuff(org) Paul Griffin(p) Joe Beck(g) Tony Levin(el b) Ray Draper(tu,vo,arr) Donald McDonald(dm) Mike Mainieri (perc).
(The Hit Factory) NYC,December 1,1970

7105	Y'all remember boogie?	BN BST84358,(Du)1A158-83401/4
7106	Ya Ya Ya Ya Ya Ya	-

Same. (The Hit Factory) NYC,December 2,1970

7107	Who's pimpin' who	
7108	Who knows what tomorrow's gonna bring	

Both titles issued on BN BST84358.

Same. (The Hit Factory) NYC,December 3,1970

7109	Wank's thang	
7110	Classic funke	

Both titles issued on BN BST84358.

DONALD BYRD - KOFI:
Donald Byrd(tp) Frank Foster(ts) Duke Pearson(el p) Wally Richardson(g) Ron Carter(b) Mickey Roker(dm) Airto Moreira,Dom Um Romao(perc).
(A & R Studios) NYC,December 4,1970

6879 tk.2	Perpetual love	BN B1-31875,CD 8-31875-2
6880 tk.7	Elmina	- -
6881 tk.15	The loud minority	-
6882 tk.18	My love waits	rejected

251

GRANT GREEN:
Clarence Thomas(ss-1,ts) Houston Person(ts) Ronnie Foster(org) Grant Green(g) Idris Muhammad(dm).
(Club Mozambique) Detroit,January 6,1971

Set #1:

	Patches	rejected
	More today than yesterday	-
	One less bell to answer -1	-
	Bottom of the barrel -1	-
	Jan Jan	-
	Make it easy on yourself -1	-
	Farid	unissued
	One more chance -1	rejected

Set #2:

	Patches	rejected
	One less bell to answer -1	-
	Bottom of the barrel -1	unissued
	I am somebody	-
	Glenda	rejected
	One more chance -1	-
	Walk on by	unissued

Set #3:

	Jan Jan	rejected
	More today than yesterday	-
	One more chance -1	unissued

Same.
(Club Mozambique) Detroit,January 7,1971

Set #1:

	One more chance -1	rejected
	Jan Jan	-
	More today than yesterday	unissued
	Farid	rejected

Set #2:

	I am somebody	rejected
	Patches	-
	Bottom of the barrel -1	-
	Walk on by	-
	Glenda	unissued
	Make it easy on yourself -1	-

Set #3:

	Jan Jan	unissued
	Patches	-
	I am somebody	rejected
	Walk on by	-
	One more chance -1	unissued

HORACE SILVER - THE UNITED STATES OF MIND,PHASE 2:TOTAL RESPONSE:
Cecil Bridgewater(tp,flh) Harold Vick(ts) Horace Silver(el p) Richie Resnicoff(g) Bob Cranshaw(el b) Mickey Roker(dm) Andy Bey,Salome Bey(vo).
Englewood Cliffs,N.J.,January 29,1971

8826	I've had a little talk (voAB)	BN 45-1975,CD 5-21152-2
7385	Soul searchin' (voSB)	
8828	Won't you open up your senses (voAB)	
7382	I'm aware of the animal within me (voSB)	
7383	Old Mother Nature calls (voAB)	CD BN 4-95576-2

All titles issued on BN BST84368,CD BN(J)TOCJ-1622.

<u>ELVIN JONES</u> - <u>GENESIS</u>:
Frank Foster(ts-1,alto fl-2,alto cl-3) Joe Farrell(ts-4,ss-5) David Liebman(ts-6,ss-7) Gene Perla(b,el b-8) Elvin Jones(dm).

Englewood Cliffs,N.J.,February 12,1971

7400	Slumber -6	BN BST84369
7402	Cecilia is love -1,4,7	-
7398 (tk.2)	P.P. Phoenix -2,4,6	-
7399 (tk.5)	For all the other times -1,4,6	-
7401	Three card Molly -1,4,5,6	-
9078	Who's afraid ... -3,5,7,8	BN BST84414

All titles also issued on CD Mosaic MD8-195.

<u>RICHARD "GROOVE" HOLMES</u> - <u>COMIN' ON HOME</u>:
Richard "Groove" Holmes(org) Gerald Hubbard(g) Chuck Rainey(el b) Darryl Washington(dm).
(A & R Studios) NYC,May 19,1971

All the way	rejected
Theme from 'Love Story'	BN 45-1967,BST84372 CD BN 8-57748-2,(J)TOCJ-4372

Richard "Groove" Holmes(org) Weldon Irvine(el p) Gerald Hubbard(g) Jerry Jemmott(el b) Darryl Washington(dm) Ray Armando(cga) James Davis(tamb,shaker,cowbell,vo).

Same session.

Groovin' for Mr. G	BN B1-99106,B1-35636,CD 7-99106-2,8-35636-2
Wave	CD BN(J)TOCJ-5740
Mr. Clean	
Down home funk	CD BN(J)TOCJ-5239
Don't mess with me (voJC)	BN 45-1967
This here (cga out)	

All titles issued on BN BST84372,CD BN(J)TOCJ-4372.
Note: On BST84372,Darryl Washington was erroneously shown as "Darryh Washington", and engineer miscredited as Rudy Van Gelder.

<u>GRANT GREEN</u> - <u>VISIONS</u>:
Billy Wooten(vb) Emanuel Riggins(el p) Grant Green(g) Chuck Rainey(el b) Idris Muhammad(dm) Ray Armando(cga).

Englewood Cliffs,N.J.,May 21,1971

7922 tk.2	Cantaloupe woman	BN B1-94705,CD 8-37741-2,4-94705-2 BN(F)45-005
7923 tk.6	Never can say goodbye	BN 45-1969
7924 tk.11	Maybe tomorrow	
7925 tk.15	Mozart symphony No.40 in G minor, K550,1st movement	
7926 tk.22	We've only just begun	
7927 tk.24	Does anybody really know what time it is	BN 45-1969,(F)45-005
7928 tk.25	Love on a two way street	
7929 tk.28	Blues for Abraham -1	

-1: Harold Caldwell(dm,perc) added.
All titles issued on BN BST84373,CD BN(J)TOCJ-4373.

JIMMY McGRIFF - BLACK PEARL:
Ronald White(tp) Joseph Morris(as) Arthur "Fats" Theus(ts) William Thorpe(bs) Jimmy McGriff(org) O'Donel "Butch" Levy(g) Willie Jenkins(dm).

	(The Golden Slipper)	Newark,N.J., 1971
	Black pearl	BN 45-1968,CD 8-57063-2
		BN(E)B1-30724,CD 8-30724-2
	Groove alley	BN 45-1968
	In a mellow tone	CD BN 4-94035-2
	C jam blues	
	Ode to Billie Joe	
	Man from bad	

All titles issued on BN BST84374.

BOBBY HUTCHERSON - HEAD ON:
Oscar Brashear(tp,flh) George Bohanon,Louis Spears(tb) Willie Ruff(frh) Harold Land(fl,ts) Fred Jackson (picc) Ernie Watts,Charles Owens,Delbert Hill,Herman Riley(reeds) Bobby Hutcherson (vb,marimba) Todd Cochran(p,arr) William Henderson(el p-1) Reggie Johnson or James Leary III-2(b) Stix Hooper,Leon Chancler,Woody Theus(dm) Warren Bryant (cga,bgo) Donald Smith(vo) with Robert Jenkins (unknown instr.)

	(Poppi Recording Studio)	LA,July 1,1971
8065 (tk.4)	Clockwork of the spirits-2	
8060 (tk.5)	At the source,pt.1: Ashes & Rust	
8063	Many thousands gone-1	

All titles issued on BN BST84376.

Oscar Brashear(tp,flh) George Bohanon,Louis Spears(tb) Harold Land(fl,ts) Fred Jackson(picc) Ernie Watts, Charles Owens,Delbert Hill,Herman Riley(reeds) Bobby Hutcherson(vb,marimba) Todd Cochran(p,arr) James Leary III(b) Stix Hooper,Leon Chancler,Woody Theus(dm) Warren Bryant(cga,bgo) Donald Smith(vo) with Robert Jenkins(unknown instr.)

	(Poppi Recording Studio)	LA,July 2,1971
	Togo land	unissued
	Jonathan	-
	Mtume	rejected

Oscar Brashear(tp,flh) George Bohanon,Louis Spears(tb) Harold Land(fl,ts) Fred Jackson(picc) Bobby Hutcherson(vb,marimba) Todd Cochran(p,arr) Reggie Johnson(b) Stix Hooper,Woody Theus(dm) Warren Bryant(cga,bgo).

	(Poppi Recording Studio)	LA,July 3,1971
	Hey Harold	unissued
8064 (tk.2)	Mtume	BN BST84376;Up Front UPF-193
8062	At the source,pt.3: Obsidian	-
8061	At the source,pt.2: Eucalyptus	-

Last three titles also issued on CD BN 4-93380-2.

LOU DONALDSON - COSMOS:
Ed Williams(tp) Lou Donaldson(el as,as-1) Leon Spencer(org,el p) Melvin Sparks(g) Gerry Jemmott (el b) Idris Muhammad(dm) Ray Armando(cga) Essence (Mildred Brown,Rosalyn Brown,Naomi Thomas)(vo) Jimmy Briggs(vocal arrangements).

Englewood Cliffs,N.J.,July 16,1971

8136	The caterpillar	BN 45-1970,B1-89907,B1-30721,CD 7-89907-2
8137	I want to make it with you -1	-
8138	If there's a hell down below	BN B1-30721,CD 8-30721-2
8139	Caracas	
8140	I'll be there -1	
8141	When you're smiling	

All titles issued on BN BST84370.

REUBEN WILSON - SET US FREE:
Jerome Richardson(ss,ts) Reuben Wilson(org) Gene Bianco(harp) David Spinozza(g,el sitar) Richard Davis(b) Jimmy Johnson(dm) Ray Armando(cga) Gordon "Specs" Powell(perc) Wade Marcus(arr).

Englewood Cliffs,N.J.,July 23,1971

8166	Tom's thumb	
8167	Right on with this mess	CD BN(J)TOCJ-5740
8168	Mercy mercy me (The ecology)-1	
8169	Sho-nuff mellow	BN B1-54360,CD 8-54360-2
8170	Set us free	
8171	Mr. Big Stuff -1	CD BN 7-99105-2
8172	We're in love -1	BN B1-94027

-1: Essence (Mildred Brown,Rosalyn Brown,Naomi Thomas)(vo) Jimmy Briggs(vocal arrangements) added.
All titles issued on BN BST84377.

GENE HARRIS & THE THREE SOUNDS:
Gene Harris(p) Albert Vescovo,Freddy Robinson(g) Luther Hughes(el b) Carl Burnett(dm) Bobbye Porter Hall (cga) Paul Humphrey(perc) Monk Higgins(org, arr).Unidentified vocals-1 overdubbed on.

(United Artists Studios) LA,July 26,1971

8173 (tk.4)	Hey girl -1	BN BST84378,B1-54357,CD 8-54357-2
(tk.10)	That's heavy	unissued
8185 (tk.3)	Did you think -1	BN BST84378
8175 (tk.3)	Your love is just too much	BN BST84378,B1-99106,CD 7-99106-2
(tk.3)	(It's) The real thing	unissued
8186 (tk.7)	What's the answer	BN BST84378
8181 (tk.6)	I'm leaving -1	-

Same.

(United Artists Studios) LA,July 27,1971

8180 (tk.3)	Put on train	BN BST84378,B1-54360,CD 8-54360-2
(tk.3)	Success	unissued
(tk.2)	Forget me not	-
8179 (tk.1)	You got to play the game -1	BN BST84378

Note: Vocal overdubs were recorded for all titles but used for title marked -1 only.

GENE HARRIS & THE THREE SOUNDS:
Gene Harris(p) Albert Vescovo,Freddy Robinson(g) Luther Hughes(el b) Carl Burnett(dm) Bobbye Porter Hall (cga) Paul Humphrey(perc) Monk Higgins(org,arr).Unidentified vocals overdubbed on.
(United Artists Studios) LA,August 2,1971

(tk.7)	The fence	unissued
(tk.2)	Turn around	-
(tk.2)	Judy blue eyes	-
(tk.5)	Loveland	-
(tk.5)	Take some time	-
(tk.7)	It's your thing	-
(tk.7)	Thank you for lovin' me	-
(tk.2)	(Since) I lost my baby	-

Same.
(United Artists Studios) LA,August 3,1971

8182 (tk.1)	Eleanor Rigby	BN BST84378

LOREZ ALEXANDRIA:
Lorez Alexandria(vo) with Freddy Hill,Melvin Moore,Harry "Sweet" Edison,Al Aarons(tp) Billy Byers, Jimmy Cleveland,George Bohanon,Lou Blackburn (tb) Buddy Collette,Bill Green(fl,as) Teddy Edwards, Clifford Scott(ts) Maurice Simon(bs) Jack Wilson(p,arr) Howard Roberts(g) Stan Gilbert(b) Jimmie Smith (dm).
(United Artists Studios) LA,August 10,1971

I wish I knew	CD BN 5-21151-2
Happiness is a thing called Joe	unissued
Medley:By myself/Alone together	-

DONALD BYRD - ETHIOPIAN KNIGHTS:
Donald Byrd(tp) Thurman Green(tb) Harold Land(ts) Bobby Hutcherson(vb) Bill Henderson III(el p) Joe Sample(org) Don Peake,Greg Poree(g) Wilton Felder(el b) Edward Greene(dm) Bobbye Porter Hall(cga, tamb).
(A & M Studios) LA,August 25,1971

8317 (tk.2)	The emperor	BN 45-1973*, B1-89606 CD 7-89606-2,4-97157-2*,(J)TOCJ-6285
8318 (tk.4)	Jamie	

Both titles issued on BN BST84380,CD 8-54328-2.
Note: Issues marked * used an edited version.

Donald Byrd(tp) Thurman Green(tb) Harold Land(ts) Bobby Hutcherson(vb) Bill Henderson III (el p) Joe Sample(org) Don Peake,David T.Walker(g) Wilton Felder(el b) Edward Greene(dm) Bobbye Porter Hall (cga,tamb).
(A & M Studios) LA,August 26,1971

8319	The little rasti	BN BST84380,B1-89606,CD 8-54328-2
	Perpetual Love (vb,el p out)	rejected

LOREZ ALEXANDRIA:
Lorez Alexandria(vo)with Teddy Edwards(ts) Ronnell Bright(p) Freddy Robinson(g) Bob Haynes(b) Harold Mason(dm) Monk Higgins(arr).
(United Artists Studios) LA,September 15,1971

Until it's time for you to go	CD BN 5-21152-2
You're gonna hear from me	unissued
We've only just begun	-
Wave	-
Something	-

LEE MORGAN:
Lee Morgan(tp-1,flh-2) Grachan Moncur III(tb) Bobbi Humphrey(fl) Billy Harper(ts,alto fl) Harold Mabern Jr. (p,el p) Jymie Merritt(el b) Reggie Workman(b,perc) Freddie Waits(dm).
Englewood Cliffs,N.J.,September 17,1971

8414 tk.7	In what direction are you headed? -1
8415 tk.11	Angela -2
8416 tk.13	Croquet Ballet -1
8417 tk.15	Inner passions-out -1

All titles were first scheduled on BN BST84381 (not released) and later issued on BN BST84901,CD 4-93401-2, (J)TOCJ-1632.

Same.
Englewood Cliffs,N.J.,September 18,1971

8418 tk.20	Capra black -1	BN BST84901,CD 4-93401-2,(J)TOCJ-1632

This title was initially scheduled on BN BST84381 (not released).

Note: The first edition of this discography listed two untitled,unissued tunes from this session because of the information on the tape boxes.After reviewing all the tapes,it turns out that no other tunes exist.

BOBBI HUMPHREY - FLUTE-IN:
Lee Morgan(tp) Bobbi Humphrey(fl) Billy Harper(ts) Hank Jones(p,el p) George Devens (vb,marimba,perc) Gene Bertoncini(g) George Duvivier(b) Idris Muhammad(dm) Ray Armando(cga) Wade Marcus(arr).
Englewood Cliffs,N.J.,Sept.30 or October 1,1971

8478	Ain't no sunshine (tp,ts out)	BN 45-1974
8481	Sad bag (tp,ts out)	BN 45-1971,45-1974
8484	Journey to Morocco	
8485	Set us free	

All titles issued on BN BST84379.

Lee Morgan(tp) Bobbi Humphrey(fl) Billy Harper(ts) Frank Owens(p,el p) George Devens (vb,marimba, perc) Gene Bertoncini(g) Gordon Edwards(el b) Jimmy Johnson(dm) Ray Armando(cga) Wade Marcus (arr).
Englewood Cliffs,N.J.,Sept.30 or October 1,1971

8479	The sidewinder	
8480	It's too late (tp,ts out)	
8482	Spanish Harlem	BN 45-1971,BN-LA699-G,CD 4-94030-2
8483	Don't knock my funk	

All titles issued on BN BST84379.

<u>GRANT GREEN</u> - <u>SHADES OF GREEN</u>:
Billy Wooten(vb) Emmanuel Riggins(el p,clavinet) Grant Green(g) Wilton Felder(el b) Stix Hooper(dm) King Errison(cga) Harold Caldwell (perc).
(United Artists Studios) LA,November 23,1971
Joe Newman,Joe Wilder,Victor Paz,Jimmy Sedlar(tp) Harry DiVito(tb) Dick Hickson(bass tb) Jimmy Buffington(frh) Phil Bodner,Romeo Penque,George Marge,John Leone(woodwinds) Wade Marcus(arr) overdubbed on.
Englewood Cliffs,N.J.,December 16 & 17,1971

8904	California Green	CD BN 8-37741-2
8907	In the middle	BN B1-89622,CD 7-89622-2
8900	Medley:	CD BN 7-99105-2
	I don't want nobody to give me nothing/	-
	Open up the door,I'll get it myself/	-
	Cold sweat	-

All titles issued on BN BST84413.

Billy Wooten(vb) Emmanuel Riggins(el p,clavinet) Grant Green(g) Wilton Felder(el b) Stix Hooper(dm) King Errison(cga) Harold Caldwell(perc).
(United Artists Studios) LA,November 24,1971
Joe Newman,Joe Wilder,Victor Paz,Jimmy Sedlar(tp) Harry DiVito(tb) Dick Hickson(bass tb) Jimmy Buffington(frh) Phil Bodner,Romeo Penque,George Marge,John Leone(woodwinds) Wade Marcus(arr) overdubbed on.
Englewood Cliffs,N.J.,December 16 & 17,1971

8905	If you really love me
8906	Cast your fate to the wind
8901	Sunrise,sunset
8902	Never my love
8903	Got to be there

All titles issued on BN BST84413.

<u>GRANT GREEN</u> - <u>THE FINAL COMEDOWN</u> (Soundtrack):
Marvin Stamm,Irving Markowitz(tp,flh) Harold Vick(as,ts) Phil Bodner(fl, picc,as,oboe) Richard Tee(p,org) Grant Green,Cornell Dupree(g) Gordon Edwards(el b) Grady Tate(dm)George Devens(vb,tympani,timbales, perc) Warren Smith(marimba,tamb) Ralph McDonald(cga,bgo) Eugene Bianco(harp) Charles McCracken, Seymour Barab(cello) Julian Barber,Harry Zaratzian(viola) Wade Marcus(comp,cond).
(A & R Studios) NYC,December 13,1971 (afternoon)

9061	Past,present and future
9064	Fountain scene
9065	Soul food-African shop
9066	Slight fear and terror
9068	Luanna's theme

All titles issued on BN BST84415.

Warren Smith out.
(A & R Studios) NYC,December 13,1971 (night)

9062	The final comedown	BN B1-89622,B1-99106,B1-94705 CD BN 7-99106-2,7-89622-2,8-37741-2,4-94705-2
9067	Afro party	BN 45-1983
9070	Traveling to get to Doc	
9071	One second after death	

All titles issued on BN BST84415.

GRANT GREEN - THE FINAL COMEDOWN (Soundtrack):
Marvin Stamm,Burt Collins(tp,flh) Harold Vick(as,ts) Romeo Penque(fl,as) Richard Tee(p,org) Grant Green,Cornell Dupree(g) Gordon Edwards(el b) Bernard Purdie(dm) George Devens(vb,tympani,timbales, perc) Warren Smith(tympani) Ralph McDonald(cga,bgo) Eugene Bianco(harp) Charles McCracken,Seymour Barab(cello) Julian Barber,Harry Zaratzian(viola) Wade Marcus(comp,cond).
(A & R Studios) NYC,December 14,1971 (afternoon)

9063 Father's lament BN 45-1983,BST84415

Alan Shulman(cello) replaces McCracken.
(A & R Studios) NYC,December 14,1971 (night)

9069 Battle scene (The battle,pts.1&2*) BN 45-1972*,BST84415

ELVIN JONES - MERRY GO ROUND:
David Liebman(ts-1,7,ss-2,6,7) Steve Grossman(ts-1,7,ss-2,6) Joe Farrell(fl-4,picc-6,ss-2,7,ts-1) Pepper Adams(bs-6) Chick Corea(p-4,7,el p-5) Jan Hammer(p-2,3,el p-1,5,glockenspiel-6) Yoshiaki Masuo(g-1,4) Gene Perla(b or el b-1,7) Elvin Jones (dm) Don Alias(cga-1,2,5,7,perc-2).
Englewood Cliffs,N.J.,December 16,1971

9071 (tk.2) 'Round town -1 BN B1-35636,CD 8-35636-2
9072 (tk.5) Brite piece -2
9073 (tk.4) Lungs -3
9074 (tk.6) A time for lov e-4
9075 (tk.2) Tergiversation -5
9077 (tk.3) The children's merry-go-round march -6
9076 (tk.2) La fiesta -7

All titles issued on BN BST84414,CD Mosaic MD8-195.
Note: Recording date was wrongly shown as December 15 on BST84414 .

BOBBY HUTCHERSON:
Blue Mitchell(tp) Thurman Green(tb) Harold Land(ts) Bobby Hutcherson(vb) Cornell Dupree,Arthur Adams (g) Clarence McDonald,Reggie Andrews(keyb) Chuck Rainey(el b) Stix Hooper(dm) King Errison(cga, bgo).
(A & M Studios) LA,December 21,1971

(tk.8) Wichita lineman unissued
(tk.6) Workin' on a groovy thing -
(tk.3) Inner city blues CD BN 5-21152-2

BOBBY HUTCHERSON:
Blue Mitchell(tp) Thurman Green(tb) Harold Land(ts) Bobby Hutcherson(vb) Arthur Adams,Mike Deasy(g) Clarence McDonald,Reggie Andrews(keyb) Stix Hooper(dm) King Errison(cga,bgo) Arthur Lewis (unknown instr.)
(A & M Studios) LA,December 22,1971

(tk.6) Family affair unissued
(tk.4) Brother Rap BN 45-1985,B1-97158,CD 4-97158-2
(tk.8) Brown eyed woman unissued

HORACE SILVER - THE UNITED STATES OF MIND PHASE 3-ALL:
Horace Silver(el p,vo) Bob Cranshaw(el b) Mickey Roker(dm) Salome Bey,Andy Bey,Gail Nelson(vo).
Englewood Cliffs,N.J.,January 17,1972

9222	Forever is a long time (voSB)	
9224	How much does matter really matter (voGN) (el b,dm out)	CD BN 4-95576-2
9221	Cause and effect (voAB)	BN 45-1978
8535	Who has the answer (voAB)	
8536	From the heart through the mind (voAB)	

All titles issued on BN BST84420.

RONNIE FOSTER - THE TWO HEADED FREAP:
Ronnie Foster(org) George Devens(vb,cabasa,shaker,cowbell) Gene Bertoncini(g) Gene Bianco(harp) George Duvivier(b) Gordon Edwards(el b) Jimmy Johnson(dm) Arthur Jenkins(cga) Wade Marcus(arr).
Englewood Cliffs,N.J.,January 20,1972

9213	Drowning in the sea of love	
9216	Let's stay together	
9217	Don't knock my love	
9218	Mystic brew	BN B1-35607,B1-54360,CD 8-54360-2

All titles issued on BN BST84382,B1-32082,CD 8-32082-2.

Same.
Englewood Cliffs,N.J.,January 21,1972

9212	Chunky	BN 45-1977,B1-99106
9214	The two headed freap	
9215	Summer song	BN 45-1977
9219	Kentucky fried chicken	CD BN(Eu) 7-89915-2

All titles issued on BN BST84382,B1-32082,CD 8-32082-2.

HORACE SILVER - THE UNITED STATES OF MIND PHASE 3-ALL:
Cecil Bridgewater(tp,flh) Harold Vick(ts) Horace Silver(el p,vo) Richie Resnicoff(g) Bob Cranshaw(el b) Mickey Roker(dm) Salome Bey,Andy Bey,Gail Nelson(vo).
Englewood Cliffs,N.J.,February 14,1972

8538	Summary (voHS,AB,SB,GN) (g out)	
9220	The merger of the minds (voHS,SB,AB,GN)	
9223	My soul is my computer (voSB) (g out)	
8534	Horn of life (g out)	BN 45-1978
8537	All (voHS,AB,GN) (tp,ts out)	CD BN 4-95576-2

All titles issued on BN BST84420.

LOU DONALDSON:
Lou Donaldson(as) Leon Spencer(org,p) Melvin Sparks(g) Jimmy Lewis(el b) Buddy Caldwell (dm).
Englewood Cliffs,N.J.,February 25,1972

	Songbird	rejected
	Coonskin	-
	Our day will come	-
	Warm breeze	-
	What now my love	-

BOBBY HUTCHERSON - NATURAL ILLUSIONS:
Bobby Hutcherson(vb) Hank Jones(p) Gene Bertoncini(g) Ron Carter(b) Jack DeJohnette(dm).
Englewood Cliffs,NJ,March 2,1972
Phil Bodner,Hubert Laws,Romeo Penque,Daniel Trimboli(fl) George Marge(oboe) John Leone(bassoon) Gene Bianco(harp) George Duvivier (b) Irving Spice,Aaron Rosand(v) Julian Barber,Seymour Berman (viola) Seymour Barab (cello) Wade Marcus(arr) overdubbed on.
Englewood Cliffs,N.J.,March 3,1972

9653-2	The folks who live on the hill	
9654-3	Lush life	CD HMV Jazz(E)5-20868-2
9655-8	Shirl	
9656-2	When you're near	BN 45-1976
9657-3	The thrill is gone	
9658-2	Sophisticated lady	
9659-5	Rain every Thursday	BN 45-1976

All titles issued on BN BST84416.

DONALD BYRD - BLACK BYRD:
Donald Byrd(tp,flh,el tp,lead vo) Fonce Mizell(tp,vo) Roger Glenn(fl,alto fl,saxes) Joe Sample(p,el p) Fred Perren(el p,synth,vo) Dean Parks(g) Wilton Felder(el b) Harvey Mason (dm) Bobbye Porter Hall(perc) Larry Mizell(vo,arr). (The Sound Factory) LA,April 3,1972

11249	Mr. Thomas	BN BN-XW309-W,BN-LA047-F CD BN 7-84466-2

Donald Byrd(tp,flh,el tp,lead vo)Fonce Mizell(tp,vo)Roger Glenn(fl,alto fl,saxes)Joe Sample(p,el p)Fred Perren(el p,synth,vo)Dean Parks(g)Wilton Felder(el b)Harvey Mason(dm) Bobbye Porter Hall(perc)Larry Mizell(vo,arr). (The Sound Factory) LA,April 4,1972

11246	Flight time	BN BN-XW309-W,BN-LA047-F,BN-LA700-G, B1-98638,(E)BN-XW623-X Lib(E)LCSP 18670213 CD BN 7-84466-2,7-98638-2
	Distant land	unissued

GRANT GREEN - LIVE AT THE LIGHTHOUSE:
Claude Bartee(ss,ts) Gary Coleman(vb) Shelton Laster(org) Grant Green(el g) Wilton Felder(el b) Greg Williams(dm) Bobbye Hall Porter(perc).
(Lighthouse Club) Hermosa Beach,Calif.,April 21,1972

	Introduction by Hank Stewart	
11225	Windjammer	BN BN-XW216-W,CD 8-37741-2
11226	Betcha by golly now	-
11227	Fancy free	
11228	Flood in Franklin Park	
11229	Jan Jan	
11230	Walk in the night	BN B1-89622,CD 7-89622-2,(J)TOCJ-6285

All titles issued on BN BN-LA037-G2,CD 4-93381-2

BOBBY HUTCHERSON:
Bobby Hutcherson(vb,marimba) Bayete (Todd Cochran)(p,el p) James Leary(b) Michael Carvin(dm).
(United Artists Studio) LA,May 24,1972

	Poem	rejected
	Unga	-
	B's thang	-
	Mr.X	-
	Twenty-five	-

GENE HARRIS OF THE THREE SOUNDS:
Gene Harris(p) Sam Brown,Cornell Dupree(g) Ron Carter(b) Freddie Waits(dm) Johnny Rodriguez(cga) Omar Clay(perc,vb).
(A & R Studios) NYC,June 29,1972

9949-8	Django	
9950-7	John Brown's body	
9951-13	A day in the life of a fool	

All titles issued on BN BST84423.

Same.
(A & R Studios) NYC,June 30,1972

9952-12	Killer Joe	
9953-4	Listen here	BN 45-1982,CD 5-21152-2
9954-8	Emily	-
9955-7	Lean on me	
9956-2	C jam blues	

All titles issued on BN BST84423.

ELVIN JONES - Mr.JONES:
David Liebman(ts-1,ss-2) Steve Grossman(ts) Pepper Adams(bs-2) Jan Hammer(p-2) Gene Perla(b) Elvin Jones(dm) Frank Ippolito(perc-2) Carlos "Patato" Valdes(cga-2).
Englewood Cliffs,N.J.,July 12,1972

9995	New Breed -1	BN BN-LA110-F;CD Mosaic MD8-195
9996	What's up-That's it -2	- -

Thad Jones(flh-2,3) David Liebman(fl-2,ts-3) Steve Grossman(ts-1,3,ss-2) Jan Hammer(p-2,3) Gene Perla (b-1,2,el b-3) Elvin Jones(dm) Frank Ippolito(perc-1,2) Albert Duffy(tympani-1,2) Carlos "Patato" Valdes (cga-2). Englewood Cliffs,N.J.,July 13,1972

9994	Soultrane -1
9992	One's native place -2
9993	G.G. -3

All titles issued on BN BN-LA110-F,CD Mosaic MD8-195.
Note: Last title was incorrectly listed as "Gee Gee" on BN -LA110F.

BOBBI HUMPHREY - DIG THIS:
Bobbi Humphrey(fl) George Marge(oboe,English h) Paul Griffin(el p,clavinet) Harry Whitaker (el p) William Fontaine,David Spinozza(g) Ron Carter(b) Wilbur Bascomb Jr.(el b) Alphonse Mouzon(dm,bell tree,arr-3) Warren Smith Jr.(perc) & strings:Julian Barber(viola) Seymour Barab(cello) Paul Winter,Paul Gershman, Seymour Berman,Irving Spice(v) Gene Bianco(harp) Wade Marcus-1,Horace Ott-2(arr).
(A & R Studios) NYC,July 20 & 21,1972

10187-12	Lonely town,lonely street -2,4	BN 45-1980
10188-8	Is this all -1	-
10189-7	Smiling faces sometimes -1	BN B1-94706,5-21147-1 CD BN 4-94211-2,4-94706-2,5-21147-2
10190-2	Virtue -3	
10191-4	I love every little thing about you -2	
10192-9	Love theme from "Fuzz" -1	
10193-2	El mundo de maravillas -3	
10194-15	Nubian lady -2	CD BN 4-97157-2

-4: Intro of this title uses take 6.
All titles issued on BN BST84421.

MARLENA SHAW - MARLENA:
Marlena Shaw(vo) with Phil Bodner(fl,oboe,English h) Paul Griffin(org,el p) Derek Smith(p,el p) Vincent Bell,Cornell Dupree,Jay Berliner(g) Gordon Edwards(el b) Richard Davis(b) Jimmy Johnson(dm) Omar Clay (perc) Johnny Pacheco(cga,bgo) Raymond Orchart(cga).
(A & R Studios) NYC,August 10,1972
Gene Bianco(harp) Irving Spice,Louis Haber,Louis Stone,Paul Winter,Harry Lookofsky,Paul Gershman(v) Charles McCracken,Seymour Barab(cello) Julian Barber,Seymour Berman(viola) Wade Marcus(arr,cond) overdubbed on. NYC,August 16,1972

10436	What are you doing the rest of your life		
10437	Somewhere	BN 45-1981	
10442	You must believe in Spring	-	CD 8-54943-2
10443	Wipe away the evil		-

All titles issued on BN BST84422,CD BN(J)TOCJ-4422.

Marlena Shaw(vo) with Phil Bodner(fl,oboe,English h) Paul Griffin(org,el p) Derek Smith(p,el p) Vincent Bell,Cornell Dupree,Jay Berliner(g) Gordon Edwards(el b) Richard Davis(b) Jimmy Johnson(dm) Omar Clay (perc) Johnny Pacheco(cga,bgo) Raymond Orchart(cga).
(A & R Studios) NYC,August 11,1972
Gene Bianco(harp) Irving Spice,Louis Haber,Louis Stone,Paul Winter,Harry Lookofsky,Paul Gershman(v) Charles McCracken,Seymour Barab(cello) Julian Barber,Seymour Berman(viola) Wade Marcus(arr,cond) overdubbed on. NYC,August 16,1972

10438	Runnin' out of fools	
10439	So far away	
10440	I'm gonna find out	
10441	Save the children	BN BN-XW209-W,CD 8-54943-2,5-21152-2
10444	Things don't never go my way	-

All titles issued on BN BST84422,CD BN(J)TOCJ-4422.

ELVIN JONES - LIVE AT THE LIGHTHOUSE:
David Liebman(fl-1,ss-2,ts-3) Steve Grossman(ss-4,ts-5) Gene Perla(b) Elvin Jones(dm).
(Lighthouse Club) Hermosa Beach,Calif.,Sept. 9,1972

Set #1:		
	Introduction by Bill Chappell & Rick Holmes#	BN BN-LA015-G2
	Brite piece -2,4,5	CD BN 7-84448-2
	New breed -3,5	BN BN-LA015-G2,CD 7-84447-2
	Sambra -3,5	- -
	My ship -1,5	- -
	Taurus people -3,5	-
	Happy birthday by Rick Holmes & audience#	BN BN-LA015-G2,CD 7-84448-2
Set #2:		
	Fancy free -2,5	BN BN-LA015-G2,CD 7-84447-2
	I'm a fool to want you -3	CD BN 7-84448-2
	Sweet Mama -3,5	BN BN-LA015-G2,CD 7-84448-2
	The children,save the children -2,5	- -
Set #3:		
	The children's merry-go-round march -1,2,3,5 (Children's merry-go-round*)	CD BN 7-84448-2*
	Small one-1,4	CD BN 7-84447-2
	P.P. Phoenix-1,5#	rejected
	For all the other times-3,5/ (For all those other times*)	CD BN 7-84447-2*
	Announcement#	-

All titles from above three sets,except those marked #,also issued on CD Mosaic MD8-195.
All titles from BN-LA015-G2 also issued on CD BN(J)TOCJ-9240/41.

263

<u>MOACIR SANTOS</u> - <u>MAESTRO</u>:
Oscar Brashear(tp) Frank Rosolino(tb) David Duke(frh) Ray Pizzi(ss,as) Don Menza(fl,ts) Moacir Santos (bs,vo, perc,arr) Hymie Lewak(p) Clare Fischer(org) Bill Henderson(el p) Joe Pass(g) John Heard(b) & dm, perc,others unknown,Sheila Wilkinson(vo) Reggie Andrews(arr-1).
(A & M Studio) LA,Sept.29 & Oct.10,1972

tk.9	The mirror's mirror (voMS,SW)	
tk.12	Kermis	
tk.15	April child (voMS)	
tk.16	Mother Iracema	

All titles issued on BN BN-LA007-F.

Same. (A & M Studio) LA,Sept. 29 & Oct. 18,1972

	Nana-1 (voMS,SW)	
tk.4	Luanne (voMS)	CD BN(J)TOCJ-5845
tk.17	Bluishmen	
	Astral whine (An elegy to any war) (voMS)	

All titles issued on BN BN-LA007-F.

<u>HORACE SILVER</u> - <u>IN PURSUIT OF THE 27th MAN</u>:
David Friedman(vb) Horace Silver(p) Bob Cranshaw(el b) Mickey Roker(dm).
Englewood Cliffs,N.J.,October 6,1972

10674	Summer in Central Park	
11480	Strange vibes	
10672	Kathy	CD BN(J)TOCJ-5845
11479	In pursuit of the 27th man	CD BN 4-95576-2,4-97157-2,(J)TOCJ-5846

All titles issued on BN BN-LA054-F.

Randy Brecker(tp,flh) Mike Brecker(ts) Horace Silver(p) Bob Cranshaw(el b) Mickey Roker(dm).
Englewood Cliffs,N.J.,November 10,1972

10671	The liberated brother	BN BN-XW325-W
11478	Nothin' can stop me now	-
10673	Gregory is here	BN B1-93206,(Du)1A158-83401/4 CD BN 7-93206-2,4-95576-2

All titles issued on BN BN-LA054-F.

DONALD BYRD - BLACK BYRD:
Donald Byrd(tp,flh,el tp,lead vo) Fonce Mizell(tp,vo) Roger Glenn(fl,alto fl) Joe Sample(el p) Fred Perren (synth,vo) David T.Walker(g) Chuck Rainey(el b) Harvey Mason(dm) Stephanie Spruill(cga,tamb) Larry Mizell(vo).
(The Sound Factory) LA,November 24,1972

11250	Sky high	BN BN-LA700-G;CD BN(J)TOCJ-5845
11247	Black byrd -1	BN BN-XW212-W,BN-LA700-G,BST2-92477, B1-98638,(E)BN-XW-623-X BN(Du)1A158-83401/4,(J)W-5515 UA UA-XW510-X CD BN 7-92477-2,7-98638-2,8-27533-2, (C)8-56508-2,(J)TOCJ-66055,Cema S21-57593, Rhino 75870-2
11251	Slop jar blues	BN BN-XW212-W
11248	Love's so far away	BN B1-98638,B1-94708;Lib(E)LCSP 18670213 CD BN 4-94708-2,(Eu)4-93994-2
11252	Where are we going?	Lib(E)LCSP 18670213;CD BN(J)TOCJ-5844

All titles issued on BN BN-LA047-F,CD 7-84466-2.

LOU DONALDSON - SOPHISTICATED LOU:
Lou Donaldson(as) Derek Smith(p,el p) Joe Venuto(vb) Jay Berliner(g,12 string g) Richard Davis(b) Grady Tate(dm) Eugene Bianco(harp) Omar Clay(perc).
(A & R Studios) NYC,December 8,1972
Joe Farrell,Paul Winter(fl,alto fl) Harry Lookofsky,Aaron Rosand,Irving Spice(v) Harry Zaratzian,Seymour Berman(viola) Seymour Barab(cello) Wade Marcus(arr) overdubbed on.
(A & R Studios) NYC,December 18,1972

11399 (tk.7) Time after time
11392 (tk.8) You've changed
11394 (tk.6) What are you doing the rest of your life
11397 (tk.5) Autumn in New York

All titles issued on BN BN-LA024-F.

Lou Donaldson(as) Derek Smith(p,el p) Joe Venuto(vb) Jay Berliner(g,12 string g) Ron Carter(b) Grady Tate (dm) Eugene Bianco(harp) Omar Clay(perc).
(A & R Studios) NYC,December 11,1972
Joe Farrell,Paul Winter(fl,alto fl) Harry Lookofsky,Aaron Rosand,Irving Spice(v) Harry Zaratzian,Seymour Berman(viola) Seymour Barab(cello) Wade Marcus(arr) overdubbed on.
(A & R Studios) NYC,December 18,1972

11393 (tk.4)	Stella by starlight	
11396 (tk.14)	You are the sunshine of my life	BN BN-XW189-W
11398 (tk.2)	Blues walk	
11395 (tk.2)	The long goodbye	BN BN-XW189-W

All titles issued on BN BN-LA024-F.

ALPHONSE MOUZON - THE ESSENCE OF MYSTERY
Buddy Terry(ss) Sonny Fortune(as) Larry Willis(p,el p) Wilbur Bascomb Jr.,Buster Williams(el b) Alphonse Mouzon(dm,tympani,tabla,perc,el p,clavinet, mellotron,vo).
(A & R Studios) NYC,December 13,14 & 15,1972

11442	The essence of mystery	CD BN(J)TOCJ-1621
11443	Funky finger	BN BN-XW261-W
11444	Crying angels	CD BN(J)TOCJ-6285
11445	Why can't we make it	BN B1-97158,CD 4-97158-2
11446	Macrobian	
11447	Spring water	BN BN-XW261-W,CD 4-97157-2
11448	Sunflower	BN B1-35607,CD 8-35607-2,5-21152-2
11449	Thank you Lord	
11450	Antonia	

All titles issued on BN BN-LA059-F,CD BN(J)TOCJ-6286.

RONNIE FOSTER - SWEET REVIVAL:
Garnett Brown(tb-1) Seldon Powell(ts-1) Ronnie Foster(org) Ernie Hayes(el p) David Spinozza,John Tropea(el g) Wilbur Bascomb Jr.(el b) Bernard Purdie(dm) unknown(perc-2) with horn section-3,strings-4, female vocal group-5,Horace Ott(arr,cond).
(Generation Sound Studios) NYC,December 14 & 15,1972

11433	Sweet revival -1,2,3	
11434 (tk.9)	Lisa's love -4	
11435	Backstabbers -3,4,5	
11436	It's just gotta be this way -2,3	
11437 (tk.1)	Alone again (Naturally) -4	
11438	Where is the love? -2,3,4,5	
11439	Me and Mrs. Jones -3,4,5	
11440 (tk.10)	Some neck	CD BN(J)TOCJ-6285
11441	Superwoman -4	
11900 (tk.1)	Inot (Enot*)	CD BN 4-97157-2*,(J)TOCJ-1621

All titles issued on BN BN-LA098-F,CD BN(J)TOCJ-1624.

THE NEW HERITAGE KEYBOARD QUARTET:
Roland Hanna(clavinet,p) Mickey Tucker(p) Richard Davis(b) Eddie Gladden(dm,perc).
(A & R Studios) NYC,January 16,17 & 18,1973

Zap carniverous	BN BN-LA099-F
Sin No.86 1/2	-
State of affairs	-
Delphi	-
Monstrosity march	-
Child of Gemini:So you will know my name	-
Man from Glad	unissued

MARLENA SHAW:
Marlena Shaw(vo) with unknown tps,ts,fls,synth,g,el b,dm,perc & strings.
(Clover Recording Studio) LA,February 12,1973

(tk.5)	Me and Mr. Jones	unissued
11635 (tk.15)	Last tango in Paris	BN BN-XW209-W CD BN 8-57748-2,EMI(E)5-20535-2

<u>LOU DONALDSON</u> - <u>SASSY SOUL STRUT</u>:
Thad Jones(tp) Garnett Brown(tb) Lou Donaldson(el as) Seldon Powell(fl,ts) Buddy Lucas(hca) Horace Ott (el p, arr,cond) Paul Griffin(el p,p,org) David Spinozza,John Tropea,Hugh McCracken(el g) Wilbur Bascomb(el b) Bernard Purdie(dm) Omar Clay,Jack Jennings(perc) (Collective personnel).
(Generation Sound Studio) NYC,April 17,1973

12066	Sanford and son theme	BN BN-XW381-W
12071	This is happiness	
12072	Inner space	

All titles issued on BN BN-LA109-F.

Same.Lou Donaldson(el as,as-1).
(Generation Sound Studio) NYC,April 18,1973

12067	Pillow talk	BN BN-XW287-W;CD BN(J)TOCJ-5844
12068	Sassy soul strut	- B1-30721
		CD BN 8-30721-2,4-97157-2,(Sp)8-53016-2
12069	Good morning heartache -1	BN BN-XW381-W
12070	City,country,city	

All titles issued on BN BN-LA109-F.

<u>MARLENA SHAW</u> - <u>FROM THE DEPTHS OF MY SOUL</u>:
Marlena Shaw(vo) with Derek Smith(clavichord,el p,p) Cornell Dupree,Carl Lynch,Hugh McCracken,Gene Bertoncini(g) Wilbur Bascomb(el b) Ron Carter(b) Grady Tate,Herbie Lovelle,Charles Collins(dm) Gene Bianco(harp) George Jenkins,George Devens(perc) Arthur Jenkins(cga)(collective personnel).
(A & R Studios) NYC,May 30,1973

12678-10	Easy evil	BN BN-XW366-W
12679-7	The laughter and the tears	CD BN 8-54943-2
12680-8	The feeling's good	BN BN-XW550-X
12682-7	I just don't want to be lonely	BN BN-XW366-W
12683-10	Waterfall	
12685-6	Time for me to go	

All titles issued on BN BN-LA143-F.

Same.
(A & R Studios) NYC,May 31,1973

12675-8	I know I love him	BN BN-LA143-F (see note to next session)
12676-7	Hum this song	BN BN-LA143-F
12677-1	But for now	BN BN-XW550-X,BN-LA143-F
		CD BN 8-54943-2,(Sp)8-56842-2
12681-10	Wildflower	BN BN-LA143-F
12684-5	Say a kind word	-
(tk.1)	Tangle in your lifeline	unissued

Unidentified strings and horns, arr. by Wade Marcus.
(A & R Studios) NYC,June 6,1973

(tk.12)	Prelude	BN BN-LA143-F (see note below)

Note: "Prelude" and "I Know I Love Him" were spliced together and issued as one piece.
The strings and horns for the rest of this album were overdubbed at this session.

267

BOBBI HUMPHREY - BLACKS AND BLUES:

Bobbi Humphrey(fl,vo) Jerry Peters(p,el p) Fonce Mizell(clavinet,tp,vo) Fred Perren (synth,vo) David T.Walker (g) Chuck Rainey(el b) Harvey Mason(dm) Stephanie Spruill(perc) Chuck Davis,Larry Mizell(vo).
(The Sound Factory) LA,June 6,1973

12693 Harlem River drive BN BN-XW455-W,BN-LA699-G,BST2-92477, B1-99106,B1-94706
BN(Du)1A158-83401/4
CD BN 7-92477-2,7-99106-2,7-80503-2, 8-54363-2, 4-94706-2,(J)TOCJ-1621,
Cema S21-57593,The Right Stuff 8-54487-2,
HMV Jazz(E)5-20881-2
12694 Just a love child BN BN-XW395-W
12695 Blacks and blues BN BN-XW455-W,B1-54360,B1-94706
CD BN 7-80503-2,4-94706-2,(J)TOCJ-5845

All titles issued on BN BN-LA142-G,CD 4-98542-2.

Bobbi Humphrey(fl,vo) Jerry Peters(p,el p) Fonce Mizell(clavinet,tp,vo) Fred Perren (synth,vo) David T. Walker(g) John Rowin(g) Chuck Rainey,Ron Brown(el b) Harvey Mason(dm) Stephanie Spruill(perc) King Errison(cga,backgr.vo) Larry Mizell(vo,arr).
(The Sound Factory) LA,June 7 & 8,1973

12692 Chicago,damn BN BN-XW395-W,BN-LA699-G,CD 7-80503-2
12696 Jasper country man BN B1-89907,CD 7-89907-2,N(J)TOCJ-6285
12697 Baby's gone

All titles issued on BN BN-LA142-G, CD 4-98542-2.

DONALD BYRD - STREET LADY:

Donald Byrd(tp,flh,vo) Roger Glenn(fl) Fonce Mizell(clavinet,tp,vo) Jerry Peters(p,el p) Fred Perren (synth,vo) David T.Walker(g) Chuck Rainey(el b) Harvey Mason(dm) King Errison(cga) Stephanie Spruill (perc) Larry Mizell(vo,arr,cond).
(The Sound Factory) LA,June 13,14 & 15,1973

12686 Lansana's priestess BN BN-LA700-G,B1-98638,B1-94708
Lib(E)LCSP 18670213
CD BN 7-98638-2,4-94708-2,(J)TOCJ-5845
12687 Miss Kane BN B1-94708,CD 4-94708-2
12688 Sister love Lib(E)LCSP 18670213
CD BN(J)TOCJ-5844
12689 Street lady BN BN-LA700-G,B1-89907,B1-98638
CD BN 7-89907-2,7-98638-2, (Eu)4-93994-2
12690 Witch hunt BN XW-445-W
12691 Woman of the world -

All titles issued on BN BN-LA140-F,B1-53923,CD 8-53923-2

GENE HARRIS - YESTERDAY,TODAY AND TOMORROW:
Gene Harris(p,arr) John Halton(b,el b) Carl Burnett(dm,perc).
(Motown Studio) Detroit,June 14 & 15,1973

12465-6	On Green Dolphin Street	BN BN-LA141-G2
12466-3	Hymn to freedom	-
12467-3	Trieste	-
12468-2	Love for sale	-
12469-15	Something	-
12470-2	How insensitive	-
12471-4	Judy,Judy,Judy	-
12472-7	After hours	-
12473-4	Sawin' wood	-
12474-2	Lil' darling	-
12475-9	Monk's tune	-

BOBBY HUTCHERSON - LIVE AT MONTREUX:
Woody Shaw(tp) Bobby Hutcherson(vb) Cecil Barnard(p) Ray Drummond(b) Larry Hancock(dm).
(Jazz Festival) Montreux(Switzerland),July 5,1973

14097	Anton's bail	BN BN-LA249-G	CD 8-27819-2
14098	The Moontrane	-	-
14099	Song of songs	-	-
	Farrallone		-

RONNIE FOSTER - LIVE AT MONTREUX:
Ronnie Foster(org) Gregory Miller(g) Marvin Chappell(dm).
(Jazz Festival) Montreux(Switzerland),July 5,1973

14100	East of ginger trees	BN BN-LA250-G
14101	Chunky	-
14102	Boogie juice	-
14103	Sameness	-

MARLENA SHAW - LIVE AT MONTREUX:
Marlena Shaw(vo) George Gaffney(p) Ed Boyer(b) Harold Jones(dm).
(Jazz Festival) Montreux(Switzerland),July 5,1973

The show has begun	
The song is you	
You are the sunshine of my life	
Twisted	
But for now	
Save the children	
Woman of the ghetto	BN B1-28965,B1-94027 CD BN 4-94027-2,(J)TOCJ-5846

All titles issued on BN BN-LA251-G,CD 8-32749-2.

DONALD BYRD - LIVE AT MONTREUX:
Donald Byrd(tp,flh) Fonce Mizell(tp) Nathan Davis(ss,ts) Allan Barnes(fl,ts) Kevin Toney(el p) Larry Mizell (synth) Barney Perry(el g) Henry Franklin(el b) Keith Killgo(dm,vo) Ray Armando(cga,perc).
(Jazz Festival) Montreux(Switzerland),July 5,1973

Poco-mania	unissued
You've got it bad,girl	-
untitled N°3	-
Black Byrd	-
Flight time	-

BOBBI HUMPHREY - LIVE AT MONTREUX
Bobbi Humphrey(fl) Kevin Toney(el p) Barney Perry(g) Henry Franklin(b) Keith Killgo(dm).
(Jazz Festival) Montreux(Switzerland),July 5,1973

14104	Virtue	CD BN(J)TOCJ-6285
14105	Sugar	CD BN 4-97157-2
14106	Sad bag	
14107	Ain't no sunshine	CD BN(J)TOCJ-6285

All titles issued on BN BN-LA252-G.

ELVIN JONES - THE PRIME ELEMENT/AT THIS POINT IN TIME:
Steve Grossman(ss) Frank Foster(ts-1,ss-2) Pepper Adams(bs) Jan Hammer(synth,p-1,el p-2) Cornell Dupree(g) Gene Perla(b) Elvin Jones(dm) Warren Smith(tympani) Candido Camero(cga) Richard "Pablo" Landrum,Omar Clay(perc,programmable rhythm box).
(A & R Studios) NYC,July 24,1973

13432 (tk.2) The whims of Bal -1
13431 (tk.2) The prime element -2

Both titles issued on BN BN-LA506-H2,CD BN 4-93385-2,Mosaic MD8-195.

Steve Grossman(ss-1,ts-2) Frank Foster(ts) Pepper Adams(bs) Jan Hammer(synth-3,p-4,el p-5) Cornell Dupree(g) Gene Perla(b,el b-6) Elvin Jones(dm) Warren Smith(tympani) Candido Camero(cga) Richard "Pablo" Landrum,Omar Clay(perc,programmable rhythm box).
(A & R Studios) NYC,July 25,1973

(tk.1) Don't cry -1,4 ,6
(tk.1) Pauke tanz -2,3
(tk.2) The unknighted nations -1,5,6

All titles issued on CD BN 4-93385-2,Mosaic MD8-195.

Steve Grossman(ss-1,ts-2) Frank Foster(ts) Pepper Adams(bs) Jan Hammer(synth-2,el p) Cornell Dupree(g) Gene Perla(b,el b-2) Elvin Jones(dm) Warren Smith(tympani) Candido Camero(cga) Richard "Pablo" Landrum,Omar Clay(perc,programmable rhythm box).
(A & R Studios) NYC,July 26,1973

13429 (tk.1) At this point in time -1
13430 (tk.1) Currents/Pollen -2

Both titles issued on BN BN-LA506-H2,CD BN 4-93385-2,Mosaic MD8-195.

ALPHONSE MOUZON - FUNKY SNAKEFOOT:
Harry Whitaker(p) Leon Pendarvis (el p,org) Richie Resnicoff(g) Mark Markowitz-2(pedal steel g,bjo) Gary King(el b) Alphonse Mouzon(vo,dm,synth,tack p) Ray Armando-3(cga,bgo) Steve Berrios,Angel Allende (perc-4)
(Electric Lady Studios) NYC,December 10,11 & 12,1973

	I've given you my love -1,3,4	
	A permanent love -1,2,3 (voAM)	
	You don't know how much I love you -3 (voAM)	
	My life is so blue (voAM)	
13733	Oh yes I do -1 (voAM)	BN BN-XW500-X

-1: Randy Brecker(tp)Barry Rogers(tb)Andy Gadsden(ts) added.
All titles issued on BN BN-LA222-G.

ALPHONSE MOUZON - FUNKY SNAKEFOOT:
Harry Whitaker(clavinet-2,p-3) Leon Pendarvis(p-2) Mike Mandel(el p-4) Gary King(el b) Alphonse Mouzon (vo,dm,synth). Same sessions.

13734	Funky snakefoot -1,2	BN BN-XW500-X,CD 4-97157-2
	ISM -1,4	
	I gotta have you -2,4 (voAM)	
	My little Rosebud -3	

-1: Randy Brecker(tp) Barry Rogers(tb) Andy Gadsden(ts) added.
All titles issued on BN BN-LA222-G.

Harry Whitaker(clavinet-2,p-3) Leon Pendarvis(org-2,el p-3) Alphonse Mouzon(vo,dm,synth).
Same sessions.

Tara tara -2 (voAM)
The beggar -3 (voAM)
Where I'm drumming from (drum solo)

All titles issued on BN BN-LA222-G.

DONALD BYRD:
Donald Byrd(tp) with The Blackbyrds: Allan Barnes(ss,ts,vo) Kevin Toney(p,el p,synth,vo) Barney Perry (el g,vo) Joe Hall(el b,vo) Keith Killgo(dm,vo) Perk Jacobs(cga,perc,vo).
(Live,The Roxy) LA,March 2,1974

tk.1	Black byrd	unissued
tk.2	Livin' For The City	-
tk.3	Lansana's Priestess	-
tk.4	Witch Hunt	-
tk.5	Poco mania	-
tk.6	You've got it bad girl	-
tk.7	Reggins	-
tk.8	A Summer love	-
tk.9	Do it fluid	-
tk.10	unknown	-
tk.11	unknown	-

MOACIR SANTOS - SAUDADE:
Steve Huffsteter(tp,flh) Sidney Muldrow(frh) Benny Powell(tb) Morris Repass(bass tb) Moacir Santos (as,bs, arr,cond) Jerome Richardson(ss,as,ts,bs,fl, alto fl) Ray Pizzi(fl,as,ts, picc,bassoon) Mark Levine (p,el p,arr-1) Lee Ritenour(g,el g) John Heard(b,el b) Harvey Mason(dm) Carmelo Garcia, Mayuto Correa (cga,perc).
(United Artists Studios) LA,March 5,6 & 12,1974

13961-3	Early morning love -2	CD BN(J)TOCJ-5845
13962-6	Suk cha	
13963-4	Kathy -2	CD BN(J)TOCJ-5844
13964-3	Off and on -2	CD BN(J)TOCJ-5846
13965-7	A saudade matta a gente -3	CD BN(J)TOCJ-5845
13966-4	What's my name -4	
13967-2	Amphibious	
13968-11	This life -2	
13969-11	The city of L.A.-1	
13970-3	Happly-happy-2,5	

-2: Petsye Powell,Mike Campbell,Donald Alves(backgr.vo) added.
-3: Petsye Powell,Mike Campbell,Jose Marino,Carmen Saveiros(backgr.vo) added.
-4: Donald Alves(backgr.vo) added.
-5: Jose Marino,Regina Werneck(backgr.vo) added.
All titles issued on BN BN-LA260-G,CD BN(J)TOCJ-6289.

271

LOU DONALDSON - SWEET LOU:
Lou Donaldson(el as,as-1) Horace Ott(keyb,synth,arr,cond) Paul Griffin(clavinet) Cornell Dupree,David Spinozza,Hugh McCracken(g) Wilbur Bascomb(el b) Bernard Purdie,Jimmie Young(dm) & unidentified cga,vb, perc.
Ernie Royal,Joe Shepley,Danny Moore(tp) Garnett Brown(tb) Seldon Powell,Arthur Clark(fl,ts) Buddy Lucas(hca) Barbara Massey,Hilda Harris,Eileen Gilbert,Carl Williams Jr,William Sample,Bill Davis,Eric Figueroa(backgr. vo) overdubbed on.
(Generation Sound Studios) NYC,March 14,1974

14049 tk.3 Hip trip
14047 tk.5 If you can't handle it,give it to me
14110 tk.7 Love eyes

All titles issued on BN BN-LA259-G.

Same.
(Generation Sound Studios) NYC,March 19,1974

14051 tk.5	Peepin'	BN BN-LA259-G
14111 tk.7	Sugar foot	unissued
14052 tk.8	Herman's mambo	BN BN-LA259-G
14048 tk.15	Lost love -1	-

Same.
(Generation Sound Studios) NYC,March 21,1974

14050 (tk.11) You're welcome,stop on by BN BN-LA259-G

DOM MINASI - WHEN JOANNA LOVED ME:
Dom Minasi(g,arr) Garry Newman(b) Bud Nealy(dm,perc) Joseph Daddiego(cga,perc) Gene Bianco(harp) Paul Winter,Peter Dimitriades(v) Harry Zaratzian,Seymour Berman(viola) Kermit Moore,Seymour Barab (cello) Wade Marcus(string arr,cond).
(A & R Studios) NYC,March 19,20 & 21,1974

14033 Spinning wheel
14034 When Joanna loved me
14035 On Green Dolphin Street
14036 With a little help from my friends
14037 What are you doing the rest of your life
14038 I'll only miss her

All titles issued on BN BN-LA258-G.

BOBBY HUTCHERSON - CIRRUS:
Woody Shaw(tp) Harold Land,Emanuel Boyd(fl,ts) Bobby Hutcherson(vb,marimba) Bill Henderson(p,el p) Ray Drummond(b) Larry Hancock(dm) Kenneth Nash(perc).
(Wally Heider Studios) LA,April 17,1974

14045	Zuri dance	BN BN-LA257-G
	Cirrus	rejected
	Even later	-

<u>BOBBY HUTCHERSON</u> - <u>CIRRUS</u>:
Woody Shaw(tp) Harold Land,Emanuel Boyd(fl,ts) Bobby Hutcherson(vb,marimba) Bill Henderson(p,el p) Ray Drummond(b) Larry Hancock(dm) Kenneth Nash(perc).
(Wally Heider Studios) LA,April 18,1974

14046	Cirrus	
14043	Even later	Up Front UPF-187
14044	Wrong or right	-
14042	Rosewood	

All titles issued on BN BN-LA257-G.

<u>RONNIE FOSTER</u> - <u>ON THE AVENUE</u>:
John E.Gatchell,Dean Robert Pratt(tp,flh) Gerald Ray Chamberlain(tb) Joel L.Kaye(bs) Ronnie Foster (org,clavinet,synth,vo) Phil Upchurch(g,el b) Marvin Chappell(dm) Alfred "Pee Wee" Ellis(horn arr).
(Electric Lady Studios) NYC,April 30,1974

14182	Serenade to a rock
14187 (tk.5)	Big farm boy goes Latin city
14183 (tk.8)	On the Alamo
14184	What happened to the sunshine
14186	To see a smile

All titles issued on BN BN-LA261-G.

Same.
(Electric Lady Studios) NYC,May 1,1974

14188 (tk.1)	First light	
14185 (tk.2)	Golden lady	CD BN(J)TOCJ-5845

Both titles issued on BN BN-LA261-G.

<u>BOBBI HUMPHREY</u> - <u>SATIN DOLL</u>:
Fonce Mizell(tp,clavinet,backgr.vo) Bobbi Humphrey(fl,vo) Jerry Peters(p,clavinet) Larry Mizell(el p,synth, backgr.vo,arr,cond) Don Preston,Phil Davis-2(synth) Melvin Ragin,John Rowin(g) Chuck Rainey(el b) Harvey Mason(dm) King Errison(cga) Stephanie Spruill,Roger Sainte(perc) Freddie Perren,Samantha Harris-1 (backgr.vo).
(The Sound Factory) LA,June 20,1974

14609	Satin doll -1	BN BN-LA344-G,BN-LA699-G
14611	Ladies day	- CD 7-80503-2
14613	My little girl	- B1-94706,CD 4-94706-2
14615	You are the sunshine of my life -2	- BN-LA699-G CD BN(J)TOCJ-5845
14618	Young warrior	unissued

Same.
(The Sound Factory) LA,July 22,1974

14612	Fun house	BN BN-XW592-X,BN-LA344-G,BN-LA699-G CD BN 7-80503-2
14614	Rain again -1	BN BN-LA344-G
14620	untitled	unissued
14621	Three dots	-
14622	High places	-

-1: Chuck Davis(backgr.vo) added.

BOBBI HUMPHREY - SATIN DOLL:
Fonce Mizell(tp,clavinet,backgr.vo) Bobbi Humphrey(fl,vo) Jerry Peters(p,clavinet) Larry Mizell (el p,synth, clavinet-1,backgr.vo,arr,cond) Chuck Davis(clavinet-1) Don Preston,Phil Davis-2(synth) Melvin Ragin,John Rowin(g) Chuck Rainey,Wayne Tweed(el b) Harvey Mason(dm) King Errison(cga) Stephanie Spruill, Roger Sainte(perc) Freddie Perren,Samantha Harris-1(backgr.vo).
(The Sound Factory) LA,August 5,1974

14608	New York times	CD BN 7-80503-2,8-54363-2, (Eu)4-93994-2
14610	San Francisco lights -1	BN BN-XW592-X,BN-LA699-G,B1-94706
		CD BN 4-94706-2

Both titles issued on BN BN-LA344-G.

GENE HARRIS - ASTRAL SIGNAL:
Oscar Brashear(tp) George Bohanon,Keg Johnson(tb,backgr.vo) Sidney Muldrow(frh) Ernie Watts(reeds) Jim Shifflett( )Gene Harris(keyboards,arr-1,lead vo-2) Jerry Peters(p,arr,backgr.vo) David T.Walker,John Rowin(g) Chuck Rainey(el b) Harvey Mason(dm,arr-3) Maxine Willard Waters,Julia Tillman Waters,Luther Waters,Oren Waters,Trisha Chamberlain,Ann Esther Davis,Lynn Mack(backgr. vo).
(The Village Recorder) LA,August 13,1974

14384	Prelude	BN B1-94027,CD 4-94027-2
14385	Summer (The first time)	BN BN-XW590-X
14386	Rubato Summer	
14387	I remember Summer	BN BN-XW551-X
14388	Don't call me nigger,whitey	BN B1-54360,CD 8-54360-2
14389	Los alamitos latin funk love song	CD BN(J)TOCJ-1621,TOCJ-5844
		BN BN-XW590-X,B1-29865,CD 8-29865-2
14390	My roots -1	
14391	Green river	
14392	Beginnings -2	CD BN(J)TOCJ-5844
14393	Higga-boom -3	BN BN-XW551-X,B1-89907,CD 7-89907-2
14394	Feeling you,feeling me too!	
14395	Love talkin'	

All titles issued on BN BN-LA313-G,CD BN(J)TOCJ-6290.

WATERS:
Maxine Waters,Julia Waters,Oren Waters,Luther Waters(vo) with Oscar Brashear(tp) George Bohanon, Maurice Spears(tb) Mike Altschul,Ernie Watts(reeds) Jerry Peters(p,keyb,arr) David T. Walker,John Rowin Jr.(g) Chuck Rainey(el b) John Guerin(dm) Mayuto Correa,Stephanie Spruill,Roger Sainte(perc) Stella Castellucci(harp) & strings.
(Music Recorders) LA,October 22-24,1974 (exact dates shown below)

14745 (22)	Stuh-born people	BN BN-LA370-G
14746 (22)	Sometime when I'm alone	unissued
14747 (22)	Trying hard to look inside	BN BN-LA370-G
14743 (23)	To be there	BN BN-XW637-X,BN-XW692-Y,BN-LA370-G
14744 (23)	Crazy about you	BN BN-LA370-G
14748 (23)	Find it	BN BN-XW637-X,BN-XW692-Y,BN-LA370-G
14749 (24)	Motherland	BN BN-LA370-G
14750 (24)	My heart just won't let you go	-
14751 (24)	Sitting here all alone	-

Similar. LA,November 10,1974

14882	You are lost in my dreams	BN BN-LA370-G

Similar. LA,November 17,1974

14881	Blinded by love	BN BN-LA370-G

DONALD BYRD - STEPPING INTO TOMORROW:
Donald Byrd(tp,flh,vo) Fonce Mizell(tp,clavinet,backgr.vo) Gary Bartz(cl,ss,as) Jerry Peters(p,org) Larry Mizell(el p,synth,backgr.vo,arr,cond) David T. Walker,John Rowin(g) Chuck Rainey(el b) Harvey Mason (dm,bata dm-1,mouth harp-1) Mayuto Correa(cga) Stephanie Spruill(perc,backgr.vo-1) Roger Sainte (perc) James Carter(whistling-2) Kay Haith(vo),Fred Perren,Margie Evans-3,Lorraine Kenner-4 (backgr.vo).
(The Sound Factory) LA,October 11,1974 to December ,1974

14883	Stepping into tomorrow -1,4	BN BN-LA700-G,B1-28263,B1-98638 Lib(E)LCSP 18670213 CD 7-98638-2,8-28263-2
14884	Harvey's tune (poss. Makin' it)	rejected
14885	You are the world -3	
14890	We're together (voKH)	BN BN-XW650-X
14893	Destination	rejected
14894	Hash & eggs,hold the eggs	unissued
14895	unknown title -6	rejected
15212	Design a nation -4	Lib(E)LCSP 18670213
15213	Rock and roll again (voDB)-2	BN-LA700-G
15214	Think twice (voDB,KH)-5	BN BN-XW650-X,B1-98638 Lib(E)LCSP 18670213 CDBN 7-98638-2,5-23559-2,(Eu)4-93994-2, (J)TOCJ-5844
15215	Makin' it -1,4	
15216	I love the girl	

-5: Ronghea Southern(g) replaces Rowin.
-6: listed in files as "10-16-74",which likely was the recording date for that title.
All titles,except 14884 & 14893/95,issued on BN BN-LA368-G,CD BN 5-23545-2,(J)TOCJ-6291.

MARLENA SHAW - WHO'S THIS BITCH ANYWAY?:
Marlena Shaw(vo) with Mike Lang(p-1) Larry Nash(el p,synth) David T.Walker,Larry Carlton(g) Chuck Rainey(el b) Harvey Mason(dm) King Errison(cga-1) & strings-2,Dale Oehler-1,Byron Olson-2 (arr).
(The Record Plant) LA,December 3,1974

15055	Loving you was like a party -1	BN BN-XW649-X,CD 8-54943-2,(J)TOCJ-5844
15056	You taught me how to speak in love -2	BN BN-XW691-Y

Both titles issued on BN BN-LA397-G,CD 7-89542-2.

Marlena Shaw(vo) with Larry Nash(el p) Dennis Budimir(g) Chuck Rainey(el b) Harvey Mason(dm,perc) with strings & horns arr. by Dale Oehler.
(The Record Plant) LA,December 4,1974

15057	You	BN BN-XW649-X,CD 8-54943-2
15058	You been away too long	CD BN(J)TOCJ-5844

Both titles issued on BN BN-LA397-G,CD 7-89542-2.

Marlena Shaw(vo)with Mike Lang(p-1) Larry Nash(el p,synth) David T.Walker,Larry Carlton(g) Chuck Rainey (el b) Harvey Mason(dm,wind chimes) King Errison(cga-1) & strings-1,Byron Olson-1,Bernard Ighner-2 (arr).
(The Record Plant) LA,December 5,1974

15059	Street walkin' woman -1	BN(Du)1A158-83401/4
15060	Feel like makin' love -2	BN BN-XW691-Y CD BN 7-99105-2,8-57463-2,5-23559-2, (J)TOCJ-6135,TOCJ-6188

Both titles issued on BN BN-LA397-G,CD 7-89542-2, 8-54943-2.

275

MARLENA SHAW - WHO'S THIS BITCH ANYWAY?:
Marlena Shaw(vo) with Bill Mays(p) Dennis Budimir(g) Chuck Domanico(b) Jim Gordon(dm) with woodwinds & strings arr. by Byron Olson.
(The Record Plant) LA,December 6,1974

15165 A prelude for Rose Marie -1
15061 Rose Marie (Mon Cherie) CD BN(J)TOCJ-5845

-1: Woodwinds and strings only.Possibly recorded on December 3,1974
Both titles issued on BN BN-LA397-G,CD 7-89542-2.

ALPHONSE MOUZON - MIND TRANSPLANT:
Jerry Peters(el p,org) Jay Graydon(g,programming) Tommy Bolin,Lee Ritenour(g) Henry Davis(b)Alphonse Mouzon(dm,vo,synth,el p-1,org,arr,cond) Elvena Mouzon(comp).
(Wally Heider Studio 3) LA,December 4,5,6,9 & 10,1974
(exact dates shown below in parentheses)

15068 (4) Happiness is loving you BN BN-XW648-X
15069 (4) Golden rainbows
15070 (4) Snow bound

15067 (5) Some of the things people do

15062 (6) Dancing vampires (see note)
15063 (6) Nitroglycerin BN BN-XW648-X
15064 (6) Carbon dioxide

15065 (9/10) Mind transplant
15066 (9/10) Ascorbic acid

All titles,except 15062,issued on BN BN-LA398-G,CD Pinnacle(E)RPM 116.
Note: 15062 was likely used and renamed for following issue which probably came from above sessions:
The real thing CD Pinnacle(E)RPM 116

MARLENA SHAW - WHO'S THIS BITCH ANYWAY?:
Marlena Shaw(vo) with Bernard Ighner(p,b,flh,arr) Dennis Budimir(g) Chuck Rainey(el b) Harvey Mason (dm) & strings.
(The Record Plant) LA,December 12,1974

15013 Davy
15172 The Lord giveth and taketh -1

-1: Marlena Shaw(vo,p) alone.
Both titles issued on BN BN-LA397-G,CD 7-89542-2.

HORACE SILVER - SILVER 'N BRASS:
Tom Harrell(tp) Bob Berg(ts) Horace Silver(p) Ron Carter(b) Al Foster(dm).
(A & R Studios) NYC,January 10,1975
Oscar Brashear,Bobby Bryant(tp,flh) Vince De Rosa(frh) Frank Rosolino(tb) Maurice Spears(bass tb) Jerome Richardson(fl,ss,as) Buddy Collette(fl,as) Wade Marcus(arr) overdubbed on.
(Wally Heider Studios) LA, 1975

15167 (tk.4) Barbara CD BN 8-33208-2,4-95576-2
15168 Dameron's dance
15170 (tk.3) Adjustment CD BN 4-95576-2
15171 (tk.3) Mysticism

All titles issued on BN BN-LA406-G.

BOBBY HUTCHERSON - LINGER LANE:
Ernie Watts(reeds) Bobby Hutcherson(marimba,arr) Jerry Peters(el p,arr-1) John Rowin(g) Chuck Rainey (el b) Harvey Mason(dm) Bobbye Porter Hall(perc) Maxine Waters,Julia Waters,Oren Waters,Luther Waters(vo).
Idylwild,Calif.,January 16,1975

15192	People make the world go round -1	
15193	Theme from M-A-S-H	Up Front UPF-187 CD BN 8-57748-2,(J)TOCJ-5844
15194	NTU	
15195	Manzanita	Up Front UPF-187
15196	Mountain caravan -1	
15197	Silver rondo	Up Front UPF-187

All titles issued on BN BN-LA369-G.

HORACE SILVER - SILVER' N' BRASS:
Tom Harrell(tp) Bob Berg(ts) Horace Silver(p) Bob Cranshaw(el b) Bernard Purdie(dm).
(A & R Studios) NYC,January 17,1975
Oscar Brashear,Bobby Bryant(tp,flh) Vince De Rosa(frh) Frank Rosolino(tb) Maurice Spears(bass tb) Jerome Richardson(fl,ss,as) Buddy Collette(fl,as) Wade Marcus(arr) overdubbed on.
(Wally Heider Studios) LA, 1975

15166 (tk.3)	Kissin' cousins	
15169	The sophisticated hippie	CD BN(J)TOCJ-5846

Both titles issued on BN BN-LA406-G.

DOM MINASI - I HAVE THE FEELING I'VE BEEN HERE BEFORE:
Bernard Ighner(tp,flh,synth,perc) Warn Luening,Jay Diversa(tp,flh) George Bohanon(tb) Keith Ighner(tb, el b) Ray Pizzi(fl,ts) Roger Kellaway(el p) Dom Minasi,John Morrell(g) Brian Magnus (el b) Bobbie Hall (cga).
(The Record Plant) LA,January ,1975

15261	Soltura	BN BN-LA426-G

Tony Terran,Ed Sheftel,Marnie Robinson,Charles Loper,Roger Bobo(brass) Bud Shank,Dave Sherr,Jack Nimitz,Ray Pizzi(reeds) Roger Kellaway(keyb) Dom Minasi(g) Carl "Chuck" Domanico(b) Ron Krasinski (dm) Harvey Mason,Victor Feldman,Gary Coleman(perc) Jackie Lustgarten,Ann Goodman,Kathleen Lustgarten,Lucille Greco(cello) Gail Levant(harp).
(The Record Plant) LA,January ,1975

15260	Sometime boogie
15262	R.K. Bossa
15263	Free
15264	I have the feeling I've been here before

All titles issued on BN BN-LA426-G.

Jim Decker(frh) Luis Ditullio(fl) Earl Dumler(oboe) Hugo Raimondi(cl) Jack Marsch(bassoon) Roger Kellaway(p) Dom Minasi,John Morrell(g) Chuck Domanico(b) Harvey Mason(dm) Mark Stevens(perc) Fred Seykora, Dennis Karmazyn,Jackie Lustgarten,Christine Ermacoff(cello) Gail Levant(harp).
(The Record Plant) LA,January ,1975

15265	Bitzy
15266	Theme from "Prisoner of 2nd Avenue"
15311	Moroccan copper
15312	You've been away too long

All titles issued on BN BN-LA426-G.

277

LOU DONALDSON:
Lou Donaldson(as) Herman Foster(p) Mark Elf(g-1) Bob Cranshaw(el b) Willie Seaberry(dm) Raymond Orchart(cga) Claudia Moore(vo).
(A & R Studios) NYC,February 4,1975

15345 (tk.5/6) Make someone happy-1 rejected
15346 (tk.2) Don't take your love from me (voCM) -1 -
15347 (tk.3) When I think about you (voCM) -1 -
15342 (tk.2) Do me like you do (voCM) -
15343 (tk.2) What now my love (voCM) -
15344 (tk.3) We'll be together again -

LOU DONALDSON:
Irvin Stokes(tp) Lou Donaldson(as) Lonnie Smith(org) Mark Elf(g-1) Bob Cranshaw(b) Willie Seaberry(dm) Raymond Orchart(cga).
(A & R Studios) NYC,February 5,1975

untitled original #1 -1 rejected
untitled original #2 -1 -
untitled original #3 -1 -
15339 (tk.3 or 8/9) Don't worry about it George -
15340 (tk.2) Funky Mama -
15341 (tk.1/2) Misty -

MOACIR SANTOS - CARNIVAL OF THE SPIRITS:
Oscar Brashear,Mike Price,Jerry Rusch(tp) J.J.Johnson,George Bohanon(tb) David Duke(frh) Don Menza (fl,alto fl,ts) Jerome Richardson(ss,alto fl) Ray Pizzi(cl,bass cl,ss) Ernie Watts(bass fl) Gary Foster(as) Moacir Santos(vo,as,bs,perc,arr-1) Larry Nash(el p, clavinet) Clare Fischer(p) Jerry Peters(org) Dennis Budimir,Dean Parks(g) Chuck Domanico(b) Harvey Mason(dm) Roberto Silva,Paulinho Da Costa,Louis Alves(perc) Lynda Lawrence(vo) Dale Oehler(arr).
(The Record Plant) LA,March 17,1975

15760 (tk.5) Tomorrow is mine BN BN-LA463-G
15759 (tk.8) Coisa No.2 -

Same.
(The Record Plant) LA,March 18,1975

15761 (tk.7) Route BN BN-LA463-G
15757 (tk.12) Kamba -

Same.
(The Record Plant) LA,March 19,1975

15755 (tk.7) Quiet carnival -1
15762 (tk.11) Anon -1

Both titles issued on BN BN-LA463-G.

Same.
(The Record Plant) LA,March 20,1975

15758 (tk.5) Sampaguita -1 CD BN(J)TOCJ-5845
15756 (tk.11) Jequie

-1: Intro of this title uses take 4.
Both titles issued on BN BN-LA463-G.

RONNIE FOSTER - CHESHIRE CAT:
Ronnie Foster(keyb,vo,arr) Joe Beck(g) William Allen(b) Dennis Davis(dm) Mtume(cga,perc) George Benson(backgr.vo).
(A & R Studios) NYC,March 21,1975

15683 (tk.2) Funky motion
15680 (tk.5) Like a child

Both titles issued on BN BN-LA425-G,CD BN(J)TOCJ-6292.

Ronnie Foster(keyb,vo,arr) Joe Beck(g) Gary King(el b) William Allen(b) Dennis Davis(dm) Mtume(cga, perc) George Benson(backgr.vo).
(A & R Studios) NYC,March 24,1975

15684 (tk.3) Cheshire cat -1 BN B1-29865,CD 4-97157-2
15685 (tk.4) Heartless

-1: George Benson(g) replaces Beck.
Both titles issued on BN BN-LA425-G,CD BN(J)TOCJ-6292.

BOBBY HUTCHERSON - INNER GLOW:
Oscar Brashear(tp) Thurman Green(tb) Harold Land(ts) Bobby Hutcherson(vb)Dwight Dickerson(p) Kent Brinkley(b) Larry Hancock(dm).
(United Artists Studios) LA,March 24,1975

(tk.7) Boodaa
(tk.4) Roses poses
(tk.2) Searchin' the Trane (horns out)

All titles issued on BN(J)GXF-3073.

Same.
(United Artists Studios) LA,March 25,1975

(tk.3) Inner glow
(tk.2) Cowboy Bob

Both titles issued on BN(J)GXF-3073.

RONNIE FOSTER - CHESHIRE CAT:
Ronnie Foster(keyb,vo,arr) Joe Beck(g) William Allen(b) Dennis Davis(dm) Mtume(cga,perc) & backgr.vo.
(A & R Studios) NYC,March 25,1975

(tk.3) Night people unissued
15681 (tk.2/8) Tuesday heartbreak BN BN-LA425-G
CD BN(J)TOCJ-5845,TOCJ-6292

Ronnie Foster(keyb,vo,arr) Joe Beck(g) Gary King(el b) William Allen(b) Dennis Davis(dm) Mtume(cga, perc) & backgr.vo.
(A & R Studios) NYC,March 27,1975

15682 (tk.1/4) Fly away BN BN-LA425-G;CD BN(J)TOCJ-6292

Note:15681 and 15682 use spliced takes.

279

EDDIE HENDERSON - SUNBURST:
Eddie Henderson(tp,flh,c) Julian Priester(tb) Bennie Maupin(ts,saxello,bass cl) George Duke(el p,clavinet, synth) Alphonso Johnson(el b) Harvey Mason(dm) Bobby Hutcherson(marimba-1).

(Wally Heider Studios) SF,March & April ,1975

15725	Sunburst	
15726	The Kumquat kids	BN B1-89907,CD 7-89907-2
15727	Galaxy -1	
15728	Explodition	
15729	Involuntary bliss	
15730	We end in a dream -2	
15731	Hop scotch	CD BN 4-97157-2

-2: Buster Williams(b) Billy Hart(dm) replace Johnson & Mason.
All titles issued on BN BN-LA464-G.

RONNIE LAWS - PRESSURE SENSITIVE:
Ronnie Laws(fl,ss,ts) Mike Cavanaugh(clavinet, el p) Joe Sample(clavinet-1,el p-2) Jerry Peters(el p-3, synth-4) John Rowin-5,Roland Bautista(g) Clint Mosley(el b) Steve Guttierez(dm) Joe Clayton(cga,tamb, Flexitone) Side Effect(backgr. vo-6).

(Angel City Sound) LA,March & April ,1975

15764	Always there	BN BN-XW738-Y,BST2-92477,5-21147-1 Cap.ST-12375;BN(Du)1A158-83401/4 CD BN 7-92477-2,7-98289-2,4-95701-2,5-21147-2 (E)8-53233-2,Cap.7-46585-2,Cema S21-57593, HMV Jazz(E)5-20881-2
15765	Momma -6	BN BN-XW777-Y,CD 4-97157-2
15766	Never be the same -2,5	
15767	Tell me something good -1,4	
15768	Nothing to lose -1,2,5	
15770	Why do you laugh at me -2,4	
15771	Miss Mary's place -1,2	BN BN-XW777-Y

All titles issued on BN LA452-G,CD 7-46554-2

Wilton Felder(el b) Michael Willers(dm) replaces Mosley & Guttierez.
Same dates.

15769	Tidal wave-3,4,5	BN BN-XW738-Y,LA452-G,B1-35607, CD 7-46554-2,8-35607-2

CARMEN McRAE - I AM MUSIC:
Carmen McRae(vo) with Dave Grusin(el p,synth,arr) Dennis Budimir(g) John Gianelli(b) Spider Webb(dm) Emil Richards(vb,perc) & string section incl.Erno Neufeld,Gerri Vinci(v) Alan Harshman(viola) Ed Lustgarten(cello).

(United Western Recorders) LA,April ,1975

15743	A letter from Anna-Lee	
15749	Like a lover	CD BN 8-33578-2

Both titles issued on BN BN-LA462-G,CD BN(J)TOCP-6690.

CARMEN McRAE - I AM MUSIC:
Carmen McRae(vo) with Roger Kellaway(p,arr) Frank Collett-1(org,synth) Dennis Budimir(g) John Gianelli (b) John Guerin(dm) Emil Richards(vb,perc) The Morgan Ames Singers(backgr.vo-1).
(United Western Recorders) LA,April ,1975

15746	I ain't here	CD BN(Sp)8-56842-2
15763	You know who you are -1	

Both titles issued on BN BN-LA462-G,CD BN(J)TOCP-6690.

Carmen McRae(vo) with Frank Collett(p,el p,synth) Dennis Budimir(g) John Gianelli(b) John Guerin(dm) Emil Richards(vb,perc), string section incl.Erno Neufeld,Gerri Vinci(v) Alan Harshman(viola) Ed Lustgarten (cello) & unidentified woodwinds-1,The Morgan Ames Singers (backgr.vo-2) Roger Kellaway,Byron Olson-3(arr).
(United Western Recorders) LA,April ,1975

15744	Trouble with hello is goodbye -2	
15745	Faraway forever	
15747	I have the feeling I've been here before	CD BN 8-33578-2
15748	Who gave you permission -1,3	
15750	I never lied to you -2	
15751	I am music -1	

All titles issued on BN BN-LA462-G,CD BN(J)TOCP-6690.

GENE HARRIS - NEXUS:
Gene Harris(keyb) with Al Aarons(tp)George Bohanon(tb) Mike Altschul,Fred Jackson(reeds) Lee Ritenour (g) John Rowin(g,el b-3) Chuck Rainey(el b) Kenneth Rice(dm) Gerald Steinholtz,Ronaldo N.Jackson(perc) Charles Veal,Wint Garvey,Rewit Koven,Julius Buffum(strings) Jerry Peters(arr,lead vo-1) Lynn Mack,John Lehman,Sigidi,Harold Clayton(vo-2) Maxine Willard Waters,Julia Tillman Waters,Lani Graves,Jerry Peters, Keg Johnson,Lynn Mack,John Lehman,Harold Clayton,Sigidi(backgr.vo).
(Music Recorders) LA,May 7,1975

15836	Game of hearts	rejected
15837	Prayer '76 -2	BN BN-LA519-G

Same.
(Music Recorders) LA,May 15,1975

15906	Love don't love nobody	BN BN-LA519-G

Same.
(Music Recorders) LA,May & June ,1975

16500	Sauda -3	
16501	Funky business -1	
16502	Koko and Lee Moe	
16503	Rushin' roulette (Don't let it backfire)	
16504	Jitterbug waltz	CD BN(J)TOCJ-5844
16505	Gettin' down country	
16506	H.R.D.(Boogie)	

-3: synth. programming by Charlotte Politte.
All titles issued on BN BN-LA519-G.

281

JOHN LEE & GERRY BROWN:
Rob Franken(el p,synth) Eef Alberts,Philip Catherine,Wah Wah Watson-3(g) John Lee(el b,synth-1, clavinet-2) Gerry Brown(dm,perc).
(Dureco Studios) Weesp,Holland,June ,1975

16382	Mango sunrise -1,3	
16383	Breakfast of champions	
16384	Keep it real -2	
16385	Ethereal cereal	BN(Du)1A158-83401/4
16386	The stop and go -4	
16387	Her celestial body	
16388	Pickin' the bone	
16389	Magnum opus -5	
16390	Haida	

-4: Eric Tagg(clavinet,synth)Mike Mandel(synth) added.
-5: Jasper Van T'Hoff(clavinet) added.
All titles issued on BN BN-LA541-G.

CHICO HAMILTON - PEREGRINATIONS:
Arthur Blythe(as) Arnie Lawrence(ss,ts-1) Barry Finnerty,Joe Beck(el g) Steve Turre(el b,tb-2) Chico Hamilton(dm,perc,arr) Abdullah(perc,cga,bgo).
(A & R Studios) NYC,July 9,1975
Jerry Peters(p,el p) Charlotte Politte(synth programming) Maxine Willard,Julia Tillman,Luther Waters, Oren Waters(vo) Keg Johnson(arr) overdubbed on.
(Sound Factory West) LA,August ,1975

16241-2	Little Lisa (no vocals)-1	
16242-4	V-O (Lawrence out)	CD BN 5-23559-2
16243-4	Peregrinations	

All titles issued on BN BN-LA520-G.

Same. (A & R Studios) NYC,July 10,1975*
Overdubs: Same as above

16244-7 *	The morning side of love (saxes out)	
16245-1 *	Andy's walk -2	
16246-3 *	Abdullah and Abraham	BN B1-35607,CD 8-35607-2
16247-1 *	Space for Stacey (no overdubs)	CD BN(J)TOCJ-1621
16248-1 *	Sweet dreams	
16249-2 *	It's about time (no overdubs)	
16409-1	On and off (no vocals)-1	

All titles issued on BN BN-LA520-G.

BOBBI HUMPHREY - FANCY DANCER:
Oscar Brashear(tp) Fonce Mizell(tp,clavinet,solina,vo) Julian Priester(tb) Bobbi Humphrey(fl,vo) Tyree Glenn Jr.(ts) Roger Glenn(vb,marimba) Larry Mizell(synth,solina,p,el p,vo) Jerry Peters(p,el p,synth) Skip Scarborough(p,el p,clavinet) Chuck Davis(p,el p) Dorothy Ashby(harp) Craig McMullen,John Rowin(g) Chuck Rainey(el b) Harvey Mason(dm) Mayuto Correa(cga) Augie Rey, Katherine Lyra,Jesse Acuna, Sonia Tavares, Rosario Davila(backgr.vo).
(The Sound Factory) LA,August 5,1975

16421	You make me feel so good	CD BN 7-80503-2,(J)TOCJ-5844
16422	The trip	-
16423	Fancy dancer	BN BN-LA699-G
16424	Please set me at ease	BN B1-94706,CD 4-94706-2,(J)TOCJ-5844

All titles issued on BN BN-LA550-G.

BOBBI HUMPHREY - FANCY DANCER:
Oscar Brashear(tp) Fonce Mizell(tp,clavinet,solina,vo) Julian Priester(tb) Bobbi Humphrey(fl,vo) Tyree Glenn Jr.(ts) Roger Glenn(vb,marimba) Larry Mizell(synth,solina,p,el p,vo) Jerry Peters(p,el p,synth) Skip Scarborough(p,el p,clavinet) Chuck Davis(p,el p) Dorothy Ashby(harp) Craig McMullen,John Rowin(g) Chuck Rainey(el b) Harvey Mason(dm) Mayuto Correa(cga) Augie Rey, Katherine Lyra,Jesse Acuna, Sonia Tavares, Rosario Davila(backgr.vo).
(The Sound Factory) LA,August 6,1975

16557 Uno esta BN BN-XW785-Y,BN-LA699-G
CD BN 5-23559-2,(Eu)4-93994-2,(J)TOCJ-5846
16558 Mestizo eyes

Both titles issued on BN BN-LA550-G,CD 7-80503-2.

Same.James Carter(whistler) added.
(The Sound Factory) LA,August 7,1975

16425 Sweeter than sugar BN BN-XW785-Y,BN-LA550-G

BOBBY HUTCHERSON - MONTARA:
Oscar Brashear(tp) Plas Johnson(fl) Ernie Watts(ts) Fred Jackson(fl,ts) Bobby Hutcherson(vb,marimba) Larry Nash(el p) Dennis Budimir(g) Chuck Domanico(el b) Harvey Mason(dm) Ralph McDonald,Bobby Matos,Victor Pantoja,Johnny Paloma(perc) Dale Oehler(arr).
(The Record Plant) LA,August 12 or 14,1975

16427 Camel rise BN BN-LA551-G;CD BN(J)TOCJ-6293
16428 Hello it's me unissued

Blue Mitchell(tp-1) Plas Johnson(ss) Ernie Watts(fl,ts) Bobby Hutcherson(vb,marimba) Larry Nash(el p) Chuck Domanico(el b) Harvey Mason(dm-2)Willie Bobo(mallets-2) Ralph McDonald,Bobby Matos,Victor Pantoja,Johnny Paloma(perc) Dale Oehler(arr).
(The Record Plant) LA,August 12 or 14,1975

16508 Little angel -1
16509 Love song -2

Both titles issued on BN BN-LA551-G,CD BN(J)TOCJ-6293.

Oscar Brashear,Blue Mitchell -2 (tp) Ernie Watts(fl,ts) Bobby Hutcherson(vb,marimba,arr-1) Larry Nash(el p) Eddie Cano(p) Dave Troncoso(el b) Bobby Matos,Victor Pantoja,Johnny Paloma,Rudy Calzado(perc) Dale Oehler(arr-2).
(The Record Plant) LA,August 12 or 14,1975

16559 Montara (p out)-1
16560 Yuyo (tp out)-1
16429 La malanga -1 CD BN 4-97156-2
16507 Oye como va (band vo)-2

All titles issued on BN BN-LA551-G,CD BN(J)TOCJ-6293.

283

DONALD BYRD - PLACES AND SPACES:
Donald Byrd(tp,flh,vo) Fonce Mizell(tp,clavinet,backgr.vo) Raymond Brown(tp) George Bohanon(tb) Tyree Glenn Jr.(ts) Larry Mizell(p,arr,backgr.vo) Skip Scarborough(el p) Craig McMullen,John Rowin(g) Chuck Rainey(el b) Harvey Mason(dm) Mayuto Correa(cga,perc) King Errison(cga) James Carter(whistler-1) Kay Haith(backgr.vo) & strings.

(The Sound Factory) LA,August 18,1975

16327	Change (makes you want to hustle)	BN BN-XW726-Y,BN-LA700-G,B1-98638 Lib(E)LCSP 18670213 CD BN 7-98638-2, (Eu)4-93994-2
16328	You and the music	BN B1-98638,B1-94708 CD BN 7-98638-2,4-94708-2
16549	Night whistler -1	

All titles issued on BN BN-LA549-G,B1-54326,CD 8-54326-2

Same.

(The Sound Factory) LA,August 20,1975

16550	Just my imagination	BN BN-XW783-Y
16551	Places and spaces	CD BN 7-98638-2
16552	Wind parade	BN B1-94708,CD 7-98638-2,4-94708-2,5-23559-2

All titles issued on BN BN-LA549-G,B1-98638,B1-54326,Lib(E)LCSP 18670213,CD 8-54326-2.

Same.

(The Sound Factory) LA,August 25,1975

16553	(Fallin' like) Dominoes	BN BN-XW783-Y,BN-LA549-G,B1-98638, B1-54326,B1-54360 Lib(E)LCSP 18670213 CD BN 8-54326-2,8-54360-2,4-95701-2, HMV Jazz(E)5-20881-2

HORACE SILVER - SILVER 'N' WOOD:
Tom Harrell(tp) Bob Berg(ts) Horace Silver(p,arr) Ron Carter(b) Al Foster(dm).
(A & R Studios) NYC,November 7,1975
Garnett Brown(tb) Buddy Collette,Fred Jackson(fl,picc) Jerome Richardson(ss) Lanny Morgan(as) Jack Nimitz(bs,fl-1) Bill Green(bass sax, fl-1) Wade Marcus(orchestrations) overdubbed on.
(Wally Heider Studios) LA,January 2 & 3,1976

	The tranquilizer suite:	
16742 (tk.3)	Pt.1: Keep on gettin' up	
16741 (tk.1)	Pt.2: Slow down	BN BN-XW905-Y,CD 4-95576-2
16740 (tk.5)	Pt.3: Time and effort -1	-
16739 (tk.8)	Pt.4: Perseverance and endurance	

All parts issued on BN BN-LA581-G.

HORACE SILVER - SILVER 'N' WOOD:
Tom Harrell(tp) Bob Berg(ts) Horace Silver(p,arr) Ron Carter(b) Al Foster(dm).
(A & R Studios) NYC,November 14,1975
Frank Rosolino(tb) Buddy Collette,Fred Jackson(fl,picc) Jerome Richardson(ss) Lanny Morgan(as) Jack Nimitz(bs) Bill Green(bass sax) Wade Marcus(orchestrations) overdubbed on.
(Wally Heider Studios) LA,January 2 & 3,1976

	The process of creation suite:	
16735 (tk.4)	Pt.1: Motivation	
16736 (tk.1)	Pt.2: Activation	CD BN 8-33208-2
16737 (tk.6)	Pt.3: Assimilation	CD BN 4-95576-2
16738 (tk.3)	Pt.4: Creation	

All parts issued on BN BN-LA581-G.

ALPHONSE MOUZON - THE MAN INCOGNITO:
Gary Grant(tp) George Bohanon(tb) Ray Pizzi(as,ts) Tom Scott(ts,bs,lyricon) George Duke (as "Dawilli Gonga ")(synth) Dave Grusin(p,el p,clavinet) Dave Benoit(p,el p) Ian Underwood(synth) Lee Ritenour(g,el g) Tim De Huff(el g) Charles Meeks(el b) Alphonse Mouzon(dm,perc,vo,synth) Victor Feldman(cga,bgo, perc) Emil Richards(cymbals,perc) Marty McCall,Jackie Ward,Caroline Willis(vo).
(Sound Labs) LA,December 2,1975

16680 Mouzon moves on
16681 New York City -1
16682 Just like the sun

-1: David T.Walker(g) added.
All titles issued on BN BN-LA584-G.

Same.
(Sound Labs) LA,December 2,1975

16702	Take your troubles away	BN BN-LA584-G
16703	Before you leave -1	-
16704	unknown title	unissued
16705	You are my dream	BN BN-LA584-G
16706	Without a reason	-
16707	Behind your mind	-

-1: John Maller(clavinet) added.

RONNIE LAWS - FEVER:
Ronnie Laws(fl,ss,ts) Donald Hepburn,Michael Hepburn(el p,clavinet,synth) Marion The Magician(g) Nathaniel Phillips(el b) Bruce Carter(dm) Bruce Smith(perc).
(Total Experience Studio) LA,December 18,1975
-1: Carroll Stephens,Murray Adler,Bonnie Douglas,Henry Ferber,Elliott Fisher,Ronald Folsom,James Getzoff,William Kurash,Joy Lyle,Gordon Marron,Paul C.Shure,Felix Sitjar(v) Jesse Ehrlich,Nathan Gershman,Raymond J. Kelley,Victor Sazer(cello) Augie Johnson,Esau Joyner,Deborah Shotlow,Douglas Thomas,Michael Miller,Ronald Coleman(backgr.vo) overdubbed on.
(Total Experience Studio) LA,c.February-March 1976

16763	Fever -1	
16764	Stay still (and let me love you) -1	
16765	Karmen -1	BN BN-LA848-Y,CD 7-98289-2
17241	Let's keep it together	-

All titles issued on BN BN-LA628-G,CD 7-89541-2.

285

RONNIE LAWS - FEVER:
Ronnie Laws(fl,ss,ts) Donald Hepburn,Michael Hepburn(el p,clavinet,synth) Marion The Magician(g) Nathaniel Phillips(el b) Bruce Carter(dm) Bruce Smith(perc).
(Total Experience Studio) LA,December 26,1975

17245 From Ronnie with love BN BN-LA628-G,CD 7-89541-2

Same.
(Total Experience Studio) LA,December 29,1975

16770 Captain midnight BN BN-LA628-G,CD 7-89541-2

EARL KLUGH:
Dave Grusin(p,el p,synth,perc) Earl Klugh(g,el g) Lee Ritenour(el g) Charles Meeks(el b) Harvey Mason (dm,perc) Laudir De Oliveira(perc).
(Kendun Recorders) LA,January 12,1976
-1: Bernard Kundell,Marcia Van Dyke,Ralph Schaeffer,Joseph Stepansky,Karen Jones,Alexander Murray, Thelma Beach,Kenneth Yerke,Edgar Lustgarten,Pamela Goldsmith,Myer Bellow,Marie Fera,Charles Veal Jr., Daniel Shindatyan (strings) overdubbed on.
-2: Chuck Findley,Oscar Brashear(tp,flh) Garnett Brown(tb) Ray Pizzi(ss) Pete Christlieb(fl,ts) Jerome Richardson(bs,fl) overdubbed on.

16841 Angelina -1 BN BST2-92477,(Du)1A158-83401/4
CD BN 7-46625-2,7-92477-2,4-95701-2,
Cema S21-57593
16842 Vonetta -2 BN(J)GP-3205;Lib(J)K22P-6116/17

Both titles issued on BN BN-LA596-G.

Dave Grusin(p,el p,synth,perc) Earl Klugh(g,el g) Lee Ritenour(el g) Charles Meeks(el b) Harvey Mason (dm,perc) Laudir De Oliveira(perc).
(Kendun Recorders) LA,January 14,1976
-1: with strings (as above) overdubbed on.
-2: with horns (as above) overdubbed on.

16844 Laughter in the rain -1 CD BN 8-53354-2
16845 Could it be I'm falling in love -2 BN(J)K28P-6045
16973 Wind and the sea -1,2 -

All titles issued on BN BN-LA596-G.

Dave Grusin(p,el p,synth,perc) Earl Klugh(g,el g) Lee Ritenour(el g) Charles Meeks,Louis Johnson(el b) Harvey Mason(dm,perc) Laudir De Oliveira(perc).
(Kendun Recorders) LA,January 16,1976
-1: with strings (same as -1 above) overdubbed on.
-2: with horns (same as -2 above) overdubbed on.

16874 Calypso unissued
16875 Los manos de fuego -1,2 BN BN-LA596-G
16876 Slippin' in the back door -2 -

Dave Grusin(p,el p,synth,perc) Earl Klugh(g,el g) Lee Ritenour(el g) Charles Meeks(el b) Harvey Mason (dm,perc) Laudir De Oliveira(perc) with strings (as above) overdubbed on.
(Kendun Recorders) LA,January 18,1976

16974 Waltz for Debby BN BN-LA596-G
CD Manhattan 8-27326-2,EMI-USA(J)TOCP-9055

286

ALPHONSE MOUZON - THE MAN INCOGNITO:
Gary Grant(tp) George Bohanon(tb) Ray Pizzi(as,ts) Tom Scott(ts,bs,lyricon) George Duke (as "Dawilli Gonga")(synth) Dave Grusin(p,el p,clavinet) Dave Benoit(p,el p) Ian Underwood(synth) Lee Ritenour (g, el g) Tim De Huff(el g) Charles Meeks(el b) Alphonse Mouzon(dm,perc,vo,synth) Victor Feldman (cga, bgo,perc) Emil Richards(cymbals,perc) Marty McCall,Jackie Ward,Caroline Willis(vo).
(Sound Labs) LA,January ,1976

17026 Snake walk BN BN-LA584-G

RONNIE LAWS - FEVER:
Ronnie Laws(fl,ss,ts) Bobby Lyle(el p,clavinet,synth) Wilton Felder(el b) Steve Guttierez (dm) Tony Ben (cga). (Total Experience) LA,January 26,1976

17242	All the time	BN BN-LA848-Y
17243	Strugglin'	
17244	Night breeze	CD BN 7-98289-2

All titles issued on BN BN-LA628-G,CD 7-89541-2.

MARLENA SHAW - JUST A MATTER OF TIME:
Marlena Shaw(vo) with Bert De Coteaux(keyb,arr) Ricky Williams,George Butcher(keyb) Lance Quinn,Jeff Mironov,Jerry Friedman,Hugh McCracken(g) Bob Babbitt(el b) Jimmy Young(dm) Ted Sommer,Dave Carey (perc) Carlos Martin(cga) (Collective personnel).

	(Media Sound Studios)	NYC,February 11,1976
17058	Love has gone away	BN BN-XW844-Y,(E)UP36163
17060	Be for real	BN BN-XW790-Y,CD 8-54943-2
17061	This time I'll be sweeter	BN BN-XW844-Y
17063	Think about me	
Same.	(Media Sound Studios)	NYC,February 16,1976
17059	You and me	CD BN 8-54943-2
17062	Brass band	
Same.	(Media Sound Studios)	NYC,February 23,1976
17057	It's better than walkin' out	BN BN-XW790-Y
Same.	(Media Sound Studios)	NYC,February ,1976
17064	Sing to me	CD BN 8-54943-2
17065	Take my body	
17090	No hiding place -1	BN(E)UP36163;CD BN 8-54943-2

-1: Marlena Shaw (vo,p) alone.
All titles from above four sessions issued on BN BN-LA606-G,CD BN(J)TOCJ-5878.

BOBBY HUTCHERSON - WAITING:
Emanuel Boyd(ss,ts) Bobby Hutcherson(vb,marimba) George Cables(p,el p) James Leary III(b) Eddie Marshall (dm) Kenneth Nash(perc,cga).

	(Different Fur Studios)	SF,February 24,1976
17092	Convergence	BN(Du)1A158-83401/4
Same.		
	(Different Fur Studios)	SF,February 25,1976
17093	Don't be afraid (to fall in love again)	
17094	Searchin' the Trane	
17095	Hangin' out (with you)-1	

-1: see note to next session.
All titles issued on BN BN-LA615-G.

287

BOBBY HUTCHERSON - WAITING:
Emanuel Boyd(ss,ts) Bobby Hutcherson(vb,marimba) George Cables(p,el p) James Leary III(b) Eddie Marshall (dm) Kenneth Nash(perc,cga).
(Different Fur Studios) SF,February 26,1976

17095 Hangin' out (with you)-1
17096 Prime thought
17097 Waiting-2
17098 Roses poses

-1: Version issued on BN BN-LA615-G is a spliced master made of recordings made on February 25 and February 26.
-2: Hadley Caliman,Mguanda Dave Johnson,Emanuel Boyd(fl) added.
All titles issued on BN BN-LA615-G.

CHICO HAMILTON AND THE PLAYERS:
Arthur Blythe(ss,as) Will Connell Jr.(as) Rodney Jones(g) Steve Turre(el b) Chico Hamilton(dm,perc) Abdullah(perc).
(Sound Ideas Studio) NYC,March 9,1976

17125 (tk.9) Ole to Miles
17126 (tk.1) Adair BN(Du)1A158-83401/4
17130 (tk.12) Hooch
17192 (tk.4) La noche de bolero

All titles issued on BN BN-LA622-G.

Same.
(Sound Ideas Studio) NYC,March 10,1976

17120 (tk.1/2) First light BN BN-LA622-G

Same.
(Sound Ideas Studio) NYC,March 11,1976

17127 (tk.2) Abdullah's delight
17129 (tk.5) Mr. Sweets
17191 (tk.1) Sex is a cymbal -1

-1: Steve Turre(el b) & Chico Hamilton(dm) only.
All titles issued on BN BN-LA622-G.

EDDIE HENDERSON - HERITAGE:
Eddie Henderson(tp,flh) Julian Priester(tb,bass tb)) Hadley Caliman(fl,ss,bass cl) Patrice Rushen(el p, clavinet, synth) Paul Jackson(el b) Mike Clarke(dm) Mtume(p,cga,perc).
(Wally Heider Studios) SF,April 2,1976

17392 Inside you BN B1-28965,B1-94027,CD 8-29865-2,4-94027-2
17393 Acuphuncture CD BN 5-23559-2
17394 Time and space
17395 Nostalgia
17396 Kudu BN B1-99106
CD BN 7-99106-2,(J)TOCJ-1621,TOCJ-5846,
TOCJ-6285
17397 Dr. Mganga -1
17398 Dark shadow -1,2

-1: Woody Theus(dm) replaces Clarke.
-2: Billy Hart(dm) added.
All titles issued on BN BN-LA636-G,CD BN(J)TOCJ-6294.

GENE HARRIS - IN A SPECIAL WAY:
George Bohanon(tb) Sidney Muldrow,Marnie Robinson(frh) Azar Lawrence(ts) Ed Green(v-1) Gene Harris keyb) Charlotte Politte(el p,synth) Jerry Peters(el p,synth,string ensemble,arr,vo-1,4) John Rowin(el g,arr-5) Al McKay(el g) Lee Ritenour(g,el g) Chuck Rainey,Verdine White(el b) James Gadson(dm) Harvey Mason (dm,perc) Mayuto Correa(perc) Philip Bailey(perc,vo-2) Ann Esther Jessica-2(vo) Denise Williams-3, Stephanie Spruill-3,D.J.Rodgers-4, Merry Clayton-4,Sigidi-1(vo,arr).
(Total Experience Studio) LA,March 29,1976

17232 Zulu -4
17233 Theme for Relana -2 BN B1-35607,CD 8-35607-2

Both titles issued on BN BN-LA634-G,CD BN(J)TOCJ-1625.

Same. (Total Experience Studio) LA,April 1,1976

17234 Naima -2
17235 Always in my mind -1

Both titles issued on BN BN-LA634-G,CD BN(J)TOCJ-1625.

Same. (Total Experience Studio) LA,April 2,1976

17236 Love for sale -3
17237 It's your love -2

Both titles issued on BN BN-LA634-G,CD BN(J)TOCJ-1625.

Same. (Total Experience Studio) LA,April 7,1976

17446 Rebop -5
17447 Soft cycles
17448 Five/Four

All titles issued on BN BN-LA634-G,CD BN(J)TOCJ-1625.

BOBBI HUMPHREY:
(session details not known).
(Sound Factory) LA,April 21-28,1976 (dates as shown below)

17338 (21) Havin' fun rejected
17339 (27) I can use it -
17340 (28) Doin' it -
17341 (28) Why aren't we friends -

CARMEN McRAE - CAN'T HIDE LOVE:
Carmen McRae(vo) with Buddy Childers,Bobby Shew,Al Aarons(tp) Lew McCreary,George Bohanon, Kenny Shroyer(tb) Bill Perkins,Lanny Morgan,Harry Klee,Abe Most,Bill Green(reeds) Artie Kane(p) Marshall Otwell (el p) Dennis Budimir(g) Joe Mondragon(b) Harvey Mason(dm) & strings dir. by Gerald Vinci
Arr. by Johnny Mandel-1,Thad Jones-2.
(A & M Studio) LA,May 3,1976

17369 The man I love -1 CD BN 7-80506-2,7-96583-2,(J)TOCJ-6135, TOCJ-6189,Toshiba-EMI(J)TOCP-65031
17370 Would you believe -1
17371 A child is born -2 CD BN(C)8-56508-2

All titles issued on BN BN-LA635-G,CD 7-89540-2,8-33578-2.

289

CARMEN McRAE - CAN'T HIDE LOVE:
Carmen McRae(vo) with Joe Sample(p,el p) Marshall Otwell(el p) Larry Carlton,Dennis Budimir(g) Chuck Berghofer(b) Wilton Felder(el b-1) Harvey Mason(dm) Victor Feldman(perc) & strings dir. by David Frisina. Arr. by Dale Oehler.

(A & M Studio) LA,May 4,1976

17372	All by myself	
17373	Music -1	BN BN-XW869-Y,CD 8-57463-2

Both titles issued on BN BN-LA635-G,CD 7-89540-2.

Carmen McRae(vo) with Dave Grusin(p,el p) Ian Underwood(synth) Dennis Budimir,Larry Carlton (g) Chuck Berghofer(b) Harvey Mason(dm) & strings dir. by Gerald Vinci.
Arr. by Dave Grusin-1,Larry Carlton-2.

(A & M Studio) LA,May 10,1976

17374	Lost up in loving you -1	
17375	Only women bleed -2	BN BN-XW869-Y

Both titles issued on BN BN-LA635-G,CD 7-89540-2.

Carmen McRae(vo) with Snooky Young,Bobby Shew,Oscar Brashear,Blue Mitchell(tp) George Bohanon, Maurice Spears,Grover Mitchell,Ernie Tack(tb) Jerome Richardson(ss,as) Ernie Watts(ts) Pete Christlieb (fl,ts) Don Menza(ss,ts) Jack Nimitz(bs) Joe Sample(p,el p) Chuck Berghofer(b) Harvey Mason(dm) Larry Bunker (perc).
Arr. by Gerald Wilson-1,Thad Jones-2.

(A & M Studio) LA,May 12,1976

17399	Can't hide love -1	BN B1-35607 CD BN 8-35607-2,5-23559-2,The Right Stuff 8-57072-2
17400	I wish you well -2	
17401	You're everything -2	BN(E)BNSLP-1 CD BN 4-97156-2,(J)TOCJ-5778

All titles issued on BN BN-LA635-G,CD 7-89540-2.

BOBBI HUMPHREY (May 14,1976): see late additions on page 301.

DONALD BYRD - CARICATURES:
Donald Byrd(tp,flh,vo,backgr.vo) Oscar Brashear(tp) Fonce Mizell(tp,keyb,backgr.vo) George Bohanon(tb) Gary Bartz,Ernie Watts(reeds) Patrice Rushen,Jerry Peters,Skip Scarborough(keyb) John Rowin,David T.Walker, Bernard Taylor(g) Scott Edwards(el b) Alphonse Mouzon(dm) Stephanie Spruill,Mayuto Correa (perc) Mildred Lane,Kay Haith(vo) Larry Mizell,Theresa Mitchell,Vernessa Mitchell(backgr. vo) & strings arr. by Wade Marcus.

(The Sound Factory) LA,April & May ,1976

17457	Dancing in the street (voML)	BN BN-LA965-Y
17458	Wild life (voML)	Lib(E)LCSP 18670213
17459	Return of the king	
17460	Onward 'til morning (voKH)	BN BN-LA965-Y,B1-98638,CD 7-98638-2 Lib(E)LCSP 18670213
17461	Caricatures (voKH)	
17462	Cartoons	rejected
17463	When love comes around	-
17464	Dance band -1	BN B1-94708,CD 4-94708-2
17683	Science funktion	
18162	Tell me	

-1: James Jameson(el b) Harvey Mason(dm) replace Edwards & Mouzon.
All titles ,except 17462 & 17463,issued on BN BN-LA633-G.

290

BARBARA CARROLL:
Barbara Carroll(p) Chuck Domanico(b) Colin Bailey(dm).
(Kendun Recorders) LA,May 25,1976

17471 Prelude to a kiss
17466 At seventeen

Same. (Kendun Recorders) LA,May 26,1976

17467 I can't get started
17468 Baubles,bangles and beads

Same. (Kendun Recorders) LA,May 27,1976

17469 Feelings
17472 Send in the clowns
17473 It never entered my mind

Victor Feldman(perc-1) Dennis Budimir(g-2) added.
(Kendun Recorders) LA,May 28,1976

17465 In some other world -1
17470 Blues for Artie -2

All titles from above four sessions issued on BN BN-LA645-G.

CARMEN McRAE AT THE GREAT AMERICAN MUSIC HALL:
Carmen McRae(vo) with Marshall Otwell(keyb) Ed Bennett(b,el b) Joey Baron(perc).
(The Great American Music Hall) SF,June 15,16 & 17,1976

18175	Them there eyes	
18176	Paint your pretty picture	
18177	On Green Dolphin Street	
18178	A song for you	
18179	On a clear day-1	
18180	Miss Otis regrets-1	CD BN 8-33578-2,5-21151-2,(C)4-94888-2
18181	Too close for comfort	-
18182	Old folks	- (J)TOCJ-6135
18183	Time after time	
18184	I'm always drunk in San Francisco	
18185	Don't misunderstand-1	
18186	A beautiful friendship-1	
18187	Star eyes	
18188	Dindi	CD BN 8-33578-2
18189	Never let me go	
18190	T'ain't nobody's bizness if I do	
18191	Only women bleed	
18192	No more blues (Chega de saudade)	CD BN 8-35283-2
18193	The folks who live on the hill	
18194	Going out music (Closing)	

-1: Dizzy Gillespie(tp) added.
All titles issued on BN BN-LA709-H2,CD BN(J)TOCJ-5880/81.

BLUE NOTE LIVE AT THE ROXY:
ALPHONSE MOUZON GROUP: Robby Robinson(synth,el p) Rex Robinson,Tim De Huff(g) Charles Fillilove(el b) Rudy Regalado(perc?) Alphonse Mouzon(dm,perc).
(The Roxy Theatre) LA,June 28,1976

17726	New York City	BN BN-LA663-J2
17727	Just like the sun	-
17728	Without a reason	-

CARMEN McRAE: Carmen McRae(vo) with Marshall Otwell(el p) Bernard Baron(b) Edward Bennett (dm).
Same concert

17729	Music	
17730	Paint your pretty picture	
17731	Them there eyes	
17732	T'ain't nobody's bizness if I do	CD BN 8-33578-2
17733	You're everything	

All titles issued on BN BN-LA663-J2.

RONNIE LAWS: Ronnie Laws(fl,ts) Bobby Lyle(el p) Bill Rogers(el g) Donald Beck(el b) Steve Guttierez (dm) Tony Ben(cga). Same concert.

17734	Captain midnight
17735	Night breeze
17736	Piano interlude -1
17737	Always there

-1: Bobby Lyle(el p)Steve Guttierez(dm) only.
All titles issued on BN BN-LA663-J2.

Dave Cunningham,George Butler(speeches). Same concert.

17738	Presentation of proclamation	BN BN-LA663-J2

EARL KLUGH: Earl Klugh(g) Robert Budson(p) Hubert Crawford(b) Ngudu Leon Chancler(dm).
Same concert.
Ron Carter(b) overdubbed later on.

17739	Medley:	BN BN-LA663-J2;Lib(J)K22P6116/17	
	Like a lover/A felicidade/	-	-
	Manha de carnaval/Samba de Orfeu	-	-

BLUE NOTE ALL STARS: Chuck Findley(tp) George Bohanon(tb) Fred Jackson(fl,ts) Gary Herbig(as) Bobby Hutcherson(marimba) Gene Harris(p,el p) Earl Klugh(g) John Lee(el b) Gerry Brown (dm,perc) Leon Chancler(perc) Jerry Peters (cond).
Same concert.

17740	Blue Note '76	BN BN-LA663-J2

<u>DONALD BYRD & THE BLACKBYRDS</u>:
Donald Byrd(tp) & prob.: Stephen Johnson(ts,vo) Kevin Toney(org-1,el p-2,synth-2,vo) Orville Saunders (el g,vo) Joe Hall(el b,vo) Keith Killgo(dm,vo).
(Live,Central Park) NYC,July 19,1976

17741	Places and spaces -1	BN BN-LA663-J2	
17742	(Fallin' like) Dominoes -2	-	B1-98638,CD 7-98638-2
	unknown titles	unissued	

<u>ROBBIE KRIEGER & FRIENDS</u>:
Gary Barone(tp-1) Jack Ellis(tb-1) Joel Peskin(saxes-1) Stu Goldberg(org,synth-1) Sal Marquez(keyb,tp-1, arr-1) Robby Krieger(g) Kenny Wild(b) Bruce Gary(dm) Perico(cga) Eddie Talamente(timbales-1).
(Devonshire Sound) LA,July 26,1976

17700	Spare changes
17701	The ally -1

Both titles issued on BN BN-LA664-G;CD World Pacific 7-96101-2.

ROBBIE KRIEGER & FRIENDS:
Sal Marquez(tp) Jack Ellis(tb) Joel Peskin(ts,picc) Greg Mathieson(org) Robby Krieger(g,arr) Kenny Wild(b) Bruce Gary(dm,tympani) Sharon Robinson,Afreeka Trees(vo).
(Devonshire Sound) LA,July 27,1976

17702 Uptown BN BN-LA664-G;CD World Pacific 7-96101-2
17703 Innocence rejected

Sal Marquez(tp,keyb,arr) Jack Ellis(tb) Joel Peskin(ts,bs) Robby Krieger(g,vo) Reggie McBride(el b) Ed Greene(dm) Sharon Robinson,Afreeka Trees(vo).
(Devonshire Sound) LA,July 28,1976

17704 Every day BN BN-LA664-G;CD World Pacific 7-96101-2

Stu Goldberg(synth) Sal Marquez(synth,arr) Robby Krieger(g,arr) Reggie McBride(el b) Bruce Gary (dm,bells,tympani,whistle,arr) Orion Crawford(arr).
(Devonshire Sound) LA,July 28,1976

17705 Low bottomy (Lobotomy) BN BN-LA664-G;CD World Pacific 7-96101-2

Sal Marquez(tp,synth,arr) Jack Ellis(tb) Joel Peskin(ts,bs) Ron Stockert(keyb) Robby Krieger(g) Reggie McBride(b) Ed Greene(dm).
(Devonshire Sound) LA,July 29,1976

17706 Gum-popper BN BN-LA664-G;CD World Pacific 7-96101-2

Sal Marquez,Stu Goldberg(synth) Jimmy Smith(org) Robby Krieger(g,vo) Reggie McBride(b) Ed Green e(dm) John Densmore(Latin perc).
(Devonshire Sound) LA,July 29,1976

17707 Marilyn Monroe BN BN-LA664-G;CD World Pacific 7-96101-2

Gary Barone(tp,arr) Sal Marquez(tp,p,synth) Jack Ellis(tb) Joel Peskin(saxes) Greg Mathieson(org) Robby Krieger(g) Bob Glaub(b) Ed Greene(dm) Eddie Talamente,Bruce Gary(shakers).
(Devonshire Sound) LA,July 30,1976

17708 Big Oak Basin BN BN-LA664-G;CD World Pacific 7-96101-2

Similar.
(Devonshire Sound) LA,July 31,1976

17709 Seven point five unissued
17710 Shuirley whirly -

BOBBY HUTCHERSON - THE VIEW FROM INSIDE:
Emanuel Boyd(ss,ts) Bobby Hutcherson(vb) Larry Nash(p,el p) James Leary(b) Eddie Marshall (dm).
(Wally Heider Studios) SF,August 4,5 & 6,1976
(exact dates shown in parentheses)

17769 (4) For heaven's sake

17766 (5) Love can be many things
17767 (5) Same shame
17768 (5) Later,even

17770 (6) Laugh,laugh again
17771 (6) Song for Annie
17772 (6) Houston St. Thursday afternoon

All titles issued on BN BN-LA710-G.

EARL KLUGH - LIVING INSIDE YOUR LOVE:
Eddie Daniels-1(fl,ss,ts) Dave Grusin(el p,synth-1) Earl Klugh(g,12-string g) Jeff Mironov(el g) Will Lee (el b) Steve Gadd(dm) Ralph McDonald(perc) Patti Austin,Vivian Cherry,Lani Groves(vo-2).
(Electric Lady Studios) NYC,July 26,1976

17887	Captain Caribe -1	Lib(J)K22P-6116/17;BN(J)GP-3205,W-5515 CD BN 7-80505-2,(J)TOCJ-6134,TOCJ-6188, Cap(J)TOCJ-6060,EMI-USA(J)TOCP-9055
17888	I heard it through the grapevine -2	BN BN-XW974-Y CD BN 7-99105-2,4-94211-2, HMV Jazz(E)5-20881-2

-2: Norman Carr,Gerald Tarack,Guy Lumia,Harold Kohon,Jean Ingraham,Tony Posk,Fred Buldrini,Doris Carr,Joseph Goodman,Ruth Buffington,Ann Barak,Noel Pointer(v) Theodore Israel,Julian Barber(viola) Charles McCracken,Richard Locker(cello) Margaret Ross(harp) overdubbed on.
(Columbia 30th Street Studio) NYC,August 5,1976

Both titles issued on BN BN-LA667-G,CD 7-48385-2.

Eddie Daniels-1(fl,ts) Dave Grusin(el p,synth) Earl Klugh(g) Francisco Centeno(el b) Steve Gadd(dm) Ralph McDonald(perc) Patti Austin,Vivian Cherry, Lani Groves(vo-2).
(Electric Lady Studios) NYC,July 26,1976

17889	Felicia -1	BN(J)K28P-6045
17890	Living inside your love -2	BN BN-XW924-Y,(J)GP-3205,W-5515 Cap.ST-12405;Lib(J)K22P-6116/17 CD BN 7-46625-2,7-48387-2, The Right Stuff 8-54487-2,EMI-USA(J)TOCP-9055

-2: strings (as above) overdubbed on.NYC,August 5,1976
Both titles issued on BN BN-LA667-G,CD 7-48385-2.

Dave Grusin(p,el p,synth,bells) Earl Klugh(g,12-string g) Eddie Gomez(b) Steve Gadd(dm).
(Electric Lady Studios) NYC,July 27,1976

17891	Another time,another place	BN BN-LA667-G,CD 7-48385-2

Earl Klugh(g).
(Electric Lady Studios) NYC,July 27,1976

17892	April fools	BN BN-LA667-G CD BN 7-48385-2,Manhattan 8-27326-2

Dave Grusin(el p,perc) Earl Klugh(g) Louis Johnson(el b) Harvey Mason(perc).
(Kendum Recorders) LA,July or August ,1976

17893	Kiko	BN BN-XW924-Y,BN-XW974-Y,BN-LA667-G, CD 7-48385-2

All titles on BN-LA667-G also issued on CD BN 7-48385-2.

JOHN LEE & GERRY BROWN - STILL CAN'T SAY ENOUGH:
Coll.:Randy Brecker(tp,flh) Jon Faddis(tp) Barry Rogers(tb) David Sanborn,Gary Bartz(as) Michael Brecker, Ernie Watts(ts) Ronnie Cuber(bs) Hubert Eaves(p,org,clavinet) Harold Ivory III(org,p) Rob Franken (synth, org) Ian Underwood(synth) Reggie Lucas,Ray Gomez(g) John Lee (el b) Gerry Brown(dm,perc, tympani) Mtume(cga,perc,vo) Donald Smith,Tawatha Agee,C.P. Alexander(vo).
(Electric Lady Studios) NYC,c. early August 1976

17957 Freeze it up
17958 Love the way you make me feel
17959 Rise on
17960 Funky row
17961 Talkin' 'bout the right one
17962 Strut 'n' get up
17963 Breakin'
17964 Down the way
17965 Out the box

All titles issued on BN BN-LA701-G.

HORACE SILVER - SILVER 'N' VOICES:
Tom Harrell(tp,flh) Bob Berg(ts) Horace Silver(p,arr) Ron Carter(b) Al Foster(dm).
(A & R Studios) NYC,September 24,1976
Monica Mancini,Avery Sommers,Joyce Copeland,Richard Page,Dale Verdugo(vo) Alan Copeland(vo,dir) overdubbed on.
(Hollywood Sound Recorders) LA,October 19 & 22,1976

18115 Togetherness BN BN-XW1032
18117 Mood for Maude
18119 New York lament
18120 All in time CD BN 4-95576-2

All titles issued on BN BN-LA708-G.

Tom Harrell(tp,flh) Bob Berg(ts) Horace Silver(p,arr) Ron Carter(b) Al Foster(dm).
(A & R Studios) NYC,October 1,1976
Monica Mancini,Avery Sommers,Joyce Copeland,Richard Page,Dale Verdugo(vo) Alan Copeland(vo,dir) overdubbed on.
(Hollywood Sound Recorders) LA,October 19 & 22,1976

18114 Out of the night (Came you) BN BN-XW1032
18116 I will always love you
18118 Incentive
18121 Freeing my mind

All titles issued on BN BN-LA708-G.

295

WILLIE BOBO - TOMORROW IS HERE:
Willie Bobo(vo,perc) with (collective personnel): Gary Grant,Ron King,Nolan Smith(tp) Thurman Green, George Bohanon(tb) Ray Pizzi,Ernie Watts(saxes) Gary Herbig(reeds) Reggie Andrews.Larry Farrow,David Garfield(keyb) Dennis Budimir,Sidney Muldrow,Craig McMullen,John Cadrecha,Curtis Robertson Jr.(g) Jim Hughart,David Troncoso,Dean Cortez(b) James Gadson,Jeff Porcaro,Gary Denton,Carlos Vega(dm) Victor Pantoja(perc) Sandi Erwin,Bernard Ighner(vo).
(Oceanway Studio) LA,October 1976-January 1977

18166	Can't stay down too long -1	
18167	Keep on walking -2	
18168	Funk de mambo -1	
18169	Dreamin' (voSE,BI)-3	BN BN-XW977-Y
18170	Wicky tobacky (The race) -3	
18171	Suitcase full of dreams -2,3	
18172	Time after time -1	
18173	Kojak theme -3	BN BN-XW977-Y,CD 8-57748-2
18174	A little tear -2	

Arranged by Reggie Andrews-1,Larry Farrow-2,Willie Bobo-3.
All titles issued on BN BN-LA711-G.

NOEL POINTER - PHANTAZIA:
Noel Pointer(v,el v) Dave Grusin(el p,synth,arr).
(Camp Columby Studio) New City,N.Y.,January 10,1977

18318	Wayfaring stranger -3	BN BN-LA736-H,CD 7-89543-2

Earl Klugh(g) Francisco Centeno(el b) Steve Gadd(dm) Ralph McDonald(perc) added.
(Camp Columby Studio) New City,N.Y.,January 10,1977

18315	Night song -2,3	BN BN-XW997-Y
18316	Living for the City	- BN-XW1114,BST2-92477 CD BN 7-92477-2,Cema S21-57593
18319	Mirabelle -1	

-1: Ian Underwood(synth) overdubbed on.
-2: Gene Cipriano,John Lowe,Justin Gordon,Bud Shank,Tom Scott(woodwinds) overdubbed on.
-3: Gerald Vinci,Jacob Krachmalnick,David Frisina,Marshall Sosson,Karen Jones,Sheldon Sanov,Bernard Kundell,Constance Pressman,David Montagu,Kathleen Lenski,Allan Harshman, Pamela Goldsmith,Edgar Lustgarten,Frederick Seykora(strings) overdubbed on.
(Kendun Recorders) LA,February ,1977

All titles issued on BN BN-LA736-H,CD 7-89543-2.

Dave Valentin(fl) Noel Pointer(v,el v) Dave Grusin(el p,synth,arr) Will Lee(el b) Steve Gadd(dm) Ralph McDonald(perc).
(Camp Columby Studio) New City,N.Y.,January 11,1977

18317	Rainstorm -2,3	BN BN-LA736-H CD BN 7-89543-2,(J)TOCJ-5845

-2,3: woodwinds and strings (as above) overdubbed on.

Noel Pointer(v,el v) Dave Grusin(el p,synth,arr) John Tropea,Lee Ritenour(el g-1) Will Lee(el b) Steve Gadd (dm) Ralph McDonald(perc).
(Camp Columby Studio) New City,N.Y.,January 11,1977

18320	Fiddler on the roof -1	BN BN-XW1114,BN-LA736-H CD BN 7-89543-2

NOEL POINTER - PHANTAZIA:
Noel Pointer(v,el v) Dave Grusin(el p,synth,arr) Will Lee(el b) Steve Gadd (dm) Ralph McDonald(perc).
(Camp Columby Studio) New City,N.Y.,January 12,1977
Ian Underwood (synth) overdubbed on.

18314 Phantazia BN BN-LA736-H,(Du)1A158-83401/4
CD BN 7-89543-2

RONNIE LAWS - FRIENDS & STRANGERS:
Ronnie Laws(alto fl,ss,ts,backgr.vo-4) Bobby Lyle(p) Larry Dunn(synth) Roland Bautista, Melvin Robinson (g) Donnie Beck or Nathaniel Phillips-2(el b) Steve Guttierez(dm) Vance "Mad Dog" Tenort-1(perc,cga) Deborah "Punkin" Shotlow-3(tamb) Eloise Laws-4, Deborah Laws-5,Saundra "Pan" Alexander-5 (backgr.vo). (ABC Studios) LA,January ,1977

18351 Good time ride -1 BN BN-LA730-H;UA UA-XW1036
CD UA(E)UAG30079

Same. (ABC Studios) LA,February ,1977

18352 Saturday evening -5 BN BN-LA730-H;Cap.ST-12375
CD BN 7-98289-2,Cap.7-46585-2,
UA(E)UAG30079

Same. (ABC Studios) LA,March ,1977

18353 Friends and strangers (Bautista out) UA UA-XW1036;Cap.ST-12375
CD BN 7-98289-2,5-23559-2,Cap.7-46585-2,
Rhino 75870-2
18354 Nuthin' 'bout nuthin' -1,2 BN BN-XW1007
18355 New day -1 CD BN 7-98289-2,(J)TOCJ-5855
18356 Life in paradise -2,4,5,6
18357 Same old story -3,6
18358 Just love -4,5 BN BN-XW1007
CD BN 7-98289-2,CD BN(J)TOCJ-5856

-6: Paul Shure,Barbara Durant,Elliot Fisher,Hyman Goodman,Bill Nuttycombe,Jerry Reisler,Carroll Stephens,Polly Sweeney(v) Leonard Selic,Barbara Simons(viola) Paul Bergstrom,Nat Gershman(cello) added.
All titles issued on BN BN-LA730-H,CD UA(E)UAG30079.

EARL KLUGH - FINGER PAINTINGS:
Dave Grusin(el p,clavinet) Earl Klugh(g) Louis Johnson(el b) Steve Gadd(dm) Steve Forman-1,Ralph McDonald-2(perc).
(Kendun Recorders) LA,February 15,1977
-3: Chuck Findley(tp) Dick Hyde(tb) Jerome Richardson,Tom Scott,Lawrence Williams(reeds) Jack Nimitz (bs) (horns arr. by Tom Scott) overdubbed on
-4: Gerald Vinci,Jacob Krachmalnick,Constance Pressman,Karen Jones,Marshall Sosson,Sheldon Sanov, Arnold Belnick,Andre Granat,Bernard Kundell,Allan Harshman,Pamela Goldsmith,Edgar Lustgarten,Dena L.Rees(strings) Ann Stockton(harp) (strings arr. by Dave Grusin) overdubbed on.
-5: Stephanie Spruill,Alexandra Brown,Lisa Roberts(backgr.vo) overdubbed on.
(Kendun Recorders) LA 1977

18500 Keep your eye on the sparrow
(Baretta's theme) -1,3,4,5 BN BN-XW1113,(J)K28P-6045
18502 Dance with me -4 - (J)GP-3205,K28P-6045
Lib(J)K22P-6116/17
CD BN 7-48387-2,EMI-USA(J)TOCP-9055
18503 Jolanta -2 CD BN 7-80505-2

All titles issued on BN BN-LA737-H,CD 7-48386-2

297

EARL KLUGH - FINGER PAINTINGS:
Dave Grusin(el p,synth) Earl Klugh(g) Lee Ritenour(el g) Anthony Jackson(el b) Harvey Mason(dm) Steve Forman-1,Ralph MacDonald-2(perc) with horns-3 & strings-4 (as above) overdubbed on.
(Kendun Recorders) LA,February 17,1977

18497	Dr. Macumba -2	BN(J)GP-3205;Lib(J)K22P-6116/17 CD BN 7-46625-2
18498	Long Ago And Far Away -2,4	-
18499	Cabo Frio -1,3,4	BN(J)GP-3205;CD BN 7-80505-2
18501	Catherine -2,4	- CD BN 8-53354-2,EMI-USA(J)TOCP-9055
18505	This Time -2	CD Manhattan 8-27326-2

All titles issued on BN BN-LA737-H,CD 7-48386-2.

Dave Grusin(el p,synth) Earl Klugh(g) Francisco Centeno(b) Steve Gadd(dm) Ralph MacDonald(perc) with strings-4 (as above) overdubbed on.
(Kendun Recorders) LA,February ,1977

18504	Summer song -4	BN BN-LA737-H,(J)K28P-6045 CD BN 7-48386-2,8-53354-2

MAXI:
Maxi Anderson(vo) with (Collective personnel): Gene Cipriano,Terry Harrington (English h) Ernie Watts(fl) Plas Johnson(as,ts) Tommy Morgan(hca) Gene Page(keyb,arr) Greg Phillinganes, Sonny Burke(keyb) David T. Walker(g) Henry Davis,Scott Edwards,Wilton Felder(el b) James Gadson(dm) Paulinho Da Costa,Jack Ashford,Tommy Vig(perc)
(Barnum Studios) LA,February 16,1977
Unknown tp,tb,Dorothy Ashby,Stella Castellucci (harp) & strings dir. by Harry Bluestone,with Jim Gilstrap, Augie Johnson,John Lehman,Gregory Marta,Danny Pearson,Julia Tillman Waters,Maxine Willard Waters (backgr.vo) overdubbed on.
(ABC Recording Studios) LA, 1977

18557	Dancin' to keep from cryin'
18558	The perfect day
18560	Let him in
18562	Delta road
18566	Music on my mind

Same. (Barnum Studios) LA,February 17,1977 (with same overdubs)

18559	Walk softly	
18561	This one's for you	
18563	Lover to lover	BN 5-21147-1,CD 5-21147-2,(J)TOCJ-5844
18564	Glory,glory	
18565	By your side	

All titles from both sessions issued on BN BN-LA738-H,CD BN(J)TOCJ-6295.

BOBBY HUTCHERSON - KNUCKLEBEAN:
Freddie Hubbard(tp) Emanuel "Manny" Boyd(fl,ss,ts) Hadley Caliman(fl,ts) Bobby Hutcherson(vb, marimba) George Cables(p,el p) James Leary(b) Eddie Marshall(dm).
(Wally Heider Studios) SF,March 1,1977

18882	Sundance knows	BN BN-LA789-H
18883	So far,so good	-

Same. (Wally Heider Studios) SF,March 2,1977

18884	Little B's poem	BN BN-LA789-H
18886	Knucklebean	-

 298

BOBBY HUTCHERSON - KNUCKLEBEAN:
Emanuel "Manny" Boyd(fl,ss,ts) Hadley Caliman(fl,ts) Bobby Hutcherson(vb, marimba) George Cables(p,el p) James Leary(b) Eddie Marshall(dm).
(Wally Heider Studios) SF,March 3,1977

18881 Why not
18885 'Til then

Both titles issued on BN BN-LA789-H.

GENE HARRIS - TONE TANTRUM:
Gene Harris(el p) Jerry Peters(el p,arr) John Rowin,Al McKay(el g) Verdine White(el b) Harvey Mason(dm) Jerry Steinholtz(perc) Ralph Beecham(vo) with Kenneth Yerke,Blanche Belnick,Harry Bluestone,Bonnie Douglas,Assa Drori,Ron Folsom,Winterton Garvey,William Henderson,Janice Gower,Mary Ann Kinggold, Rollice Dale,Denyse Buffum,Paul Pavlonick,Dennis Karmazyn,Selene Hurford,Richard Feves (strings) Dorothy Ashby(harp) Donald Byrd,Ray Jackson,George Thatcher,Maurice Spears,Donald Cook,Earl Dumler,David Crawford(horns) Venetta Fields,Maxine Waters,Julia Waters,Oren Waters,Deneice Williams, AnnEsther Davis,Gary Gairet(backgr.vo).
(Total Experience Studios) LA,March-May,1977

18762 As BN BN-LA760-H,B1-28965,CD 8-29865-2

Gene Harris(p,el p,synth) Jerry Peters(el p,synth,vo,arr) John Rowin,Al McKay(el g) Chuck Rainey(el b) Alvin Taylor(dm) Jerry Steinholtz(perc) with strings,horns & backgr.vocals as above.
(Total Experience Studios) LA,March-May,1977

18763 If you can't find love,let love find you BN BN-LA760-H

Donald Byrd(tp,flh) Gene Harris(p) Jerry Peters(el p,synth,vo,arr) John Rowin,Al McKay(el g) Harvey Mason(xyl) Leon "Ngudu" Chancler(dm) Jerry Steinholtz(perc) with strings,horns & backgr.vocals as above.
(Total Experience Studios) LA,March-May,1977

18764 A minor BN BN-XW1110,BN-LA760-H

Gene Harris(p) Jerry Peters(el p,arr) John Rowin,Al McKay(el g) Anthony Jackson(el b) Harvey Mason(dm) Jerry Steinholtz(perc) with strings,horns & backgr. vocals as above.
(Total Experience Studios) LA,March-May,1977

18765 Stranger in paradise BN BN-LA760-H

Gene Harris(el p) Jerry Peters(el p,synth,vo,arr) John Rowin,Al McKay(el g) Robert Popwell (el b) Harvey Mason(dm,marimba) Jerry Steinholtz(perc) with strings,horns & backgr. vocals as above.
(Total Experience Studios) LA,March-May,1977

18766 Peace of mind BN BN-XW1110,BN-LA760-H,CD 4-97157-2

Donald Byrd(tp,flh) Gene Harris(el p,synth) Jerry Peters(el p,synth,arr) John Rowin,Al McKay (el g) Harvey Mason(cymbal) Jerry Steinholtz(perc) D.J. Rodgers (vo) with strings, horns & backgr. vocals as above.
(Total Experience Studios) LA,March-May,1977

18767 Cristo redentor,pt.1 BN BN-LA760-H

Donald Byrd(tp,flh) Gene Harris(el p,synth) Jerry Peters(el p,synth,arr) John Rowin,Al McKay el g) Chuck Rainey(el b) Alvin Taylor(dm) Jerry Steinholtz (perc) with strings, horns & backgr. vocals as above.
(Total Experience Studios) LA,March-May,1977

18768 Cristo redentor,pt.2 BN BN-LA760-H

BLUE NOTE MEET THE L.A. PHILHARMONIC:
LOS ANGELES PHILHARMONIC ORCHESTRA: Orchestra cond. by Calvin Simmons.
(Hollywood Bowl) LA,August 13,1977

19719 National anthem BN BN-LA870-H

BOBBY HUTCHERSON: Emanuel Boyd(ss,ts) Bobby Hutcherson(vb) George Cables(p) James Leary(b) Eddie Marshall(dm) Bobbye Porter Hall(perc) & Los Angeles Philharmonic Orchestra,Dale Oehler(arr).
Same concert.

19720 Slow change
19721 Now
19722 Hello to the wind
19723 Now (Reprise)

All titles issued on BN BN-LA870-H.

CARMEN McRAE: Carmen McRae(vo) with Marshall Otwell(p) Andy Simpkins(b) Joey Baron(dm) & LA Philharmonic Orchestra,Bill Holman(arr).
Same concert.

19724 Star eyes CD BN 8-33578-2
19725 The man I love
19726 Sunday
19727 With one more look at you

All titles issued on BN BN-LA870-H.

EARL KLUGH: Onaje Allan Gumbs(keyb) Earl Klugh(g) Hubie Crawford(b) Gene Dunlap(dm) Bobbye Porter Hall(perc) & LA Philharmonic Orchestra,Dick Hazard(arr).
Same concert.

19728 Cabo frio
19729 The shadow of your smile -1
19730 Angelina

-1: Earl Klugh(solo g).
All titles issued on BN BN-LA870-H,Lib(J)K22P-6116/17.

HORACE SILVER - SILVER 'N' PERCUSSION:
Tom Harrell(tp,flh) Larry Schneider(ts) Horace Silver(p,arr) Ron Carter(b) Al Foster(dm) M.Babatunde Olatunji, Ladji Camara(perc-1).
Englewood Cliffs,N.J.,Nov.12 & 17,1977
Fred Hardy,Lee C.Thomas,Fred Gripper,Bob Barnes,Bobby Clay,Peter Oliver Norman(vo) Chapman Roberts (vo,dir) overdubbed on.
Englewood Cliffs,N.J.,November 25 & 30,1977

African ascension:
19581 Pt.1: The Gods of Yoruba -1
19582 Pt.2: The Sun God of the Masai -1
19583 Pt.3: The Spirit of the Zulu

All parts issued on BN BN-LA853-H,CD BN(J)TOCJ-1626.

HORACE SILVER - SILVER 'N' PERCUSSION:
Tom Harrell(tp,flh) Larry Schneider(ts) Horace Silver(p,arr) Ron Carter(b) Al Foster(dm) M.Babatunde Olatunji,Omar Clay(perc).
Englewood Cliffs,N.J.,Nov.12 & 17,1977

Fred Hardy,Lee C.Thomas,Fred Gripper,Bob Barnes,Bobby Clay,Peter Oliver Norman(vo) Chapman Roberts(vo,dir) overdubbed on.
Englewood Cliffs,N.J.,November 25 & 30,1977

The Great American Indian uprising:
19584 Pt.1: The idols of the Incas
19585 Pt.2: The Aztec sun God
19586 Pt.3: The Mohican and the great spirit

All parts issued on BN BN-LA853-H,CD BN(J)TOCJ-1626.

HORACE SILVER - SILVER 'N' STRINGS PLAY THE MUSIC OF THE SPHERES:
Tom Harrell(flh) Larry Schneider(ss,ts) Horace Silver(p) Ron Carter(b) Al Foster (dm) Gregory Hines(vo).
Englewood Cliffs,N.J.,November 3,1978

(The physical sphere)
The soul and its expression:
21020 Pt.1: The search for direction/ CD BN 4-95576-2
21020 Pt.2: Direction discovered -
21016 Pt.3: We all have a part to play (voGH)

All parts issued on BN LWB-1033.

Tom Harrell(flh) Larry Schneider(ss,ts) Horace Silver(p) Ron Carter(b) Al Foster(dm).
Englewood Cliffs,N.J.,November 10,1978

(The spiritual sphere)
The soul in communion with the creator:
21018 Pt.1: Communion with the creator
Pt.2: The creator guides us -1
21017? Pt.3: Progress through dedication and discipline -1
21019 Pt.4: We except positive results

-1: Guy Lumia(v,concertmaster) Aaron Rosand,Marvin Morganstern,Paul Winter,Lewis Eley,Peter Dimitriades,Louann Montesi,Harry Glickman(v) Harold Coletta,Harry Zaratzian,Seymour Berman,Theodore Israel(viola) Seymour Barab,Jonathan Abramowitz(cello) Gene Bianco(harp) Wade Marcus(arr,cond) overdubbed on. Englewood Cliffs,N.J.,December 10,1979
All parts issued on BN LWB-1033.

HORACE SILVER - SILVER 'N' STRINGS PLAY THE MUSIC OF THE SPHERES:
Tom Harrell(flh) Larry Schneider(ss,ts) Horace Silver(p) Ron Carter(b) Al Foster(dm) Brenda Alford, Chapman Roberts,Carol Lynn Maillard(vo).
Englewood Cliffs,N.J.,October 26,1979

(The physical sphere) The Pygmalion process:
20807 Pt.1: Inner feelings (voCR) -1
20810 Pt.2: Friends (voCLM)
20808 Pt.3: Empathy (voCR) -1
20809 Pt.4: Optimism (voCLM) -1
20811 Pt.5: Expansion (voBA) -1

-1: Guy Lumia(v,concertmaster) Aaron Rosand,Marvin Morganstern,Paul Winter,Lewis Eley, Peter Dimitriades,Louann Montesi,Harry Glickman(v) Harold Coletta,Harry Zaratzian,Seymour Berman,Theodore Israel(viola) Seymour Barab,Jonathan Abramowitz(cello) Gene Bianco(harp) Wade Marcus(arr,cond) overdubbed on. Englewood Cliffs,N.J.,December 10,1979
All parts issued on BN LWB-1033.

301

HORACE SILVER - SILVER 'N' STRINGS PLAY THE MUSIC OF THE SPHERES:
Tom Harrell(flh) Larry Schneider(ss,ts) Horace Silver(p) Ron Carter(b) Al Foster (dmBrenda Alford(vo).
Englewood Cliffs,N.J.,November 2,1979

	(The physical sphere)
	The soul and its progress throughout the spheres:
	Pt.1: Self portrait No.1 -1
20828	Pt.2: Self portrait No.2 -1/
20828	Pt.3: Portrait of the aspiring self -1
	(The mental sphere)
	The soul's awareness of its character:
20829	Pt.1: The soul (Character analysis) (voBA)
20830	Pt.2: Negative patterns of the sub-conscious/
20830	Pt.3: The conscious and its desire for change

-1: Guy Lumia(v,concertmaster) Aaron Rosand,Marvin Morganstern,Paul Winter,Lewis Eley,Peter Dimitriades,Louann Montesi,Harry Glickman(v) Harold Coletta,Harry Zaratzian,Seymour Berman,Theodore Israel(viola) Seymour Barab,Jonathan Abramowitz(cello) Gene Bianco(harp) Wade Marcus(cond) Dale Oehler(arr) overdubbed on. Englewood Cliffs,N.J.,December 10,1979
All parts issued on BN LWB-1033.

LATE ADDITIONS

BOBBI HUMPHREY:
(session details not known)
(Sound Factory) LA,May 14,1976

17487	Ain't no sunshine	rejected
17488	One minute to heaven	-
17489	Our day will come	-

BOBBI HUMPHREY:
(session details not known)
LA,June 28,1976

17540	Bobbi Q'lv	rejected

302

NOTES

Part 3

The EMI Era (1983–1999)

Note: This part includes sessions recorded by EMI subsidiaries in various countries and first issued on Blue Note. In each case,label of origin is mentioned.Sessions issued first on local EMI labels and reissued on Blue Note label later on are listed in part 5.

GEORGE RUSSELL & THE LIVING TIME ORCHESTRA - THE AFRICAN GAME:
Mike Peipman,Chris Passin,Roy Okutani,Mark Harvey(tp) Peter Cirelli,Chip Kaner(tb) Jeff Marsanskas(bass tb) Marshall Sealy(frh) Dave Mann,Janis Steprans(as,ss,fl) George Garzone(ts,ss) Gary Joynes(ts,ss,fl) Brad Jones(bs,bass cl,fl) Marc Rossi,Bruce Barth(keyb) Mark White(g) Bob Nieske(b) Bill Urmson(el b) Keith Copeland(dm) Dave Hagedorn(perc) George Russell(arr,cond,comp) & African percussion ensemble (5-6 perc).

(Emanuel Church) Boston,June 18,1983

Event I: Organic life on earth begins
Event II: The Paleolithic game
Event III: Consciousness
Event IV: The survival game
Event V: The human sensing of unity with great nature
Event VI: African empires
Event VII: Cartesian man
Event VIII: The mega-minimalist age
Event IX: The future?

All parts issued on BN BT 85103,CD 7-46335-2.

GEORGE RUSSELL & THE LIVING TIME ORCHESTRA - SO WHAT:
Joe Galeota(cga) replaces African percussion ensemble.Same date.

So what -1	CD BN 4-97155-2
Time spiral	

-1: arr. by George Russell & Tim Engels.
Both titles issued on BN BT 85132,CD 7-46391-2.

Mark Harvey(tp) Chip Kaner(tb) Janis Steprans(as) Gary Joynes(ts) Marc Rossi(keyb) Mark White(g) Bill Urmson(el b) Keith Copeland(dm) George Russell(arr).Same date.

Rhymes	BN BT 85132	CD 7-46391-2
War Gewesen	-	-

CHARLES LLOYD QUARTET - A NIGHT IN COPENHAGEN:
Charles Lloyd(fl,ts,oboe) Michel Petrucciani(p) Palle Danielsson(b) Sonship Theus(dm) Bobby McFerrin (vo).

(Live) Copenhagen,July 11,1983

Lotus lane (To Thakur and Trane)	BN BT 85104	
Lady Day	-	CD 4-97154-2
En encanto	-	
Third floor Richard (voBMcF)	-	
Night blooming Jasmine	-	
Of course,of course (voBMcF)		
Sweet Georgia bright		

All titles issued on CD BN 7-85104-2.

KENNY BURRELL/GROVER WASHINGTON Jr. - TOGETHERING:
Grover Washington Jr.(ss,ts-1) Kenny Burrell(g) Ron Carter(b) Jack DeJohnette(dm).
(Mastermind Studios) NYC,April 5 & 6,1984

Soulero
Daydream CD Manhattan 7-99490-2,BN 8-30493-2, (C)8-56508-2

A beautiful friendship -1
Togethering CD BN 8-30493-2
Asphalt Canyon blues CD BN 5-24271-2
What am I here for?

All titles issued on BN BT 85106,CD 7-46093-2,5-25651-2.

Grover Washington Jr.(ss) Kenny Burrell(ac g) Ron Carter(b) Jack DeJohnette(dm) Ralph McDonald(perc).
(Mastermind Studios) NYC,April 23,1984

Sails of your soul
Romance dance

Both titles issued on BN BT 85106,CD 7-46093-2,5-25651-2.

STANLEY JORDAN - MAGIC TOUCH:
Stanley Jordan(g) Sammy Figueroa(perc-1).
(Songshop Studios) NYC,September-October 1984

'Round midnight BN BT 85101,BQ 85127,(In)JAZ 3
CD BN 7-99490-2,Manhattan 7-99490-2
All the children BN BT 85101,CD 8-31502-2
Angel -
Fundance -
A child is born - CD 7-95281-2,7-96098-2
Eleanor Rigby -1 - B1-92812
CD BN 7-92812-2,7-94861-2, 8-31502-2, 8-34957-2,(C)8-56508-2,(J)CJ32-5049, TOCJ-5602,TOCJ-5874,TOCJ-6134, Cap(J)TOCJ-5201,EMI-USA(J)TOCJ-5254
New love BN B 50002

All titles issued on CD BN 7-46092-2.

Onaje Allan Gumbs(keyb) Wayne Braithwaite(el b) Omar Hakim(dm).Same dates.

The lady in my life BN B 50002,BT 85101,BST2-92477
CD BN 7-46092-2,7-92477-2,8-31502-2, 8-33878-2,4-95701-2,(Sp)8-53016-2, Cema S21-57593,Rhino 75870-2

Stanley Jordan(g) Charnett Moffett(b) Peter Erskine(dm).Same dates.

Freddie Freeloader BN BT 85101,CD 7-46092-2

Stanley Jordan(g) Charnett Moffett(b) Sammy Figueroa,Bugsy Moore(perc) Al Di Meola(cymbals).
Same dates.

Return expedition BN BT 85101,CD 7-46092-2

305

STANLEY TURRENTINE - STRAIGHT AHEAD:
Stanley Turrentine(ts) Les McCann(p,el p) Jimmy Ponder(el g) Peter Brown(el b) Gerry King(dm).
(Power Play Studios) Long Island City,N.Y.,November 24,1984

The longer you wait	BN BT 85105
Other side of time	- (In)JAZ 2

Both titles also issued on CD BN 7-46110-2.

Stanley Turrentine(ts) Jimmy Smith(org) George Benson(g) Ron Carter(b) Jimmy Madison(dm).
(Sigma Sound Studios) NYC,December 7,1984

Plum	BN B1-93201,CD 7-93201-2
A child is born	CD BN 7-95281-2
Straight ahead	
Ah,Rio	

All titles issued on BN BT 85105,CD 7-46110-2.

BILL EVANS - THE ALTERNATIVE MAN:
Note: All titles from album BT 85111 listed below were recorded in January & May 1985 at Planet Sound Studio/A & R Studios/Sound Ideas/Automated Studio,NYC.

Lew Soloff(tp) Bill Evans(fl,ss,ts,keyb,arr) Hiram Bullock(g) Marcus Miller(b) Danny Gottlieb(dm) Manolo Badrena(perc).

Let the juice loose!	BN BT 85111

Bill Evans(fl,ss,ts,keyb,arr) Hiram Bullock,Dave Hart(g) Danny Gottlieb(dm).

The cry in her eyes	BN BT 85111

Bill Evans(fl,ss,ts,keyb,arr) Mitchell Forman(keyb) Jeff Golub(g) Mark Egan(b) Danny Gottlieb(dm).

The alternative man	BN BT 85111,(In)JAZ 3

Bill Evans(fl,ss,ts,keyb,arr) Clifford Carter(keyb,vo) Sid McGinnis(g) Danny Gottlieb(dm) Manolo Badrena (perc).

The path of least resistance	BN BT 85111
Jojo	-

Bill Evans(fl,ss,ts,keyb,arr) Clifford Carter(keyb) Mitchell Forman(p) John McLaughlin(g) Mark Egan(b) Danny Gottlieb(dm) Manolo Badrena(perc).

Survival of the fittest	BN BT 85111
Flight of the falcon	-

Bill Evans(fl,ss,ts,keyb,arr) Chuck Loeb(g) Mark Egan(b) Danny Gottlieb(cymbals).

Gardiners garden	BN BT 85111

Bill Evans(fl,ss,ts,keyb,arr) Marcus Miller(b) Al Foster(dm).

Miles away	BN BT 85111,BQ 85127

All titles from BT 85111 also issued on CD BN 7-46336-2.

ONE NIGHT WITH BLUE NOTE PRESERVED:
Walter Davis(p) Reggie Workman(b) Art Blakey(dm).
(Town Hall) NYC,February 22,1985

Criss cross	rejected
Bud's bubble	-
I got rhythm	-

Freddie Hubbard(tp) Curtis Fuller(tb) Johnny Griffin(ts) added.
Same concert.

Moanin'	BN BT 85115,BTDK 85117 CD BN 7-46149-2,8-56399-2,(J)TOCJ-5946
It's only a paper moon	rejected

Stanley Jordan(g).
Same concert.

Touch of blue	unissued
When you wish upon a star	BN BT 85116,BTDK 85117 CD BN 7-46150-2,(J)TOCJ-5946
Jumping Jack	BN BT 85116,BTDK 85117 CDBN 7-46159-2, 7-96581-2,8-31502-2, HMV Jazz(E)5-20884-2

James Newton(fl-1) Bobby Hutcherson(vb) Herbie Hancock(p-2) Ron Carter(b) Tony Williams(dm-1).
Same concert.

Hat and beard -1	
Little B's poem -1,2	CD BN(J)TOCJ-5946,TOCJ-6141
Bouquet -2	

All titles issued on BN BT 85113,BTDK 85117,CD 7-46147-2,4-97811-2.

Freddie Hubbard(tp) Joe Henderson(ts) Bobby Hutcherson(vb-1) Herbie Hancock(p) Ron Carter(b) Tony Williams(dm).
Same concert

Canteloupe island	CD BN 8-56399-2,(J)CJ32-5049,TOCJ-5946, TOCJ-66063
Recorda me -1	
Maiden voyage	rejected

First two titles issued on BN BT 85113,BTDK 85117,CD 7-46147-2,4-97811-2.

Charles Lloyd(fl,ts) Michel Petrucciani(p) Cecil McBee(b) Jack DeJohnette(dm).
Same concert

The blessing	
Tone poem	
Lady Day	CD BN(J)TOCJ-5946
El encanto	
How long	

All titles issued on BN BT 85116,BTDK 85117,CD 7-46150-2.

Bennie Wallace(ts) Cecil McBee(b) Jack DeJohnette(dm).
Same concert

Broadside	BN BT 85114,BTDK 85117 CD BN 7-46148-2,(J)TOCJ-5946

ONE NIGHT WITH BLUE NOTE PRESERVED:
McCoy Tyner(p).
Same concert.

Sweet and lovely — BN BT 85114,BTDK 85117,CD 7-46148-2

Woody Shaw(tp) Jackie McLean(as) McCoy Tyner(p) Cecil McBee(b) Jack DeJohnette(dm).
(Town Hall) — NYC,February 22,1985

Appointment in Ghana
Passion dance — CD BN(J)TOCJ-5946
Blues on the corner

All titles issued on BN BT 85114,BTDK 85117,CD 7-46148-2.

Cecil Taylor(p).
Same concert

Pontos cantados — BN BT 85114,BTDK 85117,CD 7-46148-2

Alfred Lion(speaking).

Alfred Lion's speech — CD BN(J)TOCJ-5946

Grover Washington Jr.(ss-1,ts) Kenny Burrell(g) Reggie Workman(b) Grady Tate(dm).
Same concert

Nica's dream — unissued
I'm glad there is you -1 — BN BT 85115,BTDK 85117
CD BN -46149-2,5-25651-2
Summertime -1 — BN BT 85115,BTDK 85117
CD BN 7-46149-2,7-99427-2,8-30493-2,
5-20808-2,5-25651-2

Lou Donaldson(as) Jimmy Smith(org) Kenny Burrell(g) Grady Tate(dm).
Same concert

Blues walk
I'm getting sentimental over you

Both titles issued on BN BT 85115,BTDK 85117,CD 7-46149-2,(J)TOCJ-5946.

Stanley Turrentine(ts) Jimmy Smith(org) Kenny Burrell(g) Grady Tate(dm).
Same concert

The jumpin' blues — BN BT 85115,BTDK 85117,CD 7-46149-2
A child is born — - - -
Just squeeze me — unissued
Scratch my back — -

McCOY TYNER & JACKIE McLEAN - IT'S ABOUT TIME:
Jon Faddis(tp) Jackie McLean(as) McCoy Tyner(p) Ron Carter(b) Al Foster(dm).
(Right Track Studios) — NYC,April 6 & 7,1985

Spur of the moment
Hip-toe — CD BN 8-33207-2
No flower please (tp,as out)

All titles issued on BN BT 85102,CD 7-46291-2.

<u>McCOY TYNER & JACKIE McLEAN</u> - <u>IT'S ABOUT TIME</u>:
Jackie McLean(as-1) McCoy Tyner(p) Marcus Miller(el b) Al Foster(dm) Steve Thornton(perc).
(Right Track Studios) NYC,April 6 & 7,1985

It's about time -1
You taught my heart to sing
Travelin'

All titles issued on BN BT 85102,CD 7-46291-2.

<u>BENNIE WALLACE</u> - <u>TWILIGHT TIME</u>:
Ray Anderson(tb) Bennie Wallace(ts) Rabbit Edmonds(harmony ts-1) Mac Rebennack (Dr. John)(org,p) Stevie Ray Vaughan(el g) John Scofield(g) Bob Cranshaw(b) Bernard Purdie(dm).
(Skyline Studios) NYC,c.Spring 1985

All night dance -1 BN BST2-92477,CD 7-92477-2,Premier(E)CDJA 2
Trouble in mind

Both titles issued on BN BT 85107,CD 7-46293-2.

Ray Anderson(tb-2) Bennie Wallace(ts) John Scofield(g-1) Eddie Gomez(b) Jack DeJohnette(dm).
(Skyline Studios) NYC,c. Spring 1985

Is it true what they say about Dixie?
Tennessee Waltz -1
Fresh out -1,2

All titles issued on BN BT 85107,CD 7-46293-2.

Ray Anderson(tb) Bennie Wallace(ts) Dr. John(p) John Scofield(g) Eddie Gomez(b) Chris Parker(dm).
(Skyline Studios) NYC,c. Spring 1985

Sainte Fragile
Willie Mae
Saint Expedito
Twilight time (g out) BN BQ 85127,(In)JAZ 3

All titles issued on BN BT 85107,CD 7-46293-2.

<u>OUT OF THE BLUE</u> - <u>OTB</u>:
Michael Philip Mossman(tp,flh) Kenny Garrett(as) Ralph Bowen(ts) Harry Pickens(p) Robert Hurst(b) Ralph Peterson(dm).
Englewood Cliffs,N.J.,June 7,1985

	Isolation	rejected
	Feeling good	-
(tk.4)	RH factor	BN BT 85118
(tk.2)	Git in there	-

Last two titles also issued on CD BN 7-46290-2.

OUT OF THE BLUE - OTB:
Michael Philip Mossman(tp,flh) Kenny Garrett(as) Ralph Bowen(ts) Harry Pickens(p) Robert Hurst(b) Ralph Peterson(dm).

Englewood Cliffs,N.J.,June 8,1985

(tk.2)	Eastern love village	BN BT 85118
	Amoaku	rejected
	Output	BN BT 85118,BQ 85127,(In)JAZ 3
	Elevation	rejected
(tk.2)	OTB	BN BT 85118,BST2-92474 CD BN 7-92474-2,(J)CJ32-5049
(tk.2)	Blue Hughes	BN BT 85118
(tk.3)	Reunited	-
	Computer G	rejected

All titles from BT 85118 also issued on CD BN 7-46290-2.

TONY WILLIAMS - FOREIGN INTRIGUE:
Wallace Roney(tp) Donald Harrison(as) Bobby Hutcherson(vb) Mulgrew Miller(p) Ron Carter(b) Tony Williams (dm).

(M & I Studios) NYC,June 18,1985

(tk.3)	Arboretum	
(tk.2)	Takin' my time	
(tk.3)	Sister Cheryl	BN BQ 85127,(In)JAZ 3 CD BN 8-53331-2,(C)8-56508-2,(J)TOCJ-6141, Cap(J)TOCJ-5259
tk.3	Clearways	

All titles issued on BN BT 85119,CD 7-46289-2.

Same.

(M & I Studios) NYC,June 19,1985

(tk.2)	Life of the party -1	BN BT 85119,BST2-92474 CD BN 7-92474-2,8-53331-2,(J)CJ32-5049
(tk.3)	Foreign intrigue-1	BN BT 85119
(tk.2)	My Michele	-
	If you leave me now (horns out	rejected

-1: Tony Williams(electronic dm perc) overdubbed on.
First three titles also issued on CD BN 7-46289-2.

JAMES NEWTON - THE AFRICAN FLOWER:
Olu Dara(c) James Newton(fl,arr) Arthur Blythe(as) Roland Hanna(p) Jay Hoggard(vb) Rick Rozie(b) Billy Hart (dm-2) Pheeroan AkLaff(dm-1,tavil & talking dm-3) Anthony Brown(maracas,finger cymbals) John Blake(v) Milt Grayson(vo).

(RCA Studio B) NYC,June 24 & 25,1985

Black and tan fantasy -2	BN BQ 85127,(In)JAZ 3, Knitting Factory CD 249
Fleurette Africaine(The African flower)-2	
Passion flower -2	
Virgin jungle-2,3	
Strange feeling (voMG)-1	
Cottontail -1	CD BN 4-94035-2,5-20809-2
Sophisticated lady	

All titles issued on BN BT 85109,CD 7-46292-2.

310

THE OTHER SIDE OF 'ROUND MIDNIGHT:
Dexter Gordon(ts) Herbie Hancock(p) John McLaughlin(g) Pierre Michelot(b) Billy Higgins(dm).
(Studio Eclair) Paris,early July 1985

As time goes by BN BT 85135,CD 7-46397-2

Bobby Hutcherson(vb) Herbie Hancock(p) Pierre Michelot(b) Billy Higgins(dm).
(Studio Eclair) Paris,early July 1985

It's only a paper moon BN BT 85135,CD 7-46397-2

Palle Mikkelborg(tp) Dexter Gordon(ss) Cedar Walton(p) Mads Vinding(b) Billy Higgins(dm).
(Studio Davout) Paris,late August 1985

Tivoli BN BT 85135,CD 7-46397-2

Palle Mikkelborg(tp) Wayne Shorter(ss) Dexter Gordon(ts) Herbie Hancock(p) Ron Carter(b) Mads Vinding (b) Billy Higgins(dm).
(Studio Davout) Paris,late August 1985

'Round midnight BN BT 85135,(E)BNX 1
CD BN 7-46397-2,7-48337-2,(J)CJ32-5049

Wayne Shorter(ts) Herbie Hancock(p) Ron Carter(b) Billy Higgins(dm).
(Studio Davout) Paris,late August 1985

Call sheet blues BN BT 85135,CD 7-46397-2

Freddie Hubbard(tp)Herbie Hancock(p)Ron Carter(b)Tony Williams(dm).
(Studio Eclair) Paris,late August 1985

Berengere's nightmare No.2 BN BT 85135,CD 7-46397-2

Freddie Hubbard(tp) Dexter Gordon(ts) Cedar Walton(p) Ron Carter(b) Tony Williams(dm).
(Studio Eclair) Paris,late August 1985

Society red BN BT 85135,CD 7-46397-2

JOE HENDERSON - THE STATE OF THE TENOR - LIVE AT THE VILLAGE VANGUARD:
Joe Henderson(ts) Ron Carter(b) Al Foster(dm).
(Village Vanguard) NYC,November 14,1985

Set #1:
Beatrice rejected
Y ya la quiero -
Portrait -
Friday the Thirteenth -

Set #2:
Boo Boo's birthday rejected
Soulville -
Happy reunion BN BT 85123,CD 7-46296-2,8-28879-2,5-20809-2
Isotope rejected

Set #3:
Loose change rejected
Cheryl -
Ask me now -
All the things you are -

JOE HENDERSON - THE STATE OF THE TENOR - LIVE AT THE VILLAGE VANGUARD:
Joe Henderson(ts) Ron Carter(b) Al Foster(dm).

	(Village Vanguard)	NYC,November 15,1985
Set #1:		
	All the things you are	rejected
	Boo Boo's birthday	-
	Y ya la quiero	BN BT 85126,CD 7-46426-2,7-89287-2,8-28879-2
	Portrait	- - 8-28879-2,8-56692-2
	Isotope	rejected
	Stella by starlight	CD BN 7-46296-2
Set #2:		
	Loose change	rejected
	Cheryl	-
	Ask me now	BN BT 85123,CD 7-46296-2,7-95627-2,8-56692-2, (Sp)5-21755-2
	Soulville	rejected
	Friday the Thirteenth	BN BT 85123,CD 7-46296-2
	Beatrice	- BST2-92474
		CD BN 7-46296-2,7-92474-2,7-95627-2, 8-34873-2,4-95701-2

All issued takes also on CD BN 8-28879-2.

Set #3:		
	Loose change	rejected
	Boo Boo's birthday	-
	All the things you are	-
	Cheryl	-
	Happy reunion	-
	Soulville	-
Same.	(Village Vanguard)	NYC,November 16,1985
Set #1:		
	All the things you are	BN CD 7-46426-2
	Boo Boo's birthday	BN BT 85126 -
	Ask me now	rejected
	Soulville	BN BT 85126,CD 7-46426-2,8-56692-2
	Cheryl	- -
	The bead game	- -

All issued takes also on CD BN 8-28879-2.

Set #2:		
	Loose change	BN BT 85123,CD 7-46296-2,8-28879-2
	Isotope	- - 7-89287-2,8-28879-2
	Happy reunion	rejected
	Beatrice	-
	Y ya la quiero	-
	Friday the Thirteenth	-
Set #3:		
	Boo Boo's birthday	rejected
	Happy reunion	-
	Soulville	-
	All the things you are	-
Set #4:		
	Portrait	rejected
	Friday the Thirteenth	-
	Happy reunion	-

FREDDIE HUBBARD & WOODY SHAW - DOUBLE TAKE:
Freddie Hubbard(tp,flh) Woody Shaw(tp) Kenny Garrett(as,fl) Mulgrew Miller(p) Cecil McBee(b) Carl Allen (dm).
Englewood Cliffs,NJ,November 21,1985

tk.2	Desert moonlight	BN(J)BNS-17642,CD CJ32-5049
tk.5	Boperation	

Same. Englewood Cliffs,NJ,November 22,1985

tk.9	Sandu	BN B1-93202,(In)JAZ 3 CD BN 7-93202-2,Cema GSC Music 15131
tk.12	Lament for Booker	
tk.14	Just a ballad for Woody	
tk.16	Lotus blossom	
tk.17	Hub-tones	

All titles issued on BN BT 85121,CD 7-46294-2,8-32747-2

THE MICHEL PETRUCCIANI TRIO - PIANISM:
Michel Petrucciani(p) Palle Danielsson(b) Elliot Zigmund(dm).
(RCA Studio C) NYC,December 20,1985

The prayer	CD BN 4-97563-2,HMV Jazz(E)5-20873-2
Our tune	CD BN 7-89916-2
Face's face	BN(In)JAZ 3
Night and day	
Here's that rainy day	
Regina	BN BQ 85127

All titles issued on BN BT 85124,CD 7-46295-2,(F)4-97604-2.

JIMMY SMITH - GO FOR WHATCHA KNOW:
Stanley Turrentine(ts) Jimmy Smith(org) Monty Alexander(p-1) Kenny Burrell(g) Buster Williams(b) Grady Tate(dm,vo-2) Kenny Washington(dm-2) Errol "Crusher" Bennett(perc-3).
Englewood Cliffs,N.J.,January 2,1986

(tk.2)	She's out of my life -1,2
(tk.1)	We can make it work -1,3
(tk.3)	Bass face

All titles issued on BN BT 85125,CD 7-46297-2.

Stanley Turrentine(ts) Jimmy Smith(org) Kenny Burrell(g) Grady Tate(dm) Errol "Crusher" Bennett(perc-1).
Englewood Cliffs,N.J.,January 3,1986

(tk.2)	No substitute	
(tk.1)	Go for whatcha know	
(tk.1)	Fungii Mama -1	BN B1-91140,(E)BNSLP-3 CD BN 7-91140-2,(J)TOCJ-5780

All titles issued on BN BT 85125,CD 7-46297-2.

THE OTHER SIDE OF 'ROUND MIDNIGHT:
Bobby McFerrin(vo) Herbie Hancock(p).
(Studio Davout) Paris,February ,1986

What is this thing called love (voBMcF) BN BT 85135
'Round midnight -
CD BN(J)CJ28-5178,TOCJ-5637,TOCJ-5875, TOCJ-5963,TOCJ-6110,Cap(J)TOCJ-5618/19, TOCJ-5713

Both titles also issued on CD BN 7-46397-2.

BOBBY McFERRIN - SPONTANEOUS INVENTIONS:
Bobby McFerrin(vo,perc) with Robin Williams(vo) Wayne Shorter(ss-1)
(Aquarius Theatre) LA,February 28,1986

Thinkin' about your body BN BQ 85127,BST2-92477,B1-92812
CD BN 7-92477-2,7-92812-2,8-53329-2,5-20070-2
Premier(E)CDJA 1
From me to you CD BN 7-94861-2,8-53329-2
Care mia
Opportunity
Walkin'-1 CD Cema S21-56915,MFP(E)CDMFP 6303
I hear music - -
Beverly Hills blues (voRW)
Manana iguana CD Cema S21-56915,MFP(E)CDMFP 6303

All titles issued on BN BT 85110,CD 7-46298-2.

Bobby McFerrin(vo,b) with Herbie Hancock(p).
(Capitol Studios) LA,March ,1986

Turtle shoes BN BT 85110
CD BN 7-46298-2,8-53329-2,(C)8-56508-2, Cema S21-56915,MFP(E)CDMFP 6303

Bobby McFerrin(vo) solo.
(Different Fur Studio) SF,March ,1986

There ya go BN BT 85110,CD 7-46298-2

THE DON PULLEN-GEORGE ADAMS QUARTET - BREAKTHROUGH:
George Adams(ts) Don Pullen(p) Cameron Brown(b) Dannie Richmond(dm).
(RCA Studio A) NYC,April 30,1986

(tk.4) We've been here all the time BN BT 85122
(tk.1) A time for sobriety -
(tk.6) Song from the old country - BST2-92474
CD BN 7-92474-2,8-23513-2,4-95701-2, (J)CJ32-5049,TOCJ-5963,Cap(J)TOCJ-5191/92
(tk.8) Just foolin' around BN BT 85122
(tk.5) Mr. Smoothie -
(tk.1) The necessary blues
(Or thank you very much,Mr. Monk)

All titles issued on CD BN 7-46314-2.

 314

OUT OF THE BLUE - INSIDE TRACK:
Michael Philip Mossman(tp) Kenny Garrett(as) Ralph Bowen(ts) Harry Pickens(p) Bob Hurst(b) Ralph Peterson(dm).

	(RCA Studio C)	NYC,June 19,1986
	Cherry Pickens	rejected
	Nathan Jones	-
(tk.3)	Elevation	BN BT 85128,CD 7-46395-2
	Isolation	rejected

Same.	(RCA Studio C)	NYC,June 20,1986
(tk.2)	Hot house	BN BT 85128,CD 7-46395-2
(tk.7)	Isolation	- -
(tk.3)	Inside track	- -
	Feeling good	rejected
(tk.5)	E force	BN BT 85128,CD 7-46395-2
(tk.1)	Nathan Jones	- -
(tk.1)	Cherry Pickens	- -

MICHEL PETRUCCIANI - POWER OF THREE:
Wayne Shorter-1(ss,ts) Michel Petrucciani(p) Jim Hall(g).

(Jazz Festival)	Montreux,Switzerland,July 14,1986
Beautiful love	CD BN(J)TOCJ-6134
In a sentimental mood	BN BT 85133
Careful	-
Waltz new	
Limbo -1	BN BT 85133 CD BN 4-97563-2,HMV Jazz(E)5-20873-2
Morning blues -1	BN BT 85133
Bimini -1	- CD 7-89916-2

All titles issued on CD BN 7-46427-2,(F)4-97604-2.

JAMES NEWTON - ROMANCE AND REVOLUTION:
James Newton(fl) Abdul Wadud(cello) Rick Rozie(b) Pheeroan Ak Laff(dm).

(RCA Studio C)	NYC,August 20 & 21,1986
Peace	BN BT 85134
Tenderly (solo fl)	

Both titles issued on CD BN 7-46431-2.

Steve Turre,Robin Eubanks(tb) James Newton(fl) Jay Hoggard(vb) Abdul Wadud(cello) Geri Allen(p) Rick Rozie(b) Pheeroan Ak Laff(dm).

(RCA Studio C)	NYC,August 20 & 21,1986
Forever Charles (cello out)	
Meditations on integration (cello,vb out)	
The evening leans toward you (Eubanks out)	

All titles issued on BN BT 85134,CD 7-46431-2.

STANLEY JORDAN:
Stanley Jordan(el g).

(Live at The Rainbow) Denver,Colorado,August 21,1986

Fundance CD BN 7-92356-2

OTB - LIVE AT MT. FUJI:
Harry Pickens (p) Kenny Davis(b) Ralph Peterson(dm).

(Mt. Fuji Blue Note Festival) Japan,August 31,1986

Parisian thoroughfare	BN BT 85141,CD 7-46784-2
Celia	-
Over the rainbow	-
All God's children got rhythm	rejected
Blue pearl	BN BT 85141,CD 7-46784-2
Un poco loco	rejected

Michael Phillip Mossman(tp) Kenny Garrett(as) Ralph Bowen(ts) added.

Same date.

Nathan Jones
Elevation
OTB

All titles issued on BN BT 85141,CD 7-46784-2.

JAMES BLOOD ULMER - AMERICA,DO YOU REMEMBER THE LOVE?:
James Blood Ulmer(g,arr,vo) Bill Laswell(el b) Ronald Shannon Jackson(dm).

(Power Station/Quadrosonic/RPM) NYC,September 15,17,18 & 19,1986

I belong in the U.S.A.
Lady blue
After dark
Show me your love,America -1
Black sheep
Wings

-1: Nicky Skopelitis(12 string g,banjo) Bernard Fowler,Fred Fowler,Muriel Fowler (backgr.vo) added.
All titles issued on BN BT 85136,CD 7-46755-2.

JACK WALRATH - MASTER OF SUSPENSE:
Jack Walrath(tp) Steve Turre(tb) Kenny Garrett(as) Carter Jefferson(ts) James Williams(p) Anthony Cox(b) Ronnie Burrage(dm).

(Sound Ideas) NYC,September 19,1986

Meat!
Children
No mystery
A study in porcine
The Lord's calypso
I'm so lonesome I could cry,pts.1 & 3
Monk on the moon
A hymn for the discontented

All titles issued on BN BLJ-46905,CD 7-46905-2.

STANLEY JORDAN - STANDARDS,Volume 1:
Stanley Jordan(g).

	NYC,October ,1986
Moon river	BN BT 85130,CD 7-46333-2.

Stanley Jordan(g).

(Power Station)	NYC,October ,1986
The sound of silence	CD EMI-USA(J)TOCJ-5254
Sunny	
Georgia on my mind	CD BN 8-31502-2
Send one your love	
Guitar man	
One less bell to answer	
Because	
My favorite things	CD BN 8-31502-2,EMI-USA(J)TOCJ-5254
Silent night	CD BN 7-94857-2

All titles issued on BN BT 85130,CD 7-46333-2.

KENNY BURRELL - GENERATION/PIECES OF BLUE AND THE BLUES:
Kenny Burrell(g,el g,guitarjo,arr) Rodney Jones,Bobby Broome(g,el g) Dave Jackson(b) Kenny Washington (dm).

(Village Vanguard)	NYC,October 24 & 25,1986		
Announcements by Kenny Burrell	BN BT 85137,CD 7-46756-2		
Generation	-	-	
High fly	-	-	
Lover man	-	-	
Mark I	-	-	
So little time	-	-	
Fungi Mama	-	-	
The jumpin' blues	-	-	8-30493-2
Guitar medley:Dolphin dance/		-	
Naima/Star crossed lovers/Just friends		-	
Confessin' the blues	BN B1-90260,CD 7-90260-2		
Raincheck	-	-	
Blue days, blue dreams	-	-	
Salty Papa (*aka* Blues chantez)	-	-	
Jeannine	-	-	8-30493-2
'Round midnight	-	-	
No hype blues	-	-	

TONY WILLIAMS - CIVILIZATION:
Wallace Roney(tp) Billy Pierce(ss,ts) Mulgrew Miller(p) Charnett Moffett(b) Tony Williams(dm).

(Capitol Studios)	LA,November 24,25 & 26,1986
Geo Rose	CD BN 8-53331-2
Warrior	
Ancient eyes	
Soweto nights	
The slump	CD BN 8-53331-2
Civilization	
Mutants on the beach	
Citadel	

All titles issued on BN BT 85138,CD 7-46757-2.

STANLEY TURRENTINE - WONDERLAND:
Stanley Turrentine(ts) Stevie Wonder(hca-3) Don Grusin(el p-1,p-2) Ronnie Foster(p-1,el p-3,synth strings-4,arr) Mike Miller(g,el g) Abe Laboriel(el b) Harvey Mason(dm) Paulinho Da Costa(perc).
(Yamaha R & D Studios) Glendale,Calif.,December 10,11 & 12,1986

Bird of beauty -1
Boogie on reggae woman -2,3 BN BST2-92477;CD BN 7-92477-2,
Cema S21-57593,EMI-Jazz(E)8-55725-2
Rocket love -2,4

All titles issued on BN BT 85140,CD 7-46762-2.

Stanley Turrentine(ts) Ronnie Foster(keyb,synth b-1,arr) Abe Laboriel(el b-2) Harvey Mason(dm) Paulinho Da Costa(perc).
Same sessions.

Creepin'-1
Don't worry 'bout a thing -2

Both titles issued on BN BT 85140,CD 7-46762-2.

Stanley Turrentine(ts) Eddie del Barrio(keyb,arr) Ronnie Foster(arr).
Same sessions.

You and I BN BT 85140;CD BN 7-46762-2,4-94211-2,
Cema S21-57590

Stanley Turrentine(ts) Don Grusin(p) Ronnie Foster(el p-1,synth-1,vb-1,arr) Abe Laboriel (el b) Harvey Mason(dm). Same sessions.

Living for the City -1 BN BT 85140,CD 7-46762-2
Sir Duke - - 4-94211-2

FREDDIE HUBBARD - LIFE FLIGHT:
Freddie Hubbard(tp) Stanley Turrentine(ts) Larry Willis(el p,synth) George Benson(g) Wayne Braithwaite (el b) Idris Muhammad(dm,tamb).
(M & I Studios) NYC,January 23,1987

Battlescar Galorica BN BT 85139,CD 7-46898-2
Soulmates - -

Freddie Hubbard(tp) Ralph Moore(ts) Larry Willis(p) Rufus Reid(b) Carl Allen(dm).
(M & I Studios) NYC,January 24,1987

The melting pot BN BT 85139, CD 7-46898-2
Life flight - -

CHARNETT MOFFETT - NET MAN:
Kenny Kirkland(synth) Stanley Jordan(g) Charnett Moffett(b) Al Foster(dm).
(RPM Studios) NYC,March 9,1987

The dance BN BLJ-46993,CD 7-46993-2

Michael Brecker(ts) Kenny Drew Jr.(p) Charnett Moffett(b) Codaryl "Cody" Moffett(dm).
(RPM Studios) NYC,March 10,1987

Swing bass BN BLJ-46993,CD 7-46993-2

CHARNETT MOFFETT - NET MAN:
Kenny Kirkland(synth-1) Charnett Moffett(b,dm machine-2) Mino Cinelu(perc-2).
(RPM Studios) NYC,March 11,1987

Mizzom -2 BN BLJ-46993,CD 7-46993-2,(J)CJ32-5049
Mona Lisa -1 - -

Charles Moffett Jr.(ts) Kenny Drew Jr.(p) Charnett Moffett(b) Charles Moffett Sr.(dm).
(RPM Studios) NYC,March 13,1987

Softly as in a morning sunrise BN BLJ-46993,CD 7-46993-2

Kenny Kirkland(synth) Charnett Moffett(b) Mino Cinelu(perc).Same date.

For you BN BLJ-46993,CD 7-46993-2

Kenny Drew Jr.(synth) Charnett Moffett(b,el b,dm machine-1) Mino Cinelu(perc-1) Codaryl "Cody" Moffett (cymbals-1).
(RPM Studios) NYC,March 15,1987

One left over BN BLJ-46993, CD 7-46993-2
Net man -1 - -

DIANNE REEVES:
Dianne Reeves(vo) with Freddie Hubbard(flh) Billy Childs-1,George Duke-2 (p) Stanley Clarke(b) Tony Williams(dm) Airto Moreira(perc-1).
(Mama Jo's) LA,early April ,1987

Yesterdays -1
I've got it bad and that ain't good -2 CD BN 8-55221-2

Both titles issued on BN BLJ-46906,CD 7-46906-2.

THE DON PULLEN/GEORGE ADAMS QUARTET - SONG EVERLASTING:
George Adams(fl,ts) Don Pullen(p) Cameron Brown(b) Dannie Richmond(dm).
(RCA Studio C) NYC,April 21,1987

(tk.5) Sun watchers BN BLJ-46907
(tk.4) Warm up -
(tk.3) 1529 Gunn Street -
(tk.1) Serenade for Sariah -
(tk.1) Sing me a song everlasting - CD 8-23513-2
(tk.3) Another reason to celebrate

All titles issued on CD BN 7-46907-2.

DIANNE REEVES:
Dianne Reeves(vo) with Justo Almario(ts-1) Herbie Hancock(keyb) Paul Jackson Jr.(g) Freddie Washington (b) Leon "Ngudu" Chancler(dm) Paulinho Da Costa(perc) Jorge del Barrio(synclavier strings).
(Mama Jo's) LA,early May 1987

Harvest time -1 BN BLJ-46906;CD BN 7-46906-2,(J)CJ20-5029
Never said (Chan's song) - BST2-92477
CD BN 7-46906-2,7-92477-2,4-95701-2,
(J)TOCJ-5963,TOCJ-6088
Never said (Chan's song) (single mix) CD BN(J)CJ20-5029

 319

MOSE ALLISON - EVER SINCE THE WORLD ENDED:
Arthur Blythe(as-1) Bobby Malach,Bennie Wallace-2 (ts) Mose Allison(p,vo) Dennis Irwin(b) Tom Whaley (dm). (RPM Studios) NYC,May 10,1987

(tk.10)	Josephine	
(tk.2)	Gettin' there -1	CD BN 8-55230-2
(tk.3)	Ever since the world ended -1,2	-

All titles issued on BN BLJ-48015,CD 7-48015-2.

Mose Allison(p,vo) Kenny Burrell(g) Dennis Irwin(b) Tom Whaley(dm).
(RPM Studios) NYC,May 11,1987

(tk.5)	Indian Summer	CD BN(J)TOCJ-5853
(tk.3)	Tumblin' tumbleweed	
(tk.4)	I looked in the mirror	BN BLJ-48015,CD BN 8-55230-2
(tk.4)	What's your movie?	- -

All titles issued on CD BN 7-48015-2.

Bobby Malach(as) Bennie Wallace(ts) Mose Allison(p,vo) Dennis Irwin(b) Tom Whaley(dm).
(M & I Recorders) NYC,May 21,1987

(tk.4)	Tai Chi life	
(tk.4)	Trouble in mind	
(tk.8)	Top forty	CD BN 8-55230-2,5-21153-2,(C)4-94888-2

All titles issued on BN BLJ-48015,CD 7-48015-2.

DIANNE REEVES:
Dianne Reeves(vo) with Billy Childs(p) George Duke(synth-1) Tony Dumas(b) Ralph Penland(dm).
(Le Gonks West) LA,late May 1987

That's all	BN BLJ-46906
I'm O.K.-1	-

Both titles also issued on CD BN 7-46906-2.

MOSE ALLISON - EVER SINCE THE WORLD ENDED:
Mose Allison(p,vo) Dennis Irwin(b) Tom Whaley(dm).
(M & I Recorders) NYC,June 2,1987

(tk.6)	I'm alive	
(tk.4)	Puttin' up with me	CD BN 8-55230-2

Both titles issued on BN BLJ-48015,CD 7-48015-2.

DIANNE REEVES:
Dianne Reeves(vo) with George Duke(p,synth) Paul Jackson Jr.(g) Freddie Washington(b) Rickey Lawton (dm) Paulinho Da Costa(perc).
(Mama Jo's) LA,early June 1987

Sky islands	BN BLJ-46906,5-21147-1 CD BN 7-46906-2,5-21147-2,(J)CJ20-5029, TOCJ-6088
Better days	BN BLJ-46906,BST2-92477,B1-92812 CD BN 7-46906-2,7-92477-2,7-92812-2, 8-33878-2,(J)CJ32-5049,Rhino 75869-2, The Right Stuff 8-54486-2
Better days (single mix)	CD BN(J)CJ20-5029

320

BENNIE WALLACE - BORDER TOWN:
Ray Anderson(tb) Bennie Wallace(ts) Mac Rebennack (Dr. John)(p,org) John Scofield(g) Eddie Gomez(b) Herlin Riley(dm).
(Skyline Studios) NYC,June 8-13,1987

Skanctified
East Nine
Dance with a dolly (with a hole in her stocking) (g out)

All titles issued on BN B1-48014,CD 7-48014-2.

Ray Anderson(tb) Bennie Wallace(ts) Mac Rebennack (Dr. John)(p) John Scofield(g) Eddie Gomez(b) Chris Parker(dm). Same sessions.

Stormy weather
Seven sisters (tb out)

Both titles issued on BN B1-48014,CD 7-48014-2

Bennie Wallace(ts) Mac Rebennack (Dr. John)(p,org) John Scofield,Mitch Watkins(g) Will Lee(b) Chris Parker (dm) Herlin Riley(perc) Same sessions.

Border town BN B1-48014,CD 7-48014-2,(J)CJ32-5049

Bennie Wallace(ts) John Scofield(g) Eddie Gomez(b) Alvin Queen(dm)
Same sessions.

Bon-a-rue BN B1-48014,CD 7-48014-2

Bennie Wallace(ts) Mitch Watkins(g) Jay Anderson(b) Jeff Hirshfield(dm).
Same sessions.

Carolina moon BN B1-48014,CD 7-48014-2

JACK WALRATH:
Jack Walrath(tp) Willie Nelson(vo,g-1) James Williams(p).
(Pedermales Recording Studio) Spicewood,Texas,June 9,1987

A big bouquet of roses-1
I'm so lonesome I could cry,pt.2

Both titles issued on BN BLJ-46905,CD 7-46905-2.

BENNIE WALLACE - BORDER TOWN:
Bennie Wallace(ts) Mac Rebennack (Dr. John)(p) Mitch Watkins(g) Jay Anderson(b) Herlin Riley(dm).
(Skyline Studios) NYC,June 11,1987

It's only a paper moon CD BN 7-48014-2

321

FREDDIE HUBBARD-WOODY SHAW - THE ETERNAL TRIANGLE:

Freddie Hubbard,Woody Shaw(tp) Kenny Garrett(as) Mulgrew Miller(p) Ray Drummond(b) Carl Allen(dm).
Englewood Cliffs,N.J.,June 11,1987

tk.3	The Moontrane	
tk.5	Down under	CD BN 7-93202-2
tk.7	Tomorrow's destiny	
tk.8	Nostrand and Fulton	CD BN 4-95701-2
tk.9	Calling Miss Khadija	BN BST2-92474,CD 7-92474-2

All titles issued on BN B1-48017,CD 7-48017-2,8-32747-2.

Same.

Englewood Cliffs,N.J.,June 12,1987

tk.11	Reets and I	
tk.12	The eternal triangle	BN B1-48017
tk.13	Sao Paulo (as out)	

All titles issued on CD BN 7-48017-2,8-32747-2.

BIRELI LAGRENE - INFERNO:

Bill Evans(ts-1) Clifford Carter(keyb) Bireli Lagrene(g) Victor Bailey(el b) Bernard Purdie(dm) Cafe(perc-2).
(RPM Studios) NYC,July 4,1987

Rock it -1
Hips -2

Both titles issued on BN B1-48016,CD 7-48016-2.

Bill Evans(ts-1) Clifford Carter(keyb) Bireli Lagrene(g) Victor Bailey(el b) Dave Weckl-1,Danny Gottlieb-2 (dm) Cafe(perc-1).
(RPM Studios) NYC,July 5,1987

Incertitude -1
Ballade -2

All titles issued on BN BLJ-48016,CD 7-48016-2.

Bill Evans(ts-1) Clifford Carter(keyb) Bireli Lagrene(g) Victor Bailey(el b) Dave Weckl-1,Pierre Moerlen (dm-2) Cafe(perc-3).
(RPM Studios) NYC,July 6,1987

Berga -1	
Action -1,3	
Inferno -2,3	CD BN(J)TOCJ-5602

All titles issued on BN BLJ-48016,CD 7-48016-2.

Bireli Lagrene(g) solo.
(RPM Studios) NYC,July 8,1987

Rue de pierre,part two	BN BLJ-48016,CD 7-48016-2

322

MICHEL PETRUCCIANI - MICHEL PLAYS PETRUCCIANI:
Michel Petrucciani(p) John Abercrombie(g-1) Gary Peacock(b) Roy Haynes(dm).
(Clinton Studios) NYC,September 24,1987

She did it again — BN BST2-92474
CD BN 7-89916-2,7-92474-2,7-96904-2,
4-97563-2,HMV Jazz(E)5-20873-2

One for us -1
Sahara — CD Cap(J)TOCJ-5191/92
13th
Mr. K.J.

All titles issued on BN B1-48679,CD 7-48679-2,(F)4-97604-2.

Michel Petrucciani(p) John Abercrombie(g-1) Eddie Gomez(b) Al Foster(dm) Steve Thornton(perc-2).
(Clinton Studios) NYC,December 9 & 10, 1987

One night at Ken and Jessica's
It's a dance -1 — CD BN(J)CJ32-5049
La Champagne — CD BN 7-89916-2
Brazilian suite -2 — - (J)TOCJ-5187/88

All titles issued on BN B1-48679,CD 7-48679-2,(F)4-97604-2.

TONY WILLIAMS - ANGEL STREET:
Wallace Roney(tp) Billy Pierce(ss,ts) Mulgrew Miller(p) Charnett Moffet(b) Tony Williams(dm).
(Clinton Studios) NYC,April 4-6,1988

Angel street
Touch me
Red mask — CD BN 8-53331-2,4-95701-2
Kiss me
Dreamland
Only with you
Pee Wee — CD BN 8-53331-2,(J)TOCJ-6141
Thrill me
Obsession

All titles issued on BN B1 48494,CD 7-48494-2.

DIANNE REEVES:
Dianne Reeves(vo) with Greg Osby(as-1) Bobby Hutcherson(vb) Donald Brown(p) Charnett Moffett(b)
Marvin "Smitty" Smith(dm) Ron Powell(perc).
Englewood Cliffs,NJ,April 27,1988

tk.2 Softly as in a morning sunrise -1 — BN B1-90264
CD BN 7-90264-2,5-21151-2,(J)TOCJ-5855,
TOCJ-6088,TOCJ-6135
tk.3 Ancient source — CD BN(J)TOCJ-5849

Both titles issued on BN(J)RJ28-5020,CD CJ32-5020,TOCJ-5967.

Dianne Reeves(vo) with Kevin Eubanks(ac g) Ron Powell(wind chimes).
Englewood Cliffs,NJ,April 27,1988

tk.2 Like a lover — BN B1-90264,(J)RJ28-5020
CD BN 7-90264-2,7-81331-2,(J)CJ32-5020,
TOCJ-5967,TOCJ-6189

323

DIANNE REEVES:

Dianne Reeves(vo) with Greg Osby(as-1) Mulgrew Miller(p) Charnett Moffett(b) Marvin "Smitty" Smith (dm).
Englewood Cliffs,NJ,April 28,1988

(tk.2)	For all we know -1	BN B1-90264,CD 7-90264-2
(tk.2)	You taught my heart to sing	-
		CD BN 7-90264-2,7-96583-2,5-24271-2, Manhattan 7-99490-2
	How high the moon	rejected
	Do whatcha gotta do	-

First two titles also issued on BN(J)RJ28-5020,CD CJ32-5020,TOCJ-5967.

BOBBY WATSON & HORIZON - NO QUESTION ABOUT IT:

Roy Hargrove(tp) Bobby Watson(as) John Hicks(p) Curtis Lundy(b) Victor Lewis(dm).
(Skyline Studios) NYC,May 1,1988 (afternoon)

(tk.7)	Country corn flakes
(tk.5)	And then again
(tk.3)	Forty acres and a mule
(tk.3)	No question about it

All titles issued on BN B1-90262,CD 7-90262-2.

Roy Hargrove(tp) Frank Lacy(tb) Bobby Watson(as) John Hicks(p) Curtis Lundy(b) Kenny Washington (dm). (Skyline Studios) NYC,May 1,1988 (night)

(tk.1)	Blood count	BN B1-90262,CD 7-90262-2,5-20809-2
(tk.2)	What can I do for you (tp out)	- -
(tk.4)	As quiet as it's kept (tp out)	unissued
(tk.1)	Moonrise (tp out)	BN B1-90262,CD 7-90262-2

DIANNE REEVES:

Dianne Reeves(vo) with Mulgrew Miller(p) Charnett Moffett(b) Terri Lyne Carrington(dm).
Englewood Cliffs,NJ,May 9,1988

(tk.2)	Spring can really hang you up the most (b,dm out)	
(tk.2)	The nearness of you/Misty	
(tk.2)	How high the moon	BN B1-90264
		CD BN 7-90264-2,(Eu)7-89910-2,(J)TOCJ-5608

All titles issued on BN (J)RJ28-5020,CD CJ32-5020,TOCJ-5967.

BIRELI LAGRENE - FOREIGN AFFAIRS:

Bireli Lagrene(g) Koono(keyb) Jeff Andrews(el b) Dennis Chambers(dm) Cafe(perc).
(RPM Studios) NYC August 10-12,1988

Timothee -1	BN BST2-92477,B1-92812
	CD BN 7-92477-2,7-92812-2
Joseph -2	
Jack Rabbit	CD BN 7-96581-2,HMV Jazz(E)5-20884-2
Foreign affairs	
Passing through the night	
Senegal	
St. Jean	
I can't get started-3	

-1: Bireli Lagrene overdubbed vocal and el b melody and solo.
-2: Jurgen Attig(el b) replaces Andrews.
-3: Bireli Lagrene(ac g) Koono(keyb) Cafe(perc) only.
All titles issued on BN B1-90967,CD 7-90967-2.

324

BIRELI LAGRENE - FOREIGN AFFAIRS:
Bireli Lagrene(ac g).

Same sessions

Rue de Pierre,part three	BN B1-90967
Rue de Pierre,part four	
Rue de Pierre,part five	

All parts issued on CD BN 7-90967-2.

JACK WALRATH - NEOHIPPUS:
Jack Walrath(tp) Carter Jefferson(ts,cl-1) James Williams(p) John Abercrombie(g Anthony Cox(b Ronnie Burrage(dm).

(A & R Studios) NYC,August 19 & 21,1988

Village of the darned	BN B1-91101
Watch your head	-
Fright night	-
Annie Lee	-
England -1	-
Beer!	-
Future reference -2	
The smell of the blues -2	

-2: Rick Margitza(ts) added.
All titles issued on CD BN 7-91101-2.

TOMMY SMITH - STEP BY STEP:
Tommy Smith(ts) Mitchell Forman(p,keybs) John Scofield(el g) Eddie Gomez(b) Jack DeJohnette(dm).
(EMI-England) (Clinton Studios) NYC,September 7/8,1988

Ally the wallygator	BNB1-91930,B1-92812,(E)BLT 1001	
	CD BN 7-92812-2	
Step by step	BN B1-91930,(E)BLT 1001	
Ghosts	-	-
Pillow talk	-	-
Time piece	-	-
Springtime	-	-
Freetime		
Ever never land		

All titles issued on CD BN 7-91930-2,(E)CDBLT 1001.

STANLEY TURRENTINE - LA PLACE:
Freddie Hubbard(tp-1) Stanley Turrentine(ts) Bobby Lyle(keyb,arr) Paul Jackson,Jr.-2,David T. Walker-3 (g) Abe Laboriel (el b) Michael Baker(dm) Jean Carne(vo).

(Ocean Way Studios) LA,September 5-19,1988

Terrible T -1	
Touching -3,4	CD Manhattan 7-99490-2
Night Breeze -2,4,5 (voJC)	

-4: Radan Kuyumjian,Michele Zivahl,Daniel Smith,Vanesse Kibbe,Cynthia Morrow,Jean Hugo,Herschel Wise,David Shamban,Horia Moroaica(strings) Booker White(cond) added.
-5: Tony Lewis(dm) replaces Baker.

All titles issued on BN B1-90261,CD 7-90261-2.

325

STANLEY TURRENTINE - LA PLACE:
Michael Stewart(tp-1) Stanley Turrentine(ts) Bobby Lyle(keyb,arr) Paul Jackson,Jr.(g) Kevin Brandon-1, Gerald Albright-2(el b) Michael Baker(dm) Paulinho Da Costa(perc)

(Ocean Way Studios) LA,September 5-19,1988

Crusin'-1
Take 4 -2

Both titles issued on BN B1-90261,CD 7-90261-2.

Stanley Turrentine(ts) Bobby Lyle(keyb,arr) Phil Upchurch-1,Paul Jackson,Jr.-2(g) Kevin Brandon-1,Abe Laboriel-2 (el b) Michael Baker(dm)

(Aire L.A. Studios) LA,September 5-19,1988

La Place Street -1
Sparkie -2

Both titles issued on BN B1-90261,CD 7-90261-2.

McCOY TYNER - REVELATIONS:
McCoy Tyner(p).

(Merkin Hall) NYC,October 25,1988

(tk.3)	Don't blame me	
(tk.1)	You taught my heart to sing	CD BN 7-96098-2, 7-96904-2,8-37051-2, (J)TOCJ-6187
(tk.1)	Lazy bird	
(tk.2)	Contemplation	
(tk.8)	Someone to watch over me	CD BN 7-99427-2,(J)TOCJ-6190

All titles issued on BN B1-91651,CD 7-91651-2.

Same.

(Merkin Hall) NYC,October 26,1988

(tk.3)	Rio	BN B1-91651
(tk.2)	Yesterdays	-
(tk.2)	How deep is the ocean	-
(tk.1)	When I fall in love	CD BN(J)TOCJ-5875,Cap(J)TOCJ-5713
(tk.11)	In a mellow tone	BN B1-91651,CD 5-20809-2

All titles issued on CD BN 7-91651-2.

Same.

(Merkin Hall) NYC,October 27,1988

(tk.2)	Autumn leaves	CD BN(J)TOCJ-5260,Cap(J)TOCJ-5618/19
(tk.1)	View from the hill	BN B1-91651
(tk.5)	Peresins	

All titles issued on CD BN 7-91651-2.

 326

FREDDIE HUBBARD - TIMES ARE CHANGIN':
Freddie Hubbard(tp,flh) Todd Cochran(keyb,arr) Stanley Clarke(b-1) Stix Hooper(dm-2) Munyungo Jackson (perc) Michael Shrieve(cymbals,el perc-3) Ben Dowling(sound design-4) John Lehmkuhl(programming-5) Phil Perry(vo-6).
Burbank,Calif.,July-November,1988

Spanish rose -1,2,4
Back to lovin' again
Was she really there? -4,5,6
Corazon amplio (A song for Bert)
Times are changin' -2,3
Sabrosa
Fragile -3

All titles issued on BN B1-90905,CD 7-90905-2.

STANLEY JORDAN - CORNUCOPIA:
Stanley Jordan(synth g).
(PLM Hotel) Fort de France (Martinique),December 2,1988

Cornucopia BN B1-92356,CD 7-92356-2

DON PULLEN - NEW BEGINNINGS:
Don Pullen(p) Gary Peacock(b) Tony Williams(dm).
(A & R Studios) NYC,December 16,1988

(tk.2)	Once upon a time	BN B1-91785	
(tk.3)	New beginnings	-	CD 7-96904-2,8-23513-2
(tk.3)	Warriors	-	
(tk.4)	Jana's delight	-	CD 8-23513-2
(tk.3)	Silence = Death (solo p)		
(tk.2)	At the Cafe Centrale	BN B1-91785,CD 4-95981-2,(J)TOCJ-5187/88, Cap(J)TOCJ-5191/92	
(tk.3)	Reap the whirlwind	BN B1-91785	

All titles issued on CD BN 7-91785-2.

CHARNETT MOFFETT - BEAUTY WITHIN:
Kenny Garrett(as-2) Charles Moffett Jr.(ts-1) Kenny Drew Jr.(p,synth) Charnett Moffett(b,el b,keyb,perc) Codaryl "Cody" Moffett(dm).
(R.P.M. Studios) NYC,late 1988

Love never fails -1
Dancing with love -2
Eastwood -2
The message

All titles issued on BN B1-91650,CD 7-91650-2.

Bernard Wright(synth,dm programming) Stanley Jordan(el g) Charnett Moffett(el b,dm programming).
(Studio J) NYC,late 1988

Angela BN B1-91650,CD 7-91650-2

Mondre Moffett(tp,synth strings) Bernard Wright(synth) Charnett Moffett(b,keyb) Charles Moffett Sr.(dm).
(The Studio) NYC,late 1988

My little one BN B1-91650,CD 7-91650-2

CHARNETT MOFFETT - BEAUTY WITHIN:
Kenny Drew Jr.(p,synth) Charnett Moffett(b,dm programming,synth,perc) Charisa Moffett(vo)
(The Studio) NYC,late 1988

Beauty within BN B1-91650,CD 7-91650-2

GIL MELLE - MINDSCAPE:
Gil Melle(reeds,synths,arr).
(Diamondhead) Malibu,CA 1988-89

Mindscape BN B1-92168
Double exposure -
Message from Mozambique -
Shadow and substance -
Bird of paradise -
The Blue Lion -
Anti-Gravitationnal
Neon canyons BN B1-92168
Swamp girl -
The richest man in Bogota

All titles issued on CD BN 7-92168-2.

LOU RAWLS - AT LAST:
Lou Rawls(vo) with David Newman(ts-1) Richard Tee(p,org,el p) Cornell Dupree(el g) Tinker Barfield(el b) Chris Parker(dm).
(Sunset Productions) NYC,January 9,1989

Oh, what a nite -1 CD BN 8-56689-2
Room with a view -2 CD Cap.7-98306-2
Two years of torture -1,2

-2: Jack Walrath(tp) Steve Turre(tb) Bobby Watson(as) David Newman(ts) Howard Johnson(bs) overdubbed on.
All titles issued on BN B1-91937, CD 7-91937-2.

Lou Rawls(vo) with Bobby Hutcherson(vb-1) Richard Tee(p,org,el p) Steve Khan(el g) Tinker Barfield(el b) Chris Parker(dm).
(Sunset Productions) NYC,January 10,1989

You can't go home no more -3,4 CD Cap.7-98306-2
That's where it's at -3,4
She's no lady -1
If I were a magician -1,5 (g,b,dm out) CD BN 8-56689-2

-2: Ray Charles(vo) David Newman(as) overdubbed on.
-3: George Benson(g,backgr.vo) Lou Rawls,Billy Vera(backgr.vo).Strings arr.by Billy Vera & Darrell Leonard overdubbed on.
-4: Jack Walrath(tp) Steve Turre(tb) Bobby Watson(as) David Newman(ts) Howard Johnson(bs) overdubbed on.
-5: string section arr.by Bobby Scott,overdubbed on.
All titles issued on BN B1-91937,CD 7-91937-2.

<u>LOU RAWLS</u> - <u>AT LAST</u>:
Lou Rawls,Dianne Reeves-1(vo) with David Newman(ss-2) Stanley Turrentine(ts-3) Richard Tee(p,org,el p) Cornell Dupree(el g) Tinker Barfield(el b) Chris Parker(dm).

	(Sunset Productions)	NYC,January 11,1989
	After the lights go down low -4	CD BN 7-96582-2
	Fine brown frame -1	CD Cap.7-98306-2
	At last -1,3,5	- BN 7-81331-2,8-56689-2, 5-20070-2
	Good intentions-2 (g out)	

-4: Jack Walrath(tp) Robin Eubanks(tb) Bobby Watson(as,arr) David Newman(ts) Howard Johnson(bs) overdubbed on.
-5: Jack Walrath(flh) Robin Eubanks,Steve Turre(tb) arr. by Bobby Watson,with string section arr.by Bobby Scott, overdubbed on.
All titles issued on BN B1-91937,CD 7-91937-2.

<u>DIANNE REEVES</u>:
Dianne Reeves(vo) with Stanley Turrentine(ts) Richard Tee(p) Cornell Dupree(el g) Tinker Barfield(el b) Chris Parker(dm).

	(Sunset Productions)	NYC,January 12,1989
	Do whatcha gotta do	rejected
	God bless the child	-

<u>ANDREW HILL</u> - <u>ETERNAL SPIRIT</u>:
Greg Osby(as) Bobby Hutcherson(vb) Andrew Hill(p) Rufus Reid(b) Ben Riley(dm).

		Englewood Cliffs,NJ,January 30,1989	
tk.3	Pinnacle (alt.)	BN	CD 7-92051-2
tk.4	Bobby's tune	BN B1-92051,	-
tk.8	Spiritual lover (alt.)		-
	Samba rasta	rejected	
tk.10	Golden sunset (alt.)	CD BN 7-92051-2	
tk.12	Tail feather	BN B1-92051,CD 7-92051-2	

Same.		Englewood Cliffs,NJ,January 31,1989
tk.15	Pinnacle	
tk.16	Golden sunset	
tk.17	Spiritual lover	
tk.21	Samba rasta	

All titles issued on BN B1-92051,CD 7-92051-2.

<u>DON GROLNICK</u> - <u>WEAVER OF DREAMS</u>:
Randy Brecker(tp) Barry Rogers(tb) Bob Mintzer(bass cl) Michael Brecker(ts) Don Grolnick(p) Dave Holland (b) Peter Erskine(dm).

	(Skyline Studios)	NYC,February 14-16,1989
	Nothing personal	
	Taglioni	
	A weaver of dreams	
	His majesty the baby	
	I want to be happy	
	Persimmons	
	Or come fog	
	Five bars	

All titles issued on CD BN 7-94591-2,8-57197-2.

329

STANLEY JORDAN:

Kenny Kirkland(p) Stanley Jordan(el g) Charnett Moffett(b) Jeff Watts(dm).

(Live,The Manhattan Center) NYC,March 21,1989

Impressions	BN B1-92356,CD 7-92356-2,8-31502-2
Return expedition	rejected
Autumn leaves	BN B1-92356,CD 7-92356-2, EMI-USA(J)TOCJ-5254
For you	
Cousin Mary	

All titles,except the rejected one,issued on CD BN 4-97810-2.

Stanley Jordan(el g).

Same concert

Willow weep for me	BN B1-92356,CD 7-92356-2
Flying home	
Over the rainbow	CD EMI(E)5-20535-2

All titles issued on CD BN 4-97810-2.

Bernard Wright(keyb) Stanley Jordan(el g) Yossi Fine(el b) J.T. Lewis(dm).

Same concert

Still got the blues	BN B1-92356,CD 7-92356-2,8-31502-2,4-97810-2
Lady in my life	CD BN 4-97810-2
Always know	rejected
Stairway to heaven	-

RICK MARGITZA - COLOR:

Rick Margitza(ss,ts) Joey Calderazzo(p) Jim Beard(synth-1) Steve Masakowski(g,el g) Marc Johnson(b) Adam Nussbaum(dm) Airto Moreira(perc-2).

(Power Station) NYC,April-May 1989

Widow's walk -2	BN B1-92279,	CD 7-92279-2	
Color scheme	-	-	
Ferris wheel (p,g out)	-	-	
Walts -2	-	-	
Change-up		-	
Anthem -1,2	BN B1-92279	-	(J)TOCJ-5217
Brace yourself -2	-	-	
Karensong -2	-	-	
We stand adjourned -2	-	-	

Rick Margitza(ss) Jim Beard(synth) Steve Masakowski(g-1).

(Power Station) NYC,April-May 1989

Our song -1	BN B1-92279.	CD 7-92279-2
Point of view	-	-

ELIANE ELIAS - SO FAR SO CLOSE:

Randy Brecker(flh) Michael Brecker(ts) Eliane Elias(p,synth,synth b-1) Jim Beard(synth programming) Will Lee(el b) Peter Erskine(dm) Don Alias(perc).

(Skyline/Clinton/Duplex Studios) NYC,May,1989

Bluestone (perc out)
Nightimer
Straight across (to Jaco) (flh,el b out)

All titles issued on BN B1-91411,CD 7-91411-2.

 330

ELIANE ELIAS - SO FAR SO CLOSE:
Eliane Elias(p,synth,vo) Jim Beard(synth programming) Will Lee(el b) Peter Erskine (dm,perc) Cafe(perc).
(Skyline/Clinton/Duplex Studios) NYC,May,1989

At first sight (voEE)-1
Barefoot (voEE) CD BN 8-33878-2,Manhattan 7-99490-2
So close,so far
Still hidden -2
With you in mind -2
Two way street -2

-1: Lee out.Elias plays synth b.
-2: Lee,Erskine,Cafe out.

All titles issued on BN B1-91411,CD 7-91411-2

STANLEY JORDAN - CORNUCOPIA:
Bernard Wright,Robert Zantay(synth) Stanley Jordan(el g,synth g) Michael Flythe,Kenwood Dennard(dm).
(Studio J) NYC, May, 1989

What's goin' on BN B1-92356,CD 7-92356-2,7-99105-2,
EMI-USA(J)TOCJ-5254

Bernard Wright,Robert Zantay(synth) Stanley Jordan(el g,synth g) Yossi Fine(el b) Flare Funston(dm).
(Studio J) NYC, May, 1989

Always know BN B1-92356,CD 7-92356-2

Stanley Jordan(synth) Robert Zantay(synth programmer) Kenwood Dennard(dm).
(Studio J) NYC, May, 1989

Asteroids BN B1-92356,CD 7-92356-2

BOBBY WATSON - THE INVENTOR:
Melton Mustafa(tp) Bobby Watson(as) Willie Williams(ts-1) Edward Simon(p,synth) Carroll Dashiell(b,el b)
Victor Lewis(dm) Don Alias(perc-2).
(A & R Studios) NYC,June ,1989

First day:
(tk.3) For children of all ages -1,2 BN B1-91915
(tk.2) Dreams so real -1 -
(tk.3) Homemade blues (for Bo)
(tk.3) P.D. on Great Jones Street -2 BN B1-91915

All titles issued on CD BN 7-91915-2.

Melton Mustafa(tp) Bobby Watson(as) Benny Green(p) Edward Simon(synth-1) Carroll Dashiell (b,el b)
Victor Lewis(dm).
(A & R Studios) NYC, June ,1989

Second day:
(tk.2) The inventor (for Dad)-1
(tk.2) The Shaw of Newark
(tk.2) The sun
(tk.1) The long way home (tp out)
(tk.1) Heckle and Jeckle

All titles issued on BN B1-91915,CD 7-91915-2.

331

MICHEL PETRUCCIANI - MUSIC:
Michel Petrucciani(p,org,synth) Andy McKee(b) Victor Jones(dm) Frank Colon(perc-1) Tania Maria(vo).
(The Record Plant) NYC,August ,1989

My bebop tune BN B1-92563
Happy birthday Mr.K -1
Memories of Paris -2,3 BN B1-92563,CD 7-99100-2
O Nama oye (voTM)-2 - CD 7-89916-2

-2: Adam Holzman(synth) Robbie Kondor(synth programming) added.
-3: Gil Goldstein(acc) added.
All titles issued on CD BN 7-92563-2,(F)4-97604-2.

Michel Petrucciani(p,org,synth) Robbie Kondor(synth programming) Eddie Gomez(b) Victor Jones(dm) Frank Colon(perc).
(The Record Plant) NYC,August ,1989

Lullaby BN B1-92563,CD 7-92563-2,7-89916-2, (C)8-56508-2,(F)4-97604-2,(J))TOCJ-6190

Michel Petrucciani(p,org,synth,vo) Adam Holzman(synth-1) Robbie Kondor(synth programming) Anthony Jackson(b) Lenny White(dm).
(The Record Plant) NYC,August ,1989

Looking up CD BN 7-89916-2,4-97563-2,(J)TOCJ-5603
Bite-1

Both titles issued on BN B1-92563,CD 7-92563-2,(F)4-97604-2.

Joe Lovano(ss-1) Michel Petrucciani(p,org,synth,vo) Adam Holzman(synth) Robbie Kondor(synth programming) Romero Lubambo(g-2) Chris Walker(el b) Lenny White(dm).
(The Record Plant) NYC, 1989

Play me BN B1-92563,CD 7-89916-2
Brazilian suite No.2 -2 - CD Manhattan 7-99490-2
Thinking of Wayne -1

All titles issued on CD BN 7-92563-2,(F)4-97604-2.

TONY WILLIAMS - NATIVE HEART:
Wallace Roney(tp) Bill Pierce(ss,ts) Mulgrew Miller(p) Ira Coleman-1,Bob Hurst-2 (b) Tony Williams(dm, arr,dir).
(Power Station) NYC,September 11-13,1989

Native heart -1 BN B1-93170
City of lights -1 - CD BN(J)TOCJ-5608
Crystal palace -1 - CD 8-53331-2
Extreme measures -2 -
Juicy fruits -2 - CD 8-53331-2
Two worlds -2 -
Liberty -3

-3: Tony Williams(dm solo).
All titles issued on CD BN 7-93170-2.

 332

McCOY TYNER - THINGS AIN'T WHAT THEY USED TO BE:
McCoy Tyner(p).
(Merkin Hall) NYC,November 2,1989

(tk.4) What's new BN B1-93598,CD 7-93598-2
(tk.6) The greeting - -
(tk.1) Naima - -
(tk.1) Search for peace - -
(tk.4) Things ain't what they used to be - -
(tk.3) Lush life -
(tk.3) Sweet and lovely -
(tk.1) Song for my lady -

JOHN SCOFIELD - TIME ON MY HANDS:
Joe Lovano(ts) John Scofield(g) Charlie Haden(b) Jack DeJohnette(dm).
(Power Station) NYC,November 19-21,1989

Wabash III BN B1-92894;CD BN(J)TOCJ-5217
Since you asked -
So sue me - CD 8-53330-2
Let's say we did -
Flower power (ts out) -
CD BN 7-96581-2,8-53330-2,(Au)8-14808-2,
HMV Jazz(E)5-20884-2
Stranger to the light BN B1-92894
Nocturnal mission -
Farmacology -
Time and tide (ts out)
Be hear now
Fat lip CD BN 4-99257-2,(J)TOCJ-5602

All titles issued on CD BN 7-92894-2.

McCOY TYNER - THINGS AIN'T WHAT THEY USED TO BE:
McCoy Tyner(p) John Scofield(g).
(Merkin Hall) NYC,November 27,1989

(tk.3) I mean you CD BN 8-33207-2
(tk.3) Here's that rainy day
(tk.2) Joy Spring

All titles issued on BN B1-93598,CD 7-93598-2.

George Adams(ts) McCoy Tyner(p). Same date.

(tk.3) Blues on the corner BN B1-93598,CD 7-93598-2
(tk.1) My one and only love - - 8-37051-2

BOB BELDEN ENSEMBLE - THE MUSIC OF STING:
Tony Kadleck,Tim Hagans,Jim Powell(tp,flh) John Fedchock(tb) George Moran(bass tb) Peter Reit(frh) Marcus Rojas(tu) Chick Wilson(fl,cl) Mike Migliore(picc,fl,as) Rick Margitza(ts) Bob Belden(ts,arr) Ron Kozak(bass cl,Eng h) Glenn Wilson(bs) Joey Calderazzo(p) Doug Hall (synth) John Hart(g) Jay Anderson(b) Jeff Hirshfield(dm).
(Power Station) NYC,December 1,1989

(tk.1) Dream of the blue turtles
(tk.3) Roxanne
(tk.4) They dance alone

All titles issued on CD BN 7-95137-2.

333

MOSE ALLISON - MY BACKYARD:

Tony Dagradi(ts) Mose Allison(p,vo) Bill Huntington(b) John Vidacovich(dm).
(Southlake Recording Studio) NO, December 5,1989

Big brother
Sentimental fool
The gettin' paid waltz CD BN 8-55230-2
Long song
Sleepy lagoon

All titles issued on BN B1-93840,CD 7-93840-2.

Tony Dagradi(ts) Mose Allison(p,vo) Bill Huntington(b).
(Southlake Recording Studio) NO,December 6,1989

Was
My backyard

Both titles issued on BN B1-93840,CD 7-93840-2,8-55230-2.

Mose Allison(p,vo) Steve Masakowski(g) Bill Huntington(b) John Vidacovich(dm).
(Southlake Recording Studio) NO,December 7,1989

Ever since I stole the blues CD BN 8-55230-2
You call it joggin'
Stranger in my own hometown
Dr. Jekyll and Mr. Hyde
That's your red wagon

All titles issued on BN B1-93840,CD 7-93840-2.

THE MANHATTAN PROJECT:

Wayne Shorter(ss,ts) Michel Petrucciani(p) Gil Goldstein,Pete Levin(synth) Stanley Clarke(b) Lenny White (dm) Rachelle Farrell(vo).
(Chelsea Studio) NYC,December 16,1989

Old wine,new bottles CD BN 7-94204-2
Dania -
Michel's waltz -
Stella by starlight -
Goodbye porkpie hat -
Virgo rising -
Nefertiti -
Summertime -
Autumn leaves (voRF) CD BN 8-27820-2,(E)8-53231-2,
Somethin' Else(J)TOCJ-5520

LOU RAWLS - IT'S SUPPOSED TO BE FUN:

Lou Rawls(vo) with Hank Crawford(as-1) Bobby Watson(as-2,horn arr-6) Richard Tee(p,el p, org,horn arr-5) Bob Belden(string synth-3) Cornell Dupree(el g) Tinker Barfield(el b) Chris Parker(dm) Ralph MacDonald-4 (cga,perc).

(M & I Recording) NYC,January 9,1990

All around the world -1,4,5,7	CD Cap.7-98306-2
This bitter earth -1,6,7	CD BN 8-56689-2
Moonglows -2,3,4	CD Manhattan 7-99490-2
Good morning blues -5,7	CD Cap.7-98306-2,8-56689-2

-7: Jack Walrath(tp) Steve Turre(tb) Bobby Watson(as) Rick Margitza(ts) Howard Johnson(bs) added.

All titles on BN B1-93841-2,CD 7-93841-2,(J)TOCJ-5253.

Lou Rawls(vo) with Jack Walrath(tp) Steve Turre(tb) Bobby Watson(as,horn arr-1) Rick Margitza(ts) Howard Johnson(bs) Richard Tee(p,el p,org,horn arr-2) Cornell Dupree(el g) Tinker Barfield(el b) Chris Parker(dm) Ralph MacDonald-2(cga,perc).

(M & I Recording) NYC,January 10,1990

That's heaven to me	rejected
Goodnight my love-1	BN B1-93841,CD 8-56689-2
Any day now-2,3	-

-3: add Eddie Harris(ts),overdubbed at Capitol Studios,LA.
Last two titles also issued on CD BN 7-93841-2,(J)TOCJ-5253.

Lou Rawls(vo) with Jack Walrath(tp) Steve Turre(tb) Bobby Watson(as,horn arr-1) Dick Oatts(alto fl,as) Rick Margitza(ts) Howard Johnson(bs) Richard Tee(p,el p,org,horn arr-2) Bob Belden-3(string synth,horn arr) Steve Khan(el g) Tinker Barfield(el b) Chris Parker(dm) Ralph MacDonald(perc-2).

(M & I Recording) NYC,January 11,1990

I wonder where our love has gone -1	BN B1-93841,CD 8-56689-2
If you gotta make a fool of somebody -2,4	
Don't let me be misunderstood -3	BN B1-93841
	CD Cap.7-98306-2

-4: add Eddie Harris(ts),overdubbed at Capitol Studios,LA.

All titles on CD BN 7-93841-2,(J)TOCJ-5253.

TOMMY SMITH - PEEPING TOM:

Tommy Smith(ts,wind synth) Jason Rebello(p) Paul Stacey(g,el g) Terje Gewelt(b) Ian Froman(dm).

(EMI-England) (Rainbow Studios) Oslo,January 9-13,1990

The new road	BN 7-94335-1,	(E)BLT 1002
Follow your heart	-	-
Merry go round	-	-
Slip of the tongue	-	-
Interval time		
Simple pleasures		
Peeping Tom	BN 7-94335-1,	(E)BLT 1002
Quiet picnic		
Affairs,please	BN 7-94335-1,	(E)BLT 1002
Harlequin	-	-
Boats and boxes		
Biting the apple	BN 7-94335-1,	(E)BLT 1002
Naked air		

All titles issued on CD BN 7-94335-2,(E)CDBLT 1002.

BENNY GREEN - LINEAGE:
Benny Green(p) Ray Drummond(b) Victor Lewis(dm).
(A & R Studios) NYC,January 30,1990

(tk.3)	Levitation	
(tk.4)	Debo's waltz	
(tk.1)	Trust	
(tk.1)	See see rider	
(tk.2)	Dat dere	CD BN(J)TOCJ-5608,Premier(E)CDJA 2

All titles issued onCD BN 7-93670-2.

BENNY GREEN - LINEAGE:
Benny Green(p).
(A & R Studios) NYC, January 31,1990

(tk.5)	If ever I would lose you	CD BN 7-93670-2
(tk.4)	I'll wait and pray	-
(tk.8)	Glass enclosure	-
	Ask me now	-
(tk.4)	Silent night	CD BN 7-94857-2

Benny Green(p) Ray Drummond(b) Victor Lewis(dm).
(A & R Studios) NYC,February 1,1990

(tk.2)	Phoebe's samba	CD BN 7-93670-2,(J)TOCJ-5603
(tk.3)	Li'l darlin'	-
(tk.2)	Crazy	- 7-96904-2

DON PULLEN - RANDOM THOUGHTS:
Don Pullen(p) James Genus(b) Lewis Nash(dm).
(A & R Studios) NYC,March 23,1990

(tk.2)	626 Fairfax	CD BN(J)TOCJ-5603
(tk.3)	Andre's ups and downs	CD BN 7-98291-2,8-23513-2,(Du)7-99918-2
(tk.2)	Endandered species (African American youth)	
(tk.3)	The dancer	
(tk.2)	Random thoughts	
(tk.1)	Indio Gitano	CD BN 8-23513-2,Cap(J)TOCJ-5259
(tk.1)	Ode to life (solo p)	CD BN 8-23513-2

All titles issued on CD BN 7-94347-2,(J)TOCJ-5230.

LOU RAWLS - IT'S SUPPOSED TO BE FUN:
Lou Rawls(vo) with Hank Crawford(as-1) Richard Tee(p,el p,org) Cornell Dupree(el g) Tinker Barfield(el b) Chris Parker(dm).
(M & I Recording) NYC,May 8,1990

But I do -1,2	
You're the one -2	BN B1-93841
One more time -3	- 8-56689-2
The last night of the world -1,3	- 8-29095-2
The Christmas song -1	CD BN 7-94857-2

-2: Jack Walrath(tp) Steve Turre(tb) Bobby Watson(as) Rick Margitza(ts) Seldon Powell(bs) Lon Price,Billy Vera(arr) added.
-3: Bob Belden(string synth) added.
All titles,except last,issued on CD BN 7-93841-2,(J)TOCJ-5253.

<u>YULE STRUTTIN'</u>:
BOBBY WATSON: Melton Mustafa(tp) Bobby Watson(ss,as) Edward Simon(p) Carroll Dashiell(b) Victor Lewis(dm).

(Clinton Studios) NYC,June 6,1990

	Vauncing chimes	CD BN 7-94857-2

JOHN SCOFIELD: John Scofied(g) Marc Johnson(b) Adam Nussbaum(dm).
same session

	Chipmunk Christmas	CD BN 7-94857-2

JOHN HART: John Hart(g).
same session: .

	O Tannenbaum	CD BN 7-94857-2

<u>RICK MARGITZA</u> - <u>HOPE</u>:
Rick Margitza(ss,ts,keyb) Steve Masakowski(g,bjo) Marc Johnson(b) Peter Erskine(dm) Airto Moreira(perc).
(Power Station) NYC,June 9,1990

(tk.2)	We the people-1
(tk.3)	The princess
(tk.2)	Heritage-1
(tk.2)	The old country-1
(tk.2)	Mother's day (ts & b only)

-1: Richard Margitza(v) Olivia Koppell(viola) Jesse Levy(cello) Charles Pillow(oboe) Ed Calle(EWI,voice) added.
All titles issued on CD BN 7-94858-2.

Rick Margitza(ss,ts) Joey Calderazzo(p) Steve Masakowski(g,bjo) Marc Johnson(b) Peter Erskine(dm) Airto Moreira(perc). (Power Station) NYC,June 10,1990

(tk.1)	Recess -1	CD BN 7-94858-2
(tk.2)	Little drummer boy (g,perc out)	CD BN 7-94857-2
(tk.1)	Walls -2 (g out)	CD BN 7-94858-2
(tk.2)	The journey	-

-1: Michael Beza,Tai Lescinski,Jennifer Priore,Daniel Solomon(vo) added.
-2: Jeff Kievit,Danny Cahn(tp) added.

Rick Margitza(ss,ts) Joey Calderazzo(p) Steve Masakowski(g,bjo) Marc Johnson(b) Peter Erskine(dm) Airto Moreira(perc) Phil Perry(vo-1).
(Power Station) NYC,June 11,1990

(tk.1)	Stepping stone
(tk.3)	Song of hope -1
(tk.1)	Cornfed

All titles issued on CD BN 7-94858-2.

<u>BOBBY McFERRIN & CHICK COREA</u> - <u>PLAY</u>:
Bobby McFerrin(vo) Chick Corea(p).

(Live at Wolftrap)	Vienna,Va.,June 23,1990
(& Live at Carnegie Hall)	NYC,June 27,1990
Spain	CD BN 8-53329-2
Even from me	CD MFP(E)CDMFP 6303
Autumn leaves	
Blues connotation	
'Round midnight	CD BN(J)TOCJ-6135,Cema S21-56915, MFP(E)CDMFP 6303
Blue bossa	CD BN 8-53329-2,(C)4-94888-2

All titles issued on CD BN 7-95477-2.

<u>RITA REYS</u> - <u>SWING & SWEET</u>:
Rita Reys(vo) with Bernard Berkhout(cl-1) Frits Landesbergen(vb-2,arr-3) Pim Jacobs(p) Wim Overgaauw (g) Ruud Jacobs(b) Peter Ypma(dm).
(EMI-Bovema,Holland)(Studio 44) Monster,Holland,mid 1990

I thought about you
That's all
I'm old fashioned -2
The way you look tonight -1,2
Lover man -1
Just in time
Cheek to cheek -1,2
My romance (RR & vb,b only)-2,3
Just one of those things -1,2
Skylark (RR & vb only)-2
Just friends -1,2,3
So many stars -2,3
Do I love you -1,2,3

All titles issued on CD BN(Du)7-95443-2.

<u>LOU RAWLS</u> - <u>IT'S SUPPOSED TO BE FUN</u>:
Lou Rawls(vo) Ron Stallings(fl) Frank Martin,Mike Mani(keyb,synth) Ray Obiedo(g) Gary Brown(b) Narada Michael Walden(dm) Greg Gonaway(perc) Clayton Richardson,Skylar Jett,Tony Lindsay,Nikita Germaine, D'Layne Huguez(backgr.vo).

(Tarpen Studios)	San Rafael,CA,July,1990
It's supposed to be fun	BN B1-93841,CD 7-93841-2,(J)TOCJ-5253

<u>BIRELI LAGRENE</u> - <u>ACOUSTIC MOMENTS</u>:
Bireli Lagrene(ac g,el b) Michel Camilo(p-1) Koono-2(p,keyb) Loic Pontieux(dm-3) Simon Pomara(perc-4).
(EMI-France) (Studio Davout) Paris,July ,1990

Made in France	CD BN 7-99100-2,TOCJ-5602
Acoustic moments	
Rhythm thing -4	CD BN(J)TOCJ-5602
Claire Marie -1,3,4	
All the things you ar e-2,3,4	
Three views of a secret -2,3,4	
Stretch -2,3,4	
Bass ballad -2,3,4	
Impressions -2,3	

All titles issued on CD BN 7-95263-2.

BIRELI LAGRENE - ACOUSTIC MOMENTS:
Bireli Lagrene(el g) Loic Pontieux(dm).

Same sessions

Metal earthquake CD BN 7-95263-2

YULE STRUTTIN':
ELIANE ELIAS/JOEY CALDERAZZO: Eliane Elias-1,Joey Calderazzo-2 (p) Jay Anderson(b) Adam Nussbaum(dm).
(Clinton Studios) NYC,July 2,1990

I'll be home for Christmas/Sleigh ride -1 CD BN 7-94857-2
God rest ye merry gentlemen -2 -

ANDREW HILL - BUT NOT FAREWELL:
Robin Eubanks(tb) Greg Osby(ss,as) Andrew Hill(p) Lonnie Plaxico(b) Cecil Brooks III(dm).
(Clinton Studios) NYC,July 12,1990

tk.6	But not farewell	CD BN(J)TOCJ-5603
tk.10	Westbury	CD Knitting Factory CD 249
tk.12	Georgia ham	
tk.17	Nicodemus	

All titles issued on CD BN 7-94971-2.

Same. (Clinton Studios) NYC,July 13,1990

tk.18	Friends -1	CD BN 7-94971-2
	Nicodemus	rejected
	But not farewell	-
	Westbury	-

-1: Osby(as) Hill(p) only.

YULE STRUTTIN':
DIANNE REEVES: Dianne Reeves(vo) David Torkanowsky(p).
(LeGonks West) LA,July 20,1990

A merrier Christmas CD BN 7-94857-2

BENNY GREEN: Benny Green(p).
(Jim Anderson's home studio) Brooklyn,July 29,1990

A merrier Christmas CD BN 7-94857-2

BOB BELDEN ENSEMBLE - THE MUSIC OF STING:
Tony Kadleck,Tim Hagans,Jim Powell(tp,flh) John Fedchock(tb) George Moran(bass tb) Peter Reit(frh) Marcus Rojas(tu) Chick Wilson(fl,cl) Mike Migliore(fl,alto fl,as) Tim Reis(ss,ts) Rick Margitza(ts) Bob Belden(ts,arr) Ron Kozak(bass fl,bass cl,Eng h) Glenn Wilson(bs) Joey Calderazzo,Marc Copland(p) Kevin Hays(el p) Doug Hall(synth) John Scofield,Fareed Haque,John Hart(g) Jay Anderson(b) Jeff Hirshfield(dm) Jerry Gonzalez,David Earle Johnson(perc).
(Power Station) NYC,August 19,1990

tk.1	Shadows in the rain	CD BN 7-95137-2
tk.2	Straight to my heart	-
	Roxanne	rejected
tk.4	Children's crusade	CD BN 7-95137-2
	They dance alone	rejected

339

JOEY CALDERAZZO - IN THE DOOR:
Branford Marsalis(ts) Joey Calderazzo(p) Jay Anderson(b) Adam Nussbaum(dm).
(Carriage House) Stamford,Conn., September ,1990

In the door CD BN 7-95138-2

Branford Marsalis(ss) Joey Calderazzo(p) Jay Anderson(b) Peter Erskine(dm).
Same sessions

Mikell's
The missed CD BN(J)TOCJ-5603

Both titles issued on CD BN 7-95138-2.

Jerry Bergonzi(ts-1) Joey Calderazzo(p) Jay Anderson(b) Adam Nussbaum(dm) Don Alias(perc-2)
Same sessions

Spring is here -1 CD BN(J)TOCJ-5851
Dome's mode -1
Loud-Zee -1,2
Chubby's Lament -2

All titles issued on CD BN 7-95138-2.

Michael Brecker(ts) Joey Calderazzo(p) Jay Anderson(b) Adam Nussbaum(dm).
Same sessions

Pest CD BN 7-95138-2,(J)TOCJ-5712

DIANNE REEVES:
Dianne Reeves(vo) with Justo Almario(ss) Charles Mims(p,arr) Chris Severin(b) Billy Kilson(dm) Bill Summers,Luis Conte(perc).
(Madhatter Studios) LA,September 10,1990

Afro blue BN B1-80701,B1-90264
CD BN 7-90264-2,7-80701-2, (J)TOCJ-5608, TOCJ-5967

DIANNE REEVES:
Dianne Reeves(vo) with Billy Childs(p) Chris Severin(b) Billy Kilson(dm).
(Madhatter Studios) LA,September 11,1990

The nearness of you/Misty CD BN (C)4-94888-2,(J)TOCJ-5858, Cap(J)TOCP-7662
I remember sky CD BN(Du)7-99918-2,Cap(J)TOCP-7662
Love for sale CD BN(J)TOCJ-5712

All titles issued on BN B1-90264,CD BN 7-90264-2,(J)TOCJ-5967.

ANDREW HILL:
Andrew Hill(p).
(Clinton Studios) NYC,September 16,1990

Sunnyside CD BN 7-94971-2,7-96904-2
Gone -

BOBBY WATSON AND HORIZON - POST MOTOWN BOP:
Melton Mustafa(tp) Bobby Watson(ss,as) Edward Simon(p) Carroll Dashiell(b) Victor Lewis(dm).
(Power Station) NYC,September 17,1990

(tk.3)	In case you missed it	
(tk.2)	Last chance to groove	CD Premier(E)CDJA 2
(tk.5)	Slippin' and slidin'	
(tk.2)	Falling in love with love	
(tk.3)	Big girls	

All titles issued on CD BN 7-95148-2.

Same.
(Power Station) NYC,September 18,1990

(tk.1)	Bah-da-da-da-dah-dah
(tk.3)	7th Avenue
(tk.1)	Appointment in Milano
(tk.1)	In a sentimental mood
(tk.2)	The Punjab of Java Po

All titles issued on CD BN 7-95148-2.

GREG OSBY - MAN-TALK FOR MODERNS Vol. X:
Greg Osby(as,ss) Gary Thomas(ts-1) Edward Simon(p,keyb) David Gilmore-1,Chan Johnson-2(el g) Lonnie Plaxico(b) James Genus(el b-3) Billy Kilson(dm) Steve Moss(perc-4).
(Systems Two) Brooklyn,NY,November 9 & 10,1990
& December 10 1990

On a mission -1,2
Carolla -2
Lo-fi -2,4
For here to go -2,3,4
Like so... -4

All titles issued on CD BN 7-95414-2.

Gary Thomas(fl-2) Greg Osby(as,ss) Steve Coleman(as-1) Edward Simon(p,keyb) David Gilmore,Chan Johnson(el g-1) James Genus(b) Billy Kilson(dm) Steve Moss(perc).
Same sessions

Man talk -1	CD BN 7-95414-2, 7-98291-2,(Du)7-99918-2, (Eu)7-99790-2
Black moon (for Geri)-2	CD BN 7-95414-2,(Eu)7-89910-2
Man-talk (Giant step mix)-1	CD Cap(J)TOCJ-5848

Greg Osby(as,ss,keyb) Michael Cain(keyb-1) Edward Simon(p,keyb) David Gilmore-1 (el g,synth) James Genus(el b) Billy Kilson(dm) Steve Moss(perc).
Same sessions

2th (twooth)-1
Cad'lack back
Balaka -2

-2: Steve Coleman(as) Chan Johnson(el g) Steve Moss(perc Hochmad Ali Akkbar(vo) added.
All titles issued on CD BN 7-95414-2.

341

JOHN SCOFIELD - MEANT TO BE:
Joe Lovano(alto cl-1,ts) John Scofield(el g) Marc Johnson(b) Bill Stewart(dm).

	(Power Station)	NYC,December ,1990
	Big fan	CD BN 8-53330-2
	Keep me in mind	CD BN(J)TOCJ-5602
	Go blow	
	Chariots	CD BN 4-99257-2
	The Guinness spot	
	Mr. Coleman to you	
	Eisenhower	
	Meant to be	
	Some nerve	
	Lost in space -1	
	French flics -1	

All titles issued on CD BN 7-95479-2.

TOMMY SMITH - STANDARDS:
Tommy Smith(ts) Niels Lan Doky(p) Mick Hutton(b) Ian Froman(dm).

(EMI-England) (Rainbow Studio)		Oslo,January ,1991
	Star eyes	BN(E)BLT 1003
	Speak low	-
	Skylark	-
	September song	-
	Blacken blue	-
	Mil dew	-
	You've changed	-
	My secret love	-
	Night & day	-
	My old flame	-
	Julia	-
	Lover	-
	Dream scapes,pt.1	
	Silent but deadly (Dream scapes,pt.4)	

All titles issued on CD BN 7-96452-2,(E)CDBLT 1003.

McCOY TYNER - SOLILOQUY:
McCoy Tyner(p).

	(Merkin Hall)	NYC,February 19,1991
(tk.2)	Tribute to Lady Day	
(tk.2)	Crescent (alt)	
(tk.4)	Three flowers	
(tk.5)	Twilight mist	
(tk.1)	All the things you are	
(tk.1)	Willow weep for me	
(tk.3)	Crescent	
Same.	(Merkin Hall)	NYC,February 20,1991
(tk.1)	Lonnie's lament	CD BN 4-95701-2
(tk.5)	I should care	
(tk.6)	Effendi	
(tk.1)	After the rain	CD Manhattan 7-99490-2

All titles from both sessions issued on CD BN 7-96429-2.

 342

<u>McCOY TYNER</u> - <u>SOLILOQUY</u>:
McCoy Tyner(p).
(Merkin Hall) NYC,February 21,1991

(tk.2	Bouncin' with Bud	
(tk.3	Tivoli	
(tk.1	Espanola	

All titles issued on CD BN 7-96429-2.

<u>BENNY GREEN</u> - <u>GREENS</u>:
Benny Green(p) Christian McBride(b) Carl Allen(dm).
(Power Station) NYC,March 4,1991

(tk.2)	Second time around	
(tk.5)	Time after time	
(tk.3)	Greens	
(tk.2)	Decidedly	
(tk.3)	Soon	CD BN 5-20808-2
(tk.2)	You don't know what love is (solo p)	

All titles issued on CD BN 7-96485-2.

Same.
(Power Station) NYC,March 5,1991

(tk.1)	Captain Hook	CD BN 7-96485-2,(J)TOCJ-5793
(tk.3)	Shiny stockings	- Hip-O 547859-2, BN(J)TOCJ-6190
	In the wee small hours	rejected
(tk.2)	Battle hymn of the Republic	CD BN 7-96485-2
	Celia (solo p)	rejected
(tk.14)	Bish bash	CD BN 7-96485-2,4-95701-2
(tk.4)	I see your face before me	-
(tk.13)	Cute	-

<u>MICHEL PETRUCCIANI</u> - <u>PLAYGROUND</u>:
Michel Petrucciani(p) Adam Holzman(synth) Anthony Jackson(b) Omar Hakim(dm) Steve Thornton(perc).
(Clinton Studios) NYC,March 14-19,1991

September second	CD BN 7-89916-2,4-97563-2,(E)8-53228-2, (J)TOCJ-5853,HMV Jazz(E)5-20873-2
Home	CD BN 7-89916-2
P'tit Louis	
Miles Davis' licks	CD BN 7-89916-2
Rachid -1	
Brazilian suite #3	
Play school	
Contradictions	
Laws of physics	
Piango,pay the man (dm out)	
Like that	

-1: Aldo Romano(dm) replaces Hakim.
All titles issued on CD BN 7-95480-2,(F)4-97604-2.

BOB BELDEN ENSEMBLE - THE MUSIC OF STING:
Tony Kadleck,Tim Hagans,Jim Powell(tp,flh) John Fedchock(tb) George Moran(bass tb) Peter Reit(frh) Bob Stewart(tu) Chick Wilson(alto fl) Mike Migliore,Ron Kozak(bass fl) Bobby Watson(as) Tim Reis(bs) Benny Green(p) Jay Anderson(b) Jeff Hirshfield(dm) Phil Perry(vo,whistling) Bob Belden(arr).
(Giant Studio) NYC,April 24,1991

tk.2	Sister moon (voPP)	CD BN 7-95137-2,(Eu)7-89910-2

Tony Kadleck,Tim Hagans(tp) John Fedchock(tb) George Moran(bass tb) Bob Stewart(tu) Chuck Wilson (fl,alto fl) Mike Migliore(bass fl,as) Ron Kozak(bass fl,bass cl) Tim Reis(ss) Billy Childs(p) Bob Belden (synth,arr) John Scofield(g) Jimi Tunnell(g,synth,vo) Darryl Jones(el b) Dennis Chambers(dm) Ladji Camara,Abraham Adenzenya(perc) Dianne Reeves(vo).
(Power Station) NYC,May 6,1991

tk.1	Introduction/Wrapped around your finger (voDR)	CD BN 7-95137-2,(J)TOCJ-5712,TOCJ-6088
tk.2	I burn for you (voJT)	-

Chick Wilson,Mike Migliore,Ron Kozak(wooden fl) Kirk Whalum(ts) Pat Rebillot(org) Adam Holzman (synth) Darryl Jones(el b) Dennis Chambers(dm) Ladji Camara,Abraham Adenzenya(perc) Mark Ledford(vo) Bob Belden arr).
(Power Station) NYC,May 9,1991

tk.1	Every breath you take (voML)	CD BN 7-95137-2

RICK MARGITZA - THIS IS NEW:
Rick Margitza(ts) Joey Calderazzo(p) Robert Hurst(b) Jeff Watts(dm).
(Power Station) NYC,May 27,1991

(tk.3)	Just in time	CD BN 7-97196-2
(tk.4)	This is new	-
(tk.5)	Bye bye blackbird	unissued
(tk.3)	Invitation	CD BN 7-97196-2
(tk.2)	On Green Dolphin Street	-

Rick Margitza(ts) Joey Calderazzo(p) Robert Hurst(b) Jeff Watts(dm).
(Power Station) NYC,May 28,1991

(tk.1)	Stella by starlight	unissued
(tk.2)	Everything happens to me	CD BN 7-97196-2
(tk.6)	Beware of the dog -1	-
(tk.8)	Gypsies	-
	Cherokee	rejected
(tk.8)	When will the blues leave (p out)	CD BN 7-97196-2
(tk.1)	Body and soul (p out)	- 7-98291-2,(Eu)7-99790-2

-1: Tim Hagans(tp) added.

<u>CHUCHO VALDES</u> - <u>SOLO PIANO</u>:
Chucho Valdès(p).
(Ronnie Scott's Recording Facility) London,September ,1991

Isanusi
Felia
Nandy
Noliu CD World Pac.7-80599-2
Togo
Blue yes
My foolish heart
Bill (Evans)

All titles issued on CD BN 7-80597-2.

Chucho Valdès(p) Dave Green(b) Enrique Pla(dm) Miguel Diaz(perc).
(Ronnie Scott's Recording Facility) London,September ,1991

When I fall in love
Blues untitled

Both titles issued on CD BN 7-80597-2.

<u>IRAKERE</u> - <u>LIVE AT RONNIE SCOTT'S</u>:
Juan Monguia,Adalberto Moreno(tp) Caesar Lopez(ss,as) Carlos Averhoff(ts) Orlando Valle(fl,keyb) Chucho Valdes(p) Carlos Emilio Morales(g) Carlos Del Puerto(b) Enrique Pla(dm,perc) Oscar Valdes(vo,perc) Miguel "Anga" Diaz(cga).
(Ronnie Scott's Club) London,September ,1991

Neurosis
Cuando danta el corazon
Mirando arriba
Flute notes CD BN(Au)8-14710-2
Mr. Bruce
Claudia CD World Pac.7-80599-2

All titles issued on CD World Pacific 7-80598-2,BN(J)TOCJ-5832.

<u>DON PULLEN AND THE AFRICAN-BRAZILIAN CONNECTION</u> - <u>KELE MOU BANA</u>:
Carlos Ward(as) Don Pullen(p) Nilson Matta(b) Guilherme Franco(timba,berimbau,perc) Mor Thiam(djembe, tabula,rainsticks,wind chimes,vo).
(East Side Sound) NYC,September 25,1991

(tk.1) Capoeira BN B1-80701,CD 7-80701-2
(tk.1) Listen to the people CD BN(J)TOCJ-5712
(Bonnie's bossa nova)-1
(tk.1) Kele mo bana (voMT)
(tk.1) Cimili/Drum talk (voMT)
(tk.1) Doo-wop daze

-1: Keith Pullen,Tameka Pullen(vo) added.

All titles issued on CD BN 7-98166-2.

Same. (East Side Sound) NYC,September 26,1991

(tk.2) L.V.M./Directo ad assunto* *CD Knitting Factory CD 249
(tk.1) Yebino Spring

All titles issued on CD BN 7-98166-2.

345

JOEY CALDERAZZO - TO KNOW ONE:
Jerry Bergonzi(ts-1) Joey Calderazzo(p) Dave Holland(b) Jack DeJohnette(dm).
(Dreamland Recording Studio) West Hurley,NY,October ,1991

First impressions
To know one — CD BN 7-98291-2,(Du)7-99918-2,(Eu)7-99790-2
Caldo's revenge -1
Second thoughts -1
Splurge -1
Dexter -1
The code -1

All titles issued on CD BN 7-98165-2.

Branford Marsalis(ss-1,ts-2) replaces Bergonzi.Same sessions

Field of dreams -2
See saw -1
Song for Penelope -1 (b,dm out)
Reprise (solo p)

All titles issued on CD BN 7-98165-2.

ORPHY ROBINSON - WHEN TOMORROW COMES:
Rowland Sutherland(fl,picc) Leroy Osbourne(fl,g,vo)-1 Orphy Robinson(vb,marimba,perc) Tunde Jegede (kora,clo) Joe Bashorun(p,keyb) Dudley Phillips(b,el b) Winston Clifford(dm,perc).
(EMI-England) (Rainbow Studios) Oslo,October 11,12 & 13,1991

All at sixes and sevens
The bass of bad intentions
Jigsaw
Let's see what tomorrow brings
Back to the first bass
Bad means beautiful — CD BN(Du)7-99918-2
Jigsaw (reprise)
You haven't done nothing -1 — CD BN 7-99659-2,Cap(J)TOCJ-5848

All titles on CD BN 7-81212-2.
All titles,except last,issued on CD BN 7-98581-2,(E)CDBLT 1004.

T.S. MONK - TAKE ONE:
Don Sickler(tp,arr) Bobby Porcelli(as) Willie Willliams(ts) Ronnie Mathews(p) James Genus (b) T.S. Monk (dm).
Englewood Cliffs,NJ,October 16,1991

Monaco
Skippy
Infra-rae
Waiting
Boa
'Round midnight
Jodi
Bear cat
Capetown ambush
Shoutin'
Minor's holiday
Think of one

All titles issued on CD BN 7-99614-2.

346

BENNY GREEN TRIO - TESTIFYIN':
Benny Green(p) Christian McBride(b) Carl Allen(dm).
(Village Vanguard) NYC,November 8,1991

Set #1:
McThing CD BN 7-98171-2

Set #2:
Carl's blues CD BN 7-98171-2
Beautiful moons ago - (Eu)7-89910-2

Set #3:
Just a Tadd unissued

Same.
(Village Vanguard) NYC,November 9,1991

Set #1:
Spoken introduction by Green CD BN 7-98171-2
Humphrey -
Down by the riverside - (Eu)7-80703-2
I should care -
Testifyin' -

Set #2:
Don't be 'shamed CD BN 7-98171-2
Bu's march -
In the wee small hours unissued

Set #3:
The sheik of Araby CD BN 7-98171-2
Billy boy -
Me and my baby CD BN 7-98291-2,(Du)7-99918-2,(Eu)7-99790-2
Pensitiva unissued
Celia -

MICHEL PETRUCCIANI LIVE:
Michel Petrucciani(p) Adam Holzman(keyb) Steve Logan(b) Victor Jones(dm) Abdou M'Boop(perc).
(The Arsenal) Metz,France,November ,1991

Black magic
Miles Davis licks
Contradictions
Bite
Rachid
Looking up
Thank you note
Estate CD BN 4-97563-2,HMV Jazz(E)5-20873-2

All titles issued on CD BN 7-80589-2,(F)4-97604-2.

TONY WILLIAMS - THE STORY OF NEPTUNE:
Wallace Roney(tp) Bill Pierce(ss,ts) Mulgrew Miller(p) Ira Coleman(b) Tony Williams(dm).
(Power Station) NYC,November 29 & 30,1991
& December 1,1991

Neptune:Overture
Neptune:Fear not
Neptune:Creatures of conscience
Blackbird CD BN 8-53331-2
Crime scene
Poinciana
Birdlike CD BN(J)TOCJ-6141

All titles issued on CD BN 7-98169-2.

JOHN SCOFIELD- GRACE UNDER PRESSURE:
John Scofield(el g) Bill Frisell(ac g,el g) Charlie Haden(b) Joey Baron(dm).
(Power Station) NYC,December ,1991

You bet CD BN 8-53330-2
Grace under pressure CD BN(J)TOCJ-6134
Honest I do -1
Scenes from a marriage
Twang -1 CD BN 7-98291-2,4-99257-2,(Du)7-99918-2,
(Eu)7-99790-2
Pat me -1
Pretty out
Bill me
Same axe -1
Unique New York -1

-1: Randy Brecker(flh) John Clark(frh)Jim Pugh(tb) added.
All titles issued on CD BN 7-98167-2.

DON GROLNICK - NIGHTTOWN:
Randy Brecker(tp) Steve Turre(tb) Joe Lovano(ts) Marty Ehrlich(bass cl) Don Grolnick(p) Dave Holland(b)
Bill Stewart(dm).
(Skyline Studios) NYC,December ,1991

Heart of darkness
What is this thing called love
One bird,one stone
Nighttown
Genie
Spot that man
The cost of living
Blues for Pop

All titles issued on CD BN 7-98689-2,8-57197-2.

KEVIN EUBANKS - TURNING POINT:
Kent Jordan(alto fl) Kevin Eubanks(g) Dave Holland(b) Marvin "Smitty" Smith(dm).
(Sound On Sound) NYC,December 16-20,1991

Turning point
Aftermath
Initiation
Spiral ways

All titles issued on CD BN 7-98170-2.

KEVIN EUBANKS - TURNING POINT:
Kent Jordan(alto fl) Kevin Eubanks(g) Charnett Moffett(b) Mark Mondesir(dm).
(Sound On Sound) NYC,December 16-20,1991

New world order
Colors of one CD BN(J)TOCJ-6134
Freedom child
On my way to paradise
Lingering destiny (solo g)

All titles issued on CD BN 7-98170-2.

JOE LOVANO - FROM THE SOUL:
Joe Lovano(ts,ss-1,as-2) Michel Petrucciani(p) Dave Holland(b) Ed Blackwell(dm).
(Skyline Studios) NYC,December 28,1991

Evolution
Portrait of Jenny
Lines and spaces CD BN 4-95701-2
Body and soul CD BN(Sp)5-21755-2
Modern man -2 (p,b out)
Fort Worth (p out) CD BN 7-98291-2,(Du)7-99918-2,(Eu)7-99790-2
Central Park West -2
Work -1
Left behind (b,dm out)
His dreams

All titles issued on CD BN 7-98636-2.

NEW YORK STORIES:
Roy Hargrove(tp) Bobby Watson(as) Joshua Redman(ts) Franck Amsallem(p) Danny Gatton(g) Charles Farnbrough(b) Yoron Israel(dm).
(Unique Recording) NYC,February 16 & 17,1992

Dolly's ditty
Wheel within a wheel
Ice maidens
Out a day
Mike the cat
The move
A clear thought
5/4
One for Lenny

All titles issued on CD BN 7-98959-2.

TONY WILLIAMS - TOKYO LIVE:
Wallace Roney(tp) Bill Pierce(ss,ts) Mulgrew Miller(p) Ira Coleman(b) Tony Williams(dm).
(The Blue Note) Tokyo,March 3,1992

Set #1:
Civilization CD BN 7-99031-2

Same. (The Blue Note) Tokyo,March 4,1992
Set #2:
Citadel CD BN 7-99031-2
Warriors -

349

TONY WILLIAMS - TOKYO LIVE:
Wallace Roney(tp) Bill Pierce(ss,ts) Mulgrew Miller(p) Ira Coleman(b) Tony Williams(dm).

(The Blue Note) — Tokyo,March 5,1992

Set #1:

Crystal palace — CD BN 7-99031-2

Set #2:

Angel street — CD BN 7-99031-2

Same.

(The Blue Note) — Tokyo,March 7,1992

Set #1:

Mutants on the beach
Ancient eyes
The slump
Blackbird
Geo Rose
Life of the party — CD BN(J)TOCJ-6141

All titles issued on CD BN 7-99031-2.

Set #2:

Sister Cheryl — CD BN 7-99031-2
The announcements — -

STAN TRACEY OCTET - PORTRAITS PLUS:
Guy Barker(tp) Malcolm Griffiths(tb) Peter King(as) Don Weller(ts) Art Themen(ss,ts) Stan Tracey(p) Dave Green(b) Clark Tracey(dm).
(EMI-England) (EMI Abbey Road Studios) — London,March 30,1992

Newk's flute
Rocky Mount — CD BN 8-35471-2
One for Gil
Clinkscales
Spectrum No.2
Mainframe

All titles issued on CD BN 7-80696-2,(E)CDBLT 1006.

PYROTECHNICS (NEW BRITISH JAZZ FROM BLUE NOTE):
ORPHY ROBINSON: Rowland Sutherland(fl,alto fl) Orphy Robinson(marimba,perc) Joe Bashorun(p) Tunde Jegede(kora,cello) Dudley Phillips(b) Winston Clifford(dm).
(EMI-England) (Elephant Studios) — London,March 31-April 5,1992

Who fe tekit tekit — CD BN(Eu)7-99659-2

DJANGO BATES: Steve Buckley(as,tin whistle) Django Bates(E horn,p,keyb,g,vo) Michael Mondesir(b) Martin France(dm,perc).
(EMI-England) (Elephant Studios) — London,March 31-April 5,1992

Three architects called Gabrielle: just what I expected
Up up

All titles issued on CD BN(Eu)7-99659-2.

350

SYLVAN RICHARDSON JR.: Sylvan Richardson Jr.(keyb,b,vo) Nikki Iles(p,keyb) Mike Walker(g) Caroline Boaden(dm) & guests: Julian Arguelles(ts) Simon Limbrick(tabla,perc).
(EMI-England) (Elephant Studios) London,March 31-April 5,1992

Cathexis
Riccardo

Both titles issued on CD BN(Eu)7-99659-2.

TOMMY SMITH: Tommy Smith(ts) Jason Robello(p,keyb) Mike Walker(g) Mick Hutton(b) Tom Bancroft(dm).
(EMI-England) (Elephant Studios) London,March 31-April 5,1992

Why not
Children play

Both titles issued on CD BN(Eu)7-99659-2.

THE MONDESIR BROTHERS: Mo Nazam(g) Michael Mondesir(b) Mark Mondesir(dm).
(EMI-England) (Elephant Studios) London,March 31-April 5,1992

The ten worlds
The fantastic four

Both titles issued on CD BN(Eu)7-99659-2.

TONY REMY: Tony Remy(g,el g,programming) Nick E. Cohen(b) Roger Beaujolais(vb,glockenspiel) Karl Van den Bossche(perc) Cleveland Watkiss(vo).
(EMI-England) (Protocol Studios) London,April 6-8,1992

Boof!
Hazel's dream

Both titles issued on CD BN(Eu)7-99659-2.

Us3 - HAND ON THE TORCH:
Gerard Presencer(tp-1) Dennis Rollins(tb-2) Steve Williamson-3(ss,as) Ed Jones-4(ss,ts) Mike Smith(ts-5) Mel Simpson(p,keyb) Matt Cooper(p-6) Tony Remy(g-7) Roberto Pla(Latin perc-8) Kobie Powell,Rahsaan, Tukka Yoot(vo) Maria Harper(backgr.vo) Geoff Wilkenson (samples,programming).
(Flame Studios) London,Spring, 1992

*	Cantaloop (Flip fantasia) (voR)-1	BN B1-80883,(E)12CL672 CD BN 8-15892-2,8-58083-2,4-95701-2, 4-99351-2,5-20070-2,(Au)4-97893-2,(J)TOCJ-5897 TOCJ-6153,)TOCJ-6191,TOCJ-66063,TOCP-8966, (Sp)8-34712-2,Cap(J)TOCJ-5848
	Cantaloop (Flip fantasia-radio edit)	BN (E)12CL672 CD BN8-15892-2,(J)TOCJ-5860
*	I got it goin' on -1,2,5 (voKP,R)	BN B1-80883 CD BN 4-99351-2,(J)TOCJ-5897
	I got it goin' on (radio edit)-1,2,5 (voKP,R)	CD BN(J)TOCJ-5860
*	Tukka Yoot's riddim-4 (voTY)	BN B1-80883 CD BN 8-58139-2,4-99351-2,(J)TOCJ-5797, TOCJ-5897,TOCP-8966,Cap(J)TOCJ-5845
	Tukka Yoot's riddim (radio edit)-4 (voTY)	CD BN 8-27533-2,8-58139-2,(J)TOCJ-5797, TOCJ-5860

(session continued on next page)

351

*	Different rhythms,different people	BN B1-80883;CD 4-99351-2,(J)TOCJ-5897
*	It's like that (voKP)	- -
*	Just another brother -4 (voKP)	- -
*	Cruisin'-3 (voR)	- -
*	I go to work -7 (voKP)	- -
*	Knowledge of self (voR)	- -
*	Lazy day -4 (voKP,MH)	- - TOCP-65100
*	Eleven long years -1 (voTY)	- -
*	Make tracks -6 (voKP)	- -
*	The darkside (voR)	- -
*	Brand new thing -3	-
*	Just another brother (jazz mix)-4	-
*	Cruisin' (jazz mix)-3	-
*	Make tracks (jazz mix)-6	-
	Cantaloop (remix) (voR)	BN(E)12CL672;CD BN 8-15892-2
*	Cantaloop (instrumental)-1	- - 8-27533-2
	Roberto's riddim -8 (voTY)	CD BN 4-99351-2,(J)TOCJ-5797
*	Bu's riddim -4 (voTY)	-
	Blue's got it (voKP,R)	CD BN(J)TOCJ-5860
*	Bud's got it-8 (voKP,R)	-
	Cantaloop (Slain Pass mix)-1 (voR)	CD BN 8-58083-2,(J)TOCJ-5860
*	Cantaloop (groovy mix)-1 (voR)	- -
		The Right Stuff 8-33395-2
	Cantaloop (Nellee Hooper mix)-1 (voR)	CD BN 8-58083-2,4-99351-2,(C)5-20457-2,(J)TOCJ-5860
	Tukka Yoot's riddim (Manasseh Vibe Tribe mix)-4 (voTY)	CD BN(J)TOCJ-5860
	Tukka Yoot's riddim (Manasseh Vibe Tribe dub)-4 (voTY)	-
	Tukka Yoot's riddim (Extended street mix)-4 (voTY)	CD BN 8-58139-2
	Tukka Yoot's riddim (Rub-a-dub remix)-4 (voTY)	-
	Tukka Yoot's riddim (instrumental mix)-4	-

All titles on B1-80883 also issued on CD BN 7-80883-2,(J)TOCJ-5753,TOCJ-5897.
All titles from LP BN(E)12CL672 also issued on CD BN 8-15892-2,(J)TOCJ-5730
All titles marked * were also issued on CD Cap(E)8-29457-2 (CDESTX-2195).

<u>TOMMY SMITH</u> - <u>PARIS</u>:
Guy Barker(tp,monette) Julian Arguelles(ss,as) Tommy Smith(ts) Jason Rebello(p) Mick Hiuton(b) Jeremy Stacey(dm).
(EMI-England) (CBS Studios) London,May ,1992

Dischord
True sobriety
Reflections
Day light
Ping pong
Children play
Phraseology
Tear
Birth
Lost
Fragments
Occidentalism

All titles issued on CD BN 7-80612-2,(E)CDBLT 1005.

JOHN SCOFIELD QUARTET - WHAT WE DO:
Joe Lovano(ts) John Scofield(el g) Dennis Irwin(b) Bill Stewart(dm).
(Power Station) NYC,May ,1992

	Little walk	
	Camp out	CD BN 8-53330-2,4-99257-2
	Big sky	
	Easy for you	
	Call 911	CD BN 8-53330-2
	Imaginary time	
	Say the word	
	Why Nogales?	
	What they did	CD BN(J)TOCJ-5793

All titles issued on CD BN 7-99886-2.

BOB BELDEN - TURANDOT:
Tony Kadleck,Tim Hagans,Jim Powell,Phil Grenadier(tp,flh)John Fedchock(tb) Clark Gayton(bass tb) Peter Reit,John Clark(frh) George Moran(tu)Chick Wilson(fl,cl) Mike Migliore(picc,fl,as) Tim Reis(fl,ss,ts) Bob Belden(ts,arr) Ron Kozak(alto fl,bass cl,Eng h) Glenn Wilson(bs) Marc Copland(p) Kevin Hays(el p) Geoff Keezer(org) Fareed Haque(g) Jay Anderson (b) Bobby Previte,Jeff Hirshfield(dm) Joe Chambers(vb, marimba,perc) Bruce Hall(tymp,gong) Stacey Shames(harp).
(Power Station) NYC,May 26,1992 (afternoon)

tk.2	Opening	
tk.4	Calif's theme	
tk.8	Non piangere Liu	
tk.10	Del primo pianto	

All titles issued on CD BN 7-99829-2.

Jim Powell,Larry Grenadier-2(tp) Clark Gayton(tb) Bob Belden(ss,arr) Ron Kozak(bass cl) Marc Copland (org) Kevin Hays,Adam Holzman(el p) John Hart,David Miles(g)James Genus-1,Steve Logan(el b)Rocky Bryant(dm) Jerry Gonzalez,David Earle Johnson(perc).
(Power Station) NYC,May 26,1992 (evening)

tk.1	Signore Ascolta -1	CD BN 7-99829-2
	Liu's death -2	rejected

C. K. Ladzekpo(achimevu,vo) Kobla Ladzekpo(gankogui,vo) Agbi Ladzekpo(kidi,vo) Dzidzofgbe Lawluvi-Ladzekpo(axatse,vo) Adam Rudolph(kaganu) Tony Williams(dm) Ralph Penland(tymp) Bob Belden(arr).
(Capitol Studios) LA,June 1,1992 (afternoon)

tk.2	The three enigmas	CD BN 7-99829-2

Wallace Roney,Frank Szabo,Chuck Finley,Les Lovitt,Oscar Brashear,Snooky Young(tp) Bill Watrous(tb) Bill Reidenbach(bass tb) Bill Lane(frh) Bill Roper(tu) James Walker(fl) Sam Riney(fl, alto fl) Gary Herbig (bass fl, bass cl) Bob Belden(ts-1,arr) Gene Cipriano(Eng h) Ron Janelli(bassoon) Ira Coleman(b) Ralph Penland(dm) Bruce Hall(tymp).
(Capitol Studios) LA,June 1,1992 (evening)

tk.1	In questa Reggia	CD BN 7-99829-2
tk.2	In questa (reprise)-1	-

-1: Roney,Belden,Coleman,Penland only.

353

BOB BELDEN - TURANDOT:
Tim Hagans(flh) George Moran(bass tb-1) Chick Wilson(fl-1) Mike Migliore(alto fl-1) Lawrence Feldman (bass fl-1) David Liebman(ss-1) Joe Lovano(ts-2) Ron Kozak(bassoon) Marc Copland(p,el p) Kevin Hays (el p-2) Larry Goldings(org-2) Fareed Haque,John Hart(g) Gary Peacock,Jay Anderson(b-2) Joe Chambers, Paul Motian(dm-2) David Earle Johnson(perc).

(Sound On Sound) NYC,June 12,1992

tk.2	First vision -1	CD BN 7-99829-2
tk.3	The princess sleeps -1	-
tk.7	Nessun dorma -2	-

Joey Calderazzo(p)Fareed Haque(g) only.Same session.

(tk.3)	Children's song	CD BN 7-99829-2

All titles on BN 7-99829-2 also issued on CD BN(J)TOCJ-5731.
Note: BN 7-99829-2 was withdrawn soon after European release by threat of the music publisher.

BIRELI LAGRENE - STANDARDS:
Bireli Lagrene(g) Dominique Di Piazza(el b-1) Niels Henning Orsted-Pedersen(b) André Ceccarelli(dm).
(EMI-France) (Studio Davout) Paris,June ,1992

C'est si bon	CD BN(J)TOCJ-6188
Softly as in a morning sunrise	
Days of wine and roses	
Stella by starlight	
Smile	
Autumn leaves	CD BN(J)TOCJ-6134
Teach me tonight	
Donna Lee	
Body and soul	
Ornithology	
How insensitive (Insensatez)	CD BN 8-35283-2
Nuages -1	

All titles issued on CD BN 7-80251-2.

JOE LOVANO - UNIVERSAL LANGUAGE:
Tim Hagans(tp-1) Joe Lovano(ss-1,ts-2,alto cl-3) Steve Swallow(el b) Charlie Haden(b) Jack DeJohnette (dm) Judi Silvano(vo-1).

(Skyline Studios) NYC,June 26,1992

Luna Park -1
Lost nations -1,3
Hypnosis -2
This is always -2

All titles issued on CD BN 7-99830-2.

Tim Hagans(tp-2) Joe Lovano(ss-1,ts-2,alto cl-2) Scott Lee(b) Jack DeJohnette(dm) Judi Silvano(vo).
Same date.

Worship -1	CD Knitting Factory CD 249
Chelsea rendezvous -2	

Note: Lovano(gongs,perc,wood flute) overdubbed on both titles.
Both titles issued on CD BN 7-99830-2.

354

<u>JOE LOVANO</u> - <u>UNIVERSAL LANGUAGE</u>:
Tim Hagans(tp-1) Joe Lovano(as-2,ts-3) Kenny Werner(p) Charlie Haden(b) Jack DeJohnette(dm) Judi Silvano(vo-1).

	(Skyline Studios)	NYC,June 28,1992
	Sculpture -3	
	The dawn of time -3	
	Cleveland circle -1,3	
	Josie and Rosie -1,2	

All titles issued on CD BN 7-99830-2.

<u>JOEY CALDERAZZO</u> - <u>THE TRAVELER</u>:
Joey Calderazzo(p) John Patitucci(b) Peter Erskine(dm).

	(Mad Hatter Studio)	LA,August 17 & 18,1992
(tk.1)	No adults	CD BN 7-80902-2
(tk.1)	Blue in green	-
(tk.1)	What is this thing called love	-
(tk.2)	To wisdom the prize	-
(tk.2)	Love	-
(tk.1)	Giant steps	unissued
	This is the music of my people	-
	Bertha's bop	rejected
	There will never be another you	-
(tk.1)	The traveler (solo p)	CD BN 7-80902-2

Joey Calderazzo(p) Jay Anderson(b) Jeff Hirshfield(dm).

	(Skyline Studios)	NYC,September 28,1992
(tk.3)	Yesterdays	CD BN 7-80902-2
(tk.1)	Weaver of dreams	unissued
(tk.3)	My shining hour	-
(tk.4)	Lunacy	CD BN 7-80902-2
(tk.3)	Black Nile	-
(tk.1)	Dolphin dance	-

<u>GREG OSBY</u> - <u>3-D LIFESTYLES</u>:
Greg Osby(ss-2,as,mixer) Darrell Grant(p-1) Cassandra Wilson(vo-2) Bad News,RM,Lamar Supreme, Mal-Blar,Mustafo(rappers) & others unknown.

(Systems Two)	Brooklyn,October 9 & 10,1992	
Mr. Gutterman	CD BN 7-98635-2,(J)TOCJ-5757	
God-man cometh -1	-	-
3-D lifestyle -1	-	-
Honor Thy example -2	BN(J)TOJJ-5849 CD BN 7-98635-2,(J)TOCJ-5757,TOCJ-5849	
Intelligent madness	-	-
Thelonious -1	-	-
Mr. Gutterman (remix)		-
Mr. Gutterman (Subway mix)	CD Cap(J)TOCJ-5848	
Mr. Gutterman (Spare change mix)	CD BN 8-27533-2	

<u>GREG OSBY</u> - <u>3-D LIFESTYLES</u>:
Greg Osby(ss-1,as) Geri Allen(p) Bad News(rapper) Ali Shaheed Muhammed(mixer) & others unknown.

	(Sorcerer Sound)	NYC,October ,1992
	Raise -1	
	Hardcopy	
	Flow to the underculture	

All titles issued on CD BN 7-98635-2,(J)TOCJ 5757.

Greg Osby(as) Eric Sadler(mixer) & others unknown.

	(Greene Street Recording)	NYC,October .1992
	Street jazz	CD BN 7-98635-2,(J)TOCJ 5757

<u>MICHEL PETRUCCIANI</u> - <u>PROMENADE WITH DUKE</u>:
Michel Petrucciani(p).

	(Power Station)	NYC,late 1992
	Caravan	CD BN 4-97563-2
	Lush life	CD HMV Jazz(E)5-20873-2
	Take the A train	CD BN 5-20809-2
	African flower	
	In a sentimental mood	
	Hidden joy	
	One night in the hotel	
	Satin doll	
	C jam blues	CD BN(Sp)5-21755-2

All titles issued on CD BN 7-80590-2,(F)4-97604-2.

<u>THE BENNY GREEN TRIO</u> - <u>THAT'S RIGHT</u>:
Benny Green(p) Christian McBride(b) Carl Allen(dm).

	(Power Station)	NYC,December 21,1992
(tk.4)	Wiggin'	CD BN 7-84467-2
	That's right	rejected
	Cupcake	-
(tk.4)	Ain't she sweet	CD BN 7-84467-2
	Hoagie meat	rejected
	Something I dreamed last night (solo p)	-
	Altitude blues (solo p)	-
	Funky D	-
Same.	(Power Station)	NYC,December 22,1992
(tk.4)	Something I dreamed last night (solo p)	CD BN 7-84467-2
	Funky D	rejected
(tk.11)	Theme from "The Odd Couple" (solo p)	unissued
(tk.2)	Glad to be unhappy (solo p)	CD BN 7-84467-2
(tk.5)	Celia	-
	Hoagie meat	rejected
	That's right	-
(tk.5)	Cupcakes	CD BN 7-84467-2
(tk.8)	Me and my baby	-
	Altitude blues (solo p)	rejected

<u>THE BENNY GREEN TRIO</u> - <u>THAT'S RIGHT</u>:
Benny Green(p) Christian McBride(b) Carl Allen(dm).
(Power Station) NYC,December 23,1992

	Funky D (solo p)	rejected
(tk.12)	Altitude blues (solo p)	unissued
(tk.9)	Just a Tadd	CD BN 7-84467-2
(tk.12)	Hoagie meat	-
(tk.R-4)	That's right	-
	Me and my baby	rejected

<u>T.S. MONK</u> - <u>CHANGING OF THE GUARD</u>:
Don Sickler(tp,flh) Bobby Porcelli(fl,as,bs) Willie Williams(ss,ts) Ronnie Mathews(p) Scott Colley(b) T.S. Monk(dm).
(Power Station) NYC,February 8,9,10 & 13,1993

Kelo
Changing of the guard
Appointment in Milano
Monk's dream
Dark before dawn
Doublemint
Una mas
New York
Crepuscule with Nellie
K.D.
Middle of the block

All titles issued on CD BN 7-89050-2.

<u>DON PULLEN & THE AFRICAN-BRAZILIAN CONNECTION</u> - <u>ODE TO LIFE</u>:
Carlos Ward(fl,as) Don Pullen(p) Nilson Matta(b) Guilherme Franco(tumba,berimbau,perc) Mor Thiam (djembe,tabula,rainsticks,wind chimes,vo).
(Sorcerer Sound) NYC,February 18-19,1993

The third house on the right	
Paraty	
El matador	CD BN 8-23513-2
Ah George,we hardly knew ya	
Aseeko! (Get up and dance!) (voMT)	
Anastasia/Pyramid	
Variation on "Ode to life"	

All titles issued on CD BN 7-89233-2.

<u>CASSANDRA WILSON</u> - <u>BLUE LIGHT 'TIL DAWN</u>:
Cassandra Wilson(vo) with Brandon Ross(g) Charlie Burnham(v,mandocello) Lonnie Plaxico(b-1) Kevin Johnson(perc-1) Lance Carter(snares-1).
(Greene Street Studios) NYC,March ,1993

You don't know what love is	CD BN 8-54365-2,(J)TOCJ-6135,TOCJ-6187
Tupelo honey -1	CD BN 8-33878-2,5-20070-2,5-21151-2, 5-24271-2,(C)8-33908-2,4-94888-2,(Eu)5-23444-2

Both titles issued on BN(G)F671007,CD BN 7-81357-2.

STEVE MASAKOWSKI - WHAT IT WAS:
Steve Masakowski(g) Mike Pellera(p) David Torkanowsky(keyb) Bill Huntington(b) John Vidacovich(dm).
(New Orleans Recording Co.) NO,April , 1993

The big easy
Southern blue

Both titles issued on CD BN 8-80591-2.

Rick Margitza(ts-1) Steve Masakowski(g) Mike Pellera(p) David Torkanowsky(keyb-2) Larry Seiberth (keyb-3) James Genus(b) Ricky Sebastian(dm) Don Alias(perc) Hector Gallardo-4 (bgo,timbales).
(New Orleans Recording Co.) NO,April ,1993

Stepping stone -3
Budapest -1,3
Starling -1 CD Cema GSC Music 15131
Hector's lecture -1.4
What it is -2,4
Tino's blues -2
Joao -2
Alexandra -2

All titles issued on CD BN 7-80591-2.

Steve Masakowski(g)J ames Singleton(b-1) Hector Gallardo(bgo-1).
(New Orleans Recording Co.) NO,April ,1993

Quiet now -1
Jesus' last ballad

Both titles issued on CD BN 8-80591-2.

GONZALO RUBALCABA - IMAGINE:
Gonzalo Rubalcaba(p) Charlie Haden(b) Jack DeJohnette(dm) Dianne Reeves(vo).
(Alice Tully Hall) NYC,May 14,1993

Imagine rejected
You taught my heart to sing (voDR) (b,dm out)
unissued
All the things you are -
First song CD BN 8-30491-2
Airegin rejected
Ruby my dear unissued
When will the blues leave -

Reynaldo Melian(tp) Gonzalo Rubalcaba(p)Felipe Cabrera(el b) Julio Barreto(dm).
Same concert

Contagio rejected
Moose the mooche -
Transparence -
Perfidia -
Rapsodia Cubana -

<u>ANDY SHEPPARD</u> - <u>RHYTHM METHOD</u>:
Claude Deppa(tp) Gary Valente(tb-1) Andy Sheppard(ts,ss) Steve Lodder(keyb) Sylvan Richardson(el b) Dave Adams(dm).
(EMI-England) (Protocol Studios) London,May 21 & 23,1993

Sofa safari -1
Access all areas
So
Hop dreams
Undercovers -2

-2: Kevin Robinson(flh) replaces Deppa.

All titles issued on CD BN 8-27798-2,(E)CDBLT 1007.

<u>ORPHY ROBINSON</u> - <u>THE VIBES DESCRIBES</u>:
Orphy Robinson(vb,marimba,ss,g,perc) with Tunde Jegede(kora) Rowland Sutherland(alto fl) Jeffrey Durrant,Joe Bashorun(perc).
(EMI-England) (Protocol Studios) London,May ,1993

Annaves-Once upon a time (Intro) CD BN 8-29223-2,(E)CDBLT 1009

Orphy Robinson(vb,marimba,ss,g,perc) with Joe Bashorun(p,keyb,org) Leroy Osbourne(g,vo-2) Dudley Phillips(b) Winston Clifford(dm) Nana Vasconcelos-1,Jeffrey Durrant-4(perc).
(Protocol Studios) London,May ,1993

For to the power of M -1
The loneliest monk
From time to time
Monica -2
Make a change -2,3
Where's Winston
The eternal spirit
Chunky but funky -1,4
The juxtafusician (Another raggamuffin's tale)
The Krossover point

-3: Nik Cohen(el b) Andy Gangadeen(dm) replace Phillips & Clifford.
All titles issued on CD BN 8-29223-2,(E)CDBLT 1009.

Orphy Robinson(marimba) with Nana Vasconselos,Jeffrey Durrant(perc).
(Protocol Studios) London,May ,1993

Chunky but funky (interlude) CD BN 8-29223-2,(E)CDBLT 1009

Orphy Robinson(ss,g,perc) with Andy Gangadeen(dm) Jeffrey Durrant,Joe Bashorun(perc-1).
(Protocol Studios) London,May ,1993

An & Vas (interlude)
Savanna-A time once upon (Outro)-1

Both titles issued on CD BN 8-29223-2,(E)CDBLT 1009.

Orphy Robinson(vb,ss) with Joe Bashorun(p,keyb) Dudley Phillips(b,g) Andy Gangadeen(dm) Mae McKenna(vo).
(Protocol Studios) London,May ,1993

Golden brown CD BN 8-29223-2,(E)CDBLT 1009

359

EVERETTE HARP - COMMON GROUND:
Everette Harp(as,keyb,vo) Barry Eastmond(keyb,synth b,dm programming) Ira Segal,Mike Campbell(g) Eric Rehl(synth b programming) Brenda Nelson,La La Cope(backgr.vo).

(Eastbay Sound) Tarrytown,NY,May 13,1993

Where do we go CD BN 7-89297-2

CASSANDRA WILSON - BLUE LIGHT 'TIL DAWN:
Cassandra Wilson(vo,arr).

(RPM Studios) NYC,May, 1993

Sankofa BN(G)F671007;CD BN 7-81357-2

Cassandra Wilson(vo) with Gib Wharton(pedal steel g) Jeff Haynes,Cyro Baptista(perc).

(Sear Sound) NYC,May, 1993

Estrellas
Redbone
Blue light 'til dawn-1

-1: Charlie Burnham(v) Kenny Davis(b) Bill McClelland(dm) added.

All titles issued on BN(G)F671007,CD BN 7-81357-2.

Cassandra Wilson(vo) with Olu Dara(c) Brandon Ross(g).

Same sessions

Hellhound on my trail BN(G)F671007;CD BN 7-81357-2

Cassandra Wilson(vo) with Brandon Ross(g) Tony Cedras(acc) Kenny Davis(b) Lance Carter(dm).

Same sessions

Come on in my kitchen BN(G)F671007;CD BN 7-81357-2

Cassandra Wilson(vo) with Kenny Davis(b) Kevin Johnson(snare dm).

Same sessions

Tell me you'll wait for me BN(G)F671007;CD BN 7-81357-2

Cassandra Wilson(vo) with Brandon Ross(g) Vinx(perc,vo) Kevin Johnson,Lance Carter(perc).

Same sessions

Children of the night BN(G)F671007;CD BN 7-81357-2

Cassandra Wilson(vo) with Don Byron(cl) Vinx,Bill McClellan,Jeff Haynes,Cyro Baptista,Kevin Johnson, Lance Carter(perc).

Same sessions

Black Crow BN(G)F671007;CD BN 7-81357-2

ANDY SHEPPARD:
Claude Deppa(tp) Kevin Robinson(tp,flh) Gary Valente,Ashley Slater(tb) Andy Sheppard(ts,ss) Jerry Underwood(ts) Julian Arguelles(bs) Steve Lodder(keyb) Sylvan Richardson(el b) Dave Adams(dm)
(EMI-England) (Ronnie Scott's Club) London,June 12,1993

Well kept secret	CD BN 8-27798-2,(E)CDBLT 1007	
Delivery Suite:	CD BN 8-28719-2,(E)CDBLT 1008	
Pt.1: Perambulator	-	-
Pt.2: Inside information	-	-
Pt.3: Gas and air	-	-
Multi media	-	-
So	-	-

JOE LOVANO - TENOR LEGACY:
Joe Lovano,Joshua Redman(ts) Mulgrew Miller(p) Christian McBride(b) Lewis Nash(dm) Don Alias (cga-1,perc-2).
(Skyline Studio) NYC,June 18,1993

Introspection	
In the land of Ephesus	
To her ladyship	
Rounder's mood	CD BN(Eu)8-30081-2,8-36054-2
Web of fire -2	
Miss Etna -1	
Love is a many splendored thing -1	CD EMI(E)5-20535-2
Blackwell's message -1 (p out)	
Bread and wine -1 (p,b out)	
Laura -3	CD BN 8-34873-2,Cema GSC Music 15131

-3: Joe Lovano(ts)Mulgrew Miller(p) only

All titles issued on CD BN 8-27014-2.

FAREED HAQUE - SACRED ADDICTION:
Sal Marquez(tp-5) Kim Richmond-3,Doug Webb-4 (ss) Fareed Haque(ac g) Buzzy Feiten(el g) David Goldblatt-1,Patrice Rushen-2 (keyb) Charles Fambrough(b) Tom Brechtlein(dm) Luis Conte(perc).

(Mad Hatter Studios) LA,June 21-26,1993

No mystery -5 (Feiten out)	
Too much to tell	
Of a simple mind -4	
Another day in paradise -1	CD BN(J)TOCJ-6134
Mass -2	
Sacred addiction -2,3,6	
I'll be around -2,6	

-6: Fambrough out.Feiten plays el b as well as el g.
All titles issued on CD BN 7-89662-2.

Doug Webb(ss-2) Fareed Haque(ac g) Billy Childs(p-1) David Goldblatt(keyb-1) John Leftwich(b) Tom Brechtlein(dm-1) Luis Conte(perc) Bill Dickens,Bill Preskill(synth programming-3).
Same sessions

Blue people -3
Raga -1,2
The captain's refrain -1
El colibri (The hummingbird) (solo g)

All titles issued on CD BN 7-89662-2.

<u>DON PULLEN AND THE AFRICAN-BRAZILIAN CONNECTION</u> - <u>LIVE...AGAIN</u>:
Carlos Ward(as) Don Pullen(p) Nilson Matta(b) J.T. Lewis(dm) Mor Thiam(djembe,tabula,rainsticks,wind chimes,vo). (Jazz Festival) Montreux,July 13,1993

Yebino Spring
Ah George,we hardly knew ya
Capoeira — CD BN(Eu)7-99790-2
Kele mou bana (voMT)
Asseko! (Get up and dance!) (voMT)

All titles issued on CD BN 8-30271-2.

<u>CASSANDRA WILSON</u> - <u>BLUE LIGHT 'TIL DAWN</u>:
Cassandra Wilson(vo) Chris Whitley(slide g).
(Sound On Sound) NYC,July 26,1993

I can't stand the rain — BN(G)F671007;CD BN 7-81357-2,4-95701-2

<u>JAVON JACKSON</u> - <u>WHEN THE TIME IS RIGHT</u>:
Javon Jackson(ts) Jacky Terrasson(p) Chris Thomas(b) Clarence Penn(dm) Dianne Reeves(vo).
(Power Station) NYC,September 7,1993

Sweet and lovely — CD BN 8-34873-2
I waited for you (voDR) — CD BN(Eu)8-30081-2,8-36054-2
Something to remember you by
The path

All titles issued on CD BN 7-89678-2.

<u>MOSE ALLISON</u> - <u>THE EARTH WANTS YOU</u>:
Randy Brecker(tp) Joe Lovano(as) Bob Malach(ts)Mose Allison(p,vo) Ratso Harris(b) Paul Motian(dm).
(Skyline Studio) NYC,September 8,1993

Certified senior citizen — CD BN 8-55230-2
My ideal
Red wagon
Children of the future
Variation on Dixie

All titles issued on CD BN 8-27640-2.

Mose Allison(p,vo) John Scofield(g) Ratso Harris(b) Paul Motian(dm) Ray Mantilla(cga-1).
(Slyline Studio) NYC,September 9,1993

You can't push people around -1 — CD BN 8-55230-2
The earth wants you -1 — -
I don't love you -1
Who's in, who's out
Natural born malcontent

All titles issued on CD BN 8-27640-2.

Mose Allison(p,vo) Ratso Harris(b) Paul Motian(dm) Hugh McCracken(hca).
(Skyline Studio) NYC,September 10,1993

This ain't me — CD BN 8-55230-2
Cabaret card
What a shame

All titles issued on CD BN 8-27640-2.

LENA HORNE - WE'LL BE TOGETHER AGAIN:
Lena Horne(vo) with Orchestra incl. Houston Person,Jerome Richardson-1 (ts) Toots Thielemans(hca-2) Frank Owens(p,arr) Rodney Jones(g,el g) Benjamin Brown(b) Akira Tana(dm) Eli Fountain(perc) Sanford Allen (v-3) Jesse Levy(cello-4) Johnny Mathis(vo-5).
(Power Station) NYC,September-October,1993

Maybe
Something to live for CD BN 8-55221-2
Day follows day -2,5
Prelude to a kiss
Love like this can't last
A flower is a lovesome thing -4
You're the one -1,2
Do nothing till you hear from me

All titles issued on CD BN 8-28974-2.

Mike Renzi(p,arr) replaces Frank Owens.

We'll be together again
Old friend
Havin' myself a time
My mood is you -2
I'll always leave the door a little open
Forever was a day -6
I've got to have you
My buddy -3

-6: Tracy Wormworth(b) Buddy Williams(dm) replace Brown & Tana.
All titles issued on CD BN 8-28974-2.

JAVON JACKSON - WHEN THE TIME IS RIGHT:
Kenny Garrett(as-1) Javon Jackson(ts) Jacky Terrasson(p) Peter Washington(b) Carl Allen(dm).
(East Hill Studios) NYC,October 13,1993

Not yet -1 CD BN 4-95701-2
Love walked in -1
If ever I would leave you
When the time is right

All titles issued on CD BN 7-89678-2.

JOHN SCOFIELD - HAND JIVE:
Eddie Harris(ts-1) Larry Goldings(org,p-3) Dennis Irwin(b) Bill Stewart(dm) Don Alias(perc-2).
(Power Station) NYC,October ,1993

I'll take Les -1,2,3 BN B1-27327,CD 4-95701-2
Whip the mule -1,2,3
Do like Eddie -1,2 BN B1-27327,CD 8-53330-2,4-99257-2,
(Eu)8-30081-2,8-36054-2
Checkered past -1 CD BN(C)8-33908-2
Don't shoot the messenger -1
Golden daze -2 BN B1-27327
She's so lucky -2 - CD 4-99257-2,(Au)8-57460-2
Dark blue -3 -
7th floor - CD 4-99257-2
Out of the city

All titles issued on CD BN 8-27327-2.

363

EVERETTE HARP - COMMON GROUND:

Everette Harp(as,keyb,synth b,dm programming,backgr.vo,party noise) Shaun Labelle(keyb,synth b,dm programming,party noise) David Barry(g) Sheila E.(perc) Lynn Fiddmont-Lindsey,Valerie Mayo(backgr.vo) Wayne Holmes,Faith Fox(party noise)

(Le Gonks West) LA,c.late 1993

Strutt CD BN 7-89297-2

Michael "Patches" Stewart(tp) Reggie Young(tb) Everette Harp(as,keyb,synth b,dm programming) Branford Marsalis(ts) Paul Jackson,Jr.(g) Shaun Labelle(dm programming).

(Le Gonks West & Devonshire Studio) LA,c.late 1993

Common ground CD BN 7-89297-2

Everette Harp(as,EWI,keyb,dm and perc programming,arr) Ray "The Weeper" Fuller(g) Marcus Miller(solo b) Larry Kimpel(b) Caroline Perry,Lori Perry,Darlene Perry,Sharon Perry (backgr.vo).

(Le Gonks West & Devonshire Studio) LA,c.late 1993

You make me feel brand new CD BN 7-89297-2

Everette Harp(as,vo) George Duke(keyb) Paul Jackson Jr.(g) Larry Kimpell(b) Ricky Lawson(dm).

(Le Gonks West) LA,c.late 1993

I'm sorry CD BN 7-89297-2

Everette Harp(ts,EWI) George Duke(p,el p) Brian Simpson(keyb-1) Ray "The Weeper" Fuller(g) Nathan East(b) Simon Emory(dm) Paulinho Da Costa(perc).

(Mama Jo's Studio) LA,c.late 1993

Love you to the letter -1 CD BN 7-89297-2,8-34873-3
Song for Toots -

Everette Harp(as,keyb) Mark Ellis Stephens(el p-1) George Duke(p-2) Ray "The Weeper" Fuller-3,Michael Landau-4(g) Larry Kimpel(b) Ricky Lawson(dm) Brian Kilgore-5, Paulinho Da Costa-6(perc) Phil Perry, Alex Brown,Lynn Davis(backgr.vo-7) Jeffrey Osborne(vo-8).

(Studio B & Le Gonks West) LA,November, 1993

Feel so right -1,2,3,5,7
Sending my love -3,6,7
Jeri's Song -4,8

All titles issued on CD BN 7-89297-2.

Everette Harp(ss,keyb,arr) Craig Smith(el p,arr) George Duke(p) Ray "The Weeper" Fuller, Michael Landau (g) Larry Kimpel(b) Rayford Griffin(dm) Paulinho Da Costa(perc).

(Studio B & Le Gonks West) LA,November, 1993

Coming home CD BN 7-89297-2,8-33878-2

Everette Harp(EWI,keyb,synth b,dm programming,backgr.vo) Brian Simpson(p,synth b) Paul Jackson Jr.(g).

(Studio B,Le Gonks West & Devonshire Studio) LA,November, 1993

Perfect day (Tessa's smile) CD BN 7-89297-2

Everette Harp(as) Michael Beardon(keyb,synth b) Ricky Lawson(dm programming) Alex Brown,Lynn Davis,Johnny Britt(backg.vo).

(Studio B,Le Gonks West & Devonshire Studio) LA,November, 1993

Stay with me CD BN 7-89297-2

MAX ROACH WITH THE NEW ORCHESTRA OF BOSTON:
Max Roach(dm) & The New Orchestra of Boston,cond. by David Epstein.
(University of Massachusetts) Amherst,Mass.,December 2,1993

Festival journey: CD BN 8-34813-2
Movement I: Outbursts,thunder,clouds and mists
Movement II: Bells, drones and spiritual fantasy
Movement III: Strutting

TIM HAGANS - NO WORDS:
Tim Hagans(tp) Joe Lovano(ts-1) Marc Copland(p,el p) John Abercrombie(g) Scott Lee(b) Bill Stewart(dm).
(Power Station) NYC,December 3,1993

No words
Nog rhythms
Waking iris -1
Noogaloo
Immediate left -1 CD BN(Eu)8-30081-2,8-36054-2
Passing giants
For the music
Housewife from New Jersey -1
Lost in my suitcase

All titles issued on CD BN 7-89680-2.

McCOY TYNER & BOBBY HUTCHERSON - MANHATTAN MOODS:
McCoy Tyner(p) Bobby Hutcherson(vb).
(Sound On Sound) NYC,December 3,1993

(tk.3) Manhattan moods
(tk.3) Dearly beloved
(tk.1) (I loves you) Porgy

All titles issued on CD BN 8-28423-2.

Same.Bobby Hutcherson(vb or marimba-1).
(Sound On Sound) NYC,December 4,1993

(tk.6) Travelin' blues
(tk.5) Rosie
(tk.3) Isn't this my sound around me? -1
(tk.2) Soul eyes
(tk.3) Blue Monk -1 CD BN 8-35471-2,8-37051-2,(Eu)8-30081-2,
8-36054-2
(tk.2) For heaven's sake

All titles issued on CD BN 8-28423-2.

JOHN SCOFIELD & PAT METHENY - I CAN SEE YOUR HOUSE FROM HERE:
John Scofield(g,el g) Pat Metheny(g,el g,g synth) Steve Swallow(b,el b) Bill Stewart(dm).
(Power Station) NYC,December ,1993

I can see your house from here CD HMV Jazz(E)5-20884-2
The red one
No matter what
Everybody's party
Message to my friend CD BN 8-53330-2,(C)8-56508-2
No way Jose
Say the brother's name
S.C.O.
Quiet rising
One way to be
You speak my language CD BN(J)TOCJ-6134

All titles issued on CD BN 8-27765-2.

KEVIN HAYS - SEVENTH SENSE:
Seamus Blake(ts) Steve Nelson(vb) Kevin Hays(p) Doug Weiss(b) Brian Blade(dm).
(Systems Two Studio) Brooklyn,N.Y.,January 12-13 1994

Take the D flat train CD BN(Eu)8-30081-2,8-36054-2
Seventh sense
Three pillars
My man's gone now
Interlude
Space acres
Little B's poem
East of the sun
Makyo
Black narcissus

All titles issued on CD BN 7-89679-2.

SONNY FORTUNE - FOUR IN ONE:
Sonny Fortune(as) Kirk Lightsey(p) Buster Williams(b) Billy Hart(dm).
Englewood Cliffs,NJ,January 17 & 18,1994

Four in one
Criss cross
Monk's dream
Hornin' in
Coming on the Hudson
Trinkle tinkle
Hackensack
Reflections (b,dm out) CD BN(Eu)8-30081-2,8-36054-2

All titles issued on CD BN 8-28243-2.

Sonny Fortune(as,fl-1) Santi Debriano(b) Ronnie Burrage(dm-2).
Englewood Cliffs,NJ,January 27,1994

Pannonica -1
Ask me now -2

Both titles issued on CD BN 8-28243-2.

KURT ELLING - CLOSE YOUR EYES:
Kurt Elling(vo) with Laurence Hobgood(p) Eric Hochberg(b) Paul Wertico(dm,perc).
(Tone Zone Recording) Chicago,February 14,1994

Close your eyes CD BN(J)TOCJ-6135,(Sp)5-21755-2
Dolores dream
Now it is time that gods came walking out
Remembering Veronica

All titles issued on CD BN 8-30645-2.

Kurt Elling(vo) with Edward Petersen(ts-1) Laurence Hobgood(p) Rob Amster(b,el b) Paul Wertico (dm,perc).
(Tone Zone Recording) Chicago,February 15,1994

Storyteller experiencing total confusion -1
Hurricane -1
Never,never land

All titles issued on CD BN 8-30645-2.

Same. (Tone Zone Recording) Chicago,February 16,1994

Never say goodbye (for Jodi)-2 CD BN 8-33878-2,(Au)8-14808-2
These clouds are heavy, you dig? -3

-2: Dave Onderdonk(g) added.
-3: Elling(vo) Amster(b) only.

All titles issued on CD BN 8-30645-2.

JOE LOVANO QUARTET:
Tom Harrell(flh-1,tp-2) Joe Lovano(ss-3,C melody sax-4,ts-5) Anthony Cox(b) Billy Hart(dm).
(Village Vanguard) NYC,March 12,1994

Set #1:
Birds of Springtimes gone by -1,5 CD BN 8-29195-2,(C)8-52184-2
I can't get started -1,5 -
Set #2:
Fort Worth -2,5 CD BN 8-29195-2
Song and dance -2,5 -
Sail away -1,3 -
Set #3:
Blues not to lose -1,3 CD BN 8-29195-2
Uprising -2,4 -

BENNY GREEN - THE PLACE TO BE:
Benny Green(p) Christian McBride(b) Kenny Washington(dm).
Englewood Cliffs,NJ,March 22,1994

Playmate CD BN 8-32995-2
Pensativa
Concertina
The folks who live on the hill
Which came first? (dm out)
The place to be (p solo)
Noreen's nocturne (p solo)
The gravy waltz (p solo)

All titles issued on CD BN 8-29268-2.

367

BENNY GREEN - THE PLACE TO BE:
Benny Green(p) Christian McBride(b) Kenny Washington(dm) with Byron Stripling(tp) Delfayo Marsalis(tb) John Clark(frh) Herb Besson(tu) Jerry Dodgion(fl,alto fl,as) Gary Smulyan(bs) Bob Belden(arr) added.
Englewood Cliffs,NJ,March 23,1994

Nice pants
I want to talk about you
I felt that
One of another kind (horns out) CD BN(Eu)8-30081-2,8-36054-2

All titles issued on CD BN 8-29268-2.

GREG OSBY - BLACK BOOK:
Greg Osby(as) Mulgrew Miller(p) Calvin Jones(b) Bill McClellan(dm) Markita Morris,Taj McCoy(vo)
(Systems Two Studio) Brooklyn,N.Y.,March 25 & 26,1994

Intuition CD BN 8-29266-2

Greg Osby(as,keyb-1) Mulgrew Miller(p) DJ Ghetto(scratches) Sha-key(recitation-2).
Same sessions

Mr.Freeman -1
Rocking Chair -2

Both titles issued on CD BN 8-29266-2.

GREG OSBY - BLACK BOOK:
Greg Osby(as) DJ Ghetto(scratches) Riva Parker-1,Mustafo-2,Markita Morris-3,Taj McCoy-4,Bernard Collins Jr.-5 (recitation)
Same sessions

Pillars -1 CD BN(Au)4-97893-2,(E)8-53226-2,(J)TOCP-8966
Buried alive -2
Smokescreen-2
Poetry in motion -3 CD BN(C)8-52184-2 (edited)
Black book -3
Brewing poetry -1,3,4,5
Fade to Black Medley:
a.A brother and a token -1,3,4
b.In a city blues -2
c.Urbanite kodes -3,4

All titles issued on CD BN 8-29266-2.

RICHARD ELLIOT - AFTER DARK:
Richard Elliot(ts) Ron Reinhardt(keyb) Richard Smith(g) Naoki Yanai(b) Dave Reinhardt(dm.perc) Luis Conte(perc).
(Suncoast Recording) LA,c.Spring 1994

Street beat
As I sleep
After dark CD BN 8-33878-2
El Anio
Tonight
On the run
Hold me tight
The boys from the bay
Candelight

All titles issued on CD BN 8-27838-2.

RICHARD ELLIOT - AFTER DARK:
Richard Elliot(ts) Jeffrey Osborne(vo) John Andrew Schreiner(p,synth,dm,arr).
(Entourage Recording) LA,March 24 & April 19,1994

If tomorrow never comes CD BN 8-27838-2

Richard Elliot(ts) Cliff Downes(p,synth,dm,perc).
(Northbeach) Franklin,TN,Spring,1994

Song for her CD BN 8-27838-2
Bridge over troubled waters -

Richard Elliot(ts) Todd Terry(p,synth,dm machine) & unknown vocal group-1.
(No Name Studios) NYC,Spring,1994

So special CD BN 8-27838-2
Slow it down-1 -

JOE LOVANO - RUSH HOUR:
Joe Lovano(ts) Dick Oatts(fl) Ed Schuller,Mark Helias(b) George Schuller(dm) & strings: Joel Smirnoff, Matthew Raimondi,Geoff Nutall,Charles Libove,John Pintavalle,Paul Peabody,Eric Wyrick(v) Ronald Carbone,Louise Shulman(viola) Fred Sherry,Mark Shuman,Ronald Thomas(cello) Gloria Agostini(harp) Judi Silvano(vo) Gunther Schuller(arr,cond).
(Power Station) NYC,April 6,1994

Prelude to a kiss (voJS)
Lament for M

Both titles issued on CD BN 8-29269-2.

Joe Lovano(ts) James Chirillo(g) Ed Schuller,Mark Helias(b) George Schuller(dm) & strings: Joel Smirnoff, Matthew Raimondi,Geoff Nutall,Charles Libove,John Pintavalle,Paul Peabody(v) Cynthia Phelps,Toby Appel,Raymond Gniewek(viola) Fred Sherry,Mark Shuman,Ronald Thomas(cello) Gloria Agostini(harp) Gunther Schuller(arr,cond).
Same session

Angel eyes CD BN8-32995-2, 8-35282-2,(C)8-33908-2
The love I long for

Both titles issued on CD BN 8-29269-2.

Joe Lovano(ss) James Chirillo(g) Ed Schuller(b) George Schuller(dm) Fred Sherry(cello) Gloria Agostini (harp).
Same session

Kathline Gray CD BN 8-29269-2

Joe Lovano(ts) with Jack Walrath(tp) Jim Pugh(tb) Davis Taylor(bass tb,tu) John Clark,Julie Landsman(frh) Charles Russo(cl,bass cl,as,ts) Dick Oatts(fl,ts) Robert Botti(Eng h) Michael Rabinowitz(bass cl,bassoon) Dennis Smylie(contrabass cl) James Chirillo(g) Ed Schuller,Mark Helias(b) George Schuller(dm) Mark Belair (vb,perc) Judi Silvano(vo-1) Gunther Schuller(arr,cond).
(Power Station) NYC,April 7,1994

Peggy's blue skylight
Crepuscule with Nellie
Rush hour on 23th Street -1
Headin' out,movin' in -1,2

-2: Botti(Eng h) Helias(b) out.
All titles issued on CD BN 8-29269-2.

369

KEVIN EUBANKS - LIVE AT BRADLEY'S:
Kevin Eubanks(g) James Williams(p) Robert Hurst(b)
(Bradley's) NYC,May 21,1994

Set #1:

Autumn leaves	rejected
Alone together	unissued
Relaxin' at Camarillo	-
Alter ego	CD BN 8-30133-2
Mercy,mercy,mercy	rejected

Set #2:

Speak low	CD BN 8-30133-2
Stablemates	unissued
In a sentimental mood (p,b out)	CD BN 8-30133-2,4-94035-2
June in January	-
Red top	-
Mercy,mercy,mercy	-

Set #3:

Four on six	rejected
Old country	unissued
Old folks (g out)	-
June in January	rejected
Sometimes I feel like a motherless child	CD BN 8-30133-2
The theme	unissued
Mercy,mercy,mercy	rejected

JOE LOVANO - RUSH HOUR:
Joe Lovano(ts,ss,bass cl,dm) Judi Silvano(vo-1).
(Power Station) NYC,June 12,1994

Topsy turvy -1	
Juniper's garden -1	
Wildcat	
Chelsea bridge	CD BN 5-20809-2

All titles issued on CD BN 8-29269-2.

JACKY TERRASSON:
Jacky Terrasson(p) Ugonna Okegwo(b) Leon Parker(dm).
(Power Station) NYC,June 14-16,1994

I love Paris	CD BN 8-35282-2,4-95701-2,(E)8-53228-2, (Eu)8-30081-2,8-36054-2
Just a blues	
My funny Valentine	
Hommage à Lili Boulanger	
He goes on a trip	
I fall in love too easily	CD BN 5-24271-2
Time after time	CD BN(C)8-33908-2
For once in my life	

All titles issued on CD BN 8-29351-2.

GONZALO RUBALCABA - IMAGINE:
Gonzalo Rubalcaba(p).

(Live at Capitol Studios)	LA,June 23,1994
Imagine	CD BN 8-30491-2
First song	unissued
Perfidia	-
Circuito II	CD BN 8-30491-2
Prologo comienzo	unissued

Reynaldo Melian(tp) Gonzalo Rubalcaba(p) Felipe Cabrera(el b) Julio Barreto(dm).

(Wadsworth Hall,UCLA)	LA,June 24,1994
Alvecha	unissued
Contagio	CD BN 8-30491-2
Circuito II	unissued
Always say goodbye -1	-
First song-1	-
Nobody loves me -1	-
Woody 'n you	CD BN 8-30491-2
Perfidia	-
Mima (solo p)	-

-1: Gonzalo Rubalcaba(p) Charlie Haden(b) only.

KEVIN EUBANKS - SPIRITALK 2/REVELATIONS:
Robin Eubanks(tb) Kent Jordan(alto fl) Kevin Eubanks(g) Dave Holland(b) Marvin Smitty Smith(dm).
(Sound On Sound) NYC,June 25-28,1994

Earth (solo g)
Faith
Like the wind
Sun
Passing
Whispers of life -1 (alto fl out)
Revelations -1
Moon -2 (tb out)
Being -2 (alto fl out)

-1: add Gerald Moore(g)
-2: Gene Jackson(dm) replaces Smith.

All titles issued on CD BN 8-30132-2.

JACKY TERRASSON:
Jacky Terrasson(p) Ugonna Okegwo(b) Leon Parker(dm).

(Clinton Studios)	NYC,August, 1994
Bye bye blackbird	CD BN 8-32995-2
What a difference a day made	CD BN(J)TOCJ-6190
Cumba's dance	

All titles isued on CD BN 8-29351-2.

KURT ELLING - CLOSE YOUR EYES:
Kurt Elling(vo) with Laurence Hobgood(p).

(Tone Zone Recording)	Chicago,August 28,1994
Wait 'til you see her	CD BN 8-30645-2

371

PIECES OF A DREAM - GOODBYE MANHATTAN:
Vincent Calloway(tb,backgr.vo) Ron Kerber(as) James Lloyd(p) Joel Davis(keyb,programming) Gene Robinson(g Angelo Ray,Curtis Harmon(dm Eva Cassidy(vo) Annette Hardeman,Clarence Calloway,Reggie Calloway(backgr.vo).

(Ligosa Studios) Cincinnati,c. Fall 1994

Goodbye Manhattan CD BN 8-28532-2

Ron Kerber(ss) James Lloyd(p) Wesley Boatman,Steve Beckham(keyb Gene Robinson(g Curtis Harmo (dm) Keith Robertson(dm programming)Vincent Calloway,Reggie Calloway(backgr.vo).

(RTG & Crystal Clear Studios) Cincinnati,c. Fall 1994

Let's get smooth CD BN 8-28532-2

Ron Kerber(ss,keyb) James Lloyd(p) Rich Crawford(g Rob Cochran(b) Curtis Harmon(dm,perc).

(Morning Star Studios) Springhouse,PA,c. Fall,1994

Magen's Bay CD BN 8-28532-2

Ron Kerber(ss) James Lloyd(keyb,programming,synth b) Rich Crawford(programming).

(Morning Star Studios) Springhouse,PA,c. Fall,1994

Club jazz (quiet storm) CD BN 8-28532-2,8-33878-2

Ron Kerber(as) Clifford Starkey(keyb) Bennie Simms(b) Curtis Harmon(dm,synth b,programming).

(Morning Star Studios) Springhouse,PA,c. Fall,1994

Bassik instinct CD BN 8-28532-2

James Lloyd(keyb,synth b,programming) Leon Jordan(dm).

(Morning Star Studios) Springhouse,PA,c. Fall,1994

After dark CD BN 8-28532-2

Ron Kerber(ts,perc) James Lloyd(p) Stephen Scott(keyb) Rich Crawford(g,perc,dm programming) Charles Fambrough(b).

(Morning Star Studios) Springhouse,PA,c. Fall,1994

We're all alone CD BN 8-28532-2

Ron Kerber(ss) James Lloyd(p,keyb) Jeff Lee Johnson(b) Rich Crawford(dm programming,perc) Yvette Myles (backgr.vo).

(Morning Star Studios) Springhouse,PA,Fall,1994

How much I feel CD BN 8-28532-2

Ron Kerber(ss) James Lloyd(keyb) Glenn Barratt(keyb,programming) Charles Baldwin(b)

(Morning Star Studios) Springhouse,PA,c. Fall,1994

Ocean view CD BN 8-28532-2

James Lloyd(p) Curtis Dowd Jr.(keyb,synth b,dm,samples).

(Morning Star Studios) Springhouse,PA,c. Fall,1994

Lights out CD BN 8-28532-2

PIECES OF A DREAM - GOODBYE MANHATTAN:
Steven Ford(keyb,programming) Glenn Barratt(programming) Charles Baldwin(b) Eva Cassidy(vo) Yvette Myles(backgr.vo).
(Morning Star Studios) Springhouse,PA,c. Fall,1994

Have a little faith CD BN 8-28532-2

Ron Kerber(as) William Brock,Clifford Starkey(keyb) Rob Cochran(b) Curtis Harmon(dm,perc).
(Morning Star Studios) Springhouse,PA,c. Fall,1994

Love of my life CD BN 8-28532-2

STEVE MASAKOWSKI - DIRECT AXECESS:
David Torkanowsky(p) Steve Masakowski(g) James Singleton-1,Bill Huntington-2(b) Brian Blade(dm).
(The Boiler Room) NO,September ,1994

Paladia -1 CD BN 8-33878-2
Burgundy -1
Kayak -1
Headed Wes'-1
Ascending reverence -2
Lush life -2
Monk's mood (solo g)
Emily (solo g)

All titles issued on CD BN 8-31108-2.

Steve Masakowski,Hank Mackie-1(g) Bill Huntington(b) Brian Blade(dm).
(The Boiler Room) NO,September ,1994

For Django
Bayou St. John
The visit
(Voluntary) simplicity -1
New Orleans -1 (b & dm out)

All titles issued on CD BN 8-31108-2.

T.S. MONK - THE CHARM:
Don Sickler(tp) Bobby Porcelli(fl,as) Willie Williams(ss,ts) Ronnie Mathews(p) Scott Colley(b) T.S. Monk (dm).
(Ambient Recording Company) Stamford,CT,September 13-15,1994

Budini
The dealer takes four
Jean Marie
Marvelous Marvin
Bolivar blues
The highest mountain
Rejuvenate
Just waiting
Gypsy folktales

All titles issued on CD BN 7-89575-2

CAECILIE NORBY - CAECILIE:

Caecilie Norby(vo) with Rick Margitza(ss) Niels Lan Doky-1,Lars Jansson-2 (p) Ben Besiakow-3 (p,org) Jakob Fisher(el g-4) Lennart Ginman(b) Billy Hart(dm) Jacob Andersen(perc-5).

(EMI Medley/Denmark)(Focus Recording) Copenhagen,September 17 & 19,1994

Wild is the wind -4	CD BN(J)TOCJ-66071
A brand new life -1,6	
Summertime -1,5,6	CD BN(J)TOCJ-6135
Gentle is my love -1	
By the time I get to Phoenix -1,4	CD BN(J)TOCJ-6188
Man's got soul -3,7	
Girl talk -3,8	
I've been to town -2,7	
All you could ever want -2	CD Cap(J)TOCJ-6060
A feather in the wind -2,4	
So it is -9	

-6: Randy Brecker(tp) overdubbed on.(Sound On Sound) NYC ,Oct.2,1994
-7: Scott Robinson(ts) overdubbed on.(Sound On Sound) NYC,Oct.2,1994
-8: voices overdubbed on. Lan Music,Paris,August,1994 & Adaptor Studios,Copenhagen,September 18, 1994.
-9: Norby(vo) Rick Margitza(ss) Lars Jansson(p) only.

All titles issued on CD BN 8-32222-2.

LENA HORNE - AN EVENING WITH LENA HORNE:

Lena Horne(vo) with Donald Harrison(ts) Mike Renzi(p,synth) Rodney Jones(g) Benjamin Brown(b) Akira Tana (dm) & The Count Basie Orchestra-1: Bob Ojeda,Michael Williams,Derrick Gardner,Scotty Barhart (tp,flh) Clarence Banks,Melvin Wanzo,Bill Hughes(tb) Danny Turner(fl,as) Doug Miller,Kenny King(ts,fl) John Williams(bs).

(Live,The Supper Club) NYC,September 19,1994

Come runnin'-1	CD BN 8-31877-2
I'll always leave the door a little open	rejected
Got to have you	-
Maybe	CD BN 8-31877-2,(C)4-94888-2
I've got the world on a string	-
Old friend	-
How's your romance	-
Why shouldn't I	-
Ours	-
Just one of those things	-
We'll be together again -1	-
The lady is a tramp -1	-
Yesterday when I was young -1	-
Something to live for	-
Mood indigo -2	-
Just squeeze me -3	-
Do nothin' till you hear from me -1	-
Life goes on -1	rejected
Watch what happens	CD BN 8-31877-2

-2: Lena Horne(vo) Benjamin Brown(b) only.
-3: Lena Horne(vo) Benjamin Brown(b) Akira Tana(dm) only.This Ellington title is listed on CD as "Squeeze me" by Fats Waller/Clarence Williams.

<u>KURT ELLING</u> - <u>CLOSE YOUR EYES</u>:
Kurt Elling(vo) with Von Freeman(ts-1) Laurence Hobgood(p) Eric Hochberg(b) Paul Wertico(dm,perc).
(Tone Zone Recording) Chicago,September 28,1994

(Hide the) salome -1
Married blues

Both titles issued on CD BN 8-30645-2.

Kurt Elling(vo) with Laurence Hobgood(p).
(Tone Zone Recording) Chicago,November 2,1994

Ballad of the sad young men CD BN 8-30645-2,(C)8-33908-2,4-94888-2

<u>DIANNE REEVES</u> - <u>QUIET AFTER THE STORM</u>:
Dianne Reeves(vo) with Hubert Laws(fl-3) Joshua Redman(ts-1) David Torkanowsky(p) Chris Severin(b) Billy Kilson(dm) Luis Conte(cga-1,perc-2) George Duke(synclavier horns-1,synclavier strings-2) Airto Moreira(perc-3).
(Conway Studios) LA,November ,1994

Hello, haven't I seen you before -1
Sing my heart -2
When morning comes (jasmine)-3

All titles issued on CD BN 8-29511-2.

Dianne Reeves(vo) with Roy Hargrove,Gary Grant(tp) Everette Harp(as) Ron Blake(ss,ts) David Torkanowsky(p-1) George Duke(el p-2) Chris Severin(b) Billy Kilson(dm) Luis Conte(cga-3)
Same sessions

Comes love (Nothing can be done)-1,3
The benediction (Country preacher)-2,4

-4: add pre-recorded sample of Cannonball Adderley(ss)

Both titles issued on CD BN 8-29511-2.

Dianne Reeves(vo) with George Duke(p,synclavier strings-1) Chris Severin(b) Terri Lyne Carrington(dm).
Same sessions

Both sides now (vo & p only)
Jive samba
Smile -1,2 CD BN(E)8-53231-2

-2: Kevin Eubanks(g) Cherub Femmes & Two Cherub Men(backgr.vo) added.

All titles issued on CD BN 8-29511-2.

Dianne Reeves(vo) with Jacky Terrasson(p) Chris Severin(b) Billy Kilson(dm) Airto Moreira(perc-1).
Same sessions

In a sentimental mood CD Toshiba-EMI(J)TOCJ-6228
Detour ahead -1 CD BN(C)4-94888-2

Both titles issued on CD BN 8-29511-2.

375

DIANNE REEVES - QUIET AFTER THE STORM:
Dianne Reeves(vo) with Dori Cayimmi(g) Airto Moreira(perc).
Same sessions

Yemanja/Sargaco mar CD BN 8-29511-2

Dianne Reeves(vo) with John Beasley(p) Kevin Eubanks(g) Chris Severin(b) Billy Kilson(dm) Luis Conte (perc) George Duke(synclavier).
Same sessions

Nine CD BN 8-29511-2

ELIANE ELIAS - SOLOS AND DUETS:
Eliane Elias,Herbie Hancock(p)
(Hit Factory) NYC,November 18,1994

The way you look tonight CD BN 8-32073-2
Just enough - (E)8-53228-2
Messages -
Messages,pt.2 -
Messages,pt.3 -
Messages,pt.4 -

Note:An additional title from this session can be found on "Jazz To The World" CD BN 8-32127-2 (see leased masters in part 6)

ELIANE ELIAS - SOLOS AND DUETS:
Elaine Elias(p).
(Elias Studio) Sao Paulo,December,1994

Autumn leaves
The masquerade is over
All the things you are
Joy Spring/Have you met Miss Jones
Au privave

All titles issued on CD BN 8-32073-2.

MARCUS PRINTUP - SONG FOR THE BEAUTIFUL WOMAN:
Marcus Printup(tp) Walter Blanding(ts) Eric Reed(p) Reuben Rogers(b) Brian Blade(dm).
(Power Station) NYC,December 6 & 7,1994

The inquiry
I remember April
Song for the beautiful woman
Trauma
Presentation
Lonely heart
Minor ordeal
Speak low CD BN 8-32995-2,Hip-O 547897-2
Dahomey dance

All titles issued on CD BN 8-30790-2.

<u>TIM HAGANS</u> - <u>AUDIBLE ARCHITESTURE</u>:
Tim Hagans(tp) Larry Grenadier(b) Billy Kilson(dm).
(Power Station) NYC,December 17,1994

(tk.3) I hear a rhapsody CD BN 8-32995-2
(tk.4) Jasmine in three
(tk.8) Drum row (b out) CD BN(C)8-52184-2
(tk.3) You don't know what love is
(tk.7) Audible architecture
(tk.3) Whatever's next

All titles issued on CD BN 8-31808-2.

Bob Belden(ts) added.
(Power Station) NYC,December 18,1994

(tk.3) Garage bands
(tk.4) Shorts
(tk.7) Blues in my neighborhood
(tk.3) Family flowers

All titles issued on CD BN 8-31808-2.

<u>CHARLIE HUNTER</u> - <u>BING,BING,BING</u>:
Dave Ellis(ts) Charlie Hunter(el g) Jay Lane(dm).
(Mobius Music) SF,January ,1995

Greasy granny CD BN 5-20070-2
Come as you are CD BN 8-32995-2
Bullethead
Squiddlesticks
Elbo room
Lazy Susan (with a client now)-1
Scrabbling for purchase -1
Bing,bing,bing,bing -2
Fistful of haggis -2,3 CD BN 4-95701-2,(E)8-53226-2
Wornell's Yorkies -3

-1: Jeff Cressman(tb)Ben Goldberg(cl) added.
-2: David Phillips(pedal steel g) added.
-3: Scott Roberts(perc) added.

All titles issued on CD BN 8-31809-2.

<u>JAVON JACKSON</u> - <u>FOR ONE WHO KNOWS</u>:
Javon Jackson(ts) Jacky Terrasson(p) Fareed Haque(ac g-1) Peter Washington(b) Billy Drummond(dm) Cyro Baptista(perc-2).
(Sear Sound) NYC,January 18 & 19,1995

For one who knows -2
Etcetera -2
Angola CD BN(C)8-52184-2
Notes in three -1
Jane's theme -1
Paradox CD BN 8-32995-2
Useless landscape (p out)-1,2 CD BN 8-35283-2
Formosa (Gorgeous)-2

All titles issued on CD BN 8-30244-2.

377

JOE LOVANO QUARTET:
Joe Lovano(ts) Mulgrew Miller(p) Christian McBride(b) Lewis Nash(dm).

	(Village Vanguard)	NYC,January 20,1995
Set #1:		
	Miss Etna	rejected
	Reflections	-
	Sounds of joy	CD BN 8-29125-2,(J)TOCJ-6031
	This is all I ask	unissued
	Blackwell's message	-
	26-2	rejected
Set #2:		
	Lonnie's lament	CD BN 8-29125-2,(J)TOCJ-6031
	Reflections	- -
	Little Willie leaps	unissued
	This is all I ask	CD BN 8-29125-2,(J)TOCJ-6031
	Along came Betty	rejected
	What's new	-
	26-2	CD BN 8-29125-2,(J)TOCJ-6031
Set #3:		
	Duke Ellington's sound of love	CD BN 8-29125-2,(J)TOCJ-6031
	Sounds of joy	rejected
	Along came Betty	-
	The dawn of time	-
	Hot house	unissued

Same.

	(Village Vanguard)	NYC,January 22,1995
Set #1:		
	Lonnie's lament	rejected
	Reflections	-
	Little Willie leaps	CD BN 8-29125-2,(J)TOCJ-6031
	This is all I ask	rejected
	Sounds of joy	-
	The dawn of time	unissued
	26-2	rejected
Set #2:		
	Duke Ellington's sound of love	rejected
	Along came Betty	unissued
	26-2	rejected
	What's new	unissued
	Stablemates	-
	Sounds of joy	rejected

KEVIN HAYS - GO ROUND:
Seamus Blake-1(ts,ss) Steve Hall(ts-2) Kevin Hays(p,el p) Doug Weiss(b) Billy Hart(dm) Daniel Sadownick-3 (cga,perc).

(Systems Two Studio)	Brooklyn,N.Y.,January 21 & 22,1995
Early evening -1	
When I wake -1,2	
Sutra -1,2	CD BN(C)8-52184-2
Sutra (reprise)-1-2	
Daybreak -1,2,3	
Go round -1,2,3	CD BN 8-32995-2
The run -1,2,3	
Quiet -2,3	
Invitation -3	CD BN(Au)8-57460-2

All titles issued on CD BN 8-32491-2.

BOBBY McFERRIN - BANG! ZOOM:
Bobby McFerrin(vo) with Scott Wendholt(tp-1) Bob Mintzer(saxes,bass cl) Russell Ferrante(p,synth) Paul Nagel(el p-2) Paul Jackson Jr.(g) Jimmy Haslip(b) William Kennedy(dm) Paulinho da Costa(perc).
(Ocean Way Studios) LA, early 1995

Bang! Zoom -4 CD BN 8-53329-2
Remembrance
Friends -1 CD BN 8-53329-2,(C)8-52184-2,4-94888-2
Selim
Freedom is a voice -4,5 CD BN 8-53329-2,4-95701-2
Heaven's design -2
My better half -3
Kid's toys
Mere words (vo,perc only)

-3: Tower Of Power horn section (Greg Adams,David Mann,Stephen Kupka,Emilio Castillo,Lee Thornsburg) added.
-4: New Century Chamber Orchestra(strings) added.
-5: Oakland Interfaith Choir added.

All titles issued on CD BN 8-31677-2.

FAREED HAQUE-OPAQUE:
Fareed Haque(ac g,el g,sitar g,g synth) Jonathan Paul(b) Mark Walker(dm,dumbek,udu dm,perc) Hamid Drake(tabla-1).
(Bear Tracks) Suffern,NY,February 9-17,1995

Unison (b out)
Opaque
Father Dave
Duet #2 (b out)
Never ending
Tabriz
Pastoral -1
Inspiration city -1
First romance
Una limosna por el amor de dios (solo g) CD BN 8-32995-2

All titles issued on CD BN 8-29270-2.

SONNY FORTUNE - A BETTER UNDERSTANDING:
Jerry Gonzales(tp-1,flh-2,cga-3) Robin Eubanks(tb-4) Sonny Fortune(as,ss,alto fl,fl) Kenny Barron(p) Wayne Dockery(b) Billy Hart(dm) Steve Berrios(perc-5).
Englewood Cliffs,NJ,February 20 & 21,1995

It's a bird -1,4
Awakening -2,4,5
Long before our mothers cried -1,3,4,5,6
Mind games -6
Laying it down
A swing touch
It ain't what it was
Tribute to a Holiday
Never again is such a long time (fl & p only)

-6: Ronnie Burrage(dm) replaces Hart.
All titles issued on CD BN 8-32799-2.

<u>BILL STEWART</u> - <u>SNIDE REMARKS</u>:
Eddie Henderson(tp,flh) Joe Lovano(ts) Bill Carrothers(p) Larry Grenadier(b) Bill Stewart(dm).
(Sear Sound) NYC,February 21 & 22,1995

Snide remarks CD BN 8-32995-2,(C)8-52184-2
Soul's harbor
Mayberry
7.5
Shadow of the spire
Crosstalk
Space acres
Fred and Ginger
4:30 A.M.

All titles issued on CD BN 8-32489-2.

<u>DON PULLEN</u> - <u>SACRED COMMON GROUND</u>:
Don Pullen(p) & The African Brazilian Connection: Joseph Bowie(tb) Carlos Ward(as) Santi Debriano(b) Mor Thiam(perc) & The Chief Cliff Singers: Mike Kenmille(lead vo) Clifford Burke,Arteen Adams,Gina,Big Beaver,Clayton Burke,Kenny Lozeau(vo) Francis Aud(vo,perc).
(The Power Station) NYC,March 8,1995

(tk.2) Common ground (tb,as,perc out)
(tk.3) The eagle staff is first
(tk.1) River song (tb,as out)

All titles issued on CD BN 8-32800-2.

Same. (The Power Station) NYC,March 9,1995

(tk.2) Reservation blues CD BN 8-23513-2
(tk.1) Message in smoke
(tk.1) Reprise: Still here -1
(tk.2) Resting on the road (singers out)

-1: Mike Kenmille(vo) only.
All titles issued on CD BN 8-32800-2.

<u>DENISE JANNAH - I WAS BORN IN LOVE WITH YOU</u>:
Denise Jannah(vo) with John Eckert,Byron Stripling,Roger Ingram,Alan Rubin(tp) Britt Woodman,Earl McIntyre,Art Baron(tb) Howard Johnson(tu,bass cl) Dick Oatts,Paquito D'Rivera,Charlie Pillow,Craig Handy,Gary Smulyan(woodwinds) Javon Jackson(ts) John Campbell(p) Lynn Seaton(b) Dennis Mackrel (dm) Bob Belden(arr,cond).
(EMI Holland) (Clinton Studios) NYC,March 22,1995

(tk.1) You'd be so nice to come home to
(tk.3) I didn't know about you
(tk.1) They didn't believe me
Sailboat in the moonlight (vo,ts,b only)

All titles issued on CD BN 8-33390-2.

Lou Marini replaces Craig Handy. James Riggs(cl-1) Daniel Sadownick(perc-1) added.
(EMI Holland) (Clinton Studios) NYC,March 23,1995

(tk.2) Interlude (A night in Tunisia)
(tk.2) I was born in love with you -1
(tk.3) Something to live for

All titles issued on CD BN 8-33390-2.

 380

DENISE JANNAH - I WAS BORN IN LOVE WITH YOU:
Denise Jannah(vo) with Byron Stripling(tp) Art Baron(tb) Howard Johnson(tu-1,bass cl-2) Paquito D'Rivera (cl-1) James Riggs(ss-2) Gary Smulyan(bs) John Campbell(p) Lynn Seaton(b) Dennis Mackrel(dm) Bob Belden-1,Jon Schapiro-2(arr)
(Clinton Studios) NYC March 23,1995 (second session)

tk.2 Dear Ruby (Ruby my dear)-1
Bye bye blackbird -2

Both titles issued on CD BN 8-33390-2.

Denise Jannah(vo) with Javon Jackson(ts-1) Cyrus Chestnut(p) Steve Kirby(b) Yoron Israel(dm).
(Clinton Studios) NYC,March 24-25,1995

Imagination -1
That's all -1
Alone never lonely
Them there eyes
Every little snowflake
Where are the words (vo & p only)

All titles issued on CD BN 8-33390-2.

MAURIZIO GIAMMARCO HEART QUARTET - IN OUR HANDS:
Maurizio Giammarco(ts,tamb,maracas) Mauro Grossi(p,el p) Piero Leveratto(b) Andrea Melani(dm).
(EMI-Italy) (Rambler Studio) Rome,April,1995

Generation
Autumn breed
Fingers of fortune
Like a fish
One as a pair
B witch
Falling in love with love
El gordo
Outras palavras
Emanation

All titles issued on CD BN(I)8-34719-2.

CASSANDRA WILSON - NEW MOON DAUGHTER:
Cassandra Wilson(vo) with Brandon Ross(g) Kevin Breit(g,el g,bjo) Mark Anthony Peterson(b-1) Dougie Bowne(dm,perc,whistling-2) Cyro Baptista(perc,pan,jew's harp) The Peepers(backgr.vo-2).
(Turtle Creek Barn) Bearsville,NY,April 18-26,1995
and (Sound On Sound) NYC,May 3-5,1995

32-20 (Breit out)	BN LP(G)8-37183-1,CD(Eu)8-37183-2
Moon river	CD BN(J)TOCJ-5996,TOCJ-6135
Solomon's song	CD BN 8-32861-2
Death letter -1	- 4-95981-2
Harvest moon -1,2	-

All titles from CD BN 8-32861-2 also issued on BN(G)8-37183-1,CD BN(Eu)8-37183-2,(J)TOCJ-5996.

CASSANDRA WILSON - NEW MOON DAUGHTER:
Cassandra Wilson(vo) with Butch Morris(c-1) Charlie Burnham(v-2) Gary Breit(org-3) Brandon Ross(g) Kevin Breit(g,bozouki) Lonnie Plaxico(b) Dougie Bowne(dm,vb) Cyro Baptista(perc-4).
Same sessions

Love is blindness -1 — CD BN(Au)8-14808-2,(C)8-52184-2,(Sp)8-56842-2

I'm so lonesome I could cry -2
Last train to Clarksville
Memphis -3,4 (Bowne out)

All titles issued on BN(G)8-37183-1,CD BN 8-32861-2,(Eu)8-37183-2,(J)TOCJ-5996.

Cassandra Wilson(vo) with Tony Cedras(acc-1) Charlie Burnham(v-2) Brandon Ross(g) Lonnie Plaxico(b-3) Jeff Haynes(bgo,perc) Cyro Baptista(shakers,perc). Same sessions

Until -1,3
A little warm death -2 — CD BN(E)8-53231-2

Both titles issued on BN(G)8-37183-1,CD BN 8-32861-2,(Eu)8-37183-2,(J)TOCJ-5996.

Cassandra Wilson(vo) with Graham Haynes(c) Chris Whitley(g) Lonnie Plaxico(b).
Same sessions

Strange fruit — BN(G)8-37183-1;CD BN 8-32861-2,4-97154-2,(Eu)8-37183-2,(J)TOCJ-5996

Cassandra Wilson(vo) with Gib Wharton(pedal steel g) Lonnie Plaxico(b) Dougie Bowne(dm).
Same sessions

Skylark — BN(G)8-37183-1
CD BN 8-32861-2,Cap.5-23566-2,
BN(Eu)8-37183-2,(J)TOCJ-5996

Cassandra Wilson(vo) with Brandon Ross(g) Lonnie Plaxico(b).
Same sessions

Find him — BN(G)8-37183-1
CD BN 8-32861-2,(Eu)8-37183-2,(J)TOCJ-5996,
Knitting Factory CD 249

PIECES OF A DREAM - THE BEST OF:
Ron Kerber(as) James Lloyd(el p,org) Glenn Barratt(synth,programming) Darryl Johnson(g) Charles Baldwin(b) Curtis Harmon(dm,perc,backgr.vo) Yvette Myles(vo,backgr.vo).
(Morning Star Studios) — Springhouse,PA,mid 1995

Keep it smooth — CD BN 8-35800-2

Ron Kerber(as) James Lloyd(p) Steven Ford(p,el p,keyb) Glenn Barratt(synth,programming) Charles Baldwin(b) Curtis Harmon(dm,perc) Yvette Myles(vo,backgr.vo).
(Morning Star Studios) — Springhouse,PA,mid 1995

Baby it's your turn now — CD BN 8-35800-2

Ron Kerber(fl,ts) James Lloyd(el p) Rich Crawford(dm,synth programming) Steven Ford(synth strings).
(Morning Star Studios) — Springhouse,PA,mid 1995

The cool side — CD BN 8-35800-2

Ron Kerber(as,ts) Steven Ford(p,synth)Glenn Barratt(dm programming).
(Morning Star Studios) — Springhouse,PA,mid 1995

My love — CD BN 8-35800-2

JOHN SCOFIELD - GROOVE ELATION:
Larry Goldings(org,p) John Scofield(el g,g) Dennis Irwin(b) Idris Muhammad(dm).
(Power Station) NYC,June 1995

Old soul	
Soft shoe	
Lazy -1	CD BN 4-99257-2
Peculiar -1	
Let the cat out -1	
Let it shine -1	
Big top -1,2	CD BN 4-99257-2
Kool -1,2	CD BN 8-53330-2,4-99257-2,(C)8-52184-2, (E)8-53226-2,Knitting Factory CD 249
Groove elation -2	
Carlos -2	CD BN 4-99257-2

-1: Randy Brecker(tp,flh) Steve Turre(tb) Billy Drewes(ts,fl) Howard Johnson(tu,bass cl,bs) added.
-2: Don Alias (perc) added.

All titles issued on CD BN 8-32801-2.

RAY BARRETTO - MY SUMMERTIME:
Michael Philip Mossman(tp,flh,tb) Adam Kolker(ss,ts)Hector Martignon(p) Jairo Moreno(b,el b) Vince Cherico(dm) Ray Barretto(cga,vo)
(EMI-France)(Power Station) NYC,July 1,2 & 3,1995

No hay problema (No problem)
In your own sweet way
Brother Ray
When you wish upon a star
Autumn leaves
While my lady sleeps
Off minor
Fait accompli
Summertime (Guajira) (voRB)
Worlds I love

All titles issued on CD BN 8-35830-2.

JACKY TERRASSON - REACH:
Jacky Terrasson(p) Ugonna Okegwo(b) Leon Parker(dm).
(Cello Systems Studio) NYC,August 30 & 31,1995

I should care	CD BN 8-35739-2	
The rat race	-	(C)8-52184-2
Baby plum	-	
(I love you) For sentimental reasons	-	
Reach/Smoke gets in your eyes*/Reach	-	*EMI(E)5-20535-2
Happy man	-	
First affair	-	
Just one of those things	-	
All my life		
Mixed feelings -1	unissued	

-1: The beginning of "Mixed Feeling" was used for a remix project. See THE NEW GROOVE (January, 1996) for details.

All titles,except the last one,issued on CD BN 8-37570-2,(J)TOCJ 5997.

THE DOKY BROTHERS:
Michael Brecker(ts-2) Neils Lan Doky(p,keyb) Frank Stangerup(keyb-1) Ulf Wakenius(g-1) Chris Minh Doky (b) Terri Lyne Carrington(dm) Deborah Brown(vo).
(EMI-Medley,Denmark)
(Focus Recording) Copenhagen &(Sound On Sound)NYC,August-September,1995

Summertime
Teen town
You never knew
I feel pretty (voDB) CD BN(J)TOCJ-6188,Cap(J)TOCJ-6060
Hope -1
While we wait -1,2

All titles issued on CD BN 8-36909-2.

Neils Lan Doky(p) Chris Minh Doky(b) Alex Riel(dm).Same sessions

Natural woman
Children's song

Both titles issued on CD BN 8-36909 2.

Randy Brecker(tp,flh) Michael Brecker-2, Neils Lan Doky(p) Chris Minh Doky(b) Klaus Soonsaari-1, Anders Mogensen-2(dm) Terri Lyne Carrington(cymbals-1) Curtis Stigers(vo).
Same sessions:

My one and only love -1 (voCS)
Fearless dreamer -2

Both titles issued on CD BN 8-36909 2.

MAX ROACH AND THE SO WHAT BRASS QUINTET:
Max Roach(dm) & Cecil Bridgewater,Frank Gordon(tp) Steve Turre(tb) Marshall Sealy(frh) Robert Stewart (tu).
(Sound On Sound) NYC,October 5,1995

Ghost dance CD BN 8-34813-2

RENEE ROSNES - ANCESTORS:
Chris Potter(ts-1,ss-2,bass cl-3) Renee Rosnes(p) Peter Washington(b) Al Foster(dm) Don Alias(perc-4).
(EMI-Canada)(Power Station) NYC,October 9,1995

The sounds around the house
Closing spirits -1
The gift -2
Upa Neginho -2,3,4

All titles issued on CD BN 8-34634-2.

Nicolas Payton(tp) Chris Potter(ts,alto fl) Renee Rosnes(p) Peter Washington(b) Al Foster(dm) Don Alias (perc-1) Billy Drummond(cymbals-2).
(EMI-Canada)(Power Station) NYC,October 10,1995

Intuition
Life wish CD BN(C)8-52184-2
Ancestors -1
The ache of the absence -2

All titles issued on CD BN 8-34634-2.

<u>RICHARD ELLIOT</u> - <u>CITY SPEAK</u>:
Richard Elliot(ts) Ron Reinhardt(keyb) Richard Smith(g) Naoki Yanai(b) Dave Reinhardt(dm.perc) Luis Conte(perc).

(Suncoast Recording) LA,October-November,1995

City speak
Walk the walk CD BN(E)8-53226-2
Unspoken words
Amazon
I'll make love to you
Scotland
Sweet surrender
Down hill run
When the lights go out
All I need
That's all she wrote

All titles issued on CD BN 8-32620-2.

<u>LENA HORNE</u> - <u>BEING MYSELF</u>:
Lena Horne(vo) with Milt Jackson(vb-1) Bobby Forrester(org) Mike Renzi(p,keyb) Rodney Jones(g) Benjamin Brown(b) Akira Tana(dm) Jeremy Lubbock(string arr).

(Power Station) NYC,c. late 1995

Autumn in New York
Imagination-1

Both titles issued on CD BN 8-34286-2.

<u>THE CARNEGIE HALL JAZZ BAND</u>:
Jon Faddis,Lew Soloff,Byron Stripling,Earl Gardner,Ryan Kisor(tp,flh) Dennis Wilson,Steve Turre,Slide Hampton(tb) Douglas Purviance(bass tb) Dick Oatts(ss,as,ts,cl,fl) Jerry Dodgion(as,cl,fl) Ted Nash(ts,fl) Ralph Lalama (ts,cl,fl) Gary Smulyan(bs) Renee Rosnes(p) Peter Washington(b) Lewis Nash(dm).
Arr. by Jim McNeely-1,Garnett Brown-2,Slide Hampton-3,Frank Foster-4,Randy Sandke-5.

(Sony Studios) NYC,December, 1995

In the mood -1,7 CD HMV Jazz(E)5-20883-2
It never entered my mind -2
Shiny stockings -3
Giant steps -4,6
Frame for the blues -3
Sing,sing,sing -1,7
I'm gettin' sentimental over you -1
South Rampart Street parade -5

-6: Lew Tabackin(as) added.
-7: Frank Wess(ts) added.
All titles issued on CD BN 8-36728-2.

385

THE NEW GROOVE - THE BLUE NOTE REMIX PROJECT:
Note:Following titles are remixes of recordings from 1969-1977 & 1995 with added rappers and instruments recorded in January 1996

DONALD BYRD/THE ANGEL:
Donald Byrd(flh) William Campbell(tb) Lew Tabackin(fl,ts) Frank Foster(ts) Duke Pearson(el p) Ron Carter (b) Airto Moreira(dm).
(A & R Studios) NYC,December 16,1969
The Angel(remix,arr) Mystic(vo)Cokni O'Dire(scratches)
(Hollywood Sound) LA,January,1996

(4615) Kofi (The jazz master mix) BN B1-36594,CD 8-36594-2,(Au)4-97893-2
(4615) Kofi (Heavy beats mix) -

CANNONBALL ADDERLEY/LARGE PROFESSOR:
Nat Adderley(c) Cannonball Adderley(as) Joe Zawinul(el p) Walter Booker(b) Roy McCurdy(dm).
(Capitol recording)
(London House) Chicago,prob.October 17,1969
Large Professor(remix)
(Power Play Studios) NYC,January,1996

(73306) Hummin' BN B1-36594,CD 8-36594-2

NOEL POINTER/D.J. SMASH:
Noel Pointer(el v) Dave Grusin(el p,synth,arr).Earl Klugh(g) Francisco Centeno(el b) Steve Gadd(dm) Ralph McDonald(perc).
(Camp Columby Studio) New City,N.Y.,January 10,1977
D.J.Smash(remix) A. Ray Fuller(g) Nick Smith(keyb b)
(Axis & Capitol Studios) NYC & LA,January,1996

(18316) Living for the city BN B1-36594,CD 8-36594-2

GENE HARRIS/G.U.R.U.:
Gene Harris(p) Sam Brown,Cornell Dupree(g) Ron Carter(b) Freddie Waits(dm) Johnny Rodriguez(cga) Omar Clay(perc).
(A & R Studios) NYC,June 30,1972
G.U.R.U.(remix)Marcus Printup(tp).
(D & D Studio & The Crack House) NYC & LA,January,1996

(9953) Listen here BN B1-36594,CD 8-36594-2,(E)8-53233-2

RONNIE LAWS/THE L.G. EXPERIENCE:
Ronnie Laws(ss,ts) Bobby Lyle(p) Larry Dunn(synth) Melvin Robinson(g) Donnie Beck(el b) Steve Guttierez(dm).
(ABC Studios) LA,January/February/March 1977
The L.G. Experience(remix) Bill Harvey,Kenneth Staten(vo) Mark Shim(ts).
(Unique & Capitol Studios) NYC & LA,January,1996

(18353) Friends and strangers BN B1-36594,CD 8-36594-2

GRANT GREEN/THE UMMAH:
Claude Bartee(ts) William Bivens(vb) Neal Creque(org) Grant Green(g) Idris Muhammad(dm) Joseph Armstrong(cga).
(The Cliche Lounge) Newark,N.J.,August 15,1970
The Ummah(remix) Dianne Reeves(vo) Nick Smith(keyb)
(Soundtrack & Capitol Studios) NYC & LA,January,1996

Down here on the ground BN B1-36594,CD 8-36594-2,8-57748-2

RONNIE FOSTER/DIAMOND D:
Ronnie Foster(org) George Devens(vb,perc Gene Bertoncini(g) Gene Bianco(harp) George Duvivier(b) Gordon Edwards(el b) Jimmy Johnson(dm) Arthur Jenkins(cga) Wade Marcus(arr).
Englewood Cliffs,N.J.,January 21,1972
Diamond D(remix).
(The Crack House & Capitol Studios) LA,January,1996

9215 Summer song BN B1-36594,CD 8-36594-2,(Au)4-97893-2,(J)TOCP-65100

LONNIE SMITH/MICHAEL FRANTI/SPEARHEAD:
Rudy Jones(ts) Ronnie Cuber(bs) Lonnie Smith(org,vo) Larry McGee(g) Sylvester Goshay(dm).
(Club Harlem) Atlantic City,August 9,1969
Michael Franti(remix,vo) Trina Simmons, Ras I. Zulu(vo).
(The Crack House & Capitol Studios) LA,January,1996

4811 (tk.5) Move your hand BN B1-36594,CD 8-36594-2,(C)8-52184-2

HORACE SILVER/EASY MO BEE:
Tom Harrell(tp) Bob Berg(ts) Horace Silver(p) Bob Cranshaw(el b) Bernard Purdie(dm).
(A & R Studios) NYC,January 17,1975
Oscar Brashear,Bobby Bryant(tp,flh) Vince De Rosa(frh) Frank Rosolino(tb) Maurice Spears (bass tb) Jerome Richardson(fl,ss,as) Buddy Collette(fl,as) Wade Marcus(arr).
(Wally Heider Studios) LA,early 1975
Easy Mo Bee(remix).
(Unique Recording) NYC,January,1996

15169 The sophisticated hippie BN B1-36594,CD 8-36594-2,(J)TOCP-8966

BOBBY HUTCHERSON/THE ROOTS:
Oscar Brashear,Blue Mitchell(tp) Ernie Watts(fl,ts) Bobby Hutcherson(vb,marimba,arr) Eddie Cano(p) Dave Troncoso(b) Bobby Matos,Victor Pantoja,Johnny Paloma,Rudy Calzado(perc).
(The Record Plant) LA,August 12 or 14,1975
The Roots(remix) Fatin Dantzler(lead vo)Arlynne Page,Tracey Moore,Dawn Beckman,Mercedes Martinez (backgr. vo) Amir Khalib Thompson(dm)
(Sigma Sound & Platinum Island) Philadelphia & NYC,January,1996

16559 Montara BN B1-36594,CD 8-36594-2,(J)TOCP-65100

JACKY TERRASSON/THE ANGEL:
Jacky Terrasson(p) Ugonna Okegwo(b) Leon Parker(dm).
(Cello Systems Studio) NYC,August 30 or 31,1995
The Angel(remix)The Gift Of Gab(vo) Mix Master Dee(scratches) Cokni O'Dire(vocal samples) Katisse Buckingham(fl) Louis Russell(g) Jacky Terrasson(el p,org) More Rockers(jungle dm,b programming).
(Matrix Maison Rouge) London,January,1996

Mixed feelings BN B1-36594,CD 8-36594-2
Mixed feelings (Sub sonic mix) -
Mixed feelings (Dubalicious) -

<u>CHARLIE HUNTER</u> - <u>READY...SET...SHANGO!</u>:
Calder Spanier(as) Dave Ellis(ts) Charlie Hunter(el g) Scott Amendola(dm).
(The Site) Marin County,Calif.,January 3,1996

(tk.3) 911
(tk.4) Ashby man CD BN(C)8-52184-2

Both titles issued on CD BN 8-37101-2.

387

CHARLIE HUNTER - READY...SET...SHANGO!:
Calder Spanier(as) Dave Ellis(ts) Charlie Hunter(el g) Scott Amendola(dm).
(The Site) Marin County,Calif.,January 4,1996

(tk.5)	Sutton	
(tk.2)	Let's get medieval	CD BN(Au)8-57460-2
(tk.6)	Thursday the 12th	
(tk.2)	The shango, pt.III	

All titles issued on CD BN 8-37101-2.

Same. (The Site) Marin County,Calif.,January 5,1996

(tk.2)	Shango...the ballad (saxes out)	CD BN(Au)8-14808-2
(tk.2)	Dersu	
(tk.2)	Teabaggin'	

All titles issued on CD BN 8-37101-2.

BLUE NOTE ALL STARS - BLUE SPIRITS:
Tim Hagans(tp) Greg Osby(as) Javon Jackson(ts) Kevin Hays(p) Essiet Essiet(b) Bill Stewart(dm).
(Sear Sound) NYC,January 8,1996

(tk.1)	Free hop	
(tk.2)	Splash	
(tk.3)	Naaman	
(tk.1)	Theodore	
(tk.2)	Think before you think	CD BN(C)8-52184-2

All titles issued on CD BN 8-36747-2,(Eu)8-37731-2,(J)TOCJ-6058.

Same. (Sear Sound) NYC,January 9,1996

(tk.2)	Twist and out	CD BN 8-36747-2,8-56399-2
(tk.1)	Next time not	-
(tk.2)	A Caddy for daddy	
(tk.3)	Kae	CD BN 8-36747-2
(tk.5)	Our trip	-

All titles issued on CD BN (Eu)8-37731-2,(J)TOCJ-6058.

JUDI SILVANO - VOCALISE:
Judi Silvano(vo) with Dave Ballou(tp-1) Vic Juris(g) Drew Gress(b) Joe Lovano(dm,perc-2,gongs-3).
(Power Station) NYC,January 15-16,1996

Thanks for you (vo & g only)
It's so amazing -1,2
Serenity -3

All titles issued on CD BN 8-52390-2.

<u>JUDI SILVANO</u> - <u>VOCALISE</u>:
Judi Silvano(vo) with Joe Lovano(ts-1) Vic Juris(g) Drew Gress(b) Bob Meyer(dm).
Same sessions

Daydream — CD BN(Sp)8-56842-2
Pavanne — CD BN(C)4-94888-2
Vocalise
Weird nightmare (g out)
Bass space -1 (g out)
All too soon -1
Looking back (Reflections) -1,2
Heuchera Americana -2
At home (sweet home) -2
Vocalise II -2

-2: Dave Ballou(tp)Oscar Noriega(as,bass cl) added.

Note:Additional overdubs on above were done on April 13,1996 at the Power Station,NYC.
All titles issued on CD BN 8-52390-2.

<u>KURT ELLING</u> - <u>THE MESSENGER</u>:
Kurt Elling(vo) with Laurence Hobgood-1(p,keyb) Dave Onderdonk(g-2) Rob Amster(b) Paul Wertico (dm,perc).
(Tone Zone Recording) — Chicago,January 18,1996

The beauty of all things -1,2
Tne dance -2
Prayer for Mr. Davis -1,3

-3: Orbert Davis(flh) added.
All titles issued on CD BN 8-52727-2

Kurt Elling(vo) with Edward Petersen(ts) Laurence Hobgood(p,keyb) Rob Amster(b) Jim Widlowski(dm).
(Tone Zone Recording) — Chicago,January 19,1996 (afternoon)

Endless
The messenger

Both titles issued on CD BN 8-52727-2.

Kurt Elling(vo) with Laurence Hobgood(p,synth) Eric Hochberg(b) Paul Wertico(dm).
(Tone Zone Recording) — Chicago,January 19,1996 (night)

Tanya Jean
It's just a thing

Both titles issued on CD BN 8-52727-2.

389

JAVON JACKSON - A LOOK WITHIN:
Javon Jackson(ts) Lonnie Smith(org-1) Fareed Haque(g) Peter Washington(b) Billy Drummond(dm) Cyro Baptista(perc-2) Cassandra Wilson(vo-3).
(Sear Sound) NYC,February 3 & 4,1996

Assessment
Leap frog
Hamlet's favorite son
Peggy's blue skylight/
Duke Ellington's sound of love -1
Zoot allures -1,2
Memoria e fado -2
L'eau à la bouche -2
Recado bossa nova -2 (dm out)
Country girl -2,3 (dm out) CD BN 8-36736-2, (C)4-94888-2

All titles issued on CD BN 8-36490-2.

GREG OSBY - ART FORUM:
Greg Osby(ss,as) James Williams(p) Bryan Carrott(vb-1) Lonnie Plaxico(b) Jeff Tain Watts(dm).
(Systems Two Studio) Brooklyn,N.Y.,February 10-14,1996

Miss D'Meena CD BN 4-95701-2
I didn't know about you CD BN 5-20809-2
Don't explain
Dialectical interchange -1
Art forum -1
Half moon step -1
Mood for thought -1,2

-2:Robin Eubanks(tb) Cleave Guyton(alto fl) Alex Harden(bass cl) added.

All titles issued on CD BN 8-37319-2.

Cleave Guyton(fl,alto fl,ts) Greg Osby(ss) Darrell Grant(p,synth) Marvin Sewell(g) Lonnie Plaxico(b) Jeff Tain Watts(dm).
Same sessions

Perpetuity
2nd born to freedom (ss & g only)

Both titles issued on CD BN 8-37319-2.

MARCUS PRINTUP - UNVEILED:
Marcus Printup(tp) Stephen Riley(ts) Marcus Roberts(p) Reuben Rogers(b) Jason Marsalis(dm).
(Sound On Sound) NYC,February 18,1996

(tk.1) Eclipse
(tk.7) When forever is over
(tk.8) Dig
(tk.3) Say it again
(tk.2) Leave your name and number
(tk.1) Unveiled
(tk.4) Stablemates

All titles issued on CD BN 8-37302-2.

<u>MARCUS PRINTUP</u> - <u>UNVEILED</u>:
Marcus Printup(tp) Stephen Riley(ts) Marcus Roberts(p) Reuben Rogers(b) Jason Marsalis(dm).
(Sound On Sound) NYC,February 19,1996

(tk.4) Soulful J
(tk.6) M & M
(tk.7) Yes or no
(tk.3) Amazing grace (tp & p only)

All titles issued on CD BN 8-37302-2.

<u>ERIK TRUFFAZ</u> - <u>OUT OF A DREAM</u>:
Erik Truffaz(tp,flh) Cyrille Bugnon(as,ts) Patrick Muller(p) Marcello Giuliani(b) Marc Erbetta(dm).
(EMI France)(Studio Village) Montpellier,France,February ,1996

Down town
Out of a dream
Beauté bleue
Wet in Paris
Porta Comollia
Indigo
Saisir
Elégie
Samara
Uptown

All titles issued on CD BN(Eu)8-55855-2.

Same,except Bugnon out
(EMI France)(Studio Valesco) Geneva,Switzerland,February 1996

Betty CD BN 8-55855-2,5-26427-2

<u>CAECILIE NORBY</u> - <u>MY CORNER OF THE SKY</u>:
Caecilie Norby(vo) with Lars Jansson(p,org) Lennart Ginman(b) Alex Riel-1,Jeff Boudreaux-2(dm) Jacob Andersen(perc-3).
(EMI Medley-Denmark)(Focus Recording) Copenhagen, c. early March ,1996

Set them free -1,3 CD BN(J)TOCJ-6153,TOCJ-6189
Suppertime -1
What do you see in her -2

All titles on CD BN 8-53422-2.

<u>SONNY FORTUNE</u> - <u>FROM NOW ON</u>:
Eddie Henderson(tp-1) Sonny Fortune(as) Joe Lovano(ts-2) John Hicks(p) Santi Debriano(b) Jeff Watts(dm) Steve Berrios(perc-3).
Englewood Cliffs,NJ,March 11-12,1996

Glue fingers -1,2
From now on -1,3
On Second and Fifth -2
Thoughts -1,2,3
This side of infinity
Come in out of the rain
Suspension
Gift of love

All titles issued on CD BN 8-38098-2.

391

CAECILIE NORBY - MY CORNER OF THE SKY:
Caecilie Norby(vo) with Randy Brecker(tp-2) Michael Brecker(ts-1) Joey Calderazzo(p) David Kikoski(org-1) Lars Danielsson(b) Terri Lyne Carrington(dm,perc) Louise Norby(backgr.vo-1)
(EMI Medley-Denmark)(Sound On Sound) NYC,March 13-15 & 19,1996

Spinning wheel -1
Calling you CD Cap.5-21605-2
Just one of those things
Life on Mars -2 (p out)

All titles on CD BN 8-53422-2.

Caecilie Norby(vo) with Scott Robinson(fl-1) Michael Brecker(ts-2) David Kikoski(p) Lars Danielsson(b) Terri Lyne Carrington(dm,perc).
(EMI Medley-Denmark)(Sound On Sound) NYC,March 13-15 & 19,1996

The look of love -1 CD BN 8-57463-2,(C)4-94888-2,(Sp)8-56842-2
The right to love
African fairytale
Snow -2
A song for you

All titles on CD BN 8-53422-2.

DIANNE REEVES - THE GRAND ENCOUNTER:
Dianne Reeves(vo) with Harry Edison(tp) Clark Terry(tp,vo-2) Al Grey(tb) Phil Woods(as) James Moody (ts,vo-2) Kenny Barron(p) Rodney Whitaker(b) Herlin Riley(dm) Joe Williams-1,Germaine Bazzle-2, Kimberley Longstreth-2 (vo).
(Clinton Studios) NYC,April 4-6,1996
Overdubbing:(Presence Studio) Westport,CT,April 8-9,1996

Old country CD BN(Sp)8-56842-2
Tenderly CD BN(J)TOCJ-6135
Let me love you -1
Ha!-2

All titles issued on CD BN 8-38268-2.

Dianne Reeves(vo) with Harry Edison(tp-1) Bobby Watson(as-2) James Moody(ts-3) Toots Thielemans (hca-4) Kenny Barron(p) Rodney Whitaker(b) Herlin Riley(dm) Germaine Bazzle-5(vo).
Same sessions

I'm okay
Some other Spring -1 CD BN(Sp)5-21755-2
Cherokee -2 CD BN(J)TOCJ-6088,TODP-2542
After hours -3 CD BN 8-57463-2,(J)TOCJ-6187
Besame mucho -4
Side by side -5

All titles issued on CD BN 8-38268-2.

<u>KURT ELLING</u> - <u>THE MESSENGER</u>:
Kurt Elling(vo) with Orbert Davis-1(tp,flh) Eddie Johnson(ts) Laurence Hobgood(p) Rob Amster(b) Jim Widlowski(dm-1).

(Tone Zone Recording)	Chicago,May 5,1996
Prelude to a kiss	CD BN 8-52727-2
Oh my God -1	unissued

<u>SHERMAN IRBY</u> - <u>FULL CIRCLE</u>:
Sherman Irby(as) James Hurt(p) Eric Revis(b) Dana Murray(dm).

(Clinton Studios) NYC,May 17,1996

Betty the baptist
Rachaphobia
How strong is our love?
Wee -1
Mamma Faye
Crown royal
Giant steps
The choice (p out)
It's a new day
Homesick

-1: Charlie Persip(dm) replaces Murray.
All titles issued on CD BN 8-52251-2.

<u>CHARLIE HUNTER</u> - <u>NATTY DREAD</u>:
Calder Spanier(as) Kenny Brooks(ts) Charlie Hunter(g) Scott Amendola(dm).

(Mobius Music)	SF,May ,1996
Lively up yourself	
No woman, no cry	CD BN(J)TOCJ-6134,HMV Jazz(E)5-20884-2
Them belly full	
Rebel music	
So jah seh	
Natty dread	
Bend down low	
Talkin' blues	
Revolution	

All titles issued on BN(E)8-52420-1,CD BN 8-52420-2.
Note: LP was issued only in England.

LENA HORNE - BEING MYSELF:
Lena Horne(vo) with Mike Renzi(p) Bobby Forrester(org-1) Rodney Jones,George Benson-2(g)Benjamin Brown(b) Akira Tana (dm).
(Power Station) NYC,May/June,1996

As long as I live
After you
It's alright with me -1,2 CD BN 5-21151-2
How long has this been going on -1

All titles issued on CD BN 8-34286-2.

Us3 - BROADWAY & 52nd:
Alexander Pope Norris-1,Dominic Glover-2(tp) Dennis Rollins(tb-3) Mike Williams(as-4) Ed Jones-5(ss,ts) Steve Williamson-6,Mike Smith(ts-7) Jonathan Gee(melodica-8) Gherardo Catanzaro(p-9) Gareth Williams-10, Tim Vine-11(el p) Tony Remy(g-12) KCB,Shabaam Sahdee (vo) Geoff Wilkinson(samples, programming).
(Studio M & Konk) London,April-July,1996

Intro
Come on everybody (get down)-1,10 (voKCB)
CD BN 8-58610-2,4-99351-2
Caught up in a struggle -2 (voSS)
True to the game -10 (voKCB)
Snakes -5 (voKCB)
I'm thinkin' about your body -5,11 (voSS)
CD BN 8-58662-2,4-99351-2,(Au)4-97893-2
Grand groove -9 (voKCB)
Nowadays -3 (voKCB)
Sheep -12 (voSS)
Doin' a crime -6 (voSS)
Recognise and realise -2,5,7 (voKCB,SS)
Time and space -2 (voSS)
Soul brother -4 (voKCB)
Hymn for her -8

All titles issued on BN B1-30027,CD 8-30027-2.

From same sessions:

Come on everybody (get down)-1,10 (voKCB):
Radio edit CD BN 8-58610-2
Rickety raw urban remix -
Peppermint lounge remix -
Tunnel remix -
Youth in asia remix -
Q-Burns abstract message remix - 4-99351-2
I'm thinkin' about your body -5,11 (voSS):
CD BN 8-58662-2,4-99351-2
Brixton bounce remix -
Neck snappin' mix -
Blacksmith remix -
K.M.A. conclusion mix -

DENISE JANNAH - DIFFERENT COLOURS:
Denise Jannah(vo) with Klaus Gesing(ss-1) Koen van Baal(keyb) Peter Tiehuis(g-2) Marc van Wageningen (b,el b) Rene Creemers(dm) Bart Fermie(cga,chimes,udu,perc,vo) Martin Verdonk(perc-3) Lisa Boray (backgr.vo-4).
(EMI-Holland) (Studio 150) Amsterdam, mid 1996

You go to my head -1
Your eyes -1,2,3
Never meant to be -2,3
You always make me smile -2,4
Don't dream it's over (dm out)

All titles issued on CD BN(Eu)8-54729-2.

Denise Jannah(vo) with Hans Dulfer(ts-1) Bert van den Brink(p,org) Koen van Baal(keyb-2) Leonardo Amuedo(g-3) Marc van Wageningen(b) Gerhard Jelter(dm) Bart Fermie,Martin Verdonk(perc-4).
Same sessions

All blues -1
I'll always be here -2
High wire -3,4
You must believe in Spring -2,3,4 (dm out)
Have a little faith in me (vo & g only) CD BN(Sp)8-56842-2

All titles issued on CD BN(Eu)8-54729-2.

Denise Jannah(vo,skratji drum,sek'seki) with Koen van Baal(keyb) Leonardo Amuedo(g) Marc van Wageningen(b) Gregory Kranenburg(dm) Bart Fermie(backgr.vo).
Same sessions

Mi gron (my land) CD BN(Eu)8-54729-2

EVERETTE HARP - WHAT'S GOIN' ON:
Jerry Hey,Gary Grant(tp) Reggie Young(tb) Najee(fl-1) Kirk Whalum(ts-2) Everette Harp(saxes,fls,keyb, programming,backgr.vo) Mark Hollingsworth(bs) George Duke-3,Don Wyatt(p) Greg Philinganes(org-4) A. Ray "The Weeper" Fuller-5,Doc Powell(g) Larry Kimpel (b) "Li'l" John Roberts(dm) Munyungo Jackson (perc) Kim Kilgore,Charlie Bisharat,Michael James,Melissa Hasin(strings) Kenny Loggins,Howard Hewitt (vo-6) Arsenio Hall,Dawnn Lewis (recitation-7) Lynn Fiddmont-Lindsey,Lori Perry,Valerie Mayo,Maxanne Lewis,Fred White,Will Wheaton,Jessie Campbell,Cassie Bonner,Yolanda Adams(backgr.vo).
(Sunset Sound,Rambo Records,Mad Hatter & Rue Harp Studios)
June-July,1996

What's goin' on -9 CD BN(J)TOCJ-6153,HMV Jazz(E)5-20881-2
What's happening brother
Flyin' high (in the friendly sky)
Save the children -7
God is love
Mercy mercy me -3,6
Right on -1
Wholly holy -4,8
Inner city blues (makes me wanna holler)-1,2,4,5 CD BN 4-94211-2
Inner city blues (reprise)

-8: Yolanda Adams(vo) & The Kirt Carr Singers (Kirt Carr,Chaz Lamar,Edwards Tate,Sherron Bennett, Andrea Mellini,Iris Howse,Troy Clark,Yvette Williams,Jacquelyn Boyd)(gospel choir) added.
-9: Everette Harp,Darryl Porter,Jessie Campbell,Cassie Bonner,Walter Canady(party noises) added.
All titles issued CD BN 8-53068-2.

395

HELEN ERIKSEN - STANDARDS:

Helen Eriksen(ss,as,ts,vo) Jon Balke(el p-1,synth b-2) Yngve Moe(el b-3) Tommy Tee(synth,programming).
(EMI Norway)(Tee Studio) Oslo, mid 1996

Holy greed -1,3 CD BN 8-57463-2
What is this thing called love -3
City -1,2
The do don't die (x-tro) -1,2

All titles issued on CD BN(Eu)8-53325-2,(J)TOCP-50085.

Helen Eriksen(ts,vo) Helge Lilletvedt(el p-1) H.P. Gundersen(pedal steel g-2) Stefan Olsson(g) Tommy Tee(synth,programming) N-Light-N-3(rapper).
(EMI Norway)(Tee Studio) Oslo, mid 1996

Low rain in pain -1 CD BN(Eu)8-53325-2
Shake my hand -1,3 -
Slaves -2,3 -
Low rain in pain (radio edit)
Low rain in pain (remix radio edit)
Low rain in pain (remix main pass)

All titles issued on CD BN(J)TOCP-50085.

Helen Eriksen(ts,vb,vo) H.P. Gundersen-1(keyb,g) Tommy Tee(synth,programming).
(EMI Norway)(Tee Studio) Oslo, mid 1996

Arms around you -1 CD BN(Sp)8-56842-2
Cme dme
Alone

All titles issued on CD BN(Eu)8-53325-2,(J)TOCP-50085.

Helen Eriksen(ts) Helge Lilletvedt(p) Yngve Moe(b) Frank Jacobsen(dm)
(EMI Norway)(Live) c.1996

Loveskit #1
Loveskit #2
Loveskit #3

All titles issued on CD BN(Eu)8-53325-2,(J)TOCP-50085.

JOE LOVANO - CELEBRATING SINATRA:

Joe Lovano(ts) Kenny Werner(p) George Mraz(b) Al Foster(dm).
(Clinton Studios) NYC,June 2 & 3,1996

Imagination
This love of mine
South of the border (p out)
Chicago (p,b out)

All titles issued on CD BN 8-37718-2.

JOE LOVANO - CELEBRATING SINATRA:
Joe Lovano(ts) Kenny Werner(p) George Mraz(b) Al Foster(dm).
Judi Silvano(vo) Billy Drewes(ss bass cl) Dick Oatts(ts,fl) Ted Nash (ts,cl) Tom Christensen(ts,oboe,Eng h) Erik Friedlander(cello) Manny Albam(orchestrations,cond-1) added. Same sessions

	I'm a fool to want you	
	I've got the world on a string	CD BN 4-95981-2
	I've got you under my skin	
	Someone to watch over me	CD BN 5-20808-2
	One for my baby (Drewes out)	
	I'll never smile again -1	
	All the way-1	
	In other words (Fly me to the moon) -1	
	The song is you -1 (Oatts out)	

-1: John Clark(frh) Michael Rabinowitz(bassoon) Mark Feldman,Sara Perkins(v) Lois Martin(viola) Emily Mitchell(harp) added.

All titles issued on CD BN 8-37718-2.

BENNY GREEN - KALEIDOSCOPE:
Stanley Turrentine(ts) Benny Green(p) Russell Malone(g) Ron Carter(b) Lewis Nash(dm).
(Clinton Studios) NYC,June 5,1996

	M & E (ts,g out)	rejected
(tk.10)	Central Park South	CD BN 8-52037-2
	Pittsburgh shuffle	rejected
(tk.2/3)	You're my melody (ts & p only)	CD BN 8-52037-2
	The sexy Mexy (ts out)	rejected

BENNY GREEN - KALEIDOSCOPE:
Antonio Hart(as-1) Benny Green(p) Russell Malone(g) Ron Carter(b) Lewis Nash(dm).
(Clinton Studios) NYC,June 6,1996

(tk.3)	Apricot -1	CD BN 8-52037-2
(tk.1)	Soft center -1	-
(tk.3)	Kaleidoscope -1 (reprise)	-
(tk.4)	Kaleidoscope -1	-
	Benny's blues (g out)	rejected
(tk.7)	The sexy Mexy	CD BN 8-52037-2
(tk.3)	My girl Bill (dm out)	-
(tk.1)	Patience (g & dm out)	-

PAT MARTINO - ALL SIDES NOW:
Pat Martino,Mike Stern(g) Scott Colley(b) Ben Perowsky(dm).
(Sound On Sound) NYC,June 1,1996

(tk.2)	Ayako	CD BN 8-37627-2
(tk.2)	Outrider	-

Pat Martino,Tuck Andress(g).
(Musegarden) NYC,June 7,1996

	Two of a kind	CD BN 8-37627-2

Pat Martino,Les Paul(g) Lou Pollo(rhythm g) Paul Howinski(b).
(Sound On Sound) NYC,June 15.1996

(tk.4)	I'm confessin' (that I love you)	CD BN 8-37627-2,EMI Music(C)4-94893-2

PAT MARTINO - ALL SIDES NOW:
Pat Martino(g) Cassandra Wilson(vo).
(Sorcerer Sound) NYC,June 23,1996

Both sides now CD BN 8-37627-2

FAREED HAQUE - DEJA VU:
Elizabeth Conant(acc-2) Ron Perillo(el p-1) Fareed Haque,Dave Onderdonk(g) Jonathan Paul(b) Joe Bianco (dm) Tim Mulvenna(perc) Carlos Villalobos(perc-3,drum programming-4) Larry Gray(cello-5).
(War Zone Studio) Chicago,July 18-30,1996

Almost cut my hair
Everybody I love you
Carry on -1
Country girl -1
Helples s-2,3,5
Our house -4,5
Woodstock -4
Deja vu -4,6

-6: David Chelinsky(g) Joe Rendon(bgo,cga,chekere) added.
All titles issued on CD BN 8-52419-2.

Elizabeth Conant(acc-1) Fareed Haque,Dave Onderdonk(g) Carlos Villalobos(ac bass g,drum programming-2) Joe Bianco(dm) Tim Mulvenna(perc). Same sessions

Teach your children -1
4 + 20 -2

Both titles issued on CD BN 8-52419-2.

Fareed Haque(g). Same sessions

Teach your children (intro)
Teach your children (reprise)
Interlude: Farred bops
Interlude (studio talk)

All titles issued on CD BN 8-52419-2.

PAT MARTINO - ALL SIDES NOW:
Pat Martino,Joe Satriani(g) Michael Hedges-1(dm,shakers) Jeff Hirshfield(dm-2).
(Speech & Hearing Clinic) Mendacino,CA,July 27,1996

Ellipsis -1 CD BN 8-37627-2
Never and after -2 -

Pat Martino,Michael Hedges(ac g).
(Speech & Hearing Clinic) Mendacino,CA,July 30,1996

Two days old CD BN 8-37627-2

KURT ELLING - THE MESSENGER:
Kurt Elling(vo) with Laurence Hobgood(p,keyb) Rob Amster(b) Paul Wertico(dm,perc).
(Tone Zone Recording) Chicago,September 14,1996

Nature boy
Ginger bread boy

Both titles issued on CD BN 8-52727-2.

DIANNE REEVES:
Dianne Reeves(vo) with Virgil Jones(tp) Ronnie Cuber(bs) Kevin Hays(p) Ira Coleman(b) Billy Kilson(dm) Bob Belden(arr).
(Avatar Studios) NYC,September 19,1996

(tk.2)	He may be your man	CD BN 8-36736-2
(tk.3)	Sugar blues	-
(tk.2)	Jingle bells	CD BN 8-56991-2

JACKY TERRASSON:
Jacky Terrasson(p).
(Avatar Studios) NYC,September ,1996

Budism CD BN 8-36736-2

BILL STEWART - TELEPATHY:
Steve Wilson(ss,as) Seamus Blake(ts) Bill Carrothers(p) Larry Grenadier(b) Bill Stewart(dm).
(Clinton Studios) NYC,September 29,1996

(tk.1) These are they
(tk.7) Mynah
(tk.2) Calm
(tk.2) Fano

All titles issued on CD BN 8-53210-2

Steve Wilson(ss,as) Seamus Blake(ts) Bill Carrothers(p) Larry Grenadier(b) Bill Stewart (dm).
(Clinton Studios) NYC,September 30,1996

(tk.4) Lyra
(tk.6) Dwell on this
(tk.4) Happy chickens
(tk.7) Little Melonae (p & dm only)
(tk.3) Rhythm-a-ning (p,b,dm only)

All titles issued on CD BN 8-53210-2

ELIANE ELIAS - THE THREE AMERICAS:
Eliane Elias(p,vo) Oscar Castro-Neves(g-1) Cafe(perc-2).
(Avatar Studios) NYC,September/October,1996

Chega de saudade -1 (voEE) CD Cap.5-21605-2
Brigas nunca mas -1,2
Introduction to Guarani
Missing you (voEE)

All titles issued on CD BN 8-53328-2.

Dave Valentin(fl-1) Gil Goldstein(acc-2) Mark Feldman(v-2) Eliane Elias(p,vo) Marc Johnson(b) Satoshi Takeishi(dm) Manolo Badrena(perc,vo).
(Avatar Studios) NYC,September/October,1996

The time is now (voMB) -1 CD BN 4-95701-2
O Guarani
Jungle journey (voEE)
Jumping fox (perc out)
Chorango -2 (perc out)

All titles issued on CD BN 8-53328-2.

399

<u>ELIANE ELIAS</u> - <u>THE THREE AMERICAS</u>:
Dave Valentin(fl) Eliane Elias(p,vo) Oscar Castro-Neves(g-1) Marc Johnson(b,backgr.vo-1) Satoshi Takeishi (dm,backgr.vo-1) Cafe(perc,backgr.vo-1) Amanda Elias Brecker(vo).
(Avatar Studios) NYC,September/October,1996

An up dawn (voEE,AEB)-1
Caipora (voEE)
Crystal and lace

All titles issued on CD BN 8-53328-2.

<u>KURT ELLING</u> - <u>THE MESSENGER</u>:
Kurt Elling,Cassandra Wilson-1(vo) with Orbert Davis(tp-2) Laurence Hobgood(p,keyb) Rob Amster(b) Paul Wertico(dm,perc) Jim Widlowski(perc).
(Tone Zone Recording) Chicago,October 15,1996

Time of the season -1 CD BN(C)4-94888-2,5-20457-2
April in Paris -2

Both titles issued on CD BN 8-52727-2

<u>DOKY BROTHERS 2</u>:
Bill Evans(ss-3) Neils Lan Doky(p) John Scofield-1, Louis Winsberg-2(g) Chris Minh Doky(b) John Boudreaux(dm) Xavier Desandre-Navarre(perc) Trilok Gurtu(tablas-4)
(EMI-Medley,Denmark) (Focus Recording) Copenhagen,September-December,1996
(& various overdubs in NYC, LA and Paris)

Man in the mirror -1
Forever grateful -2
Sex pots -2,4
Silent prayer -3

All titles issued on CD BN 8-56458-2.

Randy Brecker(flh-4) Neils Lan Doky(p) Chris Minh Doky(b) Jeff Watts-1,Alex Riel(dm-2) Jean "Toots" Thielemans(hca-3) Same sessions

Waiting on you -1
Efter festen -2
Reminiscence -2,3
Time to say goodbye -2,4

All titles issued on CD BN 8-56458-2.

Neils Lan Doky(p) Joyce Imbesi(keyb) Chris Minh Doky(b) Al Jarreau(vo).Same sessions

How can I help you say goodbye (voAJ) CD BN 8-56458-2

Paul Mazzio(tp) Neils Lan Doky(p) Randy Cannon(keyb) Gino Vannelli(g,synth,perc,vo) Chris Minh Doky (b) Terri Lyne Carrington(dm,perc) Anders Mogensen(cymbals).
Same sessions

Tender lies (voGV) CD BN 8-56458-2

David Sanborn(as-1) Neils Lan Doky(p) Chris Parks-1(g,arr) Chris Minh Doky(b) Terri Lyne Carrington (dm) Darryl Munyungo Jackson(perc) Trilok Gurtu(tablas-2) Sanne Salomonsen-1,Dianne Reeves-2 (vo) Sharon Miller(backgr. vo-1). Same sessions

If you were my man (voSS) -1 CD BN 8-56458-2
Waiting in vain (voDR) -2 -

400

RONNIE LAWS - TRIBUTE TO THE LEGENDARY EDDIE HARRIS:
Ronnie Laws(ss,ts) Vernell Brown,Jr.(p) Craig T. Cooper(g-1) Mike Elizondo(b) Jeffrey Suttles(dm) Darryl Munyungo Jackson(perc)

(Capitol Studios) LA,October 28,30 & 31,1996
and (Mad Hatter Studio) LA,November 4-7,1996

Listen here -1
Hip hoppin'-1
Freedom jazz dance
Boogie woogie bossa nova
Cold duck -2
Sham time -1,3,4

-2: Oscar Brashear(tp) added.
-3: Patrice Rushen (p) added.
-4: Oscar Brashear,Michael Stewart(tp) Gary Bias(bs) added.

All titles issued on CD BN 8-55330-2.

Ronnie Laws(ss,ts) Vernell Brown Jr.(p,org) Larry Antonion(b) William Bryant(dm) Darryl Munyungo Jackson(perc) Andrea Coleman(vo-1).
Same dates

I don't want no one but you
Compared to what -1

Both titles issued on CD BN 8-55330-2.

PAT MARTINO - ALL SIDES NOW:
Pat Martino(g) Kevin Eubanks(ac g).
(The Complex) LA,November 13,1996

Progression CD BN 8-37627-2

Pat Martino,Charlie Hunter(g) Scott Amendola(dm)
(The Complex) LA,November 15,1996

Too high CD BN 8-37627-2,HMV Jazz(E)5-20884-2

YULE BE BOPPIN':
ELIANE ELIAS: Eliane Elias(p) Marc Johnson(b) Satoshi Takeishi(dm).
(River Sound) NYC,December 3,1996

I've got my love to keep me warm CD BN 8-56991-2

401

DREIKLANG - DREIKLANG:
Matthias Erlewein(ts) Martin Wind(b) Jochen Ruckert(dm)
(EMI-Germany) (Avatar Studios) NYC,December 19 & 20,1996

Remembering October 13th
Very early
No prisoners
As far as the moon...
Out in P.A.
In love in vain
Chorale
Beam to me -1
Will I ever learn from this -1
Nos-ex -1
A sad story -1

-1:John Abercrombie(g) added.
All titles issued on CD BN(G)8-21944-2.

KEVIN HAYS - ANDALUCIA:
Kevin Hays(p) Ron Carter(b) Jack DeJohnette(dm).
(Clinton Studios) NYC,December 21,1996

	Hart	rejected
	The breeze and I	CD BN 8-55817-2
	Chickory stick	rejected
(tk.2)	Break	unissued
	Agua	rejected
(tk.2)	Con alma	CD BN 8-55817-2

Kevin Hays(p) Ron Carter(b) Jack DeJohnette(dm).
(Clinton Studios) NYC,December 22,1996

(tk.14)	Agua
(tk.10)	And I love her
(tk.3)	That's all
(tk.7)	Mind
(tk.2)	Einbahnstrasse
(tk.9)	Chickory stick
(tk.6)	Hart

All titles issued on CD BN 8-55817-2.

LEE KONITZ - ALONE TOGETHER (57150)/ANOTHER SHADE OF BLUE (98222):
Lee Konitz(as) Brad Mehldau(p) Charlie Haden(b).
(The Jazz Bakery) LA,December 21-22,1996

Alone together	CD BN 8-57150-2,(Sp)5-21755-2
The song is you	-
Cherokee	-
What is this thing called love	-
You stepped out of a dream	-
Another shade of blue	CD BN 4-98222-2
Everything happens to me (b out)	-
What's new	-
Body and soul	-
All of us	-

Note: CD 8-57150-2 was issued as by Lee Konitz,Brad Mehldau and Charlie Haden.Year was incorrectly listed as 1997 on CD 4-98222-2.

JACKY TERRASSON & CASSANDRA WILSON - RENDEZVOUS:
Jacky Terrasson(p) Lonnie Plaxico(b) Cassandra Wilson(vo).
(Clinton Studios) NYC,January 4,1997

(tk.3)	Come rain or come shine	CD BN(Au)4)-98320-2,(J)TOCJ-6096, EMI Music(C)4-94893-2
(tk.4)	Little boy lost	CD BN 8-55484-2,(J)TOCJ-6096
(tk.3)	My ship	- -
	It might as well be Spring	rejected

Jacky Terrasson(p,el p) Lonnie Plaxico(b,el b) Mino Cinelu(perc) Cassandra Wilson(vo).
(Clinton Studios) NYC,January 5,1997

(tk.8)	It might as well be Spring	CD BN 8-55484-2,(J)TOCJ-6096
(tk.1)	I remember you	- -
	Tennessee waltz	rejected
	Baby plum	-

Same.
(Clinton Studios) NYC,January 6,1997

(tk.10)	Tennessee waltz	CD BN 8-55484-2,(J)TOCJ-6096,TOCJ-6153, TOCJ-6189,EMI(E)5-20535-2
(tk.1)	Old devil moon	CD BN 8-55484-2,(J)TOCJ-6096
	The waters of March	rejected

Same.
(Clinton Studios) NYC,January 19,1997

(tk.4)	Tea for two	CD BN 8-55484-2,(J)TOCJ-6096
(tk.2)	If ever I would leave you	- -

JOE LOVANO & GONZALO RUBALCABA - FLYING COLORS:
Joe Lovano(ts,ss,alto cl,dm,gongs) Gonzalo Rubalcaba(p).
(Sony Studios) NYC,January 11,1997

Flying colors	CD BN 8-56092-2
How deep is the ocean	-
Boss town	-
Bird food	-
Spontaneous color (solo p)	-
Phantasm	-
Ugly beauty	-
Hot house	-
Gloria's step	-
Mr. Hyde	-
I love music	-
Along came Betty	-
TTTT	unissued

MARK SHIM - MIND OVER MATTER:
Mark Shim(ts) Geri Allen(p) David Fiuczynski(g-1) Curtis Lundy(b) Ralph Peterson(dm).
(Systems Two Studio) Brooklyn,N.Y.,February 19 & 20,1997

The chosen ones
Oveida -1
Dumplin'-2

-2: Ralph Peterson(tp) overdubbed on themes.
All titles issued on CD BN 8-37628-2.

403

MARK SHIM - MIND OVER MATTER:
Mark Shim(ts) Geri Allen(p) David Fiuczynski(g,vo-1) Curtis Lundy(b) Eric Harland(dm).
Same sessions

Arrival (intro)
Mind over matter
Snake eyes (g out)
The dungeon (interlude)
Crazy
Remember Rockefeller at Attica -1 (p out)
Mass exodus (outro)

All titles issued on CD BN 8-37628-2.

YULE BE BOPPIN':
JAVON JACKSON(ts) Mulgrew Miller(p) Peter Washington(b) Billy Drummond(dm).
(Avatar Studios) NYC,February 22,1997

Santa baby CD BN 8-56991-2

YULE BE BOPPIN':
PAT MARTINO(g) James Ridl(p).
(Avatar Studios) NYC,February 25,1997

Santa Claus is coming to town CD BN 8-56991-2

PETE (LA ROCA) SIMS - SWINGTIME:
Jimmy Owens(tp) Dave Liebman(ss) Ricky Ford(ts) George Cables(p) Santi Debriano(b) Pete (LaRoca) Sims (dm).
(Clinton Studios) NYC,February 28,1997

Susan's waltz
Tomorrow's expectations
Nihon bashi
Amanda's song
Body and soul

All titles issued on CD BN 8-54876-2.

Lance Bryant(ss) replaces Liebman.
(Clinton Studios) NYC,March 1,1997

Drumtown
Candu
The candyman

All titles issued on CD BN 8-54876-2.

YULE BE BOPPIN':
FAREED HAQUE(g) Dennis Irwin(b).
(Avatar Studios) NYC,March 6,1997

You're a mean one Mr. Grinch CD BN 8-56991-2

JOE LOVANO(ts,gongs,chimes) Dennis Irwin(b,gongs,chimes) Yoron Israel(dm) Judi Silvano(vo,gongs, chimes).
Same session

Carols of the bells CD BN 8-56991-2

YULE BE BOPPIN':
JOE LOVANO: Joe Lovano(ts) Kenny Werner(p) Dennis Irwin(b) Yoron Israel(dm) Satoshi Takeishi(bgo) Tom Evered (as "Sweet Daddy Lowe")(recitation).
Same session

Be-bop Santa Claus CD BN 8-56991-2

JACKY TERRASSON: Jacky Terrasson(p,org,harpsichord,Chinese fl) Mino Cinelu(dm,bgo,cga,Indian fl).
(Avatar Studios) NYC,March 11,1997

Adeste fideles/Little drummer boy CD BN 8-56991-2

RENEE ROSNES - AS WE ARE NOW:
Renee Rosnes(p) Christian McBride(b) Jack DeJohnette(dm).
(EMI-Canada) Englewood Cliffs,NJ,March 12 & 13,1997

Abstraction blue
As we are now
Pee Wee

Chris Potter(ss,ts) Renee Rosnes(p) Christian McBride(b) Jack DeJohnette(dm).
Same sessions

Black holes
The land of five rivers
Mizmahta
Non-fiction
Bulldog's chicken run
Absinthe

All titles issued on CD BN 8-56810-2.

GREG OSBY - FURTHER ADO:
Tim Hagans(tp-1) Cleave Guyton-2(fl,alto fl,cl) Greg Osby(as) Mark Shim(ts-1) Jason Moran(p) Lonnie Plaxico(b) Eric Harland(dm) Jeff Haynes(perc-3).
(Systems Two Studio) Brooklyn,N.Y.,March 15-21,1997

Six of one
Mentor's prose
The 13th floor
Transparency -2
Of sound mind -2
Tenderly -3
Heard -1,3
Vixen's Vance -1,3
Soldan -1
The Mmental -1,4

-4: Calvin Jones(b) replaces Plaxico.

All titles issued on CD BN 8-56543-2.

405

TOMMY FLANAGAN - SUNSET AND THE MOCKINGBIRD:
Tommy Flanagan(p) Peter Washington(b) Lewis Nash(dm).
(The Village Vanguard) NYC,March 16,1997

Birdsong
With malice toward none
Let's
I waited for you
Tin tin deo
Sunset and the mockingbird
The balanced scales/The cup bearers
Good night my love

All titles issued on CD BN 4-93155-2.

PIECES OF A DREAM - PIECES:
Eddie Baccus Jr.(ss) Michael (Antonio) Thornton(keyb,dm programming) Michael Herring(ac g)
(Manhattan Beach Studio) NYC,March 19 & 20,1997

Knikki's smile CD BN 8-54052-2

Hubert Laws(fl-1) James Lloyd,Greg Phillinganes(keyb) Paul Jackson Jr.(g-1) Cedric Napoleon(b) Curtis Harmon(dm,dm programming)
(Chapel Studios/Westlake Studios) LA,March 27 & 28,1997

Epiphany CD BN 8-54052-2
Voices of wisdom -1 -

YULE BE BOPPIN':
CHARLIE HUNTER: Charlie Hunter(g).
(Mobius Music) SF,March 29,1997

Christmas time is here CD BN 8-56991-2

KURT ELLING: Kurt Elling(vo) with Art Davis(tp) Eddie Johnson(ts,closing rap) Laurence Hobgood(p) Rob Amster(b) Michael Raynor(dm).
(Chicago Recording Co.) Chicago,April 2,1997

Cool yule CD BN 8-56991-2

PIECES OF A DREAM - PIECES:
James Lloyd(keyb) Jeff Lorber(g,keyb) Cedric Napoleon(b) Curtis Harmon(dm,perc programming).
(JHL Sound) Pacific Palisades,CA,April 2 & 3,1997

Cut to the chase CD BN 8-54052-2

RAY BARRETTO - CONTACT!:
Michael Philip Mossman(tp,tb) Adam Kolker(ss,ts) John Di Martino(p) Jairo Moreno(b) Vince Cherico(dm) Ray Barretto(cga,perc) Ray Vega(perc).
(EMI France) (Systems Two Studio) Brooklyn,N.Y.,April 3,5,8 & 9,1997

Moss code
Caravan
Dance of Denial
Point of contact/Punto de contacto
La benedicion
Liberated spirit
The Summer knows
Sister Sadie
Serenata -1
Poinciana -1

-1: Hans Glawishnig(b) replaces Moreno.

All titles issued on CD BN 8-56974-2.

JACKY TERRASSON - RENDEZVOUS:
Jacky Terrasson(p,el p) Kenny Davis(b,el b) Mino Cinelu(perc).
(Clinton Studios) NYC,April 4,1997

(tk.)1	Chicago 1987	CD BN 8-55484-2,(Eu)5-23444-2,(J)TOCJ-6096
	Sister Cheryl	rejected
(tk.1)	Chan's song	CD BN 8-55484-2,(J)TOCJ-6096
(tk.1)	Medieval blues	-
	Autumn leaves	rejected

Jacky Terrasson(p,el p).
(Clinton Studios) NYC,April 5,1997

(tk.2)	Autumn leaves	CD BN 8-55484-2,(J)TOCJ-6096

PIECES OF A DREAM - PIECES:
Grover Washington Jr.(saxes-1) James Lloyd,Michael (Antonio) Thornton(keyb) Michael Herring(g-1) Bill Pearce(synth b-1) Cedric Napoleon(b) Curtis Harmon(dm)
(The Studio) Philadelphia,April 12 & 13,1997

1257	CD BN 8-54052-2
Sittin' up in my room -1	-

James Lloyd(p) Michael (Antonio) Thornton(keyb) Rohn Lawrence(g) Curtis Harmon(dm,dm programming, synth b).
(Manhattan Beach Studio) NYC,April 14 & 15,1997

The very first time	CD BN 8-54052-2

James Lloyd(p,programming,all instruments).Same session.

D'Vora	CD BN 8-54052-2

YULE BE BOPPIN':
JUDI SILVANO: Joe Locke(vb) Drew Gress(b) Bob Meyer(dm) Judi Silvano(vo).
(Unique Sound) NYC,April 20,1997

I'd like you for Christmas	CD BN 8-56991-2

BOB BELDEN - TAPESTRY:

Tim Hagans(tp) Bob Belden(ss) Kevin Hays(el p) Scott Kinsey(synth) John Hart,Bluey Maunick(g-1) David Dyson(el b) Billy Kilson(dm).

(D.K. Studios) NYC,April 28,1997

(tk.2)	Smackwater Jack -1	CD BN 8-57891-2
(tk.1)	I feel the earth move	-
(tk.1)	Venus as a boy	unissued

Tim Hagans(tp) Bob Belden(ss) Kevin Hays(el p) Scott Kinsey(synth) John Hart(g) David Dyson(el b) Billy Kilson(dm).

(D.K. Studios) NYC,April 29,1997

(tk.1)	Way down yonder	rejected
(tk.2)	Iron butterfly	unissued
(tk.1)	Home again	CD BN 8-57891-2

Tim Hagans(tp) Bob Belden(ss) Kevin Hays(p-2) Scott Kinsey(synth) John Hart(g-1) David Dyson(el b) Billy Kilson(dm).

(D.K. Studios) NYC,April 30,1997

(tk.1)	It's too late -1	CD BN 8-57891-2	
(tk.1)	You've got a friend -2	-	
(tk.1)	So far away -1	-	EMI Music(C)4-94893-2
(tk.1)	You make me feel like a natural woman	-	

BOB DOROUGH - RIGHT ON MY WAY HOME:

Bob Dorough(p.vo) Bill Takas(b) Grady Tate(dm).

(Red Rock Recordings) Saylorsburg,PA,April 29,1997

Whatever happened to love songs
Zacherly
Hodges
Up jumped a bird
Spring can really hang you up the most

All titles issued on CD BN 8-57729-2.

PIECES OF A DREAM - PIECES:

Everette Harp(saxes,keyb,synth & loop prgramming) James Lloyd(synth,keyb,dm programming) Curtis Harmon(dm programming,keyb) Shaun LaBelle(loop programming).

(Rue Harp Sounds) Saugus,CA,April 29-30,1997

...And a bag of chips CD BN 8-54052-2

YULE BE BOPPIN':

BENNY GREEN: Benny Green(p) Miles Griffith(vo,bells,tapping).

(Anderson Audio) Brooklyn,April 30,1997

Zat you Santa Claus CD BN 8-56991-2

BOB DOROUGH & BOB BELDEN: Tim Hagans(tp) Bob Belden(ss) Greg Osby(as) Bobby Watson(ts) Stefon Harris(vb) Bob Dorough(p,vo) Scott Kinsey(synth) Ira Coleman(b) Billy Kilson(dm).

(D.K. Studios) NYC,May 1,1997

tk.1	Blue Xmas (voBD)	CD BN 8-56991-2

BOB BELDEN - TAPESTRY:
Tim Hagans(tp) Bob Belden(ss) Kevin Hays(el p) Scott Kinsey(synth) John Hart(g) Ira Coleman(b) Billy Kilson (dm).

	(D.K. Studios)	NYC,May 2,1997
(tk.2)	Before	unissued
(tk.1)	Argentina	-
(tk.1)	Cambodian rhapsody pts.1-3 -1	-
(tk.2)	Tres con de o la	-
(tk.2)	Tapestry -2	CD BN 8-57891-2

-1: prerecorded music by The Royal Khmer Orchestra overdubbed on.
-2: Belden(ss) Kinsey(synth) only.

BOB DOROUGH - RIGHT ON MY WAY HOME:
Joe Lovano(ss,ts) Bob Dorough(p,vo) Christian McBride(b) Billy Hart(dm).

(Avatar Studios)	NYC May 6,1997
Moon river	CD EMI Music(C)4-94893-2
Right on my way home	
Walk on	
I get the neck of the chicken	
Something for Sidney	

All titles issued on CD BN 8-57729-2.

PIECES OF A DREAM - PIECES:
James Lloyd(keyb,backgr.vo) George Duke(synth programming) Kevin Chokan(g) Curtis Harmon(dm programming,backgr. vo) Mike Davis(vo,backgr. vo).

(Le Gonks West)	LA,May 7 & 8,1997
Anyway you want it	CD BN 8-54052-2

JAMES HURT - DARK GROOVES MYSTICAL RHYTHMS:
Antonio Hart,Abraham Burton(as) Jacques Schwartz-Bart(ts) James Hurt(p,perc) Eric Revis(b) Eric McPherson(dm) Elizabeth Kantumanou(vo).

(Avatar Studios)	NYC,May 10,1997
Waterfall	CD BN 4-95104-2

Antonio Hart(as) James Hurt(p) Eric Revis(b) Nasheet Waits(dm).
Same session.

Pyramids	CD BN 4-95104-2

Russell Gunn(tp) Robin Eubanks(tb) Sherman Irby(as) Greg Tardy(ts) James Hurt(p) Eric Revis(b) Dana Murray(dm).
Same session.

Venus	CD BN 4-95104-2

409

VIKTORIA TOLSTOY - WHITE RUSSIAN:
Viktoria Tolstoy(vo) with Peter Asplund(tp-1) Nils Landgren(tb-2) Per Johansson(as-3) Mats Oberg(hca-4) Jojje Wadenius-5(el g,vo) Esbjorn Svensson(p,keyb,vb,glockenspiel) Dan Berglund(b) Magnus Ostrom (dm,tablas, perc) Micke Littwold(backgr.vo-5).
(EMI-Sweden) (EMI Studios) Stockholm,c.Spring,1997

Solitary	CD BN(Sw) 8-21220-2
Venus & Mars -6	-
My Garden	-
I Do Care -3	-
Holy Water	-
Wonderful life -5,6	-
Invisible changes	-
High heels -1	-
For your love	-
Casablanca -2,5	-
Spring -4,6	-
My funny valentine (vo & p only)	
Solitary (single version)	

-6: Strings added,arr. by Joakim Milder.
All titles issued on CD BN(J)TOCP-50403.

DIANNE REEVES - NEW MORNING:
Dianne Reeves(vo) with David Torkanowsky(p,synth) Chris Severin(b,el b) Herlin Riley(dm).
(New Morning Club) Paris,May 14,1997

tk.1	Body and soul	CD BN(F)8-21533-2
tk.2	Yesterdays	-
tk.3	After hours	rejected
tk.4	Love for sale	CD BN(F)8-21533-2
tk.5	Nine	-
tk.6	Afro blue	unissued
tk.7	Endangered species	CD BN(F)8-21533-2
tk.8	Old souls	-
tk.9	Softly as in a morning sunrise	rejected
tk.10	Both sides now	CD BN(F)8-21533-2
tk.11	Comes love	-
tk.12	That's all	rejected
tk.13	The old country	-
tk.14	Nothing will be as it was	CD BN(F)8-21533-2
tk.15	Come to the river	rejected
tk.16	Summertime	CD BN(F)8-21533-2

DIANNE REEVES - THAT DAY...:
Dianne Reeves(vo) with Oscar Brashear(tp-1,flh-2) Bob Sheppard(ts-1,ss-2) Mulgrew Miller(p) Bob Hurst(b) Terri Lyne Carrington(dm).
(Mad Hatter Studios) LA,May 21-23 & 31,1997

Blue prelude -1
The twelfth of never -2
Close enough for love
Exactly like you

All titles on CD BN 8-56973-2.

DIANNE REEVES - THAT DAY...:
Dianne Reeves(vo) with Oscar Brashear(flh-1) Bob Sheppard(ts-1) Mulgrew Miller(p) Kevin Eubanks(g-2) Jeff Littleton(b) Terri Lyne Carrington(dm) Munyungo Jackson(perc-3).
(Mad Hatter Studios) LA,May 21-23 & 31,1997

Will you still love me tomorrow -1,3 CD EMI Music(C)4-94893-2
Morning has broken -2,3
Just a little lovin'-3
Dark truths

All titles on CD BN 8-56973-2.

Dianne Reeves(vo) with Oscar Brashear(flh) Bob Sheppard(fl) Mulgrew Miller(p) Kevin Eubanks(g) Darek Oles(b) Terri Lyne Carrington(dm) Munyungo Jackson(perc).
Same sessions

That day
Ain't nobody's business (if I do) (vo, g only)

Both titles on CD BN 8-56973-2.

RONNIE LAWS - HARVEST FOR THE WORLD:
Ronnie Laws(ts,ss,fl,backgr.vo-4) Kevin Flourney(keyb,arr,programming) Paul Jackson Jr.(g) Scott Cannady(b-1) Munyungo Darryl Jackson(perc) Michele Laws-2,Debra Laws-3(vo).
(The Mad Hatter) LA,May 27-30,1997

Prelude to harvest -5 (g,perc out)
Let me down easy -1,2
At your best you are love -5
Who loves you better -3,4
Harvest for the world -5
People of today -4
You still feel the need -5
So you wanna stay down -5

-5: Oren Waters,Maxine Waters,Julia Waters(backgr.vo) added.

All titles issued on CD BN 8-57875-2.

PIECES OF A DREAM - PIECES:
Eddie Baccus,Jr.(sax) James Lloyd,Michael (Antonion) Thornton(keyb-1) Cedric Napoleon(b) Curtis Harmon(dm,dm programming) Maxi Priest(vo-2) Paula Holloway,Charlene Holloway,Annette Hardeman (backgr.vo-3).
(The Studio) Philadelphia,June 2 & 3,1997

Pieces -1,2 CD BN 8-54052-2
Signed,sealed,delivered -3 -

JAVON JACKSON - GOOD PEOPLE:
Javon Jackson(ts) Fareed Haque(g) Vernon Reid(el g) John Medeski(org) Peter Washington(b) Billy Drummond(dm) Cyro Baptista(perc).
(Sound On Sound) NYC,June 2,1997

Flor de canela CD BN 8-56680-2

JAVON JACKSON - GOOD PEOPLE:
Javon Jackson(ts) Fareed Haque(g) Vernon Reid(el g-2) John Medeski(org-3) Peter Washington(b) Billy Drummond(dm) Cyro Baptista(perc-1).

	(Sear Sound)	NYC,June 10,1997
	Ed' oxum -1	
	Diane -1	
	Emergency	
	Exotica	
	Good people -2,3	
	Naaman -3	CD Hip-O 547897-2

All titles issued on CD BN 8-56680-2.

JACKY TERRASSON - ALIVE:
Jacky Terrasson(p) Ugonna Okegwo(b) Leon Parker(dm).

	(The Iridium)	NYC,June 14,1997
Set #1:		
tk.1	Nardis	rejected
tk.2	I love playing	-
tk.3	The way you look tonight	unissued
tk.4	Nature boy	rejected
tk.5	Baby plum	unissued
tk.6	Things ain't what they used to be	CD BN 8-59651-2,(Au)4-98320-2
tk.7	Cumba's dance	-
Set #2:		
tk.8	Autumn leaves	unissued
tk.9	Sister Cheryl	CD BN 8-59651-2
tk.10	Happy man	rejected
tk.11	Simple things	CD BN 8-59651-2
tk.12	I love playing	unissued
tk.13	Nature boy	CD BN 8-59651-2
tk.14	Love for sale	-
Set #3:		
tk.15	Fog taking over one valley	CD BN 8-59651-2
tk.16	You'd be so nice to come home to	unissued
tk.17	Cumba's dance	-
tk.18	Chan's song	-
tk.19	'Round midnight/Ruby my dear	-
tk.20	There's no disappointment in heaven (solo p)	-
tk.21	All blues	-
tk.22	The theme	CD BN 8-59651-2

BOB BELDEN - TAPESTRY:
Bob Belden(ss) Stefon Harris(vb) Kevin Hays(el p) John Hart(g) David Dyson(el b) Billy Kilson(dm).

	(D.K. Studios)	NYC,July 14,1997
(tk.2)	Will you still love me tomorrow	
(tk.2)	Where you lead	
(tk.1)	Beautiful	

All titles issued on CD BN 8-57891-2.

PRYSM - PRYSM 2:
Pierre De Bethmann(p) Christophe Wallemme(b) Benjamin Henocq(dm,perc).
(EMI-France)(La Buissonne Studios) Pernes Les Fontaines,France,July-August,1997

The way
The stone cutter
Temps dense
Come's peace
Extension
Suspended time
False roots
Hope
Secret world CD BN(C)5-20457-2
Tao of Chloe
Upside down
Eliot

All titles issued on CD BN 4-93565-2

TIM HAGANS & MARCUS PRINTUP - HUBSONGS:
Tim Hagans,Marcus Printup(tp) Vincent Herring(as-1) Javon Jackson(ts-2) Benny Green(p) Peter Washington(b) Kenny Washington(dm).
(Avatar Studios) NYC,August 1 & 2,1997

Backlash -1 CD BN(Au)4-98320-2
On the que-tee -1
Life flight -1
Happy times -2
Crisis -2
Thermo -2
Hub cap
Byrd like
Lament for Booker -3 CD EMI Music(C)4-94893-2
Up jumped Spring -4

-3: Marcus Printup(tp) Benny Green(p) only.
-4: Tim Hagans(tp) Benny Green(p) only.

All titles issued on CD BN 8-59509-2.

LENA HORNE - BEING MYSELF:
Lena Horne(vo) with Houston Person-1,Donald Harrison-2(ts) Bobby Forrester(org) Rodney Jones(g,arr) Benjamin Brown(b) Akira Tana(dm).
(Nola Studios) NYC,September ,1997

Some of my best friends are the blues -1
Willow weep for me -1
Sleepin' Bee -2
What am I here for -2

All titles issued on CD BN 8-34286-2.

BOB BELDEN - TAPESTRY:
Tim Hagans(tp) Bob Belden(ss) Greg Osby(as) Kevin Hays(p).
(D.K. Studios) NYC,September 14,1997

tk.5 Way over yonder CD BN 8-57891-2

JOE LOVANO - TRIO FASCINATION:
Joe Lovano(ss-1,as-2,ts-3,alto cl-4) Dave Holland(b) Elvin Jones(dm).
(Avatar Studios) NYC,September 16 & 17,1997

New York fascination -3	
Sanctuary park -3	
Eternal joy -1	CD BN(C)5-20457-2
Ghost of a chance -3	
Studio Rivbea -2	
Cymbalism -3	
Impressionistic -1,4	
Villa Paradiso -3	
4 on the floor -2	
Days of yore -3	
Alexander the great -3	unissued

All titles,except last,issued on CD BN 8-33114-2.

CHARLIE HUNTER - RETURN OF THE CANDYMAN:
Stefon Harris(vb) Charlie Hunter(g) Scott Amendola(dm) John Santos(perc).
(Mobius Sound) SF,September 15-18,1997

Bongo confront	
Enter the dragon	
Fly like an eagle	CD BN(Au)4-97893-2
Dope-a-licious	
Mystic relaxation	CD BN(Au)4-98320-2
Return of the candyman	-
Pound for pound	
Grinch comfort	
People	CD BN 5-24271-2
Shake, shake it, baby	
Turn me loose	
Huggy bear	CD EMI Music(C)4-94893-2
Of things to come	

All titles issued on BN(E)8-23108-1,CD BN 8-23108-2.
Note: LP was issued only in England.

BRIAN BLADE - FELLOWSHIP:
Myron Weldon(as) Melvin Butler(ts,ss) Jon Cowherd(p,el p) Jeff Parker(g) Dave Easley(pedal steel g) Daniel Lanois(mando g-1,el g-2) Christopher Thomas(b) Brian Blade(dm)
(The Teatro) Oxnard,CA,September 23-29,1997

Red river revel -1	CD BN(Au)4-98320-2
The undertow	
Folklore	
In spite of everything	CD EMI Music(C)4-94893-2
Lifeline	
Mohave -2	
If you see Lurah	
Loving without asking	

All titles issued on CD BN 8-59417-2.

JEAN-PIERRE COMO - September 1997: see late additions on page 445.

<u>STEFON HARRIS</u> - <u>A CLOUD OF RED DUST</u>:
Stefon Harris(vb,baliphone,orchestral bells,perc) Jason Moran(p-2) Dwayne Burno(b-1) Alvester Garnett (dm-1) Kimati Dinizulu(perc,one-string harp).
(Avatar Studios) NYC,October 6 & 7,1997

One string blues CD BN 8-23487-2
Sacred forest -1 -
Nature music -1,2 -
Drum storn -1,2 -

Steve Turre(tb,shells) Steve Wilson(ss-1,as-2) Stefon Harris(vb) Jason Moran(p) Dwayne Burno(b) Alvester Garnett(dm) June Gardner(vo-3). Same dates

Jamo CD BN 8-23487-2,Hip-O 547859-2
In the garden of thought -1,3 -
The prophet -2,4 -

-4: Kaoru Watanabe(fl) Greg Osby(as) Kimati Dinizulu(perc) added.

Kaoru Watanabe(fl) Greg Osby(as-1) Steve Wilson(ss-2,as-3) Stefon Harris(vb) Mulgrew Miller(p) Dwayne Burno(b) Alvester Garnett(dm) Kimati Dinizulu(perc). Same dates

Sophistry -1 CD BN 8-23487-2
And this too shall pass -1 -
A cloud of red dust -1,2 -
For you mom and dad -3 -

<u>ONDER FOCAN</u> - <u>BENEATH THE STARS</u>:
John Nugent(ts-1) Sam Yahel(org) Onder Focan(g) Bill Stewart(dm).
(EMI-Turkey) (RPM Studios) NYC,November 16,1997

Denizle
Smoke gets in your eyes
Beneath the stars
Can't cure
Ballad for two guitarists
Peshrev, 2nd part
Nardis
O.K. Bob -1
Grey haired waltzer -1
Sunburst cat -1

All titles issued on CD BN(Turkey)100301-2.

<u>IRAKERE - YEMAYA</u>:
Mario Fernandez,Basilio Marquez(tp) Cesar Lopez(as) Alfredo Thompson(ts) Chucho Valdès(p,arr) Carlos Emilio Morales(g) Carlos Del Puerto(b) Enrique Pla(dm) Andres Miranda(cga) Jose Miguel Melendez (timbales) Mayra Caridad Valdes(vo).
(EMI-Canada)(Studio Egrem) Havana,late 1997

Yemaya (voMCV)
Mister Bruce
Santa Amalia
La explosion
San Francisco
Son montuno
Chorrino

All titles issued on CD BN 4-98239-2.

415

DON BYRON - LULU ON THE BRIDGE:
Steve Wilson(as) Brian Carrott(marimba) Uri Caine(org) Nioka Workman(cello) Leo Traversa(b) Ben Wittman (dm) Johnny Almendra,Rodney Holmes(perc) Don Byron(arr,comp).
(Mastersound) Astoria,NY,November-December, 1997

Izzy's last jam CD BN 4-95317-2

JOE LOVANO:
Joe Lovano(ts-1,ss-2) Kenny Werner(p) Dennis Irwin(b) Yoron Israel(dm).
(Live,Avatar Studios) NYC,December 7,1997

Set #1:

The dawn of time -1	unissued
Sanctuary park -2	-

Set #2:

Alexander the great -1	unissued
Chelsea bridge -1	-
I'm s fool to want you -2	-
Prelude to a kiss -1	-
Topsy turvy -1	-

MEDESKI,MARTIN & WOOD - COMBUSTICATION:
John Medeski(keyb) Chris Wood(b,el b,bass drum) Billy Martin(dm,perc) DJ Logic(turntables-1) Steve Cannon(spoken word-2).
(The Magic Shop) NYC,December 15-21,1997

Sugarcraft -1	BN B1-93011,CD 4-93011-2,4-95317-2		
Just like I pictured it	-	-	
Start-stop -1	-	-	
Church of logic -1	-	-	
No ke ano ahiaki	-	-	
Nocturne	-	-	
Hey-hee-hi-ho	-	-	
Whatever happened to Gus -2	-	-	
Latin shuffle	-	-	CD BN(Au)4-97893-2
Everyday people	-	-	
Coconut Boogaloo	-	-	CD BN(Au)4-98320-2
Hypnotized	-	-	
Ligeti			
First day wurli			

All titles issued on CD BN(J)TOCJ-6229.

Same tracks as above,remixed September-October,1998.

Hey-hee-hi-ho (Billy Martin remix)	CD BN 4-99503-2
Whatever happened to Gus (Guru remix)	-
Start-stop (DJ Logic remix)	-
Nocturne (Automator remix)	-
Satan's church of hypnotized logic (Bill Laswell reconstruction and remix)	-
Sugarcraft (Yuka Honda Remix) -3	-

-3: Yuka Honda(dm programming,synth,samples) Sean Lennon(synth,clav) Mino Hatori(vo) overdubbed on.
(Greene Street Studios) NYC,May 29,1998.

416

KURT ELLING - THIS TIME IT'S LOVE:
Kurt Elling(vo) with Laurence Hobgood(p) Rob Amster(b) Michael Raynor(dm,perc).
(Hinge Studio) Chicago,December 8,1997

My foolish heart
Freddie's yen for Jen
My love, effendi CD BN 5-21153-2

All titles on CD BN 4-93543-2.

Kurt Elling(vo) with Eddie Johnson(ts-1) Johnny Frigo(v-2) Laurence Hobgood(p) Dave Onderdonk(g-3) Rob Amster(b) Michael Raynor(dm,perc).
(Hinge Studio) Chicago,December 9,1997

Too young to go steady -1 CD BN 4-93543-2
I feel so smoochie -2.3 -

Kurt Elling(vo) with Brad Wheeler(ss) Laurence Hobgood(p) Dave Onderdonk(g) Rob Amster(b) Paul Wertico(dm).
(Hinge Studio) Chicago,December 15,1997

A time for love
Where I belong

Both titles on CD BN 4-93543-2.

Kurt Elling(vo) with Laurence Hobgood(p) Rob Amster(b-1) Michael Raynor(dm-1).
(Hinge Studio) Chicago,December 16,1997

The very thought of you -1
She's funny that way
Everytime we say goodbye

All titles on CD BN 4-93543-2.

GREG OSBY - BANNED IN NEW YORK:
Greg Osby(as) Jason Moran(p) Atsushi Osada(b) Rodney Green(dm).
(Sweet Basil) NYC,December ,1997

The 13th floor
Pent up house
I didn't know about you
Big foot
Big foot (excerpt)
52nd street theme

All titles issued on CD BN 4-96860-2

CASSANDRA WILSON - TRAVELING MILES:
Cassandra Wilson(vo) with Steve Coleman(as-2) Eric Lewis(p-5) Marvin Sewell(g,el g) Doug Wamble(g) Lonnie Plaxico(b) Cecilia Smith(marimba-1) Perry Wilson(dm) Mino Cinelu-3,Jeffrey Haynes-4(perc).
(The Hit Factory) NYC,December ,1997

Resurrection blues (Tutu) -1 CD BN 8-54123-2
Right here, right now -1,4 -
Traveling Miles -2,3 - BN 4-95317-2
Prancing (Pfrancing) -4,5

All titles on BN(G)8-54123-1,CD BN(J)TOCJ-66020.

417

GEORGE HOWARD - THERE'S A RIOT GOIN' ON:
George Howard(ss) Eric Daniels(keyb,dm programming) Li'l John Roberts(dm) Tammy Thomas,Adarryl Perry,Keith Robinson,Terence Marks(backgr. vo).
LA,December ,1997

Luv 'n haight (no vocal)
Family affair — CD HMV Jazz(E)5-20881-2
(You caught me) Smilin' -2
Thank you for talkin' to me Africa -1

-1: Sam Sims(el b) Alexandra Brown,Phillip Ingram,Mortonette Jenkins(backgr. vo) added.
-2: Tammy Thomas (lead vo) on this title.
All titles issued on CD BN 8-21431-2.

George Howard(ss) Darryl Smith(keyb) Tommy Organ,Ron Smith(el g) Sam Sims(el b,dm programming) Munyungo Jackson(cga,timbales,perc) Tammy Thomas(vo).
LA,December ,1997

Runnin' away (voTT)
Africa talks to you "The Asphalt Jungle"
Poet

All titles issued on CD BN 8-21431-2.

George Howard(ss) Darryl Smith(keyb) Sam Sims(el b,dm programming) Li'l John Roberts(dm) Munyungo Jackson-1 (timbales,perc).
LA,December ,1997

Brave & strong -1
Just like a baby

Both titles issued on CD BN 8-21431-2.

George Howard(ss) Eric Daniels(keyb) Ron Smith(el g) Sam Sims(el b) Munyungo Jackson(cga).
LA,December ,1997

Time — CD BN 8-21431-2

DON BYRON - NU BLAXPLOITATION:
Don Byron(cl) Uri Caine(p,org) Reggie Washington(b) Ben Wittman(dm) Sadiq(recitation) Dean Bowman (vo-1)
(Bearsville Studios) — Woodstock,NY,December 27,1997-January 5,1998

Alien
Blinky
I cannot commit
If 6 was 9 -1 (Caine out)
Furman

All titles issued on CD BN 4-93711-2.

James Zollar(tp,backgr.vo) Curtis Fowkles(tb,backgr.vo) Don Byron(cl,bs-1,perc-2,backgr.vo) Uri Caine (p,org,clavinet) David Gilmore(g) Reggie Washington(b) Ben Wittman(dm) Johnny Almendra(perc, backgr.vo) Sadiq(recitation) Dean Bowman(vo).Same sessions

Mango meat -1,2
I'm stuck
Fencewalk -1
Hagalo (g out) — CD BN(Au)4-98320-2

All titles issued on CD BN 4-93711-2.

DON BYRON - NU BLAXPLOITATION:
Don Byron(cl,b cl) David Gilmore(g) Ben Wittman(dm) Sadiq(recitation).
Same sessions

Dodi — CD BN 4-93711-2

Don Byron,Reggie Washington,Uri Caine,Monique Curnen,Sadiq,Danny Kapilian(spoken word).
Same sessions

Domino theories,pt.1
Domino theories,pt.2
Interview

All titles issued on CD BN 4-93711-2.

ERIK TRUFFAZ - THE DAWN:
Erik Truffaz(tp) Patrick Muller(p,el p) Marcello Giuliani(b,el b) Marc Erbetta(dm) Nya(vo).
(EMI-France) (Studio de Flon) — Lausanne,December 29-31,1997

Bukowsky-chapter 1 (p out)	BN(F)4-93916-1		
Yuri's choice	-	CD BN 5-26427-2	
The dawn (instr.)	-	-	(Au)4-97893-2
Wet in Paris	-		
Slim pickings (vo only)	-		
Round-trip (instr.)	-		
The mask (instr.)	-	CD BN 5-26427-2	
Free stylin'			

All titles issued on CD BN(F)4-93916-2.

KURT ELLING - THIS TIME IT'S LOVE:
Kurt Elling(vo) with Laurence Hobgood(p-1) Dave Onderdonk(g-2) Rob Amster(b) Michael Raynor(dm, perc).
(Hinge Studio) — Chicago,January , 1998

The best things happen when you're dancing-1
Rosa Moreno-2

Both titles on CD BN 4-93543-2.

GREG OSBY - ZERO:
Greg Osby(sopranino s,ss,as) Jason Moran(p) Kevin McNeal(g-3) Lonnie Plaxico-1,Dwayne Burno-2(b) Rodney Green(dm).
(Systems Two Studio) — Brooklyn,N.Y.,January 9-11,1998

Minstrale -1
Two over one -1
Ozthetica -1
Nekide-1 (p out)
Sea of illusion -2
Interspacial affair -2
Extreme behavior -2
Savant cycles -2,3

All titles issued on CD BN 4-93760-2.

<u>GREG OSBY</u> - <u>ZERO</u>:
Greg Osby(ss,as) Jason Moran(org) Kevin McNeal(g) Rodney Green(dm).Same sessions

Deuce ana quota
Penetrating stare
Concepticus in C

All titles issued on CD BN 4-93760-2.

<u>PHIL WOODS</u> - <u>THE REV AND I</u>:
Phil Woods(as) Johnny Griffin(ts) Cedar Walton(p) Peter Washington(b) Ben Riley(dm).
(Red Rock Recording Studio) Saylorsburg,PA,January 10 & 11,1998

The Rev and I -1
We could make such beautiful music together
Hand in glove
All too soon
Red top
I'm so scared of girls when they're good looking
Loose change
Dutch morning
Before I left

-1: Phil Woods(el p) Bill Goodwin(perc) overdubbed on.

All titles issued on CD BN 4-94100-2

<u>CHUCHO VALDES</u> - <u>BELE BELE EN LA HABANA</u>:
Chucho Valdes(p) Alain Perez Rodriguez(b,vo) Raul Pineda Roque(dm) Roberto Vizcaino Guillot(cga,bata dm,chimes,guiro,cowbell,chekere).
(EMI Canada)(McClear Pathe Studio) Toronto,January 12 & 13,1998

Son Montuno CD BN(Au)4-98320-2,(C)5-20457-2
Lorraine CD EMI Music(C)4-94893-2
But not for me
Con poco coco
El cumbanchero
Tres lindas Cubanas
La sitiera
Los caminos

All titles issued on CD BN 8-23082-2.

<u>DON BYRON</u> - <u>NU BLAXPLOITATION</u>:
James Zollar(tp,backgr.vo) Curtis Fowkles(tb,backgr.vo) Don Byron(cl) Uri Caine(p) David Gilmore(g) Reggie Washington(b) Ben Wittman(dm) Johnny Almendra(perc,backgr.vo) Sadiq(recitation) The Diabolical Bizmarkie(vo).
(The Knitting Factory) NYC,January 14,1998

Schizo jam CD BN 4-93711-2

<u>CHUCHO VALDES SOLO</u> - <u>LIVE IN NEW YORK</u>:
Chucho Valdes(p).
(EMI Canada)(Kaplan Penthouse,Lincoln Center) NYC,January 16,1998

A mi madre
Munequita Linda
Besame mucho
El maisero
Over the rainbow
Son
Novia mia
Delirio
Tres lindas Cubanos
La negra Tomasa

All titles issued on CD BN 4-93456-2.

<u>MARCUS PRINTUP</u> - <u>NOCTURNAL TRACES</u>:
Marcus Printup(tp) Kevin Bales(p) Ricky Ravelo(b) Woody Williams(dm).
(Avatar Studios) NYC,January 24 & 25,1998

Woody's beat
Have you met Miss Jones
Shertzing along
Body and soul
Black coffee
Pier pressure
Nocturnal traces
Ain't misbehavin'
How do you keep the music playing?
Freddie's inferno

All titles issued on CD BN 4-93676-2.

<u>PAT MARTINO</u> - <u>STONE BLUE</u>:
Eric Alexander(ts) Delmar Brown(keyb) Pat Martino(g) James Genus(el b) Kenwood Dennard(dm,perc).
(Avatar Studios) NYC,February 14,1998

(tk.6) Uptown down
(tk.2) Stone blue CD BN(Au)4-98320-2
(tk.4) With all the people

All titles issued on CD BN 8-53082-2.

Same.
(Avatar Studios) NYC,February 15,1998

(tk.3) 13 to go
(tk.2) Boundaries
(tk.2) Joyous Lake
(tk.1) Mac tough
(tk.2) Two weighs out
(tk.1) Never say goodbye (g & keyb only)

All titles issued on CD BN 8-53082-2.

SHERMAN IRBY - BIG MAMA'S BISCUITS:
Sherman Irby(as) Ed Cherry(g-1) Gerald Cannon(b) Clifford Barbaro(dm).
(Sear Sound) NYC,February 28,1998

Conversing with Cannon
'Bama
Passage of time
Aunt Dorothy
Take the A train
Lake Tuscaloosa -1
Too high -1
We're gonna be alright -1
Away from home -2
Big Mama's biscuits -2,3

-2: Dana Murray(dm,perc) replaces Barbaro.
-3: Roy Hargrove(tp) James Hurt(p) added.

All titles issued on CD BN 8-56234-2.

DIANNE REEVES - BLUE NOTE SALUTES MOTOWN:
Dianne Reeves(vo) with Jim Beard(el p,org,perc) Tony Cedras(ac g,acc) Todd Reynolds(v) Anthony Jackson (el b).
(Unique Studios) NYC,March ,1998

Tracks of my tears CD BN 4-94211-2

JACKY TERRASSON - LULU ON THE BRIDGE:
Jacky Terrasson(p)
(Anderson Audio) Brooklyn,April 6,1998

Cumba's dance CD BN 4-95317-2

LENA HORNE - LULU ON THE BRIDGE:
Lena Horne(vo) with Donald Harrison(ts) Mark Sherman(vb) Mike Renzi(p) Bobby Forrester(org) Rodney Jones(g,arr) Benjamin Brown(b) Lewis Nash(dm).
(Nola Recording) NYC,April 29,1998

Singin' in the rain CD BN 4-95317-2

DAVE KOZ - BLUE NOTE SALUTES MOTOWN:
Dave Koz(as) Jim Beard(el p,synth,perc) Jon Herington(g).
(Jimsong Studios) NYC,April ,1998

I'll be there CD BN 4-94211-2

EVERETTE HARP - BETTER DAYS:
Everette Harp(as) Michael Beardon(keyb,synth and dm programming) Paul Jackson Jr.(g) Larry Kimpel(b) "Li'l" John Roberts(dm).
(Rue Harp & Westlake Studios) LA,April ,1998

Modern religion CD BN 8-33588-2

Everette Harp(ss,keyb,programming) A. Ray "The Weeper" Fuller(g) Wayman Tisdale(b).
(Rue Harp & Westlake Studios) LA,April ,1998

Better days CD BN 8-33588-2

422

EVERETTE HARP - BETTER DAYS:
Everette Harp(EWI,keyb and rhythm programming,backgr.vo) Brian Simpson(p) Doc Powell,Paul Jackson Jr.(g) "Li'l" John Roberts(dm)Valerie Pinkston,Kevin Wyatt,Lynn Fiddmont-Lindsey(backgr.vo).
(Rue Harp & Westlake Studios) LA,April ,1998

I just can't stop thinking about you CD BN 8-33588-2

Everette Harp(ss,keyb) Wayne Holmes(keyb,clay fl,vo,backgr.vo) George Duke(p,el p) Michael Landau(g) Marc Antoine(ac g) Jimmy Haslip(b) Will Kennedy(dm) Valerie Pinkston,Kevin Wyatt,Lynn Fiddmont-Lindsey,Will Wheaton,Tessa Harp,Jeri Harp(backgr.vo).
(Rue Harp & Westlake Studios) LA,April ,1998

We will answer CD BN 8-33588-2

Everette Harp(ss,ts,p) Marc Antoine(ac g) Jimmy Haslip(b) Will Kennedy(dm) Kevin Ricard(perc) Valerie Pinkston,Kevin Wyatt,Lynn Fiddmont-Lindsey,Will Wheaton(backgr.vo).
(Rue Harp & Westlake Studios) LA,April ,1998

Norwegian lillies CD BN 8-33588-2

Everette Harp(as,saxes) Bobby Lyle(p) DeWayne "Smitty" Smith(b) Michael White(dm) Valerie Pinkston, Kevin Wyatt(backgr.vo).
(Rue Harp & Westlake Studios) LA,April ,1998

Mutual admiration society CD BN 8-33588-2

Rick Braun(flh-1) Everette Harp(as,keyb and rhythm programming) Paul Jackson Jr.(g) Michael White(dm) Valerie Pinkston,Kevin Wyatt,Lynn Fiddmont-Lindsey,Will Wheaton(backgr.vo).
(Rue Harp & Westlake Studios) LA,April, 1998

Stand up! -1
When next we meet (we will reminisce)-2

-2: Brian Simpson(el p) George Duke(synth) Marcus Miller(b) Kevin Ricard(perc) added.
Both titles issued on CD BN 8-33588-2.

Everette Harp(ss,keyb,dm programming) Kevin Ricard(perc) Cassie Bonner(backgr.vo).
(Rue Harp & Westlake Studios) LA,April ,1998

For you always CD BN 8-33588-2

Everette Harp(ts,keyb,programming) George Duke(p) Dwight Sills(g) Larry Kimpel(b) "Li'l" John Roberts (dm) Kevin Ricard(perc) Valerie Pinkston,Kevin Wyatt,Lynn Fiddmont-Lindsey,Will Wheaton(backgr.vo).
(Rue Harp & Westlake Studios) LA,April ,1998

Circle of friends CD BN 8-33588-2

CHARLIE HUNTER - BLUE NOTE SALUTES MOTOWN:
Charlie Hunter(g,b) Monte Croft(vb) Willard Dyson(dm).
(Hip Pocket Studios) NYC,May ,1998

You keep me hangin' on CD BN 4-94211-2

RAY BARRETTO - BLUE NOTE SALUTES MOTOWN:
Adam Kolker(ts,shaker) John Martino(p) Hans Glawischnig(b) Vince Cherico(dm) Ray Barretto(cga,vo).
(Systems Two Studio) Brooklyn,N.Y.,May ,1998

What's goin' on CD BN 4-94211-2

TIM HAGANS - ANIMATION/IMAGINATION:
Tim Hagans(tp) Bob Belden(ss-2) Kurt Rosenwinkel(g-3) Scott Kinsey(synth,programming) David Dyson (el b) Billy Kilson(dm).
(Sony Studios) NYC,May 5,1998

(tk.1)	Hud Doyle-1	
(tk.1)	French girl-2	
(tk.2)	Trumpet sandwich (tp,el b,dm only)	
(tk.1)	Animation/imagination-3	CD BN(C)5-20457-2

-1: Kevin Hays(el p) DJ Kingsize(programming) added.

All titles issued on CD BN 4-95198-2.

Tim Hagans(tp) Bob Belden(ss) Scott Kinsey(synth) Kevin Hays(el p,programming-2) Ira Coleman(b) Billy Kilson(dm).
(Avatar Studios) NYC,May 6,1998

(tk.1)	What they don't tell you about jazz	CD BN 4-95198-2	
(tk.1)	Are you threatening me? -1	-	
(tk.1)	Far West -2	-	(Au)4-97893-2
(tk.2)	The original bass and drums (tp,b,dm only)	-	
(tk.1)	Killer instinct	unissued	
(tk.2)	Love's lullaby (tp,el p,synth only)	CD BN 4-95198-2	

-1: DJ Kingsize(programming) added.
-2: Alfred Lion(sampled narration) added.

Tim Hagans(tp) Kurt Rosenwickel(g-2) David Dyson(el b-1) Matthew Brecker-1,DJ Kingsize (programming).
(Sony Studios) NYC,May 7,1998

(tk.1) Snake kisses -1
(tk.1) 28 IF -1

Both titles issued on CD BN 4-95198-2.

Tim Hagans(tp) Bob Belden(p) DJ Smash(synth,programming)
(Sonny Studios) NYC, May 7 & 8,1998

(tk.1) I heard you were dropped
(tk.1) Slo mo

Both titles issued on CD BN 4-95198-2.

CASSANDRA WILSON - TRAVELING MILES:
Cassandra Wilson(vo) with Olu Dara(c-1) Eric Lewis(p) Marvin Sewell(el g-1) Pat Metheny(ac g-3) Kevin Breit(el g,as g mandolin)) Dave Holland(b) Marcus Baylor(dm-1) Jeffrey Haynes(perc) Angelique Kidjo (vo-2).
(Bearsville Studio) Bearsville,NY,May & September,1998

Run the voodoo down -1
Voodoo reprise -1,2
Sky and sea (Blue in green)

All titles on BN(G)8-54123-1,CD BN 8-54123-2,(J)TOCJ-66020.

CASSANDRA WILSON - TRAVELING MILES:
Cassandra Wilson(vo,ac g) with Marvin Sewell(ac g,el g,bazouki) Lonnie Plaxico(b-1) Jeffrey Haynes perc-1) Vincent Henry(hca-1). Same sessions

Piper
When the sun goes down -1

Both titles on BN(G)8-54123-1,CD BN 8-54123-2,(J)TOCJ-66020.

Cassandra Wilson(vo) with Marvin Sewell(ac g) Kevin Breit(el g,bazouki) Lonnie Plaxico (b) Jeffrey Haynes (perc). Same sessions

Time after time BN(G)8-54123-1
CD BN 8-54123-2,(J)TOCJ-66020

Cassandra Wilson(vo) with Regina Carter(v) Stefon Harris(vb-1) Eric Lewis(p-4) Marvin Sewell(ac g) Kevin Breit(stereophonic g,mand) Lonnie Plaxico(b) Marcus Baylor-3(dm,perc) Jeffrey Haynes(perc-2).
Same sessions

Never broken (ESP) -1,2
Someday my prince will come -2,3 CD BN(C)5-20457-2
Seven steps -1,3,4 (guitars out)

All titles on BN(G)8-54123-1,CD BN 8-54123-2, (J)TOCJ-66020.

ELIANE ELIAS - BLUE NOTE SALUTES MOTOWN:
Elaine Elias(p,el p,b,vo) Jim Beard(programming,perc)Jon Herington(g).
(Jimsong Studios) NYC,June ,1998

Bird of beauty CD BN 4-94211-2

RICHARD ELLIOT - BLUE NOTE SALUTES MOTOWN:
Richard Elliot(saxes) Mitch Forman(keyb) Tony Maiden(g) Steve Dubin(programming).
(Dubie Grooves Studio) LA,June ,1998

Ain't nothin' like the real thing CD BN 4-94211-2,8-57491-2

JOE CHAMBERS - MIRRORS:
Eddie Henderson(tp) Vincent Herring(ss-1.as-2.ts-3) Mulgrew Miller(p)Ira Coleman(b) Joe Chambers(dm).
(Sound On Sound) NYC,July 7,1998

Tu-way-pock-e-way -3
Mirrors -3
Caravanserail -3
Ruth-2 (tp out)
Mariposa -1
Come back to me -1

All titles issued on CD BN 4-96685-2.

425

JOE CHAMBERS - MIRRORS:
Mulgrew Miller(p) Ira Coleman(b) Joe Chambers(dm-1,vb-2).
(Sound On Sound) NYC,July 8,1998

The lady in my life -1,2
Ruthless -1
Circles -1,2 (p,b out) CD BN(C)5-20457-2

All titles issued on CD BN 4-96685-2.

STEFANO DI BATTISTA - A PRIMA VISTA:
Flavio Boltro(tp,flh) Stefano Di Battista(as,ss) Eric Legnini(p) Rosario Bonaccorso(b) Benjamin Henocq (dm).
(EMI-France)(Gil Evans Studio) Amiens,France,August 27-29,1998

Spirit of messengers
Funny moon
Aiova
Ne'll acqua
Buffo
Another time
Dina
T-Tonic
Miccettina
First smile
Benji
Lush life

All titles issued on CD BN(F)4-97945-2.

JASON MORAN - SOUNDTRACK TO HUMAN MOTION:
Greg Osby-1(ss,as) Stefon Harris(vb-2) Jason Moran(p) Lonnie Plaxico(b) Eric Harland(dm).
(Systems Two Studio) Brooklyn,N.Y.,August 29 & 30,1998

Gangsterism on canvas -1,2
Still moving -1,2
Aquanaut -1,2
Snake stance -1 CD BN(C)5-20457-2
Retrograde -1
Le tombeau de Couperin/States of art
JAMO meets SAMO
Release from suffering
Root progression (as & p only)-1
Kinesics (solo p)

All titles issued on CD BN 4-97431-2.

RODNEY JONES - THE UNDISCOVERED FEW:
Mark Sherman(vb) Mike Renzi(p) Rodney Jones(g) Benjamin Brown(b) Lewis Nash(dm) Robert Allende (perc-1).
(Nola Recording Studio) NYC,October 2,1998

Tradewinds -1
Dreamers in love

Both titles issued on CD BN 4-96902-2.

426

DIANNE REEVES - BRIDGES:

Dianne Reeves(vo) with Mulgrew Miller(p) Romero Lubambo(g) Reginald Veal(b) Brian Blade (dm) Manolo Barena(perc,bgo).

(Right Track Studios) NYC,October 5-8,1998

I remember
Goodbye (perc out)
Bridges
River -1,2
Suzanne -2,3

-1: Joe Locke(vb,bass marimba) added.
-2: Kenny Garrett(as) added.
-3 Billy Childs(p) replaces Mulgrew Miller.

All titles issued on CD BN 8-33060-2.

Dianne Reeves(vo) with Billy Childs-1,Eddie Del Barrio-2,George Duke-3(p) Romero Lubambo(g) Reginald Veal(b) Terri Lyne Carrington(dm) Munyungo Jackson(perc).

(Conway Studio C) LA,October 12-16,1998

In your eyes -1 CD BN(C)5-20457-2
1863 -2
Mista -3,4
Make someone happy -3,5 (perc out)

-4: Jimmy Zavala(harmonica) added.
-5: Marcus Printup(tp) added.

All titles issued on CD BN 8-33060-2.

Dianne Reeves(vo) with Billy Childs(p).

(Le Gonks West) LA,late October,1998

Olokun CD BN 8-33060-2

Dianne Reeves(vo) with George Duke(p) Stanley Clarke(b) Munyungo Jackson(perc).

(Le Gonks West) LA,late October,1998

Testify CD BN 8-33060-2

RODNEY JONES - THE UNDISCOVERED FEW:

Tim Hagans(tp) Greg Osby(as) Donald Harrison(ts) Mark Sherman(vb) Shedrick Mitchell(p) Rodney Jones (g) Lonnie Plaxico(b) Eric Harland(dm) Robert Allende(perc-1).

(Nola Recording Studio) NYC,November 16,1998

The undiscovered few -1,2
The message -1
3rd orbit -1
Light & shadows
Circus wheel

-2: Earl Gardner(tp) Charles Gordon(tb) Morris Goldberg(as) Tim Reis(ts) overdubbed on.

All titles issued on CD BN 4-96902-2.

427

RODNEY JONES - THE UNDISCOVERED FEW:
Mark Sherman(vb-1) Mulgrew Miller(p-1) Rodney Jones(g) Lonnie Plaxico(b) Eric Harland(dm) Robert Allende(perc).
(Nola Recording Studio) NYC,November 16,1998

Lesson time
My favorite things -1
Oliver & Thad -2

-2: Earl Gardner(tp) Charles Gordon(tb) Morris Goldberg(as) Tim Reis(ts) overdubbed on.
All titles issued on CD BN 4-96902-2.

JACKY TERRASSON - WHAT IT IS:
Jay Collins(fl-2) Gregoire Maret(hca-2) Jacky Terrasson(p,el p) Richard Bona(el b-1) Ugonna Okegwo(b-2) Jaz Sawyer(dm) Mino Cinelu(perc,sound effects)
(Avatar Studios) NYC,November 16,1998

Better world-1
Toot-too's tune-2
Money-2

All titles issued on CD BN 4-98756-2.

Michael Brecker(ts) Jacky Terrasson(p,el p) Richard Bona(el b-1) Ugonna Okegwo(b-2) Jaz Sawyer(dm-2) Mino Cinelu(perc).
(Avatar Studios) NYC,November 17,1998

Baby plum -1
What's wrong with you? -2

Both titles issued on CD BN 4-98756-2.

Jacky Terrasson(p,el p,chekere) Ugonna Okegwo(b) Jaz Swayer(dm) Mino Cinelu(perc,g).
Same session
Rick Centalonzo(fl,oboe) Fernando Saunders(el b) overdubbed on.
NYC,November 27,1998

Ravel: Bolero CD BN 4-98756-2

Jacky Terrasson(p) Ugonna Okegwo(b) Mino Cinelu(dm).
(Avatar Studios) NYC,November 18,1998

Little red ribbon CD BN 4-98756-2

RODNEY JONES - THE UNDISCOVERED FEW:
Rodney Jones(g) Regina Carter(v-1) Jesse Levy(cello-2).
(Nola Recording Studio) NYC,November 23,1998

Tears of a forgotten child -1
Through the eyes of a child -2

Both titles issued on CD BN 4-96902-2.

<u>FRANK EMILIO Y LOS AMIGOS</u> - <u>ANCESTRAL REFLECTIONS</u> <u>(REFLEJOS ANCESTRALES)</u>:
Joaquin Olivero Gavilan(13-key wooden fl) Lazaro Jesus Ordonez Enriquez(v,solo on 1) Pablo A. Mesa Suarez(v) Frank Emilio Flynn(p) William Rubalcaba(b) Jose Luis "Changuito" Quintana(timbales) Federico Aristides "Tata Guines" Soto(cga) Enrique Lazaga Varona(guiro,claves,tom-tom) Juan Crespo Masa, Enrique Contreras Orama(chorus) with Orlando "Maraca" Valle(fl-1) Barbaro Torres Delf-gado(lute-2).
(EMI-Canada)(Abdala Studios) Havana,Cuba,November 20-24,1998

Guerra de flautas (War of the flutes) -1
Rico melao (Delicious sugar cane syrup)
La mulata rumbera (The mulata rumba dancer)
La conga se va (The passing carnival procession)
Ru^ba elegante (The elegant rumba)
Bilongo (Black magic spell) -1
El arroyo que murmura (The murmuring brook) -2
Juventud de Pueblo Nuevo (The youth of Pueblo Nuevo neighborhood)
Reflejos ancestrales (Ancestral reflections)

All titles issued on CD BN 4-98918-2.

<u>CHUCHO VALDES</u>- <u>BRIYUMBA PALO CONGO (RELIGION OF THE CONGO)</u>:
Chucho Valdes(p,chorus vo-2) Francisco Rubio Pampin(b,chorus vo-2) Raul Pineda Roque(dm,chorus vo-2) Roberto Vizcaino Guillot(cga,bata dm,chorus vo-2).
(EMI Canada) (Abdala Studios) Havana,Cuba,November 23 & 24,1998

El Rumbon (The party)
Bolero (Ballad)
Caravan
Embraceable you
Ponle la clave (Put the time on it)
Rhapsody in blue-1
Briyumba palo Congo (Congolese religion)-2

-1: Joaquin Olivero Gavilan (13 key Cuban wooden fl) added.
-2: Mayra Caridad Valdes(vocalization,chorus vo) Juan "Chan" Campo Cardenas(vo,chorus vo) Haila Mompie Gonzalez(chorus vo) added.

All titles issued on CD BN 4-98917-2.

<u>GONZALO RUBALCABA</u> - <u>INNER VOYAGE</u>:
Gonzalo Rubalcaba(p) Jeff Chambers(b) Ignacio Berroa(dm).
(Avatar Studios) NYC,November 24,1998

(tk.2) Sandyken
(tk.2) Promenade
(tk.2) Joan
(tk.2) Joao
(tk.2) Yolanda
(tk.2) Here's that rainy day
(tk.2) Caravan

All titles issued on CD BN 4-99241-2.

Michael Brecker(ts) Gonzalo Rubalcaba(p) Jeff Chambers(b) Ignacio Berroa(dm).
(Avatar Studios) NYC,November 25,1998

(tk.3) Hard one
(tk.4) Blues Lundvall

Both titles issued on CD BN 4-99241-2.

<u>JACKY TERRASSON</u> - <u>WHAT IT IS</u>:
Rick Centalonzo(fl-1) Jacky Terrasson(p) Adam Rogers(g) Fernando Saunders(el b) Mino Cinelu(dm.perc)
(Avatar Studios) NYC,November 27,1998

Sam's song -1
Le Roi Basil

Both tunes issued on CD BN 4-98756-2.

<u>RICHARD ELLIOT</u> - <u>CHILL FACTOR</u>:
Rick Braun(flh-1) Richard Elliot(ts) Tim Heintz,Leon Bisquera-2(keyb) Wah Wah Watson(g-3) Alex Al(b-4) Li'l John Roberts(dm) Lenny Castro(perc).
(Schnee Studios/Alpha Studios/Pacifique Studios)
LA,November & December ,1998

Chill factor -1,3,4
Moomba -2

Both titles issued on CD BN 8-57491-2.

Richard Elliot(ts) Tim Heintz(keyb) Tony Maiden-1,Michael Sims-2(g) Peter White(ac g-3) Alex Al(b-4) Li'l John Roberts(dm) Lenny Castro-5,Luis Conte-6(perc). Same sessions

On the fly -1,5,6
Kick it up -1,4,6
Like butter -2,3,4

All titles issued on CD BN 8-57491-2.

Richard Elliot(ts) Tim Heintz(p,keyb) Steven Dubin(programming) Paul Jackson Jr.(g) Alex Al(b) Luis Conte (perc). Same sessions

Deep touch CD BN 8-57491-2

Richard Elliot(ts) Tim Heintz(keyb) Robbie Nevil(g,backgr. vo) Steven Dubin(dm programming) Li'l John Roberts(dm) Luis Conte(perc) Siedah Garrett(vo). Same sessions

This could be real CD BN 8-57491-2

Richard Elliot(ts) Tim Heintz(org) Steven Dubin(synth).Same sessions

Who? CD BN 8-57491-2

Richard Elliot(ts) Mitch Forman(keyb) Michael Sims(g) Steven Dubin(dm programming) Luis Conte(perc).
Same sessions

Adia CD BN 8-57491-2

Richard Elliot(ts) Dwight Sills(g).Same sessions.

Mikayla's smile CD BN 8-57491-2

<u>CHARLIE HUNTER & LEON PARKER</u> - <u>DUO</u>:
Charlie Hunter(8-string g) Leon Parker(dm,perc,cymbals).
(Beat Tracks) Suffern,NY,December 8 & 9,1998

Mean streeak
Belief
Do that then
You don't know what love is
Recess
Don't talk (Put your head on my shoulder)
CD BN(C)5-20457-2
The last time
Dark corner
The spin seekers
Calypso for grandpa

All titles issued on CD BN 4-99187-2.

<u>BOB DOROUGH</u> - <u>TOO MUCH COFFEE MAN</u>:
Bob Dorough(p,el p,vo) Joe Cohn(g) Tony Marino(el b)Jamey Haddad(dm).
(Red Rock Recording) Sailorsburg,Pennsylvania,December 14,1998

(tk.4) Too much coffee man -1
(tk.2/3) Webster's definition of love
(tk.6) I've got just about everything -2
(tk.3) Marilyn,queen of lies

-1: Craig Kastelnik(org) Hui Cox(rh g) Marc Holen(perc) overdubbed on.
-2: Phil Woods(as) overdubbed on.
All titles issued on CD BN 4-99239-2.

<u>JOE LOVANO & GREG OSBY</u> - <u>FRIENDLY FIRE</u>:
Greg Osby(ss-1,as-2) Joe Lovano(ss-1,ts-3,fl-4) Jason Moran(p) Cameron Brown(b) Idris Muhammad(dm).
(Avatar Studios) NYC,December 15 & 16,1998

Geo J Lo -2,3
The wild East -2,3
Serene -2,4
Broad way blues -2,3
Monk's mood -5
Idris-1
Truth be told -2,3
Silence -2,3
Alexander the great -2,3

-5:Joe Lovano(ts) Jason Moran(p) only.
All titles issued on CD BN 4-99125-2.

<u>JAVON JACKSON</u> - <u>PLEASANT VALLEY</u>:
Javon Jackson(ts) Larry Goldings(org) Dave Stryker(g) Billy Drummond(dm).
(Sear Sound) NYC,January 4,1999

Sunswept Sunday
Pleasant valley
Hippodelphia
Don't you worry 'bout a thing
Jim jam
In the pocket
Brother "G"
Love and happiness
For one who knows

All titles issued on CD BN 4-99697-2.

<u>BENNY GREEN</u> - <u>THESE ARE SOULFUL DAYS</u>:
Benny Green(p) Russell Malone(g) Christian McBride(b).
(Avatar Studios) NYC,January 16,1999

	Hub's nub	rejected
(tk.6)	Tale of the fingers	CD BN 4-99527-2
	Tom thumb	rejected
(tk.3)	Ernie's tune	CD BN 4-99527-2
(tk.4)	Hocus pocus	

<u>BENNY GREEN</u> - <u>THESE ARE SOULFUL DAYS</u>:
Benny Green(p) Russell Malone(g) Christian McBride(b).
(Avatar Studios) NYC,January 17,1999

(tk.10)	Come on home
(tk.7)	Virgo
(tk.9)	Bellarosa
(tk.9)	Summer nights
(tk.3)	These are soulful days
(tk.5)	Punjab

All titles issued on CD BN 4-99527-2.

<u>STEPHANE HUCHARD</u> - <u>TRIBAL TRAQUENARD (TRIBAL TRAP)</u>:
Stephane Guillaume(fl,cl,bass cl,ss,as,ts,flh,vo,mouth dm) Pierre de Bethmann(el p) Olivier Louvel(g) Linley Marthe(b) Stephane Huchard(dm,perc,synth programming).
(EMI France)(Studio Sous La Ville) Paris,January , 1999

Margaux 96
Love for sale (el p,b out)
African jerk (el p out) -1,4
Le Voyage de Yangdol -3
Welcom e-2,5
Casse a Caracas
Kiss a Kirikis
Batbouche au pays des babouches (el p,b out)
Tutoyer les anges -5
Lady Zab -4,5
Mes soleils
Premier cri classe
Un ange passe -6

-1: Alain Debiossat(bs) added.
-2: Stefano di Battista(ss) added.

-3: Jean-Pierre Como(keyb) added.
-4: Marc Berthoumieux(acc) added.
-5: Louis Winsberg(g) added.
-6: Stephane Guillaume(cl,bass cl,fl) alone.

All titles issued on CD BN(F)4-99908-2.

DON BYRON - ROMANCE WITH THE UNSEEN
Don Byron(cl) Bill Frisell(g) Drew Gress(b) Jack DeJohnette(dm)
(Bearsville Studios) Bearsville,NY,January 23-25,1999

A mural from two perspectives
Sad twilight
Bernard Goetz,James Ramseur and me
I'll follow the sun
'Lude
Homegoing
One finger snap
Basquiat
Perdido
Closer to home

All titles issued on CD BN 4-99545-2

JAMES HURT - DARK GROOVES MYSTICAL RHYTHMS:
Jacques Schwartz-Bart(ts-1) James Hurt(p) François Moutin(b) Ari Hoenig(dm).
(Avatar Studios) NYC,February 1,1999

(tk.2)	Eleven dreams (dm out)	CD BN 4-95104-2
(tk.3)	Neptune	-
(tk.3)	Orion's view	-
(tk.2)	Jupiter -1	-
(tk.1)	Mars -1	-
(tk.3)	The tree of life -1	-
	African 7 -1	unissued
(tk.2)	Dark nines -1	CD BN 4-95104-2
(tk;2)	Faith	-
(tk.1)	Sun day -1	-
	untitled solo piano piece	unissued

MARK SHIM - TURBULENT FLOW:
Mark Shim(ts,ss-1) Edward Simon(p,el p-2) Drew Gress(b) Eric Harland(dm).
(Systems Two Studio) Brooklyn,N.Y.,February 3 & 4,1999

Emminence (For Betty Carter) -1,2	CD BN 8-23392-2
Don't wake the violent baby -2	-
Turbulent flow -2	-
Christal gazing	-
Scorpio	-
Jive ones	-
If I should lose you (p out)	unissued

Stefon Harris(vb-3,marimba-4) added.Same sessions.

Recorda me -3
Survival tactics -4
Dirty Bird -1,4

All titles issued on CD BN 8-23392-2.

STEFON HARRIS - BLACK ACTION FIGURE:
Stefon Harris(vb) Jason Moran(p) Tarus Mateen(b) Eric Harland(dm).
(Systems Two Studio) Brooklyn,N.Y.,February 14 & 15,1999

	You stepped out of a dream (solo vb)	CD BN 4-99546-2
	Bass vibes (p,dm out)	-
	Conversations at the mess (p,b out)	-
	There is no greater love (p out)	-
	After the day is done	-
	My little black action figure	-

Steve Turre(tb) Greg Osby(as) Gary Thomas(ts,alto fl) added.Same sessions.

	Collage (tb,as out)	CD BN 4-99546-2
	Of things to come	-
	Feine blues	-
	Alovi	-
	The alchemist	-
	Chorale	-
	Faded beauty	-

Note: Above CD opens with "Clud madness" which is made of voices and sound effects and closes with "Musical silence" which is a track of silence.

RENEE ROSNES - ART & SOUL:
Renee Rosnes(p) Scott Colley(b) Billy Drummond(dm)Richard Bona(perc-1) Dianne Reeves(vo).
(EMI Canada)(Bear Tracks) Sufern,NY,February 16-18,1999

tk.2	Little spirit	CD BN 4-99997-2,(C)5-20457-2
tk.11	Blues connotation	-
tk.12/13	Fleurette Afraicaine -1	-
tk.17	Children's song #3	-
tk.19	So in love	
tk.27	With a little help from my friends	CD BN 4-99997-2
tk.29	Sonfona	-
tk.31	Romp	-
tk.32	Goodbye	-
tk.34	Lazy afternoon (voDR)	-
tk.38	Ancient footprints (voDR) -1	-

All titles issued on CD BN(J)TOCJ-66062.

BOB DOROUGH - TOO MUCH COFFEE MAN:
Bob Dorough(p,vo).
(Red Rock Recording) Sailorsburg,Pennsylvania,March 16,1999

tk.2	Yesterday I made you breakfast	CD BN 4-99239-2

MEDESKI,MARTIN & WOOD - TONIC:
John Medeski(p,melodica) Chris Wood(b) Billy Martin(dm,perc,mbira).
(Live at Tonic) NYC,March ,1999

	Invocation	CD BN 5-25271-2
	Afrique	-
	Seven deadlies	-
	Your lady	-
	Rise up	-
	Buster rides again	-
	Thaw	-
	Hay Joe	-

CAECILIE NORBY - QUEEN OF BAD EXCUSES:
Caecilie Norby(vo,mouth perc) with Hans Ulrik(ts) Ben Besiakov(p) Lars Danielsson(g,cello,strings,b,dm) Xavier Desandre-Navarre(perc) Anders Kjellberg(cymbals).
(EMI-Denmark)(Focus Recording Studios) Copenhagen,Denmark,March ,1999

Cuban cigars CD BN 5-22342-2,(J)TOCJ-66067

Caecilie Norby(vo) with Ben Besiakov(p) Aske Jacoby(g) Lars Danielsson(b,cello,strings) Anders Kjellberg (dm).
Same sessions.

Fly CD BN 5-22342-2,(J)TOCJ-66067

Caecilie Norby(vo) with John Scofield(g) Lars Jansson(p) Lars Danielsson(b,keyb,p,dm) Anders Kjellberg (dm) Xavier Desandre-Navarre(perc).
Same sessions.

Psyko Pippi CD BN 5-22342-2,(J)TOCJ-66067

Caecilie Norby(vo) with Lars Moller(ts) John Scofield(g) Lars Danielsson(b,el p,keyb,dm) Billy Hart(dm).
Same sessions.

Everyone beneath the sun CD BN 5-22342-2,(J)TOCJ-66067

Caecilie Norby(vo) with Hans Ulrik(fl) Ben Besiakov(p) John Scofield(g) Lars Danielsson(g,b,cello,keyb) Per Lindvall(dm) Xavier Desandre-Navarre(perc).
Same sessions.

You CD BN 5-22342-2,(J)TOCJ-66067

Caecilie Norby(vo) with Anders Bergcrantz(tp) Ben Besiakov(el p) Lars Danielsson(g,p,b,keyb) Anders Kjellberg(dm) Xavier Desandre-Navarre(perc).
Same sessions.

Thick blue grass CD BN 5-22342-2,(J)TOCJ-66067

Caecilie Norby(vo) with Anders Bergcrantz(flh) Lars Danielsson(p,b,cello,strings).
Same sessions.

Newborn broken CD BN 5-22342-2,(J)TOCJ-66067

Caecilie Norby(vo) with Anders Bergcrantz(flh-1) Lars Moller,Hans Ulrik-1(ts) Ben Besiakov(p) John Scofield(g) Lars Danielsson(b) Billy Hart (dm).
Same sessions.

Milkman CD BN 5-22342-2,(J)TOCJ-66067
Naked in the dark -1 -

Caecilie Norby(vo) with Anders Bergcrantz(tp) Lars Jansson(p) John Scofield(g) Lars Danielsson(b,keyb) Per Lindvall(dm) Xavier Desandre-Navarre(perc).
Same sessions.

Remember Rosa CD BN 5-22342-2,(J)TOCJ-66067

Caecilie Norby(vo) with Lars Jansson(p) John Scofield(g) Lars Danielsson(b) Anders Kjellberg(cymbals, chimes).
Same sessions.

Himalaya's bijou CD BN 5-22342-2,(J)TOCJ-66067

435

CAECILIE NORBY - QUEEN OF BAD EXCUSES:
Caecilie Norby(vo) with Hans Ulrik(ss) Lars Danielsson(el p,b,keyb) John Scofield(g) Billy Hart & Anders Kjellberg(dm) Xavier Desandre-Navarre(perc).
(EMI-Denmark)(Focus Recording Studios) Copenhagen,Denmark,March ,1999

Meet the monotone	CD BN 5-22342-2,(J)TOCJ-66067

Caecilie Norby(vo) with Lars Danielsson(p,b,cello,strings).Same sessions.

Our day will come	CD BN 5-22342-2,(J)TOCJ-66067

Caecilie Norby(vo with Aske Jacoby(g) Lars Danielsson(rh g,b,dm).Same sessions.

A bad girl's dream	CD BN(J)TOCJ-66067

ERIK TRUFFAZ - BENDING NEW CORNERS:
Erik Truffaz(tp) Patrick Muller(el p,p-1) Marcello Giuliani(b) Marc Erbetta(dm) Nya(vo).
(EMI France)(Studio du Flon) Lausanne (Switzerland),April 3-6,1999

Sweet mercy	CD BN 5-26427-2,(F)5-22123-2	
Arroyo	-	-
More	-	-
Less	-	-
Siegfried (voN)		-
Bending new corners	CD BN 5-26427-2	-
Betty		-
Minaret	CD BN 5-26427-2	-
Minaret #2		
Friendly fire (voN)-1	CD BN(F)5-22123-2	
And	CD BN 5-26427-2,(F)5-22123-2	

All titles issued on BN(F)5-22123-1.

CHUCHO VALDES - LIVE AT THE VILLAGE VANGUARD:
Chucho Valdes(p) Francisco Rubio Pampin(b) Raul Pineda Roque(dm) Roberto Vizcaino Guillot(cga,bata dm) Mayra Caridad Valdes(vo).
(EMI-Canada)(Live,The Village Vanguard) NYC,April 9 & 10,1999

Anabis
Son XXI para pia
Punto Cubano
My funny Valentine
To Bud Powell
Drume negrita
Como traigo la yuca
Ponle la Clave
Encore - Lorraine's habanera

All titles issued on CD BN 5-20730-2.

BOB DOROUGH - TOO MUCH COFFEE MAN:
Phil Woods(as) Bob Dorough(p,vo) Ray Drummond(b) Billy Hart(dm).
(Red Rock Recording) Sailorsburg,Pennsylvania,April 18,1999

(tk.4)	The coffee song (They've got a lot of coffee in Brazil) -1
(tk.4)	Fish for supper
(tk.1)	Where is the song?

-1: Ken Brader III(tp,flh) Rick Chamberlain(tb) Jim Daniels(bass tb,tu) Mark Holen(perc) overdubbed on.
All titles issued on CD BN 4-99239-2.

GREG OSBY - THE INNER CIRCLE:
Greg Osby(as) Stefon Harris(vb) Jason Moran(p) Tarus Mateen(b) Eric Harland(dm).
(Systems Two Studio) Brooklyn,N.Y.,April 22 & 23,1999

Entruption
Stride logic
Diary of the same dream
Equalatogram
All neon like
Fragmatic decoding
The inner circle (principle)
Sons of the confidential
Self portrait in 3 colors

All titles scheduled for issue on CD BN 4-99871-2 (not released yet).

PRYSM - TIME:
Pierre De Bethmann(p,synth-1) Christophe Wallemme(b,el b-1) Benjamin Henocq(dm).
(BN-France) (Studio La Buissonne) Pernes-les-Fontaines (France),April ,1999

Keystone
Dream on
X-Ray
Voice of angels
The circle
Light
Exit
Outlines
Jacques's song
Scratch...-1

All titles issued on CD BN(F) 5-21886-2.

BOB DOROUGH - TOO MUCH COFFEE MAN:
Bob Dorough(p,vo) Hui Cox(g-1) Steve Gilmore(b) Bill Goodwin(dm).
(Red Rock Recording) Sailorsburg,Pennsylvania,May 6,1999

(tk.3) There's never been a day
(tk.2) Wake up Sally -4
(tk.1) Oklahoma toad -2,4,5
(tk.2) Late in the century -1,2,3

-2: Craig Kastelnik(org) overdubbed on.
-3: Craig Kastelnik,Pat Flaherty,Lois Brownsey(backgr. vo) overdubbed on.
-4: Ken Brader III(tp,flh) Rick Chamberlain(tb) Jim Daniels(bass tb,tu) overdubbed on.
-5: Mark Holen(perc) overdubbed on.
All titles issued on CD BN 4-99239-2.

PIECES OF A DREAM - AHEAD TO THE PAST:
Eddie Baccus Jr.(ss) Larry Gold(cello) Randy Bowland(g) Pablo Batista Jr.(perc).
(The Studio) Philadelphia,May ,1999

Bella voce (Beautiful voice) CD BN 4-98488-2

Eddie Baccus Jr.(sax) James K. Lloyd(keyb,dm programming) Randy Bowland(g) Cedric Napoleon(b) Curtis Harmon(cymbals) Dr. Leonard Gibbs(perc).
(The Studio) Philadelphia,May ,1999

Took so long CD BN 4-98488-2

437

PIECES OF A DREAM - AHEAD TO THE PAST:

Eddie Baccus Jr.(ss) James K. Lloyd(p,keyb) Michael Antonio Thornton(keyb) Randy Bowland(g) Bill Pierce(b) Curtis Harmon(dm,perc).

(The Studio) Philadelphia,May ,1999

Malibu nights CD BN 4-98488-2

Eddie Baccus Jr.(ss) James K. Lloyd(p,keyb) Michael Antonio Thornton(keyb) Randy Bowland(g) Cedric Napoleon(b) Curtis Harmon(dm,perc).

(The Studio) Philadelphia,May ,1999

Love you for life CD BN 4-98488-2

James K. Lloyd,Michael Antonio Thornton-1 (keyb,programming) Randy Bowland(g-1).

(The Studio) Philadelphia,May ,1999

Driving it home -1 CD BN 4-98488-2
Cry of the lonely -

Cherie Mitchell(el p) James K. Lloyd(keyb bass) Curtis Harmon(dm) Maysa Leak(lead vo,backgr. vo).

(The Studio) Philadelphia,May ,1999

You and I CD BN 4-98488-2

Eddie Baccus Jr.(sax-2) James K. Lloyd(keyb,dm programming,vo-2) Ronny Jordan(b-1,g-1,ac g-2) Curtis Harmon (dm-1,vo-2) Charles Baldwin(dm programming-2).

(The Studio) Philadelphia,May ,1999

Philly high -1
It's you that I want -2

Both titles issued on CD BN 4-98488-2.

Eddie Baccus Jr.(ss-1) Bennie Sims(keyb,dm programming) Curtis D. Harmon(keyb,dm programming, backgr. vo) Calvin Richardson(lead vo-2).

(Sigma Sound Studios) Philadelphia,May ,1999

You -1 CD BN 4-98488-2
Why don't you let me love you -2 -

Eddie Baccus Jr.(ss,dm programming) Michael Antonio Thornton(keyb) Randy Bowland(g) Cedric Napoleon(b) Pablo Batista Jr.(perc).

(Sigma Sound Studios) Philadelphia,May ,1999

The good life (La feliz vida) CD BN 4-98488-2

ELIANE ELIAS - EVERYTHING I LOVE:

Eliane Elias(p,vo) Marc Johnson(b) Jack DeJohnette(dm).

(Avatar Studios) NYC,May 29 & 30,1999

I fall in love too easily (voEE)
They say it's wonderful (voEE)
Everything I love
Introduction #1/If I should lose you
I love you
That's all it was
Introduction #2/Alone together
Introduction #3/Autumn leaves

All titles issued on CD BN 5-20827-2.

<u>ELIANE ELIAS</u> - <u>EVERYTHING I LOVE</u>:
Eliane Elias(p,vo) Christian McBride(b) Carl Allen(dm).
(Avatar Studios) NYC,May 31,1999

Bowing to Bud	CD BN 5-20827-2
Nostalgia in Times Square	-
Woody'n you	-
Blah,blah,blah (voEE)	-

<u>FLAVIO BOLTRO</u> - <u>ROAD RUNNER</u>:
Flavio Boltro(tp,flh,arr) Stefano Di Battista(ss,as,ts) Louis Winsberg(g) Eric Legnini(p,keyb,arr) Pippo Matino(el b) Stephane Huchard(dm).
(EMI-France) (Gimmick Studio) Yerres (France),May 31-June 6,1999

Matteo
Duo
Little room -1
Flaviosphere
Hey! Papa -2
Vucciria -3
Tea in the Sahara
Ajo
Call -4

-1: Daniele Scannapieco(ts) added.
-2: Paco Sery(dm,perc) replaces Huchard.
-3: Nantha Kumar(tablas) added.
-4: Marcello Giuliani(g,el b) replaces Winsberg & Matino.
All titles issued on CD BN(F)5-23342-2.

<u>RONNY JORDAN</u> - <u>A BRIGHTER DAY</u>:
Joel Campbell(keyb,arr) Ronny Jordan(g) Steve Lewinson(b) Poogie Bell(dm) Stephanie McKay(vo).
(Unique Studios) NYC,May-July 1999
Bass and keyboards overdubbed on.(Timeless Studios) London,c. 1999

A brighter day	BN B1-20208,CD 5-20208-2,(J)TOCP-65391

Same recording,with Mos Def(rapper) DJ Spinna(mixer) added.

A brighter day (remix)	CD BN 5-20208-2

Stefon Harris(vb) Bruce Flowers(p) Ronny Jordan(g,synth g) Ian Martin(b) Jeff "Tain" Watts(dm).
Same sessions.

5/8 in flow	CD BN 5-20208-2,(J)TOCP-65391

Todd Hinton(tp-1)Bruce Flowers(p,el p,keyb) Ronny Jordan(ac g,g,synth,dm programming) Ian Martin(b) Poogie Bell(dm) Café(perc) Stephanie McKay-1,Philip Hamilton-2 (backgr.vo).
Same sessions.

Seeing is beieving	CD BN 5-20208-2,(J)TOCP-65391
Aftermath (perc out)-1	BN B1-20208,CD 5-20208-2,(J)TOCP-65391
Rio-2	CD BN 5-20208-2,(J)TOCP-65391
Two worlds (b out)	BN B1-20208,CD 5-20208-2,(J)TOCP-65391

Bruce Flowers(el p-1) Ticklah-2 (keyb,sound effects) Ronny Jordan(g,b,synth g,synth) DJ Spinna(dm programming,scratches) Jill Jones(vo-2).
(Unique Studios/Skyelab Studios) NYC,March-July 1999

Mackin' -1	BN B1-20208,CD 5-20208-2,(J)TOCP-65391
Why -2	- - -

RONNY JORDAN - A BRIGHTER DAY:
Roy Ayers(vb-1) Bruce Flowers(el p-1) Bran Mitchell(org-2) Ronny Jordan(g,b,dm programming,g,synth, keyb) Neil Clarke(perc).
(Unique Studios/Skyelab Studios) NYC,March-July 1999

Mystic voyage -1 BN B1-20208,CD 5-20208-2,(J)TOCP-65391
London lowdown -2 - - -

Marcus Persiani(p) Ronny Jordan(g,sub b,dm synth,synth) Andy Gonzalez(b) Café(perc).
(Unique Studios/Skyelab Studios) NYC,March-July 1999

Mambo inn CD BN 5-20208-2,(J)TOCP-65391

Steve Wilson(fl) Onaje Allan Gumbs(p) Ronny Jordan(ac g,synth g,b & dm programming) Ian Martin(b) Clarence Penn(dm).
(Unique Studios/Skyelab Studios) NYC,March-July 1999
Shivas Shanker(tablas) Sivashakti Sivanesan(vo) overdubbed on.
(Hear No Evil Studios) London, 1999

New Delhi BN B1-20208,CD 5-20208-2,(J)TOCP-65391

Ronny Jordan(all instruments).
(Unique Studios/Skyelab Studios) NYC,March-July 1999

State of grace CD BN(J)TOCP-65391

Ronny Jordan(g) Zachary Breaux(sampled rhythm g)-1.
(Unique Studios) NYC,May-June 1999

Breauxlude CD BN(J)TOCP-65391

-1: sample from the track "West side worry" in album "Laidback" (NYC Records).

DENISE JANNAH - THE MADNESS OF OUR LOVE:
Denise Jannah(vo) with Bert Van den Brink(p) Ira Coleman(b) Carl Allen(dm).
(EMI-Holland)(Avatar Studios) NYC,June 1,1999

(tk.2) Wide awake
(tk.2) My favorite things
(tk.3) Dearly beloved
(tk.1) Le sourire de mon amour (The shadow of your smile) -1
(tk.2) Harlem nocturne
(tk.1) Teach me tonight
(tk.1) The madness of our love
(tk.1) 'Round midnight

-1: Khalil Bell(shaker) added.
All titles issued on CD BN 5-22642-2.

Same. (Avatar Studios) NYC,June 2,1999

(tk.1) Medley: My foolish heart/ CD BN 5-22642-2
I fall in love too easily -
Turn out the stars rejected
(tk.3) Just you,just me CD BN 5-22642-2
(tk.2) Softly as in a morning sunrise -
(tk.2) If only -
God bless the child rejected

ELIANE ELIAS - EVERYTHING I LOVE:
Eliane Elias(p,vo) Rodney Jones(g) Marc Johnson(b) Carl Allen(dm).
(Avatar Studios) NYC,June 2,1999

	The beat of my heart (voEE)	CD BN 5-20827-2

TIM HAGANS - LIVE IN MONTREAL:
Tim Hagans(tp) Bob Belden(ss) Scott Kinsey(synth) David Dyson(el b) Billy Kilson(dm) DJ Kingsize (Stephen Hindman)(turntables).
(Montreal Jazz Festival,Salle de Jesu) Montreal,Canada,July 3,1999

tk.1	Drum and trumpet thing	rejected
tk.2	Animation/Imagination	CD BN 5-27544-2
tk.3	Kingsize	-
tk.4	Hud Doyle	-
tk.5	Killer instinct	-
tk.6	28 IF	-
tk.7	Dark city	-
tk.8	French girl	rejected
tk.9	Are you threatening me?	CD BN 5-27544-2
tk.10	Love's lullaby	-
tk.11	Trumpet sandwich	-

KURT ELLING:
Kurt Elling(vo) with Laurence Hobgood(p) Rob Amster(b) Mike Raynor(dm) Kahil El' Zabar(hand dm,vo)-1
(Live,The Green Mill) Chicago,July 14,1999

Set #1:		
	Downtown	rejected
	Resolution	-
	Smoke gets in your eyes	CD BN 5-22211-2
	My foolish heart	rejected
	On my God -1	CD BN 5-22211-2
	Dolores dream	rejected
	Renaissance of the resistance -1	CD BN(Au)5-25494-2
	Esperanto (Esperança)	rejected
Set #2:		
	Tanya Jean	rejected
	Moon & sand	-
	Dolores dream -1	-
	On my God -1	-
	Downtown	-
	Straight no chaser	-

Kurt Elling(vo) with Laurence Hobgood(p) Rob Amster(b) Mike Raynor(dm).
(Live,The Green Mill) Chicago,July 15,1999

Set #1:		
	Oleo (Elling out)	rejected
	My foolish heart	CD BN 5-22211-2
	Smoke gets in your eyes	rejected
	Esperanto (Esperança)	-
	Downtown	-
	Resolution	-
	Rent party -1	-
	I feel so smoochie -1	-

-1: Elling out.Von Freeman,Eddie Johnson,Ed Petersen(ts) added.

441

KURT ELLING:

Kurt Elling(vo) with Laurence Hobgood(p) Rob Amster(b) Mike Raynor(dm).

(Live,The Green Mill) Chicago,July 15,1999

Set #2:

Moanin'-1	rejected
Intro/Rent party -1	CD BN 5-22211-2
I feel so smoochie -1	rejected
Downtown	-
Night dream (Night dreamer)	CD BN 5-22211-2
Esperanto (Esperança)	rejected
Blues closer	-

-1: Von Freeman,Eddie Johnson,Ed Petersen(ts) added.

Same. (Live,The Green Mill) Chicago,July 16,1999

Set #1:

Solar (Elling out)	rejected
Smoke gets in your eyes	-
Downtown	CD BN 5-22211-2
Resolution	CD BN(Au)5-25494-2
What I meant to say was... (solo p)	-
All is quiet	rejected
Night dream (Night dreamer)	CD BN 5-22211-2
(I love you) For sentimental reasons	-
Intro/Esperanto (Esperança)	-
Moanin'-1	rejected
Intro/Goin' to Chicago -1	CD BN 5-22211-2
Don't get scared -1	rejected

-1: Jon Hendricks(vo) added.

Set #2:

Tanya Jean	rejected
Moon and sand	CD BN(Au)5-25494-2
Dolores dream	-
Smoke gets in your eyes	rejected
Everybody's boppin'-1	-
Goin' to Chicago -1	-
Don't get scared -1	CD BN 5-22211-2
Straight no chaser	rejected

-1: Jon Hendricks(vo) added.

THE JAZZ MANDOLIN PROJECT - XENOBLAST :

Jamie Masefield(mand,mandola) Chris Dahlgren(b,el b) Ari Hoenig(dm,perc).

(The Barn) Burlington,Vermont,August 16 & 17,1999

Xenoblast
Double agent
The Milliken way
Spiders
Jovan
Dromedary
Shaker Hill
Igor
Hang ten -1

-1: Troy Anastasio(g) added.
All titles issued on CD BN 5-25251-2.

<u>GREG OSBY</u> - <u>THE INVISIBLE HAND</u>:
Greg Osby(as) Gary Thomas(fl-1,alto fl-2,ts-3) Andrew Hill(p) Jim Hall(g) Scott Colley(b) Terri Lyne Carrington(dm).

(Systems Two Studio)	Brooklyn,N.Y.,September 8,1999
Ashes	CD BN 5-20134-2
Sanctus -2	-
Nature boy (p out) -1,4	-
With son (g out) -1,3,4	-
(Back home in) Indiana (p,g out) -3	rejected

-4: Gary Thomas(alto fl) Greg Osby(cl,bass cl) overdubbed on.

Greg Osby(as) Andrew Hill(p) Scott Colley(b) Terri Lyne Carrington(dm).

(Systems Two Studio)	Brooklyn,N.Y.,September 9,1999
(Back home in) Indiana (p out) -1	
Tough love	
Jitterbug waltz	
The watcher (as & p only)	
The watcher 2 (as & p only)	
Who needs forever (p out) -2	

-1: Greg Osby(cl) overdubbed on.
-2: Gary Thomas (fl,alto fl) Greg Osby(cl,bass cl) overdubbed on.
All titles issued on CD BN 5-20134-2.

<u>BRIAN BLADE FELLOWSHIP</u> - <u>PERPETUAL</u>:
Myron Walden(as,bass cl) Melvin Butler(ss,ts) Jon Cowherd(p,el p,pump org) Dave Easley(pedal steel g) Kurt Rosenwinkel(el g,g) Christopher Thomas(b,grunting) Brian Blade(dm).

(Avatar Studios)	NYC,September 24-27, 1999
Perceptual	
Evinrude-Fifty (Trembling)	
Reocnciliation	
Crooked creek	
Patron saint of girls	
The Sunday boys (Improvisation)	
Variations of a bloodline:	
a. From the same blood	
b. Fellowship (Like brothers)	
c. Mustangs (Class of 1988)	
Steadfast -1	

-1: Brian Blade (ac g) Daniel Lanois(el g) Joni Mitchell(vo) overdubbed on.

(Teatro)	Oxnard,Calif.,October ,1999

All titles issued on CD BN 5-23571-2.

Brian Blade(ac g,vo) Daniel Lanois (pedal steel g).

(Teatro)	Oxnard,Calif.,October ,1999
Trembling	CD BN 5-23571-2

443

THE JOE LOVANO NONET - 52nd STREET THEMES:
Tim Hagans(tp) Conrad Herwig(tb) Steve Slagle(as) Joe Lovano(ts,arr) Ralph Lamama(ts) Gary Smulyan (bs) John Hicks(p) Dennis Irwin(b) Lewis Nash(dm) Willie Smith(orchestrations).
(Avatar Studios) NYC,November 3,1999

(tk.2)	On a misty night	CD BN 4-96667-2
(tk.2)	Whatever possess'd me	-
(tk.3)	Tadd's delight	(see note at end of Nov. 4 session))
(tk.3)	Deal	CD BN 4-96667-2
	Embraceable you	rejected
(tk.1)	Charlie Chan -1	CD BN 4-96667-2
(tk.2)	Sippin' at bells -2	-
(tk.2)	Passion flower -3	-

-1: George Garzone(ts) added with Lovano,Lamama,Garzone,Hicks,Irwin & Nash only.
-2: Hagans,Slagle,Lovano,Hicks,Irwin & Nash only.
-3: Lovano & Hicks only.

Tim Hagans(tp) Conrad Herwig(tb) Steve Slagle(as) Joe Lovano(ts,arr) George Garzone(ts) Gary Smulyan (bs) John Hicks(p) Dennis Irwin(b) Lewis Nash(dm) Willie Smith(orchestrations).
(Avatar Studios) NYC,November 4,1999

(tk.1)	Abstractions on 52nd Street -1	CD BN 4-96667-2
(tk.4)	Embraceable you	-
	On a misty night	rejected
(tk.4)	Tadd's delight	CD BN 4-96667-2 (see note)
(tk.3)	52nd Street theme	-
(tk.3)	Theme for Ernie -2	-
(tk.3)	The scene is clean -3	-

-1: Lovano only.
-2: Lovano,Hicks,Irwin & Nash only.
-3: Lovano,Irwin & Nash only.

Note: The issued version of "Tadd's delight" consists mainly of tk. 4 from Nov. 4 session with the closing ensemble from tk. 3 of Nov. 3 and an insert from Nov. 4 .

BOB DOROUGH & DAVE FRISHBERG - WHO'S ON FIRST:
Bob Dorough,Dave Frishberg(vo,p).
(Live,The Jazz Bakery) LA,November 5,6 & 7,1999

Two hands too many (instr.)	
Rockin' in rhythm (instr.)	CD BN 5-23403-2
Health food nut (voBD)	-
Conjunction junction (voBD)	-
Who's on first? (voBD,DF)	-
Just about everything (voBD,DF)	
Alone together (voBD,DF)	
I'm hip (voBD,DF)	CD BN 5-23403-2
Saturday dance (voBD,DF)	-
Where you at? (voBD,DF)	-
Yardbird suite (voBD,DF)	

BOB DOROUGH & DAVE FRISHBERG - WHO'S ON FIRST:
Dave Frishberg(vo on all titles,p).Same sessions.

I want to be a sideman	unssued
Too long in LA	CD BN 5-23403-2
You are there	-
Medley:	unissued
I'm just a bill/	-
Dollars and sense/	-
7:50 Once a week/	-
Wall Street	-
Zoot walked in (Red door)	-
The Christy Matheson song	-
Do you miss New York	-
The underdog	CD BN 5-23403-2
Lookin' good	-

Bob Dorough(vo on all titles,p).Same sessions.

Oklahoma toad	unissued
Devil may care	CD BN 5-23403-2
Lament for Lady Day	unissued
Hong Kong blues	CD BN 5-23403-2
'Tis Autumn	unissued
Baltimore oriole	-
Nothing like you	CD BN 5-23403-2
If it lasts till then	unissued

Note: Recordings were made on two sets on the nights of November 5 & 6,and one matinee set on November 7.

SUPERGENEROUS:
Kevin Breit(g) Cyro Baptista(perc) Cassandra Wilson (vo).
(J.B. Music Studio) NYC,December 2-4,6,7 & 9,1999

Johnny cactus
Sao Paolo Slim
Dreamin' of the A train
Home in the range (voCW)
God's parking lot
Steinbeck
Marissa O'Brien
Brohemia
Ghosts
Caravan
Bandito's horse
Mary
Interloop

All titles issued on CD BN 5-24633-2.

PAUL JACKSON Jr. - THE POWER OF THE STRING:

LA,December 1999 - January 2000

(no details) CD BN 5-21477-2

445

LATE ADDITIONS

JEAN-PIERRE COMO - EMPREINTE:
Emmanuelle Cisi(ts,vo) Jean-Pierre Como(p,vo) Zool Fleischer(keyb,arr) Marc Bertaux(el b) Paco Sery(dm) Minino Garay(perc,vo).
(EMI-France) (Studio Harry Son) Pantin (France),August ,1997

Resonnances CD BN(F)5-20907-2

Emanuelle Cisi(ts,vo) Jean-Pierre Como(p,keyb,arr,vo) Jean-Marie Ecay(el g) Marc Bertaux(el b) Stephane Huchard(dm) Minino Garay(perc,vo).
Omar Tolure,Guila Tchiam(vo-1) Karim Ziad(perc,vo)-2 Sylvain Luc-3 (g,mandolin) Miguel Sanchez(perc-4) Zool Fleischer(el p-5) Eric Chevalier(programming-5) Didier Lockwood(v-6) Michael Allibo(el b-6) added.
(EMI-France) (Studio Gimmick) Yerres (France),September ,1997

Anatole Frtance -1
Tontine (de Leon case)
Marguax
Ange Michel -2,3
Three views of a secret -4
Boulougnou -5
Empreinte -1,6
Alpicoise -3
Milestrone
Giant steps

All titles issued on CD BN(F)5-20907-2.

Dario Dedda,Emanuel Binet(el b) Paco Sery(dm,perc) Jean-Pierre Como,Oumar Ba,Weuz Kaly,Aurélie Guiller(vo).
(EMI-France) (Studio Gimmick) Yerres (France),September ,1997

Liberty City CD BN(F)5-20907-2

HELEN ERIKSEN - LOVE VIRGIN:
Helen Eriksen(vo,ts) Helge Lilletvedt(p,keyb,synth) Martin Hedstrom-1 (g,b) Tommy Tee (b,dm,samples, programming) Opaque-2,N-Light N-3 (rappers).
(EMI Norway) (Tee Studios) Oslo,c. early 1998

Mind is new -1
Heroine
You are my star
Main minority -1,2
Boys and girls -1
Brave heart -1
Cosmis comedian
Let love
Greeted creatures -2,3
Wild eyes -4
Wild eyes (Shawn J. Periode remix)-4
Wild eyes (instr.)

-4: Mike Zoot and Words(rappers) overdubbed at D & D Studios,NYC.

All titles issued on CD BN(Norway)4-96968-2.

KURT ELLING:
Remix of Horace Silver 1956 recording of "Senor blues" (see page 58):
Kurt Elling,Tess Marsalis(vo) Matthew Brecker(tape sounds, mixer).
(2 Ton Sound Studio) NYC,c. Spring 1999

Senor blues 2000 CD BN(Au)5-25494-2

PACO SERY - VOYAGES:
Paco Sery(dm,perc,keyb,rh g,comp,arr,programming) with various groups including brass,saxes/cl,rhythm & choir,feat. Dianne Reeves(vo-1) (see complete details in addendum - page 907).
(EMI France) (Gimmick Studio) France,c. Summer/Fall 1999

Donne-moi une chance
Partage
Lucie
Nasty girl
Pygmee rap
Dialogue
Wi
Maghreb
Bassam
Guerini blues
Thank full
Senza univers -1
Jungle
Break interlude
Faut pas nous blaguer
Salt peanuts

All titles issued on CD BN(F)5-21758-2.

Part 4
Purchased Sessions

T-BONE WALKER:
T-Bone Walker(vo) with Les Hite and his Orchestra: Paul Campbell,Walter Williams,Forrest Powell(tp) Britt Woodman,Allen Durham(tb) Les Hite(as,dir) Floyd Turnham(as) Quedillis "Que" Martyn,Roger Hurd(ts) Sol Moore(bs) Nat Walker(p) Frank Pasely(g) Al Morgan(b) Oscar Bradley(dm).
(purchased from Varsity label) NYC,June ,1940

US1852-1	T-Bone blues	BN 530

GEORGE LEWIS & HIS NEW ORLEANS STOMPERS:
Jim Robinson(tb) Sidney "Little Jim" Brown(tu) George Lewis(cl) Lawrence Marrero(bjo) Edgar Mosley (dm).
(purchased from Bill Russell) NO,May 15,1943

CD 101	Climax rag	Dan(J)VC-7021,YB-1005
CD 102	New Orleans hula	-
CD 103	Don't go 'way nobody	BN BLP1206,(J)K23P-9289
CD 104	Two Jim blues	Climax 102;BN BLP7013,BLP1206 BN(J)K23P-9289;Vogue(E)EPV1066,LAE12005

All titles also issued on Mosaic MR5-132,CD MD3-132.

Avery "Kid" Howard(tp,vo) Jim Robinson(tb) George Lewis(cl) Lawrence Marrero(bjo) Chester Zardis(b) Edgar Mosley(dm).(purchased from Bill Russell) NO,May 16,1943

CD 105 °	Climax rag BST89902,BN-LA158-G2	Climax 101;BN BEP404,BLP7010,BLP1206, Vogue(E)EPV1066,LAE 12005
CD 106	Climax rag	
CD 107 °	Just a closer walk with Thee	Climax 103;BN BLP7010,BLP1206 Vogue(E)EPV1081,LAE12005
CD 108	Just a closer walk with Thee	Dan(J)VC-7021,YB-1005
CD 109	I ain't gonna give nobody none of my jelly roll	
CD 110	I ain't gonna give nobody none of my jelly roll	
CD 111 °	Careless love blues (Careless love *)	Climax 105;BN BEP404*,BLP7013* Vogue(E)EPV1081*,LAE12005*
CD 112	Careless love blues	Dan(J)VC-7007,YB-1005;Storyville(Dk)SLP201
CD 113 °	Dauphine Street blues	Climax 104;BN BLP7010,BLP1206 Vogue(E)LAE12005
CD 114 °	Just a little while to stay here	Climax 103;BN BEP404,BLP7013,BLP1206 Vogue(E)EPV1081,LAE12005
CD 115	Just a little while to stay here	Dan(J)VC-7021
CD 116	Just a closer walk with Thee	-
CD 117	Milenburg joys	
CD 118 °	Milenburg joys	Climax 102;BN BLP7010,BLP1206 Vogue(E)EPV1066,LAE12005
CD 119 °	Fidgety feet	Climax 104;BN BLP7010,BLP1206 Vog(E)LAE12005
CD 120 °	Fidgety feet N°2	BN BLP1206
CD 121	Don't go 'way nobody	
CD 122 °	Don't go 'way nobody	Climax 105;BN BLP7013 Vogue(E)EPV1081,LAE12005
CD 123 °	Deep bayou blues	Climax 101;BN BLP7010,BLP1206 Vogue(E)EPV1066,LAE12005

(session continued on next page)

CD 124	When you're lonesome,telephone me	Dan(J)VC-7021
CD 125	Just a closer walk with thee	
CD	Old man Mose (voKH)	unissued (lost master)
CD	You rascal you (voKH)	- -

All titles, except last two, issued on Mosaic MR5-132,CD MD3-132.
All titles marked ° also issued on BN(J)K23P-9289.

ERROLL GARNER (all titles purchased from Timme Rosenkrantz - see reissues at bottom of page):
Erroll Garner(p). NYC,November 16,1944

The clock stood still	BN BLP5016;CD Classics(F)802

Erroll Garner(p). NYC,November 18,1944

Floating on a cloud	BN BLP5008,(F)BNP25101;CD Classics(F)802

Erroll Garner(p). NYC,November 22,1944

Autumn mood	BN BLP5008,(F)BNP25101;CD Classics(F)802

Erroll Garner(p). NYC,November 24,1944

On the sunny side of the street	BN BLP5014,(F)BNP25102;CD Classics(F)802

Note: This recording featured a part by Vic Dickenson(tb),which is not included in the issued records.

Erroll Garner(p) George Wettling(dm). NYC,December ,1944

I surrender dear	BN BLP5008,(F)BNP25102;CD Classics(F)802

Note: This recording featured parts by Bobby Pratt(tb) and Barney Bigard(cl),which are not included in the issued records.

Erroll Garner(p). NYC,December 10-12,1944

Overture to dawn	BN BLP5007,(F)BNP25101
Erroll's concerto	BN BLP5008 -
Yesterdays	BN BLP5014,(F)BNP25102

All titles also issued on CD Classics(F)802.

Erroll Garner(p). NYC,December 14,1944

All the things you are	BN BLP5016;CD Classics(F)802
I hear a rhapsody	BN BLP5007,(F)BNP25101;CD Classics(F)818
Erroll's reverie	BN BLP5015;CD Classics(F)818
You were born to be kissed	BN BLP5007,(F)BNP25101;CD Classics(F)818

Erroll Garner(p) unknown(g-1). NYC,December 20,1944

The fighting cocks	BN BLP5015,(F)BNP25102
A lick and a promise	-
Opus I	BN BLP5016
Gaslight	-
Fast company-1	BN BLP5014,(F)BNP25102

-1: This title was issued on Selmer(F)Y7086 as "Twistin" the cat's tail".
All titles also issued on CD Classics(F)818.

All Garner titles listed above also issued on Official(Dk) 3016-3,CD 83016-2.

ERROLL GARNER:
Erroll Garner(p). NYC,December 23-25,1944

	Duke for dinner	BN BLP5015,(F)BNP25102
	I got rhythm	BN BLP5014 -

Both titles also issued on Official(Dk) 3016-3,CD Classics(F)850,Official(Dk)83016-2.

BOBBY HACKETT:
Bobby Hackett(tp) Vernon Brown(tb) Joe Dixon(cl) Deane Kincaide(bs) Dave Bowman(p) Carl Kress(g) Bob Haggart(b) George Wettling(dm).
(purchased from Melrose label)
(WOR Studios) NYC,May 31,1945

(101-1)	Pennies from heaven (alt.)	
(101-)	Pennies from heaven	Melrose 1401, CD BN 4-95981-2
(102-1)	Rose of the Rio Grande (alt.)	
(102-2)	Rose of the Rio Grande	Melrose 1401
(103-1)	Body and soul	
(103-4)	Body and soul (alt.)	
(104-2)	I want to be happy	

All titles, except 102-1, were scheduled on BN LT-1055, which was not released.
All 7 titles were issued on Mosaic MQ19-170,CD MD12-170.

ALBERT NICHOLAS SEXTET:
George Poor(tp) Bob Hendrick(tb) Albert Nicholas(cl) Beth Hendrick(p) Bill Learoyd(b) Bob Saltmarsh(dm).
Marblehead,Mass.,late Summer 1947

	Dawn at Marblehead	BN BLP7013

SARAH VAUGHAN & LESTER YOUNG - TOWN HALL CONCERT:
Shorty McConnell(tp) Lester Young(ts) Sadik Hakim(p) Freddie Lacey(g) Rodney Richardson(b) Roy Haynes(dm).
(Town Hall) NYC,November 8,1947

	Lester leaps in	CD BN 8-32139-2
	Just you,just me	-
	Jumpin' with Symphony Sid	-
	Sunday	-
	Lester's bebop boogie	-
	These foolish things	-
	Movin' with Lester	-

Sarah Vaughan(vo) Sammy Benskin(p) Freddie Lacey(g) Rodney Richardson(b) Roy Haynes(dm).
Same concert

	Don't blame me	
	My kinda love	
	I cover the waterfront	
	A ghost of a chance	
	The man I love	
	Time after time	
	Mean to me	
	Body and soul	
	I cried for you-1	CD BN 8-23517-2

-1: Shorty McConnell(tp) Lester Young(ts) added.
All titles issued on CD BN 8-32139-2.

GIL MELLE SEXTET:
Eddie Bert (as "X.Kentonite")(tb) Gil Melle(ts) Joe Manning(vb) George Wallington(p) Red Mitchell(b) Max Roach(dm) Monica Dell(vo).
(purchased from Triumph label) Hackensack,N.J.,March 2,1952

BN 461-3 (tk.4)	Four moons	BN 1606	
BN 462-3 (tk.8)	The gears (voMD)	-	BST2-84433
BN 463-0 (tk.9)	Mars (voMD)	BN 1607	
BN 464-0 (tk.10)	Sunset concerto (voMD)	-	

All titles issued on BN BLP5020,(J)K18P-9275, CD BN 4-95718-2.

CHARLIE PARKER - THE WASHINGTON CONCERTS:
Charlie Parker(as) Bill Shanahan(p) Charlie Byrd(g) Mert Oliver(b) Don Lamond(dm) unknown(cga).
(Howard Theater) Washington,D.C.,October 18,1952

Scrapple from the apple
Medley: Out of nowhere/
Now's the time -1

-1: Charlie Walp(tp) Kai Winding,Earl Swope(tb) Zoot Sims(ts) added.
All titles issued on CD BN 5-22626-2.

Charlie Parker(as) Jack Holliday(p) Franklin Skeete(b) Max Roach(dm).
(Howard Theater) Washington,D.C.,March 7,1953

Ornithology
Out of nowhere
Cool blues
Anthropology

All titles issued on CD BN 5-22626-2.

CHARLIE PARKER AT STORYVILLE:
Charlie Parker(as) Red Garland(p) Bernie Briggs(b) Roy Haynes(dm).
(Storyville Club) Boston,March 10,1953

Moose the mooche	
I'll walk alone	
Ornithology	CD BN(E)8-53230-2,(Eu)8-29964-2, (Sp)8-34712-2,8-53016-2
Out of nowhere	CD Cema GSC Music 15131

All titles issued on BN BT 85108,CD 7-85108-2.

Herb Pomeroy(tp) Charlie Parker(as) Sir Charles Thompson(p) Jimmy Woode(b) Kenny Clarke(dm).
(Storyville Club) Boston,September 22,1953

Now's the time	
Don't blame me	
Dancing on the ceiling	
Cool blues	
Groovin' high	CD BN 7-89032-2,8-57742-2

All titles issued on BN BT 85108, CD 7-85108-2.

CHARLIE PARKER - BIRD AT THE HI HAT:
Herbie Williams(tp) Charlie Parker(as) Rollins Griffith(p) Jimmy Woode(b) Marquis Foster(dm).
(Hi-Hat Club) Boston,December 18 & 20,1953

Now's the time
Ornithology (version 1)
My little suede shoes (version 1)
Groovin' high
Cheryl
Ornithology (version 2)

All titles issued on CD BN 7-99787-2.

Herbie Williams(tp) Charlie Parker(as) Rollins Griffith(p) Jimmy Woode(b) Marquis Foster(dm).
(Hi-Hat Club) Boston,January 24,1954

Cool blues
My little suede shoes (version 2)
Interview & announcement
Ornithology (version 3)
Interview & announcement
Out of nowhere
Jumpin' with Symphony Sid

All titles issued on CD BN 7-99787-2.

JUTTA HIPP AND HER QUINTET:
Emil Mangelsdorff(as) Joki Freund(ts) Jutta Hipp(p) Hans Kresse(b) Karl Sanner(dm).
(Franz Althoff Bau) Frankfurt-am-Main (Germany),April 24,1954

100-3	Blue skies (Frankfurt bridges*)	L+R(G)LR41006*;CD BN 7-99095-2
100-4	Mon petit	-
100-6	Cleopatra (Chloe-Patra*)	-*
100-7	Variations	-
101-3	Ghost of a chance (ts out)	-
101-4	Laura (as out)	-
102-2	Don't worry 'bout me (ts,as out)	-
102-3	What's new? (ts,as out)	

All titles issued on BN BLP5056,(J)BN0014,CD TOCJ-9227.

GEORGE LEWIS AND HIS NEW ORLEANS STOMPERS:
Avery "Kid" Howard(tp,vo) Jim Robinson(tb) George Lewis(cl) Alton Purnell(p) Lawrence Marrero(bjo) Alcide "Slow Drag" Pavageau(b) Joe Watkins(dm,vo).
(Studio radio performance) Bakersfield,Calif.,May 28,1954

Gettysburg march	BN BLP1208
Bill Bailey (voKH,JW)	-
Burgundy Street blues	- CD 8-35811-2
Old Man Moses (voKH)	
Walking with the King (voKH)	BN BLP1208

All titles issued on Mosaic MR5-132,CD MD3-132.

<u>GEORGE LEWIS AND HIS NEW ORLEANS STOMPERS</u>:
Avery "Kid" Howard(tp,vo) Jim Robinson(tb) George Lewis(cl) Alton Purnell(p) Lawrence Marrero(bjo) Alcide "Slow Drag" Pavageau(b) Joe Watkins(dm,vo).
(Seven Arts Club) Bakersfield, Calif.,May 28,1954

George Lewis' spoken introduction	BN BLP1208	
Over the waves	-	CD 8-35811-2
Canal Street blues	-	
Red wing	-	
Just a closer walk with Thee (voKH,JW)*	-*	
Ice cream (voKH,JW)	-	
Mama don't allow it (voJW)	-	

All titles issued on Mosaic MR5-132,CD MD3-132.
Note: Track * was edited to 5:26 on BLP1208.The full 9:43 version appears on the Mosaic issues.
The remainder of this concert was sold to and issued on Storyville Records,Denmark.

<u>WARDELL GRAY</u> - <u>BEEHIVE '55</u>:
Poss. John Jenkins(as) Wardell Gray(ts) Norman Simmons(p) Victor Sproles(b) Bert Dahlander(dm).
(private recording)(Live,The Beehive Club) Chicago,c. March 1955

Billie's bounce-1
I can't get started
What is this thing called love-1
Keen and peachy-2
The squirrel
Southside
Pennies from heaven-2

-1: prob. Ira Sullivan or E. Parker MacDougal(ts) added.
-2: poss. Nicky Hill or Jay Peters(ts) added.
All titles to be issued on CD BN 8-33329-2.

<u>HERB POMEROY</u> - <u>JAZZ IN A STABLE</u>:
Herb Pomeroy(tp) Varty Haroutunian(ts) Ray Santisi(p) John Neves(b) Jim Zitano(dm).
(purchased from Transition Records) Boston,March 13,1955

It might as well be Spring	Transition/BN(J)GXF-3125
Honey bunny	-
Moten swing	-
Porta desks & tuxedos	-
One bass hit	-
Off minor	-
Sweet and lovely	-
Ray's idea	-
Dear old Stockholm	-
Tiny's blues	Transition/BN(J-GXF-3126

All titles to be issued on the Blue Note label

<u>JAY MIGLIORI</u>:
Tommy Ball(tp) Jay Migliori(ts) Danny Kent(p) Paul Morrison(b) Floyd Williams(dm).
(purchased from Transition Records) Boston,November 7,1955

Something's's gotta give	Transition/BN(J) GXF-3126

<u>DONALD BYRD JAZZ GROUP</u>:
Donald Byrd,Joe Gordon(tp) Hank Mobley(ts) Horace Silver(p) Doug Watkins(b) Art Blakey(dm).
(purchased from Transition Records) Cambridge,Mass,December 2,1955

Everything happens to me-1	Transition/BN(J)GXF-3123,BN(J)LNJ-70104
Hank's other tune (Late show)-1	- -
Doug's blues	- -
Hank's tune	- -
El Sino-2	- -
Crazy rhythm-2	Transition/BN(J)GXF-3126

-1: Joe Gordon out; -2: Hank Mobley out.
All titles to be issued on Blue Note label.

<u>PAUL CHAMBERS/JOHN COLTRANE</u>:
Curtis Fuller(tb) John Coltrane(ts) Pepper Adams(bs) Roland Alexander(p-1) Paul Chambers(b) Philly Joe Jones(dm).
(purchased from Transition Records) Boston,April 20,1956

High step	
Nixon,Dixon and Yates blues	
Trane's strain-1	Transition/BN(J)GXF-3126

All titles issued on BN BN-LA451-H2, CD 7-84437-2.
Note: This session was first intended to be released as by Curtis Fuller & Pepper Adams.

<u>DONALD BYRD</u> - <u>BYRD BLOWS ON BEACON HILL</u>:
Donald Byrd(tp) Ray Santisi(p) Doug Watkins(b) Jim Zitano(dm).
(purchased from Transition Records) Boston,May 7,1956

If I love again
Little rock getaway
Polka dots and moonbeams
People will say we're in love (Byrd out)
Stella by starlight
What's new? (Byrd out)

All titles issued on Transition/BN(J)GXF-3124,BN(J)LNJ70109.

<u>SUN RA</u>:
Dave Young,Art Hoyle(tp) Julian Priester(tb) James Scales(as) John Gilmore(ts) Pat Patrick(bs) Sun Ra(p) Richard Evans(b) Wilbur Green(el b) Bob Barry(dm) Jim Hearndon(tympani).
(purchased from Transition Records) Chicago,July 12,1956

Swing with a little taste	Transition/BN(J)GXF-3126

<u>CECIL TAYLOR IN TRANSITION</u> (BN-LA458-H2)/<u>JAZZ ADVANCE</u> (CD 7-84462-2):
Steve Lacy(ss-1) Cecil Taylor(p) Buell Neidlinger(b) Dennis Charles(dm).
(purchased from Transition Records) Boston,September 14,1956

Bemsha swing	CD BN(J)TOCJ-5187/88
Charge 'em blues -1	
Azure	
Song -1	BN(J)K23P-6725
You'd be so nice to home to (p solo)	
Rick Kick shaw	CD BN 7-96904-2
Sweet and lovely	Transition/BN(J)GXF-3126

All titles issued on BN BN-LA458-H2,CD 7-84462-2.
All titles,except last,also issued on Transition/BN(J)GXF-3121.

DAVE COLEMAN:
Tommy Ball(tp) Bud Pearson(as) Pepper Adams(bs) Dick Wetmore(v) Pat Petracco(g) Everett Evans(b) Paul Drummond(dm) Dave Coleman(comp,arr).
(purchased from Transition Records) Boston,November 7,1956

Backstreet	Transition/BN(J)GXF-3126

DOUG WATKINS - WATKINS AT LARGE:
Donald Byrd(tp) Hank Mobley(ts) Duke Jordan(p) Kenny Burrell(g) Doug Watkins(b) Art Taylor(dm).
(purchased from Transition Records) prob. NYC,December 8,1956

Return to paradise	
Phinupi	
Phil T. McNasty's blues	CD BN(J)TOCJ-5710
More of the same	
Panonica (ts,g out)	

All titles issued on Transition/BN (J)GXF-3122;BN(J)LNJ70088.

LOUIS SMITH - HERE COMES LOUIS SMITH:
Louis Smith(tp)Julian "Cannonball" Adderley (as "Buckshot La Funke")(as) Duke Jordan(p) Doug Watkins (b) Art Taylor(dm).
(purchased from Transition Records) NYC,February 4,1957

Tribute to Brownie	BN 45-1701,BLP1584;CD BN 8-52438-2
Brill's blues	BN 45-1700 - -
South side	- -

Louis Smith(tp) Julian "Cannonball" Adderley (as "Buckshot La Funke")(as) Tommy Flanagan(p) Doug Watkins(b) Art Taylor(dm).
(purchased from Transition Records) NYC,February 9,1957

Ande	
Stardust (as out)	BN 45-1701,CD BN(J)TOCJ-5300,TOCJ-6133
Val's blues	

All titles issued on BN BLP 1584,CD 8-52438-2

THELONIOUS MONK QUARTET - DISCOVERY! LIVE AT THE FIVE SPOT:
John Coltrane(ts) Thelonious Monk(p) Ahmed Abdul-Malik(b) Roy Haynes(dm).
(Five Spot Cafe) NYC,September 11,1958

Crepuscule with Nellie	CD BN 8-23518-2
Trinkle tinkle	
In walked bud	
I mean you	
Epistrophy	CD BN 8-23518-2

All titles issued on CD BN 7-99786-2, CD 8-30363-2.
Note: On CD 7-99786-2,the recording date is incorrectly given as late summer 1957.

FRANK SINATRA - LIVE IN AUSTRALIA,1959:
Frank Sinatra(vo) Jerry Dodgion(as,fl) Red Norvo(vb) Bill Miller(p) Jimmy Wyble(g) Red Wooten(b) John Markham(dm) & unidentified orchestra-1.
(West Melbourne Stadium) Melbourne,Australia,March 31,1959

Perdido (instr.)	CD BN 8-37513-2
Between the devil and the deep blue sea (instr.)	-
One for my baby	-
Night and day-1	-

455

FRANK SINATRA - LIVE IN AUSTRALIA,1959:

Frank Sinatra(vo) Jerry Dodgion(as,fl) Red Norvo(vb) Bill Miller(p) Jimmy Wyble(g) Red Wooten(b) John Markham(dm) & unidentified orchestra-1.

(West Melbourne Stadium) Melbourne,Australia,April 1,1959

I could have danced all night
Just one of those things
I get a kick out of you
At long last love
Willow weep for me
I've got you under my skin
Moonlight in vermont
The lady is a tramp
Angel eyes
Come fly with me
All the way
Dancing in the dark
All of me-1
On the road to Mandalay -1

All titles issued on CD BN 8-37513-2.

ERIC DOLPHY - OTHER ASPECTS:

Eric Dolphy(fl) Gina Lalli(tablas) Roger Mason(tamboura).

(Stereo Sound Studios) NYC,July 8,1960

Improvisation and tukras BN BT 85131,CD 7-48041-2

Eric Dolphy(fl,as-1) Ron Carter(b-1).

(Esoteric Sound Studio) NYC,November ,1960

Inner flight No.1
Inner flight No.2
Dolphy-N -1

All titles issued on BN BT 85131, CD 7-48041-2.

KENNY CLARKE - FRANCY BOLAND & Co. - THE GOLDEN EIGHT:

Dusko Gojkovic(tp) Raymond Droz(alto h) Christian Kellens(bar h) Derek Humble(as) Karl Drevo(ts) Francy Boland(p,arr) Jimmy Woode(b) Kenny Clarke(dm).

(purchased from Gigi Campi) Cologne,Germany,May 18 & 19,1961

La Campimania
Gloria
High notes
Softly as in a morning sunrise
The golden eight
Strange meeting
You'd be so nice to come home to CD BN 7-89914-2,(J)TOCJ-5934
Dorian 04-37
Poor butterfly
Basse cuite

All titles issued on BN BLP4092/BST84092.

Note: One further title from these sessions (A ball for Othello) was issued by Columbia Records.

ORNETTE COLEMAN AT THE TOWN HALL:
Ornette Coleman(as) Dave Izenzon(b) Charles Moffett(dm).
(see note at end of session)(Town Hall) NYC,December 21,1962

Dedication to poets and writers -1	BN BLP4211
Story teller	BN BLP4210
Sadness	BN BLP4211
The ark	-
Taurus (b only)	unissued
I don't love you	BN BLP4210
Children's books	-
Blues misused -2	unissued
Architecture	BN BLP4210
Play it straight	unissued
Doughnut	BN BLP4211
Just for you	unissued

-1: String Quartet; -2: Chris Towns(p) Napoleon Allen(g) Barney Richardson(b) added.
Note: This session was purchased,but then sold back to Ornette Coleman.BLP4210/11 were never issued

ERIC DOLPHY - ILLINOIS CONCERT:
Eric Dolphy(as,bass cl,fl) Herbie Hancock(p) Eddie Khan(b) J.C. Moses(dm).
(University Of Illinois) Champaign,Illinois,March 10,1963

Softly as in a morning sunrise
Medley: Something sweet, something tender/God bless the child
South street exit
Iron man
Red planet (aka Miles' mode)-1
G.W. -2

-1: add University of Illinois Brass Ensemble: Cecil Bridgewater,Ralph Woodward,Carol Holden(tp) 3 unknowns (frh),2 unknowns(baritone h) Aaron Johnson(tu).
-2:add University of Illinois Big Band: Cecil Bridgewater,Dick Montz,Bruce Scafe,Joe Kennon,Roman Popowycz,Larry Franklin(tp) Dick Sporny,Jon English,Paul Barthelmy,Bob Edmondson(tb) Kim Richmond,Nick Henson,Ron Scalise,Vince Johnson,Bob Huffington(reeds).
All titles issued on CD BN 4-99826-2.

ERIC DOLPHY:
Eric Dolphy(fl,as,bass cl) Bob James(p) Ron Brooks(b) Bob Pozar(dm,perc) David Schwartz(vo).
(Live,University of Michigan) Ann Arbor,March 1 or 2,1964

Jim Crow (*aka* A personal statement) BN BT 85131,CD 7-48041-2

Note: This is actually a Bob James composition and was performed and recorded under his leadership.

DEXTER GORDON - THE SQUIRREL:
Dexter Gordon(ts) Kenny Drew(p) Bo Stief(b) Art Taylor(dm).
(Jazzhus Monmartre) Copenhagen,June 29,1967

The squirrel
Cheese cake
You've changed
Sonnymoon for two

All titles issued on CD BN 8-57302-2.

<u>DEXTER GORDON</u> - <u>NIGHTS AT THE KEYSTONE</u>:
Dexter Gordon(ts,ss) George Cables(p) Rufus Reid(b) Eddie Gladden(dm).
(Live,Keystone Korner) SF,May 13,1978

Antabus	BN BABB 85112,CD 7-94848-2

Same.
(Live,Keystone Korner) SF,May 16,1978

It's you or no one	BN BABB 85112,CD 7-94848-2
Tangerine	- CD 7-94849-2
Come rain or come shine	- -

Same.
(Live,Keystone Korner) SF,Sept.16,1978

Body and soul	CD BN 7-94850-2, 7-96579-2

Same.
(Live,Keystone Korner) SF,Sept.17,1978

Ginger bread boy	CD BN 7-94849-2
I told you so	CD BN 7-94850-2

Same.
(Live,Keystone Korner) SF,March 23,1979

Sophisticated lady	BN BABB 85112,CD 7-94848-2
The panther	CD BN 7-94849-2

Same.
(Live,Keystone Korner) SF,March 24,1979

Easy living	BN BABB 85112,CD 7-94848-2
Backstairs/LTD	-
You've changed	CD BN 7-94850-2
As time goes by	- (J)TOCJ-5713

Same.
(Live,Keystone Korner) SF,March 27,1979

More than you know	BN BABB 85112,CD 7-94849-2

<u>DIANNE REEVES</u> - <u>THE PALO ALTO SESSIONS</u>:
Ernie Watts(ts-1)Billy Childs(p,synth,arr) Billy Carroll,Larry Klein-2(el b) Joe Heredia,Harvey Mason-3 (dm) Luis Conte(perc) Dianne Reeves(vo).
(purchased from the Palo Alto label)
(Mad Hatter Studios) LA, 1982

My funny Valentine
Better days
Mi vida
Hesitations
Welcome to my love-3
Perfect love-1
Lullaby-2
Passageway
Siren serenade

All titles issued on CD BN 8-36545-2.

 458

DIANNE REEVES - THE PALO ALTO SESSIONS:
Charlie Davis,Larry Hall(tp) Jon Bonine,Bruce Paulson(tb) Don Menza(reeds) Richard Cummings(keyb) Dan Carillo(g) Angel Nunes(el b) Kenwood Dennard(dm) Neil Clarke(perc) Charles Veal Jr., Jeremy Cohen(v) Linda Lipsett,Barbara Tomason(viola) Nancy Stein(cello) Dianne Reeves,Jon Lucien-1(vo).
(purchased from the Palo Alto label)
(Green Street Studio) NYC, 1984

Sitting in limbo CD BN 8-36545-2
Be my husband -
Separate vacations -1 -

Note: Horns and strings were overdubbed in LA.

WOODY SHAW:
Woody Shaw(tp) Geri Allen(p) Robert Hurst(b) Roy Brooks(dm).
(purchased from Roy Brooks)
(Baker's Keyboard Lounge) Detroit,February 26,1986

Bemsha swing
Nutty
In a capricornian way
Star eyes
Theloniously speaking

All titles issued on CD BN 8-29029-2.

Same.
(Baker's Keyboard Lounge) Detroit,February 27,1986

Ginseng people
Well you needn't
Eric
United

All titles issued on CD BN 8-29029-2.

PRYSM - PRYSM 1:
Pierre De Bethmann(p) Christophe Wallemme(b) Benjamin Henocq(dm,perc).
(from Harmonia Mundi label-EMI-France)
(La Buissonne Studios) Pernes Les Fontaines,France,July ,1995

Reflection
Double Face
Obsession
Masque Arabe
Trait neuf
L'Apothepse d'Homer
Le pas suspendu
Body and soul
Un des sens
La voie du silence
D'ici demain
Patience

All titles issued on CD BN(F)4-95588-2.

Part 5
Reissues from EMI Labels

ALADDIN

Note: IM- master numbers shown on these sessions were assigned by Imperial label.

LESTER YOUNG:
Lester Young(ts) Nat Cole(p) Red Callender(b).
LA,July 15,1942

Van1000 (IM-3691) Indiana
Van1001 (IM-3692) I can't get started — CD BN 8-54365-2
Van1002 (IM-3690) Tea for two
Van1003 (IM-3689) Body and soul

All titles issued on CD BN 8-32787-2.

ILLINOIS JACQUET:
Russell Jacquet(tp) Henry Coker(tb) Illinois Jacquet(ts) Arthur Dennis(bs) Sir Charles Thompson(p) Ulysses Livingston(g) Billy Hadnott(b) Johnny Otis(dm).
LA,July ,1945

3A Flying home,part one — CD BN 8-54364-2

HELEN HUMES:
Helen Humes(vo) with Bill Doggett Octet: Ross Butler(tp) John Brown(as) Wild Bill Moore(ts) Ernest Thompson (bs) Bill Doggett(p) Elmer Warner(g) Alfred Moore(b) Charles Harris(dm).
LA,c.Summer ,1945

A2123 (IM-4855) He may be your man — CD BN 8-54364-2

LESTER YOUNG:
Vic Dickenson(tb) Lester Young(ts) Dodo Marmarosa(p) Red Callender(b) Henry Tucker (Green) (dm).
LA,December ,1945

(IM-3563) D.B. Blues — CD BN 4-95981-2
(IM-3564) Lester blows again
(IM-3565) These foolish things (tb out)
(IM-3566) Jumpin' at Mesner's

Note: Freddie Green,though listed in most discographies,does not appear on this session.
All titles issued on BN BN-LA456-H2,CD 8-32787-2

HELEN HUMES:
Helen Humes(vo) Snooky Young(tp) Willie Smith(as) Lester Young,Maxwell Davis(ts) Jimmy Bunn(p) Dave Barbour(g) Junior Rudd(b) Henry Tucker(dm).
LA,December 22,1945

Please let me forget
He don't love me anymore
Pleading man blues
(IM-5048) See see rider
It's better to give than receive
Riffin' without Helen (Humes out)

All titles issued on CD BN 8-32787-2.

460

LESTER YOUNG:
Howard McGhee(tp) Vic Dickenson(tb) Willie Smith(as) Lester Young(ts) Wesley Jones(p) Curtis Counce(b) Johnny Otis(dm).
LA,January ,1946

(IM-3567) It's only a paper moon
(IM-3568) After you've gone (tp & tb out)
(IM-3569) Lover come back to me
(IM-3583) Jammin' with Lester

All titles issued on BN BN-LA456-H2,CD 8-32787-2.

Dr. JO JO ADAMS:
Dr.Jo Jo Adams(vo) with Maxwell Davis's Orchestra.
LA,June 11,1946

tk.2 When I'm in my tea CD BN 8-54364-2

AL HIBBLER:
Al Hibbler(vo) with Taft Jordan,Shorty Baker(tp) Russell Procope(as) Jack McVea(ts) Harry Carney(bs) Lady Will Carr(p) Ralph Hamilton(g) Red Callender(b) Doc West(dm).
(Radio Recorders) LA,July/August, 1946

RR 2700-5 (IM-1708) Don't take your love from me CD BN 7-96582-2

LESTER YOUNG:
Lester Young(ts) Joe Albany(p) Irving Ashby(g) Red Callender(b) Chico Hamilton(dm).
LA,August ,1946

(IM-3584) You're driving me crazy
(IM-3585) New Lester leaps in
(IM-3586) She's funny that way
(IM-3587) Lester's be bop boogie

All titles issued on BN BN-LA456-H2, CD 8-32787-2.

LESTER YOUNG:
Shorty McConnell(tp) Lester Young(ts) Argonne Thornton (Sadik Hakim)(p) Fred Lacey(g) Rodney Richardson(b) Lyndell Marshall(dm).
Chicago,October ,1946

46 Sunday
47 (IM-3588) S.M. Blues
48 (IM-3571) Jumpin' with Symphony Sid (tp out)
49 (IM-3573) No eyes blues
50 Sax-O-be-bop
51 On the sunny side of the street (tp out)

Note: Masters 49 and 50 are switched on BN-LA456-H2.
All titles issued on BN BN-LA456-H2,CD 8-32787-2.

LESTER YOUNG:
Shorty McConnell(tp) Lester Young(ts) Argonne Thornton(p) Fred Lacey(g) Ted Briscoe(b) Roy Haynes (dm).
(Radio Recorders) LA,February 18,1947

121-1 (IM-3577)	Easy does it	BN BN-LA456-H2
121	Easy does it (alt.)	
122-1	Movin' with Lester	BN BN-LA456-H2
123-5	One O'Clock Jump	
124-3 (IM-3575)	Jumpin' at the Woodside	BN BN-LA456-H2

All titles issued on CD BN 8-32787-2.

LESTER YOUNG:
Shorty McConnell(tp) Lester Young(ts) Argonne Thornton(p) Nasir Barakaat(g) Rodney Richardson(b) Lyndell Marshal(dm).
NYC,April 2,1947

141-1 (IM-3578)	I'm confessin' (tp out)
142-1	Lester smooths it out
143-1 (IM-3582)	Just cooling

All titles issued on BN BN-LA456-H2,CD 8-32787-2.

ILLINOIS JACQUET:
Illinois Jacquet(ts) Sir Charles Thompson(p) John Collins(g) Al Lucas(b) Shadow Wilson(dm).
(WOR Studios) NYC,September 10,1947

WOR 264-1	It's wild	CD BN 5-21052-2

LESTER YOUNG:
Lester Young(ts) Gene Di Novi(p) Chuck Wayne(g) Curly Russell(b) Tiny Kahn(dm).
(WOR Studios) NYC,December 29,1947

25-1020	Tea for two	
25-1021 (IM-3579)	East of the sun	BN BN-LA456-H2
25-1022 (IM-3580)	The Sheik of Araby	-
25-1023 (IM-3581)	Something to remember you by	-

All titles issued on CD BN 8-32787-2.

CHARLES BROWN:
Charles Brown(p,vo) Chuck Norris(g) Eddie Williams(b).
(Radio Recorders) LA,November 11,1948

RR 611-1	In the evening when the sun goes down	CD BN 7-96582-2

AMOS MILBURN:
Don Wilkerson,Willie Smith(ts) Willie Simpson(bs) Amos Milburn(vo,p) Johnny Brown(g) Harper Crosby (b) Lawrence Norman(dm) Maxwell Davis(arr).
(Radio Recorders) LA,January 4,1950

1506-2	Sax shack boogie	CD BN 8-54364-2

CALVIN BOZE:
Calvin Boze(vo) with prob. Don Wilkerson,Maxwell Davis(ts) & others unknown.
(Radio Recorders) LA,January 13,1950

1512-2 (IM-4169)	Safronia B	CD BN 8-54364-2

 462

THE FIVE KEYS:
Rudy West,Bernie West,Ripley Ingram,Maryland Pierce,Dickie Smith(vo) with others unknown.
(RCA Studios) NYC,March 22,1951

1640-B (IM-3618) Hucklebuck with Jimmy CD BN 8-54364-2

BILLIE HOLIDAY:
Billie Holiday(vo) Heywood Henry(ts,bs) Bobby Tucker(p) Tiny Grimes(g) & unknown b,dm.
(WOR Studios) NYC,April 29,1951

1681-4 (IM-3694) Be fair to me
1682-1 (IM-3695) Rocky mountain blues
1683-5 (IM-3693) Blue turning grey over you
1684-5 (IM-3696) Detour ahead CD BN 7-96583-2,8-32994-2,4-95981-2,
(C)4-94888-2,(Sp)8-56842-2

All titles issued on CD BN 7-48786-2.

PEPPERMINT HARRIS:
Peppermint Harris(vo) with Maxwell Davis Orchestra.
(Radio Recorders) LA,June 16,1951

1698-3 (IM-4934) I got loaded CD BN 8-54364-2

PEE WEE CRAYTON:
Pee Wee Crayton(vo,g) with Jake Porter(tp) Jack McVea(as) Maxwell Davis(ts,arr) Maurice Simon(bs)
Austin McCoy(p) Red Callender(b) Lee Young(dm).
(Radio Recorders) LA,November 5,1951

1794-1 Daybreak CD BN 8-54364-2

FLOYD DIXON:
Maxwell Davis(ts) Floyd Dixon(vo,p) Roy Hayes(g) Eddie Williams(b) Nathaniel "Monk" McFadden(dm).
(Radio Recorders) LA,May 12,1952

RR 1931-4 Wine,wine,wine CD BN 8-54364-2

JACK "THE BEAR" PARKER:
Jack "The Bear" Parker(dm) Emmett Davis(vo) & others unknown.
(7-11 label) (WOR Studios) NYC,October 7,1952

WOR 52-3 (IM-4723) I need you,I want you CD BN 8-54364-2

LOWELL FULSON:
Lowell Fulson(vo,g) & others unknown.
(J & M Studios) NO,October 19,1953

NO 2232-3 Don't leave me baby CD BN 8-54364-2

LOUIS JORDAN:
Louis Jordan(as,vo) & others unknown.
(Audio-Video Studios) NYC,January ,1954

AV 16-7 (IM-3732) Messy Bessy CD BN 8-54364-2

JIMMY LIGGINS:
Jimmy Liggins(vo,g) & others unknown.
(Radio Recorders) LA,June 29,1954

2295-7 (IM-4580) I ain't drunk CD BN 8-54364-2,4-97222-2

Note: CD incorrectly credits this track to Jimmy and Joe Liggins.

KENNY DREW TALKIN' & WALKIN':
Joe Maini(as,ts) Kenny Drew(p) Leroy Vinnegar(b) Lawrence Marable(dm).
(from Jazz West label)(Capitol Studios) LA,December ,1955

(IM-4021) Talkin'-walkin'
(IM-4022) In the prescribed manner
(IM-4023) Prelude to a kiss
(IM-4024) Wee dot
(IM-4025) Hidden channel
(IM-4026) Deadline
(IM-4027) I'm old fashioned
(IM-4028) Minor blues (Blues in a cardboard box)
(IM-4029) Walkin'-talkin'

All titled issued on CD BN 7-84439-2

PAUL CHAMBERS/JOHN COLTRANE:
John Coltrane(ts) Kenny Drew(p) Paul Chambers(b) Philly Joe Jones(dm).
(from Jazz West label)(Western Recorders) LA,March ,1956

(IM-3532) Dexterity CD BN 7-99175-2
(IM-3533) Stablemates
(IM-3534) Easy to love (ts out)
(IM-3535) Visitation (ts out)
(IM-3536) John Paul Jones (Trane's blues) CD BN 7-99175-2,4-98240-2
(IM-3537) Eastbound

All titles issued on BN BN-LA451-H2,CD 7-84437-2.

SHIRLEY & LEE:
Shirley Goodman,Leonard Lee(vo) with poss. Dave Bartholomew(tp) Joe Harris(as) Lee Allen,Clarence Hall,Herb Hardesty(ts) Alvin "Red" Tyler(bs) Edward Frank(p) Justin Adams or Ernest McLean(g) Frank Fields(b) Earl Palmer(dm).
(poss. Cosimo Studio) NO,May ,1956

NO 2688 (IM-3589) Let the good times roll CD BN 8-54364-2

LAWRENCE MARABLE QUARTET - TENORMAN:
James Clay(ts) Sonny Clark(p) Jimmy Bond(b) Lawrence Marable(dm).
(from Jazz West label)(Capitol Studios) LA,August ,1956

(IM-4602) Between the devil and the deep blue sea
(IM-4603) Easy living CD BN(J)TOCJ-5712
(IM-4604) Minor meeting CD BN(J)TOCJ-5710
(IM-4605) Airtight
(IM-4606) Willow weep for me
(IM-4607) Three fingers north
(IM-4608) Lover man CD BN 8-54365-2
(IM-4609) Marbles

All titles issued on CD BN 7-84440-2.

464

ART PEPPER QUINTET - THE RETURN OF ART PEPPER:
Jack Sheldon(tp) Art Pepper(as) Russ Freeman(p) Leroy Vinnegar(b) Shelly Manne(dm).
(from Jazz West label)(Capitol Studios) LA,August ,1956

(IM-3827) Pepper returns CD 8-33244-2,(J)TOCJ-5631,TOCJ-6107
(IM-3828) Broadway - -
(IM-3829) You go to my head (tp out) CD 8-33244-2,8-57460-2,(J)TOCJ-5631, TOCJ-6107,TOCJ-5300
(IM-3830) Angel wings
(IM-3831) Funny blues
(IM-3832) Five more
(IM-3833) Minority
(IM-3834) Patricia (tp out)
(IM-3835) Mambo de la Pinta BN B1-57745,CD 7-80707-2,8-33244-2,8-57745-2
(IM-3836) Walkin' out blues

All titles issued on BN BN-LA591-H2,CD 7-46863-2.

CHARLES BROWN:
Charles Brown(p,vo) with prob.: Lee Allen(ts) Alvin "Red" Tyler(bs) Justin Adams(g) Frank Fields(b) Earl Palmer (dm).
NO,September 4,1956

Merry Christmas baby CD BN(J)TOCJ-5854

KING PLEASURE:
King Pleasure(vo) with John Anderson(tp) Dave Wells(tb) Plas Johnson(ts) Jewell Grant(bs) Ernie Freeman (p,arr) Irving Ashby(g) Curtis Counce(b) Jimmy Miller(dm).
(Capitol Studios) LA,October 11,1956

2754 (IM-4594) Blues I like to hear
2755 (IM-4595) At your beck and call
2756 (IM-4596) D.B. blues
2557 (IM-4597) I'm in the mood for love

All titles issued on CD BN 7-84463-2.

ART PEPPER QUARTET:
Art Pepper(as) Russ Freeman(p) Ben Tucker(b) Chuck Flores(dm).
(from Intro label)(Radio Recorders) LA,December 28,1956

RR 2783 (IM-3837) What is this thing called love? CD BN(J)CJ28-5021,TOCJ-5631,TOCJ-6107
RR 2784 (IM-3838) Stompin' at the Savoy - -
RR 2785 (IM-3841) Blues in -1
RR 2785 (IM-3841) Blues out -1 CD BN(J)CJ28-5030
RR 2786 (IM-3840) Bewitched,bothered and bewildered CD BN(J)CJ28-5179,TOCJ-5631,TOCJ-6107

-1: Freeman & Flores out.
All titles issued on BN BN-LA591-H2,CD 7-46848-2,(J)TOCJ-5664.

465

JOE MORELLO/ART PEPPER QUINTET:
Art Pepper(as,ts) Red Norvo(vb) Gerald Wiggins(p) Ben Tucker(b)Joe Morello(dm).
(from Intro label)(Western Recorders) LA,January 3,1957

(IM-3845)	Tenor blooz	CD BN(J)TOCJ-5710
(IM-3846)	You're driving me crazy	
(IM-3849)	Pepper steak	
	Yardbird suite -1	CD BN 8-57742-2
	Straight life -1	CD BN (J)TOCJ-5631,TOCJ-6107

-1: Norvo out.
All titles issued on BN BN-LA591-H2,CD-7-46863-2.

ART PEPPER QUARTET:
Art Pepper(as) Russ Freeman(p) Ben Tucker(b) Chuck Flores(dm).
(from Intro label)(Master Recorders) LA,January 14,1957

MR 2804 (IM-3842)	When you're smiling	BN BN-LA591-H2,CD(J)TOCJ-5631,TOCJ-6188
MR 2805 (IM-3843)	Cool Bunny	- CD 8-33244-2
MR 2806 (IM-3844)	Diane's dilemma	-
	Diane's dilemma (alt.)-1	
MR 2807	Summertime	

-1: mistakenly issued as "Blues out" on some pressings of BN-LA591-H2.
All titles issued on CD BN 7-46848-2.First three titles also issued on CD BN(J)TOCJ-5664.

ART PEPPER QUARTET - OMEGA ALPHA:
Art Pepper(as) Carl Perkins(p) Ben Tucker(b) Chuck Flores(dm).
(Audio Arts Studio) LA,April 1,1957

AA 2871-4	Holiday flight	CD BN 7-46853-2,(J)TOCJ-5852
AA 2872-1	Too close for comfort	BN LT-1064,CD 7-46853-2
AA 2873-1	Long ago and far away	- - 8-33244-2
AA 2874-5	Begin the beguine	BN LT-1064 - (J)TOCJ-6107
AA 2874	Begin the beguine (alt.)	CD BN 7-46848-2
AA 2875-3	I can't believe that you're in love with me	CD BN 7-46853-2,(J)TOCJ-5631
AA 2876	Webb City	BN LT-1064,CD 7-46853-2
AA 2876-2	Webb City (alt.)	CD BN 7-46848-2
AA 2877-1	Summertime	BN LT-1064,CD 7-46853-2,(J)TOCJ-6107
AA 2879	Fascinatin' rhythm	- - 7-80706-2, (J)TOCJ-5631,TOCJ-6107
AA 2879-10	Fascinatin' rhythm (alt.)	CD BN 7-46848-2
AA 2880-3	Body and soul	BN LT-1064,(J)W-5503 CD BN 7-46853-2,(J)CJ28-5023,TOCJ-5631, TOCJ-6107
AA 2881-7	Without a song	CD BN 7-46853-2
AA 2884-2	The breeze and I	- (J)TOCJ-6107
AA 2885-6	Surf ride	BN LT-1064,(J)W-5503 CD BN 7-46853-2,(J)TOCJ-5631

BIG "T" TYLER:
Big T Tyler(vo) & others unknown.
(Master Recorders) LA,April 25.1957

2908-6	King Kong	CD BN 8-54364-2

466

CAPITOL

PAUL WHITEMAN AND HIS ORCHESTRA:
Monty Kelly,Larry Neil,Don Waddilove(tp) Skip Layton,Murray McEachern(tb) Alvy West,Danny d'Andrea, Lenny Hartman,King Guion,Tommy Mace(saxes) Buddy Weed(p) Mike Pingitore(g) Art Shapiro(b) Willie Rodriguez(dm) Harry Azen,Sol Blumenthal,David Newman(strings-1) Jimmy Mundy(arr) Billie Holiday, Johnny Mercer,Jack Teagarden(vo).
LA,June 12,1942

30	Trav'lin' light (voBH)-1	CD BN 7-48786-2,(Sp)8-53016-2
31	The old music maker (voJM,JT)	CD BN 7-96582-2

BENNY CARTER AND HIS ORCHESTRA:
Claude Dunson,Jake Porter,Teddy Buckner,Freddie Webster(tp) Shorty Haughton,J.J. Johnson,Alton Moore (tb) Benny Carter(as,arr) Porter Kilbert(as) Gene Porter,Bumps Myers(ts) Willard Brown(as,bs) Teddy Brannon(p) Ulysses Livingston(g) Curly Russell(b) Oscar Bradley(dm).
SF,October 25,1943

96-1	Love for sale	CD BN 8-33146-2

THE CAPITOL JAZZMEN:
Billy May(tp) Jack Teagarden(tb,vo) Jimmie Noone(cl) Dave Matthews(ts) Joe Sullivan(p) Dave Barbour(g) Artie Shapiro(b) Zutty Singleton(dm).
(Radio Recorders) LA,November 16,1943

105-2	Casanova's lament	CD BN 5-21052-2

THE KING COLE TRIO:
Nat "King" Cole(p,vo) Oscar Moore(g) Johnny Miller(b).
(Radio Recorders) LA,November 30,1943

123-4	Straighten up and fly right	CD BN(Sp) 8-53016-2,5-21755-2

THE KING COLE TRIO:
Nat "King" Cole(p,vo) Oscar Moore(g) Johnny Miller(b).
(Radio Recorders) LA,December 15,1943

139-1	Sweet Lorraine	CD BN 7-96582-2,8-32994-2

BENNY CARTER AND HIS ORCHESTRA:
John Carroll,Karl George,Edwin Davis,Milton Fletcher(tp) Shorty Haughton,J.J. Johnson, Alton Moore, Bart Varsalona(tb) Benny Carter(as-1,tp-2,arr) Porter Kilbert(as) Gene Porter,Bumps Myers(ts) Willard Brown(as,bs) Gerald Wiggins(p) Jimmy Edwards(g) Charlie Drayton(b) Max Roach(dm).
(Radio Recorders) LA,May 21,1944

254-3	I can't escape from you -1	CD BN 8-33146-2
256-3	I can't get started -1	-
257-3	I surrender dear -2	-

ANITA O'DAY:
Anita O'Day(vo) with Charlie Griffith(tp) Jimmy Skyles(tb) Heinie Beau,Manny Gershman(as) Herbie Haymer(ts) Harry Schuman(bs) Milt Raskin(p) Dave Barbour(g) Phil Stephens(b) Zutty Singleton(dm) Lowell Martin(arr,cond).
(Radio Recorders) LA,January 18,1945

553-3	I can't believe that your in love with me	CD BN 7-96583-2

COLEMAN HAWKINS:
Howard McGhee(tp) Coleman Hawkins(ts) Sir Charles Thompson(p) Allan Reuss(g) John Simmons(b) Denzil Best(dm)
(Radio Recorders) LA,March 9,1945

595-3 Someone to watch over me CD BN 7-80706-2,8-34873-2

THE CAPITOL INTERNATIONAL JAZZMEN:
Bill Coleman(tp) Buster Bailey(cl) Benny Carter(as,arr) Coleman Hawkins(ts) Nat "King" Cole(p) Oscar Moore(g) John Kirby(b) Max Roach(dm) Kay Starr(vo).
(Radio Recorders) LA,March 30,1945

600-3 If I could be with you (voKS) CD BN 7-96583-2
602-5 Riffamarole CD BN 8-33146-2

BENNY CARTER AND HIS ORCHESTRA:
Irving Lewis,Fred Trainer,Gerald Wilson,Emmett Berry,Paul Cohen(tp) Henry Coker,George Washington, Louis Taylor,Alton Moore(tb) Benny Carter(as,arr) Porter Kilbert,Jewell Grant(as) Bumps Myers,Harold Clark(ts) John Taylor(bs) Rufus Webster(p) Herman Mitchell (g) Charlie Drayton(b) Max Roach(dm).
(Radio Recorders) LA,April 9,1945

611-3 Malibu CD BN 8-33146-2

STAN KENTON AND HIS ORCHESTRA:
John Carroll,Buddy Childers,John Anderson,Gene Roland,Mel Green(tp) Freddie Zito,Milt Kabak,Marshall Ocker(tb) Bart Varsalona(bass tb) Bob Lively,Boots Mussulli(as) Joe Magro,Dave Madden(ts) Bob Gioga (bs) Stan Kenton(p,arr) Bob Ahern(g) Max Wayne(b) Bob Varney(dm).
(Universal Studios) Chicago,May 4,1945

342-4 Southern scandal CD BN 8-33243-2

STAN KENTON AND HIS ORCHESTRA:
Buddy Childers,Ray Wetzel,John Anderson,Russ Burgher,Bob Lymperis(tp) Freddie Zito,Milt Kabak, Jimmy Simms(tb) Bart Varsalona(bass tb) Al Anthony,Boots Mussulli(as) Vido Musso,Bob Cooper(ts) Bob Gioga(bs) Stan Kenton(p) Bob Ahern(g) Eddie Safranski(b) Ralph Collier(dm) June Christy(vo) Gene Roland(arr).
(Radio Recorders) LA,October 30,1945

777-2 Just a-sittin' and a-rockin' CD BN 8-33243-2

BENNY CARTER AND HIS ORCHESTRA:
Louis Gray,Wallace Jones,Dupree Bolton,Idrees Sulieman(tp) Al Grey,Charley Johnson,Johnny Morris, Alton Moore(tb) Benny Carter(as,arr) Porter Kilbert,Joe Epps(as) Bumps Myers,Harold Clark(ts) Willard Brown(as,bs) Rufus Webster(p) James Cannady(g) Thomas Moultrie(b) Percy Brice(dm).
(WMCA Studios) NYC,December 12,1945

838-5 Cuttin' Time CD BN 8-33146-2

Note: This tune was incorrectly titled "Forever Blue" in the Capitol master listings and on album Capitol M-11057.

JUNE CHRISTY:
June Christy(vo) with Ray Wetzel(tp) Gene Roland(vtb) Boots Mussulli(as) Fred Zito(p) Dave Barbour(g) Eddie Safranski(b) Eddie Spanier(dm).
(Radio Recorders) LA,December 13,1945

ET 490-2 I can't believe that you're in love with me CD BN 5-21052-2

468

<u>JO STAFFORD</u>:
Jo Stafford (vo) with Ray Linn(tp) Heinie Beau,Fred Stulce(reeds) Herbie Haymer(ts) Harry Schuchman(bs) Nat Cole(p) Dave Barbour(g) Artie Shapiro(b) Nick Fatool(dm) Paul Weston(arr).
(Radio Recorders) LA,March 28,1946

1054-3 Baby won't you please come home CD BN 7-96583-2

<u>STAN KENTON AND HIS ORCHESTRA</u>:
Buddy Childers,Ray Wetzel,John Anderson,Chico Alvarez,Ken Hanna(tp) Kai Winding,Miff Sines,Milt Kabak(tb) Bart Varsalona(bass tb) Al Anthony,Boots Mussulli(as) Vido Musso,Bob Cooper(ts) Bob Gioga (bs) Stan Kenton(p) Bob Ahern(g) Eddie Safranski(b) Shelly Manne(dm) Pete Rugolo(arr).
(Radio Recorders) LA,July 12,1946

1197-1 Artistry in bolero CD BN 8-33243-2

<u>PEGGY LEE</u>:
Peggy Lee(vo) with Orchestra cond. by Dave Barbour(g).
(Radio Recorders) LA,July 23,1946

1212 Aren't you kind of glad we did? CD BN 7-80506-2

<u>JOHNNY MERCER</u>:
Johnny Mercer(vo) with Orchestra arr. & cond. by Paul Weston.
(Radio Recorders) LA,July 25,1946

1221-5 One for my baby
(and one more for the road) CD BN 7-89914-2,(C)4-94888-2

<u>BENNY GOODMAN AND HIS ORCHESTRA</u>:
Nate Kazebier,Mannie Klein,Rubin "Zeke" Zarchy,Joe Triscari(tp) Tommy Pederson,Lou McGarity,Ed Kusby(tb) Benny Goodman(cl) Gus Bivona,Heinie Beau(as) Babe Russin,Jack Chaney(ts) Chuck Gentry (bs) Jess Stacy(p) Allan Reuss(g) Larry Breen(b) Sammy Weiss(dm) Mary Lou Williams(arr).
(Radio Recorders) LA,January 28,1947

1609-5 Lonely moments CD BN(J)TOCJ-6147

<u>STAN KENTON AND HIS ORCHESTRA</u>:
Buddy Childers,Ray Wetzel,John Anderson,Chico Alvarez,Ken Hanna(tp) Kai Winding,Skip Layton,Milt Bernhart,Harry Forbes(tb) Bart Varsalona(bass tb) Eddie Meyers,Boots Mussulli(as) Vido Musso,Bob Cooper(ts) Bob Gioga(bs) Stan Kenton(p) Bob Ahern(g) Eddie Safranski(b) Shelly Manne(dm) Ivan Lopez(bgo) Eugenio Keyes(maracas) Pete Rugolo(arr).
(Radio Recorders) LA,March 31,1947

1805-1 Machito CD BN 8-33243-2

<u>NELLIE LUTCHER AND HER RHYTHM</u>:
Nellie Lutcher(p,vo) Ulysses Livingston(g) Billy Hadnott(b) Lee Young(dm).
(Radio Recorders) LA,April 10,1947

1823-2 The one I love (belongs to somebody else)
CD BN(Sp)8-56842-2

<u>THE KING COLE TRIO</u>:
Nat "King" Cole(p,vo) Oscar Moore(g) Johnny Miller(b).
(Radio Recorders) LA,July 2,1947

2085-5 Honeysuckle rose CD BN(J)TOCJ-5187/88
2093-2 It's kind of lonesome out tonight (voNKC)
CD BN 8-55221-2

THE KING COLE TRIO:
Nat "King" Cole(p) Oscar Moore(g) Johnny Miller(b).
(Radio Recorders) LA,August 13,1947

2155-2 How high the moon CD BN 7-96580-2

NAT KING COLE:
Nat "King" Cole(vo) with Orchestra arr. & cond. by Frank DeVol.
(Radio Recorders) LA,August 22,1947

2193-1 Nature boy CD BN(J)TOCJ-5875

RED NORVO'S NINE:
Bobby Sherwood(c) Benny Carter(as) Dave Cavanaugh,Eddie Miller(ts) Red Norvo(vb) Arnold Ross(p) Dave Barbour(g) Billy Hadnott(b) Jesse Price(dm).
(Radio Recorders) LA,October 14,1947

2345-5 Hollyridge Drive CD BN 8-33146-2

STAN KENTON AND HIS ORCHESTRA:
Buddy Childers,Ray Wetzel,Al Porcino,Chico Alvarez,Ken Hanna(tp) Eddie Bert,Milt Bernhart,Harry Forbes(tb) Bart Varsalona(bass tb) George Weidler,Art Pepper(as) Bob Cooper,Warren Weidler(ts) Bob Gioga(bs) Stan Kenton(p) Laurindo Almeida(g) Eddie Safranski(b) Shelly Manne(dm) Jack Costanzo (bgo) Pete Rugolo(arr).
(Radio Recorders) LA,October 22,1947

2361-1 Unison riff CD BN(J)TOCJ-6147

JO STAFFORD:
Jo Stafford(vo) with orchestra arr. & cond. by Paul Weston.
(Radio Recorders) LA,October,31,1947

2403-4 Autumn in New York CD BN(J)TOCJ-5853

JULIA LEE AND HER BOYFRIENDS:
Benny Carter(as) Dave Cavanaugh(ts) Vic Dickenson(tb) Julia Lee(p,vo) Jack Marshall(g) Billy Hadnott(b) 'Sam Baby' Lovett(dm).
(Radio Recorders) LA,November 13,1947

2458-3 I didn't like it the first time
(The spinach song) CD BN 8-33146-2

PEGGY LEE:
Peggy Lee(vo) with orchestra incl. Dave Barbour(g,arr).
(Radio Recorders) LA,November 19.1947

2493-3 Why don't you do right CD BN(C) 4-94888-2

RED NORVO-JESSE PRICE:
Ray Linn(tp) Dexter Gordon,Jimmy Giuffre(ts) Red Norvo(vb-1,p-2) Dodo Marmarosa(p-1) Barney Kessel (g) Red Callender(b) Jackie Mills(dm) Jesse Price(vo-2).
(Radio Recorders) LA,November 28,1947

2644-4 Bop-1 CD BN 8-23514-2,(J)TOCJ-6147
2627-2 Baby, let's be friends-2 -

 470

STAN KENTON AND HIS ORCHESTRA:
Buddy Childers,Ray Wetzel,Al Porcino,Chico Alvarez,Ken Hanna(tp) Eddie Bert,Milt Bernhart,Harry Betts, Harry Forbes(tb) Bart Varsalona(bass tb) George Weidler,Art Pepper(as) Bob Cooper,Warren Weidler(ts) Bob Gioga(bs) Stan Kenton(p,arr) Laurindo Almeida(g) Eddie Safranski(b) Shelly Manne(dm) Jack Costanzo (bgo) Carlos Vidal(cga) Jose Mangual(timbales,cowbell) Machito(maracas).
(RKO Pathe Studios) NYC,December 6,1947

2668-2 The peanut vendor CD BN(E)8-53227-2

STAN HASSELGARD:
Stan Hasselgard(cl) Red Norvo(vb) Arnold Ross(p) Barney Kessel(g) Rollo Garberg(b) Frank Bode(dm).
(Radio Recorders) LA,December 18,1947

2872-1 Swedish pastry CD BN(J)TOCJ-6147

METRONOME ALL-STARS:
Dizzy Gillespie(tp) Bill Harris(tb) Buddy De Franco(cl) Flip Phillips(ts) Nat "King" Cole(p) Billy Bauer(g) Eddie Safranski(b) Buddy Rich(dm).
(RKO Pathe Studios) NYC,December 21,1947

2933-4 Leap here CD BN 7-89032-2

Same,with members of Kenton Orchestra: Buddy Childers,Ray Wetzel,Al Porcino,Ken Hanna(tp) Milt Bernhart,Harry Betts,Harry Forbes(tb) Bart Varsalona(bass tb) George Weidler,Art Pepper(as) Bob Cooper, Warren Weidler(ts) Bob Gioga(bs) Shelly Manne(dm) Pete Rugolo(arr) Stan Kenton(dir).
Same session.

2934-4 Metronome Riff CD BN(J)TOCJ-6147

STAN KENTON AND HIS ORCHESTRA:
Buddy Childers,Ray Wetzel,Al Porcino,Chico Alvarez,Ken Hanna(tp) Eddie Bert,Milt Bernhart,Harry Betts,Harry Forbes(tb) Bart Varsalona(bass tb) George Weidler,Art Pepper(as) Bob Cooper,Warren Weidler (ts) Bob Gioga(bs) Stan Kenton(p) Laurindo Almeida(g) Eddie Safranski(b) Shelly Manne(dm) Jack Costanzo (bgo) June Christy(vo).
(RKO Pathe Studios) NYC,December 21,1947

2937-2 How high the moon (voJC) CD BN(J)TOCJ-6147

Same: (RKO Pathe Studios) NYC,December 22,1947

2942-3 Harlem holiday CD BN 8-33243-2

NELLIE LUTCHER:
Nellie Lutcher(p,vo) Hurley Ramey(g) Truck Parham(b) Alvin Burroughs(dm).
Chicago,December 27,1947

3034 Fine brown frame CD BN 8-54364-2

T-BONE WALKER:
George Orendorff(tp) Bumps Myers(ts) Willard McDaniel(p) T-Bone Walker(g,vo) Billy Hadnott(b) Oscar Lee Bradley(dm).
(purchased from Black & White label) LA,December 29,1947

BW 696-1 I'm still in love with you CD BN 7-96582-2

BENNY GOODMAN:
Fats Navarro(tp) Benny Goodman(cl) Wardell Gray(ts) Gene Di Novi(p) Mundell Lowe(g) Clyde Lombardi (b) Mel Zelnick(dm).

NYC September 9, 1948

2974-3 Stealin' apples CD BN 8-33373-2

WOODY HERMAN AND HIS ORCHESTRA:
Stan Fishelson,Bernie Glow,Red Rodney,Shorty Rogers,Ernie Royal(tp) Bill Harris,Earl Swope, Ollie Wilson(tb) Bob Swift(bass tb) Woody Herman(cl) Sam Marowitz(as) Al Cohn,Stan Getz, Zoot Sims(ts) Serge Chaloff(bs) Terry Gibbs(vb) Lou Levy(p) Chubby Jackson(b) Don Lamond (dm).

LA,December 30,1948

3831-2 Early Autumn BN(J)W-5502
CD BN(E)8-53227-2,(J)CJ28-5023,TOCJ-5853

MEL TORME:
Mel Torme(vo) with Orchestra arr. & cond. by Sonny Burke.
(Capitol Studios) LA,January 13,1949

3866-4 Do do do CD BN 7-80506-2

MEL TORME:
Mel Torme(vo) with Orchestra arr. & cond. by Sonny Burke: Ziggy Elman,Paul Geil,Ray Linn,George Seaberg(tp) Walter Benson,Joe Howard,Ed Kusby,Si Zentner(tb) Skeets Herfurt,Harry Klee(as,fl) Don Raffell,Babe Russin(ts) Bob Lawson(bs) Walter "Moe" Wechsler(p) Barney Kessel(g) Larry Breen(b) Alvin Stoller(dm).
(Capitol Studios) LA,January 17,1949

3871-2 Stompin' at the Savoy CD BN(C)4-94888-2

TADD DAMERON AND HIS ORCHESTRA:
Fats Navarro(tp) Kai Winding(tb) Sahib Shihab(as) Dexter Gordon(ts) Cecil Payne(bs) Tadd Dameron(p,arr) Curley Russell(b) Kenny Clarke(dm) Diego Iborra(bgo) Carlos Vidal Bolado (cga) Rae Pearl(vo).

NYC,January 18,1949

3391-3 Sid's delight BN(J)W-5501;CD BN 8-23514-2
3392-3 Casbah (voRP)

Both titles issued on CD BN 7-81531-2,8-33373-2.

BABS GONZALES AND HIS ORCHESTRA:
Bennie Green,J.J. Johnson(tb) Julius Watkins(frh) Jordan Fordin(as) Sonny Rollins(ts) Linton Garner(p) Art Phipps(b) Jack "The Bear" Parker(dm) Babs Gonzales(vo).

NYC,January 20,1949

3393-3 Capitolizing
3394-4 Professor bop BN(J)W-5501;CD BN 8-57742-2

Both titles issued on CD BN 7-84464-2.

MILES DAVIS AND HIS ORCHESTRA:
Miles Davis(tp) Kai Winding(tb) Junior Collins(frh) John Barber(tu) Lee Konitz(as) Gerry Mulligan(bs,arr-1) Al Haig(p) Joe Shulman(b) Max Roach(dm) John Lewis(arr-2).
NYC,January 21,1949

3395-3	Jeru -1	
3396-3	Move -2	BN(J)W-5502;CD BN 7-99287-2,8-34957-2, 8-36736-2,(J)TOCJ-5632,TOCJ-5657,TOCJ-6102
3397-2	Godchild -1	BN(J)W-5502;CD BN 7-99287-2
3398-1	Budo -2	CD BN 7-99287-2,Cema GSC Music 15131

BENNY GOODMAN AND HIS ORCHESTRA:
Al Stewart,Howard Reich,Doug Mettome,Nick Travis(tp) Milt Bernhart,Eddie Bert,George Monte(tb) Benny Goodman(cl) Mitch Goldberg,Angelo Cicalese(as) Wardell Gray,Eddie Wasserman(ts) Larry Molinelli(bs) Buddy Greco(p) Francis Beecher(g) Clyde Lombardi(b) Sonny Igoe(dm) Chico O'Farrill(arr).
(Capitol Studios) LA,February 10,1949

3958-7	Undercurrent blues	BN(J)W-5501

LENNIE TRISTANO SEXTETTE:
Lee Konitz(as-1) Warne Marsh(ts-1) Lennie Tristano(p) Billy Bauer(g) Arnold Fishkin(b) Harold Granowsky (dm).
NYC,March 4,1949

3413-3	Wow -1	BN(J)W-5502
3714-1	Yesterdays	CD BN 7-96580-2,(J)TOCJ-5187/88

BABS GONZALES AND HIS ORCHESTRA:
J.J. Johnson(tb) Art Pepper(as) Herbie Steward(ts) Wynton Kelly(p) Pee Wee Tinney(g,group vo) Bruce Lawrence(b,group vo) Jackie Mills(dm) Babs Gonzales(vo)
(Capitol Studios) LA,March 15,1949

4099-4	The Continental
4100-1	Prelude to a nightmare

Both titles issued on CD BN 7-84464-2
Note: CD incorrectly states the recording date as March 20.

BENNY GOODMAN AND HIS ORCHETRA:
Howard Reich,Doug Mettome,Al Stewart,Ziggy Schatz(tp) Billy Byers,Eddie Bert,George Monte(tb) Benny Goodman(cl) Mitch Goldberg,Angelo Cicalese(as) Wardell Gray,Eddie Wasserman(ts) Bob Dawes(bs) Buddy Greco(p) Francis Beecher(g) Clyde Lombardi(b) Sonny Igoe(dm).
(Capitol Studios) LA,April 12,1949

4195-2	Bop hop	CD BN (E)8-53227-2

BENNY GOODMAN SEPTET:
Doug Mettome(tp) Benny Goodman(cl) Wardell Gray(ts) Buddy Greco(p) Francis Beecher(g) Clyde Lombardi(b) Sonny Igoe(dm).
(Capitol Studios) LA,April 14,1949

4203-5	Bedlam	BN(J)W-5501 CD BN 4-95981-2

TADD DAMERON AND HIS ORCHESTRA:
Miles Davis(tp) J.J. Johnson(tb) Sahib Shihab(as) Benjamin Lundy(ts) Cecil Payne(bs) Tadd Dameron(p,arr) John Collins(g) Curly Russell(b) Kenny Clarke (dm) Kay Penton(vo).
NYC,April 19,1949

3760-4	John's delight	BN(J)W-5501
3761-1	What's New	
3762-3	Heaven's Doors Are Wide Open (voKP)	
3763-2	Focus	

All titles on CD BN 7-81531-2,8-33373-2.

MILES DAVIS:
Miles Davis(tp) J.J.Johnson(tb) Sandy Siegelstein(frh) Bill Barber(tu) Lee Konitz(as) Gerry Mulligan(bs, arr-1) John Lewis(p) Nelson Boyd(b) Kenny Clarke(dm) Gil Evans-2,John Carisi-3(arr).
NYC,April 22,1949

3764-7	Venus de Milo -1	BN(I)JAZ 1
3766-2	Boplicity -2	BN(J)W-5502;CD BN 8-23515-2,4-95981-2, 8-21381-2,(C)8-33908-2
3767-2	Israel -3	CD BN 8-23515-2,(J)CJ28-5030,TOCJ-5632, TOCJ-6102

BABS GONZALES AND HIS ORCHESTRA:
J.J. Johnson(tb) Alberto Socarras(fl) Don Redman(ss) Sonny Rollins(ts) Wynton Kelly(p) Bruce Lawrence (b,group vo) Roy Haynes(dm) Babs Gonzales(vo).
NYC,April 27,1949

3776-3	Real crazy	
3777-4	Then you'll be boppin' too	
3778-1	When lovers they lose -1	
3779-2	St. Louis blues	BN(J)W-5501

-1: unknown(v) added (not Ray Nance as stated on CD).
All titles issued on CD BN 7-84464-2

LENNIE TRISTANO SEXTETTE:
Lee Konitz(as) Warne Marsh(ts) Lennie Tristano(p) Billy Bauer(g) Arnold Fishkin(b) Denzil Best(dm).
NYC,May 16,1949

3785	Sax of a kind	BN(J)W-5502

ART TATUM:
Art Tatum(p).
(Capitol Studios) LA,July 13,1949

5038	Willow weep for me	CD BN 7-96580-2
5041	Aunt Hagar's blues	CD BN 7-99099-2

WOODY HERMAN AND HIS ORCHESTRA:
Stan Fishelson,Al Porcino,Shorty Rogers,Ernie Royal,Charlie Walp(tp) Bill Harris,Earl Swope,Bart Varsalona,Ollie Wilson(tb) Woody Herman(cl) Sam Marowitz(as) Gene Ammons,Jimmy Giuffre,Buddy Savitt(ts) Serge Chaloff(bs) Terry Gibbs(vb) Lou Levy(p) Joe Mondragon(b) Shelly Manne(dm).
(Capitol Studios) LA,July 21,1949

4679-3	Rhapsody in wood	BN(J)W-5502

ART TATUM:
Art Tatum(p).

(Capitol Studios) LA,July 25,1949

5046 Sweet Lorraine CD BN(J)TOCJ-5187/88

CHARLIE BARNET AND HIS ORCHESTRA:
Rolf Ericson,Maynard Ferguson,Johnny Howell,Doc Severinsen,Ray Wetzel(tp) Harry Betts,Herbie Harper, Dick Kenny(tb) Kenny Matlock(bass tb) Charlie Barnet(ss,ts) Vinnie Dean,Reuben Leon(as) Kurt Bloom, Dick Hafer(ts) Manny Albam(bs,arr) Claude Williamson(p) Eddie Safranski(b) Tiny Kahn(dm) Carlos Vidal (cga).

(Capitol Studios) LA,August 16,1949

4903-3 Really? BN(J)W-5501

BUDDY DE FRANCO SEXTET:
Buddy De Franco(cl) Teddy Charles(vb) Harvey Leonard(p) Jimmy Raney(g) Bob Carter(b) Max Roach (dm).

NYC,August 24,1949

4273-3 Penthouse serenade BN(J)W-5502
4276-2 Aishie -

ART TATUM:
Art Tatum(p).

(Capitol Studios) LA,September 29,1949

5055 Blue Skies CD BN 7-99095-2,4-95981-2,(J)TOCJ-5851

CLEO BROWN:
Cleo Brown(vo) with Nappy Lamare(g) Leonard Bibbs(b) Zutty Singleton(dm).

(Capitol Studios) LA,September 30,1949

4936-3 Cleo's boogie CD BN 8-54364-2

DIZZY GILLESPIE:
Dizzy Gillespie,Willie Cook,Don Slaughter,Elmon Wright(tp) Matthew Gee,Sam Hurt,Charles Greenlea(tb) Jimmy Heath,John Coltrane(as) Jesse Powell,Paul Gonsalves(ts) Al Gibson(bs) John Acea(p) Floyd Smith (g) Al McKibbon(b) Specs Wright(dm) Buster Harding(arr).

NYC,January 10,1950

4330-3 Coast to coast CD BN 8-57742-2

STAN KENTON AND HIS ORCHESTRA:
Buddy Childers,Maynard Ferguson,Shorty Rogers,Chico Alvarez(tp) Milt Bernhart,Harry Betts,Bob Fitzpatrick,Bill Russo(tb) Bart Varsalona(bass tb) John Graas,Lloyd Otto(frh) Gene Englund(tu) Bud Shank (as,fl) Art Pepper(as,cl) Bob Cooper(ts,oboe,Eng h) Bart Calderall(ts,bassoon) Bob Gioga(bs,bass cl) George Kast,Lew Elias,Jim Holmes,Jim Cathcart,Earl Cornwell,Anthony Doria,Alex Law,Herbert Offner, Carl Ottobrino,Dave Schackner(v) Stan Harris,Leonard Selic,Sam Singer(viola) Gregory Bemko,Zachary Bock,Jack Wulfe(cello) Stan Kenton(p) Laurindo Almeida(g) Don Bagley(b) Shelly Manne(dm) Carlos Vidal(cga) Franklyn Marks(arr).

(Capitol Studios) LA,February 4,1950

5487-1 Evening in Pakistan (single version) CD BN 8-33243-2

475

MILES DAVIS:
Miles Davis(tp) J.J.Johnson(tb) Gunther Schuller(frh) Bill Barber(tu) Lee Konitz(as) Gerry Mulligan(bs, arr-1) John Lewis(p) Al McKibbon(b) Max Roach(dm) Gil Evans(arr-2).
NYC,March 9,1950

4346-1	Deception-1	CD BN 8-23515-2
4347-4	Rocker-1	CD BN(Eu) 8-29964-2
4348-2	Moon dreams-2	CD BN 7-89910-2,8-36633-2,(J)TOCJ-5658, TOCJ-5858

MEL TORME:
Mel Torme(vo) with The Dave Lambert Octet(vocal group) & Pete Rugolo's Orchestra: Louis Mucci,Tony Faso(tp) Kai Winding(tb) Al Richman(frh) Sid Cooper,Milt Yaner,Eddie Brown,Manny Thaler(reeds) Teddy Napoleon(p) Barry Galbraith(g) Eddie Safranski(b) Mel Zelnick(dm) & strings: Leo Kruczek,Morris Leibowitz,Lew Stone,Stan Karpenia,George Zornig,Phil Solomon,Ray Sabinsky,Tom Alonje,Maurice Brown,Sandor Szatmery.Arr. & dir. by Pete Rugolo.
NYC,April 3,1950

5710-2	Bewitched,bothered and bewildered	CD BN (J)TOCJ-5851

STAN KENTON AND HIS ORCHESTRA:
Buddy Childers,Maynard Ferguson,Chico Alvarez(tp) Shorty Rogers(tp,arr) Milt Bernhart, Harry Betts,Bob Fitzpatrick,Bill Russo(tb) Clyde Brown(bass tb) John Graas,Lloyd Otto(frh) Gene Englund(tu) Bud Shank, Art Pepper(as) Bob Cooper,Bart Calderall(ts) Bob Gioga(bs) George Kast,Lew Elias,Jim Holmes,Jim Cathcart,Earl Cornwell,Anthony Doria,Alex Law,Herbert Offner,Carl Ottobrino,Dave Schackner(v) Stan Harris,Leonard Selic,Sam Singer(viola) Gregory Bemko,Zachary Bock,Jack Wulfe(cello) Stan Kenton(p) Laurindo Almeida(g) Don Bagley(b) Shelly Manne(dm) Carlos Vidal(cga).
(Capitol Studios) LA,May 18,1950

6045-1	Art Pepper	CD BN 8-33244-2

MEL TORME:
Mel Torme(vo) with Red Norvo(vb) Tal Farlow(g) Charles Mingus(b).
(Capitol Studios) LA,August 31,1950

6553-3	I've got a feeling I'm falling	CD BN 7-96582-2,CD 7-81331-2

Note: On both of these CDs,the recording date is wrongly given as August 11,1949.

JUNE CHRISTY:
June Christy(vo) with Shorty Rogers(tp,arr) John Graas(frh) Gene Englund(tu) Art Pepper(as) Bud Shank, Bob Cooper(ts) Bob Gioga(bs) Claude Williamson(p) Don Bagley(b) Shelly Manne(dm).
(Capitol Studios) LA,September 11,1950

6564-4	Do it again	CD BN(E)8-53232-2

STAN KENTON AND HIS ORCHESTRA:
Al Porcino,Maynard Ferguson,Chico Alvarez,John Howell(tp) Shorty Rogers(tp,arr) Milt Bernhart,Harry Betts,Bob Fitzpatrick,Eddie Bert(tb) Bart Varsalona(bass tb) Bud Shank, Art Pepper(as) Bob Cooper,Bart Calderall(ts) Bob Gioga(bs) Stan Kenton(p) Ralph Blaze(g) Don Bagley(b) Shelly Manne(dm).
(Capitol Studios) LA,September 12,1950

6581-2	Round robin	CD BN 8-33243-2

METRONOME ALL-STARS:
Miles Davis(tp) Kai Winding(tb) John LaPorta(cl) Lee Konitz(as) Stan Getz(ts) Serge Chaloff(bs) Terry Gibbs(vb) George Shearing(p) Billy Bauer(g) Eddie Safranski(b) Max Roach(dm) Ralph Burns(arr).
NYC,January 23,1951

6252-4	Early Spring	CD BN (J)TOCJ-5851

STAN KENTON AND HIS ORCHESTRA:
Maynard Ferguson,John Howell,Conte Candoli,Stu Williamson,John Coppola(tp) Harry Betts,Bob Fitzpatrick,Bill Russo,Dick Kenney(tb) George Roberts(bass tb) Stan Fletcher(tu) Bud Shank,Art Pepper(as) Bob Cooper,Bart Calderall(ts) Bob Gioga(bs) Stan Kenton(p,arr) Ralph Blaze(g) Don Bagley(b) Shelly Manne(dm).
(Capitol Studios) LA,September 20,1951

9052-3 Street of dreams CD BN 8-33243-2

SHORTY ROGERS AND HIS GIANTS:
Shorty Rogers(tp) John Graas(frh) Gene Englund(tu) Art Pepper(as) Jimmy Giuffre(ts) Hampton Hawes(p) Don Bagley(b) Shelly Manne(dm).
(Capitol Studios) LA,October 8,1951

9117 Popo BN(J)W-5503
9120 Over the rainbow CD BN 8-33244-2
9121 A propos BN(J)W-5503
9122 Sam and the lady CD BN 8-33244-2

LOUIS BELLSON JUST JAZZ ALL STARS:
Clark Terry(tp) Juan Tizol(vtb) John Graas(frh) Willie Smith(as) Wardell Gray(ts) Harry Carney(bs) Billy Strayhorn(p,arr) Wendell Marshall(b) Louis Bellson(dm).
LA,May 23,1952

9939 The jeep is jumpin' BN(J)W-5501
9940 Passion flower CD BN 4-95981-2

NAT KING COLE:
Nat "King" Cole(p) John Collins(g) Charlie Harris(b) Bunny Shawker(dm).
NYC,July 18,1952

9474-21 Polka dots and moonbeams CD BN(J)CJ28-5178

ART TATUM:
Art Tatum(p) Everett Barksdale(g) Slam Stewart(b).
LA,December 20,1952

10936 September song CD BN(J)TOCJ-5853
10938 Tea for two CD BN(Sp) 8-34712-2,8-53016-2

STAN KENTON AND HIS ORCHESTRA:
Buddy Childers,Maynard Ferguson,Conte Candoli,Don Dennis,Ruben McFall(tp) Bob Burgess,Frank Rosolino,Keith Moon(tb) Bill Russo(tb,arr) George Roberts(bass tb) Vinnie Dean,Lee Konitz(as) Bill Holman,Richie Kamuca(ts) Bob Gioga(bs) Stan Kenton(p) Sal Salvador(g) Don Bagley(b) Stan Levey(dm).
(Capitol Studios) LA,January 28,1953

11080-5 Lover man CD BN 7-81331-2

Same.
(Capitol Studios) LA,January 30,1953

11090-6 Fascinating rhythm CD BN 8-33243-2

GERRY MULLIGAN AND HIS TENTETTE:
Chet Baker,Pete Candoli(tp) Bob Enevoldsen(vtb) John Graas(frh) Ray Siegel(tu) Bud Shank(as) Don Davidson,Gerry Mulligan(bs) Joe Mondragon(b) Chico Hamilton(dm).
(Capitol Studios) LA,January 29,1953

11117 Walkin' shoes BN(J)W-5502;CD BN 8-54905-2

477

DUKE ELLINGTON AND HIS ORCHESTRA:
Clark Terry,Cat Anderson,Willie Cook,Ray Nance(tp) Quentin Jackson,Britt Woodman(tb) Juan Tizol(vtb) Russell Procope(cl,as) Rick Henderson(as) Paul Gonsalves(ts) Jimmy Hamilton(cl,ts) Harry Carney (bass cl,bs) Duke Ellington(p) Wendell Marshall(b) Butch Ballard(dm).

	(Capitol Studios)	LA,April 6,1953
11398-1	Satin doll	CD BN 8-54900-2,8-21381-2,(Sp)8-34712-2, 8-53016-2

Same.

	(Capitol Studios)	LA April 7,1953
11417-5	Stormy weather	CD BN 8-54900-2
11418-8	Star dust	- (J)CJ28-5024

DUKE ELLINGTON:
Duke Ellington(p) Wendell Marshall(b) Butch Ballard(dm).

	(Capitol Studios)	LA,April 13,1953
11434-3	Passion flower	CD BN 4-95981-2
11438-2	Prelude to a kiss	CD BN(J)CJ28-5178

Same.	(Capitol Studios)	LA,April 14,1953
11439-2	In a sentimental mood	CD BN(J)CJ28-5023
11440-5	Things ain't what they used to be	CD BN(J)TOCJ-5187/88
11442-2	Janet	CD BN 8-54900-2

Note: A Gloria Wood title issued on CD is not the April 1953 original version,but a remake recorded in 1961 (see details on page 490).

JUNE CHRISTY:
June Christy(vo) with Orchestra arr. & cond. by Pete Rugolo: Maynard Ferguson,Conrad Gozzo,Shorty Rogers,Jimmy Zito(tp) Milt Bernhart,Herbie Harper,Tommy Pederson(tb) George Roberts(bass tb) Gus Bivona,Bud Shank(as) Bob Cooper,Ted Nash(ts) Chuck Gentry(bs) Jeff Clarkson(p) Barney Kessel(g) Joe Mondragon(b) Frank Carlson(dm).

	(Capitol Studios)	LA,August 14,1953
11706	Something cool	CD BN 7-80707-2,8-32994-2,(C)8-33908-2, 4-94888-2,(J)TOCJ-5852

DUKE ELLINGTON:
Duke Ellington(p) Wendell Marshall(b) Dave Black(dm) Jimmy Grissom(vo).

		NYC,December 3,1953
20249-2	I'm just a lucky so and so	CD BN 8-55221-2

DUKE ELLINGTON:
Ray Nance(v-1,vo-2) Duke Ellington(p) Wendell Marshall(b) Dave Black(dm).

		NYC,December 15,1953
20275-7	Chile bowl -1	CD BN 8-54900-2
20278-2	Just a-sittin' and a-rockin'-2	CD BN 8-55221-2

JUNE CHRISTY:
June Christy(vo) with Orchestra arr. & cond. by Pete Rugolo: Frank Beach,Conrad Gozzo, Ray Linn,Ray Triscari,Uan Rasey(tp) Nick Di Maio,Dick Noel,Tommy Pederson,Dick Reynolds(tb) Skeets Herfurt,Willie Schwartz(as) Fred Falensby,Ted Nash(ts) Chuck Gentry(bs) Paul Smith(p) Tony Rizzi(g) Joe Mondragon(b) Alvin Stoller(dm).
(Capitol Studios) LA,December 27,1953

12181 Midnight sun CD BN(Sp)8-56842-2

DUKE ELLINGTON AND HIS ORCHESTRA:
Clark Terry,Cat Anderson,Willie Cook,Ray Nance(tp) Quentin Jackson,Britt Woodman,George Jean(tb) Russell Procope,Rick Henderson(as) Paul Gonsalves,Jimmy Hamilton(ts) Harry Carney(bs) Duke Ellington (p) Wendell Marshall(b) Dave Black(dm).
(Universal Studios) Chicago,January 2,1954

12253-4 One o'clock jump CD BN 8-54900-2

STAN KENTON AND HIS ORCHESTRA:
Buddy Childers,Vic Minichiello,Sam Noto,Stu Williamson,Don Smith(tp) Bob Fitzpatrick,Frank Rosolino, Milt Gold,Joe Clavardone(tb) George Roberts(bass tb) Dave Schildkraut,Charlie Mariano(as) Bill Perkins, Mike Cicchetti(ts) Tony Ferina(bs) Stan Kenton(p) Bob Lesher(g) Don Bagley(b) Stan Levey(dm) Bill Holman(arr).
(Capitol Studios) LA,March 2,1954

12445-12 Fearless Finlay CD BN 8-33243-2

FRANK SINATRA:
Frank Sinatra(vo) wih Orchestra arr. & cond. by Nelson Riddle: Harry "Sweets" Edison(tp) Ray Sims, Tommy Pederson(tb) George Roberts(bass tb) Eddie Miller(cl) Skeets Herfurt,Mahlon Clark(as) Babe Russin(ts) Joe Koch(bs) Frank Flynn(vb) Bill Miller(p) Allan Reuss (g) Joe Comfort(b) Alvin Stoller(dm).
(Capitol Studios) LA,April 7,1954

12433 Wrap your troubles in dreams CD BN 4-95981-2

DUKE ELLINGTON AND HIS ORCHESTRA:
Clark Terry,Cat Anderson,Willie Cook,Ray Nance(tp) Quentin Jackson,Britt Woodman,John Sanders(tb) Russell Procope,Rick Henderson(as) Paul Gonsalves,Jimmy Hamilton(ts) Harry Carney(bs) Duke Ellington (p) Wendell Marshall(b) Dave Black(dm).
SF,April 26,1954

12584-4 C jam blues CD BN (E)8-53227-2

SAL SALVADOR:
Eddie Costa(p,vb-1) Sal Salvador(g) Kenny O'Brien(b) Joe Morello(dm).
(Muzak Studios) NYC,July 21,1954

20413 Yesterdays -1
20427 Round trip
20428 See
20429 Cabin in the sky -1

All titles issued on CD BN 4-96548-2.

NAT KING COLE:
Nat "King" Cole(vo) with Nelson Riddle and his Orchestra.
(Capitol Studios) LA,July 27,1954

12854 Smile CD BN(J)TOCJ-5875

479

SAL SALVADOR:

Eddie Costa(p,vb-1) Sal Salvador(g) Jimmy Gannon(b) Jimmy Campbell(dm).
(Muzak Studios) NYC,October 9,1954

20462 Wheels
20463 Nothin' to do -1
20484 Autumn in New York -1
20485 Boo boo be doop-1 CD BN 7-96581-2
20486 Down home
20487 Violets for your furs -1
20488 Salutations
20489 Now see here,man (*aka* Toot #2)

All titles issued on CD BN 4-96548-2.

FRANK ROSOLINO:

Sam Noto(tp) Frank Rosolino(tb) Charlie Mariano(as) Pete Jolly(p) Max Bennett(b) Mel Lewis(dm).
(Muzak Studios) NYC,November 6,1954

20508-4 Embraceable you CD BN 7-80706-2
20510-6 Besame mucho CD BN(J)TOCJ-5296

BENNY GOODMAN:

Chris Griffin,Ruby Braff,Bernie Privin,Carl Poole(tp) Will Bradley,Cutty Cutshall,Vernon Brown(tb) Hymie Schertzer,Paul Ricci(as) Boomie Richman,Al Klink(ts) Sol Schlinger(bs) Mel Powell(p) Steve Jordan(g) George Duvivier(b) Bobby Donaldson(dm).
(Riverside Plaza Hotel) NYC,November 9,1954

20536 Stompin' at the Savoy CD BN(Sp) 8-34712-2,8-53016-2

NAT KING COLE:

Nat "King" Cole(vo) with Orchestra arr. & cond. by Nelson Riddle.
(Capitol Studios) LA,December 20,1954

13327-14 A blossom fell CD BN(J)TOCJ-5851

JIMMY GIUFFRE:

Jack Sheldon(tp) Jimmy Giuffre(cl) Ralph Pena(b) Artie Anton(dm).
(Capitol Studios) LA,January 31,1955

13528-6 Iranic CD BN 7-80707-2,5-21052-2

Note: Above title was mistitled "Ironic" on CD 7-80707-2.

SERGE CHALOFF:

Herb Pomeroy(tp) Boots Mussulli(as) Serge Chaloff(bs) Ray Santisi(p) Everett Evans(b) Jim Zitano(dm)
NYC,April 4,1955

20631-1 Body and soul CD BN(Sp)8-34712-2

BOB COOPER OCTET:

Stu Williamson(tp,vtb) Bob Enevoldsen(vtb,ts,bass cl) Bud Shank(fl,as,ts) Bob Cooper(ts,oboe,English h,arr) Jimmy Giuffre(ts,bs) Claude Williamson(p) Max Bennett(b) Stan Levey(dm).
(Capitol Studios) LA,April 26,1955

13747-10 Strike up the band CD BN 7-80706-2
13748-2 Sunset CD BN(J)TOCJ-5855

<u>CLAUDE WILLIAMSON</u>:
Claude Williamson(p) Buddy Clark(b) Mel Lewis(dm).
(Capitol Studios) LA,May 19,1955

13888 Get happy CD BN(J)TOCJ-5187/88

<u>DUKE ELLINGTON</u>:
Ray Nance(tp) Quentin Jackson(tb) Russell Procope(cl) Duke Ellington(el p) Jimmy Woode(b) Dave Black (dm).
(Universal Studios) Chicago,May 19,1955

14102-7 Discontented blues CD BN 5-21052-2

<u>BOB COOPER OCTET</u>:
Bob Enevoldsen(vtb,ts,bass cl) John Graas(frh) Bud Shank(fl,as,ts) Bob Cooper(ts,oboe,English h,arr) Jimmy Giuffre(cl,ts,bs) Claude Williamson(p) Joe Mondragon(b) Shelly Manne(dm).
(Capitol Studios) LA,June 13,1955

13966-10 It's de-lovely CD BN(J)TOCJ-5856

<u>NAT KING COLE</u>:
Nat "King" Cole(p) John Collins(g) Charlie Harris(b) Lee Young(dm).
(Capitol Studios) LA,July 14,1955

14192-9 It could happen to you CD BN(J)CJ28-5022

<u>STAN KENTON AND HIS ORCHESTRA</u>:
Al Porcino,Ed Leddy,Sam Noto,Stu Williamson,Bob Clark(tp) Bob Fitzpatrick,Carl Fontana,Gus Chappell, Kent Larsen(tb) Don Kelly(bass tb) Lennie Niehaus,Charlie Mariano(as) Bill Perkins,Dave Van Kriedt(ts) Don Davidson(bs) Stan Kenton(p) Ralph Blaze(g) Max Bennett(b) Mel Lewis(dm) Gerry Mulligan(arr).
(Universal Studios) Chicago,July 20,1955

20822-10 Limelight CD BN 8-33243-2

<u>THE FOUR FRESHMEN</u>:
Ross Barbour,Don Barbour,Ken Errair,Bob Flanigan(vo) with Frank Rosolino,Harry Betts,Milt Bernhart, Tommy Pederson(tb) George Roberts(bass tb) Claude Williamson(p) Barney Kessel(g) Joe Mondragon(b) Shelly Manne(dm) Pete Rugolo(arr).
(Capitol Studios) LA,August 23,1955

14351 You stepped out of a dream CD BN(J)TOCJ-5858

<u>NAT KING COLE</u>:
Nat "King" Cole(p,vo) with Orchestra arr. & cond. by Nelson Riddle: Conrad Gozzo(tp) Francis Howard, James Priddy,Murray McEachern(tb) Juan Tizol(vtb) George Roberts(bass tb) Willie Smith(as) Willie Schwartz,Harry Klee(saxes) & strings: Dan Lube,Erno Neufeld,Marshall Sosson,Victor Bay,Alex Beller, Harold Dicterow,Nathan Ross,Eudice Shapiro(v) David Sterkin,Stanley Spiegelman(viola) Eleanor Slatkin, Victor Gottlieb,Raphael Kramer(cello).
(Capitol Studios) LA,August 23,1955

14344 Autumn leaves CD BN(J)TOCJ-5853

<u>JUDY GARLAND</u>:
Judy Garland(vo) with Orchestra cond. by Jack Cathcart.
(Capitol Studios) LA,August 25.1955

14374 Over the rainbow CD BN(J)TOCJ-6152

481

NAT KING COLE:
Nat "King" Cole(vo) with Orchestra arr. & cond. by Nelson Riddle.
(Capitol Studios) LA,August 25,1955

14380 Love is a many splendered thing CD BN(J)TOCJ-5203

BENNY GOODMAN:
Harry James,Chris Griffin,Billy Butterfield,Bernie Privin(tp) Urbie Green,Will Bradley(tb) Benny Goodman (cl) Hymie Schertzer,Phil Bodner(as) Al Klink,Peanuts Hucko(ts) Dick Hyman(p) Tony Mottola(g) Milt Hinton(b) Bobby Donaldson(dm).
(Riverside Plaza Hotel) NYC,December 7,1955

20935/6 Sing,sing,sing CD BN(J)CJ28-5021

Ruby Braff,Jimmy Maxwell,Carl Poole(tp) replace James & Privin.
(Riverside Plaza Hotel) NYC,December 8,1955

20937 Bugle call rag CD BN(J)TOCJ-5750

BENNY GOODMAN:
Benny Goodman(cl) Lionel Hampton(vb) Mel Powell(p) George Duvivier(b) Bobby Donaldson(dm).
(Riverside Plaza Hotel) NYC,December 14,1955

20954 Moonglow CD BN(J)TOCJ-5858

JUNE CHRISTY:
June Christy(vo) with Orchestra arr. & dir. by Pete Rugolo: John Graas(frh) Bud Shank(fl,as) Bob Cooper (ts,oboe) Bernie Mattinson (vb,bells,perc) Ann Mason Stockton(harp) Howard Roberts(g)Joe Mondragon(b) Shelly Manne(dm) & strings: Dan Lube,Erno Neufeld,Nick Pisani(v) David Sterkin(viola) Edgar Lustgarten (cello).
(Capitol Studios) LA,January 16,1956

14955 Day dream CD BN 8-55221-2

June Christy(vo) with Orchestra arr. & cond. by Pete Rugolo: Milt Bernhart,Frank Rosolino(tb) George Roberts(bass tb) John Graas(frh) Bud Shank(as,fl) Bob Cooper(ts,oboe) Bernie Mattinson(vb,perc,bells) Ann Mason Stockton(harp) Claude Williamson(p) Howard Roberts(g) Joe Mondragon(b) Shelly Manne(dm) & strings: Dan Lube,Erno Neufeld,Nick Pisani(v) David Sterkin(viola) Edgar Lustgarten(cello).
(Capitol Studios) LA,January 23,1956

14612 I didn't know about you CD BN 8-55221-2

GEORGE SHEARING:
Johnny Rae(vb) George Shearing(p) Jean "Toots" Thielemans(g) Al McKibbon(b) Bill Clark(dm) & unidentified orchestra,incl. strings,arr. & cond. by Dennis Farnon.
(Capitol Studios) LA,January 24,1956

14909 'Round midnight CD BN(J)TOCJ-5857

BILLY MAY AND HIS ORCHESTRA:
John Best,Conrad Gozzo,Mannie Klein,Uan Rasey(tp) Ed Kusby,Murray McEachern,Lloyd Ulyate,Joe Howard(tb) Skeets Herfurt,Wilbur Schwartz(as) Ted Nash,Fred Falensby(ts) Chuck Gentry (bs) Paul Smith (p) Al Hendrickson(g) Phil Stephens(b) Alvin Stoller(dm) & The Jud Conlon's Rhythmaires (Jud Conlon, Loulie Jean Norman,Gloria Wood,Charles Parlato,Mack McLean,Robert Wacker)(vo) Billy May (arr,dir).
(Capitol Studios) LA,January 30,1956 (20:30-24:00)

14936 Main title from "The man with the golden arm"
CD BN 7-80707-2

STAN KENTON AND HIS ORCHESTRA:
Ed Leddy,Maynard Ferguson,Pete Candoli,Vinnie Tano,Don Paladino(tp) Bob Fitzpatrick,Milt Bernhart,Carl Fontana,Kent Larsen(tb) Don Kelly(bass tb) Lennie Niehaus,Skeets Herfurt(as) Bill Perkins,Spencer Sinatra, Vido Musso(ts) Jack Nimitz(bs) Stan Kenton(p) Ralph Blaze(g) Don Bagley(b) Mel Lewis(dm) Chico Guerrero(timbales-1) Pete Rugolo(arr-2).
(Goldwyn Studios) LA,February 12,1956

15043 Peanut vendor -1 CD BN 8-33243-2
15046 Lover -2 CD BN(Sp)8-53016-2

SERGE CHALOFF:
Serge Chaloff(bs) Sonny Clark(p) Leroy Vinnegar(b) Philly Joe Jones(dm).
(Capitol Studios) LA,March 14,1956

15157-3 A handful of stars CD BN 7-80707-2

LOUIS PRIMA:
Louis Prima(vo) with James Blount, Jr.(tb) Sam Butera(ts) Willie McCumber(p) Jack Marshall(g) Amado Robriguez(b) Bobby Morris(dm).
(Capitol Studios) LA,April 19,1956

15372 Medley:Just a gigolo/I ain't got nobody CD BN(C)4-94888-2

LOUIS ARMSTRONG & BING CROSBY:
Louis Armstrong(tp,vo) Trummy Young(tb) Edmond Hall(cl) Billy Kyle(p) Arvell Shaw(b) Barrett Deems (dm) Bing Crosby(vo).
LA,April 20,1956

15720 Now you has jazz CD BN 7-96582-2,(C)4-94888-2

NAT KING COLE:
Harry "Sweets" Edison(tp) Nat "King" Cole(p,vo) John Collins(g) Charlie Harris(b) Lee Young(dm).
(Capitol Studios) LA,August 15,1956

15789-8 Candy CD BN(J)TOCJ-6189
15791-5 It's only a paper moon CD BN(J)TOCJ-5858,TOCJ-66071
15792-3 Route 66 CD BN(J)TOCJ-5296

NAT KING COLE:
Stuff Smith(v) Nat "King" Cole(p,vo) John Collins(g) Charlie Harris(b) Lee Young(dm).
(Capitol Studios) LA,September 24,1956

15937-3 I know that you know CD BN 4-95981-2

GEORGE SHEARING:
Emil Richards(vb) George Shearing(p) Jean "Toots" Thielemans(g,hca) Al McKibbon(b) Percy Brice(dm) & Orchestra arr. & cond. by Billy May: Vince De Rosa(frh) Jules Kinsler,Jules Jacob,Pete Terry,Joe Krechter (saxes) Jacques Gasselin,Felix Slatkin,Paul Shure,Marshall Sosson,Erno Neufeld,Eudice Shapiro,William Weiss,Nathan Ross(v) Alvin Dinkin,David Sterkin(viola) Eleanor Slatkin,Edgar Lustgarten,Victor Gottlieb (cello) Meyer Rubin(b).
(Capitol Studios) LA,December 19,1956 (20:00-23:30)

16305 One morning in May CD BN(J)TOCJ-5855

NAT KING COLE:
Nat "King" Cole(vo) with Gordon Jenkins and his Orchestra.
(Capitol Studios) LA,December 19,1956

16308 Star Dust CD BN(J)TOCJ-5875

483

PAUL SMITH:
Paul Smith(p) Barney Kessel(g) Joe Mondragon(b) Stan Levey(dm).
(Capitol Studios) LA,January 22,1957

16491 Invitation CD BN(J)TOCJ-6190

COLEMAN HAWKINS:
Coleman Hawkins(ts) with string Orchestra arr. & dir. by Glenn Osser.
(Capitol Studios) NYC,February 7,1957

21393 Autumn leaves CD BN 8-54365-2

JUDY GARLAND:
Judy Garland(vo) with Orchestra cond. by Gordon Jenkins.
(Capitol Studios) LA,February 22,1957

16627 By myself CD BN(Sp)8-56842-2

DAKOTA STATON:
Dakota Staton(vo) with Orchestra cond. by Van Alexander,incl. fl,vb,p,g,b,dm.
NYC,February 28,1957

21432 Misty CD BN(Sp)8-56842-2

DAKOTA STATON:
Dakota Staton(vo) with Jonah Jones(tp) Hank Jones(p) & others unknown.
(Capitol Studios) NYC,March 2,1957

21436 The late,late show CD BN 7-96583-2
21438 A foggy day CD BN 7-80506-2

Dakota Staton(vo) & unknown tb,vb,g,b,dm. Same session.

21440 Broadway CD BN 8-54363-2

ELLA MAE MORSE:
Ella Mae Morse(vo) with Billy May and his Orchestra: John Best,Conrad Gozzo,Mannie Klein(tp) Murray McEachern,George Roberts,Si Zentner(tb) Harry Klee(as,fl) Les Robinson(as) Gene Cipriano,Fred Falensby (ts) Justin Gordon(bs) Jimmy Rowles(p) Al Hendrickson(g) Joe Mondragon(b) Alvin Stoller(dm) David Grupp(vb) Billy May(arr,cond).
(Capitol Studios) LA,June 5,1957

17138 My funny Valentine CD BN(Sp)8-56842-2

JUNE CHRISTY:
June Christy(vo) with Orchestra arr. & cond. by Pete Rugolo: Milt Bernhart,Herbie Harper,Tommy Pederson,Frank Rosolino(tb) George Roberts(bass tb) Bernie Mattinson(vb) Benny Aronov(p) Howard Roberts(g) Red Mitchell(b) Alvin Stoller(dm).
(Capitol Studios) LA,July 2,1957

17274 It's a most unusual day CD BN(J)TOCJ-5855
17276 Love turns Winter to Spring CD BN(J)TOCJ-5854

THE KING SISTERS:
Yvonne,Luise,Marilyn & Alyce King(vo) with Orchestra cond. by Alvino Rey.
(Capitol Studios) LA,August 19,1957

17481 Take the A train CD BN 8-54363-2,(Sp)8-56842-2

484

STAN KENTON AND HIS ORCHESTRA:
Ed Leddy,Billy Catalano,Sam Noto,Lee Katzman,Phil Gilbert(tp) Kent Larsen,Archie LeCoque,Don Reed, Jim Amlotte(tb) Kenny Shroyer(bass tb) Lennie Niehaus(as) Bill Perkins,Wayne Dunstan(ts) Bill Robinson, Steve Perlow(bs) Stan Kenton(p) Red Kelly(b) Jerry McKenzie(dm) Joe Coccia(arr).
(Rendezvous Ballroom) Balboa Beach,Calif.,October 8,1957

17672-7 Two shades of Autumn CD BN(J)TOCJ-5853

KEELY SMITH:
Keely Smith(vo) with Orchestra cond. by Nelson Riddle: Pete Candoli,Conrad Gozzo,George Seaberg, Shorty Sherock(tp) Dick Noel,Tommy Pederson,Jimmy Priddy,George Roberts(tb) Buddy Collette,Joe Cook,Lee Elliott,Wilbur Schwartz,Willie Smith(saxes) Bill Miller(p) Bobby Gibbons(g) Joe Comfort(b) Bill Richmond(dm) & strings: Kathryn Julye(harp) Alex Beller,Victor Bay,Ben Gill,Paul Nero,Erno Neufeld, Eudice Shapiro,Paul Shure,Felix Slatkin(v) Alvin Dinkin,David Sterkin(viola) Cy Bernard,Eleanor Slatkin (cello).
(Capitol Studios) LA,November 7,1957

17896 Don't take your love from me CD BN(Sp)8-56842-2
17897 When your lover has gone CD BN(Sp)8-53016-2

PEGGY LEE:
Peggy Lee(vo) with Orchestra arr. & cond. by Nelson Riddle.
(Capitol Studios) LA,December 20,1957

18085 Old devil moon CD BN(Sp)8-56842-2

HANK JONES:
Hank Jones(p) Barry Galbraith(g) Milt Hinton(b) Osie Johnson(dm).
(Capitol Studios) NYC,February 7,1958

22008 My one and only love CD BN(J)TOCJ-5187/88

GEORGE SHEARING:
Emil Richards(vb) George Shearing(p) Jean "Toots" Thielemans(g) Al McKibbon(b) Percy Brice(dm).
(Claremont College) Claremont,Calif.,March 8,1958

31128C September in the rain CD BN (J)TOCJ-5853

GLEN GRAY AND THE CASA LOMA ORCHESTRA:
Shorty Sherock,Conrad Gozzo,Mannie Klein,Pete Candoli(tp) Walt Benson,Joe Howard,Si Zentner(tb) Murray McEachern(tb,as) Skeets Herfurt(as) Gus Bivona(cl,as) Babe Russin,Jules Jacob(ts) Chuck Gentry (bs) Ray Sherman(p) Jack Marshall(g) Mike Rubin(b) Nick Fatool(dm) Gene Gifford,Larry Wagner(arr) Glen Gray(leader).
(Capitol Studios) LA,March ,1958

18564 Snowfall CD BN(J)TOCJ-5854

NAT KING COLE:
Nat "King" Cole(vo) with string orchestra arr. & cond. by Gordon Jenkins.
(Capitol Studios) LA,May 8,1958

19093 For all we know CD BN(J)TOCJ-5300

PEGGY LEE:
Peggy Lee(vo) with Jack Marshall's Music: Conrad Gozzo,Don Fagerquist,Mannie Klein(tp) Bob Enevoldsen(vtb) Milt Bernhart(tb) Justin Gordon,George Smith(reeds) Joe Harnell(p) Howard Roberts(g) Joe Mondragon(b) Shelly Manne(dm).
(Capitol Studios) LA,May 19,1958

19145 Fever CD BN 5-21151-2,(Sp)8-53016-2

485

PEGGY LEE:

Peggy Lee(vo) with Jack Marshall's Music: Conrad Gozzo,Don Fagerquist,Mannie Klein(tp) Bob Enevoldsen(vtb) Milt Bernhart(tb) Justin Gordon,George Smith(reeds) Joe Harnell(p) Howard Roberts(g) Joe Mondragon(b) Shelly Manne(dm).
(Capitol Studios) LA,May 25,1958

19202 All right,okay,you win CD BN(J)TOCJ-5296

Peggy Lee(vo) with Jack Marshall's Music: Uan Rasey,Pete Candoli,Mannie Klein(tp) Bob Enevoldsen(vtb) Milt Bernhart(tb) Justin Gordon,George Smith(reeds) Joe Harnell(p) Barney Kessel(g) Joe Mondragon(b) Shelly Manne(dm).
(Capitol Studios) LA,May 30,1958

19233 Alone together CD BN 7-96583-2

JUNE CHRISTY:

June Christy(vo) with Russ Freeman(p) Monte Budwig(b) Shelly Manne(dm).
(Capitol Studios) LA,June 16,1958

19389 It don't mean a thing CD BN(J)CJ28-5021

NAT KING COLE:

Nat "King" Cole(vo) with Wendell Culley,Snooky Young,Thad Jones,Joe Newman(tp) Henry Coker,Al Grey, Benny Powell(tb) Frank Wess(as,fl) Marshall Royal(as) Frank Foster,Billy Mitchell(ts) Charles Fowlkes(bs) Gerald Wiggins(p) Freddie Green(g) Eddie Jones(b) Sonny Payne(dm) Dave Cavanaugh(arr).
(Capitol Studios) LA,June 30,1958

19553 Mood indigo CD BN 4-94035-2

KEELY SMITH:

Keely Smith(vo) with Orchestra arr. & cond. by Billy May: Uan Rasey(tp) Francis "Joe" Howard,Ed Kusby, Murray McEachern,Si Zentner(tb) Justin Gordon,Jules Jacob,Harry Klee,Wilbur Schwartz(saxes) Paul Smith(p) Howard Roberts(g) Ralph Pena(b) Irving Cottler(dm) Larry Bunker(perc) Verlye Mills(harp) & strings: Victor Arno,Israel Baker,Ben Gill,Dan Lube,Erno Neufeld,Lou Raderman,Paul Shure, Marshall Sosson(v) Alvin Dinkin,Paul Robyn(viola) Edgar Lustgarten,Kurt Reher(cello).
(Capitol Studios) LA,June 30,1958

19557 Cocktails for two CD BN (J)TOCJ-5857

JUNE CHRISTY:

June Christy(vo) with Ed Leddy(tp) Frank Rosolino(tb) Red Callender(tu) Bud Shank(as) Bob Cooper(ts,arr) Russ Freeman(p) Monte Budwig(b) Mel Lewis(dm).
(Capitol Studios) LA,July 3,1958

19620 They can't take that away from me CD BN 7-80506-2

June Christy(vo) with Orchestra arr. & cond. by Pete Rugolo: John Cave,Vince De Rosa(frh) Paul Horn,Bob Cooper,Marty Berman(reeds) Tony Rizzi(g) Kathryn Julye(harp) Red Mitchell(b) Frank Flynn,Larry Bunker (perc) & strings: Dan Lube,Lou Raderman,Victor Arno,Ben Gill,Sam Freed,Lou Klass,Ambrose Russo, Alfred Lustgarten,Erno Neufeld(v) Virginia Majewski,Stanley Harris,Alexander Niemann(viola) Edgar Lustgarten,Raphael Kramer,Kurt Reher(cello).
(Capitol Studios) LA,August 15,1958

19758 Spring can really hang you up the most CD BN 7-96583-2

LOUIS PRIMA:

Louis Prima(tp,vo) Lou Sineaux(tb) Sam Butera(ts) Willie McCumber(p) Bobby Roberts(g) Tony Liuzza(b) Paul Ferrara(dm).
(Capitol Studios) LA,August 25,1958

30002 Sing,sing,sing CD BN(C)4-94888-2

GLEN GRAY AND THE CASA LOMA ORCHESTRA:
Cappy Lewis,Conrad Gozzo,Mannie Klein,Pete Candoli(tp) Tommy Pederson,Joe Howard,Si Zentner(tb) Murray McEachern(tb,as) Skeets Herfurt(as) Gus Bivona(cl,as) Babe Russin,Jules Jacob(ts) Chuck Gentry (bs) Ray Sherman(p) Jack Marshall(g) Mike Rubin(b) Nick Fatool(dm) Gene Gifford,Larry Wagner(arr) Glen Gray(leader).
(Capitol Studios) LA,September 17,1958

30134 In the mood CD BN(J)TOCJ-5203

LES BROWN:
Dick Collins,Wes Hensel,Ray Triscari,Jerry Kadowitz,Mickey McMahan(tp) Dick Kenney,Roy Main(tb) Jim Hill,Stumpy Brown(bass tb) Abe Most(cl) Les Brown(as) Matt Utal,Ralph Lapolla(fl,cl,as) Billy Usselton(ts) Butch Stone(cl,bs,vo) Abe Aaron(ss,ts,bs) Don Trenner(p) Tony Rizzi(g) Bob Berteaux(b) Lloyd Morales (dm) Laurie Johnson(vo) Skip Martin(arr).
(Capitol Studios) LA,October 13,1958

30352 I've got my love to keep me warm CD BN(J)TOCJ-5854

PEGGY LEE:
Peggy Lee(vo) with Orchestra arr. & cond. by Jack Marshall.
(Capitol Studios) LA,October 19,1958

30438 So in love CD BN 7-81331-2

MARK MURPHY:
Mark Murphy(vo) with Conte Candoli,Pete Candoli(tp) Jimmy Rowles(p) Bobby Gibbons(g) Joe Mondragon (b) Mel Lewis(dm) Carlos Mejia(cga) Bill Holman(arr).
(Capitol Studios) LA,December 15,1958

30780 Day in,day out CD BN 7-96582-2
30781 This could be the start of something big CD BN 7-80707-2,(C)4-94888-2
30782 The lady is a tramp CD BN 7-89914-2

JUNE CHRISTY:
June Christy(vo) with Orchestra arr. & cond. by Pete Rugolo: Buddy Childers,Al Porcino,Don Fagerquist, Ollie Mitchell(tp) Milt Bernhart,Bob Fitzpatrick,Frank Rosolino(tb) Ken Shroyer(bass tb) Red Callender(tu) Bud Shank,Harry Klee(as) Bob Cooper,Paul Horn(ts) Chuck Gentry(bs) Joe Castro(p) Jim Hall(g) Ralph Pena(b) Irv Kluger(dm).
(Capitol Studios) LA,January 21,1959

31030 How high the moon CD BN(Sp)8-53016-2

STAN KENTON AND HIS ORCHESTRA:
Frank Huggins,Bud Brisbois,Jack Sheldon,Joe Burnett,Roger Middleton(tp) Archie LeCoque,Kent Larsen, Jim Amlotte(tb) Bob Olson,Bill Smiley(bass tb) Lennie Niehaus(as) Richie Kamuca,Bill Trujillo(ts) Billy Root,Sture Swenson(bs) Stan Kenton(p) Red Kelly(b) Jerry McKenzie(dm) Gene Roland(arr).
(Blue Room,Tropicana Hotel) Las Vegas,February 2,1959

31179 It's all right with me CD BN 4-97155-2
31191 Don't get around much anymore CD BN 4-94035-2

HANK JONES:
Hank Jones(p) Kenny Burrell(g) Milt Hinton(b) Elvin Jones(dm).
(Capitol Studios) NYC,February 4,1959

22561 Summertime CD BN 7-80706-2,(J)CJ28-5178,
TOCJ-5852,TOCJ-5873

GEORGE SHEARING:

Emil Richards(vb) George Shearing(p) Jean "Toots" Thielemans(g) James Bond(b) Ray Mosca (dm) with Orchestra arr. & cond. by Billy May: Vincent De Rosa(frh) Hugo Raimondi(cl) Arthur Gleghorn(fl) Wilbur Schwartz(as) Jules Jacob(oboe) Art Fleming(bassoon) & strings: Victor Arno,Israel Baker,Jacques Gasselin, James Getzoff,Murray Kellner,Erno Neufeld,Mischa Russell,Eudice Shapiro,Gerald Vinci(v) Virginia Majewski,Alex Niemann,David Sterkin(viola) Victor Gottlieb,Ray Kramer,Edgar Lustgarten(cello).
(Capitol Studios) LA,February 26,1959

31238 Moonlight becomes you CD BN(J) TOCJ-5858
31240 There'll never be another Spring CD BN(J) TOCJ-5851
31262 Laura CD BN(Sp) 8-53016-2

GEORGE SHEARING TRIO:

George Shearing(p) Jimmy Bond(b) Ray Mosca(dm).
(Capitol Studios) LA,March 27,1959

31429 What's new CD BN(J)CJ28-5022,TOCJ-5187/88,TOCJ-5873
31431 Heart of Winter CD BN(J)TOCJ-5854

PEGGY LEE & GEORGE SHEARING:

Peggy Lee(vo) with Ray Ellington(vb) George Shearing(p) Toots Thielemans(g) Carl Pruitt(b) Ray Mosca (dm). (Live at the Americana Hotel) Miami,Florida,April 28,1959

31807 Do I love you? CD BN 7-80707-2,(E)8-53232-2

Note: Although Warren Chiasson(vb),Jimmy Bond(b) and Roy Haynes(dm) have often been credited for this session,Ray Ellington has confirmed the above personnel as correct.

DINAH SHORE-ANDRE PREVIN:

Dinah Shore(vo) with Andre Previn(p).
(Capitol Studios) LA, June 2,1959

31774 My funny Valentine CD BN 7-81331-2,(Sp)8-53016-2
31782 April in Paris CD BN 7-99100-2,(J)TOCJ-5853
31783 I'll be seeing you CD BN(J)TOCJ-6189,TOCJ-66071

JERI SOUTHERN AT THE CRESCENDO:

Jeri Southern(vo) with Dick Hazard(p,arr) John Kitzmiller(b) Frankie Capp(dm) Edgar Lustgarten(cello).
(Live,Crescendo Club) LA,June 8,1959

31834 I get a kick out of you CD BN 5-21151-2

DINAH SHORE-ANDRE PREVIN:

Dinah Shore(vo) with Andre Previn(p) Red Mitchell(b) Frank Capp(dm).
(Capitol Studios) LA, June 12,1959

31881 That old feeling CD BN(J)CJ28-5179
31883 My melancholy baby CD BN(J)TOCJ-5300

MARK MURPHY:

Mark Murphy(vo) with Orchestra arr. & cond. by Bill Holman: Conte Candoli,Pete Candoli(tp) Bill Holman (bs) Jimmy Rowles(p) Bobby Gibbons(g) Joe Mondragon(b) Mel Lewis(dm) Larry Bunker(vb).
(Capitol Studios) LA,August 28,1959

32281 Witchcraft CD BN 5-21153-2

STAN KENTON AND HIS ORCHESTRA:

Bud Brisbois,Dalton Smith,Bill Mathieu,Rolf Ericson,Roger Middleton(tp) Archie LeCoque,Kent Larsen, Don Sebesky(tb) Jim Amlotte,Bob Knight(bass tb) Charlie Mariano(as) Bill Trujillo,Ronnie Rubin(ts) Jack Nimitz,Marvin Holladay(bs) Stan Kenton(p,arr) Pete Chivily(b) Jimmy Campbell(dm) June Christy,The Four Freshmen(vo).
(Purdue University) Lafayette,Indiana,October 10,1959

102720 September song CD BN 8-33243-2

KAY STARR:
Kay Starr(vo) with Orchestra arr. & cond. by Van Alexander.
(Capitol Studios) LA,March 5, 1960

33398 You're just in love CD BN 4-95981-2

GEORGE SHEARING/BILLY MAY:
George Shearing(p) Joe Mondragon,Myer Rubin(b) Mel Lewis(dm) with strings arr. & cond. by Billy May: Jacques Gasselin,Ben Gill,Mort Herbert,Anatol Kaminsky,Joseph Livoti,Dan Lube,Emanuel Moss,Lou Raderman,Nathan Ross,Felix Slatkin,Marshall Sosson,Gerald Vinci(v) Alvin Dinkin,Cecil Figelski,Alex Niemann,Paul Robyn(viola) Naoum Benditsky,Virgil Gates,Armand Kaproff,Eleanor Slatkin(cello).
(Capitol Studios) LA,March 15,1960

33454 Autumn nocturne CD BN (J)TOCJ-5853

CANNONBALL ADDERLEY:
Nat Adderley(c) Cannonball Adderley(as) Bobby Timmons(p) Sam Jones(b) Louis Hayes(dm).
(purchased from Riverside Records) Chicago,March 29,1960

Work song CD BN(J)TOCJ-5203,TOCJ-5298,TOCJ-5638, TOCJ-6152

JUNE CHRISTY:
June Christy(vo) with Orchestra arr. & cond. by Pete Rugolo: Conrad Gozzo,Conte Candoli,Frank Beach, Ollie Mitchell(tp) Milt Bernhart,Frank Rosolino,Harry Betts(tb) George Roberts(bass tb) Bud Shank,Harry Klee,Paul Horn,Bob Cooper,Chuck Gentry(saxes) Joe Castro(p) Jack Marshall(g) Joe Mondragon(b) Larry Bunker(dm).
(Capitol Studios) LA,April 26,1960

33685 Something cool CD BN 5-24271-2

DEAN MARTIN:
Dean Martin(vo) with Orchestra cond. by Nelson Riddle: Pete Candoli,Conrad Gozzo,Carroll Lewis,Shorty Sherock(tp) Russell Brown,Dick Noel,Tommy Pederson,Tommy Shepard(tb) Buddy Collette,Plas Johnson, Harry Klee,Joe Koch,Wilbur Schwartz(saxes) Bill Miller(p) Al Hendrickson(g) Joe Comfort(b) Alvin Stoller (dm) & strings: Victor Bay,Alex Beller, Dan Lube,Felix Slatkin,Marshall Sosson,Gerald Vinci(v) Alvin Dinkin,Paul Robyn(viola) Edgar Lustgarten,Eleanor Aller Slatkin(cello).
(Capitol Studios) LA,May 10,1960

33807 Ain't that a kick in the head CD BN(C)4-94888-2

NANCY WILSON:
Nancy Wilson(vo) with Orchestra arr. & cond. by Billy May.
(Capitol Studios) LA,May 11,1960

33811 Guess who I saw today CD BN(C)4-94888-2

CANNONBALL ADDERLEY:
Cannonball Adderley(as) Wes Montgomery(g) Victor Feldman(p) Ray Brown(b) Louis Hayes(dm).
(purchased from Riverside Records)
(Fugazi Hall) SF,May 21,1960

Au Privave CD BN 8-54898-2

NANCY WILSON & GEORGE SHEARING:
Nancy Wilson(vo) with Eddie Costa(vb) George Shearing(p) Dick Garcia(g) prob. George Duvivier(b) prob. Walter Bolden(dm).
(Capitol Studios) NYC,June 29,1960

23192 The things we did last Summer CD BN(J) TOCJ-5854
23195 Born to be blue CD BN(Sp) 8-53016-2

489

MARK MURPHY:

Mark Murphy(vo) with Jimmy Rowles(p) Joe Mondragon(b) Shelly Manne(dm).
(Capitol Studios) LA,July 7,1960

34161 Honeysuckle rose CD BN(J)TOCJ-5851

CANNONBALL ADDERLEY:

Nat Adderley(c) Cannonball Adderley(as) Victor Feldman(p) Sam Jones(b) Louis Hayes(dm).
(purchased from Riverside Records)
(Live,The Lighthouse) Hermosa Beach,Calif.,October 16,1960

Sack O' Woe CD BN 8-54898-2

THE FOUR FRESHMEN:

Bob Flanigan,Bill Comstock,Ross Barbour,Ken Albers(vo) with Orchestra arr. & cond. by Billy May: Frank Beach,Conrad Gozzo,Mannie Klein,Vito "Mickey" Mangano(tp) Dick Noel,Tommy Pederson,William Schaefer,Si Zentner(tb) Harry Klee,Wilbur Schwartz,Ted Nash,Jules Jacob,Chuck Gentry(saxes) Paul Smith(p) Bobby Gibbons(g) Ralph Pena(b) Irving Cottler,Hugh Anderson(dm) Verlye Brilhart(harp).
(Capitol Studios) LA,November 7,1960

34870 On the sunny side of the street CD BN(J)CJ28-5021

GEORGE SHEARING:

Eddie Costa(vb) George Shearing(p) Dick Garcia(g) prob. George Duvivier(b) prob. Walter Bolden(dm).
NYC,January 7,1961

23455 Lullaby of Birdland CD BN 8-54363-2,(J)CJ28-5178,TOCJ-6152

STAN KENTON AND HIS ORCHESTRA:

Dalton Smith,Larry McGuire,Bob Rolfe,Sanford Skinner,Ernie Bernhardt(tp) Bob Fitzpatrick,Paul Heydorff (tb) Jim Amlotte,Dave Wheeler(bass tb) Dwight Carver,Gene Roland,Keith LaMotte,Gordon Davison (mell) Clive Acker(tu) Gabe Baltazar(as) Sam Donahue,Paul Renzi(ts) Marvin Holladay,Wayne Dunstan(bs) Stan Kenton(p,arr) Pete Chivily(b) Jerry Lestock McKenzie(dm).
(Goldwyn Sound Stage) LA,March 13,1961

35523 Say it isn't so CD BN 7-99095-2

STAN KENTON AND HIS ORCHESTRA:

Dalton Smith,Bud Brisbois, Conte Candoli,Larry McGuire,Bob Rolfe,Sanford Skinner,Ernie Bernhardt(tp) Bob Fitzpatrick,Paul Heydorff(tb) Jim Amlotte,Dave Wheeler(bass tb) Dwight Carver,Gene Roland,Joe Burnett,Gordon Davison(mellophonium) Clive Acker(tu) Gabe Baltazar(as) Sam Donahue,Paul Renzi(ts) Marvin Holladay(bs) Wayne Dunstan(bs,bass sax) Stan Kenton(p,arr) Pete Chivily(b) Jerry Lestock McKenzie(dm) Larry Bunker(tymp) George Acevedo(cga).
(Goldwyn Sound Stage) LA,March 15,1961

35529 Maria CD BN 8-29095-2

NAT KING COLE:

Nat "King" Cole(p,vo) John Collins(g) Charlie Harris(b).
NYC,March 23,1961

23565-12 (I love you) For sentimental reasons CD BN 5-24271-2
23566-10 Embraceable you CD BN 7-80506-2

DINAH SHORE:

Dinah Shore(vo) with Orchestra arr. & cond. by Jack Marshall: Shorty Sherock,Uan Rasey(tp) Lew McCreary,Ed Kusby,George Roberts(tb) Phil Stephens(tu) Abe Most,Babe Russin,Chuck Gentry(reeds) Milt Raskin(p) Bob Bain(g) Mike Rubin(b) Irv Cottler(dm).
(Capitol Studios) LA,May 24,1961

35961 Mississippi mud CD BN(Sp)8-56842-2

PEGGY LEE:
Peggy Lee(vo) with Benny Carter(as) Victor Feldman(p) Dennis Budimir(g) Max Bennett(b) Shelly Manne (dm) & strings arr. by Quincy Jones.
(Capitol Studios) LA,June 22,1961

36070 As time goes by CD BN(J)TOCJ-5853,TOCJ-6189,TOCJ-66071

Peggy Lee(vo) with Victor Feldman(vb) Dennis Budimir(g) Max Bennett(b) Shelly Manne(dm) & flutes, trombones,French horns,strings arr. by Quincy Jones.
(Capitol Studios) LA,June 23,1961

36093 Here's that rainy day CD BN(J)TOCJ-5855

Peggy Lee(vo) with Ted Nash,Justin Gordon(fl) Victor Feldman(vb) Dennis Budimir,Al Hendrickson(g) Max Bennett(b) Shelly Manne(dm) Mike Gutierrez,Melvin Zelnick(perc) Quincy Jones(arr).
(Capitol Studios) LA,June 24,1961

36096 Maybe it's because (I love you too much) CD BN 7-99095-2

NANCY WILSON & CANNONBALL ADDERLEY:
Nancy Wilson(vo) with Nat Adderley(c-1) Cannonball Adderley(as-1) Joe Zawinul(p) Sam Jones(b) Louis Hayes(dm).
(Capitol Studios) NYC,June 27,1961

23769 Save your love from me -1 CD BN 5-24271-2
23770 Happy talk -1 CD BN 8-29095-2
23772 The masquerade is over CD BN 7-96583-2,8-32994-2

CANNONBALL ADDERLEY:
Cannonball Adderley(as) Joe Zawinul(p) Sam Jones(b) Louis Hayes(dm).
(Capitol Studios) NYC,August 24,1961

23779 I can't get started CD BN(J)TOCJ-5638,TOCJ-6187

VIC DAMONE:
Vic Damone(vo) with Jack Marshall's Music (Orchestra arr. & cond. by Jack Marshall).
(Capitol Studios) LA,October 6,1961

36533 Let's face the music and dance CD BN(J)TOCJ-5296
36536 Deep night CD BN(J)TOCJ-6189

NAT KING COLE:
Nat "King" Cole(vo,org) with Orchestra arr. & cond. by Billy May: Reunald Jones,Conrad Gozzo,John Best,Uan Rasey(tp) Ed Kusby,Milt Bernhart,Lloyd Ulyate,William Schaefer(tb) Red Callender(tu) Willie Schwartz,Harry Klee(as) Plas Johnson, Buddy Collette(ts) Chuck Gentry(bs) Emil Richards(vbs,perc) Jimmy Rowles(p) John Collins(g) Charlie Harris(b)Lee Young(dm) & string section.
(Capitol Studios) LA,November 21,1961

36706-12 Let's face the music and dance CD BN(Sp)8-34712-2

GLORIA WOOD & PETE CANDOLI:
Gloria Wood(vo) & Pete Candoli,Uan Rasey,Frank Beach,Conrad Gozzo,Ray Triscari(tp) Joe Howard,Milt Bernhart,Dick Leith(tb) Justin Gordon,Ted Nash,Ronnie Lang,Frank Albright(saxes) Mike Melvoin(p) Bob Bain(g) Gary Peacock(b) Shelly Manne(dm) Larry Bunker(perc,vb,bell).
(Capitol Studios) LA,November 21,1961

36709 Hey,bellboy CD BN 7-80707-2

NAT KING COLE:
Nat "King" Cole(vo) with Billy May and his Orchestra: Reunald Jones,Conrad Gozzo,John Best,Vito "Mickey" Mangano(tp) Ed Kusby,Tommy Pederson,Tom Shepard,William Schaefer(tb) Red Callender(tu) Harry Klee(as) Plas Johnson,Buddy Collette,Ted Nash(ts) Chuck Gentry(bs) Jimmy Rowles(p) John Collins (g) Charlie Harris(b) Lee Young(dm) Emil Richards(vb,perc) Isadore Roman,David Frisina,Marshall Sosson, Gerald Vinci,Victor Arno,Emanuel Moss,Joseph Livoti,Rickey Marino,Jacques Gasselin(v) Alan Harshman, Alvin Dinkin,Virginia Majewski,Gareth Nuttycombe(viola) Joseph DiTullio,David Pratt,William Vandenburg,Hyman Gold(cello) Kathryn Julye(harp) Billy May(arr,cond).
(Capitol Studios) LA,November 22,1961

36737-5	Bidin' my time	CD BN 7-80706-2

KAY STARR:
Kay Starr(vo) with Ben Webster(ts) Gerald Wiggins(p) Al Hendrickson(g) Joe Comfort(b) Lee Young(dm).
(Capitol Studios) LA,December 1,1961

36801	It had to be you	CD BN(Sp)8-56842-2

STAN KENTON AND HIS ORCHESTRA:
Dalton Smith,Bob Behrendt,Marvin Stamm,Bob Rolfe,Norman Baltazar(tp) Bob Fitzpatrick, Dee Barton,Bud Parker(tb) Jim Amlotte(bass tb) Dave Wheeler(bass tb,tu) Ray Starling,Dwight Carver,Carl Saunders,Keith LaMotte(mellophonium) Gabe Baltazar(as) Buddy Arnold,Paul Renzi(ts) Allan Beutler(bs) Joel Kaye(bs,bass sax) Stan Kenton(p) Pat Senatore(b) Jerry Lestock McKenzie(dm).
(Capitol Studios) LA,December 7,1961

36832	Just in time	CD BN 8-33243-2

Same as above,with Gene Roland(mellophonium,ss,arr) added:
(Capitol Studios) LA,December 13,1961

36876	The blues story	CD BN 8-33243-2

NAT KING COLE & GEORGE SHEARING:
Nat "King" Cole(vo) with George Shearing(p) Emil Richards(vb) Al Hendrickson(g) Al McKibbon(b) Shelly Manne(dm) & strings arr. by Ralph Carmichael.
(Capitol Studios) NYC,December 20,1961

36944	Let there be love	CD BN 7-81331-2
Same.	(Capitol Studios)	NYC,December 21,1961
36953	Fly me to the moon	CD BN 7-89910-2,8-54365-2

LOU RAWLS & LES McCANN:
Lou Rawls(vo) with Les McCann(p) Leroy Vinnegar(b) Ron Jefferson(dm).
(Capitol Studios) LA,February 5,1962

37123	(They call it) Stormy Monday	BN B1-91441,CD 7-98306-2	
37123	(They call it) Stormy Monday (alt)		
37125	Sweet love	BN B1-91441	
37126	Lost and lookin'	-	
37127	God bless the child	-	CD 5-21153-2
37128	Willow weep for me	-	
37130	Blues is a woman		
37131	A little Les of Lou's blues		

All titles issued on CD BN 7-91441-2.

492

LOU RAWLS & LES McCANN:
Lou Rawls(vo) with Les McCann(p) Leroy Vinnegar(b) Ron Jefferson(dm).
(Capitol Studios) LA,February 12,1962

37142 I'd rather drink muddy water
37143 I'm gonna move to the outskirts of town
37148 See see rider
37181 In the evening when the sun goes down
37182 T'ain't nobody's business if I do

All titles issued on BN B1-91441,CD 7-91441-2.

PEGGY LEE:
Peggy Lee(vo) with Jack Sheldon(tp) Lou Levy(p) Herb Ellis,Al Hendrickson(g) Max Bennett(b) Mel Lewis (dm) Benny Carter(arr).
(Capitol Studios) LA,March 30,1962

37427 Whisper not CD BN(J)CJ28-5176

GEORGE SHEARING TRIO:
George Shearing(p) Israel Crosby(b) Vernel Fournier(dm)
(Capitol Studios) NYC,June 20,1962

24337 Like someone in love CD BN(J)TOCJ-5856

Same.
(Capitol Studios) NYC,June 21,1962

24339 What is this thing called love CD BN 7-81331-2,(J)TOCJ-6190

CANNONBALL ADDERLEY:
Nat Adderley(c) Cannonball Adderley(as) Yusef Lateef(fl,ts) Joe Zawinul(p) Sam Jones(b) Louis Hayes(dm).
(purchased from Riverside Records)
(International Jazz Festival) Comblain-La-Tour,Belgium,August 5,1962

Gemini CD BN 8-54898-2

LAURINDO ALMEIDA:
Don Fagerquist(tp) Justin Gordon(fl) Bob Cooper(ts) Jimmy Rowles(p,org) Laurindo Almeida,Howard Roberts,Al Viola(g) Max Bennett(b) Shelly Manne(dm) Milt Holland,Chico Guerrero(perc).
(Capitol Studios) LA.September 26,1962

38444 Moon river CD BN(J)TOCJ-5875

LOU RAWLS:
Lou Rawls(vo) with Orchestra arr. & cond. by Onzy Matthews; Bob Bryant,Bud Brisbois,Bob Rolfe,James Dalton Smith,Freddy Hill (tp) Horace Tapscott,Lou Blackburn,Richard Hyde,Ronald Smith(tb) Curtis Amy (ss,ts) Joe Maini(as) Clifford Solomon(ts) Clifford Scott,Jay Migliori(ts,fl) Sidney Miller(bs) ?Onzy Matthews (p) Richard "Groove" Holmes(org) Gene Edwards(g) Leroy Johnson(dm).
(Capitol Studios) LA,October 1,1962

38470 St. James Infirmary CD BN(C)4-94888-2

CANNONBALL ADDERLEY:
Cannonball Adderley(as) Sergio Mendes(p) Durual Ferreira(g) Octavio Bailly Jr.(b) Dom Um Romao(dm).
(purchased from Riverside Records)
(Plaza Sound Studios) NYC,December 7,1962

tk.7 Clouds CD BN(J)TOCJ-5638,TOCJ-5851

CANNONBALL ADDERLEY:
Cannonball Adderley(as) Sergio Mendes(p) Durual Ferreira(g) Octavio Bailly Jr.(b) Dom Um Romao(dm). with Pedro Paulo(tp-1) Paulo Moura(as-1).
(purchased from Riverside Records)
(Plaza Sound Studios) NYC,December 10,1962

tk.8 Corcovado CD BN(J)TOCJ-5638,TOCJ-5852
Sambop -1 CD BN 7-95590-2

GEORGE SHEARING:
Don Shelton,John Lowe,Bernie Fleisher,Bud Shank,Skeets Herfurt(woodwinds) Larry Bunker(vb) Clare Fischer(org,arr,cond) George Shearing(p) Laurindo Almeida(g) Ralph Pena(b) Bob Neel(dm) Chico Guerrero(perc).
(Capitol Studios) LA,December 17,1962

38806 Samba da borboleta CD BN(J)TOCJ-5852

PEGGY LEE:
Peggy Lee(vo) with Orchestra arr. & cond. by Dick Hazard: Mannie Klein(tp) Dave Wells(tb) Paul Horn (reeds) Mike Melvoin(p) John Pisano,Al Hendrickson(g) Max Bennett(b) Stan Levey (dm) Francisco Aguabella(perc).
(Capitol Studios) LA,January 5,1963

38931-12 Mack the knife CD BN(J)CJ28-5021

JUNE CHRISTY:
June Christy(vo) with Al Viola(g).
(Capitol Studios) LA,April 24,1963

39592 Misty CD BN(J)CJ28-5023

NANCY WILSON:
Nancy Wilson(vo) with Orchestra arr. & cond. by Jimmy Jones.
(Capitol Studios) NYC,June 11,1963

24664 Moon river CD BN 8-57748-2,(J)CJ28-5024

Nancy Wilson(vo) with orchestra arr. & cond. by Jimmy Jones.
(Capitol Studios) NYC,June 13,1963

24675 You'd be so nice to come home to CD BN(J)TOCJ-5203,TOCJ-6152

LOU RAWLS:
Lou Rawls(vo) with Orchestra arr & cond. by Onzy Matthews, incl. tps,tbs,saxes,Onzy Matthews(p) Ray Crawford(g) Jim Crutcher(b) Charles "Chiz" Harris(dm).
(Capitol Studios) LA,August 7,1963

50267 Stormy weather CD BN(C)4-94888-2

NANCY WILSON:
Nancy Wilson(vo) with Orchestra arr. & cond. by Gerald Wilson:Jack Wilson(p,celeste) Joe Pass(g) Jimmy Bond(b) Kenny Dennis(dm) & strings,incl. George Poole,Edgar Lustgarten(cello) & others,probably taken from the following: Felix Slatkin,Eleanor Slatkin, Gerald Vinci,Israel Baker,Jacques Gasselin,Thelma Breach,Bonnie Douglas,Marshall Sosson,Lou Raderman,Paul Shure,James Getzoff(v) Virginia Majewski, Paul Robyn,Alvin Dinkin,Stan Harris(viola) Ann Goodman(cello).
(Capitol Studios) LA,October 9,1963

50706 Someone to watch over me CD BN 7-80506-2

<u>BILLY TAYLOR</u>:
Billy Taylor(p) Ben Tucker(b) Grady Tate(dm) & unidentified big band arr. by Oliver Nelson.
(Capitol Studios) NYC,November 16,1963

24760 I wish I knew how it felt to be free CD BN 8-35472-2

<u>BLOSSOM DEARIE</u>:
Blossom Dearie(vo) with Jack Sheldon(tp) Joe Mondragon(b) Shelly Manne(dm) Jack Marshall(arr) & others unknown.
(Capitol Studios) LA,January 15,1964

51232 Corcovado (Quiet Nights) CD BN(J)TOCJ-5852

<u>NANCY WILSON</u>:
Nancy Wilson(vo) with Orchestra cond. by Kenny Dennis: Lou Levy(p) John Gray(g) Bill Plummer(b) Kenny Dennis(dm) Milt Holland(perc).
(Capitol Studios) LA,February 18,1964

51395 Wives and lovers CD BN 8-57749-2

<u>NAT KING COLE</u>:
Nat "King" Cole(vo) with Orchestra arr. & cond. by Ralph Carmichael,feat. Bobby Bryant(tp).
(Capitol Studios) LA,June 3,1964

52144-9 L-O-V-E CD BN(J)TOCJ-5856,TOCJ-6152

<u>BOBBY DARIN</u>:
Bobby Darin(vo) with Orchestra arr. & cond. by Richard Wess.
(Capitol Studios) LA,September 17,1964

52859-9 Hello Dolly CD BN 8-29095-2

<u>CANNONBALL ADDERLEY</u>:
Nat Adderley(c) Cannonball Adderley(as) Charles Lloyd(fl,ts) Joe Zawinul(p) Sam Jones(b) Louis Hayes (dm).
(Capitol Studios) NYC,October 19,1964

26047 Fiddler on the roof CD BN 8-29095-2

<u>PEGGY LEE</u>:
Peggy Lee(vo) with Orchestra arr. & cond. by Lou Levy,incl. Lou Levy(p) Bob Bain,John Pisano,Bill Pitman,Dennis Budimir(g) Bob Whitlock(b) John Guerin(dm) Francisco Aguabella(cga,bgo).
(Capitol Studios) LA,February 17,1965

53393 A hard day's night CD BN(J)TOCJ-5874

<u>NANCY WILSON</u>:
Nancy Wilson(vo) with Orchestra arr. & cond. by Sid Feller.
(Capitol Studios) LA,March 30,1965

53595 You've lost that loving feeling CD BN(Eu)4-93993-2
53596 Reach out for me -

CANNONBALL ADDERLEY:
Nat Adderley(c) Jimmy Maxwell,Jimmy Nottingham,Clark Terry,Snooky Young(tp) Jimmy Cleveland,Willie Dennis,J.J. Johnson(tb) Tony Studd(bass tb) Don Butterfield(tu) Cannonball Adderley(as) Phil Woods, Marshall Royal,Budd Johnson,Bob Ashton,Danny Bank(reeds) Joe Zawinul(p) Richard Davis(b) Grady Tate(dm) Oliver Nelson(arr,cond).
(Capitol Studios) NYC,April 26,1965

27089 Shake a lady BN B1-30725, CD 8-30725-2

WANDA DE SAH:
Wanda De Sah(vo) with Orchestra arr. by Jack Marshall.
(Capitol Studios) LA,April 26,1965

53653 Agua de Beber CD BN(J)CJ28-5177

NANCY WILSON:
Nancy Wilson(vo) with Orchestra arr. & cond. by Billy May: Uan Rasey,Al Porcino,Joe Graves,Jimmy Salko(tp) Lew McCreary,Dick Noel,Tommy Pederson,William Schaefer(tb) Vincent De Rosa,Arthur Frantz, Dick Perissi,James Decker(frh) Red Callender(tu) Ronnell Bright(p) John Collins(g) Buster Williams(b) Shelly Manne(dm).
(Capitol Studios) LA,January 26,1966

55582 Gee baby,ain't I good to you? CD BN 5-21151-2

LOU RAWLS:
Lou Rawls(vo) with Tommy Strode(p) Herb Ellis(g) Jimmy Bond(b) Earl Palmer(dm).
(Capitol Studios) LA,January 31,1966

55649 The girl from Ipanema CD BN(Eu)4-93995-2,4-97156-2

NANCY WILSON:
Nancy Wilson(vo) with Orchestra cond. by Oliver Nelson.
(Capitol Studios) LA,March 16,1966

55819 And I love him CD BN(J)TOCJ-5874

Nancy Wilson(vo) with Orchestra cond. by Oliver Nelson.
(Capitol Studios) LA,March 17,1966

55826 Call me CD BN(Eu)4-93993-2

Nancy Wilson(vo) with Orchestra cond. by Oliver Nelson.
(Capitol Studios) LA,March 18,1966

55836 Uptight CD BN(Eu)4-93993-2

Nancy Wilson(vo) with Orchestra cond. by Oliver Nelson.
(Capitol Studios) LA,March 22,1966

55863 The power of love CD BN(Eu)4-93993-2

BILLY PRESTON:
Billy Preston(org) & others unknown.
LA,March 30,1966

55879 Uptight BN B1-54357, CD 8-54357-2

LOU RAWLS:
Lou Rawls(vo) with Orchestra arr. & cond. by H. B. Barnum.
(Capitol Studios) LA,July 6,1966

56206 Love is a hurtin' thing CD BN(Eu)4-93995-2

NANCY WILSON:
Nancy Wilson(vo) with Orchestra arr. & cond. by Billy May: Ray Triscari,Don Fagerquist,John Audino, Anthony Terran(tp) Tommy Pederson,Lew McCreary,Vernon Friley,William Schaefer(tb) Willie Smith, Wilbur Schwartz(as) Harry Klee,Justin Gordon(ts) Chuck Gentry(bs) Ronnell Bright(p) Mike Melvoin(org) John Collins,Howard Roberts(g) Buster Williams,Chuck Berghofer(b) Earl Palmer(dm).
(Capitol Studios) LA,July 13,1966

56253 My babe CD BN(Eu)4-93993-2

Nancy Wilson(vo) with Orchestra arr. & cond. by Billy May: Ray Triscari,Don Fagerquist,John Audino,John Fowler(tp) Tommy Pederson,Lew McCreary,Vernon Friley,Joe Howard(tb) Willie Smith,Wilbur Schwartz (as) Harry Klee,Justin Gordon(ts) Chuck Gentry(bs) Ronnell Bright(p) Mike Melvoin(org) John Collins, Herb Ellis(g) Buster Williams,Chuck Berghofer(b) Earl Palmer(dm) Sid Feller(dir).
(Capitol Studios) LA,July 14,1966

56257 Ten years of tears CD BN(Eu)4-93993-2

PEGGY LEE:
Peggy Lee(vo) with Orchestra arr. by Dave Grusin.
(Capitol Studios) LA,July 18,1966

56272 Strangers in the night CD BN(J)CJ28-5024

CANNONBALL ADDERLEY:
Nat Adderley(c) Cannonball Adderley(as) Joe Zawinul(p) Victor Gaskin(b) Roy McCurdy(dm).
(Sankei Hall) Tokyo,August 26,1966

56955 Bohemia after dark CD BN 8-54898-2
56958 Jive samba CD BN(J)TOCJ-5638

CANNONBALL ADDERLEY:
Nat Adderley(c) Cannonball Adderley(as) Joe Zawinul(el p) Victor Gaskin(b) Roy McCurdy(dm).
(Capitol Studios) LA,October 20,1966

56778 Mercy,mercy,mercy BN B1-30725, CD 8-30725-2, 8-54898-2,
(J)TOCJ-5638,EMI-Jazz(E)4-93469-2
56779 Games BN B1-30725, CD 8-30725-2
56782 The sticks - -

LOU RAWLS:
Lou Rawls(vo) with Tommy Strode(p) Jimmy Bond(b) Earl Palmer(dm).
(Capitol Studios) LA,November 16,1966

56856 On Broadway CD BN(Eu)4-93995-2

LOU RAWLS:
Lou Rawls(vo) with large orchestra arr. & cond. by H.B. Barnum,incl. Freddy Hill,Tony Terran(tp) Teddy Edwards,Jim Horn(sax) Gerald Wiggins(p) Barney Kessel(g) Jimmy Bond(b) Earl Palmer(dm).
(Capitol Studios) LA,February 16,1967

57143 Dead end street CD BN(Eu)4-93995-2

NANCY WILSON:
Nancy Wilson(vo) with Orchestra arr. & cond. by Billy May: Pete Candoli,John Audino,Ray Triscari,Bub Brisbois(tp)Vernon Friley,Lew McCreary,Dick Noel,William Schaefer(tb) Skeets Herfurt,Ernest Green, Justin Gordon,Plas Johnson,Jack Nimitz(saxes) Don Trenner(p) Mike Melvoin(org) John Collins(g) Buster Williams(b) Earl Palmer(dm,Latin perc,bells).
(Capitol Studios) LA,February 20,1967

57163 Mercy,mercy,mercy CD BN (Eu)-93993-2
57165 Alfie CD BN 8-57749-2

CANNONBALL ADDERLEY:
Nat Adderley(c) Cannonball Adderley(as) Joe Zawinul(el p) Victor Gaskin(b) Roy McCurdy(dm).
(Capitol Studios) LA,March 6,1967

57231 Why am I treated so bad? BN B1-30725, CD 8-30725-2
57232 I'm on my way - -

BOBBIE GENTRY:
Bobbie Gentry(vo) with Orchestra arr. by Jimmie Haskell.
(Capitol Studios) LA,April 3,1967

57421 Mississippi delta BN B1-54357,CD 8-54357-2

LOU RAWLS:
Lou Rawls(vo) with Orchestra arr. & cond. by H. B. Barnum.
(Capitol Studios) LA,May 14,1967

57583 (How do I say) I don't love you anymore CD BN(Eu)4-93995-2

NANCY WILSON:
Nancy Wilson(vo) with Orchestra arr. & cond. by H.B. Barnum.
(Capitol Studios) LA,May 10,1967

57611 The end of our love CD BN(Eu)4-93993-2

NANCY WILSON:
Nancy Wilson(vo) with Orchestra arr. & cond. by Billy May: Phillip Teele(tb)Vincent De Rosa,Henry Sigismonti,Richard Mackey(frh) Ted Nash,Abe Most(cl,fl) Justin Gordon(cl,bass cl,fl,English horn) Bob Hardaway(cl,bassoon,English horn,fl) Don Trenner(p) John Collins(g) Buster Williams(b) Shelly Manne (dm) Larry Bunker(perc,tympani,mallets) Ann Stockton(harp) & strings: Erno Neufeld,Harry Bluestone,Dan Lube,Gerald Vinci,Victor Arno,Jacques Gasselin,Marshall Sosson,Louis Kaufman,Anatol Kaminsky,James Getzoff,Mischa Russell,Edward Bergman(v) Raphael Kramer,Justin Di Tullio,Frederick Seykora,Nathan Gershman (cello).
(Capitol Studios) LA,May 13,1967

57619-10 Lush life CD BN 8-55221-2,(E)8-53232-2

Nancy Wilson(vo) with Orchestra arr. & cond. by Billy May: Phillip Teele(tb)Vincent De Rosa,Henry Sigismonti,William Alfred Hinshaw(frh) Harry Klee(fl,bass fl,cl) Abe Most(fl,alto fl,bass fl,cl) Justin Gordon(fl,cl,bass cl) Bob Hardaway(alto fl,cl,oboe) Don Trenner(p) John Collins(g) Buster Williams(b) Shelly Manne(dm) Larry Bunker(perc,mallets,tympani) Catherine Gotthoffer(harp) & strings: Erno Neufeld, Carl LaMagna,Harry Bluestone,Gerald Vinci,Victor Arno,Jacques Gasselin,Marshall Sosson,Alfred Lustgarten,Nathan Kaproff,John De Voogt,Mischa Russell,Edward Bergman(v) Raphael Kramer,Justin Di Tullio,Frederick Seykora,Armand Kaproff(cello).
(Capitol Studios) LA,May 16,1967

57625-6 Sunny CD BN(Eu)4-93993-2

LOU RAWLS:
Lou Rawls(vo) with Orchestra arr. & cond. by H. B. Barnum.
(Capitol Studios) LA,May 25,1967

57696	They don't give medals (to yesterday's hereos)	CD BN 8-57749-2
57701	When love goes wrong	CD BN(Eu)4-93995-2

CANNONBALL ADDERLEY:
Nat Adderley(c) Cannonball Adderley(as) Joe Zawinul(el p) Victor Gaskin(b) Roy McCurdy(dm).
(Capitol Studios) LA,June 12,1967

57804	Do do do (what is next)	BN B1-37025,CD 8-30725-2

HOWARD ROBERTS:
Victor Feldman(el p) Dave Grusin(org) Howard Roberts(g) Chuck Berghofer(b) John Guerin(dm) unknown(perc).
(Capitol Studios) LA,September 22,1967

58357	Walk tall	BN B1-97158,CD 4-97158-2

STAN KENTON AND HIS ORCHESTRA:
Dalton Smith,Clyde Reasinger,Jay Daversa,Carl Leach,Jack Laubach(tp) Dick Shearer,Tom Whittaker,Tom Senff(tb) Jim Amlotte(bass tb) Graham Ellis(bass tb,tu) Ray Reed(as) Alan Rowe,Bob Dahl(ts) John Mitchell (bs) Bill Fritz(bs,bass sax) Stan Kenton(p,arr) Don Bagley(b) Dee Barton(dm).
(Capitol Studios) LA,October 3,1967

58394	Gloomy Sunday	CD BN 8-33243-2

LOU RAWLS:
Lou Rawls(vo) with unidentified Orchestra.
(Capitol Studios) LA,October 24,1967

58505	For what it's worth	BN B1-54357,CD 8-54357-2, (Eu)4-93995-2
58507	The letter	-

NANCY WILSON:
Nancy Wilson(vo) with Orchestra arr. & cond. by Oliver Nelson: Eddie "Lockjaw" Davis(ts) Ralph Sharon (p) John Collins,Charles Wright(g) Buster Williams(b) Shelly Manne(dm) Victor Feldman(vb, tympany) Lou Raderman,Erno Neufeld,Marshall Sosson,Louis Kaufman,Harry Bluestone,Myron Sandler,Nathan Kaproff, Anatol Kaminsky,Sidney Sharp(v) Alvin Dinkin,Alan Harshman,Virginia Majewski(viola) Raphael Kramer, Ann Goodman,Frederick Seykora,Igor Roroshevsky(cello) Ann Stockton(harp).
(Capitol Studios) LA,November 3,1967

58590-6	Ode to Billy Joe	BN B1-54357,CD 8-54357-2,(Eu) 4-93993-2
58591-2	For once in my life	-

ELLA FITZGERALD:
Ella Fitzgerald with Orchestra arr. & cond. by Sid Feller.
(Capitol Studios) LA,December 21,1967

58937	Born to lose	CD BN(Sp)8-53016-2
58939	Misty blue	CD BN 5-21151-2

499

JIMMY CARAVAN TRIO:
Details unknown.
(from Tower label)(purchased) c.1968

61888 Look into the flower BN B1-54357,CD 8-54357-2

BENNY GORDON:
Details unknown.
(from Hot Biscuit label) LA?,March 21,1968

59560 Tighten up BN B1-54357,CD 8-54357-2

LOU RAWLS:
Lou Rawls(vo) with Orchestra arr. & cond. by H. B. Barnum.
(Capitol Studios) LA,March 25,1968

59431 You're good for me CD BN(Eu)4-93995-2
59432 Soul serenade -

NANCY WILSON:
Nancy Wilson(vo) with Orchestra cond. by Jimmy Jones.
(Capitol Studios) LA,April 1,1968

59414 The look of love CD BN(Eu)4-93993-2

BILLY TAYLOR:
Billy Taylor(p) Ben Tucker(b) Grady Tate(dm).
(from Tower label) NYC,April 13,1968

62067 I wish I knew how it felt to be free CD BN 8-57748-2

LOU RAWLS:
Lou Rawls(vo) with Orchestra arr. & cond. by H. B. Barnum.
(Capitol Studios) LA,April 30,1968

59668 Down here on the ground CD BN(Eu)4-93995-2

Lou Rawls(vo) with Orchestra arr. & cond. by H. B. Barnum.
(Capitol Studios) LA,May 2,1968

59691 One for my baby CD BN(Eu)4-93995-2

JACKIE AND ROY:
Ray de Sito(tb) George Young,Artie Shroeck(saxes) Roy Kral(el p,vo) Stuart Scharf(g) Andy Musin(el b) Jim Molinor(dm) Jackie Cain(vo).
NYC,May 8,1968

26896 Lady Madonna CD BN(J)TOCJ-5874

ARTIE SHAW:
Bernie Privin,Mel Davis(tp) Buddy Morrow(tb) Walt Levinsky(cl) Toots Mondello(as) Al Klink,Billy Slapin (ts) Bernie Leighton(p) Don Lamond(dm) Artie Shaw(cond) & others unknown.
NYC,May 17,1968

26898 Begin the beguine CD BN (J)TOCJ-5203

ELLA FITZGERALD:
Ella Fitzgerald(vo) with Harry "Sweets" Edison(tp) Benny Carter(as,arr) George Auld(ts) Jimmy Jones(p) Bob West(b) Panama Francis(dm).
(Capitol Studios) LA,May 28,1968

59799 Medley: CD BN(C)4-94888-2,(Sp)8-56842-2
On Green Dolphin Street/How am I to know/
Just friends/I cried for you/Seems like
old times/You stepped out of a dream

DAVID AXELROD:
Orchestra arr. & cond. by David Alexrod.
(Capitol Studios) LA,June 4,1968

59898 Holy Thursday BN B1-94027,CD 4-94027-2

CANNONBALL ADDERLEY:
Nat Adderley(c) Freddy Hill,Jack Laubach,Ollie Mitchell,Anthony Terran(tp) Bob Pring,Dick Leith(tb) Vincent DeRosa(frh) Cannonball Adderley(as) Jackie Kelso,Jules Jacob, Buddy Collette,Plas Johnson,Jim Horn(reeds) Gene Estes(vbs,tymp) Don Randi(p) Howard Roberts(g) Ray Brown(b,tamb) Earl Palmer (dm,perc) Joe Clayton,Frank Guerrero(perc) H.B. Barnum(arr,cond) & unknown vocal chorus.
(Capitol Studios) LA,June 13,1968

59919 Up and at it BN B1-30725, CD 8-30725-2

Same.
(Capitol Studios) LA,June 14,1968

70010 Marabi CD BN 4-94031-2

PATTI DREW:
Patti Drew(vo) with unknown accompaniment.
(purchased master) Chicago?, 1968

71293 Fever BN B1-97158,CD 4-97158-2

LOU RAWLS:
Lou Rawls(vo) with Orchestra arr. & cond. by Benny Golson: Harry "Sweets" Edison,Freddy Hill(tp,flh) Dick Leith(tb) Jim Horn(as,fl,bass cl) Bill Green(as,ts,fl) Plas Johnson(ts,fl,alto fl) Gildo Mahones(p,org) Howard Roberts,Walter Namuth(g) Robert Haynes(b,el b) Melvin Lee(dm) Joe Clayton(cga,perc) Dale Anderson(vb,marimba).
(Capitol Studios) LA,November 26,1968

71540 Just squeeze me CD BN 4-94035-2

LOU RAWLS:
Lou Rawls(vo) with Orchestra arr. & cond. by Phil Wright.
(Capitol Studios) LA,February 25,1969

71907 Season of the witch BN 5-21147-1,CD 5-21147-2,(Eu)4-93995-2

NANCY WILSON:
Nancy Wilson(vo) with unidentified orchestra.
(Capitol Studios) LA,March 28,1969

72144 Son of a preacher man CD BN(Eu)4-93993-2

LOU RAWLS:
Lou Rawls(vo) with Orchestra arr. & cond. by Phil Wright.
(Capitol Studios) LA,May 29,1969

72278 Your good thing (is about to end) CD BN(Eu)4-93995-2

MEL TORME:
Mel Torme(vo) with Orchestra arr. & cond. by Jimmy Jones.
(Capitol Studios) LA,June 2,1969

72545 Midnight swinger CD BN 5-21153-2

MEL TORME:
Mel Torme(vo) with Orchestra arr. & cond. by by Jimmy Jones.
(Capitol Studios) LA,June 3,1969

72548 A time for us CD BN(J)TOCJ-5875
72551 She's leaving home CD BN(J)TOCJ-5874

THE FOURTH WAY:
Michael White(v) Mike Nock(p,el p) Ron McClure(b) Eddie Marshall(dm).
(Capitol Studios) LA,July 22,1969

72679 Everyman's your brother BN B1-94027

THE FAME GANG:
Details unknown.
(Fame label) (Fame Studios) Muscle Shoals,Alabama,c.mid 1969

72741 Grits and gravy BN B1-54357,CD 8-54357-2

THE SONS OF CHAMPLIN:
Details unknown.
LA,July 28,1969

72851 Boomp,boomp,chomp BN B1-94027,CD 4-94027-2

NANCY WILSON:
Nancy Wilson(vo) with Orchestra arr. & cond. by Phil Wright.
(Capitol Studios) LA,August 27,1969

73073 Spinning wheel
73074 Willie & Laura Mae Jones BN B1-54357,CD 8-54357-2
73077 You're all I need to get by

All titles issued on CD BN(Eu)4-93993-2

LOU RAWLS:
Lou Rawls(vo) with Orchestra arr. & cond. by Phil Wright.
(Capitol Studios) LA,August 29,1969

73105 Give me your love CD BN(Eu)4-93995-2

LOU RAWLS:
Lou Rawls(vo) with Orchestra arr. & cond. by Dave Axelrod.
(Capitol Studios) LA,August 30,1969

73107 I can't make it alone CD BN(Eu)4-93995-2

CANNONBALL ADDERLEY:
Nat Adderley(c) Cannonball Adderley(as) Joe Zawinul(el p) Walter Booker(b) Roy McCurdy(dm).
(Live in a Church) Chicago,prob.October 17,1969

73306 Hummin' BN B1-30725

Same.
(Live in a Church) Chicago,October 18,1969

73813 Walk tall BN B1-30725,B1-54360
CD BN 8-30725-2,8-54360-2

NANCY WILSON:
Nancy Wilson(vo) with Hank Jones(p) Gene Bertoncini(g) Ron Carter(b) Grady Tate(dm).
(Capitol Studios) NYC,November 4,1969

73355 Prelude to a kiss CD BN 8-55221-2,(J)CJ28-5023,TOCJ-5856

Same.
(Capitol Studios) NYC,November 5,1969

73360 But beautiful CD BN(J)CJ28-5179

Same.
(Capitol Studios) NYC,November 6,1969

73363 In a sentimental mood CD BN(J)TOCJ-6189
73366 Do it again CD BN 7-80706-2

PATTI DREW:
Patti Drew(vo) with unknown accompaniment.
Chicago?,c.1969

73592 Beggar for the blues BN B1-35607,CD 8-35607-2

LOU RAWLS:
Lou Rawls(vo) with Orchestra arr. & cond. by H.B. Barnum.
(Capitol Studios) LA,December 15,1969

73729 Mama told me not to come
73730 You've made me so very happy BN B1-54360,CD 8-54360-2

Both titles issued on CD BN(Eu)4-93995-2.

LOU RAWLS:
Lou Rawls(vo) with Orchestra arr. & cond. by H.B. Barnum.
(Capitol Studios) LA,December 16,1969

73742 Feelin' Alright CD BN(Eu)4-93995-2

PAUL NERO:
details unknown.
c.1970

This is soul BN B1-94027,CD 4-94027-2

DAVID AXELROD:
Incl. tps,tbs,reeds,vb,p,b,dm & vocal chorus. LA,February 6,1970

73963 The signs,pt.1 BN 5-21147-1,CD 5-21147-2

NANCY WILSON:
Nancy Wilson(vo) with Orchestra arr. & cond. by Bobby Martin.
(Capitol Studios) LA,August 25,1970

75363 The real me CD BN(Sp)8-56842-2

NANCY WILSON:
Nancy Wilson(vo) with unidentified orchestra.
(Capitol Studios) LA,August 26,1970

75366 The long and winding road CD BN(Eu)4-93993-2

JIMMY McGRIFF:
Larry Frazier(g) Jimmy McGriff(org) & unknown horns,el b,dm,cga.
(purchased masters) NYC,November 2,1970

27435 Fat cakes BN(E)8-30724-1,CD BN 8-57063-2,(E)8-30724-2
27528 Ain't it funky now - - -

BEN SIDRAN:
Ben Sidran(el p,vo) Curley Cooke(g) John Pisano(rhythm g) Willie Ruff(b) Judy Sidran(vo).
LA,May 12,1971

76789 About love BN B1-29865,CD 8-29865-2

CANNONBALL ADDERLEY:
Nat Adderley(c) Cannonball Adderley(as-1) Ernie Watts(ts) George Duke(el p) Mike Deasy(g) Walter Booker (el b) Roy McCurdy(dm) Rick Holmes(narr).
LA,January 14,1972

77981 Aries-1 BN B1-30725, CD 8-30725-2
77983 Capricorn BN B1-94027
77992 Taurus BN B1-30725, CD 8-30725-2

BILLY MAY AND HIS ORCHESTRA:
John Audino,John Best,Pete Candoli,Uan Rasey,George Werth(tp) Joe Howard,Lloyd Ulyate,Lew McCreary,Dick Nash(tb) Les Robinson,Wilbur Schwartz(as)Justin Gordon,Don Raffell(ts) Chuck Gentry (bs) Ray Sherman(p) Bob Bain(g) Morty Corb(b) Nick Fatool(dm) Bob Grabeau,Eileen Wilson(vo) Sue Allen,Bernie Parke,Jerry Whitman,Allan Davies,William Brown(vocal group) Billy May(cond) Bill Finegan (arr).
(Capitol Studios) LA,January 31,1972

78044 Rhapsody in blue CD BN 7-80706-2

PEGGY LEE:
Peggy Lee(vo) with Victor Feldman(vb) Artie Butler(p,arr) Louis Shelton(g) Reinhold Preiss(b) Earl Palmer(dm).
(Capitol Studios) LA,April 27,1972

78552 Just for a thrill CD BN(C) 4-94888-2

BILLY MAY:
Studio Orchestra,arr. & cond. by Billy May.
(Capitol Studios) LA,July 17,1972

78851 Mission impossible CD BN 8-57748-2

CANNONBALL ADDERLEY:
Nat Adderley(c) Cannonball Adderley(as) George Duke(el p) Walter Booker(b) Roy McCurdy(dm) Airto Moreira(vo,perc) Mayuto,Octavio(perc) Flora Purim,Olga James(backgr. vo).
(Live) LA,July 31,1972

78960 The happy people BN B1-30725, CD 8-30725-2
78962 Ela -

NAT ADDERLEY:
Nat Adderley(c) Cannonball Adderley(as) George Duke(p,el p) Walter Booker(b) Roy McCurdy(dm) Airto Moreira(perc) Stephanie Spruill(vcl).
LA,October 14,1972

79238 Space Spiritual BN B1-35607,CD 8-35607-2

SUPERSAX:
Conte Candoli(tp) Med Flory,Joe Lopes(as) Warne Marsh,Jay Migliori(ts) Jack Nimitz(bs) Ronnell Bright(p) Buddy Clark(b) Jake Hanna(dm).
(Capitol Studios) LA,January 12,1973

79617 Star eyes CD BN (J)TOCJ-5858

BOB DOROUGH:
Bob Dorough(vo) & others unknown.
NYC,February ,1973

79891 Three is the magic number BN B1-94027,CD 4-94027-2

BARRETT STRONG:
Barrett Strong(vo) with ?
(purchased master)(Crystal Sound Studios) LA,February ,1973

91868 Is it true? BN 5-21147-1,CD 5-21147-2

MARGO THUNDER:
Margo Thunder(vo) with unknown accompaniment.
(from Haven label) LA?,March ,1974

91171 Expressway to your heart BN B1-35607,CD 8-35607-2,4-97222-2

NANCY WILSON:
Nancy Wilson(vo) with unidentified orchestra.
(Sound Factory) LA,July 2,1974

91458 My love CD BN(Eu)4-93993-2

SUPERSAX:
Conte Candoli(tp) Frank Rosolino(tb) Med Flory,Joe Lopes(as) Warne Marsh,Jay Migliori(ts) Jack Nimitz (bs) Lou Levy(p) Buddy Clark(b) Jake Hanna(dm) Roger Kellaway(string arr).
(Capitol Studios) LA,October 14,1974

91697 Cool blues CD BN(J)TOCJ-5298

Same.
(Capitol Studios) LA,November 1,1974

91716 I didn't know what time it was CD BN(J)TOCJ-5857

NANCY WILSON:
Nancy Wilson(vo) with Orchestra arr. & cond. by Gene Page.
LA,February 12,1975

91889 Come get to this CD BN(Eu)4-93993-2

THE REFLECTIONS:
Details unknown.

LA,July 16,1975

92432 She's my Summer breeze BN B1-29865,CD 8-29865-2

DAVE GRUSIN:
Music comp. and cond. by Dave Grusin.
(purchased master) 1975

92560 Condor! (Theme from "3 days from the condor")
BN 5-21147-1

HENRY COLE:
Details unknown.

prob. mid '70s

Shake a lady BN B1-97158,CD 4-97158-2

WILLARD BURTON:
Details unknown.

prob. mid '70s

Funky in here BN B1-97158,CD 4-97158-2

JIMMY CASTOR:
Jimmy Castor(ts,vo) & others unknown.

prob. mid '70s

Psycho man BN B1-97158

100% PURE POISON:
details unknown.

mid '70s

Windy C BN B1-35607,CD 8-35607-2

Note: This may have appeared on a subsidiary label.

STRATAVARIOUS:
Guido Basso(tp) & others unknown.

mid '70s

Nightfall BN B1-35607,CD 8-35607-2

HARLEM RIVER DRIVE:
Details unknown. mid '70s

Idle hands BN B1-35607

BANBARA:
Details unknown. c.1975

Shack Up,pts 1 & 2 BN B1-94027, CD 4-94027-2

WILLIE HOBO:

LA,February 6,1976

93006 Funky sneakers BN B1-97158,CD 4-97158-2

FRANKIE BEVERLY AND MAZE:
Details unknown.

November 23,1976

93626 While I'm alone BN B1-29865,CD 8-29865-2

RANCE ALLEN GROUP:
Rance Allen(vo) & others unknown.

LA,December 23,1976

93689 Truth is marching on CD BN(Eu)4-93994-2

Similar. LA,January 22,1977

93806 Peace of mind BN B1-29865,CD 8-29865-2,(Eu)4-93994-2

GARY BARTZ:
Gary Bartz(as,vo) Larry Mizell(keyb,vo) David T.Walker,Wah Wah Watson,John Rowin,Juewett Bostwick (g) Curtis Robinson Jr. or Welton Gite(b) Nat Neblet,James Gadson or Howard King(dm) Mtume(cga) Bill Summers(perc) Syreeta Wright,Sigidi(vo).

LA March 25,1977

93893 Carnaval de l'esprit (Carnival de l'esprit) BN B1-35607,CD 8-35607-2

Similar. LA,March ,1977

93910 Music is my sanctuary BN B1-29865,CD 8-29865-2,5-23559-2,
(Eu)4-93994-2

BOBBY LYLE:
Bobby Lyle(el p) Bill Rogers,Roland Bautista(g) Donnie Beck(b) Steve Guttierez(dm) Babatunde(cga).

LA,April 7,1977

93939 The genie BN B1-29865, CD 8-29865-2
93941 Pisces CD BN 7-89284-2

Oscar Brashear(tp) Ernie Watts(ts) Bobby Lyle(el p,synth) Roland Bautista(g) Donnie Beck (b) Steve Guttierez(dm).

Same date.

93944 Night breeze
93945 Mother Nile
93946 I didn't know what time it was (solo p)

All titles issued on CD BN 7-89284-2.

CALDERA:
Steve Tavaglione(fl,alto fl,ss,as,ts) Eduardo del Barrio(p,el p,synth) Larry Dunn(synth) Jorge Strunz(g) Dean Cortez(el b) Mike 'Baiano' Azevedo(cga,perc) Hector Andrade(timbales,cga,perc) Dianne Reeves(vo).

LA,April 1,1977

94168 Sky islands BN B1-29865, CD 8-29865-2
94169 Ancient source CD BN 8-36545-2

NATALIE COLE:
Natalie Cole(vo) with unknown accompaniment.

LA,August 30,1977

94403 La costa BN B1-35607,CD 8-35607-2
94407 Annie Mae BN B1-29865,CD 8-29865-2

A TASTE OF HONEY:
A Taste Of Honey(vo) & others unknown.

LA October 26,1977

94605 Boogie oogie oogie CD BN(Eu)4-93994-2

RAUL DE SOUZA:
Raul De Souza(tb) George Duke (as "Dawilli Gonga")(p,synth,arr) Roland Bautista,Charles Icarus Johnson (g) Byron Miller(el b) Leon Ngudu Chancler(dm).
(Paramount Studios) LA,December 27,1977

94748 Daisy Mae BN 5-21147-1,CD 5-21147-2

BOBBY LYLE:
Bobby Lyle(org,el p,p) Nathaniel Phillips(b) Harvey Mason(dm) Joe Blocker(synth dm) Sunship,Paulinho Da Costa(perc).

LA,June 29,1978

95101 New warrior BN 5-21147-1
95108 Star traveler
95109 What is this thing called love (solo p)

All titles issued on CD BN 7-89284-2.

EDDIE HENDERSON:
Eddie Henderson(tp) Julian Priester(tb) Hubert Laws(fl) Bennie Maupin(ts) Herbie Hancock(el p,synth) Ray Obiedo(g) Paul Jackson(el b) Howard King(dm) Bill Summers(cga) John Bowen(string synth).
(Wally Heider Studios) SF,June 29,1978

95178 Butterfly BN 5-21147-1,CD 5-21147-2

A TASTE OF HONEY:
A Taste Of Honey(vo) & others unknown.

LA,February 9,1979

95771 I love you BN B1-29865,CD 8-29865-2

NANCY WILSON:
Nancy Wilson(vo) with Orchestra arr. & cond. by Larry Farrow.

LA,March 7,1979

95831 Sunshine BN B1-29865,CD 8-29865-2

MINNIE RIPPERTON:
Minnie Ripperton(vo) with unknown accompaniment.

LA,May 21,1979

96137 Inside your love BN B1-35607,CD 8-35607-2
96238 Here we go BN B1-94027

BOBBY LYLE:
Bobby Lyle(p,el p,org) John Shykun(synth prog) Michael McGloiry,L.Mario Henderson(g) Nathaniel Watts (b) Kenneth Rice(dm) Bobbye Hall(perc).
(Crystal Sound) LA,June 11,1979

96048-4 For love
96049-2 Blues for Scott Joplin (solo p)

Both titles issued on CD BN 7-89284-2.

"HEART BEAT" (soundtrack):
Feat. Art Pepper(as) & others unknown.Jack Nitzsche(comp,arr)
LA,January ,1980

96472 On the road CD BN 8-33244-2

NATALIE COLE:
Natalie Cole(vo) with ?
LA,,February 29,1980

96733 Stairway to the stars CD BN(Sp)8-56842-2

GENE DUNLAP:
Gene Dunlap(dm) Gloria Ridgeway(vo) Esther Ridgeway,Gracie Ridgeway(backgr.vo),others unknown.
? Detroit,March 4 1980

97171 Before you break my heart BN B1-35607,CD 8-35607-2

MAZE:

LA?,April 3,1980

97019 Roots BN 5-21147-1,CD 5-21147-2

SHEREE BROWN:
Sheree Brown(vo) with unknown accompaniment.
LA?,December 17,1980

97344 It's a pleasure BN B1-35607,CD 8-35607-2

EARL KLUGH:
Greg Phillinganes(keyb,synth) Earl Klugh(g,keyb) Paul Jackson Jr.(el g) Charles Meeks-1,Louis Johnson-2 (el b) Raymond Pounds(dm) Paulinho Da Costa(perc) Frank Floyd,Merle Miller,Dana Kral(backgr.vo-4) Clare Fischer(orchestration-3)
(A & M Studios) LA,January-February,1982
Horns arranged by Dave Matthews overdubbed on.
(Media Sound Studios) NYC,May,1982.

98736 Back in Central Park-1,4 CD BN 7-80505-2
98742 Christina-1,3 CD BN 7-46625-2
98743 Night drive-2 CD BN 7-80505-2

EARL KLUGH & BOB JAMES:
Bob James(keyb) Earl Klugh(g) Gary King(el b) Harvey Mason(dm) Dr.Gibbs,Sammy Figueroa(perc).
(Minor Studios) White Plains,N.Y.,February ,1982

98501 Whiplash CD BN 8-33878-2

EARL KLUGH:
Barry Eastmond(keyb) Earl Klugh(g) Carlos Rios-1,Joe Beck-2(el g) Luico Hopper(el b) Ted Thomas Jr. (dm) Sammy Figueroa(perc)
(Media Sound Studio) NYC,October 13,1983

99109 Tropical Legs-1 CD BN 7-46625-2,8-34957-2,(J)TOCJ-5602
99110 Wishful thinking-2 - (J)TOCJ-5602

Brian Blake(dm) replaces Thomas Jr.Dave Matthews(orchestration).
(Media Sound Studios) NYC,October 20,1983

99113 Right from the start CD BN 7-80505-2

509

EARL KLUGH:
Earl Klugh(g) Dave Matthews(orchestration).
(Media Sound Studios) NYC,October 24,1983

99116 A natural thing CD BN 7-80505-2

EARL KLUGH:
Barry Eastmond(p) Earl Klugh(g) Ron Carter(b) Grady Tate(dm).
(Media Sound Studios) NYC,January 23,1984

99271 The shadow of your smile CD BN 7-96581-2,5-24271-2,(J)TOCJ-6187

Note: Original Capitol album erroneously lists Sammy Figueroa(perc) present on this track.

EARL KLUGH:
Toots Thielemans(hca) Barry Eastmond(keyb) Earl Klugh(g) Joe Beck(el g) Luico Hopper(el b) Brian Blake (dm) Sammy Figueroa(perc) Dave Matthews(orchestration)
(Media Sound Studios) NYC,January 25,1984

99268 Night song CD BN 8-53354-2

MAZE:

LA,April 10,1985

99818 Twilight BN 5-21147-1,CD 5-21147-2

FREDDIE JACKSON:
Freddie Jackson(vo) with Najee(sax) & others unknown.
LA,May 26,1986

100487 Have you ever loved somebody CD BN 8-23735-2

NORMAN CONNORS:
Freddie Hubbard(tp) Norman Connors(dm) & others unknown.
LA,September 14,1987

100941 Samba for Maria BN B1-54357,CD 8-54357-2

DAVE KOZ:
Dave Koz(as) & others unknown.
LA,April 30,1990

102412 Endless Summer nights CD BN(J)TOCJ-5852

BEASTIE BOYS:
Mark Ramos Nishita(keyb) Adrock(g) MCA(b) Mike D(dm) Juanito Vazquez(cga,cuica)Beastie Boys(vo).
(G Son Studios) Atwater,Calif., 1992

103211 Groove Holmes CD BN 8-27533-2

MELLOW MAN ICE:
Mellow Man Ice(vo) Senen Reyes(backgr. vo)
(Digital Sound & Picture Studios) LA,January 6,1992

103243 Babalu bad boy CD BN(J)TOCP-65100

510

RACHELLE FERRELL:
Rachelle Ferrell(p,vo) Will Downing(vo) Barry Eastmond(keyb) Kevin Eubanks,Mike Campbell(g) Anthony Jackson(el b) Buddy Williams(dm) Steve Thornton(perc)
(Skyline & East Bay Studios) NYC,March 10,1992

103375 Nothing has ever felt like this CD BN(C)4-94888-2

RACHELLE FERRELL:
Rachelle Ferrell(p,vo).
(Le Gonks West) LA,March 16,1992

103380 Peace on earth CD BN 7-99918-2,8-56991-2

RACHELLE FERRELL:
George Duke,Brian Simpson(keyb) Paul Jackson Jr.(g) Larry Kimpel(b) Ricky Lawson(dm) Lori Perry,Jim Gilstrap,Lynn Fiddmont-Lindsay(backgr.vo) Rachelle Ferrell(vo).
(Le Gonks West) LA,March 18,1992

103373 'Til you come back to me CD BN 8-57463-2

DAVE KOZ:
Dave Koz(as) & others unknown.
LA, c.1992

103924 Piece of my wish CD BN(J)TOCJ-6153

SPEARHEAD:
details unknown.
early-mid '90s

104276 Positive CD BN(J)TOCP-8966

THE PHARCYDE:
details unknown.
early-mid '90s

Runnin' (Jay Dee redio mix) CD BN (J)TOCP-8966

CHANNEL LIVE:
Salaam Remi(arr,mixer).
(The Crib Recording/Palm Tree Studios) LA, 1995

104508 Homicide ride CD BN(J)TOCP-65100

ACEYALONE:

(Kitchen Sync Studios/Hollywood Sound Recorders)
LA, 1995

Deep and wide CD BN(J)TOCP-65100

CHRYSALIS

GURU:
details unknown. c. early '90s

Loungin' CD BN 8-27533-2

GANG STARR:
details unknown. c. early '90s

Jazz music CD BN 8-27533-2

GURU'S JAZZAMATAZZ:
details unknown. c. early '90s

Down the backstreets CD BN(J)TOCP-8966

THE SOLSONICS:
details unknown. c. early-mid '90s

Jazz in the present tense CD BN(J)TOCP-8966

GANG STARR:
DJ Premier & The Guru(mixers)
(D & D Studio) NYC, 1992

24-7/365 CD BN(J)TOCP-65100

GURU & MC SOLAAR:
Guru(mixer) & MC Solaar(rapper)
(Studio Ferber) Paris, 1993

Le bien,le mal CD BN(J)TOCP-65100

GANG STARR:
DJ Premier & The Guru(mixers)
(D & D Studio) NYC, 1994

Code on the streets CD BN(J)TOCP-65100

GURU & CHAKA KHAN:
Guru(rapper) Chaka Khan(vo,backgr.vo) Carl Chucky Thompson(remixer).
NYC, 1995

Watch what you say (Chucky remix) CD BN(J)TOCP-65100

COLPIX

NINA SIMONE:
Nina Simone(p,vo) Jimmy Bond(b) Al "Tootie" Heath(dm).
(Town Hall) NYC,September 12,1959

Summertime CD BN 7-80506-2
Wild is the wind CD BN(E)8-53232-2,(Sp)8-56842-2

NINA SIMONE:
Nina Simone(p,vo) Al Schackman(g) Chris White(b) Bobby Hamilton(dm).
(Newport Jazz Featival) Newport,Rhode Island,June 30,1960

(I loves you) Porgy CD BN 8-32994-2,(C)4-94888-2

Nina Simone(p,vo) Al Schackman(g) Chris White(b) Bobby Hamilton(dm).
NYC, 1961

Work song CD BN(Sp)8-53016-2

Same. (Village Gate) NYC, 1961

Children,go where I send Thee CD BN 5-21151-2,(C) 4-94888-2

Nina Simone(p,vo) Malcolm Dodd Singers(backgr.vo) & others unknown.
NYC, 1962

It don't mean a thing CD BN 4-94035-2

RANDY WESTON:
Ray Copeland(tp) Quentin Jackson(tb) Julius Watkins(frh) Aaron Bell(tu) Budd Johnson(ss,ts) Booker Ervin (ts) Randy Weston(p) Peck Morrison(b) Charlie Persip(dm) Archie Lee(cga) Frankie Dunlop,George Young(perc) Melba Liston(arr,cond)
NYC,April or August, 1963

Caban bamboo highlife CD BN 4-95981-2
Zulu CD BN 4-94031-2

EMI-AMERICA

NAJEE:
Najee(as,ss,fl,keyb) Charles Elgart,Rahni Song(p,keyb,synth & drum programming) Fareed(g) Wayne Braithwaite,Barry Johnson(el b) Regis Branson,Kris Kellow(keyb b) Richie Ruiz-1, Omar Hakim-2(dm) Pete Tateo,Zachary Harris(perc) Regis Branson,Tanya Willoughby,Vanessa Anderson,Andrika,John White, Scott White,Zachary Harris,Rahni Song,Karen Marshall,Tracey Clay,Billy Rucker(vo).
(EMI America) (Celestial Sounds/Unique Recording/Bayside Sounds)
NYC, 1985

For the love of you-1
Najee's theme
Sweet love
Can't hide love-2
Betcha don't know

All titles issued on CD BN 8-23735-2.

Najee(ts) Morris Pleasure(keyb) Denzil Miller(p) Fareed,Rohn Lawrence(g) James Calloway(el b) Paul Mills (dm). (FAN Studios) Springfield Gardens,NY,c.1989-90

Tokyo blue CD BN 8-23735-2

Najee(fl) Morris Pleasure(keyb,b) Robert Damper(synth) Fareed,Steve Horton(g) Mark Ledford,Barry Johnson(vo). (FAN Studios) Springfield Gardens,NY,c.1989-90

My old friend CD BN 8-23735-2

513

NAJEE:
Najee(ts,keyb) Donald Blackman(keyb)Fareed(g) Barry "Sunjon" Johnson(el b) Omar Hakim(dm) Audrey Wheeler(backgr. vo).
(FAN Studios) Springfield Gardens,NY,c.1989-90

Stay CD BN 5-23547-2

AZ:
AZ(rapper) (Green Street Studio/Chung King Studio) NYC,c. early '90s

Your world don't stop CD BN(J)TOCP-65100

NAJEE:
Najee(ss,keyb,dm programming).
(EMI Records Group) (FAN Studios) Springfield Gardens,NY,1991-92

Noah's ark CD BN 8-23735-2

Najee(as,dm) Alec Shantzis(keyb,b).
(FAN Studios) Springfield Gardens,NY,c.1991-92

Until we meet again CD BN 5-23547-2

Najee(ss) Morris Pleasure(keyb,strings) Victor Bailey(b) Bernard Davis(dm).
(FAN Studios) Springfield Gardens,NY,c.1991-92

Now that I've found you CD BN 5-23547-2

Najee(ss) Steve Skinner(keyb,programming) Omar Hakim(hi-hat) Paul Pesco(g) Freddie Jackson(lead vo) Gerry Barnes,Katresse Barnes,Rachelle Capelli,Reggie Griffin(backgr. vo).
(FAN Studios) Springfield Gardens,NY,c.1991-92

All I ever ask CD BN 5-23547-2

Najee(ss) Mitchell Forman(keyb) Paul Jackson Jr.(g) Steve Dubin(dm,perc) Brenda Lee Eager,Jeffrey Pescetto,Angel Rogers(backgr. vo).
(Oceanway Studios/Record One) LA,c.1991-92

I adore mi amore CD BN 5-23547-2

THE JAZ:
(D & D Studios) NYC, 1993

A nation divided CD BN(J)TOCP-65100

NAJEE:
Jerry Hey,Gary Grant(tp) Najee(as) Daniel Higgins(as,ts) Greg Phillinganes(el p) George Duke(org,arr) David T. Walker,Ray Fuller(g) Byron Miller,Chuck Rainey(el b) Michael White(dm) Sheila E(tamb).
(O'Henry Studios) LA,c. Summer,1995

I wish CD BN(J)TOCJ-6153

Najee(alto fl) Paul Jackson Jr.(ac g,mand) George Duke(synth b,arr) Paulinho Da Costa(perc).
(O'Henry Studios) LA,Summer,1995

Nigiculela es una historia/I am singing CD BN 8-23735-2

NAJEE:

Najee(ss,alto fl) George Duke(clavinet,el p,synth,vocoder,arr) Wah Wah Watson(g) Chuck Rainey(el b).
(O'Henry Studios) LA,c. Summer 1995
Strings arr. by Paul Riser ovedrdubbed on.
(Oceanway Studios) LA,c. Summer 1995

Easy going evening CD BN 5-23547-2

Najee(ss) Ronnie Foster(el p,clavinet,arr) Ray Fuller(g) Chuck Rainey(el b) James Gadson(dm) Sheila E. (perc) & strings arr. by Jorge Del Barrio.
(O'Henry Studios) LA,c. Summer 1995

Love's in the need of love CD BN 5-23547-2

Najee(alto fl) George Duke(p,synth,string synth,arr).
(LeGanks Studio) LA,c. Summer 1995

If it's magic CD BN 5-23547-2

EMI AUSTRALIA

VINCE JONES:

Vince Jones(vo,tp) Barney McAll(p) Jonathan Zwartz(b) Peter Jones(dm).
Australia,mid 1990s

Luncheon with the president CD BN 8-57460-2

EMI BOVEMA (HOLLAND)

BEN WEBSTER:

Ben Webster(ts) Frans Wieringa(p) Gerard Holdgrefe(b) Tom van Steenderen(dm).
(Bovema Studios) Heemstede,Holland,January 12,1969

Benny's tune
Once in a while
Ben's blues
Sweet Lorraine
Hymn to freedom
St. Louis blues

All titles issued on CD BN 8-57371-2.

Ben Webster(ts) Cees Slinger(p) Jacques Schols(b) John Engels(dm).
(Bovema Studios) Heemstede,Holland,May 26,1969

I got it band (and that ain't good)
Drop me off in Harlem
One for the guv'nor
Prelude to a kiss
In a sentimental mood
Rockin' in rhythm

All titles issued on CD BN 8-57371-2.

BEN WEBSTER:
Ben Webster(ts) Irv Rocklin(p) Henk Haverhoek(b) Peter Ypma(dm).
(Cafe Societeit De Twee Spieghels) Leiden,Holland,September 6,1973

Pennies from heaven
I got rhythm
My romance
Autumn leaves
For all we know
Sunday
Just you, just me
How high the moon
Straight, no chaser
Short speech by Ben Webster

All titles issued on CD BN 8-57371-2.

EMI CANADA

DREAM WARRIORS & GANG STARR:
No details. Toronto or NYC, 1991

I've lost my ignorance CD BN(J)TOCP-65100

DREAM WARRIORS:

(Wellesly Sound) Toronto, 1995

I wouldn't wanna be ya CD BN(J)TOCP-65100

EMI CLASSICS

GIOVANNI BATTISTA PERGOLESI:
Barbara Frittoli(soprano vo) Anna Caterina Antonacci(contralto vo) Francesco Catena(org) & soloists from the Orchestra Filarmonica Della Scala,cond. by Riccardo Muti.
Milano,January/February,1996

Dolorosa (from Stabat Mater) CD BN 4-95317-2

EMI ENGLAND
(HMV,PARLOPHONE)

LOUIS ARMSTRONG & HIS HOT FIVE:
Louis Armstrong(tp) Kid Ory(tb) Johnny Dodds(cl) Lil Hardin(p) Johnny St. Cyr(bjo).
Chicago,December 11,1925

Muskrat ramble CD BN(Sp)8-34712-2

FATS WALLER:
Dave Wilkins(tp) George Chisholm(tb) Alan Ferguson(cl) Alfie Kahn(ts) Ian Sheppard(ts,v)Fats Waller (p,vo) Len Harrison(b) Edmundo Ros(dm).
London,August 21,1938

OEA-6704-1 A-tisket, a-tasket CD BN 4-95981-2

EVE BOSWELL:
Eve Boswell(vo) with Reg Owen and his Orchestra: Laddie Busby,George Chisholm,Jackie Armstrong,Ken Goldie(tb)Phil Goody(alto fl,reeds) & reeds,p,g,b,dm,strings,Reg Owen (arr).
(from Parlophone label) London,March 10,1957

Sentimental journey CD BN(Sp)8-56842-2

SHIRLEY BASSEY:
Shirley Bassey(vo) with Geoff Love and his Orchestra.
London, 1959

'S wonderful CD BN(Sp)8-56842-2

BRIAN BENNETT:
details unknown. c.1969

Soul mission BN B1-54357,CD 8-54357-2

TRINIDAD OIL COMPANY:
details unknown.
(Harvest label) mid '70s

Feelin' allright BN B1-97158,CD 4-97158-2

GONZALEZ:
details unknown. mid '70s

Funky Frith Street BN B1-97158,CD 4-97158-2

THE UMC'S:
details unknown. c. early '90s

One to grow on CD BN 8-27533-2

LABI SIFFRE:
details unknown.

The vulture BN 5-21147-1,CD 5-21147-2

Dr. JOHN - DUKE ELEGANT:
Dr. John (Mac Rebennack)(p,el p,org,vo) with Bobby Broom(g) David Barard(el b) Herman Ernest III(dm).
Cyro Baptista(bgo-1) Ronnie Cuber(bs-2) added.
(Parlophone label)(RPM Sound Studios) NYC,c. late May 1999

I'm beginning to see the light (voDJ)
Solitude (voDJ)
Satin doll (voDJ)-1
Do nothin' till you hear from me (voDJ)
Mood indigo (voDJ)
On the wrong side of the tracks (voDJ)
Flaming sword
Caravan
I'm gonna go fishin' (voDJ & band vocal)
Perdido (voDJ)-2
Things ain't what they used to be
It don't mean a thing (voDJ & band vocal)
Don't get around much anymore (voDJ)-2

All titles issued on CD BN (J)TOCP-65367.All titles,except first,also issued on CD BN 5-23220-2.

EMI FRANCE
(COLUMBIA/SWING/DUCRETET-THOMSON/PATHE MARCONI)

QUINTETTE DU HOT CLUB DE FRANCE:
Stephane Grappelli(v) Django Reinhardt(g) Joseph Reinhardt,Pierre Ferret(rh g) Lucien Simoens(b).
Paris,May 4,1936

OLA 1062 Limehouse blues CD BN 8-37138-2

Stephane Grappelli(v) Django Reinhardt(g) Marcel Bianchi,Pierre Ferret(rh g) Louis Vola(b).
Paris,April 22,1937

OLA 1711 When day is done CD BN 8-37138-2

COLEMAN HAWKINS:
Benny Carter(tp,arr) Andre Ekyan(as) Alix Combelle(cl) Coleman Hawkins(ts) Stephane Grappelli(v) Django Reinhardt(g) Eugène d'Hellemmes(b) Tommy Benford(dm).
Paris,April 28,1937

OLA 1744-1 Out of nowhere CD BN 4-95981-2

DJANGO REINHARDT:
Django Reinhardt(g) Louis Gasté(rh g) Eugène d'Hellemmes(b).
Paris,September 9,1937

OLA 1952 St. Louis blues CD BN 8-37138-2

QUINTETTE DU HOT CLUB DE FRANCE:
Stephane Grappelli(v) Django Reinhardt(g) Joseph Reinhardt,Eugène Vees(rh g) Louis Vola(b).
Paris,November 25,1937

OLA 1990 Minor swing CD BN 8-37138-2

Same. Paris,December 14,1937

OLA 1998 My serenade CD BN 8-37138-2

DJANGO REINHARDT:
Django Reinhardt(g) Louis Vola(b).
Paris,December 21,1937

OLA 2215 You rascal,you CD BN 8-37138-2

REX STEWART AND HIS FEETWARMERS:
Rex Stewart(c) Barney Bigard(cl) Django Reinhardt(g) Billy Taylor(b).
Paris,June 5,1939

OSW 63 Montmartre CD BN 8-37138-2

DJANGO REINHARDT:
Django Reinhardt(g) Pierre Ferret(rh g-1) Emmanuel Soudieux(b-1).
Paris,June 30,1939

OPG 1721 I'll see you in my dreams -1 CD BN 8-37138-2
OPG 1725 Naguine -

CHARLES TRENET:
Charles Trenet(vo) with unidentified orchestra.
Paris,February ,1940

Boom! CD BN 7-99100-2

GUS VISEUR ET SON ORCHESTRE:
Gus Viseur(acc) with ?
Paris,August 9,1940

CL 7330-1 Swing valse CD N 7-99100-2

DJANGO REINHARDT ET LE QUINTETTE DU HOT CLUB DE FRANCE:
Alix Combelle,Hubert Rostaing(cl) Django Reinhardt(g) Joseph Reinhardt(rh g) Tony Rovira(b) Pierre Fouad(dm).
Paris,December 13,1940

OSW 146 Nuages CD BN 7-99100-2,8-37138-2

DJANGO REINHARDT:
Django Reinhardt(g) Eugène Vees(rhythm g) Jean Storne(b) Gaston Leonard(dm).
Paris,February 26,1943

OSW 328 Blues clair CD BN 8-37138-2

DJANGO REINHARDT ET SON ORCHESTRE:
Alex Renard,Alex Caturegli,Maurice Moufflard(tp) Maurice Gladieu,Pierre Remy(tb) Max Blanc,Robert Merchez,Robert Mavounzy(as) André Louis,Charles Hary(ts) Django Reinhardt (g) Eugène Vees(rhythm g) Jean Storne(b) Pierre Fouad(dm).
Paris,July 7,1943

OSW 359 Place De Brouckere CD BN 8-37138-2

DJANGO REINHARDT AND HIS AMERICAN SWING BAND:
Herb Bass,Jerry Stephan,Lonnie Wilfong(tp) Bill Decker,Don Gardner,Sheldon Heath,John Kirkpatrick(tb) Jim Hays(cl,as) Joe Moser(as) Bernie Cavaliere,Bill Zickefoose(ts) Ken Lowther(bs) Larry Mann(p) Django Reinhardt(g) Bob Decker(b) Bill Bethel(dm) Jack Platt(dir).
Paris,November 6,1945

OSW 410 Manoir des mes rêves (*aka* Django's castle) CD BN 8-37138-2

DJANGO REINHARDT ET LE QUINTETTE DU HOT CLUB DE FRANCE:
Stephane Grappelli(v) Django Reinhardt(g) Jack Llewelin,Allan Hodgkiss(rh g) Coleridge Goode(b).
London,January 31,1946

OEF 26	Django's tiger	CD BN 8-37138-2
OEF 28	Echoes of France	CD BN 7-99100-2

Stephane Grappelli(v) Django Reinhardt(g) Joseph Reinhardt,Eugene Vees(rh g) Fred Ermelin(b).
Paris,November 14,1947

OSW 483	Ol' man river	CD BN 8-37138-2
OSW 486	Diminishing	-

Stephane Grappelli(v) Django Reinhardt(g) Joseph Reinhardt,Challin Ferret(rhythm g-1) Emmanuel Soudieux (b).
Paris,March 10,1948

OSW 501	Lady be good-1	CD BN 8-37138-2
OSW 506	To each his own symphony	-

JACK DIEVAL AVEC STEPHANE GRAPPELLI:
Stephane Grappelli(v) Jack Dieval(p) Benoit Quersin(b) Jean-Louis Viale(dm).
Paris,September 17,1954

Pennies from heaven CD BN(Sp)8-53016-2

ZOOT SIMS:
Joe Eardley(tp) Zoot Sims(ts) Henri Renaud(p) Eddie De Haas(b) Charles Saudrais(dm).
Paris,March 15,1956

Charlie went to Cherbourg
Crazy rhythm
I found a new baby
Charlie was in Rouen

All titles to be issued on the Blue Note label.

ZOOT SIMS:
Jon Eardley(tp) Zoot Sims(ts) Henri Renaud(p) Benoit Quersin(b) Charles Saudrais(dm).
(Studio Thorens) Paris,March 16,1956

Captain Jetter
Nuzzolese blues
Everything I love
On the alamo
Evening in Paris CD BN 7-99100-2
My old flame
Little Jon special

All titles to be issued on the Blue Note label.

KENNY CLARKE:
Lucky Thompson(ts) Martial Solal(p) Pierre Michelot(b) Kenny Clarke(dm).
Paris,September 26,1957

Now's the time CD BN 8-57742-2

 520

<u>EDITH PIAF</u>:
Edith Piaf(vo) with unknown accompaniment.
Paris,September 4,1958

Je me souviens d'une chanson CD BN 4-95317-2

<u>ROGER GUERIN</u>:
Roger Guerin(tp) Benny Golson(ts) Bobby Timmons(p) Pierre Michelot(b) Christian Garros(dm).
Paris,December 12,1958

Blues march
I remember Clifford
Moanin'
Stablemates

All titles issued under Benny Golson's name on CD BN 4-94104-2.

<u>EARL HINES</u>:
Earl Hines(p).
Paris,May 27,1965

I surrender dear CD BN(J)TOCJ-5187/88

<u>PHIL WOODS AND HIS EUROPEAN RHYTHM MACHINE</u>:
Phil Woods(as) George Gruntz(p) Henri Texier(b) Daniel Humair(dm).
(Pathe Marconi Studios) Paris,November 14 & 15,1968

And when we were young
Alive and well
Freedom jazz dance
Stolen moments CD BN(J)CJ28-5176
Doxy

All titles to be issued on Blue Note.

<u>ART ENSEMBLE OF CHICAGO</u>:
Lester Bowie(tp) Roscoe Mitchell,Joseph Jarman(ts) Malachi Favors(el b) Don Moye(dm) Fontella Bass(vo, tamb).
(Pathe Studios) Boulogne-Billancourt (France) July 22,1970

Theme for Yo Yo CD BN 8-35414-2

<u>ANNETTE BANNEVILLE</u>:
Annette Banneville(vo) with unidentified orchestra.
Paris, 1990

Rendez-vous à Saint-Germain CD BN 7-99100-2

<u>EMMANUELLE TORENTE</u>:
Emmanuelle Torente(vo) with unidentified orchestra.
Paris, 1990

Sous le ciel de Prris CD BN 7-99100-2

<u>SOON E MC</u>:
Soon e MC(vo) Jimmy Jay(samples) J.F. Delfour(mixer).
(Studio Palais des Congrès/Jimmy's Studio)
Paris,February-October,1992

Elucide ce mystere CD BN 8-27533-2

521

GEORGES GARVARENTZ:
details unknown.

Haschisch party — BN 5-21147-1,CD 5-21147-2

EMI ITALIANA

MANDRAKE SOM:
details unknown.

Italy,1975

Berimbau — BN B1-29196,CD 8-29196-2,(Au)8-14710-2

EMI ODEON (BRAZIL)

JOAO GILBERTO:
Joao Gilberto(g,vo) & unknown tps,fls,b,dm,perc,strings,Antonio Carlos Jobim(arr,cond).
Brazil,November 10,1958

Desafinado — CD BN 8-35283-2, (Au)8-14710-2

Joao Gilberto(g,vo) & unknown tp,fl,as,oboe,b,dm,perc,strings,Antonio Carlos Jobim(p,arr,cond).
Brazil,April 4,1960

Samba De Uma Nota So — CD BN 8-35283-2

Joao Gilberto(g,vo) with Orchestra arr. & cond. by Antonio Carlos Jobim.
Brazil,August 2,1961

O barquinho — CD BN(J)TOCJ-5852

WILSON SIMONAL:
details unknown. — Brazil,June 17,1964

Nana — BN B1-57741,CD 8-57741-2

MILTON BANANA TRIO:
unknown(p),(b)Milton Banana(dm).
Brazil,December 14-15,1964

Primitivo — BN B1-29196,CD 8-29196-2
Noa,noa — - -

SILVIO CEZAR & MEIRELLES:
details unknown. — Brazil,September 15,1965

Sambo do Carioca — BN B1-57741,CD 8-57741-2

PERY RIBIERO & BOSSA 3:
Luiz Carlos Vinhas(p) & unknown b,dm,Pery Ririero(vo).
Brazil,September 29,1965

Deus Brasiliero — BN B1-29196,CD 8-29196-2

LENY ANDRADE:
details unknown. Brazil,September 29,1965

Estamos ai BN B1-57741,CD 8-57741-2

BOSSA 3:
Luiz Carlos Vinhas(p)unknown b,dm,escola da samba(perc).
Brazil,November 11,1965

Nao me diga adeus BN B1-29196,CD 8-29196-2,(Au)8-14710-2

ELZA SOARES:
details unknown,Elza Soares(vo).
Brazil,April 13,1966

Deixa a nega gingar BN B1-57741,CD 8-57741-2

MARCOS VALLE:
unknown big band. Brazil July 26,1966

Batucada sergiu BN B1-29196,CD 8-29196-2,(Au)8-14710-2

LUIZ ARRUDA PAEZ:
details unknown. Brazil,October 25,1966

Upa neguinho BN B1-29196,CD 8-29196-2

QUARTETO NOVO:
Hermeto Pascoal(fl,p,g) Theo de Barros(g) Heraldo de Monte(b) Airto Moreira(dm,perc).
Brazil,June 20-21,1967

Vim de Santana BN B1-29196,CD 8-29196-2
Mistrurada - -
Ponteio BN B1-57741,CD 8-57741-2

ELZA SOARES:
Unknown big band,Wilson des Neves(dm) Elza Soares(vo).
Brazil,September 29,1967

Deixa isso pra la BN B1-29196,CD 8-29196-2

MILTON BANANA TRIO:
Unknown p,b & Milton Banana(dm).
Brazil,January 23,1968

Procissao BN B1-57741,CD 8-57741-2

SOM TRES:
Unknown big band. Brazil,May 23,1968

Jungle BN B1-57741,CD 8-57741-2

ELZA SOARES:
Details unknown,Elza Soares(vo)
Brazil,June 21,1968

Mas que nada BN B1-54357,B1-57741,CD 8-54357-2,8-57741-2

SOM TRES:
Unknown big band. Brazil, May 19,1969

Homenagen a Mongo BN B1-29196,CD 8-29196-2,(Au)8-14710-2

OS TRES MORAIS:
details unknown. Brazil,September 17,1970

Freio aerodinamico BN B1-57741,CD 8-57741-2

ANTONIO ADOLPHO & A BRAZUCA:
details unknown. Brazil,November 11,1970

Transamozonica BN B1-57741,CD 8-57741-2

MILTON NASCIMENTO:
Wagner Tiso(org) Tavito(g) Luis Alves(b) Rubinho(dm) Robertinha Silva,Beto Guedes,Toninho Horta, Nelson Angelo(perc) Milton Nascimento(vo).
Rio De Janeiro, c.1972

Lilia CD BN(Au)8-14710-2

EUMIR DEODATO:
Unknown big band with Eumir Deodato(p,synth,arr).
Brazil or NYC,November 23,1971

Bebe BN B1-29196,CD 8-29196-2

QUINTETO VILLA LOBOS & LUIS ECA:
details unknown. Brazil,June 5,1972

Reflexos BN B1-57741,CD 8-57741-2

QUARTETO EM CY:
details unknown. Brazil,July 4,1972

Todo que voce podia ser BN B1-57741,CD 8-57741-2

EDU LOBO:
Unknown orchestra. Brazil,November 8,1972

Libera nos BN B1-57741,CD 8-57741-2

Unknown big band with Edu Lobo(vo). Brazil,November 23,1972

Vento brava BN B1-57741,CD 8-57741-2

EDU LOBO:
Unknown orchestra. Brazil,January 16,1973

Viola fora de moda BN B1-29196,CD 8-29196-2

JOAO DONATO:
details unknown. Brazil, c.1973

Me deixa BN B1-29196
Cala boca menino - B1-54357,CD 8-54357-2

<u>LUIS GONZAGA Jr.</u>:
details unknown. Brazil,May 5,1973

Moleque BN B1-57741,CD 8-57741-2

<u>JOHNNY ALF</u>:
details unknown. Brazil,December 3,1973

Um tema p'ro Simon BN B1-29196,CD 8-29196-2

<u>MEIRELLES</u>:
details unknown.
Brazil,December 20,1973

Also sprach Zarathustra BN B1-57741,CD 8-57741-2

<u>MILTON BANANA</u>:
Unknown fl,el p ,g,(b with Milton Banana(dm).
Brazil,April 1,1974

Ladeira da preguice BN B1-57741,CD 8-57741-2

<u>DI MELO</u>:
details unknown.
Brazil,June 25,1975

A vida en seus metodos Diz Calma BN B1-57741,CD 8-57741-2

<u>ALAIDE COSTA</u>:
Incl. Joao Donato,Nelson Angelo,Toninho Horta,Ivan Lins(vo).
Brazil,May 17,1976

Catavento BN B1-29196,CD 8-29196-2

<u>DJAVAN</u>:
Djavan(vo,g) & others unknown.
Brazil, c.1979

Serrado CD BN 8-14710-2
Samba Dobrado -

<u>LO BORGES</u>:
Lo Borges(g,vo) & others unknown.
Brazil,June 19,1979

Tudo que voce podia ser BN B1-29196,CD 8-29196-2

<u>JOYCE</u>:
Joyce(vo) & others unknown.
Brazil,January 14,1980

Aldeia de ogum BN B1-29196,8-29196-2

<u>VICTOR ASSIS BRASIL</u>:
details unknown.
Brazil, c.1980

Night and day BN B1-29196

MARISA MONTE:
Luis Claudio Ramos(viola) Eduardo Souto Neto(p,arr) Luis Alves(b) Theo Lima(dm) Marisa Monte(vo) & 20 strings.

Brazil,October 24,1988

Speak low — CD BN(Au)8-14808-2

Bernie Worrell(keyb) Marc Ribot(g,v) Melvin Gibbs(b) Dougie Bowne(dm) Marisa Monte(vo).
NYC, 1990

Beija eu — CD BN 7-99790-2

MARINA LIMA:
Marcio Miranda(keyb,programming) William Magalhaes(keyb,backgr.vo) Marina Lima(steel g,vo) Fernando Vidal(g) Nilo Romero(el b) Cesinho(dm) Cecilia Spyer,Veronica Magalhaes(backgr.vo) Jota Moraes(string arr) & 8 strings.
(Nas Nuvens Studio) — Rio De Janeiro, 1993

It's not enough — CD BN 8-57463-2

MARISA MONTE:
Marisa Monte(vo) with Bernie Worrell(org) Gilberto Gil(ac g) Nando Reis(el g) Arthur Maia(b) Jorginho Gomes(dm) Marcos Suzano(talking dm).
(Nas Nuvens Studio) — Rio De Janeiro
& (Skyline Studio) — NYC,March-May,1994

O ceu — CD BN(E)8-53231-2

Marisa Monte(vo) with Peter Ecklund(tp) Waldonys Menezes(accordion) Davi Moraes,Fernando Caneca (el g) Dadi(ac g,b) Cesinho(dm) Marco Lobo(perc).
(Impressao Digital Studios) — Rio De Janeiro,June 1996
10 strings overdubbed on,arr. by Greg Cohen.
(Kampos Audio/Video, Studios) — NYC, July 1996

Tempos modernos — CD BN 8-57463-2

EMI ODEON (India)

ANANDA SHANKAR:
details unknown.

c.1975

Streets of Calcutta — BN B1-54357,CD 8-54357-2
Dancing drums — - -

EMI SOUTH AFRICA

ABDULLAH IBRAHIM - TOWNSHIP ONE MORE TIME:
Faya Faku(tp) David Roubain(as) Basil "Manenberg" Cotzee(ts) Abdullah Ibrahim(bs) Lionel Beukes(b) Denver Furness(dm)
(Milestone Studios) — Capetown,SA, c.1998

Lekker lekkers — (poss. to be issued on BN)

ABDULLAH IBRAHIM - TOWNSHIP ONE MORE TIME:
Abdullah Ibrahim(p,bs-1) Gary Kriel(el b) Denver Furness(dm)
(Milestone Studios) Capetown,SA, c.1998

Shosholoza (trio version)	(poss. to be issued on BN)
Timer (trio version)	-
The minstrel (trio version)	-
Genadendal -1	-
Timer (with sax) -2	-
	-

-2: Jimmy Adams or Harold Jefta(as) added.

Faya Faku(tp) Jimmy Adams,Harold Jefta(as) David Roubain(ts,fl) Abdullah Ibrahim(p,bs-1) Gary Kriel (el b) Denver Furness(dm)
(Milestone Studios) Capetown,SA, c.1998

Township one more time	(poss. to be issued on BN)
Chisa	-
Someday soon sweet samba	-
Medley: Shosholoza/Oudtshoorn -1	-
Minstrel	-
Genadendal	-
Chisa (with baritone) -1	-

EMI SWEDEN

DORIS:
Doris(vo) & others unknown.
c.1970

You never come closer	BN B1-54357,CD 8-54357-2
Beatmaker	BN 5-21147-1,CD 5-21147-2

REBECKA TORNQVIST:
Rebecka Tornqvist(vo) with Niklas Medin(Hammond org) Anders Widmarl(p) Max Schultz(g) Pal Svenre(el b) Hans Backenroth(b) Jan Robertson(dm) René Martinez(perc) Andre De Lange,Max Schultz,Jean-Paul Wall(backgr. vo) & horns arr. by Joaquin Milder. Stockholm, 1993

Easy come,easy go	CD BN(Sp)8-56842-2

EMI VALENTIM DE CARVALHO (PORTUGAL)

AMALIA RODRIGUES:
Amalia Rodrigues(vo) with Jose Nunes(Portuguese 12-string g) Castro Nota(ac g).
Lisbon, 1962

Estranha forma de vida	CD BN 4-95317-2

MADREDEUS:
Gabriel Gomes(acc) Rodrigo Leao(keyb) Jose Peixoto,Pedro Ayres Magalhaes(g) Francisco Ribeiro (cello) Teresa Salgueiro(vo)
(Great Linford Manor & Lansdowne Recording Studios)
England,March-May 1994

O Pastor	CD BN 8-52184-2

HISPAVOX (EMI SPAIN)

NURIA FELIU:
Nuria Feliu(vo) with orchestra arr. & cond. by Leon Borrell.
Madrid, 1967

Mai non goses (On a clear day you can see forever)
Potser mai (I should care)
La verge inutil
Alfie
Un dia de pluja (Here's that rainy day)
Crec en tu (I believe in you)
En San Francisco (I left my heart in San Francisco)
Ja estic bé aixi
Recordare l'Abril (I'll remember April)

All titles issued on CD BN(Sp)8-53973-2.

PEDRO ITURRALDE - JAZZ FLAMENCO VOLS. 1 & 2:
Pedro Iturralde(ss,ts) Paul Grassl(p) Paco de Antequera(g) Eric Peter(b) Peer Wyboris(dm).
(Hispavox Studios) Madrid,June 30,1967

Las morillas de jaen CD BN(Sp)8-53933-2
El zorongo gitano -

Pedro Iturralde(ss,ts) Paul Grassl(p) Paco de Algeciras(g) Eric Peter(b) Peer Wyboris(dm).
(Hispavox Studios) Madrid,September 14,1967

El Cafe de Chinitas CD BN(Sp)8-53933-2
Soleares (omit p,b,dm) -

PEDRO ITURRALDE QUARTET FEATURING HAMPTON HAWES:
Pedro Iturralde(fl-1,ss-2,ts-3,bs-4) Hampton Hawes(p) Eric Peter(b) Peer Wyboris(dm).
(Hispavox Studios) Madrid,late February,1968

On Green Dolphin Street -3
Black Forest Blues (Hampton Hawes Blues)-1
Autumn leaves -4
Oleo -3
Moonlight in Vermont -3
My funny Valentine -2

All titles issued on CD BN(Sp)8-55850-2.

PEDRO ITURRALDE - JAZZ FLAMENCO VOLS. 1 & 2:
Dino Piana(vtb) Pedro Iturralde(ss,ts) Paul Grassl(p) Paco de Algeciras(g) Eric Peter(b) Peer Wyboris(dm).
(Hispavox Studios) Madrid,August 5,1968

Bulerias
Adios Granada
Anda jaleo!
Homenaje a Granados

All titles issued on CD BN(Sp)8-53933-2.

JUAN CALDERON Y SU ORQUESTA DE JAZZ:
Arturo Fornes,Joe Moro,Juan Cano,José Luis Medrano(tp) José Chenoll,Jesus Pardo(tb) Sigfrido Vidaurreta(bass tb) Vlady Bas(as,cl,bass cl) Pedro Itturalde(ts,ss,fl) Lincoln Barcelo(ts,fl) Lin Barto(bs,fl) Juan Carlos Calderon(p,arr,cond) Carlos Casanovas(b) Pepe Nisto(dm).
Madrid, 1968

Milestones
Bad feeling
Sambando
Stolen moments
Straight no chaser
Bloque 6 (Cano out)

All titles issued on CD BN(Sp) 8-53934-2.

NURIA FELIU:
Nuria Feliu(vo) with orchestra arr. & cond. by Leon Borrell.
Madrid, 1972

Applaudiments (Applause)
Que tal Dolly? (Hello Dolly)
Si en aquest moment tornes (If he walked into my life)

All titles issued on CD BN(Sp)8-53973-2.

Same.
Madrid, 1973

Soleament et puc donar amor,baby (I can't give you anything but love)
Es facil estimar (I'm in the mood for love)
Quan tu somrius (When you're smiling)
Te per dos (Teas for two)
No sé pas com t(ho fas (You do something to me)
Pepa suro (I want to be happy)
Soc sentimental (I'm gettin' sentimental over you)
Pot explicar-ho algu? (Can anyone explain?)

All titles issued on CD BN(Sp)8-53973-2.

529

IMPERIAL

T-BONE WALKER:
Eddie Hutcherson(tp) Edward Hale(as) Eddie Davis(ts) Jim Wynn(ts,bs) Zell Kindred(p) T-Bone Walker (g,vo) Buddy Woodson(b) Robert "Snake" Sims(dm).

LA,April 5,1950

IM-175-3	Strollin' with the bones	CD BN 7-96581-2
IM-176	The sun went down	
IM-177	You don't love me	

All titles issued on BN BN-LA533-H2.

Same.

LA,April 6, 1950

IM-179	The hustle is on (LP take)
IM-180	Baby you broke my heart (LP take)
IM-181	Evil hearted woman

All titles issued on BN BN-LA533-H2.

BIG JOE TURNER:
Big Joe Turner(vo) with Dave Bartholomew's orchestra.
(J & M Studios) NO,April ,1950

IM-191	Jumpin' tonight (Midnight rockin')	CD BN 8-54364-2

T-BONE WALKER:
Unknown(tp) Edward Hale(as) Maxwell Davis(ts) Willard McDaniel(p) T-Bone Walker(g,vo) Billy Hadnott (b) Oscar Lee Bradley(dm).

LA,August 15,1951

IM-329	Alimony blues
IM-330	Life is too short
IM-331	You don't understand

All titles issued on BN BN-LA533-H2

Same.

LA,August 20,1951

IM-333	I get so weary
IM-335	Tell me what's the reason
IM-336	I'm about to lose my mind

All titles issued on BN BN-LA533-H2.

BIG JAY McNEELY:
Britt Woodman,John Ewing(tb) Big Jay McNeely(ts) Bob McNeely(bs) Jimmy O'Brien(p) Ted Shirley(b) Leonard Hardiman(dm).

LA,November or December,1951

IM-375	Deacon rides again	CD BN 8-54364-2

T-BONE WALKER:
T-Bone Walker(vo) with Edward Hale(as) Maxwell Davis(ts) prob Jim Wynn(bs) Willard McDaniel(p) Billy Hadnott(b) Oscar Lee Bradley(dm).
LA,January 5,1952

IM-383-4 Cold,cold feeling
IM-384-2 News for you baby
IM-385-3 Get these blues off me
IM-386-3 I got the blues again
IM-387-1 Through with women
IM-388-3 Street walking woman
IM-389-5 Blues is a woman
IM-390-5 I got the blues

All titles issued on BN BN-LA533-H2.

T-BONE WALKER:
T-Bone Walker(vo,g) with prob. Smith(tp) Edward Hale(as) Maxwell Davis(ts) Jim Wynn(bs) Zell Kindred or Willard McDaniel(p) R.S.Rankin(g) Buddy Woods(b) Robert "Snake" Sims or Oscar Lee Bradley (dm).
LA,March ,1952

IM-404 Blue Mood
IM-405 Every Time

Both titles issued on BN BN-LA533-H2.

Same.
LA,March 10,1952

IM-410 Party girl
IM-411-4 Love is a gamble (omit horns)
IM-412-6 High society

All titles issued on BN BN-LA533-H2.

ARCHIBALD:
Archibald(vo) & others unknown.
NO,September ,1952

IM-483 Great big eyes (*aka* Soon as I go home) CD BN 8-54364-2

T-BONE WALKER:
T-Bone Walker(vo,g) with Dave Bartholomew's band (tp,as,ts,bs,p,b,dm) Baby Davis or Tiny Brown(vo-1)
NO,March 20,1953

IM-520 Got no use for you -1
IM-521 Railroad station blues

Both titles issued on BN BN-LA533-H2.

John Lawton(tp) Walter Cox(ts) T-Bone Walker(vo,g) T.J.Fowler(p) Henry Ivory(b) Clarence Stamp(dm).
Detroit,October 21,1953

IM-647 Bye bye baby BN BN-LA533-H2

T-Bone Walker(vo,g) & others unknown.
LA,June 20,1954

IM-740 Teenage baby CD BN 8-54364-2

531

DAVE BARTHOLOMEW:
Dave Bartholomew(vo) with Fats Domino's orchestra.
(J & M Studio) NO,August 13,1954

IM-751	Jump children	CD BN 8-54364-2

SONNY CRISS - JAZZ U.S.A.:
Sonny Criss(as) Kenny Drew(p) Barney Kessel(g) Bill Woodson(b) Chuck Thompson(dm).
LA,January 26,1956

IM-981	Easy living
IM-982	Criss cross
IM-983	Willow weep for me
IM-984	Alabamy bound

All titles issued on CD BN 5-24564-2,(J)TOCJ-6127.

Sonny Criss(as) Kenny Drew(p) Bill Woodson(b) Chuck Thompson(dm).
LA,February 24,1956

IM-1012	Something's gotta give	
IM-1013	These foolish things	
IM-1014	West coast blues	CD BN 7-80707-2,(J)TOCJ-5298
IM-1015	Blue Friday	

All titles issued on CD BN 5-24564-2,(J)TOCJ-6127.

Same. LA,March 23,1956

IM-1034	More than you know
IM-1035	Sunday
IM-1036	Sweet Georgia Brown
IM-1037	Ham's blues

All titles issued on CD BN 5-24564-2,(J)TOCJ-6127.

SONNY CRISS - GO MAN!:
Sonny Criss(as) Sonny Clark(p) Leroy Vinnegar(b) Lawrence Marable(dm).
(Master Recorders) LA,July 10,1956

IM-1084	Summertime	CD BN(J)TOCJ-5710
IM-1085	Memories of you	CD BN(J)CJ28-5179
IM-1086	Wailin' with Joe	
IM-1087	How deep is the ocean	
IM-1088	The blues for Rose	
IM-1089	The man I love	

All titles issued on CD BN 5-24564-2.

Same. (Master Recorders) LA,July 31,1956

IM-1090	Until the real thing comes along	
IM-1091	Blue prelude	
IM-1092	After you've gone	
IM-1093	Come rain or come shine	CD BN(J)TOCJ-5296
IM-1094	How high the moon	
IM-1095	If I had you	

All titles issued on CD BN 5-24564-2.

532

SONNY CRISS PLAYS COLE PORTER:
Sonny Criss(as) Larry Bunker(vb) Sonny Clark(p) Buddy Clark(b) Lawrence Marable(dm).
(Master Recorders) LA,August 26,1956

IM-1101	What is this thing called love	CD BN(J)TOCJ-5299
IM-1102	Night and day	
IM-1103	Love for sale	
IM-1104	Just one of those things	
IM-1105	Anything goes	CD BN(J)CJ28-5177
IM-1106	I get a kick out of you	

All titles issued on CD BN 5-24564-2.

Same. (Master Recorders) LA,October 3,1956

IM-1155	Easy to love
IM-1156	It's all right with me
IM-1157	I love you
IM-1158	In the still of the night

All titles issued on CD BN 5-24564-2.

WARNE MARSH - JAZZ OF TWO CITIES:
Warne Marsh,Ted Brown(ts) Ronnie Ball(p) Ben Tucker(b) Jeff Morton(dm).
(Radio Recorders) LA,October 3,1956

IM-1159	Quintessence
IM-1160	Smog eyes
IM-1161	Lover man (mono master)
IM-1162	Ear conditioning (mono master)

All titles issued on BN(F)BNP25106.

Same.
(Radio Recorders) LA,October 11,1956

IM-1201	Dixie's dilemma	
IM-1202	Jazz of two cities (mono take)	CD BN(J)TOCJ-5710
IM-1203	I never knew (mono take)	
IM-1204	Tchaikovsky's opus 42,3rd mvt-1	

-1:previously issued as "These are the things I love".
All titles issued on BN(F)BNP25106.

ROY BROWN:
Roy Brown(vo) prob. with Lee Allen,Clarence Hall,Herb Hardesty(saxes) Edward Frank(p) Justin Adams(g) Frank Fields(b) Charles Williams(dm).
NO,January 22,1957

IM-1243	Let the four winds blow	CD BN 8-54364-2

HAROLD LAND:
Carmell Jones(tp) Harold Land(ts) John Houston(p) Jimmy Bond(b) Mel Lewis(dm).
LA,July 3,1963

IM-5652	Kisses sweeter than wine
IM-5653	Tom Dooley
IM-5654	Scarlet ribbons

All titles to be issued on the Blue Note label.

HAROLD LAND:
Carmell Jones(tp) Harold Land(ts) John Houston(p) Jimmy Bond(b) Mel Lewis(dm).
LA,July 17,1963

IM-5655 Take this hammer
IM-5656 Foggy,foggy dew
IM-5657 Hava nagila
IM-5660 On top of Old Smokeu
IM-5661 Blue tail fly

All titles to be issued on the Blue Note label.

ALBERT COLLINS:
Albert Collins(g,vo) & others unknown.
Nashville,July ,1968

Trash talkin' CD BN(J)TOCJ-5712
Things that I used to do -1 -

-1: mistitled "Talking Slim Blues" in its original issue.

SANDY NELSON:
Sandy Nelson(dm) & others unknown.
LA, 1968

IM-6434 Alligator bogaloo BN B1-97158,CD 4-97158-2

JUBILEE

KING PLEASURE:
King Pleasure(vo) Sid Bass(arr) & others unknown
NYC, 1955

All of me
Blame the comdition
Evening blues
Diaper pin

All titles issued on CD BN 7-84463-2.

DELLA REESE:
Della Reese(vo) with Orchestra arr. & dir. by Sid Bass: Billy Taylor(p) Billy Moore(g) Al Hall(b) Osie Johnson(dm).
NYC, 1956

They can't take that away from me CD BN(Sp)8-56842-2

ART BLAKEY & SABU MARTINEZ:
Bill Hardman(tp) Johnny Griffin(ts) Sam Dockery(p) Spanky De Brest(b) Art Blakey(dm) Sabu Martinez (cga).
NYC,May 13,1957

Sakeena CD BN 5-21688-2

JACKIE McLEAN:
Webster Young(c) Ray Draper(tu) Jackie McLean(as) Gil Coggins(p) George Tucker(b) Larry Ritchie(dm).
NYC,December 27,1957

Tune up CD BN 8-57742-2

DELLA REESE:
Della Reese(vo) with Charlie Shavers,Shorty Baker,Emmett Berry(tp) Frank Saracco,Bobby Byrne,Dick Hixson(tb) George Dorsey,Seymour Press,Sam Taylor,Dave McRae(reeds) Dave Martin(p) George Barnes(g) Joe Benjamin(b) Bobby Donaldson(dm) Sy Oliver(arr,cond).
NYC,September 24,1958

Stormy weather CD BN 5-21151-2

BOBBY MONTEZ:
Bobby Montez(vb) Carlos Ortega Avelar(p) Jimmy Baiz(b) Miguel Guttierez(timbales) Luis Miranda(cga).
1958

African fantasy CD BN 5-21688-2

LOU LEVY TRIO:
Lou Levy(p) Max Bennett(b) Gus Johnson(dm).
LA, 1958

Under Paris skies CD BN 7-99100-2

LIBERTY

JIMMY ROWLES:
Jimmy Rowles(p) Red Mitchell(b) Art Mardigan(dm).
(Western Recorders) LA,September,1954

Serenade in blue CD BN 4-95981-2
Chloe CD BN(J)TOCJ-5710

JULIE LONDON:
Barney Kessel(g) Ray Leatherwood(b) Julie London(vo).
LA,October,1955

Gone with the wind CD BN(J)TOCJ-5853
I'm in the mood for love CD BN(J)TOCJ-5856
Cry me a river CD BN 5-24271-2,(Au)8-14808-2,(J)TOCJ-6189
No moon at all CD BN 7-89910-2

JULIE LONDON:
Julie London(vo) with orchestra arr. by Pete King.
(Capitol Studios) LA,May ,1956

June in January CD BN (J)TOCJ-5854

ABBEY LINCOLN:
Abbey Lincoln(vo) with orchestra arr. & cond. by Benny Carter.
LA,July ,1956

Warm valley CD BN 8-55221-2
Do nothing till you hear from me - , 8-32994-2
Lonesome cup of coffee CD BN(C)4-94888-2

<u>BILL PERKINS</u> - <u>TENORS HEAD-ON</u>:
Bill Perkins,Richie Kamuca(ts) Pete Jolly(p) Red Mitchell(b) Stan Levey(dm).
(Radio Recorders) LA,July ,1956

Cottontail
I want a little girl
Blues for two
Indian Summer
Don't be that way
Oh look at me now
Spain
Pick a dilly

All titles issued on BN(F)BNP25114.

<u>ABBEY LINCOLN</u>:
Abbey Lincoln(vo) with Orchestra incl. strings arr. by Marty Paich.
LA, November 5-6,1956

Love walked in	CD BN 7-80506-2
Crazy he calls me	CD BN 7-96583-2

Abbey Lincoln(vo) with Orchestra incl. woodwinds arr. by Benny Carter.Same sessions.

This can't be love	CD BN(Sp)8-56842-2

<u>BOBBY TROUP</u>:
Bob Enevoldsen(tb) Buddy Collette(ts) Red Norvo(vb) Jimmy Rowles(p) Al Viola(g) Mike Rubin(b) Don Heath(dm) Bobby Troup(vo).
(Capitol Studios) LA,November 6 or 7,1956

Route 66	CD BN 7-80707-2,(Eu)5-23444-2

<u>JACK COSTANZO</u>:
Jay Corre(ts) Eddie Cano(p) Tony Reyes(b) Ray Rivera(dm) Jack Costanzo(bgo).
LA, 1958

Latin fever	CD BN 5-21688-2

<u>JULIE LONDON</u>:
Julie London(vo) with orchestra arr. & cond. by Andre Previn.
LA, ?1959

They can't take that away from me	CD BN 7-80706-2

Julie London(vo) with Bob Flanigan(tb) Emil Richards(vb) Jimmy Rowles(p) Al Viola(g) Don Bagley(b) Earl Palmer(dm). (Capitol Studios) LA,March 4,1960

You'd be so nice to come home to	CD BN(C)4-94888-2

Julie London(vo) with Orchestra arr. by Dick Reynolds,incl. fl,p,b,dm.
(Capitol Studios) LA,August,1960

Misty	CD BN 8-57463-2

Julie London(vo) with string orchestra arr. by Bobby Troup.
LA,March 15 & 16,1962

Love letters	CD BN 7-81331-2
What a diff'rence a day makes	CD BN(J)TOCJ-5855

JULIE LONDON:

Julie London(vo) with Pete King sextet.

(Universal Studios) Chicago,August 28-30,1962

What's new CD BN(J)TOCJ-6152

Julie London(vo) with Orchestra arr. & cond. by Ernie Freeman.

LA, 1963

Fly me to the moon CD BN 5-21151-2

Julie London(vo) with orchestra arr. & cond. by Richard Wess.

(RCA Studios) LA,October 9,1964

As time goes by CD BN(J)TOCJ-5875

Julie London(vo) with Bud Shank(as,fl) Russ Freeman(p) Joe Pass(g) Monte Budwig(b) Colin Bailey(dm).

(Pacific Jazz Studios) LA,July ,1965

My heart belongs to Daddy CD BN(C) 4-94888-2

MEL TORME:

Mel Torme(vo) with orchestra arr. by Lincoln Mayorga.

LA, c.1970

I concentrate on you CD BN(J)TOCJ-5854

IKE & TINA TURNER:

Tina Turner(lead vo) Ike Turner(p,g) The Ikettes (Esther Burton,Jane Burks,Vera Hamilton)(vo) with Allen Deville(tp) Edward Burks(tb) Ronald Miller(ts) Harold Freddie(bs) Leon Blue(p,org) Jackie Clark(lead g) Byron Ridge(rh g) John Lillyn(el b) Soko Richardson(dm) & perc.

Las Vegas & LA,August/September 1970

Game of love BN 5-21147-1,CD 5-21147-2

EARL KLUGH - DREAM COME TRUE:

Note: On following album,all tracks were recorded at Electric Lady Studios in NYC,with some additional parts recorded at Young'un Sound in Nashville.Strings & flutes were recorded later on at Columbia 30th Street Studio in NYC and overdubbed on.

Greg Philllinganes(synth) Darryl Dybka(el p) Mickie Roquemore(p,clavinet) Earl Klugh(g) Perry Hughes (el g) Marcus Miller(el b) Gene Dunlap(dm) Dr. Gibbs(perc) with strings & flutes arr. by Dave Matthews.

NYC,September 19,1979

20782 Amazon BN(J)GP-3225;CD BN 7-46625-2

Phillinganes out. Hubie Crawford(el b) replaces Miller.

NYC,September 21,1979

20784 If it's in your heart,it's in your smile BN(J)GP-3225

Greg Phillinganes(keyb) Earl Klugh(g) David Saltman(el b) James Bradley,Jr.(dm) Dr. Gibbs(perc) & strings arr. by Dave Matthews.

NYC,September 24,1979

20785 Dream come true BN(J)GP-3225,W-5515

Saltman & Gibbs out. NYC,September 25,1979

20786 Spellbound BN(J)GP-3225

David Briggs(p) Mickie Roquemore(el p) Earl Klugh(g) Reggie Young(el g) Lloyd Green(pedal steel g) Mike Leech(el b) Gene Dunlap(dm) Dr.Gibbs(perc) Frank Floyd,Krystal Davis,Yvonne Lewis(backgr.vo) with strings & flutes arr. by Dave Matthews.

NYC,October 1,1979

20787 I don't want to leave you alone anymore BN(J)GP-3225;CD BN 7-46625-2

David Briggs(p) Mickie Roquemore(el p) Earl Klugh(g) Reggie Young(el g) Lloyd Green(pedal steel g) Mike Leech(el b) Gene Dunlap(dm) Dr.Gibbs(perc).

NYC,October 3,1979

20789 Sweet rum and starlight BN(J)GP-3225;CD BN 8-53354-2

EARL KLUGH - DREAM COME TRUE:
Darryl Dybka(el p) Mickie Roquemore(synth,tack p) Earl Klugh(g) Perry Hughes (el g) Hubie Crawford(el b) Gene Dunlap(dm) Dr. Gibbs(perc) with strings & flutes arr. by Dave Matthews.
NYC,October 24,1979

20815 Doc BN(J)GP-3225,K28P-6045,W-5515

Mickie Roquemore(p,el p) Earl Klugh(g) Reggie Young(el g) Lloyd Green(pedal steel g) Mike Leech(el b) Gene Dunlap(dm) Dr.Gibbs(perc) with strings & flutes arr. by Dave Matthews.
NYC,October 29,1979

20814 Message to Michael BN(J)GP-3225

EARL KLUGH - LATE NIGHT GUITAR:
Earl Klugh(g).
(Electric Lady Studios) NYC,April 4,1980
Phil Bodner,Walter Kane(woodwinds) David Friedman(perc,vb) with strings arr. & cond. by Dave Matthews,overdubbed on at a later date.
(Columbia 30th Street Studio) NYC, 1980

21038 I'll never say goodbye
21039 Two for the road
21040 Nice to be around
21041 Like a lover CD BN 8-53354-2
21042 Mona Lisa

All titles issued on CD BN 4-98573-2.

John Gatchell,Joe Shepley(tp) Sam Burtis(tb) David Tofani(ts) Ronnie Cuber(bs) Ken Ascher(el p) Earl Klugh(g) David Spinozza(rhythm g) Marcus Miller(el b) Jose Madera,Michael Collazo(Latin perc).
-1: Earl Klugh(g) Gloria Agostini(harp).
(Electric Lady Studios) NYC,July 23,1980

21278 Lisbon antigua CD BN 4-98573-2
21279 A time for love -1 -

Earl Klugh(g) Dr.Gibbs(perc-1).
(Electric Lady Studios) NYC,July 24,1980

21347 Triste CD BN 8-35283-2
21348 Mirabella CD BN 8-53354-2
21349 Smoke gets in your eyes
21350 Laura
21351 Jamaica farewell -1
21352 Tenderly

All titles issued on CD BN 4-98573-2.

EARL KLUGH - CRAZY FOR YOU:
Ronnie Foster(el p,vocoder) Earl Klugh(g) Phil Upchurch,Donald Griffin-2(el g) Nathan East(el b) Ricky Lawson(dm) Paulinho Da Costa(perc) & strings arr. by Patrick Williams-1,Johnny Mandel-2.
(A & M Studios) LA,January 14,1981

21611 Soft stuff (and other delights)-1 CD BN 7-48387-2
21612 Calypso getaway-2 CD BN 7-46625-2,7-48387-2

Ronnie Foster(el p) Greg Phillinganes(synth) Earl Klugh(g) Phil Upchurch,Donald Griffin(el g) Charles Meeks(el b) James Bradley Jr.(dm) Paulinho Da Costa(perc) & strings arr. by Clare Fischer.
(A & M Studios) LA,January 15,1981

21613 Crazy for you CD BN 7-48387-2,7-80505-2

Ronnie Foster(el p) Earl Klugh(g) Phil Upchurch(el g) Charles Meeks(el b) James Bradley Jr. (dm) Paulinho Da Costa(perc) & strings arr. by Clare Fischer.
(A & M Studios) LA,January 23,1981

21620 Balladina (Ballad in A) CD BN 7-48387-2,8-53354-2

EARL KLUGH - CRAZY FOR YOU:
Silvester Rivers(el p) Greg Phillinganes(synth) Earl Klugh(g) Ray Parker Jr.(el g,b,dm,arr) Jack Ashford (tamb).

(A & M Studios) LA,January 17 or 26,1981

21773 I'm ready for your love CD BN 7-48387-2,8-53354-2

Greg Phillinganes(el p,synth,arr) Earl Klugh(g) Louis Johnson(el b) Raymond Pounds(dm) Paulinho Da Costa(perc).

LA,February 4,1981

21774 Twinkle CD BN 7-48387-2

RONNIE LAWS - SOLID GROUND:
Ronnie Laws(as,vo) Barnaby Finch(p) Larry Dunn(synth) Pat Kelly(g) Leon Johnson(el b) William Bryant (dm).

(Indigo Ranch) LA,February 9,1981

21662 Stay awake CD BN 4-98544-2

Ronnie Laws(sopranino sax,ts,p) Barnaby Finch(p) Larry Dunn(synth) Roland Bautista(g) Leon Johnson(el b) William Bryant(dm).

(Indigo Ranch) LA,February 19,1981

21664 Solid ground BN(J)W-5515;CD BN 7-98289-2,4-98544-2

Ronnie Laws(ss,vo) Barnaby Finch(p) Pat Kelly(g) Leon Johnson(el b) William Bryant (dm) Marlena Jeter, Gwenche Machu(backgr.vo).

(Indigo Ranch) LA,March 30,1981

21703 There's a way CD BN 4-98544-2

Ronnie Laws(ss,vo) Barnaby Finch(p) Larry Dunn(synth) Pat Kelly(g) Leon Johnson(el b) William Bryant (dm) Marlena Jeter,Gwenche Machu,Debra Laws(backgr.vo).

(Indigo Ranch) LA,April 9,1981

21753 Summer fool CD BN 4-98544-2

Ronnie Laws(ss,p) Denzil Miller(el p) Larry Dunn(synth) Leon Johnson(el b) Raymond Pounds(dm).

(Indigo Ranch) LA,April 9,1981

21754 Just as you are CD BN 7-98289-2,4-98544-2

Hubert Laws(fl) Ronnie Laws(sopranino sax,ss,vo) Denzil Miller(p,synth) William Bryant(dm) Marlena Jeter,Gwenche Machu(backgr.vo).

(Indigo Ranch) LA,April 10,1981

21755 Your stuff CD BN 4-98544-2

Ronnie Laws(alto fl,ss) Barnaby Finch(p) Larry Dunn(synth) Roland Bautista(g) Leon Johnson(el b) William Bryant(dm) Darryl Munyungo Jackson(perc).

(Indigo Ranch) LA,April 17,1981

21772 Heavy on easy CD BN 4-98544-2

EARL KLUGH - CRAZY FOR YOU:
Hubie Crawford(hca) Darryl Dybka(synth voice,el p) Earl Klugh(g) Perry Hughes(el g) Mickie Roquemore (synth b) Gene Dunlap(dm).

(Media Sound) NYC,May 15,1981

21816 Broadway ramble CD BN 7-48387-2

539

RONNIE LAWS - SOLID GROUND:
Ronnie Laws(as) Barnaby Finch(p) Pat Kelly(g) Leon Johnson(el b) William Bryant(dm) Marlena Jeter, Eloise Laws,Maxi Anderson(backgr.vo) Frank Kavelin(string arr).
(Indigo Ranch) LA,May 19,1981

21829 Good feelings CD BN 4-98544-2

EARL KLUGH - CRAZY FOR YOU:
Jon Faddis,Lew Soloff,Joe Shepley,John Gatchell(tp) Jim Pugh,Sam Burtis(tb) Dave Taylor(bass tb) George Young(ts) Onaje Allan Gumbs(el p) Earl Klugh(g) Hiram Bullock(el g) Gary King(el b) Brian Blake(dm) Sammy Figueroa,Manolo Badrena(perc).
(Media Sound) NYC,May 22,1981

21818 The Rainmaker CD BN 7-48387-2,7-80505-2

RONNIE LAWS - SOLID GROUND:
Unknown el p,g,el b,dm.
LA,August 20,1981

22030 Segue CD BN 4-98544-2

MANHATTAN

AL DI MEOLA:
Al Di Meola(g). NYC, 1984

Coral CD BN 7-96581-2
Atavism of twilight CD BN(J)TOCJ-5602

Phil Markowitz(synth) Al Di Meola(g) Chip Jackson(b) Danny Gottlieb(dm) Airto Moreira(perc,vo).
(Right Track Recording Studio) NYC,late 1985

July BN(In)JAZ 3

PIECES OF A DREAM:
James Lloyd(keyb) Rhett Lawrence(synth programming) Marlon McLain(g) Cedric Napoleon(b) Curtis Harmon(dm) Paulinho Da Costa(perc).
(Bill Schnee's Studio) LA,late 1985

Outside in BN(In)JAZ 3

James Lloyd,Bernard Wright(keyb) Jason Miles,Jamie Lawrence,Lenny White(synth programming) Cedric Napoleon(b,vo) Curtis Harmon(dm) Chude Mondiane,Sybil Thomas,Dennis Collins(backgr.vo).
(House Of Music) NYC, late 1985

Say la la CD BN 8-35800-2

James Lloyd(keyb) Cedric Napoleon(b)Curtis Harmon(dm) Lance Webb(vo) Cliff Dawson (backgr.vo,arr) Preston Glass(keyb & dm programming,arr).
(One On One Studios) LA,c.1987

Rising to the top CD BN 8-35800-2

PIECES OF A DREAM:
James Lloyd,Vincent Evans(keyb) Pete Levin(keyb programming) Randall Bowland(g) Cedric Napoleon(b) Curtis Harmon(dm).
(Kajem Studios) NYC,c.1987

'Round Midnight CD BN 8-35800-2

TANIA MARIA:
Tania Maria(keyb,vo) Eddie Gomez(b) Steve Gadd(dm) Steve Thornton(perc)
NYC,c.1987

Valeu CD BN 8-57463-2

AL DI MEOLA:
Kei Akagi(keyb) Al Di Meola(g) Anthony Jackson(el b) Harvey Swartz(b) Tommy Brechtlein(dm) Mino Cinelu,Carlos "Beluba" Da Silva Pinto,Roberto "Lusa" Bastos Pinheiro,Elizeu Felix(perc) Jose Renato(vcl).
NYC,April ,1987

Rhapsody of fire CD BN(J)TOCJ-5602

NAJEE:
Najee(ss) Eric Rehl(keyb,synth programming) Wayne Braithwaite(el b,synth,dm programming) Yogi Lee(vo)
(39th Street Music/Unique Recording) NYC,c.1987-88

Day by day CD BN 8-23735-2

NAJEE:
Najee(ss,keyb) Fareed(keyb,dm programming) Alex Bugnon,Robert Damper(keyb) Cindy Mizell,Audrey Wheeler(backgr. vo).
(Celestial recording/Unique Recording) NYC,c. 1987-88

Gina CD BN 5-23547-2

NAJEE:
Najee(ts,keyb) Robert Damper(keyb) Fareed(g,perc) Barry Johnson(b) Judy Jones,Barry Johnson,Cindy Gomes(backgr. vo).
(Celestial recording/Unique Recording) NYC,c. 1987-88

That's the way of the world CD BN 5-23547-2

TANIA MARIA:
Tania Maria(keyb,vo) Ted Lo(synth) Anthony Jackson(el b) Buddy Williams(dm) Airto Moreira,Steve Thornton(perc).
NYC, 1988

It's only love CD BN(J)TOCJ-5217

BOBBY McFERRIN:
Bobby McFerrin(vo).
(Power Station) NYC, 1988

Don't worry, be happy CD BN(J)TOCJ-6152,
Good lovin'
Drive my car CD BN 5-21153-2,(J)TOCJ-5874,
Cap(J)TOCJ-5201

All titles issued on CD BN 8-53329-2.

RICHARD ELLIOT:
Richard Elliot(ts) Tom Kellock(keyb) Alan Hinds(g) Naoki Yanai(b) Bob Harsen(dm,perc).
LA, 1988

When a man loves a woman	CD BN 7-99105-2.(J)TOCJ-5856
In your arms	CD BN(J)TOCJ-5857

Note: Above titles originally from the Intima label.

STANLEY JORDAN:
Stanley Jordan(g).
(Village Recorders) LA, 1988

Flying home	CD BN 8-31502-2

STANLEY JORDAN:
Preston Glass(keyb) Stanley Jordan(g) Larry Graham(el b) Cody Moffett(dm).
(Village Recorders) LA, 1988

Stairway to heaven	CD BN 8-31502-2

RICHARD ELLIOT:
Richard Elliot(ts,lyricon) Tom Kellock(keyb) Richard Smith(g) Naoki Yanai(b).
LA, 1989

Rise and shine	CD BN(J)TOCJ-5855
Sea Breeze	CD BN(J)TOCJ-5851

Note: Above titles originally from the Intima label.

DIANNE REEVES:
Dianne Reeves(vo) with George Duke(keyb) Ray Fuller(g) Abraham Laboriel(el b) Ricky Lawson(dm) Claude McKnight III,Mark Kibble,Mervyn Warren,David Thomas(backgr.vo).
LA, 1989

Hello (haven't I seen you before)	CD BN(J)TOCJ-6088

PIECES OF A DREAM:
James Lloyd(p.synth,programming).
(Morning Star Studios) Ambler,Penn.,c.1989

For you	CD BN 8-35800-2

TANIA MARIA:
Lew Soloff(tp) Jay Ashby(tb) Jim Clouse(ts) Tania Maria(keyb,perc,vo) Robbie Kondor(synth) Dan Carillo (g) Tom Barney(b) Kim Plainfield(dm) Manolo Badrena,Luis Conte(perc).
NYC,c. 1990-91

210 West	CD BN(E)8-53231-2,(J)TOCJ-5603

Lew Soloff(tp) Jay Ashby(tb) Jim Clouse(ts) Tania Maria(keyb,perc,vo) Robbie Kondor(synth) Will Lee(el b) Steve Gadd(dm) Sammy Figueroa(perc).
NYC,c.1990-91

Satisfaction	CD BN(J)TOCJ-6189

HOLLY COLE TRIO:
Aaron Davis(p) David Piltch(b) Holly Cole(vo).
(Eastern Sound) Toronto,June-July,1991

Trust in me CD B(C) 8-33908-2,(J)TOCJ-6189
Calling you CD BN 5-21151-2,(J)TOCJ-5875.TOCJ-6135, TOCJ-6153,TOCJ-6187

Similar. Date unknown

Me and my shadow CD BN(C)8-33908-2

ELIANE ELIAS:
Eliane Elias(p,vo) John Herington(g) Marc Johnson(b) Peter Erskine(dm) Mino Cinelu(perc) Mark Ledford (vo).
NYC, 1991

Back in time CD BN 8-57463-2

EVERETTE HARP:
Everette Harp(as,keyb,arr) Morris Pleasure(keyb) Doc Powell(g) Larry Kimpel(el b) Herman Mathews(dm) George Duke(perc).
LA, 1992

Full circle CD BN (E) 8-53226-2

PIECES OF A DREAM:
Ron Kerber(as) James Lloyd(keyb,synth b,programming) Jeff Lee(g).
(Morning Star Studios) Ambler,Penn., 1992

Club jazz (club mix) CD BN 8-35800-2

RICHARD ELLIOT:
Richard Elliot(ss,ts) Sam Mims(keyb,arr) Naoki Yanai(el b) Craig Yamek(perc).
(Suncoast Recording) Brandon,Florida, 1992

I'm not in love CD BN(J)TOCJ-6188

LOU RAWLS - PORTRAIT OF THE BLUES:
Lou Rawls(vo) with Richard Tee(p,el p,org) Steve Khan(el g) Tinker Marfield(el b) Chris Parker(dm).
(M & I Studios) NYC,April 13-16,1992

My babe-1
I'm still in love with you -2,5 CD BN 8-56689-2
I just want to make love to you-3
Since I met you baby-4,5

-1: Houston Person(ts) added. (M & I Studios) NYC,October 3,1992 &
Buddy Guy(solo g) added.(Streeterville Studio) Chicago,June 11,1992.
-2: Joe Lovano(ts) Cornell Dupree(obbligato g) added.(M & I Studios) NYC,May 27,1992.
-3: Junior Wells(hca) added.(Streeterville Studio) Chicago,June 11,1992 &
Tom Pomposello(slide g) added.(M & I Studios) NYC,July 15,1992.
-4: Plas Johnson(ts) added.(Capitol Studios) LA,August 25,1992.
-5: Jon Faddis(tp) Jimmy Knepper(tb Jerome Richardson(as) Ron Blake(ts) Seldon Powell(bs) Benny Golson (arr) overdubbed on. (M & I Studios) NYC,October 2,1992.

All titles issued on Manhattan CD 7-99548-2,to be reissued on the Blue Note label.

LOU RAWLS - PORTRAIT OF THE BLUES:
Lou Rawls(vo) with Richard Tee(p,el p,org) Steve Khan(el g) Tinker Marfield(el b) Chris Parker(dm).
(M & I Studios) NYC,April 14,1992

Hide nor hair -1,6
Snap your fingers -2
Save your love for me -5 CD BN 8-56689-2
Saturday night fish fry -3

-1: Hank Crawford(as) added.(M & I Studios) NYC,April 17,1992.
-2: Plas Johnson(ts) added.(Capitol Studios) LA,August 25,1992.
-3: Joe Williams(vo) added.(Capitol Studios) LA,August 25,1992 &
Lionel Hampton(vb) added.(M & I Studios) NYC,April 17,1992
-5: Jon Faddis(tp) Jimmy Knepper(tb Jerome Richardson(as) Ron Blake(ts) Seldon Powell(bs) Benny Golson (arr) overdubbed on. (M & I Studios) NYC,October 2,1992.
-6: Tim Hagans(tp) Wayne Andre(tb)Hank Crawford(as,arr) David Newman(ts) Seldon Powell(bs) overdubbed on. (M & I Studios) NYC,October 3,1992.

All titles issued on Manhattan CD 7-99548-2,to be reissued on the Blue Note label.

LOU RAWLS - PORTRAIT OF THE BLUES:
Lou Rawls(vo) with Richard Tee(p,el p,org) Steve Khan(el g) Tinker Marfield(el b) Chris Parker(dm).
(M & I Studios) NYC,April 15,1992

Baby, what you want me to do -1
A lover's qesution -2
Chains of love -3,6 CD BN 8-56689-2
Person to person -4,6

-1: Junior Wells(hca) added.(Streeterville Studio) Chicago,June 11,1992.
-2: Joe Lovano(fl) added.(M & I Studios) NYC,May 27,1992 &
Tom Pomposello(slide g) Phoebe Snow(vo) added.(M & I Studios) NYC,July 15,1996
-3: Hank Crawford(as) added.(M & I Studios) NYC,April 17,1992, &
Cornell Dupree(obbligato g) added.(M & I Studios) NYC,May 27,1992
-4: Hank Crawford(as) added.(M & I Studios) NYC,April 17,1992.
-6: overdubs as shown in session above.

All titles issued on Manhattan CD 7-99548-2,to be reissued on the Blue Note label.

LOU RAWLS - PORTRAIT OF THE BLUES:
Lou Rawls(vo) with Richard Tee(p,el p,org) Steve Khan(el g) Tinker Marfield(el b) Chris Parker(dm).
(M & I Studios) NYC,April 16,1992

Sweet slumber -1,5 CD BN 8-56689-2
Suffering with the blues -2,6
I ain't got nothing but the blues -3,5 CD BN 8-55221-2

-1: Hank Crawford(as) added.(M & I Studios) NYC,April 17,1992.
-2: Cornell Dupree(obbligato g) added.(M & I Studios) NYC,May 27,1992.
-3: Hank Crawford(as) added.(M & I Studios) NYC,April 17,1992 &
Joe Lovano(ts) Cornell Dupree(obbligato g) added.(M & I Studios) NYC,May 27,1992.
5,6: overdubs as shown in session above (April 14).

All titles issued on Manhattan CD 7-99548-2,to be reissued on the Blue Note label.

RICHARD ELLIOT:
Richard Elliot(ts) Ron Reinhardt(keyb)
(Suncoast Recording) Brandon,Florida,September ,1992

Because I love you CD BN 5-20070-2

METRO BLUE

HOLLY COLE:

Holly Cole(vo) with Howard Levy(hca-1) Aaron Davis(p) Kevin Breit(el g-1) Rob Piltch(ac g-1) David Piltch(b) Dougie Bowne(dm) Cyro Baptista(perc-1) The Colettes(backgr.vo-2).

(Grand Avenue Studio) Hamilton,Ontario, 1995

(Looking for) The heart of Saturday night -1
CD BN(Au)8-14808-2,(E)8-53231-2

Jersey girl-2 CD BN 8-54363-2

Holly Cole(vo) with Aaron Davis(p) Kevin Breit(g) David Piltch(b) Dougie Bowne(dm,perc).

(Live) Montreal,June 28,1995

Get out of town CD BN(Sp)8-56842-2

Holly Cole(vo) with Aaron Davis(org) Jim Cox(el p) Kevin Breit(g) Greg Leisz(pedal steel g) David Piltch(b) Mark Kelso(dm).

(McClear Pathe Studio) Toronto, 1996

Make it go away CD BN 4-95317-2

545

PACIFIC JAZZ

Note: This section also includes recordings originally issued on World Pacific & World Pacific Jazz labels.

GERRY MULLIGAN:
Gerry Mulligan(bs,p) Red Mitchell(b) Chico Hamilton(dm).
(Phil Turetsky's home studio) LA,June 10,1952

Get happy BN LT-1101

GERRY MULLIGAN QUARTET:
Chet Baker(tp) Gerry Mulligan(bs) Jimmy Rowles(p) Joe Mondragon(b).
(Phil Turetsky's home studio) LA,July 9,1952

She didn't say yes BN LT-1101,(F)BNP25103

GERRY MULLIGAN QUARTET:
Chet Baker(tp) Gerry Mulligan(bs) Bob Whitlock(b) Chico Hamilton(dm).
(Phil Turetsky's home studio) LA,August 16 or 29,1952

Bernie's tune CD BN(E)8-53224-2
Lullaby of the leaves BN(J)FCPA6212,W-5503,CD TOCJ-5853

Both titles issued on BN LT-1101,(F)BNP25103.

GERRY MULLIGAN QUARTET:
Same.
(Gold Star Studios) LA,October 15,1952

Nights at the turntable
Frenesi
Aren't you glad you're you
Walkin' shoes
Soft shoe
Freeway

All titles issued on BN LT-1101,(F)BNP25103.

AL HAIG:
Al Haig(p) Harry Babasin(b) Larry Bunker(dm)
LA, September 6,1952

Takin' a chance on love CD BN 7-96580-2

GERRY MULLIGAN:
Chet Baker(tp) Lee Konitz(as) Gerry Mulligan(bs) Joe Mondragon(b) Larry Bunker(dm).
(Phil Turetsky's home studio) LA,late January 1953

235 I can't believe that you're in love with me BN BN-LA532-H2
238 Lady be good -

546

GERRY MULLIGAN:
Chet Baker(tp) Lee Konitz(as) Gerry Mulligan(bs) Carson Smith(b) Larry Bunker(dm).
LA,late January 1953

	Broadway	
237	Sextet	
	Almost like being in love	

All titles issued on BN BN-LA532-H2.

GERRY MULLIGAN:
Chet Baker(tp) Lee Konitz(as) Gerry Mulligan(bs) Carson Smith(b) Larry Bunker(dm).
(The Haig) LA,late January 1953

236	Lover man	CD BN 7-80707-2
	These foolish things	
	I'll remember April	
	All the things you are	
	Too marvelous for words	CD BN 7-89914-2

All titles issued on BN BN-LA532-H2.

GERRY MULLIGAN QUARTET:
Chet Baker(tp) Gerry Mulligan(bs) Carson Smith(b) Larry Bunker(dm).
(Gold Star Studios) LA,February 24,1953

Cherry	BN(F)BNP25103
Carson City stage	-
Makin' whoopee	-

Chet Baker(tp) Gerry Mulligan(bs) Carson Smith(b) Larry Bunker(dm).
(Radio Recorders) LA,April 27,1953

Jeru	BN(J)FCPA6212,W-5503

Chet Baker(tp) Gerry Mulligan(bs) Carson Smith(b) Larry Bunker(dm).
LA,April 29-30,1953

The nearness of you	BN(J)FCPA6212
Tea for two	-

Chet Baker(tp) Gerry Mulligan(bs) Carson Smith(b) Larry Bunker(dm).
(The Haig) LA,May 20,1953

Five brothers	
My funny Valentine	BN(J)W-5503;CD BN(E)8-53224-2

Both titles issued on CD BN 8-54905-2.

CHET BAKER-STAN GETZ:
Chet Baker(tp) Stan Getz(ts) Carson Smith(b) Larry Bunker(dm).
(The Haig) LA,June 12,1953

My funny Valentine	CD BN(Sp)5-21755-2

547

CHET BAKER:
Chet Baker(tp) Russ Freeman(p) Joe Mondragon(b) Shelly Manne(dm).
(Radio Recorders) LA,October 3,1953

Happy little Sunbeam CD BN(J)TOCJ-5852
Bea's flat CD BN (E) 8-53224-2

CHET BAKER:
Chet Baker(tp) Russ Freeman(p) Joe Mondragon(b) Shelly Manne(dm).
(Radio Recorders) LA,October 27,1953

Winter wonderland CD BN 7-94857-2

CHET BAKER:
Chet Baker(tp) Herb Geller(as) Jack Montrose(ts,arr) Bob Gordon(bs) Russ Freeman(p) Joe Mondragon(b) Shelly Manne(dm).
LA, December 14,1953

Bockhanal CD BN 8-54902-2

RUSS FREEMAN:
Russ Freeman(p) Joe Mondragon(b) Shelly Manne(dm).
LA,December 22,1953

Bock's tops CD BN(J)TOCJ-5187/88

CHET BAKER:
Chet Baker(tp,vo) Russ Freeman(p) Carson Smith(b) Bob Neel(dm).
(Capitol Studios) LA,February 15,1954

PJ 358 But not for me CD BN 7-80506-2,7-80706-2,7-80707-2, 8-32994-2,8-54902-2,8-21381-2,5-21153-2, (C) 4-94888-2,(E) 8-53224-2,(J)CJ28-5177, TOCJ-66071
PJ 360 I get along without you very well CD BN 8-54902-2
PJ 363 My funny Valentine CD BN 7-81331-2,8-34957-2,5-24271-2, (C)8-33908-2,4-94888-2
PJ 364 I fall in love too easily CD BN 8-54902-2,(C)4-94888-2,(J)TOCJ-5299

LAURINDO ALMEIDA-BUD SHANK QUARTET:
Bud Shank(as) Laurindo Almeida(g) Harry Babasin(b) Roy Harte(dm).
LA,April 15 or 22,1954

Speak low BN(J)W-5511,CJ28-5023

BOB GORDON:
Jack Montrose(ts) Bob Gordon(bs) Paul Moer(p) Joe Mondragon(b) Billy Schneider(dm).
(Radio Recorders) LA,May 6,1954

Meet Mr.Gordon CD BN(J)TOCJ-5710

Same.
(Radio Recorders) LA, May 27,1954

Two can play CD BN 7-80707-2

CLIFFORD BROWN ENSEMBLE:
Clifford Brown(tp) Stu Williamson(tp,vtb) Zoot Sims(ts) Bob Gordon(bs) Russ Freeman(p) Joe Mondragon (b) Shelly Manne(dm) Jack Montrose(arr).

(Capitol Studios) LA,July 12,1954

Daahoud CD BN 8-23373-2
Finders keepers
Joy Spring CD BN 8-23373-2

All titles issued on CD BN 8-34195-2.

CHET BAKER:
Chet Baker(tp) Russ Freeman(p) Carson Smith(b)Bob Neel(dm).

(Live at the Tiffany Club) LA,August 10,1954

Russ Job CD BN 8-54902-2

CLIFFORD BROWN ENSEMBLE:
Clifford Brown(tp) Stu Williamson(tp,vtb) Zoot Sims(ts) Bob Gordon(bs) Russ Freeman(p) Carson Smith(b) Shelly Manne(dm) Jack Montrose(arr).

(Capitol Studios) LA,August 13,1954

Gone with the wind
Bones for Jones
Blueberry hill
Tiny capers CD BN 8-23373-2
Tiny capers (alt.)

All titles and takes issued on CD BN 8-34195-2.

CHET BAKER:
Chet Baker(tp) Bob Brookmeyer(vtb) Bud Shank(bs) Russ Freeman(p) Carson Smith(b) Shelly Manne(dm) Jack Montrose-1,Johnny Mandel-2 (arr).

LA,September 9,1954

Dot's Groovy -1 CD BN 8-54902-2
Stella by starlight -2 CD BN(J)TOCJ-5854

RICHARD TWARDZICK TRIO:
Richard Twardzick(p) Carson Smith(b) Peter Littman(dm).

Hackensack,N.J.,October 27,1954

'Round midnight B(J)W-5510

GERRY MULLIGAN:
Jon Eardley(tp-1)Bob Brookmeyer(vtb-1,p-2) Zoot Sims(ts) Gerry Mulligan(bs) Red Mitchell(b) Larry Bunker(dm).

(Hoover High School) San Diego,Calif.,December 14,1954

The red door -1 BN(J)W-5503
Western Union -2

Both titles issued on CD BN 8-54905-2.

549

CHET BAKER:
Chet Baker(tp,vo) Bud Shank(fl) Russ Freeman(p) Red Mitchell(b) Bob Neel(dm) Corky Hale(harp) & strings arr. by Johnny Mandel or Marty Paich.
(Capitol Studios) LA,February 28,1955

	This is always	CD BN 7-96582-2
	Someone to watch over me	CD BN(J)TOCJ-5750

CHET BAKER:
Chet Baker(tp,vo) Russ Freeman(p) Carson Smith(b) Bob Neel(dm).
(Capitol Studios) LA,March 7,1955

1730	Daybreak	CD BN(J)TOCJ-5855
1732	I remember you	CD BN(J)TOCJ-6189
1733	Let's get lost	CD BN 8-29964-2,(E)8-53224-2,(J)CJ28-5176,(Sp)8-34712-2,8-53016-2

BUD SHANK-BILL PERKINS:
Bud Shank,Bill Perkins(fl) Hampton Hawes(p) Red Mitchell(b) Mel Lewis(dm).
(Capitol Studios) LA,May 2,1955

Fluted columns	BN B2S 5256

HAMPTON HAWES:
Hampton Hawes(p) Red Mitchell(b) Mel Lewis(dm).
(Capitol Studios) LA,May 2,1955

I hear music	CD BN 7-80707-2,(J)TOCJ-5187/88

JACK MONTROSE SEXTET:
Conte Candoli(tp) Jack Montrose(ts) Bob Gordon(bs) Paul Moer(p) Ralph Pena(b) Shelly Manne(dm).
(Radio Recorders) LA,June 24,1955

Bewitched,bothered and bewildered	CD BN 8-29095-2

CHICO HAMILTON QUINTET:
Buddy Collette(fl) Jim Hall(g) Fred Katz(cello) Carson Smith(b) Chico Hamilton(dm).
(Radio Recorders) LA,August 23,1955

My funny Valentine	CD BN 7-81331-2
Blue sands	BN(J)W-5503

JACK SHELDON QUINTET:
Jack Sheldon(tp) Joe Maini(as) Kenny Drew(p) Leroy Vinnegar(b) Lawrence Marable(dm).
(Forum Theatre) LA,November 18,1955

It's only a paper moon	CD BN 7-89910-2,Cap(J)TOCJ-5229
Leroy's blues	
Contour	

All titles issued on CD BN 7-84439-2 under Kenny Drew's name.

BUD SHANK QUARTET:
Bud Shank(as) Claude Williamson(p) Don Prell(b) Chuck Flores(dm).
(Capitol Studios) LA,January 25,1956

Bag of blues	BN(J)FCPA6212,W-5503
Carioca	- CD TOCJ-5852

JOHN LEWIS-BILL PERKINS QUINTET:
Bill Perkins(ts) John Lewis(p) Jim Hall(g) Percy Heath(b) Chico Hamilton(dm).
('Music Box Theatre) LA,February 10,1956

2 degrees East,3 degrees West	BN(J)W-5503
I can't get started (p,b,dm only)	BN(J)W-5510;CD BN 7-80706-2, (J)TOCJ-5187/88,TOCJ-5300,TOCJ-5873
Easy living	CD BN 8-57460-2
Almost like being in love	CD BN(J)CJ28-5177

CHICO HAMILTON QUINTET:
Buddy Collette(reeds) Fred Katz(cello) Jim Hall(g) Carson Smith(b) Chico Hamilton(dm).
(Music Box Theatre) LA,February 10 or 13,1956

The squimp	CD BN 7-80707-2
Takin' a chance on love	CD BN(J)TOCJ-5856

CHET BAKER:
Chet Baker(vo,tp) Russ Freeman(p) Jimmy Bond(b) Peter Littman(dm).
(Forum Theatre) LA,July 23,1956

That old feeling	CD BN 8-54902-2

Chet Baker(tp) Phil Urso(ts) Bobby Timmons(p) Jimmy Bond(b) Peter Littman(dm).
(Forum Theatre) LA,July 24,25 or 31,1956

Lucius Lu	CD BN 8-54902-2
Halema	-
I can't get started (omit ts)	CD BN(E)8-53229-2

BOBBY TIMMONS:
Bobby Timmons(p) Jimmy Bond(b) Peter Littman(dm).
(Forum Theatre) LA,July 24,25 or 31 or October 18,1956

Autumn in New York	CD BN(J)TOCJ-5187/88

JAMES CLAY:
James Clay(ts) Bobby Timmons(p) Jimmy Bond(b) Peter Littman(dm).
(Forum Theatre) LA,July 25,1956

In a sentimental mood	CD BN 7-84440-2

CHET BAKER:
Chet Baker(tp) Art Pepper(as) Richie Kamuca(ts) Pete Jolly(p) Leroy Vinnegar(b) Stan Levey(dm).
(Forum Theatre) LA,July 26,1956

The route	CD BN 8-54902-2

Chet Baker(vo,tp) Russ Freeman(p) Jimmy Bond(b) Lawrence Marable(dm).
(Forum Theatre) LA,July 30,1956

My ideal	CD BN(J)TOCJ-5300

HOAGY CARMICHAEL:
Hoagy Carmichael(vo) with Orchestra arr. & cond. by Johnny Mandel: Harry "Sweets" Edison,Conrad Gozzo (tp) Jimmy Zito(bass tp) Harry Klee,Art Pepper(as) Mort Friedman(ts) Marty Berman(bs) Jimmy Rowles(p) Al Hendrickson(g) Joe Mondragon(b) Irv Cottler(dm).
(Forum Theatre) LA,September 10,1956

Georgia on my mind	CD BN 5-21153-2

HOAGY CARMICHAEL:
Don Fagerquist(tp) Art Pepper(as) Jimmy Rowles(p,celeste) Al Hendrickson(g) Joe Mondragon(b) Nick Fatool(dm) Hoagy Carmichael(vo).
-1: Ray Linn(tp) Harry Klee(fl) Mort Friedman(cl) Marty Berman(bass cl) added.Same session.

(Forum Theatre)	LA September 13,1956
Winter moon	CD BN 7-89910-2,(C)4-94888-2,(J)TOCJ-5854
Skylark -1	CD BN(J)TOCJ-5851

JIMMY ROWLES:
Jimmy Rowles(p) Al Hendrickson(g) Joe Mondragon(b) Nick Fatool(dm).

(Forum Theatre)	LA September 13,1956
We'll be together again	CD BN(J)TOCJ-5187/88

CHET BAKER:
Chet Baker(tp) Bob Burgess(tb) Fred Waters(as) Phil Urso,Bob Graf(ts) Bill Hood(bs) Bobby Timmons(p) Jimmy Bond(b) Peter Littman(dm) Pierre Michelot(arr).

	LA,October 18,1956
Chet	CD BN 4-97155-2

BILL PERKINS & RICHIE KAMUCA:
Bill Perkins(ts,bass cl) Richie Kamuca(ts) Hampton Hawes(p) Red Mitchell(b) Mel Lewis(dm).

(Radio Recorders)	LA,October 29,1956
Sweet and lovely	CD BN 8-54365-2
All of me	CD BN(J)TOCJ-6152

CHET BAKER & ART PEPPER:
Chet Baker(tp) Art Pepper(as) Phil Urso(ts) Carl Perkins(p) Curtis Counce(b) Lawrence Marable(dm).

(Radio Recorders)	LA,October 31,1956
For Miles and Miles	BN(J)FCPA6212
Picture of Heath	CD BN 8-54902-2
Minor yours	CD BN 8-33244-2
For minors only	BN(J)FCPA6212

CHET BAKER:
Chet Baker(tp) Russ Freeman(p) Leroy Vinnegar(b) Shelly Manne(dm).

	LA,November 6,1956
Love nest	BN(J)FCPA6212
Lush life	-
Summer sketch	-

Chet Baker,Don Fagerquist,Ray Linn(tp) Milt Bernhart(tb) Bud Shank,Charlie Mariano,Herbie Steward(as) Bill Holman,Richie Kamuca(ts) Pepper Adams(bs) Claude Williamson(p) Monty Budwig(b) Mel Lewis(dm) Mike Pacheco(bgo) Johnny Mandel(arr).

	LA,November 8,1956
Jimmy's theme	CD BN 7-80707-2

BUD SHANK & BOB COOPER:
Bud Shank(fl) Bob Cooper(oboe) Howard Roberts(g) Don Prell(b) Chuck Flores(dm).

	LA,November 29.1956
What'll I do	CD BN 7-99095-2

<u>GERRY MULLIGAN QUARTET</u>:
Bob Brookmeyer(vtb) Gerry Mulligan(bs) Bill Crow(b) Dave Bailey(dm).
(The Storyville Club) Boston,December 6,1956

Open country CD BN 8-54905-2

<u>BILL PERKINS & ART PEPPER</u>:
Art Pepper(as) Bill Perkins(ts) Jimmy Rowles(p) Ben Tucker(b) Mel Lewis(dm).
LA,December 11,1956

What is this thing called love CD BN 8-33244-2

<u>JIM HALL TRIO</u>:
Carl Perkins(p) Jim Hall(g) Red Mitchell(b).
LA,January 10 & 24,1957

Stompin' at the Savoy	BN(J)W-5511;CD BN 8-54363-2
Stella by starlight	-
Seven comes eleven	CD BN 7-96581-2
Tangerine	CD BN(J)CJ28-5177
Things ain't what they used to be	CD BN(J)CJ28-5030

<u>ART BLAKEY</u> - <u>ONCE UPON A GROOVE/RITUAL</u>:
Bill Hardman(tp) Jackie McLean(as) Sam Dockery(p) Spanky De Brest(b) Art Blakey(dm).
NYC,January 14,1957

Little T	CD BN 7-97190-2
Once upon a groove	
Sam's tune	
Touché	

All titles issued on BN LT-1065,CD 7-46858-2.

<u>ART BLAKEY</u> - <u>ONCE UPON A GROOVE/RITUAL</u>:
Bill Hardman(tp) Jackie McLean(as) Sam Dockery(p) Spanky De Brest(b) Art Blakey(dm).
NYC,February 11,1957

Exhibit A	BN LT-1065
Scotch blues	-
Wake up	-
Ritual -1	

-1: Hardman,McLean and Dockery play also percussion on this title. The spoken intro to this title has been issued as "Comment on ritual" on BN B1-28263,CD BN 8-28263-2.
All titles issued on CD BN 7-46858-2.

<u>BOB BROOKMEYER</u>:
Jimmy Giuffre(ts) Bob Brookmeyer(vtb) Jim Hall(g) Joe Benjamin(b) Dave Bailey(dm).
LA,July 13,1957

Some sweet day CD BN(J)TOCJ-5855

<u>ART PEPPER NINE</u>:
Don Fagerquist(tp) Stu Williamson(vtb) Red Callender(tu) Art Pepper(as) Bill Holman(ts) Bud Shank(bs) Russ Freeman(p) Monty Budwig(b) Shelly Manne(dm) Shorty Rogers(arr,cond).
LA,August 12,1957

Diablo's Dance	CD BN 7-80707-2
Bunny	CD BN 8-33244-2

ELMO HOPE QUINTET:
Stu Williamson(tp) Harold Land(ts) Elmo Hope(p) Leroy Vinnegar(b) Frank Butler(dm).
LA,October 31,1957

	So nice	CD BN 7-84438-2
	St. Elmo's fire	-
	Vaun ex	-

DAVID ALLYN:
David Allyn(vo) with orchestra arr. by Johnny Mandel.
LA,November ,1957

	Sure thing	CD BN 7-96582-2

CHET BAKER:
Chet Baker(vo) David Wheat(g) Russ Savakus(b).
NYC,December 9,1957

	Come rain or come shine	CD BN(E) 8-53224-2

GERRY MULLIGAN/LEE KONITZ:
Lee Konitz(as) Allen Eager,Zoot Sims(as,ts) Gerry Mulligan(bs) Freddie Green(g) Henry Grimes(b) Dave Bailey(dm) Bill Holman(arr).
(Fulton Studios) NYC,December 3,11 & 17,1957

	Disc jockey jump	CD BN 8-54905-2
	Crazy day	BN(E)UALP 17
	Revelation	CD BN 8-54905-2
	Venus de Milo	-
	Four and one more	
	Turnstile	
	Sextet No.2	

All titles issued on BN BN-LA532-H2.

GERRY MULLIGAN:
Chet Baker(tp) Gerry Mulligan(bs) Henry Grimes(b) Dave Bailey(dm).
(Fulton Studios) NYC,December 3,11 or 17,1957

	I got rhythm	CD BN 8-57742-2

ANNIE ROSS:
Annie Ross(vo) with Chet Baker(tp) Gerry Mulligan(bs) Henry Grimes(b) Dave Bailey(dm).
(Fulton Studios) NYC,December 11 or 17,1957

	How about you`	CD BN 7-96583-2
	I've grown accustomed to your face (alt.)	CD BN 8-57460-2
	It don't mean a thing	CD BN 8-55221-2

Annie Ross(vo) with Art Farmer(tp) Gerry Mulligan(bs) Bill Crow(b) Dave Bailey(dm).
(Fulton Studios) NYC,December ,1957

	I feel pretty	CD BN(C)4-94888-2,(J)TOCJ-5299,TOCJ-5857

WES MONTGOMERY:
Freddie Hubbard(tp) Wayman Atkinson,Alonzo Johnson(ts) Buddy Montgomery(vb) Joe Bradley(p) Wes Montgomery(g) Monk Montgomery(el b) Paul Parker(dm).
Chicago,December 30,1957

2021	Finger pickin' (g,p,b,dm only)	BN BN-LA531-H2
2023	Bock to Bock	-
	Billie's bounce	-

DAVID ALLYN:
David Allyn(vo) Jimmy Rowles(p) with orchestra arr. by Bill Holman or Johnny Mandel.
LA, 1958

They all laughed CD BN 7-80506-2

LAURINDO ALMEIDA & BUD SHANK:
Bud Shank(as) Laurindo Almeida(g) Gary Peacock(b) Chuck Flores(dm).
(Radio Recorders) LA,March, 1958

Gershwin Prelude No.2 CD BN 7-80706-2

BUD SHANK:
Bud Shank(as,fl) with Len Mercer Strings: Giulio Libano(tp) Glauco Masetti(as) Appio Squajella (fl,frh) Eraldo Volonte(ts) Fausto Papetti(bs) Bruno de Filippi(g) Don Prell(b) Jimmy Pratt(dm) with strings & harp arr. & cond. by Ezio Lenni (as "Len Mercer"). Milan,April 4-5,1958

Smoke gets in your eyes CD BN 8-54365-2

Note: Above title was originally recorded and issued by the Italian Music label and later purchased by Pacific Jazz.

GIL EVANS:
Johnny Coles,Louis Mucci,Ernie Royal(tp) Joe Bennett,Frank Rehak,Tom Mitchell(tb) Julius Watkins(frh) Harvey Phillips(tu) Julian "Cannonball" Adderley(as) Jerry Sanfino(reeds) Gil Evans(p,arr,cond) Chuck Wayne(g) Paul Chambers(b) Art Blakey(dm).
NYC,April 9,1958

Saint Louis blues
King Porter stomp
'Round midnight CD BN 8-35471-2
Lester leaps in BN(E)UALP 19

All titles issued on BN BN-LA461-H2.

WES MONTGOMERY:
Harold Land(ts) Buddy Montgomery(p) Wes Montgomery(g) Monk Montgomery(el b) Tony Bazley (dm).
LA,April 18,1958

4321 Far Wes
4322 Leila
4323 Old folks
Wes' tune CD BN 7-96581-2
Hymn for Carol
4326 Montgomeryland funk CD BN 4-94032-2
Stompin' at the Savoy

All titles issued on BN BN-LA531-H2.

Buddy Montgomery(vb) Richie Crabtree(p) Wes Montgomery(g) Monk Montgomery(el b) Benny Barth(dm).
(Forum Theatre) LA,April 22,1958

Stranger in paradise
Baubles,bangles and beads CD BN 8-29095-2

Both titles issued on BN BN-LA531-H2.

GIL EVANS:
Johnny Coles,Louis Mucci,Ernie Royal(tp) Joe Bennett,Frank Rehak,Tom Mitchell(tb) Julius Watkins(frh) Bill Barber(tu) Julian "Cannonball" Adderley(as) Phil Bodner(reeds) Gil Evans (p,arr,cond) Chuck Wayne(g) Paul Chambers(b) Philly Joe Jones(dm). NYC,May 2,1958

Willow tree BN BN-LA461-H2

JIMMY WITHERSPOON:
Jimmy Witherspoon(vo) with Harry "Sweets" Edison(tp)Teddy Edwards,Jimmy Allen(ts) Henry McDode(p) Herman Mitchell(g) Jimmy Hamilton(b) Jimmy Miller(dm).
(Radio Recorders) LA,May 16,1958

Then the lights go out CD BN 5-21153-2

GIL EVANS:
Johnny Coles,Louis Mucci,Ernie Royal(tp) Joe Bennett,Frank Rehak,Tom Mitchell(tb) Julius Watkins(frh) Bill Barber(tu) Julian "Cannonball" Adderley(as) Phil Bodner(reeds) Gil Evans(p,arr,cond) Chuck Wayne(g) Paul Chambers(b) Art Blakey(dm).
NYC,May 21,1958

Struttin' with some barbecue BN BN-LA461-H2

Clyde Raesinger(tp) replaces Ernie Royal. NYC,May 26,1958

Manteca CD BN 7-89032-2,4-97155-2
Bird feathers CD BN 8-57742-2

Both titles issued on BN BN-LA461-H2.

ANNIE ROSS:
Annie Ross(vo) with Conte Candoli,Pete Candoli(tp) Frank Rosolino(tb) Herb Geller(as) Richie Kamuca or Stan Getz(ts) Bill Perkins(bs) Russ Freeman(p) Jim Hall(g) Monty Budwig(b) Mel Lewis(dm).
LA,September 25,1958

Some people CD BN (E)8-53232-2

CHICO HAMILTON:
Paul Horn(fl) Buddy Collette(as) Jim Hall(g) Fred Katz(cello) Carson Smith(b,arr) Chico Hamilton(dm).
(Sound Enterprises) LA,January 9 or 12,1959

In a mellow tone CD BN 5-21052-2,(J)CJ28-5177

ANNIE ROSS:
Annie Ross(vo) with Orchestra arr. by Buddy Bregman:Conte Candoli,Pete Candoli(tp) Frank Rosolino(tb) Herb Geller(as) Richie Kamuca,Stan Getz(ts) Bill Perkins(bs) Russ Freeman(p) Jim Hall(g) Monty Budwig (b) Mel Lewis(dm). LA, 1959

Small world CD BN(Sp)8-56842-2

GIL EVANS:
Johnny Coles,Louis Mucci,Allan Smith(tp) Bill Elton,Curtis Fuller,Dick Lieb(tb) Bob Northern(frh) Bill Barber(tu) Steve Lacy(ss) Al Block(reeds) Gil Evans(p,arr,cond) Chuck Wayne(g) Dick Carter(b) Dennis Charles(dm).
NYC,c. early 1959

Davenport blues
Straight no chaser BN(J)W-5502
Django

All titles issued on BN BN-LA461-H2.

<u>GIL EVANS</u>:
Johnny Coles,Louis Mucci,Danny Styles(tp) Jimmy Cleveland,Curtis Fuller,Rod Levitt(tb) Earl Chapin(frh) Bill Barber(tu) Steve Lacy(ss) Budd Johnson(cl,ts) Eddie Caine(woodwinds) Gil Evans(p,arr,cond) Ray Crawford(g) Tommy Potter(b) Elvin Jones(dm).
NYC,February 5,1959

Chant of the Weed
Ballad of the sad young men
Joy Spring
Theme

All titles issued on BN BN-LA461-H2.

<u>ANNIE ROSS & ZOOT SIMS</u>:
Annie Ross(vo) with Zoot Sims(ts) Russ Freeman(p) Jim Hall(g) Monte Budwig(b) Mel Lewis(dm).
LA,February ,1959

I was doing all right — CD BN 7-80506-2

<u>ANNIE ROSS</u>:
Annie Ross(vo) with Bill Perkins(ts) Russ Freeman(p) Jim Hall(g) Monte Budwig(b) Mel Lewis(dm).
LA,February ,1959

I'm just a lucky so and so — CD BN 5-21151-2

<u>LENNY McBROWNE & THE 4 SOULS</u>:
Don Sleet(tp) Daniel L. Jackson(ts) Terry Trotter(p) Herbie Lewis(b) Lenny McBrowne(dm).
(Pacific Jazz Studios) LA, mid 1959

Soul sisters — CD BN 4-94032-2

<u>TEDDY EDWARDS & LES McCANN LTD</u>:
Teddy Edwards(ts) Les McCann(p) Leroy Vinnegar(b) Ron Jefferson(dm).
(Pacific Jazz Studios) LA,August ,1959

Our love is here to stay — CD BN 7-80707-2

<u>WES MONTGOMERY</u>:
Pony Poindexter(as) Buddy Montgomery(p) Wes Montgomery(g) Monk Montgomery(el b) Louis Hayes (dm). LA,October 1,1959

6555	Summertime (as out)	BN(J)W-5511, CD BN(Sp)8-53016-2
	Monk's shop	
6557	Falling in love with love	
	Renie	

All titles issued on BN BN-LA531-H2.

<u>LES McCANN</u>:
Les McCann(p) Leroy Vinnegar(b) Ron Jefferson(dm).
(Pacific Jazz Studios) LA,February ,1960

PJ 6161	(13186)	Vacushna	CD BN(J)TOCJ-5187/88
PJ 6330	(13183)	Fish this week	
PJ 6708/9	(13185)	The truth	
	(13187)	A little 3/4 for God and Co.	
	(13188)	For Carl Perkins	

All titles issued on BN BN-LA171-G2.

557

LES McCANN:
Les McCann(p) Leroy Vinnegar(b) Ron Jefferson(dm).
(The Bit) LA,June ,1960

PJ 6594 (13191) The shout BN BN-LA171-G2

LES McCANN:
Les McCann(p) Herbie Lewis(b) Ron Jefferson(dm).
(The Jazz Workshop) SF,December ,1960

(13193) Come on and get that church
(13194) We'll see y'all after awhile,ya heah
(13198) Big Jim

All titles issued on BN BN-LA171-G2.

PAUL BRYANT:
Paul Bryant(org) Jim Hall(g) Jimmy Bond(b) Jimmy Miller(dm).
(Pacific Jazz Studios) LA, 1961

Burnin' CD BN 4-94032-2

CURTIS AMY & PAUL BRYANT:
Roy Brewster(vtb) Curtis Amy(ts) Paul Bryant(org) Clarence Jones(b) Jimmy Miller(dm)
(Pacific Jazz Studios) LA 1961

Meetin' here BN B1-29092, CD 8-29092-2

RICHARD GROOVE HOLMES:
Lawrence "Tricky" Lofton(tb) Ben Webster(ts) Richard Groove Holmes(org) Les McCann(p) George Freeman(g) Ron Jefferson(dm).
(Pacific Jazz Studios) LA,March 1961

Satin doll CD BN 4-94035-2

LES McCANN:
Les McCann(p) Herbie Lewis(b) Ron Jefferson(dm).
(Pacific Jazz Studios) LA,Spring ,1961

(13184) Dorene don't cry,I
(13189) Pretty lady

Both titles issued on BN BN-LA171-G2.

BUD SHANK:
Carmell Jones(tp) Bud Shank(as) Dennis Budimir(g) Gary Peacock(b) Mel Lewis(dm).
(Pacific Jazz Studios) LA,May ,1961

Liddledablldnya CED BN 5-21052-2

THE JAZZ CRUSADERS:
Wayne Henderson(tb) Wilton Felder(ts) Joe Sample(p) Roy Gaines(g-1) Jimmy Bond(b) Stix Hooper(dm).
(Pacific Jazz Studios) LA,May ,1961

E7912 Freedom sound -1
M.J.S. Funk
That's it

All titles issued on BN BN-LA170-G2.

CARMELL JONES:
Carmell Jones(tp) Harold Land(ts) Frank Strazzeri(p) Gary Peacock(b) Leon Pettis(dm).
(Pacific Jazz Studios) LA,June,1961

Full moon and empty arms CD BN 7-89910-2
Sad march CD BN 4-94032-2

RICHARD GROOVE HOLMES & GENE AMMONS:
Gene Ammons(ts) Richard Groove Holmes(org) Gene Edwards(g) Leroy Henderson(dm).
(Pacific Jazz Studios) LA, August 15,1961

Morris the minor BN B1-29092, 8-29092-2

KENNY DORHAM - INTA SOMETHIN':
Kenny Dorham(tp) Jackie McLean(as) Walter Bishop(p) Leroy Vinnegar(b) Art Taylor(dm).
(The Jazz Workshop) SF,November ,1961

Us (*aka* Una mas)
It could happen to you
Let's face the music
No two people
Lover man
San Francisco beat

All titles issued on CD BN 7-84460-2.

LES McCANN:
Les McCann(p) Herbie Lewis(b) Ron Jefferson(dm).
(Village Gate) NYC,December 28,1961

(13195) The shampoo
(13196) Someone stole my chitlins

Both titles issued on BN BN-LA171-G2.

RICHARD GROOVE HOLMES:
Richard Groove Holmes(org) Joe Pass(g) Lawrence Marable(dm).
(Pacific Jazz Studios) LA,late 1961-early 1962

This here CD BN 4-94032-2

THE JAZZ CRUSADERS:
Wayne Henderson(tb,euph) Wilton Felder(as,ts) Joe Sample(p) Jimmy Bond(b) Stix Hooper(dm).
(Pacific Jazz Studios) LA,January ,1962

(16544) The young rabbits
(16547) Big hunk of funk
(16548) Till all ends

All titles issued on BN BN-LA530-H2.

CLARE FISCHER TRIO:
Clare Fischer(p) Gary Peacock(b) Gene Stone(dm).
(Pacific Jazz Studios) LA,April 12,1962

I love you BN(J)W-5510

THE JAZZ CRUSADERS:
Wayne Henderson(tb,euph) Wilton Felder(ts) Joe Sample(p) Victor Gaskin(b) Stix Hooper(dm).
(The Lighthouse) Hermosa Beach,Calif.,August 5 & 6,1962

(16541)	Congolese sermon	
(16543)	Appointment in Ghana	CD BN 4-94031-2

Both titles issued on BN BN-LA530-H2.

GERALD WILSON:
Carmell Jones,Jules Chaikin,John Audino,Freddy Hill(tp) Bob Edmondson,Lou Blackburn,Frank Strong, Bob Knight(tb) Bud Shank,Joe Maini(as) Teddy Edwards,Harold Land(ts) Don Raffell(bs) Jack Wilson(p) Joe Pass(g) Jimmy Bond(b) Mel Lewis(dm) Modesto Duran(cga) Gerald Wilson(arr,cond).
(Pacific Jazz Studios) LA,August 27,1962

	Viva Tirado	BN B1-89907, CD 7-89907-2

Same.
LA,September ,1962

	Milestones	CD BN 4-97155-2

THE JAZZ CRUSADERS:
Wayne Henderson(tb,euph) Wilton Felder(ts) Joe Sample(p) Bobby Haynes(b) Stix Hooper(dm).
(Pacific Jazz Studios) LA,February ,1963

	Turkish black	BN BN-LA170-G2, CD 4-94032-2
	Lazy canary	-
	Tough talk	-
	No name samba	-
	Lonely horn	-
(16534)	Boopie	BN BN-LA530-H2

LES McCANN:
Charles Kynard(org) Les McCann(p) Stanley Gilbert(b) Paul Humphrey(dm).
LA, 1963

(13190)	The gospel truth	
(13192)	Sent it down to me	

Both titles issued on BN BN-LA171-G2.

JOE PASS - CATCH ME:
Clare Fischer(p,org-3) Joe Pass(g,ac g-4) Ralph Pena(b) Larry Bunker(dm).
(Pacific Jazz Studios) LA,January 30,1963

	Catch me (alt.version)-1,2	
	Days of wine and roses -2,3,4	CD BN(J)TOCJ-5296
	You stepped out of a dream	
	But beautiful -4	

-1: Entitled "Forward Pass" on its original 45 issue.
-2: Albert Stinson & Colin Bailey were miscredited for Pena & Bunker on BN LT-1053.
All titles issued on BN LT-1053.

Same. LA,February 4,1963

	Mood indigo	BN LT-1053

560

CURTIS AMY with DUPREE BOLTON:
Dupree Bolton(tp) Curtis Amy(ts) Jack Wilson(p) Ray Crawford(g) Victor Gaskin(b) Doug Sides(dm).
(Pacific Jazz Studios) LA,March ,1963

Katanga CD BN 7-80707-2,4-94031-2

JOE PASS - CATCH ME:
Clare Fischer(p,org-1) Joe Pass(g) Albert Stinson(b) Colin Bailey(dm).
(Pacific Jazz Studios) LA,July 18,1963

Walking up BN LT-1053
Just friends -1 - (J)W-5511
No cover no minimum -

Same. (Pacific Jazz Studios) LA,July 19,1963

Catch me -1 BN LT-1053
Summertime -
Falling in love with love -1 -

CHARLES KYNARD:
Clifford Scott(ts) Charles Kynard(org) Howard Roberts(g) Milt Turner(dm).
(Pacific Jazz Studios) LA, 1963

Where's it at CD BN 4-94032-2

THE JAZZ CRUSADERS:
Wayne Henderson(tb,euph) Wilton Felder(ts) Joe Sample(p) Bobby Haynes(b) Stix Hooper(dm).
(Pacific Jazz Studios) LA,September ,1963

Close shave
Some samba
Stix march
Purple onion
Free sample

All titles issued on BN BN-LA170-G2.

LES McCANN:
Les McCann(p) Joe Pass(g-1) Paul Chambers(b) Paul Humphrey(dm).
(Pacific Jazz Studios) LA,October 29/30,1963

Sack o'woe -1 CD BN 4-94032-2
(13197) Kathleen's theme BN BN-LA171-G2

GERALD WILSON AND HIS ORCHESTRA:
Al Porcino,Carmell Jones,Jules Chaikin,Freddy Hill(tp) Bob Edmondson,John Ewing,Don Switzer,Lester Robertson(tb) Joe Maini,Jimmy Woods(as) Teddy Edwards,Harold Land(ts) Jack Nimitz(bs) Jack Wilson(p) Joe Pass(g) Leroy Vinnegar(b) Chuck Carter(dm) Gerald Wilson(arr,cond).
(Pacific Jazz Studios) LA,December 2,1963

Paco CD BN 4-94032-2

LES McCANN & THE JAZZ CRUSADERS:
Wayne Henderson(tb-1,euph-2) Wilton Felder(ts) Joe Sample(org-1,p-2) Les McCann(p-1,el p-2) Bobby Haynes(b) Stix Hooper(dm).
(Pacific Jazz Studios) LA,December ,1963

Spanish castles-1 CD BN 4-94032-2
All blue-2 -

LES McCANN:
Les McCann(p) Victor Gaskin(b) William Correa(cga,bgo,timbales)
(Pacific Jazz Studios) LA, 1964

McCanna BN B1-97158,CD 4-97158-2

CHARLES KYNARD:
Buddy Collette(fl) Charles Kynard(org) John Rae(vb,timbales) Al McKibbon(b) Doug Sides(dm) Nicholas (Nick) "Cuco" Martinez(timbales,perc) Bill Fitch(cga) Armando Peraza(cga,bgo)
LA 1964

Mamblues BN B1-29092
Blue sands CD BN 5-21688-2

BILLY LARKIN & THE DELEGATES:
Billy Larkin(org) Hank Swann(g) Mel Brown(dm).
(Pacific Jazz Studios) LA, 1964

Pygmy CD BN 4-94032-2

JOE PASS - JOY SPRING:
Mike Wofford(p) Joe Pass(g) Jim Hughart(b) Colin Bailey(dm).
(Encore Theatre) LA,February 6,1964

Joy Spring BN LT-1103;CD BN(J)TOCJ-5851
Some time ago -
The night has a thousand eyes -
Relaxin' at the Camarillo -
There is no greater love -

THE JAZZ CRUSADERS:
Wayne Henderson(tb,euph) Wilton Felder(ts) Joe Sample(p) Joe Pass(g-1) Monk Montgomery(el b) Stix Hooper(dm).
(Pacific Jazz Studios) LA,July ,1964

(16537) Out back -1 BN BN-LA530-H2
(16535) Robbins' nest -
(16545) Polka dots and moonbeams -1 -
I'll remember tomorrow -1 BN BN-LA170-G2
Long John -

CLARE FISCHER:
Clare Fischer(p,org) Dennis Budimir(g) Bob West(b) Colin Bailey(dm).
LA,August ,1964

Quiet nights (Corcovado) CD BN(J)CJ28-5179
How insensitive CD BN(J)TOCJ-6190

JOE PASS - DJANGO:
Joe Pass,John Pisano(g) Jim Hughart(b) Colin Bailey(dm).
(Pacific Jazz Studios) LA,September 2,1964

Django BN(J)W-5511
CD BN 7-99100-2,(J)CJ28-5024
Rosetta BN(In)JAZ 2
Nuages CD BN(J)TOCJ-5853
For Django
Night and day CD BN 7-96581-2,(J)TOCJ-5855

All titles issued on BN(F)BNP25100.

 562

<u>JOE PASS</u> - <u>DJANGO</u>:
Joe Pass,John Pisano(g) Jim Hughart(b) Colin Bailey(dm).
(Pacific Jazz Studios) LA,October 18,1964

Fleur d'ennui BN(F)BNP25100
Insensiblement -
Cavalerie -
Manoir de mes rêves (as "Django's castle") -
Limehouse blues -
-

<u>MONTY ALEXANDER</u>:
Monty Alexander(p) Victor Gaskin(b) Paul Humphrey(dm).
(Esquire Theatre) LA, 1964-65

Autumn leaves BN(J)K23P-6726
If I were a bell -
Spirit of Foo Foo BN(J)W-5510

<u>THE JAZZ CRUSADERS</u>:
Wayne Henderson(tb,euph) Wilton Felder(ts) Joe Sample(p) Monk Montgomery(b) Stix Hooper(dm).
LA,February ,1965

(16538) New time shuffle BN BN-LA530-H2

Wayne Henderson(tb) Hubert Laws(fl) Wilton Felder(ts) Clare Fischer(org) Joe Sample(p) Al McKibbon(b) Stix Hooper(dm) Carlos Vidal(cga) Hungaria "Carmelo" Garcia(timbales,cowbell).
(Pacific Jazz Studios) LA,July 1,1965

(13167) Tough talk BN BN-LA530-H2,(E)UALP 19
(16546) Latin bit -

Same. (Pacific Jazz Studios) LA,July 2,1965

(16539) Dulzura BN BN-LA530-H2
Agua dulce BN BN-LA170-G2,CD 5-21688-2

<u>DIZZY GILLESPIE/GIL FULLER</u>- <u>THE MONTEREY JAZZ FESTIVAL ORCHESTRA</u>:
Dizzy Gillespie,Freddy Hill,Harry Edison,Melvin Moore,John Audino(tp) Lester Robertson, Francis Fitzpatrick,Jim Amlotte(tb) Herman Lebow,Sam Cassano,David Duke,Alan Robinson(frh) Buddy Collette, Gabe Baltazar,Bill Green,Carrington Visor Jr.,Jack Nimitz(reeds) Phil Moore III(p) Dennis Budimir(g) Jimmy Bond(b) Earl Palmer(dm) Gil Fuller(arr,cond).
(Pacific Jazz Studios) LA,September ,1965

Man from Monterey CD BN 8-57460-2
Angel city
Love theme from "The Sandpiper"
Groovin' high CD BN 7-89032-2
Be's that way CD BN 4-97155-2
Big Sur
Moontide
Things are here

All titles issued on CD BN 7-80370-2.

<u>CLARE FISCHER</u>:
Clare Fischer(p) Ralph Pena or Richard West(b) Nicholas "Cuco" Martinez(timbales) Chino Valdes,Carlos Vidal(cga) Rudy Calzado(perc). LA,October ,1965

Favela CD BN 5-21688-2

563

BUD SHANK:
Chet Baker(flh) Bud Shank(as,fl) Bob Florence(arr,cond) & others unknown.
LA,December ,1965

	Michelle	CD BN(J)TOCJ-5874
	Girl	-

THE JAZZ CRUSADERS:
Wayne Henderson(tb) Wilton Felder(ts) Joe Sample(p) Leroy Vinnegar(b) Stix Hooper(dm).
(The Lighthouse) Hermosa Beach,Calif.,January 14-16,1966

(16542)	Blues up tight	BN BN-LA530-H2,B2S 5256
Same.	(Pacific Jazz Studios)	LA,February 7,1966
	Uptight (Everything's alright)	CD BN 4-94032-2

BUD SHANK:
Bud Shank,Bill Perkins(as) Bob Hardaway,Bob Cooper(ts) Jack Nimitz,John Lowe(bs) Dennis Budimir(g) Ray Brown(b) Larry Bunker(dm) Bob Florence(arr).
LA,July or August ,1966

	Take five	CD BN 7-80707-2,(J)CJ28-5177,TOCJ-5203, TOCJ-6152
	Work song	CD BN(J)CJ28-5176

BUDDY RICH BIG BAND:
Bobby Shew,John Sottile,Yoshito Murakami,Walter Battagello(tp) Jim Trimble,John Boice(tb) Dennis Good, Mike Waverley(bass tb) Gene Quill(as,cl) Pete Yellin(as,fl) Jay Corre,Marty Flax(ts,cl,fl) Steve Perlow (bs,bass cl) John Bunch(p) Barry Zweig(g) Carson Smith(b) Buddy Rich(dm) Don Rader(arr).
(Chez Club) LA,September 29,1966

	Chicago	CD BN(Sp) 8-34712-2,8-53016-2

THE DON ELLIS ORCHESTRA:
Don Ellis,Glenn Stuart,Alan Weight,Ed Warren,Bob Harmon(tp) Dave Wells,Ron Meyers,Terry Woodson (tb) Reuben Leon(ss,as,fl) Tom Scott(saxello,as,fl,cl) Ira Schulman,Ron Starr(ts,fl,cl) John Magruder (bs,fl,cl,bass cl) Dave Mackay(p) Ray Neapolitan,Frank De La Rosa,Chuck Domanico(b) Steve Bohannon, Alan Estes(dm) Chino Valdes(bgo,cga).
(Pacific Jazz Festival) Costa Mesa,Calif.,October 8,1966

	Freedom jazz dance	CD BN 4-97155-2

BUDDY RICH BIG BAND:
Same as on September 29,1966 (see above). Bill Reddie(arr).
(RCA Studios) LA,October 10,1966

	West side story medley	CD BN(E) 8-53227-2

BILLY LARKIN & THE DELEGATES:
Leonide Flowers(tp) Arthur "Fats" Theus,Eugene Hemsley(reeds) Billy Larkin(org) James Daniels(g) John Boudreaux Jr.(dm).
LA,October or November ,1966

	Don't stop	BN B2S 5256

JOHNNY LYTLE:
Johnny Lytle(vb) Jimmy Foster(org) Major Holley(b) Peppy Hinant(dm) Don Alias(cga).
NYC,November ,1966

	Done it again	CD BN 4-94032-2

BOOKER ERVIN:
Charles Tolliver(tp) Booker Ervin(ts) John Hicks(p) Red Mitchell(b) Lennie McBrowne(dm).
(Pacific Jazz Studios) LA,December 14,1966

	Boo's blues	CD BN 5-27545-2
	You're my everything	-
	Shiny stockings	-

Same. (Pacific Jazz Studios) LA,December 15,1966

	Berkshire blues	CD BN 5-27545-2
(tk.3)	Franess (alt.)	-
	Franess	-
	Take the A train	CD BN 4-94035-2,5-27545-2

Charles Tolliver(tp-1) Booker Ervin(ts) John Hicks(p) Red Mitchell(b) Lennie McBrowne(dm).
(Pacific Jazz Studios) LA,December 16,1966

	Stolen moments -1	CD BN 5-27545-2
	Dancing in the dark	-
	Deep night	-
(tk.3)	Deep night (alt.)	-
(tk.4)	White Chtistmas	-

VICTOR FELDMAN:
Victor Feldman(keyb,perc).
LA 1966-67

	Sunshine superman	BN B1-97158,CD 4-97158-2

BUDDY RICH BIG BAND:
Bobby Shew,John Sottile,Yoshito Murakami,Chuck Findley(tp) Jim Trimble,Ron Meyers(tb) Bill Wimberly (bass tb) Quinn Davis(as) Ernie Watts(as,fl) Jay Corre,Robert Keller(ts,cl, fl) Marty Flax(bs) Ray Starling(p) Richard Resnicoff(g) James Gannon(b) Buddy Rich(dm).Arr. by Bill Holman.
(Chez Club) LA,February 22,1967

	Norwegian wood	CD BN(J)TOCJ-5874

Same.Arr. by Harry Betts.
(Chez Club) LA,February 24,1967

	Mexicali nose-1	CD BN 4-97155-2

-1: mistitled "Mexicali Noise" on European pressings of this CD.

Same.Arr. by Shorty Rogers
(Chez Club) LA,February 25,1967

	The beat goes on-1	BN B1-94027,CD 4-94027-2

-1: Cathy Rich(vo) overdubbed on. (United Recorders) LA,March 10,1967.

THE JAZZ CRUSADERS:
Wayne Henderson(tb) Wilton Felder(ts) Joe Sample(p) Buster Williams(b) Stix Hooper(dm).
(Pacific Jazz Studios) LA,May 15,1967

(16536)	Watts happening	BN BN-LA530-H2, CD 8-35472-2

565

PAUL HORN IN INDIA:
Paul Horn(fl) Satya Dev Pawar(v) Gaffar Hyder Khan(tabla) Gopal Verma(tamboura).
New Delhi (India),April or May 1967

Raga Desh BN BN-LA529-H2

Gopal Krishan(vichitraveena) Gaffar Hyder Khan(tabla) Satya Dev Pawar(v).
New Delhi (India),April or May 1967

Raga Bihag BN BN-LA529-H2

Paul Horn(fl) Gopal Krishan(vichitraveena) Gaffa Hyder Khan(tabla) Gopal Verma-1(tamboura).
New Delhi (India),April or May 1967

Raga Vibhas -1 BN BN-LA529-H2
Raga Filang -

Paul Horn(fl) Gopal Verma (tamboura). New Delhi (India),April or May 1967

Alap BN BN-LA529-H2

Vinay Bharat-Ram(vo) Satya Dev Pawar(v) Gaffa Hyder Khan(tabla) Gopal Verma (tamboura).
New Delhi (India),April or May 1967

Manj-Kamaj BN BN-LA529-H2

Paul Horn(fl) Satya Dev Pawar(v) Gopal Krishan(vichitraveena) Gopal Verma(tamboura) Gaffa Hyder Khan (tabla).
New Delhi (India),April or May 1967

Raga Shivaranjani BN BN-LA529-H2

Paul Horn(fl) J.N.Shivpuri(sitar) Shri Chunilal Kaul(dilruba,tamboura,vo) Rajinder Raina(tabla).
New Delhi (India),April or May 1967

Arti
Raga Ahir Bhairao
Tabla solo in Teental
Raga Puria Dhanashri
Alap in Raga Bhairav
Raga Kerwani

All titles issued on BN BN-LA529-H2.

JOHNNY LYTLE:
Johnny Lytle(vb) Jimmy Foster(org Larry Gales(b) Josell Carter(dm) Carlos Valdes(cga)
(Top Of The Gate) NYC, 1967

Minor soul BN B1-29092, CD 8-29092-2

BOOKER ERVIN:
Booker Ervin(ts) with Charles Tolliver,Ray Copeland,Freddie Hubbard,Richard Williams(tp,flh) Britt Woodman,Bennie Green(tb) Benny Powell(bass tb) Kenny Barron(p) Reggie Johnson(b) Lennie McBrowne (dm) Teddy Edwards(arr).
(Webster Hall) NYC,September 12,1967

tk.6 L.A. after dark CD BN 4-94032-2

Martin Banks,Johnny Coles(tp,flh) replace Tolliver and Hubbard.
(Webster Hall) NYC,September 13,1967

tk.8 East Dallas special CD BN 4-94032-2

BUD SHANK:
Chet Baker,Gary Barone(flh) Bud Shank(as,fl) Dennis Budimir,Herb Ellis(g) Bob West(b) John Guerin(dm) Victor Feldman(perc).
LA,November 3 & 8,1967

Hello,goodbye CD BN(J)TOCJ-5874

THE JAZZ CRUSADERS - LIVE SIDES:
Wayne Henderson(tb) Wilton Felder(ts) Joe Sample(p) Buster Williams(b) Stix Hooper(dm).
(The Lighthouse) Hermosa Beach,Calif.,November 10-12,1967

Impressions
The emperor
Native dancer

All titles issued on BN LT-1046.

BUDDY RICH BIG BAND:
Bill Prince,Al Porcino,Dave Culp,Ken Faulk(tp) Rick Stepton,Jimmy Trimble(tb) Peter Greaves(bass tb) Art Pepper,Charlie Owens(as) Don Menza,Pat LaBarbera(ts) John Laws(bs) Joe Azarello(p) Walt Namuth(g) Gary Walters(b) Buddy Rich(dm).
(Caesar's Palace) Las Vegas,July 6,1968

Alfie CD BN 8-33244-2

THE JAZZ CRUSADERS:
Wayne Henderson(tb) Wilton Felder(ts) Joe Sample(p,el p) Buster Williams(b,el b) Stix Hooper (dm).
(Pacific Jazz Studios) LA,July 9-11,1968

(16533)	Fancy dance	BN BN-LA530-H2
(16540)	Fire water	-
	Hey Jude	CD BN 7-94861-2,(J)TOCJ-5874
	Promises,promises	CD BN 8-57749-2

GERALD WILSON AND HIS ORCHESTRA:
Ollie Mitchell,Dalton Smith,Alex Rodrigues,Tony Rusch(tp) Frank Strong,Lester Robertson,Thurman Green (tb) Mike Wimberly(bass tb) Jim McGee,George Hyde(frh) Anthony Ortega(as,fl,picc) Ramon Borjorquez (as) Hadley Caliman,Harold Land(ts) Richard Aplanalp(bs) Henry De Vega,Pete Terry,Bill Perkins(reeds) Bobby Hutcherson(vb) Mike Wofford,Jimmy Rowles(p,org,hpsc) Mike Anthony(g) Wilton Felder(el b) Carl Lott(dm) Hugh Anderson,Joe Porcaro(perc) Gerald Wilson(arr,cond).
(Liberty Studios) LA,August 16,1968

tk.5 California soul BN B1-97158,CD 4-97158-2
BN 45-1985

GERALD WILSON AND HIS ORCHESTRA:
Bobby Bryant,Larry McGuire,Alex Rodrigues,Tony Rusch(tp) Frank Strong,Lester Robertson,Thurman Green(tb) Mike Wimberly(bass tb) Dave Duke(frh) Anthony Ortega(as,fl,picc) Ramon Borjorquez(as) Hadley Caliman,Harold Land(ts) Allan Beutler(bs) Henry De Vega,Pete Terry(reeds) Mike Wofford,Jimmy Rowles (p,org,hpsc) Mike Anthony(g) Wilton Felder(el b) Stan Gilbert(b) Carl Lott(dm) Hugh Anderson,Joe Porcaro(perc) Gerald Wilson(arr,cond).
(Liberty Studios) LA,September 2,1968

tk.9 Sunshine of your love CD BN 5-21152-2

WILBERT LONGMIRE:
Gary Barone,Gray Reins(tp) George Bohanon(tb) Anthony Ortega(as,fl Wilton Felder(ts) Leon Spencer Jr. (org,p) Wilbert Longmire,Cal Green(g) Ron Johnson(el b) Larry Gales(b) Paul Humphrey(dm) Marshall Sosson,Myron Sandler,David Burk,Jesse Erlich,Harry Bluestone(strings) Joe Sample(arr).
LA, 1968

Give it up or turn it loose BN B1-97158,CD 4-97158-2

JOE TORRES:
Gary Barone-1 or Steve Huffsteter-2 (tp) Bill Hood(ts) Victor Feldman(p) Max Bennett(b) Joe Torres (timbales) Bobby Torres,Orlando Lopez,Marion Tholmer(perc).
(World Pacific) LA, 1968

Soul cha -1 CD BN 5-21688-2
La bruja negra -2 BN B1-97158,CD 4-97158-2,5-21688-2

RICHARD GROOVE HOLMES:
William Peterson(el tp)Jerome Rusch,Larry McGuire,Herbert Anderson(tp) Frank Strong(tb) Mike Wimberly(bass tb) Ernie Watts,Anthony Ortega(as) Richard Aplanalp(bs) Richard Groove Holmes(org) Dennis Budimir(g) Wilton Felder(el b) Paul Humphrey(dm) Gerald Wilson(arr).
(Liberty Studios) LA,October ,1968

Do you know the way to San Jose CD BN 8-57749-2

FREDDY ROBINSON:
Bud Brisbois(tp) Allen Butler(fl) Plas Johnson(ts) Ernie Williams(bs) Alan C. Estes(vb) Joe Sample(el p) Monk Higgins(org) Freddy Robinson(g) Sid Sharp(v,viola) Bob West(el b) Paul Humphrey(dm) King Errison(cga) Dee Ervin(perc) Mamie Galore,Alexandra Brown,Patricia Dunn,Difosco Ervin,Adrienne Williams(backgr.vo).
LA, 1968-69

Coming to Atlantis CD BN 4-94032-2

WILTON FELDER:
Wilton Felder(ts) Wayne Henderson(arr) & others unknown.
LA, 1968-69

Theme from Bullit CD BN 8-57748-2

BUD SHANK:
Bud Shank(as) Michel Legrand(arr,cond) & others unknown.
LA,January ,1969

The windmills of your mind CD BN 8-57748-2

ERNIE WATTS:
Ernie Watts(ts) Clarence MacDonald(p) Stan Gilbert(b) Robert Marin(dm).
(Pacific Jazz Studios) LA,March ,1969

Knowing when to leave CD BN 8-57749-2

JEAN-LUC PONTY - LIVE AT DONTE'S:
Jean-Luc Ponty(v) George Duke(p) John Heard(b) Al Cecchi(dm).
(Live at Donte's) LA,March 11 & 12,1969

	Hypomode del sol	BN LT-1102
	People	-
	California	-
	Eighty-one	-
	Foosh	
	Sara's theme	
	Pamukkale	
	Cantaloupe island	

All titles issued on Pacific Jazz CD 8-35635-2.

BOBBY BRYANT AND HIS ORCHESTRA:
Bobby Bryant,Buddy Childers,Freddy Hill,Paul Hubinon(tp) George Bohanon,John Ewing,Bill Tole(tb) David Duke(frh) Don Waldrop(tu) Herman Riley,Ernie Watts,Pete Christlieb(saxes) Donald Bailey(hca) Melvin Moore(v) Joe Sample(p) Mike Anthony(g) Wilton Felder(el b) John Duke(b) Carl Lott(dm) Chino Valdes,Bob Norris(cga).
LA, 1969

	I wanna testify	CD BN 5-21152-2

THE JAZZ CRUSADERS - LIVE SIDES:
Wayne Henderson(tb) Wilton Felder(ts) Joe Sample(p) Buster Williams(b) Stix Hooper (dm).
(Lighthouse Club) Hermosa Beach,CA.,July 26-27,1969

	It's gotta be real	BN LT-1046
	Inside the outside	-
	Reflections	-
	It's your thing	BN B1-97158,CD 4-97158-2

THE JEAN-LUC PONTY EXPERIENCE:
Jean Luc Ponty(v) George Duke(el p) John Heard(el b) Dick Berk(dm).
(Thee Experience) LA,September 24,1969

(17316)	Foosh	
(17317)	Pamukkale	
(17318)	Contact	Lib(F)LBS83442/43
(17319)	Cantaloupe island	
(17320)	Starlight,starbright	

All titles issued on BN BN-LA632-H2.

JEAN-LUC PONTY - KING KONG:
Ian Underwood(as,ts) Jean-Luc Ponty(v,baritone violectra) Gene Estes(vb,perc) George Duke(p,el p) Buell Neidlinger(b) Arthur Dyne Tripp III(dm) Frank Zappa(arr,cond).
LA,October 6,1969

(17310)	King Kong	BN BN-LA632-H2
(17315)	America drinks and goes home	- (E)UALP 17

<u>JEAN-LUC PONTY</u> - <u>KING KONG</u>:
Ernie Watts(as,ts) Jean-Luc Ponty(v,baritone violectra) George Duke(el p) Wilton Felder(el b) John Guerin (dm) Frank Zappa(arr,cond,g-1). LA,October 7,1969

(17312) Twenty small cigars
(17313) How would you like to have a head like that -1
BN(In)JAZ 1;CD BN(J)TOCJ-1621
(17311) Idiot bastard son

All titles issued on BN BN-LA632-H2.

Vince De Rosa(frh) Arthur Maebe(frh,tu) Jonathan Meyer(fl) Gene Cipriano(oboe,English h) Donald Christlieb(bassoon) Jean-Luc Ponty(v) Milton Thomas(viola) Harold Bemko(cello) George Duke(p,el p) Buell Neidlinger(b) Arthur Dyne Tripp III(dm) Ian Underwood(cond) Frank Zappa (arr).
LA,October 8,1969

(17314) Music for electric violin and low-budget orchestra
BN BN-LA632-H2

<u>HANK DIAMOND</u>:
details unknown.
(World Pacific) prob. late '60s

Soul sauce BN B1-97158,CD 4-97158-2

<u>PENDULUM</u>

<u>DIGABLE PLANETS</u>:
details unknown.
early '90s

Rebirth of slick (cool like dat) CD BN(J)TOCP-8966

<u>BOOGIE MONSTERS</u>:
Bahamadia(rapper) John Adams(el p) Ron Long(b).
1997

Say word CD BN(J)TOCP-65100

ROOST

BUD POWELL:
Bud Powell(p) Curly Russell(b) Max Roach(dm).
NYC,January 10,1947

2991	I'll remember April	CD BN(J)TOCJ-5640,TOCJ-6105
2992	Indiana	CD BN 8-54906-2,(J)TOCJ-5640,TOCJ-5873
2993	Somebody loves me	CD BN(J)TOCJ-5640,TOCJ-6105,TOCP-50060
2994	I should care	- - -
2995	Bud's bubble	CD BN 8-54906-2,8-21381-2
2996	Off minor	CD BN(J)TOCJ-6147
2997	Nice work if you can get it	CD BN 7-89914-2
2998	Everything happens to me	CD BN(J)TOCJ-5640,TOCJ-6105,TOCP-50060

All titles issued on CD BN 8-30083-2

CHARLIE PARKER AND DIZZY GILLESPIE:
Dizzy Gillespie(tp) Charlie Parker(as) John Lewis(p) Al McKibbon(b) Joe Harris(dm).
(Carnegie Hall) NYC,September 29,1947

A night in Tunisia CD BN 4-95981-2
Dizzy atmosphere
Groovin' high
Confirmation
Koko

All titles on Roost/Blue Note CD 8-57061-2.

DIZZY GILLESPIE BIG BAND:
Dizzy Gillespie(tp,vo) Elmon Wright,Matthew McKay,Dave Burns,Ray Ore(tp) Taswell Baird,William Shepherd(tb) John Brown,Howard Johnson(as) James Moody,Joe Gayles(ts) Cecil Payne(bs) Milt Jackson (vb) John Lewis(p,arr-4) Al McKibbon(b) Joe Harris(dm) Chano Pozo(cga) Lorenzo Salan (bgo) Kenny "Pancho" Hagood(vo) Tadd Dameron-1,George Russell-2,Gil Fuller-3 (arr).
(Carnegie Hall) NYC,September 29,1947

Cool breeze -1
Relaxin' at Camarillo -2
One bass hit -3
Nearness -1
Salt peanuts
Cubano-be,Cubano-bop -2
Hot house-1
Toccata for trumpet -4
Oop-pop-a-da (voKH,DG)
Things to come -3

All titles issued on Roost/Blue Note CD 8-57061-2.

STAN GETZ:
Stan Getz(ts) Al Haig(p)Tommy Potter(b) Roy Haynes(dm).
NYC,May 17,1950

R 1030	Gone with the wind	CD BN 8-34873-2
R 1031	Yesterdays	CD BN(J)TOCJ-5853

<u>STAN GETZ</u>:
Stan Getz(ts) Jimmy Raney(g) Al Haig(p) Teddy Kotick(b) Tiny Kahn(dm).
(Storyville Club) Boston,October 28,1951

	Mosquito kness	CD BN 4-95981-2

<u>JOHNNY SMITH</u>:
Stan Getz(ts) Johnny Smith(g) Sanford Gold(p) Eddie Safranski(b) Don Lamond(dm).
NYC,March 11,1952

R 1108	Moonlight in Vermont	CD BN 7-89910-2

<u>JOHNNY SMITH</u>:
Johnny Smith(g) Sanford Gold(p) Arnold Fishkin(b) Don Lamond(dm).
NYC,August ,1953

R 1194	What's new	CD BN(J)TOCJ-5853

<u>BUD POWELL</u>:
Bud Powell(p) George Duvivier(b) Art Taylor(dm).
NYC,September ,1953

	Embraceable you	CD HMV Jazz(E)5-20874-2
	Burt covers Bud	CD BN 8-54906-2 -
	My heart stood still	
	You'd be so nice to come home to	
	Bags' groove	
	My devotion	
	Stella by starlight (omit b,dm)	CD BN(J)TOCP-50060
	Woody 'n you	

All titles issued on CD BN 8-30083-2.

<u>SONNY STITT</u>:
Sonny Stitt(as) Dean Earl(p) Bernie Griggs(b) Marquis Foster(dm)
(The Hi-Hat Club) Boston,February 11,1954

	I'm in the mood for love	CD BN 8-57742-2

<u>BEVERLY KENNEY & JOHNNY SMITH</u>:
Beverly Kenney(vo) with Bob Panecost(p) Johnny Smith(g) George Roumanis(b) Jerry Segal(dm).
NYC, 1955

	This little town is Paris	CD BN 7-99100-2
	Snuggled on your shoulder	CD BN(J)TOCJ-5710

<u>SONNY STITT</u>:
Thad Jones,Joe Newman(tp) Jimmy Cleveland(tb) Anthony Ortega(as,fl) Sonny Stitt(as) Seldon Powell(ts) Cecil Payne(bs) Hank Jones(p) Freddie Green(g) Oscar Pettiford(b) Jo Jones(dm) Quincy Jones(arr).
NYC,October 17.1955

	Star dust	CD BN(J)TOCJ-6187

<u>BEVERLY KENNEY</u>:
Beverly Kenney(vo) with Don Lamond or Ted Sommer(bgo).
NYC,May ,1956

	It ain't necessarily so	CD BN 7-80506-2

BEVERLY KENNEY:
Beverly Kenney(vo) with Joe Newman(tp) Frank Wess(ts,fl) Jimmy Jones(p,arr) Freddie Green(g) Eddie Jones(b) Jo Jones(dm).

NYC, 1956

Makin' whoopee CD BN 7-89914-2

SONNY STITT:
Sonny Stitt(ts) Hank Jones(p) Wendell Marshall(b) Shadow Wilson(dm).

NYC,June 28,1957

It might as well be Spring CD BN(J)TOCJ-5851

JOHNNY HARTMAN:
Johnny Hartman(vo) with orchestra arr. & cond. by Rudy Traylor.

NYC, 1958

How long has this been going on CD BN 7-80506-2
But beautiful CD BN(J)TOCJ-5856

SONNY STITT:
Thad Jones(tp) SonnyStitt(as) Chick Corea(p) Larry Gales(b) Willie Bobo(timbales) Carlos "Patato" Valdes (cga) Osvaldo "Chihuahua" Martinez(perc).

NYC,June 11,1963

Ritmo Bobo CD BN 5-21688-2

573

ROULETTE

SARAH VAUGHAN & THE COUNT BASIE ORCHESTRA:
Sarah Vaughan(vo) with Wendell Culley,Reunald Jones,Thad Jones,Joe Newman(tp) Henry Coker,Bill Hughes,Benny Powell(tb) Frank Wess(as,fl) Marshall Royal(as) Ernie Wilkins,Frank Foster(ts) Charles Fowlkes(bs) Jimmy Jones(p) Joe Benjamin)b) Roy Haynes(dm).
(Carnegie Hall) NYC,September 25,1954

	Perdido	CD BN 8-23517-2

JOE WILLIAMS:
Joe Williams(vo) with Jimmy Jones(p) Jimmy Mundy(arr) & others unknown.
NYC,October 11/12,1957

12442	A man ain't supposed to cry	CD BN 8-21146-2

BUD POWELL:
Bud Powell(p) George Duvivier(b) Art Taylor(dm).
NYC,October 14,1957

12451-1	Yardbird suite	CD BN(J)TOCJ-6105

THE COUNT BASIE ORCHESTRA:
Wendell Culley,Snooky Young,Thad Jones,Joe Newman(tp) Henry Coker,Al Grey,Benny Powell(tb) Frank Wess(as,fl) Marshall Royal(as) Eddie Lockjaw Davis,Frank Foster(ts) Charles Fowlkes(bs) Count Basie(p) Freddie Green(g) Eddie Jones(b) Sonny Payne(dm) Neal Hefti(arr).
(Capitol Studios) NYC,October 21,1957

12470-8	Li'l Darlin'	CD BN 4-97155-2
12473-7	The kid from Red Bank	CD BN 8-29964-2,(Sp)8-34712-2,8-53016-2, (E)8-53227-2

Same. (Capitol Studios) NYC,October 22,1957

12480-6	Splanky	CD BN 4-97155-2
12482-6	After supper	CD BN(J)TOCJ-5857

BUD POWELL:
Bud Powell(p) Paul Chambers(b) Art Taylor(dm).
NYC,December 2,1957

12523-3	Ornithology	CD BN 8-57742-2

Note: Although George Duvivier is credited for this session, it is most likely Paul Chambers on bass.

MACHITO AND HIS ORCHESTRA:
Mario Bauza(musical dir) Francis Williams,Doc Cheatham,Paul Cohen,Paquito Davila,Joe Livramento,Joe Newman(tp) Santos Russo,Eddie Bert,Bart Varsalona(tb) Julian "Cannonball" Adderley(as) Ray Santos Jr., Jose Madera(ts) Leslie Johnakins(bs) Rene Hernandez(p) Roberto Rodriguez(b) Jose Mangual (bgo) Umbaldo Nieto(timbales) Candido Camero,Carlos "Patato" Valdes(cga) prob. Jose Silva,Nilo Siera,Pedro Boulong(perc) A.K. Salim(arr) Machito(leader).
(Metropolitan Studios) NYC,December 24,1957

	Congo Mulence	CD BN 5-21688-2

EDDIE DAVIS & JOE NEWMAN:
Joe Newman(tp) Eddie 'Lockjaw' Davis(ts) Count Basie(p) Shirley Scott(org) George Duvivier(b) Butch Ballard(dm). NYC,December 19,1957

12557	Save your love for me	CD BN(J)TOCJ-5856
12560	Marie	CD BN 7-99095-2

BUD POWELL:
Bud Powell(p) George Duvivier(b) Art Taylor(dm). NYC,January 30,1958

12580-1	Relaxin' at Camarillo	CD BN(J)TOCJ-6105

COUNT BASIE AND HIS ORCHESTRA:
Wendell Culley,Snooky Young,Thad Jones,Joe Newman(tp) Henry Coker,Al Grey,Benny Powell(tb) Frank Wess(as,fl) Marshall Royal(as) Frank Foster,Billy Mitchell(ts) Charles Fowlkes(bs) Count Basie(p) Freddie Green(g) Eddie Jones(b) Sonny Payne(dm) Jimmy Mundy(arr).
(Capitol Studios) NYC,April 28,1958

12823-4	Ol' man river	CD BN 8-29095-2

COUNT BASIE AND HIS ORCHESTRA:
Wendell Culley,Snooky Young,Thad Jones,Joe Newman(tp) Henry Coker,Al Grey,Benny Powell(tb) Frank Wess(as,fl) Marshall Royal(as) Frank Foster,Billy Mitchell(ts) Charles Fowlkes(bs) Count Basie(p) Freddie Green(g) Eddie Jones(b) Sonny Payne(dm) Joe Williams,Dave Lambert,Jon Hendricks,Annie Ross(vo).
(Capitol Studios) NYC,May 26,1958

13067	Goin' to Chicago	CD BN 8-21146-2

COUNT BASIE-JOE WILLIAMS:
Harry "Sweets" Edison(tp) Count Basie(org) Freddie Green(g) George Duvivier(b) Jimmy Crawford(dm) Joe Williams(vo). (Capitol Studios) NYC,December 29,1958

13469-6	If I could be with you	CD BN 8-21146-2

TONY BENNETT & THE COUNT BASIE ORCHESTRA:
Tony Bennett(vo) with Wendell Culley,Thad Jones,Joe Newman,Snooky Young(tp) Henry Coker,Al Grey, Benny Powell(tb) Marshall Royal(cl,as) Frank Wess(fl,as,ts) Frank Foster,Billy Mitchell(ts) Charlie Fowlkes(bs) Ralph Sharon(p) Freddie Green(g) Eddie Jones(b) Sonny Payne(dm).
(Capitol Studios) NYC,January 5,1959

13476	Chicago	CD BN 7-89914-2
13477	I've grown accustomed to your face	CD BN 7-96582-2,8-32994-2
13483	With plenty of money and you	CD BN(C)4-94888-2

BILLY ECKSTINE & THE COUNT BASIE ORCHESTRA:
Billy Eckstine(vo) with Wendell Culley,Thad Jones,Joe Newman,Snooky Young(tp) Henry Coker,Al Grey, Benny Powell(tb) Marshall Royal(cl,as) Frank Wess(fl,as,ts) Frank Foster,Billy Mitchell(ts) Charlie Fowlkes(bs) Bobby Tucker(p) Freddie Green(g) George Duvivier(b) Sonny Payne(dm).
(Capitol Studios) NYC,May 23,1959

13865	Drifting blues	CD BN 8-32994-2
13869	Jelly jelly	CD BN 7-96582-2,(C) 4-94888-2

MAYNARD FERGUSON AND HIS ORCHESTRA:
Maynard Ferguson(tp,vtb,euph) Don Ellis,Bill Chase,Larry Moser(tp) Don Sebesky(tb,bass tb) Slide Hampton(tb,tu) Jimmy Ford(as) Carmen Leggio,Willie Maiden(ts) John Lanni(bs) Bob Dogan(p) Jimmy Rowser(b) Frankie Dunlop(dm).
(Capitol Studios) NYC,March 31,1959

13652-5	It might as well be Spring	CD BN(C)8-33908-2

COUNT BASIE AND HIS ORCHESTRA:
Wendell Culley,Thad Jones,Joe Newman,Snooky Young(tp) Henry Coker,Al Grey,Benny Powell(tb) Marshall Royal(cl,as) Frank Wess(fl,as,ts) Frank Foster,Billy Mitchell(ts) Charlie Fowlkes(bs) Count Basie (p) Freddie Green(g) Eddie Jones(b) Sonny Payne(dm) Joe Williams(vo).

(Live,Americana Hotel) Miami, May 31,1959

Set #1:

	The deacon	CD BN 8-33273-2
	No moon at all (voJW)	-
	Roll 'em Pete (voJW)	CD BN 8-21146-2

Set t#2:

	Every day I have the blues(voJW)	CD BN 8-33273-2
	Back to the apple	-

PHINEAS NEWBORN:
Phineas Newborn(p) John Simmons(b) Roy Haynes(dm).

NYC,June 18,1959

13974	Chelsea Bridge	CD BN 4-94035-2

JOE WILLIAMS:
Joe Williams(vo) with Harry "Sweets" Edison(tp) Ben Webster(ts) Hank Jones(p) Freddie Green(g) Milt Hinton(b) Don Lamond(dm) & unidentified strings,woodwinds arr. by Jimmy Jones.

(Capitol Studios) NYC,July 14,1959

14153	I was telling her all about you	CD BN 8-21146-2
14154	When did you leave heaven?	-

COUNT BASIE-JOE WILLIAMS:
John Anderson,Thad Jones,Joe Newman,Snooky Young(tp) Henry Coker,Al Grey,Benny Powell(tb) Marshall Royal(cl,as) Frank Wess(fl,as,ts) Frank Foster,Billy Mitchell(ts) Charlie Fowlkes(bs) Count Basie (p) Freddie Green(g) Eddie Jones(b) Sonny Payne(dm) Joe Williams(vo).

(Universal Studios) Chicago,September 24,1959

14372-5	Every day I have the blues	CD BN 7-96582-2,8-21146-2,8-32994-2, (C)4-94888-2

RAY BRYANT:
Ray Bryant(p) Tommy Bryant(b) Oliver Jackson(dm).
(purchased from Signature Records) NYC,October 29,1959

	Now's the time	CD BN(J)TOCJ-5873

Same: NYC,November 6,1959

	Misty	CD BN(J)TOCJ-5299,TOCJ-5855
	Whisper not	CD BN(J)TOCJ-6190

JOE WILLIAMS:
Joe Williams(vo) with Orchestra cond. by Jimmy Jones & arr. by Frank Foster.

NYC,December 29,1959

14677	Cherry	CD BN 8-21146-2

PEARL BAILEY:
Pearl Bailey(vo) with Orchestra cond. by Don Redman.

NYC, 1959

14764	Between the devil and the deep blue sea	CD BN(Sp)8-56842-2

SARAH VAUGHAN:
Sarah Vaughan(vo) with Orchestra arr. & cond. by Jimmy Jones: Harry Edison(tp) Gerald Sanfino(fl,ts) Ronnell Bright(p) Barry Galbraith(g) Richard Davis or George Duvivier(b) Percy Brice(dm) Janet Soyer (harp) & strings.
(Capitol Studios) NYC,April 19,1960

14952	You've changed	CD BN(J)TOCJ-66071
14960	Dreamy	CD BN 8-23517-2

THAD JONES:
Thad Jones(tp) Al Grey(tb) Billy Mitchell(ts) Frank Wess(fl-1,ts-2,as-3) Hank Jones(p) Richard Davis(b) Osie Johnson(dm).
(Capitol Studios) NYC,May 12,1960

15018-2	Subtle rebuttal (alt.)-1.2
15018-5	Subtle rebuttal -1,2
15019-5	Tip toe (alt.)-1
15019-9	Tip toe -1
15020-4	H & T blues -2
15021-5	Friday the 13th -3

All titles issued on Mosaic MQ5-172,CD MD3-172.
To be issued on the Blue Note label.

LEE MORGAN:
Lee Morgan(tp) Wayne Shorter(ts) Bobby Timmons(p) Jimmy Rowser(b) Art Taylor(dm).
(prob. Capitol Studios) NYC,June 1960

15140-6	Suspended sentence
15141-5	Minor strain
15142-2	A bid for Sid

All titles to be issued on the Blue Note label.

COUNT BASIE-SARAH VAUGHAN:
Sonny Cohn,Thad Jones,Joe Newman,Snooky Young(tp) Henry Coker,Al Grey,Benny Powell(tb) Marshall Royal(cl,as) Frank Wess(fl,as,ts) Frank Foster,Billy Mitchell(ts) Charlie Fowlkes(bs) Count Basie(p) Freddie Green(g) Eddie Jones(b) Sonny Payne(dm) Sarah Vaughan,Joe Williams(vo).
(Capitol Studios) NYC,July 14,1960

15285	Until I met you (voSV)	CD BN(C)4-94888-2
15286	If I were a bell (voSV,JW)	CD BN 8-21146-2
15287	Teach me tonight (voSV,JW)	CD BN 8-23517-2

COUNT BASIE-JOE WILLIAMS:
Same.Joe Williams(vo) replaces Vaughan.
(Universal Recording) Chicago,August 24,1960

15321-7	Confessin' the blues (voJW)	CD BN 8-21146-2

BILLY ECKSTINE:
Billy Eckstine(vo) with The Bucky Manieri Orchestra: Charlie Walp(tp) Bucky Manieri(tb) Charlie McLean, Buddy Balboa(saxes) Bobby Tucker(p,arr) Buddy Grievey(dm) & others unknown.
(Cloud Nine Lounge,New Frontier Hotel)
Las Vegas,August 30,1960

15336	It might as well be Spring	CD BN 5-21153-2
	Medley:Prelude to a kiss/ I'm beginning to see the light	CD BN 8-55221-2
15338	You'll never walk alone	CD BN 8-29095-2

COUNT BASIE AND HIS ORCHESTRA:
Sonny Cohn,Thad Jones,Joe Newman,Snooky Young(tp) Henry Coker,Al Grey,Benny Powell(tb) Marshall Royal(cl,as) Frank Wess(fl,as,ts) Frank Foster,Billy Mitchell(ts) Charlie Fowlkes(bs) Count Basie(p) Freddie Green(g) Eddie Jones(b) Sonny Payne(dm) Benny Carter(arr).
(United/Western Recorders) LA,September 6,1960

15341 Meetin' time CD BN(J)TOCJ-5857

JOHN COLTRANE:
John Coltrane(ts) McCoy Tyner(p) Steve Davis(b) Billy Higgins(dm).
(United/Western Recorders) LA,September 8,1960

15543 One and four (*aka* Mr.Day) CD BN 4-98240-2,(J)TOCJ-5630,TOCJ-6104
15544 Exotica - -
15545 Simple like (*aka* Like Sonny) CD BN 4-95981-2

SARAH VAUGHAN:
Sarah Vaughan(vo) with orchestra arr. & cond. by Billy May.
(United/Western Recorders) LA,October 8,1960

15494 Them there eyes CD BN 8-23517-2

SARAH VAUGHAN:
Sarah Vaughan(vo) with Orchestra arr. & cond. by Jimmy Jones.
NYC,October ,1960

15468 Jump for joy CD BN 8-55221-2
15476 When your lover has gone CD BN 8-23517-2

JOE WILLIAMS:
Joe Williams(vo) with Orchesra arr. & cond. by Jimmy Jones.
(Capitol Studios) NYC,January 16 or 23,1961

15665 Ev'ry time we say goodbye CD BN 8-21146-2

CHRIS CONNOR & MAYNARD FERGUSON:
Maynard Ferguson,Chet Ferretti,Rolf Ericson,Bill Berry(tp) Ray Winslow,Kenny Rupp(tb) Lanny Morgan (as,fl) Joe Farrell(ts,ss,fl) Willie Maiden(ts,fl) Frank Hittner(bs) Jaki Byard(p) Charlie Sanders(b) Rufus Jones(dm) Chris Connor(vo).
(Capitol Studios) NYC,January 30,1961

15654 Can't get out of this mood CD BN 7-96583-2

JOE WILLIAMS:
Joe Williams(vo) with Harry "Sweets" Edison(tp)Jimmy Forrest(ts) Sir Charles Thompson(p) unknown(g) Tommy Potter(b) Clarence Johnston(dm).
(The Cloisters) LA,February 2,1961

15850 Alone together CD BN 8-21146-2

LOUIS ARMSTRONG & DUKE ELLINGTON:
Louis Armstrong(tp,vo) Trummy Young(tb) Barney Bigard(cl) Duke Ellington(p) Mort Herbert(b) Danny Barcelona(dm).
(RCA Studios) NYC, April 3,1961

15969-9/10/12
It don't mean a thing CD BN 4-95981-2,(Sp) 8-34712-2,(C) 4-94888-2
15976-2 Duke's place CD BN 4-94035-2,(Sp)8-53016-2
15979-1 The beautiful American CD BN 4-95981-2

LOUIS ARMSTRONG & DUKE ELLINGTON:
Louis Armstrong(tp,vo) Trummy Young(tb) Barney Bigard(cl) Duke Ellington(p) Mort Herbert(b) Danny Barcelona(dm).
(RCA Studios) NYC,April 4,1961

15980-4	Drop me off in Harlem	CD BN 7-96582-2,8-55221-2
15981-4	I'm just a lucky so and so	CD BN 5-21153-2

COUNT BASIE AND HIS ORCHESTRA:
Sonny Cohn,Thad Jones,Lennie Johnson,Snooky Young(tp) Henry Coker,Quentin Jackson,Benny Powell (tb) Marshall Royal(cl,as) Frank Wess(fl,as,ts) Frank Foster,Budd Johnson(ts) Charlie Fowlkes(bs) Count Basie(p) Freddie Green(g) Eddie Jones(b) Sonny Payne(dm) Jon Hendricks(vo).
(Live,Birdland Club) NYC, June 27,1961

Set #1:		
	A little tempo please	CD BN 8-33273-2
	Segue in C	- 4-95981-2
Set #2:		
	I needs to be bee'd with	CD BN 8-33273-2,5-21052-2
	Whirly bird	-
	One o'clock jump	-
Set #3:		
	Easin' it	CD BN 8-33273-2

COUNT BASIE AND HIS ORCHESTRA:
Sonny Cohn,Thad Jones,Lennie Johnson,Snooky Young(tp) Henry Coker,Quentin Jackson,Benny Powell (tb) Marshall Royal(cl,as) Frank Wess(fl,as,ts) Frank Foster,Budd Johnson(ts) Charlie Fowlkes(bs) Count Basie(p) Freddie Green(g) Eddie Jones(b) Sonny Payne(dm) Jon Hendricks(vo).
(Live,Birdland Club) NYC June 28,1961

Set #1:		
	Jingle bells	CD BN 7-94857-2
Set #2:		
	Whirly bird (voJH)	CD BN 7-96582-2
Set #3:		
	Corner pocket	CD BN 8-33273-2,8-21381-2

JOE WILLIAMS:
Joe Williams(vo) with Harry "Sweets" Edison(tp) unknown(saxes) Jimmy Jones(p) unknown(g) Joe Benjamin(b) Charlie Persip(dm) Ernie Wilkins(arr). NYC,July ,1961

16202	Until I met you	CD BN 8-21146-2
16203	Sometimes I'm happy	-
16210	Summertime	CD BN 5-21153-2

SARAH VAUGHAN:
Sarah Vaughan(vo) with Mundell Lowe(g) George Duvivier(b).
NYC,July 18,1961

16158	My favorite things	CD BN 8-23517-2,(J)TOCJ-6152
16161	Ev'ry time we say goodbye	CD BN(C)4-94888-2,(Sp) 8-53016-2
16160	Sophisticated lady	CD BN 7-80506-2,8-55221-2
16165	Easy to love	CD BN(Sp)8-34712-2

CANDIDO:
Jimmy Cleveland(tb) unknown(ts) Jay Cameron(bs) Lalo Schifrin(p,arr) Milt Hinton or George Duvivier(b) Charlie Persip(dm) Candido Camero(cga,bgo) & others unknown.
NYC,October ,1961

16079	Toccata	CD BN 5-21688-2
16082	Long,long Summer	-

579

SARAH VAUGHAN:
Sarah Vaughan(vo) with Orchestra arr. & cond. by Quincy Jones.
NYC,January-February,1962

16498	I could write a book	CD BN(Sp)8-56842-2
16505	You're mine you	CD BN 8-23517-2

DINAH WASHINGTON:
Dinah Washington(vo) with Orchestra arr. & cond. by Fred Norman.
(Capitol Studios) NYC,March ,1962

16684	Destination moon	CD BN 8-54907-2,(Sp)8-56842-2
16689	Coquette	-
16692	A handful of stars	-
16693	Miss you	-
16694	I'll never stop loving you	-
16696	You're nobody 'til someone loves you	CD BN(C)4-94888-2,(Sp)8-53016-2

DINAH WASHINGTON:
Dinah Washington(vo) with Orchestra arr. & cond. by Don Costa.
NYC,May 8 & 9,1962

16732	Lover man	CD BN 8-54907-2,8-21381-2
16737	The man that got away	-
16738	Baby, won't you please come home	CD BN (E)8-53232-2

JOE WILLIAMS:
Joe Williams(vo) with Harry "Sweets" Edison(tp) Jimmy Forrest(ts) Hugh Lawson(p) Ike Isaacs(b) Clarence Johnston(dm).
(Birdland Club) NYC,June , 1962

	Alright,okay,you win	CD BN 8-21146-2,(Sp)8-34712-2

SARAH VAUGHAN:
Sarah Vaughan(vo) with Orchestra arr. & cond. by Don Costa.
NYC,July ,1962

16878	Snowbound	CD BN 8-23517-2
16904	Blah! blah! blah!	CD BN 7-80506-2

SARAH VAUGHAN:
Sarah Vaughan(vo) with Barney Kessel(g) Joe Comfort(b).
LA,August 7,1962

16914	Key Largo	CD BN 8-23517-2
16923	Goodnight sweetheart	CD BN 4-95981-2

SARAH VAUGHAN:
Sarah Vaughan(vo) with Orchestra arr. & cond. by Benny Carter.
(United/Western Recorders) LA,August 8,1962

16925	Nobody else but me	CD BN 8-23517-2,8-21381-2

DINAH WASHINGTON:
Dinah Washington(vo) with Orchestra arr. & cond. by Don Costa.
NYC,August 22,1962

17003	Just one more chance	CD BN 8-54907-2

580

DINAH WASHINGTON:
Dinah Washington(vo) with Orchestra arr. & cond. by Fred Norman,incl. Eddie Chamblee(ts) Billy Butler(g) & others unknown.
NYC,November 27 & 28,1962

17160-4 Don't say nothin' at all CD BN 8-54907-2
17165-5 The blues ain't nothin' but a woman cryin' for her man CD BN 8-54907-2,4-95981-2
17170-5 Key to the highway CD BN 5-21151-2

SARAH VAUGHAN:
Sarah Vaughan(vo) with Orchestra arr. & cond. by Marty Manning.
NYC February 27,1963

17255 Star eyes CD BN 8-23517-2

Same NYC March 5 or 8,1963

17267 Once upon a Summertime CD BN 8-23517-2,(J)TOCJ-5852

Same NYC,March 11,1963

17284 Intermezzo CD BN 8-23517-2

DINAH WASHINGTON:
Dinah Washington(vo) with Orchestra arr. & cond. by Fred Norman.
NYC,May ,1963

17502 I wanna be around CD BN 7-96583-2,8-32994-2,8-54907-2

SARAH VAUGHAN:
Sarah Vaughan(vo) with Carmell Jones(p) Teddy Edwards(ts) Ernie Freeman(org) John Collins(g) Al McKibbon(b) Milt Turner(dm) Gerald Wilson(arr).
(United Studios) LA,May 29,1963

17529 'Round midnight CD BN 7-96583-2,8-32994-2,5-24271-2,(J)TOCJ-5300

Sarah Vaughan(vo) with Carmell Jones(p) Teddy Edwards(ts) Jack Wilson(org) John Collins(g) Al McKibbon(b) Milt Turner(dm) Gerald Wilson(arr).
(United Studios) LA,May 31,1963

17531 Easy street CD BN 8-57463-2
17533 A taste of honey CD BN 5-21151-2

Sarah Vaughan(vo) with Carmell Jones(p) Teddy Edwards(ts) Jack Wilson(org) John Collins(g) Al McKibbon(b) Earl Palmer(dm) Gerald Wilson(arr).
(United Studios) LA,June 10,1963

17534 Moanin' CD BN 8-23517-2

SARAH VAUGHAN:
Sarah Vaughan(vo) with Orchestra arr. & cond. by Benny Carter.
LA,June 13-16,1963

17547 The lonely hours CD BN 8-23517-2

SARAH VAUGHAN:
Sarah Vaughan(vo) with Orchestra arr. & cond. by Lalo Schifrin.
(Universal Studios) Chicago, June, 1963

17552 More than you know CD BN 8-23517-2
17554 Lazy afternonn CD BN(J)TOCJ-5855
17558 I got rhythm CD BN 7-80506-2

DINAH WASHINGTON:
Dinah Washington(vo) with Orchestra arr. & cond. by Marty Manning.
NYC,October 13 & 18,1963

17823 A stranger on earth CD BN 8-54907-2
17825 Funny thing -
17826 To forget about you -

WILLIE BOBO:
Willie Bobo(timbales) & tp,tb,ts,bs,p,g,b,dm. NYC,c. early 1964

18112 Trinidad CD BN 5-21688-2

BUD POWELL:
Bud Powell(p)John Ore(b)J.C. Moses(dm). NYC,October ,1964

18230 On Green Dolphin Street CD BN(J)TOCJ-6105

Bud Powell(p) John Ore(b) J.C. Moses(dm). NYC,October 21,1964

18235 I remember Clifford CD BN(J)TOCJ-6105,TOCP-50060
18236 The best thing for you CD BN 7-99095-2
18237 Someone to watch over ne CD BN(J)TOCP-50060

CHRIS CONNOR:
Chris Connor(vo) with unidentified orchestra.
(purchased from FM label) c.1964

Hum drum blues CD BN(J)TOCJ-5298
I wish you love CD BN 7-99100-2

BETTY CARTER:
Betty Carter(vo) Norman Simmons(p) Lisle Atkinson(b) Al Harewood(dm).
(Live,Judson Hall) NYC,December 6,1969

'Round midnight CD BN(Sp)8-34712-2
Girl talk CD BN(C)4-94888-2

ART BLAKEY AND THE JAZZ MESSENGERS:
Valery Ponomarev(tp) Bobby Watson(as) Dave Schnitter(ts) Walter Davis Jr.(p) Dennis Irwin(b) Art Blakey (dm). (Sound Ideas) NYC,February ,1977

20611 Jodi CD BN 7-97190-2,8-54899-2

BOBBY WATSON:
Sinclair Acey(tp) Clifford Adams(tb) Arthur White(as) Bobby Watson(as,keyb) Bill Saxton(ts) Charles Davis(bs) Pamela Watson(keyb) Joe Caro(g) Curtis Lundy(el b) Wilby Fletcher(dm) Monty Ellison(cga).
NYC,June ,1977

20624 Reachin' searchin' BN 5-21147-1,CD 5-21147-2

Note: Personnel for this title was quoted by Bobby Watson.

SOLID STATE

JIMMY McGRIFF:
Thornel Schwartz(g) Jimmy McGriff(org) Willie Jenkins(dm).
NYC, 1966

	See see rider	BN(E)8-30724-1 CD BN 8-57063-2,(E)8-30724-2

THAD JONES-MEL LEWIS ORCHESTRA:
Thad Jones(flh,arr-1) Richard Williams,Danny Stiles,Bill Berry,Jimmy Nottingham(tp) Bob Brookmeyer (vtb,arr-2) Jack Rains(tb) Tom McIntosh(tb,arr-3) Cliff Heather(bass tb) Jerome Richardson(ss,as,fl,cl,bass cl) Jerry Dodgion(as,fl.cl) Joe Farrell(ts,fl,cl) Eddie Daniels(ts,cl,bass cl) Pepper Adams(bs) Hank Jones(p) Sam Herman(g) Richard Davis(b) Mel Lewis(dm).
(A & R Studios) NYC,May 4,1966

(tk.4)	ABC blues -2	
(tk.11)	Kids are pretty people -1	
Same.	(A & R Studios)	NYC,May 5,1966
(tk.12)	Don't ever leave me -1	
(tk.8)	Once around -1	
Same.	(A & R Studios)	NYC,May 6,1966
(tk.7)	Three and one -1	
(tk.4)	Balanced scales = justice -3	
(tk.13)	Willow weep for me -2	
(tk.6)	Mean what you say -1	BN BN-LA392-H2

All titles issued on Mosaic MQ7-151,CD MD5-151.

PRESENTING JOE WILLIAMS AND THE THAD JONES/MEL LEWIS JAZZ ORCHESTRA:
Thad Jones(flh,arr) Snooky Young,Jimmy Nottingham,Bill Berry,Richard Williams(tp) Bob Brookmeyer, Garnett Brown,Tom McIntosh(tb) Cliff Heather(bass tb) Jerome Richardson(ss,as) Jerry Dodgion(as) Eddie Daniels,Joe Farrell(ts) Pepper Adams(bs) Roland Hanna(p) Sam Herman(g) Richard Davis(b) Mel Lewis(dm) Joe Williams(vo).
(A & R Studios) NYC,September 30,1966

455	Woman's got soul	BN BN-LA392-H2
457	Get out of my life	- B1-54360,CD 8-54360-2
	Nobody knows the way I feel this morning	
	Gee baby, ain't I good to you	
	How sweet it is to be loved by you	CD BN(C)4-94888-2
	Keep your hand on your heart	
	Evil man blues	
(14978)	Come Sunday	BN BN-LA392-H2, CD 8-55221-2
	Smack dab in the middle	CD BN 5-21153-2
	It don't mean a thing	CD BN 8-21146-2
	Hallelujah I love her so	
	Night time is the right time	

All titles issued on CD BN 8-30454-2.

583

THAD JONES & MEL LEWIS:
Thad Jones(flh,arr-1) Snooky Young,Marvin Stamm,Richard Williams,Jimmy Nottingham(tp) Bob Brookmeyer(vtb,arr-2) Tom McIntosh(tb) Garnett Brown(tb,arr-3) Cliff Heather(bass tb) Phil Woods(as,cl) Jerry Dodgion(as,fl) Joe Farrell(ts,fl,cl) Eddie Daniels(ts,cl) Pepper Adams(bs,cl) Roland Hanna(p) Sam Herman(g,shaker) Richard Davis(b) Mel Lewis(dm).
(A & R Studios) NYC,January 24,1967

(tk.6) Sophisticated lady -3
(tk.3) Willow tree -2
(tk.11) Hawaii -1

All titles on Mosaic MQ7-151,CD MD5-151.

JOE WILLIAMS:
Joe Williams(vo) & members of the Thad Jones/Mel Lewis Orchestra,Thad Jones(arr)
(A & R Studios) NYC,April 22-27,1967

Young man on the way up
Hurry on down CD BN 8-21146-2
Everybody loves my baby
When I take my sugar to tea
Did I really live
Honeysuckle rose
Imagination
If I were a bell
Everybody wants to be loved (by someone)
Lonliness, sorrow and grief
One for my baby

All titles to be issued on the Blue Note label.

THAD JONES & MEL LEWIS:
Thad Jones(c,arr-1) Snooky Young,Jimmy Nottingham,Marvin Stamm,Richard Williams,Bill Berry(tp) Bob Brookmeyer(vtb,arr-2) Tom McIntosh(tb) Garnett Brown(tb,arr-3) Cliff Heather(bass tb) Jerome Richardson (ss,as,fl,cl) Jerry Dodgion(as,fl) Joe Farrell(ts,fl,arr-4) Eddie Daniels(ts,cl) Pepper Adams(bs,cl) Roland Hanna(p) Sam Herman(g,shaker) Richard Davis(b) Mel Lewis(dm).
(Village Vanguard) NYC,April 28,1967

974 The little pixie -1 BN BN-LA392-H2
A-that's freedom -1
The second race -1
Willow tree -2
Quietude -1
Bachafillen (Bacha feelin') -3
Lover man -4
Mornin' reverend-1 (first version)
Samba con getcha -2
Willow tree (alt.)-2
Don't git sassy -1

All titles on Mosaic MQ7-151,CD MD5-151.

JIMMY McGRIFF:
Joe Newman(tp) Jerome Richardson(ts,ss) Jimmy McGriff(org) Barry Galbraith,Wally Richardson(g) Richard Davis(b) Mel Lewis(dm).
NYC, mid 1967

A long day's night CD BN(J)TOCJ-5239

DIZZY GILLESPIE - LIVE AT THE VILLAGE VANGUARD:
Dizzy Gillespie(tp) Ray Nance(v) Pepper Adams(bs) Chick Corea(p) Richard Davis(b) Elvin Jones-1,Mel Lewis-2(dm). (Village Vanguard) NYC,October 1,1967

Birks' works (Dizzy's blues*)-1,3	BN(E)BNS40035*
Lullaby of the leaves -1,3	CD BN(J)TOCJ-5633
Lover come back to me -2	
Blues for Max -2	BN(E)BNS40035

-3: edited on all previous LP issues.
All titles issued on CD BN 7-80507-2.

Garnett Brown(tb) replaces Nance.Same date.

Tour de force -2,3	BN(E)BNS40035,UALP 19
On the trail -2,3	
Sweet Georgia Brown -2	

-3: edited on all previous LP issues.
All titles issued on CD BN 7-80507-2.

JAZZ FOR A SUNDAY AFTERNOON:
Marvin Stamm(tp) Garnett Brown(tb) Joe Farrell(ts) Chick Corea(p) Richard Davis(b) Elvin Jones(dm).
(Village Vanguard) NYC,October 1,1967

13 Avenue B-1	
Stella by starlight -1	CD BN (J)TOCJ-5633
Bachafillen	

-1: edited on all previous LP issues.
All titles issued on CD BN 7-89280-2.

JIMMY McGRIFF:
Fats Theus(ts) Thornel Schwartz(g) Jimmy McGriff(org) Willie Jenkins(dm).
NYC,c. late 1967

I've got a woman (Kiko*)	BN(E)8-30724-1*; CD BN 8-57063-2*,(E)8-30724-2*

Note: This track appears in place of "Kiko" on all pressings of 30724-1 & 30724-2 and on most pressings of 57063-2 (see page 616).

CHICO HAMILTON:
Danny Bank(fl) Steve Potts(as) Russ Andrews(ts) Jimmy Cleveland,Britt Woodman,Bill Campbell(tb) Jimmy Cheatham(bass tb,arr) Jan Arnett(b) Chico Hamilton(dm),
(A & R Studios) NYC,c. early 1968

MSP	BN B1-54357,CD 8-54357-2

CHICK COREA:
Chick Corea(p) Miroslav Vitous(b) Roy Haynes(dm).
(A & R Studios) NYC,March 14,1968

(tk.1) The law of falling and catching up BN BN-LA395-H2,B1-90055
(tk.2) Bossa BN BN-LA472-H2
(tk.3) Matrix BN BN-LA395-H2,B1-90055,
BN(In)JAZ 1,(J)K23P-6725,W-5510
CD BN 7-89282-2,7-96904-2,(J)CJ28-5030,
TOCJ-5633,TOCJ-5187/88,GRP GRD5-9819
(tk.3) My one and only love BN BN-LA472-H2;Lib(J)K22P-6092/93
CD 7-89282-2,(J)CJ28-5022,TOCJ-5633,
TOCJ-5856,TOCJ-5873,(Sp)8-34712-2,8-53016-2
(tk.1) Step - What was (intro) BN B1-90055
(tk.1) Now he beats the drum - now he stops (body of tune) -

All titles also issued on CD BN 7-90055-2.

Same. (A & R Studios) NYC,March 19,1968

Gemini BN BN-LA472-H2
(tk.3) Now he sings,now he sobs BN BN-LA395-H2,B1-90055,CD 7-89282-2,
(C)8-56508-2,(J)TOCJ-5633
Fragments BN BN-LA472-H2
(tk.4) Steps - What was (body of tune) BN B1-90055
(tk.3) Now he beats the drum - now he stops (intro) -

All titles also issued on CD BN 7-90055-2.

Same. (A & R Studios) NYC,March 27,1968

I don't know
Pannonica BN(Du)1A158-83401/4
CD BN 7-89282-2,(J)CJ28-5178,TOCJ-5633
Samba Yantra -
Windows - (J)TOCJ-5633

All titles issued on BN BN-LA472-H2,CD 7-90055-2.

RUTH BROWN WITH THAD JONES & MEL LEWIS:
Thad Jones(flh,arr) Snooky Young,Jimmy Nottingham,Danny Moore,Richard Williams,Bill Berry(tp) Garnett Brown,Jimmy Cleveland,Jimmy Knepper(tb) Cliff Heather(bass tb) Jerome Richardson(ss,as) Jerry Dodgion(as) Eddie Daniels,Seldon Powell(ts) Pepper Adams(bs) Roland Hanna(p) Richard Davis(b) Mel Lewis(dm) Ruth Brown(vo).
(Plaza Sound Studios) NYC,June 18,1968

Yes sir, that's my baby CD BN(Sp)8-56842-2
2597 Be anything (but be mine) BN BN-LA392-H2

Same. (Plaza Sound Studios) NYC,July 2,1968

Trouble in mind
Sonny Boy
Bye, bye, blackbird
I'm gonna move to the outskirts of town
Black coffee
2595 Fine Brown frame BN BN-LA392-H2
2596 You won't let me go -

All titles issued on CD Capitol Jazz 7-81200-2.

THAD JONES & MEL LEWIS:
Thad Jones(flh,arr-1) Snooky Young,Jimmy Nottingham,Danny Moore,Richard Williams(tp) Garnett Brown,Jimmy Cleveland,Jimmy Knepper(tb) Cliff Heather(bass tb) Jerome Richardson (ss,as,fl) Jerry Dodgion(as,fl) Eddie Daniels,Seldon Powell(ts,cl) Pepper Adams(bs,cl) Roland Hanna(p) Richard Davis(b) Mel Lewis(dm).
(Village Vanguard) NYC,October 17,1968

	Say it softly-1	
2983	Mornin' reverend-1	BN BN-LA392-H2
	Kids are pretty people-1	
	The second race-1	
	St. Louis blues-2	
	The waltz you swang for me-1	

-2: arr. by Bob Brookmeyer.
All titles on Mosaic MQ7-151,CD MD5-151.

JIMMY McGRIFF:
Blue Mitchell(tp) Danny Turner(as) Fats Theus(ts) Bob Ashton(bs) Jimmy McGriff(org) Thornel Schwartz(g) Bob Bushnell(el b)Mel Lewis or Grady Tate(dm). NYC,c. Autumn 1968

The worm	BN 45-1963,B1-89907,CD 7-89907-2
	Lib.C-1027
Blue Juice	B1-99106, CD 7-99106-2

Both titles issued on BN(E)8-30724-1,CD BN 8-57063-2,(E)8-30724-2.

Blue Mitchell(tp) Danny Turner(as) Fats Theus(ts) Bob Ashton(bs) Jimmy McGriff(org) Larry Frazier(g) Jesse Kilpatrick Jr.(dm). NYC,December 17-19,1968

Step one	BN 45-1963
South Wes	

Both titles issued on BN(E)8-30724-1,CD BN 8-57063-2,(E)8-30724-2.

MONK HIGGINS:
Thomas Scott,William Peterson(tp) David A. Duke(frh) Monk Higgins(ts,org,arr) Jim Horn(fl) Alan Estes (vb,perc) Miles Grayson(p) Dee Ervin(org) Freddy Robinson,Arthur Adams,Al Vescovo(g) Bob West or Ron Brown(b) John Guerin(dm) Jerry Williams(cga) Sid Sharp(concert master) & strings.
LA,c.1969

Little green apples	BN B1-94027,CD 4-94027-2

JOHNNY LYTLE:
Johnny Lytle(vb) & others unknown.
NYC,c.1969

Killiano	BN B1-54357,CD 8-54357-2

RANDY BRECKER - SCORE:
Randy Brecker(tp,flh) Michael Brecker(ts) Jerry Dodgion(alto fl-2) Hal Galper(p-1) Larry Coryell(g) Eddie Gomez(b) Mickey Roker(dm). Englewood Cliffs,N.J.,January 24,1969

Bangalore -1
Name game -1
Morning song -2
Pipe dream -2
The marble sea -2

All titles issued on CD BN 7-81202-2.

RANDY BRECKER - SCORE:
Randy Brecker(tp) Michael Brecker(ts) Hal Galper(el p) Larry Coryell(g) Chuck Rainey(el b) Bernard Purdie (dm). Englewood Cliffs,N.J.February 3,1969

The weasel goes out to lunch
The vamp
Score

All titles issued on CD BN 7-81202-2.

CHICK COREA:
Woody Shaw(tp) Hubert Laws(fl,picc) Bennie Maupin(ts) Chick Corea(p-1,el p-2) Dave Holland(b) Jack DeJohnette,Horace Arnold(dm,perc).
(Bell Sound Studios) NYC,May 11,12 & 13,1969

This -2
Jamala -1,2
Is -1

All titles issued on BN BN-LA395-H2.

THAD JONES & MEL LEWIS:
Thad Jones(flh,arr) Snooky Young,Danny Moore,Jimmy Nottingham,Richard Williams(tp) Eddie Bert, Jimmy Knepper,Benny Powell(tb) Cliff Heather(bass tb) Jerome Richardson(ss,as,fl) Jerry Dodgion(as,cl) Joe Farrell,Eddie Daniels(ts,cl) Joe Temperley(bs,bass cl) Roland Hanna(p) Barry Galbraith,Sam Brown(g) Richard Davis(b) Mel Lewis(dm).
(A & R Studios) NYC,June 17,1969

(tk.3) (4458) Central Park North
(tk.5) (4455) Jive samba

Both titles on BN BN-LA392-H2,Mosaic MQ7-151,CD BN(J)TOCJ-5419,Mosaic MD5-151.

Same. (A & R Studios) NYC,June 18,1969

(tk.8)	Quietude-1	
(tk.5) (4457)	Big dipper-1	BN BN-LA392-H2
(tk.3)	Tow away zone	
(tk.9) (4456)	The groove merchant	BN BN-LA392-H2

-1: omit Sam Brown(g).
All titles issued on Mosaic MQ7-151,CD BN(J)TOCJ-5419,Mosaic MD5-151.

CANDIDO:
Pat Russo,Jimmy Sedlar(tp) Alan Raph(tb,bass tb) Joe Grimm(sax,fl,picc) Frank Anderson(p,org) Dave Spinozza(g) Chuck Rainey(el b) Herbie Lovelle(dm) Candido Camero(cga,bgo) Joe Cain(arr).
(A & R Studios) NYC,September 4,1969

5058	Tony's theme	CD BN 5-22664-2
5059	Hallelujah! I'm comin' home	-

Gerry Jemmott(el b) replaces Rainey.
(A & R Studios) NYC,September 9,1969

5060	Soul limbo	BN 45-1959
5061	Come on choo-choo train	
5062	Thousand finger man	BN B1-97158,CD 4-97158-2
5063	Jump back	BN 45-1959

All titles issued on CD BN 5-22664-2.

SOMETHIN' ELSE

RENEE ROSNES:
Wayne Shorter(ss) Renee Rosnes(p,synth).
(Montmartre Club) Copenhagen,April 18,1988

Diana BN B1-93561, CD 7-93561-2

RALPH PETERSON QUINTET - V:
Terence Blanchard(tp) Steve Wilson(ss-1,as) Geri Allen(p) Phil Bowler(b) Ralph Peterson(dm).
(A & R Studios) NYC,April 19 & 20,1988

Enemy within
Monief -1
The short end of the stick
Soweto 6
Viola's dance -1
Bebopskerony

All titles issued on BN B1-91730,CD 7-91730-2.

RALPH PETERSON - TRIANGULAR:
Geri Allen(p) Phil Bowler(b) Ralph Peterson(dm).
(A & R Studios) NYC,April 20,1988

Just you,just me BN B1-92750,CD 7-92750-2

SUPERBLUE
Don Sickler(tp) Roy Hargrove(tp,flh) Frank Lacy(tb) Bobby Watson(as) Bill Pierce(ts) Mulgrew Miller(p) Bob Hurst(b) Kenny Washington(dm). Englewood Cliffs,N.J.,April 26,1988

Open sesame
Summertime
Marvelous Marvin
Time off
I remember Clifford
Conservation
Once forgotten
M & M

All titles issued on BN B1-91731, CD 7-91731-2.

GEORGE ADAMS - NIGHTINGALE:
George Adams(fl-1,ss-2,ts) Hugh Lawson(p) Sirone(b) Victor Lewis(dm).
(A & R Studios) NYC,August 19 & 20,1988

Bridge over troubled water	BN B1-91984;CD BN(J)TOCJ-5608
What a wonderful world (omit b,dm)	- CD BN(J)TOCJ-5203, TOCJ-5217,TOCJ-5793,TOCJ-6152
Cry me a river	
A nightingale sang in Berkeley Square -1	BN B1-91984;CD BN(J)TOCJ-5750
Moon river	-
Precious Lord,take my hand	-
Ol' man river	-
Going home-2	-
Besame mucho	

All titles issued on CD BN 7-91984-2.

589

RALPH PETERSON - TRIANGULAR:
Geri Allen(p) Essiet Okon Essiet(b) Ralph Peterson(dm).

	(A & R Studios)	NYC,August 21 & 22,1988
	Bemsha swing	CD BN 8-35471-2
	Water colors	
	Princess	
	Move	CD BN(J)TOCJ-5187/88
	Splash	
	Smoke rings	

All titles issued on BN B1-92750,CD 7-92750-2.

RENEE ROSNES:
Renee Rosnes,Herbie Hancock(p).

		Englewood Cliffs,NJ,December 11,1988
	Fleur-de-lis	BN B1-93561,CD 7-93561-2

JOHN HART - ONE DOWN:
Tim Hagans(tp-1) Rick Margitza(ts-2) John Hart(g) Chuck Bergeron(b) John Riley(dm).

	(Manhattan Studios)	NYC,December 21,1988	
	Take no prisoners -1,2	BN B1-93476	
	One down -1,2	-	
	It could happen to you -1		
	Deborah	BN B1-93476	
	Transcendence	-	CD BN(J)TOCJ-5602
	Lamar	-	
	90 minute cigarette	-	CD BN 7-96581-2
	Stoned on video	-	

All titles issued on CD BN 7-93476-2.

OUT OF THE BLUE - SPIRAL STAIRCASE:
Michael Philip Mossman(tp)Steve Wilson(as) Ralph Bowen(ts) Renee Rosnes(p) Kenny Davis(b) Billy Drummond(dm).

	(A & R Studios)	NYC,January 24,1989
(tk.3)	Gerri-Ann	BN B1-93006
(tk.2)	Samba La Rue	-
(tk.1)	Spiral staircase	-
(tk.3)	North of the border	-
Same	(A & R Studios)	NYC,January 25,1989
(tk.5)	Ika Sashi	
(tk.2)	Input	BN B1-93006
(tk.3)	The perpetrator	-

All titles issued on CD BN 7-93006-2.

590

RENEE ROSNES:
Ralph Bowen(ts-1) Branford Marsalis(ss,ts)-2 Renee Rosnes(p) Ron Carter(b) Lewis Nash(dm).
Englewood Cliffs,N.J.,February 4,1989

The storyteller -1
I.A. blues -1 — CD BN(J)TOCJ-5603
Punjab -1
Playground for the birds -2
Bright Mississippi -2
Everything I love

All titles issued on BN B1-93561, CD 7-93561-2.

RALPH PETERSON - VOLITION:
Terence Blanchard(tp) Steve Wilson(as,ss) Geri Allen(p) Phil Bowler(b) Ralph Peterson(dm).
(Clinton Studios) NYC,February 27 & 28,1989

Volition
Seven of swords
On my side
Forth and back
Back to stay
In step
The benevolent one
Sasquatch

All titles issued on CD BN 7-93894-2.

JOHN HART - ONE DOWN:
John Hart(g).
(Manhattan Studios) NYC,April 23,1989

Denise's smile — BN B1-93476
Ruby my dear — -
Stairway to the stars
No more blues

All titles issued on CD BN 7-93576-2.

SUPERBLUE - SUPERBLUE 2:
Don Sickler(tp,arr) Wallace Roney(tp) Robin Eubanks(tb) Bobby Watson(as) Ralph Moore(ts) Renee Rosnes(p) Robert Hurst(b) Marvin "Smitty" Smith(dm).
Englewood Cliffs,NJ,April 24-25,1989

Flight to Jordan
Nica's dream
'Round midnight
Take your pick
Blue minor
Autumn leaves
Blue bossa
Desert moonlight
Low tide
Cool struttin'

All titles issued on CD BN 7-92997-2.

591

GIL GOLDSTEIN - CITY OF DREAMS:
John Clark(frh-1) Gil Goldstein(p,synth.acc-2) John Patitucci(b,el b) Lenny White(dm) Don Alias(perc) Bruce Martin(tabla).

(Centerfield Productions)	NYC,March-July 1989
2BE-balloon song	
Lucky you.lucky me	CD BN(J)TOCJ-5603
In my life	CD BN 7-94861-2,(J)TOCJ-5874
Loro -2	
Corner sports	
City lights	
Casa blu -1	
Nobody's heart	
Three views of a secret	
Lucky you, lucky me (solo p)	

All titles issued on CD BN 7-93893-2.

ELLIS MARSALIS:
Tony Dagradi,Rick Margitza(ts) Ellis Marsalis(p) Bill Huntington(b) David Lee(dm).

(Live at Snug Harbor)	NO,April 30,1989
Nothin' but the blues	CD BN(J)TOCJ-5217

GEORGE ADAMS - AMERICA:
George Adams(fl-1,ts,vo) Hugh Lawson(p) Cecil McBee(b) Mark Johnson(dm).

(A & R Studios)	NYC,May,June & July 1989
America the beautiful	CD BN 7-93896-2
Tennessee waltz	-
Motivation (voGA)	-
Old folks at home (Swanee)-1	-
Gee baby,ain't I good to you? (voGA)	-
You are my sunshine	-
Have you thanked America? (voGA)	-
Nothing ever changed my love for you	

George Adams(ts) Hugh Lawson(p-1).

	Same sessions
Georgia on my mind -1	CD BN 7-93896-2
Come Sunday -1	
How deep is the ocean? -1	
Take me out to the ball game	CD BN 7-93896-2
The star spangled banner	-

HUGH LAWSON:
Hugh Lawson(p) Cecil McBee(b) Marvin 'Smitty' Smith(dm).

	NYC,August 3-4,1989
As time goes by	CD BN 7-81331-2
When you wish upon a star	CD BN(J)TOCJ-6152

TERUMASA HINO - BLUESTRUCK:
Terumasa Hino(c) Rob Scheps(ts) Onaje Allan Gumbs(p) Bob Hurst(b) Victor Lewis(dm).
(A & R Studios) NYC,September 19,1989

Alone,alone and alone (omit ts)	CD BN 7-93671-2,(J)TOCJ-5712
Melody for C	rejected
Bluestruck	CD BN 7-93671-2
Autumn leaves	-

Terumasa Hino(c) Bobby Watson(as-1) Rob Scheps(ts) Onaje Allan Gumbs(p) John Scofield(g) Michael Formanek(b) Victor Lewis(dm).
(A & R Studios) NYC,September 21,1989

Hugo	
Sweet love of mine	
Time-outing -1	
Romancero Gitano	CD BN(J)TOCJ-5217,TOCJ-5963
Rain again	

All titles issued on CD BN 7-93671-2.

JERRY BERGONZI - STANDARD GONZ:
Jerry Bergonzi(ts) Joey Calderazzo(p) Dave Santoro(b) Adam Nussbaum(dm).
(Outpost Studio) Stoughton,Mass.,October 19,1989 & April 5.1990

If I were a bell
Come rain or come shine
McCoy
Just friends
Jab
Arbonius unt
Here's that rainy day
Night and day
Conjunction

All titles issued on CD BN 7-96256-2.

ELIANE ELIAS PLAYS JOBIM:
Eliane Elias(p,vo) Eddie Gomez(b) Jack DeJohnette(dm) Nana Vasconcelos(perc).
(Power Station) NYC,December ,1989

Waters of March/Agua de beber	CD BN 7-95590-2,8-35283-2,(Au)8-14710-2 CD BN(J)TOCJ-5217,TOCJ-6188
Sabia	
Passarim	CD BN(J)TOCJ-5603
Don't ever go away	CD BN(C)4-94888-2
Desafinado	CD BN(Au)4-98320-2
Angela	
Children's games	
Dindi	
Zingaro	
One note samba	
Don't ever go away	

All titles issued on CD BN 7-93089-2.

RALPH PETERSON PRESENTS THE FO'TET:
Don Byron(cl,bass cl-1) Bryan Carrott(vb) Melissa Slocum(b) Ralph Peterson(dm).
(A & R Studios) NYC,December 22 & 23,1989

Urban omen
Homegoing
Axis mundi -1
Ballad for Queen Tiye -1
I can dream,can't I?
Johnny come lately

All titles issued on CD BN 7-95475-2.

Frank Lacy(tb-2,flh-3) David Murray(ts-4,bass cl-5) added.
Same sessions

Thabo -1,2,4
Miss Lady -1,2,4
Confrontation -2,3,4,5

All titles issued on CD BN 7-95475-2.

GERI ALLEN - THE NURTURER:
Marcus Belgrave(tp,flh) Kenny Garrett(as) Geri Allen(p) Robert Hurst(b) Jeff Watts(dm) Eli Fountain(perc).
(Sound On Sound) NYC,January 5 & 6,1990

Night's shadow	CD BN(J)TOCJ-5603
N° 3	
It's good to be home again	
Batista's groove	
Night of power (for my daughter Laila)	
Our gang	CD BN 7-98291-2,7-99790-2
Silence and song/The Nurturer	
Le goo wop	
Lullaby of Isfahan	

All titles issued on CD BN 7-95139-2.

RACHELLE FERRELL - FIRST INSTRUMENT:
Rachelle Ferrell(vo) with Alex Foster(ss-1) Eddie Green(p) Tyrone Brown(b) Doug Nally(dm).
(Kajem Victory) Gladwynne,PA,January-February,1990

You send me	CD BN 7-99105-2,(J)TOCJ-5217
You don't know what love is	CD BN 4-95701-2
Bye bye blackbird	CD BN 7-96583-2
Prayer dance	
Inchworm -1	
What is this thing called love -2	CD BN 4-95701-2,(J)TOCJ-5856
My funny Valentine	CD BN(J)TOCJ-5963,TOCJ-6135,TOCJ-6189
Don't waste your time	
Extensions -3	

-2: Ferrell(vo) Nally(dm) only.
-3: Ferrell(vo,p).
All titles issued on CD BN 8-27820-2.

Rachelle Ferrell(vo) with Terence Blanchard(tp) Gil Goldstein(p) Kenny Davis(b) Lenny White(dm).
(Sound On Sound) NYC,February,1990

With every breath I take	CD BN 8-27820-2

594

<u>RENEE ROSNES</u> - <u>FOR THE MOMENT</u>:
Joe Henderson(ts) Renee Rosnes(p) Ira Coleman(b) Billy Drummond(dm).
(A & R Recording Studios) NYC,February 15 & 16,1990

Summer night CD BN 7-89287-2
For the moment -1
Four in one
Malaga moon -1 CD BN(C)8-33908-2
Nemesis -1
Thinking to myself
The organ grinder
Homeward (ts out)

-1: Steve Wilson(ss,as) added.
All titles issued on CD BN 7-94859-2.

<u>ELLIS MARSALIS TRIO</u>:
Ellis Marsalis(p) Robert Hurst(b) Jeff Watts(dm).
(RCA Studios) NYC,March 18,1990

Syndrome
Emily
Just squeeze me
Little Niles
Limehouse blues
A moment alone
Li'l boy man
Jitterbug waltz
The garden
Chapter one
I thought about you

All titles issued on CD BN 7-96107-2.

<u>RICHIE BEIRACH</u> - <u>SUNDAY SONGS</u>:
Richie Beirach(p).
(RCA Studios) NYC,June 29 & 30,1990

Full circle
Inamorata
Chopin: Prelude (Opus 28,N°20 in C minor)
Debussy: Des pas sur la neige (Prelude book 1,N°.6)
Wisteria
Anse des flamands

All titles issued on CD BN 7-80511-2.

<u>GONZALO RUBALCABA</u> - <u>DISCOVERY</u>:
Gonzalo Rubalcaba(p) Charlie Haden(b) Paul Motian(dm).
(Jazz Festival) Montreux,July 15,1990

Well you needn't CD BN 8-35471-2,4-95701-2,(J)TOCJ-5608
Velas CD BN(J)TOCJ-5603
Prologo comienzo
First song
Once around the park
Joao
All the things you are

All titles issued on CD BN 7-95478-2.

<u>RALPH PETERSON</u> - <u>ORNETTOLOGY</u>:
Don Byron(cl,bass cl-1) Bryan Carrott(vb) Melissa Slocum(b) Ralph Peterson(dm).
(Clinton Studios) NYC,August 7,8 & 9,1990

Ornettology
The substance of things hoped for -1 CD BN 7-98291-2,7-99790-2
Nemesis
Iris -1
Status flux
I mean you
Sneak attack
Congeniality
There is no greater love -2

-2: Ralph Peterson(c)Melissa Slocum(b) only.
All titles issued on CD BN 7-98290-2.

<u>JOE LOVANO</u> - <u>LANDMARKS</u>:
Joe Lovano(ts) Ken Werner(p) John Abercrombie(g) Marc Johnson(b) Bill Stewart(dm).
(Sorcerer Sound) NYC,August 13 & 14,1990

The owl and the fox
Primal dance
Emperor Jones
Landmarks
Along the way
Street talk
Here and now
I love music
Where hawks fly
Thanksgiving

All titles issued on CD BN 7-96108-2.

<u>LOU RAWLS</u>:
Lou Rawls(vo) with Orchestra arr. & cond. by H.B. Barnum: Jeffrey W. Colella(p) David T. Walker(g) Curtis Robinson Jr.(b) Kenny Eliott(dm) Carl Vincent Rigolo(perc) Dimitri J. Leivici(v,concertmaster) Suzie Katamaya,Daniel W. Smith,Michele K. Richards,Denyse Nadeau Buffum,Patricia Ann Johnson,Michael B. Markman(strings).
LA,August 22/23,1990

Love me tender CD BN(J)TOCJ-5253

<u>GEOFF KEEZER</u> - <u>HERE AND NOW</u>:
Donald Harrison(as-1) Steve Nelson(vb) Geoff Keezer(p) Peter Washington(b) Billy Higgins(dm).
(Clinton Studios) NYC,October 3 & 4,1990

There but for the grace of..
Headed off at the pass
Leilani's mirror -1
Agra
Just one of those things
It's the thought that counts -1
Feeling of jazz
Turning point
It never entered my mind
If that's the way you feel
Scandal in Shinjuku -1

All titles issued on CD BN 7-96691-2.

STANLEY JORDAN - STOLEN MOMENTS:
Stanley Jordan(el g) Charnett Moffett(b,el b-1) Kenwood Dennard(dm).

	(Blue Note Club)	Tokyo,November 7,8 & 9,1990
	Stairway to heaven	CD BN(J)TOCJ-5602,TOCJ-5608
	Impressions	
	Lady in my life -1	
	Autumn leaves	
	Stolen moments	
	Return expedition	
	Over the rainbow (b,dm out)	CD BN 8-31502-2

All titles issued on CD BN 7-97159-2.

TERUMASA HINO - FROM THE HEART:
Terumasa Hino(c,tp-1) Roger Byam(ts) Onaje Allan Gumbs(p) John Hart(g) Michael Formanek(b) Michael Carvin(dm).

	(RPM Studios)	NYC,January 17,1991
(tk.1)	T for three	CD BN 7-96688-2
	Kimiko -1	rejected
(tk.1)	Lava dance	CD BN 7-96688-2
(tk.5)	Sage	-
(tk.3)	There's always time for peace (ts,g out)	-

Same.

	(RPM Studios)	NYC,January 18,1991
(tk.1)	Free Mandela	CD BN 7-96688-2
(tk.6)	Why knot	-
(tk.5)	Kimiko -1	-
(tk.4)	Over the rainbow (ts,g out)	-
	Sage	rejected

GEORGE ADAMS - OLD FEELING:
Hannibal Marvin Peterson(tp) George Adams(ts) Jean-Paul Bourelly(g) Ray Gallon(p-1) Santi DeBriano(b) Lewis Nash(dm).

	(Clinton Studios)	NYC,March 11 & 12,1991
	Better git hit in yo' soul	
	That old feeling	
	The wanderer	
	As time goes by -1	
	Melody for Monet	
	The cry	
	Teamwork -1	
	Just the way you are	

All titles on CD BN 7-96689-2.

JOHN HART - TRUST:
John Hart(g) Michael Formanek(b) Victor Lewis(dm).

	(Power Station)	NYC,April 28,1991
	The arrival	
	Dressin' up the Johnson	
	What does it mean?	
	Trust	
	The evolution of a joke	
	Everything I love	
	Forbidden fruit	

All titles issued on CD BN 7-95206-2.

JOHN HART - TRUST:
John Hart(g) solo. Same session.

Embraceable you
All the things you are
Michael's turn

All titles issued on CD BN 7-95206-2.

GONZALO RUBALCABA - THE BLESSING:
Gonzalo Rubalcaba(p) Charlie Haden(b) Jack DeJohnette(dm).
(McClear Place) Toronto,Canada,May 12-15,1991

Circuito
Sandino
Besame mucho CD BN(J)TOCJ-5608
Giant steps
Sin remedio,el mar
Silver hollow
The blessing
Blue in green
Sinpunto y contracopa
Mima
Airegin CD BN 7-98291-2,7-99790-2,7-99918-2

All titles,except last one,issued on CD BN 7-97197-2.

JACK DeJOHNETTE'S SPECIAL EDITION - EARTH WALK:
Greg Osby(as,ss) Gary Thomas(ts,fl) Michael Cain(p,synth) Lonnie Plaxico(b,el b) Jack DeJohnette(dm) Joan Henry(vo-1).
(Dreamland Studios) West Hurley,NY,June ,1991

It's time to wake up and dream
Blue
Where or Wayne
Priestesses of the mist
Earth walk -1
On golden beams CD BN 7-98291-2,7-99790-2,7-99918-2
One on one
Lydia
Monk's plumb
It's time to wake up and dream

All titles issued on CD BN 7-96690-2.

GONZALO RUBALCABA - IMAGES:
Gonzalo Rubalcaba(p) John Patitucci(b) Jack DeJohnette(dm).
(Mount Fuji Jazz Festival) Japan,August 23,1991

No name rejected
Autumn leaves -
Peace and quiet time -
Ebony -
Imagine -
Giant steps -

GONZALO RUBALCABA - IMAGES:
Gonzalo Rubalcaba(p).
(Mount Fuji Jazz Festival) Japan,August 24,1991

Gaby	CD BN 7-99492-2	
Joao	-	
Prologo/Cimienza	rejected	

Gonzalo Rubalcaba(p) John Patitucci(b) Jack DeJohnette(dm).
(Mount Fuji Jazz Festival) Japan,August 25,1991

No name	CD BN 7-99492-2	
Imagine	-	(J)TOCJ-5712,(J)TOCJ-5963
Autumn leaves	-	
Peace and quiet time	-	
Ebony	-	
Giant steps	-	
Mima	-	

THE BOYS CHOIR OF HARLEM - CHRISTMAS CAROLS AND SACRED SONGS:
James Williams(p) Peter Washington(b) Tony Reedus(dm) Boys Choir Of Harlem(vo).
(The Power Station) NYC,September 4-6,1991

O Holy night -1
I wonder as I wander
Winter wonderland
The Christmas song -1
Let it snow,let it snow!
White Christmas
O Tannenbaum
Go tell it on the mountain -1
Sweet little Jesus boy
Silent night

-1: add Dianne Reeves(vo) overdubbed at Le Gonks West,LA,September 9,1991.

All titles issued on CD BN 7-99965-2.

RON CARTER - RON CARTER MEETS BACH:
Ron Carter(b,piccolo b - all parts overdubbed).
(Clinton Studios) December 15-17,1991

Air
Christ lag in Todesbanden
Wachet auf,ruft uns die stimme
Arioso
Jesu,joy of man's desiring
Es woll uns Gott genadig sein
Gavotte en rondeau
Prelude,interlude and fugue
Siciliano
Praeludium,interlude,praeludium
Komm susser Tod,komm sel'ge Ruh

All titles issued on CD BN 7-80510-2.

599

RICHIE BEIRACH - SUNDAY SONGS:
Richie Beirach(p).
(Master Sound) Astoria,NY,December 21 & 22,1991

Chopin: Prelude (opus 28, no.4 in E minor)
Schumann: From foreign lands and people (Scenes from childhood no.1)
Peace piece
Sunday song
Mompou: Musica callada no.1
Chopin: Etude (opus 10, no.3 in E major)

All titles issued on CD BN 7-80511-2.

RENEE ROSNES - WITHOUT WORDS:
Renee Rosnes(p) Buster Williams(b) Billy Drummond(dm) & strings: Gene Orloff,Matthew Raimondi, Sandra Park,Louann Montesi,Mark Feldman,Mary Rowell,Laura Seaton(v) Lamar Alsop,Lois Martin, Maureen Gallagher(viola) Frederick Zlotkin,Erik Friedlander(cello) Robert Friedman(arr,cond).
(Power Station) NYC,January 8,1992

tk.2/6	Dear old Stockholm	
tk.2	Estate	
tk.3	Jitterbug waltz	
tk.2	In a sentimental mood	
tk.2	I've got you under my skin	CD BN 7-89914-2

All titles issued on CD BN 7-98168-2.

Same.	(Power Station)	NYC,January 9,1992
tk.3	You and the night and the music	CD BN 7-98168-2
tk.1	Little B's poem	-
tk.3	Misty	-
tk.3	It ain't necessarily so	unissued
tk.5	Solar	CD BN 7-98168-2

GERI ALLEN - MAROONS:
Wallace Roney-1,Marcus Belgrave-2 (tp) Geri Allen(p) Dwayne Dolphin(b) Tani Tabbal(dm)
(Sound On Sound) NYC,February 11-14,1992

No more Mr. Nice Guy
Feed the fire III
Brooklyn bound A
Bed-Sty
Laila's house -1
Maroons-1
Dolphy's dance -1,2
Number four (b,dm out)-2
For John Malachi (b,dm out)-1

All titles issued on CD BN 7-99493-2.

Wallace Roney(tp) Geri Allen(p) Anthony Cox(b) Pheeroan AkLaff(dm).
Same sessions.

A prayer for peace
Mad money

Both titles issued on CD BN 7-99493-2.

GERI ALLEN - MAROONS:
Wallace Roney(tp-3) Geri Allen(p) Anthony Cox,Dwayne Dolphin(b-1) Pheeroan Aklaff,Tani Tabbal(dm-2).
Same sessions

Two brothers -1
Feed the fire I -2 BN(J)TOJJ-5849,CD TOCJ-5849
Feed the fire II -1,2
And they partied -1,2,3

All titles issued on CD BN 7-99493-2.

ELIANE ELIAS - FANTASIA:
Eliane Elias(p) Eddie Gomez(b) Jack DeJohnette(dm) Nana Vasconselos(perc-1) Ivan Lins(vo).
(Sound On Sound) NYC,March ,1992

The girl from Ipanema -1 CD BN 8-35283-2
Wave
Sabe voce
Fantasia (dm out)
No more blues
Ivan Lins medley (voIL)-1:
Coragem mulher/
Choro das aguas/
Doce presenca/
Coragem mulher

All titles issued on CD BN 7-96146-2.

Eliane Elias(vo,p) Marc Johnson(b) Peter Erskine(dm) Nana Vasconselos(perc,vo) Amanda Elias Brecker (vo).
(Sound On Sound) NYC,March ,1992

Milton Nascimiento medley (voEE,AEB):
Ponta de arela/
Cancao do sal/
Cravo e canela
Bahia (voEE,NV)

All titles issued on CD BN 7-96146-2.

RALPH PETERSON - ART:
Graham Haynes(c) Ku-umba Frank Lacy(tb-1) Steve Wilson(ss,as) Craig Handy(ts-1) Michelle Rosewoman (p) Phil Bowler(b) Ralph Peterson(dm).
(Power Station) NYC,March 18-20,1992

Free for all -1
Sonora
Art of Blakey
Central Park West
When you wish upon a star
Bon Marie
I remember Bu
Where it's come from
People make the world go round

All titles issued on CD BN 8-27645-2.

601

TERUMASA HINO - UNFORGETTABLE:
Terumasa Hino(c) Cedar Walton(p) David Williams(b) Michael Carvin(dm).
(M & I Studios) NYC,April 21,1992

(tk.1) Alfie
(tk.1) Smile
(tk.4) My one and only love
(tk.1) Blue smiles
(tk.2) Body and soul
(tk.1) Bye, bye blackbird

All titles issued on CD BN 7-81191-2.

Terumasa Hino(c) Cedar Walton(p) David Williams(b) Michael Carvin(dm).
(M & I Studios) NYC,April 22,1992

(tk.1) Unforgettable
(tk.1) All the things you are
(tk.3) You are so beautiful
(tk.3) I've never been in love before (b,dm out)
(tk.1) My funny Valentine (b,dm out)

All titles issued on CD BN 7-81191-2.

GONZALO RUBALCABA - SUITE 4 Y 20:
Reynaldo Melian(tp) Gonzalo Rubalcaba(p) Felipe Cabrera(el b) Julio Barreto(dm).
(Estudio Quarzo) Madrid,Spain,May 7-12,1992

Preludio proyecto Latino
Here,there and everywhere
Tres palabras
Comienzo
Nuestro balance
4 y 20
Siempra Maria
Quizas,quizas,quizas

All titles issued on CD BN 7-80054-2.

Reynaldo Melian(tp) Gonzalo Rubalcaba(p) Charlie Haden(b) Julio Barreto(dm).
(Estudio Quarzo) Madrid,Spain,May 7-12,1992

Transparence
Our Spanish love song
Love letters
Perfidia
Nadie me ama

All titles issued on CD BN 7-80054-2.

JUNKO ONISHI:
Junko Onishi(p) Tomoyuki Shima(b) Dairiki Hara(dm).
(Sound City) Tokyo,September 3-5,1992

Ko ko CD BN(J)TOCJ-5793
Rockin' in rhythm -

<u>GONZALO RUBALCABA</u> - <u>RAPSODIA</u>:
Reynaldo Melian(tp-1) Gonzalo Rubalcaba(p,keyb) Felipe Cabrera(el b) Julio Barreto(dm).
(Woodstock Karuizawa Studio) Japan,November 15-21,1992

Contagio -1
Circuito 11 -1
Tributo
Santo canto (Holy chant)
Moose the mooche -1
Chancletera -1
Rapsodia Cubana -1

All titles issued on CD BN 8-28264 2.

<u>RON CARTER</u> - <u>FRIENDS</u>:
Hubert Laws(fl) Kenny Barron/Stephen Scott(p) Alison Dean(p,harpsichord) Ron Carter(b,piccolo b) Leon Maleson(b) Lewis Nash(dm) Kermit Moore,Caryl Paisner,Carol Buck,Marisol Espada(cello).
(Clinton Studios) NYC,December 27-29,1992

Minuet in Central Park (Liebeslied)
Minor mood (Vocalise)
Friends
Django
Freefall (Gymnopedie)
The beginning (Prelude #4 in E minor)
Ack varmeland du Skona
Opus one point five
Vagabond vision (Après un rêve/After a dream)

All titles issued on CD BN 7-89548-2.

<u>ELIANE ELIAS</u> - <u>PAULISTANA</u>:
Eliane Elias(p,vo).
(Skyline Studios) NYC,late 1992,early 1993

Jazz influence (Influencia do jazz)
Who knows? (Quem diz que sabe)
Old companion (Velho companheiro) (voEE)

All titles issued on CD BN 7-89544-2

Eliane Elias(p,synth,vo) Marc Johnson(b) Peter Erskine(dm) Cafe-1,Nana Vasconselos-2 (perc) Portinho (shaker-3) Amanda Elias Brecker,Malcolm Pollack(vo).
(Sound On Sound) NYC,late 1992 or early 1993

Brazil (Aquarela do Brasil)-1,3
Paulistana -1
Carioca nights (Noites Cariocas)-1
Jet samba (Samba do aviao) (voAEB,MP)
Wild flower -3

All titles issued on CD BN 7-89544-2.

Eliane Elias(p,vo) Eddie Gomez(b) Jack DeJohnette(dm) Ivan Lins(vo).
(Power Station) NYC,c. early 1993

Black Orpheus (Manha de carnaval) CD BN 7-89544-2
Iluminados (voIL)-1 -
So in love -

-1: Jim Beard(synth) added.

603

BENNY GREEN - BLUE NOTES:
Benny Green(p) Christian McBride(b) Carl Allen(dm).
(Power Station) NYC,April 16 & 17,1993

The sidewinder
Tokyo blues
Cool struttin'
Song for my father
Watermelon man
The Preacher
Softly as in a morning sunrise
Moanin'
Doodlin'
Blues march

All titles to be issued on Blue Note in the future.

JUNKO ONISHI TRIO - CRUISIN':
Junko Onishi(p) Rodney Whitaker(b) Billy Higgins(dm).
(Power Station) NYC,April 21-22,1993

Eulogia
The shepherd CD BN 5-20809-2,(J)TOCJ-6190
Summertime
Congeniality
Melancholia (omit dm)
Caravan
Roz
Switchin' in
Blue seven

All titles issued on CD BN 8-28447-2.

BOB BELDEN:
Cassandra Wilson(vo) with Greg Osby(ss) Bob Belden(p,arr) Adam Holzman(synth) Richard Patterson(el b) Ricky Wellman(dm) Loris Diran(backgr.vo).
(DK Studios) NYC May 12,1993

When doves cry CD BN(C)4-94888-2

GONZALO RUBALCABA - DIZ:
Gonzalo Rubalcaba(p) Ron Carter(b) Julio Barreto(dm).
(McClear Pathe) Toronto,December 14 & 15,1993

Hot house
Woody'n you CD BN 8-32995-2
I remember Clifford
Donna Lee CD BN 8-30081-2,8-35471-2
Bouncing with Bud
Smooch
Ah-leu-cha
A night in Tunisia
Con alma

All titles issued on CD BN 8-30490-2.

JIMMY SMITH - THE MASTER:
Jimmy Smith(org,vo) Kenny Burrell(g) Jimmie Smith(dm).
(Kirin Plaza) Osaka,Japan,December 24 & 25,1993

Chitlins con carne	CD BN 8-30451-2
It's alright with me	-
The organ grinder's swing	-
The preacher	-
All day long	-
I got my mojo working	-
When Johnny comes marching home	-
Back at the chicken shack	-
The cat	-
Summertime	CD BN 8-55466-2
Laura	-
My romance	-
Mack the Knife	-
A child is born	-
Stormy Monday	-

RON CARTER - JAZZ,MY ROMANCE:
Kenny Barron(p) Herb Ellis(g) Ron Carter(b).
(Clinton Studios) NYC,January 4 & 5,1994

Blues for D.P.
My romance
Airegin
Quiet times
Summertime
I fall in love too easily
For toddlers only
Sweet Lorraine

All titles issued on CD BN 8-30492-2.

JACK DeJOHNETTE - EXTRA SPECIAL EDITION:
Gary Thomas(ss,ts,alto fl) Michael Cain(p,keyb,vo) Marvin Sewell(g) Lonnie Plaxico(b) Jack DeJohnette (dm,log dm) Paul Grassi(perc) Bobby McFerrin(vo,whistling).
(Dreamland Studios) West Hurley,NY,early 1994

Numoessence (voBM)
Inside the kaleidoscope (voBM)
You can get there (voBM)
Ha chik kah voBM)
Speaking in tongues (voBM)
Rituals of Spring

All titles issued on CD BN 8-30494-2.

Paul Grassi(perc) Bobby McFerrin(vo,whistling) out.
Same sessions.

Seventh D
Summer time

Both titles issued on CD BN 8-30494-2.

605

JACK DeJOHNETTE - EXTRA SPECIAL EDITION:
Michael Cain(p,keyb)-1,Lonnie Plaxico(b-2) Jack DeJohnette(dm,log dem,ocarina,keyb)-3,Bobby McFerrin (vo).

(Dreamland Studios) West Hurley,NY,early 1994

Elmer Wudd? -1,3,4
Then there was light -1,4
Liquid over tones -3
Memories of Sedone -1,2,3

All titles issued on CD BN 8-30494-2.

GERI ALLEN - TWENTY ONE:
Geri Allen(p) Ron Carter(b) Tony Williams(dm).

(Manhattan Center Studio) NYC,March 23 & 24,1994

RTG
If I should lose you
Drummer's song
Medley:Introspection/Thelonious
A beautiful friendship
In the morning (For Sister Leola)
Tea for two
Lullaby of the leaves
Feed the fire CD BN 8-32995-2
Old folks
A place of power
In the middle

All titles issued on CD BN 8-30028-2.

TERUMASA HINO - SPARK:
Terumasa Hino(tp) Jay Hoggard(marimba,vb) Don Alias,Tatsuji Yokoyama,Mark DeRose(perc).

(Crescente Studios) Tokyo,March 9-11,1994

Obatala (Rumba Yeza) CD BN 8-30450-2

Tatsuya Satoh(ts) Benisuke Sakai(b) Kenji Hino(el b) Motohiko Hino(dm) added.
Same sessions.

Song for my father
Tribe
Suavemente (ts out)-1
Monday night Village Gate (el b out)
Culcutta cutie (el b out)
Art Blakey
Moonbow (ts out)
Camelback

-1: Hiromasa Suzuki(synth) Takeaki Sugiyama(synth programming) added.
All titles issued on CD BN 8-30450-2.

606

JUNKO ONISHI - LIVE AT THE VILLAGE VANGUARD:
Junko Onishi(p) Reginald Veal(b) Herlin Riley(dm).
(Village Vanguard) NYC,May 6-8,1994

So long Eric	CD BN 8-31886-2
Blue skies	-
Concorde	-
How long has the been goin' on	-
Darn that dream	- ,8-32995-2
Congeniality	-
The house of blue lights	CD BN 8-33418-2
Never let me go	-
Brilliant corners	-
Ringo Oiwake	-
Tea for two	- ,(J)TOCJ-5963

MICHELLE ROSEWOMAN - SPIRIT:
Michelle Rosewoman(p,vo) Kenny Davis(b) Gene Jackson(dm).
(International Jazz Festival) Montreal,July 9,1994

Dolphin dance
In a mood
Indepenence day
When Sunny gets blue
For Agayu
Where it comes from
Passion dance blues
For Monk
Spirit

All titles issued on CD BN 8-36777-2.

BOB BELDEN'S SHADES OF BLUE:
Note: Bob Belden selected and, in most cases, arranged the tunes on these sessions.The musician whose name is in capital letters is the leader of each ensemble.

ELIANE ELIAS(p) Nico Assumpao(el b) Paulo Braga(dm).
(DK Studios) NYC,November 9,1994

tk.7	Una mas	CD BN 8-32166-2, 4-95704-2

JACKY TERRASSON(p) Ugonna Okegwo(b) Leon Parker(dm).
(Systems II Studio) Brooklyn,November 21,1994

tk.2	Un poco loco	CD BN 8-32166-2, 4-95704-2

LONNIE SMITH: Dominic Glover(tp) Dennis Koffa(as) Ed Jones(ts) Jim Mullin(g) Lonnie Smith(org) Winston Clifford (dm).
(Angle Studios) London,December 3,1994

tk.2	Move your hand	CD BN 4-95704-2

JOE LOVANO & GERI ALLEN: Wallace Roney(tp) Joe Lovano(as,ts) Geri Allen(p) Clarence Seay(b) Paul Motian(dm).
(Power Station) NYC,December 5,1994

tk.4	Good old days	CD BN 4-95704-2

FAREED HAQUE(g) Ira Coleman(b).
(Power Station) NYC,December 7,1994

tk.3 Soul lament CD BN 4-95704-2

DIANNE REEVES & GERI ALLEN: Dianne Reeves(vo) Steve Hall(ts) Geri Allen(p)Fareed Haque(g) Peter Washington(b) Joe Chambers(dm).
(Power Station) NYC,December 7,1994

tk.5 Maiden voyage CD BN 8-32166-2,4-95704-2,(J)TOCJ-6088

KEVIN HAYS: Myron Walden(as) Steve Nelson(vb) Kevin Hays(p) Dwayne Burno(b) Dion Parson(dm)
(Power Station) NYC,December 8,1994

tk.3 Omega CD BN 4-95704-2

JOHN SCOFIELD(el g) Larry Goldings(org) Dennis Irwin(b) Bill Stewart(dm).
(Sound On Sound) NYC,December 8,1994

tk.1 Tom Thumb CD BN 8-32166-2,4-95704-2
tk.2 Tom Thumb CD BN 8-53330-2

MARCUS PRINTUP(tp) Eric Reed(p) Reuben Rogers(b) Will Terrill III(dm).
(Sound On Sound) NYC,December 8,1994

tk.2 You've changed CD BN 8-32166-2,4-95704-2

KURT ELLING(vo) Lawrence Hobgood(p Eric Hochberg(b) Paul Wertico(dm).
(Chicago Recording Co) Chicago,December 16,1994

tk.3 Tanganyika dance CD BN 8-32166-2,4-95704-2

RENEE ROSNES: Jerry Dodgion(alto fl) Erik Friedlander(cello) Renee Rosnes(p) Fareed Haque(g) Peter Washington(b) Billy Drummond(dm).
Englewood Cliffs,NJ,December 17,1994

tk.5 Song for my father CD BN 8-32166-2,4-95704-2

T.S. MONK: Don Sickler(tp) Ron Carter(b) T.S. Monk(dm).
Englewood Cliffs,NJ,December 17,1994

tk.2 Evidence CD BN 8-32166-2,4-95704-2

CASSANDRA WILSON(vo) Ron Carter(b).
Englewood Cliffs,NJ,December 17,1994

tk.2 Joshua fit de battle of Jericho CD BN 8-32166-2,4-95704-2

BOB BELDEN: Tim Hagans(tp) Bob Belden(ts) Charles Pillow(English horn) Kevin Hays,Marc Copland (el p) Scott Kinsey(synth) Larry Grenadier(b) Billy Kilson(dm).
(Power Station) NYC,December 18,1994

tk.3 Siete ocho CD BN 8-32166-2,4-95704-2

GEOFF KEEZER(p) David Ephross(b) Billy Drummond(dm).
(Power Station) NYC,December 18,1994

tk.3 2300 Skidoo CD BN 8-32166-2, 4-95704-2

 608

JACK WALRATH(tp) & BOBBY WATSON(as) Franck Amsallem(p) Jeff Andrews(el b) Tony Reedus(dm) Judi Silvano(vo).
(Systems II Studio) Brooklyn,December 19,1994

tk.2 Christo Redentor CD BN 8-56991-2
tk.3 Christo Redentor CD BN 4-95704-2

KEVIN HAYS(el p) Doug Weiss(b) Billy Drummond(dm).
(Systems II Studio) Brooklyn,December 19,1994

tk.3 Inner Urge CD BN 4-95704-2

HOLLY COLE & JAVON JACKSON: Holly Cole(vo) Tim Hagans(tp) Javon Jackson(ts) Mulgrew Miller(p) Jay Anderson(b) Bill Stewart(dm).
(Power Station) NYC,January 5,1995

tk.6 Hum drum blues CD BN 8-32166-2,4-95704-2,(C)4-94888-2

REUBEN WILSON: Davis Weiss(tp) Ronnie Cuber(bs) John Hart(g) Reuben Wilson(org) Carl Allen(dm).
(Power Station) NYC,January 5,1995

tk.5 Love bug CD BN 4-95704-2

BLUE NOTE DETROIT LEGACY: Peven Everette(tp) J.D. Allen III(ts) Carlos McKinney(p) Tssili Bond(b) Ali Muhammed Jackson(dm).
(Sound On Sound) NYC January 5,1995

tk.8 Spellbound CD BN 4-95704-2

KEVIN EUBANKS(g) Buddy Montgomery(p) Richard Reid(b) Billy Higgins(dm).
(O'Henry Studios) LA,January 13,1995

tk.3 Little B's poem CD BN 4-95704-2

GREG OSBY(as) Edward Simon(p) DJ Ghetto(scratches) Bernard Collins(vo) with samples from original John Coltrane recording of September 15,1957.
(Systems Two) Brooklyn,NY,January 16-17,1995

tk.1 Blue train CD BN(J)TOCP-8966

GONZALO RUBALCABA(p) Eddie Gomez(b) Greg Hutchinson(dm) Jerry Gonzalez(cga).
(Clinton Studios) NYC,February 17,1995

tk.4 Recado bossa nova CD BN 4-95704-2

609

RON CARTER - MR. BOW-TIE:
Edwin Russel(tp) Javon Jackson(ts) Gonzalo Rubalcaba(p) Ron Carter(b) Lewis Nash(dm) Steve Kroon (perc).

(Clinton Studios) NYC,February 17 & 18,1995

Mr. Bow-tie (tp,ts out) CD BN(J)TOCJ-6190
Well, you needn't
I thought about you
Stablemates
St. Thomas
Nearly (perc out)
Fill in the blanks (p,perc out)
Cut and paste (p out)
Wait for the beep (p out)
M.S.R.P. (p out)

All titles issued on CD BN 8-35407-2.

TERUMASA HINO & MASABUMI KIKUCHI - ACOUSTIC BOOGIE:
Terumasa Hino(tp) Greg Osby(as) Masabumi Kikuchi(p) James Genus(b) Billy Kilson(dm).

(Clinton Studios) NYC,May 2 & 3,1995

Monk's dilemma
Summer mist
The moon dog
The pain's the killer
Shape of the window
Thump
Sliced wild potatoes

All titles issued on CD BN 8-36259-2.

JUNKO ONISHI - PIANO QUINTET SUITE:
Marcus Belgrave(tp,vo) Eiichi Hayashi(as) Junko Onishi(p) Rodney Whitaker(b) Tony Rabeson(dm).

(Woodstock Karuizawa) Japan,July 7-11,1995

Piano quintet suite
Peggy's blue skylight
Interlude 1
Naturally
Interlude 2
The tropic of capricorn
Tony
Orange was the color of her dress,the blue silk
Take the A train (voMB)

All titles issued on CD BN 8-36483-2.

<u>GONZALO RUBALCABA</u> - <u>ANTIGUO</u>:
Reynaldo Melian(tp) Dagoberro Gonzalez(el v-2) Gonzalo Rubalcaba(p,keyb,perc,synth-5) Mario Garcia (programming) Felipe Cabrera(el b) Julio Barreto(dm) Giovanni Hidalgo-1(cga,perc) Apwan Lazaro Ros (vo).
(Klangstudio) Leyh,Germany,July 24-28,1995

Circuito III
Ellioko -3,4 (voALR)
Intermitencia
Circuito IV -2
Oddi lobbe
Eshun agwe -1,3
Homenaje -1

-3: Jose M. Crego(tp,tb) Roman Filiu(as) Alfredo Thompson(ts) overdubbed on.
(Estudio Egrem) Havana,Cuba, October 17-21,1995
-4: Carlos Aldama,Alexander Martinez,Michael Aldama(perc) Gerardo Reyes,Maria del Carmen Argudin, Lazaro Campillo(choir) overdubbed on. (Estudio Egrem) Havana,Cuba,October 17-21,1995
-5: synthesizer overdubs.
(Estudios Viva) Santa Domingo,late 1995 and (Soundtrack Studio) NYC, July 16, 1996.
All titles issued on CD BN 8-37717-2.

Gonzalo Rubalcaba(p,keyb,perc) Mario Garcia(programming) Julio Barreto(dm-1)Maridalia Hernandez(vo)
Same sessions

Opening
Deserto-1
Coral Negro (voMH)
Closing

All titles issued on CD BN 8-37717-2.

<u>GERI ALLEN</u> - <u>EYES...IN THE BACK OF YOUR HEAD</u>:
Wallace Roney(tp-1) Geri Allen(p,synth) Cyro Baptista(perc-2).
(Clinton Studios) NYC,December 14 & 15,1995

FMFMF (for my family,for my friends)
New eyes opening for little Wallace
In the back of your head -1
Windows to the soul -1
M.O.P.E.-1,2
Dark eyes -1,2
Mother wit -2
Little waltz -2

All titles issued on CD BN 8-38297-2

<u>RON CARTER</u> - <u>BRANDENBURG CONCERTO</u>:
Ron Carter (b,picc b-1,arr) & string orchestra: Sanford Allen,Charles Libove,John Pintavalle,Rebekah Johnson,Winterton Garvey,Dale Stuckenbruck,Robert Chausow,Cecilia Hobbs Gandner,Mary Whitaker(v) Jesse Levine,Julian Barber,Richard Brile(viola) Caryl Paisner,Carol Buck,Marisol Espada,Maximow Neuman-2(cello)Leon Maleson(b) Kermit Moore(cond).
(Clinton Studios) NYC,December 27,1995

Brandenburg Concerto No.3
Pavana -1
Joc Cu Bata -2
Aria (from alis holberg zeit)-1
Ventos del deserto
Ombra mai fu

All titles on CD BN 8-54559-2.

JACKIE McLEAN - HAT TRICK:
Jackie McLean(as) Junko Onishi(p) Nat Reeves(b) Lewis Nash(dm).
(Power Station) NYC,January 28-31,1996

	Little Melonae	
	A cottage for sale	
	Solar	
	Bags' groove	
	Will you still be mine	
	Left alone	CD BN(J)TOCJ-6187
	Jackie's hat	
	Sentimental journey	
	Bluesnik	

All titles issued on CD BN 8-38363-2.

GERI ALLEN - EYES...IN THE BACK OF YOUR HEAD:
Ornette Coleman(as) Geri Allen(p).
(Clinton Studios) NYC,March 1,1996

	Vertical flowing	CD BN 8-38297-2
	The eyes have it	- , 4-95981-2

BOB BELDEN - STRAWBERRY FIELDS:
Jim Anderson(frh-1) Charlie Pillow(Eng h-1) Jack Lee-1,Fareed Haque(g) Joe Chambers(p-1) Kevin Hays (el p) Bob Belden(synth,tympani) David Dyson(el b) Billy Kilson(dm) Tomas Ulrich(cello-1) Stacey Shames (harp-1) Cassandra Wilson(vo).
(Power Station) NYC,April 8,1996

tk.1	Strawberry fields -1 (voCW)	CD BN 8-53920-2
tk.2	And I love her	rejected

Tim Hagans(tp-2) Jim Anderson(frh-1) Charlie Pillow(Eng h-1) Javon Jackson(ts-1) Mike "Dino" Campbell, Fareed Haque(g) Kevin Hays(el p) Bob Belden(synth,tympani) David Dyson(el b) Billy Kilson(dm) Tomas Ulrich(cello-1) Stacey Shames(harp-1) Dianne Reeves,Cassandra Wilson(vo).
(Power Station) NYC,April 8,1996

tk.1	The fool on the hill-1	CD BN 8-53920-2,(J)TOCJ-6088
tk.2	Tomorrow never knows -2 (voDR)	- - TOCJ-6153
tk.2	Come together -2 (voDR,CW)	- 8-57463-2

Kevin Breit,Fareed Haque(g) Aaron Davis(p) Ira Coleman(b) Billy Kilson(dm) Holly Cole(vo).
(Power Station) NYC,April 9,1996

tk.1	I've just seen her face (voHC)	CD BN 8-53920-2,(C)4-94888-2
tk.1	I'm only sleeping	- 8-57463-2

Bob Belden(ss) Junko Onishi(p-1) Scott Kinsey(synth) Fareed Haque(g) David Dyson(el b) Billy Kilson(dm) Jahlisa(vo).
(Village Recorders) LA,April 24,1996

tk.2	Hey Jude	CD BN 8-53920-2
tk.1	Get back -1 (voJ)	-

Bob Belden(ss) Sam Riney(as-1) Scott Kinsey(synth) Fareed Haque(g) David Dyson(el b) Billy Kilson(dm) Penny Ford,Sylvia Shemwell(vo).
(Village Recorders) LA, April 25,1996

tk.1	Lady Madonna (voPF)	CD BN 8-53920-2
tk.2	Let it be -1 (voSS)	-

 612

JOE LOVANO - TENOR TIME:
Joe Lovano(ts) Junko Onishi(p) Rodney Whitaker(b) Al Foster(dm).
(Avatar Studios) NYC,September 29,1996

tk.1 Paradox
tk.2 Bye bye blackbird
tk.3 Why don't I
tk.2 Ruby my dear
tk.2 Walkin'
tk.2 Budo
tk.2 Like Sonny
tk.1 Invitation
tk.2 Dewey said

All titles to be issued on Blue Note

DIANNE REEVES:
Dianne Reeves(vo) with Tim Pierce(g) Tom Keane(synth) Carlos Vega(cymbals) Assa Drori(concert master) Eric Smith(cond) Taro Iwashiro(arr) Phillip Ingram,Lynn Davis,Yvonne Williams(backgr.vo) & unidentified orchestra.
prob.LA,c. Fall 1996

When I cry CD BN(J)TOCJ-6088
When I cry (edit) CD BN(J)TODP-2542
When I cry (instrumental) -

Note: This recording was made for the film "The Dog Of Flanders".

RON CARTER - THE BASS AND I:
Stephen Scott(p) Ron Carter(b) Lewis Nash(dm) Steve Kroon(perc).
Englewood Cliffs,NJ,January 14,1997

You and the night and the music
Someday my prince will come
Blues for O.P.
The shadown of your smile
Mr. bow-tie
Double bass
I remember Clifford

All titles on CD BN 8-59698-2.

JACKIE McLEAN - FIRE AND LOVE:
Raymond Williams(tp,flh-1) Steve Davis(tb) Jackie McLean(as) Rene McLean(ts) Alan Jay Palmer(p) Phil Bowler(b) Eric McPherson(dm).
(Avatar Studios) NYC July 15 & 16,1997

Mr. E
Optimism
Cryptography
The griot
Entrapment -1
Excursions
Rites of passage-2
Beautiful majestic one
I found you

-2: Jackie McLean, Rene Mclean, Steve Davis also play perc.
All titles issued on CD BN 4-93254-2.

<u>GONZALO RUBALCABA</u> - <u>THE TRIO</u>:
Gonzalo Rubalcaba(p) Brian Bromberg(b) Dennis Chambers(dm).
(Avatar Studios) NYC,August 6,1997

tk.1	Morse code	unissued
tk.1	Yesterdays	CD BN/Somethin' Else(Eu) 4-94442-2
	Hot house	rejected
	Black Orpheus	-

Gonzalo Rubalcaba(p) Brian Bromberg(b) Dennis Chambers(dm).
(Avatar Studios) NYC,August 7,1997

tk.1	Improvisation	unissued
tk.2	Caravan	CD BN/Somethin' Else(Eu) 4-94442-2
tk.2	On Green Dolphin Street	-
tk.1	Maiden voyage	-
tk.2	Woody 'n you	-
tk.4	Hot house	-
tk.5	Black Orpheus	-

<u>ELIANE ELIAS</u> - <u>SINGS JOBIM</u>:
Eliane Elias(p,vo) Oscar Castro-Neves(g-1) Paulo Braga(bgo-2).
(Sony Studios) NYC,late 1997

For all of my life (Por toda a minha vida) (voEE)
Modinha (voEE)
Pois e (voEE)-1
Falando de amor (voEE)-1
Looks like December (Anos Dourados)(voEE)-1,2

All titles issued on CD BN 4-95050-2.

Michael Brecker(ts-1) Eliane Elias(p,vo) Oscar Castro-Neves(g,vo) Marc Johnson(b) Paulo Braga(dm) Cafe (perc).
(Sony Studios) NYC,late 1997

Girl from Ipanema
(Garota de Ipanema) -1 (voEE) CD BN 5-20070-2
One note samba (Samba de uma nota so) (voEE)
Jazz 'n samba (So danco samba) (voEE,OC)
She's a Carioca (Ela e carioca) (voEE)
Desafinado -1 (voEE)
Song of the jet (Samba do aviao) (voEE)
A felicidade -1,2 (voEE)
How insensitive (voEE)
Forgetting you (Esquecendo voce) (voEE)
Once I loved (Amor em paz) (voEE)
Caminhos cruzados (voEE)
The Continental -1,3 (voEE)

-2: Eliane Elias,Oscar Castro-Neves,Amanda Brecker,Marc Johnson,Paulo Braga,Christine Martin,Elza Silva (backgr. vo) added.
-3: Nilson Natta(b) replaces Marc Johnson.
All titles, except last tune, issued on CD BN 4-95050-2.

RON CARTER - SO WHAT:
Kenny Barron(p) Ron Carter(b) Lewis Nash(dm).
(Avatar Studios) NYC,January 4,1998

So what
You'd be so nice to come home to
It's about time
My foolish heart
Hi-fly
3 more days
Eddie's theme
The third plane

All titles issued on CD BN 4-94976-2.

JUNKO ONISHI - FRAGILE:
Jumko Onishi(p,el p,org,synth) Reginald Veal(b,el b) Karriem Riggins(dm) Peace(vo) & Motohiko Hino-1, Tamaya Honda-2 (dm).
(Toshiba-EMI Studios) Tokyo,July 5-7,1998

Phaethon
Complexions -1
You've lost that lovin' feelin'
Compared to what -1 (voP)
Hey Joe -2
Eulogia variation
Sunshine of your love -2 CD BN(C)5-20457-2

All titles issued on CD BN 4-98108-2.

KURT ELLING:
Kurt Elling(vo) with Orchestra arr. by Akira Senju & cond. by Eddie Karam,incl. fls,strings,harp,p,b.
(Ocean Way Studios) LA,August 15,1998
& (O'Henry Studios) LA,August 16,1998

A world away CD BN(J)TOCJ-66001

PHIL WOODS:
Phil Woods(as,cl-1) Junko Onishi(p) Ron Carter(b) Bill Goodwin(dm)
(Right Track Studios) NYC,January 4,1999

tk.2 All the things you are
tk.1 You don't know what love is
tk.1 The L.B. blues
tk.1 Lullaby of the leaves
tk.2 Someone to watch over me -1
tk.1 Stella by starlight

Same. (Right Track Studios) NYC,January 5,1999

tk.1 Bye bye blackbird (p out)
tk.1 Embraceable you
tk.1 Come rain or come shine
tk.1 As time goes by -1
tk.1 What are you doing the rest of your life
tk.1 Samba du bois
tk.1 'Round midnight

Some or all titles to be issued on Blue Note.

615

RON CARTER - ORFEU:
Houston Person(ts) Bill Frisell(g) Stephen Scott(p) Ron Carter(b) Payton Crossley(dm) Steve Kroon(perc).
(Avatar Studios) NYC,February 1,1999

Saudade
Manha de carnaval
Por-do-sol
Goin' home
1:17 special
Obrigado
Samba de Orfeu (ts,p out)

All titles issued on CD BN 5-22490-2.

THE BLUE NOTE NEW DIRECTIONS BAND:
Greg Osby(as) Mark Shim(ts) Stefon Harris(vb) Jason Moran(p) Tarus Mateen(b) Nasheet Waits(dm).
Englewood Cliffs,N.J.,May 10,1999

(tk.3) The sidewinder
(tk.1) Song for my father CD BN(J)TOCJ-66060
(tk.1) Theme from "Blow Up"
(tk.3) No room for squares
(tk.2) Tom Thumb
(tk.1) Big Bertha
(tk.3) Ping pong

All titles issued on CD BN 5-22978-2.

Same.
Englewood Cliffs,N.J.,May 11,1999

(tk.2) Song of the whispering banshee
20 questions (false start)
(tk.2) 20 questions
(tk.1) Commentary on electrical switches (p,b,dm only)
(tk.2) Recorda-me
(tk.2) Beatrice (vb,p only)

All titles issued on CD BN 5-22978-2.

JACKIE McLEAN - NATURE BOY:
Jackie McLean(as) Cedar Walton(p) David Williams(b) Billy Higgins(dm).
(Avatar Studios) NYC,June 12,1999

What is this thing called love
I fall in love too easily
You don't know what love is
A nightingale sang in Berkele Square

All titles issued on CD B 5-23273-2.

Same. (Avatar Studios) NYC,June 13,1999

Star eyes
I can't get started
Nature boy
Smoke gets in your eyes

All titles issued on CD B 5-23273-2.

616

SUE

IKE AND TINA TURNER:
Tina Turner(vo) Ike Turner(b) & others unknown.
1960

A fool in love CD BN 8-54364-2

JIMMY McGRIFF:
Morris Dow(g) Jimmy McGriff(org) Jackie Mills(dm).
NYC, 1962

All about the girl BN B1-96563, CD 7-96563-2,(E)8-53234-2
I got a woman, pts. 1 & 2

Both titles issued on BN(E)8-30724-1,CD BN 8-57063-2,(E)8-30724-2.

JIMMY McGRIFF:
Morris Dow or Larry Frazier(g) Jimmy McGriff(org) Willie Jenkins(dm).
NYC 1963

The Last Minute
Gospel Time

Both titles issued on BN(E)8-30724-1,CD BN 8-57063-2,(E)8-30724-2.

Larry Frazier(g) Jimmy McGriff(org) Jimmy Smith(dm).
NYC, 1963

Discotheque U.S.A.
Cash Box

Both titles issued on BN(E)8-30724-1,CD BN 8-57063-2,(E)8-30724-2.

Rudolph Johnson(ss) Larry Frazier(g) Jimmy McGriff(org) Jimmy Smith(dm).
NYC, 1964

Kiko* BN(E)8-30724-1*
CD BN 8-57063-2*,(E)8-30724-2*

Note: On all copies of 30724 (LP & CD) and most copies of 8-57063-2, McGriff's 1967 remake of "I've Got a woman" mistakenly was used in place of "Kiko" (see page 584).

TOSHIBA-EMI (JAPAN)

JOHNNY HARTMAN:
Johnny Hartman(vo) with Terumasa Hino(tp-1) Mikio Masuda(p) Yoshio Ikeda(b) Motohiko Hino(dm).
Tokyo,November 29,1972

Summertime
Why did I choose you
The nearness of you -1 — CD BN 8-54365-2,(C) 4-94888-2
I'm glad there is you -1
On Green Dolphin Street -1
My funny Valentine -1
Sometimes I'm happy -1
S'posin' -1

All titles issued on CD BN 8-35346-2.

Johnny Hartman(vo) with Masahiko Kikuchi(p) Yoshio Suzuki(dm) Hiroshi Murakami(dm).
Tokyo.December 1, 1972

My favorite things
Violets for your furs
Nature boy — CD BN 5-21153-2

All titles issued on CD BN 8-35346-2.

ERNESTINE ANDERSON:
Ernestine Anderson(vo) with Norman Simmons(p) George Mraz(b) Tim Horner(dm).
(East World label) (Toshiba EMI Studios) Tokyo,April 25 or 27,1983

Someday my prince will come — CD BN(J)TOCJ-6189

DEEJAY COOL CUTS BLUE:
DAZZLE-T & QUICKY: Dazzle-T & Quicky(programming,mixing) Yuki(sax) Kiyomi(vo) sampling of "Places and Spaces" by Donald Byrd (see page 283).
(E Quick Studio) Tokyo, 1998

Place is the space — CD BN(J)TOCP-65099

DJ HASEBE: DJ Hasebe(programming,mixing) Ryousoke Imai(p) sampling of "The Trip" by Bobbi Humphrey (see page 281).
(Little Bach Aoyama Studio) Tokyo, 1998

The trip — CD BN(J)TOCP-65099

KYOTO JAZZ MASSIVE: Yasushi Kurobane(programming) Hajime Yoshizawa (p,clavinet,synth,synth b) sampling of "Another night in Tunisia" by Bobby McFerrin (see page 649)
(Hal Studio/Toshiba-EMI Studio) Tokyo, 1998

Speedom — CD BN(J)TOCP-65099

FANTASTIC PLASTIC MACHINE: Masayuki Kumahara(programming) Tomoyuki Tanaka(mixing) sampling of "Early morning love",by Moacir Santos (see page 270),"Moon rappin'" by Jack McDuff (see page 234),"Sandalia dela" by Duke Pearson (see page 226),"Street walkin' woman" & "Rose Marie (Mon cherie)" by Marlena Shaw (see pages 274/275).
(Azabuu West Studio) Tokyo, 1998

Bossa for Duke — CD BN(J)TOCP-65099

CALM: Farr(programming) Moonage Electric Ensemble Horns: Michell(fl) Yuichiro Kato(ss) K.T.(as) sampling of "Peregrinations" by Chico Hamilton (see page 281),"Inner passions expelled" by Lee Morgan (see page 256),"Move your hand" by Lonnie Smith (see page 230) & "Calm" by Wayne Shorter (see page 247).

(Delicious Paper Studio) Tokyo, 1998

Quo Vadis CD BN(J)TOCP-65099

DJ KRUSH: DJ Krush(beats,programming) sampling of "When you're near" & "Sophisticated lady" by Bobby Hutcherson (see page 260),"Cara mia" by Bobby McFerrin((see page 313) & "Please set me at ease" By Bobbi Humphrey (see page 281).

(Toshiba-EMI Studio) Tokyo, 1998

Deep in Ill-Usion CD BN(J)TOCP-65099

SLEEP WALKER: Masato Nakamura(as) Hajime Yoshizawa(p,org,synth) Toshitaka Shiratri(b,synth) Nobuaki Fujii(dm,synth) sampling of "His blessings" by McCoy Tyner (see page 238) & "Poppin'" by Hank Mobley (see page 72).

(Studio Terra) Tokyo, 1998

The gate CD BN(J)TOCP-65099

CHILD'S VIEW: Child's View(mixing) sampling from "Sound gravitations" by Ornette Coleman (see page 195) & "The all seeing eye" by Wayne Shorter (see page 186).

(Moonlit Studio) Kyoto, 1998

Shift CD BN(J)TOCP-65099

UNITED ARTISTS

BILLIE HOLIDAY:
Billie Holiday(vo) with Carl Drinkard(p) Red Mitchell(b) Elaine Leighton(dm)
(concert) Cologne,Germany,January 5, 1954

Announcement	
Blue moon	CD BN(SP)8-34712-2
All of me	CD BN 5-21151-2
My man	
Them there eyes	
I cried for you	
What a little moonlight can do	
I cover the waterfront	

All titles issued on CD BN 7-48786-2,(J)TOCJ-6243.

Billie Holiday(vo) Buddy DeFranco(cl) Red Norvo(vb) Jimmy Raney(g) Sonny Clark,Beryl Booker(p) Red Mitchell(b) Elaine Leighton(dm).
Same concert.

Billie's blues	
Lover come back to me	CD BN 4-97154-2

Both titles issued on CD BN 7-48786-2,(J)TOCJ-6243.

BENNY CARTER:
Benny Carter(as) Teddy Charles(vb) Hal Schaefer(p) John Drew(b) Gus Johnson(dm)
NYC, 1958

Anything goes	CD BN 8-33146-2

GERRY MULLIGAN:
Art Farmer(tp) Frank Rosolino(tb) Bud Shank(as) Gerry Mulligan(bs) Pete Jolly(p) Red Mitchell(b) Shelly Manne(dm).
LA, May 24,1958

Black nightgown	CD BN 7-80707-2

BENNY CARTER:
Al Porcino,Stu Williamson,Ray Triscari,Joe Gordon(tp) Frank Rosolino,Tommy Pederson,Russ Brown(tb) Benny Carter(as,arr) Buddy Collette,Bill Green,Jewell Grant,Plas Johnson(reeds) Gerald Wiggins(p) Barney Kessel(g) Joe Comfort(b) Shelly Manne(dm).
(Capitol Studios) LA,late summer,1958

March wind	CD BN 8-33146-2
June is busting out all over (mono take)	-

Conrad Gozzo,Shorty Sherock,Pete Candoli,Uan Rasey(tp) Tommy Pederson,Herbie Harper,George Roberts(tb) Benny Carter(as,arr) Buddy Collette,Bill Green,Justin Gordon,Chuck Gentry(reeds) Arnold Ross(p) Bobby Gibbons(g) Joe Comfort(b) Shelly Manne(dm) Larry Bunker(perc).
(Capitol Studios) LA,late summer,1958

September song	CD BN 8-33146-2

<u>ART FARMER</u> - <u>MODERN ART</u>:
Art Farmer(tp) Benny Golson(ts) Bill Evans(p) Addison Farmer(b) Dave Bailey (dm).
(Nola Studios) NYC,September 10,11 & 14,1958

Mox nix	BN(J)FCPA 6210
Fair weather	- CD(J)CJ28-5176
Darn that dream	-
The touch of your lips	
Jubilation	BN(J)FCPA 6210
Like someone in love	
I love you	BN(J)W-5512,CDTOCJ-6188
Cool breeze	

All titles issued on BN(F)BNP25108,CD BN 7-84459-2.

<u>JOHN COLTRANE</u> - <u>COLTRANE TIME</u>:
Kenny Dorham(tp) John Coltrane(ts) Cecil Taylor(p) Chuck Israels(b) Louis Hayes(dm).
NYC,October 13,1958

Shifting down	CD BN 7-99175-2,4-98240-2
Just friends	CD BN(J)TOCJ-5630,TOCJ-6104
Like someone in love	- -
Double clutching	

All titles issued on CD BN 7-84461-2.
Note: This session was originally issued as by Cecil Taylor.

<u>BOOKER LITTLE 4 PLUS MAX ROACH</u> - <u>MILESTONES</u>:
Booker Little(tp) George Coleman(ts) Tommy Flanagan(p) Art Davis(b) Max Roach(dm).
(Nola Studios) NYC,October ,1958

Milestones
Sweet and lovely (ts out)
Rounders mood
Dungeon waltz
Jewel's tempo
Moonlight becomes you (ts out)

All titles issued on BN(F)BNP25107,CD BN 7-84457-2.

<u>BOOKER LITTLE</u>:
Booker Little,Louis Smith(tp) Frank Strozier(as) George Coleman(ts) Phineas Newborn(p) Calvin Newborn (g) Jamil Nasser(b) Charles Crosby(dm).
(Olmsted Studios) NYC, 1958

Things ain't what they used to be
Blue 'n boogie

Both titles issued on CD BN 7-84457-2.

621

RANDY WESTON - LITTLE NILES:
Ray Copeland(tp) Melba Liston(tb,arr) Johnny Griffin(ts) Randy Weston(p) George Joyner (Jamil Nasser)(b) Charlie Persip(dm).

(RCA Studios) NYC,October ,1958

Little Niles
Pam's waltz
Let's climb a hill
Earth birth
Nice ice
Little Susan

All titles issued on BN BN-LA598-H2.

Idris Sulieman(tp) Melba Liston(tb,arr) Johnny Griffin(ts) Randy Weston(p) George Joyner (Jamil Nasser) (b) Charlie Persip(dm).

(RCA Studios) NYC,October ,1958

Babe's blues BN BN-LA598-H2

BENNY GOLSON AND THE PHILADELPHIANS:
Lee Morgan(tp) Benny Golson(ts) Ray Bryant(p) Percy Heath(b) Philly Joe Jones(dm).

(Nola Studios) NYC,November 17,1958

You're not the kind
Blues on my mind
Stablemates
Thursday's theme
Afternoon in Paris
Calgary

All titles issued on CD BN 4-94104-2.

DIAHANN CARROLL:
Diahann Carroll(vo) with Andre Previn(p) Joe Mondragon(b) Larry Bunker(dm).

LA, 1958

Summertime CD BN(Sp)8-56842-2

MILT JACKSON - BAGS' OPUS:
Art Farmer(tp) Benny Golson(ts) Milt Jackson(vb) Tommy Flanagan(p) Paul Chambers(b) Connie Kay(dm).

(Nola Studios) NYC,December 28/29,1958

Ill wind	BN BN-LA590-H2	
Blues for Diahann	-	
Afternoon in Paris	-	CD 7-99100-2
I remember Clifford	-	CD(J)TOCJ-6187
Thinking of you		
Whisper not	BN BN-LA590-H2, CD(J)TOCJ-5299	

All titles issued on CD BN 7-84458-2.

 622

CHARLES MINGUS - JAZZ PORTRAITS (MINGUS IN WONDERLAND):
John Handy(as) Booker Ervin(ts) Richard Wyands(p) Charles Mingus(b) Dannie Richmond(dm).
(Nonagon Art Gallery) NYC,January 16,1959

Nostalgia in Times Square
I can't get started (ts out)
No private income blues
Alice's wonderland

All titles issued on CD BN 8-27325-2.

BILL POTTS BIG BAND:
Art Farmer,Harry Edison,Bernie Glow,Marky Markowitz,Charlie Shavers(tp) Bob Brookmeyer,Frank Rehak,Jimmy Cleveland,Earl Swope,Rod Levitt(tb) Gene Quill,Phil Woods(as) Zoot Sims,Al Cohn(ts) Sol Schlinger(bs) Bill Evans(p) Herbie Powell(g) George Duvivier(b) Charlie Persip(dm) Bill Potts(arr,dir).
(Webster Hall) NYC,January 13-15,1959

Summertime
A woman is a sometime thing
My man's gone now
It takes a long pull to get there
I got plenty o' nuttin' CD BN 7-80706-2
Bess,you is my woman now
It ain't necessarily so
Medley:Prayer/Strawberry/
Honey man/Crab man
I loves you Porgy
Clara Clara
There's a boat dat's leavin' soon
Bess,oh where is my Bess
Oh Lawd,I'm on my way

All titles scheduled on BN(F)BNP25109 (probably never released).

ZOOT SIMS & AL COHN-JAZZ ALIVE! - A NIGHT AT THE HALF NOTE:
Phil Woods(as-1) Al Cohn,Zoot Sims(ts) Mose Allison(p) Knobby Totah(b) Paul Motian(dm).
(Half Note Cafe) NYC,February 6 & 7,1959

Lover come back to me
It had to be you
Wee dot-1
After you've gone -1

All titles issued on BN(F)BNP25105,CD BN 4-94105-2.

TOMMY FLANAGAN - LONELY TOWN:
Tommy Flanagan(p) Joe Benjamin(b) Elvin Jones(dm).
NYC,March 10,1959

America
Lonely town
Tonight CD BN(J)CJ28-5022,TOCJ-5875
It's love
Lucky to be me Lib(J)K22P-6092/93
Glitter and be gay
Make our garden grow

All titles issued on BN(J)GP-3186,CD TOCJ-66081.
Note: This session was not issued on the United Artists label.

623

CURTIS FULLER - SLIDING EASY:
Lee Morgan(tp) Curtis Fuller(tb) Hank Mobley(ts) Tommy Flanagan(p) Paul Chambers(b) Elvin Jones(dm) Gigi Gryce-1,Benny Golson-2(arr).
(Nola Studios) NYC,March 12,1959

tk.5 Down home -1
tk.6 Down home (alt.)-1
tk.7 C.T.A. -1
tk.17 When lights are low -2
tk.4 I wonder where our love has gone -2
tk.5 Bongo bop -2
tk.6 Bit of heaven -2

All titles issued on Mosaic MQ5-166,CD MD3-166.
All titles to be reissued on the Blue Note label.

BILL EVANS-BOB BROOKMEYER QUARTET - AS TIME GOES BY:
Bill Evans,Bob Brookmeyer(p) Percy Heath(b) Connie Kay(dm).
(Olmsted Studios) NYC,March 12,1959

Honeysuckle rose
As time goes by CD BN(J)CJ28-5023
The way you look tonight
It could happen to you
The man I love
I got rhythm CD BN 7-80706-2,7-99427-2

All titles issued on BN LT-1100,CD 8-27324-2.

CECIL TAYLOR - LOVE FOR SALE:
Cecil Taylor(p) Buell Neidlinger(b) Rudy Collins(dm).
(Nola Studios) NYC,April 15,1959

Get out of town
I love Paris
Love for sale

All titles issued on BN BN-LA458-H2, CD 4-94107-2.

Ted Curson(tp) Bill Barron(ts) added.Same session.

Little Lees (Louise)
Motystrophe CD BN 8-35414-2
Carol/Three points

All titles issued on BN BN-LA458-H2,CD 4-94107-2.
Note: Bass player on above titles was erroneously listed as Chris White on BN-LA458-H2

RANDY WESTON:
Bennie Green,Slide Hampton,Frank Rehak(tb) Melba Liston(tb,arr) Randy Weston(p) Peck Morrison(b) Elvin Jones(dm) Willie Rodriguez(cga).
NYC,May ,1959

I know your kind
Every once in a while
Once knew a fella
I say hello

All titles issued on BN BN-LA598-H2.

624

ART FARMER:
Art Farmer,Lee Morgan,Ernie Royal(tp) Jimmy Cleveland,Curtis Fuller(tb) James Haughton(baritone h) Julius Watkins(frh) Don Butterfield(tu) Percy Heath(b) Philly Joe Jones(dm) Benny Golson(arr).
(Nola Studioz) NYC,May 14,1959

Five Spot after dark CD BN(J)TOCJ-5203,TOCJ-5298,TOCJ-5857, TOCJ-6152

THE MODERN JAZZ QUARTET - ODDS AGAINST TOMORROW:
Milt Jackson(vb) John Lewis(p) Percy Heath(b) Connie Kay(dm).
(Olmsted Studios) NYC,October 9,1959

Skating in Central Park CD BN 8-54363-2,(J)TOCJ-5854
No happiness for Slater
A social call
Cue #9
Cold wind is blowing
Odds against tomorrow CD BN 4-95981-2

All titles issued on CD BN 7-93415-2.

RANDY WESTON:
Kenny Dorham(tp) Coleman Hawkins(ts) Randy Weston(p) Wilbur Little(b) Clifford Jarvis(dm).
(Five Spot Cafe) NYC,October 26,1959

High fly
Beef blues stew
Star crossed lovers
Spot Five blues
Lisa lovely -1
Where -2

-1: Roy Haynes(dm) replaces Jarvis.
-2: Brock Peters(vo) added.
All titles issued on BN BN-LA598-H2.

THAD JONES:
Thad Jones(flh,c) Al Grey(tb) Billy Mitchell(ts) Tommy Flanagan(p) Paul Chambers(b) Elvin Jones(dm).
(Nola Studios) NYC,December 24 & 31,1959

Let's play one
Minor on top
Like old times
No refill

All titles issued on Mosaic MQ5-172,CD MD3-172.
All titles to be reissued on the Blue Note label.

BENNY CARTER - BENNY ON THE COAST:
Benny Carter(as,ss-2) Jimmy Rowles(p) Leroy Vinnegar(b) Mel Lewis(dm).
(Radio Recorders) LA,February 5,1960

And the angels sing CD BN 8-33146-2
Everything I have is yours
I understand
All or nothing at all
I'll never smile again
If I loved you
Far away places CD BN 8-33146-2
(session continued on next page)

625

	I should care	
	For all we know	
	I don't stand a ghost of a chance	
	The one I love	
(tk.3)	Moon of Manakoora -1	CD BN 8-33146-2
(tk.5)	Ennui -2	unissued
(tk.5)	Friendly island	-

-1: Benny Carter(ts) part overdubbed on.
All titles,except last two,issued on BN(F)BNP25112.
All titles to be issued on a Blue Note CD.

THE CLOVERS:
John "Buddy" Bailey(lead tenor vo) Billy Mitchell(1st tenor vo) Matthew McQuater(2nd tenor vo) Harold Lucas(baritone vo) Harold Winley(bass vo) with King Curtis(ts) & p,g,b,dm,tamb.
(Bell Sound Studios) NYC,October 12,1960

711	Yes,it's you	CD BN 8-54364-2

SAUTER-FINEGAN ORCHESTRA:
Bobby Nichols,Joe Ferrante,Nick Travis(tp) Urbie Green,Sonny Russo(tb) Tommy Mitchell(bass tb) John Barrows(frh) Harvey Phillips(tu) Joe Soldo,Walt Kane(cl,as) Al Klink(fl,ts) Al Block,Ray Shriner(ts,reeds) Gene Allen(bs) Buddy Weed or Bernie Leighton(p) Mundell Lowe(g) Dave Seyer(cello) Don Lamond(dm) Eddie Costa,Arnold Goldberg,Art Marottla,Bradley Spindley(perc) Janet Putnam(harp) Florence Blumberg (vo) Eddie Sauter,Bill Finegan(arr).
NYC,December ,1960

Midnight sleighride	CD BN(J)TOCJ-5854
A foggy day (voFB)	CD BN(J)TOCJ-5855

BILLY STRAYHORN:
Billy Strayhorn(p) Michel Gaudry(b).
(Barclay Studios) Paris,January ,1961

Passion flower	CD BN 4-94035-2

MORGANA KING:
Morgana King(vo) with Chauncey Welsh(tb) Sam Most(fl) Jimmy Jones(p) Chuck Wayne(g) Ernie Furtado (b) Johnny Cresci(dm).
NYC, 1961

All or nothing at all	CD BN(Sp)8-56842-2

ZOOT SIMS IN PARIS:
Zoot Sims(ts) Henri Renaud(p) Bob Whitlock(b) Jean-Louis Viale(dm).
(The Blue Note) Paris,December ,1961

Zoot's blues	
Spring can really hang you up the most	CD BN 8-34873-2,(J)TOCJ-5851
Once in a while	
These foolish things	
On the alamo	
Too close for comfort	
A flat blues	
You got to my head	
Stompin' at the Savoy	

All titles to be issued on the Blue Note label.

JEROME RICHARDSON:
Jerome Richardson(bs) Les Spann(fl,g) Richard Wyands(p) Henry Grimes(b) Grady Tate(dm).
NYC, 1962

	No problema	BN B1-54357,CD 8-54357-2

ART BLAKEY'S JAZZ MESSENGERS:
Freddie Hubbard(tp) Curtis Fuller(tb) Wayne Shorter(ts) Cedar Walton(p) Jymie Merritt(b) Art Blakey(dm).
(Renaissance Club) LA,March 18,1962

tk.1	Three blind mice	BN(J)FCPA 6205,W-5512 CD BN 7-84451-2.7-97190-2
tk.2	The theme	rejected
tk.3	Up jumped Spring	CD BN 7-84451-2,7-97190-2,8-54899-2
tk.4	Arabia	rejected
tk.5	Brother, can you spare a dime	-
tk.6	When lights are low	BN(J)FCPA 6205;CD BN 7-84451-2
tk.7	Blue moon	CD BN 7-84451-2
tk.8	Up jumped Spring (alt.)	BN BN-LA573-J2,(J)GXF-3021 CD BN 7-84451-2
tk.9	That old feeling	BN(J)FCPA 6205;CD BN 7-84451-2
tk.10	Plexus (see note)	- -
tk.11	It's only a paper moon	BN BN-LA573-J2,(J)GXF-3021 CD BN 7-84452-2
tk.12	Mosaic	BN BN-LA573-J2,(J)GXF-3021 CD BN 7-84452-2
tk.13	Ping pong	BN BN-LA573-J2,(J)GXF-3021 CD BN 7-84452-2
tk.14	Plexus/the theme	rejected
tk.15	Children of the night	CD BN 7-84451-2
tk.16	When lights are low (alt.)	rejected

Note: "Plexus" was listed as "Plexis" on all BN releases.

KENNY DORHAM - MATADOR:
Kenny Dorham(tp) Jackie McLean(as) Bobby Timmons(p) Teddy Smith(b) J.C. Moses(dm).
(Sound Makers) NYC,April 15,1962

(tk.7)	El matador
(tk.5)	Melanie
(tk.4)	Prelude (tp & p only)
(tk.7)	There goes my heart
(tk.3)	Beautiful love
(tk.6)	Smile

Note: All previous issues of "El Matador" were edited.
All titles issued on CD BN 7-84460-2.

BILL EVANS/JIM HALL - UNDERCURRENT:
Bill Evans(p) Jim Hall(g).
(Sound Makers) NYC,April 24,1962

I hear a rhapsody	
Stairway to the stars	
I'm getting sentimental over you	CD BN(J)CJ28-5178

All titles issued on BN B1-90583,CD 7-90583-2.

627

BILL EVANS/JIM HALL - UNDERCURRENT:
Bill Evans(p) Jim Hall(g).
(Sound Makers) NYC,May 14,1962

My funny Valentine	BN B1-90583,(J)W-5510 CD BN(J)CJ28-5022,TOCJ-5187/88
My funny Valentine (alt.)	
Dream gypsy	BN B1-90583,(J)K23P-6725, CD BN(J)TOCJ-5873,TOCJ-6190
Romain	BN B1-90583
Romain (alt.)	
Skatin' in Central Park	BN B1-90583
Darn that dream	- CD BN 7-96904-2

All titles issued on CD BN 7-90583-2.

KEN McINTYRE:
John Mancebo Lewis(tb) Ken McIntyre(as-1,fl-2) Ed Stoute(p) Ahmad Abdul-Malik(b) Warren Smith(dm).
(Sound Makers) NYC,June 11, 1962

(tk.2) Undulation -1
(tk.2) Turbospacey -1
(tk.2) Bootsie -1
(tk.1) New time -1
(tk.1) Naomi -2
(tk.2) Someday -2 (tb out)
(tk.3) Mercedes -2

All titles issued on CD BN 8-57200-2.

KING PLEASURE:
King Pleasure(vo) Seldon Powell(ts) Teacho Wilshire(arr) & others unknown.
(Sound Mixers) NYC,July 26,1962

Swan blues	
Jazz jump	CD BN 5-21153-2
That old black magic (Diaper pin)	
It might as well be spring	

All titles issued on CD BN 7-84463-2.

KEN McINTYRE:
Ken McIntyre(as-1,oboe-2) Jaki Byard(p) Ron Carter(b) Louis Hayes(dm).
(Sound Makers) NYC,August 31, 1962

(tk.5) Sendai -2
(tk.3) Cosmos -1

All titles issued on CD BN 8-57200-2.

Ken McIntyre(as-1,fl-2) Jaki Byard(p) Ron Carter(b) Ben Riley(dm).
(Sound Makers) NYC,September 4, 1962

(tk.2) Say what -1
(tk.2) 96.5 -2
(tk.1) Arisin'-1
(tk.3) Laura -1
(tk.1) Speak low -1

All titles issued on CD BN 8-57200-2.

KING PLEASURE:
King Pleasure,Jon Hendricks-1(vo) Seldon Powell(ts) Teacho Wilshire(arr) & others unknown.
(Sound Makers) NYC,September 4, 1962

Sometimes I'm happy	CD BN 7-84463-2
Blues I like to hear	-
Don't get scared -1	-

King Pleasure(vo) Seldon Powell(ts) Teacho Wilshire(arr) & others unknown.
(Sound Makers) NYC,September 5,1962

Mean to me	
This is always	
I'm in the mood for love	CD BN 7-81331-2,7-96582-2

All titles issued on CD BN 7-84463-2.

DUKE ELLINGTON - MONEY JUNGLE:
Duke Ellington(p) Charles Mingus(b) Max Roach(dm).
(Sound Makers) NYC,September 17,1962

Very special	BN BT85129,(F)BNP25113
A little Max (Parfait)(alt.)	
A little Max (Parfait)	BN BT85129
Fleurette Africaine (African flower)	- (F)BNP25113
Rem blues	-
Wig wise	- (F)BNP25113
	CD BN 7-96904-2,8-54900-2
Switch blade	BN BT85129
Caravan	- (F)BNP25113
	CD BN 8-29964-2,8-54900-2
Money jungle	BN BT85129,(F)BNP25113,(J)W-5510
Solitude (alt.)	
Solitude	BN BT85129,(F)BNP25113
Warm valley	- -
Backward country boy blues	-

All takes shown issued on CD BN 7-46398-2.
All titles from BNP25113 also issued on CD BN(J)TOCJ-6247.

CHARLES MINGUS - TOWN HALL CONCERT:
Clark Terry,Ernie Royal,Snooky Young,Richard Williams,Rolf Ericson,Ed Armour,Lonnie Hillyer(tp) Eddie Bert,Jimmy Cleveland,Willie Dennis,Quentin Jackson,Britt Woodman,Jimmy Knepper,Paul Faulise(tb) Don Butterfield(tu) Buddy Collette,Charlie Mariano, Charles McPherson,Eric Dolphy(as) Zoot Sims,George Berg (ts) Romeo Penque(oboe) Jerome Richardson,Pepper Adams(bs) Danny Bank (contrabass cl) Warren Smith (vb,perc) Toshiko Akiyoshi,Jaki Byard(p) Les Spann(g) Charles Mingus(b,narr-1) Milt Hinton(b) Dannie Richmond(dm) Grady Tate(perc) Melba Liston(arr,cond-1) Bob Hammer(arr-2) Gene Roland (arr).
Band vocal on -3.
(Town Hall) NYC,October 12,1962

Set #1

Freedom,pt.2 (Clark in the dark*)-4	BN(E)BNS40034
Osmotin'	
Epitaph,pt.1 -4	BN(E)BNS40034
Freedom,pt.1	-
Peggy's blue skylight -1	
Epitaph,pt.2 -1,3,4	BN(E)BNS40034
My search -2,4	

All titles issued on CD BN 8-28353-2
All titles on BN(E)BNS40034 also issued on BN(P)8E074-60106,1601061.

CHARLES MINGUS - TOWN HALL CONCERT:
Same.

(Town Hall) NYC,October 12,1962

Set #2

	Portrait	
	Duke's choice (Don't come back*)-2,4	BN(E)BNS40034*
	Please don't come back from the moon	
	In a mellotone (Finale*)-4	BN(E)BNS40034*
	Epitaph,pt.1 (alt.)	

-4: These titles edited on all LP issues. Titles in parentheses are as they appeared on LP.
Note: Most likely, Akiyoshi is the pianist on set one and Byard on set two.

All titles issued on CD BN 8-28353-2
All titles on BN(E)BNS40034 also issued on BN(P)8E074-60106,1601061.

HOWARD McGHEE:
Howard McGhee(tp) Phil Porter(org) Larry Ridley(b) Dave Bailey(dm).
(Regent Sound Studios) NYC,February 19,1963

(tk.10)	Blue bell
(tk.3)	Lonely town
(tk.4)	Satin doll
(tk.3)	Fly me to the moon
(tk.6)	Secret love
(tk.11)	Nobody knows you when you're down and out

All titles issued on CD BN(J)TOCJ-6302.

HOWARD McGHEE:
Howard McGhee(tp) Jimmy Jones(p) Ron Carter(b) Art Taylor(dm).
(Regent Sound Studios) NYC,March 1,1963

(tk.11)	Blues duende
(tk.9)	Way run away
(tk.3)	Tenderly
(tk.5)	Canadian sunset

All titles issued on CD BN(J)TOCJ-6302.

RENE THOMAS:
Jacques Pelzer(ss,as,fl) Charlie Rouse(ts) Kenny Drew(p) René Thomas(g) Gilbert Rovere(b) Frankie Dunlop (dm).

Paris,March 8,1963

I remember Sonny
Theme for Freddy
Theme
Short bridge
Meeting
B like Bud
Crepuscule with Nellie (solo g)
When I fall in love (omit Pelzer)

All titles to be issued on Blue Note.
Note: This session was not issued on the United Artists label.

KEN McINTYRE:
Ken McIntyre(as-1,fl-2,oboe-3) Bob Cummingham(b) Edgar Bateman(dm) & strings dir. by Selwart Clarke.
(Regent Sound) NYC,May.27,1963

(tk.3) Kajee -3
(tk.6) Reflections -1
(tk.2) Miss Ann -2
(tk.3) Lois Marie -3
(tk.7) Permanentity -1
(tk.3) Tip top -2
(tk.3) Chitlins and cavyah -1

All titles issued on CD BN 8-57200-2.

BETTY CARTER:
Betty Carter(vo) with Harold Mabern(p) Bob Cranshaw(b) Roy McCurdy(dm).
(Sound Makers) NYC,April ,1964

My favorite things CD BN 7-96583-2,8-29095-2,5-21151-2
This is always CD BN 8-57460-2,(Sp)8-56842-2
Beware my heart CD BN(C)4-94888-2

LEROY HOLMES:
Unidentified orchestra,arr. & cond. by Leroy Holmes.
NYC, c.1965

James Bond theme CD BN 8-57748-2

COUNT BASIE AND HIS ORCHESTRA:
Al Aarons,Sonny Cohn,Wallace Davenport,Phil Guilbeau(tp) Henderson Chambers,Al Grey,Grover Mitchell (tb) Bill Hughes(bass tb) Marshal Royal,Bobby Plater(as) Eric Dixon,Eddie "Lockjaw" Davis(ts) Charles Fowlkes(bs) Count Basie(p) Freddie Green(g) Norman Keenan(b) Sonny Payne(dm) George Williams(arr).
NYC,December 27,1965

From Russia with love CD BN 8-57748-2

JIMMY McGRIFF:
Jimmy McGriff(org) Thornel Schwartz(g) Willie Jenkins(dm).
(from Veep label) (The Club) Newark,N.J.,December 30,1965

Where it's at BN B1-29092,(E)8-30724-1
CD BN 8-29092-2,8-57063-2,(E),8-30724-2

LENA HORNE:
Lena Horne(vo) with Orchestra arr. & cond. by Ray Ellis.
NYC?,March ,1966

A taste of honey CD BN(Sp)8-56842-2

LENA HORNE:
Lena Horne(vo) with unidentified orchestra.
NYC,August 1,1966

What are you doing New Year's Eve CD BN(J)TOCJ-5854

TINA BRITT:
Tina Britt(vo & others unknown.
(from Veep label) c.1967

Sookie,Sookie BN B1-54357,CD 8-54357-2

631

<u>TRUMAN THOMAS</u>:
details unknown.
(from Veep label) c.late '60s

Respect BN B1-97158,CD 4-97158-2

<u>JANET LAWSON</u>:
Janet Lawson(vo) with trio.
c.late '60s

Dindi BN B1-29865,CD 8-29865-2

<u>DUKE ELLINGTON</u> - <u>70th BIRTHDAY CONCERT</u>:
Cat Anderson,Cootie Williams,Mercer Ellington,Rolf Ericson(tp) Lawrence Brown,Chuck Connors(tb) Russell Procope(cl,as) Johnny Hodges(as) Norris Turney(as,cl,fl) Harold Ashby(ts,cl) Paul Gonsalves(ts) Harry Carney(bs,cl, bass cl) Duke Ellington(p) Wild Bill Davis(org) Victor Gaskin(b) Rufus Jones(dm).
(Colston Hall) Bristol,England,November 25,1969

Satin doll CD BN 8-32746-2

<u>DUKE ELLINGTON</u> - <u>70th BIRTHDAY CONCERT</u>:
Cat Anderson,Cootie Williams,Mercer Ellington,Rolf Ericson(tp) Lawrence Brown,Chuck Connors(tb) Russell Procope(cl,as) Johnny Hodges(as) Norris Turney(as,cl,fl) Harold Ashby(ts,cl) Paul Gonsalves(ts) Harry Carney(bs,cl, bass cl) Duke Ellington(p) Wild Bill Davis(org) Victor Gaskin(b) Rufus Jones(dm).
(Free Trade Hall) Manchester,England,November 26,1969

Rockin' in rhythm	CD BN 4-94035-2
B.P. blues	
Take the A train	CD BN 8-54900-2
Tootie for Cootie	
4:30 blues	CD BN 8-54900-2
El gato	CD BN 4-97155-2
Black butterfly	CD BN 4-95981-2
Things ain't what they used to be	
Layin' on mellow	
Azure te	
In triplicate	CD BN 8-54900-2
Perdido	
Fife	
Medley:	
Don't you know I care/	
In a sentimental mood/	
Prelude to a kiss/	
I'm just a lucky so and so/	
I let a song go out of my heart/	
Do nothin' till you hear from me/	
Just squeeze me/	
Don't get around much anymore/	
Mood indigo/	
Sophisticated lady/	
Caravan	
Black swan	
Final Ellington speech	

All titles issued on CD BN 8-32746-2.

SHIRLEY BASSEY MEETS BOOSTER - LIGHT MY FIRE:
Shirley Bassey(vo) with Orchestra arr. & cond. by Johnny Harris.
1970

	Light my fire	BN B1-54360, CD 8-54360-2 BN(F)8-87504-1,8-87504-2

Booster (mixer) Nicoas Gueguen(el p,clavinet) Rob (synth) added.
Paris,c. Spring 1998

	Light my fire (Booster mix edit)	BN(F)8-87504-1,8-87504-2
	Light my fire (Booster remix)	- -
	Light my fire (Booster jungle mix)	- -

DUKE ELLINGTON - TOGO BRAVA SUITE:
Cootie Williams,Johnny Coles,Mercer Ellington,Eddie Preston,Harold Johnson(tp) Chuck Connors, Malcolm Taylor,Booty Wood(tb) Russell Procope(cl,as) Harold Minerve(as) Norris Turney(as,fl) Harold Ashby(ts) Paul Gonsalves(ts) Harry Carney(bs,bass cl) Duke Ellington(p) Joe Benjamin(b) Rufus Jones (dm).
(Odeon Theatre) Bristol,England,October 22,1971

	C jam blues	
	Togo brava suite,pt.1 & 2	
	Togo brava suite,pt.3 & 4	
	Happy reunion -1	CD BN 8-54900-2
	Addi	
	Lotus blossom (solo p)	
	La plus belle africaine	
	In a mellotone	
	Soul flute	

-1: Gonsalves,Ellington,Benjamin,Jones only.
All titles on CD BN 8-30082-2.

DUKE ELLINGTON - TOGO BRAVA SUITE:
Cootie Williams(tp,vo) Johnny Coles,Mercer Ellington,Eddie Preston,Harold Johnson(tp) Chuck Connors, Malcolm Taylor,Booty Wood(tb) Russell Procope(cl,as) Harold Minerve(as) Norris Turney(as,fl) Harold Ashby(ts) Paul Gonsalves(ts) Harry Carney(bs,bass cl) Duke Ellington(p) Joe Benjamin(b) Rufus Jones(dm) Nell Brookshire(vo).
(Birmingham Theatre) Birmingham,England,October 24,1971

Cotton tail
Checkered hat
I got it bad (voNB,CW)
Melancholia -1 (solo p)

-1: mistitled "Goof" on all LP issues.
All titles on CD BN 8-30082-2.

MONK HIGGINS:
Details unknown.
LA, c.1972

UA-10010	Walking in my sleep	CD BN 4-97157-2

IKE AND TINA TURNER:
Tina Turner(vo) Ike Turner(g) & others unknown.
LA,March 15,1975

15899	Whole lotta love	BN B1-94027,CD 4-94027-2

NOEL POINTER - HOLD ON:
Noel Pointer(v) Dave Grusin(el p,synth,kalimba,African & bass marimba) Eric Gale(g) Francisco Centeno-1, Anthony Jackson-2(b) Steve Gadd(dm) Sammy Figueroa(lujon,cga,perc) Patti Austin,Gwen Guthrie, Yolanda McCullough,Bill Eaton,Frank Floyd,Milt Grayson(backgr. vo).
(Electric Lady Studios) NYC, 1977

19436 Roots suite:
a. Introduction & pastoral -1
b. Mama aifambeni -2
c. Oluwa (many rains ago)-1,3

-3: String section (David Nadien,Barry Finclair,Theodore Israel,Ulysses Kirksey,Julian Barber,Charles McCracken,Lewis Eley,Diana Halpern,Carl Ector,Max Ellen,Marvin Morganstern,Robert Rozek,Tony Posk,LaMar Alsop,Sanford Allen,Max Pollikoff) overdubbed on.

All titles issued on BN(J)GP-3155,CD BN 4-98543-2.

Noel Pointer(v,vo) Dave Grusin(p,el p,synth) Onaje Allan Gumbs-7(p,el p) Eric Gale(g) Francisco Centeno-1,Anthony Jackson-2 (b) Steve Gadd(dm) Ralph McDonald-3,Sammy Figueroa-4(perc) Patti Austin,Vivian Cherry,Gwen Guthrie(backgr. vo-5),Louvinia Pointer(backgr. vo-6).
(Electric Lady Studios) NYC, 1977

19434	Hold on -1,3,5,8	BN(J)W-5515
19435	Stardust lady -2,6 (voNP)	
19437	Where were you -2,3,5,8	
19438	Staying with you -2,3,5,8 (voNP,PA)	
19439	Movin' in -1,4,7,8	
19440	Cappriccio stravagante -2,3,9	

-8 : string section (as above) overdubbed on.
-9: David Nadien,Barry Finclair(v) Theodore Israel(viola) Ulysses Kirksey(cello) added.
All titles issued on BN(J)GP-3155,CD BN 4-98543-2.

EARL KLUGH - MAGIC IN YOUR EYES:
Earl Klugh,Chet Atkins(g) Lloyd Green(pedal steel g) Hubie Crawford(el b) Gene Dunlap(dm) & strings arr. by Booker T. Jones.
(C.A.Workshop) Nashville,Tenn.,October 18,1977

19759	Good time Charlie's got the blues	BN(J)GP-3160,GP-3205 CD BN 7-48389-2,7-80505-2

Darryl Dybka(el p-1) Earl Klugh(g) Lloyd Green(pedal steel g) Hubie Crawford(el b) Gene Dunlap(dm,perc) & strings arr. by Booker T. Jones.
(Music City Music Hall) Nashville,Tenn.,October 19,1977

19755	Julie -1	CD BN 8-53354-2
19761	Cry a little while	BN(J)K28P-6045

Both titles issued on BN(J)GP-3160,CD BN 7-48389-2.

Greg Phillinganes(p,el p,synth,arr) Earl Klugh(g) Scott Edwards(el b) Gene Dunlap(dm) Paulinho Da Costa (perc-1) & strings arr. by Booker T. Jones-2.
(Sound Factory) LA January 30,1978

19753	Magic in your eyes -1,2	CD BN 7-46625-2
19754	Alicia	CD BN 8-53354-2

Both titles also issued on BN(J)GP-3160,CD BN 7-48389-2.

EARL KLUGH - MAGIC IN YOUR EYES:
Greg Phillinganes(p,el p,synth,arr) Earl Klugh(g) Scott Edwards(el b) Gene Dunlap(dm) Paulinho Da Costa (perc-1).
(Sound Factory) LA,January 31,1978

19756	Lode star	BN(J)GP-3160,CD BN 7-48389-2
19760	Mayagues -1	- -

Same. LA,February 1,1978

19758	Rose hips	BN(J)GP-3160,K28P-6045;CD BN 7-48389-2

Booker T. Jones(chimes) & strings arr. by Booker T .Jones added.Prob. same date.

19757	Cast your fate to the wind -1	BN(J)GP-3160,CD BN 7-48389-2,7-80505-2

RONNIE LAWS:
Ronnie Laws(ss,ts,vo) Barnaby Finch(el p) Melvin Robinson,Roland Bautista(g) Bobby Vega(el b) Raymond Pounds(dm) Andrew Acosta(perc) Sylvia St.James,Debra Thomas(backgr.vo).
(Indigo Ranch) LA,June 6,1978

20186	Love is here	CD BN 7-98289-2

Ronnie Laws(ss,fl) Larry Dunn(el p,synth) Pat Kelly(g) Louis Satterfield(el b) Fred White(dm) Lovely Hardy,Dianne Reeves,Philip Bailey(backgr. vo).
(Indigo Ranch) LA,June 20,1978

20185	Living love	CD BN 7-98289-2

Ronnie Laws(ts,el p) Barnaby Finch(el p) Larry Dunn(synth) Pat Kelly(g) Bobby Vega(b) Art Rodriguez (dm) Andrew Acosta(perc).
(Indigo Ranch) LA,July 10,1978

20184	Flame	BN(J)W-5515, CD BN 7-98289-2

EARL KLUGH - HEART STRING:
Greg Phillinganes(el p,clav,arr) Mickey Roquemore(clavinet-1) Earl Klugh(g) Phil Upchurch(el g-2) Charles Meeks(el b) Victor Lewis(dm) Ralph McDonald(perc) & strings arr. by Dave Matthews-3.
(Electric Lady Studios) NYC,October 1978

20348	Heart string -2	BN(J)GP-3205,W-5515 CD BN 7-46625-2,8-53354-2
20349	I'll see you again -1,2,3	BN(J)K28P-6045;CD BN 7-80505-2
20351	Spanish night	-
20354	Rayna -2	

All titles issued on BN(J)GP-3181,CD BN 5-23546-2.

Mickey Roquemore(p,clavinet) Darryl Dybka(el p) Earl Klugh(g) Hubie Crawford,Roland Wilson(el b) Gene Dunlap(dm) Ralph McDonald(perc) & strings arr. by Dave Matthews-1.Same sessions

20350	Acoustic lady, pt I -1	
20363	Acoustic lady, pt II -1	
20352	Pretty world	BN(J)GP-3205

All titles issued on BN(J)GP-3181,CD BN 5-23546-2.

Earl Klugh(g) & strings arr. by Dave Matthews-1.Same sessions

20353	Waiting for Cathy	BN(J)GP-3181,CD BN 5-23546-2
20355	Heart string (reprise) -1	- -

<u>NOEL POINTER</u> - <u>FEEL IT</u>:
Noel Pointer(v,p,vo) Onaje Allan Gumbs-1(p,el p)Richard Tee(clavinet-2) Patrice Rushen(el p-3) Michael Boddicker(synth-4) Hiram Bullock-5,Barry Finnerty-6(g) Will Lee-7,Neil Jason-8 (el b) Quentin Dennard (dm) Neil A. Clarke(perc) Eddie Bongo Brown-9,Lionel Job-10(perc) Warren Smith-11(orchestra bells,wind chimes) The Jones Girls-12,Louvinia Pointer-13,vocal group (Noel Pointer,Jon Lucien,Gwen Guthrie, Yvonne Lewis, Brenda White,Frank Floyd,Ray Simpson)-14 (backgr.vo).
(Sound Ideas & Electric Lady Studios) NYC,February - March 1979
(exact dates listed below when known)

Earl Gardner,Virgil Jones(tp) Wayne Andre,Daniel Cahn(tb) George Marge,Lou Marini,Romeo Penque, Seldon Powell,David Taylor(reeds) and string section overdubbed on all titles.

20536 Niteroi -1,5,7,11,14

Feb. 19,1979:

20539 For you -3,5,6,8,9,10,11,12

March 1,1979:

20541 Feel it -1,2,4,5,6,7,8,12

March 2,1979:

20537 Captain Jarvis -1,2,4,5,7,9
20538 There's a feeling -4,12,13 (voNP)

All titles issued on BN(J)GP-3200.

<u>RONNIE LAWS</u>:
(session details unknown)
LA,July 24,1979

20674 Every generation BN B1-29865,CD 8-29865-2

(see Liberty and Capitol sections for later recordings by Earl Klugh and Ronnie Laws)

VIRGIN

<u>HADDA BROOKS</u>:
Hadda Brooks(p,vo) Al Viola(g) Richard Dodd(cello) Eugene Wright(b).
c.1995

Time was when CD BN(C) 4-94888-2

<u>THE JAZZ PASSENGERS WITH DEBORAH HARRY</u>:
Deborah Harry(vo) Marc Ribot(g) & others unknown.
c.1997

Il n'y a plus d'après CD BN(C) 4-94888-2

 636

NOTES

Part 6
Leased Sessions

DUKE ELLINGTON AND HIS ORCHESTRA:
Bubber Miley,Arthur Whetsol(tp) Joe "Tricky Sam" Nanton(tb) Barney Bigard(cl) Johnny Hodges(as) Harry Carney(bs) Duke Ellington(p) Lonnie Johnson(g) Fred Guy(bjo) Wellman Braud(b) Sonny Greer(dm) Baby Cox(vo).
(leased from Okeh label) NYC,October 1,1928

W401175-A The mooche CD BN(Sp)8-53016-2

RAYMOND SCOTT:
Russ Case(tp) Pete Pumiglio(cl) Dave Harris(ts) Raymond Scott(p) Fred Whiting(b) Johnny Williams(dm).
(leased from Stash Records) (CBS Radio Studios) NYC,June 15,1939

Devil drums CD BN 4-95317-2

GLENN MILLER AND HIS ORCHESTRA:
Clyde Hurley,Legh Knowles,Dale McMickle(tp) Glenn Miller(tb,arr) Al Mastren,Paul Tanner(tb) Wilbur Schwartz(cl,as) Hal McIntyre(as) Harold Tennyson(cl,as,bs) Tex Beneke,Al Klink(ts) Chummy McGregor (p) Richard Fisher(g) Rowland Bundock(b) Maurice Purtill(dm).
(leased from RCA Victor) NYC,August 1,1939

038170-1 In the mood CD BN(Sp)8-34712-2

ELLA FITZGERALD:
personnel and location unknown
(leased from Drive Entertainment) mid '40s

A-tisket,a-tasket CD BN 8-36736-2

DIZZY GILLESPIE & CHARLIE PARKER:
personnel and location unknown.
(leased from Jazz Classics, Inc.) mid '40s

Shaw 'nuff CD BN 8-36736-2

THE ANDREWS SISTERS:
Personnel and location unknown.
(leased from Radio Yesteryear) mid '40s

Heartbreaker CD BN 8-36736-2

HOWARD McGHEE:
Howard McGhee(tp) Jimmy Bunn(p) Bob Kesterson(b) Roy Porter(dm).
(leased from Dial/Spotlite Records) LA,July 29,1946

D 1025-B Trumpet at tempo CD BN(J)TOCJ-5710

CHARLIE PARKER:
Charlie Parker(as) Erroll Garner(p) Red Callender(b) Harold West(dm).
(leased from Dial/Spotlite Records) LA,February 19,1947

D 1054 Cool blues CD BN(J)TOCJ-6147

DEXTER GORDON:
Melba Liston(tb) Dexter Gordon(ts) Charles Fox(p) Red Callender(b) Chuck Thompson(dm).
(leased from Dial/Spotlite Records) LA,June 5,1947

D 1081 Mischievious lady CD BN(J)TOCJ-6147

ERROLL GARNER:
Erroll Garner(p).
(leased from Dial/Spotlite Records) LA,June 10,1947

D 1091-C Play,piano,play CD BN(J)TOCJ-6147

DEXTER GORDON/WARDELL GRAY:
Dexter Gordon,Wardell Gray(ts) Jimmy Bunn(p) Red Callender(b) Chuck Thompson(dm).
(leased from Dial/Spotlite Records) LA,June 12,1947

D 1083 The chase CD BN(J)TOCJ-6147

CHARLIE PARKER:
Miles Davis(tp) Charlie Parker(as) Duke Jordan(p) Tommy Potter(b) Max Roach(dm).
(leased from Dial/Spotlite Records) NYC,October 28,1947

D 1104 (tk.8) Superman (The hymn) CD BN(J)TOCJ-6147
D 1105 (tk.8) Bird of paradise -

DODO MARMAROSA:
Dodo Marmarosa(p) Harry Babasin(cello) Jackie Mills(dm).
(leased from Dial/Spotlite Records) LA,December 3,1947

D 1131-C Bopmatism CD BN(J)TOCJ-6147

HOWARD McGHEE:
Howard McGhee(tp) James Moody(ts) Milt Jackson(vb) Hank Jones(p) Ray Brown(b) J.C. Heard(dm).
(leased from Dial/Spotlite Records) NYC,December 3,1947

D 1121 Dorothy CD BN(J)TOCJ-6147

DEXTER GORDON/TEDDY EDWARDS:
Dexter Gordon,Teddy Edwards(ts) Jimmy Rowles(p) Red Callender(b) Roy Porter(dm).
(leased from Dial/Spotlite Records) LA,December 4,1947

D 1143 The duel CD BN(J)TOCJ-6147

CHARLIE PARKER:
Miles Davis(tp) J.J.Johnson(tb) Charlie Parker(as) Duke Jordan(p) Tommy Potter(b) Max Roach(dm).
(leased from Dial/Spotlite Records) NYC,December 17,1947

D 1151-E Air conditioning (Drifting on a reed) CD BN(J)TOCJ-6147

JAMES MOODY QUARTET:
James Moody(ts) Art Simmons(p) Buddy Banks(b) Clarence Terry(dm).
(leased from Vogue label) Lausanne,Switzerland,April 30,1949

3004 Just Moody BN 1570,BLP5010

MAX ROACH QUINTET:
Kenny Dorham(tp) James Moody(ts) Al Haig(p) Tommy Potter(b) Max Roach(dm).
(leased from Vogue label) Paris,France,May 15,1949

3010	Prince Albert,pts. 1 & 2	BN 1569
3012	Tomorrow,pts. 1 & 2	BN 1571
3013	Maximum	BN 1570

All titles issued on BN BLP5010.

SIDNEY BECHET & CLAUDE LUTER:
Pierre Dervaux(tp) Claude Philippe(tp,bjo) Mowgli Jospin(tb) Claude Luter(cl) Sidney Bechet(cl,ss) Christian Azzi(p) Roland Bianchini(b) François "Moustache" Galepides(dm).
(leased from Vogue label) Paris,October 14,1949

V3015-2	Ce mossieu qui parle	BN 569,BLP7014
V3016-2	Buddy Bolden story	BN 570,BLP7001
V3017-1	Bechet's creole blues	BN 569,BLP7014
V3019-2	The onions	BN 570,BLP7001
V3020-1	See see rider	BN 566,BEP402,BLP7005

Note: BN 569 was never issued.

SIDNEY BECHET & CLAUDE LUTER:
Pierre Dervaux(tp) Bernard Zacharias(tb) Claude Luter(cl) Sidney Bechet(ss) Christian Azzi(p) Roland Bianchini(b) François "Moustache" Galepides(dm).
(leased from Vogue label) Paris,November 15,1949

V3029-2	Temptation rag	BN 567,BEP402,BLP7009
V3030-1	Riverboat shuffle	BN 568 -
V3031-2	Sobbin' and cryin'	BN 567
V3033-1	Struttin' with some barbecue	BN 566,BEP402,BLP7005
V3034-2	Saw mill blues	BN 568

THE COOL BRITONS:
Jimmy Deuchar(tp) Eddie Harvey(tb) Johnny Dankworth(as) Don Rendell(ts) Bill Le Sage(p) Eric Dawson (b) Tony Kinsey(dm).
(leased from Esquire label) London,July 29,1950

SSS7-126	Birdland bounce	BN 1611,BLP5019
SSS7-127	Leapin' in London	- -
116	Tea for me	BN 1612 -
117	Cherokee	- -

JAMES MOODY WITH STRINGS:
James Moody(as,ts) Rene Reumont(frh) Max Porret(fl) Robert Jeannoutot(oboe) Henri Bellicourt(cl,bass cl) Lionel Gali,Jean Gaunet,Charles Vaudevoir,Marcel Beaujojan(v) Robert Jadoux,Guy Rogne(cello) Bernard Gallais(harp) Raymond Fol(p) Pierre Michelot(b) Pierre Lemarchand(dm) Pepito Riebe(bgo) André Hodeir (arr,cond).
(leased from Vogue label) Paris,July 13,1951

V4055	Loving you the way I do	BN 1588,BLP5005
V4056	Bedelia	BN 1587 -
V4057	Autumn leaves	BN 1588 -
V4058	So very pretty	BN 1586 -
V4059	Singing for you	BN 1585 -
V4060	Shades of blonde	- -
V4061	Jackie my little cat	BN 1587 -
V4062	September serenade	BN 1586 -

THE SWINGING SWEDES:
Rolf Ericson(tp) Ake Persson(tb) Putte Wickman(cl) Arne Domnerus(as) Carl-Henrik Norin(ts) Lars Gullin (bs) Ulf Linde(vb) Bengt Hallberg(p) Sten Carlberg(g) Simon Brehm(b) Jack Noren(dm).
(leased from Cupol label) Stockholm,September 5,1951

2186 Cream of the crop,pt.1 BN 1604
2187 Cream of the crop,pt.2 -
2188 Summertime BN 1605
2189 Pick yourself up -

All titles also issued on BN BEP201,BLP5019.

MEZZ MEZZROW AND HIS BAND:
Lee Collins(tp) Mowgli Jospin(tb) Mezz Mezzrow(cl) Guy Lafitte(ts,cl) André Persiany(p) Zutty Singleton (dm).
(leased from Vogue label) Paris,November 15,1951

51V4147 If I could be with you BN BLP7023
51V4148 Struttin' with some barbecue -

Same.(leased from Vogue label) Paris,November 16,1951

51V4150 Blues Jam BN BLP 7023
51V4152 Blues no one dug -
51V4153 Mezzerola blues -
51V4155 Blues of the twenties -

BECHET-LUTER - PLEYEL JAZZ CONCERT:
Guy Longnon,Claude Rabanit(tp) Bernard Zacharias(tb) Claude Luter(cl) Sidney Bechet(ss) Christian Azzi(p) Roland Bianchini(b) François "Moustache" Galepides(dm).
(leased from Vogue label)(Live,Salle Pleyel) Paris,January 31,1952

Sweet Georgia Brown BN BLP7025
South BN BLP7024
In the streets of Antibes -
Petite fleur BN BLP7025
St. Louis blues BN BLP7024
Royal garden blues -
Maryland,my Maryland BN BLP7025
Frankie and Johnny BN BLP7024

Guy Longnon,Claude Rabanit(tp) Bernard Zacharias(tb) Claude Luter(cl) Sidney Bechet(ss) Raymond Fol(p) Roland Bianchini(b) François "Moustache" Galepides(dm).
(leased from Vogue label)(Live,Salle Pleyel) Paris,March 12,1952

September song BN BLP7024
High society BN BLP7025
I found a new baby -
Casey Jones -

Note: Master numbers shown in parentheses in the next two sessions were assigned by Blue Note.

DIZZY GILLESPIE QUINTET:
Dizzy Gillespie(tp,vo) Don Byas(ts) Arnold Ross(p) Joe Benjamin(b) Bill Clark(dm) Umberto Canto (cga-1).
(leased from Vogue label)(Studio Jouvenet) Paris,March 27,1952

52V4210 (BN 2003) Hurry home BN 1614,BEP202,BLP5017
52V4211 (BN 2004) Afro-Paris -1 - - -
52V4212 (BN 2008) Say Eh (voDG) BN 1615
52V4227 (BN 2006) She's funny that way BN 1616,BLP5017

641

DIZZY GILLESPIE SEXTET:
Dizzy Gillespie(tp,vo) Bill Tamper(tb) Hubert Fol(as) Don Byas(ts) Raymond Fol(p) Pierre Michelot(b) Pierre Lemarchand(dm).
(leased from Vogue label)(Schola Cantorum) Paris,April 11,1952

52V4224 (BN 2010)	CCC blues (voDG)	BN 1617
52V4225 (BN 2002)	Lady Bird	BN 1613,BEP202,BLP5017
52V4226 (BN 2009)	Somebody loves me	BN 1617 -
52V4228 (BN 2005)	Wrap your troubles in dreams	BN 1616 -
52V4229 (BN 2001)	Sweet Lorraine	BN 1613,BEP202 -
52V4230 (BN 2007)	Everything happens to me	BN 1615 -

CHARLIE PARKER - THE WASHINGTON CONCERTS:
Charlie Parker(as) with Ed Leddy,Marky Markowitz,Charlie Walp,Bob Carey(tp) Earl Swope,Rob Swope, Dan Spiker(tb) Jim Riley(as) Jim Parker,Angelo Tompros,Ben Lary(ts) Jack Nimitz(bs) Jack Holliday(p) Mert Oliver(b) Joe Timer(dm,dir) Willis Conover(m.c.).
Arr. by Al Cohn-1,Joe Timer-2,Bill Potts-3,Johnny Mandel-4,Jack Holliday-5,Gerry Mulligan-6
(leased from Elektra label)(Club Kavakos) Washington,D.C.,February 22,1953

Fine and dandy -1
These foolish things -2
Light green -3
Thou swell -4
Willis -3
Don't blame me -5
Something to remember you by/Blue room -2
Roundhouse -6

All titles issued on CD BN 5-22626-2.

WADE LEGGE TRIO:
Wade Legge(p) Lewis Hackney(b) Al Jones(dm).
(leased from Vogue label) Paris,February 27,1953

Perdido
Dream a little of me
Wade leg's blues
A Swedish folksong
Dance of the infidels
Aren't you glad you're you
These foolish things
Why don't you believe me

All titles issued on BN BLP5031.

GIGI GRYCE ENSEMBLE:
Jimmy Cleveland(tb) Anthony Ortega(fl,as) Gigi Gryce(as) Clifford Solomon(ts) William Boucaya(bs) Henri Renaud(p) Pierre Michelot(b) Alan Dawson(dm) Quincy Jones(arr-1).
(leased from Vogue label) Paris,September 26,1953

53V4650-1	Paris the beautiful	BN BLP5050
53V4651-1	Purple shades -1	-

Art Farmer(tp) Jimmy Cleveland(tb) Anthony Ortega(fl) Clifford Solomon(ts) Quincy Jones(p) Pierre Michelot(b) Alan Dawson(dm).
(leased from Vogue label) Same date.

53V4652-1	La rose noire	BN BLP5049

642

LIONEL HAMPTON AND HIS PARIS ALL STARS:
Walter Williams(tp) Al Hayse,Jimmy Cleveland(tb) Mezz Mezzrow(cl) Clifford Scott(ts) Lionel Hampton (vb) Claude Bolling(p) Billy Mackel(g) Monk Montgomery(b) Curley Hamner(dm).
(leased from Vogue label) Paris,September 28,1953

Real crazy
Real crazy (More and more)

Both titles issued on BN BLP5046.

LIONEL HAMPTON AND HIS PARIS ALL STARS:
Lionel Hampton(vb) Billy Mackel(g) Monk Montgomery(b).
(leased from Vogue label) Same date.

Always
September in the rain

Both titles issued on BN BLP5046.

GIGI GRYCE AND HIS ORCHESTRA:
Clifford Brown,Art Farmer,Walter Williams,Fernand Verstraete,Fred Gerard(tp) Quincy Jones(tp,arr) Jimmy Cleveland,Bill Tamper,Al Hayse(tb) Gigi Gryce,Anthony Ortega(as) Clifford Solomon,Henri Bernard(ts) Henri Jouot(bs) Henri Renaud(p) Pierre Michelot(b) Alan Dawson(dm).
(leased from Vogue label) Paris,September 28,1953

53V4655-2	Brown skins	BN BLP5049
53V4656-1	Deltitnu -2	-
53V4657-1	Strike up the band -1	BN BLP5050
53V4658-1	Keeping up with Jonesy -2	BN BLP5049

-1: Art Farmer(tp) Jimmy Cleveland(tb) Anthony Ortega(as) Clifford Solomon(ts) Henri Renaud(p) Alf Masselier(b) Alan Dawson(dm) only.
-2: Gerard out.

CLIFFORD BROWN SEXTET:
Clifford Brown(tp) Gigi Gryce(as) Henri Renaud(p) Jimmy Gourley(g) Pierre Michelot(b) Jean-Louis Viale (dm).
(leased from Vogue label) Paris,September 29,1953

53V4659-1	Blue conception
53V4660-1	All the things you are
53V4661-1	I cover the waterfront (g out)
53V4662-1	Goofin' with me (g out)

All titles were scheduled on BN BLP5051 (not released).

GIGI GRYCE-CLIFFORD BROWN SEXTET:
Clifford Brown(tp) Gigi Gryce(as) Henri Renaud(p) Jimmy Gourley(g) Pierre Michelot(b) Jean-Louis Viale (dm).
(leased from Vogue label) Paris,October 8,1953

tk.1	Minority
tk.1	Salute to the Bandbox
tk.1	Strictly romantic (g out)
tk.1	Baby (g out)

All titles issued on BN BLP5048.

GIGI GRYCE AND HIS ORCHESTRA:
Clifford Brown,Art Farmer,Walter Williams(tp) Quincy Jones(tp,arr) Jimmy Cleveland,Al Hayse,Benny Vasseur(tb) Gigi Gryce(as,arr) Anthony Ortega(as) Clifford Solomon,André Dabonneville(ts) William Boucaya(bs) Henri Renaud(p) Pierre Michelot(b) Jean-Louis Viale(dm).
(leased from Vogue label) Paris,October 9,1953

Quick step
Bum's rush

Both titles issued on BN BLP5049.

ART FARMER:
Art Farmer(tp) Jimmy Cleveland(tb) Anthony Ortega(as) Henri Renaud(p) Marcel Dutrieux(b) Jean-Louis Viale(dm). (leased from Vogue label) Paris,October 10,1953

tk.1	Serenade to Sonny	BN BLP5051 (not released)

GIGI GRYCE-CLIFFORD BROWN OCTET:
Clifford Brown(tp) Jimmy Cleveland(tb) Gigi Gryce(as) Clifford Solomon(ts) William Boucaya(bs) Henri Renaud(p) Jimmy Gourley(g) Pierre Michelot(b) Jean-Louis Viale(dm).
(leased from Vogue label) Paris,October 10,1953

	Chez moi	BN BLP5050
	Hello	-

Gigi Gryce(as) Quincy Jones(p) Jimmy Gourley(g) Marcel Dutrieux(b) Jean-Louis Viale(dm).
(leased from Vogue label) Same date

tk.1	Evening in Paris	BN BLP5051 (not released)

Clifford Brown(tp) Jimmy Cleveland(tb) Gigi Gryce,Anthony Ortega(as) Clifford Solomon(ts) William Boucaya(bs) Quincy Jones(p) Marcel Dutrieux(b) Jean-Louis Viale(dm).
(leased from Vogue label) Same date.

tk.1	All weird	BN BLP5050

CLIFFORD BROWN QUARTET:
Clifford Brown(tp) Henri Renaud(p) Pierre Michelot(b) Benny Bennett(dm).
(leased from Vogue label) Paris,October 15,1953

53V4718-1	Blue and Brown	BN BLP5047
53V4719-1	I can't dream,can't I?	-
53V4720-1	The song is you	-
53V4721-1	Come rain or come shine	-
53V4722-1	It might as well be Spring	-
53V4723-1	You're a lucky guy	-

FATS SADI'S COMBO:
Roger Guerin(tp) Nat Peck(tb) Bobby Jaspar(ts) Jean Aldegon(bass cl) Fats Sadi(vb) Maurice Vander(p) Pierre Michelot(b Jean-Louis Viale(dm).
(leased from Vogue label) Paris,May 8,1954

	Sadisme	BN BLP5061
	Sweet feeling	-
	Thanks a million	-
	Big Baloony	-
	Karin	-
	Laguna leap	-
	Ad libitum	-
	Ridin' high	-

THE COOL BRITONS - NEW SOUNDS FROM OLDE ENGLAND:
Albert Hall(tp) Johnny Dankworth(as) Don Rendell(ts) Ralph Dollimore(p) Johnny Hawksworth(b) Alan Ganley(dm).
(leased from Atlantic-Golden Bell label) London,May 13,1954

Quick return
Deep purple
Jazz Club U.S.A.

All titles issued on BN BLP5052.

Albert Hall(tp) Don Rendell(ts) Harry Klein(bs) Ralph Dollimore(p) Johnny Hawksworth(b) Tony Kinsey (dm).
(leased from Atlantic-Golden Bell label) London,May 15,1954

Crystal
I'm putting all my eggs
Nom de plume
Epigram (Klein out)

All titles issued on BN BLP5052.

BECHET-LUTER - OLYMPIA CONCERT:
Pierre Dervaux,Gilles Thibaut(tp) Benny Vasseur(tb) Claude Luter(cl) Sidney Bechet(ss) Yannick St. Gery(p) Claude Philippe(bjo) Roland Bianchini(b) Marcel Blanche(dm).
(leased from Vogue label)
(Live,Olympia Theatre) Paris,December 8,1954

Buddy Bolden stomp	BN BLP7029
Have you got the blues?	-
Riverboat shuffle	-
Temperamental	-
Halle hallelujah	-
Montmartre boogie woogie	BN BLP7030 (never issued)
When the Saints go marchin' in	-
Muskrat ramble	-
Sobbin' and cryin' blues	-
On the sunny side of the street	-

MEL TORME:
Mel Torme(vo) with Marty Paich Dek-Tette: Pete Candoli,Don Fagerquist(tp) Bob Enevoldsen(vtb) Vince De Rosa,John Cave(frh) Al Pollan(tu) Bud Shank(as) Bob Cooper,Jack Montrose(ts) Jack Dulong(bs) Marty Paich(p) Red Mitchell(b) Mel Lewis(dm).
(leased from Bethlehem label) LA,January 20,1956

Lullaby of Birdland CD BN(J)TOCJ-66071

ELLA FITZGERALD:
Ella Fitzgerald(vo) with Ben Webster(ts Oscar Peterson(p) Herb Ellis(g) Ray Brown(b) Alvin Stoller(dm).
(leased from Verve Records) LA,October 17,1957

21773-5 In a mellow tone CD BN(Sp)8-34712-2

<u>MILES DAVIS</u>:
Miles Davis(tp) with Orchestra arr. & cond. by Gil Evans: Ernie Royal,Bernie Glow,Johnny Coles,Louis Mucci(tp) Dick Hixson,Frank Rehak,Jimmy Cleveland,Joe Bennett(tb) Willie Ruff,Julius Watkins,Gunther Schuller(frh) Bill Barber(tu) Jerome Richardson,Romeo Penque(fl,cl) Julian "Cannonball" Adderley(as) Danny Bank(bass cl,fl) Paul Chambers(b) Jimmy Cobb(dm).
(leased from Columbia Records)
(Columbia 30th Street Studio) NYC,August 4,1958

CO 61421 Summertime CD BN(Sp)8-34712-2

<u>CHARLES MINGUS</u>
Jimmy Knepper(tb) John Handy(as) Booker Ervin,Shafi Hadi(ts) Horace Parlan(p) Charles Mingus(b) Dannie Richmond(dm).
(leased from Columbia Records)
(Columbia 30th Street Studio) NYC,May 5,1959

CO 63154-6 Better get it in your soul CD BN 8-36736-2

<u>DAVE BRUBECK</u>:
Paul Desmond(as) Dave Brubeck(p) Gene Wright(b) Joe Morello(dm)
(leased from Columbia Records) NYC,July 1,1959

CO 62578 Take five CD BN(Sp)8-34712-2

<u>BOB BROOKMEYER</u>:
Bob Brookmeyer(vtb) Stan Getz(ts) Gary Burton(vb) Herbie Hancock(p) Ron Carter(b) Elvin Jones(dm).
(leased from Columbia Records) NYC,May ,1964

CO 82279 Misty CD BN(Sp)8-34712-2

<u>STAN TRACEY</u> - <u>JAZZ SUITE INSPIRED BY DYLAN THOMAS' UNDER MILK WOOD</u>:
Bobby Wellins(ts) Stan Tracey(p) Jeff Clyne(b) Jackie Dougan(dm).
(leased from Steam Records)
(Lansdowne Studio) London,May 8,1965

Cockle row
Starless and bible black
I lost my step in Nantucket
No good boys
Penpals
Llareggub
Under milk wood
A. M. mayhem

All titles issued on CD BN(E) 7-89449-2.

<u>HERBIE HANCOCK</u> - <u>BLOW UP</u> (Film Soundtrack):
Prob.: Joe Henderson(ts) Paul Griffin(org) Jim Hall(g) Ron Carter(b) Jack DeJohnette(dm) Herbie Hancock (comp,arr).
(leased from MGM/UA films) NYC,December 8,1966

101892 Bring down the birds BN B1-94027,CD 4-94027-2

<u>DICK HYMAN</u>:
Dick Hyman(synth).
(leased from ABC/Command label) NYC, 1969

Give it up or turn it loose BN B1-54357,CD 8-54357-2

ART BLAKEY AND THE JAZZ MESSENGERS:
Woody Shaw(tp) Carter Jefferson(ts) Cedar Walton(p) Mickey Bass(b) Art Blakey(dm) Tony Waters(cga).
(leased from Prestige) (Fantasy Studios) SF,March,1973

	Gertrude's bounce	CD BN 7-97190-2

JIMMY WITHERSPOON - SPOONFUL:
Jimmy Witherspoon(vo) with Benny Powell(tb) Seldon Powell,Delbert Hill,Don Menza(ts) Arthur Clark(bs) Buddy Lucas(hca) Richard Tee(org) Horace Ott(el p,arr) Joe Sample(clavinet) Robben Ford,Cornell Dupree, Freddy Robinson(el g) Chuck Rainey(el b) Bernard Purdie(dm) Gene Estes,King Errison,Omar Clay(perc) Hilda Harris,Ella Winston,Barbara Massey(backgr.vo).
(leased from Far Out Productions)
(Wally Heider Studios) LA,May 21,1973

12892	Sign on the building	BN BN-XW716-Y,	BN-LA534-G
12893	Spoonful		-
12894	Big boss man		-
12895	Inflation blues		-
12896	Pearly whites	BN BN-XW716-Y	-
12897	Nothing's changed		-

Same. (Wally Heider Studios) LA,May 22,1973

12898	Gloomy Sunday	BN BN-LA534-G
12899	Take out some insurance	-
12900	Reds and whiskey	-
12901	The moon is rising	-

TONY BENNETT:
Tony Bennett(vo) with Ruby Braff(c) George Barnes,Wayne Wright(g) John Giuffrida(b).
(leased from Improv label) NYC,September 28-30,1973

	The lady is a tramp	CD BN(C)4-94888-2

AL HAIG:
Al Haig(p) Gilbert Rovere(b) Kenny Clarke(dm).
(leased from Spotlite label) London,January 7,1974

	Holyland	CD BN(J)TOCJ-6190

JOHNNY HAMMOND SMITH:
Johnny Hammond Smith(el p,synth) Jerry Peters(p) Fonce Mizell(clavinet,vo) Mel Bolton,Melvin "Wah Wah" Ragin, John Rowin(g) Tony Dumas or Henry Franklin(el b) Harvey Mason or Fritz Wise(dm) Stephanie Spruill(perc,vo) King Erisson(cga) Larry Mizell(solina,vo) Fred Perren(vo).
(leased from Salvation label) LA, c.1974

	Starborne	CD BN(Eu)4-93994-2

STAN TRACEY DUETS - TNT/SONATINAS:
Stan Tracey(p) Keith Tippett(p).
(leased from Steam label)
(Wigmore Hall) London,December 21,1974

Dance 1
Dance 2
Skipover
Biformis
TNT

All titles issued on CD BN(E)7-89450-2.

647

JOHNNY HAMMOND SMITH:
Roger Glenn(fl) Michael White(v) Johnny Hammond Smith(el p,synth) Larry Mizell(solina,vo) Fonce Mizell (clavinet,vo) John Rowin,Craig McMullen(g) Chuck Rainey(el b) Harvey Mason(dm) Kenneth Nash(perc).
(leased from Fantasy Records) LA or SF, c.1975

	Shifting gears	CD BN(Eu)4-93994-2

RICO - MAN FROM WAREIKA:
Eddie Thornton(tp) Rico Rodrigues(tb,arr) Keith Gemmel(fl?,ts) Tony Washington(keyb) Junior Hanson Marvin(lead g)Phillip Chen(rhythm g) Benny McKenzie(b) Jacko(dm)Tony Utah,Satch Dixon(perc) Djahman,Candi McKenzie(backgr.vo).
(leased from Island label) London,May ,1976

(19150)	Africa	BN BN-LA819-H

Viv Talent Hall,Bobby Ellis(tp) Dick Cathell(flh) Rico Rodrigues(tb,arr) Herman Marquis,Ray Allen(as) Dirty Harry,George Lee(ts) Touter Harvey/Ansel Collins/Tarzan Nelson(keyb) Karl Pitterson(keyb,lead g, perc) Duggie Bryan(lead g) Lloyd Parker(rhythm g) Ras Robbie Shakespeare(b Sly Dunbar(dm) Skully(wood dm) Flick(tambourine).
(leased from Island label) Kingston,Jamaica,September ,1976

(19147)	This day	BN BN-LA819-H2	
(19148)	Ramble	-	
(19149)	Lumumba	-	
(19151)	Man from Wareika	-	CD BN(J)TOCJ-5846
(19152)	Rasta	-	
(19153)	Over the mountain	-	
(19154)	Gunga Din	-	
(19155)	Dial Africa	-	

Note: Master numbers shown were assigned by United Artists.

WAR - PLATINUM JAZZ:
Charles Miller(fl,ss,as,ts,bs,perc) Lonnie Jordan(p,el p,org,synth) Lee Oskar(hca,perc) Howard Scott(g) B.B. Dickerson(b) Harold Brown(dm) Dee Allen(timbales,perc,cga,bgo) & vocal group.
(leased from Far Out Productions) June 14,1977

(17955)	River Niger	
(17956)	H2 overture	
(17966)	Deliver the word	
(17967)	City Country City	
(17968)	Smile happy	
(17969)	Four cornered room	
(17970)	Nappy head	
(18652)	L.A. sunshine	BN BN-XW1009
(18653)	Slowly we walk together	-
(18656)	I got you	
(18657)	War is coming!War is coming!	
(18658)	Platinum jazz	

All titles issued on BN BN-LA690-J2.

648

STAN TRACEY DUETS - TNT/SONATINAS:
John Surman(bs,ss,bass cl,tenor recorder,synth) Stan Tracey(p,synth).
(leased from Steam label)
(South Hill Park Arts Centre) Bracknell,U.K.,April 24/25,1978

Three against one
Still on the run
Murphy's dream
Fleeting glances
Summer hobo
Chalk blue
Ominoso

All titles issued on CD BN(E)7-89450-2.

DEXTER GORDON:
Dexter Gordon(ts) Kirk Lightsey(p) David Eubanks(b) Eddie Gladden(dm).
(leased from Columbia Records)
(Columbia 30th Street Studio) NYC,November 4,1980

Have yourself a merry little Christmas (alt.)
CD BN 7-94857-2

ART BLAKEY AND THE JAZZ MESSENGERS BIG BAND:
Valery Ponomarev,Wynton Marsalis(tp) Robin Eubanks(tb) Bobby Watson(as,arr) Bill Pierce(ts) Branford Marsalis(bs) James Williams(p) Kevin Eubanks(g) Charles Fambrough(b) Art Blakey,John Ramsey(dm).
(leased from Timeless label) (Jazz Festival) Montreux (Switzerland),July 17, 1980

A wheel within a wheel CD BN 7-97190-2

PIECES OF A DREAM:
Grover Washington Jr.(ss) James Lloyd(p,synth) Dexter Wanzel(synth) Cedric Napoleon(b) Curtis Harmon (dm) Ralph McDonald(cga,perc) Barbara Walker(vo).
(leased from Elektra label)
(Sigma Sound Studios) Philadelphia, 1981

Warm weather CD BN 8-35800-2

ART BLAKEY AND THE JAZZ MESSENGERS:
Wynton Marsalis(tp) Bobby Watson(as) Bill Pierce(ts) James Williams(p) Charles Fambrough(b) Art Blakey (dm).
(leased from Timeless label)
(Studio Davout) Paris,April 12,1981

Ms. B.C. CD BN 7-97190-2

MAX ROACH QUARTET:
Cecil Bridgewater(tp) Odeon Pope(ts) Calvin Hill(b) Max Roach(dm).
(leased from Soul Note Records) Milano,July 22/23,1982

Straight no chaser CD BN 8-36736-2

PIECES OF A DREAM:
James Lloyd(p,el p,synth) Cedric Napoleon(b) Curtis Harmon(dm) Ralph McDonald(perc).
(leased from Elektra label) (Sigma Sound) Philadelphia, 1982

Mt.Airy groove CD BN 8-35800-2

PIECES OF A DREAM:
Grover Washington Jr.(ss,as,ts) James Lloyd(p,el p,synth) Richard Lee Stracker,Roy R. Smith-1 (g) Cedric Napoleon(b,vo) Curtis Harmon(dm) Dr.Gibbs(cga,perc) Marilyn Ashford,Charlene Jones(backgr.vo-1).
(leased from Elektra label)
(Sigma Sound) Philadelphia, 1983

Fo-fi-fo -1 CD BN 8-35800-2
The shadow of your smile -

BOBBY McFERRIN:
Bobby McFerrin(vo,b,perc) Jon Hendricks(vo) The Manhattan Transfer (Cheryl Bentyne,Tim Hauser,Alan Paul,Janis Siegel)(vo).(Vocal arrangement by Bobby McFerrin & Cheryl Bentyne)
(leased from Atlantic Records) NYC, 1984-85

Another night in Tunisia BN BT 85110,CD 7-46298-2,8-53329-2

HELEN MERRILL:
Helen Merrill(vo) with Stephane Grappelli(v) Steve Lacy(ss) Gordon Beck(p).
(leased from Owl Records) Paris,March ,1986

'Round midnight CD BN(Sp)8-56842-2

ELIANE ELIAS - ILLUSIONS:
Toots Thielemans(hca) Eliane Elias(p) Eddie Gomez(b) Al Foster(dm).
(leased from Denon label)(RPM Studios) NYC,October 22-24,1986

Falling in love with love
Iberia
Sweet Georgia fame
Chan's song

All titles issued on BN BLJ-46994.

Eliane Elias(p) Stanley Clarke(b,el b) Lenny White(dm).Same sessions.

Choro
Through the fire

Both titles issued on BN BLJ-46994.

Eliane Elias(p) Eddie Gomez(b) Steve Gadd(dm).Same sessions.

Illusions
Loco motif

Both titles issued on BN BLJ-46994.

ELIANE ELIAS - CROSS CURRENTS:
Eliane Elias(p) Eddie Gomez(b) Jack DeJohnette(dm).
(leased from Denon label)(RPM Studios) NYC,March 16-21,1987

Hallucinations
One side of you
East coastin'
Beautiful love
When you wish upon a star
Impulsive

All titles issued on BN B1-48785.

<u>ELIANE ELIAS</u> - <u>CROSS CURRENTS</u>:
Eliane Elias(p) Barry Finnerty(g-1) Eddie Gomez(b) Peter Erskine(dm) Cafe(perc-1).
(leased from Denon label)(RPM Studios) NYC,March 16-21,1987

Coming and going -1	BN B1-48785
Cross currents	-
Campari & soda	-

<u>DIANNE REEVES</u>:
Dianne Reeves(vo) with Gerald Albright(ts) David Torkanowsky(keyb) Tony Dumas(el b) Michael Baker (dm) Ron Powell(perc) Joe Blacker(synth programming) Charles Mims(arr).
(leased from artist) (Madhatter Studios) LA, February 3 & 5,1988

Oh what a freedom	BN(J)RJ28-5020,CD CJ32-5020, CJ20-5029,TOCJ-5967,TOCJ-6088

<u>PABLO MILANES</u>:
Ricardo Miralles(arr) Pablo Milanes(vo) & others unknwon.
(leased from Polygram Mexico) Havana,c.1990

Te quiero pro que te quiero	CD BN 8-14710-2

<u>CHARLIE HADEN & THE LIBERATION ORCHESTRA</u> - <u>DREAM KEEPER</u>:
Tom Harrell(tp,flh) Earl Gardner(tp) Ray Anderson(tb) Sharon Freeman(frh) Joe Daley(tu) Ken McIntyre(as) Dewey Redman(ts) Joe Lovano(ts,fl) Amina Claudine Myers(p) Mick Goodrick(g) Charlie Haden(b) Paul Motian(dm) Don Alias(perc) Juan Lazzaro Mendolas-1(pan pipes,wood fls) Carla Bley(arr,cond) Karen Mantler(arr-2).
(leased from Disk Union/DIW)(Clinton Studios) NYC,April 4 & 5,1990

Rabo de nube -1,2	
Nkosi Sikelel'i Afrika	
Sandino	CD BN 7-98291-2

All titles issued on CD BN 7-95474-2.

Branford Marsalis(ts) replaces Dewey Redman.The Oakland Youth Chorus(vo) added.
Same dates

Spiritual
Dream keeper (suite):
  Dream keeper,part one
  Feliciano ama
  Dream keeper,part two
  Canto del pilon (1)-1
  Dream keeper,part three
  Canto del pilon (2)-1
  Hymn of the anarchist women's movement
  Dream keeper,part four

Note: Chorus overdubbed at Fantasy Studios, San Francisco at a later date.

All titles on CD BN 7-95474-2.

<u>JAZZ TO THE WORLD</u>:
(leased from Special Olympics International,Inc.)

HOLLY COLE(vo) Aaron Davis(p) David Piltch(b).
(Inception Sound) Toronto,October,1991

Christmas blues	CD BN 8-32127-2

651

XXL:
Details unknown.
(leased from Street Beat label) Germany,1991-92

Agua De Beber CD BN(J)TOCJ-6153
Summertime CD BN(J)TOCP-8966
Take five -

KEVIN EUBANKS - SPIRIT TALK:
Robin Eubanks(tb-1) Kent Jordan(alto fl-2) Kevin Eubanks(g) Dave Holland(b) Mark Mondesir(dm).
(leased from artist) (Sound On Sound) NYC,April 19-23,1993

Landing -1,2
Contact -1,2
Union -1
Spirit talk -2

All titles on CD BN 7-89286-2.

Robin Eubanks(tb-1) Kent Jordan(alto fl-2) Kevin Eubanks(g) Dave Holland(b) Marvin 'Smitty' Smith (dm,perc,vo).
(leased from artist) (Sound On Sound) NYC,April 19-23,1993

Earth party
Going outside -2
Living -1,2

All titles on CD BN 7-89286-2.

Robin Eubanks(tb-1) Kevin Eubanks(g) Dave Holland(b-1).
(leased from artist) (Sound On Sound) NYC,April 19-23,1993

Inside -1
Journey

Both titles on CD BN 7-89286-2.

GARY LE MEL - ROMANCING THE SCREEN:
Gary LeMel(vo) with Jim Thatcher(frh) Randy Waldman(p,synth,vb,fl,tp,dm-1,dm programming,arr,cond) Chuck Domanico(b) John Guerin(dm)
(leased from artist) (Capitol Studios) LA, 1993
String orchestra : Stuart Canin,Charlie Bisharat,Darius Campo,Assa Drori,Bruce Dukow,Juliann French,Julie Gigante,Rene Mandel,Robin Olson,Rachel Robinson,Anatoly Rosinsky, Robert Sanov(v) Brian Dembow, Allison French,Carrie Holzman-Little,Simon Oswell(viola) Larry Corbett,Paula Hochhalter,Dennis Karmazyn,Sachi McHenry(cello) overdubbed on at Andora Studios,LA.

I'm old fashioned
Nice to be around
She's funny that way
Once upon a time
How do you keep the music playing -1
A lovely way to spend an evening
Alfie
The way you look tonight
All the things you are
When I fall in love

All titles issued on CD BN 8-29479-2.

<u>STAN TRACEY</u> - <u>LIVE AT THE QEH</u>:
Gerard Presencer(tp-1) Stan Tracey(p).
(leased from the BBC) (Queen Elizabeth Hall) London,November 30,1993

Sophisticated lady
Some other blues -1
Easy living -1

All titles issued on CD BN(E)8-31139-2.

Stan Tracey(p) Dave Green(b) Clark Tracey(dm). Same concert

Come Sunday -1
Triple celebration -2
Devil's acre -3
Mary Rose -3
The Cuban connection -4

-1: Peter King(as) added.
-2: Art Themen(ts) added.
-3: Guy Barker(tp) Jamie Talbot(as) Art Themen(ts) added.
-4: Guy Barker(tp) Malcolm Griffiths(tb) Peter King(as) Art Themen,Don Weller(ts) added.
All titles issued on CD BN(E)8-31139-2.

Derek Watkins,Tony Fisher,Guy Barker,Henry Lowther(tp) Pete Beachill,Malcolm Griffiths,Geoff Perkins (tb) Peter King,Jamie Talbot(as) Alan Skidmore(ss,ts) Art Themen(ts) Dave Bishop(bs) Stan Tracey(p) Dave Green(b) Clark Tracey(dm). Same concert

The sixth day CD BN(E)8-31139-2

<u>PATRICIA BARBER</u> - <u>CAFE BLUE</u>:
Patricia Barber(p,vo) John McLean(g) Michael Arnopol(b) Mark Walker(dm,perc).
(Chicago Recording Company) Chicago,June 28-30 & July 1,1994
(leased from Premonition label)

What a shame
Mourning grace
The thrill is gone
Romanesque
Yellow car III
Wood is a pleasant thing to think about
Inch worm
Ode to Billy Joe
Too rich for my blood
A taste of hney
Manha de carnaval

All titles issued on CD BN/Premonition 5-21810-2.

<u>JAZZ TO THE WORLD</u>: (all titles: leased from Special Olympics International,Inc.)
HERBIE HANCOCK,ELIANE ELIAS(p).
(The Hit Factory) NYC,November 18,1994

I'll be home for Christmas CD BN 8-32127-2

ANITA BAKER(vo) with orchestra arr. by Billy Byers & cond. by Ian Frasier.
NYC,December 25,1994

The Christmas song CD BN 8-32127-2

DAVID KOZ(ss,as) Don Wyatt(keyb) Tony Maiden(g) Bill Sharpe(b) Gerry Brown(dm) Steve Reid(perc).
(Kingsound Studios) LA, 1995

Winter wonderland CD BN 8-32127-2

RANDY BRECKER(flh) MICHAEL BRECKER(ts) STEVE KHAN(ac g) Nestor Sanchez,Doris Eugenio (vo).
(Lightstream Studio) NYC,March,1995

The Christmas waltz CD BN 8-32127-2

Dr. JOHN: Lew Soloff(tp) Birch Johnson(tb) Marcus Rojas(tu) Ronnie Cuber(bs) Dr.John (Mac Rebennack) (p) Richard Crooks(dm).
(Studio 900) NYC,March 6,1995

Il est né,le divin enfant CD BN 8-32127-2

CASSANDRA WILSON(vo) Cyro Baptista(perc).
(Bearsville Studio) Bearsville,NY,April,1995

The little drummer boy CD BN 8-32127-2

STEPS AHEAD: Donny McCaslin(ss) Mike Mainieri(vb) Rachel Z(p) Victor Bailey(b) Clarence Penn(dm).
(Power Station) NYC,April,1995

Angels we have heard on high CD BN 8-32127-2

CHICK COREA(p).
(Mad Hatter Studios) LA,April, 1995

What child is this CD BN 8-32127-2

MICHAEL FRANKS(vo) with Carla Bley(p) Artie Traum(ac g) Steve Swallow(b) Danny Gottlieb (dm) Veronica Nunn(backgr.vo).
(The Make Believe Ballroom) West Shokan,N.Y.,April 6,1995

Let it snow! Let it snow! Let it snow! CD BN 8-32127-2

EVERETTE HARP/GEORGE DUKE/STANLEY CLARKE: Oscar Brashear(tp) Everette Harp(as) George Duke(p) Stanley Clarke(b) Ralph Penland(dm).
(Studio 1) LA,April 24,1995

O Tannenbaum CD BN 8-32127-2

JOHN McLAUGHLIN: Jim Beard(synth,string synth,arr) John McLaughlin(ac g) Ben Perowsky(cymbals).
(Jimsong Studios) NYC,May ,1995
and (Studio Ygmas) Beausoleil,France,May ,1995

O come, O come Emmanuel CD BN 8-32127-2

FOURPLAY: Bob James(keyb,arr) Lee Ritenour(g) Nathan East(b,Santa scat) Harvey Mason(dm).
(Sunset Sound) LA,May 8,1995

It came upon a midnight clear CD BN 8-32127-2

DIANNE REEVES,LOU RAWLS(vo) with Teddy Edwards(ts) Gerald Wiggins(p) Andy Simpkins(b) Sherman Ferguson(dm)
(Clearlake Audio) Burbank,Calif.,May 10,1995

Baby, it's cold outside CD BN 8-32127-2

HERB ALPERT(tp) JEFF LORBER(p,keyb,arr) DeWayne "Smitty" Smith(b) Harvey Mason(dm,sleigh bells).

(H.A. Studio) Santa Monica,CA, June,1995

Winter wonderland CD BN 8-32127-2

DIANA KRALL(vo,p) Russell Malone(g) James Genus(b).

(Power Station) NYC,June 12,1995

Have yourself a merry little Christmas CD BN 8-32127-2

WOULDN'T IT BE NICE - A JAZZ PORTRAIT OF BRIAN WILSON:
(leased from HoriPro, Inc, Japan)
All titles: LA & NYC, early 1996

Tollak Ollestad(hca,vo) Don Grusin(p,keyb,vo,arr) Tim Weston(g) Armand Sabal-Lecco(el b, vo) Alex Acuna(dm,perc).

Surfer girl CD BN 8-33092-2

Ralf Rickert(flh,tp) Don Grusin(p,keyb,arr) Tim Weston(g) Armand Sabal-Lecco(el b) Walfredo Reyes Jr. (dm,perc) Jeffrey Osborne(vo).

Wouldn't it be nice CD BN 8-33092-2

Elements: Bill Evans(ss,ts) Clifford Carter(keyb) Mark Egan(el b) Danny Gottlieb(dm).

'Til I die CD BN 8-33092-2

Mitch Forman(keyb) Tim Weston(g,arr) Jimmy Haslip(b) Peter Erskine(dm) Luis Conte(perc) Shelby Flint (vo).

The warmth of the sun CD BN 8-33092-2

Mitch Forman(keyb,arr) Larry Carlton(g) Abraham Laboriel(el b) Bernie Dresel(dm) Luis Conte (perc) Tim Weston(arr).

I just wasn't made for these time CD BN 8-33092-2

Russell Ferrante(p) Jimmy Haslip(el b) William Kennedy(dm) Vince Mendoza(arr) Marilyn Scott(vo).

In my room CD BN 8-33092-2

Don Grusin(keyb) Dori Cayimmi(g,vo,arr) Tim Weston(g) Abraham Laboriel(el b) Claudio Slon(dm) Luis Conte(perc) Shelby Flint(vo).

Caroline no CD BN 8-33092-2

Elaine Elias(p).

Medley: Our sweet love/Friends CD BN 8-33092-2

Rob Mounsey(keyb) Steve Khan(g,arr) Ruben Rodriguez(el b) Marc Quinones(timbales,guiro) Papo Pepin (cga).

Don't worry baby CD BN 8-33092-2

Yellowjackets: Bob Mintzer(ts,arr) Russell Ferrante(p,keyb) Jimmy Haslip(el b) William Kennedy(dm).

God only knows CD BN 8-33092-2

John Abercrombie(g) Steve Carpenter(b) Joe La Barbera(dm) & strings arr. by Vince Mendoza.

Don't talk (put your head on my shoulder)
CD BN 8-33092-2

Clark Burroughs(vo,arr) Shelby Flint,Michelle Weir,Mary Hylan,Bob Joyce,Gene Morford (vo).

'Til I die CD BN 8-33092-2

JANE BUNNETT AND THE SPIRITS OF HAVANA - CHAMALONGO:
Larry Cramer(tp) Jane Bunnett(ss,fl) Yosvanny Terry(ts-3) Hilario Duran,Frank Emilio(p-1) Carlitos del Puerto(b)Tata Guines(cga,vo) Raulito Hernandez(timbales) Merceditas Valdes(vo-2) with the Cuban Folkloric All-Stars: Rodolfo Chacon,Gregorio Hernandez, Ernesto Gatell,Amado Dedeu,Pedro Martinez(vo) Pancho Quinto,Maximino Duquesne, Aspirina,Marcos Diaz Scull,Lazaro Rizo Cuevas(perc).
(leased from Bunnett-Cramer) (Studio Egrem) Havana,February 20-24,1996

Mondongo
Yambu
Inolvidable -2
Amor por ti -2
Descarga a la Hindemith -1 CD BN(Au)4-98320-2
San Lazaro
Chamalongo
Avisale
Freedom at last -3
Coco -2

All titles issued on CD BN 8-23684-2

THIERRY LANG:
Thierry Lang(p) Heiri Känzig(b) Marcel Papaux(dm).
(leased from I.D. Records) November,1996

Yellow story
Comrade Conrad
Angels fly
If I should lose you
My foolish heart
The blue peach
Oliver's song
Bop boy
'Round midnight

All titles issued on CD BN(Eu)8-56254-2,(J)TOCJ 6094.

"THE LAST TIME I COMMITTED SUICIDE" (Soundtrack):
(leased from Tapestry Films)
Film dialogue:Kevin Bacon(vo). LA,late 1996

It's a metaphor CD BN 8-36736-2
Right back where I started -
Woody wagon -
The wild stuff -
Carry on, my brother -

Red Fish Blue Fish: Brad Goode(tp) Jeb Bishop(tb) Ken Vandermark(ts) Jamie Passman(p) Tyler Bates(g) Kent Kessler(b) Alex LoCascio(dm)
(Uber Studios) Chicago,late 1996

The suicide suite CD BN 8-36736-2

"<u>THE LAST TIME I COMMITTED SUICIDE</u>" (Soundtrack):
Pet: Rick Baptist(tp) Tyler Bates(g) John Alderete(b) Alex LoCascio(dm) Lisa Papineau(vo).
(Stagg Street Studios) LA, late 1996

Ride my heart CD BN 8-36736-2

<u>PAUL JACKSON Jr.</u> - <u>NEVER ALONE-DUETS</u>:
(leased from Pony Canyon label)
All titles: (Mankind Recording Studios) LA, 1996-97

Harvey Mason(vb) Joe Wolf(synth programming) Paul Jackson Jr.(g,keyb,arr) Cornelius Mims(el b,keyb, arr) James Allen(dm programming).

Da boardwalk CD BN 8-37630-2

Paul Jackson Jr.(g)Michael Norfieet(keyb programming) Cornelius Mims(el b,arr) James Allen(dm, percussion programming) Tim Owens,Sharlotte Gibson(vo).

Let's start again CD BN 8-37630-2

Paul Jackson Jr.(el g) Earl Klugh(g) Roman Johnson(keyb,bass synth) Ollie E. Brown(dm,perc).

Reunited CD BN 8-37630-2

Kirk Whalum(ts) Paul Jackson Jr.,Ray Parker Jr.(g) Roman Johnson(keyb,bass synth,arr) Ollie E. Brown (dm,perc,arr).

Soulful Strut CD BN 8-37630-2

Najee(ss) Tom Scott(as,bass cl) Gerald Albright(ts) Paul Jackson Jr.(g,arr) Fortune Reed(bass & dm programming,arr) Harvey Mason(dm).

Wind beneath my strings CD BN 8-37630-2

Ced "C"(keyb) Paul Jackson Jr.(g) Vic "C"(bass g) James D.Blair(dm) Ali Ollie Woodson(vo) The Katinas (backgr. vo).

People get ready CD BN 8-37630-2

George Bohanon(tb) Wilton Felder,Gerald Albright(ts) Joe Sample(p,keyb) Paul Jackson Jr.(g,arr) Cornelius Mims(el b,synth,arr) Harvey Mason(dm) Sheila E.(perc).

Knighttime CD BN 8-37630-2

Paul Jackson Jr.(g) Greg Phillinganes(p,el p) Chuck Cymone(keyb,bass synth,arr) Ollie E. Brown(dm,perc, arr) Howard Hewitt,Jasmin(vo).

Where is the love CD BN 8-37630-2

Najee(fl) Jeff Lorber(keyb) Paul Jackson Jr.(g,keyb,el b,arr) Michael White(dm) Sheila E.(perc).

End to a perfect day CD BN 8-37630-2

Kevin Toney(p,org) George Duke(clavinet) Jeff Lorber(synth) Paul Jackson Jr.(g) Neil Stubenhaus(el b) Alphonse Mouzon(dm) Sheila E.(perc).

Short and suite CD BN 8-37630-2

<u>AMEDEO</u> - <u>THE RHYTHM OF LIFE</u>:
Amedeo(ss,as,ts) Arturo Sandoval(tp-1) Keith Morrison(flh-3) Bruno Di Filippi(hca-4) Ivar Gastaminza (keyb) Paquito Hechavarria(p-1) Pablo Manavello(ac g,mand) Brian Monroney (ac g-2,el g) Eris Ramazotti (el g-3) Julio Hernandez(el b) Papito Hernandez(b-2) Beppe Gemelli(dm) Carlos Nene Quintero(perc) Wendy Pederson,Raoul Midon,Rita Quintero,George Noriega,Tony Lamendola(backgr. vo).
(leased from Pelago)
(Criteria Recording/Kokopelli Sound) Miami,Florida,c. 1996-97

Beyond the clouds
Like water (still)
Summer in October
In my dreams -2
Going South -1
Lonely steps -5
Coffee,milk and soda -6
Tantra -3,4,6
The rhythm of life (voDP)
Smiling ladies -4 (voRM)

-5: overdubbed string section arr. by Ricardo Eddy Martinez.
-6: overdubbed horn section: Tony Conception(tp) Dana Taboe(tb) Amedeo(as,arr) Ed Calle(fl,ts,bs).

All titles issued on Blue Note Contemporary CD 8-33135-2.

<u>MOSE ALLISON</u> - <u>GIMCRACKS AND GEWGAWS</u>:
Mark Shim(ts-1) Russell Malone(g-2) Mose Allison(p,vo) Ratso Harris(b) Paul Motian(dm)
(leased from artist)(Sony Studios) NYC, May 17 & 18,1997

MJA Jr. -1
Gimcracks and gewgaws -1
Numbers on paper
Cruise control -2
St. Louis blues -2
Mockingbird
The more you get
Texanna
What will it be -2
So tired -1
Somebody gonna have to move
Fires of Spring
What's with you -1
Old man blues (b,dm out) CD EMI-Music(C) 4-94893-2

All titles issued on CD BN 8-23211-2.

PATRICIA BARBER - MODERN COOL:
Dave Douglas(tp-1) Patricia Barber(p,vo) John McLean(g) Michael Arnopol(b) Mark Walker(dm,perc).
(Chicago Recording Company) Chicago,January 6-8,1998
(leased from Premonition label)

Touch of trash -1
Winter -1
You and the night and the music
Constantinople -1,2
Light my fire -1
Silent partner -1
Company -1
Let it rain
She's a lady
Love,put on your faces -3
Postmodern blues
Let it rain,vamp -3

-2: Jeff Stitely(udu) added.
-3: Choral Thunder Vocal Choir added,arr. by Bryan P. Johnson,Lucy Smith & Shelby Webb Jr.
All titles issued on CD BN/Premonition 5-21811-2.

D.I.G.:
Rick Robertson(sax,fl) Scott Saunders(keyb) Tim Rollinson(g) Samuel Dixon(b) Terepai Richmond (dm,perc) Dana Diaz-Tutaan,Trey,Shorti(vo-1)
(leased from Directions In Groove Ltd) Australia, 1998

Upside (alt)-1 CD BN(Au)4-97893-2
Antimatter -

"LULU ON THE BRIDGE":
(Original score leased from Redeemable Pictures)
Mira Sorvino(vo).
(Pilot Recording) NYC,June,1998

Close your eyes CD BN 4-95317-2

Paul Auster(sound effects)

Voices from box CD BN 4-95317-2

Unknown orchestra,Graeme Revell(arr,cond,comp).

The blue light
On the roof
Goodbye, celia
Finale

All titles issued on CD BN 4-95317-2.

CHRIS MINH DOKY - MINH:
Chris Minh Doky(arr) with (coll.): David Sanborn,Michael Brecker,Randy Brecker,Hiram Bullock,Mike Stern,David Gilmore,Louis Winsberg,Joe Caro,Chris Parks,St. Paul,Ricky P.,Lalah Hathaway,Dianne Reeves,Joey Calderazzo,Jim Beard,Larry Goldings,Lasse Jansson,Lenny White,Alex Riel,Norbert Lucarain, Adam Nussbaum,Michael Bland (see details below).

(leased from Horipro,Inc.)		1998
(Focus Recording)	Copenhagen,	1998
(Seedy Underbelly)	Minneapolis,	1998
(Intermedia)	NYC,	1998
(C.P. Productions)	NYC,	1998
(Sound on Sound)	NYC,	1998

Ricky P.(Hammond org,keyb) St. Paul(g,cymbals) Chris Minh Doky(b) Michael Bland(dm).
1998

I told you so — CD EMI/BN 4-94664-2

Michael Brecker(ts)Ricky P.(p,keyb) Chris Minh Doky(b) St. Paul(dm) Dianne Reeves(vo).

Every breath you take — CD EMI/BN 4-94664-2
Welcome — -

Joey Calderazzo(p) Chris Parks(keyb,programming) Chris Minh Doky(b,keyb) Lenny White(dm).

Waiting on you — CD EMI/BN 4-94664-2

Louis Winsberg(g) Chris Minh Doky(b) Norbert Lucarain(clay pot).

Sleepless dream — CD EMI/BN 4-94664-2

Larry Goldings(p) Chris Parks(g,dm,keyb,programming) Chris Minh Doky(b),keyb) Vivian Sessoms(vo)

Lean on me — CD EMI/BN 4-94664-2
Chhaya (voVS) — -

David Sanborn(as) Joey Calderazzo(p) Joe Caro(g) Chris Minh Doky(b) Lenny White(dm) Lalah Hathaway (vo).Arr. by Gino Vannelli.

I just wanna stop — CD EMI/BN 4-94664-2

Larry Goldings(p) Mike Stern(el g) David Gilmore(g) Chris Minh Doky(b) Adam Nussbaum(dm).

A new day — CD EMI/BN 4-94664-2
Ken & Mai — -

Lasse Jansson(p) Chris Minh Doky(b) Alex Riel(dm).
(Focus Recording) — Copenhagen, 1998

It once was — CD EMI/BN 4-94664-2

Jim Beard(synth) Louis Winsberg(g) Chris Minh Doky(b) Norbert Lucarain(wood box).

Mardi chez Lionel — CD EMI/BN 4-94664-2
Messages — -

Ricky P.(p,Hammond org,keyb) Hiram Bullock(g) Chris Minh Doky(b) St. Paul(dm,programming).

Home sweet home — CD EMI/BN 4-94664-2
New York City — -

CHRIS MINH DOKY - MINH:
Randy Brecker(tp,lead vo) Larry Goldings(p) Chris Parks(g,dm,programming) Chris Minh Doky(el b,b,vo) Vivian Sessoms(vo) Kayoko Suzuki Lange(Japanese voice).

Don't get funny with my money CD EMI/BN 4-94664-2

THIERRY LANG - NAN:
Hugo Read(sax) Daniel Pezzotti(cello) Thierry Lang(p) Heiri Känzig(b) Marcel Papaux(dm).
(leased from I.D. Records)
(Rainbow Studio) Oslo,November 8,9 & 11,1998

Nan
The long and winding road
Requiem
The moon under water
Oslo
Only wood
Tchoo-tchoo
Softly as in a morning sunrise
A star to my father

All titles issued on CD BN(Eu)4-98492-2.

MARC JORDAN - THIS IS HOW MEN CRY:
(all titles leased from Cafe Productions,Inc.)
Marc Jordan(vo) with Don Byron(cl) Hugh Marsh(el v) Steven MacKinnon(keyb) Richard Armin(cello) Aruna Narayan Kalle(sarang).
(Reaction Studios) Toronto,Canada,December 14-20,1998

This is how men cry CD BN(C)5-20419-2

Marc Jordan(vo) with David Travers-Smith(tp) John Capek(p,b,keyb) Richard Armin(cello) Kevan McKenzie (dm) Sue-Ann Carwell(backgr. vo). Same sessions

Charlie Parker loves me CD BN(C)5-20419-2

Marc Jordan(vo) with Phil Dwyer(p) Tom Szczesniak(acc) Kieran Overs(b) Archie Alleyne(dm).
Same sessions

Crazy CD BN(C)5-20419-2

Marc Jordan(vo) with Chase Sanborn(tp) Guido Basso(flh) Josh Brown(tb) John Johnson(alto fl) Bob Leonard(bass cl) Colleen Allen,Kirk MacDonald(ts) Phil Dwyer(p,bs,ss) James McCollum (nylon string g) Kevin Breit(g) Kieran Overs(b) Kevan McKenzie(dm).
Same sessions

Slow bombing the world CD BN(C)5-20419-2

Marc Jordan(vo) with Toots Thielemans(hca) Phil Dwyer(p) Tom Szczesniak(acc) Scott Alexander(b) Kevan McKenzie(dm). Same sessions

I must have left my heart CD BN(C)5-20419-2

Marc Jordan(vo) with Kevin Turcotte(tp) Michael White(ambient tp) Hugh Marsh(el v) Steven MacKinnon(p) Kevin Breit(g) Scott Alexander(b) Kevan McKenzie(dm).
Same sessions

Let's get lost CD BN(C)5-20419-2

MARC JORDAN - THIS IS HOW MEN CRY:
(all titles leased from Cafe Productions,Inc.)
Marc Jordan(vo) with Chase Sanborn(tp) Guido Basso(frh) Josh Brown(tb) John Johnson(alto fl) Phil Dwyer(ss) Colleen Allen(ts) Kirk MacDonald(ts solo) Bob Leonard(bass cl) Steven MacKinnon(p) Kevin Breit(guit-organ) James McCollum(nylon string g)George Koller(b) Mark Kelso(dm).
Same sessions

London in the rain CD BN(C)5-20419-2

Marc Jordan(vo) with Tom Szczesniak(p,acc) Scott Alexander(b).
(Inception Sound Studio) Toronto,Canada,c. early 1999

Let it be me CD BN(C)5-20419-2

Marc Jordan(vo) with Kirk MacDonald(ts) Dave Restivo(p) George Koller(b) Mark Kelso(dm,djembe).
(McClear Studios) Toronto,Canada,c. early 1999

Almost blue CD BN(C)5-20419-2

MALCOLM BRAFF - TOGETHER:
Mattthieu Michel(tp,flh) Malcolm Braff(p) Banz Oester(b) Olivier Clerc(dm) Yaya Ouattara(perc,vo).
(leased from Kameleon Music) 1999

Rhetorical dance
Koka Nyami (voYO)
Nyouman
Nakan
Lelwa
Together
Djougou
Djougou ya

All titles issued on CD BN(F) 5-20676-2.

PATRICIA BARBER - COMPANION:
Patricia Barber(p,org,vo) John McLean(g) Michael Arnopol(b) Eric Montzka(dm) Ruben P. Alvarez(perc) Jason Narducy(vo-1).
(Live,The Green Mill) Chicago,July 17-19,1999

The best goes on
Use me
So what
Rhythming
Touch of trash -1
If this isn't jazz
Black magic woman

All titles issued on CD BN/Premonition 5-22963-2.

662

ST. GERMAIN - TOURIST:
Coll.: Ludovic Navarre (as "St. Germain")(mixer,vo) Pascal Ohze(tp) Edouard Labor(fl,ts) Claudio De Geiro (bs) Alexandre Destrez (keyb) Edmondo Carneiro(dm,perc) with vb-1,cga-2 & guest artist Idrissa Diop (talking dm).
(leased from Primary Society)(Magic House Studio) Paris,August-December 1999

Rose rouge
Montego Bay spleen -3
So flute
Land of...
Latin note -1,2
Sure thing -3
Pont des Arts -3
La Goutte d'Or -1

-3: Ernest Ranglin(g) unknown(cga) added.
All titles issued on BN(F)5-25114-2,CD 5-25114-2,5-26201-2.

JANE BUNNETT AND THE SPIRITS OF HAVANA - RITMO & SOUL:
Larry Cramer(tp) Jane Bunnett(fl,bass fl,ss) Hilario Duran(p,vo) Roberto Occhipinti(b) Dafnis Prieto(dm) Pancho Quinto(cajones,cga,bata dm,vo) Lucumi(cga,bata dm) Ernesto "El Gato" Gatell(bata dm-1,vo) Jacko Backo(kalimba-2,vo) Dean Bowman(vo).
(leased from Bunnett-Cramer)(Wellesley Sound Studio) Toronto,Canada,September 19-21,1999

Joyful noise (voEG,DB,JB) (p,Lucumi out)
The river/El rio (voEG,DB)
Osain (tp out)
Drume negrita (voEG)-1
Journey back (voDB)-1
Three voices,one spirit (voEG,JB)-2
Hebioso (voHD,EG)
Francisco's dream (Prieto out)-1

All titles issued on CD BN 5-24456-2.

Part 7
Single Numerical Listings

78 RPM SERIES

BLUE NOTE label (12 in. Series)

Issue Number	Artist	Title Number	Master	Page
BN-				
1	MEADE LUX LEWIS	Melancholy	443-12	1
		Solitude	444-11	1
2	ALBERT AMMONS	Boogie woogie stomp	441-5	1
		Boogie woogie blues	442-8	1
3	PORT OF HARLEM JAZZMEN	Mighty blues	GM 516-2	2
		Rocking the blues	GM 517-1	2
4	ALBERT AMMONS	Chicago in mind	GM 535	1
	A. AMMONS & MEADE LUX LEWIS	Two and fews	GM 537-17	2
5	EARL 'FATHA' HINES	The Father's getaway	GM 301x3	3
		Reminiscing at Blue Note	GM 302x2	3
6	SIDNEY BECHET QUINTET	Summertime	GM 533-14	3
	PORT OF HARLEM SEVEN	Pounding heart blues	GM 536-11	3
7	PORT OF HARLEM SEVEN	Blues for Tommy	GM 532x10	2
	J.C.HIGGINBOTHAM QUINTET	Basin Street blues	GM 532B	2
8	MEADE LUX LEWIS	The blues,pt.1	486A-1	1
		The blues,pt.2	486A-2	1
9	MEADE LUX LEWIS	The blues,pt.3	486A-3	1
		The blues,pt.4	486A-4	1
10	PETE JOHNSON BLUES TRIO	Barrelhouse breakdown	RS 659-7	4
		Kansas City farewell	RS 660-8	4
11	PETE JOHNSON BLUES TRIO	Vine Street bustle	RS 653-1	4
		Some day blues	RS 655-3	4
12	PETE JOHNSON	Holler stomp	RS 658-6	4
		You don't know my mind	RS 662-10	4
13	SIDNEY BECHET QUARTET	Lonesome blues	RS 709B	4
		Dear old Southland	RS 710A	4
14	PORT OF HARLEM JAZZMEN	Port of Harlem blues	GM515-A5	2
	FRANK NEWTON QUINTET	After hour blues	GM 531	2
15	MEADE LUX LEWIS	Honky tonk train blues	RS 791B	5
		Tell your story	RS 794A	5
16	MEADE LUX LEWIS	Bass on top	RS 792C	5
		Six wheel chaser	RS 793A	5
17	EDMOND HALL CELESTE QT.	Profoundly blue	R 3461	5
		Celestial express	R 3462A	5
18	EDMOND HALL	Jamming in four	R 3459A	5
		Edmond Hall blues	R 3460	5
19	MEADE LUX LEWIS	19 ways of playing a chorus	RS 934B	5
		Self portrait	RS 937A	5
20	MEADE LUX LEWIS	School of rhythm	RS 935B	5
		Feeling tomorrow like I feel	RS 938A	5
21	ALBERT AMMONS	Suitcase blues	1007	1
		Bass goin' crazy	1014	1
22	MEADE LUX LEWIS	Tell your story No.2	RS 794B	5
		Rising tide blues	BN 639	5

23	JOSH WHITE TRIO	Careless love blues	RS 671A	4
		Milk cow blues	RS 672	4
24	JAMES P.JOHNSON	J.P.Boogie	BN 777	6
		Gut stomp	BN 780	6
25	JAMES P.JOHNSON	Backwater blues	BN 778	6
		Carolina Balmoral	BN 779	6
26	JAMES P.JOHNSON	Caprice rag	BN 783	6
		Improvisation on Pinetop's..	BN 784	6
27	JAMES P.JOHNSON	Mule walk	BN 781	6
		Arkansas blues	BN 782	6
28	EDMOND HALL'S BLUE NOTE	High society	BN 901-2	6
	JAZZMEN	Blues at Blue Note	BN 903-1	6
29	EDMOND HALL'S BLUE NOTE	Night shift blues	BN 905-2	6
	JAZZMEN	Royal garden blues	BN 907-2	6
30	EDMOND HALL'S ALL STAR FIVE	Romping in 44	BN 908-2	7
		Smooth sailing	BN 910-2	7
31	EDMOND HALL'S ALL STAR FIVE	Blue interval	BN 909	7
		Seeing red	BN 911	7
32	JAMES P.JOHNSON'S BLUE NOTE	Blue mizz	BN 950-1	7
	JAZZMEN	Victory stride	BN 951-3	7
33	JAMES P.JOHNSON'S BLUE NOTE	Joy mentin'	BN 952-2	7
	JAZZMEN	After you've gone	BN 953-2	7
34	ART HODES' BLUE NOTE	Sweet Georgia Brown	BN 977	9
	JAZZMEN	Sugar foot stomp	BN 979-1	9
35	ART HODES' BLUE NOTE	Squeeze me	BN 978	9
	JAZZMEN	Bugle call rag	BN 980-1	9
36	EDMOND HALL'S SWINGTET	Big city blues	BN 975-1	8
		Steamin' and beamin'	BN 976-1	8
37	IKE QUEBEC FIVE	Tiny's exercise	BN 985-1	10
		Blue Harlem	BN 988-1	10
38	IKE QUEBEC FIVE	She's funny that way	BN 986	10
		Indiana	BN 987-2	10
39	MEADE LUX LEWIS	Chicago flyer	BN 1202	10
		Blues whistle	BN 1203	10
40	SIDNEY DE PARIS' BLUE NOTE	Everybody loves my baby	BN 981	9
	JAZZMEN	The call of the blues	BN 984	9
41	SIDNEY DE PARIS' BLUE NOTE	Ballin' the jack	BN 982	9
	JAZZMEN	Who's sorry now	BN 983-1	9
42	IKE QUEBEC SWINGTET	Mad about you	BN 991	10
		Facin' the face	BN 992-1	10
43	SIDNEY BECHET BLUE NOTE	Blue horizon	BN 208	12
	JAZZMEN	Muskrat ramble	BN 209	12
44	SIDNEY BECHET BLUE NOTE	Saint Louis blues	BN 206-1	12
	JAZZMEN	Jazz me blues	BN 207-3	12
45	ART HODES' BLUE FIVE	Apex blues	BN 201-1	11
		Shake that thing	BN 202-1	11
46	BENNY MORTON'S ALL STARS	Conversing in blue	BN 220	13
		The Sheik of Araby	BN 221	13
47	BENNY MORTON'S ALL STARS	My old flame	BN 219	13
		Limehouse blues	BN 222	13
48	"PIGMEAT" ALAMO MARKHAM	Blues before sunrise	BN 254-2	15
		How long,how long blues	BN 256	15
49	SIDNEY BECHET'S BLUE NOTE	Salty dog	BN 216-2	12
	JAZZMEN	Weary blues	BN 217-1	12
50	SIDNEY BECHET'S BLUE NOTE	High society	BN 215-1	12
	JAZZMEN	Jackass blues	BN 218-2	12
51	ART HODES TRIO	K.M.H. Drag	BN 230	13
		Funny feathers	BN 231-1	13
52/53: not released				
54	BECHET-NICHOLAS BLUE FIVE	Old stack o'Lee blues	BN 277-1	17
		Bechet's fantasy	BN 278-3	17

665

BLUE NOTE label (10 in. Series)

501	FRANK NEWTON QUINTET	Daybreak blues	GM 512A-6	2
	J.C.HIGGINBOTHAM QUINTET	Weary land blues	GM 513-A-5	2
502	SIDNEY BECHET'S	Bechet's steady river	RS 711A	4
	BLUE NOTE QUARTET	Saturday night blues	RS 712A	4
503	TEDDY BUNN	King Porter stomp	RS 713A	4
		Bachelor blues	RS 714A	4
504	TEDDY BUNN	Blues without words	RS 715B	4
		Guitar in high	RS 716A	4
505	ART HODES	Maple leaf rag	BN 960	7
	and his Chicagoans	Yellow dog blues	BN 962	7
506	ART HODES	She's crying for me	BN 961-1	7
	and his Chicagoans	Slow 'em down blues	BN 963-1	7
507	ART HODES	Doctor Jazz	BN 964-2	8
	and his Chicagoans	Shoe shiner's drag	BN 965	8
508	ART HODES	There'll be some changes made	BN 966-4	8
	and his Chicagoans	Clark and Randolph	BN 967	8
509	PIGMEAT ALAMO MARKHAM	You've been a good ol' wago	BN 255-1	15
	with Rev. O.Mesheux	See see rider	BN 257-1	15
510	IKE QUEBEC SWINGTET	Hard tack	BN 989	10
		If I had you	BN 990-1	10
511	EDMOND HALL SWINGTET	It's been so long	BN 973-3	8
		I can't believe that you're in love with me	BN 974-1	8
512	ORIGINAL ART HODES TRIO	Eccentric	BN 229-4	13
		Blues 'n' booze	BN 232	13
513	JOHN HARDEE'S SWINGTET	Tired	BN 280	17
		Blue skies	BN 281	17
514	JOHN HARDEE'S SWINGTET	Hardee's party	BN 282	17
		Idaho	BN 283-5	17
515	IKE QUEBEC SWING SEVEN	Topsy	BN 248-1	15
		Cup-mute Clayton	BN 249	15
516	IKE QUEBEC QUINTET	Dolores	BN 234-1	14
		Sweethearts on parade	BN 236-3	14
517	BECHET-NICHOLAS BLUE FIVE	Quincy Street stomp	BN 276-1	17
		Weary way blues	BN 279-2	17
518	BABY DODDS' JAZZ FOUR	Careless love	BN 273-1	16
		Winin' boy blues	BN 275	16
519	BABY DODDS' JAZZ FOUR	Feelin' at ease	BN 272-2	16
		High society	BN 274-2	16
520	JOHN HARDEE'S SEXTET	What is this thing called love	BN 284-1	17
		Nervous from the service	BN 285-1	17
521	JOHN HARDEE'S SEXTET	Sweet and lovely	BN 287	17
		River edge rock	BN 286-4	17
522	SAMMY BENSKIN TRIO	Cherry	BN 250-2	15
		The world is waiting for the sunrise	BN 252	15
523	not released			
524	TINY GRIMES' SWINGTET	Flying home,pt.1	BN 289-1	18
		Flying home,pt.2	BN 290-1	18
525	TINY GRIMES' SWINGTET	C jam blues	BN 288-3	18
		Tiny's boogie woogie	BN 291-2	18
526	ART HODES BACK ROOM BOYS	Low down blues	BN 969	8
		Back room blues	BN 972	8
527	ART HODES BACK ROOM BOYS	M.K. Blues	BN 968-1	8
		Jug head boogie	BN 970-1	8
528	ART HODES' BLUE FIVE	Gutbucket blues	BN 200	11
		Nobody's sweetheart	BN 204	11
529	not released			

530	JIMMY SHIRLEY	Jimmy's blues	BN 214	12
	T-BONE WALKER	T-Bone blues	1852-1	445
531	ART HODES' HOT FIVE	Save it pretty Mama	BN 262-1	16
		Darktown strutter's ball	BN 267	16
532	ART HODES' HOT FIVE	Memphis blues	BN 264-1	16
		Shine	BN 265	16
533	ART HODES' HOT FIVE	Way down yonder in N.O.	BN 263-1	16
		Saint James infirmary	BN 266-1	16
534	BABS' THREE BIPS AND A BOP	Oop-pop-a-da	BN 297-1	18
		Stomping at the Savoy	BN 298-3	18
535	BABS' THREE BIPS AND A BOP	Lop-pow	BN 296-1	18
		Pay dem blues	BN 299-2	18
536	BABS' THREE BIPS AND A BOP	Dob bla bli	BN 302-3	18
		Weird lullaby	BN 303-1	18
537	BABS' THREE BIPS AND A BOP	Runnin' around	BN 300-3	18
		Babs' dream	BN 301-5	18
538	IKE QUEBEC SWING SEVEN	Someone to watch over me	BN 294-1	18
		Zig billion	BN 295-4	18
539	IKE QUEBEC SWING SEVEN	The masquerade is over	BN 292-4	18
		Basically blue	BN 293-2	18
540	TADD DAMERON SEXTET	The squirrel	BN 305-1	19
		Our delight	BN 306-5	19
541	TADD DAMERON SEXTET	The chase	BN 304-2	19
		Dameronia	BN 307-2	19
542	THELONIOUS MONK SEXTET	Suburban eyes	BN 310-1	19
		Thelonious	BN 311	19
543	THELONIOUS MONK SEXTET	Well you needn't	BN 314	20
		Round about midnight	BN 321-1	21
544	IKE QUEBEC	Blue Harlem,pt.1	BN 1206	10
		Blue Harlem,pt.2	BN 1207	10
545	ART BLAKEY'S MESSENGERS	The thin man	BN 322-3	21
		Musa's vision	BN 325-1	21
546	ART BLAKEY'S MESSENGERS	Bop alley	BN 323-1	21
		Groove Street	BN 324-2	21
547	THELONIOUS MONK SEXTET	Evonce	BN 309-4	19
	THELONIOUS MONK TRIO	Off minor	BN 317-1	20
548	THELONIOUS MONK QUINTET	In walked Bud	BN 318-3	21
	THELONIOUS MONK QUARTET	Epistrophy	BN 330	22
549	THELONIOUS MONK TRIO	Ruby my dear	BN 313-1	20
	THELONIOUS MONK QUARTET	Evidence	BN 28	22
550	ART HODES' HOT SEVEN	Wolverine blues	BN 241	14
		Bujie blues	BN 245	14
551	ART HODES' HOT SEVEN	I never knew what a gal could do	BN 238-3	14
		Mr.Jelly Lord	BN 239-1	14
552	ART HODES' HOT SEVEN	Chacgo gal	BN 237-1	14
		Willie the weeper	BN 244-2	14
553	JAMES MOODY'S MODERNISTS	The Fuller bop man	BN 340-4	23
		Tropicana	BN 344	23
554	JAMES MOODY'S MODERNISTS	Moodamorphosis	BN 343-2	23
		Cu-ba	BN 345-1	23
555	JAMES MOODY'S MODERNISTS	Oh,Henry	BN 342-2	23
		Tin tin deo	BN 347	23
556	JAMES MOODY'S MODERNISTS	Workshop	BN 341	23
		Moody's all frantic	BN 346	23
557	HOWARD McGHEE BOPTET	Double talk,pt.1	BN 338A	23
		Double talk,pt.2	BN 338B	23
558	HOWARD McGHEE BOPTET	The skunk	BN 336-2	23
		Boperation	BN 337-1	23
559	TADD DAMERON SEPTET	Jahbero	BN 332-1	22
		Lady Bird	BN 333-0	22

667

560	THELONIOUS MONK	Humph	BN 308-2	19
		Misterioso	BN 329	22
561	SIDNEY BECHET'S BLUE NOTE JAZZMEN	Tin roof blues	BN 350	24
		At the jazz band ball	BN 357-2	24
562	SIDNEY BECHET'S BLUE NOTE JAZZMEN	Tiger rag	BN 349-2	24
		Cake walking babies	BN 355-1	24
563	SIDNEY BECHET'S BLUE NOTE JAZZMEN	When the Saints go marching in	BN 353-1	24
		Basin Street blues	BN 354	24
564	BUNK JOHNSON & SIDNEY BECHET	Milenberg joys	BN 223-1	13
		Days beyond recall	BN 226	13
565	BUNK JOHNSON & SIDNEY BECHET	Lord let me in the lifeboat	BN 225	13
		Up in Sidney's flat	BN 28-1	13
566	SIDNEY BECHET & CLAUDE LUTER ORCH.	Struttin' with some barbecue	V3033	639
		See see rider	V3020	639
567	SIDNEY BECHET & CLAUDE LUTER ORCH.	Temptation blues	V3029	639
		Sobbin' and cryin'	V3031	639
568	SIDNEY BECHET & CLAUDE LUTER ORCH.	Riverboat shuffle	V3030	639
		Saw mill blues	V3034	639
569 (not released)	SIDNEY BECHET & CLAUDE LUTER ORCH.	Ce mossieu qui parle	V3015	639
		Bechet creole blues	V3034	639
570	SIDNEY BECHET & CLAUDE LUTER ORCH.	Buddy Bolden's story	V3016	639
		The onions	V3019	639
571	SIDNEY BECHET'S BLUE NOTE JAZZMEN	Nobody knows you when you're down & out	BN 352-1	24
		Fidgety feet	BN 359	24
572	SIDNEY BECHET'S BLUE NOTE JAZZMEN	Copenhagen	BN 376-4	26
		Shim-me-sha-wabble	BN 381-2	26
573	SIDNEY BECHET'S BLUE NOTE JAZZMEN	China boy	BN 377-1	26
		Sister Kate	BN 348-2	24
1201	THELONIOUS MONK	All the things you are	BN 326-3	22
		I should care	BN 327-2	22
1202	CLYDE BERNHARDT	Cracklin' bread	BN 366	25
		Meet me on the corner	BN 367	25
1203	CLYDE BERNHARDT	Don't tell it	BN 368	25
		Chattanooga	BN 369	25
1564	THELONOUS MONK QUARTET	I mean you	BN 331-1	22
	TADD DAMERON SEPTET	Symphonette	BN 334-1	22
1565	THELONIOUS MONK QUINTET	Monk's moods	BN 319	21
		Who knows	BN 320	21
1566	BUD POWELL TRIO	You go to my head	BN 364	25
		Ornithology	BN 365	25
1567	BUD POWELL QUINTET	Bouncing with Bud	BN 360-2	25
		Wail	BN 361-3	25
1568	BUD POWELL QUINTET	Dance of the infidels	BN 362-1	25
		52nd Street theme	BN 363-1	25
1569	MAX ROACH QUINTET	Prince Albert,pt.1	V3010A	639
		Prince Albert,pt.2	V3010B	639
1570	MAX ROACH QUINTET	Maximum	V3013	639
	JAMES MOODY QUARTET	Just Moody	V3004	638
1571	MAX ROACH QUINTET	Tomorrow,pt.1	V3012A	639
		Tomorrow,pt.2	V3012B	639
1572	HOWARD McGHEE ALL STARS	Fuguetta	BN 371-1	26
		I'll remember April	BN 375-1	26
1573	HOWARD McGHEE ALL STARS	Fluid drive	BN 372	26
		Donellon Square	BN 374	26
1574	HOWARD McGHEE ALL STARS	Lo-flame	BN 370-2	26
		Meciendo	BN 373	26
1575	THELONIOUS MONK TRIO	Nice work if you can get it	BN 312-1	20
		April in Paris	BN 315-1	20

1576	BUD POWELL TRIO	Over the rainbow	BN 383	27
		Night in Tunisia	BN 384	27
1577	BUD POWELL TRIO	Un poco loco	BN 382-4	27
		It could happen to you	BN 385-1	27
1578	WYNTON KELLY	Born to be blue	BN 403-1	29
		Where or when	BN 404	29
1579	WYNTON KELLY	Moonglow	BN 405	29
		Cherokee	BN 402-1	29
1580	WYNTON KELLY	Summertime	BN 412-1	29
		Crazy he calls me	BN 414-1	29
1581	WYNTON KELLY	Goodbye	BN 408	29
		Blue moon	BN 399-1	29
1582/84:not released				
1585	JAMES MOODY WITH STRINGS	Singing for you	51V4059	639
		Shades of blonde	51V4060	639
1586	JAMES MOODY WITH STRINGS	So very pretty	51V4058	639
		September serenade	51V4062	639
1587	JAMES MOODY WITH STRINGS	Bedelia	51V4056	639
		Jackie my little cat	51V4061	639
1588	JAMES MOODY WITH STRINGS	Loving you the way I do	51V4055	639
		Autumn leaves	51V4057	639
1589	THELONIOUS MONK QUINTET	Four in one	BN 392-1	28
		Straight no chaser	BN 395-1	28
1590	THELONIOUS MONK QUINTET	Criss cross	BN 393	28
		Eronel	BN 394	28
1591	THELONIOUS MONK	Ask me now	BN 396-1	28
		Willow weep for me	BN 397-2	28
1592	MILT JACKSON QUINTET	Tahiti	BN 422	30
		What's new	BN 425-3	30
1593	MILT JACKSON QUINTET	Bags' groove	BN 424-2	30
		Lillie	BN 423-1	30
1594	LOU DONALDSON QUINTET	Don't get around	BN 426	30
		On the scene	BN 427	30
1595	MILES DAVIS AND HIS SEXTET	Dear old Stockholm	BN 428-1	31
		Woody'n you	BN 431-3	31
1596	MILES DAVIS AND HIS SEXTET	Chance it	BN 429-3	31
		Yesterdays	BN 432	31
1597	MILES DAVIS AND HIS SEXTET	Donna	BN 430-1	31
	TADD DAMERON	The squirrel	BN 305	19
1598	LOU DONALDSON QUARTET	Roccus	BN 440-1	32
		Cheek to cheek	BN 442-4	32
1599	LOU DONALDSON QUARTET	The things we did last Summer	BN 441-2	32
		Lou's blues	BN 443-1	32
1600	VIC DICKENSON	Lion's den	BN 446-3	32
		Tenderly	BN 444-2	32
1601	VIC DICKENSON	In a mellow tone	BN 447-3	32
		Gettin' sentimental over you	BN 445-1	32
1602	THELONIOUS MONK	Skippy	BN 434-1	32
		Let's cool one	BN 438	32
1603	THELONIOUS MONK	Hornin' in	BN 435-3	32
		Carolina moon	BN 437	32
1604	SWINGIN' SWEDES	Cream of the crop,pt.1	2186	640
		Cream of the crop,pt.2	2187	640
1605	SWINGIN' SWEDES	Summertime	2188	640
		Pick yourself up	2189	640
1606	GIL MELLE SEXTET	The gears	BN 461-3	450
		Four moons	BN 462-3	450
1607	GIL MELLE SEXTET	Sunset concerto	BN 464	450
		Mars	BN 463	450

 669

1608	HORACE SILVER	Safari	BN 449-1	33
		Thou swell	BN 450-6	33
1609	LOU DONALDSON	Sweet juice	BN 457	33
		The best things in life are free	BN 460-1	33
1610	LOU DONALDSON	If I love again	BN 458-5	33
		Down home	BN 459-1	33
1611	THE COOL BRITONS	Birdland bounce	SSS 7-126	639
		Leapin' in London	SSS 7-127	639
1612	THE COOL BRITONS	Cherokee	117	639
		Tea for me	116	639
1613	DIZZY GILLESPIE JAZZ ENSEMBLE	Lady Bird	52V4225	641
		Sweet Lorraine	52V4229	641
1614	DIZZY GILLESPIE JAZZ ENSEMBLE	Hurry home	52V4210	640
		Afro Paris	52V4211	640
1615	DIZZY GILLESPIE	Everything happens to me	52V4230	641
		Say eh	52V4212	640
1616	DIZZY GILLESPIE	Wrap your troubles in dreams	52V4228	641
		She's funny that way	52V4227	640
1617	DIZZY GILLESPIE	C C C blues	52V4224	641
		Somebody loves me	52V4226	641
1618	MILES DAVIS	Tempus fug it	BN 480	34
		Enigma	BN 478-2	34
1619	MILES DAVIS	Ray's idea	BN 479-2	34
		I waited for you	BN 482	34
1620	MILES DAVIS	Kelo	BN 477-2	34
		C.T.A.	BN 481-3	34
1621	JAY JAY JOHNSON	Capri	BN 503-3	36
		Turnpike	BN 505	36
1622	LOU DONALDSON	Brownie speaks	BN 492	35
		You go to my head	BN 494	35
1623	LOU DONALDSON	Cookin'	BN 491-1	35
		Bellarosa	BN 489-1	35
1624	LOU DONALDSON	Carving the rock	BN 490-3	35
		Dee-dah	BN 493	35
1625	HORACE SILVER	Opus de funk	BN 534-2	39
		Day in,day out	BN 535-1	39
1626	ART BLAKEY	Nothing but the soul	BN 536	39
		Message from Kenya	BN 533	39
1627	URBIE GREEN	Skylark	BN 543	39
		Dansero	BN 545-2	39
1628	BUD POWELL	I want to be happy	BN 514-1	37
		The glass enclosure	BN 516	37
1629	BUD POWELL	Sure thing	BN 511-2	37
		Collard greens & black-eyed peas	BN 512-2	37

CLIMAX label

101	GEORGE LEWIS AND HIS NEW ORLEANS STOMPERS	Climax rag	CD 105	447
		Deep bayou blues	CD 123	448
102	GEORGE LEWIS AND HIS NEW ORLEANS STOMPERS	Milenberg joys	CD 118	447
		Two Jim blues	CD 104	447
103	GEORGE LEWIS AND HIS NEW ORLEANS STOMPERS	Just a closer walk with Thee	CD 107	447
		Just a little while to stay here	CD 114	447
104	GEORGE LEWIS AND HIS NEW ORLEANS STOMPERS	Fidgety feet	CD 119	447
		Dauphine Street blues	CD 113	447
105	GEORGE LEWIS AND HIS NEW ORLEANS STOMPERS	Don't go 'way nobody	CD 122	448
		Careless love blues	CD 111	447

670

78 RPM ALBUMS

BLUE NOTE label

BN 8/9	Meade Lux Lewis - The Blues (folder including BN 8 & BN 9)	1
101	John Hardee,Tenor Sax (= BN 514/520/521)	17
102	Ike Quebec Album,Tenor Sax (= BN 510/515/516)	10,14,15
103	Art Hodes' Hot Five (= BN 531/532/533)	16
104	A Monday Date At Blue Note - Art Hodes' Hot Seven (= BN 550/551/552)	14
105	Sidney Bechet and His Blue Note Jazzmen (= BN 561/562/563)	24

671

45 RPM SERIES

BLUE NOTE label

Note: Numbers marked nr were probably not released.
45-1626,1630 through 1955,1958 and 1963 were issued in mono.All others were released in stereo. Some of the later 45s (1945-1983) were issued with no prefix or with prefix BN or SBN (for stereo) rather than 45-, or with the suffix -S to denote stereo.There was no consistency to the practice.

Issue number	Artist	Title	Master number	Page
45-				
1626	ART BLAKEY	Nothing but the soul	BN 536	39
		Message from Kenya	BN 533	39
1630	HORACE SILVER & THE JAZZ MESSENGERS	The preacher		45
		Doodlin'		44
1631	HORACE SILVER & THE JAZZ MESSENGERS	Room 608		44
		Creepin' in		44
1632	JAY JAY JOHNSON	Pennies from heaven		48
		Groovin'		48
1633	MILES DAVIS	Well you needn't	BN 551	41
		Donna	BN 430	31
1634	CHARLIE CHRISTIAN-ED HALL	Profoundly blue	R 3461	5
	IKE QUEBEC	Blue Harlem	BN 988-1	10
1635	JIMMY SMITH	The high and the mighty		50
		You get 'cha		50
1636	JIMMY SMITH	Midnight sun		50
		The preacher		50
1637	JIMMY SMITH	Tenderly		50
		Joy		50
1638	BABS GONZALES with JIMMY SMITH TRIO	You need connections		51
		'Round about midnight		51
1639	JOHNNY GRIFFIN	Mil dew		52
		Chicago calling		52
1640	JOHNNY GRIFFIN	Nice and easy		52
		The boy next door		52
1641	JIMMY SMITH	The champ,pts.1 & 2		51
1642	JIMMY SMITH	Bubbis		51
		Bayou		51
1643	JIMMY SMITH	Judo mambo		55
		Autumn leaves		54
1644	JIMMY SMITH	Fiddlin' the minors		55
		Willow weep for me		54
1645	MILT JACKSON	What's new	BN 425-3	30
		Bags' groove	BN 424-2	30
1646	MILT JACKSON	Lillie	BN 423-1	30
		Willow weep for me	BN 397-2	28
1647	CLIFFORD BROWN	Brownie speaks	BN 492	35
		You go to my head	BN 494	35
1648	CLIFFORD BROWN	Hymn of the Orient	BN 524-1	38
		Easy living	BN 527	38
1649	MILES DAVIS	Tempus fug it	BN 480	34
		Lazy Susan		41
1650	MILES DAVIS	The leap		41
		Weirdo		41
1651	JAY JAY JOHNSON	Jay		43
		Old devil moon		43

1652	JIMMY SMITH	I cover the waterfront		55
		I can't give you anything but love		55
1653	KENNY BURRELL	Delilah		53
		This time the dream's on me		53
1654	HORACE SILVER QUINTET	Enchantment		58
		Camouflage		58
1655	HORACE SILVER QUINTET	Senor blues		58
		Cool eyes		58
1656	ART BLAKEY-CLIFFORD BROWN	Quicksilver		41
		Once in a while		40
1657	BLAKEY-BROWN-DONALDSON	Wee dot		41
		If I had you		40
1658	JULIUS WATKINS	Linda Delia		43
		I had known		43
1659	THAD JONES	April in Paris		55
		If someone had told me		55
1660	JIMMY SMITH	The new preacher,pts.1 & 2		56
1661	LEE MORGAN	Gaza strip		57
		Reggie of Chester		57
1662	LOU DONALDSON	Caravan		59
		Old folks		59
1663	LOU DONALDSON	L.D. Blues		59
		That good old feeling		59
1664	THELONIOUS MONK	'Round midnight	BN 321-1	21
		In walked Bud	BN 318-3	21
1665	JIMMY SMITH	Where or when,pts.1 & 2		56
1666	JIMMY SMITH	Love is a many splendored thing,pts.1 & 2		56
1667	JIMMY SMITH with	How high the moon		61
	LOU DONALDSON	Summertime		60
1668	JIMMY SMITH-LOU DONALDSON	Plum Nellie		60
		I'm getting sentimental over you		60
1669	SONNY ROLLINS	Decision,pts.1 & 2		59
1670	SONNY ROLLINS	Plain Jane,pts.1 & 2		59
1671	HANK MOBLEY	Lower stratosphere		59
		Reunion		59
1672	HORACE SILVER QUINTET	Home cookin'		64
		The back beat		64
1673	HORACE SILVER QUINTET	Soulville		64
		No smokin'		64
1674	KENNY BURRELL	D.B. blues		60
		K.B. blues		60
1675	HANK MOBLEY	Funk in deep freeze		62
		End of the affair		62
1676	JIMMY SMITH	All day long,pts.1 & 2		61
1677	JIMMY SMITH	Funk's oats,pts. 1 & 2		60
1678	BLAKEY-BROWN-DONALDSON	Now's the time,pts.1 & 2		40
1679	ART BLAKEY	Ya ya		62
		Meet me tonight		62
1680	LOU DONALDSON	Dorothy		65
		Peck time		65
1681	LOU DONALDSON	Herman's mambo		65
		Grits and gravy		65
1682	JIMMY SMITH	Penthouse serenade		64
		I can't get started		64
1683	JIMMY SMITH	East of the sun		64
		The very thought of you		64
1684	HANK MOBLEY	Bass on balls		62
		Stellawise		62
1685	JIMMY SMITH	Blue moon,pts.1 & 2		61
1686	JIMMY SMITH	There'll never be another you		61
		Jitterbug waltz		64

673

1687	SONNY ROLLINS	You stepped out of a dream	63
		Why don't I	63
1688 nr	HANK MOBLEY	Easy to love	63
		Time after time	63
1689 nr	CURTIS FULLER	Algonquin	68
		Pickup	68
1690	CURTIS FULLER	Oscalypso	66
		Hugore	66
1691	JOHN COLTRANE	Blue train,pts.1 & 2	71
1692	LEE MORGAN	A night in Tunisia,pts.1 & 2	72
1693	THE JAZZ MESSENGERS	Soft winds,pts.1 & 2	49
1694	not used		
1695	THE JAZZ MESSENGERS	Avila & Tequila,pts.1 & 2	49
1696	ART BLAKEY	Abdallah's delight	62
		Elephant walk	62
1697	SONNY CLARK	Sonny's crib,pts.1 & 2	70
1698	SONNY ROLLINS	Sonnymoon for two,pts.1 & 2	73
1699 nr	CLIFF JORDAN	Soul-lo blues,pts. 1 & 2	74
1700	LOUIS SMITH	Brill's blues,pts. 1 & 2	454
1701	LOUIS SMITH	Tribute to Brownie	454
		Star dust	454
1702 nr	CURTIS FULLER	Quantrale	75
		Two quarters of a mile	75
1703	JIMMY SMITH AT "SMALL'S PARADISE"	After hours,pts.1 & 2	74
1704	JIMMY SMITH AT "SMALL'S PARADISE"	Just friends	74
		Lover man	74
1705	HORACE SILVER QUINTET	Safari	76
		The outlaw	76
1706	BENNIE GREEN	I love you	80
		You're mine you	80
1707	BENNIE GREEN	Just friends	80
		Melba's mood	80
1708	BENNIE GREEN	Soul stirrin'	81
		That's all	81
1709	BENNIE GREEN	We wanna cook	81
		Lullaby of the doomed	81
1710	BILL HENDERSON SINGS with HORACE SILVER QUINTET	Senor blues	82
		Tippin'	82
1711	JIMMY SMITH	The swingin' shepherd blues	82
		Cha cha J	67
1712	BUD POWELL	Buster rides again	82
		Dry soul	82
1713	LOU DONALDSON	Sputnik,pts.1 & 2	76
1714	SONNY CLARK	Cool struttin',pts.1 & 2	76
1715	LOUIS SMITH	Smithville,pts.1 & 2	80
1716	KENNY BURRELL	Yes baby,pts.1 & 2	81
1717	KENNY BURRELL	Rock salt,pts.1 & 2	81
1718	JOHN COLTRANE	Moment's notice,pts.1 & 2	66
1719	JOHN COLTRANE-SONNY CLARK	Speak low	70
		Softly as in a morning sunrise	70
1720	LOU DONALDSON	Blues walk	83
		The masquerade is over	83
1721	LOU DONALDSON	Play Ray	83
		Autumn nocturne	83
1722	THE THREE SOUNDS	Tenderly	83
		Willow weep for me	83
1723	THE THREE SOUNDS	Both sides	83
		Mo-Ge	83
1724	THE THREE SOUNDS	It's nice	83
		Angel eyes	83

1725	THE THREE SOUNDS	Blue bells	84
		O sole mio	84
1726	THE THREE SOUNDS	Goin' home	84
		Time after time	84
1727	BILL HENDERSON sings with JIMMY SMITH TRIO	Ain't no use	84
		Angel eyes	84
1728	BILL HENDERSON sings with JIMMY SMITH TRIO	Ain't that love	84
		Willow weep for me	84
1729	SONNY CLARK TRIO	I can't give you anything but love	86
		The breeze and I	86
1730	SONNY CLARK TRIO	Lucky so and so	86
		Ain't no use	86
1731	SONNY CLARK TRIO	Gee baby	86
		Black velvet	86
1732	BENNIE GREEN	Bye bye blackbird	86
		On the street where you live	86
1733	BENNIE GREEN	Encore	86
		Ain't nothing but the blues	86
1734	BENNIE GREEN	Minor revelation	86
		Can't we be friends	86
1735	ART BLAKEY'S JAZZ MESSENGERS	Moanin',pts.1 & 2	85
1736	ART BLAKEY'S JAZZ MESSENGERS	Blues march	85
		Along came Betty	85
1737	CANNONBALL ADDERLEY'S FIVE STARS	Autumn leaves,pts.1 & 2	79
1738	CANNONBALL ADDERLEY'S FIVE STARS	Somethin' else,pts.1 & 2	79
1739	CANNONBALL ADDERLEY'S FIVE STARS	One for Daddy-O,pts.1 & 2	79
1740	HORACE SILVER QUINTET	Come on home	89
		Finger poppin'	89
1741	HORACE SILVER QUINTET	Juicy Lucy	89
		Cookin' at the Continental	89
1742	HORACE SILVER QUINTET	Swingin' the samba	89
		Mellow D	89
1743	THE THREE SOUNDS	Besame mucho	89
		Jenny Lou	89
1744	THE THREE SOUNDS	I could write a book	89
		Nothing ever changes my love for you	89
1745	LEON EASON	I'm in the mood for love	91
		Lazy river	91
1746 nr	LEON EASON	Song of the Islands	91
		Because of you	91
1747 nr	LEON EASON	That's my home	91
		I'm just a gigolo	91
1748	IKE QUEBEC	Dear John	92
		Blue Monday	92
1749	IKE QUEBEC	The buzzard lope	92
		Blue Friday	92
1750	HORACE SILVER QUINTET	Sister Sadie	94
		Break city	94
1751	HORACE SILVER QUINTET	Blowin' the blues away	94
		The Baghdad blues	94
1752	LOU DONALDSON	Mack the knife	96
		The nearness of you	96
1753	LOU DONALDSON	Be my love	96
		Lou's blues	96
1754	DUKE PEARSON	Gate city blues	96
		Black coffee	96

675

1755	DUKE PEARSON	Taboo	96
		Like someone in love	96
1756	THE THREE SOUNDS	Tracy's blue	91
		Don't blame me	91
1757	THE THREE SOUNDS	Down the track	91
		Robbin's nest	91
1758	THE THREE SOUNDS	That's all	91
		St. Thomas	91
1759	DIZZY REECE	The rake	97
		The rebound	97
1760	JACKIE McLEAN	What's new	96
		116th and Lenox	96
1761	SONNY RED	Stay as sweet as you are	97
		Bluesville	97
1762	SONNY RED	Alone too long	97
		Blues in the pocket	97
1763	DONALD BYRD	Here am I,pts.1 & 2	92
1764	DONALD BYRD	Fuego	95
		Amen	95
1765	JIMMY SMITH	Makin' whoopee	98
		What's new	98
1766	JIMMY SMITH	Mack the knife	98
		When Johnny comes marchin' home	98
1767	JIMMY SMITH	I got a woman	92
		Alfredo	98
1768	JIMMY SMITH	See see rider	92
		Come on baby	92
1769	JIMMY SMITH	Motorin' along	82
		Since I fell for you	82
1770	HORACE PARLAN	C jam blues	100
		Up in Cynthia's room	100
1771	HORACE PARLAN	Bags' groove	100
		There is no greater love	100
1772	LOU DONALDSON	Blue moon	89
		Smooth groove	89
1773	LOU DONALDSON	The truth	100
		Goose grease	99
1774	LOU DONALDSON	Politely	99
		Blues for J.P.	100
1775	ART BLAKEY'S JAZZ MESSENGERS	The chess players,pts.1 & 2	101
1776	JACKIE McLEAN	Greasy,pts.1 & 2	91
1777	DIZZY REECE	Ghost of a chance	103
		Blue streak	103
1778	HORACE PARLAN QUINTET	Wadin'	107
		Borderline	107
1779	FREDDIE HUBBARD	One mint julep	104
		Gypsy blue	104
1780	STANLEY TURRENTINE	Look out	104
		Journey into melody	104
1781	STANLEY TURRENTINE	Little Sheri	104
		Minor chant	104
1782	TINA BROOKS	Good old soul,pts.1 & 2	105
1783 nr	TINA BROOKS	True blue	105
		Theme for Doris	105
1784	HORACE SILVER QUINTET	Strollin'	106
		Nica's dream	106
1785	HORACE SILVER QUINTET	Me and my baby	106
		Where you at	106
1786	ART BLAKEY'S JAZZ MESSENGERS	Hipsippy blues,pts.1 & 2	90

1787	ART BLAKEY'S JAZZ MESSENGERS	Close your eyes,pts.1 & 2	90
1788	ART BLAKEY'S JAZZ MESSENGERS	Chicken 'n dumplins	90
		Hi-fly	90
1789	ART BLAKEY'S JAZZ MESSENGERS	It's only a paper moon	101
		Lester left town	101
1790	ART BLAKEY'S JAZZ MESSENGERS	Dat dere,pts.1 & 2	101
1791	THE THREE SOUNDS	Li'l darlin'	105
		Loose walk	105
1792	THE THEEE SOUNDS	I'm beginning to see the light	105
		Tammy's breeze	105
1793	THE THEEE SOUNDS	On Green Dolphin Street	105
		Love for sale	105
1794	THE THREE SOUNDS	Things ain't what they used to be,pts.1 & 2	105
1795	ART BLAKEY'S JAZZ MESSENGERS	So tired	109
		Yama	108
1796	ART BLAKEY'S JAZZ MESSENGERS	A night in Tunisia,pts.1 & 2	109
1797	HANK MOBLEY	Remember	99
		Dig this	99
1798	DONALD BYRD	Little boy blue	106
		Gate city	98
1799	DONALD BYRD	Bo	106
		Ghana	99
1800	ART TAYLOR	Cookoo & fungi	108
		Epistrophy	108
1801 nr	DUKE JORDAN	Starbrite	108
		Flight to Jordan	108
1802	IKE QUEBEC	I've got the world on a string	111
		What a difference a day made	111
1803	IKE QUEBEC	If I could be with you	111
		Me 'n Mabe	111
1804	IKE QUEBEC	Everything happens to me	111
		Mardi-Gras	111
1805 nr	IKE QUEBEC	For all we know	111
		Ill wind	111
1806	LOU DONALDSON	Hog maw	87
		Day dreams	87
1807	LOU DONALSON	Here 'Tis,pts.1 & 2	116
1808	LOU DONALSON	Watusi jump,pts.1 & 2	116
1809	FREDDIE HUBBARD	The changing scene	111
		I wished I knew	111
1810	FREDDIE HUBBARD	Osie Mae	120
		Cry me not	120
1811	GRANT GREEN	Miss Ann's tempo	116
		Ain't nobody's business if I do	116
1812	GRANT GREEN	A wee bit o' Green,pts.1 & 2	116
1813	STANLEY TURRENTINE	Gee baby,ain't I good to you	114
		Blue riff	114
1814	STANLEY TURRENTINE	Wee hour theme	124
		Baia	124
1815	"BABY FACE" WILLETTE	Swingin' at Sugar Ray's	117
		Something strange	117
1816	"BABY FACE" WILLETTE	Goin' down,pts.1 & 2	117
1817	HORACE SILVER QUINTET	Filthy McNasty,pts.1 & 2	122
1818	HORACE SILVER QUINTET	Doin' the thing,pts.1 & 2	122
1819	JIMMY SMITH	Midnight special,pts.1 & 2	103
1820	JIMMY SMITH	Jumpin' the blues	103
		One o'clock jump	103

677

1821	ART BLAKEY'S JAZZ MESSENGERS	What know,pts.1 & 2	110
1822	LEO PARKER	Blue Leo	126
		Let me tell you 'bout it	126
1823	LEO PARKER	Parker's pals	126
		Low Brown	126
1824	THE THREE SOUNDS	When I fall in love	105
		Parker's pad	105
1825	THE THREE SOUNDS	Here we come	114
		Our love is here to stay	114
1826	THE THREE SOUNDS	Now's the time	114
		Just squeeze me	114
1827	THE THREE SOUNDS	Broadway	114
		Summertime	114
1828	DEXTER GORDON	Soul sister,pts.1 & 2	122
1829	DEXTER GORDON	Ernie's tune	122
		Modal mood	122
1830	LOU DONALDSON	Gravy train,pts.1 & 2	121
1831	LOU DONALDSON	Polka dots and moonbeams	121
		South of the border	121
1832	LOU DONALDSON	Glory of love	121
		Avalon	121
1833 nr	LEO PARKER	The Lion's roar	128
		Bad girl	128
1834 nr	LEO PARKER	Rollin' with Leo	128
		Talkin' the blues	128
1835	HORACE PARLAN QUINTET	On the spur of the moment	119
		Ray C	119
1836 nr	IKE QUEBEC	Acquitted	129
		Just one more chance	129
1837	IKE QUEBEC	The man I love	129
		Heavy soul	129
1838	IKE QUEBEC	Nature boy	129
		Brother can you spare a dime	129
1839 nr	IKE QUEBEC	Que's dilemma	129
		I want a little girl	129
1840	IKE QUEBEC	Intermezzo	135
		All of me	135
1841 nr	IKE QUEBEC	All the way	135
		But not for me	135
1842	FRED JACKSON	Dippin' in the bag	134
		Hootin' and tootin'	134
1843	FRED JACKSON	Preach brother	134
		Easing on down	134
1844 nr	FRED JACKSON	Southern exposure,pts.1 & 2	134
1845	STANLEY TURRENTINE	Smile,Stacey,pts.1 & 2	132
1846	STANLEY TURRENTINE	Soft pedal blues,pts.1 & 2	132
1847 nr	STANLEY TURRENTINE	Pia	132
		Dorene don't cry,I	132
1848	STANLEY TURRENTINE	We'll see yaw'll after while,ya heah,pts.1 & 2	132
1849	ART BLAKEY AND THE AFRO DRUM ENSEMBLE	Ife L'ayo	133
		Obirin African	133
1850	ART BLAKEY'S JAZZ MESSENGERS	Contemplation	130
		Backstage Sally	131
1851	JIMMY SMITH	Ain't she sweet	133
		Everybody loves my baby	133
1852	JIMMY SMITH	Lulu's back in town	133
		Honeysuckle rose	133
1853	DONALD BYRD	Hush	127
		6 M's	127
1854 nr	DONALD BYRD	Jorgie's,pts.1 & 2	127

678

1855	THE THREE SOUNDS	You are my sunshine	125
		Nothin' but the blues	125
1856	THE THREE SOUNDS	Sermonette	125
		Dap's groove	125
1857	DODO GREENE	My hour of need	137
		I won't cry anymore	137
1858 nr	DODO GREENE	Trouble in mind	136
		Let there be love	136
1859	DODO GREENE	You are my sunshine	137
		Little things mean a lot	136
1860	DODO GREENE	Lonesome road	137
		There must be a way	137
1861 nr	DODO GREENE	I'll never stop lovin' you	137
		Down by the riverside	136
1862	HERBIE HANCOCK	Watermelon man	139
		Three bags full	139
1863	HERBIE HANCOCK	Driftin'	139
		Alone and I	139
1864	DON WILKERSON	Homesick blues	140
		Camp meeting	140
1865 nr	DON WILKERSON	Jeanie-Weanie	140
		Dem tambourines	140
1866 nr	IKE QUEBEC	Lover man	130
		A light reprieve	130
1867 nr	IKE QUEBEC	Easy don't hurt	130
		It might as well be Spring	130
1868	LOU DONALDSON	Funky Mama,pts.1& 2	138
1869 nr	LOU DONALDSON	That's all,pts.1 & 2	138
1870 nr	GRANT GREEN	Mambo inn	137
		Besame mucho	137
1871	HORACE SILVER	The Tokyo blues,pts.1 & 2	141
1872	HORACE SILVER	Sayonara blues,pts.1 & 2	141
1873	HORACE SILVER	Too much saki,pts.1 & 2	141
1874	IKE QUEBEC	Loie	143
		Lloro tu despedita	143
1875	IKE QUEBEC	Liebestraum	143
		Shu shu	143
1876	IKE QUEBEC	Blue samba,pts.1 & 2	143
1877	JIMMY SMITH	Back at the chicken shack,pts.1 & 2	103
1878	JIMMY SMITH	Minor chant,pts.1 & 2	102
1879	JIMMY SMITH	The sermon,pts.1 & 2	78
1880 nr	FREDDIE ROACH	De bug	141
		Lion down	141
1881	CHARLIE ROUSE	Back in the tropics	145
		Velhos tempos	145
1882	CHARLIE ROUSE	Aconteceu	145
		In Martinique	145
1883 nr	CHARLIE ROUSE	Un dia,pts.1 & 2	145
1884	KENNY BURRELL	The good life	151
		Loie	151
1885	KENNY BURRELL	Chitlins con carne,pts.1 & 2	147
1886	KENNY BURRELL	Wavy gravy,pts.1 & 2	147
1887	HERBIE HANCOCK	Blind man,blind man,pts.1 & 2	151
1888	JOHN PATTON	The silver meter,pts. 1 & 2	152
1889	JOHN PATTON	I'll never be free	152
		Along came John	152
1890	FREDDIE ROACH	I know	148
		Googa mooga	151
1891	FREDDIE ROACH	Blues in the front room	148
		Mo' greens please	151

679

1892	FREDDIE ROACH	Party time		148
		Nada bossa		151
1893 (1)	STANLEY TURRENTINE	Trouble,pts.1 & 2		150
1893 (2)	STANLEY TURRENTINE	Trouble No.2,pts. 1 & 2		162
1894	STANLEY TURRENTINE	Major's minor		150
		Never let me go		148
1895	LOU DONALDSON	Spaceman twist,pts.1 & 2		138
1896 nr	LOU DONALDSON	Good gracious		148
1897	HAROLD VICK	Our Miss Brooks		154
		Vicksville		154
1898	THE THREE SOUNDS	One for Renee		114
		The nearness of you		114
1899	SOLOMON ILORI	Yaba E (Farewell),pts.1 & 2		153
1900	SOLOMON ILORI	Follow me to Africa		153
		Jojolo (Look at this beautiful girl)		153
1901	JOE HENDERSON	Blue bossa		155
		Recorda me		155
1902	HORACE SILVER	Silver's serenade		153
		Let's go to the Nitty Gritty		153
1903	HORACE SILVER	Sweet sweetie dee		153
		The dragon lady		153
1904	JIMMY SMITH	When my dreamboat comes home,pts.1 & 2		149
1905	JIMMY SMITH	Can heat		149
		Matilda,Matilda		149
1906	JIMMY SMITH	Porkshop,pts.1 & 2		149
1907	DONALD BYRD	Elijah		147
		Cristo redentor		147
1908	FREDDIE HUBBARD	Blue frenzy	1348	166
		Mirrors	1349	166
1909	JIMMY SMITH	Prayer meetin',pts.1 & 2		149
1910	JIMMY SMITH	Red top,pts.1 & 2		149
1911	LEE MORGAN	The sidewinder,pts.1 & 2		161
1912	HORACE SILVER	Song for my father,pts.1 & 2	1457	173
1913	HORACE SILVER	Que pasa,pts.1 & 2	1455	173
1914	FREDDIE ROACH	Brown sugar	1315	164
		Next time you see me	1314	164
1915	HANK MOBLEY	The turnaround,pts.1 & 2	1455	177
1916	DONALD BYRD	Brother Isaac	1495	175
		I've longed and searched for my mother	1496	176
1917	STANLEY TURRENTINE	River's invitation,pts.1 & 2	1569	181
1918	LEE MORGAN	The rumproller,pts.1 & 2	1571	181
1919	GRANT GREEN	I want to hold your hand	1554	179
		Corcovado	1550	179
1920	JOHN PATTON	Fat Judy (1541),pts.1 & 2		178
1921	BLUE MITCHELL	Fungii Mam (1391),pts. 1 & 2		169
1922	KENNY DORHAM	Mamacita,pts.1 & 2		172
1923	HORACE SILVER	The Cape Verdean blues(	1663	185
		Pretty eyes	1661	185
1924	HORACE SILVER	The African queen (1662),pts.1 & 2		185
1925	JIMMY SMITH	I cover the waterfront		55
		I can't give you anything but love		55
1926	JOHN PATTON	Ain't that peculiar	1733	192
		Amanda	1731	192
1927	JIMMY SMITH	Bucket		149
		Sassy Mae		149
1928	THE THREE SOUNDS	The frown		196
		It was a very good year		196
1929	STANLEY TURRENTINE	And satisfy	1756	193
		Walk on by	1755	193
1930	LEE MORGAN	Cornbread,pts.1 & 2	1654	185

680

1931	DUKE PEARSON	Sweet honey bee	1807	198
		Ready Rudy?	1804	198
1932	HORACE SILVER	The Jody grind,pts. 1 & 2	1781	196
1933	STANLEY TURRENTINE	What would I do without you	1752	193
		Feeling good	1753	193
1934	LOU DONALDSON	Alligator bogaloo		201
		Reverend Moses		201
1935	THE THREE SOUNDS	Makin' bread again		203
		Still I'm sad		203
1936	STANLEY TURRENTINE	Spooky	2033	209
		Love is blue	2035	209
1937	LOU DONALDSON	Peepin'	1972	206
		Humpback	1975	206
1938	HANK MOBLEY	Reach out,I'll be there	2032	209
		Goin' out of my head	2029	209
1939	HORACE SILVER	Psychedelic Sally	2051	210
		Serenade to a soul sister	2050	210
1940	STANLEY TURRENTINE	The look of love	2093	212
		This guy's in love with you	3012	213
1941	LOU DONALDSON	Midnight creeper		211
		Love power		211
1942	THE THREE SOUNDS	Elegant soul	2956	218
		Harper Valley P.T.A.	2959?	218
1943	LOU DONALDSON	Say it loud		220
		Snake bone		220
1944	BLUE MITCHELL	Swahili suite		218
		Collision in black		218
1945	LONNIE SMITH	Think	3068	216
		Son of ice bag	3066	216
1946	HORACE SILVER	You gotta take a little love	3394	222
		Down and out	3399	222
1947	LEE MORGAN	Sweet honey bee	1797	195
		Hey Chico	1799	195
1948	STANLEY TURRENTINE	Always something there	4028	220
		When I look into your eyes	4043	220
1949	LOU DONALDSON	Hot dog		226
		Who's making love		226
1950	THE THREE SOUNDS	Sugar hill	2960	218
		Sittin' duck	2958	218
1951	LEE MORGAN	Midnight cowboy	4377	227
		Popi	4378	227
1952	EDDIE GALE	Black rhythm happening	4222	226
		Ghetto Summertime	4219	226
1953	BROTHER JACK McDUFF	Down home style	4468	228
		Theme from Electric Surfboard	4470	228
1954	BLUE MITCHELL	H.N.I.C.,pts.1 & 2		227
1955	LONNIE SMITH	Move your hand,pts.1 & 2	4811	230
1956	LOU DONALDSON	Everything I do gonh be funky	5761	236
		Minor bash	5763	236
1957	BROTHER JACK McDUFF	Oblighetto	5834	234
		The vibrator	4467	228
1958	BROTHER JACK McDUFF	Hunk o' funk	6155	240
		Mystic John	6153	239
1959	CANDIDO	Jump back	5063	587
		Soul limbo	5060	587
1960	GRANT GREEN	Ain't it funky now,pts.1 & 2	5886	237
1961	REUBEN WILSON	Orange peel		238
		Knock on wood		238
1962	THAD JONES/MEL LEWIS	Ahunk,ahunk	5859	242
		Us	5858	242

Year	Artist	Title	Matrix	Page
1963	JIMMY McGRIFF	The worm		586
		Step one		586
1964	HORACE SILVER	The show has begun		241
		There's much to be done		243
1965	GRANT GREEN	Sookie sookie		246
		Time to remember		247
1966	BOBBY HUTCHERSON	Ummh,pts.1 & 2		245
1967	RICHARD GROOVE HOLMES	Love story		252
		Don't mess with me		252
1968	JIMMY McGRIFF	Groove alley		253
		Black pearl		253
1969	GRANT GREEN	Does anybody know what time it is?	7927	252
		Never can say goodbye	7923	252
1970	LOU DONALDSON	Caterpillar		254
		I want to make it with you		254
1971	BOBBI HUMPHREY	Spanish Harlem	8482	256
		Sad bag	8481	256
1972	GRANT GREEN	The battle,pts.1 & 2	9069A/B	258
1973	DONALD BYRD	The emperor,pts.1 & 2		255
1974	BOBBI HUMPHREY	Ain't no sunshine	8478	256
		Sad bag	8481	256
1975	HORACE SILVER	I've had a little talk	8826	251
		Acid,pot or pills	8829	250
1976	BOBBY HUTCHERSON	Rain every Thursday	9659	260
		When you're near	9656	260
1977	RONNIE FOSTER	Summer song	9215	259
		Chunky	9212	259
1978	HORACE SILVER	Horn of life	8534	259
		Cause and effect	9221	259
1979	JOE WILLIAMS	Baby		241
		Bridges		241
1980	BOBBI HUMPHREY	Lonely town,lonely streets	10187	261
		Is this all	10186	261
1981	MARLENA SHAW	You must believe in Spring	10442	262
		Somewhere	10437	262
1982	GENE HARRIS	Listen here	9953	261
		Emily	9954	261
1983	GRANT GREEN	Afro party	9067	257
		Father's lament	9063	258
1984				

1985: see U.K. issues

(series discontinued)

<u>BLUE NOTE label</u> (United Artists Series):

BN-XW

Issue	Artist	Title	Matrix	Page
189-W	LOU DONALDSON	The long goodbye	11395	264
		You are the sunshine of my life	11396	264
209-W	MARLENA SHAW	Save the children	10441	262
		Last tango in Paris	11635	265
212-W	DONALD BYRD	Black Byrd	11247	264
		Slop jar blues	11251	264
216-W	GRANT GREEN	Windjammer	11225	260
		Betcha by golly now	11226	260
261-W	ALPHONSE MOUZON	Funky finger	11443	265
		Spring water	11447	265
287-W	LOU DONALDSON	Pillow talk	12067	266
		Sassy soul strut	12068	266

682

309-W DONALD BYRD	Flight time	11246	260
	Mr.Thomas	11249	260
325-W HORACE SILVER	Nothing can stop me now	11478	263
	The liberated brother	10671	263
366-W MARLENA SHAW	Easy evil	12678	266
	Just don't want to be lonely	12682	266
381-W LOU DONALDSON	Sanford and son theme	12066	266
	Good morning heartache	12069	266
395-W BOBBI HUMPHREY	Chicago,damn	12692	267
	Just a love child	12694	267
445-W DONALD BYRD	Witch hunt	12690	267
	Woman of the world	12691	267
455-W BOBBI HUMPHREY	Harlem River drive	12693	267
	Blacks and blues	12695	267
500-X ALPHONSE MOUZON	Oh yes I do	13733	269
	Funky snakefoot	13734	270
550-X MARLENA SHAW	But for now	12677	266
	The feeling's good	12680	266
551-X GENE HARRIS	I remember Summer	14387	273
	Higga-boom	14393	273
590-X GENE HARRIS	Summer (The first time)	14385	273
	Los Alamitos (Latin funk love song)	14389	273
592-X BOBBI HUMPHREY	San Francisco lights	14610	263
	Fun house	14612	262
623-X: see U.K. issues			
637-X WATERS	To be there	14743	273
	Find it	14748	273
648-X ALPHONSE MOUZON	Nitroglycerin	15063	275
	Happiness is loving you	15068	275
649-X MARLENA SHAW	Loving you was like a party	15055	274
	You	15057	274
650-X DONALD BYRD	Think twice	15214	274
	We're together	14890	274
691-Y MARLENA SHAW	You taught me how to speak in love	15056	274
	Feel like makin' love	15060	274
692-Y WATERS	To be there	14743	273
	Find it	14748	273
716-Y JIMMY WITHERSPOON	Sign on the building	12892	646
	Pearly whites	12896	646
726-Y DONALD BYRD	Change (makes you want to hustle),pts.1 & 2	16327	283
738-Y RONNIE LAWS	Always there	15764	279
	Tidal wave	15769	279
777-Y RONNIE LAWS	Momma	15765	279
	Miss Mary's place	15771	279
783-Y DONALD BYRD	Just my imagination	16550	283
	(Fallin' like)Dominoes	16553	283
785-Y BOBBI HUMPHREY	Sweeter than sugar	16425	282
	Uno esta	16557	282
790-Y MARLENA SHAW	It's better than walkin' out	17057	286
	Be for real	17060	286
844-Y MARLENA SHAW	Love has gone away	17058	286
	This time I'll be sweeter	17061	286
848-Y RONNIE LAWS	Karmen	16765	284
	All the time	17242	286
869-Y CARMEN McRAE	Only women bleed	17375	289
	Music	17373	289

683

BN-XW				
905-Y	HORACE SILVER	Slow down	16741	283
		Time and effort	16740	283
924-Y	EARL KLUGH	Kiko	17893	293
		Living inside your love	17890	293
965-Y	DONALD BYRD	Dancing in the street	17457	289
		Onward 'til morning	17460	289
974-Y	EARL KLUGH	I heard it through the grapevine	17888	293
		Kiko	17893	293
977-Y	WILLIE BOBO	Dreamin'	18169	295
		Kojak theme	18173	295
997-Y	NOEL POINTER	Night song	18315	295
		Living for the city	18316	295
1007	RONNIE LAWS	Just love	18358	296
		Nuthin' but nuthin'	18354	296
1009	WAR	L.A. Sunshine	18652	647
		Slowly we walk together	18653	647
1032	HORACE SILVER	Togetherness	18115	294
		Out of the night came you	18114	294
1110	GENE HARRIS	A minor	18764	298
		Peace of mind	18766	298
1113	EARL KLUGH	Baretta's theme	18500	296
		Dance with me	18502	296
1114	NOEL POINTER	Fiddler on the roof	18320	295
		Living for the city	18316	295
B-50002	STANLEY JORDAN	The lady in my life		304
		New love		304

<u>CLASSIC label</u>

BST81595-45	CANNONBALL ADDERLEY	Autumn leaves		79
		Alison's uncle		79

<u>UNITED ARTISTS label</u>

UA-XW				
134	JOHN COLTRANE	Blue train,pts.1 & 2		71
136	LEE MORGAN	The sidewinder,pts.1 & 2		161
137	HORACE SILVER	The Jody grind (1781),pts.1 & 2		196
510-X	DONALD BYRD	Black Byrd	11247	264
		Cristo redentor	14283-E	147
1036	RONNIE LAWS	Friends & strangers	18353	296
		Goodtime ride	18351	296

 684

33 RPM (7 IN.)

Note: These 7-inch 33rpm "Little LPs" (stereo) were made for jukebox use only and not issued commercially.

BLUE NOTE label

L1593	LOU DONALDSON	Blues walk		83
		The masquerade is over		83
L1595	CANNONBALL ADDERLEY with Miles Davis	Autumn leaves		79
		One for Daddy-O		79
L4003	ART BLAKEY AND THE JAZZ MESSENGERS	Moanin'		85
		Blues march		85
L4011	JIMMY SMITH	The sermon,pt.1		78
		The sermon,pt.2		78
L4044	THE THREE SOUNDS	Love for sale		105
		On Green Dolphin Street		105
L4078	JIMMY SMITH	Midnight special		103
		One o'clock jump		103
L4118	DONALD BYRD	Pentecostal feelin'		131
		Nai Nai		131
L4124	DONALD BYRD	Elijah		147
		Cristo redentor		147
L4157	LEE MORGAN	The sidewinder		161
		Gary's notebook		161
L4169	LEE MORGAN	Mr. Kenyatta	1304	163
		The joker	1306	163
L4171	GEORGE BRAITH	Sweetville	1326	164
		Ev'ry time we say goodbye	1330	164
L4185	HORACE SILVER	Song for my father	1457	173
		Que pasa	1455	173
L4193	ART BLAKEY	When love is new		165
		Calling Miss Khadija	1353	166
L4201	STANLEY TURRENTINE	River's invitation	1569	181
		Mattie T	1564	181
L4202	GRANT GREEN	I want to hold your hand	1554	179
		Corcovado (Quiet nights)	1550	179
L4222	LEE MORGAN	Cornbread	1654	185
		Most like Lee	1653	185
L4229	JOHN PATTON	The yodel	1734	192
		Ain't that peculiar	1733	192
L4235	JIMMY SMITH	Bucket		149
		Sassy Mae/John Brown's body		149
L4240	STANLEY TURRENTINE	And satisfy	1756	193
		Walk on by	1755	193
L4248	THE THREE SOUNDS	The frown/Let's go get stoned		196
		It was a very good year/Something you got		196
L4250	HORACE SILVER	The jody grind	1781	196
		Blue silver	1795	197
L4337	LOU DONALDSON	Everything I do gonh be funky	5761	236
		(further titles unknown)		
UAS 2300	JIMMY McGRIFF	Something to listen to/Indiana		248
		Satin doll/Shiny stockings		248
2301	LOU DONALDSON	Donkey walk	5027	231
		West Indian daddy	5029	231
		Hamp's hump	5764	236
		Minor bash	5763	236

FOREIGN SERIES

Note: Numbers shown in second column are U.S. equivalent when applicable.Full details appear in session listings under original number and pages in parentheses refer to the original issue.

ENGLAND/UNITED KINGDOM

BLUE NOTE label (45 rpm)

SBN					
1956	45-1956	Lou Donaldson (236)			
45-1985		Bobby Hutcherson	Brother Rap (258)		
		Gerald Wilson	California soul (566)		
BNXW-					
623-X		Donald Byrd	Blackbyrd (264)		
			Flight time (260)		
4003	BN-XW726-Y	Donald Byrd (283)			
LBF					
15062	45-1935	The Three Sounds (203)			
UP					
35517	BN-XW209-W	Marlena Shaw (262,265)			
36125	BN-XW790-Y	Marlena Shaw (286)			
36163		Marlena Shaw	Love has gone away	17058	(286)
			No hiding place	17090	(286)
36251	BN-XW974-Y	Earl Klugh (293)			
36535		Sidney Bechet	Summertime	GM533	(3)
			Muskrat ramble	BN 209	(12)

VOGUE label (78 rpm - see note)

Note: All numbers shown were released as 78 rpm.Numbers marked +,and possibly some others in the list, were also released as 45 rpm with prefix 45V.

V2017	BN 1566	Bud Powell (25)			
V2045	BN 29	Edmond Hall's Blue Note Jazzmen (6)			
V2051+	Climax 101	George Lewis New Orleans Stompers (447,448)			
V2052+	Climax 102	George Lewis New Orleans Stompers (447)			
V2053+	Climax 103	George Lewis New Orleans Stompers (447)			
V2054+	Climax 104	George Lewis New Orleans Stompers (447)			
V2055+	Climax 105	George Lewis New Orleans Stompers (447,448)			
V2062	BN 531	Art Hodes' Hot Five (16)			
V2063	BN 532	Art Hodes' Hot Five (16)			
V2064	BN 533	Art Hodes' Hot Five (16)			
V2084	BN 565	Bunk Johnson-Sidney Bechet Orchestra (13)			
V2109	BN 2	Albert Ammons (1)			
V2123	BN 39	Meade Lux Lewis (10)			
V2161		Milt Jackson	Willow weep for me	BN 397-2	(28)
			Criss cross	BN 393-2	(28)
V2201	BN 4	Albert Ammons & Meade Lux Lewis (1,2)			

686

V2202		Miles Davis	Dear old Stockholm	BN 428	(31)
			How deep is the ocean	BN 433	(31)
V2213	BN 21	Albert Ammons (1)			
V2222		Miles Davis	Donna	BN 430	(31)
			Would'n you	BN 431	(31)
V2227	BN 1596	Miles Davis (31)			
V2229	BN 16	Meade Lux Lewis (5)			
V2246		Sidney Bechet's Blue Note Jazzmen:			
			Tailgate ramble	BN 356	(24)
			Joshua fit the battle of Jericho	BN 358	(24)
V2247	BN 22	Meade Lux Lewis (5)			
V2265		Sidney Bechet's Blue Note Jazzmen:			
			Jelly Roll	BN 379-2	(26)
			I've found a new baby	BN 351	(24)
V2303		Milt Jackson's New Group:			
			Lillie	BN 423-1	(30)
			Eronel	BN 394	(28)
V2307		Horace Silver:	Safari	BN 449	(33)
			Ecaroh	BN 453-2	(33)
V2336		Thelonious Monk:	Off minor	BN 317-1	(20)
			Well you needn't	BN 314	(20)
V2347		Gil Melle	Spellbound		(38)
			Gingersnaps		(38)
V2363		Art Hodes Trio	Blues 'n booze	BN 232	(13)
			KMH drag	BN 230	(13)
V2371+	BN 54	Bechet-Nicholas Blue Five (17)			

FRANCE

JAZZ SELECTION label (78 rpm):

JS 521	BN 517	Sidney Bechet Blue Note Jazzmen (17)		
JS 522	BN 43	Sidney Bechet Blue Note Jazzmen (12)		
JS 523	BN 543	Thelonious Monk (20,21)		
JS 532	BN 44	Sidney Bechet Blue Note Jazzmen (12)		
JS 533	BN 13	Sidney Bechet Blue Note Jazzmen (4)		
JS 534	BN 49	Sidney Bechet Blue Note Jazzmen (12)		
JS 535	BN 50	Sidney Bechet Blue Note Jazzmen (12)		
JS 539	BN 557	Fats Navarro - Howard McGhee (23)		
JS 541	BN 32	James P. Johnson Blue Note Jazzmen (7)		
JS 542	BN 560	Thelonious Monk (19,22)		
JS 544	BN 40	Sidney De Paris & His Blue Note Jaazzmen (9)		
JS 545		Sidney Bechet & His Blue Note Jazzmen:		
		Summertime	GM 533	(3)
		Blues for Tommy	GM 532	(3)
JS 547	BN 33	James P. Johnson Blue Note Jazzmen (7)		
JS 548	BN 548	Thelonious Monk (21,22)		
JS 551	BN 46	Benny Morton Blue Note Jazzmen (13)		
JS 553	BN 41	Sidney De Paris Blue Note Jaazzmen (9)		
JS 554	BN 549	Thelonious Monk (20,22)		
JS 555	BN 1566	Bud Powell Trio (25)		
JS 557	BN 547	Thelonious Monk (19,20)		
JS 562	BN 540	Tadd Dameron with Fats Navarro (19)		
JS 570	BN 525	Tiny Grimes & His Orchestra (18)		
JS 573	BN 54	Sidney Bechet - Albert Nicholas (17)		
JS 580		Jimmy Hamilton & The Duke's Men:		
		Blues in my music room	BN 271-1	(16)
		Old uncle Bud	BN 268-1	(16)
JS 586	BN 563	Sidney Bechet Blue Note Jazzmen (24)		
JS 588	BN 1568	Bud Powell's Modernists (25)		
JS 590	BN 1567	Bud Powell's Modernists (25)		
JS 592	BN 561	Sidney Bechet Blue Note Jazzmen (24)		
JS 596	BN 562	Sidney Bechet Blue Note Jazzmen (24)		
JS 643	BN 515	Ike Quebec Swing Seven (15)		
JS 644	BN 514	John Hardee Swingtet (17)		
JS 646	BN 29	Sidney De Paris Blue Note Jazzmen (6)		
JS 647	BN 25	James P. Johnson (6)		
JS 790	BN 531	Sidney Bechet Blue Note Jazzmen (16)		
JS 792	BN 532	Sidney Bechet Blue Note Jazzmen (16)		
JS 795	BN 533	Sidney Bechet Blue Note Jazzmen (16)		
JS 800	BN 565	Sidney Bechet's Jazz Band (13)		
JS 818		Sidney Bechet Blue Note Jazzmen:		
		Jelly Roll	BN 379-2	(26)
		I've found a new baby	BN 351	(24)
JS 819		Sidney Bechet Blue Note Jazzmen:		
		Tailgate ramble	BN 356	(24)
		Joshua fit the battle of Jericho	BN 358	(24)
JS 820		Sidney Bechet Blue Note Jazzmen:		
		Runnin' wild	BN 378-1	(26)
		Mandy	BN 380-2	(26)

SWING label (78 rpm):

SW403		Miles Davis & His Orchestra.	Dear old Stockholm	BN 428	(31)
			How deep is the ocean	BN 433	(31)
SW404		Miles Davis & His Orchestra.	Wouldn't you	BN 431	(31)
			Donna	BN 430	(31)
SW405	BN 1596	Miles Davis & His Orchestra (31)			
SW407		Milt Jackson And His Group:	Tahiti	BN 422	(30)
			Lillie	BN 423	(30)
SW408		Milt Jackson And His Group:	Criss cross	BN 393	(28)
			Willow weep for me	BN 397	(28)
SW409		Milt Jackson And His Group:	What's new	BN 425	(30)
			On the scene	BN 427	(30)
SW427		Milt Jackson And His Group:	Bags' groove	BN 424	(30)
			Eronel	BN 394	(28)

VOGUE label (78 rpm):

V3096	BN 16	Meade Lux Lewis (5)
V3097	BN 2	Albert Ammons (1)
V3098	BN 39	Meade Lux Lewis (10)
V3101	BN 22	Meade Lux Lewis (5)
V3158	BN 21	Albert Ammons (1)
V3159	BN 4	Albert Ammons & Meade Lux Lewis (1,2)

BLUE NOTE label (45 rpm)

BN				
45-001	45-1879	Jimmy Smith (78)		
45-002		Art Blakey & The Jazz Messengers: Blues march/Moanin' (85)		
45-003	45-1968	Jimmy McGriff (253)		
45-004	45-1966	Bobby Hutcherson (245)		
45-005		Grant Green	Does anybody really knows what time it is?	(252)
			Canteloupe woman	(252)
8-87504-1 (12 in.)		Shirley Bassey Meets The Booster (632)		

GERMANY

CLIMAX label (78 rpm - all probably 10 in.)

6	BN 6	Sidney Bechet/Port of Harlem Seven (3)
36	BN 36	Edmond Hall's Swingtet (8)
43	BN 43	Sidney Bechet Blue Note Jazzmen (12)
44	BN 44	Sidney Bechet Blue Note Jazzmen (12)
49	BN 49	Sidney Bechet Blue Note Jazzmen (12)
101	Climax 101	George Lewis And His New Orleans Stompers (445,446)
102	Climax 102	George Lewis And His New Orleans Stompers (445)
103	Climax 103	George Lewis And His New Orleans Stompers (445)
104	Climax 104	George Lewis And His New Orleans Stompers (445)
105	Climax 105	George Lewis And His New Orleans Stompers (445,446)
502	BN 502	Sidney Bechet (4)
505	BN 505	Art Hodes and his Chicagoans (4,7)
506	BN 506	Art Hodes and his Chicagoans (7)
561	BN 561	Sidney Bechet's Blue Note Jazzmen (24)
562	BN 562	Sidney Bechet's Blue Note Jazzmen (24)
563	BN 563	Sidney Bechet's Blue Note Jazzmen (24)
564	BN 564	Bunk Johnson & Sidney Bechet (13)
571	BN 571	Sidney Bechet's Blue Note Jazzmen (24)
572	BN 572	Sidney Bechet's Blue Note Jazzmen (26)
573	BN 573	Sidney Bechet's Blue Note Jazzmen (24,26)

689

JAPAN

BLUE NOTE label (45 rpm)

NP		
2001	45-1911	Lee Morgan - The Sidewinder,pts. 1 & 2 (161)
2002	45-1735	Art Blakey's Jazz Messengers - Moanin',pts. 1 & 2 (85)
2003	45-1736	Art Blakey's Jazz Messengers - Blues march/Along came Betty (85)
2004	45-1737	Cannonball Adderley - Autumn leaves,pts. 1 & 2 (79)
2005	45-1750	Horace Silver - Sister Sadie/Break City (94)
2006		Horace Silver - Senor blues/Blowin' the bl:ues away (58,94)
2007	45-1912	Horace Silver - Song for my father,pts. 1 & 2 (173)
2008		Sonny Clark - Blue minor,pts. 1 & 2 (76)
2009		Bud Powell - Cleopatra's dream/The scene changes (88)
2010	45-1934	Stanley Turrentine - What would I do without you?/Feeling good (193)
2011	45-1796	Art Blakey's Jazz Messengers - A night in Tunisia,pts. &1 & 2 (109)
2012		Herbie Hancock - Watermelon man,pts. 1 & 2 (139)
2013	45-1738	Cannonball Adderley - Somethin' else,pts. 1 & 2 (79)
2014	45-1691	John Coltrane - Blues train,pts. 1 & 2 (71)
2015	45-1764	Donald Byrd - Fuego/Amen (92,95)
2016	45-1714	Sonny Clark - Cool struttin',pts. 1 & 2 (76)
2017		Horace Silver Trio - Opus de funk/Ecaroh (33,39)
2018	45-1630	Horace Silver & The Jazz Messengers - Room 608/Creepin' in (44)
2019		The Three Sounds - The frown/Still I'm sad (196,203)
2020		Lou Donaldson - Midnight creeper/The humpback (206,211)

BNS-			
17642	Freddie Hubbard & Woody Shaw		
		Desert moonlight,pts.1 & 2	(312)

(45 rpm-12 in.):

BNJ			
27001	Cannonball Adderley	Allison's uncle	(79)
		Autumn leaves	(79)
27002	Bud Powell	Blue pearl (2 takes)	(68)
		Cleopatra's dream	(88)

SWEDEN

GAZELL label(78 rpm):

2012 BN 1567 Bud Powell Quintet (25)

45 EPs

BLUE NOTE label

Modern Jazz Series (mono):
BEP

201	The Swinging Swedes (640)
202	Dizzy Gilllespie - Horn of Plenty (640,641)
203	Gil Melle Quintet (33)
204	Miles Davis (31)

Dixieland Series (mono):
BEP

401	Sidney Bechet with Wild Bill Davison & Sidney De Paris (24,30)
402	Sidney Bechet (639)
403	Art Hodes' Chicagoans (7)
404	George Lewis' New Orleans Stompers (447)

Stereo Issue:
BN-EP-
45-8001 Jimmy Smith (149)

FOREIGN SERIES

ENGLAND/UNITED KINGDOM

VOGUE label

EPV

1033	Bud Powell's Modernists (25)
1048	Thelonious Monk (20,21,22)
1058	Milt Jackson Quartet (30)
1065	Meade Lux Lewis (5,10)
1066	George Lewis (447,448)
1071	Albert Ammons (1)
1075	Miles Davis (31)
1081	George Lewis (447,448)
1087	Art Hodes Blue Note Jazzmen (16)
1105	Fats Navarro (19,23)
1116	Gil Melle (38)
1164	Edmond Hall Blue Note Jazzmen (6,9)

FRANCE

VOGUE label

Note: Following issues are equivanlent to U.K. issues shown in second column.

EPV

7064	EPV1075	Miles Davis (31)
7082	EPV1058	Milt Jackson Quartet (30)
7181	EPV1033	Bud Powell's Modernists (25)
7183	EPV1048	Thelonious Monk (20,21,22)

Part 8
Album Numerical Listings

10 in. LPs

Note: Albums marked nr were not released.

BLUE NOTE label (Modern Jazz Series)

BLP

5001 Mellow the Mood - Jazz in a Mellow Mood:
Charlie Christian (5) Benny Morton (13)
Ike Quebec (10,15) John Hardee (17)

5002 Thelonious Monk - Genius of Modern Music (19,20,21)

5003 The Amazing Bud Powell (25,27)

5004 Fats Navarro Memorial Album:
Tadd Dameron (19,22) Bud Powell (25)
Fats Navarro (23)

5005 James Moody with Strings conducted by Andre Hodeir (639)

5006 James Moody and his Modernists with Chano Pozo (23)

5007 Erroll Garner - Overture to Dawn,Volume 1 (448)

5008 Erroll Garner - Overture to Dawn,Volume 2 (448)

5009 Thelonious Monk - Genius of Modern Music,Volume 2 (19,20,28)

5010 New Sounds - Max Roach Quintet/Art Blakey and his Band:
Art Blakey (21) Max Roach (639)

5011 Milt Jackson - Wizard of the Vibes:
Thelonious Monk (28) Milt Jackson (30)

5012 Howard McGhee's All Stars (23,26)

5013 Miles Davis - Young Man with a Horn (31)

5014 Erroll Garner - Overture to Dawn,Volume 3 (448,449)

5015 Erroll Garner - Overture to Dawn,Volume 4 (448,449)

5016 Erroll Garner - Overture to Dawn,Volume 5 (449)

5017 Dizzy Gillespie - Horn of Plenty (640,641)

5018 New Faces - New Sounds: Introducing the Horace Silver Trio (33)

5019 New Sounds from the Old World:The Swinging Swedes/The Cool Britons:
The Swinging Swedes (640) The Cool Britons (639)

5020 New Faces - New Sounds: Gil Melle Quintet/Sextet (33,450)

5021 New Faces - New Sounds: Lou Donaldson Quintet/Quartet (32,33)

5022 Miles Davis,Volume 2 (34)

5023 New Faces - New Sounds: Introducing the Kenny Drew Trio (34)

5024 Howard McGhee,Volume 2 (35)

5025 New Faces - New Sounds: Piano Interpretations by Wynton Kelly (29)

5026 Memorable Sessions:
Edmond Hall-Charlie Christian (5) Edmond Hall-Red Norvo (7)

5027 Swing Hi - Swing Lo:
Benny Morton (13) Ike Quebec (15,18)
Jimmy Hamilton (16)

5028 Jay Jay Johnson (36)

5029 New Faces - New Sounds: Elmo Hope Trio (36)

5030 New Faces - New Sounds: Lou Donaldson-Clifford Brown (35)

5031 New Faces - New Sounds: Wade Legge Trio (641)

5032 Clifford Brown - New Star on the Horizon (38)

5033 Gil Melle Quintet,Volume 2 (38)

5034 Horace Silver Trio,Volume 2/Art Blakey-Sabu (39)

5035 Sal Salvador Quintet (39)

5036 Urbie Green Septet (39)

5037 A Night at Birdland with The Art Blakey Quintet,Volume 1 (40,41)

BLP
5038 A Night at Birdland with The Art Blakey Quintet,Volume 2 (40,41)
5039 A Night at Birdland with The Art Blakey Quintet,Volume 3 (40,41)
5040 Miles Davis,Volume 3 (41)
5041 The Amazing Bud Powell,Volume 2 (37)
5042 Tal Farlow Quartet (41)
5043 New Faces - New Sounds: Frank Foster - Here Comes Frank Foster (42)
5044 New Faces - New Sounds: Elmo Hope Quintet,Volume 2 (42)
5045 George Wallington and his Band - Showcase (42)
5046 Lionel Hampton in Paris (642)
5047 Clifford Brown Quartet (643)
5048 Clifford Brown - Gigi Gryce Sextet (642)
5049 Gigi Gryce and his Big Band,Volume 1 (641,642,643)
5050 Gigi Gryce and his Little Band,Volume 2 (641,642,643)
5051 nr Gigi Gryce Quintet/Sextet,Volume 3 (642,643)
5052 New Sounds from the Ole England - The Cool Britons (644)
5053 New Faces - New Sounds:Julius Watkins Sextet (43)
5054 The Gil Melle Quartet,Volume 3 (43)
5055 Lou Donaldson Sextet,Volume 2 (43)
5056 New Faces - New Sounds from Germany:Jutta Hipp Quintet (451)
5057 The Eminent Jay Jay Johnson,Volume 2 (43)
5058 Horace Silver Quintet (44)
5059 Best from The West - Modern Sounds from California,Volume 1 (44)
5060 Best from The West - Modern Sounds from California,Volume 2 (44)
5061 The Swinging Fats Sadi Combo (643)
5062 Horace Silver Quintet,Volume 2 (45)
5063 Gil Melle Quintet,Volume 4 (45)
5064 Julius Watkins Sextet,Volume 2 (45)
5065 Afro-Cuban: Kenny Dorham (46)
5066 Hank Mobley Quartet (46)
5067 Lou Mecca Quartet (46)
5068 The Prophetic Herbie Nichols,Volume 1 (47)
5069 The Prophetic Herbie Nichols,Volume 2 (48)
5070 The Eminent Jay Jay Johnson,Volume 3 (48)

BLUE NOTE label (Dixieland Series)

BLP
7001 Sidney Bechet's Blue Note Jazzmen with "Wild Bill" Davison (24,26,639)
7002 Sidney Bechet Jazz Classics,Volume 1 (3,4,12)
7003 Sidney Bechet Jazz Classics,Volume 2 (3,12)
7004 The Best in 2 Beat - Art Hodes and his Chicagoans (7,8)
7005 Art Hodes' Hot Five with Sidney Bechet and "Wild Bill" Davison:
Art Hodes (16) Sidney Bechet (639)
7006 Dixieland Jubilee with Art Hodes and his Blue Note Jazz Men (9,11)
7007 Jamming in Jazz - Edmond Hall-De Paris' Blue Note Jazzmen:
Edmond Hall (6) Sidney De Paris (9)
7008 Days Beyond Recall - Sidney Bechet and Bunk Johnson (13,17)
7009 Giant of Jazz - Sidney Bechet and his Blue Note Jazzmen with "Wild Bill" Davison (24,639)
7010 Echoes of New Orleans - George Lewis and his New Orleans Stompers,Volume 1 (447,448)
7011 Rent Party Piano - James P.Johnson (6)
7012 Jazz Band Ball - James P.Johnson's Blue Note Jazzmen (7,9,11)
7013 Echoes of New Orleans - George Lewis and his New Orleans Stompers,Volume 2:
Albert Nicholas (16,449) George Lewis (447,448)
7014 Sidney Bechet's Blue Note Jazzmen,Volume 2 (24,26,639)
7015 Dixieland Clambake - Art Hodes' Hot Seven (14)
7016 Sidney De Paris' Blue Note Stompers (27)
7017 Boogie Woogie Classics - Albert Ammons Memorial Album (1,2)
7018 Boogie Woogie Classics - Meade 'Lux' Lewis (5,10)
7019 Boogie Woogie,Blues and Skiffle - Pete Johnson (4)
7020 The Fabulous Sidney Bechet and his Hot Six with Sidney De Paris (30)

693

BLP
7021 Out of the Back Room - Art Hodes' Back Room Boys (8,13,15,16)
7022 Sidney Bechet - Port of Harlem Six (2,4,17)
7023 Mezz Mezzrow and his Band:
Art Hodes (11) Mezz Mezzrow (640)
7024 Sidney Bechet - Jazz Festival Concert,Paris 1952 (640)
7025 Sidney Bechet - Jazz Festival Concert,Paris 1952,Volume 2 (640)
7026 Dixie by the Fabulous Sidney Bechet (37)
7027 George Lewis and His New Orleans Stompers,Volume 3 (47)
7028 George Lewis and His New Orleans Stompers,Volume 4 (47)
7029 Sidney Bechet - Olympia Concert,Paris 1954,Volume 1 (644)
7030 nr Sidney Bechet - Olympia Concert,Paris 1954,Volume 2 (644)

694

FOREIGN SERIES

ENGLAND/UNITED KINGDOM

VOGUE label

Note:Second column shows equivalent US album,when applicable.

LDE		
025		Sidney Bechet and his Blue Note Jazzmen (17,24,26)
028	BLP5013	Miles Davis - Young Man with a Horn (31)
042	BLP5047	Clifford Brown Quartet (643)
044	BLP5011	Milt Jackson and his New Group: Thelonious Monk (28) Milt Jackson (30)
064	BLP5022	Miles Davis and his Orchestra (34)
065	BLP5018	Horace Silver Trio (33)
086	BLP7005	Sidney Bechet's Blue Note Jazzmen (16,639)
121	BLP5032	Clifford Brown Sextet (38)
124	BLP5028	J.J.Johnson Sextet (26)
127	BLP7026	Sidney Bechet Hot Six (37)
138	BLP7020	Sidney Bechet Hot Six (30)
139	BLP5044	Elmo Hope Quintet (42)
141	BLP5033	Gil Melle Quintet (38)
162	BLP5057	The Eminent Jay Jay Johnson (43)
174	BLP7021	Art Hodes Back Room Boys (8,13,15,16)

FRANCE

JAZZ SELECTION label

JSLP		
50008	BLP5028	Jay Jay Johnson Sextet (36)
50016	BLP7026	Sidney Bechet and his Blue Note Jazzmen,Volume 3 (37)
50017	BLP5032	Clifford Brown Sextet (38)
50037	BLP5033	Gil Melle Quintet (38)
50038	BLP5044	Elmo Hope Quintet (42)
50039	BLP7020	Sidney Bechet and his Blue Note Jazzmen (30)
50040	BLP5057	Jay Jay Johnson Quintet,Volume 2 (43)
50044	BLP7021	Blues Session at Blue Note (8,13,15,16)

VOGUE label

LD		
026	BLP7005	Sidney Bechet Blue Note Jazzmen,Volume 1: Art Hodes (16) Sidney Bechet (639)
066		Kings of Boogie Woogie: Albert Ammons (1) Meade Lux Lewis (5) Albert Ammons & Meade Lux Lewis (1) (& one further Blind John Davis title,not from BN)
091	(LDE025)	Sidney Bechet Blue Note Jazzmen,Volume 2 (17,24,26)
122	BLP5013	Miles Davis - Young Man with a Horn (31)
138	BLP5011	Milt Jackson and his New Group - Wizard of the Vibes: Thelonious Monk (28) Milt Jackson (30)
172	BLP5022	Miles Davis & his Orchestra,Volume 2 (34)
176	BLP5018	Horace Silver Trio (33)

695

JAPAN

Note:Following albums are reissues of original albums shown in second column.
Reissues 5001 & 5027 were bonus LPs for buyers of more than 20 LPs in the series,and used prefix BN- in place of TOJJ.

TOJJ-	BLP	
5001	5001	Mellow the Mood - Jazz in a Mellow Mood:
		Charlie Christian (5) Benny Morton (13)
		Ike Quebec (10,15) John Hardee (17)
5002	5002	Thelonious Monk - Genius of Modern Music (19,20,21)
5003	5003	The Amazing Bud Powell (25,27)
5004	5004	Fats Navarro Memorial Album:
		Tadd Dameron (19,22) Bud Powell (25)
		Fats Navarro (23)
5006	5006	James Moody and his Modernists with Chano Pozo (23)
5009	5009	Thelonious Monk - Genius of Modern Music,Volume 2 (19,20,28)
5011	5011	Milt Jackson - Wizard of the Vibes:
		Thelonious Monk (28) Milt Jackson (30)
5012	5012	Howard McGhee's All Stars (23,26)
5013	5013	Miles Davis - Young Man with a Horn (31)
5018	5018	New Faces - New Sounds: Introducing the Horace Silver Trio (33)
5020	5020	New Faces - New Sounds: Gil Melle Quintet/Sextet (33,450)
5021	5021	New Faces - New Sounds: Lou Donaldson Quintet/Quartet (32,33)
5022	5022	Miles Davis,Volume 2 (34)
5023	5023	New Faces - New Sounds: Introducing the Kenny Drew Trio (34)
5024	5024	Howard McGhee,Volume 2 (35)
5025	5025	New Faces - New Sounds: Piano Interpretations by Wynton Kelly (29)
5026	5026	Memorable Sessions:
		Edmond Hall-Charlie Christian (5) Edmond Hall-Red Norvo (7)
5027	5027	Swing Hi-Swing Lo:
		Benny Morton (13) Ike Quebec (15,18)
		Jimmy Hamilton (16)
5028	5028	Jay Jay Johnson (36)
5029	5029	New Faces - New Sounds: Elmo Hope Trio (36)
5030	5030	New Faces - New Sounds: Lou Donaldson-Clifford Brown (35)
5032	5032	Clifford Brown - New Star on the Horizon (38)
5033	5033	Gil Melle Quintet,Volume 2 (38)
5034	5034	Horace Silver Trio,Volume 2/Art Blakey-Sabu (39)
5035	5035	Sal Salvador Quintet (39)
5036	5036	Urbie Green Septet (39)
5037	5037	A Night at Birdland with The Art Blakey Quintet,Volume 1 (40,41)
5038	5038	A Night at Birdland with The Art Blakey Quintet,Volume 2 (40,41)
5039	5039	A Night at Birdland with The Art Blakey Quintet,Volume 3 (40,41)
5040	5040	Miles Davis,Volume 3 (41)
5041	5041	The Amazing Bud Powell,Volume 2 (37)
5042	5042	Tal Farlow Quartet (41)
5043	5043	New Faces - New Sounds: Frank Foster Quintet (42)
5044	5044	New Faces - New Sounds: Elmo Hope Quintet,Volume 2 (42)
5045	5045	George Wallington and his Band - Showcase (42)
5053	5053	New Faces - New Sounds: Julius Watkins Sextet (43)
5054	5054	The Gil Melle Quartet,Volume 3 (43)
5055	5055	Lou Donaldson Sextet,Volume 2 (43)
5056	5056	New Faces - New Sounds from Germany: Jutta Hipp Quintet (451)
5057	5057	The Eminent Jay Jay Johnson,Volume 2 (43)
5058	5058	Horace Silver Quintet (44)
5059	5059	Best from The West - Modern Sounds from California,Volume 1 (44)
5060	5060	Best from The West - Modern Sounds from California,Volume 2 (44)
5062	5062	Horace Silver Quintet,Volume 2 (45)

696

TOJJ-	BLP	
5063	5063	Gil Melle Quintet,Volume 4 (45)
5064	5064	Julius Watkins Sextet,Volume 2 (45)
5065	5065	Afro-Cuban: Kenny Dorham (46)
5066	5066	Hank Mobley Quartet (46)
5067	5067	Lou Mecca Quartet (46)
5068	5068	The Prophetic Herbie Nichols,Volume 1 (47)
5069	5069	The Prophetic Herbie Nichols,Volume 2 (48)
5070	5070	The Eminent Jay Jay Johnson,Volume 3 (48)

Note: Some of BLP5000 albums were also reissued in Japan as 12 in. LPs (see 12 in. LP Section).

697

12 in. LPs

BLUE NOTE label (Traditional Jazz Series)

BLP

1201 Sidney Bechet Jazz Classics,Volume 1 (3,4,12,13,17)
1202 Sidney Bechet Jazz Classics,Volume 2 (3,12,13,17,30)
1203 Sidney Bechet - Giant of Jazz,Volume 1:
Art Hodes (16) Sidney Bechet(24,26)
1204 Sidney Bechet - Giant of Jazz,Volume 2 (24,26)
1205 George Lewis and his New Orleans Stompers,Volume 1 (47)
1206 Echoes of New Orleans - George Lewis and his New Orleans Stompers,Volume 2 (447,448)
1207 The Fabulous Sidney Bechet (30,37)
1208 Concert! - George Lewis and his New Orleans Stompers (451,452)
1209: see French issues on page 730.

Note: BLP1201 to 1208 were reissued in pseudo stereo as BST81201 to BST81208.

BLUE NOTE label (Modern Jazz Series)

Notes: ps denotes albums issued in the BLP mono series and reissued in pseudo stereo in the BST81000 series.Albums with mention nr were not released.
Album marked + were recorded in stereo and were issued in both BLP mono series and the equivalent BST81500/84000 stereo series. Albums marked * were issued in stereo only.
Some albums have been reissued using same number and new prefix BLJ- (for albums marked J) or BN1- (for albums marked 1).
Many albums have also been listed in various catalogues with new Liberty prefixes LT or LW in place of BST or BN, but records may have retained the original BN prefix.

BLP

1501 ps Miles Davis,Volume 1 (31,34)
1502 ps Miles Davis,Volume 2 (31,34,41)
1503 ps The Amazing Bud Powell,Volume 1 (25,27)
1504 ps The Amazing Bud Powell,Volume 2 (25,27,37)
1505 ps The Eminent Jay Jay Johnson,Volume 1 (36,43)
1506 ps The Eminent Jay Jay Johnson,Volume 2 (36,43,48)
1507 ps The Jazz Messengers at the Cafe Bohemia,Volume 1 (49,50)
1508 ps The Jazz Messengers at the Cafe Bohemia,Volume 2 (49,50)
1509 psJ Milt Jackson (22,28,30)
1510 ps Thelonious Monk,Volume 1 (20,21,22)
1511 ps Thelonious Monk,Volume 2 (20,21,28,32)
1512 ps A New Star - A New Sound: Jimmy Smith at the Organ,Volume 1 (50)
1513 Detroit - New York Junction: Thad Jones (51)
1514 ps A New Star - A New Sound: Jimmy Smith at the Organ,Volume 2 (51)
1515 Jutta Hipp at the Hickory House,Volume 1 (52)
1516 Jutta Hipp at the Hickory House,Volume 2 (52)
1517 Gil Melle - Patterns in Jazz (51)
1518 ps Horace Silver and The Jazz Messengers (44,45)
1519 Herbie Nichols Trio (48,49,53)
1520 ps Horace Silver Trio and Spotlight on Drums: Art Blakey-Sabu (33,39)
1521 ps A Night at Birdland with The Art Blakey Quintet,Volume 1 (40,41)
1522 ps A Night at Birdland with The Art Blakey Quintet,Volume 2 (40,41)
1523 ps Introducing Kenny Burrell Guitar (53)
1524 Kenny Dorham - 'Round Midnight at the Cafe Bohemia (54)
1525 ps Jimmy Smith at the Organ,Volume 3 (54,55)
1526 ps Clifford Brown Memorial Album (35,38)
1527 The Magnificent Thad Jones (55)
1528 ps The Incredible Jimmy Smith at Club 'Baby Grand',Wilmington,Delaware Volume 1 (56)

BLP
1529 ps The Incredible Jimmy Smith at Club 'Baby Grand',Wilmington,Delaware Volume 2 (56)
1530 Jutta Hipp (56)
1531 The Fabulous Fats Navarro,Volume 1 (19,23,25)
1532 The Fabulous Fats Navarro,Volume 2 (22,23,25)
1533 Introducing Johnny Griffin,Tenor Sax (52)
1534 ps Paul Chambers Sextet - Whims of Chambers (57)
1535 Kenny Dorham Octet/Sextet (45,46)
1536 J.R.Monterose (57)
1537 Lou Donaldson Quartet/Quintet/Sextet (32,33,43)
1538 Lee Morgan Indeed! (57)
1539 ps 6 Pieces of Silver - Horace Silver Quintet (58)
1540 Hank Mobley Sextet (58)
1541 ps Lee Morgan,Volume 2 (58)
1542 ps Sonny Rollins (59)
1543 ps Kenny Burrell,Volume 2 (50,53,54)
1544 ps Hank Mobley and his All Stars (59)
1545 Lou Donaldson,Volume 2 - Wailin' With Lou (59)
1546 The Magnificent Thad Jones,Volume 3 (55,59)
1547 ps A Date with Jimmy Smith,Volume 1(60,61)
1548 ps A Date with Jimmy Smith,Volume 2 (60)
1549 Blowing in from Chicago - Cliff Jordan and John Gilmore (61)
1550 Hank Mobley Quintet (62)
1551 ps Jimmy Smith at the Organ,Volume 1: All Day Long (61)
1552 ps Jimmy Smith at the Organ,Volume 2 (60,61)
1553 nr not used
1554+ Art Blakey - Orgy in Rhythm,Volume 1 (62)
1555+ Art Blakey - Orgy in Rhythm,Volume 2 (62)
1556 ps The Sounds of Jimmy Smith (60,61)
1557 Lee Morgan,Volume 3 (62)
1558 ps Sonny Rollins,Volume 2 (62)
1559 Johnny Griffin - A Blowing Session (63)
1560 Hank Mobley Sextet - Hank (63)

Note:All subsequent issues were recorded in stereo,but stereo versions were not all issued on LP.

BLP
1561 Sabu - Palo Congo (64)
1562+ Horace Silver Quintet - The Stylings of Silver (64)
1563+ Jimmy Smith at the Organ plays Pretty Just for You (64)
1564 Paul Chambers Quintet (65)
1565 Cliff Jordan (65)
1566+ Lou Donaldson - Swing and Soul (65) (Note: Stereo and mono issues are slightly different)
1567 Curtis Fuller,Trombone - The Opener (66)
1568 Hank Mobley (66)
1569 + Paul Chambers Quartet - Bass on Top (67)
1570 Sonny Clark - Dial S for Sonny (67)
1571+ The Amazing Bud Powell,Volume 3 - Bud! (68)
1572 Curtis Fuller,Volume 2 - Bone & Bari (68)
1573 John Jenkins with Kenny Burrell (69)
1574 Hank Mobley - Peckin' Time (77)
1575+ Lee Morgan - City Lights (69)
1576+ Sonny Clark - Sonny's Crib (70)
1577+ John Coltrane - Blue Train (71)
1578+ Lee Morgan - The Cooker (72)
1579+ Sonny Clark Trio (72)
1580 Johnny Griffin - The Congregation (73)
1581 ps Sonny Rollins - A Night at The Village Vanguard (73)
1582 Cliff Jordan,Volume 2 - Cliff Craft (74)
1583 Curtis Fuller - Art Farmer (70)
1584 Here Comes Louis Smith (454)

 699

BLP
1585 Jimmy Smith - Groovin' at Smalls' Paradise,Volume 1 (74)
1586 Jimmy Smith - Groovin' at Smalls' Paradise,Volume 2 (74)
1587+ Bennie Green - Back on the Scene (80)
1588 J Sonny Clark - Cool Struttin' (76)
1589+ Further Explorations by the Horace Silver Quintet (76)
1590 Lee Morgan - Candy (75,77)
1591 Lou Donaldson - Lou Takes Off (76)
1592 nr Sonny Clark Quintets (Issued in Japan as BN LNJ70093) (75,76)
1593+ Lou Donaldson - Blues Walk (83)
1594 Louis Smith - Smithville (80)
1595+ Cannonball Adderley with Miles Davis - Somethin' Else (79)
1596+ Kenny Burrell - Blue Lights,Volume 1 (81)
1597+ Kenny Burrell - Blue Lights,Volume 2 (81)
1598+ The Amazing Bud Powell,Volume 4 - Time Waits (82)
1599+ Bennie Green - Soul Stirrin' (81)(stereo issue slightly different from mono issue)
1600+ Introducing The Three Sounds (83,84)

4001+ Sonny Rollins - Newk's Time (71)
4002+ Jimmy Smith - House Party (70,77,78)
4003+ Art Blakey and The Jazz Messengers - Moanin' (85)
4004+ A Message from Blakey - Holiday for Skins,Volume 1 (86)
4005+ A Message from Blakey - Holiday for Skins,Volume 2 (86)
4006 Dizzy Reece - Blues in Trinity (83)
4007+ Donald Byrd - Off to the Races (87)
4008+ Finger Poppin' with the Horace Silver Quintet (89)
4009+ The Amazing Bud Powell,Volume 5 - The Scene Changes (88)
4010+ Bennie Green - Walkin' and Talkin' (88)
4011+ Jimmy Smith - The Sermon (70,78)
4012+ Lou Donaldson with The Three Sounds (89)
4013+ Jackie McLean - New Soil (91)
4014+ The Three Sounds - Bottoms Up! (83,84,89)
4015+ Art Blakey and The Jazz Messengers at the Jazz Corner of the World,Volume 1 (90)
4016+ Art Blakey and The Jazz Messengers at the Jazz Corner of the World,Volume 2 (90)
4017+ Horace Silver Quintet & Trio - Blowin' the Blues Away (94,95)
4018+ Walter Davis Jr. - Davis Cup (93)
4019+ Donald Byrd - Byrd in Hand (92)
4020+ The Three Sounds - Good Deal (91)
4021+ Kenny Burrell with Art Blakey - On View at the Five Spot Cafe (93,94)
4022+ Duke Pearson - Profile (96)
4023+ Dizzy Reece - Star Bright (97)
4024+ Jackie McLean - Swing,Swang,Swingin' (96)
4025+ Lou Donaldson - The Time is Right (96,97)
4026+ Donald Byrd - Fuego (95)
4027+ Freddie Redd Quartet - Music from 'The Connection' (100)
4028+ Horace Parlan - Movin' and Groovin' (100)
4029+ Art Blakey and The Jazz Messengers - The Big Beat (101)
4030+ The Incredible Jimmy Smith - Crazy Baby (98)
4031+J Hank Mobley - Soul Station (99)
4032+ Sonny Red - Out of the Blue (97,99)
4033 Dizzy Reece - Soundin' Off (103)
4034+ Lee Morgan - Leeway (103)
4035+ Duke Pearson - Tender Feelin's (98)
4036+ Lou Donaldson - Sunny Side up (99,100)
4037+ Horace Parlan - Us Three (102)
4038+ Jackie McLean - Capuchin' Swing (102)
4039+ Stanley Turrentine - Look Out! (104)
4040+ Freddie Hubbard - Open Sesame (104)
4041 Tina Brooks - True Blue (105)
4042+ Horace Silver - Horace-Scope (106)
4043+ Horace Parlan Quintet - Speakin' my Piece (107)

BLP
4044+ The Three Sounds - Moods (105)
4045+ Freddie Redd Quintet - Shades of Redd (109)
4046+ Duke Jordan - Flight to Jordan (108)
4047+ Art Taylor - A.T.'s Delight (108)
4048+ Donald Byrd - Byrd in Flight (98,99,106)
4049+ Art Blakey and The Jazz Messengers - A Night in Tunisia (108,109)
4050+ The Incredible Jimmy Smith - Home Cookin' (82,92)
4051+ Jackie McLean - Jackie's Bag (88,110)
4052 nr Tina Brooks - Back to the Tracks (110,111)
4053+ Lou Donaldson - Light Foot (87)
4054+ Art Blakey and The Jazz Messengers - Meet You at the Jazz Corner of theWorld, Vol. 1 (110)
4055+ Art Blakey and The Jazz Messengers - Meet You at the Jazz Corner of the World,Vol. 2 (110)
4056+ Freddie Hubbard - Goin' Up (111)
4057+ Stanley Turrentine with The Three Sounds - Blue Hour (114)
4058+ Hank Mobley - Roll Call (113)
4059+ Kenny Drew - Undercurrent (113)
4060+ Donald Byrd at The Half Note Cafe,Volume 1 (112)
4061+J Donald Byrd at The Half Note Cafe,Volume 2 (112)
4062+ Horace Parlan Trio plus Ray Barretto - Headin' South (113)
4063+ Kenny Dorham - Whistle Stop (115)
4064+ Grant Green - Grant's First Stand(116)
4065 nrJ Stanley Turrentine - Comin' Your Way (issued as BLJ-84065 only and as part of BN BN-LA883-J2) (116)
4066+ Lou Donaldson - Here 'Tis (116)
4067+ Jackie McLean - Bluesnik (115)
4068+ 'Baby Face' Willette - Face to Face (117)
4069+ Stanley Turrentine - Up at Minton's,Volume 1 (118)
4070+ Stanley Turrentine - Up at Minton's,Volume 2 (118)
4071+ Grant Green - Green Street (120)
4072+ The Three Sounds - Feelin' Good (105)
4073+ Freddie Hubbard - Hub Cap (120)
4074+ Horace Parlan - On the Spur of the Moment (119)
4075+ Donald Byrd - The Cat Walk (121)
4076+ The Horace Silver Quintet at The Village Gate - Doin' the Thing (122,123)
4077+ Dexter Gordon - Doin' Allright (121)
4078+ Jimmy Smith - Midnight Special (102,103)
4079+ Lou Donaldson - Gravy Train (121)
4080+ J Hank Mobley - Workout (119)
4081+ Stanley Turrentine - Dearly Beloved (124)
4082+ Horace Parlan - Up and Down (124)
4083+ Dexter Gordon - Dexter Calling (122)
4084+ Baby Face Willette - Stop and Listen (123)
4085+ Freddie Hubbard - Ready for Freddie (126)
4086+ Grant Green - Grantstand (125)
4087+ Leo Parker - Let Me Tell You 'bout It (126)
4088+ The Three Sounds - Here We Come (114)
4089+ Jackie McLean - A Fickle Sonance (128)
4090+ Art Blakey and The Jazz Messengers - Mosaic (127)
4091+ Sonny Clark - Leapin' and Lopin' (129)
4092 Kenny Clarke - Francy Boland & Co. - The Golden Eight (455)
4093+ Ike Quebec - Heavy Soul (129)
4094+ Fred Jackson - Hootin' 'n Tootin' (134)
4095* Leo Parker - Rollin' with Leo (128)
4096+ Stanley Turrentine - That's Where It's At (132)
4097+ Art Blakey and The Afro-Drum Ensemble - The African Beat (133)
4098+ Ike Quebec - Blue and Sentimental (131)
4099+ Grant Green - Sunday Mornin' (124)
4100+ Jimmy Smith plays Fats Waller (133)
4101+ Donald Byrd - Royal Flush (127)
4102+ The Three Sounds - Hey There! (125)

BLP
4103*nr Ike Quebec Sextet - Easy Living (133)
4104+ Art Blakey and The Jazz Messengers - Buhaina's Delight (130,131)
4105+ Ike Quebec - It Might as Well be Spring (130)
4106+ Jackie McLean - Let Freedom Ring (136)
4107+ Don Wilkerson - Preach Brother! (140)
4108+ Lou Donaldson - The Natural Soul (138)
4109+ Herbie Hancock - Takin' Off (139)
4110+ The Horace Silver Quintet - The Tokyo Blues (141)
4111+ Grant Green - The Latin Bit (137)
4112+ Dexter Gordon - Go! (142)
4113+ Freddie Roach - Down To Earth (141)
4114+ Ike Quebec - Soul Samba (Bossa Nova) (143)
4115+ Freddie Hubbard - Hub-Tones (144)
4116 nr Jackie McLean Quintet (Issued as part of BN BN-LA483-J2 and in Japan as BN LNJ80118)(139)
4117+ Jimmy Smith - Back at The Chicken Shack (102,103)
4118+ Donald Byrd - Free Form (131)
4119+ Charlie Rouse - Bossa Nova Bacchanal (145)
4120+ The Three Sounds - It Just Got To Be (114)
4121+ Don Wilkerson - Elder Don (137)
4122* Stanley Turrentine - Jubilee Shout!!! (145)
4123+ Kenny Burrell - Midnight Blue (147)
4124+ Donald Byrd - A New Perspective (147)
4125+ Lou Donaldson - Good Gracious! (148)
4126+ Herbie Hancock - My Point of View (151)
4127+ Kenny Dorham - Una Mas (One More Time) (152)
4128+ Freddie Roach - Mo' Greens Please (148,151)
4129+ Stanley Turrentine - Never Let Me Go (150)
4130+ John Patton - Along Came John (152)
4131+ The Horace Silver Quintet - Silver's Serenade (153)
4132+ Grant Green - Feelin' The Spirit (146)
4133+ Dexter Gordon - A Swingin' Affair (142)
4134* Horace Parlan - Happy Frame of Mind (150)
4135* Freddie Hubbard - Here to Stay (146)
4136+ Solomon Ilori and His Afro-Drum Ensemble - African High Life (153)
4137+ Jackie McLean - One Step Beyond (153)
4138+ Harold Vick - Steppin' Out (154)
4139+ Grant Green - Am I Blue (154)
4140+ Joe Henderson - Page One (155)
4141+ Jimmy Smith - Rockin' the Boat (149)
4142 nr Blue Mitchell Quintet (Issued as BN LT-1082) (157)
4143* John Patton - Blue John (155,156)
4144+ Johnny Coles - Little Johnny C (156)
4145+ Don Wilkerson - Shoutin' (156)
4146+ Dexter Gordon - Our Man in Paris (154)
4147+ Herbie Hancock - Inventions and Dimensions (157)
4148+ George Braith - Two Souls in One (157)
4149+ Hank Mobley - No Room for Squares (151,158)
4150+ Stanley Turrentine - A Chip Off the Old Block (158)
4151+ Andrew Hill - Black Fire (159)
4152+ Joe Henderson - Our Thing (157)
4153+ Grachan Moncur III - Evolution (160)
4154+ Grant Green - Idle Moments (159)
4155+ The Three Sounds - Black Orchid (136)
4156+ Art Blakey and The Jazz Messengers - The Freedom Rider (117,123)
4157+ Lee Morgan - The Sidewinder (161)
4158+ Freddie Roach - Good Move (160)
4159+ Andrew Hill - Judgment! (162)
4160+ Andrew Hill - Smoke Stack (160)
4161+ George Braith - Soul Stream (161)
4162+ Stanley Turrentine - Hustlin' (162)

702

BLP

4163+ Eric Dolphy - Out to Lunch! (163)
4164+ 1 Jimmy Smith - Prayer Meetin' (149)
4165+ Jackie McLean - Destination...Out! (158)
4166+ Joe Henderson - In 'n Out (165)
4167+ Andrew Hill - Point Of Departure (164)
4168+ Freddie Roach - Brown Sugar (164)
4169+ Lee Morgan - Search for The New Land (163)
4170+ Art Blakey and The Jazz Messengers - Free for All (162)
4171+ George Braith - Extension (164)
4172+ Freddie Hubbard - Breaking Point! (166)
4173+ Wayne Shorter - A Night Dreamer (165)
4174+ 'Big' John Patton - The Way I Feel (168)
4175+ Herbie Hancock - Empyrean Isles (168)
4176+ Dexter Gordon - One Flight up (167)
4177+ Grachan Moncur III - Some Other Stuff (169)
4178+ Blue Mitchell - The Things to Do (169)
4179+ Jackie McLean - It's Time! (169)
4180+ Anthony Williams - Life Time (171)
4181+ Kenny Dorham - Trompeta Toccata (172)
4182+ Wayne Shorter - Ju Ju (169)
4183+ Grant Green - Talkin' About! (172)
4184+ Sam Rivers - Fuchsia Swing Song (175)
4185+ The Horace Silver Quintet - Song for My Father (159,173)
4186+ Hank Mobley - The Turnaround! (151,177)
4187+ Larry Young - Into Somethin' (174)
4188+ Donald Byrd - I'm Tryin' To Get Home (175,176)
4189+ Joe Henderson - Inner Urge (175)
4190+ Frederick Roach - All That's Good (172)
4191+ Duke Pearson - Wahoo! (175)
4192+ Big John Patton - Oh Baby! (178)
4193+ Art Blakey and The Jazz Messengers - Indestructible (165,166)
4194+ Wayne Shorter - Speak No Evil (176)
4195+ Herbie Hancock - Maiden Voyage (179)
4196+ Freddie Hubbard - Blue Spirits (177)
4197+ The Three Sounds - Out Of This World (134,135,136)
4198+ J Bobby Hutcherson - Dialogue (179)
4199+ Lee Morgan - The Rumproller (181)
4200+ Jimmy Smith - Softly As A Summer Breeze (78)
4201+ Stanley Turrentine - Joyride (181)
4202+ Grant Green - I Want To Hold Your Hand (179)
4203+ Andrew Hill - Andrew!! (168)
4204+ Dexter Gordon - Gettin'Around (182)
4205+ Pete La Roca - Basra (181)
4206+ Sam Rivers - Contours (182)
4207+ The Night of the Cookers - Live at Club La Marchal with Freddie Hubbard, Volume 1 (180)
4208+ The Night of the Cookers - Live at Club La Marchal with Freddie Hubbard, Volume 2 (180)
4209+ Hank Mobley - Dippin' (183)
4210 nr Ornette Coleman at The Town Hall,Volume 1 (456)
4211 nr Ornette Coleman at The Town Hall,Volume 2 (456)
4212* Lee Morgan - The Gigolo (183,184)
4213+ Bobby Hutcherson - Components (183)
4214+ The Blue Mitchell Quintet - Down With It!(184)
4215+ Jackie McLean - Right Now! (176)
4216+ Anthony Williams - Spring (184)
4217+ Andrew Hill - Compulsion (186)
4218+ Jackie McLean - Action (172)
4219+ Wayne Shorter - The All Seeing Eye (186)
4220+ The Horace Silver Quintet - The Cape Verdean Blues (185,186)
4221+ Larry Young - Unity (186)
4222+ 1 Lee Morgan - Cornbread (185)

BLP
4223 nr Jackie McLean - Jacknife (Issued as part of BN BN-LA457-H2) (185)
4224+ The Ornette Coleman Trio at The "Golden Circle",Stockholm,Volume 1 (187,188)
4225+ The Ornette Coleman Trio at The "Golden Circle",Stockholm,Volume 2 (187,188)
4226+ Don Cherry - Complete Communion (189)
4227+ Joe Henderson - Mode For Joe (189)
4228+ Blue Mitchell - Bring it Home (189)
4229+ Big John Patton - Got a Good Thing Goin' (192)
4230+ Hank Mobley - A Caddy for Daddy (188)
4231+ Bobby Hutcherson - Happenings (190)
4232+ Wayne Shorter - Adam's Apple (190)
4233 nr Andrew Hill - One for One (Issued as part of BN BN-LA453-H2) (191)
4234 nr Stanley Turrentine (167,171)
4235+ Jimmy Smith - Bucket (149)
4236 nr Jackie McLean - High Frequency (Issued as part of BN BN-LA457-H2) (192)
4237+ Cecil Taylor - Unit Structures (192)
4238+ Donald Byrd - Mustang (193)
4239+ Big John Patton - Let 'em Roll (188)
4240+ Stanley Turrentine - Rough 'n Tumble (193)
4241 nr Hank Mobley (191,193)
4242+ Larry Young - Of Love and Peace (194)
4243+ DelightfuLee Morgan (191,192)
4244+ Bobby Hutcherson - Stick Up! (194)
4245+ Art Blakey and The Jazz Messengers - Like Someone in Love (108,109)
4246+ Ornette Coleman - The Empty Foxhole (195)
4247+ Don Cherry - Symphony for Improvisers (195)
4248+ The Three Sounds - Vibrations (196)
4249+ Sam Rivers - A New Conception (196)
4250+ Horace Silver Quintet/Sextet - The Jody Grind (196,197)
4251+ Jack Wilson - Something Personal (194)
4252+ Duke Pearson - Sweet Honey Bee (198)
4253+ Grant Green - Street of Dreams (174)
4254* Lou Donaldson - Lush Life (199)
4255+ Jimmy Smith - I'm Movin' On (148)
4256+ Stanley Turrentine - The Spoiler (195)
4257+ Blue Mitchell - Boss Horn (197)
4258* Art Blakey and The Jazz Messengers - The Witch Doctor (119)
4259+ Donald Byrd - Blackjack (198)
4260+ Cecil Taylor - Conquistador (196)
4261* Sam Rivers - Dimensions & Extensions (200)
4262+ Jackie McLean - New and Old Gospel (201)
4263+ Lou Donaldson - Alligator Bogaloo (201)
4264+ McCoy Tyner - The Real McCoy (201)
4265+ The Three Sounds - Live at The Lighthouse (203)
4266* Larry Young - Contrasts (205)
4267* Duke Pearson - The Right Touch (205)
4268+ Stanley Turrentine - Easy Walker (193)
4269* Jimmy Smith - Open House (101)
4270* Jack Wilson - Easterly Winds (206)
4271* Lou Donaldson - Mr. Shin -A-Ling (206)
4272* Blue Mitchell - Heads Up! (207)
4273* Hank Mobley - Hi Voltage (206)
4274* Tyrone Washington - Natural Essence (208)
4275* McCoy Tyner - Tender Moments (207)
4276* Introducing Duke Pearson's Big Band (208)
4277+ Horace Silver Quintet - Serenade to a Soul Sister (210,214)
4278+ Frank Foster - Manhattan Fever (211)
4279+ Herbie Hancock - Speak Like A Child (210)
4280* Lou Donaldson - Midnight Creeper (211)
4281+ John Patton - That Certain Feeling (210)
4282+ Elvin Jones Trio - Puttin' it Together (212)

Note:All subsequent albums were issued in stereo only.

BST
84283 Booker Ervin - The In Between (208)
84284 Jackie McLean - 'Bout Soul (205)
84285 The 3 Sounds - Coldwater Flat (212)
84286 Stanley Turrentine - The Look of Love (212,213,214)
84287 Ornette Coleman - New York is Now! (213,214)
84288 Hank Mobley - Reach Out! (209)
84289 Lee Morgan - Caramba! (213)
84290 Lonnie Smith - Think! (216)
84291 Bobby Hutcherson - Total Eclipse (215)
84292 Donald Byrd - Slow Drag (202)
84293 Duke Pearson Quintet - The Phantom (215,217)
84294 Eddie Gale - Ghetto Music (219)
84295 Reuben Wilson - On Broadway (219)
84296 Jimmy Smith - Plain Talk (101)
84297 Wayne Shorter - Schizophrenia (200)
84298 Stanley Turrentine - Always Something There (220)
84299 Lou Donaldson - Say It Loud (220)
84300 Blue Mitchell - Collision in Black (218)
84301 Gene Harris & his Three Sounds - Elegant Soul (218)
84302 Introducing Kenny Cox and The Contemporary Jazz Quintet (221)
84303 Andrew Hill - Grass Roots (216)
84304 Larry Young - Heaven on Earth (209)
84305 The Ultimate Elvin Jones (217)
84306 John Patton - Understanding (220)
84307 McCoy Tyner - Time for Tyner (214)
84308 Duke Pearson Big Band - Now Hear This! (221)
84309 The Horace Silver Quintet - You Gotta Take a Little Love (222)
84310 Grant Green - Goin' West (146)
84311 Don Cherry - Where is Brooklyn (197)
84312 Lee Morgan - Charisma (195)
84313 Lonnie Smith - Turning Point (222)
84314 nr Booker Ervin (Issued as part of BN BN-LA488-H2) (215)
84315 Stanley Turrentine - The Common Touch (217)
84316 nr Frank Foster (222)
84317 Reuben Wilson - Love Bug (224)
84318 Lou Donaldson - Hot Dog (226)
84319 Donald Byrd - Fancy Free (227,228)
84320 Eddie Gale - Black Rhythm Happening (226)
84321 Herbie Hancock - The Prisoner (225)
84322 Jack McDuff - Down Home Style (228)
84323 Duke Pearson - Merry Ole Soul (223,230)
84324 Blue Mitchell - Bantu Village (227)
84325 The Best of Horace Silver (44,45,58,94,122,141)
84326 Lonnie Smith - Move Your Hand (230)
84327 Grant Green - Carryin' On (233)
84328 Jack Wilson - Song for my Daughter (219,222,226,228,229)
84329 Hank Mobley - The Flip (229)
84330 Andrew Hill - Lift Every Voice (227)
84331 Elvin Jones - Poly-Currents (232)
84332 1 Wayne Shorter - Super Nova (231)
84333 Bobby Hutcherson - Now (232,233)
84334 Jack McDuff - Moon Rappin' (234)
84335 Lee Morgan - The Sixth Sense (207)
84336 Stanley Turrentine - Another Story (223)
84337 Lou Donaldson - Everything I Play is Funky (231,236)
84338 McCoy Tyner - Expansions (217)
84339 Kenny Cox & The Contemporary Jazz Quintet - Multidirection (234)
84340 John Patton - Accent on the Blues (230)

705

BST

84341 The Three Sounds - Soul Symphony (231)
84342 Grant Green - Green is Beautiful (237)
84343 Reuben Wilson - Blue Mode (235)
84344 Duke Pearson - How Insensitive (224,225,226)
84345 Jackie McLean - Demon's Dance (208)
84346 Thad Jones-Mel Lewis - Consummation (236,237,242)
84347 Art Blakey and The Jazz Messengers - Roots and Herbs (117,123)
84348 Brother Jack McDuff - To Seek a New Home (239,240)
84349 Donald Byrd - Electric Byrd (242)
84350 Jimmy McGriff - Electric Funk (232)
84351 Lonnie Smith - Drives (236)
84352 Horace Silver Quintet - That Healin' Feelin' (241,243)
84353 Chick Corea - The Song of Singing (240)
84354 Jeremy Steig - Wayfaring Stranger (238)
84355 Joe Williams - Worth Waiting For... (241)
84356 Ornette Coleman - Love Call (213,214)
84357 Candido - Beautiful (249)
84358 Brother Jack McDuff - Who Knows what Tomorrow's Gonna Bring? (250)
84359 Lou Donaldson - Pretty Things (243)
84360 Grant Green - Alive! (246,247)
84361 Elvin Jones - Coalition (245)
84362 Bobby Hutcherson - San Francisco (245)
84363 Wayne Shorter - Odyssey of Iska (247)
84364 Jimmy McGriff - Something to Listen to (248)
84365 Reuben Wilson - A Groovy Situation (248)
84366 nr John Patton (Transferred to BST84418) (248)
84367 nr Hank Mobley (Transferred to BST84417 and actually issued as BN LT-1045) (246)
84368 Horace Silver - Total Response (250,251)
84369 Elvin Jones - Genesis (252)
84370 Lou Donaldson - Cosmos (254)
84371 nr Lonnie Smith
84372 Richard Groove Holmes - Comin' on Home (252)
84373 Grant Green - Visions (252)
84374 Jimmy McGriff - Black Pearl (253)
84375 nr not used
84376 Bobby Hutcherson - Head on (253)
84377 Reuben Wilson - Set Us Free (254)
84378 Gene Harris & The Three Sounds (254,255)
84379 Bobbi Humphrey - Flute In (256)
84380 Donald Byrd - Ethiopian Knights (255)
84381 nr Lee Morgan (Issued as BN BST84901) (256)
84382 Ronnie Foster - The Two Headed Freap (259)
84383:see French issues on page 730.

84384 to 84412: not used.

84413 Grant Green - Shades of Green (257)
84414 Elvin Jones - Merry Go Round (258)
84415 Grant Green - The Final Comedown (257,258)
84416 Bobby Hutcherson - Natural Illusions (260)
84417 nr Hank Mobley - Thinking of Home (Issued as BN LT-1045) (246)
84418 nr Big John Patton - Memphis to New York Spirit (248)
84419 nr McCoy Tyner - Extensions (Issued as BN BN-LA006-F) (238)
84420 Horace Silver - The United States of Mind,Phase 3: All (259)
84421 Bobbi Humphrey - Dig This (261)
84422 Marlena Shaw - Marlena (262)
84423 Gene Harris of The Three Sounds (261)
84424 Stanley Turrentine - Z.T.'s Blues (127)
84425 Hank Mobley - Far Away Lands (202)
84426 Lee Morgan - The Rajah (197)

706

BST
84427 Jackie McLean - Tippin' The Scales (143)
84428 Clifford Brown - Alternate Takes (35,36,38)
84429:see 2-LP Sets on page 707
84430 Bud Powell - Alternate Takes (25,37,68,82,88,154)
84431 Hank Mobley - Another Workout (130)
84432 Grant Green - Born to be Blue (132,135)
84433:see 2-LP Sets on page 707
84434 The Three Sounds - Babe's Blues (125,136)
84435 Hank Mobley - Straight No Filter (151,177,193)

84901 Lee Morgan (256)

SPECIAL ISSUES

BLP
1001 25 Years Blue Note Anniversary Album - Modern Jazz Series:
Miles Davis (34) Thelonious Monk (21)
Bud Powell (27) Tadd Dameron (19)
James Moody (23) Horace Silver (33)
J.J.Johnson (36) Clifford Brown (38)
Milt Jackson (30) Art Blakey & Sabu (39)

2001 (& Stereo BST82001) Blue Note Gems of Jazz (Same contents as BN BLP1001 above)

JAZZ CLASSICS SERIES (mono issues)

B6501 Sidney De Paris - De Paris Dixie (9,27)
B6502 The Funky Piano of Art Hodes (7,8,11,13,14,15)
B6503 The Beginning and End of Bop:
James Moody (23) George Wallington (42)
B6504 Original Blue Note Jazz,Volume 1:
Edmond Hall (6) Art Hodes (9)
B6505 Edmond Hall - Celestial Express (5,7)
B6506 Original Blue Note Jazz,Vol.2:
James P.Johnson (7,11) Sidney De Paris (9)
B6507 Swing Hi Swing Lo:
Ike Quebec (10,15) Jimmy Hamilton (16)
Benny Morton (13) John Hardee (17)
B6508 Sittin' In - Art Hodes,Volume 1 (7,8,11,13)
B6509 Classics,Volume 1:
Port of Harlem Six (2) Art Hodes (7,9,14,15)
Edmond Hall (6) Baby Dodds (16)

VOCAL SERIES

BLP
9001+ Dodo Greene - My Hour of Need (136,137)
9002+ Sheila Jordan - A Portrait of Sheila (142,144)

Note: These albums were also issued in stereo as BST 89001/89002.

2 LP SETS

BST2-
84429 The Best of Blue Note:

Bud Powell (27) | Miles Davis (34)
James Moody (23) | John Coltrane (71)
Thelonious Monk (28) | Herbie Hancock (179)
Milt Jackson (90) | Donald Byrd (147)
Clifford Brown (38)

Art Blakey & The Jazz Messengers (85) | Jimmy Smith (103)
Lou Donaldson (83) | Kenny Burrell (147)
Horace Silver (173) | Lee Morgan (161)

84433 The Best of Blue Note, Volume 2:

Ike Quebec (10) | Horace Silver (58)
Tadd Dameron (19) | Sonny Rollins (59)
Thelonious Monk (21) | Clifford Brown & Lou Donaldson (35)
Gil Melle (450) | Dexter Gordon (142)
Bud Powell (37) | Lou Donaldson (96)

Art Blakey (85) | Cannonball Adderley (79)
Horace Parlan (107) | Joe Henderson (155)
Lee Morgan (181) | Herbie Hancock (139)

BST
89901 Jimmy Smith's Greatest Hits (51,61,78,98,103,149)
89902 Three Decades of Jazz, Volume 1: 1939-1949:

Albert Ammons (1) | Sidney De Paris (9)
Port Of Harlem Jazzmen (2) | Art Hodes (7)
Sidney Bechet (3,12) | Ike Quebec (10)
Earl Hines (3) | Benny Morton (13)
Meade Lux Lewis (5) | Bunk Johnson-Sidney Bechet (13)
Edmond Hall (5,6) | Tadd Dameron (19)
George Lewis | Thelonious Monk (21,22)
Josh White (4) | James Moody (23)
James P.Johnson (6,7)

89903 Three Decades of Jazz, Volume 2: 1949-1959:

Bud Powell (27) | Clifford Brown (38)
Thelonious Monk (28) | Miles Davis (41)
Milt Jackson (30) | Horace Silver (58)
J.J. Johnson (36) | Jimmy Smith (61)

Sonny Clark (70) | Art Blakey (85)
John Coltrane (71) | Lou Donaldson (83)
Sonny Rollins (71)

89904 Three Decades of Jazz, Volume 3: 1959-1969:

Jimmy Smith (103) | Donald Byrd (147)
Ike Quebec (131) | Lee Morgan (161)
Kenny Burrell (147)

Eric Dolphy (163) | Ornette Coleman (187)
Horace Silver (173) | Lou Donaldson (206)
Stanley Turrentine (181)

89905 Jazz Wave Ltd. on Tour, Volume 1 (235,236)
89906 Lee Morgan - Live at the Lighthouse (245)
89907 The Best of Herbie Hancock (139,151,157,168,179,210,225)

B2S-5256 World of Jazz:

Jazz Crusaders (563)	John Patton (168)
Bud Shank (549)	Duke Pearson (96)
Billy Larkin (563)	Horace Silver (173)
Jack Wilson (194)	Lou Donaldson (100)
Joe Henderson (157)	Donald Byrd (87)
Jimmy Smith (149)	Stanley Turrentine (124)
Bobby Hutcherson (190)	The Three Sounds (91)
Lee Morgan (192)	

<u>BLUE NOTE label</u> (United Artists Series)

Note: Following albums were issued as part of the United Artists label album series.
Suffixes G2,H2 and J2 were used for 2-LP sets.Missing numbers in the series were not on Blue Note label.

BN-LA
006-F McCoy Tyner - Extensions (238)
007-F Moacir Santos - Maestro (263)
014-G Wayne Shorter - Moto Grosso Feio (240)
015-G2 Elvin Jones - Live at the Lighthouse (262)
024-F Lou Donaldson - Sophisticated Lou (264)
037-G2 Grant Green - Live at the Lighthouse (260)
047-F Donald Byrd - Black Byrd (260,264)
054-F Horace Silver - In Pursuit of the 27th Man (263)
059-F Alphonse Mouzon - The Essence of Mystery (265)
098-F Ronnie Foster - Sweet Revival (265)
099-F The New Heritage Keyboard Quartet (265)
109-F Lou Donaldson - Sassy Soul Strut (266)
110-F Elvin Jones - Mr.Jones (232,261)
140-F Donald Byrd - Street Lady (267)
141-G2 Gene Harris - Yesterday,Today & Tomorrow (268)
142-G Bobbi Humphrey - Blacks and Blues (267)
143-F Marlena Shaw - From The Depths of My Soul (266)
152-F Herbie Hancock - Succotash (=BN BLP4147) (157)
158-G2 A Decade of Jazz,Volume 1 (= BN BST89902) (see page 707)
159-G2 A Decade of Jazz,Volume 2 (= BN BST89903) (see page 707)
160-G2 A Decade of Jazz,Volume 3 (= BN BST89904) (see page 707)
169-F Cannonball Adderley - Somethin' Else (= BN BLP1595) (79)
170-G2 The Jazz Crusaders - Tough Talk (557,559,560,561,562)
171-G2 Les McCann - Fish This Week (556,557,558,559,560)
222-G Alphonse Mouzon - Funky Snakefoot (269,270)
223-G McCoy Tyner - Asante (247)
224-G Lee Morgan Memorial Album (72,161,184,185)
249-G Bobby Hutcherson - Live at Montreux (268)
250-G Ronnie Foster - Live at Montreux (268)
251-G Marlena Shaw - Live at Montreux(268)
252-G Bobbi Humphrey - Live at Montreux (269)
257-G Bobby Hutcherson - Cirrus (271,272)
258-G Dom Minasi - When Joanna Loved Me (271)
259-G Lou Donaldson - Sweet Lou (271)
260-G Moacir Santos - Saudade (270)
261-G Ronnie Foster - On the Avenue (272)
267-G Clifford Brown - Brownie Eyes (35,36,38)
313-G Gene Harris - Astral Signal (273)
317-G Duke Pearson - It Could Only Happen With You (238,241)
344-G Bobbi Humphrey - Satin Doll (272,273)
356-H2 Freddie Hubbard (104,111,120,126,166,177)
368-G Donald Byrd - Stepping into Tomorrow (274)
369-G Bobby Hutcherson - Linger Lane (276)
370-G Waters (273)
392-H2 Thad Jones & Mel Lewis (237,242,582,583,585,586,587)

709

BN-LA
393-H2 Dexter Gordon (121,122,142,167,182)
394-H2 Stanley Turrentine (158,162,199,204,212,219,220)
395-H2 Chick Corea (240,585,587)
397-G Marlena Shaw - Who is This Bitch,Anyway? (274,275)
398-G Alphonse Mouzon - Mind Transplant (275)
399-H2 Herbie Hancock (139,151,157,168,179,210,215)
400-H2 Jimmy Smith (50,51,61,77,78,98,108,149)
401-H2 Sonny Rollins (59,63,71,74)
402-H2 Horace Silver (39,64,89,94,106,153,173,185,186,196,210,222)
406-G Horace Silver - Silver 'n Brass (275,276)
425-G Ronnie Foster - Cheschire Cat (278)
426-G Dom Minasi - I Have The Feeling I've Been Here Before (276)
451-H2 Paul Chambers/John Coltrane - High Step (57,453,463)
452-G Ronnie Laws - Pressure Sensitive (279)
453-H2 Sam Rivers - Involution (= BN BLP4233 + BST84261) (191,200)
456-H2 Lester Young - The Aladdin Sessions (459,460,461)
457-H2 Jackie McLean - Jacknife (= BLP4223 + BLP4236) (185,192)
458-H2 Cecil Taylor in Transition (453,623)
459-H2 Andrew Hill - One for One (177,229,237)
460-H2 McCoy Tyner - Cosmos (221,224,246)
461-H2 Gil Evans - Pacific Standard Time (554,555,556)
462-G Carmen McRae - I Am Music (279,280)
463-G Moacir Santos - Carnival of the Spirits (277)
464-G Eddie Henderson - Sunburst (279)
472-H2 Chick Corea - Circling In (246,247,585)
473-J2 Art Blakey's Jazz Messengers - Live Messengers (40,41,125,626)
474-H2 Horace Silver - The Trio Sides (33,39,58,76,89,95,141,159,211)
475-H2 Sonny Rollins - More from the Vanguard (73,74)
483-J2 Jackie McLean - Hipnosis (139,199)
485-H2 Herbie Nichols - The Third World (47,48,49)
488-H2 Booker Ervin - Back from the Gig (150,215)
496-H2 Freddie Hubbard - Here to Stay (= BLP4073 + BST84135) (120,146)
506-H2 Elvin Jones - The Prime Element (224,269)
507-H2 Fats Navarro - Prime Source (19,22,23,25)
519-G Gene Harris - Nexus (280)
520-G Chico Hamilton - Peregrinations (281)
521-H2 Johnny Griffin/John Coltrane/Hank Mobley - Blowin' Sessions (= BLP1549 + BLP1559) (61,63)
529-H2 Paul Horn in India (565)
530-H2 The Jazz Crusaders - The Young Rabbits (558,559,561,562,563,564,566)
531-H2 Wes Montgomery - Beginnings (553,554,556)
532-H2 Gerry Mulligan/Lee Konitz - Revelation (545,546,553)
533-H2 T-Bone Walker - Classics of Modern Blues (529,530)
534-G Jimmy Witherspoon - Spoonful (646)
541-G John Lee & Gerry Brown (281)
549-G Donald Byrd - Places and Spaces (283)
550-G Bobbi Humphrey - Fancy Dancer (281,282)
551-G Bobby Hutcherson - Montara (282)
579-H2 Thelonious Monk - The Complete Genius (19,20,21,28,32)
581-G Horace Silver - Silver 'n Wood (283,284)
582-J2 Lee Morgan - The Procrastinator (204,231,233)
584-G Alphonse Mouzon - The Man Incognito (284,286)
590-H2 Milt Jackson - All Star Bags (30,59,621)
591-H2 Art Pepper - Early Art (464,465)
596-G Earl Klugh (285)
598-G2 Randy Weston - Little Niles (621,623,624)
606-G Marlena Shaw - Just a Matter of Time (286)
615-G Bobby Hutcherson - Waiting (286,287)
622-G Chico Hamilton and the Players (287)
628-G Ronnie Laws - Fever (284,285)
632-H2 Jean-Luc Ponty - Canteloupe Island (568,569)

BN-LA
633-G Donald Byrd - Caricatures (289)
634-G Gene Harris - In a Special Way (288)
635-G Carmen McRae - Can't Hide Love (288,289)
636-G Eddie Henderson - Heritage (287)
645-G Barbara Carroll (290)
663-J2 Blue Note Live at the Roxy (290,291)
664-G Robbie Krieger and Friends (291,292)
667-G Earl Klugh - Living Inside Your Love (293)
690-J2 War - Platinum Jazz (647)
699-G The Best of Bobbi Humphrey (256,267,272,273,281,282)
700-G The Best of Donald Byrd (260,264,267,274,283)
701-G John Lee & Gerry Brown - Still Can't Say Enough (294)
708-G Horace Silver - Silver 'n Voices (294)
709-H2 Carmen McRae at the Great American Music Hall (290)
710-G Bobby Hutcherson - The View from the Inside (292)
711-G Willie Bobo - Tomorrow is Here (295)
730-H Ronnie Laws - Friends & Strangers(296)
736-H Noel Pointer - Phantazia (295,296)
737-H Earl Klugh - Finger Paintings (296,297)
738-H Maxi (297)
760-H Gene Harris - Tone Tantrum (298)
789-H Bobby Hutcherson - Knucklebean (297,298)
819-H Rico - Man from Wareika (647)
853-H Horace Silver - Silver 'n Percussion (299,300)
870-H Blue Note Meet the L.A. Philharmonic (299)
882-J2 Chick Corea - Circulus (240,247)
883-J2 Stanley Turrentine - Jubilee Shouts (= BN BLP4065 + BST84122) (116,145)
945-H Horace Silver - Sterling Silver (58,82,94,122,123,159,162)

Jazz Classics Series:

LT-
987 Lee Morgan - Sonic Boom (201,202)
988 Wayne Shorter - The Soothsayer (178)
989 Dexter Gordon - Clubhouse (182)
990 Grant Green - Solid (167)
991 Donald Byrd - Chant (120)
992 Jimmy Smith - Confirmation (70,78)
993 Stanley Turrentine - New Time Shuffle (199,204)
994 Jackie McLean - Consequence (187)
995 Hank Mobley - A Slice of the Top (191)
996 Bobby Hutcherson - Spiral (179,221)
1028 Lou Donaldson - Midnight Sun (107)
1030 Andrew Hill - Dance with Death (219)
1031 Lee Morgan - Taru (209)
1032 Grant Green - Nigeria (132)

LWB-
1033 Horace Silver - Silver and Strings Play the Music of the Spheres (300,301)

LT-
1037 Stanley Turrentine - In Memory of (167)
1038 Larry Young - Mother Ship (213)
1044 Bobby Hutcherson - Patterns (211)
1045 Hank Mobley - Thinking of Home(246)
1046 The Jazz Crusaders - Live Sides (566,568)
1051 Dexter Gordon - Landslide (122,137,140)
1052 Ike Quebec - With a Song in my Heart (135)
1053 Joe Pass,Jazz Guitar No.1 - Catch me (559,560)
1054 Jimmy Smith - Cool Blues (80)

711

LT
1055 nr Mainstreamin': Vic Dickenson (32) / Bobby Hackett (449)
1056 Wayne Shorter - Et Cetera (183)
1057 Harold Land - Take Aim (107)
1058 Lee Morgan - Tom Cat (170)
1064 Art Pepper - Omega Alpha (465)
1065 Art Blakey - Once Upon a Groove (552)
1075 Stanley Turrentine - Mr. Natural (171)
1076 Leo Parker - Rollin' with Leo (= BN BST84095) (128)
1081 Hank Mobley - Third Season (200)
1082 Blue Mitchell - Step Lightly (157)
1085 Jackie McLean - Vertigo (91,149)
1086 Bobby Hutcherson - Medina (230)
1088 Art Blakey and The Jazz Messengers - Africaine (97)
1089 Ike Quebec - Congo Lament (133)
1091 Lee Morgan - Infinity (187)
1092 Jimmy Smith - On the Sunny Side (70,82,103)
1095 Stanley Turrentine - Ain't no Way (214,229)
1096 Donald Byrd - The Creeper (206)
1100 Bill Evans - Bob Brookmeyer Quintet (623)
1101 Gerry Mulligan - Freeway (545)
1102 Jean-Luc Ponty - Live at Donte's (568)
1103 Joe Pass - Joy Spring (561)

BLUE NOTE label (New Series)

BT
85101 Stanley Jordan - Magic Touch (304)
85102 McCoy Tyner & Jackie McLean - It's About Time (307,308)
85103 George Russell & The Living Time Orchestra - The African Game (303)
85104 Charles Lloyd Quartet - A Night in Copenhagen (303)
85105 Stanley Turrentine - Straight Ahead (305)
85106 Kenny Burrell/Grover Washington Jr. - Togethering (304)
85107 Bennie Wallace - Twilight Time (308)
85108 Charlie Parker at Storyville (450)
85109 James Newton - The African Flower (309)
85110 Bobby McFerrin - Spontaneous Inventions (313,649)
85111 Bill Evans - The Alternative Man (305)

BABB
85112 Dexter Gordon - Nights at the Keystone (2 LP Set) (457)

BT
85113 One Night with Blue Note,Volume 1 (306)
85114 One Night with Blue Note,Volume 2 (306,307)
85115 One Night with Blue Note,Volume 3 (306,307)
85116 One Night with Blue Note,Volume 4 (306)

BTDK
85117 One Night with Blue Note Preserved (4 LP Box Set)(same contents as BT 85113/4/5/6) (306,307)

BT
85118 OTB - Out of the Blue (308,309)
85119 Tony Williams - Foreign Intrigue (309)
85120 not used
85121 Freddie Hubbard -Woody Shaw - Double Take (312)
85122 The Don Pullen/George Adams Quartet - Breakthrough (313)
85123 The State of the Tenor - Joe Henderson Live at the Village Vanguard,Volume 1 (310,311)
85124 The Michel Petrucciani Trio - Pianism (312)
85125 Jimmy Smith - Go for Whatcha Know (312)
85126 The State of the Tenor - Joe Henderson Live at the Village Vanguard,Volume 2 (311)

712

BQ

85127	Blue Note 86 - A New Generation of Jazz:	
	Michel Petrucciani (312)	Tony Williams (309)
	Bobby McFerrin (313)	OTB (309)
	Stanley Jordan (304)	Bill Evans (305)
	Bennie Wallace(308)	James Newton (309)

BT

85128 Out of The Blue - Inside Track (314)
85129 Duke Ellington - Money Jungle (628)
85130 Stanley Jordan - Standards,Vol.1 (316)
85131 Eric Dolphy - Other Aspects (455,456)
85132 George Russell - So What (303)
85133 Michel Petrucciani - Power of Three (314)
85134 James Newton - Romance and Revolution (314)
85135 The Other Side of 'Round Midnight - Dexter Gordon (310,313)
85136 James Blood Ulmer - America,Do You Remember The Love? (315)
85137 Kenny Burrell - Generation (316)
85138 Tony Williams - Civilization (316)
85139 Freddie Hubbard - Life Flight (317)
85140 Stanley Turrentine - Wonderland (317)
85141 Out of The Blue - Live at Mt. Fuji (315)

BLUE NOTE label (International Series - Produced by EMI)

Note: This series include issues produced in various European countries. Prefixes used were mostly B1- for U.S. issues and prefixes similar to CD issues in Europe (for example,B1-35221 was issued in Europe as 7243 8-35221-1).
Albums marked ** were also produced as 180-gram vinyl issues,released in 1997/98 in US and Europe,using prefix B1-ST or B1-BST.

B1-46094 BST84112 ** Dexter Gordon - Go! (142)
B1-46095 BST81577 ** John Coltrane - Blue Train (71)
B1-46137 BST84157 ** Lee Morgan - The Sidewinder (161)
B1-46338 BST81595 ** Cannonball Adderley - Somethin' Else (79)
B1-46339 BST84195 ** Herbie Hancock - Maiden Voyage (179)
B1-46509 BST84194 ** Wayne Shorter - Speak No Evil (176)
B1-46516 BST84003 ** Art Blakey - Moanin' (85)
B1-46523 BST84090 ** Art Blakey - Mosaic (127)
B1-46524 BST84163 ** Eric Dolphy - Out To Lunch (163)
B1-46528 BST84031 ** Hank Mobley - Soul Station (99)
B1-46548 BST84185 ** Horace Silver - Song For My Father (159,173)

BLJ-
46905 Jack Walrath - Master of Suspense (315,320)
46906 Dianne Reeves (318,319)
46907 The Don Pullen/George Adams Quartet - Song Everlasting (318)
46993 Charnett Moffett - Net Man (317,318)
46994 Eliane Elias - Illusions (649,650)

BLJ- (or BN1- on *)
48014 * Bennie Wallace - Border Town (320)
48015 Mose Allison - Ever Since The World Ended (319)
48016 Bireli Lagrene - Inferno (321)
48017 * Freddie Hubbard/Woody Shaw - The Eternal Triangle (321)
B1-48494 Tony Williams - Angel Street (322)
B1-48679 Michel Petrucciani - Michel Plays Petrucciani (322)

713

B1-80679	(U.K.)	Blue 'N Groovy (2 LP Set):
		Duke Pearson (205) · Tina Brooks (105)
		Jack Wilson (206) · Donald Byrd (112)
		Stanley Turrentine (193) · Bobby Hutcherson (194)
		Don Wilkerson (140) · Wayne Shorter (200)
		Lee Morgan (161) · Blue Mitchell (184)
		Herbie Hancock (168) · Grant Green (166)
		Jazz Messengers (117) · Horace Silver (58)
B1-80701	(U.K.)	Afro Blue (2 LP Set):
		Dianne Reeves (339) · McCoy Tyner (207)
		Don Pullen (344) · Jackie McLean (110)
		Horace Parlan (150) · Art Blakey (86)
		Art Blakey (133) · Lee Morgan (163)
		James Moody (23) · Horace Silver (39)
		Bud Powell (27) · Sabu Martinez (64)
B1-80883		Us 3 - Hand On The Torch (350,351)
B1-81558	BLP1558 **	Sonny Rollins,Volume Two (63)
B1-84115	BST84115 **	Freddie Hubbard - Hub-Tones (144)
B1-84140	BST84140 **	Joe Henderson - Page One (155)
B1-84154	BST84154 **	Grant Green - Idle Moments (159)
B1-84344	BST84344	Duke Pearson - How Insensitive (224,225,226)
B1-84357	BST84357	Candido - Beautiful (249)
B1-89383	BLP1580	Johnny Griffin - The Congregation (73)
B1-89392	BLP4027	Freddie Redd Quartet - The Music From "The Connection" (100)
B1-89606	(U.K.)	Donald Byrd - Early Byrd - The Best Of The Jazz Soul Years (2 LP Set) (193,198,202,227,242,255)
B1-89622	(U.K.)	The Best Of Grant Green - Street Funk And Jazz Grooves (2 LP Set) (125,159,166,167,172,174,233,237,246,257,260)
B1-89907		Blue Break Beats,Volume Two:
		Donald Byrd (198,267) · Grant Green (237)
		Bobbi Humphrey (267) · Bobby Hutcherson (245)
		Eddie Henderson (279) · Blue Mitchell (207)
		Gene Harris (273) · Gerald Wilson (559)
		Reuben Wilson (235) · Lonnie Smith (236)
		Jimmy McGriff (586) · Duke Pearson (217)
		Lou Donaldson (243,254)
B1-90055		Chick Corea - Now He Thinks,Now He Sobs (585)
B1-90260		Kenny Burrell And The Jazz Guitar Band - Piece Of Blue And The Blues (316)
B1-90261		Stanley Turrentine - La Place (324,325)
B1-90262		Bobby Watson & Horizon - No Question About It (323)
B1-90264		Dianne Reeves - I Remember (322,323,339)
B1-90905		Freddie Hubbard - Times Are Changin' (326)
B1-90967		Bireli Lagrene - Foreign Affairs (323,324)
B1-91101		Jack Walrath - Neohippus (324)
B1-91138		The Best Of Lee Morgan - The Blue Note Years (72,75,161,181,184,185)
B1-91139		The Best Of Dexter Gordon - The Blue Note Years (121,122,142)
B1-91140		The Best Of Jimmy Smith - The Blue Note Years (78,98,103,312)
B1-91141		The Best Of Wayne Shorter - The Blue Note Years (176,178,190,200)
B1-91142		The Best Of Herbie Hancock - The Blue Note Years (139,168,179,210)
B1-91143		The Best Of Horace Silver - The Blue Note Years (39,44,45,58,64,89,94)
B1-91411		Eliane Elias - So Far,So Close (329,330)
B1-91441		Lou Rawls With Les McCann Ltd. - Stormy Monday (491,492)
B1-91650		Charnett Moffett - Beauty Within (326,327)
B1-91651		McCoy Tyner - Revelations (325)
B1-91730		Ralph Peterson Quintet - V (588)
B1-91731		Superblue (588)
B1-91785		Don Pullen - New Beginnings (326)
B1-91915		Bobby Watson - The Inventor (330)
B1-91930	BLT1001§	Tommy Smith - Step By Step (§:original U.K. issue)(324)
B1-91937		Lou Rawls At Last (327,328)
B1-91984		George Adams - Nightingale (584)

B1-92051 Andrew Hill - Eternal Spirit (328)
B1-92168 Gil Melle - Mindscape (327)
B1-92279 Rick Margitza - Color (329)
B1-92356 Stanley Jordan - Cornucopia (326,329,330)

BLUE NOTE 50th ANNIVERSARY COLLECTION (2 LP sets):

BST2-
92465 Vol.1: From Boogie To Bop (1939-1956):

Albert Ammons & Meade Lux Lewis (1)	Thelonious Monk(28)
Sidney Bechet (3)	Milt Jackson (30)
Edmond Hall (5)	Bud Powell (37)
Ike Quebec (10)	Miles Davis (34)
Thelonious Monk (21)	Clifford Brown (38)
Tadd Dameron with Fats Navarro (22)	Horace Silver (45)
James Moody (23)	Hank Mobley (49)
Bud Powell (27)	Sonny Rollins (59)
	Jimmy Smith (51)

92468 Vol.2: The Jazz Message (1956-1965)

John Coltrane (71)	Art Blakey & The Jazz Messengers (127)
Jackie McLean (110)	Wayne Shorter (176)
Cannonball Adderley & Miles Davis (79)	Herbie Hancock (179)
Dexter Gordon (142)	Bobby Hutcherson (183)
	Larry Young (186)

92471 Vol.3: Funk & Blues (1956-1967)

Horace Silver (58)	Joe Henderson with Kenny Dorham (155)
Art Blakey & The Jazz Messengers (85)	Horace Silver (173)
Jimmy Smith (103)	Blue Mitchell (169)
Donald Byrd (147)	Lee Morgan (261)
	Lou Donaldson (201)

92474 Vol.4: Outside In (1964-1989)

Eric Dolphy (163)	Tony Williams (309)
Andrew Hill (159)	Freddie Hubbard & Woody Shaw (321)
Ornette Coleman (214)	Don Pullen-George Adams Quartet (313)
McCoy Tyner (201)	Joe Henderson (311)
OTB (309)	Michel Petrucciani (322)

92477 Vol.5: Lightning The Fuse (1970-1989)

Grant Green (237)	Stanley Jordan (304)
Earl Klugh (285)	Stanley Turrentine (317)
Noel Pointer (295)	Benny Wallace (308)
Donald Byrd (264)	Bobby McFerrin (313)
Bobbi Humphrey (267)	Dianne Reeves (318,319)
Ronnie Laws (279)	Bireli Lagrene (323)

B1-92547 Blue Note 50th Anniversary Collection (5x2LP box)
(same contents as previous 5 sets)
B1-92563 Michel Petrucciani - Music '89 (331)
B1-92750 Ralph Peterson - Triangular (588,589)
B1-92812 Special 50th Anniversary Sampler (in UK: Blue Note Sampler,Vol.2)

Dianne Reeves (319)	Albert Ammons & Meade Lux Lewis (2)
Bireli Lagrene (323)	Miles Davis (31)
Tommy Smith (324)	Bud Powell (37)
Stanley Jordan (304)	Lou Donaldson (201)
Bobby McFerrin (313)	Horace Silver (173)

B1-92894 John Scofield - Time On My Hands (332)
B1-93006 Out Of The Blue - Spiral Staircase (589)
B1-93170 Tony Williams - Native Heart (331)
B1-93201 The Best Of Stanley Turrentine - The Blue Note Years
(104,114,132,150,181,305)
B1-93202 The Best Of Freddie Hubbard - The Blue Note Years (104,120,126,144,166,312)
B1-93203 The Best Of Sonny Rollins - The Blue Note Years (69,63,71,73)
B1-93204 The Best Of Bud Powell - The Blue Note Years (25,27,37,68,82,88)

715

B1-93205 The Best Of Art Blakey And The Jazz Messengers - The Blue Note Years (85,101,109)
B1-93206 The Best Of Horace Silver,Vol.2 - The Blue Note Years (173,185,196,210,263)
B1-93476 John Hart - One Down (589,590)
B1-93561 Renee Rosnes (588,589,590)
B1-93598 McCoy Tyner - Things Ain't What They Used To Be (332)
B1-93840 Mose Allison - My Backyard (333)
B1-93841 Lou Rawls - It's Supposed To Be Fun (334,335,337)
7-94335-1 (U.K.) Tommy Smith - Peeping Tom (334)
B1-96563 (U.K.) So Blue So Funky,Vol.1 - Heroes of The Hammond (2 LP Set):

Jimmy McGriff (616) Big John Patton (163)
Big John Patton (152) Larry Young (174)
Jimmy Smith (148) George Braith (161)
Freddie Roach (160,164) Lou Donaldson (236)
Fred Jackson (134) Jack McDuff (228)
Baby Face Willette (117) Grant Green (237)
Reuben Wilson (224)

B1-98635 Greg Osby - 3-D Lifestyles (354,355)
B1-98638 (U.K.) The Best of Donald Byrd (2 LP Set) (260,264,267,274,283,289,291)
B1-99106 (2 LP Set) Blue Break Beats,Volume One:

Richard "G." Holmes (252) Jimmy McGriff (586)
Grant Green (246) Grant Green (257)
Lou Donaldson (226) Lou Donaldson (226)
Donald Byrd (227) The Three Sounds (254)
Eddie Henderson (287) Donald Byrd (198)
Bobbi Humphrey 267) Herbie Hancock (168)
Ronnie Foster (259) Lonnie Smith (230)
Ike Quebec (143)

8-23108-1 (U.K.) Charlie Hunter - Return Of The Candyman (413)
B1-27206 BN-LA260-G Moacir Santos - Saudade (U.K. issue) (270)
B1-27327 John Scofield - Hand Jive (362)
B1-28263 (2 LP Set) Straight No Chaser:

Pee Wee Marquette (40) Lou Donaldson (116)
Herbie Hancock (151,168) Thelonious Monk (28)
Reuben Wilson (219) Grant Green (246)
Art Blakey (127,552) Donald Byrd (112,274)
John Patton (220) Horace Silver (122,173)
Bobby Hutcherson (245)

B1-28265 BST84342 Grant Green - Green Is Beautiful (237)
B1-28266 BST84351 Lonnie Smith - Drives (236)
B1-28267 BST84318 Lou Donaldson - Hot Dog (226)
B1-28268 BST84362 Bobby Hutcherson - San Francisco (245)
B1-28269 BST84267 Duke Pearson - The Right Touch (205)
B1-28975 BLP4041 (Connoisseur Series) Tina Brooks - True Blue (105)
B1-28976 BST84247 (Connoisseur Series) Don Cherry - Symphony For Improvisers (195)
B1-28977 BLP1549 (Connoisseur Series) Clifford Jordan/John Gilmore - Blowing In From Chicago (61)
B1-28978 BST84063 (Connoisseur Series) Kenny Dorham - Whistle Stop (115)
B1-28981 BST84159 (Connoisseur Series) Andrew Hill - Judgment (162)
B1-28982 BST84246 (Connoisseur Series) Ornette Coleman - The Empty Foxhole (195)
B1-28998 BST84084 (Connoisseur Series) Baby Face Willette - Stop And Listen (123)
B1-29027 BST84213 (Connoisseur Series) Bobby Hutcherson - Components (183)
B1-29092 (U.K.) So Blue So Funky - Heroes Of The Hammond,Vol.2 (2 LP Set):

LP1:
Jimmy McGriff (630) Jimmy Smith (149)
Curtis Amy & Paul Bryant (557) Richard "Groove" Holmes (558)
Fred Jackson (134)
Freddie Roach (160) Johnny Lytle (565)
George Braith (157)

LP2:
Baby Face Willette (117) Charles Kynard (561)
Big John Patton (210) Lou Donaldson (206)
Larry Young (223) Reuben Wilson (219)

B1-29100 BST84219 (Connoisseur Series) Wayne Shorter - The All Seeing Eye (186)
B1-29102 BLP1536 (Connoisseur Series) J.R. Monterose (57)
B1-29196 (U.K.) Blue Brazil - Blue Note In A Latin Groove (2 LP Set):

LP 1:
Luiz Arruda Paez (522) Milton Banana (521)
Alaide Costa (524) Edu Lobo (523)
Mandrake Som (521) Bossa 3 (522)
Quarteto Novo (522) Marcos Valle (522)
Perry Ribiero (521)

LP2:
Joyce (524) Eumir Deodato (523)
Lo Borges (524) Johnny Alf (524)
Som Tres (523) Joao Donato (523)
Elza Soares (522) Victor Assis (524)
Quarteto Novo (522

B1-29865 (U.K.) Capitol Rare - Funky Notes From The West Coast (2 LP Set):
Gene Harris (273,298) Caldera (506)
Eddie Henderson (287) Nancy Wilson (507)
Ben Sidran (503) Natalie Cole (506)
Gary Bartz (506) Frankie Beverley & Maze (506)
Rance Allen (506) Janet Lawson (631)
Bobby Lyle (506) Ronnie Laws (635)
A Taste Of Honey (507) The Reflections (505)
Marlena Shaw (268) Ronnie Foster (278)

B1-29905 BST84317 Reuben Wilson - Love Bug (224)
B1-29906 BST84343 Reuben Wilson - Blue Mode (235)
B1-29907 BST84352 Horace Silver - That Healin' Feelin' (U.K. issue)(241,243)
B1-29908 BST84268 Stanley Turrentine - Easy Walker (193,204,229)
B1-30027 (2 LP Set) Us3 - Broadway & 52nd (393)
B1-30721 (U.K.) Lou Donaldson - The Righteous Reed! The Best Of Poppa Lou (2 LP Set) (96,121,201,206,211,220,226,236,254,266)
B1-30724 (U.K.) Pullin' Out The Stops! The Best Of Jimmy McGriff (2 LP Set) (232,253,503,582,584,586,616,630)
B1-30725 (U.K.) Deep Groove! The Best Of Cannonball Adderley (2 LP Set) (495,496,497,498,500,502,503)
B1-30728 (U.K.) The Best Of Big John Patton - The Organization (2 LP Set) (152,156,178,188,192,210,216,228,248)
B1-31223 BST84306 John Patton - Understanding (220)
B1-31247 BST84327 Grant Green - Carryin' On (233)
B1-31248 BST84337 Lou Donaldson - Everything I Play Is Funky (236)
B1-31249 BST84326 Lonnie Smith - Move Your Hand (230)
B1-31875 Donald Byrd - Kofi (235,250)
B1-31876 Lou Donaldson - The Scorpion/Live At The Cadillac Club (249,250)
B1-31878 John Patton - Boogaloo (216)
B1-31880 Lonnie Smith - Live at Club Mozambique (242)
B1-31883 (2 LP Set) The Lost Grooves:
Reuben Wilson (233) John Patton (230)
Grant Green (246) Stanley Turrentine (204,209)
Lou Donaldson (220,249) Lonnie Smith (230)

B1-32082 BST84382 Ronnie Foster - The Two-Headed Freap (259)
B1-32087 BST84165 (Connoisseur Series) Jackie McLean - Destination Out (158)
B1-32088 BST84071 (Connoisseur Series) Grant Green - Green Street (120)
B1-32089 BST84034 (Connoisseur Series) Lee Morgan - Lee Way (103)
B1-32090 BST84093 (Connoisseur Series) Ike Quebec - Heavy Soul (129)
B1-32091 BST84205 (Connoisseur Series) Pete La Roca - Basra (181)
B1-32092 BST84177 (Connoisseur Series) Grachan Moncur III - Some Other Stuff (169)
B1-32093 BST84006 (Connoisseur Series) Dizzy Reece - Blues In Trinity (83)
B1-32094 BST84085 (Connoisseur Series) Freddie Hubbard - Ready For Freddie (126)
B1-32095 BST84036 (Connoisseur Series) Lou Donaldson - Sunny Side Up (99,100)
B1-32096 BST84297 (Connoisseur Series) Wayne Shorter - Schizophrenia (200)
B1-32097 BST84160 (Connoisseur Series) Andrew Hill - Smokestack (160)
B1-32098 BST84018 (Connoisseur Series) Walter Davis Jr. - Davis Cup (93)
B1-33579 GXF-3023 Lee Morgan - The Procrastinator (204)

717

B1-33580 LT-990 Grant Green - Solid (167)
B1-33581 LT-1056 Wayne Shorter - Etcetera (183)
B1-33582 LT-995 Hank Mobley - A Slice Of The Top (191)
B1-33583 LT-1044 Bobby Hutcherson - Patterns (211)
B1-35220 Duke Pearson - I Don't Care Who Knows It (215,226,232,234,238)
B1-35221 John Patton - Memphis To New York Spirit (248)
B1-35338 Gene Harris And The Three Sounds - Live At The "It" Club (239)
B1-35607 (U.K.) Capitol Rare,Vol.2 (2 LP Set):

LP1:	Sheree Brown (508)	Gary Bartz (506)
	Gene Dunlap (508)	Alphonse Mouzon (265)
	Natalie Cole (506)	Chico Hamilton (281)
	Harlem River Drive (505)	Ronnie Laws (279)
		Carmen McRae (289)
LP2:	Nat Adderley (504)	Gene Harris (288)
	Margo Thunder (504)	Ronnie Foster (259)
	Patti Drew (502)	Minnie Riperton (507)
	100% Pure Poison (505)	Stratavarious (505)

B1-35636 (2 LP Set) Rare Grooves:

Reuben Wilson (224,235)	John Patton (210)
Jack McDuff (240)	Richard "Groove" Holmes (252)
Jimmy McGriff (232)	Elvin Jones (258)
Stanley Turrentine (217)	Andrew Hill (213)
Larry Young (209)	Donald Byrd (198)
Eddie Gale (226)	Candido (249)

B1-36594 (2 LP Set) The New Groove - The Blue Note Remix Project,Volume 1 (385,386)
8-37183-1 (Germany) Cassandra Wilson - New Moon Daughter (380,381)

8-52420-1 (U.K.) Charlie Hunter - Natty Dread (392)
B1-53923 BN-LA140-G Donald Byrd - Street Lady (267)
B1-53924 BST84340 John Patton - Accent On The Blues (230)
8-54123-1 (2 LP Set) (Germany) Cassandra Wilson - Traveling Miles (416,423,424)
B1-54325 BST84125 Lou Donaldson - Good Gracious! (148)
B1-54326 BN-LA549-G Donald Byrd - Places And Spaces (283)
B1-54327 BST84214 Blue Mitchell - Down With It (184)
B1-54329 BST84322 Jack McDuff - Down Home Style (228)
B1-54357 (U.K.) Blue Juice (2 LP Set):

LP1:	Ananda Shankar(525)	Tina Britt (630)
	Brian Bennett (516)	Benny Gordon (499)
	Lou Rawls (498)	The Fame Gang (501)
	Nancy Wilson (501)	Billy Preston (495)
	Bobbie Gentry (497)	Jimmy Caravan (499)
		Dick Hyman (645)
LP2:	Johnny Lytle (586)	Joao Donato (523)
	Jerome Richardson (626)	Doris (526)
	Norman Connors (509)	Nancy Wilson (498)
	Elza Soares (522)	Gene Harris & The Three Sounds (254)
		Chico Hamilton (584)

B1-54360 (2 LP Set) Blue Break Beats,Volume 3

LP1:	Cannonball Adderley (502)	Shirley Bassey (632)
	Lou Rawls (502)	Lou Donaldson (226)
	Lou Donaldson (206)	Gene Harris & The 3 Sounds (254)
	Reuben Wilson (254)	Blue Mitchell (227)
	Jeremy Steig (238)	Grant Green (247)
LP2:	Gene Harris (273)	Joe Williams (582)
	Bobbi Humphrey (267)	Bobby Hutcherson (245)
	Donald Byrd (283)	Duke Pearson (208)
	Ronnie Foster (259)	Jackie McLean (205)

B1-57741 (U.K.)	Blue Brazil #2 - Blue Note In A Latin Groove (2 LP Set):	
LP1:	Antonio Adolfo (523)	Quinteto Villa Lobos (523)
	Silvio Cezar (521)	Elza Soares (522)
	Wilson Simonal (521)	Quarteto Em Cy (523)
	Os Tres Morais (523)	Di Melo (524)
		Luis Gonzaga Jr. (524)
LP2:	Milton Banana (522,524)	Edu Lobo (523)
	Elza Soares (522)	Meirelles (524)
	Som Tres (522)	Leny Andrade (522)
		Quarteto Novo (522)
B1-57745 (U.K.)	Blue 'N Groovy,Vol.2 - Mostly Modal (2 LP Set):	
LP1:	Hank Mobley (229)	Jackie McLean (91)
	Stanley Turrentine (193)	Art Blakey (119)
	Donald Byrd (193)	Art Pepper (464)
		Blue Mitchell (157)
LP2:	Don Wilkerson (137)	Bobby Hutcherson (194)
	Horace Parlan (113)	Duke Pearson (175)
	Lee Morgan (207)	McCoy Tyner (238)
B1-93011 (2 LP Set)	John Medeski,Billy Martin & Chris Wood - Combustication (415)	
4-93916-1 (France)	Erik Truffaz - The Dawn (417)	
B1-94027 (2 LP Set)	Blue Break Beats,Vol.4:	
	Gene Harris (273)	Ike & Tina Turner (632)
	David Axelrod (500)	The Three Sounds (231)
	Gene Harris/3 Sounds(218)	Reuben Wilson (254)
	Buddy Rich (564)	Eddie Henderson (287)
	Bob Dorough (504)	Marlena Shaw (267)
	Banbara (505)	Minnie Riperton (507)
	The Sons (501)	Lonnie Smith (222)
	Cannonball Adderley (503)	Paul Nero (502)
	Monk Higgins (586)	The Fourth Way (501)
	Herbie Hancock (645)	
B1-94704	Lee Morgan - Blue Breakbeats (161,185,192,213)	
B1-94705	Grant Green - Blue Breakbeats (233,237,246,252,257)	
B1-94706	Bobbi Humphrey - Blue Breakbeats (261,267,272,273,281)	
B1-94707	Reuben Wilson - Blue Breakbeats (219,224,235)	
B1-94708	Donald Byrd - Blue Breakbeats (202,264,267,283,289)	
B1-94709	Lou Donaldson - Blue Breakbeats (148,201,220,226,236,243)	
B1-97158 (U.K.)	Blue Juice,Vol.2 (2 LP Set):	
(4-97158-1)	Duke Pearson (241)	Trinidad Oil Company (516)
	Lonnie Smith (242)	Sandy Nelson (533)
	Bobby Hutcherson (258)	Les McCann (561)
	Alphonse Mouzn (265)	Victor Feldman (564)
	Howard Roberts (498)	Gerald Wilson (566)
	Henry Cole (505)	Wilbert Longmire (567)
	Patti Drew (500)	The Jazz Crusaders (568)
	Willie Hobo (505)	Joe Torres (567)
	Willard Burton (505)	Hank Diamond (569)
	Jimmy Caster (505)	Candido (587)
	Gonzalez (516)	Truman Thomas (631)

719

B1-20208 Ronny Jordan - A Brighter Day (438,439)

5-21147-1 (U.K.) Capitol Rare,Vol.3 (2 LP Set):

Ronnie Laws (279)	Dave Grusin (505)
Raul De Souza (507)	Eddie Henderson (507)
Dianne Reeves (319)	Bobby Watson (581)
Maze (509)	Bobby Lyle (507)
Labi Siffre (516)	Georges Garvarentz (521)
Ike & Tina Turner (536)	Maze (508)
Bobbi Humphrey (261)	Barrett Strong (508)
Lou Rawls (500)	Maxi (297)
Doris (526)	David Axelrod (502)

5-22123-1 (France) (2 LP) Erik Truffaz - Bending New Corners (435)

5-25114-1 (France) (2 LP) St. Germain - Tourist (446)

 720

APPLAUSE label

Note: Second column shows BN equivalent album.

2301	BST84416	Bobby Hutcherson - Natural Illusion (260)
2302	BLP4164	Jimmy Smith - Prayer Meetin' (149)
2303	BST84296	Jimmy Smith - Plain Talk (101)
2304	BST84254	Lou Donaldson - Lush Life (199)
2305	BST84286	Stanley Turrentine - Look of Love (212,213,214)
2306	BLP4057	Stanley Turrentine - Blue Hour (114)
2307	BST84298	Stanley Turrentine - Always Something There (220)
2308	BST84379	Bobbi Humphrey - Flute In (256)
2309	BST84280	Lou Donaldson - Midnight Creeper (211)
2310	BST84338	McCoy Tyner - Expansions (217)
2311/2312/2313		The Jazz Crusaders (not Blue Note material)
2314	BN-LA267-G	Clifford Brown - Brownie Eyes (35,36,38)
2315	BST84258	Art Blakey - The Witch Doctor (119)
2316	BLP4147	Herbie Hancock - Inventions and Dimensions (157)
2317	BLP4244	Bobby Hutcherson - Stick Up (194)
2318	BLP4100	Jimmy Smith Plays Fats Waller (133)
2319	BLP4139	Grant Green - Am I blue (154)
2320	BLP4001	Sonny Rollins - Newk's Time (71)
2321	BST84325	The Best of Horace Silver (44,45,58,94,122,141)
2322	BLP4077	Dexter Gordon - Doin' Alright (121)

CAPITOL label

ST-12375	Ronnie Laws - Classic Masters (279,296) (& further titles not from BN)
ST-12405	Earl Klugh - Key Notes (293) (& further titles not from BN)

CLASSIC label

Following BN albums were remastered for issue on the Classic label:

BST 1577	John Coltrane - Blue Train (71)
BST 81582	Clifford Jordan - Cliff Craft (74)
BST 81588	Sonny Clark - Cool Struttin' (76)
BST 81591	Lou Donaldson - Lou Takes Off (76)
BST 81595	Cannonball Adderley - Somethin' Else (79)
BST 84040	Freddie Hubbard - Open Sesame (104)
BST 84052	Tina Brooks - Back To The Tracks (110,111)
BST 84058	Hank Mobley - Roll Call (113)
BST 84059	Kenny Drew - Undercurrent (113)
BST 84074	Horace Parlan - On The Spur Of The Moment (119)
BST 84114	Ike Quebec - Soul Samba (143)
BST 84133	Dexter Gordon - A Swingin' Affair (142)

BA-1588-45 Sonny Clark - Cool Struttin' (4 LP set - 45 rpm-12 in.) (76)

EPITAPH label

E-4000	BST84335	Lee Morgan - The Sixth Sense (207)

721

LIBERTY label

LN-10054	BN-LA140-F	Donald Byrd - Street Lady (267)
LN-10075	BST84157	Lee Morgan - The Sidewinder (161)
LN-10163	BN-LA596-G	Earl Klugh (285)
LN-10164	BN-LA452-G	Ronnie Laws - Pressure Sensitive (279)
LN-10200		Donald Byrd - The Dude (98,99,147,198,242)
LN-10233	BN-LA667-G	Earl Klugh - Living Inside Your Love (293)
LN-10236	BN-LA736-H	Noel Pointer - Phantazia (295,296)
LN-10255	BN-LA628-G	Ronnie Laws - Fever (284,285)
LN-10257	BN-LA737-H	Earl Klugh - Finger Paintings (296,297)
LN-10266	BN-LA730-H	Ronnie Laws - Friends And Strangers (296)

MOBILE FIDELITY label

AMOBU/UHQ-1025	BN-LA737-H	Earl Klugh - Finger Paintings (296,297)

MOSAIC label (Box sets)

Note:Number shown as prefix is the number of LPs in box.

MR

4-101 The Complete Blue Note Recordings of Thelonious Monk (19,20,21,28,32,63)

3-103 The Complete Blue Note Recordings of Albert Ammons and Meade Lux Lewis:
Albert Ammons (1,2) Meade Lux Lewis (1,2,5,10)
(& 1 further title from Decca label)

5-104 The Complete Blue Note and Pacific Jazz Recordings of Clifford Brown:
(35,36,34,38,40,41) (& further titles from Pacific Jazz label)

4-106 The Complete Blue Note Recordings of The Tina Brooks Quintets (79,105,110,111,118)

4-107 The Complete Blue Note Forties Recordings of Ike Quebec and John Hardee:
John Hardee (17) Ike Quebec (10,14,15,18)
Tiny Grimes (18)

1-108 The Complete Recordings of The Port of Harlem Jazzmen (2,3)

6-109 The Complete Edmond Hall/James P.Johnson/Sidney De Paris/Vic Dickenson Blue Note Sessions:
James P.Johnson 6,7,11) Sidney De Paris (9,27)
Edmond Hall (5,6,7,8) Vic Dickenson (32)

6-110 The Complete Blue Note Recordings of Sidney Bechet:
Port of Harlem Seven (3) Bunk Johnson & Sidney Bechet (13)
Josh White (4) Art Hodes (16)
Sidney Bechet (3,4,12,24,26,30,37) Bechet-Nicholas (17)

5-114 The Complete Blue Note Recordings of Art Hodes:
Art Hodes (7,8,11,13,14,15,16) Baby Dodds (16)

1-115 Blue Note Swingtets:
Benny Morton's All Stars (13) Jimmy Hamilton and the Duke's Men (16)
The Sammy Benskin Trio (15)

5-116 The Complete Blue Note Recordings of Bud Powell (25,27,37,68,82,88)

5-118 The Complete Blue Note Recordings of Herbie Nichols (47,48,49,53)

1-119 The Pete Johnson-Earl Hines-Teddy Bunn Blue Note Sessions:
Pete Johnson (4) Earl Hines (3) Teddy Bunn (4)

3-121 The Complete Blue Note 45 Sessions of Ike Quebec (92,111,135)

3-124 The Complete Blue Note Recordings Of Freddie Redd (100,109,115)

5-132 The Complete Blue Note Recordings Of George Lewis (47,447-448,451,452)

6-133 The Complete Blue Note Recordings Of Grant Green With Sonny Clark (132,134,135,142)

9-137 The Complete Blue Note Recordings Of Larry Young (172,174,179,186,194,205,209,223)

10-141 The Complete Blue Note Recordings Of The 1960 Jazz Messengers (101,108,109,117,119,123)

3-145 The Complete Blue Note Recordings Of Don Cherry (189,195,197)

6-150 The Complete Blue Note 1964-66 Jackie McLean Sessions (169,172,176,176,185,187,192)

5-154 The Complete February 1957 Jimmy Smith Blue Note Sessions (60,61)

10-161 The Complete Blue Note Andrew Hill Sessions (159,160,162,164,168,177,186,191)

MQ

6-162	The Complete Blue Note Lee Morgan Fifties Sessions (57,58,62,69,72,75,77)
5-166	The Complete Blue Note/UA Curtis Fuller Sessions (66,68,75,77,623)
5-167	The Complete Blue Note Sam Rivers Sessions (175,182,196,200)
19-170	Classic Capitol Jazz Sessions: Bobby Hackett (449) (& further titles not from BN)
5-172	The Complete Blue Note/UA/Roulette Recordings Of Thad Jones (51,55,59, 576,624)
6-178	The Complete Blue Note Blue Mitchell Sessions (157,169,184,189,197,207)
10-181	The Complete Blue Note Hank Mobley Fifties Sessions (46,58,59,62,63,66,69,72,77)
8-197	The Complete Blue Note Horace Parlan Sessions (100,102,107,113,119,124,150)

PAUSA label

9000	BLP4123	Kenny Burrell - Midnight Blue (147)
9001		
9002	BN-LA152-G	Herbie Hancock & Willie Bobo - Succotash (157)
9003	BN-LA635-G	Carmen McRae - Can't Hide Love (288,289)
9004/5/6:not from Blue Note label		
9007	BST84307	McCoy Tyner - Time for Tyner (214)
9008	BST84355	Joe Williams - Worth Waiting for... (241)

SMITHSONIAN label

P6-11891 The Smithsonian Collection of Classic Jazz (6 LP Set):
Sidney Bechet and His Blue Note Jazzmen (12)
Tadd Dameron's Sextet (22)
(& further titles not from BN)
Thelonious Monk (22,28)
Cecil Taylor (192)

SUNSET label

Mono SUM	Stereo SUS	BN equiv.	
1175	5175		Jimmy Smith (50,51,55)
	5246	BST84079	Lou Donaldson (121)
	5255	BLP4039	The Soul of Stanley Turrentine (98)
	5258	BLP1537	Lou Donaldson (32,33,43)
	5263	BLP1590	Lee Morgan - All the Way (75,77)
	5316	BLP4002	Jimmy Smith - Just Friends (70,77,78)
	5318	BST81566	Lou Donaldson Quintet - I Won't Cry Anymore (65)

UNITED ARTISTS label

UAS
9952 BLP1501+BLP1502 Miles Davis (2 LP Set) (31,34,41)

UP FRONT label

UPF-	
187	Bobby Hutcherson (272,276)
188	Dexter Gordon (122)
193	Bobby Hutcherson (245,253)

FOREIGN SERIES

BRAZIL

BLUE NOTE label (2 LP Sets)

Note: Second column shows equivalent BN albums.

31 C 152-		
53698-9	BST84101 + BST84048	Donald Byrd (98,99,106,127)
53710-1	BLP1503 + BLP1504	Bud Powell (25,27,37)
53712-3	BST81577 + BST84163	John Coltrane/Eric Dolphy (71,163)
82830-1	BLP1201 + BLP1202	Sidney Bechet (3,4,12,13,17,30)
82832-3	BLP1205 + BLP1206	George Lewis (47,447,448)
82834-5	BLP1505 + BLP1506	J.J.Johnson (36,43,48)
82836-7	BLP1510 + BLP1511	Thelonious Monk (20,21,22,28,32)
82838-9	BN-LA399-H2	Herbie Hancock (139,151,157,168,179,210,225)
82840-1	BN-LA531-H2	Wes Montgomery (553,554,556)
82842-3	BN-LA401-H2	Sonny Rollins (59,63,71,74)
82844-5	BST84115 + BST84172	Freddie Hubbard (144,166)
82846-7	BST84015 + BST84016	Art Blakey (90)

DENMARK

OFFICIAL label

3016-3 (3 LP Set) Erroll Garner - Overture To Dawn (448,449)

THE NETHERLANDS (DUTCH ISSUES)

BLUE NOTE label

Note: Box 1 in the following series was issued in Germany (see page 730).

1A158-83385/8 40 Years of Jazz:History of Blue Note - Box 2 (4 LP Set):

83385:	Babs Gonzales (18) James Moody (23)	
	Art Blakey & The Jazz Messengers (21)	Kenny Dorham (46)
	Tadd Dameron (19,22)	
83386:	Bud Powell (25,27)	Elmo Hope (36,42)
	Thelonious Monk (21,32)	Jutta Hipp (56)
	Wynton Kelly (29) Herbie Nichols (48)	
83387:	Howard McGhee & Fats Navarro (23)	Clifford Brown (38)
	Howard McGhee (26)	Lou Donaldson-Clifford Brown (35)
	Miles Davis (34,41)	J.J.Johnson (36)
	Milt Jackson(30)	
83388:	Johnny Griffin (52)	Horace Silver(44,58)
	Lou Donaldson (32)	The Jazz Messengers (50)
	Kenny Dorham (45)	Lee Morgan (57)
	Hank Mobley (62)	

724

1A158-83391/4 40 Years of Jazz:History of Blue Note-Box 3 (4 LP Set):

83391: Bud Powell (68); John Coltrane (71); Cannonball Adderley (79); Sonny Rollins (63); Hank Mobley (66,99)

83392: Lou Donaldson (65); Jimmy Smith (51); The Three Sounds (83); Horace Silver (89,162); Art Blakey & The Jazz Messengers (85,130)

83393: Jimmy Smith(103); Stanley Turrentine (104,118); Horace Parlan (107); Louis Smith (80); Donald Byrd (92); Jackie McLean (110); Freddie Hubbard (120)

83394: Johnny Griffin (63); Jimmy Smith (101); Bennie Green(86); Leo Parker (126); Ike Quebec (129); Sonny Clark (129); Dexter Gordon (121)

1A158-83395/8 40 Years of Jazz:History of Blue Note - Box 4 (4 LP Set):

83395: Joe Henderson (155); Horace Silver (173,196); Blue Mitchell (189); Lee Morgan (161,163)

83396: Donald Byrd (147); Stanley Turrentine (181); Kenny Burrell (147); Jimmy Smith (149); John Patton (178); Freddie Roach (160); Larry Young (186,205)

83397: Bobby Hutcherson (183); Joe Henderson (189); Freddie Hubbard (190); Herbie Hancock (168,179); Wayne Shorter (176)

83398: Jackie McLean (158); Eric Dolphy (163); Sam Rivers (175); Andrew Hill (159,164); Don Cherry (197); Cecil Taylor (192)

1A158-83401/4 40 Years of Jazz:History of Blue Note - Box 5 (4 LP Set):

83401: Hank Mobley (209); Booker Ervin (215); Elvin Jones (224); Kenny Cox & The Contemporary Jazz Quintet (221); Horace Silver (263); Herbie Hancock (225); Frank Foster (222); The Thad Jones-Mel Lewis Orchestra(242)

83402: Chick Corea (585); Bobby Hutcherson (215,286); Wayne Shorter (231); McCoy Tyner (224); Ornette Coleman(214)

83403: Chico Hamilton (287); Grant Green (237); Donald Byrd (228); John Patton (210); Lou Donaldson (201); Jack McDuff (250)

83404: Marlena Shaw (274); Donald Byrd (264); Bobbi Humphrey (267); Noel Pointer (296); John Lee & Gerry Brown (281); Ronnie Laws (279); Earl Klugh (285)

5C038-

60085	BST84085	Freddie Hubbard - Ready For Freddie (126)
60092	BLP1502	Miles Davis (31,34,41)
60094	BLP1577	John Coltrane - Blue Train (71)
60106	BNS40034	Charlie Mingus - Town Hall Concert (628,629)
98574	BST84003	Art Blakey & The Jazz Messengers - Moanin' (85)
98576S	BST81523	Introducing Kenny Burrell Guitar (53)
98598S	BST84109	Herbie Hancock - Takin' Off (139)
98656	BST81578	Lee Morgan - The Cooker (72)

<u>OLDIE BLUES label</u>

Note: Albums listed below include further titles from other labels.

OL 2805 Meade Lux Lewis 1905-1964 - Tell Your Story (2,5,10)
OL 2807 Albert Ammons-King of Blues and Boogie Woogie 1907-1949 (1)
OL 2822 Albert Ammons (2)

725

ENGLAND/UNITED KINGDOM

BLUE NOTE label

BLT	(Europe)	
1001	7-91930-1	Tommy Smith - Step By Step (324)
1002	7-94335-1	Tommy Smith - Peeping Tom (335)
1003		Tommy Smith - Standards (341)

BNS		
40001	BLP1201	Sidney Bechet - Jazz Classics,Vol.1 (3,4,12,13,17)
40002	BLP1202	Sidney Bechet - Jazz Classics,Vol.2 (3,12,13,17,30)
40003	BLP1501	Miles Davis,Vol.1 (31,34)
40004	BLP1502	Miles Davis,Vol.2 (31,34,41)
40005	BLP1503	The Amazing Bud Powell,Vol.1 (25,27)
40006	BLP1504	The Amazing Bud Powell,Vol.2 (25,27,37)
40007	BLP1521	Art Blakey Quintet - A Night at Birdland,Vol.1 (40,41)
40008	BLP1522	Art Blakey Quintet - A Night at Birdland,Vol.2 (40,41)
40009	BLP1577	John Coltrane - Blue Train (71)
40010	BLP1581	Sonny Rollins - A Night at the Village Vanguard (73)
40011	BLP4001	Sonny Rollins - Newk's Time (71)
40012	BLP4003	Art Blakey & The Jazz Messengers - Moanin' (85)
40013	BLP4058	Hank Mobley - Roll Call (113)
40014	BLP4077	Dexter Gordon - Doin' Alright (121)
40015	BLP4123	Kenny Burrell - Midnight Blue (147)
40016	BLP4157	Lee Morgan - The Sidewinder (161)
40017	BLP4163	Eric Dolphy - Out to Lunch (163)
40018	BLP4180	Tony Williams - Lifetime (171)
40019		no information (possibly not BN material)
40020	BLP4195	Herbie Hancock - Maiden Voyage (179)
40021	BLP4224	Ornette Coleman at the Golden Circle,Vol.1 (187,188)
40022	BLP4225	Ornette Coleman at the Golden Circle,Vol.2 (187,188)
40023	BLP4237	Cecil Taylor - Unit Structures (192)
40024	BST84275	McCoy Tyner - Tender Moments (207)
40025	BST84279	Herbie Hancock - Speak like a Child (210)
40026	BST84297	Wayne Shorter - Schizophrenia (200)
40027	BST84311	Don Cherry - Where is Brooklyn (197)
40028	BST84332	Wayne Shorter - Supernova (231)
40029	BST84347	Art Blakey & The Jazz Messengers - Roots and Herbs (117,123)
40030	BST84353	Chick Corea - The Song of Singing (240)
40031	BST84380	Donald Byrd - Ethiopian Knights (255)
40032	BLP4112	Dexter Gordon - Go! (142)
40033		no information (possibly not BN material)
40034	UAJ14024	Charlie Mingus - Town Hall Concert (from United Artists label) (628,629)
40035	SS18034	Dizzy Gillespie - Live at the Village Vanguard (from Solid State label) (584)
40036	BLP1595	Cannonball Adderley with Miles Davis - Somethin' Else (79)

BNSLP-

1 Blue Bossa:

Horace Parlan (113)
Charlie Rouse (145)
Big John Patton (188)
Duke Pearson (226)
Kenny Dorham (46)
Grant Green (137)
Horace Silver (185)
Carmen McRae (289)

2 Blue Bop:

Don Wilkerson (140,156)
Tina Brooks (105)
Donald Byrd (112)
Art Blakey (109)
Horace Silver (106)

726

3 The Baptist Beat:

Lou Donaldson (148,201)
Horace Silver (196)
Big John Patton (188)
Jimmy Smith (312)
Hank Mobley (113)
Stanley Turrentine (150)
Freddie Roach (148)

4 Blue Bossa 2:

Hank Mobley (183)
Charlie Rouse (145)
Andrew Hill (216)
Duke Pearson(241)
Lou Donaldson (121)
Grant Green (137)
Donald Byrd (99)
J.J. Johnson (43)

BNX

1 Blue Note Sampler,Vol.1:

Horace Silver (94)
Stanley Turrentine (114)
Jimmy Smith (78)
The Jazz Messengers (49)
Dexter Gordon (142)
All Stars (310)
Lou Donaldson (83)
Herbie Hancock (179)
Cannonball Adderley (79)
Hank Mobley (99)
Kenny Burrell (147)
Lee Morgan (161)

2 B1-92812 Blue Note Sampler,Vol.2:

Dianne Reeves (319)
Bireli Lagrene (323)
Tommy Smith (324)
Stanley Jordan (304)
Bobby McFerrin (313)
Albert Ammons & Meade Lux Lewis (2)
Miles Davis (31)
Bud Powell (37)
Lou Donaldson (201)
Horace Silver (173)

<u>BLUE NOTE label</u> (2 LP Sets)

BND		
4004	BN-LA392-H2	Thad Jones & Mel Lewis (237,242,582,583,585,586,587)
4006	BN-LA394-H2	Stanley Turrentine (158,162,199,203,212,219,220)
4008	BN-LA400-H2	Jimmy Smith (50,51,61,77,78,98,103,149)
4010	BN-LA451-H2	Paul Chambers/John Coltrane - High Step (57,453,463)
4016	BN-LA532-H2	Gerry Mulligan & Lee Konitz - Revelation (545,546,553)
4018	BN-LA632-H2	Jean-Luc Ponty - Canteloupe Island (568,569)
4022	BN-LA456-H2	Lester Young - The Aladdin Sessions (459,460,461)
4024	BN-LA461-H2	Gil Evans - Pacific Standard Time (54,555,556)
4028	BN-LA530-H2	The Jazz Crusaders - The Young Rabbits (558,559,561,562,563,564,566)
4032	BN-LA579-H2	Thelonious Monk - The Complete Genius (19,20,21,28,32)

Note: Missing numbers in above series were presumably not used for BN material.

<u>BLUE NOTE label</u>

LBR		
1020	LT-987	Lee Morgan - Sonic Boom (201,202)
1021	LT-988	Wayne Shorter - The Soothsayer (178)
1022	LT-989	Dexter Gordon - Clubhouse (182)
1023	LT-990	Grant Green - Solid (167)
1024	LT-991	Donald Byrd - Chant (120)
1025	LT-992	Jimmy Smith - Confirmation (70,78)
1026	LT-993	Stanley Turrentine - New Time Shuffle (199,203)
1027	LT-994	Jackie McLean - Consequences (187)
1028	LT-995	Hank Mobley - A Slice of the Top (191)
1029	LT-996	Bobby Hutcherson - Spiral (179,221)
1035	LT-1053	Joe Pass,Jazz Guitar Vol.1 - Catch me (559,560)
1037	LT-1056	Wayne Shorter - Et Cetera (183)
1038	LT-1057	Harold Land - Take Aim (107)
1039	LT-1064	Art Pepper - Omega Alpha (465)

 727

BLUE NOTE label

UAG

20001	BN-LA549-G	Donald Byrd - Places and Spaces (283)
20002	BN-LA452-G	Ronnie Laws - Pressure Sensitive (279)
20003	BN-LA550-G	Bobbi Humphrey - Fancy Dancer (281,282)
20004	BN-LA541-G	John Lee & Gerry Brown - Mango Sunrise (281)
20005	BN-LA584-G	Alphonse Mouzon - The Man Incognito (284,286)
20006	BN-LA606-G	Marlena Shaw - Just a Matter of Time (286)
20007	BN-LA628-G	Ronnie Laws - Fever (284,285)
20008	BN-LA633-G	Donald Byrd - Caricatures (289)
20009	BN-LA667-G	Earl Klugh - Living Inside Your Love (293)
20010		
20011	BN-LA737-G	Earl Klugh - Finger Paintaings (296,297)
20012		
20013	BN-LA853-H	Horace Silver - Silver 'n Percussion (299,300)
20014	BN-LA870-H	Blue Note Meet the L.A. Philharmonic (299)

UALP

17 Blue Note Sampler,Vol.1 (one-sided LP - all tracks are edited versions):

Hank Mobley (113)	Gerry Mulligan/Lee Konitz (553)
Art Blakey & The Jazz Mess. (117)	Herbie Hancock (179)
John Coltrane (71)	Jean-Luc Ponty (568)

19 Blue Note Sampler,Vol.2 (all tracks are edited versions)

The Jazz Crusaders (562)	Sidney Bechet (3)
Kenny Burrell (147)	Art Blakey & The Jazz Messengers (85)
Thelonious Monk (20)	Bud Powell (25)
Dizzy Gillespie (584)	Stanley Turrentine (162)
Sonny Rollins (71)	Thad Jones/Mel Lewis (242)
Dexter Gordon (142)	Cannonball Adderley/Miles Davis (79)
Gil Evans (554)	

21 Blue Note Sampler,Vol.3 (probably edited versions):

Lee Morgan (202)	Donald Byrd (120)
Dexter Gordon(182)	Wayne Shorter (178)
Grant Green (167)	Jimmy Smith (70)
Jackie McLean (187)	Hank Mobley (191)
Stanley Turrentine (204)	Bobby Hutcherson (179)

BOPLICITY LABEL

BOP

1		John Coltrane - Coltrane Time (not from Blue Note)
2	BLP4024	Jackie McLean - Swing Swang Swingin' (96)
3		Chet Baker/Art Pepper Sextet - Playboys (not from Blue Note)
4	BLP4027	Freddie Redd Quartet - Music from 'The Connection' (100)

EMI-LIBERTY label

LCSP101 BST89902 Three Decades of Jazz,Vol.1:1939-1949 (see page 707)

LIBERTY label

LCSP 18670213 Donald Byrd - Blue Note Collection (260,264,267,274,283,289)

VOGUE label

LAE12005 George Lewis and His New Orleans Stompers (447,448)

728

EUROPE

Note: Following series has been used in various European countries.Country of issue is listed in parenthesis.

LIBERTY label

Note: Issues marked * were also issued on Blue Note label with prefix BST in place of LBS.

LBS
83135/6 *(E) BST89901 Jimmy Smith's Greatest Hits! (51,61,78,98,103,149)
83249 *(Du,E) The Soul of Jazz:
Jackie McLean (205)
Horace Silver (196)
Larry Young (205)
Cannonball Adderley (79)
Lou Donaldson (201)
The Three Sounds (203)
Lee Morgan (161)
Art Blakey (85)
Herbie Hancock (139)
83367/8 *(E) (2 LP Set) Jimmy Smith Greatest Hits,Vol.2 (78,98,101,103,148,149)
83442/3 (F) (2 LP Set) Entrez Dans Le Monde du Jazz :
Albert Ammons (1)
Sidney Bechet (12)
Charlie Christian (5)
Billie Holiday (UA title)
Milt Jackson (30)
Lee Morgan (161)
Art Blakey & The Jazz Messengers (85)
Kenny Burrell (147)
Thelonious Monk (21)
Modern Jazz Quartet (UA title)
Miles Davis (79)
John Coltrane (71)
Jean-Luc Ponty (568)
Ornette Coleman (187)

SUNSET label

SLS
50006 (E) Jimmy Smith plays the Standards (= Sunset SUM1175) (50,51,55)
50190 (E) Art Blakey's Jazz Messengers (109,117,123 + ?)
50226 (G) Jimmy Smith - House Party (= BST84002) (70,77,78)
50228 (F) Sidney Bechet (3,12,16,24,26,30)
50229 (E) Jazz Highlights: John Coltrane (71 + ?)

UNITED ARTISTS label

UAS
29573 (E) BN-LA534-G Jimmy Witherspoon - Spoonful (646)
29814 BST84002 Jimmy Smith - House Party (70,77,78)

729

FRANCE

BLUE NOTE label

BLP
1209 Boogie Woogie Classics: Albert Ammons - Pete Johnson:
Albert Ammons (1) / Albert Ammons & Meade Lux Lewis (2) /Pete Johnson (4)

BNP		
25100		Joe Pass - For Django (561,562)
25101		Erroll Garner - Overture to Dawn (448)
25102		Erroll Garner - Yesterdays (448,449)
25103		Gerry Mulligan Quartet,Vol.1 (545)
25104	BLP5024 +BLP5042	Tal Farlow - Early Tal (35,41)
25105	UAL4046	Zoot Sims - Jazz Alive!A Night at the Half Note (622)
25106	LP9027	Warne Marsh - Jazz of Two Cities (532)
25107	UAL4034	Booker Little - Milestones (620)
25108	UAL4007	Art Farmer - Jubilation (620)
25109 nr	UAL4043	Bill Potts Big Band (622)
25110	BLP1590	Lee Morgan - Candy Lee (75,77)
25111		
25112	UAL4054	Benny Carter - Benny on the Coast (624-625)
25113	UAJ14017	Duke Ellington - Money Jungle (628)
25114	LRP3051	Bill Perkins - Tenors Head-On (535)

BST
84383 Art Blakey and The Jazz Messengers - Greatest Hits (85,101,109)

2S062-
61900 Chick Corea - Circulus,No.2 (part of BN BN-LA882-J2) (240,247)
61901 Chick Corea - Circulus,No.1 (part of BN BN-LA882-J2) (247)

THE JAZZ CLUB label

2M056-
64846 Sidney Bechet - Live in New York 1945-1949 (16) (& further titles not from BN)

MODE label

MDINT
9852 The Many Faces of Jazz,Vol.45 - Thelonious Monk (Reissue of Vogue LD503-30 - See below)

SWING label

CLD869 Thelonious Monk - Monk (Reissue of Vogue LD503-30 - See below)

VOGUE label

LD483-30 L'Unique Mr. Bechet - Petite Fleur (24) (& further titles not from BN)
LD503-30 Thelonious Monk - The Prophet (19,21,22) (& further titles not from BN)

GERMANY

BLUE NOTE label

Note:Albums marked " were 2 LP sets.

BST		
84424	BN-LA006-F	McCoy Tyner - Extensions (238)
84428"	BN-LA015-G2	Elvin Jones - Live at the Lighthouse (262)
84429	BN-LA024-F	Lou Donaldson - Sophisticated Lou (264)
84431"	BN-LA037-G2	Grant Green - Live at the Lighthouse (260)
84432	BN-LA047-F	Donald Byrd - Black Byrd (260,264)
84433	BN-LA054-F	Horace Silver - In Pursuit of the 27th Man (263)
84435	BN-LA098-F	Ronnie Foster - Sweet Revival (265)
84436	BN-LA099-F	The New Heritage Keyboard Quartet (265)
84437	BN-LA109-F	Lou Donaldson - Sassy Soul Strut (266)
84438	BN-LA110-F	Elvin Jones - Mr. Jones (232,261)
84439	BN-LA140-F	Donald Byrd - Street Lady (267)
84441"	BN-LA141-G2	Gene Harris - Yesterday,Today and Tomorrow (268)
84442	BN-LA142-G	Bobbi Humphrey - Blacks and Blues (267)
84443	BN-LA143-F	Marlena Shaw - From the Depths of my Soul (266)
84445	BN-LA223-G	McCoy Tyner - Asante (247)
84446	BN-LA224-G	Lee Morgan Memorial Album (72,161,184,185)
84456	BN-LA249-G	Bobby Hutcherson - Live at Montreux (268)
84457	BN-LA250-G	Ronnie Foster - Live at Montreux (268)
84458	BN-LA251-G	Marlena Shaw - Live at Montreux (268)
84459	BN-LA252-G	Bobbi Humphrey - Live at Montreux (269)
84460	BN-LA257-G	Bobby Hutcherson - Cirrus (271,272)
84461	BN-LA258-G	Dom Minasi - When Joanna Loved Me (271)
84462	BN-LA259-G	Lou Donaldson - Sweet Lou (271)
84465	BN-LA014-G	Wayne Shorter - Moto Grosso Feio (240)
84471	BN-LA398-G	Alphonse Mouzon - Mind Transplant (275)
84472	BN-LA406-G	Horace Silver - Silver 'n Brass (275,276)
84473	BN-LA369-G	Bobby Hutcherson - Linger Lane (276)
84474	BN-LA368-G	Donald Byrd - Stepping into Tomorrow (274)
84477	BN-LA425-G	Ronnie Foster - Cheshire Cat (278)
84480	BN-LA464-G	Eddie Henderson - Sunburst (279)
84482"	BN-LA451-H2	Paul Chambers/John Coltrane (57,453,463)
84484"	BN-LA456-H2	Lester Young - The Aladdin Sessions (459,460,461)
84486"	BN-LA457-H2	Jackie McLean - Jacknife (185,192)
84488"	BN-LA458-H2	Cecil Taylor in Transition (453,623)
84490"	BN-LA459-H2	Andrew Hill - One for One (177,229,237)
84492"	BN-LA453-H2	Sam Rivers - Involution (191,200)
84494"	BN-LA461-H2	Gil Evans - Pacific Standard Time (554,555,556)
84496"	BN-LA356-H2	Freddie Hubbard (104,111,120,126,166,177)
84498"	BN-LA392-H2	Thad Jones & Mel Lewis (237,242,582,583,585,586,587)
84502"	BN-LA393-H2	Dexter Gordon (121,122,142,167,182)
84504"	BN-LA395-H2	Chick Corea (240,585,587)
84506"	BN-LA394-H2	Stanley Turrentine (158,162,199,203,212,219,220)
84508"	BN-LA401-H2	Sonny Rollins (59,63,71,74)
84510"	BN-LA402-H2	Horace Silver (39,64,89,94,106,153,173,185,186,196,210,222)
84512"	BN-LA399-H2	Herbie Hancock (139,151,157,168,179,210,225)
84514"	BN-LA400-H2	Jimmy Smith (50,51,61,77,78,98,103,149)
84519	BN-LA541-G	John Lee & Gerry Brown (281)
84521	BN-LA520-G	Chico Hamilton - Peregrinations (281)
84524	BN-LA549-G	Donald Byrd - Places and Spaces (283)
84545	BN-LA534-G	Jimmy Witherspoon - Spoonful (646)
84546	BN-LA584-G	Alphonse Mouzon - The Man Incognito (284,286)

731

BST

84547"	BN-LA521-H2	Johnny Griffin/John Coltrane/Hank Mobley - Blowin' Sessions (61,63)
84548"	BN-LA532-H2	Gerry Mulligan/Lee Konitz - Revelation (545,546,553)
84549"	BN-LA531-H2	Wes Montgomery - Beginnings (554,556)
84550"	BN-LA533-H2	T-Bone Walker - Classics of Modern Blues (529,530)
84551"	BN-LA529-H2	Paul Horn in India (564,565)
84552"	BN-LA485-H2	Herbie Nichols - The Third World (47,48,49,53)
84553"	BN-LA530-H2	Jazz Crusaders - The Young Rabbits (558,559,561,562,563,564,566)
84554"	BN-LA507-H2	Fats Navarro - Prime Source (19,22,23,25)
84555"	BN-LA472-H2	Chick Corea - Circling in (246,247,585)
84556"	BN-LA475-H2	Sonny Rollins - More from the Vanguard (73,74)
84557	BN-LA628-G	Ronnie Laws - Fever (284,285)
84560"	BN-LA663-J2	Blue Note Live at the Roxy (290,291)

F671007		Cassandra Wilson - Blue Light 'Til Dawn (356,359,361)
F671097		Herbie Hancock - Cantaloupe Island (139,151,168,179)

<u>ELECTROLA/BLUE NOTE label</u>

F667786/9* 40 Years of Jazz:History of Blue Note-Box 1 (4 LP Set):

667786:	Port of Harlem Jazzmen (3)	Frankie Newton Quintet (2)
	Sidney Bechet (3,4,17)	Art Hodes (11)
	Port of Harlem Seven (3)	
667787:	Albert Ammons & Meade Lux Lewis (2)	Pete Johnson (4)
	Albert Ammons (1)	Edmond Hall (6)
	Meade Lux Lewis (10)	James P.Johnson (6,11)
667788:	Edmond Hall (8)	Jimmy Hamilton (16)
	Bennie Morton (13)	
667789:	Earl Hines (3)	John Hardee (17)
	Teddy Bunn (4)	Jimmy Shirley (12)
	Ike Quebec (10,14)	Tiny Grimes (18)

Note: See Dutch issues (page 723) for Boxes 2/5 in the same series.

<u>L+R Records label</u>

LR41006 Jutta Hipp Quintet - Cool Dogs & Two Oranges (451) (& further titles not from Blue Note)

GREECE

<u>BLUE NOTE label</u>

14C 062-

2400081	BST84175	Herbie Hancock - Empyrean Isles (168)
2613491	BST84095	Leo Parker - Rollin' With Leo (128)
2613621	BST84428	Clifford Brown - Alternate Takes (35,36,38)

 732

INDIA

BLUE NOTE label

JAZ 1 Greatest Jazz Tunes:
- Jean-Luc Ponty (569)
- Sonny Rollins (71)
- Miles Davis (473)
- Herbie Hancock (210)
- Chick Corea (585)
- Wayne Shorter (165)
- McCoy Tyner (207)
- Art Blakey(40)

JAZ 2 Greatest Jazz Tunes,Vol.II:
- Lou Donaldson (83)
- Horace Silver (173)
- Miles Davis (34)
- Bud Powell (27)
- Freddie Hubbard (120)
- Stanley Turrentine (305)
- Jimmy Smith (103)
- Lee Morgan (161)
- Joe Pass (561)

JAZ 3 Greatest Jazz Tunes,Vol.3:
- Pieces of a Dream (539)
- Bill Evans (305)
- Bennie Wallace (308)
- James Newton (309)
- Michel Petrucciani (312)
- Tony Williams (309)
- Freddie Hubbard & Woody Shaw (312)
- OTB (309)
- Stanley Jordan (304)
- Al Di Meola (539)

ITALY

BLUE NOTE label

BNST

36052	BLP1507	The Jazz Messengers at the Cafe Bohemia,Vol.1 (49,50)
36057	BLP4049	Art Blakey & The Jazz Messengers - A Night in Tunisia (108,109)

ABNST

2-36520	BN-LA579-H2	Thelonious Monk - The Complete Genius (2 LP Set) (19,20,21,28,32)

733

JAPAN

<u>BLUE NOTE label</u> (produced by King Records)

DY		
5801-01	BST84139	Grant Green - Am I Blue (154)
5801-02	BLP4087	Leo Parker - Let Me Tell You 'Bout It (126)
5805-01		Art Blakey at The Cafe Bohemia,Vol.3 (49,50)
5806-01	BLP5056	Jutta Hipp (451)
5806-02		Port of Harlem Jazzmen (2,3)/James P. Johnson (7)

Note: Above albums were bonus albums given to buyers of some Blue Note albums reissue series.

GP-		
534	BN-LA664--G	Robbie Krieger And Friends (291,292)
3120	BN-LA737-H	Earl Klugh - Finger Paintings (296,297)
3121	BN-LA736-H	Noel Pointer - Phantazia (295,296)
3122	BN-LA730-H	Ronnie Laws - Friends and Strangers (296)
3123	BN-LA596-G	Earl Klugh (285)
3124	BN-LA667-G	Earl Klugh - Living Inside your Love (293)
3125	BN-LA047-F	Donald Byrd - Black Byrd (260,264)
3126	BN-LA628-G	Ronnie Laws - Fever (284,285)
3137	BN-LA789-H	Bobby Hutcherson - Knucklebean (297,298)
3143	BN-LA701-G	John Lee & Gerry Brown - Can't Say Enough (294)
3144	BN-LA551-G	Bobby Hutcherson - Montara (282)
3145	BN-LA344-G	Bobbi Humphrey - Satin Doll (272,273)
3146	BN-LA452-G	Ronnie Laws - Pressure Sensitive (279)
3149	BN-LA462-G	Carmen McRae - I Am Music (279,280)
3150	BN-LA635-G	Carmen McRae - Can't Hide Love (288,289)
3151	BN-LA397-G	Marlena Shaw - Who is this Bitch Anyway? (274,275)
3152	BN-LA251-G	Marlena Shaw - Live at Montreux (268)
3155	UA-LA848-H	Noel Pointer - Hold On (633)
3157	BN-LA853-H	Horace Silver - Silver 'n' Percussion (299,300)
3160	UA-LA877-H	Earl Klugh - Magic In Your Eyes (633,634)
3170	BN-LA870-H	Blue Note Meet Los Angeles Philharmonic (299)
3177	BN-LA628-G	Ronnie Laws - Fever (284,285)
3181	UA-LA942-H	Earl Klugh - Heart String (634)
3186		Tommy Flanagan Trio - Lonely Town (622)
3200	UA-LA973-H	Noel Pointer - Feel It (635)
3205		Earl Klugh - Captain Caribe (285,293,296,297,633,634,635)
3225	LT-1026	Earl Klugh - Dream Come True (from Liberty label) (536,537)

GXF-		
3001	BLP1595	Cannonball Adderley - Somethin' Else (79)
3002	BLP4003	Art Blakey - Moanin' (85)
3003	BLP1521	Art Blakey - A Night at Birdland (40,41)
3004	BLP1588	Sonny Clark - Cool Struttin' (76)
3005	BLP1579	Sonny Clark Trio (72)
3006	BLP1526	Clifford Brown Memorial Album (35,38)
3007	BLP1581	Sonny Rollins - Live at the Village Vanguard (73)
3008	BLP4264	The Real McCoy Tyner (201)
3009	BLP4163	Eric Dolphy - Out to Lunch (163)
3010	BLP1577	John Coltrane - Blue Train (71)
3011	BLP1501	Miles Davis,Vol.1 (31,34)
3012	BLP1502	Miles Davis,Vol.2 (31,34,41)
3013	BLP4009	Bud Powell - The Scene Changes (88)
3014	BLP1510	Thelonious Monk - Genius of Modern Music,Vol.1 (20,21,22)

GXF-

3015	BLP4157	Lee Morgan - The Sidewinder (161)
3016	BLP1569	Paul Chambers - Bass on Top (67)
3017	BLP4185	Horace Silver - Song for my Father (159,173)
3018	BLP4224	Ornette Coleman at the Gyllene Cirkeln (187,188)
3019	BST84332	Wayne Shorter - Super Nova (231)
3020	BLP4195	Herbie Hancock - Maiden Voyage (179)
3021		Art Blakey - Live at the Renaissance Club (= part of BN-LA473-J2) (626)
3022		Jackie McLean - Hipnosis (= part of BN BN-LA483-J2) (199)
3023	BN-LA582-J2/1	Lee Morgan - The Procrastinator,Vol.1 (204)
3024	BN-LA582-J2/2	Lee Morgan - The Procrastinator,Vol.2 (231,233)
3025	BN-LA883-J2/1	Stanley Turrentine - Jubilee Shout (145)
3026	BN-LA882-J2/1	Chick Corea - Circulus,Vol.1 (240,247)
3027	BN-LA882-J2/2	Chick Corea - Circulus,Vol.2 (247)
3037	BST84346	Thad Jones-Mel Lewis - Consummation (236,237,242)
3051		Sonny Clark - Blues in the Night (86,87)
3052		Kenny Burrell - K.B. Blues (60)
3053		Grant Green - Matador (166)
3054	LT-988	Wayne Shorter - The Soothsayer (178)
3055	LT-989	Dexter Gordon - Clubhouse (182)
3056		Sonny Clark - My Conception (90)
3057		Kenny Burrell - Freedom (151,173)
3058		Grant Green - Gooden's Corner (132)
3059		Wayne Shorter - The Collector (183,190)
3060		Art Blakey's Jazz Messengers - Pisces (117,123,165)
3061		Bobby Hutcherson - Oblique (204)
3062	BST84427	Jackie McLean - Tippin' the Scales (143)
3063		Bennie Green - Minor Revelation (86)
3064		Curtis Fuller - Two Bones (77)
3065		Grant Green - Oleo (134)
3066		Hank Mobley - Poppin' (72)
3067		Jackie McLean/Tina Brooks - Street Singer (110)
3068	BST84254	Lou Donaldson - Sweet Slumber (199)
3069		Sonny Clark - The Art of the Trio (72,86)
3070		Kenny Burrell - Swingin' (50,81,93)
3071		Grant Green - Remembering (126)
3072		Tina Brooks - Minor Move (79)
3073		Bobby Hutcherson - Inner Glow (278)
3074 nr	DY 5805-01	Art Blakey's Jazz Messengers at Cafe Bohemia,Vol.3 (49,50)
3075 nr	BST84432	Grant Green - Born to be Blue (132,135)
3076 nr		The Three Sounds - D.B. Blues
3077 nr	(J)BNJ61003	Kenny Dorham at Cafe Bohemia,Vol.2 (54)
3078 nr		Jimmy Smith - Lonesome Road (75)
3079 nr	BST84431	Hank Mobley - Another Workout (130)
3080 nr		Andrew Hill - Chained (202)
3121*	TRLP 19	Cecil Taylor - Jazz Advance (453)
3122*	TRLP 20	Doug Watkins - Watkins At Large (454)
3123*	TRLP 4	Donald Byrd - Byrd's Eye View (452)
3124*	TRLP 17	Donald Byrd - Byrd Blows On Beacon Hill (453)
3125*	TRLP 1	Herb Pomeroy - Jazz In A Stable (452)
3126*	TRLP 30	Jazz In Transition:
		Donald Byrd (453) — Jay Migliori (452)
		Herb Pomeroy (452) — Sun Ra (453)
		Paul Chambers/John Coltrane (453) — Dave Coleman (454)
		Cecil Taylor (453)

(*: those albums were issued by King as on Transition/BN label,both names appearing on the LPs.)

3143	BLP4114	Ike Quebec - Soul Samba (143)
3149	BN-LA317-G	Duke Pearson - It Could Only Happen with You (238,241)
3151	BLP5023+ BLP5025	Kenny Drew/Wynton Kelly (29,34)
3152	BLP1600	Introducing The Three Sounds (83,84)

GXF-

3153	BLP4044	The Three Sounds - Moods (105)
3154	BLP4037	Horace Parlan - Us Three (102)
3171	BLP5035 + BLP5042	Sal Salvador/Tal Farlow (39,41)
3172	BLP1596	Kenny Burrell - Blue Lights,Vol.1 (81)
3173	BLP4099	Grant Green - Sunday Mornin' (124)
3177	BLP1597	Kenny Burrell - Blue Lights,Vol.2 (81)
3178	BLP4154	Grant Green - Idle Moments (159)

GXH-

3001/02	BN-LA663-J2	Blue Note Live at The Roxy (2 LP Set) (290,291)
3501/02	BN-LA709-H2	Carmen McRae at The Great American Music Hall (2-LP Set) (290)
3503	BLP9002	Sheila Jordan - Portrait of Sheila (142,144)

GXK-

8001	BST84279	Herbie Hancock - Speak Like a Child (210)
8002	BLP4175	Herbie Hancock - Empyrean Isles (168)
8003	BLP4173	Wayne Shorter - Night Dreamer (165)
8004	BLP4219	Wayne Shorter - The All Seeing Eye (186)
8005	BLP4073	Freddie Hubbard - Hub Cap (120)
8006	BST84172	Freddie Hubbard - Breaking Point! (166)
8007	BST84216	Anthony Williams - Spring (184)
8008	BST84338	McCoy Tyner - Expansions (217)
8009	BLP4231	Bobby Hutcherson - Happenings (190)
8010	BLP4189	Joe Henderson - Inner Urge (175)
8011	BLP1523	Introducing Kenny Burrell Guitar (53)
8012	BLP1570	Sonny Clark - Dial S for Sonny (67)
8013	BLP1524	Kenny Dorham - 'Round Midnight at The Cafe Bohemia (54)
8014	BLP4140	Joe Henderson - Page One (155)
8015	BLP1533	Introducing Johnny Griffin (52)
8016	BLP1542	Sonny Rollins (59)
8017	BLP1538	Lee Morgan Indeed! (57)
8018	BLP1534	Paul Chambers Sextet - Whims of Chambers (57)
8019	BST84282	Elvin Jones - Puttin' it Together (212)
8020	BLP4184	Sam Rivers - Fuchsia Swing Song (175)
8021	BLP4109	Herbie Hancock - Takin' Off (139)
8022	BLP4040	Freddie Hubbard - Open Sesame (104)
8023	BLP4151	Andrew Hill - Black Fire (159)
8024	BLP4198	Bobby Hutcherson - Dialogue (179)
8025	BLP1512	Jimmy Smith at the Organ,Vol.1 (50)
8026	BLP4180	Anthony Williams - Life Time (171)
8027	BLP1520	Horace Silver Trio and Spotlight on Drums (33,39)
8028	BLP4013	Jackie McLean - New Soil (91)
8029	BLP1537	Lou Donaldson Quartet/Quintet/Sextet (32,33,43)
8030	BLP4007	Donald Byrd - Off to the Races (87)
8031	BLP1513	Thad Jones - Detroit-New York Junction (51)
8032	BLP1505	The Eminent Jay Jay Johnson,Vol.1 (36,43)
8033	BLP1506	The Eminent Jay Jay Johnson,Vol.2 (36,43,48)
8034	BLP1509	Milt Jackson (22,28,30)
8035	BLP1558	Sonny Rollins,Volume 2 (63)
8036	BST84017	Horace Silver - Blowin' the Blues Away (94,95)
8037	BST84026	Donald Byrd - Fuego (95)
8038	BLP4106	Jackie McLean - Let Freedom Ring (136)
8039	BLP1583	Curtis Fuller - Art Farmer (75)
8040	BLP1518	Horace Silver and The Jazz Messengers (44,45)
8041	BLP4049	Art Blakey and The Jazz Messengers - A Night in Tunisia (108,109)
8042	BLP1595	Cannonball Adderley with Miles Davis - Somethin' Else (79)
8043	BLP1588	Sonny Clark - Cool Struttin' (76)
8044	BLP4003	Art Blakey and The Jazz Messengers - Moanin' (85)

736

GXK-		
8045	BST84157	Lee Morgan - The Sidewinder (161)
8046	BST84163	Eric Dolphy - Out to Lunch! (163)
8047	BLP4185	The Horace Silver Quintet - Song for my Father (159,173)
8048	BST84332	Wayne Shorter - Super Nova (231)
8049	BST84264	McCoy Tyner - The Real McCoy (201)
8050	BST84195	Herbie Hancock - Maiden Voyage (179)
8051	BLP1579	Sonny Clark Trio (72)
8052	BLP4146	Dexter Gordon - Our Man in Paris (154)
8053	BLP1569	Paul Chambers - Bass on Top (67)
8054	BLP1526	Clifford Brown Memorial Album (35,38)
8055	BLP1577	John Coltrane - Blue Train (71)
8056	BLP1501	Miles Davis,Vol.1 (31,34)
8057	BLP1502	Miles Davis,Vol.2 (31,34,41)
8058	BLP1510	Thelonious Monk - Genius of Modern Music,Vol.1 (20,21,22)
8059	BLP1511	Thelonious Monk - Genius of Modern Music,Vol.2 (20,21,28,32)
8060	BLP1531	The Fabulous Fats Navarro,Vol.1 (19,23,25)
8061	BLP1532	The Fabulous Fats Navarro,Vol.2 (22,23,25)
8062	BLP1539	Horace Silver - 6 Pieces of Silver (58)
8063	BLP1562	Horace Silver Quintet - The Stylings of Silver (64)
8064	BLP1589	Further Explorations by the Horace Silver Quintet (76)
8065	BLP4008	Finger Poppin' with the Horace Silver Quintet (89)
8066	BLP4042	Horace Silver - Horace-Scope (106)
8067	BLP4076	The Horace Silver Quintet at the Village Gate - Doin' the Thing (122,123)
8068	BST84275	McCoy Tyner - Tender Moments (207)
8069	BST84307	McCoy Tyner - Time for Tyner (214)
8070	BN-LA006-F	McCoy Tyner - Extensions (238)
8071	BLP1503	The Amazing Bud Powell,Vol.1 (25,27)
8072	BLP1504	The Amazing Bud Powell,Vol.2 (25,27,37)
8073	BLP1571	The Amazing Bud Powell,Vol.3 - Bud! (68)
8074	BLP1598	The Amazing Bud Powell,Vol.4 - Time Waits (82)
8075	BLP4009	The Amazing Bud Powell,Vol.5 - The Scene Changes (88)
8076	BLP4182	Wayne Shorter - Ju Ju (169)
8077	BLP4194	Wayne Shorter - Speak No Evil (176)
8078	BLP4232	Wayne Shorter - Adam's Apple (190)
8079	BST84297	Wayne Shorter - Schizophrenia (20)
8080	BST84363	Wayne Shorter - Odyssey of Iska (247)
8081	BLP4024	Jackie McLean - Swing Swang Swingin' (96)
8082	BLP4051	Jackie McLean - Jackie's Bag (88,110)
8083	BLP4137	Jackie McLean - One Step Beyond (153)
8084	BLP4165	Jackie McLean - Destination...Out! (158)
8085	BLP4179	Jackie McLean - It's Time! (169)
8086	BLP4215	Jackie McLean - Right Now (176)
8087	BLP4218	Jackie McLean - Action (172)
8088	BST84262	Jackie McLean - New and Old Gospel (201)
8089	BLP4001	Sonny Rollins - Newk's Time (71)
8090	BLP4204	Dexter Gordon - Gettin' Around (182)
8091	BLP1559	Johnny Griffin Vol.2 (63)
8092	BLP1580	Johnny Griffin - The Congregation (73)
8093	BLP1536	J.R. Monterose (57)
8094	BLP1545	Lou Donaldson Quintet - Wailing with Lou (59)
8095	BLP1574	Hank Mobley - Peckin' Time (77)
8096	BLP4031	Hank Mobley - Soul Station (99)
8097	BLP4058	Hank Mobley - Roll Call (113)
8098	BST84080	Hank Mobley - Workout (119)
8099	BLP1521	Art Blakey - A Night at Birdland,Vol.1 (40,41)
8100	BLP1522	Art Blakey - A Night at Birdland,Vol.2 (40,41)
8101	BLP1581	Sonny Rollins - A Night at The Village Vanguard (73)
8102	BLP1507	The Jazz Messengers at the Cafe Bohemia,Vol.1 (49,50)
8103	BLP1508	The Jazz Messengers at the Cafe Bohemia,Vol.2 (49,50)
8104	BLP4060	Donald Byrd at the Half Note Cafe - Jazz at the Waterfront,Vol.1 (112)

GXK-		
8105	BLP4061	Donald Byrd at the Half Note Cafe - Jazz at the Waterfront,Vol.2 (112)
8106	BLP4021	Kenny Burrell - On View at The Five Spot Cafe (93,94)
8107	BST84224	The Ornette Coleman Trio at the "Golden Circle",Stockholm,Vol.1 (187,188)
8108	BST84225	The Ornette Coleman Trio at the "Golden Circle",Stockholm,Vol.2 (187,188)
8109	BLP1527	The Magnificent Thad Jones (55)
8110	BLP1546	The Magnificent Thad Jones,Vol.3 (55,59)
8111	BLP1584	Here Comes Louis Smith (454)
8112	BLP1549	Clifford Jordan & John Gilmore - Blowing in from Chicago (61)
8113	BLP1582	Cliff Jordan - Cliff Craft (74)
8114	BLP4071	Grant Green - Green Street (120)
8115	BLP1543	Kenny Burrell,Vol.2 (50,53,54)
8116	BST84123	Kenny Burrell - Midnight Blue (147)
8117	BST84132	Grant Green - Feelin' The Spirit (146)
8118	BLP1576	Sonny Clark - Sonny's Crib (70)
8119	BLP4046	Duke Jordan - Flight to Jordan (108)
8120	BLP4059	Kenny Drew - Undercurrent (113)
8121	BLP1519	Herbie Nichols Trio (48,49,53)
8122	BLP4020	The Three Sounds - Good Deal (91)
8123	BLP4028	Horace Parlan - Movin' and Groovin' (100)
8124	BLP4019	Donald Byrd - Byrd in Hand (92)
8125	BLP4048	Donald Byrd - Byrd in Flight (98,99,106)
8126	BLP4056	Freddie Hubbard - Goin' Up (111)
8127	BLP4101	Donald Byrd - Royal Flush (127)
8128	BLP4127	Kenny Dorham - Una Mas (152)
8129	BST84205	Pete La Roca - Basra (181)
8130	BST84090	Art Blakey and The Jazz Messengers - Mosaic (127)
8131	BLP1590	Lee Morgan - Candy (75,77)
8132	BLP1578	Lee Morgan - The Cooker (72)
8133	BLP4034	Lee Morgan - Leeway (103)
8134	BLP1541	Lee Morgan,Vol.2 (58)
8135	BLP1557	Lee Morgan,Vol.3 (62)
8136	BLP4147	Herbie Hancock - Inventions and Dimensions (157)
8137	BLP4126	Herbie Hancock - My Point of View (151)
8138	BST84321	Herbie Hancock - The Prisoner (225)
8139	BLP4167	Andrew Hill - Point of Departure (164)
8140	BST84291	Bobby Hutcherson - Total Eclipse (215)
8141	BST84319	Donald Byrd - Fancy Free (227,228)
8142	BLP1514	Jimmy Smith at the Organ,Vol.2 (51)
8143	BLP1564	Paul Chambers Quintet (65)
8144	BLP4027	Freddie Redd - The Connection (100)
8145	BLP4030	Jimmy Smith - Crazy Baby! (98)
8146	BLP4035	Duke Pearson - Tender Feelin's (98)
8147	BLP4237	Cecil Taylor - Unit Structures (192)
8148	BST84260	Cecil Taylor - Conquistador (196)
8149	BLP4246	Ornette Coleman - The Empty Foxhole (195)
8150	BLP4247	Don Cherry - Symphony for Improvisers (195)
8151	GXF-3060	Art Blakey - Pisces (117,123,165)
8152	LT-988	Wayne Shorter - The Soothsayer (178)
8153	GXF-3059	Wayne Shorter - The Collector (183,190)
8154	GXF-3052	Kenny Burrell - K.B. Blues (60)
8155	GXF-3070	Kenny Burrell - Swingin' (50,81,93)
8156	GXF-3051	Sonny Clark - Blues in the Night (86,87)
8157	GXF-3069	Sonny Clark - The Art of The Trio (72,86)
8158	GXF-3056	Sonny Clark - My Conception (90)
8159	GXF-3053	Grant Green - Matador (166)
8160	BST84427	Jackie McLean - Tippin' the Scales (143)
8161	GXF-3067	Jackie McLean - Street Singer (110)
8162	GXF-3072	Tina Brooks - Minor Move (79)
8163	GXF-3066	Hank Mobley - Poppin' (72)
8164	BST84254	Lou Donaldson - Sweet Slumber (199)

GXK-		
8165	GXF-3063	Bennie Green - Minor Revelation (86)
8166	GXF-3064	Curtis Fuller - Two Bones (77)
8167	GXF-3071	Grant Green - Remembering (126)
8168	GXF-3058	Grant Green - Gooden's Corner (132)
8169	GXF-3065	Grant Green - Oleo (134)
8170	GXF-3057	Kenny Burrell - Freedom (151,173)
8171	LT-987	Lee Morgan - Sonic Boom (201,202)
8172	LT-994	Jackie McLean - Consequences (187)
8173	LT-1028	Lou Donaldson - Midnight Sun (107)
8174	LT-1057	Harold Land - Take Aim (107)
8175	LT-1051	Dexter Gordon - Landslide (122,137,140)
8176	LT-1075	Stanley Turrentine - Mr. Natural (171)
8177	LT-995	Hank Mobley - A Slice of the Top (191)
8178	LT-996	Bobby Hutcherson - Spiral (179,221)
8179	LT-992	Jimmy Smith - Conformation (70,78)
8180	LT-1032	Grant Green - Nigeria (132)
8181	LT-1058	Lee Morgan - Tom Cat (170)
8182	LT-1082	Blue Mitchell - Step Lightly (157)
8183	LT-991	Donald Byrd - Chant (120)
8184	LT-1030	Andrew Hill - Dance with Death (219)
8185	LT-1044	Bobby Hutcherson - Patterns (211)
8186	LT-1054	Jimmy Smith - Cool Blues (80)
8187	LT-990	Grant Green - Solid (167)
8188	LT-1045	Hank Mobley - Thinking of Home (246)
8189	LT-993	Stanley Turrentine - New Time Shuffle (199,203)
8190	LT-1052	Ike Quebec - With a Song in my Heart (135)
8201	BLP4209	Hank Mobley - Dippin' (183)
8202	BLP4041	Tina Brooks - True Blue (105)
8203	BLP4085	Freddie Hubbard - Ready for Freddie (126)
8204	BST84144	Johnny Coles - Little Johnny C (156)
8205	BST84221	Larry Young - Unity (186)
8206	BST84119	Charlie Rouse - Bossa Nova Bacchanal (145)
8207	BLP1575	Lee Morgan - City Lights (69)
8208	BLP1591	Lou Donaldson - Lou Takes Off (76)
8209	BST84111	Grant Green - The Latin Bit (137)
8210	BLP4011	Jimmy Smith - The Sermon (70,78)
8211	BST84345	Jackie McLean - Demon's Dance (208)
8212	BST84022	Duke Pearson - Profile (96)
8213	BLP1530	Jutta Hipp (56)
8214	BLP1573	John Jenkins (69)
8215	BLP4110	Horace Silver - The Tokyo Blues (141)
8216	BST84091	Sonny Clark - Leapin' and Lopin' (129)
8217	BLP4010	Bennie Green - Walkin' & Talkin' (88)
8218	BST84263	Lou Donaldson - Alligator Bogaloo (201)
8219	BLP4067	Jackie McLean - Bluesnik (115)
8220	BLP4100	Jimmy Smith Plays Fats Waller (133)
8221	BLP4064	Grant Green - Grant's First Stand (116)
8222	BLP4176	Dexter Gordon - One Flight Up (167)
8223	BLP1594	Louis Smith - Smithville (80)
8224	BLP4214	Blue Mitchell - Down with It (184)
8225	BLP1568	Hank Mobley Sextet (66)
8226	BLP4057	Stanley Turrentine with The Three Sounds - Blue Hour (114)
8227	BLP4002	Jimmy Smith - House Party (70,77,78)
8228	BLP4105	Ike Quebec - It Might as Well be Spring (130)
8229	BLP4012	Lou Donaldson + The Three Sounds (89)
8230	BLP4202	Grant Green - I want to Hold Your Hand (179)

739

K16P-
9031/32 Modern Jazz Double Gold Super Disc (2 LP Set) (same as K22P-6096/97 - see page 741):

9031: Cannonball Adderley (79)
Horace Silver (173)
Herbie Hancock (139)
Art Blakey & The Jazz Messengers (85)
Sonny Clark (72)
Kenny Burrell (147)
Grant Green (146)
Jimmy Smith (51)
Lee Morgan (62)

9032: Sonny Clark (76)
John Coltrane (71)
Joe Henderson (155)
Miles Davis (31)
Clifford Brown (38)
Thelonious Monk (21)
Bud Powell (88)
Lou Donaldson (59)
Sonny Rollins (73)

K18P-
9124 Round About Midnight (1947-1956):
Miles Davis (31)
Bud Powell (27)
J.J.Johnson (43)
The Jazz Messengers (49)
Milt Jackson (30)
Thelonious Monk (21)
Jimmy Smith (50)
Thad Jones (51)
Horace Silver & The Jazz Messengers (45)
Horace Silver Trio (39)
The Art Blakey Quintet (40)
Kenny Burrell (53)
Kenny Dorham (54)
Clifford Brown (38)
Fats Navarro (19)
Lou Donaldson (32)

9125 Yesterdays (1956-1957):
Paul Chambers (57)
J.R. Monterose (57)
Johnny Griffin (52)
Lee Morgan (57)
Sonny Rollins (59,63)
Johnny Griffin (52)
Horace Silver (64)
Paul Chambers (67)
Bud Powell (68)
John Coltrane (71)

9126 Autumn Leaves (1957-1958):
Sonny Clark Trio (72)
Johnny Griffin (73)
Sonny Rollins (73)
Sonny Clark (76)
Cannonball Adderley (79)
The Horace Silver Quintet (76)
Sonny Rollins (71)
Art Blakey (85)

9127 A Night in Tunisia (1958-1962):
Bud Powell (88)
Horace Silver (94)
Jackie McLean (96)
Kenny Burrell (93)
Donald Byrd (95)
Art Blakey (109)
Donald Byrd (112)
Freddie Hubbard (120)
Herbie Hancock (139)

9128 Blue Bossa (1963-1965):
Joe Henderson (155)
Freddie Hubbard (166)
Dexter Gordon (154)
Andrew Hill (159)
Eric Dolphy (163)
Jackie McLean (153)
Wayne Shorter (165)
Herbie Hancock (168)
Anthony Williams (184)

K18P-

9201	BST84015	Art Blakey and The Jazz Messengers - At The Jazz Corner of the World,Vol.1 (90)
9202	BST84016	Art Blakey and The Jazz Messengers - At The Jazz Corner of the World,Vol.2 (90)
9203	BST84089	Jackie McLean - A Fickle Sonance (128)
9204	BLP1593	Lou Donaldson - Blues Walk (83)
9205	BST84252	Duke Pearson - Sweet Honey Bee (198)
9206	BST84082	Horace Parlan - Up and Down (124)
9207	BLP4045	Freddie Redd - Shades of Redd (109)
9208	BLP4047	Art Taylor - A.T.'s Delight (108)
9209	BLP1567	Curtis Fuller - The Opener (66)
9210	BLP1599	Bennie Green - Soul Stirrin' (81)
9211	BLP1540	Hank Mobley featuring Donald Byrd and Lee Morgan (58)
9212	BST84183	Grant Green - Talkin' About (172)

K18P-

9213	BST84078	Jimmy Smith - Midnight Special (102,103)
9214	BST84361	Elvin Jones - Coalition (245)
9215	BN-LA014-G	Wayne Shorter - Moto Grosso Feio (240)

9226	BST84054	Art Blakey and The Jazz Messengers - Meet You at the Jazz Corner of the World, Vol.1 (110)
9227	BST84055	Art Blakey and The Jazz Messengers - Meet You at the Jazz Corner of the World, Vol.2 (110)
9228	BLP1515	Jutta Hipp at The Hickory House,Vol.1 (52)
9229	BLP1516	Jutta Hipp at The Hickory House,Vol.2 (52)
9230	BLP4018	Walter Davis Jr. - Davis Cup (93)
9231	BST84220	The Horace Silver Quintet - The Cape Verdean Blues (185,186)
9232	BST84115	Freddie Hubbard - Hub Tones (144)
9233	BST84181	Kenny Dorham - Trompeta Toccata (172)
9234	BST84212	Lee Morgan - The Gigolo (183,184)
9235	BST84187	Larry Young - Into Somethin' (174)
9236	BLP4036	Lou Donaldson - Sunny Side Up (99,100)
9237	BST84098	Ike Quebec - Blue and Sentimental (131)
9238	BST84186	Hank Mobley - The Turnaround (151,177)
9239	BST84069	Stanley Turrentine - Up at Minton's,Vol.1 (118)
9240	BST84070	Stanley Turrentine - Up at Minton's,Vol.2 (118)
9241	BST84038	Jackie McLean - Capuchin' Swing (102)
9242	BLP1566	Lou Donaldson - Swing and Soul (65)
9243	BLP4032	Sonny Red - Out of The Blue (97,99)
9244	BST84075	Donald Byrd - The Cat Walk (121)
9245	BLP4006	Dizzy Reece - Blues in Trinity (83)
9246	BST84169	Lee Morgan - Search for the New Land (163)
9247	BST84077	Dexter Gordon - Doin' Allright (121)
9248	BLP4039	Stanley Turrentine - Look Out! (104)
9249	BLP1572	Curtis Fuller - Bone & Bari (68)
9250	BST84159	Andrew Hill - Judgment (162)

9271	BLP5029 + BLP5044	Elmo Hope - Trio & Quintet (36,42)
9272	BLP5068 + BLP5069	Herbie Nichols Trio (47,48)
9273	BLP5053 + BLP5064	Julius Watkins (43,45)
9274	BLP5012 + BLP5024	Howard McGhee Sextet (23,26,35)
9275	BLP5020 + BLP5033	Gil Melle (33,38,450)
9276	BLP5045 + BLP5066	George Wallington (42) / Hank Mobley (46)
9277	BN BN-LA475-H2/1	Sonny Rollins - A Night at The Village Vanguard,Vol.2 (73)
9278	BN BN-LA475-H2/2	Sonny Rollins - A Night at The Village Vanguard,Vol.3 (73,74)
9279	BLP1592	Sonny Clark - Cool Struttin',Vol.2 (= BN(J)LNJ70093) (75,76)
9280		Jimmy Smith - The Singles (51,55,60,67)

Note: Albums marked L below were on Liberty Label.

K22P-

6074/75 L The World of Jazz Giants (2 LP Set):
- Miles Davis (31,34,41,79)
- Sonny Rollins (63,71,73)
- (& further titles not from BN: Charles Mingus/Bill Evans)

6092/93 L The World of Jazz Piano (2 LP Set):

6092:
- James P.Johnson (6)
- Earl Hines (3)
- Albert Ammons (1)
- Meade Lux Lewis (5)
- Thelonious Monk (19,20)
- Bud Powell (28,68,82,88)
- Horace Silver (33,39)

6093:
- Sonny Clark (87)
- Wynton Kelly (29)
- Kenny Drew (34)
- Tommy Flanagan (622)
- Horace Parlan (100)
- McCoy Tyner (214)
- Andrew Hill (159)
- Herbie Hancock (210)
- Chick Corea (585)
- (& further titles not from BN: Russ Freeman/Cecil Taylor)

K22P-
6094/95 L The World of Jazz Guitar (2 LP Set):

6094: Charlie Christian (5) | Tal Farlow (41)
Jimmy Shirley (12) | Sal Salvador (39)
Tiny Grimes (18)
(& further titles not from BN: Jim Hall-Jimmy Raney/Jim Hall/Joe Pass/Laurindo Almeida)

6095: Kenny Burrell (53,81) | Grant Green (116,132,159)
(& further titles not from BN: Wes Montgomery)

6096/97 The World of Modern Jazz (2 LP Set)(= K16P-9031/32)

6096: Cannonball Adderley (79) | Sonny Clark (72)
Horace Silver (173) | Kenny Burrell (147)
Herbie Hancock (139) | Grant Green(146)
Art Blakey & The Jazz Messengers (85) | Jimmy Smith (51)
Lee Morgan (62)

6097: Sonny Clark (76) | Thelonious Monk (21)
John Coltrane(71) | Bud Powell (88)
Joe Henderson (155) | Lou Donaldson (59)
Miles Davis (31) | Sonny Rollins (73)
Clifford Brown (38)

6116/17 L The World of Earl Klugh (2 LP Set) (285,291,293,296,297,299) (& further Liberty/UA titles)

6125/26 The World of Jazz Organ (2 LP Set):
Jimmy Smith (54,56,60,74,101,103,133,149)
John Patton (220) | Larry Young (209)
Freddie Roach (151) | Baby Face Willette (123)
Lonnie Smith (222,230)

6131/32 L The World of Jazz Sax (2 LP Set):

6131: Sonny Rollins (73) | Johnny Griffin (52)
Joe Henderson (175) | Dexter Gordon (154,182)
Hank Mobley (119)

6132: Jackie McLean (96,143) | Cannonball Adderley (79)
Lou Donaldson (32,199) | (& further titles not from BN:Art Pepper/Bud Shank)

K23P-
6722 Thelonious Monk - The Genius of Monk (20,21,28)
6723 Bud Powell - Cleopatra's Dream (27,37,68,82,88)
6724 Art Blakey - The Art of Blakey (40,49,85,90,110)
6725 Jazz Time Now - History of Jazz Piano:
James P.Johnson (6) | Bill Evans (627)
Albert Ammons & Meade Lux Lewis (2) | Cecil Taylor (453)
Earl Hines (3) | McCoy Tyner (217)
Thelonious Monk (20) | Herbie Hancock (210)
Bud Powell (27) | Chick Corea (585)
Horace Silver (95)

6726 Jazz Time Now - Jazz Piano Standards:
Sonny Clark (72) | Monty Alexander (562)
The Three Sounds (83,91) | Duke Pearson (96,98)

K23P-
9281 Jazz Piano Classics on Blue Note/Omnibus:
James P.Johnson (6) | Albert Ammons (1,2)
Earl Hines (3) | Meade Lux Lewis (2,5)

9282 B6505 Edmond Hall & Charlie Christian - Memorable Sessions on Blue Note (5,9)

9283 Sidney Bechet - Basin Street Blues (4,17,24)
9284 Sidney Bechet - Saint Louis Blues (12,13)
9285 Sidney Bechet - Blues My Naughty Sweetie Gives to Me (30,37)

K23P-
9286 Blue Note Jazzmen - Swing Sessions:
James P.Johnson (7) Benny Morton (13)
Edmond Hall (8)
9287 Blue Note Jazzmen - Jammin' in Jazz:
Edmond Hall (6) Sidney De Paris (9)
James P.Johnson (11)
9288 Art Hodes - Back Room Sessions (8,11,13,15,16)
9289 George Lewis & His New Orleans Stompers (447-448)
9290 George Lewis and His Ragtime Band - Memorable Concert (= BLP1208) (451,452)
9291 George Lewis and His New Orleans Stompers - New Orleans Stompers '55 (47)
9292 Mainstream Jazz at Blue Note:
Ike Quebec (10,15) John Hardee (17)
Jimmy Hamilton (16) Tiny Grimes (18)
K28P-
6045 Earl Klugh - Portrait of Earl Klugh (285,293,296,297,537,633,634)

BLUE NOTE/CBS-SONY label

FCPA
6201 Sonny Rollins (= BN BLP1581) (73)
6202 Cannonball Adderley and John Coltrane:
Cannonball Adderley (79) John Coltrane (71)
6203 Bud Powell (25,27,37,68,82,88)
6204 The Jazz Messengers (49,50)
6206 Horace Silver (44,45,58,94,141,173)
6207 Sonny Clark (72,76)
6208 Duke Jordan and Kenny Drew: Duke Jordan (108) / Kenny Drew (113)
6209 Kenny Burrell and Grant Green: Grant Green (124) / Kenny Burrell (147)
6210 Donald Byrd and Art Farmer: Donald Byrd (95) / Art Farmer (620)
6211 The Blowin' Sessions:
Johnny Griffin (63) Dexter Gordon (154)
Cliff Jordan (74) Joe Henderson (155)
Hank Mobley (119) Wayne Shorter (165)
6212 The West Coast Jazz Sessions (Pacific Jazz label):
Gerry Mulligan (545,546) Chet Baker & Art Pepper (551)
Bud Shank (549) Chet Baker (551)
6213 Lee Morgan and Jackie McLean:
Lee Morgan (77,103,161) Jackie McLean (88,91,96,110)
6214 Herbie Hancock and McCoy Tyner:
Herbie Hancock (139,179,210) McCoy Tyner (201)
6215 Ornette Coleman (187,188)

Note: These FCPA records were issued in a 15 LP set as "The Great Modern Jazz Collection" (CBS-Sony FCPO 901).

BLUE NOTE/COLUMBIA RECORD CLUB LABEL

CRC
LP 8119 7-94857-2 Yule Struttin' (A Blue Note Christmas) (various artists)
(same contents as CD 7-94857-2 - see page 780)

SOLID STATE label (King Series)

GXC-3167 BST 84353 Chick Corea - The Song Of Singing (240)

LAX-3153 BST 84353 Chick Corea - The Song Of Singing (240)

BLUE NOTE label (produced by Toshiba) (Old Series)

NR-
8101 B6505 Memorable Sessions - Charlie Christian & Edmond Hall (5,7)
8102 Jamming in Jazz - Edmond Hall,Sidney De Paris & James P.Johnson:
Edmond Hall (6) James P.Johnson (11)
Sidney De Paris (9)
8103 (Toshiba label - not BN)
8104 Swing Sessions/Blue Note All Star Jazzmen:
James P.Johnson (7) Benny Morton (13)
Edmond Hall (8)

8830	BLP1501	Miles Davis,Vol.1 (31,34)
8831	BLP1502	Miles Davis,Vol.2 (31,34,41)
8832	BLP1503	The Amazing Bud Powell (25,27)
8833	BLP1507	The Jazz Messengers at The Cafe Bohemia,Vol.1 (49,50)
8834	BLP1508	The Jazz Messengers at The Cafe Bohemia,Vol.2 (49,50)
8835	BLP1509	Milt Jackson (22,28,30)
8836	BLP1510	Thelonious Monk - Genius of Modern Music,Vol.1 (20,21,22)
8837	BLP1518	Horace Silver and The Jazz Messengers (44,45)
8838	BLP1521 +1	A Night at Birdland with Art Blakey,Vol.1 (40,41)
8839	BLP1522 +1	A Night at Birdland with Art Blakey,Vol.2 (40,41)
8840	BLP1542	Sonny Rollins (59)
8841	BLP1558	Sonny Rollins,Vol.2 (63)
8842	BLP1569	Paul Chambers - Bass On Top (67)
8843	BLP1581	Sonny Rollins - A Night at The Village Vanguard (73)
8844	BLP4009	The Amazing Bud Powell - The Scene Changes (88)
8845	BLP1590	Lee Morgan - Candy (75,77)

9020C Blue Note Jazz,Vol.1:
Lee Morgan (77,161) Horace Silver (94,173)
Art Blakey (85,109) Cannonball Adderley (79)
Bud Powell (88)
9021 Blue Note Jazz,Vol.2:
Cannonball Adderley (79) Paul Chambers (67)
Art Blakey (85) Jimmy Smith (78)
Horace Silver (94) Sonny Clark (76)
9022 Blue Note Jazz,Vol.3:
Herbie Hancock (179) John Coltrane (71)
Sonny Clark (76) Herbie Hancock (139)
Bobby Hutcherson (190) Eric Dolphy (163)
Donald Byrd (95)

ECJ-
60006 BLP9002 Sheila Jordan - Portrait of Sheila (142,144)

LNJ-

70067	BLP1523	Kenny Burrell (53)
70068	BLP1583	Curtis Fuller - Art Farmer (75)
70071	BLP1531	Fats Navarro,Vol.1 (19,23,25)
70074	BLP1532	Fats Navarro,Vol.2 (22,23,25)
70075	BLP1505	J.J. Johnson,Vol.1 (36,43)
70076	BLP1504	Bud Powell,Vol.2 (25,27,37)
70077	BLP1526	Clifford Brown Memorial (35,38)
70078	BLP1545	Lou Donaldson - Wailin' with Lou (59)
70079		Sonny Clark/Wynton Kelly: Sonny Clark (86) / Wynton Kelly (29)
70081	BLP1569	Paul Chambers - Bass on Top (67)
70082	BLP1501	Miles Davis,Vol.1 (31,34)
70083	BLP1502	Miles Davis,Vol.2 (31,34,41)
70084	BLP1542	Sonny Rollins,Vol.1 (59)
70085	BLP1503	Bud Powell,Vol.1 (25,27)

LNJ-		
70086	BLP1558	Sonny Rollins,Vol.2 (63)
70087	BLP1590	Lee Morgan - Candy (76)
70088	TRLP 20	Doug Watkins - Doug at Large (from Transition label) (454)
70089	BLP1509	Milt Jackson (22,28,30)
70090	BLP1510	Thelonious Monk,Vol.1 (20,21,22)
70091	BLP1521 +1	Art Blakey's Jazz Messengers at Birdland,Vol.1 (40,41)
70092	BLP1522 +1	Art Blakey's Jazz Messengers at Birdland,Vol.2 (40,41)
70093	BLP1592	Sonny Clark (75,76)
70094	BLP1574	Hank Mobley - Peckin' Time (77)
70096	BLP1511	Thelonious Monk - Genius of Modern Music,Vol.2 (20,21,28,32)
70097	BLP1581	Sonny Rollins at The Village Vanguard (73)
70098	BLP1524?	Kenny Dorham (54)
70102	BLP1506	J.J.Johnson,Vol.2 (36,43,48)
70104	TRLP 4	Donald Byrd - Byrd's Eye View (453)
70108	BLP1520 +2	Horace Silver Trio (33,39)
70109	TRLP 17	Donald Byrd - Byrd Blows on Beacon Hill (from Transition label) (453)
70112	BLP1576	Sonny Clark - Sonny's Crib (70)
70113	BLP1541	Lee Morgan Sextet (58)
70125	BLP1507	Art Blakey's Jazz Messengers at Cafe Bohemia,Vol.1(49,50)
70126	BLP1508	Art Blakey's Jazz Messengers at Cafe Bohemia,Vol.2 (49,50)
70127	BLP1539	Horace Silver - Six Pieces of Silver (58)
70128	BLP1534	Paul Chambers - Whims of Chambers (57)
70129	BLP1523	Introducing Kenny Burrell (53)
70130	BLP1540	Hank Mobley Sextet (58)
80035	BN-LA344-G	Bobbi Humphrey - Satin Doll (272,273)
80056	BN-LA462-G	Carmen McRae - I Am Music (279,280)
80064	BLP1595	Cannonball Adderley - Somethin' Else (79)
80065	BN-LA550-G	Bobbi Humphrey - Fancy Dancer (281,282)
80066	BLP4163	Eric Dolphy - Out to Lunch (163)
80067	BLP1577	John Coltrane - Blue Train (71)
80068	BLP1598	The Amazing Bud Powell - Time Waits (82)
80071	BLP4003	Art Blakey's Jazz Messengers - Moanin' (85)
80072	BLP1588	Sonny Clark - Cool Struttin' (76)
80073	BLP4013	Jackie McLean - New Soil (91)
80075	BLP4185	Horace Silver - Song for My Father (159,173)
80076	BLP4157	Lee Morgan - The Sidewinder (161)
80077	BLP4195	Herbie Hancock - Maiden Voyage (179)
80079	BN-LA549-G	Donald Byrd - Places and Spaces (283)
80080	BLP4031	Hank Mobley - Soul Station (99)
80086	BLP4001	Sonny Rollins - Newk's Time (71)
80087	BLP4017	Horace Silver - Blowing the Blues Away (94,95)
80088	BLP4049	Art Blakey's Jazz Messengers - A Night in Tunisia (108,109)
80091	BLP4109	Herbie Hancock - Takin' Off (139)
80092	BLP4059	Kenny Drew (113)
80093	BLP4019	Donald Byrd - Byrd in Hand (92)
80095	BLP4146	Dexter Gordon - Our Man in Paris (154)
80096	BLP4123	Kenny Burrell (147)
80097	BLP4009	The Amazing Bud Powell,Vol.5 - The Scene Changes (88)
80099	BLP4264	McCoy Tyner - The Real McCoy (201)
80100	BLP4073	Freddie Hubbard - Hub Cap (120)
80101	BLP4099	Grant Green - Sunday Morning (124)
80103	BN-LA635-G	Carmen McRae - Can't Hide Love (288,289)
80104	BLP4047	Art Taylor - A.T.'s Delight (108)
80105	BLP4102	The Three Sounds - Hey There (125)
80112	BN-LA645-G	Barbara Carroll (290)
80118	BLP4116	Jackie McLean Quintet (139)
80124	BST84279	Herbie Hancock - Speak Like a Child (210)
80125	BLP1579	Sonny Clark Trio (72)
80126	BLP4035	Duke Pearson - Tender Feelin's (98)

745

LNJ-

80133	BLP4037	Horace Parlan - Us Three (102)
80139	BLP4046	Duke Jordan - Flight to Jordan (108))
80146	BLP1571	The Amazing Bud Powell,Vol.3 - Bud! (68)
80147	BLP4132	Grant Green - Feelin' The Spirit (146)
80156	BLP4091	Sonny Clark - Leapin' and Lopin' (129)
80157	BLP4089	Jackie McLean - A Fickle Sonance (128)
80158	BLP4179	Jackie McLean - It's Time (169)

LBN

80259 Art Blakey's Jazz Messengers - All About The Messengers (85,109,127,130,162)

LNJ

80574	BN-LA628-G	Ronnie Laws - Fever (284,285)
80810	BN-LA633-G	Donald Byrd - Caricatures (289)

LNS-

80842 BN-LA701-G John Lee & Gerry Brown - Still Can't Say Enough (294)

LNP-

88046		The Best of Jimmy Smith (51,78,92,98,103,148,149)
88137	BN-LA047-F	Donald Byrd - Black Byrd (260,264)

LNS

90031 Blue Note Best Selections:

Cannonball Adderley (79)
Lee Morgan (161)
Art Blakey (85)
Sonny Clark (76)
Bud Powell (88)
John Coltrane (71)
Herbie Hancock (139)

LNP-

95059B Blue Note Jazz Golden Disk,Vol.1:

Lee Morgan (161)
Art Blakey (85,109)
Horace Silver (94,173)
Herbie Hancock (139)
Cannonball Adderley (79)

95060 Blue Note Jazz Golden Disk,Vol.2:

Bud Powell (88)
Sonny Clark (76)
John Coltrane (71)
Cannonball Adderley (79)
Horace Silver (94)
Donald Byrd (95)
Bobby Hutcherson (190)
Eric Dolphy (163)

 746

BLUE NOTE label (produced by Toshiba) (New Series)

Reissues of 10 in. LPs as 12 in. LPs (no extra tracks):

BN-	BLP	
0001	5003	The Amazing Bud Powell (25,27)
0002	5041	The Amazing Bud Powell,Volume 2 (37)
0003	5004	Fats Navarro Memorial Album:
		Tadd Dameron (19,22) Bud Powell (25)
		Fats Navarro (23)
0004	5006	James Moody and his Modernists with Chano Pozo (23)
0005	5005	James Moody with Strings Conducted by Andre Hodeir (639)
0006	5012	Howard McGhee's All Stars (23,26)
0007	5024	Howard McGhee,Volume 2 (35)
0008	5018	New Faces - New Sounds: Introducing the Horace Silver Trio (33)
0009	5034	Horace Silver Trio,Volume 2/Art Blakey - Sabu (39)
0010	5021	New Faces - New Sounds: Lou Donaldson Quintet/Quartet (32,33)
0011	5055	Lou Donaldson Sextet,Volume 2 (43)
0012	5032	Clifford Brown - New Star on the Horizon (38)
0013	5043	New Faces - New Sounds: Frank Foster Quintet (42)
0014	5056	New Faces - New Sounds from Germany: Jutta Hipp Quintet (451)
0015	5058	Horace Silver Quintet (44)
0016	5062	Horace Silver Quintet,Volume 2 (45)
0017	5065	Afro - Cuban: Kenny Dorham (46)
0018	5066	Hank Mobley Quartet (46)
0019	5068	The Prophetic Herbie Nichols,Volume 1 (47)
0020	5069	The Prophetic Herbie Nichols,Volume 2 (48)

Reissues of 12 in. LPs:

BN-		
0047	BNLA-047F	Donald Byrd - Black Byrd (260,264)
0549	BNLA-549G	Donald Byrd - Places And Spaces (283)

Reissues of 10 in. LPs as 12 in. LPs (no extra tracks):

BN-	BLP	
5023	5023	New Faces - New Sounds: Introducing the Kenny Drew Trio (34)
5025	5025	New Faces - New Sounds: Piano Interpretations by Wynton Kelly (29)
5029	5029	New Faces - New Sounds: Elmo Hope Trio (36)
5035	5035	Sal Salvador Quintet (39)
5036	5036	Urbie Green Septet (39)
5042	5042	Tal Farlow Quartet (41)
5044	5044	New Faces - New Sounds: Elmo Hope Quintet,Volume 2 (42)
5045	5045	George Wallington and his Band (42)
5053	5053	New Faces - New Sounds: Julius Watkins Sextet (43)
5064	5064	Julius Watkins Sextet,Volume 2 (45)

Reissues of 12 in. LPs (mono issues)

BN-	BLP	
1501	1501	Miles Davis,Volume 1 (31,34)
1502	1502	Miles Davis,Volume 2 (31,34,41)
1503	1503	The Amazing Bud Powell,Volume 1 (25,27)
1504	1504	The Amazing Bud Powell,Volume 2 (25,27,37)
1507	1507	The Jazz Messengers at the Cafe Bohemia,Volume 1(49,50)
1508	1508	The Jazz Messengers at the Cafe Bohemia,Volume 2 (49,50)
1512	1512	A New Star - A New Sound: Jimmy Smith at the Organ,Volume 1 (50)
1513	1513	Detroit-New York Junction: Thad Jones (51)
1514	1514	A New Star - A New Sound: Jimmy Smith at the Organ,Volume 2 (51)
1515	1515	Jutta Hipp at the Hickory House,Volume 1 (52)

BN-	BLP	
1516	1516	Jutta Hipp at the Hickory House,Volume 2 (52)
1518	1518	Horace Silver and The Jazz Messengers (44,45)
1519	1519	Herbie Nichols Trio (48,49,53)
1520	1520	Horace Silver Trio and Spotlight on Drums: Art Blakey-Sabu (33,39)
1521	1521	A Night at Birdland with The Art Blakey Quintet,Volume 1 (40,41)
1522	1522	A Night at Birdland with The Art Blakey Quintet,Volume 2 (40,41)
1523	1523	Introducing Kenny Burrell Guitar (53)
1524	1524	Kenny Dorham - 'Round Midnight at the Cafe Bohemia (54)
1526	1526	Clifford Brown Memorial Album (35,38)
1527	1527	The Magnificent Thad Jones (55)
1530	1530	Jutta Hipp (56)
1533	1533	Introducing Johnny Griffin,Tenor Sax (52)
1534	1534	Paul Chambers Sextet - Whims of Chambers (57)
1535	1535	Kenny Dorham Octet/Sextet (45,46)
1536	1536	J.R.Monterose (57)
1537	1537	Lou Donaldson Quartet/Quintet/Sextet (32,33,43)
1538	1538	Lee Morgan Indeed! (57)
1539	1539	6 Pieces of Silver - Horace Silver Quintet (58)
1540	1540	Hank Mobley Sextet (58)
1541	1541	Lee Morgan,Volume 2 (58)
1542	1542	Sonny Rollins (59)
1543	1543	Kenny Burrell,Volume 2 (50,53,54)
1544	1544	Hank Mobley and his All Stars (59)
1545	1545	Lou Donaldson,Volume 2 - Wailin' With Lou (59)
1550	1550	Hank Mobley Quintet (62)
1557	1557	Lee Morgan,Volume 3 (62)
1558	1558	Sonny Rollins,Volume 2 (62)
1559	1559	Johnny Griffin - A Blowing Session (63)
1560	1560	Hank Mobley Sextet - Hank (63)
1561	1561	Sabu - Palo Congo (64)
1562	1562	Horace Silver Quintet - The Stylings of Silver (64)
1568	1568	Hank Mobley (66)
1569	1569	Paul Chambers Quartet - Bass on Top (67)
1570	1570	Sonny Clark - Dial S for Sonny (67)
1571	1571	The Amazing Bud Powell,Volume 3 - Bud! (68)
1573	1573	John Jenkins with Kenny Burrell (69)
1574	1574	Hank Mobley - Peckin' Time (77)
1575	1575	Lee Morgan - City Lights (69)
1577	1577	John Coltrane - Blue Train (71)
1578	1578	Lee Morgan - The Cooker (72)
1579	1579	Sonny Clark Trio (72)
1580	1580	Johnny Griffin - The Congregation (73)
1581	1581	Sonny Rollins - A Night at The Village Vanguard (73)
1582	1582	Cliff Jordan,Volume 2 - Cliff Craft (74)
1584	1584	Here Comes Louis Smith (454)
1587	1587	Bennie Green - Back On The Scene (80)
1588	1588	Sonny Clark - Cool Struttin' (76)
1589	1589	Further Explorations by the Horace Silver Quintet (76)
1590	1590	Lee Morgan - Candy (75,77)
1591	1591	Lou Donaldson - Lou Takes Off (76)
1593	1593	Lou Donaldson - Blues Walk (83)
1594	1594	Louis Smith - Smithville (80)
1595	1595	Cannonball Adderley with Miles Davis - Somethin' Else (79)
1596	1596	Kenny Burrell - Blue Lights,Volume 1 (81)
1597	1597	Kenny Burrell - Blue Lights,Volume 2 (81)
1598	1598	The Amazing Bud Powell,Volume 4 - Time Waits (82)
1599	1599	Bennie Green - Soul Stirrin' (81)(stereo issue slightly different from mono issue)
1600	1600	Introducing The Three Sounds (83,84)

Reissues of 12 in . LPs (stereo issues):

BN-	BST/BLP	
4001	84001	Sonny Rollins - Newk's Time (71)
4002	84002	Jimmy Smith - House Party (70,77,78)
4003	84003	Art Blakey and The Jazz Messengers - Moanin' (85)
4004	84004	A Message from Blakey - Holiday for Skins,Volume 1 (86)
4005	84005	A Message from Blakey - Holiday for Skins,Volume 2 (86)
4006	4006	Dizzy Reece - Blues in Trinity (83)
4007	84007	Donald Byrd - Off to the Races (87)
4008	84008	Finger Poppin' with the Horace Silver Quintet (89)
4009	84009	The Amazing Bud Powell,Volume 5 - The Scene Changes (88)
4010	84010	Bennie Green - Walkin' and Talkin' (88)
4011	84011	Jimmy Smith - The Sermon (70,78)
4012	84012	Lou Donaldson with The Three Sounds (89)
4013	84013	Jackie McLean - New Soil (91)
4014	84014	The Three Sounds - Bottoms Up! (83,84,89)
4015	84015	Art Blakey and The Jazz Messengers at the Jazz Corner of the World,Volume 1 (90)
4016	84016	Art Blakey and The Jazz Messengers at the Jazz Corner of the World,Volume 2 (90)
4017	84017	Horace Silver Quintet & Trio - Blowin' the Blues Away (94,95)
4018	84018	Walter Davis Jr. - Davis Cup (93)
4019	84019	Donald Byrd - Byrd in Hand (92)
4020	84020	The Three Sounds - Good Deal (91)
4021	84021	Kenny Burrell with Art Blakey - On View at the Five Spot Cafe (93,94)
4022	84022	Duke Pearson - Profile (96)
4023	84023	Dizzy Reece - Star Bright (97)
4024	84024	Jackie McLean - Swing,Swang,Swingin' (96)
4025	84025	Lou Donaldson - The Time is Right (96,97)
4026	84026	Donald Byrd - Fuego (95)
4027	84027	Freddie Redd Quartet - Music from 'The Connection' (100)
4028	84028	Horace Parlan - Movin' and Groovin' (100)
4029	84029	Art Blakey and The Jazz Messengers - The Big Beat (101)
4030	84030	The Incredible Jimmy Smith - Crazy Baby (98)
4031	84031	Hank Mobley - Soul Station (99)
4032	84032	Sonny Red - Out of the Blue (97,99)
4033	4033	Dizzy Reece - Soundin' Off (103)
4034	84034	Lee Morgan - Leeway (103)
4035	84035	Duke Pearson - Tender Feelin's (98)
4036	84036	Lou Donaldson - Sunny Side up (99,100)
4037	84037	Horace Parlan - Us Three (102)
4038	84038	Jackie McLean - Capuchin' Swing (102)
4039	84039	Stanley Turrentine - Look Out! (104)
4040	84040	Freddie Hubbard - Open Sesame (104)
4041	4041	Tina Brooks - True Blue (105)
4042	84042	Horace Silver - Horace -Scope (106)
4043	84043	Horace Parlan Quintet - Speakin' My Piece (107)
4044	84044	The Three Sounds - Moods (105)
4045	84045	Freddie Redd Quintet - Shades of Redd (109)
4046	84046	Duke Jordan - Flight to Jordan (108)
4047	84047	Art Taylor - A.T.'s Delight (108)
4048	84048	Donald Byrd - Byrd in Flight (98,99,106)
4049	84049	Art Blakey and The Jazz Messengers - A Night in Tunisia (108,109)
4050	84050	The Incredible Jimmy Smith - Home Cookin' (82,92)
4051	84051	Jackie McLean - Jackie's Bag (88,110)
4053	84053	Lou Donaldson - Light Foot (87)
4054	84054	Art Blakey & The Jazz Messengers - Meet You at the Jazz Corner of the World, Vol. 1 (110)
4055	84055	Art Blakey & The Jazz Messengers - Meet You at the Jazz Corner of the World,Vol. 2 (110)
4056	84056	Freddie Hubbard - Goin' Up (111)
4057	84057	Stanley Turrentine with The Three Sounds - Blue Hour (114)

BN-	BST/BLP	
4058	84058	Hank Mobley - Roll Call (113)
4059	84059	Kenny Drew - Undercurrent (113)
4060	84060	Donald Byrd at The Half Note Cafe,Volume 1 (112)
4061	84061	Donald Byrd at The Half Note Cafe,Volume 2 (112)
4062	84062	Horace Parlan Trio plus Ray Barretto - Headin' South (113)
4063	84063	Kenny Dorham - Whistle Stop (115)
4064	84064	Grant Green - Grant's First Stand(116)
4065	84065	Stanley Turrentine - Comin' Your Way (116)
4066	84066	Lou Donaldson - Here 'Tis (116)
4067	84067	Jackie McLean - Bluesnik (115)
4068	84068	'Baby Face' Willette - Face to Face (117)
4069	84069	Stanley Turrentine - Up at Minton's,Volume 1 (118)
4070	84070	Stanley Turrentine - Up at Minton's,Volume 2 (118)
4071	84071	Grant Green - Green Street (120)
4072	84072	The Three Sounds - Feelin' Good (105)
4073	84073	Freddie Hubbard - Hub Cap (120)
4074	84074	Horace Parlan - On the Spur of the Moment (119)
4075	84075	Donald Byrd - The Cat Walk (121)
4076	84076	The Horace Silver Quintet at The Village Gate - Doin' the Thing (122,123)
4077	84077	Dexter Gordon - Doin' Allright (121)
4078	84078	Jimmy Smith - Midnight Special (102,103)
4079	84079	Lou Donaldson - Gravy Train (121)
4080	84080	Hank Mobley - Workout (119)
4081	84081	Stanley Turrentine - Dearly Beloved (124)
4082	84082	Horace Parlan - Up and Down (124)
4083	84083	Dexter Gordon - Dexter Calling (122)
4084	84084	Baby Face Willette - Stop and Listen (123)
4085	84085	Freddie Hubbard - Ready for Freddie (126)
4086	84086	Grant Green - Grantstand (125)
4087	84087	Leo Parker - Let Me Tell You 'Bout It (126)
4088	84088	The Three Sounds - Here We Come (114)
4089	84089	Jackie McLean - A Fickle Sonance (128)
4090	84090	Art Blakey and The Jazz Messengers - Mosaic (127)
4091	84091	Sonny Clark - Leapin' and Lopin' (129)
4092	4092	Kenny Clarke-Francy Boland & Co. - The Golden Eight (455)
4093	84093	Ike Quebec - Heavy Soul (129)
4094	84094	Fred Jackson - Hootin' 'n Tootin' (134)
4095	4095	Leo Parker - Rollin' with Leo (128)
4096	84096	Stanley Turrentine - That's Where It's At (132)
4097	84097	Art Blakey and The Afro-Drum Ensemble - The African Beat (133)
4098	84098	Ike Quebec - Blue and Sentimental (131)
4099	84099	Grant Green - Sunday Mornin' (124)
4100	84100	Jimmy Smith Plays Fats Waller (133)
4101	84101	Donald Byrd - Royal Flush (127)
4102	84102	The Three Sounds - Hey There! (125)
4103	84103	Ike Quebec Sextet - Easy Living (133)
4104	84104	Art Blakey and The Jazz Messengers - Buhaina's Delight (130,131)
4105	84105	Ike Quebec - It Might As Well Be Spring(130)
4106	84106	Jackie McLean - Let Freedom Ring (136)
4107	84107	Don Wilkerson - Preach Brother! (140)
4108	84108	Lou Donaldson - The Natural Soul (138)
4109	84109	Herbie Hancock - Takin' Off (139)
4110	84110	The Horace Silver Quintet - The Tokyo Blues (141)
4111	84111	Grant Green - The Latin Bit (137)
4112	84112	Dexter Gordon - Go! (142)
4113	84113	Freddie Roach - Down To Earth (141)
4114	84114	Ike Quebec - Soul Samba (Bossa Nova) (143)
4115	84115	Freddie Hubbard - Hub-Tones (144)
4117	84117	Jimmy Smith - Back at The Chicken Shack (102,103)
4118	84118	Donald Byrd - Free Form (131)

BN-	BST	
4119	84119	Charlie Rouse - Bossa Nova Bacchanal (145)
4120	84120	The Three Sounds - It Just Got To Be (114)
4121	84121	Don Wilkerson - Elder Don (137)
4122	84122	Stanley Turrentine - Jubilee Shout!!! (145)
4123	84123	Kenny Burrell - Midnight Blue (147)
4124	84124	Donald Byrd - A New Perspective (147)
4125	84125	Lou Donaldson - Good Gracious! (148)
4126	84126	Herbie Hancock - My Point of View (151)
4127	84127	Kenny Dorham - Una Mas(One More Time) (152)
4128	84128	Freddie Roach - Mo' Greens Please (148,151)
4129	84129	Stanley Turrentine - Never Let Me Go (150)
4130	84130	John Patton - Along Came John (152)
4131	84131	The Horace Silver Quintet - Silver's Serenade (153)
4132	84132	Grant Green - Feelin' The Spirit (146)
4133	84133	Dexter Gordon - A Swingin' Affair (142)
4134	84134	Horace Parlan - Happy Frame of Mind (150)
4135	84135	Freddie Hubbard - Here to Stay (146)
4136	84136	Solomon Ilori and His Afro-Drum Ensemble - African High Life (153)
4137	84137	Jackie McLean - One Step Beyond (153)
4138	84138	Harold Vick - Steppin' Out (154)
4139	84139	Grant Green - Am I Blue (154)
4140	84140	Joe Henderson - Page One (155)
4141	84141	Jimmy Smith - Rockin' The Boat (149)
4142	84142	Blue Mitchell Quintet (issued in U.S. as BN LT-1082) (157)
4143	84143	John Patton - Blue John (155,156)
4144	84144	Johnny Coles - Little Johnny C (156)
4145	84145	Don Wilkerson - Shoutin' (156)
4149	84149	Hank Mobley - No Room for Squares (151,158)
4169	84169	Lee Morgan - Search For The New Land (163)
4170	84170	Art Blakey and The Jazz Messengers - Free For All (162)
4172	84172	Freddie Hubbard - Breaking Point! (166)
4173	84173	Wayne Shorter - A Night Dreamer (165)
4179	84179	Jackie McLean - It's Time! (169)
4187	84187	Larry Young - Into Somethin' (174)
4189	84189	Joe Henderson - Inner Urge (175)
4192	84192	Big John Patton - Oh Baby! (178)
4214	84214	The Blue Mitchell Quintet - Down With It! (184)
4215	84215	Jackie McLean - Right Now! (176)
4220	84220	The Horace Silver Quintet - The Cape Verdean Blues (185,186)
4222	84222	Lee Morgan - Cornbread (185)
4229	84229	Big John Patton - Got A Good Thing Goin' (192)
4230	84230	Hank Mobley - A Caddy For Daddy (188)
4245	94245	Art Blakey and The Jazz Messengers - Like Someone In Love (108,109)
4248	84248	The Three Sounds - Vibrations (196)
4263	84263	Lou Donaldson - Alligator Bogaloo (201)
4267	84267	Duke Pearson - The Right Touch (205)
4269	84269	Jimmy Smith - Open House (101)
4271	84271	Lou Donaldson - Mr. Shing-A-Ling (206)
4274	84274	Tyrone Washington - Natural Essence (208)
4288	84288	Hank Mobley - Reach Out! (209)
4293	84293	Duke Pearson Quintet - The Phantom (215,217)
4342	84342	Grant Green - Green is Beautiful (237)
4416	84416	Bobby Hutcherson - Natural Illusions (260)

BNJ		
50101		Jimmy Smith - Special Guests (70,103,148)

BNJ		
61001	BST84428	Memorable Tracks by Clifford Brown - More Memorable Tracks(35,36,38)
61002		A Night at Birdland with The Art Blakey Quintet,Vol.3 (40,41)
61003		Kenny Dorham - 'Round about Midnight at The Cafe Bohemia,Vol.2 (54)
61004		Kenny Dorham - 'Round about Midnight at The Cafe Bohemia,Vol.3 (54)
61005		Horace Silver - Senor Blues (33,39,58,62,82)
61006		Hank Mobley - Curtain Call (69)
61007	DY-5805-01	Art Blakey & The Jazz Messengers at The Cafe Bohemia,Vol.3 (49,50)
61008/9/10		The Other Side of Blue Note 1500 Series (3 LP Set):
61008:		Tadd Dameron Septet (22); H.McGhee-Fats Navarro Boptet (23); Lou Donaldson Quartet (32); Bud Powell Trio (37); Lou Donaldson Sextet (43); Kenny Dorham Sextet (45); Kenny Burrell Quintet 50); Johnny Griffin Quartet(52)
61009:		Herbie Nichols Trio (53); Thad Jones & Kenny Burrell (55); Jutta Hipp Quintet (56); Lou Donaldson Quintet(65); Paul Chambers Quartet (67); Bud Powell Trio (68); Johnny Griffin Quartet (73)
61010:		Lee Morgan Quartet (75); Louis Smith Quintet (80); Bennie Green Sextet (81); Cannonball Adderley Quintet (79); Kenny Burrell Septet (81); Bud Powell Trio (82)
61011		More Genius of Thelonious Monk (19,20,21,32)
61012		Thelonious Monk/Milt Jackson (22,28,30)
61013		Jimmy Smith Trio + L.D. (67)
61014		Sonny Rollins at The Village Vanguard,Vol.2 (73)
61015		Sonny Rollins at The Village Vanguard,Vol.3 (73,74)
61016	BLP1592	Sonny Clark Quintet (= BN(J)LNJ70093) (75,76)
61017	GXF-3069 +1	Sonny Clark Trio,Vol.2 (72,86)
61018	GXF-3051 -1	Sonny Clark Trio,Vol.3 (87)
61019		Introducing The Three Sounds,Vol.2 (83,84)
61020	GXF-3063 +1	Bennie Green - The 45 Session (86)
NNJ-		
70211	BN-LA737-H	Earl Klugh - Finger Paintings (296,297)
70212	BN-LA596-G	Earl Klugh (285)
70213	BN-LA667-G	Earl Klugh - Living Inside Your Love (293)
BNJ-		
71001	BLP5025 +11	Wynton Kelly - Piano Interpretations (29)
71002	BLP5023 +1	Introducing Kenny Drew (34)
71003	BLP5045 +4	George Wallington Showcase (42)
71004	BST84009	Bud Powell - The Scene Changes (88)
71005	BST84022	Duke Pearson - Profile (96)
71006	BST84046	Duke Jordan - Flight to Jordan (108)
71007	BST84062	Horace Parlan - Headin' South (113)
71008	BST84076	Horace Silver - Doin' The Thing (122,123)
71009	BST84088	The Three Sounds - Here We Come (114)
71010	BST84091	Sonny Clark - Leapin' and Lopin' (129)
71011	BST84003	Art Blakey and The Jazz Messengers - Moanin' (85)
71012	BST84026	Donald Byrd - Fuego (95)
71013	BST84040	Freddie Hubbard - Open Sesame (104)
71014	BST84106	Jackie McLean - Let Freedom Ring (136)
71015	BST84109	Herbie Hancock - Takin' Off (139)
71016	BST84127	Kenny Dorham - Una Mas (152)
71017	BST84157	Lee Morgan - The Sidewinder (161)
71018	BST84185	Horace Silver - Song for My Father (159,173)
71019	BST84205	Pete La Roca - Basra (181)
71020	BST84231	Bobby Hutcherson - Happenings (190)
71021	BST84001	Sonny Rollins - Newk's Time (71)

752

BNJ-		
71022	BST84008	Horace Silver - Finger Poppin' (89)
71023	BST84049	Art Blakey's Jazz Messengers - A Night in Tunisia (108,109)
71024	BST84140	Joe Henderson - Page One (155)
71025	BST84154	Grant Green - Idle Moments (159)
71026	BST84173	Wayne Shorter - Night Dreamer (165)
71027	BST84175	Herbie Hancock - Empyrean Isles (168)
71028	BST84199	Lee Morgan - The Rumproller (181)
71029	BST84204	Dexter Gordon - Gettin' Around (182)
71030	BST84209	Hank Mobley - Dippin' (183)
71031	BST84025	Lou Donaldson - The Time is Right (96,97)
71032	BST84033	Dizzy Reece - Soundin' Off (103)
71033	BST84043	Horace Parlan - Speakin' my Piece (107)
71034	BST84074	Horace Parlan - On the Spur of the Moment (119)
71035	BST84092	Kenny Clarke - The Golden Eight (455)
71036	BST84128	Freddie Roach - Mo' Greens Please (148,151)
71037	BST84161	George Braith - Soul Stream (161)
71038	BST84270	Jack Wilson - Easterly Winds (206)
71039	BST84283	Booker Ervin - The In-Between (208)
71040	BST84304	Larry Young - Heaven on Earth (209)
71041	BST84163	Eric Dolphy - Out to Lunch (163)
71042	BST84167	Andrew Hill - Point of Departure (164)
71043	BST84180	Anthony Williams - Life Time (171)
71044	BST84184	Sam Rivers - Fuschia Swing Song (175)
71045	BST84224	Ornette Coleman at The Golden Circle,Vol.1 (187,188)
71046	BST84225	Ornette Coleman at The Golden Circle,Vol.2 (187,188)
71047	BST84237	Cecil Taylor - Unit Structures (192)
71048	BST84247	Don Cherry - Symphony for Improvisers (195)
71049	BST84260	Cecil Taylor - Conquistador (196)
71050	BST84262	Jackie McLean - New and Old Gospel (201)
71051	BST84011	Jimmy Smith - The Sermon (70,78)
71052	BST84029	Art Blakey And The Jazz Messengers - The Big Beat (101)
71053	BST84073	Freddie Hubbard - Hub Cap (120)
71054	BST84112	Dexter Gordon - Go! (142)
71055	BST84124	Donald Byrd - A New Perspective (147)
71056	BST84182	Wayne Shorter - Ju Ju (169)
71057	BST84195	Herbie Hancock - Maiden Voyage (179)
71058	BST84201	Stanley Turrentine - Joy Ride (181)
71059	BST84227	Joe Henderson - Mode for Joe (189)
71060	BST84243	Lee Morgan - DelightfuLee (191,192)
71061	BST84338	McCoy Tyner - Expansions (217)
71062	BST84353	Chick Corea - The Song of Singing (240)
71063	BST84353	Hank Mobley - Far Away Lands (202)
71064	BST84426	Lee Morgan - The Rajah (197)
71065	BST84427	Jackie McLean - Tippin' The Scales (143)
71066	BST84428	Clifford Bown - Alternate Takes (35,36,38)
71067/8	BST2-84429	The Best of Blue Note (2 LP Set):
71067:		Bud Powell (27) · Miles Davis (34)
		James Moody (23) · John Coltrane (71)
		Thelonious Monk (28) · Herbie Hancock (179)
		Milt Jackson (30) · Donald Byrd (147)
		Clifford Brown (38)
71068:		Art Blakey & The Jazz Messengers (85) · Jimmy Smith (103)
		Lou Donaldson (83) · Kenny Burrell (147)
		Horace Silver (173) · Lee Morgan (161)
71069	BST84002	Jimmy Smith - House Party (70,77,78)
71070	BST84019	Donald Byrd - Byrd in Hand (92)
71071	BST84051	Jackie McLean - Jackie's Bag (88,110)
71072	BST84077	Dexter Gordon - Doin' Allright (121)
71073	BST84135	Freddie Hubbard - Here To Stay (146)

BNJ-		
71074	BST84181	Kenny Dorham - Trompeta Toccata (172)
71075	BST84216	Anthony Williams - Spring (184)
71076	BST84275	McCoy Tyner - Tender Moments (207)
71077	BST84279	Herbie Hancock - Speak Like A Child (210)
71078	BST84291	Bobby Hutcherson - Total Eclipse (225)
71079	BST84430	Bud Powell - Alternate Takes (25,37,68,82,88,154)
71080	BST84424	Stanley Turrentine - Z.T.'s Blues (127)
71081	BST84431	Hank Mobley - Another Workout (130)
71082	BST84432	Grant Green - Born To Be Blue (132,135)
71083	BST84017	Horace Silver - Blowin' The Blues Away (94,95)
71084	BST84047	Art Taylor - A.T.'s Delight (108)
71085	BST84057	Stanley Turrentine With The Three Sounds - Blue Hour (114)
71086	BST84115	Freddie Hubbard - Hub Tones (144)
71087	BST84117	Jimmy Smith - Back at The Chicken Shack (102,103)
71088	BST84123	Kenny Burrell - Midnight Blue (147)
71089	BST84152	Joe Henderson - Our Thing (157)
71090	BST84178	Blue Mitchell - The ThingTo Do (169)
71091	BST84193	Art Blakey and The Jazz Messengers - Indestructible (165,166)
71092	BST84212	Lee Morgan - The Gigolo (183,184)
71093	BST84232	Wayne Shorter - Adam's Apple (190)
71094	BST84273	Hank Mobley - High Voltage (206)
71095	BST84331	Elvin Jones - Poly-Currents (232)
71096/7	BABB 85112	Dexter Gordon - Nights At The Keystone (2 LP Set) (456,457)
71098	BT85108	Charlie Parker At Storyville (450)
71099	BST84021	Kenny Burrell with Art Blakey - On View At The Five Spot Cafe (93,94)
71100	BST84060	Donald Byrd At The Half Note Cafe - Jazz At The Waterfront (112)
71101	BST84146	Dexter Gordon - Our Man in Paris (154)
71102	BST84153	Grachan Moncur III - Evolution (160)
71103	BST84176	Dexter Gordon - One Flight Up (167)
71104	BST84221	Larry Young - Unity (186)
71105	BST84307	McCoy Tyner - Time For Tyner (214)
71106		Soho Blue:
		Wayne Shorter (190)
		Kenny Dorham (46)
		Art Blakey-Clifford Brown (40)
		Jackie McLean (115)
		Stanley Turrentine (181)
		Don Wilkerson (140)
		Jimmy Smith (103)
		Donald Byrd (202)
		Horace Silver (141)

BNJ-		
91001	BT 85101	Stanley Jordan - Magic Touch (304)
91002	BT 85106	Kenny Burrell/Grover Washington Jr. - Togethering (304)
91003	BT 85104	Charles Lloyd Quartet - A Night in Copenhagen (303)
91004	BT 85105	Stanley Turrentine - Straight Ahead (304,305)
91005	BT 85103	George Russell & The Living Time Orchestra - The African Game (303)
91006	BT 85113	One Night with Blue Note,Vol.1 (306)
91007	BT 85114	One Night with Blue Note,Vol.2 (306,307)
91008	BT 85115	One Night with Blue Note,Vol.3 (306,307)
91009	BT 85116	One Night with Blue Note,Vol.4 (306)
91006/9	BTDK85117	One Night with Blue Note Preserved (4 LP Box) (306,307)
91010	BT 85118	OTB - Out Of The Blue (308,309)
91011	BT 85102	McCoy Tyner & Jackie McLean - It's About Time (307,308)
91012	BT 85107	Bennie Wallace - Twilight Time (308)
91013	BT 85109	James Newton - The African Flower (309)
91014	BT 85111	Bill Evans - The Alternative Man (305)
91015	BT 85119	Tony Williams - Foreign Intrigue (309)
91016	BT 85121	Freddie Hubbard/Woody Shaw - Double Take (312)
91017	BT 85123	Joe Henderson - The State of The Tenor - Live At The Village Vanguard,Vol.1 (310,311)
91018	BT 85124	The Michel Petrucciani Trio - Pianism (312)
91019	BT 85125	Jimmy Smith - Go For Whatcha Know (312)

BNJ-		
91020	BQ 85127	Blue Note '86 - A New Generation of Jazz: Michel Petrucciani (312) / Tony Williams (309) Bobby McFerrin (313) / OTB (309) Stanley Jordan (304) / Bill Evans (305) Bennie Wallace (308) / James Newton (309)
91021	BT 85128	Out of The Blue - Inside Track (314)
91022	BT 85110	Bobby McFerrin - Spontaneous Inventions (313,649)
91023	BT 85122	The Don Pullen-George Adams Quartet - Breakthrough (313)
91024	BT 85135	Dexter Gordon - The Other Side of 'Round Midnight (310,313)
91025	BT 85130	Stanley Jordan - Standards,Volume 1 (316)
91026	BT 85133	Michel Petrucciani - Power of Three (314)
91027	not used	
91028	BT 85141	OTB - Live at Mt. Fuji (315)
91029	BT 85138	Tony Williams - Civilization (316)
91030	BT 85137	Kenny Burrell - Generation (316)
91031	BT 85140	Stanley Turrentine - Wonderland (317)
91032	BT 85139	Freddie Hubbard - Life Flight (317)
91033	BLJ-46906	Dianne Reeves (318,319)
91034	BLJ-46907	The Don Pullen/George Adams Quartet - Song Everlasting (318)

BRP-		
8033	BLP4052	Tina Brooks - Back To The Tracks (110,111)

Note: This LP was a bonus album offered to buyers of a certain amount of other albums.

RJ28-		
5001	BLJ-46993	Charnett Moffett - Net Man (317,318)
5002	BLJ-48016	Bireli Lagrene - Inferno (321)
5003	BLJ-48015	Mose Allison - Ever Since The World Ended (319)
5004	B1-48014	Bennie Wallace - Border Town (320)
5014	B1-48679	Michael Petrucciani - Michel Plays Petrucciani (322)
5020		Dianne Reeves - The Nearness Of You (322,323,650)

SGD-		
67	BLP1521	A Night At Birdland With The Art Blakey Quintet,Vol.1 (40,41)
68	BLP1522	A Night At Birdland With The Art Blakey Quintet,Vol.2 (40,41)
69	BST81600	Introducing The Three Sounds (83,84)
70	BST84216	Tony Williams - Spring (184)

TOJJ-5849 Mo' Deep Mo' Phunky:
- Geri Allen (600)
- Charlie Rouse (145)
- Horace Parlan (113)
- The Three Sounds (196)
- Grant Green (172)
- Greg Osby (354)
- Wayne Shorter (183)
- Bobby Hutcherson (183)

W-5501/15 The Ages of Jazz (15 LP Set):

W-5501 Vol.1: 52nd Street Theme - Into Be Bop:
- Bud Powell (25)
- Thelonious Monk (21)
- Tadd Dameron (19,22,471,473)
- Babs Gonzales (471,473)
- Benny Goodman (472)
- Charlie Barnet (474)
- Louis Bellson (476)

W-5502 Vol.2: Yesterdays - Birth of The Cool:
- Miles Davis (31,472,473)
- Gil Evans (555)
- Woody Herman (471,473)
- Lennie Tristano (472,473)
- Gerry Mulligan (476)
- Buddy De Franco (474)

W-5503 Vol.3: Blue Sands - Jazz From The West:
- Gerry Mulligan (545,546,548)
- Bud Shank (549)
- Art Pepper (465)
- Shorty Rogers (476)
- Chico Hamilton (549)
- John Lewis (550)

755

W-5504 Vol.4: Tempus Fugit - Hard Bop Movement:
Miles Davis (34,41) Clifford Brown (35,38)
J.J. Johnson (43,48) Thelonious Monk (28,32)
W-5505 Vol.5: 'Round Midnight - Live at The Night Clubs:
Art Blakey (40) Sonny Rollins (73)
Kenny Dorham (54) Donald Byrd (112)
Horace Silver (122)
W-5506 Vol.6: Moanin' - Funky Jazz No.1:
Art Blakey (85,109) Horace Silver (45,58,94,173)
W-5507 Vol.7: Whisper Not - Funky Jazz No.2:
Lee Morgan (58) Donald Byrd (95)
Sonny Rollins (59) Hank Mobley (119)
Jimmy Smith (51) Lou Donaldson (83)
W-5508 Vol.8: Cool Struttin - The Best of Hard Bop:
Sonny Clark (76) Kenny Drew (113)
Dexter Gordon (154) Hank Mobley (59)
Johnny Griffin (63) Thad Jones (55)
Duke Jordan (108)
W-5509 Vol.9: Cleopatra's Dream - Modern Jazz Piano No.1:
Bud Powell (27,88) Sonny Clark (72)
Thelonious Monk (20) Elmo Hope (36)
Herbie Nichols (48) Kenny Drew (34)
Horace Silver (33,39) Wynton Kelly (29)
W-5510 Vol.10: My Funny Valentine - Modern Jazz Piano No.2:
Bill Evans (627) Duke Ellington (628)
Herbie Hancock (210) John Lewis (550)
Chick Corea (585) The Three Sounds (83)
Duke Pearson (96) Richard Twardzick (548)
Horace Parlan (102) Clare Fisher (558)
Monty Alexander (562)
W-5511 Vol.11: Django - Modern Jazz Guitar:
Wes Montgomery (556) Kenny Burrell (81,147)
Jim Hall (552) Grant Green (124)
Joe Pass (560,561) Tal Farlow (41)
Laurindo Almeida (547)
Sal Salvador (39)
W-5512 Vol.12: Autumn Leaves - Modern Main Stream No.1:
Cannonball Adderley (79) John Coltrane (71)
Art Farmer (620) Art Blakey (626)
Herbie Hancock (139)
W-5513 Vol.13: Maiden Voyage - Modern Main Stream No.2:
Herbie Hancock (179) Lee Morgan (161)
Anthony Williams (171) Freddie Hubbard (104)
Joe Henderson (155) Jackie McLean (96)
Blue Mitchell (184) Wayne Shorter (165)
W-5514 Vol.14: Super Nova - New Wave in Jazz:
Ornette Coleman (188) Wayne Shorter (231,247)
McCoy Tyner (217) Elvin Jones (245)
W-5515 Vol.15: Captain Caribé - New Sound Scene:
Donald Byrd (264) Noel Pointer (633)
Ronnie Laws (538,634) Earl Klugh (293,536,537,634)

756

PORTUGAL

BLUE NOTE label

1601061	(8E074-60106)	BNS40034	Charlie Mingus - Town Hall Concert (628,629)
1618981	(11C076-61898)	BST84279	Herbie Hancock - Speak Like a Child (210)
1827861	(8E074-82786)	BST84195	Herbie Hancock - Maiden Voyage (179)
1828301	(11C076-82830)	BLP1201	Sidney Bechet - Jazz Classics,Vol.1 (3,4,12,13,17)
1828311	(11C080-82831)	BLP1202	Sidney Bechet - Jazz Classics,Vol.2 (3,12,13,17,30)
1829511	(11C076-82951)	LT-987	Lee Morgan - Sonic Boom (201,202)
1830021	(11C076-83002)	LT-1053	Joe Pass - The Complete "Catch Me!" Sessions (559,560)
1830351	(11C074-83035)	BST84226	Don Cherry - Complete Communion (189)
1830361	(11C074-83036)	BST84297	Wayne Shorter - Schizophrenia (200)
1830391	(11C074-83039)	BST84347	Art Blakey and The Jazz Messengers - Roots and Herbs (117,123)
1830681		LT-1064	Art Pepper - Omega Alpha (465)
1831191	(11C076-83119)	BST84247	Don Cherry - Symphony for Improvisers (195)
1831221	(11C076-83122)	BST84353	Chick Corea - The Song of Singing (240)
1831251	(11C076-83125)	BST84167	Andrew Hill - Point of Departure (164)
1831271	(11C076-83127)	BST84332	Wayne Shorter - Super Nova (231)
1833311	(11C078-83331)	BST84275	McCoy Tyner - Tender Moments (207)
1867181	(11C080-86718)	BST84218	Jackie McLean - Action,Action,Action (172)
1867421		LT-1102	Jean-Luc Ponty - Live at Donte's (568)
1985751	(11C074-98575)	BST81595	Cannonball Adderley - Somethin' Else (79)
1985771	(11C078-98577)	BLP1526	Clifford Brown Memorial Album (35,38)
2403091		BT85101	Stanley Jordan (304)

SPAIN

BLUE NOTE label

BLP
5059/5060 (054 2600191) Best from The West - Modern Sounds from California (44)

HBNS-

451-01	BLP2001	Gems of Jazz (see page 706)
451-02	BLP4255	Jimmy Smith - I'm Movin' On (148)
451-03	BLP4245	Art Blakey - Like Someone In Love (108,109)
451-04	BLP4246	Ornette Coleman - The Empty Foxhole (195)
451-05	BLP4247	Don Cherry - Symphony For Improvisers (195)
451-06	BLP1595	Julian Cannonball Adderley - Somethin' Else (79)
451-07	BLP4017	Horace Silver - Blowin' The Blues Away (94,95)
451-08	BLP4188	Donald Byrd - Tryin' To Get Home (175,176)
451-09	BLP4230	Hank Mobley - A Caddy For Daddy (188)
451-10	BLP4232	Wayne Shorter - Adam's Apple (190)
451-11	BLP1558	Sonny Rollins,Vol.2 (62)
451-12	BLP4117	The Incredible Jimmy Smith - Back At The Chicken Shack (102,103)
451-13	BLP4269	Jimmy Smith - Open House (101)
451-14	BLP4200	The Incredible Jimmy Smith with Kenny Burrell and Philly Joe Jones (78)

500-7-8 BLP1501 + BLP1502 Miles Davis (2 LP Set) (31,34,41)

Part 9
Compact Disc Numerical Listings

U.S. ISSUES

BLUE NOTE label (International series)

Note: Following series list Blue Note CDs which were produced primarily in U.S. and also foreign releases which were numbered in the same series.
Prefixes shown are abbreviated from those actually appearing on CDs.Early issues in series 7- used prefix CDP7,which was replaced by 0777 7- later on.Other series (4-, 5- & 8-) use prefix 7243 4,7243 5 or 7243 8.
Series are listed in prefix numerical order,although chronological order was different: series 7- was used first, followed by series 8-,4- and 5- in that order.
Second column shows equivalent LP number,with number of additional or omitted tracks in CD issue,when applicable, or equivalent older CD issue, or label/country of origin when not produced in U.S..

4-93011-2		Medeski,Martin & Wood - Combustication (415)
4-93072-2		Blakey '60 - The Best Of Art Blakey & The Jazz Messengers (101,109,117,119,123)
4-93155-2		Tommy Flanagan - Sunset And The Mockingbird (405)
4-93254-2		Jackie McLean - Fire And Love (612)
4-93381-2	BN-LA037-G2	Grant Green - Live At The Lighthouse (260)
4-93384-2	BN-LA223G +3	McCoy Tyner - Asante (246,247)
4-93385-2	BN-LA506-H2+3	Elvin Jones - At This Point In Time (269)
4-93401-2	BST84901	Lee Morgan - The Last Session (256)
4-93456-2		Chucho Valdes Solo - Live In New York (420)
4-93466-2	(EMI Jazz-U.K.)	Horace Silver - Jazz Masters (44,45,58,94,173,185,196)
4-93467-2	(EMI Jazz-U.K.)	Art Blakey - Jazz Masters (85,101,109)
4-93469-2	(EMI Jazz-U.K.)	Jazz Superhits Of The 60s: Donald Byrd (147) / Lou Donaldson (201) Horace Silver (173) / Cannonball Adderley (496) Art Blakey & The J.M. (85) / Lee Morgan (161)
4-93543-2		Kurt Elling - This Time It's Love (416,418)
4-93565-2		Prysm Second Rhythm (412)
4-93676-2		Marcus Printup - Nocturnal Traces (420)
4-93711-2		Don Byron - Nu Blaxploitation (417,418,419)
4-93760-2		Greg Osby - Zero (418,419)
4-93916-2	(France)	Erik Truffaz - The Dawn (418)
4-93991-2	(Europe)	Easy - Stanley Turrentine Plays The Pop Hits (171,195,204,209,212,214,217,219,220,229)
4-93993-2	(Europe)	Outta Sight! - Nancy Wilson Sings The Hits (494,495,496,497,498,499,500,501,503,504)
4-93994-2	(Europe)	Sky High - The Mizell Brothers: Johnny Hammond Smith (646,647) / A Taste Of Honey (507) Gary Bartz (506) / Donald Byrd (264,267,274,283) Rance Allen (506) / Bobbi Humphrey (273,282)
4-93995-2	(Europe)	Brother Man! - Lou Rawls Sings The Hits (495,496,497,498,499,500,501,502)
4-94027-2	B1-94027 -5	Blue Break Beats,Vol.4: Gene Harris (273) / Monk Higgins (586) David Axelrod (500) / Herbie Hancock (645) Gene Harris/3 Sounds (218) / Ike & Tina Turner (632) Buddy Rich (564) / The Three Sounds (231) Bob Dorough (504) / Eddie Henderson (287) Banbara (505) / Marlena Shaw (267) The Sons (501) / Paul Nero (502)

4-94030-2	(Europe)	Blue 45s (The Ultimate Jukebox):	
		Art Blakey & The J.M.(101)	Horace Silver (210)
		Don Wilkerson (140)	Blue Mitchell (169)
		Lou Donaldson (138)	Jimmy Smith (149)
		Kenny Burrell (147)	Lonnie Smith (230)
		Herbie Hancock (151)	Bobbi Humphrey (256)
		Freddie Roach (148,164)	Hank Mobley (177)
		Donald Byrd (175)	Lee Morgan (181)
		John Patton (178)	Stanley Turrentine (150)
		Horace Silver (196)	Joe Henderson (155)
		Lou Donaldson (201)	Lou Donaldson (201)
4-94031-2		Afro Blue Vol.2 (The Roots of Rhythm & Jazz):	
		Art Blakey (39,133)	McCoy Tyner (247)
		Solomon Ilori (153)	Candido (249)
		Wayne Shorter (165)	The Jazz Crusaders (559)
		Stanley Turrentine (167)	Curtis Amy & Dupree Bolton (560)
		Lee Morgan (191)	Randy Weston (512)
		Blue Mitchell (227)	Cannonball Adderley (500)
4-94032-2	(Europe)	Blue Pacific Funk (Walkin' On The West Coast):	
		Booker Ervin (566)	Gerald Wilson (560)
		Johnny Lytle (563)	The Jazz Crusaders (563)
		Richard Groove Holmes (558)	Billy Larkin & The Delegates (561)
		Les McCann (560)	Freddy Robinson (567)
		Carmell Jones (558)	The Jazz Crusaders (559)
		Les McCann & The Jazz Crusaders (560)	Lenny McBrowne & 4 Souls (556)
			Wes Montgomery (554)
		Charles Kynard (560)	Paul Bryant & Jim Hall (557)
4-94035-2	(Europe)	Azure Ellington - Blue Note Plays The Duke:	
		Nat King Cole (485)	Billy Strayhorn (625)
		Stan Kenton (486)	Duke Ellington (631)
		Lou Rawls (500)	Clifford Jordan (74)
		Nina Simone (512)	Kenny Burrell (81)
		Richard Groove Holmes (557)	Jimmy McGriff (253)
		Booker Ervin (563)	James Newton (309)
		Phineas Newborn (575)	Joe William (241)
		Armstrong/Ellington (577)	Kevin Eubanks (369)

Note: First issues of 4-94030/31/32/35-2 were issued as 94030/31/32/35-0 in a enhanced version with graphics.

4-94100-2		Phil Woods - The Rev And I (419)	
4-94104-2		Benny Golson And The Philadelphians (520,621)	
4-94105-2		Zoot Sims - Jazz Alive - A Night At The Half Note (622)	
4-94107-2		Cecil Taylor - Love For Sale (623)	
4-94211-2		Blue Note Salutes Motown:	
		John Patton (192)	Dave Koz (421)
		Bobbi Humphrey (261)	Charlie Hunter (422)
		Earl Klugh (293)	Ray Barretto (422)
		Stanley Turrentine (317)	Eliane Elias (424)
		Everette Harp (394)	Richard Elliot (424)
		Dianne Reeves (421)	Stanley Turrentine (317)
4-94442-2	(Europe)	Gonzalo Rubalcaba - The Trio (613) (BN/Somethin' Else label)	
4-94508-2	BST84276 +6	Duke Pearson - Introducing Duke Pearson's Big Band (208,221)	

Following block was issued in France only (see U.S. equivalents shown in second column):

4-94589-2	4-95324-2	Art Blakey And The Jazz Messengers - Moanin' (85)
4-94590-2	4-95338-2	Kenny Burrell - Midnight Blue (147)
4-94591-2	7-89795-2	John Patton - Let 'em Roll (188)
4-94592-2	7-81501-2	Miles Davis,Volume 1 (31,41)
4-94593-2	4-98794-2	Dexter Gordon - Go! (142)
4-94594-2	4-97809-2	Sonny Rollins Volume 2 (63)

759

4-94595-2	7-81510-2	Thelonious Monk - Genius Of Modern Music,Vol.1 (19,20,21)
4-94596-2	7-81503-2	The Amazing Bud Powell,Vol.1 (25,27)
4-94597-2	7-81577-2	John Coltrane - Blue Train (71)
4-94598-2	7-46506-2	Herbie Hancock - Takin' Off (139)
4-94599-2	7-84185-2	The Horace Silver Quintet - Song For My Father (159,162,173)
4-94600-2	4-95329-2	Cannonball Adderley - Somethin' Else (79)
4-94601-2	7-84356-2	Ornette Coleman - Love Call (213,214)
4-94602-2	4-98793-2	Eric Dolphy - Out To Lunch (163)
4-94603-2	7-84263-2	Lou Donaldson - Alligator Boogaloo (201)
4-94604-2	7-46815-2	Kenny Dorham - Afro Cuban (45,46)
4-94605-2	8-29156-2	Joe Henderson - In 'n Out (165)
4-94606-2	7-84073-2	Freddie Hubbard - Hub Cap (120)
4-94607-2	7-84067-2	Jackie McLean - Bluesnik (115)
4-94608-2	4-95332-2	Lee Morgan - The Sidewinder (161)
4-94609-2	7-46097-2	Jimmy Smith - The Sermon! (70,78)
4-94610-2	4-97807-2	McCoy Tyner - The Real McCoy (201)
4-94611-2	7-84080-2	Hank Mobley - Workout (119)
4-94612-2	7-84098-2	Ike Quebec - Blue And Sentimental (131)
4-94613-2	4-99001-2	Wayne Shorter - Speak No Evil (176)

4-94664-2	BN/EMI (Europe)	Chris Minh Doky (659,660)
4-94704-2	B1-94704	Lee Morgan - Blue Breakbeats (161,185,192,213)
4-94705-2	B1-94705	Grant Green - Blue Breakbeats (233,237,246,252,257)
4-94706-2	B1-94706	Bobbi Humphrey - Blue Breakbeats (261,267,272,273,281)
4-94707-2	B1-94707	Reuben Wilson - Blue Breakbeats (219,224,235)
4-94708-2	B1-94708	Donald Byrd - Blue Breakbeats (202,264,267,283,289)
4-94709-2	B1-94709	Lou Donaldson - Blue Breakbeats (148,201,220,226,236,243)
4-94888-2	(Canada)	Blue Box II (4 CD Box):

Tony Bennett (646)
Billie Holiday (462)
Johnny Mercer (468)
Peggy Lee (469)
Mel Torme (471)
June Christy (477)
Louis Prima (482)
Bing Crosby (482)
Louis Prima (485)
Mark Murphy (486)
Dean Martin (488)
Nancy Wilson (488)
Lou Rawls (492,493)
Ella Fitzgerald (500)
Peggy Lee (503)
Rachelle Ferrell (510)
Nina Simone (512)
Abbey Lincoln (534)
Julie London (535)
Chet Baker (547)
Hoagy Carmichael (551)
Annie Ross (553)
Tony Bennett (574)
Billy Eckstine (574)
Joe Williams (575)
Sarah Vaughan (576)
Louis Armstrong & Duke Ellington (577)
Sarah Vaughan (578)
Dinah Washington (579)
Betty Carter (581)
Joe Williams (582)
Eliane Elias (592)
Bob Belden/Cassandra Wilson (603)
Bob Belden/Holly Cole (608,611)
Johnny Hartman (617)
Betty Carter (630)
Hadda Brooks (635)
The Jazz Passengers (635)
Sheila Jordan (142)
Carmen McRae (290)
Mose Allison (319)
Dianne Reeves (339)
Bobby McFerrin (337)
Kurt Elling (374)
Caecilie Norby (391)
Lena Horne (373)
Dianne Reeves (374)
Kurt Elling/Cassandra Wiilson (399)
Bobby McFerrin (378)
Judi Silvano (388)
Javon Jackson/Cassandra Wilson (389)
Cassandra Wilson (356)

4-94893-2 (EMI Music)(Canada) CBS's After Hours Jazz Collections,Vol.3:
Pat Martino (296) | Brian Blade (413)
Charlie Hunter (413) | Grant Green (246)
Bob Dorough (408) | Mose Allison (657)
Dianne Reeves (410) | Bob Belden (407)
Chucho Valdes (419) | Marcus Printup (412)
Jacky Terrasson & Cassandra Wilson (402) | Cassandra Wilson (not from BN)

4-94976-2 Ron Carter - So What (614)
4-95050-2 Eliane Elias Sings Jobim (613)
4-95104-2 James Hurt - Dark Grooves Mystical Rhythms (432)
4-95198-2 Tim Hagans - Animations/Imagination (423)
4-95317-2 (Europe) Lulu On The Bridge (Soundtrack):
Raymond Scott (637) | Don Byron (415)
Mira Sorvino (658) | Jacky Terrasson (421)
Paul Auster (658) | Lena Horne (421)
Graeme Revell (658) | Giovanni Battista Pergolesi (515)
Ike Quebec (130) | Edith Piaf (520)
Cassandra Wilson (416) | Amalia Rodrigues (526)
Medeski/Martin/Wood (415) | Holly Cole (544)

4-95324-2 7-46516-2 +1 (RVG Series) Art Blakey - Moanin' (85)
4-95327-2 7-46513-2 (RVG Series) Sonny Clark - Cool Stuttin' (76)
4-95329-2 7-46338-2 (RVG Series) Cannonball Adderley - Somethin' Else (79)
4-95331-2 7-46339-2 (RVG Series) Herbie Hancock - Maiden Voyage (179)
4-95332-2 7-84157-2 (RVG Series) Lee Morgan - The Sidewinder (161)
4-95338-2 7-46399-2 (RVG Series) Kenny Burrell - Midnight Blue (147)
4-95342-2 7-46526-2 (RVG Series) Horace Silver - Blowin' The Blues Away (94,95)
4-95343-2 7-46528-2 (RVG Series) Hank Mobley - Soul Station (99)
4-95569-2 Herbie Hancock - The Complete Blue Note Sixties Sessions (6 CD Set)
(131,139,151,157,168,179,190,194,204,210,225)
4-95576-2 The Horace Silver Retrospective (4 CD Box):
(33,39,44,45,58,64,76,82,89) (173,185,186,196,210,222,241,251)
(94,106,122,141,153) (259,263,275,283,284,294,300)
4-95588-2 (Europe) Prysm - Prysm 1 (458)
4-95697-2 The Blue Note Swingtets:
Tiny Grimes (18) | Benny Morton (13)
John Hardee (17) | Jimmy Hamilton (16)
Ike Quebec (10,14,15,18)

4-95698-2 (2 CD Set) The Blue Note Years,Vol.1 - Boogie,Blues And Bop:
Albert Ammons (1) | Thelonious Monk (20,21,28)
Meade Lux Lewis (10) | Bud Powell (25,27,37)
Earl Hines (3) | Wynton Kelly (29)
Sidney Bechet (3) | Milt Jackson (30)
Edmond Hall (5) | Miles Davis (34)
James P. Johnson (7) | Horace Silver (33)
Bechet-Nicholas (17) | Lou Doinaldson/Clifford Brown (35)
Jimmy Hamilton (16) | J.J. Johnson (36)
Ike Quebec (10,15) | Clifford Brown (38)
Tiny Grimes (18) | Gil Melle (38)
Babs Gonzales (18) | Art Blakey (39)
Tadd Dameron (19,22) | Herbie Nichols (48)
McGhee/Navarro (23) | Art Blakey (41)
James Moody (23)

761

4-95701-2 (2 CD Set) The Blue Note Years,Vol.6 - The New Era:
Donald Byrd ((283) Joe Henderson (311)
Earl Klugh (285) Freddie Hubbard/Woody Shaw (321)
Ronnie Laws (279) McCoy Tyner (341)
Bobby McFerrin (378) Tony Williams (322)
Stanley Jordan (304) Don Pullen/George Adams (313)
Dianne Reeves (318) Benny Green (342)
Eliane Emias (398) Joe Lovano (348)
Rachelle Ferrell (593) Gonzalo Rubalcaba (594)
John Scofield (362) Javon Jackson (362)
Cassandra Wilson (361) Jacky Terrasson (369)
Charlie Hunter (376) Greg Osby (389)
Us3 (350)

4-95704-2 (2 CD Set) The Blue Note Years,Vol.7 - Then As Now:
Bob Belden Presents Various Artists (606,607,608)

4-95718-2 (2 CD Set) (Connoisseur Series) Gil Melle - The Complete 50s Sessions (33,38,43,45,51,450)

4-95747-2 BLP5012 +1 + BLP5023 +2 (Connoisseur Series) Howard McGhee/Introducing Kenny Drew Trio:
Howard McGhee (26) Kenny Drew (34)

4-95748-2 BLP5024 +1 + BLP5042 (Connoisseur Series) Howard McGhee,Vol.2/Tal Farlow Quartet:
Howard McGhee (35) Tal Farlow (41)

4-95749-2 BLP5053+5064 (Connoisseur Series) Julius Watkins Sextet,Vol.1 & 2 (43,45)

4-95750-2 BLP5045 +4 + BLP5043 +1 (Connoisseur Series) George Wallington/Frank Foster:
George Wallington (42) Frank Foster (42)

4-95981-2 (2 CD Set) Visions Of Jazz - The First Century:
Lester Young (459) Count Basie (578)
Billie Holiday (462) Sarah Vaughan (579)
Benny Goodman (472) Dinah Washington (580)
Miles Davis (473) Modern Jazz Quartet (624)
Art Tatum (474) Duke Ellington (631)
Louis Bellson (476) Bobby Hackett (449)
Duke Ellington (477) Art Hodes (14,16)
Frank Sinatra (478) Thelonious Monk (19)
Nat King Cole (482) Bud Powell (25)
Kay Starr (488) Horace Silver (44)
Randy Weston (512) George Lewis (47)
Fats Waller (516) Sonny Rollins (73)
Coleman Hawkins (517) Dexter Gordon (142)
Jimmy Rowles (534) Cecil Taylor (192)
Ch. Parker/D. Gillespie (570) Don Pullen (326)
Stan Getz (571) Cassandra Wilson (380)
John Coltrane (577) Joe Lovano (396)
L. Armstrong/D. Ellington (577) Geri Allen 611)

4-96365-2 (Australia) Jazz Ballads (4 CD Box) - includes the following CDs:
8-56689-2 Lou Rawls 8-56691-2 Freddie Hubbard
8-56690-2 Ike Quebec 8-56692-2 Joe Henderson

4-96375-2 (2 CD Set) The Blue Note Years,Vol.2 - The Jazz Message (US reissue of 8-54185-2)
4-96378-2 (2 CD Set) The Blue Note Years,Vol.3 - Organ And Soul (US reissue of 8-54188-2)
4-96381-2 (2 CD Set) The Blue Note Years,Vol.4 - Hard Bop And Beyond (US reissue of 8-54191-2)
4-96384-2 (2 CD Set) The Blue Note Years,Vol.5 - The Avant Garde (US reissue of 8-54194-2)
4-96427-2 (14 CD Box) The Blue Note Years (= Vol.1-7 (= 4-95698-2 + 4-95701-2 + 4-95704-2 + 4-96375-2 + 4-96378-2 + 4-96381-2 + 4-96384-2)
4-96548-2 BLP5035+T6505 Sal Salvador Quintet/Quartet (39,478,479)
4-96667-2 The Joe Lovano Nonet - 52nd Street Themes (442,443)
4-96685-2 Joe Chambers - Mirrors (424,425)
4-96860-2 Greg Osby - Banned In New York (416)
4-96902-2 Rodney Jones - The Undiscovered Few (425,426,427)
4-96968-2 (Norway) Helen Eriksen - Love Virgin (445)

762

4-97154-2 (Europe) Lady Day & John Coltrane - True Blue:
Billie Holiday (619) Larry Young (186)
Lee Morgan (198) Wayne Shorter (178)
J.J. Johnson (36) Grant Green (166)
Herbie Nichols (48) McCoy Tyner (207)
John Coltrane (71) Charles Lloyd (303)
Ike Quebec (135) Cassandra Wilson (381)

4-97155-2 Blue Big Bands:
Stan Kenton (486) Count Basie (573)
Chet Baker (551) Duke Ellington (631)
Gil Evans (555) Stanley Turrentine (181)
Gerald Wilson (559) Duke Pearson (208)
Gil Fuller (562) Thad Joes/Mel Lewis (242)
Don Ellis (563) George Russell (303)
Buddy Rich (564)

4-97156-2 Blue Bossa,Vol.2:
Lou Rawls (495) Horace Parlan (113)
J.J. Johnson (43) Lee Morgan (181)
Duke Pearson (226) Bobby Hutcherson (282)
Stanley Turrentine (195) Dexter Gordon (142)
Donald Byrd (202) Grant Green (137)
Carmen McRae (289) Ike Quebec (143)
Charlie Rouse (145) Joe Henderson (155)

4-97157-2 (Europe) Electric Blue (not reissued on U.S.):
Monk Higgins (632) Bobbi Humphrey (261)
Alphonse Mouzon (276) Eddie Henderson (279)
Donald Byrd (255) Ronnie Foster (278)
Horace Silver (263) Gene Harris (298)
Ronnie Foster (265) Alphonse Mouzon (265)
Lou Donaldson (266) Bobbi Humphrey (269)
Ronnie Laws (279)

4-97158-2 (Europe) Blue Juice,Vol.2
Duke Pearson (241) Sandy Nelson (533)
Bobby Hutcherson (258) Les McCann (561)
Alphonse Mouzon (265) Victor Feldman (564)
Howard Roberts (498) Gerald Wilson (566)
Henry Cole (505) Wilbert Longmire (567)
Patti Drew (500) The Jazz Crusaders (568)
Willie Hobo (505) Joe Torres (567)
Willard Burton (505) Hank Diamond (569)
Gonzalez (516) Candido (587)
Trinidad Oil Company (516) Truman Thomas (631)

Following block is made of French reissues of previous U.S. CDs:

4-97171-2 4-97808-2 Larry Young - Unity (186)
4-97178-2 7-89392-2 Freddie Redd - Music From "The Connection" (100)
4-97179-2 7-84057-2 Stanley Turrentine - Blue Hour (114)
4-97180-2 7-81502-2 Miles Davis Volume 2 (34)
4-97181-2 4-95331-2 Herbie Hancock - Maiden Voyage (179)
4-97182-2 4-99005-2 Wayne Shorter - Ju Ju (169)
4-97183-2 7-81511-2 Thelonious Monk - Genius Of Modern Music,Volume 2 (28,32)
4-97184-2 7-81504-2 The Amazing Bud Powell,Volume 2 (27,37)
4-97185-2 7-81542-2 Sonny Rollins Volume 1 (59)
4-97186-2 4-95327-2 Sonny Clark - Cool Struttin' (76)
4-97187-2 7-81505-2 The Eminent J.J. Johnson Volume 1 (36)
4-97188-2 7-84442-2 Grant Green - The Matador (166,167)
4-97189-2 7-81526-2 Clifford Brown Memorial Album (35,38)
4-97190-2 7-81559-2 Johnny Griffin - A Blowing Session (63)
4-97191-2 7-84049-2 Art Blakey - A Night In Tunisia (108,109)

4-97222-2		Blue Sampler II:
		Jimmy Liggins (463) / Stanley Turrentine (167)
		Margo Thunder (504) / Horace Silver (89)
		Jeremy Steig (238) / Lee Morgan (227)
		John Patton (178) / Stanley Turrentine (213)
		Jackie McLean (91)
4-97367-2	7-46819-2	Sonny Clark - Sonny's Crib (70)
4-97399-2	(Korea)	Jazz On Cinema (see 5-20535-2)
4-97431-2		Jason Moran - Soundtrack To Human Motion (425)
4-97504-2	LT-1091	Lee Morgan - Infinity (187)
4-97505-2	BST84200 +4	Jimmy Smith - Softly As A Summer Breeze (78,84)
4-97506-2	LT-1081	Hank Mobley - Third Season (200)
4-97507-2	LT-1088	Art Blakey - Africaine (97)
4-97508-2	LT-1086 +5	Bobby Hutcherson - Medina (221,230)
4-97517-2	(France)	Herbie Hancock - Dr. Jazz (127,139,151,157,168,179,185,204,210,225)
4-97563-2		The Best Of Michel Petrucciani - The Blue Note Years (312,314,322,331,342,346,355)
4-97604-2	(France)	The Complete Recordings Of Michel Petrucciani On Blue Note (7 CD Box): (= 7-46295-2 + 7-46427-2 + 7-48679-2 + 7-80589-2 + 7-80590-2 + 7-92563-2 + 7-95480-2)
4-97807-2	7-46512-2	(RVG Series) McCoy Tyner - The Real McCoy (201)
4-97808-2	BST 84221	(RVG Series) Larry Young - Unity (186)
4-97809-2	7-81558-2	(RVG Series) Sonny Rollins - Volume Two (63)
4-97810-2		Stanley Jordan - Live In New York (329)
4-97811-2	7-46147-2	Town Hall Concert (306)
4-97870-2	(Aladdin)	Jump 'N' Jive:
		Clyde Bernhardt (23) / (& further titles not from BN)
4-97893-2	(Australia)	Groove Hip - Hop:
		Us3 (350) / Erik Truffaz (418)
		Greg Osby (367) / Medeski,Martin & Wood (415)
		Charlie Hunter (413) / Us3 (393)
		Diamond D/R. Foster (386) / Tim Hagans (423)
		The Angel/.D.Byrd (385) / D.I.G. (658)
4-97945-2		Stefano Di Battista Quintet - A Prima Vista (425)
4-98108-2		Junko Onishi - Fragile (614)
4-98222-2		Lee Konitz - Another Shade Of Blue (401)
4-98239-2		Irakere - Yemaya (414)
4-98240-2		John Coltrane - Trane's Blues:
		Paul Chambers (57,463) / Johnny Griffin (63)
		Sonny Clark (70) / John Coltrane/Cecil Taylor (620)
		John Coltrane (71) / John Colrane (577)
4-98320-2	(Australia)	Funk + Latin + Jazz = Blue Note:
		Medeski,Martin & Wood (415) / Jane Bunnett (655)
		Pat Martino (420) / Eliane Elias (592)
		Charlie Hunter (413) / Jacky Terrasson (411)
		Brian Blade (413) / Tim Hagans & Marcus Printup (412)
		Don Byron (417) / Jacky Terrasson & Cassandra Wilson (402)
		Chucho Valdes (419)
4-98488-2		Pieces Of A Dream - Ahead To The Past (436,437)
4-98492-2	(Europe)	Thierry Lang - Nan (660)
4-98542-2	BN-LA142-G	Bobbi Humphrey - Blacks And Blues (267)
4-98543-2		Noel Pointer - Hold On (633)
4-98544-2		Ronnie Laws - Common Ground (537)
4-98573-2		Earl Klugh - Late Night Guitar (537)
4-98756-2		Jacky Terrasson - What It Is (427,429)
4-98793-2	7-46524-2	(RVG Series) Eric Dolphy - Out To Lunch (163)
4-98794-2	7-46094-2	(RVG Series) Dexter Gordon - Go! (142)
4-98795-2	7-84140-2	(RVG Series) Joe Henderson - Page One (155)
4-98796-2	7-84175-2	(RVG Series) Herbie Hancock - Empyrean Isles (168)

4-98899-2	EMI Music (Special Markets)	Blue Note Essentials,Vol.1:	
		Herbie Hancock (168)	Horace Silver (58)
		Art Blakey (101)	John Coltrane (71)
		Donald Byrd (147)	
4-98900-2	EMI Music (Special Markets)	Blue Note Essentials,Vol.2:	
		Art Blakey (85)	Kenny Burrell (147)
		Cannonball Adderley (79)	Herbie Hancok (139)
		Lee Morgan (161)	Horace Silver (173)
4-98917-2		Chucho Valdes - Briyumba Palo Congo (428)	
4-98918-2		Frank Emilio Y Los Amigos - Ancestral Reflections (Reflejos Ancestrales) (428)	
4-99001-2	BST84194 +1	(RVG Series) Wayne Shorter - Speak No Evil (176)	
4-99002-2	7-84185-2	(RVG Series) Horace Silver - Song For My Father (159,162,173)	
4-99003-2	7-84154-2	(RVG Series) Grant Green - Idle Moments (159)	
4-99004-2	7-84180-2	(RVG Series) Tony Williams - Life Time (171)	
4-99005-2	BST84182 +2	(RVG Series) Wayne Shorter - Ju Ju (169)	
4-99006-2	7-84124-2	(RVG Series) Donald Byrd - A New Perspective (147)	
4-99007-2	BST84167 +3	(RVG Series) Andrew Hill - Point Of Departure (164)	
4-99008-2	7-84115-2	(RVG Series) Freddie Hubbard - Hub-Tones (144)	
4-99009-2	BLP1559 +1	(RVG Series) Johnny Griffin - Blowin' Session (63)	
4-99125-2		Joe Lovano & Greg Osby - Friendly Fire (430)	
4-99158-2	EMI-Jazz (U.K.)	Miles Davis - Jazz Masters (31,34,41)	
4-99159-2	EMI-Jazz (U.K.)	Dexter Gordon - Jazz Masters (121,142,154,182)	
4-99187-2		Charlie Hunter & Leon Parker - Duo (430)	
4-99239-2		Bob Dorough - Too Much Coffee Man (430,433,435,436)	
4-99241-2		Gonzalo Rubalcaba - Inner Voyage (428)	
4-99257-2		John Scofield - Steady Groovin': The Blue Note Groove Sides (332,341,347,352,362,382)	
4-99351-2		Us3 - Flip Fantasia: Hits And Remixes (350,351,393)	
4-99503-2		Medeski,Martin & Wood - Combustication Remixes (415)	
4-99527-2		Benny Green - These Are Soulful Days (431)	
4-99545-2		Don Byron - Romance With The Unseen (432)	
4-99546-2		Stefon Harris - Black Action Figure (433)	
4-99697-2		Javon Jackson - Pleasant Valley (431)	
4-99777-2	BLP1585/86 +4	(RVG Series) Jimmy Smith - Groovin' At Small's (2 CD Set) (74)	
4-99795-2	(2 CD Set)	(RVG Series) Sonny Rollins - A Night At The Village Vanguard (73,74) (= BLP1581+ BN-LA475-H2)	
4-99826-2		Eric Dolphy - Illinois Concert (456)	
4-99871-2	(not released yet)	Greg Osby - The Inner Circle (436)	
4-99908-2	(France)	Stéphane Huchard - Tribal Traquenard (431-432)	
4-99997-2		Renee Rosnes - Art & Soul (433)	
5-20070-2	(2 CD Set)	The Best Blue Note Album In The World ... Ever:	
		Horace Silver (173)	Us3 (350)
		John Coltrane (71)	John Patton (188)
		Art Blakey (85)	Charlie Hunter (376)
		Lou Donaldson (83)	Jimmy Smith (103)
		Cannonball Adderley (79)	Dexter Gordon (142)
		Kenny Burrell (147)	Eliane Elias (613)
		Lee Morgan (161)	Bobby McFerrin (313)
		Herbie Hancock (139)	Cassandra Wilson (356)
		Donald Byrd (95)	Lou Rawls (328)
		Grant Green (135)	Richard Elliot (544)
5-20134-2		Greg Osby - The Invisible Hand (442)	
5-20208-2		Ronny Jordan - A Brighter Day (438,439)	
5-20419-2	(Canada)	Marc Jordan - This Is How Men Cry (660,661)	

5-20457-2	(Canada)	Blue Note Festival '99:	
		Dianne Reeves (426)	Chucho Valdes (419)
		Renee Rosnes (433)	Charlie Hunter/Leon Parker (429)
		Cassandra Wilson (424)	Jason Moran (425)
		Prysm (412)	Tim Hagans (423)
		Kurt Elling (399)	Us3 (351)
		Joe Chambers (425)	Junko Onishi (614)
		Joe Lovano (413)	
5-20535-2	EMI (2 CD Set)	Jazz On Cinema:	
	(U.K. only)	Thelonious Monk (21)	Joe Lovano (360)
		Jacky Terrasson	Sidney Bechet (3)
		& Cassandra Wilson (402)	Jacky Terrasson (382)
		Stanley Jordan (329)	Marlena Shaw (265)
		The Three Sounds (212)	(& further titles not from BN)
5-20676-2	(France)	Malcolm Braff - Together (661)	
5-20730-2		Chucho Valdes - Live At The Village Vanguard (435)	
5-20808-2		Blue Note Plays Gershwin:	
		Stanley Turrentine (148)	Ike Quebec (133)
		Jimmy Smith (101)	Sonny Clark (67)
		Dexter Gordon (154)	Lou Donaldson (100)
		Benny Green (342)	Herbie Nichols (53)
		Kenny Burrell (307)	Joe Lovano (396)
5-20809-2		Blue Note Plays Ellington And Strayhorn:	
		James Newton (309)	McCoy Tyner (325)
		Clifford Jordan (74)	Horace Silver (33)
		Junko Onishi (603)	Sonny Clark (86)
		Joe Henderson (310)	Greg Osby (389)
		Horace Parlan (100)	Michel Petrucciani (355)
		Bobby Watson (323)	Joe Lovano (369)
5-20827-2		Eliane Elias - Everything I Love (437,438,440)	

Following block is made of U.K. issues on HMV Jazz label,which were released only for HMV stores.Most of them are equivalent to CDs from the Jazz Profile series (numbers shown in second column).Those marked + have additional titles as shown.

5-20858-2	8-54898-2	Cannonball Adderley	
5-20862-2	8-54899-2	Art Blakey	
5-20863-2	8-23515-2	Miles Davis	
5-20865-2	8-23514-2	Dexter Gordon	
5-20866-2	8-33205-2	Grant Green	
5-20867-2	8-54904-2	Herbie Hancock	
5-20868-2	HMV Jazz (UK)	Bobby Hutcherson (183,190,194,204,245,260)	
5-20870-2	8-23518-2	Thelonious Monk	
5-20871-2 +	8-54901-2 +1	Lee Morgan (77,161,170,183,185,204) + (195)	
5-20873-2	HMV Jazz (UK)	Michel Petrucciani (312,314,322,331,342,346,355)	
5-20874-2 +	8-54906-2 +2*	Bud Powell (25,27,37,68,82,88,570,571) (*extra titles not from BN)	
5-20875-2	8-23516-2	Sonny Rollins	
5-20877-2	8-59072-2	Wayne Shorter	
5-20878-2	8-33208-2	Horace Silver	
5-20879-2	8-33206-2	Jimmy Smith	
5-20880-2	8-33207-2	McCoy Tyner	
5-20881-2	HMV Jazz (UK)	Soul Jazz:	
		Everette Harp (394)	Earl Klugh (293)
		Bobbi Humphrey (267)	Stanley Turrentine (213)
		Ronnie Laws (279)	George Howard (417)
		Donald Byrd (283)	Reuben Wilson (235)
		(& further titles not from BN)	

766

5-20882-2 HMV Jazz (UK) Dinner Jazz:
Stanley Turrentine (181) John Coltrane (71)
Ike Quebec (131) Dexter Gordon (142)
Kenny Burrell (147) Hank Mobley (99)
Cannonball Adderley (79) Grant Green (134)
Sonny Rollins (63) (& further titles not from BN)

5-20883-2 HMV Jazz (UK) Big Bands:
Carnegie Hall Jazz Band (384) Stanley Turrentine (181)
Sidney Bechet (12) (& further titles not from BN)

5-20884-2 HMV Jazz (UK) Guitar Jazz:
Edmond Hall (5) Grant Green (124)
Charlie Hunter (392) Bireli Lagrene (323)
Pat Martino (400) John Scofield (332)
Tal Farlow (41) John Scofield & Pat Metheny (365)
Kenny Burrell (147) Stanley Jordan (306)
(& further titles not from BN)

5-20885-2 HMV Jazz (UK) Latin Jazz:
Charlie Rouse (145) Joe Henderson (155)
Grant Green (137) Kenny Dorham (46)
Horace Silver (185) Lee Morgan (213)
(& further titles not from BN)

5-20907-2 (France) Jean-Pierre Como - Empreinte (445)

5-21052-2 The Mosaic Sampler:
The Capitol Jazzmen (466) Count Basie (578)
Illinois Jacquet (461) Hank Mobley (66)
Duke Ellington (480) Lee Morgan (58)
Chico Hamilton (555) Bud Shank (557)
Jimmy Giuffre (479) Andrew Hill (159)
June Christy (467)

Following block is made of French reissues of previous U.S. CDs:

5-21127-2 7-84147-2 Herbie Hancock - Inventions And Dimensions (157)
5-21128-2 7-81506-2 The Eminent J.J. Johnson - Volume 2 (43,48)
5-21129-2 7-48786-2 Billie Holiday - Billie's Blues (462,466,619)
5-21130-2 7-84078-2 Jimmy Smith - Midnight Special (102,103)
5-21131-2 7-84189-2 Joe Henderson - Inner Urge (175)
5-21132-2 7-84220-2 Horace Silver - Cape Verdean Blues (185,186)
5-21133-2 7-84133-2 Dexter Gordon - A Swingin' Affair (142)
5-21134-2 7-90055-2 Chick Corea - Now He Sings,Now He Sobs (585)
5-21135-2 7-90583-2 Bill Evans/Jim Hall - Undercurrent (626,627)
5-21136-2 7-81531-2 The Fabulous Fats Navarro,Volume 1:
Fats Navarro (19,25) Tadd Dameron (471,473)

5-21147-2 5-21147-1 -2 Capitol Rare,Vol.3 (Europe):
Ronnie Laws (279) Doris (526)
Raul De Souza (507) Eddie Henderson (507)
Dianne Reeves (319) Bobby Watson (581)
Maze (509) Georges Garvarentz (521)
Labi Siffre (516) Maze (508)
Ike & Tina Turner (536) Barrett Strong (508)
Bobbi Humphrey (261) Maxi (297)
Lou Rawls (500) David Axelrod (502)

5-21151-2 (Europe) Misty Blue:
Holly Cole (542) Betty Carter (630)
Dianne Reeves (322) Dinah Washington (580)
Sheila Jordan (142) Carmen MacRae (290)
Cassandra Wilson (356) Dodo Greene (136)
Sarah Vaughan (580) Lorez Alexandria (255)
Ella Fitzgerald (498) Annie Ross (556)
Billie Holiday (619) Della Reese (534)
Peggy Lee (484) Nancy Wilson (495)
Julie London (536) Jeri Southern (487)
Lena Horne (393) Nina Simone (512)

5-21152-2 (Europe) Deep Blue:
Andrew Hill (229) Alphonse Mouzon (265)
Lonie Smith (236) Gene Harris & The 3 Sounds (218)
Bobby Hutcherson (258) Hank Mobley (193)
Horace Silver (251) Duke Pearson (224)
Gene Harris (261) Lorez Alexandria (256)
Lee Morgan (231) Gerald Wilson (567)
Duke Pearson (175) Bobby Bryant (568)
Marlena Shaw (262)

5-21153-2 (Europe) Blue Velvet:
Mark Murphy (487) Lou Rawls (491)
Johnny Hartman (617) Mel Torme (501)
King Pleasure (627) Bill Henderson & Horace Silver (82)
Horace Silver (241) Leon Eason (91)
Louis Armstrong (578) Bobby McFerrin (540)
Joe Williams (578,582) Jimmy Witherspoon (555)
Billy Eckstine (576) Mose Allison (319)
Kurt Elling (416) Chet Baker (547)
Babs Gonzales (51) Hoagy Carmichael (550)

5-21226-2 7-84126-2 +1 (RVG Series) Herbie Hancock - My Point Of View (151)
5-21227-2 7-46820-2 (RVG Series) Bud Powell - Time Waits (82)
5-21228-2 7-46515-2 (RVG Series) Kenny Dorham - Una Mas (152)
5-21229-2 7-46428-2 (RVG Series) Lee Morgan - The Rumproller (180,181)

5-21426-2 EMI (U.K.) Jazz Cafe:
Herbie Hancock (168) Grant Green (137)
Art Blakey & The Jazz Messengers(85) Bud Powell (25)
Kenny Burrell (147)
Horace Silver (44) John Coltrane (71)
Lou Donaldson (201) (& further titles not from BN)

5-21427-2 EMI Gold (UK) Smooth Jazz:
Miles Davis (31) Lou Donaldson (83)
John Coltrane (71) Stanley Turrentine (114)
Dexter Gordon (142) (& further titles not from BN)

5-21435-2 (Connoisseur Series) Jimmy Smith - Six Views Of The Blues (82)
5-21436-2 (Connoisseur Series) Lou Donaldson - Man With A Horn (127,155)
5-21437-2 (Connoisseur Series) Bobby Hutcherson - The Kicker (161)
5-21438-2 (Connoisseur Series) Grant Green - Blue For Lou (150,155)
5-21455-2 (Connoisseur Series) Art Blakey - Drums Around The Corner (85,90)
5-21477-2 Paul Jackson Jr. - The Power Of The String (444)
5-21484-2 (Connoisseur Series) The Lost Sessions:
Charlie Rouse (176) Ike Quebec & The 3 Sounds (134)
Tadd Dameron (131) Fred Jackson (140)
Duke Pearson (105) Herbie Hancock (194)
Sonny Stitt & Dexter Gordon (138)

5-21605-2 Capitol Sophisticated Dames (U.K. only):
Caecilie Norby (391) Eliane Elias (398)
(& further titles not from BN)

5-21688-2		Latino Blue:
		Jack Costanzo (535) — Kenny Dorham (46)
		Willie Bobo (581) — Candido (578)
		Machito (573) — Charles Kynard & Buddy Collette (561)
		Joe Torres (567) — Clare Fischer (562)
		The Jazz Crusaders (562) — Sonny Stitt (572)
		Bobby Montez (534) — Art Blakey & Sabu Martinez (533)
5-21755-2	(2 CD)(Spain)	Un Toque De Jazz (Y Una Nota Azul) - A Touch Of Jazz (And A Blue Note)
Disc 1:		Art Blakey (127) — Sonny Clark (72)
		Jimmy Smith (92) — Freddie Hubbard (120)
		Sonny Rollins (74) — Joe Henderson (157)
		Kenny Dorham (115) — Jacke McLean (208)
		Dexter Gordon (122) — Bobby Hutcherson (215)
		Lee Morgan (183) — Horace Silver (196)
		Hank Mobley (99)
Disc 2:		Cannonball Adderley (79) — Herbie Hancock (168)
		Chet Baker/Stan Getz (546) — Joe Henderson (311)
		Kenny Burrell (147) — Konitz/Haden/Mehldau (401)
		Nat King Cole Trio (466) — Joe Lovano (348)
		John Coltrane (71) — Thelonious Monk (20)
		Kurt Elling (366) — Michel Petrucciani (355)
		Dexter Gordon (182) — Dianne Reeves (391)
		Bobby Watson (323) — Joe Lovano (369)
5-21758-2	(France)	Paco Sery - Voyages (446)
5-21810-2		Patricia Barber - Cafe Blue (652)
5-21811-2		Patricia Barber - Modern Cool (658)
5-21886-2	(France)	Prysm - Time (436)
5-21956-2	BST84347 +3	Art Blakey - Roots And Herbs (117,123)
5-21957-2	BST84258 +1	Art Blakey's Jazz Messengers - The Witch Doctor (119)
5-21958-2	BST84183	Grant Green - Talkin' About (172)
5-21959-2	BST84064	Grant Green - Grant's First Stand (116)
5-22019-2		(Connoisseur Series) Dizzy Reece - Comin' On (102,107)
5-22123-2	(France)	Erik Truffaz - Bending New Corners (435)
5-22211-2		Kurt Elling - Live In Chicago (440,441)
5-22342-2		Caecilie Norby - Queen Of Bad Excuses (434,435)
5-22467-2	BST84335 +3	Lee Morgan - The Sixth Sense (207,218)
5-22490-2		Ron Carter - Orfeu (615)
5-22626-2		Charlie Parker - The Washington Concerts (450,641)
5-22642-2		Denise Jannah - The Madness of Our Love (439)
5-22664-2		Candido - Thousand Finger Man (587)
5-22665-2	BLP1561	Sabu - Palo Congo (stereo version) (64)
5-22666-2	BST84097	Art Blakey - The African Beat (133)
5-22669-2	LT-1085 -1+6	(Connoisseur Series) Jackie McLean - Vertigo (139,149)
5-22670-2	LT-1031	(Connoisseur Series) Lee Morgan - Taru (209)
5-22671-2	GXF-3072 +1	(Connoisseur Series) Tina Brooks - Minor Move (79)
5-22672-2	BST84303 +5	(Connoisseur Series) Andrew Hill - Grass Roots (213,216)
5-22673-2	BT84226	(Connoisseur Series) Don Cherry - Complete Communication (189)
5-22674-2	GXF-3056 +3	(Connoisseur Series) Sonny Clark - My Conception (75,90)
5-22963-2	BN/Premonition	Patricia Barber - Companion (661)
5-22978-2		The Blue Note New Directions Band (615)
5-23182-2	(4 CD Set)	Blue Break Beats Vol.1-4 (= 7-99106-2 + 7-89907-2 + 8-54360-2 + 4-94027-2)
5-23220-2		Dr. John - Duke Elegant (517)
5-23273-2		Jackie McLean - Nature Boy (615)
5-23342-2	(France)	Flavio Boltro - Road Runner (438)
5-23403-2		Bob Dorough & Dave Frishberg - Who's On First? (443,444)

769

5-23444-2	(Europe)	Blunited States: Bobby Troup (535) Kenny Dorham (115) Thelonious Monk (32) Donald Byrd (198) Gil Melle (43) Jacky Terrasson (406) Leonard Feather (44) Duke Pearson (208) Hank Mobley (72) Cassandra Wilson (356) Jimmy Smith (78) John Patton (248) Don Wilkerson (137) Wynton Kelly (29) Sheila Jordan (142) The Three Sounds (212)
5-23545-2	BN-LA368-G	Donald Byrd - Stepping Into Tomorrow (274)
5-23546-2	(J)GP-3181	Earl Klugh - Heart String (634)
5-23547-2		Najee - Love Songs (513,514,540)
5-23559-2		Blue '70s: Carmen McRae (289) Lonnie Smith (236) Donald Byrd (274) Donald Byrd (283) Bobbi Humphrey (282) Ronnie Laws (296) Eddie Henderson (287) Chico Hamilton (281) Marlena Shaw (274) Grant Green (247) Gary Bartz (506)
5-23566-2	(Capitol)	The Great Jazz Vocalists Sing Hoagy Carmichael: Sheila Jordan (142) Cassandra Wilson (381) (& further titles not from BN)
5-23571-2		Brian Blade Fellowship - Perpetual (442)
5-23995-2	BST84265 +8	The Three Sounds - Live At The Lighthouse (203)
5-23997-2		Gene Harris And The Three Sounds - Live At The It Club,Vol.2 (239)
5-24271-2		Pure Cool: Chet Baker (547) Sarah Vaughan (580) Miles Davis (41) John Coltrane (71) Nat King Cole (489) Earl Klugh (509) Dexter Gordon (142) Dianne Reeves (323) June Christy (488) Charlie Hunter with Stefon Harris (413) Jacky Terrasson (369) Nancy Wilson & C. Adderley (480) Julie London (534) Kenny Burrell & Gr. Washington Jr.(304) Stanley Turrentine (150) Cassandra Wilson (356)
5-24456-2		Jane Bunnett And The Spirits Of Havana - Ritmo & Soul (662)
5-24539-2	BST84149 +2)	(RVG Series) Hank Mobley - No Room For Squares (151,158)
5-24540-2	BST84186	(RVG Series) Hank Mobley - The Turnaround (151,177)
5-24541-2	BST84011	(RVG Series) Jimmy Smith - The Sermon (70,78)
5-24542-2	BST84002 +1	(RVG Series) Jimmy Smith - House Party (70,77,78)
5-24543-2	BST84219	(RVG Series) Wayne Shorter - The All Seeing Eye (186)
5-24544-2	BST84089	(RVG Series) Jackie McLean - A Fickle Sonance (128)
5-24549-2	BST84280	Lou Donaldson - The Midnight Creeper (211)
5-24550-2	BST84235 +2	Jimmy Smith - Bucket (149)
5-24551-2	BST84158	Freddie Roach - Good Move (160)
5-24552-2	BST84240	Stanley Turrentine - Rough 'N Tumble (193)
5-24555-2	(2 CDs)	(Connoisseur Series) Don Wilkerson - The Complete Blue Note Sessions (= BST84107 + BST84121 + BST84145) (137,140,156)
5-24558-2	(2 CDs)	(Connoisseur Series) George Braith - The Complete Blue Note Sessions (= BST84148 + BST84161 + BST84171) (157,161,164)
5-24561-2	(2 CDs)	(Connoisseur Series) Kenny Burrell - Introducing Kenny Burrell - The First Blue Note Sessions (50,53,60)
5-24564-2	(2 CDs)	(Connoisseur Series) Sonny Criss - The Complete Imperial Sessions (531,532)
5-24586-2	(2 CDs)	(Connoisseur Series) Stanley Turrentine & The 3 Sounds - Blue Hour - The Complete Sessions (106,114)
5-24633-2		Supergenerous (444)
5-25114-2	5-25114-1	St. Germain - Tourist (662)
5-25251-2		The Jazz Mandolin Project - Xenoblast (441)
5-25271-2		Medeski,Martin & Wood - Tonic (433)
5-25494-2	(Australia)	Kurt Elling - Live In Chicago - The Out-Takes (440,441,446)
5-25646-2	BST84063	(RVG Series) Kenny Dorham - Whistle Stop (115)

770

5-25647-2	BST84152 +1	(RVG Series) Joe Henderson - Our Thing (157)
5-25648-2	BLP1539 +3	(RVG Series) Horace Silver - Six Pieces Of Silver (58,82)
5-25649-2	BST84321 +2	(RVG Series) Herbie Hancock - The Prisoner (225)
5-25650-2	BST84360 +3	Grant Green - Alive (246,247)
5-25651-2	BT 85106 +2	Kenny Burrell & Grover Washington Jr. - Togethering (304,307)
5-26201-2	5-25114-2	St. Germain - Tourist (jewel box) (662)
5-26427-2		Erik Truffaz - The Mask (390,418,435)
5-27544-2		Tim Hagans - Live In Montreal (440)
5-27545-2		(Connoisseur Series) Booker Ervin - Structurally Sound (563,564)
5-27546-2	BST84330 +6	(Connoisseur Series) Andrew Hill - Lift Every Voice (227,238,239)
5-27548-2		(Connoisseur Series) Grant Green - First Session (113,128)
5-27549-2	BST84435 +3	(Connoisseur Series) Hank Mobley - Straight No Filter (151,158,177,193)
5-30607-2	BLP1207 +7	The Fabulous Sidney Bechet (30,37)

771

7-46092-2	BT 85101 +1	Stanley Jordan - Magic Touch (304)
7-46093-2	BT 85106	Kenny Burrell/Grover Washington - Togethering (304)
7-46094-2	BST84112	Dexter Gordon - Go! (142)
7-46095-2	BST81577	John Coltrane - Blue Train (71)
7-46097-2		Jimmy Smith - The Sermon (70,78)
7-46100-2	BST84201 +2	Stanley Turrentine - Joyride (181)
7-46110-2	BT 85105	Stanley Turrentine - Straight Ahead (305)
7-46135-2	BST84216	Anthony Williams - Spring (184)
7-46136-2	BST84279	Herbie Hancock - Speak Like a Child (210)
7-46137-2	BST84157	Lee Morgan - The Sidewinder (161)
7-46140-2	BST81518	Horace Silver and The Jazz Messengers (44,45)
7-46142-2	BST84051 +3	Jackie McLean - Jackie's Bag (88,110)
7-46147-2	BT 85113	One Night with Blue Note,Volume 1 (306)
7-46148-2	BT 85114	One Night with Blue Note,Volume 2 (306,307)
7-46149-2	BT 85115	One Night with Blue Note,Volume 3 (306,307)
7-46150-2	BT 85116	One Night with Blue Note,Volume 4 (306)
7-46289-2	BT 85119	Tony Williams - Foreign Intrigue (309)
7-46290-2	BT 85118	Out of The Blue - OTB (309)
7-46291-2	BT 85102	McCoy Tyner & Jackie McLean - It's About Time (308)
7-46292-2	BT 85109	James Newton - The African Flower (309)
7-46293-2	BT 85107	Bennie Wallace - Twilight Time (308)
7-46294-2	BT 85121	Freddie Hubbard/Woody Shaw - Double Take (312)
7-46295-2	BT 85124	The Michel Petrucciani Trio - Pianism (312)
7-46296-2	BT 85123 +1	Joe Henderson-The State of the Tenor - Live at The Village Vanguard,Vol. 1 (310,311)
7-46297-2	BT 85125	Jimmy Smith - Go for Whatcha Know (312)
7-46298-2	BT 85110	Bobby McFerrin - Spontaneous Inventions ((313,649)
7-46314-2	BT 85122 +1	The Don Pullen-George Adams Quartet - Breakthrough (313)
7-46333-2	BT 85130	Stanley Jordan - Standards,Volume 1 (316)
7-46335-2	BT 85103	George Russell & The Living Time Orchestra - The African Game (303)
7-46336-2	BT 85111	Bill Evans - The Alternative Man (305)
7-46338-2	BLP1595 +1	Cannonball Adderley - Somethin' Else (79)
7-46339-2	BST84195	Herbie Hancock - Maiden Voyage (179)
7-46391-2	BT 85132	George Russell & The Living Time Orchestra - So What (303)
7-46394-2	BST84146 +2	Dexter Gordon - Our Man In Paris (154)
7-46395-2	BT 85128	Out Of The Blue - Inside Track (314)
7-46397-2	BT 85135	Dexter Gordon - The Other Side of 'Round Midnight (310,313)
7-46398-2	BT 85129 +2	Duke Ellington - Money Jungle (628)
7-46399-2	BST84123 +2	Kenny Burrell - Midnight Blue (147)
7-46400-2	BST84029 +1	Art Blakey & The Jazz Messengers - The Big Beat (101)
7-46401-2	BST84353 +2	Chick Corea - The Song of Singing (240)
7-46402-2	BST84117 +1	Jimmy Smith - Back at The Chicken Shack (102,103)
7-46403-2	BST84232 +1	Wayne Shorter - Adam's Apple (190)
7-46426-2	BT 85126 +2	Joe Henderson-The State of The Tenor - Live at the Village Vanguard,Vol.2 (311)
7-46427-2	BT 85133 +2	Michel Petrucciani - Power of Three (314)
7-46428-2	BST84199 +1	Lee Morgan - The Rumproller (180,181)
7-46429-2	BST84193 +1	Art Blakey and The Jazz Messengers - Indestructible (165,166)
7-46430-2	BST84086 +1	Grant Green - Grandstand (125)
7-46431-2	BT 85134 +1	James Newton - Romance & Revolution (314)
7-46506-2	BST84109	Herbie Hancock - Takin' Off (139)
7-46507-2	BST84115	Freddie Hubbard - Hub-tones (144)
7-46508-2	BST81590 +1	Lee Morgan - Candy (75,77)
7-46509-2	BST84194	Wayne Shorter - Speak No Evil (176)
7-46510-2	BST84166	Joe Henderson - In 'N Out (165)
7-46511-2	BST84209	Hank Mobley - Dippin' (183)
7-46512-2	BST84264	McCoy Tyner - The Real McCoy (201)
7-46513-2	BST81588 +2	Sonny Clark - Cool Struttin' (76)
7-46514-2	BST84182	Wayne Shorter - Juju (169)
7-46515-2	BST84127 +1	Kenny Dorham - Una Mas (152)
7-46516-2	BST84003 +1	Art Blakey and The Jazz Messengers - Moanin' (85)

7-46517-2		Sonny Rollins - Live at The Village Vanguard,Vol.1 (73)
7-46518-2		Sonny Rollins - Live at The Village Vanguard,Vol.2 (73,74)
7-46519-2	BST81521 +2	Art Blakey Quintet - A Night at Birdland,Vol.1 (40,41)
7-46520-2	BST81522 +2	Art Blakey Quintet - A Night at Birdland,Vol.2 (40,41)
7-46521-2	BST81507 +3	Art Blakey At Cafe Bohemia with The Jazz Messengers,Vol.1 (49,50)
7-46522-2	BST81508 +3	Art Blakey At Cafe Bohemia with The Jazz Messengers,Vol.2 (49,50)
7-46523-2	BST84090	Art Blakey and The Jazz Messengers - Mosaic (127)
7-46524-2	BST84163	Eric Dolphy - Out to Lunch (163)
7-46525-2	BST81593	Lou Donaldson - Blues Walk (83)
7-46526-2	BST84017 +1	Horace Silver - Blowin' the Blues Away (94,95)
7-46527-2	BST84106	Jackie McLean - Let Freedom Ring (136)
7-46528-2	BST84031	Hank Mobley - Soul Station (99)
7-46529-2	BST84009 +1	The Amazing Bud Powell - The Scene Changes (88)
7-46530-2	BST84231	Bobby Hutcherson - Happenings (190)
7-46531-2	BST81600 +6	Introducing The Three Sounds (83,84)
7-46532-2	BST84049	Art Blakey and The Jazz Messengers - A Night in Tunisia (108,109)
7-46533-2	BST81569 +1	Paul Chambers - Bass on Top (67)
7-46534-2	BST84026	Donald Byrd - Fuego (95)
7-46535-2	BST84260	Cecil Taylor - Conquistador (196)
7-46536-2	BST81533 +2	Introducing Johnny Griffin (52)
7-46537-2	BST84198 +1	Bobby Hutcherson - Dialogue (179)
7-46538-2	BST84021 +3	Kenny Burrell at The Five Spot Cafe (93,94)
7-46539-2	BST84060 +2	Donald Byrd at The Half Note Cafe,Vol.1 (112)
7-46540-2	BST84061 +2	Donald Byrd at The Half Note Cafe,Vol.2 (112)
7-46541-2	BLP1524 +3	Kenny Dorham - 'Round Midnight at the Cafe Bohemia,Vol.1 (54)
7-46542-2		Kenny Dorham - 'Round Midnight at the Cafe Bohemia,Vol.2 (54)
7-46543-2	BST84039 +3	Stanley Turrentine - Look Out! (104)
7-46544-2	BST84083 +1	Dexter Gordon - Dexter Calling...(122)
7-46545-2	BST84196 +2	Freddie Hubbard - Blue Spirits (177,190)
7-46546-2		Jimmy Smith - House Party (70)
7-46547-2	BST81579 +3	Sonny Clark Trio (72)
7-46554-2	BN-LA452-G	Ronnie Laws - Pressure Sensitive (279)
7-46585-2	(Capitol)	Ronnie Laws - Classic Masters (279,296) (& further titles not from BN)
7-46625-2		The Best of Earl Klugh,Vol.1 (285,293,297,508,536,537,633,634)
7-46681-2	BST84204 +2	Dexter Gordon - Gettin' Around (182)
7-46755-2	BT 85136	James Blood Ulmer - America,Do You Remember The Love? (315)
7-46756-2	BT 85137 +4	Kenny Burrell - Generation (316)
7-46757-2	BT 85138	Tony Williams - Civilization (316)
7-46762-2	BT 85140	Stanley Turrentine - Wonderland (317)
7-46784-2	BT 85141 +2	OTB - Live at Mt. Fuji (315)
7-46814-2	BLP1527 +2	The Magnificent Thad Jones (55)
7-46815-2	BLP1535 +2	Kenny Dorham - Afro Cuban (45,46)
7-46816-2	BLP1550 +2	The Hank Mobley Quintet (62)
7-46817-2	BLP1557 +1	Lee Morgan,Vol.3 (62)
7-46818-2	BLP1558	Sonny Rollins,Vol.2 (63)
7-46819-2	BLP1576 +3	Sonny Clark - Sonny's Crib (70)
7-46820-2	BST81598 +1	Bud Powell - Time Waits (82)
7-46821-2	BST84137 +1	Jackie McLean - One Step Beyond (153)
7-46822-2	BST84132 +1	Grant Green - Feelin' The Spirit (146)
7-46823-2	BST84058 +1	Hank Mobley - Roll Call (113)
7-46824-2	BST8407-46 +2	Duke Jordan - Flight to Jordan (108)
7-46845-2	BST84321	Herbie Hancock - The Prisoner (225)
7-46846-2	BST84103 +2	Ike Quebec - Easy Living (133)
7-46848-2		The Complete Art Pepper Aladdin Recordings,Vol.2 - Modern Art (464,465)
7-46853-2		The Complete Art Pepper Aladdin Recordings,Vol.3 - The Art Of Pepper (465)
7-46858-2	LT-1065 +1	Art Blakey - Once Upon A Groove (310,311,552)
7-46863-2		The Complete Art Pepper Aladdin Recordings,Vol.1 (464,465)
7-46898-2	BT 85139	Freddie Hubbard - Life Flight (317)
7-46905-2	BLJ-7-46905	Jack Walrath - Master of Suspense (315,320)
7-46906-2	BLJ-7-46906	Dianne Reeves (318,319)

773

7-46907-2	BLJ-46907+1	The Don Pullen/George Adams Quartet - Song Everlasting (318)	
7-46993-2	BLJ-46993	Charnett Moffett - Net Man (318)	
7-48014-2	BN1-48014+1	Bennie Wallace - Border Town (320)	
7-48015-2	BLJ-48015+2	Mose Allison - Ever Since The World Ended (319)	
7-48016-2	BLJ-48016	Bireli Lagrene - Inferno (321)	
7-48017-2	BN1-48017+2	Freddie Hubbard/Woody Shaw - The Eternal Triangle (321)	
7-48041-2	BT 85131	Eric Dolphy - Other Aspects (455,456)	
7-48337-2	(E)CDBNX 1	Sampling Of Blue Notes:	
	(U.K. only)	Horace Silver (94)	Lou Donaldson (83)
		Stanley Turrentine (114)	Herbie Hancock (179)
		Jimmy Smith (78)	Cannonball Adderley (79)
		The Jazz Messengers (49)	Hank Mobley (99)
		Dexter Gordon (142)	Kenny Burrell (147)
		All Stars (310)	Lee Morgan (161)
7-48385-2	BNLA-667-G	Earl Klugh - Living Inside Your Love (293)	
7-48386-2	BNLA-737-H	Earl Klugh - Finger Paintings (296,297)	
7-48387-2		Earl Klugh - Crazy For You (293,296,537,538,539)	
7-48389-2		Earl Klugh - Magic In Your Eyes (633,634)	
7-48494-2	B1-48494	Tony Williams - Angel Street (322)	
7-48679-2	B1-48679	Michel Petrucciani - Michel Plays Petrucciani (322)	
7-48786-2		Billie Holiday - Billie's Blues (462,466,619)	
7-80054 2		Gonzalo Rubalcaba - Suite 4 y 20 (601)	
7-80251-2		Bireli Lagrene - Standards (353)	
7-80370-2		Dizzy Gillespie/Gil Fuller - The Monterey Jazz Festival Orchestra (562)	
7-80503-2		The Best Of Bobbi Humphrey (267,272,273,281,282)	
7-80505-2		The Best Of Earl Klugh,Vol.2 (293,296,297,508,509,537,539,633,634)	
7-80506-2		The Great Jazz Vocalists Sing The Gershwin Songbook:	
		Carmen MacRae (288)	David Allyn (554)
		Nat King Cole (489)	Mel Torme (471)
		Chet Baker (547)	Peggy Lee (468)
		Sarah Vaughan (579,581)	Dakota Staton (483)
		Annie Ross (556)	Johnny Hartman (572)
		Nancy Wilson (493)	Abbey Lincoln (534)
		June Christy (485)	Nina Simone (511)
		Beverley Kenny (571)	
7-80507-2	(2 CD Set)	Dizzy Gillespie - Live At The Village Vanguard (584)	
7-80510-2		Ron Carter Meets Bach (508)	
7-80511-2		Richie Beirach - Sunday Songs (594,599)	
7-80589-2		Michel Petrucciani Live (316)	
7-80590 2		Michel Petrucciani - Promenade With Duke (355)	
7-80591-2		Steve Masakowski - What It Was (357)	
7-80597-2		Chucho Valdès - Solo Piano (344)	
7-80598-2	(Pacific Jazz)	Irakere - Live At Ronnie Scott's (344)	
7-80599-2	(World Pacific)	El Jazz Cubano:	
		Irakere (344)	Chucho Valdes (344)
		(& further titles not from BN)	
7-80612-2	(E)CDBLT 1005	Tommy Smith - Paris (Europe only - see U.K. issues) (351)	
7-80679-2	B1-80679 -3	Blue 'N' Groovy (Blue Note Connects With The Good Vibes):	
		Duke Pearson (205)	The Jazz Messengers (117)
		Jack Wilson (206)	Tina Brooks (105)
		Stanley Turrentine (193)	Donald Byrd (112)
		Don Wilkerson (140)	Bobby Hutcherson (194)
		Lee Morgan (161)	Wayne Shorter (200)
		Herbie Hancock (168)	(see LP issue for 3 bonus tracks)
7-80696-2	(E)CDBLT 1006	Stan Tracey Octet - Portraits Plus (Europe only - see U.K. issues) (349)	

7-80701-2	B1-80701 -2	Afro Blue:	
		Dianne Reeves (339)	McCoy Tyner (207)
		Don Pullen (344)	Jackie McLean (110)
		Horace Parlan (150)	Art Blakey (86)
		Art Blakey (133)	Lee Morgan (163)
		James Moody (23)	Sabu Martinez (64)
		Art Blakey (86)	(see LP issue for 2 bonus tracks)
7-80703-2	(Europe)	Blue Testament - Blue Note Plays The Good Book:	
		Benny Green (346)	Dodo Greene (136)
		Johnny Griffin (73)	Grant Green (146)
		Horace Silver (45)	Hank Mobley (113)
		Fred Jackson (134)	Donald Byrd (131)
		Lou Donaldson (201)	Duke Pearson (224)
		Andrew Hill (227)	Donald Byrd (95)
7-80706-2		Rhapsody In Blue - Blue Note Plays The Music of George & Ira Gershwin:	
		Billy May (503)	Bill Potts (622)
		L. Almeida/B. Shank (554)	Kenny Burrell (81)
		Bob Cooper (479)	Jimmy Smith (70)
		Chet Baker (546)	Nat Cole (491)
		Frank Rosolino (479)	Coleman Hawkins (467)
		Julie London (535)	John Lewis (550)
		Thelonious Monk (20)	Nancy Wilson (502)
		Evans/Brookmeyer (623)	Ike Quebec (135)
		Hank Jones 5486)	Art Pepper (465)
7-80707-2		California Cool:	
		Mark Murphy (486)	Bobby Troup (535)
		Billy May (481)	Bob Gordon & Jack Montrose (547)
		Gerry Mulligan (619)	Bud Shank (563)
		Chico Hamilton (550)	Chet Baker & Bud Shank (551)
		Chet Baker (547)	June Christy (477)
		Jimmy Giuffre (479)	Art Pepper (464)
		Hampton Hawes (549)	Peggy Lee & G. Shearing (487)
		Konitz/Mulligan (546)	Curtis Amy & Dupree Bolton (560)
		Gloria Wood (490)	Serge Chaloff (482)
		Art Pepper/Sh. Rogers (552)	Sonny Criss (531)
		Teddy Edwards/Les McCann (556)	
7-80883-2	B1-80883	Us 3 - Hand On The Torch (350,351)	
7-80902-2		Joey Calderazzo - The Traveler (354)	
7-81191-2		Terumasa Hino - Unforgettable (601)	
7-81200-2	(Capitol Jazz)	Ruth Brown With The Thad Jones-Mel Lewis Orchestra - Fine Brown Frame (585)	
7-81202-2		Randy Brecker - Score (586,587)	
7-81212-2		Orphy Robinson - When Tomorrow Comes (345)	
7-81331-2		Blue Valentines:	
		Dinah Shore & A. Previn (487)	Lou Rawls (328)
		Nat Cole & G. Shearing (491)	Dianne Reeves (322)
		Sonny Clark (76)	Chico Hamilton (549)
		Hank Mobley (66)	King Pleasure (628)
		Peggy Lee (486)	Duke Pearson (96)
		George Shearing (492)	Hugh Lawson (591)
		Julie London (535)	Mel Torme (475)
		Stan Kenton (476)	Chet Baker (547)
7-81357 2	(G)F671007	Cassandra Wilson - Blue Light 'Til Dawn (356,359,361)	
7-81501-2		Miles Davis,Volume One (31,41)	
7-81502-2		Miles Davis,Volume 2 (34)	
7-81503-2		The Amazing Bud Powell,Vol.1 (25,27)	
7-81504-2		The Amazing Bud Powell,Vol.2 (27,37)	
7-81505-2		The Eminent Jay Jay Johnson,Vol.1 (36)	
7-81506-2		The Eminent Jay Jay Johnson,Vol.2 (43,48)	
7-81509-2		Milt Jackson (22,28,30)	

775

7-81510-2		Thelonious Monk - Genius Of Modern Music,Vol.1 (19,20,21)
7-81511-2		Thelonious Monk - Genius Of Modern Music,Vol.2 (28,32)
7-81520-2	BLP1520 +4	Horace Silver/Art Blakey - Sabu (33,39)
7-81526-2	BLP1526 + BST84428	Clifford Brown - Memorial Album (35,38)
7-81531-2		The Fabulous Fats Navarro,Vol.1: Fats Navarro (19,25) Tadd Dameron (471,473)
7-81532-2		The Fabulous Fats Navarro,Vol.2 (22,23,25)
7-81537-2		Lou Donaldson Quartet/Quintet/Sextet (32,33,43)
7-81539-2	BLP1539 +3	Horace Silver - 6 Pieces Of Silver (58,82)
7-81542-2	BLP1542	Sonny Rollins,Volume 1 (59)
7-81558-2	BLP1558	Sonny Rollins,Volume 2 (63)
7-81559-2	BLP1559	Johnny Griffin - A Blowing Session (63)
7-81571-2	BST84571 +1	Bud Powell - Bud! (The Amazing Bud Powell,Vol.3) (68)
7-81574-2	BLP1574 +3	Hank Mobley - Peckin' Time (77)
7-81596-2		Kenny Burrel - Blue Lights,Vol.1 (81)
7-81597-2		Kenny Burrell - Blue Lights,Vol.2 (81)
7-84001-2	BST84001	Sonny Rollins - Newk's Time (71)
7-84008-2	BLP4008	Fingerpoppin' With The Horace Silver Quintet (89)
7-84013-2	BST84013 +1	Jackie McLean - New Soil (91)
7-84019-2	BST84019	Donald Byrd - Byrd In Hand (92)
7-84030-2	BST84030 +2	Jimmy Smith - Crazy Baby (98)
7-84040-2	BST84040 +2	Freddie Hubbard - Open Sesame (104)
7-84042-2	BST84042	Horace Silver - Horace-Scope (106)
7-84047-2	BST84047	Art Taylor - A.T.'s Delight (108)
7-84049-2	BST84049 +2	Art Blakey & The Jazz Messengers - A Night In Tunisia (108,109)
7-84057-2	BST84057	Stanley Turrentine - Blue Hour (114)
7-84059-2	BST84059	Kenny Drew - Undercurrent (113)
7-84065-2	BLJ-84065 +2	Stanley Turrentine - Comin' Your Way (116)
7-84067-2	BST84067 +2	Jackie McLean - Bluesnik (115)
7-84073-2	BST84073 +1	Freddie Hubbard - Hub Cap (120)
7-84076-2	BST84076 +2	The Horace Silver Quintet - Doin' The Thing (122,123)
7-84077-2	BST84077 +2	Dexter Gordon - Doin' Alright (121)
7-84078-2	BST84078	Jimmy Smith - Midnight Special (102,103)
7-84080-2	BST84080 +1	Hank Mobley - Workout (119)
7-84087-2	BST84087 +3	Leo Parker - Let Me Tell You 'Bout It (126)
7-84091-2	BST84091 +2	Sonny Clark - Leapin' and Lopin' (129)
7-84095-2	BST84095	Leo Parker - Rollin' with Leo (128)
7-84096-2	BST84096 +1	Stanley Turrentine - That's Where It's At (132)
7-84098-2	BST84098 +2	Ike Quebec - Blue And Sentimental (131)
7-84104-2	BST84104 +4	Art Blakey And The Jazz Messengers - Buhaina's Delight (130,132)
7-84108-2	BST84108 +1	Lou Donaldson - The Natural Soul (138)
7-84115-2	BST84115 + 3	Freddie Hubbard - Hub-Tones (144)
7-84118-2	BST84188 + 1	Donald Byrd - Free Form (131)
7-84122-2	BST84122	Stanley Turrentine - Jubilee Shout!! (145)
7-84124-2	BST84124	Donald Byrd - A New Perspective (147)
7-84126-2	BST84126	Herbie Hancock - My Point of View (151)
7-84129-2	BST84129 + 1	Stanley Turrentine - Never Let Me Go (148,150)
7-84133-2	BST84133	Dexter Gordon - A Swingin' Affair (142)
7-84134-2	BST84134	Horace Parlan - Happy Frame Of Mind (150)
7-84135-2	BST84135	Freddie Hubbard - Here To Stay (146)
7-84140-2	BST84140	Joe Henderson - Page One (155)
7-84143-2	BST84143	Big John Patton - Blue John (155,156)
7-84147-2	BST84147	Herbie Hancock - Inventions and Dimensions (157)
7-84149-2		Hank Mobley - No Room For Squares (158)
7-84151-2	BST84151 +2	Andrew Hill - Black Fire (159)
7-84152-2	BST84152 +1	Joe Henderson - Our Thing (157)
7-84153-2	BST84153	Grachan Moncur III - Evolution (160)
7-84154-2	BST84154 +2	Grant Green - Idle Moments (159)
7-84157-2	BST84157 +1	Lee Morgan - The Sidewinder (161)

776

7-84164-2	BST84164 +2	Jimmy Smith - Prayer Meetin' (103,149)
7-84167-2	BST84167 +2	Andrew Hill - Point Of Departure (164)
7-84169-2	BST84169	Lee Morgan - Search For The New Land (163)
7-84170-2	BST84170	Art Blakey and The Jazz Messengers - Free For All (162)
7-84172-2	BST84172 +2	Freddie Hubbard - Breaking Point (166)
7-84173-2	BST84173 +1	Wayne Shorter - Night Dreamer (165)
7-84175-2	BST84175 +2	Herbie Hancock - Empyrean Isles (168)
7-84176-2	BST84176 +1	Dexter Gordon - One Flight Up (167)
7-84178-2	BST84178	Blue Mitchell - The Thing To Do (169)
7-84180-2	BST84180	Tony Williams - Life Time (171)
7-84181-2	BST84181	Kenny Dorham - Trompeta Toccata (172)
7-84185-2	BST84185 +4	Horace Silver - Song For My Father (159,162,173)
7-84186-2		Hank Mobley - The Turnaround (177)
7-84188-2	BST84188	Donald Byrd - I'm Trying To Get Home (175,176)
7-84189-2	BST84189	Joe Henderson - Inner Urge (175)
7-84191-2	BST84191	Duke Pearson - Wahoo! (175)
7-84212-2	BST84212 +1	Lee Morgan - The Gigolo (183,184)
7-84215-2	BST84215 +1	Jackie McLean - Right Now (176)
7-84220-2	BST84220	Horace Silver - The Cape Verdean Blues (185,186)
7-84221-2	BST84221	Larry Young - Unity (186)
7-84222-2	BST84222	Lee Morgan - Cornbread (185)
7-84224-2	BST84224	Ornette Coleman at The Golden Circle,Vol.1 (187,188)
7-84225-2	BST84225	Ornette Coleman at The Golden Circle,Vol.2 (187,188)
7-84227-2	BST84227 +1	Joe Henderson - Mode For Joe (189)
7-84230-2	BST84230	Hank Mobley - A Caddy For Daddy (188)
7-84237-2	BST84237 +1	Cecil Taylor - Unit Structures (192)
7-84243-2	BST84243 +4	Lee Morgan - Delightfulee Morgan (191,192)
7-84245-2	BST84245 +1	Art Blakey & The Jazz Messengers - Like Someone In Love (108,109)
7-84250-2	BST84250	Horace Silver - The Jody Grind (196,197)
7-84254-2	BST84254	Lou Donaldson - Lush Life (199)
7-84260-2	BST84260 +1	Cecil Taylor - Conquistador (196)
7-84261-2	BST84261	Sam Rivers - Dimensions And Extensions (200)
7-84263-2	BST84263	Lou Donaldson - Alligator Bogaloo (201)
7-84269-2	BST84269 + BST84296	Jimmy Smith - Open House/Plain Talk (101)
7-84271-2	BST84271	Lou Donaldson - Mr. Shing-A-Ling (206)
7-84273-2	BST84273	Hank Mobley - Hi Voltage (206)
7-84275-2	BST 84275	McCoy Tyner - Tender Moments (207)
7-84277-2	BST84277	Horace Silver - Serenade To A Soul Sister (210,211)
7-84282-2	BST84282	Elvin Jones - Puttin' It Together (212)
7-84287-2	BST84287	Ornette Coleman - New York Is Now (213,214)
7-84290-2	BST84290	Lonnie Smith - Think (216)
7-84291-2	BST84291	Bobby Hutcherson - Total Eclipse (215)
7-84307-2	BST84307	McCoy Tyner - Time for Tyner (214)
7-84331-2	BST84331	Elvin Jones - Poly-Currents (232)
7-84332-2	BST84332	Wayne Shorter - Super Nova (231)
7-84338-2	BST84338	McCoy Tyner - Expansions (217)
7-84345-2	BST84345	Jackie McLean - Demon's Dance (208)
7-84350-2	BST84350	Jimmy McGriff - Electric Funk (232)
7-84353-2	BST84353 +2	Chick Corea - The Song Of Singing (240)
7-84356-2	BST84356 +3	Ornette Coleman - Love Call (213,214)
7-84363-2	BST84363	Wayne Shorter - Odyssey of Iska (247)
7-84424-2	BST84424	Stanley Turrentine - Z.T.'s Blues (127)
7-84425-2	BST84425	Hank Mobley - Far Away Lands (202)
7-84426-2	BST84426	Lee Morgan - The Rajah (197)
7-84427-2	BST84427 +3	Jackie McLean - Tippin' The Scales (143)
7-84431-2	BST84431	Hank Mobley - Another Workout (130)
7-84432-2	BST84432 +3	Grant Green - Born To Be Blue (132,135)
7-84434-2	BST84434	The Three Sounds - Babe's Blues (125,136)
7-84435-2	BST84435 +5	Hank Mobley - Straight No Filter (151,193)

7-84436-2	BLP5006 +6	Art Blakey/James Moody - New Sounds:
		Art Blakey (21) James Moody (23)
7-84437-2		Paul Chambers - Chambers' Music (453,463)
7-84438-2	BLP5029 +1 + BLP5044 +1	Elmo Hope Trio and Quintet (36,42,553)
7-84439-2		Kenny Drew - Talkin' & Walkin' (463)
7-84441-2	LT-1054 +3	Jimmy Smith - Cool Blues (80)
7-84442-2	GXF-3053 +1	Grant Green - Matador (166,167)
7-84443-2	LT-988 +1	Wayne Shorter - The Soothsayer (178)
7-84444-2	GXF-3061	Bobby Hutcherson - Oblique (204)
7-84445-2	LT-989	Dexter Gordon - Clubhouse (182)
7-84446-2	LT-1058	Lee Morgan - Tom Cat (170)
7-84447-2		Elvin Jones - Live At The Lighthouse,Vol.1 (262)
7-84448-2		Elvin Jones - Live At The Lighthouse,Vol.2 (262)
		(Note: Vol. 1 & 2 = BN-LA-015-G2 + 5)
7-84451-2		Art Blakey And The Jazz Messengers - Three Blind Mice,Vol.1 (626)
7-84452-2		Art Blakey And The Jazz Messengers - Three Blind Mice,Vol.2 (126,626)
7-84456-2	BLP5025 +11	Wynton Kelly - Piano Interpretations (29)
7-84457-2		Booker Little 4 Plus Max Roach (620)
7-84458-2		Milt Jackson - Bags' Opus (621)
7-84459-2	BNP25108	Art Farmer - Modern Art (620)
7-84460-2		Kenny Dorham - Matador/Inta Somethin' (558,626)
7-84461-2		John Coltrane - Coltrane Time (620)
7-84462-2		Cecil Taylor - Jazz Advance (from Transition) (453)
7-84463-2		King Pleasure - Moody's Mood For Love (64,533,627,628)
7-84464-2		Babs Gonzales - Weird Lullaby (18,51,86,471,472,473)
7-84465-2		Chick Corea - Early Circle (246,247)
7-84466-2	BN-LA047-F	Donald Byrd - Black Byrd (260,264)
7-84467-2		The Benny Green Trio - That's Right (355,356)
7-85108-2	BT 85108	Charlie Parker At Storyville (450)
7-89002-2	BST89002	Sheila Jordan - Portrait of Sheila (142,144)
7-89032-2		Birks' Works (The Music Of Dizzy Gillespie):
		Kenny Burrell (93) Jimmy Smith (51)
		Art Blakey (109) Charlie Parker (450)
		Gil Fuller (562) Sonny Rollins (73)
		Sonny Clark (72) Clifford Jordan (74)
		Miles Davis (34) Metronome All Stars (470)
		Gil Evans (555)
7-89050-2		T.S. Monk - Changing Of The Guard (356)
7-89233-2		Don Pullen & The African-Brazilian Connection - Ode To Life (356)
7-89280-2		Jazz For A Sunday Afternoon - Live From The Village Vanguard (584)
7-89282-2		The Best Of Chick Corea (197,240,585)
7-89284-2		The Best Of Bobby Lyle (506,507)
7-89286-2		Kevin Eubanks - Spirit Talk (651)
7-89287-2		Joe Henderson - The Blue Note Years (4 CD set):
		Disc 1: (152,155,157,159,161,164)
		Disc 2: (164,165,172,173,175)
		Disc 3: (177,181,186,189,192,194)
		Disc 4: (194,198,201,225,235,311,594)
7-89297-2	(BN Contemp)	Everette Harp - Common Ground (359,363)
7-89383-2	BLP1580 +1	Johnny Griffin - The Congregation (73)
7-89384-2	BLP1201 (F)	Sidney Bechet - Jazz Classics,Vol.1 (3,4,12,13,17)
7-89385-2	BLP1202 (F)	Sidney Bechet - Jazz Classics,Vol.2 (3,12,13,17,30)
7-89390-2	BLP1554 (F)	Art Blakey - Orgy In Rhythm,Vol.1 (62)
7-89392-2	BST84027	Freddie Redd - The Connection (100)
7-89449-2	(U.K. only)	Stan Tracey - Jazz Suite: Under Milk Wood (645)
7-89450-2	(U.K. only)	Stan Tracey Duets - TNT/Sonatinas (646,648)
7-89540-2	BN-LA635-G	Carmen McRae - Can't Hide Love (288,289)
7-89541-2	BN-LA628-G	Ronnie Laws - Fever (284,285)
7-89542-2	BN-LA397-G	Marlena Shaw - Who Is This Bitch,Anyway? (274,275)

778

7-89543-2	BN-LA736-G	Noel Pointer - Phantazia (295,296)	
7-89544-2		Eliane Elias - Paulistana (602)	
7-89548-2		Ron Carter - Friends (602)	
7-89575-2		T.S. Monk - The Charm (372)	
7-89606-2	B1-89606 -1	Donald Byrd - Early Byrd (193,198,202,227,242,255)	
7-89622-2	B1-89622 -4	The Best Of Grant Green - Street Funk & Jazz Grooves (125,172,174,233,237,246,257,260)	
7-89662-2		Fareed Haque - Sacred Addiction (360)	
7-89678-2		Javon Jackson - When The Time Is Right (361,362)	
7-89679-2		Kevin Hays - Seventh Sense (365)	
7-89680-2		Tim Hagans - No Words (364)	
7-89792-2	BST84252	Duke Pearson - Honey Bee (198)	
7-89793-2	BST84360	Grant Green Alive! (246,247)	
7-89794-2	BST84359	Lou Donaldson - Pretty Things (236,243)	
7-89795-2	BST84329	Big John Patton - Let 'Em Roll (188)	
7-89796-2	BST84319	Donald Byrd - Fancy Free (227,228)	
7-89872-2	BLP1534 (Italy)	Paul Chambers - Whims of Chambers (57)	
7-89907-2	B1-89907 -3	Blue Break Beats,Volume Two:	
		Donald Byrd (267)	Lou Donaldson (254)
		Bobbi Humphrey (267)	Grant Green (237)
		Eddie Henderson (279)	Bobby Hutcherson (245)
		Gene Harris (273)	Blue Mitchell (207)
		Reuben Wilson (235)	Donald Byrd (198)
		Jimmy McGriff (586)	Gerald Wilson (559)
7-89910-2	(Europe)	Blue Moon:	
		Bob Belden (343)	Kenny Drew (with Jack Sheldon) (549)
		Greg Osby (340)	Dizzy Reece (97)
		Lou Donaldson (121)	Miles Davis (475)
		Johnny Smith (571)	Grant Green (132)
		Julie London (534)	Nat King Cole & George Shearing (491)
		Wynton Kelly (29)	Hoagy Carmichael (551)
		Carmell Jones (558)	Benny Green (346)
		Dianne Reeves (323)	
7-89914-2	(Europe)	Blue Eyes - Sinatra Songs The Blue Note Way:	
		Mark Murphy (486)	Ike Quebec (131)
		Renee Rosnes (599)	Duke Pearson (96)
		The Three Sounds (135,196)	Kenny Clarke-Francy Boland (455)
		Sonny Clark (87)	Sonny Rollins (73)
		Bud Powell (570)	Hank Mobley ((119)
		Lou Donaldson (32)	Gerry Mulligan & Lee Konitz (546)
		Tony Bennett (574)	Johnny Mercer (468)
		Beverley Kenney (572)	
7-89915-2	(Europe)	Cordon Blue - Savour The Soul Sauce With Blue Note:	
		Big John Patton (152)	Lou Donaldson (226)
		Lee Morgan (185)	Ronnie Foster (259)
		Kenny Burrell (147)	Freddie Roach (151)
		Lou Donaldson (65)	Freddie Hubbard (104)
		Stanley Turrentine (171)	Andrew Hill (219)
		Art Blakey & Jazz Mess. (90)	Bud Powell (37)
7-89916-2		The Best Of Michel Petrucciani - The Blue Note Years (312,314,322,331,342)	
7-90055-2	B1-90055 +8	Chick Corea - Now He Sings,Now He Sobs (585)	
7-90260-2	B1-90260	Kenny Burrell And The Jazz Guitar Band - Pieces Of Blue And The Blues (316)	
7-90261-2	B1-90261	Stanley Turrentine - La Place (323,325)	
7-90262-2	B1-90262	Bobby Watson & Horizon - No Question About It (323)	
7-90264-2	B1-90264	Dianne Reeves - I Remember (322,323,329)	
7-90583-2	UAJ 14003 +4	Bill Evans/Jim Hall - Undercurrent (626,627)	
7-90905-2	B1-90905	Freddie Hubbard - Times Are Changin' (326)	
7-90967-2	B1-90267 +2	Bireli Lagrene - Foreign Affairs (323,324)	
7-91101-2	B1-91101 +2	Jack Walrath - Neohippus (324)	

7-91138-2	B1-91138 +3	The Best Of Lee Morgan - The Blue Note Years (62,72,75,161,163,181,184,185)
7-91139-2	B1-91139 +1	The Best Of Dexter Gordon - The Blue Note Years (121,122,142,167)
7-91140-2	B1-91140 +2	The Best Of Jimmy Smith - The Blue Note Years (51,61,78,98,103,312)
7-91141-2	B1-91141 +3	The Best Of Wayne Shorter - The Blue Note Years (165,169,176,178,190,200,231)
7-91142-2	B1-91142 +2	The Best Of Herbie Hancock - The Blue Note Years (139,151,168,179,210)
7-91143-2	B1-91143 +4	The Best Of Horace Silver - The Blue Note Years (39,44,45,58,64,89,94)
7-91411-2	B1-91411	Eliane Elias - So Far So Close (329,330)
7-91441-2	B1-91441 +3	Lou Rawls & Les McCann Ltd. - Stormy Monday (491,492)
7-91650-2	B1-91650	Charnett Moffett- Beauty Within (326,327)
7-91651-2	B1-91651 +3	McCoy Tyner - Revelations (325)
7-91730-2	B1-91730	Ralph Peterson Quintet - V (588)
7-91731-2	B1-91731	Superblue (588)
7-91785-2	B1-91785 +1	Don Pullen - New Beginnings (326)
7-91915-2	B1-91915 +1	Bobby Watson - The Inventor (330)
7-91930-2	(E)CDBLT1001*	Tommy Smith - Step By Step (*original U.K. issue) (324)
7-91937-2	B1-91937	Lou Rawls - At Last (327,328)
7-91984-2	B1-91984 +1	George Adams - Nightingale (588)
7-92051-2	B1-92051 +3	Andrew Hill - Eternal Spirit (328)
7-92168-2	B1-92168 +2	Gil Melle - Mindscape (327)
7-92279-2	B1-92279 +1	Rick Margitza - Color (329)
7-92356-2	B1-92356 +1	Stanley Jordan - Cornucopia (315,326,329,330)

<u>BLUE NOTE 50th ANNIVERSARY COLLECTION</u>: (CDs & 2 LP Sets)

7-92465-2 BST2-92465 Vol.1: From Boogie To Bop (1939-1956):

Albert Ammons & Meade Lux Lewis (1)	Thelonious Monk(28)
Sidney Bechet (3)	Milt Jackson (30)
Edmond Hall (5)	Bud Powell (37)
Ike Quebec (10)	Miles Davis (34)
Thelonious Monk (21)	Clifford Brown (38)
Tadd Dameron with Fats Navarro (22)	Horace Silver (45)
James Moody (23)	Hank Mobley (49)
Bud Powell (27)	Sonny Rollins (59)
	Jimmy Smith (51)

7-92468-2 BST2-92468 Vol.2: The Jazz Message (1956-1965):

John Coltrane (71)	Art Blakey & The Jazz Messengers (127)
Jackie McLean (110)	Wayne Shorter (176)
Cannonball Adderley & Miles Davis (79)	Herbie Hancock (179)
Dexter Gordon (142)	Bobby Hutcherson (183)
	Larry Young (186)

7-92471-2 BST2-92471 Vol.3: Funk & Blues (1956-1967):

Horace Silver (58)	Joe Henderson with Kenny Dorham (155)
Art Blakey & The Jazz Messengers (85)	Horace Silver (173)
Jimmy Smith (103)	Blue Mitchell (169)
Donald Byrd (147)	Lee Morgan (261)
	Lou Donaldson (201)

7-92474-2 BST2-92474 Vol.4: Outside In (1964-1989):

Eric Dolphy (163)	Tony Williams (309)
Andrew Hill (159)	Freddie Hubbard & Woody Shaw (321)
Ornette Coleman (214)	Don Pullen-George Adams Quartet (313)
McCoy Tyner (201)	Joe Henderson (311)
OTB (309)	Michel Petrucciani (322)

7-92477-2 BST2-92477 Vol.5: Lighting The Fuse (1970-1989):

Grant Green (237)	Stanley Jordan (304)
Earl Klugh (285)	Stanley Turrentine (317)
Noel Pointer (295)	Benny Wallace (308)
Donald Byrd (264)	Bobby McFerrin (313)
Bobbi Humphrey (267)	Dianne Reeves (318,319)
Ronnie Laws (279)	Bireli Lagrene (323)

7-92547-2	(5 CD Box)	Blue Note 50th Anniversary Collection (same contents as Vol.1-5 shown above)
7-92563-2	B1-92563 +2	Michel Petrucciani - Music (331)
7-92750-2		Ralph Peterson Jr. - Triangular (588,589)
7-92812-2	B1-92812 (CDBNX 2*)	Special 50th Anniversary Sampler (*in UK: Blue Note Sampler,Vol.2): Dianne Reeves (319) — Albert Ammons & Meade Lux Lewis (2) Bireli Lagrene (323) — Miles Davis (31) Tommy Smith (324) — Bud Powell (37) Stanley Jordan (304) — Lou Donaldson (201) Bobby McFerrin (313) — Horace Silver (173)
7-92894-2	B1-92894 +3	John Scofield - Time On My Hands (332)
7-92997-2		Superblue 2 (590)
7-93006-2	B1-93006 +1	Out Of The Blue - Spiral Staircase (589)
7-93089-2		Eliane Elias Plays Jobim (592)
7-93170-2	B1-93170 +1	Tony Williams - Native Heart (331)
7-93201-2	B1-93201 +3	The Best Of Stanley Turrentine - The Blue Note Years (104,114,132,150,167,181,193,195,305)
7-93202-2	B1-93202 +1	The Best Of Freddie Hubbard - The Blue Note Years (104,120,126,144,166,312,321)
7-93203-2	B1-93203 +3	The Best of Sonny Rollins - The Blue Note Years (59,63,71,73,74)
7-93204-2	B1-93204 +4	The Best of Bud Powell - The Blue Note Years (25,27,37,68,82,88,154)
7-93205-2	B1-93205 +2	The Best Of Art Blakey And The Jazz Messengers - The Blue Note Years (85,101,109,127,162)
7-93206-2	B1-93206 +2	The Best of Horace Silver,Vol.2 - The Blue Note Years (173,185,186,196,210,263)
7-93415-2	UA	The Modern Jazz Quartet - Odds Against Tomorrow (624)
7-93476-2	B1-93476 +3	John Hart - One Down (589,590)
7-93561-2	B1-93561	Renée Rosnes (588,589,590)
7-93598-2	B1-93598 +3	McCoy Tyner - Things Ain't What They Used to Be (332)
7-93670-2		Benny Green - Lineage (335)
7-93671-2		Terumasa Hino - Bluestruck (592)
7-93840-2	B1-93840	Mose Allison - My Backyard (333)
7-93841-2	B1-93841 +2	Lou Rawls - It's Supposed To Be Fun (334,335,337)
7-93893-2		Gil Goldstein - City Of Dreams (591)
7-93894-2		Ralph Peterson - Volition (590)
7-93896-2		George Adams - America (591)
7-94204-2		The Manhattan Project (333)
7-94335-2	(E)CDBLT1002*	Tommy Smith - Peeping Tom (*original U.K. issue) (334)
7-94347-2		Don Pullen - Random Thoughts (335)
7-94591-2		Don Grolnick - Weaver of Dreams (328)
7-94848-2		Dexter Gordon - Nights At The Keystone,Vol.1 (457)
7-94849-2		Dexter Gordon - Nights At The Keystone,Vol.2 (457)
7-94850-2		Dexter Gordon - Nights At The Keystone,Vol.3 (457)
7-94857-2		Yule Struttin' (A Blue Note Christmas): Bobby Watson & Horizon (336) — John Hart (336) Stanley Jordan (316) — Count Basie (578) Lou Rawls (335) — John Scofield (336) Eliane Elias (338) — Joey Calderazzo (338) Chet Baker (547) — Dexter Gordon (648) Bennie Green (338) — Bennie Green (335) Dianne Reeves (338) — Rick Margitza (336)
7-94858-2		Rick Margitza - Hope (336)
7-94859-2		Renee Rosnes - For The Moment (594)
7-94861-2		Blue Beat - Blue Note Plays The Music Of Lennon & McCartney (US) Love Me Blue (The Music Of Lennon & McCartney) (U.K.): Stanley Turrentine (171,220) — Gil Goldstein (591) Stanley Jordan (304) — The Three Sounds (239) Grant Green (179) — Lonnie Smith (222) Lee Morgan (191) — The Jazz Crusaders (566) Bobby McFerrin (313)
7-94971-2		Andrew Hill - But Not Farewell (338,339)

781

7-95137-2 Bob Belden - Straight To My Heart (The Music Of Sting) (332,338,343)
7-95138-2 Joey Calderazzo - In The Door (339)
7-95139-2 Geri Allen - The Nurturer (593)
7-95148-2 Bobby Watson And Horizon - Post-Motown Bop (340)
7-95206-2 John Hart - Trust (596,597)
7-95263-2 Bireli Lagrene - Acoustic Moments (337,338)
7-95281-2 Stanley Turrentine - Ballads (114,116,127,150,193,229,305)
7-95414-2 Greg Osby - Man-Talk For Moderns Volume X (340)
7-95443-2 (The Netherlands) Rita Reys - Swing & Sweet (337)
7-95474-2 Charlie Haden & The Liberation Music Orchestra - Dream Keeper (650)
7-95475-2 Ralph Peterson Presents The Fo'tet (593)
7-95477-2 Bobby McFerrin/Chick Corea - Play (337)
7-95478-2 Gonzalo Rubalcaba - Discovery (594)
7-95479-2 John Scofield - Meant To Be (341)
7-95480-2 Michel Petrucciani - Playground (342)
7-95590-2 Blue Bossa:
Horace Parlan (113) Grant Green (137)
Charlie Rouse (145) Horace Silver (185)
John Patton (188) Eliane Elias (592)
Duke Pearson (226) Andrew Hill (216)
Ike Quebec (143) Hank Mobley (183)
Cannonball Adderley (493) Lou Donaldson (121)
Kenny Dorham (46) Donald Byrd (99)
7-95591-2 Blue Porter (US) /
Jazz Hot & Blue - Blue Note Plays The Music Of Cole Porter (U.K.):
Cannonball Adderley (79) Jackie McLean (96)
Dexter Gordon (142) Lee Morgan (72)
Paul Chambers (67) Hank Mobley (63)
Grant Green (179) Johnny Griffin (52)
Joe Henderson (175) Ike Quebec (131)
7-95627-2 The Best Of Joe Henderson - The Blue Note Years (155,157,165,175,189,311)
7-95636-2 The Best Of Thelonious Monk - The Blue Note Years (19,20,21,22,28,32)
7-96098-2 Blue Ballads (U.S.) /
Ballads In Blue - Big Sounds For The Small Hours (U.K.):
Stanley Turrentine (304) Bobby Hutcherson (190)
Lee Morgan (75) Pete La Roca (181)
Dexter Gordon (142) Clifford Brown (38)
Cannonball Adderley (79) Ike Quebec (129)
John Coltrane (71) McCoy Tyner (325)
Freddie Hubbard (120)
7-96101-2 BN-LA664-G Robbie Krieger And Friends (291,292)(World Pacific label)
7-96107-2 Ellis Marsalis Trio (594)
7-96108-2 Joe Lovano - Landmarks (595)
7-96110-2 The Best Of Blue Note,Vol.1 (also in box 8-36054-2):
John Coltrane (71) Lou Donaldson (83)
Herbie Hancock (179) Horace Silver (173)
Donald Byrd (147) Jimmy Smith (103)
Art Blakey & The Jazz Messengers (85) Kenny Burrell (147)
Lee Morgan (161)
7-96146-2 Eliane Elias - Fantasia (600)
7-96256-2 Jerry Bergonzi - Standard Gonz (592)
7-96429-2 McCoy Tyner - Soliloquy (341,342)
7-96452-2 (E)CDBLT 1003 Tommy Smith - Standards (Europe only - see U.K. issues) (341)
7-96485-2 Benny Green - Greens (342)

7-96563-2	(Europe)	So Blue So Funky,Vol.1 - Heroes Of The Hammond:	
	(reissued in U.S.)	Jimmy McGriff (616)	Big John Patton (163)
		Big John Patton (152)	Larry Young (174)
		Jimmy Smith (148)	George Braith (161)
		Freddie Roach (164)	Lou Donaldson (236)
		Fred Jackson (134)	Jack McDuff (228)
		Baby Face Willette (117)	Grant Green (237)

Note: A first U.S. release of above CD was entitled "Blue Funk"

7-96579-2	Dexter Gordon g- Ballads (121,122,142,154,167,182,457)	
7-96580-2	Blue Piano:	
	Albert Ammons (1)	Art Hodes (8)
	Meade Lux Lewis (10)	Bud Powell (27)
	Pete Johnson (4)	Lennie Tristano (472)
	Earl Hines (3)	Thelonious Monk (20)
	James P. Johnson (6)	Wynton Kelly (27)
	Nat Cole (469)	Al Haig (545)
	Art Tatum (473)	Horace Silver (39)
7-96581-2	Blue Guitar:	
	Charlie Christian (5)	Joe Pass (561)
	Jimmy Shirley (12)	Grant Green (124)
	Tiny Grimes (18)	Earl Klugh (509)
	T-Bone Walker (529)	Bireli Lagrene (323)
	Tal Farlow (41)	Al Di Meola (539)
	Sal Salvador (479)	John Scofield (332)
	Jim Hall (552)	John Hart (589)
	Kenny Burrell (50)	Stanley Jordan (306)
	Wes Montgomery (554)	
7-96582-2	Blue Vocals,Vol.1:	
	J.Mercer/J.Teagarden (466)	David Allyn (553)
	Louis & Bing (482)	King Pleasure (628)
	Nat King Cole (466)	Jon Hendricks (578)
	Charles Brown (461)	Billy Eckstine (574)
	Al Hibbler (460)	Joe Williams (575)
	T-Bone Walker (470)	Tony Bennett (574)
	Mel Torme (475)	Lou Rawls (328)
	Chet Baker (549)	Bill Henderson (84)
	Mark Murphy (486)	L. Armstrong & D.Ellington (578)
7-96583-2	Blue Vocals,Vol.2:	
	Anita O'Day (466)	Chris Connor (577)
	Jo Stafford (468)	Betty Carter (630)
	Kay Starr (467)	Nancy Wilson (490)
	Billie Holiday (462)	Dinah Washington (580)
	Abbey Lincoln (535)	Sarah Vaughan (580)
	Dakota Staton (483)	Sheila Jordan (142)
	Annie Ross (553)	Carmen MacRae (288)
	June Christy (485)	Dianne Reeves (323)
	Peggy Lee (485)	Rachelle Ferrell (593)
7-96688-2	Terumasa Hino - From The Heart (596)	
7-96689-2	George Adams - Old Feeling (596)	
7-96690-2	Jack DeJohnette's Special Edition - Earth Walk (597)	
7-96691-2	Geoff Keezer - Here And Now (595)	
7-96904-2	Blue Piano,Vol.2:	
	Duke Ellington (628)	Chick Corea (585)
	Herbie Nichols (48)	Michel Petrucciani (322)
	Cecil Taylor (453)	Benny Green (335)
	Sonny Clark (72)	McCoy Tyner (325)
	Bill Evans (627)	Don Pullen (326)
	Herbie Hancock (210)	Andrew Hill (339)
7-97159-2	Stanley Jordan - Stolen Moments (596)	

7-97190-2 The History Of Art Blakey & The Jazz Messengers (3 CD Set):
Disc 1: (21,41,44,49,85,552)
Disc 2: (90,101,109,117,127)
Disc 3: (162,165,166,581,646,648)
7-97196-2 Rick Margitza - This Is New (343)
7-97197-2 Gonzalo Rubalcaba - The Blessing (343)
7-97960-2 The Best Of Blue Note,Vol.2 (also in box 8-36054-2):
Horace Silver (58) Lee Morgan (181)
Sonny Rollins (59) Cannonball Adderley-Miles Davis (79)
Dexter Gordon (142) Joe Henderson (155)
Art Blakey (85) Herbie Hancock (139)
Horace Parlan (107)
7-98165-2 Joey Calderazzo - To Know One (345)
7-98166-2 Don Pullen And The African-Brazilian Connection - Kele Mou Bana (344)
7-98167-2 John Scofield - Grace Under Pressure (347)
7-98168-2 Renee Rosnes - Without Words (599)
7-98169-2 Tony Williams - The Story Of Neptune (347)
7-98170-2 Kevin Eubanks - Turning Point (347)
7-98171-2 Benny Green Trio - Testifyin' (346)
7-98287-2 Miles Davis - The Best Of The Capitol/Blue Note Years (31,34,41,79,472)
7-98289-2 The Best Of Ronnie Laws (279,284,286,296,537,634)
7-98290-2 Ralph Peterson - Ornettology (595)
7-98291-2 Critic's Choice (U.S. version - see 7-99790-2 for U.K. Version):
Benny Green (346) Ralph Peterson (595)
Joe Lovano (348) Don Pullen (335)
Greg Osby (340) John Scofield (347)
Jack DeJohnette (597) Gonzalo Rubalcaba (597)
Joey Calderazzo (345) Geri Allen (593)
Rick Margitza (343) Charlie Haden (650)
7-98306-2 (Capitol) The Legendary Lou Rawls (327,328,334) (& further titles not from BN)
7-98450-2 Albert Ammons/Meade Lux Lewis - The First Day (1,2)
7-98581-2 (Europe only) Orphy Robinson - When Tomorrow Comes (345)
(see 7-81212-2 for U.S. version)
7-98635-2 (B1-98635) Greg Osby - 3-D Lifestyles ((354,355)
7-98636-2 Joe Lovano - From The Soul (348)
7-98638-2 The Best Of Donald Byrd (260,264,267,274,274,283,289,291)
7-98689-2 Don Grolnick - Nighttown (347)
7-98959-2 New York Stories (348)
7-99031-2 (2 CD) Tony Williams - Tokyo Live (348,349)
7-99095-2 Blue Berlin:
Jackie McLean (96) Jutta Hipp (451)
Horace Parlan (113) Hank Mobley (99)
Peggy Lee (490) Stan Kenton (489)
Lou Donaldson (32) Bud Shank (551)
Elmo Hope (36) Joe Newman/Eddie Davis (574)
Lee Morgan (77) Bud Powell (581)
Miles Davis (31) Paul Chambers-Art Blakey (90)
Art Tatum (474) Sheila Jordan (144)
7-99099-2 Blue Boogie (Boogie Woogie Stride And The Piano Blues):
Albert Ammons (1,2) Sidney De Paris (9)
Meade Lux Lewis (1,2,5) Sammy Benskin (15)
Pete Johnson (4) Art Hodes (8,13)
James P. Johnson (6) Earl Hines (3)
Edmond Hall (6) Art Tatum (473)

7-99100-2	(Europe)	Le Paris Bleu:	
		Charles Trenet (518)	Django Reinhardt (518)
		Dexter Gordon (182)	Joe Pass (561)
		Milt Jackson (621)	Beverley Kenney (571)
		Lou Levy (534)	Thad Jones (55)
		Dinah Shore (487)	Larry Young (174)
		Annette Banneville (520)	Zoot Sims-Henri Renaud (519)
		Michel Petrucciani (331)	Chris Connor (581)
		Bud Powell (27)	Emmanuelle Torente (520)
		Gus Viseur (518)	Django & Quintet du HCF (519)
		Bireli Lagrene (337)	
7-99105-2		Blue 'n Soul - Blue Note Plays The Soul Hits:	
		Rachelle Ferrell (593)	Lonnie Smith (216)
		Blue Mitchell (184)	Earl Klugh (293)
		Stanley Turrentine (193)	Grant Green (257)
		Big John Patton (192,220)	Reuben Wilson (254)
		Richard Elliott (541)	Stanley Jordan (330)
		Hank Mobley (209)	Marlena Shaw (274)
7-99106-2		Blue Break Beats,Volume One:	
		Richard "G." Holmes (252)	Jimmy McGriff (586)
		Grant Green (246)	Grant Green (257)
		Lou Donaldson (226)	Lou Donaldson (226)
		Donald Byrd (227)	The Three Sounds (254)
		Eddie Henderson (287)	Donald Byrd (198)
		Bobbi Humphrey (267)	Herbie Hancock (168)
7-99175-2		The Art Of John Coltrane (57,70,71,620)	
7-99176-2		The Art Of Herbie Nichols (47,48,49,53)	
7-99177-2		The Art Of Larry Young (172,174,186,194,205,223)	
7-99178-2		The Art Of Ike Quebec (129,130,131,133,135,143)	
7-99427-2		Blue Gershwin:	
		Ike Quebec (135)	Stanley Turrentine (148)
		Thad Jones (55)	Jimmy Smith (101)
		Thelonious Monk (20)	Lou Donaldson (100)
		Dexter Gordon (154)	McCoy Tyner (325)
		Sonny Clark (67)	Curtis Fuller (66)
		Herbie Nichols (53)	Bill Evans (623)
		Kenny Burrell (307)	
7-99490-2	(Manhattan label)	Moonlight Love:	
		Eliane Elias (330)	Lou Rawls (334)
		Kenny Burrell & Grover Washington (304)	Stanley Jordan (304)
			Stanley Turrentine (324)
		Dianne Reeves (323)	McCoy Tyner (341)
		Michel Petrucciani (331)	(& further titles not from BN)
7-99492-2		Gonzalo Rubalcaba - Images (598)	
7-99493-2		Geri Allen - Maroons (599,600)	
7-99548-2	(Manhattan label)	Lou Rawls - Portrait Of The Blues (542,543)	
7-99614-2		T.S. Monk - Take One (345)	
7-99659-2	(Europe only)	Pyrotechnics (New British Jazz From Blue Note) (349,350)	
7-99786-2		Thelonious Monk Live At The Five Spot - Discovery! (454)	
7-99787-2		Charlie Parker - Bird At The Hi Hat (451)	
7-99790-2		Critics' Choice (U.K. edition - see 7-98291-2 for U.S. version):	
		Benny Green (346)	Don Pullen (361)
		Joe Lovano (348)	John Scofield (347)
		Greg Osby (340)	Geri Allen (593)
		Jack DeJohnette (597)	Gonzalo Rubalcaba (597)
		Rick Margitza (343)	Marisa Monte (525)
		Ralph Peterson (595)	
7-99829-2		Bob Belden - Turandot (352)	
7-99830 2		Joe Lovano - Universal Language (353,354)	
7-99886-2		John Scofield - What We Do (352)	

7-99918-2 (Holland only) Jaavanse Jonsens Jazz Collection '92:
Benny Green (346) Don Pullen (335)
Joe Lovano (348) John Scofield (347)
Greg Osby (340) Gonzalo Rubalcaba (597)
Jack DeJohnette (597) Rachelle Ferrell (510)
Joey Calderazzo (345) Orphy Robinson (345)
Dianne Reeves (339)
7-99965-2 The Boys Choir Of Harlem - Christmas Carols And Sacred Songs (578)

8-14710-2 (Australia only) Salsa Blue:
Bossa 3 (522) Milton Nascimento (523)
Djavan(524) Mandrake Som (521)
Marcos Valle (522) Eliane Elias (592)
Som Tres (523) Irakere (344)
Joao Gilberto (521) Pablo Milanes (650)
Duke Pearson (232)
8-14808-2 (Australia only) Ice Blue:
Grant Green (159) Cassandra Wilson (381)
Stanley Turrentine (114) Kurt Elling (366)
Kenny Burrell (147) Charlie Hunter (387)
Lou Donaldson (83) Julie London (534)
John Scofield (332) Holly Cole (544)
Marisa Monte (525)
8-15892-2 (CD Single) Us3 - Cantaloop (350,351)

8-21146-2 The Best Of Joe Williams (241,573,574,575,576,577,578,579,582,583)
8-21220-2 (Sweden only) Viktoria Tolstoy - White Russian (408)
8-21259-2 Sidney Bechet - Runnin' Wild (24,26)
8-21260-2 Edmond Hall - Profoundly Blue (5,7,8)
8-21261-2 George Lewis And His New Orleans Stompers (47)
8-21262-2 The Blue Note Jazzmen:
Ed Hall (6) James P. Johnson (7,11)
Sidney De Paris (9)
8-21280-2 (3 CD Box) Low And Slow - The Blue Note Tenor Sax Ballads Collection:
Stanley Turrentine - Ballads (7-95281-2)
Dexter Gordon - Ballads (7-96579-2)
Ike Quebec - Ballads (8-56690-2)
8-21281-2 Gene Harris & The Three Sounds - Standards (95,134,140,141)
8-21282-2 Jimmy Smith - Standards (70,82,92)
8-21283-2 Sonny Clark - Standards (86,87)
8-21284-2 Grant Green - Standards (126)
8-21286-2 BST84259 +1 Donald Byrd - Blackjack (154,198)
8-21287-2 BST84156 +3 Art Blakey & The Jazz Messengers - The Freedom Rider (117,123)
8-21288-2 BST84131 Horace Silver - Silver's Serenade (153)
8-21289-2 BST84155 +7 The Three Sounds - Black Orchid (134,135,136,140)
8-21290-2 BST84253 Grant Green - Street Of Dreams (174)
8-21371-2 Sonny Rollins - The Complete Blue Note Recordings (5 CD Slip case, containing 7-46517-2,7-46518-2,7-81542-2,7-81558-2 & 7-84001-2) (59,63,71,73,74)
8-21381-2 Jazz Profile - Introduction Sampler:
Miles Davis (473) Sarah Vaughan (579)
Dinah Washington (579) Duke Ellington (477)
Count Basie (578) Thelonious Monk (28)
Bud Powell (570) Sonny Rollins (63)
Chet Baker (547) Dexter Gordon (142)
8-21431-2 George Howard - There's A Riot Goin' On (417)
8-21533-2 Dianne Reeves - New Morning (409)
8-21734-2 BST84187 +1 (Connoisseur Series) Larry Young - Into Somethin' (174)
8-21735-2 BST84074 +2 (Connoisseur Series) Horace Parlan - On The Spur Of The Moment (119)
8-21736-2 BST84105 (Connoisseur Series) Ike Quebec - It Might As Well Be Spring (130)
8-21737-2 BLP4052 (Connoisseur Series) Tina Brooks - Back To The Tracks (110,111)

8-21738-2 BST84045 +2 (Connoisseur Series) Freddie Redd - Shades Of Redd (109)
8-21819-2 BST84094 +7 (Connoisseur Series) Fred Jackson - Hootin' 'N Tootin' (134,136)
8-21944-2 (Germany only) Dreiklang (401)

8-23082-2 Chucho Valdes - Bele Bele En La Habana (419)
8-23108-2 Charlie Hunter - Return Of The Candyman (413)
8-23211-2 Mose Allison - Gimcracks And Gewgaws (657)
8-23213-2 Lee Morgan - Standards (198)
8-23372-2 The Best Of Ornette Coleman - The Blue Note Years (187,188,195,201,214)
8-23373-2 The Best Of Clifford Brown (35,36,38,40,41,548)
8-23392-2 Mark Shim - Turbulent Flow (432)
8-23487-2 Stefon Harris- A Cloud of Red Dust (414)
8-23513-2 Don Pullen - The Best Of The Blue Note Years (313,318,326,335,356,379)
8-23514-2 Jazz Profile - Dexter Gordon (121,122,142,154,182,469,471)
8-23515-2 Jazz Profile - Miles Davis (31,34,41,79,473,475)
8-23516-2 Jazz Profile - Sonny Rollins (59,63,71,73,74)
8-23517-2 Jazz Profile - Sarah Vaughan (449)
8-23518-2 Jazz Profile - Thelonious Monk (19,20,21,28,32,454)
8-23684-2 Jane Bunnett And The Spirits Of Havana - Chamalongo (655)
8-23735-2 The Best Of Najee:
Freddie Jackson (509) Najee (512,513,540)

Following block is made of French issues in Jazz Profile Series: (see equivalents shown in second column):
8-23967-2 8-54906-2 Jazz Profile 8 - Bud Powell
8-23968-2 8-59072-2 Jazz Profile 20 - Wayne Shorter
8-23969-2 8-33146-2 Jazz Profile 17 - Benny Carter (Capitol)
8-23970-2 8-59071-2 Jazz Profile 18 - Freddie Hubbard
8-23971-2 8-33207-2 Jazz Profile 13 - McCoy Tyner
8-23972-2 8-54902-2 Jazz Profile 1 - Chet Baker (Pacific Jazz)
8-23973-2 8-54905-2 Jazz Profile 10 - Gerry Mulligan
8-23974-2 8-54899-2 Jazz Profile 3 - Art Blakey
8-23975-2 8-54901-2 Jazz Profile 7 - Lee Morgan
8-23976-2 8-54904-2 Jazz Profile 2 - Herbie Hancock
8-23977-2 8-54898-2 Jazz Profile 4 - Cannonball Adderley (Capitol)
8-23978-2 8-54900-2 Jazz Profile 6 - Duke Ellington (Capitol)
8-23979-2 8-33243-2 Jazz Profile 19 - Stan Kenton (Capitol)
8-23980-2 8-54907-2 Jazz Profile 5 - Dinah Washington (Roulette)
8-23982-2 8-55230-2 Jazz Profile 9 - Mose Allison

8-27014-2 Joe Lovano - Tenor Legacy (360)
8-27298-2 The Best Of Lou Donaldson,Vol.1 (65,76,83,87,96,116,138,199,201)
8-27312-2 The Best Of Grant Green (116,120,125,159,167,179)
8-27323-2 The Best Of The Three Sounds (83,84,91,105,114,125,136)
8-27324-2 LT-1000 Bob Brookmeyer & Bill Evans (623)
8-27325-2 Charles Mingus - Jazz Portraits (Mingus In Wonderland) (622)
8-27326-2 (Manhattan) Earl Klugh - Ballads (285,293,297) (& further titles not from BN)
8-27327-2 John Scofield - Hand Jive (362)
8-27475-2 Miles Davis - The Blue Note And Capitol Recordings (4 CD Set)
(= 7-81501-2 + 7-81502-2 + 7-46638-2 + 7-92862-2)
8-27533-2 Giant Steps:
Us3 (351) Reuben Wilson (224)
Greg Osby (354) Us3 (350)
Donald Byrd (264) Lou Donaldson (226)
Soon e MC (520 Gang Starr (511)
Guru (511) The UMC's (516)
Beastie Boys (509)
8-27640-2 Mose Allison - The Earth Wants You (361)
8-27645-2 Ralph Peterson Quintet - Art (600)
8-27765-2 John Scofield & Pat Metheny - I Can See Your House From Here (365)
8-27798-2 (E)CDBLT 1007 Andy Sheppard - Rhythm Method (Europe only - see U.K. issues) (358,360)
8-27819-2 BN-LA249-G +1 Bobby Hutcherson - Live At Montreux (268)

8-27820-2		Rachelle Ferrell - First Instrument (333,593)
8-27838-2		Richard Elliott - After Dark (367,368)
8-28243-2		Sonny Fortune - Four In One (365)
8-28263-2	(2 CD Set)	Straight No Chaser - The Original Sources of Us3's Hand On The Torch: Pee Wee Marquette (40) Lou Donaldson (116) Herbie Hancock (151,168) Thelonious Monk (28) Reuben Wilson (219) Grant Green (246) Art Blakey (127,552) Donald Byrd (112,274) John Patton (220) Horace Silver (122,173) Bobby Hutcherson (245)
8-28264-2		Gonzalo Rubalcaba - Rapsodia (602)
8-28265-2	BST84342	Grant Green - Green Is Beautiful (237)
8-28266-2	BST84351	Lonnie Smith - Drives (236)
8-28267-2	BST84318	Lou Donaldson - Hot Dog (226)
8-28268-2	BST84362	Bobby Hutcherson - San Francisco (245)
8-28269-2	BST84267 +1	Duke Pearson - The Right Touch (205)
8-28353-2	UA	Charles Mingus - The Complete Town Hall Concert (628,629)
8-28423-2		McCoy Tyner & Bobby Hutcherson - Manhattan Moods (364)
8-28447-2		Junko Onishi Trio - Cruisin' (603)
8-28532-2		Pieces Of A Dream - Goodbye Manhattan (371,372)
8-28719 2	(E)CDBLT 1008	Andy Sheppard - Delivery Suite (Europe only - see U.K. issues) (360)
8-28879 2	BT85123 + 85126	Joe Henderson - The State Of The Tenor:Live At The Village Vanguard (2 CD Set) (310,311)
8-28882-2	BST84207 + 84208	Freddie Hubbard - Night Of The Cookers (2 CD Set) (180)
8-28885-2	BST84069 + 84070	Stanley Turrentine - Up At Minton's (2 CD Set) (118)
8-28888-2	(2 CD Set)	Art Blakey & The Jazz Messengers At The Jazz Corner Of The World (= BST84015 + BST84016)(90)
8-28891-2		The Best Of Sidney Bechet (3,12,13,16,17,24,26,37)
8-28892-2		The Port Of Harlem Jazzmen: The Port Of Harlem Jazzmen (2,3) Sidney Bechet/Teddy Bunn (4)
8-28893-2		Reminiscing At Blue Note: Earl Hines (3) James P. Johnson (6) Pete Johnson (4)
8-28974-2		Lena Horne - We'll Be Together Again (362)
8-28975-2	BLP4041+2	(Connoisseur Series) Tina Brooks - True Blue (105)
8-28976-2	BST84247	(Connoisseur Series) Don Cherry - Symphony For Improvisers (195)
8-28977-2	BLP1549 +1	(Connoisseur Series) Clifford Jordan-John Gilmore - Blowin' In From Chicago (61)
8-28978-2	BST84063	(Connoisseur Series) Kenny Dorham - Whistle Stop (115)
8-28981-2	BST84159 +1	(Connoisseur Series) Andrew Hill - Judgment (162)
8-28982-2	BST84246	(Connoisseur Series) Ornette Coleman - The Empty Foxhole (195)
8-28998-2	BST84084 +1	(Connoisseur Series) Baby Face Willette - Stop And Listen (123)
8-29027-2	BST84213	(Connoisseur Series) Bobby Hutcherson - Components (183)
8-29029-2	(2 CD Set)	Woody Shaw - Live/Bemsha Swing (458)
8-29092-2		So Blue So Funky,Vol.2 - Heroes Of The Hammond: Jimmy McGriff (630) Jimmy Lytle (565) Curtis Amy & Paul Bryant (557) Baby Face Willette (117) Freddie Roach (160) Big John Patton (210) George Braith (157) Larry Young (223) Jimmy Smith (149) Lou Donaldson (206) Richard Groove Holmes (558)
8-29095-2	(Europe)	Blue Broadway - Show Tunes Blue Note Style: Bobby Darin (494) Ike Quebec (129) Bennie Green (86) The Three Sounds (114) Lee Morgan (77) Horace Parlan (113) Jutta Hipp (56) Wes Montgomery (554) Cannonball Adderley (494) McCoy Tyner (214) Nancy Wilson (490) Betty Carter (630) Stan Kenton (489) Count Basie (574) Jack Montrose (549) Billy Eckstine (576) Lou Rawls (335)

8-29100-2	BST84219	(Connoisseur Series) Wayne Shorter - The All Seeing Eye (186)
8-29102-2	BLP1536 +1	(Connoisseur Series) J.R. Monterose (57)
8-29125-2	(2 CD Set)	Joe Lovano Quartets Live At The Village Vanguard (366,377)
8-29156-2	BST84166 +1	Joe Henderson - In 'n Out (165)
8-29196-2		Blue Brazil (Blue Note in A Latin Groove):
		Luiz Arruda Paez (522) — Joyce (524)
		Alaide Costa (524) — Lo Borges (524)
		Mandrake Som (521) — Som Tres (523)
		Quarteto Novo (522) — Elza Soares (522)
		Perry Ribiero (521) — Quarteto Novo (522)
		Milton Banana (521) — Eumir Deodato (523)
		Edu Lobo (523) — Johnny Alf (524)
		Bossa 3 (522) — Joao Donato (523)
		Marcos Valle (522) — Victor Assis (524)
8-29223-2	(E)CDBLT 1009	Orphy Robinson - The Vibes Describes (Europe only)(see U.K. issues)(358)
8-29266-2		Greg Osby - Black Book (367)
8-29268-2		Benny Green - The Place To Be (366,367)
8-29269-2		Joe Lovano - Rush Hour (368,369)
8-29270-2		Fareed Haque - Opaque (378)
8-29331-2		Herbie Hancock - Cantaloupe Island (139,151,168,179)
8-29351-2		Jacky Terrasson (369,370)
8-29457-2	(Capitol U.K.)	Hand On The Torch/The Jazz Mixes (2 CD Set) (350,351)
8-29479-2		Gary Le Mel - Romancing The Screen (651)
8-29511-2		Dianne Reeves - Quiet After The Storm (374,375)
8-29865-2		Capitol Rare - Funky Notes From The West Coast:
		Gene Harris (273,298) — Caldera (506)
		Eddie Henderson (287) — Nancy Wilson (507)
		Ben Sidran (503) — Natalie Cole (506)
		Gary Bartz (506) — Frankie Beverley & Maze (506)
		Rance Allen (506) — Janet Lawson (631)
		Bobby Lyle (506) — Ronnie Laws (635)
		A Taste Of Honey (507) — The Reflections (505)
8-29905-2	BST84317 +1	Reuben Wilson - Love Bug (224,233)
8-29906-2	BST84343	Reuben Wilson - Blue Mode (235)
8-29908-2	BST84268 +5	Stanley Turrentine - Easy Walker (193,204,229)
8-29964-2	(Europe)	The Best Of Blue Note - A Selection From 25 Best Albums:
		Art Blakey (85) — Dexter Gordon (142)
		Kenny Burrell (147) — Chet Baker (549)
		Duke Ellington (628) — Sonny Rollins (71)
		Count Basie (573) — Thelonious Monk (28)
		Bud Powell (27) — John Coltrane (71)
		Charlie Parker (450) — Herbie Hancock (179)
		Miles Davis (475) — Horace Silver (159)
8-30027-2	B1-30027	Us3 - Broadway & 52nd (393)
8-30028-2		Geri Allen - Twenty One (605)
8-30081-2	(Europe)	Blue Note Now!:
		John Scofield (362) — Benny Green (367)
		McCoy Tyner/Hutcherson (364) — Sonny Fortune (365)
		Tim Hagans (364) — Gonzalo Rubalcaba (603)
		Javon Jackson (361) — Joe Lovano (360)
		Kevin Hays (365) — Jacky Terrasson (369)
8-30082-2		Duke Ellington - Togo Brava Suite (632)
8-30083-2	(4 CD Set)	Bud Powell - The Complete Blue Note And Roost Recordings (25,27,37,68,82,88,154,570,571)
8-30132-2		Kevin Eubanks - Spirit Talk 2/Revelations (370)
8-30133-2		Kevin Eubanks - Live At Bradley's (369)
8-30244-2		Javon Jackson - For One Who Knows (376)
8-30271-2		Don Pullen & The African Brazilian Connection - Live...Again (361)
8-30363-2	(4 CD Set)	The Complete Blue Note Recordings of Thelonious Monk (19,20,21,22,28,32,63,454)
8-30450-2		Terumasa Hino - Spark (605)

8-30451-2		Jimmy Smith - The Master (604)
8-30454-2		Presenting Joe Williams And Thad Jones/Mel Lewis Orchestra (582)
8-30490-2		Gonzalo Rubalcaba - Diz (603)
8-30491-2		Gonzalo Rubalcaba In The U.S.A. - Imagine (357,357,370)
8-30492-2		Ron Carter - Jazz,My Romance (604)
8-30493-2		The Best Of Kenny Burrell (50,60,81,147,151,304,307,316)
8-30494-2		Jack DeJohnette - Extra Special Edition (604)
8-30645-2		Kurt Elling - Close your Eyes (366,370,374)
8-30721-2	B1-30721 -4	Lou Donaldson - The Righteous Reed! The Best Of Poppa Lou (U.K. issue) (201,206,211,220,226,236,254,266)
8-30724-2	(E)8-30724-1	Pullin' Out The Stops! The Best Of Jimmy McGriff (UK issue) (232,253,503,582,584,586,616,630,636)
8-30725-2	B1-30725 -2	Deep Groove! - The Best Of Cannonball Adderley (UK issue) (495,496,497,498,500,502,503)
8-30728-2	#B1-30728	Best Of Big John Patton - The Organization (#not identical to LP set) (U.K. issue) (152,156,168,178,188,192,220,230,248)
8-30790-2		Marcus Printup - Song For The Beautiful Woman (375)
8-31108-2		Steve Masakowski - Direct Axecess (372)
8-31139-2	(E)CDBLT 1010	Stan Tracey - Live At The Q.E.H. (Europe only - see U.K issues) (652)
8-31223-2	BST84306	John Patton - Understanding (220)
8-31247-2	BST84327	Grant Green - Carryin' On (233)
8-31248-2	BST84337	Lou Donaldson - Everything I Play Is Funky (236)
8-31249-2	BST84326 +1	Lonnie Smith - Move Your Hand (230)
8-31502-2		The Best Of Stanley Jordan - The Blue Note Years (304,306,316,329,541,596)
8-31677-2		Bobby McFerrin - Bang! Zoom (378)
8-31808-2		Tim Hagans - Audible Architecture (376)
8-31809-2		Charlie Hunter Trio - Bing,Bing,Bing! (376)
8-31875-2	B1-31875 +1	Donald Byrd - Kofi (235,250)
8-31876-2	B1-31876 +2	Lou Donaldson - The Scorpion/Live At The Cadillac Club (249,250)
8-31877-2		An Evening With Lena Horne (373)
8-31878-2	B1-31878	John Patton - Boogaloo (216)
8-31880-2	B1-31880	Lonnie Smith - Live At Club Mozambique (242)
8-31883-2	B1-31883	The Lost Grooves: Reuben Wilson (233) John Patton (230) Grant Green (246) Stanley Turrentine (204,209) Lou Donaldson (220,249) Lonnie Smith (230)
8-31886-2		Junko Onishi - Live At The Village Vanguard (606)

Following block is made of South African reissues:

8-31915-2	BST84130	John Patton - Along Came John (152) (reissued in US & Europe -May 2000)
8-31916-2	BST84174	John Patton - The Way I Feel (168)
8-31917-2	BST84341	The Three Sounds - Soul Symphony (231)
8-31918-2	BST84301	The Three Sounds - Elegant Soul (218)

8-32073-2		Eliane Elias - Solos And Duets (375)
8-32082-2	BST8438	Ronnie Foster - The Two-Headed Freap (259)
8-32087-2	BST84165	(Connoisseur Series) Jackie McLean - Destination Out (158)
8-32088-2	BST84071 +2	(Connoisseur Series) Grant Green - Green Street (120)
8-32089-2	BST84034	(Connoisseur Series) Lee Morgan - Lee Way (103)
8-32090-2	BST84093 +1	(Connoisseur Series) Ike Quebec - Heavy Soul (129)
8-32091-2	BST84205	(Connoisseur Series) Pete La Roca - Basra (181)
8-32092-2	BST84177	(Connoisseur Series) Grachan Moncur III - Some Other Stuff (169)
8-32093-2	BST84006 +2	(Connoisseur Series) Dizzy Reece - Blues In Trinity (83)
8-32094-2	BST84085 +2	(Connoisseur Series) Freddie Hubbard - Ready For Freddie (126)
8-32095-2	BST84036+1	(Connoisseur Series) Lou Donaldson - Sunny Side Up (99,100)
8-32096-2	BST84297	(Connoisseur Series) Wayne Shorter - Schizophrenia (200)
8-32097-2	BST84160+2	(Connoisseur Series) Andrew Hill - Smokestack (160)
8-32098-2	BST84018	(Connoisseur Series) Walter Davis Jr. - Davis Cup (93)

 790

8-32127-2 Jazz To The World:
Herb Alpert (654) Herbie Hancock/Eliane Elias (652)
Dianne Reeves (653) John McLaughlin (653)
Fourplay (653) Holly Cole (650)
Diana Krall (654) Steps Ahead (653)
Stanley Clarke (653) Anita Baker (652)
Michael Franks (653) Chick Corea (653)
The Brecker Bothers (653) Dave Koz (653)
Cassandra Wilson (653) Dr. John (653)
8-32129-2 BST84144 (Connoisseur Series) Johnny Coles - Little Johnny C (156)
8-32139-2 Sarah Vaughan & Lester Young - One Night Stand/Town Hall Concert (449)
8-32166-2 Bob Belden's Shades Of Blue:
Dianne Reeves (607) Holly Cole (608)
Jacky Terrasson (606) Geoff Keezer (607)
John Scofield (607) Jerry Dodgion (607)
Cassandra Wilson (607) Kurt Elling (607)
Tim Hagans (607) Don Sickler (607)
Marcus Printup (607) Eliane Elias (606)
8-32222-2 Caecilie Norby - Caecilie (373)
8-32489-2 Bill Stewart - Snide Remarks (379)
8-32491-2 Kevin Hays - Go Round (377)
8-32620-2 Richard Elliot - City Speak (384)
8-32746-2 (2 CD Set) Duke Ellington - 70th Birthday Concert (631)
8-32747-2 (2 CD Set) The Freddie Hubbard-Woody Shaw Sessions (312,321)
(= BT 85121 + BN2-48017)
8-32749-2 BN-LA251-G Marlena Shaw - Live At Montreux (268)
8-32750-2 BST84255 +2 Jimmy Smith - I'm Movin' On (148)
8-32787-2 (2 CD set) The Complete Aladdin Sessions Of Lester Young (459,460,461)
8-32799-2 Sonny Fortune - A Better Understanding (378)
8-32800-2 Don Pullen - Sacred Common Ground (379)
8-32801-2 John Scofield - Groove Elation (382)
8-32861-2 (US Version) Cassandra Wilson - New Moon Daughter (380,381)
8-32993-2 Esquire Jazz Collection: Toward The Light:
Herbie Hancock (168) Freddie Hubbard (120)
Joe Henderson (155) Art Blakey (162)
Larry Young (186) Stanley Turrentine (162)
Dexter Gordon (122) Jackie McLean (153)
Lee Morgan (161)
8-32994-2 Esquire Jazz Collection: The Voice Of The Soul:
Billie Holiday (462) Chet Baker (547)
Nat Cole (466) Joe Williams (575)
June Chrusty (477) Dinah Washington (580)
Nancy Wilson (490) Tony Bennett & Count Basie (574)
Nina Simone (512) Billy Eckstine & Count Basie (574)
Abbey Lincoln (534) Sarah Vaughan (580)
8-32995-2 Esquire Jazz Collection: Breakthrough!:
Jacky Terrasson (370) Tim Hagans (376)
Marcus Printup (375) Kevin Hays (377)
Benny Green (366) Joe Lovano (368)
Javon Jackson (376) Fareed Haque (378)
Gonzalo Rubalcaba (603) Bill Stewart (379)
Junko Onishi (606) Charlie Hunter (376)
Geri Allen (605)
8-33060-2 Dianne Reeves - Bridges (426)
8-33092-2 Wouldn't It Be Nice - A Jazz Portrait Of Brian Wilson (654,655)
8-33114-2 Joe Lovano - Trio Fascination (413)
8-33135-2 Amadeo - The Rhythm Of Life (657)
8-33146-2 Jazz Profile 17 - Benny Carter (466,467,469,619,624,625)
8-33205-2 Jazz Profile 11 - Grant Green (116,137,146,166,172,174)
8-33206-2 Jazz Profile 14 - Jimmy Smith (50,56,60,70,78,101,102,148)
8-33207-2 Jazz Profile 13 - McCoy Tyner (201,207,214,217,221,247,307,332)

791

8-33208-2 Jazz Profile 12 - Horace Silver (58,76,89,106,173,197,275,284)
8-33243-2 Jazz Profile 19 - Stan Kenton
(467,468,470,474,475,476,478,480,482,487,491,498)
8-33244-2 Jazz Profile 16 - Art Pepper (464,465,475,476,508,551,552,566)
8-33273-2 Jazz Profile 15 - Count Basie (575,578)
8-33329-2 Wardell Gray - Beehive '55 (452)
8-33373-2 (2 CD Set) The Complete Blue Note And Capitol Recordings Of Fats Navarro And Tadd Dameron (19,22,23,25,471,473)
8-33390-2 Denise Jannah - I Was Born In Love With You (379,390)
8-33395-2 (The Right Stuff) PsycheFunkaJazzadelic 2nd Edition:
Us3 (351) (& further titles not from BN)
8-33418-2 Junko Onishi - Live At The Village Vanguard II (606)
8-33576-2 (2 CD Set) Kenny Dorham - 'Round About Midnight At The Cafe Bohemia
(= 7-46541-2 + 7-46542-2) (54)
8-33578-2 The Best Of Carmen McRae (279,280,288,290,291,299)
8-33579-2 GXF-3023 (Connoisseur Series) Lee Morgan - The Procrastinator (204)
8-33580-2 LT-990 +1 (Connoisseur Series) Grant Green - Solid (167)
8-33581-2 LT-1056 (Connoisseur Series) Wayne Shorter - Et Cetera (183)
8-33582-2 LT-995 (Connoisseur Series) Hank Mobley - A Slice Of The Top (191)
8-33583-2 LT-1044 +1 (Connoisseur Series) Bobby Hutcherson - Patterns (211)
8-33588-2 Everette Harp - Better Days (421,422)
8-33878-2 Esquire Jazz Collection: Crosstown Traffic:
Earl Klugh & Bob James (508) Steve Masakowski (372)
Pieces of A Dream (371) Kurt Elling (366)
Richard Elliot (367) Eliane Elias (330)
Dianne Reeves (319) Cassandra Wilson (356)
Stanley Jordan (304) Everette Harp (363)
8-33908-2 (Canada) CBC's After Hours Blue Note Collection:
Chet Baker (547) Herbie Hancock (179)
Joe Lovano (368) Miles Davis (473)
Holly Cole (542) John Scofield (362)
Jacky Terrasson (369) Cassandra Wilson (356)
June Christy (477) Dexter Gordon (142)
Maynard Ferguson (574) Holly Cole (542)
Renee Rosnes (594) Thelonious Monk (21)
Kurt Elling (374)
8-34195-2 (4 CD Set) The Complete Blue Note And Pacific Jazz Recordings Of Clifford Brown
(35,36,38,40,41,548)
8-34200-2 (6 CD Box) Dexter Gordon - The Complete Blue Note Sixties Sessions
(121,122,137,138,140,142,154,167,182)
8-34286-2 Lena Horne - Being Myself (384,393,412)
8-34634-2 Renee Rosnes - Ancestors (383)
8-34712-2 (Spain)(2 CD) Jazz Classics:
Art Tatum (476) Charlie Parker (450)
Duke Ellington (477) Glenn Miller (637)
Benny Goodman (479) Ella Fitzgerald (644)
Serge Chaloff (479) Miles Davis (645)
Nat Cole (490) Dave Brubeck (645)
Louis Armstrong (516) Bob Brookmeyer (645)
Chet Baker (549) Thelonious Monk (28)
Buddy Rich (563) Bud Powell (27)
Count Basie (573) John Coltrane (71)
Armstrong/Ellington (577) Sonny Rollins (71)
Sarah Vaughan (578) Art Blakey (85)
Joe Williams (579) Lou Donaldson (96)
Betty Carter (581) Horace Silver (173)
Chick Corea (585) Herbie Hancock (179)
Billie Holiday (619) Us3 (350)
8-34719-2 (Italy) Maurizio Giammarco Heart Quartet - In Our Hands (380)
8-34813-2 Max Roach With The New Orchestra Of Boston (364,383)

8-34873-2		Bedroom Tenors - Romantic Ballads: Dexter Gordon (142) · Sonny Rollins (71) Stanley Turrentine (150) · Joe Lovano (360) Stan Getz (570) · Joe Henderson (311) Wayne Shorter (176) · Coleman Hawkins (467) Ike Quebec (129) · Everette Harp (363) Zoot Sims (625) · Hank Mobley (151) Javon Jackson (361)
8-34957-2		The Best Of Blue Note Best Of's: Earl Klugh (508) · Miles Davis (472) Jimmy Smith (103) · Stanley Jordan (304) Dexter Gordon (142) · Kenny Burrell (151) Grant Green (116) · Horace Silver (196) Art Blakey (85) · Chet Baker (547)
8-35220-2	B1-35220 +3	Duke Pearson - I Don't Care Who Knows It (215,226,232,234,238)
8-35221-2	B1-35221 +3	John Patton - Memphis To New York Spirit (228,248)
8-35282-2		Blue Note Plays Sinatra: Jazz Messengers (85) · Jacky Terrasson (369) Freddie Hubbard (104) · Miles Davis (41) Dexter Gordon (142) · Ike Quebec (133) Cannonball Adderley (79) · Bennie Green (88) Sonny Rollins (73) · Joe Lovano (368) The Three Sounds (141) · The Three Sounds (196)
8-35283-2		Blue Note Plays Jobim: Joao Gilberto (521) · Javon Jackson (376) Eliane Elias (592) · Carmen McRae (290) Stanley Turrentine (229) · Stanley Turrentine (199) Bireli Lagrene (353) · Jack Wilson (219) Duke Pearson (232) · Earl Klugh (537) Grant Green (179) · Eliane Elias (600) Joao Gilberto (521)
8-35338-2	B1-35338 +2	Gene Harris And The Three Sounds - Live At The "It" Club (239)
8-35346-2		Johnny Hartman - For Trane (617)
8-35407-2		Ron Carter - Mr. Bow-Tie (609)
8-35414-2	(Europe)	Out Of The Blue - The Art Of The Improvisers: Art Ensemble Of Chicago (520) · Andrew Hill (236) Jackie McLean (201) · Eric Dolphy (163) Cecil Taylor (623) · Larry Young (205) Sam Rivers (182) · Ornette Coleman (213) Bobby Hutcherson (215)
8-35471-2		Blue Monk - Blue Note Plays Monk's Music: Ralph Peterson (589) · Gil Evans (554) Stan Tracey (349) · Babs Gonzales (51) Larry Young (186) · Art Taylor (108) Grachan Moncur (160) · The Three Sounds (105) McCoy Tyner (364) · Gonzalo Rubalcaba (594) Eric Dolphy (163)
8-35472-2	(Europe)	Blue 60s: Herbie Hancock (225) · Eddie Gale(226) Grant Green (233) · Jazz Crusaders (564) Horace Silver (250) · Stanley Turrentine (217) Lee Morgan (207) · Billy Taylor (494) Bobby Hutcherson (233) · Lou Donaldson (220) Don Cherry (197)

793

8-35607-2	B1-35607 -2	Capitol Rare,Vol.2:
		Ronnie Laws (279) / Natalie Cole (506)
		Carmen McRae (289) / Shere Brown (508)
		Alphonse Mouzon (281) / Gene Dunlap (508)
		Chico Hamilton (281) / Margo Thunder (504)
		Nat Adderley (504) / Patti Drew (502)
		Gary Bartz (506) / 100 % Pure Poison (505)
		Minnie Riperton (507) / Gene Harris (288)
		Stratavarious (505)
8-35636-2	B1-35636	Rare Grooves:
		Reuben Wilson (224,235) / John Patton (210)
		Jack McDuff (240) / Richard "Groove" Holmes (252)
		Jimmy McGriff (232) / Elvin Jones (258)
		Stanley Turrentine (217) / Andrew Hill (213)
		Larry Young (209) / Donald Byrd (198)
		Eddie Gale (226) / Candido (249)
8-35739-2		Jacky Terrasson - Reach (382)
8-35800-2		The Best Of Pieces Of A Dream (381,540,541,542,648,649)
8-35811-2	(4 CD set)	Hot Jazz On Blue Note:
Disc 1:		Meade Lux Lewis (10) / Sidney Bechet (12,17)
		Josh White (4) / Art Hodes (8,14)
		Edmond Hall (5) / Baby Dodds (16)
		George Lewis (47,451,452) / Sidney De Paris (27)
		Bunk Johnson (13)
Disc 2:		Art Hodes (7,8,9,13,16) / Edmond Hall (6)
		Sidney Bechet (12,24,30) / James P. Johnson (11)
Disc 3:		Sidney Bechet (12,24,26,30) / Edmond Hall (6)
		Art Hodes (8,9,11,16) / Sidney De Paris (9,27)
Disc 4:		James P. Johnson (11) / Art Hodes (7,8,9,13,16)
		Edmond Hall (5,6) / Sidney Bechet (12,26,30)
		Sidney De Paris (9) / Baby Dodds (16)
8-35830-2		Ray Barretto - My Summertime (382)
8-36054-2	(U.K.4 CD Box)	The Blue Note Box (= 7-96110-2 + 7-97960-2 + 8-30081-2 + 8-31883-2)
8-36195-2	BST84349	Donald Byrd - Electric Byrd (242)
8-36259-2		Terumasa Hino & Masaumi Kikuchi - Acoustic Boogie (609)
8-36483-2		Junko Onishi - Piano Quintet Suite (609)
8-36490-2		Javon Jackson - A Look Within (389)
8-36545-2		Dianne Reeves - The Palo Alto Sessions 1981-85 (457,458,506)
8-36594-2	B1-36594 -3	The New Groove - The Blue Note Remix Project,Volume 1 (385,386)
8-36633-2		Miles Davis - Ballads & Blues (31,34,41,79,475)
8-36728-2		The Carnegie Hall Jazz Band (384)
8-36736-2		The Last Time I Committed Suicide (Soundtrack):
		Charles Mingus (645) / Jacky Terrasson (398)
		Max Roach (648) / Cassandra Wilson (389)
		Miles Davis (472) / The Andrews Sisters (637)
		Dianne Reeves (398) / Red Fish,Blue Fish:Suicide Suite (655)
		Ch. Parker & D. Gillespie (637) / Javon Jackson (389)
		Ella Fitzgerald (637) / Pet (656)
		Thelonious Monk (32) / Film Dialogues (655)
		Art Blakey & The J.M. (21)
8-36747-2		Blue Note All Stars - Blue Spirit (387)
8-36777-2		Michelle Rosewoman - Spirit (606)
8-36909-2		The Doky Brothers (383)
8-37051-2		The Best Of McCoy Tyner - The Blue Note Years (201,207,217,224,238,325,332,364)
8-37052-2		The Best Of Hank Mobley - The Blue Note Years (46,62,99,113,119,158,177,183,188)
8-37101-2		Charlie Hunter - Ready...Set...Shango! (386,387)
8-37138-2		The Best Of Django Reinhardt (517,518,519)
8-37183-2	(Europe)	Cassandra Wilson - New Moon Daughter (= 8-32861-2 +1) (380,381)

8-37302-2		Marcus Printup - Unveiled (389,390)
8-37319-2		Greg Osby - Art Forum (389)
8-37513-2		Frank Sinatra - Live In Australia 1959 (454,455)
8-37570-2	8-35739-2 +1 (Europe)	Jacky Terrasson - Reach (382)
8-37627-2		Pat Martino - All Sides Now (396,397,400)
8-37628-2		Mark Shim - Mind Over Matter (402,403)
8-37630-2		Paul Jackson Jr. - Never Alone/Duets (656)
8-37643-2	BST84109 +3	Herbie Hancock - Takin' Off (139)
8-37644-2	BST84182 +2	Wayne Shorter - Juju (169)
8-37645-2	BST84111+3	Grant Green - The Latin Bit (137,142)
8-37646-2	BN-LA006-F	McCoy Tyner - Extensions (238)
8-37647-2	BLP1534	Paul Chambers - Whims Of Chambers (57)
8-37668-2	BLP1544	Hank Mobley And His All Stars (59)
8-37717-2		Gonzalo Rubalcaba & Cuban Quartet - Antiguo (610)
8-37718-2		Joe Lovano - Celebrating Sinatra (395,396)
8-37731-2	(Europe)	Blue Note All Stars - Blue Spirits (387)
8-37741-2		The Best Of Grant Green - The Blue Note Years,Vol.2 (224,233,237,246,252,257,260)
8-37745-2		The Best Of Lou Donaldson - The Blue Note Years,Vol. 2 (206,211,220,226,236,243)
8-38098-2		Sonny Fortune - From Now On (390)
8-38268-2		Dianne Reeves - The Grant Encounter (391)
8-38297-2		Geri Allen - Eyes...In The Back Of Your Head (610,611)
8-38363-2		Jackie McLean/Junko Onishi - Hat Trick (611)
8-52037-2		Benny Green - Kaleidoscope (396)
8-52051-2	Capitol (2 CD)	Capitol Blues Collection: Cool Cats & Hip Chicks - Jumpin' Like Mad: Babs Gonzalez (18) (& further titles not from BN)
8-52184-2	(Canada)	Canada Blue Note Festival '96: Charlie Hunter (386) / Blue Note All Stars (387) Bobby McFerrin (378) / Tim Hagans (376) Cassandra Wilson (381) / Kevin Hays (377) Renee Rosnes (383) / Javon Jackson (376) Joe Lovano (366) / Greg Osby (367) Jacky Terrasson (382) / Bill Stewart (379) John Scofield (382) / Lonnie Smith/M. Franti (remix) (386) Madre Deus (526)
8-52251-2		Sherman Irby - Full Circle (392)
8-52390-2		Judi Silvano - Vocalise (387,388)
8-52419-2		Fareed Haque - Deja Vu (397)
8-52420-2	B1-52420	Charlie Hunter - Natty Dread (392)
8-52433-2	BST84138	(Connoisseur Series) Harold Vick - Steppin' Out (154)
8-52434-2	BST84099 +1	(Connoisseur Series) Grant Green - Sunday Mornin' (124)
8-52435-2	BST84048 +3	(Connoisseur Series) Donald Byrd - Byrd In Flight (98,99,106)
8-52436-2	BST84251 +1	(Connoisseur Series) Jack Wilson - Something Personal (194)
8-52437-2	BLP1573 +2	(Connoisseur Series) John Jenkins With Kenny Burrell (69)
8-52438-2	BLP1584	(Connoisseur Series) Here Comes Louis Smith (454)
8-52439-2	BLP1530 +2	(Connoisseur Series) Jutta Hipp With Zoot Sims (56)
8-52440-2	BST84032 +5	(Connoisseur Series) Sonny Red - Out Of The Blue (97,99)
8-52441-2	BST81564 +1	(Connoisseur Series) Paul Chambers Quintet (65)
8-52442-2	BST89001 +6	(Connoisseur Series) Dodo Greene - My Hour Of Need (136,137,143,145)
8-52443-2	BST84114 +3	Ike Quebec - Soul Samba (143)
8-52727-2		Kurt Elling - The Messenger (388,392,397,399)

8-53016-2 (Spain)(2 CD) Ahora Jazz:

Duke Ellington (637) | Peggy Lee (484)
Count Basie (573) | Louis Armstrong & Duke Ellington (577)
Wes Montgomery (556) | Bud Powell (27)
Stephane Grappelli (519) | Benny Goodman (479)
Billie Holiday (466) | June Christy (486)
Miles Davis (31) | Dexter Gordon (122)
Art Tatum (476) | Sonny Rollins (71)
Herbie Hancock (139) | Stanley Jordan (304)
Thelonious Monk (28) | Dinah Shore (487)
Nat King Cole (466) | Ella Fitzgerald (498)
Dinah Washington (579) | Stan Kenton (482)
Lou Donaldson (266) | Horace Silver (173)
Chick Corea (585) | John Coltrane (71)
Sarah Vaughan (578) | Keely Smith (484)
Charlie Parker (450) | Buddy Rich (563)
Art Blakey (85) | George Shearing (487)
Nina Simone (512) | Duke Ellington (477)
Chet Baker (549) | Nancy Wilson & George Shearing (488)

8-53068-2 Everette Harp - What's Going On (394)
8-53082-2 Pat Martino - Stone Blue (420)
8-53210-2 Bill Stewart - Telepathy (398)

Blue Note Notables Series (U.K. only):

8-53223-2 The Three Tenors:
Dexter Gordon (121,142) | John Coltrane (71)
Sonny Rollins (59,63)

8-53224-2 Chet Baker - Mr. Cool (545,546,547,549,553)

8-53225-2 Blue Note's Blue Bloods:
Art Blakey (85) | Cannonball Adderley (79)
Hank Mobley (99) | Dexter Gordon (154)
Grant Green (159) | Lou Donaldson (211)

8-53226-2 Blue Note's New Bloods:
Everette Harp (542) | Greg Osby (367)
Richard Elliott (384) | Charlie Hunter (376)
John Scofield (382)

8-53227-2 Bands On The Run:
Count Basie (573) | Woody Herman (471)
Duke Ellington (478) | Benny Goodman (472)
Stan Kenton (470) | Buddy Rich (563)

8-53228-2 Blue Ivory:
Thelonious Monk (21) | Michel Petrucciani (342)
Bud Powell (27) | Jacky Terrasson (369)
Herbie Hancock (139) | Eliane Elias (375)
Horace Silver (173)

8-53229-2 Blue In The Night:
Chet Baker (550) | Stanley Turrentine (150)
Ike Quebec (131) | McCoy Tyner (201)
Miles Davis (41) | Lee Morgan (197)

8-53230-2 Blue Bebop:
Charlie Parker (450) | Bud Powell (25)
Miles Davis (34) | Tadd Dameron (22)
Thelonious Monk (28) | Milt Jackson (30)

8-53231-2 Blue Moods:
Dianne Reeves (374) | Holly Cole (544)
Cassandra Wilson (381) | Tania Maria (541)
Rachelle Ferrell (333) | Marisa Monte (525)

8-53232-2 Blue Divas:
Peggy Lee (487) | Nina Simone (511)
June Christy (475) | Annie Ross (555)
Nancy Wilson (497) | Dinah Washington (579)

8-53233-2		Six Shades Of Blue Funk:	
		Herbie Hancock (168)	Lee Morgan (161)
		Gene Harris (385)	Donald Byrd (193)
		Ronnie Laws (279)	Horace Silver (122)
8-53234-2		Blue Note's Six Vital Organs!:	
		Jimmy McGriff (616)	Baby Face Willette (123)
		John Patton (188)	Jack McDuff (240)
		Jimmy Smith (103)	Larry Young (174)
8-53325-2	(Europe)	Helen Eriksen - Standards (395)	
8-53328-2		Eliane Elias - The Three Americas (398,399)	
8-53329-2		The Best Of Bobby McFerrin (313,337,378,540,649)	
8-53330-2		The Best Of John Scofield - The Best Of The Blue Note Years (332,341,347,352,362,365,382,607)	
8-53331-2		Tony Williams - The Best Of The Blue Note Years (309,316,322,331,347)	
8-53354-2		Earl Klugh - Love Songs (285,297,509,536,537,538,633,634)	
8-53355-2	BST84110	Horace Silver - The Tokyo Blues (141)	
8-53356-2	BST84262	Jackie McLean - New And Old Gospel (201)	
8-53357-2	BST84079 +2	Lou Donaldson - Gravy Train (121)	
8-53358-2	BST84289 +1	Lee Morgan - Caramba! (213)	
8-53359-2	BST84256 +1	Stanley Turrentine - The Spoiler (195)	
8-53360-2	BST84050 +5	Jimmy Smith - Home Cookin' (82,92)	
8-53422-2		Caecilie Norby - My Corner Of The Sky (390,391)	
8-53428-2	BST81577 +2	John Coltrane - The Ultimate Blue Train (71)	
8-53648-2		Kenny Dorham - Best Of The Blue Note Years (46,54,115,152,155,165,172)	
8-53920-2		Bob Belden - Strawberry Fields:	
		Dianne Reeves (611)	Dianne Reeves/Javon Jackson (611)
		Cassandra Wilson (611)	Jahlisa/Greg Osby (611)
		Holly Cole (611)	Penny Ford (611)
		Jahlisa/J.Onishi (611)	Sylvia Shemwell (611)
8-53923-2	BN-LA140-G	Donald Byrd - Street Lady (267)	
8-53924-2	BST84340 +3	John Patton - Accent On The Blues (228,230)	
8-53933-2	(Spain)	Pedro Iturralde - Jazz Flamenco,Volumes 1 & 2 (527)	
8-53934-2	(Spain)	Juan Carlos Calderon (528)	
8-53973-2	(Spain)	Nuria Feliu (528)	
8-54052-2		Pieces Of A Dream - Pieces (405,406,407,408,410)	
8-54123-2		Cassandra Wilson - Traveling Miles (416,423,424)	

Following block of 2 CD sets was issued in France only (U.S. equivalents are shown in second column):

8-54185-2	4-96375-2	Les Années Blue Note 1955-1960: The Jazz Message:	
Disc 1 (8-54186-2):		The Jazz Messengers (49)	Sonny Rollins (59)
		Horace Silver (45)	Johnny Griffin (52)
		Clifford Brown (38)	John Coltrane (71)
		Horace Silver (58)	Cannonball Adderley with Miles Davis (79)
		Hank Mobley (62)	
Disc 2 (8-54187-2):		Sonny Clark (76)	Art Blakey & The Jazz Messengers (85)
		Bud Powell (82)	Stanley Turrentine (104)
		Lee Morgan (62)	Freddie Hubbard (104)
		Lou Donaldson (83)	Dexter Gordon (121)
		Jackie McLean (110)	
8-54188-2	4-96378-2	Les Années Blue Note 1956-1967: Organ & Soul:	
Disc 1 (8-54189-2):		Jimmy Smith (78)	Ike Quebec (130)
		Baby Face Willette (117)	Freddie Roach (160)
		Fred Jackson (134)	John Patton (188)
		Don Wilkerson (156)	Grant Green (125)
Disc 2 (8-54190-2):		Kenny Burrell (147)	Wayne Shorter (190)
		Lou Donaldson (87)	Hank Mobley (177)
		Donald Byrd (147)	Donald Byrd (202)
		Stanley Turrentine (181)	Lou Donaldson (201)
		Lee Morgan (161)	

 797

8-54191-2	4-96381-2	Les Années Blue Note 1963-1967: Hard Bop & Beyond:	
Disc 1 (8-54192-2):		Dexter Gordon (142)	Horace Silver (173)
		Joe Henderson (155)	Pete La Roca (181)
		Herbie Hancock (168)	Wayne Shorter (190)
		Blue Mitchell (169)	Kenny Dorham (152)
Disc 2 (8-54193-2):		Herbie Hancock (179)	Art Blakey & The Jazz Messengers (127)
		Joe Henderson (189)	Lee Morgan (184)
		Wayne Shorter (176)	Bobby Hutcherson (183)
		Freddie Hubbard (144)	McCoy Tyner (201)
		Hank Mobley (158)	
8-54194-2	4-96384-2	Les Années Blue Note 1963-1967: The Avant Garde:	
Disc 1 (8-54195-2):		Larry Young 186)	Tony Williams (171)
		Andrew Hill (159,162)	Sam Rivers (175)
		Jackie McLean (153,158)	Grachan Moncur III (169)
Disc 2 (8-54196-2):		Eric Dolphy (163)	Ornette Coleman (213)
		Grachan Moncur III (160)	Don Cherry (197)
		Andrew Hill (164)	Cecil Taylor (192)
		Eric Dolphy (163)	
8-54197-2	(2 CD Set)	Les Années Blue Note - The Finest In Jazz :	
		Pee Wee Marquette (90)	John Patton (188)
		Art Blakey (85)	John Coltrane (71)
		Kenny Burrell (147)	Cannonball Adderley (79)
		Horace Silver (58)	Lou Donaldson (83)
		Hank Mobley (62)	Freddie Hubbard (104)
		Sonny Rollins (59)	Bud Powell (82)
		Jimmy Smith (103)	Dexter Gordon (142)
		Herbie Hancock (168)	Wyne Shorter (190)
		Donald Byrd (202)	Joe Henderson (189)
		Lee Morgan (161)	Eric Dolphy (163)
8-54325-2	BST84125	Lou Donaldson - Good Gracious! (148)	
8-54326-2	BN-LA549-G	Donald Byrd - Places and Spaces (283)	
8-54327-2	BST84214	Blue Mitchell - Down With It (184)	
8-54328-2	BST84380	Donald Byrd - Ethiopian Knights (255)	
8-54329-2	BST84322	Jack McDuff - Down Home Style (228)	
8-54357-2	B1-54357	Blue Juice:	
	(Europe)	Bobbie Gentry (497)	Joao Donato (523)
		Billy Preston (495)	Ananda Shankar (525)
		Nancy Wilson (498)	Doris (526)
		Lou Rawls (498)	Johnny Lytle (586)
		Jimmy Caravan (499)	Chico Hamilton (584)
		Benny Gordon (499)	Jerome Richardson (626)
		The Fame Gang (500)	Tina Britt (630)
		Norman Connors (509)	Dick Hyman (645)
		Brian Bennett (516)	The Three Sounds (254)
		Elza Soares (522)	
8-54360-2	B1-54360 -4	Blue Break Beats,Vol.3:	
		Cannonball Adderley (502)	Gene Harris & The 3 Sounds (254)
		Lou Rawls (502)	Gene Harris (273)
		Lou Donaldson (206)	Donald Byrd (283)
		Reuben Wilson (254)	Ronnie Foster (259)
		Jeremy Steig (238)	Joe Williams (582)
		Shirley Bassey (632)	Duke Pearson (208)
		Lou Donaldson (226)	Jackie McLean (205)
8-54363-2	(Europe)	Blue York Blue York:	
		Dakota Staton (483)	Bud Powell (25)
		The King Sisters (483)	Lee Morgan (69)
		George Shearing (489)	Jackie McLean (96)
		Holly Cole (544)	Jimmy Smith (78)
		Jim Hall (552)	Reuben Wilson (219)
		Modern Jazz Quartet (624)	The Three Sounds (218)
		Ike Quebec (10)	Bobbi Humphrey (267,273)

8-54364-2 Jump Blue - Rockin' The Jooks:
Pigmeat Markham (15) Jimmy Liggins (463)
Illinois Jacquet (459) Shirley & Lee (463)
Helen Humes (459) Big "T" Tyler (465)
Jo Jo Adams (460) Nellie Lutcher (470)
Amos Milburn (461) Cleo Brown (474)
Calvin Boze (461) Big Joe Turner (529)
The Five Keys (462) Big Jay McNeely (529)
Peppermint Harris (462) Archibald (530)
Pee Wee Crayton (462) T-Bone Walker (530)
Floyd Dixon (462) Dave Bartholomew (531)
Jack "The Bear" Parker (462)Roy Brown (532)
Lowell Fulson (462) Ike & Tina Turner (616)
Louis Jordan (462) The Clovers (625)
8-54365-2 Midnight Blue - The Bewitching Hour:
Lester Young (459) Ike Quebec (111)
Lawrence Marable (463) Stanley Turrentine & The 3 Sounds (114)
Coleman Hawkins (483) Grant Green (132)
Nat King Cole (491) Dexter Gordon (142)
Bill Perkins (551) Jimmy Smith (149)
Bud Shank (554) Duke Pearson (198)
Johnny Hartman (617) Cassandra Wilson (356)
8-54486-2 (The Right Stuff) Slow Jams/On The Jazz Tip,Volume One:
Dianne Reeves (319) (& further titles not from BN)
8-54487-2 (The Right Stuff) Slow Jams/On The Jazz Tip,Volume Two:
Bobbi Humphrey (267) Earl Klugh (293)
(& further titles not from BN)
8-54719-2 BST84315 +1 Stanley Turrentine - The Common Touch (214,217)
8-54729-2 (Europe) Denise Jannah - Different Colors (394)
8-54876-2 Pete (La Roca) Sims - SwingTime (403)
8-54898-2 Jazz Profile 4 - Cannonball Adderley (79,488,489,492,496)
8-54899-2 Jazz Profile 3 - Art Blakey (41,85,127, 581,626)
8-54900-2 Jazz Profile 6 - Duke Ellington (477,478,628,631,632)
8-54901-2 Jazz Profile 7 - Lee Morgan (77,161,170,183,185,204)
8-54902-2 Jazz Profile 1 - Chet Baker (547,548,550,551)
8-54904-2 Jazz Profile 2 - Herbie Hancock (139,149,157,168,179,210,225)
8-54905-2 Jazz Profile 10 - Gerry Mulligan (476,548,552,553)
8-54906-2 Jazz Profile 8 - Bud Powell (25,27,37,68,82,88,570,571)
8-54907-2 Jazz Profile 5 - Dinah Washington (579,580,581)
8-54943-2 The Best Of Marlena Shaw (262,266,274,286)
8-55221-2 The Great Jazz Vocalists Sing Ellington And Strayhorn:
Dianne Reeves (318) Annie Ross/Gerry Mulligan (553)
Lou Rawls (544) June Christy (481)
Lena Horne (362) Nat King Cole Trio (468)
Nancy Wilson (497,502) Joe Williams (582)
Abbey Lincoln (534) Sarah Vaughan (577,578)
Ray Nance/D.Ellington (477)Billy Eckstine (576)
Jimmy Grissom (477) Louis Armstrong (578)
8-55230-2 Jazz Profile 9 - Mose Allison (319,333,361)
8-55330-2 Ronnie Laws - Tribute To The Legendary Eddie Harris (400)
8-55466-2 Jimmy Smith - The Master II (604)
8-55484-2 Jacky Terrasson & Cassandra Wilson - Rendezvous (402,406)
8-55720-2 EMI-Jazz (U.K.) Jazz Masters - Thelonious Monk (= CDMFP6300) (20,21,22,28)
8-55725-2 EMI-Jazz (U.K.) Totally Jazz:
Thelonious Monk (21) Stanley Turrentine (317)
(& further titles not from BN)
8-55817-2 Kevin Hays - Andalucia (401)
8-55850-2 (Spain) Pedro Itturalde Quartet Feat. Hampton Hawes (527)
8-55855-2 (Europe) Erik Truffaz - Out Of A Dream (390)
8-56092-2 Joe Lovano & Gonzalo Rubalcaba - Flying Colors (402)
8-56234-2 Sherman Irby - Big Mama's Biscuits (421)

8-56254-2 (Europe) Thierry Lang (655)
8-56399-2 (2 CD Set) Blue Note - A Story Of Modern Jazz:

McGhee/Navarro (23) BN All Stars (306)
Bud Powell (27) Art Blakey (127)
Elmo Hope (42) John Coltrane (71)
Miles Davis (41) Lee Morgan (163)
Thelonious Monk (32) Hank Mobley (119)
Kenny Burrell (147) Grachan Moncur III (160)
Lee Morgan (161) BN All Stars (387)
Joe Henderson (155)

8-56458-2 The Doky Brothers - Doky Brothers Two (399)
8-56508-2 (Canada) The Blue Box (4 CD Box):

Art Blakey (101) John Scofield (365)
Herbie Hancock (179) The Three Sounds (125)
Kenny Burrell (304) Donald Byrd (202)
Sidney Bechet (3) Jimmy Smith (103)
Kenny Dorham (152) Wayne Shorter (176)
McCoy Tyner (238) Grant Green (246)
Lou Donaldson (83) Joe Henderson (155)
Donald Byrd (264) Michel Petrucciani (331)
Stanley Jordan (304) Miles Davis (34)
Miles Davis (41) Sonny Rollins (59)
Bobby McFerrin (313) Stanley Turrentine (150)
Herbie Hancock (168) Horace Silver (173)
Dexter Gordon (142) Wayne Shorter (190)
Thelonious Monk (28) Chick Corea (585)
John Coltrane (71) Lou Donaldson (236)
Carmen McRae (288) Freddie Hubbard (104)
J.J. Johnson (48) Grant Green (179)
Horace Silver (58) J.J. Johnson (36)
Bud Powell (37) Bud Powell (27)
Hank Mobley (46) Dexter Gordon (142)
Lee Morgan (161) Tony Williams (309)
Thelonious Monk (21)

8-56543-2 Greg Osby - Further Ado (404)
8-56581-2 BLP4037 (Connoisseur Series) Horace Parlan - Us Three (102)
8-56582-2 BST84024 (Connoisseur Series) Jackie McLean - Swing,Swang,Swingin' (96)
8-56583-2 BST81589 (Connoisseur Series) Horace Silver - Further Explorations By The Horace Silver Quintet (76)
8-56584-2 BLP1582 (Connoisseur Series) Clifford Jordan - Cliff Craft (74)
8-56585-2 BLP1570 (Connoisseur Series) Sonny Clark - Dial S For Sonny (67)
8-56586-2 BLP1554/55 (Connoisseur Series) Art Blakey - Orgy In Rhythm (62)
8-56680-2 Javon Jackson - Good People (411)
8-56689-2 Lou Rawls - Ballads (327,328,334,335,542,543)
8-56690-2 Ike Quebec - Ballads (111,129,130,133,135)
8-56691-2 Freddie Hubbard - Ballads (104,111,120,126,144,146,166)
8-56692-2 Joe Henderson - Ballads And Blues (155,175,181,311)
8-56810-2 Renee Rosnes - As We Are Now (404)
8-56842-2 (Spain) Ahora - Las Chicas (2 CD Set):
Disc 1 (8-56843-2)

Dinah Washington (579) Nancy Wilson (502)
Sarah Vaughan (579) Carmen McRae (280)
Billie Holiday (462) June Christy (478)
Dakota Staton (483) Annie Ross (555)
Judy Garland (483) Helen Merrill (649)
Abbey Lincoln (535) Dinah Shore (489)
Lena Horne (630) Pearl Bailey (575)
Ruth Brown (585) Shirley Bassey (516)
Peggy Lee (484) Nina Simone (511)
Betty Carter (630) Ella Fitzgerald (500)

Disc 2 (8-56844-2)		Dianne Reeves (391)	Eve Boswell (516)
		Holly Cole (544)	Dodo Greene (143)
		Cassandra Wilson (381)	Ella Mae Morse (483)
		Rebecka Tornqvist (526)	Kay Starr (491)
		Helen Eriksen (395)	The King Sisters (483)
		Caecilie Norby (391)	Keely Smith (484)
		Judi Silvano (388)	Nellie Lutcher (468)
		Denise Jannah (394)	Della Reese (533)
		Natalie Cole (508)	Morgana King (624)
		Diahann Carroll (621)	Marlena Shaw (266)
8-56973-2		Dianne Reeves - That Day... (409,410)	
8-56974-2		Ray Barretto - Contact! (406)	
8-56991-2		Yule Be Boppin':	
		Kurt Elling (405)	Judi Silvano (406)
		Pat Martino (403)	Jacky Terrasson (404)
		Dianne Reeves (398)	Benny Green (407)
		Eliane Elias (400)	Bobby Watson/Jack Walrath (608)
		Bob Dorough (407)	Rachelle Ferrell (510)
		Fareed Haque (403)	Charlie Hunter (405)
		Javon Jackson (403)	Joe Lovano (403 404)
		BN Ad Hoc Orch. (404)	
8-57061-2		Charlie Parker & Dizzy Gillespie - Diz 'N Bird At Carnegie Hall (570)	
8-57063-2		Jimmy McGriff Greatest Hits (232,253,523,582,584,586,616,630)	
8-57071-2	(The Right Stuff)	Slow Jams/On The Jazz Tip,Volume Three:	
		Herbie Hancock (179)	Lee Morgan (161)
		Horace Silver (173)	(& further titles not from BN)
8-57072-2	(The Right Stuff)	Slow Jams/On The Jazz Tip,Volume Four:	
		Art Blakey (85)	Herbie Hancock (168)
		Donald Byrd (228)	Carmen McRae (289)
		(& further titles not from BN)	
8-57150-2		Lee Konitz/Brad Mehldau/Charlie Haden - Alone Together (401)	
8-57184-2	BLP1596/97 +1	Kenny Burrell - Blue Lights (2 CD Set) (81)	
8-57187-2	7-46539/40-2?	Donald Byrd At The Half Note Cafe (2 CD Set) (112)	
8-57191-2		Jimmy Smith - A New Sound,A New Star (2 CD Set) (50,51,54,55)	
8-57194-2		Grant Green - Complete Quartets With Sonny Clark (2 CD Set) (132,134)	
8-57197-2	(2 CD Set)	Don Grolnick - The Blue Note Sessions (328,347)	
		(= 7-94591-2 + 7-98689-2)	
8-57200-2		Ken McIntyre - The Complete United Artists Sessions (627,630)	
8-57302-2		Dexter Gordon - The Squirrel (456)	
8-57371-2	(2 CD Set)	Ben Webster - The Holland Sessions (514,515)	
8-57460-2	(Australia)	Basement Sydney Australia:	
		Vince Jones (514)	Johnny Griffin (73)
		Annie Ross (553)	Jimmy Smith (103)
		Art Pepper (464)	Freddie Hubbard (166
		Betty Carter (630)	John Scofield (362)
		Dizzy Gillespie (562)	Kevin Hays (377)
		John Lewis (550)	Charlie Hunter (387)
8-57463-2	(Australia)	Women In Blue:	
		Julie London (535)	Carmen McRae (289)
		Tania Maria (540)	Eliane Elias (542)
		Rachelle Ferrell (510)	Caecilie Norby (391)
		Marisa Monte (525)	Helen Eriksen (395)
		Marima Lima (525)	Dianne Reeves (391)
		Sarah Vaughan (580)	Dianne Reeves/Cassandra Wilson (611)
		Marlena Shaw (274)	Holly Cole (611)
8-57491-2		Richard Elliot - Chill Factor (424,429)	
8-57729-2		Bob Dorough - Right On My Way Home (407,408)	

8-57741-2 B1-57741 Blue Brazil,Vol.2 - Blue Note In A Latin Groove:
Antonio Adolfo (523) Milton Banana (522,524)
Silvio Cazar (521) Elza Soares (522)
Wilson Simonal (521) Som Tres (522)
Os Tres Morais (523) Edu Lobo (523)
Quinteto Villa Lobos (523) Meirelles (524)
Elza Soares (522) Leny Andrade (522)
Quarteto Em Cy (523) QuartetoNovo (522)
Di Meio (524) Edu Lobo (523)
Luis Gonzaga Jr.(524)

8-57742-2 (Europe) Blue Bop - Great Goatees And Blazing Berets:
Gil Evans (555) Art Blakey (21)
Babs Gonzales (471) Howard McGhee (23)
Kenny Clarke (519) Jackie McLean (534)
Gerry Mulligan (553) Art Pepper (465)
Charlie Parker (450) Dizzy Gillespie (474)
Th. Monk & M. Jackson (28) Elmo Hope (36)
Bud Powell (573) Thelonious Monk (22)
Fats Navarro/Dameron (19) Miles Davis (34)
Cl:ifford Brown (38) Sonny Stitt (474)
James Moody (23)

8-57745-2 B1-57745 -3 Blue 'N' Groovy,Vol.2 - Mostly Modal:
Hank Mobley (229) Blue Mitchell (157)
Stanley Turrentine (193) Don Wilkerson (137)
Donald Byrd (193) Lee Morgan (207)
Jackie McLean (91) Duke Pearson (175)
Art Blakey (119) McCoy Tyner (238)
Art Pepper (464)

8-57748-2 Blue Movies - Scoring For The Studios:
Billy Taylor (499) Billy May (503)
Leroy Holmes (630) John Patton (220)
Willie Bobo (295) Lee Morgan (227)
Wilton Felder (567) Marlena Shaw (265)
Count Basie (630) Nancy Wilson (493)
Lou Donaldson (206) Richard "Groove" Holmes (252)
Grant Green/Remix (385) Bobby Hutcherson (276)
Bobby Hutcherson (204) Bud Shank (567)
The Three Sounds (212)

8-57749-2 Blue Bacharach - A Cooler Shaker:
Stanley Turrentine (213) Richard "Groove" Holmes (567)
Nancy Wilson (494) Stanley Turrrentine (193)
Reuben Wilson (224) The Jazz Crusaders (566)
The Three Sounds (212) Ernie Watts (567)
Stanley Turrentine (193) Stanley Turrentine (220)
Lou Rawls (498) Grant Green (169)
Grant Green (237) Nancy Wilson (497)

8-57875-2 Ronnie Laws - Harvest For The World (410)
8-57891-2 Bob Belden - Tapestry (407,408,411,412)
8-58083-2 (CD Single) Us3 - Cantaloop (350,351)
8-58139-2 (CD Single) Us3 - Tukka Yoot's Riddim (350,351)
8-58610-2 (CD Single) Us3 - Come On Everybody (Get Down) (393)
8-58662-2 (CD Single) Us3 - I'm Thinkin' About Your Body (393)
8-59071-2 Jazz Profile 18 - Freddie Hubbard (104,111,120,126,144,162,166,177)
8-59072-2 Jazz Profile 20 - Wayne Shorter (165,169,176,186,190,200,231,247)
8-59229-2 (France) Blue Note - A Story Of Modern Jazz (2 CD Set) (same as 8-56399-2):
Disc 1 (8-59230-2):
McGhee/Navarro (23) Kenny Burrell (147)
Bud Powell (27) Lee Morgan (161)
Elmo Hope (42) Joe Henderson (155)
Miles Davis (41) BN All Stars (306)
Thelonious Monk (32) Art Blakey (85)

Disc 2 (8-59231-2):		Art Blakey (127) John Coltrane (71) Lee Morgan (163)	Hank Mobley (119) BN All Stars (387) Grachan Moncur III (160)

8-59352-2	(3 CD Set)	The Complete Blue Note Recordings Of Herbie Nichols (47,48,49,53)
8-59378-2	BST84244	(Connoisseur Series) Bobby Hutcherson - Stick Up (194)
8-59379-2	BST84283	(Connoisseur Series) Booker Ervin - The In Between (208)
8-59380-2	BST84056	(Connoisseur Series) Freddie Hubbard - Goin' Up (111)
8-59381-2	BST81599 +1	(Connoisseur Series) Bennie Green - Soul Stirrin' (81)
8-59382-2	BST84068 +2	(Connoisseur Series) Baby Face Willette (117)
8-59383-2	BST84284 +1	(Connoisseur Series) Jackie McLean - 'Bout Soul (205)
8-59417-2		Brian Blade - Fellowship (413)
8-59509-2		Tim Hagans & Marcus Printup - Hubsongs (412)
8-59651-2		Jacky Terrrasson Alive (411)
8-59698-2		Ron Carter - The Bass And I (612)
8-59961-2	BST84312	Lee Morgan - Charisma (195)
8-59962-2	BST84202	Grant Green - I Want To Hold Your Hand (179)
8-59963-2	BST84238 +2	Donald Byrd - Mustang (174,193)
8-59964-2	BST84288	Hank Mobley - Reach Out (209)
8-87504-2	(France)	Shirley Bassey Meets The Booster (632) (CD maxi single)

CEMA SPECIAL MARKETS label

S21-56914 Art Blakey - Blakey's Best (85,101,109)
S21-56915 Bobby McFerrin - Don't Worry,Be Happy (313,337)
(& further titles not from BN)
S21-57588 Thelonious Monk - 'Round Midnight And Other Jazz Classics (20,21,22,28)
S21-57589 Horace Silver Greatest Hits (44,45,58,94,173,185,196)
S21-57590 The Soulful Saxophone Of Stanley Turrentine (114,150,181,193,195,317)
S21-57592 Jazz Super Hits Of The '60s:
Art Blakey (85) Lee Morgan (161)
Donald Byrd (147) Lou Donaldson (201)
Horace Silver (173) (& further titles not from BN)
S21-57593 Jazz Super Hits Of The '70s and '80s:
Earl Klugh (285) Ronnie Laws (279)
Noel Pointer (295) Stanley Jordan (304)
Donald Byrd (264) Stanley Turrentine (317)
Bobbi Humphrey (267) (& further titles not from BN)
S21-57610 The Ballad Artistry Of Miles Davis (31,34,41,79)

GSC Music Series:

15131 (3 CDs) The Very Best Of Blue Note Jazz:
Disc 1:
Stanley Turrentine (150) Art Blakey (49)
Freddie Hubbard/Woody Shaw (312) Horace Silver (39)
Jackie McLean (172) Jimmy Smith/Grant Green (148)
(& further titles not from BN)
Disc 2:
Joe Lovano (360) Kenny Burrell (50)
Lou Donaldson (96) Thelonious Monk (21)
Miles Davis (472) Charlie Parker (450)
Steve Masakowski (357) (& further titles not from BN)
Disc 3:
Kenny Dorham (54) J.J. Johnson/Clifford Brown (36)
Bud Powell (27) (& further titles not from BN)

GRP label

GRD5-9819 (5 CD Set) Chick Corea - Music Forever And Beyond (includes 3 BN tracks only)
(169,247,585) (& further titles not from BN)

HIP-O label

HIPD-64557 Late Night Jazz Essentials:
Dexter Gordon (167) Herbie Hancock (168)
(& further titles not from BN)

CD 547859-2 Essential Young Lions,Vol.1:
Stefon Harris (414) Benny Green (342)
(& further titles not from BN)
CD 547897-2 Essential Young Lions,Vol.2:
Marcus Printup (375) Javon Jackson (411)
(& further titles not from BN)

KNITTING FACTORY label

CD 249 Future Jazz:
Eric Dolphy (163) Joe Lovano (353)
James Newton (309) John Scofield (382)
Andrew Hill (338) Cassandra Wilson (381)
Don Pullen (344) (& further titles not from BN)

MOBILE FIDELITY label:

UDCD 547	7- 81577-2	John Coltrane - Blue Train (71)
UDCD 549	7-48386-2	Earl Klugh - Finger Paintings (296,297)
UDCD 563	BST81595	Cannonball Adderley - Somethin' Else (79)
UDCD 601	BST84049	Art Blakey - A Night In Tunisia (108,109)

MOSAIC label

Note: Number shown in MD prefix denotes the number of CDs in box.Second column shows equivalent LP set.

MD2-103	MR3-103	The Complete Blue Note Recordings Of Albert Ammons And Meade Lux Lewis : Albert Ammons (1,2) Meade Lux Lewis (1,2,5,10) (& one further title from Decca)
MD3-107	MR4-107	The Complete Blue Note Forties Recordings Of Ike Quebec And John Hardee: John Hardee (17) Tiny Grimes (18) Ike Quebec (10,14,15,18)
MD4-109	MR6-109	The Complete Edmond Hall/James P. Johnson/Sidney DeParis/Vic Dickenson Blue Note Sessions: James P. Johnson (6,7,11) Sidney De Paris (9,27) Edmond Hall (5,6,7,8) Vic Dickenson (32)
MD4-110	MR6-110	The Complete Blue Note Recordings of Sidney Bechet: Port of Harlem Seven (3) Josh White (4) Sidney Bechet (3,4,12,24,26,27,30,37)
MD4-114	MR5-114	The Complete Art Hodes Blue Note Sessions: Art Hodes (7,8,9,11,13,14,15,16) Baby Dodds (16)
MD3-118	MR5-118	The Complete Blue Note Recordings of Herbie Nichols (47,48,49,53)
MD2-121	MR3-121	The Complete Blue Note 45 Sessions of Ike Quebec (92,111,135)
MD2-124	MR3-124	The Complete Blue Note Recordings of Freddie Redd (100,109,115)
MD3-132	MR5-132	The Complete Blue Note Recordings Of George Lewis (47,447-448,451,452)
MD4-133	MR6-133	Grant Green-The Complete Blue Note Recordings with Sonny Clark (132,134,135,142)
MD6-137	MR9-137	The Complete Blue Note Recordings Of Larry Young (172,174,179,186,194,205,209,223)
MD6-141	MR10-141	The Complete Blue Note Recordings Of The 1960 Jazz Messengers (101,108,109,110,117,119,123)
MD2-145	MQ3-145	The Complete Blue Note Recordings of Don Cherry (189,195,197)
MD4-150	MQ6-150	The Complete Blue Note 1964-66 Jackie McLean Sessions (169,172,176,185,187,192)
MD3-154	MQ5-154	The Complete February 1957 Jimmy Smith Blue Note Sessions (60,61)
MD7-161	MQ10-161	The Complete Blue Note Andrew Hill Sessions (1963-66): (159,160,162,164,168,177,186,191)
MD4-162	MQ6-162	The Complete Blue Note Lee Morgan Fifties Sessions (57,58,62,69,72,75,77)
MD3-166	MQ5-166	The Complete Blue Note/UA Curtis Fuller Sessions (66,68,75,77,623)
MD3-167	MQ5-167	The Complete Blue Note Sam Rivers Sessions (175,182,196,200)
MD12-170	MQ19-170	Classic Capitol Jazz Sessions: Bobby Hackett (449) (& further titles not from BN)
MD3-172	MQ5-172	The Complete Blue Note/United Artists/Roulette Recordings of Thad Jones (51,55,59,576,624)
MD4-178	MQ6-178	The Complete Blue Mitchell Blue Note Sessions (1963-67) (157,169,184,189,197,207)
MD6-181	MQ10-181	The Complete Blue Note Hank Mobley Fifties Sessions (46,58,59,62,63,66,69,72,77)
MD4-194		The Complete Donald Byrd-Pepper Adams Blue Note Studio Sessions (87,92,120,121,127,206)
MD8-195		The Complete Blue Note Elvin Jones Sessions (212,217,224,232,245,252,258,261,262,269)
MD5-197	MQ8-197	The Complete Blue Note Horace Parlan Sessions (100,102,107,113,119,124,150)

805

ONE WAY label

S21-17373 BN-LA014-G Wayne Shorter - Moto Grosso Feio (240)

RHINO label

75869-2	Billboard's Top Contemporary Jazz Vocals:	
	Dianne Reeves (319) (& further titles not from BN)	
75870-2	Billboard's Top Contemporary Urban Jazz:	
	Donald Byrd (264)	Stanley Jordan (304)
	Ronnie Laws (296)	(& further titles not from BN)

32 Jazz label

32025-2	Hit Jazz:	
	Art Blakey (85)	Lee Morgan (161)
	Horace Silver (173)	(& further titles not from BN)
32039-2	Woody Shaw - Two More Pieces Of The Puzzle:	
	Horace Silver (186)	Larry Young (186)
	(& further titles not from BN)	

DVD-CDs

CLASSIC label (U.S.)

DAD		
1016	BST84058	Hank Mobley - Roll Call (113)
1019	BST84040	Freddie Hubbard - Open Sesame (104)
1022	BST81595	Cannonball Adderley - Somethin' Else (79)
1024	BST84059	Kenny Drew - Undercurrent (113)
1026	BLP1591	Lou Donaldson - Lou Takes Off (76)
1028	BST81577	John Coltrane - Blue Train (71)

FOREIGN ISSUES

DENMARK

OFFICIAL label

83016-2 (2 CD Set) Erroll Garner - Overture To Dawn (448,449)

ENGLAND/UNITED KINGDOM

BLUE NOTE label

Note:Second column shows equivalent US CD (or LP) when applicable.

BNZ		
1	7-46338-2	Cannonball Adderley - Somethin' Else (79)
2	7-46400-2	Art Blakey - The Big Beat (101)
3	7-46429-2	Art Blakey - Indestructible (165,166)
4	7-46516-2	Art Blakey - Moanin' (85)
5	7-84170-2	Art Blakey & The Jazz Messengers - Free For All (162)
6	7-46532-2	Art Blakey & The Jazz Messengers - A Night In Tunisia (108,109)
7	7-46523-2	Art Blakey & The Jazz Messengers - Mosaic (127)
8	7-46519-2	Art Blakey Quintet - A Night At Birdland,Vol.1 (40,41)
9	7-46520-2	Art Blakey Quintet - A Night At Birdland,Vol.2 (40,41)
10	7-46399-2	Kenny Burrell - Midnight Blue (147)
11	7-46538-2	Kenny Burrell - On View At The Five Spot Cafe,Vol.1 (93,94)
12	7-46756-2	Kenny Burrell - Generation (316)
13	7-46534-2	Donald Byrd - Fuego (95)
14	7-46539-2	Donald Byrd - At The Half Note Café,Vol.1 (112)
15	7-46540-2	Donald Byrd - At The Half Note Café,Vol.2 (112)
16	7-46533-2	Paul Chambers - Bass On Top (67)
17	7-84091-2	Sonny Clark - Leapin' & Lopin' (129)
18	7-46819-2	Sonny Clark - Sonny's Crib (70)
19	7-46513-2	Sonny Clark - Cool Struttin' (76)
20	7-46547-2	Sonny Clark Trio (72)
21	7-46095-2	John Coltrane - Blue Train (71)
22	7-46401-2	Chick Corea - The Song Of Singing (240)
23	7-46524-2	Eric Dolphy - Out To Lunch (163)
24	7-46525-2	Lou Donaldson - Blues Walk (83)
25	7-46541-2	Kenny Dorham - Round About Midnight At The Café Bohemia,Vol.1 (54)
26	7-46542-2	Kenny Dorham - Round About Midnight At The Café Bohemia,Vol.2 (54)
27	7-46515-2	Kenny Dorham - Una Mas (152)
28	7-46815-2	Kenny Dorham - Afro-Cuban (45,46)
29	7-46398-2	Duke Ellington - Money Jungle (628)
30	7-46336-2	Bill Evans - The Alternative Man (305)
31	7-84133-2	Dexter Gordon - A Swingin' Affair (142)
32	7-46681-2	Dexter Gordon - Gettin' Around (182)
33	7-46094-2	Dexter Gordon - Go! (142)
34	7-46394-2	Dexter Gordon - Our Man In Paris (154)
35	7-46397-2	Dexter Gordon - The Other Side Of Round Midnight (310,313)
36	7-46544-2	Dexter Gordon - Dexter Calling (122)
37	7-46430-2	Grant Green - Grantstand (125)
38	7-46822-2	Grant Green - Feelin' The Spirit (146)

39	7-46536-2	Introducing Johnny Griffin (52)
40	7-46339-2	Herbie Hancock - Maiden Voyage (179)
41	7-46136-2	Herbie Hancock - Speak Like A Child (210)
42	7-46506-2	Herbie Hancock - Takin' Off (139)
43	7-46845-2	Herbie Hancock - The Prisoner (225)
44	7-84126-2	Herbie Hancock - My Point Of View (151)
45	7-46510-2	Joe Henderson - In 'n Out (165)
46	7-46426-2	Joe Henderson - State Of The Tenor/Live At The Village Vanguard,Vol.2 (311)
47	7-46545-2	Freddie Hubbard - Blue Spirits (177,190)
48	7-46507-2	Freddie Hubbard - Hub Tones (144)
49	7-46537-2	Bobby Hutcherson - Dialogue (179)
50	7-46530-2	Bobby Hutcherson - Happenings (190)
51	7-46521-2	Art Blakey & The Jazz Messengers At The Café Bohemia, Vol.1 (49,50)
52	7-46522-2	Art Blakey & The Jazz Messengers At The Café Bohemia, Vol.2 (49,50)
53	7-46814-2	The Magnificent Thad Jones (55)
54	7-46824-2	Duke Jordan - Flight To Jordan (108)
55	7-46092-2	Stanley Jordan - Magic Touch (304)
56	7-46333-2	Stanley Jordan - Standards,Vol.1 (316)
57	7-46298-2	Bobby McFerrin - Spontaneous Inventions (313,649)
58	7-46527-2	Jackie McLean - Let Freedom Ring (136)
59	7-46142-2	Jackie McLean - Jackie's Bag (88,110)
60	7-46821-2	Jackie McLean - One Step Beyond (153)
61	7-84345-2	Jackie McLean - Demon's Dance (208)
62	7-46511-2	Hank Mobley - Dippin' (183)
63	7-46528-2	Hank Mobley - Soul Station (99)
64	7-46823-2	Hank Mobley - Roll Call (113)
65	7-46816-2	The Hank Mobley Quintet (62)
66	7-46137-2	Lee Morgan - The Sidewinder (161)
67	7-46508-2	Lee Morgan - Candy (75,77)
68	7-46817-2	Lee Morgan,Volume 3 (62)
69	7-46428-2	Lee Morgan - The Rumproller (180,181)
70	7-46431-2	James Newton - Romance & Revolution (314)
71	7-46292-2	James Newton - The African Flower (309)
72	7-46395-2	Out Of The Blue - Inside Track (314)
73	7-46784-2	Out Of The Blue - Live At Mt. Fuji (315)
74	7-46427-2	Michel Petrucciani - Power Of Three (314)
75	7-46529-2	Bud Powell - The Scene Changes (88)
76	7-46820-2	Bud Powell - Time Waits (82)
77	7-46907-2	Don Pullen - Song Everlasting (318)
78	7-46846-2	Ike Quebec - Easy Living (133)
79	7-46517-2	Sonny Rollins - A Night At The Village Vanguard,Vol.1 (73)
80	7-81558-2	Sonny Rollins Volume 2 (63)
81	7-46518-2	Sonny Rollins - A Night At The Village Vanguard,Vol.2 (73,74)
82	7-46335-2	George Russell - The African Game (303)
83	7-46391-2	George Russell - So What (303)
84	7-46403-2	Wayne Shorter - Adam's Apple (190)
85	7-46514-2	Wayne Shorter - Ju-Ju (169)
86	7-46509-2	Wayne Shorter - Speak No Evil (176)
87	7-84173-2	Wayne Shorter - Night Dreamer (165)
88	7-46140-2	Horace Silver & The Jazz Messengers (44,45)
89	7-46526-2	Horace Silver - Blowin' The Blues Away (94,95)
90	7-46402-2	Jimmy Smith - Back At The Chicken Shack (102,103)
91	7-46546-2	Jimmy Smith - House Party (70)
92	7-46097-2	Jimmy Smith - The Sermon (70,78)
93	7-46297-2	Jimmy Smith - Go For Whatcha Know (312)
94	7-46535-2	Cecil Taylor - Conquistador (196)
95	7-46531-2	Introducing The Three Sounds (83,84)
96	7-46100-2	Stanley Turrentine - Joyride (181)
97	7-46762-2	Stanley Turrentine - Wonderland (The Music Of Stevie Wonder) (317)
98	7-46543-2	Stanley Turrentine - Look Out! (104)
99	7-84275-2	McCoy Tyner - Tender Moments (207)

100	7-46512-2	McCoy Tyner - The Real McCoy (201)
101	7-46291-2	McCoy Tyner - It's About Time (308)
102	7-46755-2	James "Blood" Ulmer - America/Do You Remember The Love (315)
103	7-46905-2	Jack Walrath - Master Of Suspense (315,320)
104	7-46135-2	Tony Williams - Spring (184)
105	7-46757-2	Tony Williams - Civilization (316)
106	7-84282-2	Elvin Jones - Puttin' It Together (212)
107	7-90055-2	Chick Corea - Now He Sings,Now He Sobs (585)
108	7-48679-2	Michel Petrucciani - Michel Plays Petrucciani (322)
109	7-84222-2	Lee Morgan - Cornbread (185)
110		
111	7-81501-2	Miles Davis,Vol.1 (31,41)
112	7-48017-2	Freddie Hubbard - The Eternal Triangle (321)
113	7-84077-2	Dexter Gordon - Doin' Alright (121)
114	7-81542-2	Sonny Rollins,Volume 1 (59)
115	7-84154-2	Grant Green - Idle Moments (159)
116	7-84080-2	Hank Mobley - Workout (119)
117	7-84332-2	Wayne Shorter - Super Nova (231)
118	7-46858-2	Art Blakey - Ritual (552)
119	7-46853-2	Art Pepper - Complete Aladdin Recordings, Vol.III (465)
120	7-46863-2	Art Pepper - Complete Aladdin Recordings, Vol.I (464,465)
121	7-84164-2	Jimmy Smith - Prayer Meetin' (103,149)
122	7-48014-2	Bennie Wallace - Border Town (320)
123		
124	7-84254-2	Lou Donaldson - Lush Life (199)
125	7-84135-2	Freddie Hubbard - Here To Stay (146)
126		
127	7-84178-2	Blue Mitchell - The Thing To Do (169)
128	7-84273-2	Hank Mobley - Hi Voltage (206)
129	7-84425-2	Hank Mobley - Far Away Lands (202)
130	7-84431-2	Hank Mobley - Another Workout (130)
131	7-84426-2	Lee Morgan - The Rajah (197)
132	7-84095-2	Leo Parker - Rollin' With Leo (128)
133	7-84134-2	Horace Parlan - Happy Frame Of Mind (150)
134	7-84191-2	Duke Pearson - Wahoo (175)
135	7-84261-2	Sam Rivers - Dimensions And Extensions (200)
136	7-84290-2	Lonnie Smith - Think (216)
137	7-84434-2	The Three Sounds - Babe's Blues (125,136)
138	7-84057-2	Stanley Turrentine - Blue Hour (114)
139	7-84122-2	Stanley Turrentine - Jubilee Shout (145)
140	7-84424-2	Stanley Turrentine - Z.T.'s blues (127)
141	7-84338-2	McCoy Tyner - Expansions (217)
142	7-91139-2	The Best Of Dexter Gordon - The Blue Note Years (121,122,142,167)
143	7-91142-2	The Best Of Herbie Hancock - The Blue Note Years (139,151,168,179,210)
144	7-91138-2	The Best Of Lee Morgan - The Blue Note Years (62,72,75,61,163,181,184,185)
145	7-91141-2	The Best Of Wayne Shorter - The Blue Note Years (165,169,176,178,190,200,231)
146	7-91143-2	The Best Of Horace Silver - The Blue Note Years (39,44,45,58,64,89,94)
147	7-91140-2	The Best Of Jimmy Smith - The Blue Note Years (51,61,78,98,103,312)
148	7-81505-2	The Eminent Jay Jay Johnson,Volume 1 (36)
149	7-81506-2	The Eminent Jay Jay Johnson,Volume 2 (43,48)
150	7-81520-2	Horace Silver Trio (33,39)
151	7-84149-2	Hank Mobley - No Room For Squares (158)
152	7-84186-2	Hank Mobley - The Turnaround (177)
153	7-84435-2	Hank Mobley - Straight No Filter (151,193)
154	7-84147-2	Herbie Hancock - Inventions And Dimensions (157)
155	7-84167-2	Andrew Hill - Point Of Departure (164)
156	7-84245-2	Art Blakey - Like Someone In Love (108,109)
157	7-84124-2	Donald Byrd - A New Perspective (147)
158	7-84013-2	Jackie McLean - New Soil (91)
159	7-81537-2	Lou Donaldson Quartet/Quintet/Sextet (32,33,43)
160	7-84040-2	Freddie Hubbard - Open Sesame (104)

161	7-84076-2	Horace Silver Quartet - Doin' The Thing (At The Village Gate) (122,123)
162	7-84078-2	Jimmy Smith - Midnight Special (102,103)
163	7-84073-2	Freddie Hubbard - Hub Cap (120)
164		
165	7-84019-2	Donald Byrd - Byrd In Hand (92)
166	7-84181-2	Kenny Dorham - Trompeta Toccata (172)
167	7-90583-2	Bill Evans/Jim Hall - Undercurrent (626,627)
168	7-81559-2	Johnny Griffin - A Blowin' Session (63)
169	7-84140-2	Joe Henderson - Page One (155)
170	7-81574-2	Hank Mobley - Peckin' Time (77)
171	7-84153-2	Grachan Moncur III - Evolution (160)
172	7-84169-2	Lee Morgan - Search For The New Land (163)
173	7-81571-2	The Amazing Bud Powell,Vol.3 (68)
174	7-84098-2	Ike Quebec - Blue And Sentimental (131)
175	7-81539-2	Horace Silver - Six Pieces Of Silver (58,82)
176	7-84008-2	Finger Poppin' With The Horace Silver Quintet (89)
177		
178	7-84096-2	Stanley Turrentine - That's Where It's At (132)
179	7-46093-2	Kenny Burrell/Grover Washington - Togethering (304)
180	7-84224-2	Ornette Coleman At The Golden Circle,Vol.1 (187,188)
181	7-84225-2	Ornette Coleman At The Golden Circle,Vol.2 (187,188)
182	7-48041-2	Eric Dolphy - Other Aspects (455,456)
183	7-84263-2	Lou Donaldson - Alligator Boogaloo (201)
184	7-84059-2	Kenny Drew - Undercurrent (113)
185	7-84175-2	Herbie Hancock - Empyrean Isles (168)
186	7-84151-2	Andrew Hill - Black Fire (159)
187	7-46898-2	Freddie Hubbard - Life Flight (317)
188	7-84243-2	Lee Morgan - Delightfulee Morgan (191,192)
189		
190	7-84363-2	Wayne Shorter - Odyssey Of Iska (247)
191	7-84065-2	Stanley Turrentine - Comin' Your Way (116)
192	7-84307-2	McCoy Tyner - Time For Tyner (214)
193	7-84118-2	Donald Byrd - Free Form (131)
194	7-84108-2	Lou Donaldson - The Natural Soul (138)
195	7-84176-2	Dexter Gordon - One Flight Up (167)
196	7-84432-2	Grant Green - Born To Be Blue (132,135)
197	7-84152-2	Joe Henderson - Our Thing (157)
198	7-84427-2	Jackie McLean - Tippin' The Scales (143)
199	7-84212-2	Lee Morgan - The Gigolo (183,184)
200	7-84185-2	Horace Silver - Song For My Father (159,162,173)
201		
202	7-81526-2	Clifford Brown Memorial Album (35,38)
203	7-84291-2	Bobby Hutcherson - Total Eclipse (215)
204	7-81531-2	The Fabulous Fats Navarro,Vol.1: Fats Navarro (19,25) Tadd Dameron (471,473)
205	7-81532-2	The Fabulous Fats Navarro,Vol.2 (22,23,25)
206	7-81503-2	The Amazing Bud Powell,Vol.1 (25,27)
207	7-81504-2	The Amazing Bud Powell,Vol.2 (27,37)
208	7-46430-2	Grant Green - Grantstand (125)
209	7-84227-2	Joe Henderson - Mode For Joe (189)
210	7-46296-2	Joe Henderson - State Of The Tenor/Live At The Village Vanguard,Vol.1 (310,311)
211	7-46294-2	Freddie Hubbard/Woody Shaw - Double Take (312)
212	7-46537-2	Bobby Hutcherson - Dialogue (179)
213		
214	7-46993-2	Charnett Moffett - Net Man (318)
215	7-46848-2	Modern Art - Art Pepper Complete Aladdin Recordings, Vol.II (464,465)
216	7-46295-2	Michel Petrucciani - Pianism (312)
217	7-46314-2	Don Pullen-George Adams Quartet - Breakthrough (313)
218	7-84237-2	Cecil Taylor - Unit Structures (192)
219	7-46110-2	Stanley Turrentine - Straight Ahead (305)
220	7-46293-2	Bennie Wallace - Twilight Time (308)

 810

221	7-46289-2	Tony Williams - Foreign Intrigue (309)
222		
223	7-81596-2	Kenny Burrell - Blue Lights,Vol.1 (81)
224	7-81597-2	Kenny Burrell - Blue Lights,Vol.2 (81)
225	7-84067-2	Jackie McLean - Bluesnik (115)
226	7-84143-2	Big John Patton - Blue John (155,156)
227	7-84188-2	Donald Byrd - I'm Tryin' To Get Home (175,176)
228	7-84189-2	Joe Henderson - Inner Urge (175)
229	7-84220-2	Horace Silver - The Cape Verdean Blues (185,186)
230	7-89002-2	Sheila Jordan - Portrait Of Sheila Jordan (142,144)
231	7-93201-2	The Best Of Stanley Turrentine (104,114,132,150,167,181,193,195,305)
232	7-93205-2	The Best Of Art Blakey & The Jazz Messengers (85,101,109,127,162)
233	7-93206-2	The Best Of Horace Silver,Vol.2 (173,185,186,196,210,263)
234	7-93204-2	The Best Of Bud Powell (25,27,37,68,82,88,154)
235	7-93203-2	The Best Of Sonny Rollins (59,63,71,73,74)
236	7-93202-2	The Best Of Freddie Hubbard (104,120,126,144,166,312,321)
237	7-91441-2	Lou Rawls & Les McCann Ltd. - Stormy Monday (491,492)
238	7-84001-2	Sonny Rollins - Newk's Time (71)
239	7-93415-2	Modern Jazz Quartet - Odds Against Tomorrow (624)
240	7-81502-2	Miles Davis,Vol.2 (34)
241	7-84087-2	Leo Parker - Let Me Tell You 'Bout It (126)
242	7-84287-2	Ornette Coleman-New York Is Now (213,214)
243	7-84356-2	Ornette Coleman - Love Call (213,214)
244	7-81510-2	Thelonious Monk - Genius Of Modern Music,Vol.1 (19,20,21)
245	7-81511-2	Thelonious Monk - Genius Of Modern Music,Vol.2 (28,32)
246	7-84445-2	Dexter Gordon - Clubhouse (182)
247	7-84442-2	Grant Green - Matador (166,167)
248	7-84444-2	Bobby Hutcherson - Oblique (204)
249	7-84446-2	Lee Morgan - Tom Cat (170)
250	7-84443-2	Wayne Shorter - The Soothsayer (178)
251	7-84441-2	Jimmy Smith - Cool Blues (80)
252	7-84230-2	Hank Mobley - A Caddy For Daddy (188)
253	7-84042-2	Horace Silver - Horace-Scope (106)
254	7-84451-2	Art Blakey & The Jazz Messsengers - Three Blind Mice,Vol.1 (626)
255	7-84452-2	Art Blakey & The Jazz Messsenger s- Three Blind Mice,Vol.2 (126,626)
256	7-84447-2	Elvin Jones - Live At The Lighthouse,Vol.1 262)
257	7-84448-2	Elvin Jones - Live At The Lighthouse,Vol.2 (262)
258	7-94848-2	Dexter Gordon - Nights At The Keystone,Vol.1 (457)
259	7-94849-2	Dexter Gordon - Nights At The Keystone,Vol.2 (457)
260	7-94850-2	Dexter Gordon - Nights At The Keystone,Vol.3 (457)
261	7-95636-2	The Best Of Thelonious Monk (19,20,21,22,28,32)
262		
263	7-95627-2	The Best Of Joe Henderson (155,157,165,175,189,311)
264	7-46625-2	The Best Of Earl Klugh,Vol.1 (285,293,297,508,536,537,538,634)
265	7-94861-2	Love Me Blue (The Music Of Lennon & McCartney) (see page 780)
266	7-96098-2	Ballads In Blue - Big Sounds For The Small Hours (see page 781)
267	7-96563-2	So Blue So Funky,Vol.1 (Heroes Of The Hammond) (see page 782)
268	7-95591-2	Jazz Hot And Blue - Blue Note Plays The Music Of Cole Porter (see page 781)
269	7-95590-2	Blue Bossa (see page 781)
270		
271		
272		
273		
274		
275	7-96579-2	Dexter Gordon - Ballads (121,122,142,154,167,182)
276		
277		
278		
279	7-84458-2	Milt Jackson-Bags' Opus (621)
280	7-84457-2	Booker Little 4 Plus Max Roach (620)
281		

282
283
284
285 7-98638-2 The Best Of Donald Byrd (260,264,267,274,283,289,291)
286 7-98287-2 The Best Of Miles Davis (31,34,41,79,472)
287 7-98289-2 The Best Of Ronnie Laws (279,284,286,296,537,633)
288 7-99106-2 Blue Break Beats,Vol.1 (see page 784)
289 7-99095-2 Blue Berlin (see page 783)
290 7-99105-2 Blue 'N' Soul - Blue Note Plays The Soul Hits (see page 784)
291 7-99100-2 Le Paris Bleu (see page 784)
292 7-99099-2 Blue Boogie - Boogie Woogie Stride And The Piano Blues (see page 783)
293 7-99790-2 Critic's Choice (see page 784)
294 7-84466-2 Donald Byrd - Blackbyrd (260,264)
295
296
297
298
299
300 7-80679-2 Blue 'N' Groovy (see page 773)
301 7-80703-2 Blue Testament: (see page 774)
302 7-80706-2 Rhapsody In Blue - The Music Of George And Ira Gershwin (see page 774)
303 7-80707-2 California Cool (see page774)
304 7-80701-2 Afro-Blue (see page 774)
305
306
307 7-80505-2 The Best Of Earl Klugh,Vol.2 (293,296,297,508,509,538,633,634)
308 7-97960-2 Best Of Blue Note,Vol.2 (see page 783)
309 7-81331-2 Blue Valentines (see page 774)
310 7-89032-2 Birks' Works - The Music Of Dizzy Gillespie (see page 777)
311 7-89907-2 Blue Break Beats,Vol.2 (see page 778)
312 7-89910-2 Blue Moon (see page 778)
313 7-89914-2 Blue Eyes - Sinatra Songs The Blue Note Way (see page 778)
314 7-89915-2 Cordon Blue (see page 778)
315
316 7-89606-2 Donald Byrd - Early Byrd (193,198,202,227,242,255)
317 7-89622-2 The Best Of Grant Green - Street Funk And Jazz Grooves
(125,159,172,174,233,237,246,257,260)

CDBLT (Europe)
1001 7-91930-2 Tommy Smith - Step By Step (324)
1002 7-94335-2 Tommy Smith - Peeping Tom (334)
1003 7-96452-2 Tommy Smith - Standards (341)
1004 7-98581-2 Orphy Robinson - When Tomorrow Comes (345)
1005 7-80612-2 Tommy Smith - Paris (351)
1006 7-80696-2 Stan Tracey - Portraits Plus (349)
1007 8-27798-2 Andy Sheppard - Rhythm Method (358,360)
1008 8-28719-2 Andy Sheppard - Delivery Suite (360)
1009 8-29223-2 Orphy Robinson - The Vibes Describe (358)
1010 8-31139-2 Stan Tracey - Live At The QEH (652)

CDBNX
1 7-48337-2 Sampling Of Blue Notes:
Horace Silver (94)
Stanley Turrentine (114)
Jimmy Smith (78)
The Jazz Messengers (49)
Dexter Gordon (142)
All Stars (310)
Lou Donaldson (83)
Herbie Hancock (179)
Cannonball Adderley (79)
Hank Mobley (99)
Kenny Burrell (147)
Lee Morgan (161)

2 7-92812-2 Blue Note Sampler,Vol.2:

Dianne Reeves (319)	Albert Ammons & Meade Lux Lewis (2)
Bireli Lagrene (323)	Miles Davis (31)
Tommy Smith (324)	Bud Powell (37)
Stanley Jordan (304)	Lou Donaldson (201)
Bobby McFerrin (313)	Horace Silver (173)

CDEST
2230 7-80883-2 Us3 - Hand On The Torch (350,351)

CZ
40 7-48385-2 Earl Klugh - Living Inside Your Love (293)
95 7-84164-2 Jimmy Smith - Prayer Meetin' (103,149)
447 7-96101-2 Robbie Krieger (290,291)

3 CD Sets:

CDOMB 007 Miles Davis-Birth Of The Cool/Miles Davis,Vol.1/Miles Davis,Vol.2 (The Originals) (= BLP1501 +BLP1502 + Cap.T 762)
CDOMB 008 Sonny Rollins/Sonny Rollins Vol.2/Newk's Time (= BLP1542 + BLP1558 + BLP4001)
CDOMB 009 Herbie Hancock-Takin' Off/Inventions and Dimensions/Empyrean Isles (= BLP4109 + BLP4147 + BLP4175)

CAPITOL label

BU 6 7-46585-2 Ronnie Laws - Classic Masters (279,396) (& further titles fnot from BN)

CDESTX
2195 8-29457-2 Us3 - Hand On The Torch/The Jazz Mixes (2 CD Set) (350,351)

DORMOUSE label

CDX-04 Art Hodes-Sessions At Blue Note (7,8,11,13,14,15)

EMI Label

CZ 40 7-48385-2 Earl Klugh - Living Inside Your Love (293)
CZ 44 7-48386-2 Earl Klugh - Finger Paintings (296,297)
CZ 59 7-48387-2 Earl Klugh - Crazy For You (293,538)
CZ 61 7-48389-2 Earl Klugh - Magic In Your Eyes (633,634)

PARLOPHONE label

CDPCDS 7367 BN 8-27533-2 Giant Steps (see page 786)

PINNACLE label

RD 116 BN-LA398-G +1 Alphonse Mouzon - Mind Transplant (275)

PREMIER (MFP) label

CDJA 1 Travellin' Light:

Horace Parlan Trio (100)	Jimmy Smith (98)
Jutta Hipp & Zoot Sims (56)	Horace Silver (94)
Bobby McFerrin (313)	(& further titles not from BN)

CDJA 2 Last Chance To Groove:

Horace Silver Quintet (45)	Bennie Wallace (308)
Benny Green (335)	Bobby Watson with Victor Lewis (340)
Horace Silver Quintet (185)	(& further titles not from BN)

813

CDJA 3	Sentimental Over You: Vic Dickenson Quartet (32)	(& further titles not from BN)
CDPR 127	Original Jazz Classics: Joe Henderson (161) (& further titles not from BN)	Kenny Burrell (147)

UNITED ARTISTS label

UAG 30079	BN-LA730-H	Ronnie Laws - Friends & Strangers (296)

FRANCE

CLASSICS label

Note:(+) mark is used for CDs including further titles from other labels.

538	The Chronological Earl Hines 1937-1939 (3) (+)
608	The Chronological Sidney Bechet 1938-1940 (3) (+)
619	The Chronological Sidney Bechet 1940 (4) (+)
643	The Chronological Frankie Newton 1937-1939 (2) (+)
656	The Chronological Pete Johnson 1938-1939 (4) (+)
665	The Chronological Pete Johnson 1939-1941 (4) (+)
715	The Chronological Albert Ammons 1936-1939 (1,2) (+)
722	The Chronological Meade Lux Lewis 1927-1939 (1) (+)
743	The Chronological Meade Lux Lewis 1939-1941 (1,2,5) (+)
802	The Chronological Erroll Garner 1944 (448) (+)
818	The Chronological Erroll Garner 1944,Vol.2 (448) (+)
824	The Chronological James P. Johnson 1943-1944 (6,7)
830	The Chronological Edmond Hall 1937-1944 (5,6,7) (+)
850	The Chronological Erroll Garner 1944,Vol.3 (449) (+)
860	The Chronological Sidney Bechet 1941-1944 (12) (+)
872	The Chronological Edmond Hall 1944-1945 (8) (+)
906	The Chronological Benny Morton 1934-1945 (13) (+)
954	The Chronological Sidney Bechet 1945-1946 (12,13,17) (+)
957	The Chronological Ike Quebec 1944-1946 (10,14,15) (+)
1027	The Chronological James P. Johnson 1944-1945 (11) (+)
1112	The Chronological Sidney Bechet 1947-1949 (24) (+)
1116	The Chronological James Moody 1948-1949 (23) (+)
1118	The Chronological Thelonious Monk 1947-1948 (19,20,21,22)
1124	The Chronological Bobs Gonzales 1947-1949 (18) (+)
1136	The Chronological John Hardee 1946-1948 (17) (+)
1140	The Chronological Sidney Bechet 1949 (24) (+)

JAPAN

BLUE NOTE label

Note:In following series,second column shows US equivalent CD (or LP) when applicable.

28WD-1001 BST84323 Duke Pearson - Merry Old Soul (223,230)

CJ20-5029 Dianne Reeves - Oh What A Freedom (318,319,650)

CJ25-5181/84(4 CD Set) Swing Journal Presents The Blue Note Years:

Albert Ammons & Meade Lux Lewis (2)
Sidney Bechet (3)
Edmond Hall (5)
Ike Quebec (10)
Thelonious Monk (20)
Tadd Dameron (22)
James Moody (23)
Bud Powell (25,27)
Thelonious Monk (28)
Milt Jackson (30)
Miles Davis (31)
Clifford Brown (38)
Horace Silver (39)
Kenny Dorham (46)
Jimmy Smith (51)
Johnny Griffin (52)
Horace Silver (58)
John Coltrane (71)
Sonny Rollins (73)
Curtis Fuller (75)
Sonny Clark (76)
Hank Mobley (77)
Cannonball Adderley (79)
Art Blakey (85)
Bud Powell (88)
Lou Donaldson (89)
Donald Byrd (95)
Jimmy Smith (98)
Hank Mobley (99)
Stanley Turrentine (104)
Horace Silver (106)
Freddie Hubbard (120)
Grant Green (124)
Art Blakey (130)
Dexter Gordon (142)
Donald Byrd (147)
Lee Morgan (161)
Eric Dolphy (163)
Herbie Hancock (168)
Wayne Shorter (169)
Jackie McLean (169)
Tony Williams (171)
Bobby Hutcherson (179)
Larry Young (186)
Ornette Coleman (187)

CJ28-5021 Sunday Afternoon Jazz:

Bobby Hutcherson (190)
Hank Mobley (183)
The Three Sounds (89)
Sonny Clark (72)
Lee Morgan (161)
Art Pepper (464)
Benny Goodman (481)
June Christy (485)
The Four Freshmen (489)
Peggy Lee (493)

5022 Midnight Jazz Piano:

Thelonious Monk (21)
Sonny Clark (72)
Bud Powell (88)
Duke Jordan (108)
Kenny Drew (113)
McCoy Tyner (214)
Herbie Hancock (210)
Nat King Cole (480)
George Shearing (487)
Chick Corea (585)
Tommy Flanagan (622)
Bill Evans (627)

5023 Lullabies For Lovers:

Miles Davis (31)
John Coltrane (71)
Duke Pearson (98)
Ike Quebec (143)
Lee Morgan (191)
Art Pepper (465)
Woody Herman (471)
Duke Ellington (477)
June Christy (493)
Nancy Wilson (502)
Laurindo Almeida (547)
Bill Evans (623)

CJ28-

5024 Twilight Time Jazz:

Lee Morgan (58) | Dexter Gordon (182)
Sonny Clark (76) | Duke Ellington (477)
Cannonball Adderley (79) | Nancy Wilson (493)
Ike Quebec (143) | Peggy Lee (496)
Joe Henderson (155) | Joe Pass (561)

5030 Jazzlife Presents The Heart Of Jazz:

Bud Powell (25) | Kenny Burrell (93)
Thelonious Monk (28) | Herbie Hancock (179)
Milt Jackson (30) | McCoy Tyner (201)
Horace Silver (39) | Art Pepper (464)
Sonny Rollins (59) | Miles Davis (473)
Sonny Clark (72) | Jim Hall (552)
Art Blakey (85) | Chick Corea (585)

5031 The Best Of Art Blakey -The Blue Note Years (49,85,101,109,127,130,166)
5032 The Best Of Bud Powell - The Blue Note Years (25,27,37,68,82,88,154)
5033 The Best Of Horace Silver - The Blue Note Years (39,45,58,64,89,94,106,122,141,173)
5034 The Best Of Jimmy Smith - The Blue Note Years (50,54,55,60,64,70,74,98,103,133)
5035 The Best Of Hank Mobley - The Blue Note Years (46,63,77,99,113,119,130,183)
5036 The Best Of Sonny Clark - The Blue Note Years (67,70,72,75,76,86,87,129)
5037 The Best Of Lee Morgan - The Blue Note Years (58,62,72,77,161,181,184,185,191)
5038 The Best Of Dexter Gordon - The Blue Note Years (121,122,142,154,182)
5039 The Best Of Wayne Shorter - The Blue Note Years (165,169,176,186,190,200,231)
5040 The Best Of Herbie Hancock - The Blue Note Years (139,151,157,168,179,210,225)
5051 7-46338-2 Cannonball Adderley/Miles Davis - Somethin' Else (79)
5052 7-46516-2 Art Blakey & The Jazz Messengers (85)
5053 7-46529-2 The Amazing Bud Powell,Vol. 5 - The Scene Changes (88)
5054 7-46394-2 Dexter Gordon - Our Man In Paris (154)
5055 7-46339-2 Herbie Hancock - Maiden Voyage (179)
5056 7-81501-2 Miles Davis (31,41)
5057 7-81542-2 Sonny Rollins,Vol.1 (59)
5058 7-81571-2 Bud Powell - Bud! (68)
5059 7-46513-2 Sonny Clark - Cool Struttin' (76)
5060 7-84008-2 Finger Poppin' With The Horace Silver Quintet (89)
5061 7-46547-2 Sonny Clark Trio (72)
5062 7-84073-2 Freddie Hubbard - Hup Cap (120)
5063 7-84076-2 The Horace Silver Quintet At The Village Gate - Doin' The Thing (122,123)
5064 7-84157-2 Lee Morgan - The Sidewinder (161)
5065 7-46511-2 Hank Mobley - Dippin' (183)
5066 7-81539-2 Horace Silver - 6 Pieces Of Silver (58,82)
5067 7-81559-2 Johnny Griffin - A Blowing Session (63)
5068 BST84028 Horace Parlan - Movin' And Groovin' (100)
5069 7-84049-2 Art Blakey & The Jazz Messengers - A Night In Tunisia (108,109)
5070 7-84077-2 Dexter Gordon - Doin' Allright (121)
5071 7-84013-2 Jackie McLean - New Soil (91)
5072 7-84019-2 Donald Byrd - Byrd In Hand (92)
5073 7-84140-2 Joe Henderson - Page One (155)
5074 7-46509-2 Wayne Shorter - Speak No Evil (176)
5075 7-84245-2 Art Blakey And The Jazz Messengers - Like Someone In Love (108,109)
5076 7-81577-2 John Coltrane - Blue Train (71)
5077 BST84014 +3? The 3 Sounds - Bottoms Up! (83,84,89)
5078 7-84078-2 The Incredible Jimmy Smith - Midnight Special (102,103)
5079 8-37643-2 Herbie Hancock - Takin' Off (139)
5080 7-46429-2 Art Blakey & The Jazz Messengers - Indestructible (165,166)

CJ28-

5081	7-81574-2	Hank Mobley-Lee Morgan - Peckin' Time (77)
5082	7-46508-2	Lee Morgan - Candy (75,77)
5083	7-84047-2	Art Taylor - A.T.'s Delight (108)
5084	7-84167-2	Andrew Hill - Point Of Departure (164)
5085	7-46136-2	Herbie Hancock - Speak Like A Child (210)
5086	7-46517-2	Sonny Rollins-Vol.1 (73)
5087	7-46518-2	Sonny Rollins,Vol.2 (73,74)
5088	7-84040-2	Freddie Hubbard - Open Sesame (104)
5089	7-84147-2	Herbie Hancock - Inventions And Dimensions (157)
5090	7-84154-2	Grant Green - Idle Moments (159)
5091	7-46533-2	Paul Chambers - Bass On Top (67)
5092	BST84022	Duke Pearson - Profile (96)
5093	7-46523-2	Art Blakey & The Jazz Messengers - Mosaic (127)
5094	7-84153-2	Grachan Moncur III - Evolution (160)
5095	7-46100-2	Stanley Turrentine - Joyride (181)
5096	7-81537-2	Lou Donaldson Quartet/Quintet/Sextet (32,33,43)
5097	7-46528-2	Hank Mobley - Soul Station (99)
5098	7-46142-2	Jackie McLean - Jackie's Bag (88,110)
5099	7-46399-2	Kenny Burrell - Midnight Blue (147)
5100	7-46524-2	Eric Dolphy - Out To Lunch (163)
5101	7-46526-2	Horace Silver - Blowin' The Blues Away (94,95)
5102	7-46534-2	Donald Byrd - Fuego (95)
5103	7-46527-2	Jackie McLean - Let Freedom Ring (136)
5104	7-46094-2	Dexter Gordon - Go! (142)
5105	7-46514-2	Wayne Shorter - Ju Ju (169)
5106	7-46428-2	Lee Morgan - The Rumproller (180,181)
5107	7-46135-2	Anthony Williams - Spring (184)
5108	7-46512-2	McCoy Tyner - The Real McCoy (201)
5109	7-46845-2	Herbie Hancock - The Prisoner (225)
5110	7-84332-2	Wayne Shorter - Super Nova (231)
5111	7-81502-2	Miles Davis - Second Session On Blue Note (34)
5112	7-81503-2	The Amazing Bud Powell,Vol.1 (25,27)
5113	7-81504-2	The Amazing Bud Powell,Vol.2 (25,27,37)
5114		Thelonious Monk - First And Second Sessions On Blue Note (19,20)
5115		Thelonious Monk - Third And Fourth Sessions On Blue Note (21,22)
5116	7-81511-2	Thelonious Monk - Fifth And Final Sessions On Blue Note (28,32)
5117	7-46519-2	Art Blakey - A Night At Birdland,Vol.1 (40,41)
5118	7-46520-2	Art Blakey - A Night At Birdland,Vol.2 (40,41)
5119	7-81526-2	Clifford Brown Memorial Album (35,38)
5120		The Tadd Dameron Sextet/Septet Feat. The Fabulous Fats Navarro (19,22)
5121	7-84436-2	New Sounds Of Art Blakey And James Moody (21,23)
5122	7-84456-2	Wynton Kelly - Piano Interpretations (29)
5123	7-81520-2	Horace Silver Trio & Art Blakey-Sabu (33,39)
5124	BNJ-71002	Introducing The Kenny Drew Trio (34)
5125	7-84438-2	Elmo Hope Trio/Quintet (36,42,553)
5126	BNJ-71003	George Wallington (42)
5127		The Great Guitars: Tal Farlow/Sal Salvador/Lou Mecca (39,41,46)
5128	BLP5066 +2	Hank Mobley Quartet (46)
5129	7-81505-2	The Eminent Jay Jay Johnson,Vol.1 (36)
5130	7-81506-2	The Eminent Jay Jay Johnson,Vol.2 (43,48)
5131	7-46525-2	Lou Donaldson - Blues Walk (83)
5132	7-46531-2	Introducing The Three Sounds (83,84)
5133	7-84030-2	Jimmy Smith - Crazy Baby (98)
5134	7-84042-2	Horace Silver - Horace-Scope (106)
5135	7-46539-2	Donald Byrd At The Half Note,Vol.1 (112)
5136	7-46540-2	Donald Byrd At The Half Note,Vol.2 (112)
5137	7-84096-2	Stanley Turrentine - That's Where It's At (132)
5138	7-84098-2	Ike Quebec - Blue And Sentimental (131)
5139	7-46515-2	Kenny Dorham - Una Mas (152)
5140	8-59962-2	Grant Green - I Want To Hold Your Hand (179)

CJ28-		
5141	7-46521-2	Art Blakey At the Cafe Bohemia,Vol.1 (49,50)
5142	7-46522-2	Art Blakey At the Cafe Bohemia,Vol.2 (49,50)
5143	7-46140-2	Horace Silver & The Jazz Messengers (44,45)
5144	BLP 1523 +2	Introducing Kenny Burrell (53)
5145	BLP1541	Lee Morgan,Volume Two (58)
5146	BLP1568	Hank Mobley (66)
5147	BLP1570	Sonny Clark - Dial S For Sonny (67)
5148	BLP1583	Curtis Fuller-Art Farmer (75)
5149	BLP1591	Lou Donaldson - Lou Takes Off (76)
5150	7-84001-2	Sonny Rollins - Newk's Time (71)
5160	7-84437-2	Paul Chambers - Chambers Music Plus (453,463)
5161		The Best Of Sidney Bechet - The Blue Note Years (3,4,12,17,24,30,37)
5162		The Best Of Thelonious Monk - The Blue Note Years (19,20,21,22,28,32,63)
5163		The Best Of Jackie McLean - The Blue Note Years (91,96,110,136,139,143,153,169,187,208)
5164		The Best Of Freddie Hubbard - The Blue Note Years (104,111,120,126,144,146,166,177)
5165		The Best Of McCoy Tyner - The Blue Note Years (201,207,214,217,238,247)
5166		The Best Of Miles Davis - The Blue Note Years (31,34,41,79)
5167		The Best Of Sonny Rollins - The Blue Note Years (59,63,71,73,74)
5168		The Best Of The Three Sounds - The Blue Note Years (83,89,91,105,114,125)
5169		The Best Of Grant Green - The Blue Note Years (116,120,124,132,137,146,159,179)
5170		The Best Of Stanley Turrentine - The Blue Note Years (114,116,124,127,150,158,171,181,193,199)
5171		Blue Note For You - Originals: Art Blakey (85) / John Coltrane (71) Sonny Clark (76) / Horace Silver (173) Bud Powell (88) / Joe Henderson (155) Lee Morgan (161) / Herbie Hancock (179) Duke Jordan (108)
5172		Blue Note For You - Standards: Cannonball Adderley (79) / Jackie McLean (96) Hank Mobley (183) / Miles Davis (31) Sonny Clark (72) / Lee Morgan (77) Thad Jones (55) / Paul Chambers (67) Dexter Gordon (182) / John Coltrane (71)
5173	7-91785-2	Don Pullen - New Beginning (326)
5174	7-91411-2	Eliane Elias - So Far So Close (329,330)
5175	7-90261-2	Stanley Turrentine - La Place (324,325)
5176		Jazz Cruise At The Seaside: John Coltrane (71) / Phil Woods (520) Sonny Clark (76) / Chet Baker (549) Grant Green (124) / Bud Shank (563) Duke Jordan (108) / Art Farmer (620) Peggy Lee (492)
5177		Jazz On A Sunny Afternoon: Horace Silver (58) / Sonny Criss (532) Lee Morgan (77) / Chet Baker (547) Hank Mobley (99) / John Lewis (550) Herbie Hancock (139) / Jim Hall (552) Grant Green (137) / Chico Hamilton (555) Wanda De Sah (495) / Bud Shank (563)

CJ28-			
5178		Jazz Piano For Swingin' Lovers:	
		Bud Powell (27)	Herbie Hancock (313)
		Wynton Kelly (29)	Nat King Cole (476)
		Kenny Drew (34)	Duke Ellington (477)
		Sonny Clark (87)	Hank Jones (486)
		The Three Sounds (91)	George Shearing (489)
		Duke Pearson (98)	Chick Corea (585)
		Horace Parlan (100)	Bill Evans (626)
5179		Jazz Ballads In A Midnight Mood:	
		Clifford Brown (38)	Dexter Gordon (154)
		Miles Davis (41)	Art Pepper (464)
		Lee Morgan (62)	Dinah Shore (487)
		Jimmy Smith (64)	Nancy Wilson (502)
		Stanley Turrentine (127)	Sonny Criss (531)
		Sonny Clark (129)	Clare Fisher (561)
5186	7-92279-2	Rick Margitza - Color (329)	
CJ32-			
5001	7-46993-2	Charnett Moffett - Net Man (318)	
5002	7-48016-2	Bireli Lagrene - Inferno (321)	
5003	7-48015-2	Mose Allison - Ever Since The World Ended (319)	
5004	7-48014-2	Bennie Wallace - Border Town (320)	
5009	7-90055-2	Chick Corea - Now He Sings,Now He Sobs (585)	
5010	7-48786-2	Billie Holiday - Billie's Blues (462,466,619)	
5014	7-48679-2	Michel Petrucciani - Michel Plays Petrucciani (322)	
5016		The Blue Note Jazz Story II:	
		Freddie Hubbard (104)	Bobby Hutcherson (190)
		Dexter Gordon (122)	Wayne Shorter (190)
		Art Blakey (127)	Lee Morgan (191)
		Jackie McLean (153)	Elvin Jones (212)
		Hank Mobley (183)	McCoy Tyner (214)
		Larry Young (186)	Herbie Hancock (210)
5017	7-90260-2	Kenny Burrell - Piece Of Blue And The Blues (316)	
5018	7-48017-2	Freddie Hubbard & Woody Shaw - The Eternal Triangle (321)	
5020	RJ28-5020	Dianne Reeves - The Nearness of You (322,323,650)	
5027	7-90262-2	Bobby Watson - No Question About It (323)	
5028	7-48494-2	Tony Williams - Angel Street (322)	
5047	7-91651-2	McCoy Tyner - Revelations (325)	
5048	7-90905-2	Freddie Hubbard - Times Are Changin' (326)	
5049		The Blue Note Jazz Story III - Blue Note Into The '90s:	
		Don Pullen/George Adams (313)	Dexter Gordon (310)
		Michel Petrucciani (322)	Out Of The Blue (309)
		Bennie Wallace (320)	Stanley Jordan (304)
		Tony Williams (309)	Freddie Hubbard/Woody Shaw (312)
		Dianne Reeves (319)	Blue Note All Stars (306)
		Charnett Moffett (318)	
5050	7-91937-2	Lou Rawls - At Last (327,328)	
CP28-5864 (Capitol)		I Love New York:	
		Bud Powell (37)	Thelonious Monk (21)
		The Three Sounds (114)	Duke Pearson (96)
		Kenny Drew (34)	(& further titles not from BN)

CP32-
5052 7-46092-2 Stanley Jordan - Magic Touch (304)
5053 7-46093-2 Kenny Burrell/Grover Washington Jr. - Togethering (304)
5054 7-46110-2 Stanley Turrentine - Straight Ahead (305)
5056 The Best Of Blue Note,Vol.1:
Bud Powell (27) Miles Davis (34)
James Moody (23) John Coltrane (71)
Thelonious Monk (28) Herbie Hancock (179)
Milt Jackson (30) Donald Byrd (147)
Clifford Brown (38)
5057 The Best Of Blue Note,Vol.2:
Art Blakey (85) Jimmy Smith (103)
Lou Donaldson (83) Kenny Burrell (147)
Horace Silver (173) Lee Morgan (161)
5062 7-46147-2 One Night with Blue Note,Vol.1 (306)
5063 7-46148-2 One Night with Blue Note,Vol.2 (306,307)
5064 7-46149-2 One Night with Blue Note,Vol.3 (306,307)
5065 7-46150-2 One Night with Blue Note,Vol.4 (306)

5186 7-46398-2 Duke Ellington - Money Jungle (628)
5187 7-90583-2 Bill Evans/Jim Hall - Undercurrent (626,627)

5196 7-46397-2 Dexter Gordon - The Other Side of 'Round Midnight (310,313)
5197 7-46333-2 Stanley Jordan-Standards,Volume 1 (316)

(Super 50 Series)
CP32-
5201 7-46519-2 A Night at Birdland with Art Blakey and The Jazz Messengers, Vol.1 (40,41)
5202 7-46520-2 A Night at Birdland with Art Blakey and The Jazz Messengers, Vol.2 (40,41)
5203 7-46533-2 Paul Chambers - Bass on Top (67)
5204 7-46547-2 Sonny Clark Trio (72)
5205 7-46338-2 Cannonball Adderley - Somethin' Else (79)
5206 7-46531-2 Introducing The Three Sounds (83,84)
5207 7-46529-2 The Amazing Bud Powell,Vol.5 - The Scene Changes (88)
5208 7-46534-2 Donald Byrd - Fuego (95)
5209 7-46523-2 Art Blakey and The Jazz Messengers - Mosaic (127)
5210 7-46507-2 Freddie Hubbard - Hub Tones (144)
5211 7-46524-2 Eric Dolphy - Out to Lunch (163)
5212 7-46510-2 Joe Henderson - In 'n Out (165)
5213 7-84185-2 Horace Silver - Song for My Father (159,162,173)
5214 7-46509-2 Wayne Shorter - Speak No Evil (176)
5215 7-46428-2 Lee Morgan - The Rumproller (180,181)
5216 7-46511-2 Hank Mobley - Dippin' (183)
5217 7-46530-2 Bobby Hutcherson - Happenings (190)
5218 7-46535-2 Cecil Taylor - Conquistador (196)
5219 7-46136-2 Herbie Hancock - Speak Like a Child (210)
5220 7-46845-2 Herbie Hancock - The Prisoner (225)
5221 BLP1501 Miles Davis,Vol.1 (31,34)
5222 BLP1502 Miles Davis,Vol.2 (31,34,41)
5223 7-46140-2 Horace Silver and The Jazz Messengers (44,45)
5224 7-46517-2 Sonny Rollins - A Night at The Village Vanguard,Vol.1 (73)
5225 7-46518-2 Sonny Rollins - A Night at The Village Vanguard,Vol.2 (73,74)
5226 7-46508-2 Lee Morgan - Candy (75,77)
5227 7-46532-2 Art Blakey and The Jazz Messengers - A Night in Tunisia (108,109)
5228 7-46506-2 Herbie Hancock - Takin' Off (139)
5229 7-46399-2 Kenny Burrell - Midnight Blue (147)
5230 7-46394-2 Dexter Gordon - Our Man in Paris (154)
5231 7-46095-2 John Coltrane - Blue Train (71)
5232 7-46525-2 Lou Donaldson - Blues Walk (83)
5233 7-46516-2 Art Blakey and The Jazz Messengers - Moanin' (85)
5234 7-46528-2 Hank Mobley - Soul Station (99)

CP32-

5235	7-46527-2	Jackie McLean - Let Freedom Ring (136)
5236	7-46137-2	Lee Morgan - The Sidewinder (161)
5237	7-46339-2	Herbie Hancock - Maiden Voyage (179)
5238	7-46135-2	Anthony Williams - Spring (184)
5239	7-46512-2	McCoy Tyner - The Real McCoy (201)
5240	7-84332-2	Wayne Shorter - Super Nova (231)
5241		The Amazing Bud Powell,Vol.1 (25,27)
5242	7-46521-2	The Jazz Messengers at The Cafe Bohemia,Vol.1 (49,50)
5243	7-46522-2	The Jazz Messengers at The Cafe Bohemia,Vol.2 (49,50)
5244	BLP1526 +2	Clifford Brown Memorial Album (35,38)
5245	7-46513-2	Sonny Clark - Cool Struttin' (76)
5246	7-46526-2	Horace Silver - Blowin' the Blues Away (94,95)
5247	7-84057-2	Stanley Turrentine with The Three Sounds - Blue Hour (114)
5248	7-46094-2	Dexter Gordon - Go! (142)
5249	7-46515-2	Kenny Dorham - Una Mas (152)
5250	7-46514-2	Wayne Shorter - Ju Ju (169)
5251	7-46395-2	Out of The Blue - Inside Track (314)
5252	7-46290-2	OTB - Out of The Blue (309)
5253	7-46289-2	Tony Williams - Foreign Intrigue (309)
5254	7-46295-2	The Michel Petrucciani Trio - Pianism (312)
5255	7-46292-2	James Newton - The African Flower (309)
5256	7-46293-2	Bennie Wallace - Twilight Time (308)
5257	7-46294-2	Freddie Hubbard/Woody Shaw - Double Take (312)
5258	7-46296-2	Joe Henderson - The State of The Tenor - Live at The Village Vanguard,Vol. 1 (310,311)
5259	7-46314-2	The Don Pullen-George Adams Quartet - Breakthrough (313)
5260	7-46298-2	Bobby McFerrin - Spontaneous Inventions (313,649)
5261	7-46297-2	Jimmy Smith - Go For Whatcha Know (312)
5262	7-46291-2	McCoy Tyner & Jackie McLean - It's About Time (308)
5263	7-46391-2	George Russell & The Living Time Orchestra - So What (303)
5336	7-46427-2	Michel Petrucciani - Power of Three (314)
5337	7-46426-2	Joe Henderson - The State of The Tenor-Live at The Village Vanguard,Vol. 2 (311)
5345	7-46431-2	James Newton - Romance and Revolution (314)
5346	7-48041-2	Eric Dolphy - Other Aspects (455,456)
5406	7-46784-2	OTB - Live at Mt. Fuji (315)
5438	7-46757-2	Tony Williams - Civilization (316)
5439	7-46756-2	Kenny Burrel - Generation (316)
5440	7-46762-2	Stanley Turrentine - Wonderland (317)
5441	7-46848-2	The Complete Art Pepper Aladdin Recordings,Vol.1 - The Return Of Art Pepper (464,465)
5442	7-46853-2	The Complete Art Pepper Aladdin Recordings,Vol.2 - Modern Art (465)
5443	7-46863-2	The Complete Art Pepper Aladdin Recordings,Vol.3 (464,465)
5445	7-46898-2	Freddie Hubbard - Life Flight (317)
5446	7-46906-2	Dianne Reeves (318,319)
5447	7-46907-2	The Don Pullen/George Adams Quartet - Song Everlasting (318)
5448		The Blue Note Jazz Story: Albert Ammons (1) Sidney Bechet (3,12) Edmond Hall (5) Ike Quebec (10) Thelonious Monk (21) James Moody (23) Bud Powell (27) Miles Davis 31 Horace Silver (45) Kenny Dorham (46) Jimmy Smith (50) Lee Morgan (62) Sonny Clark (72) Art Blakey (85)
5513	7-93476-2	John Hart - One Down (589,590)

(CD Treasury Series):

CP32-		
9501	7-46541-2	Kenny Dorham - 'Round About Midnight at The Cafe Bohemia (54)
9502	7-46542-2	Kenny Dorham - 'Round About Midnight at The Cafe Bohemia,Vol.2 (54)
9503	7-46814-2	The Magnificent Thad Jones (55)
9504	7-46536-2	Introducing Johnny Griffin (52)
9505	7-46815-2	Kenny Dorham Afro Cuban (45,46)
9506	7-46816-2	Hank Mobley (62)
9507	7-46817-2	Lee Morgan,Vol.3 (62)
9508	7-46818-2	Sonny Rollins,Vol.2 (63)
9509	7-46819-2	Sonny Clark - Sonny's Crib (70)
9510	7-46820-2	The Amazing Bud Powell (82)
9511	7-46546-2	Jimmy Smith's House Party,Volume 1 (70)
9512	7-46097-2	Jimmy Smith,Volume 2 - The Sermon! (70,78)
9513	7-46538-2	Kenny Burrell with Art Blakey - On View at The Five Spot Cafe (93,94)
9514	7-46400-2	Art Blakey & The Jazz Messengers - The Big Beat (101)
9515	BST84035	Duke Pearson - Tender Feelin's (98)
9516	8-56581-2	Horace Parlan - Us Three (102)
9517	7-46543-2	Stanley Turrentine - Look Out! (104)
9518	BST84044	The 3 Sounds - Moods (105)
9519	7-46824-2	Duke Jordan - Flight to Jordan (108)
9520	7-46823-2	Hank Mobley - Roll Call (113)
9521	7-84059-2	Kenny Drew - Undercurrent (113)
9522	7-84080-2	Hank Mobley - Workout (119)
9523	7-46544-2	Dexter Gordon - Dexter Calling... (122)
9524	7-84091-2	Sonny Clark - Leapin' and Lopin' (129)
9525	7-46402-2	The Incredible Jimmy Smith - Back at The Chicken Shack (102,103)
9526	7-84126-2	Herbie Hancock - My Point of View (151)
9527	7-46822-2	Grant Green - Feelin' The Spirit (146)
9528	7-84133-2	Dexter Gordon - A Swingin' Affair (142)
9529	7-46821-2	Jackie McLean - One Step Beyond (153)
9530	7-84151-2	Andrew Hill - Black Fire (159)
9531	7-84170-2	Art Blakey & The Jazz Messengers - Free For All (162)
9532	7-84173-2	Wayne Shorter - Night Dreamer (165)
9533	7-84175-2	Herbie Hancock - Empyrean Isles (168)
9534	7-84180-2	Anthony Williams - Life Time (171)
9535	7-46545-2	Freddie Hubbard - Blue Spirits (177,190)
9536	7-46537-2	Bobby Hutcherson - Dialogue (179)
9537	7-46681-2	Dexter Gordon - Gettin' Around (182)
9538	7-84221-2	Larry Young - Unity (186)
9539	7-84224-2	The Ornette Coleman Trio at The Golden Circle,Stockholm,Vol.1 (187,188)
9540	7-84225-2	The Ornette Coleman Trio at The Golden Circle,Stockholm,Vol.2 (187,188)
9541	7-46403-2	Wayne Shorter - Adam's Apple (190)
9542	7-84237-2	Cecil Taylor - Unit Structures (192)
9543	7-84243-2	Lee Morgan - DelightfuLee Morgan (191,192)
9544	7-84263-2	Lou Donaldson - Alligator Bogaloo (201)
9545	7-84275-2	McCoy Tyner - Tender Moments (207)
9546	7-84282-2	The New Elvin Jones Trio - Puttin' It Together (212)
9547	7-84307-2	McCoy Tyner - Time For Tyner (214)
9548	7-84345-2	Jackie McLean - Demon's Dance (208)
9549	7-46401-2	Chick Corea - The Song of Singing (240)
9550	7-84363-2	Wayne Shorter - Odyssey of Iska (247)

CP35-		
3069	7-46137-2	Lee Morgan - The Sidewinder (161)
3070	BLP1595	Cannonball Adderley - Somethin' Else (79)
3071	7-46339-2	Herbie Hancock - Maiden Voyage (179)
3088	7-46095-2	John Coltrane - Blue Train (71)
3089	BLP1588	Sonny Clark - Cool Struttin' (76)
3090	BLP4003	Art Blakey & The Jazz Messengers - Moanin' (85)

Note: In following series,all numbers are equivalent to BLP issues with same number.Numbers marked # have no equivalent US CD issue.Numbers 1501 to 1561 are in mono,all others are in stereo.

TOCJ-	CD/LP equiv.	
1501	CP32-5221	Miles Davis,Volume 1 (31,34)
1502	CP32-5222	Miles Davis,Volume 2 (31,34,41)
1503	BLP1503	The Amazing Bud Powell,Volume 1 (25,27)
1504	BLP1504	The Amazing Bud Powell,Volume 2 (25,27,37)
1505	BLP1505	The Eminent Jay Jay Johnson,Volume 1 (36,43)
1506	BLP1506	The Eminent Jay Jay Johnson,Volume 2 (36,43,48)
1507	BLP1507	The Jazz Messengers at the Cafe Bohemia,Volume 1 (49,50)
1508	BLP1508	The Jazz Messengers at the Cafe Bohemia,Volume 2 (49,50)
1509	BLP1509	Milt Jackson (22,28,30)
1510	BLP1510	Thelonious Monk,Volume 1 (20,21,22)
1511	BLP1511	Thelonious Monk,Volume 2 (20,21,28,32)
1512	BLP1512	A New Star - A New Sound: Jimmy Smith at the Organ,Volume 1 (50)
1513#	BLP1513	Detroit-New York Junction: Thad Jones (51)
1514	BLP1514	A New Star - A New Sound: Jimmy Smith at the Organ,Volume 2 (51)
1515#	BLP1515	Jutta Hipp at the Hickory House,Volume 1(52)
1516#	BLP1516	Jutta Hipp at the Hickory House,Volume 2 (52)
1517	BLP1517	Gil Melle - Patterns in Jazz (51)
1518	7-46140-2	Horace Silver and The Jazz Messengers (44,45)
1519	BLP1519	Herbie Nichols Trio (48,49,53)
1520	BLP1520	Horace Silver Trio and Spotlight on Drums: Art Blakey-Sabu (33,39)
1521	BLP1521	A Night at Birdland with The Art Blakey Quintet,Volume 1 (40,41)
1522	BLP1522	A Night at Birdland with The Art Blakey Quintet,Volume 2 (40,41)
1523	BLP1523	Introducing Kenny Burrell Guitar (53)
1524	BLP1524	Kenny Dorham - 'Round Midnight at the Cafe Bohemia (54)
1525	BLP1525	Jimmy Smith at the Organ,Volume 3 (54,55)
1526	BLP1526	Clifford Brown Memorial Album (35,38)
1527	BLP1527	The Magnificent Thad Jones (55)
1528#	BLP1528	The Incredible Jimmy Smith at Club 'Baby Grand',Wilmington,Delaware Vol. 1 (56)
1529#	BLP1529	The Incredible Jimmy Smith at Club 'Baby Grand',Wilmington,Delaware Vol. 2 (56)
1530	BLP1530	Jutta Hipp (56)
1531	BLP1531	The Fabulous Fats Navarro,Volume 1 (19,23,25)
1532	BLP1532	The Fabulous Fats Navarro,Volume 2 (22,23,25)
1533	BLP1533	Introducing Johnny Griffin,Tenor Sax (52)
1534	8-37647-2	Paul Chambers Sextet - Whims of Chambers (57)
1535	BLP1535	Kenny Dorham Octet/Sextet (45,46)
1536	BLP1536	J.R.Monterose (57)
1537	BLP1537	Lou Donaldson Quartet/Quintet/Sextet (32,33,43)
1538#	BLP1538	Lee Morgan Indeed! (57)
1539	BLP1539	6 Pieces of Silver - Horace Silver Quintet (58)
1540#	BLP1540	Hank Mobley Sextet (58)
1541	CJ28-5145	Lee Morgan,Volume 2 (58)
1542	7-81542-2	Sonny Rollins (59)
1543#	BLP1543	Kenny Burrell,Volume 2 (50,53,54)
1544	8-37668-2	Hank Mobley and his All Stars (59)
1545#	BLP1545	Lou Donaldson,Volume 2 - Wailin' With Lou (59)
1546#	BLP1546	The Magnificent Thad Jones,Volume 3 (55,59)
1547#	BLP1547	A Date with Jimmy Smith,Volume 1 (60,61)
1548#	BLP1548	A Date with Jimmy Smith,Volume 2 (60)
1549	BLP1549	Blowing in from Chicago - Cliff Jordan and John Gilmore (61)
1550	BLP1550	Hank Mobley Quintet (62)
1551#	BLP1551	Jimmy Smith at the Organ,Volume 1: All Day Long (61)
1552#	BLP1552	Jimmy Smith at the Organ,Volume 2 (60,61)
1554	BLP1554	Art Blakey - Orgy in Rhythm,Volume 1 (62)
1555	BLP1555	Art Blakey - Orgy in Rhythm,Volume 2 (62)
1556#	BLP1556	The Sounds of Jimmy Smith (60,61)

TOCJ-		
1557	BLP1557	Lee Morgan,Volume 3 (62)
1558	7-81558-2	Sonny Rollins,Volume 2 (62)
1559	7-81559-2	Johnny Griffin - A Blowing Session (63)
1560#	BLP1560	Hank Mobley Sextet - Hank (63)
1561#	BLP1561	Sabu - Palo Congo (64)
1562#	BLP1562	Horace Silver Quintet - The Stylings of Silver (64)
1563#	BLP1563	Jimmy Smith at the Organ Plays Pretty Just For You (64)
1564	BLP1564	Paul Chambers Quintet (65)
1565#	BLP1565	Cliff Jordan (65)
1566#	BLP1566	Lou Donaldson - Swing and Soul (65)
1567#	BLP1567	Curtis Fuller,Trombone - The Opener (66)
1568	CJ28-5146	Hank Mobley (66)
1569	BLP1569	Paul Chambers Quartet - Bass on Top (67)
1570	CJ28-5147	Sonny Clark - Dial S for Sonny (67)
1571	BLP1571	The Amazing Bud Powell,Volume 3 - Bud! (68)
1572#	BLP1572	Curtis Fuller,Volume 2 - Bone & Bari (68)
1573	BLP1573	John Jenkins with Kenny Burrell (69)
1574	BLP1574	Hank Mobley - Peckin' Time (77)
1575#	BLP1575	Lee Morgan - City Lights (69)
1576	BLP1576	Sonny Clark - Sonny's Crib (70)
1577	7-81577-2	John Coltrane - Blue Train (71)
1578#	BLP1578	Lee Morgan - The Cooker (72)
1579	BLP1579	Sonny Clark Trio (72)
1580	BLP1580	Johnny Griffin - The Congregation (73)
1581	BLP1581	Sonny Rollins - A Night at The Village Vanguard (73)
1582	BLP1582	Cliff Jordan,Volume 2 - Cliff Craft (74)
1583#	CJ28-5148	Curtis Fuller - Art Farmer (70)
1584	8-52438-2	Here Comes Louis Smith (454)
1585#	BLP1585	Jimmy Smith - Groovin' at Smalls' Paradise,Volume 1 (74)
1586#	BLP1586	Jimmy Smith - Groovin' at Smalls' Paradise,Volume 2 (74)
1587#	BLP1587	Bennie Green - Back on the Scene (80)
1588	CP35-3089	Sonny Clark - Cool Struttin' (76)
1589	8-56583-2	Further Explorations by the Horace Silver Quintet (76)
1590	BLP1590	Lee Morgan - Candy (75,77)
1591#	CJ28-5149	Lou Donaldson - Lou Takes Off (76)
1592	LNJ70093	Sonny Clark Quintets (75,76)
1593	7-46525-2	Lou Donaldson - Blues Walk (83)
1594#	BLP1594	Louis Smith - Smithville (80)
1595	CP35-3070	Cannonball Adderley with Miles Davis - Somethin' Else (79)
1596	BLP1596	Kenny Burrell - Blue Lights,Volume 1 (81)
1597	BLP1597	Kenny Burrell - Blue Lights,Volume 2 (81)
1598	BLP1598	The Amazing Bud Powell,Volume 4 - Time Waits (82)
1599	BLP1599	Bennie Green - Soul Stirrin' (81)
1600	BLP1600	Introducing The Three Sounds (83,84)
1601		Blue Trails - The Rare Tracks: John Coltrane (71), Johnny Griffin (52), Lee Morgan (72), Cannonball Adderley (79), Horace Silver (58), Kenny Dorham (45), Tina Brooks (79), J.R. Monterose (57), Bud Powell (68)
1602	BNJ-61002	Art Blakey - A Night At Birdland,Vol.3 (40,41)
1603	BNJ-61007	Art Blakey - A Night At The Cafe Bohemia,Vol.3 (49,50)
1604	BNJ-61011 +5	Thelonious Monk - More Genius Of The High Priest Of Bebop (19,20,21,22,28,32)
1605	BNJ-61001	Clifford Brown - More Memorable Tracks (35,36,38)
1606	BNJ-61003	Kenny Dorham - 'Round Midnight At The Cafe Bohemia,Vol.2 (54)
1607	BNJ-61004	Kenny Dorham - 'Round Midnight At The Cafe Bohemia,Vol.3 (54)
1608		The Herbie Nichols Trio,Vol.2 (48,49,53)
1609		Kenny Burrell,Vol.3 (50,60,81,93)

TOCJ-		
1610	BNJ-61013	Jimmy Smith Trio + Lou Donaldson (67)
1611	BNJ-61006	Hank Mobley - Curtain Call (69)
1612		Jimmy Smith - Cherokee (64,66)
1613	BNJ-61014	Sonny Rollins - A Night At The Village Vanguard,Vol.2 (73)
1614	BNJ-61015	Sonny Rollins - A Night At The Village Vanguard,Vol.3 (73,74)
1615	GXF-3078	Jimmy Smith - Lonesome Road (75)
1616	GXF-3072	Tina Brooks - Minor Move (79)
1617	BNJ-61017	Sonny Clark - The 45 Sessions (72,86)
1618	BNJ-61018	Sonny Clark Vol.3 - Blues In The Night (87)
1619	BNJ-61020	Bennie Green - The 45 Session (86)
1620	GXF-3066	Hank Mobley - Poppin' (72)
1621		A Head Like That: Alphonse Mouzon (265) Jack McDuff (234) Bobby Hutcherson (233) Ronnie Foster (265) McCoy Tyner (247) Gene Harris (273) Chico Hamilton (281) Bobbi Humphrey (267) Jean-Luc Ponty (569) Freddie Hubbard (177) Eddie Henderson (287) Donald Byrd (131)
1622	BT84368	Horace Silver - Total Response (250,251)
1623	8-54328-2	Donald Byrd - Ethiopian Knights (255)
1624	BN-LA098-F	Ronnie Foster - Sweet Revival (265)
1625	BN-LA634-G	Gene Harris - In A Special Way (288)
1626	BN-LA853-H	Horace Silver - Silver 'N' Percussion (299,300)
1627	LT-1091	Lee Morgan - Infinity (187)
1628	7-84426-2	Lee Morgan - The Rajah (197)
1629	LA-582-J2	Lee Morgan - The Proscratinator (231,233)
1630	LT-987	Lee Morgan - Sonic Boom (201,202)
1631	LT-1031	Lee Morgan - Taru (209)
1632	4-93401-2	Lee Morgan - The Last Session (256)

Note: In following series,all numbers are equivalent to U.S. LPs with same number in the BST84000 series. Equivalent CD issue is shown when applicable.

TOCJ-	CD/LP equiv.	
4001	7-84001-2	Sonny Rollins - Newk's Time (71)
4002	BST84002	Jimmy Smith - House Party (70,77,78)
4003	CP35-3090	Art Blakey and The Jazz Messengers - Moanin' (85)
4004#	BST84004	A Message from Blakey - Holiday for Skins,Volume 1 (86)
4005#	BST84005	A Message from Blakey - Holiday for Skins,Volume 2 (86)
4006	BST84006	Dizzy Reece - Blues in Trinity (83)
4007#	BST84007	Donald Byrd - Off to the Races (87)
4008	7-84008-2	Finger Poppin' with the Horace Silver Quintet (89)
4009	BST84009	The Amazing Bud Powell,Volume 5 - The Scene Changes (88)
4010#	BST84010	Bennie Green - Walkin' and Talkin' (88)
4011	BST84011	Jimmy Smith - The Sermon (70,78)
4012#	BST84012	Lou Donaldson with The Three Sounds (89)
4013	BST84013	Jackie McLean - New Soil (91)
4014#	CJ28-5077	The Three Sounds - Bottoms Up! (83,84,89)
4015	BST84015	Art Blakey and The Jazz Messengers at the Jazz Corner of the World, Vol. 1 (90)
4016	BST84016	Art Blakey and The Jazz Messengers at the Jazz Corner of the World, Vol. 2 (90)
4017	BST84017	Horace Silver Quintet & Trio - Blowin' the Blues Away (94,95)
4018	8-32098-2	Walter Davis Jr. - Davis Cup (93)
4019	7-84019-2	Donald Byrd - Byrd in Hand (92)
4020#	BST84020	The Three Sounds - Good Deal (91)
4021	BST84021	Kenny Burrell with Art Blakey - On View at the Five Spot Cafe (93,94)
4022#	CJ28-5092	Duke Pearson - Profile (96)
4023#	BST84023	Dizzy Reece - Star Bright (97)
4024	8-56582-2	Jackie McLean - Swing,Swang,Swingin' (96)
4025#	BST84025	Lou Donaldson - The Time is Right (96,97)
4026	7-46534-2	Donald Byrd - Fuego (95)

 825

TOCJ-		
4027	7-89392-2	Freddie Redd Quartet - Music from 'The Connection' (100)
4028#	CJ28-5068	Horace Parlan - Movin' and Groovin' (100)
4029	BST84029	Art Blakey and The Jazz Messengers - The Big Beat (101)
4030	BST84030	The Incredible Jimmy Smith - Crazy Baby (98)
4031	4-95343-2	Hank Mobley - Soul Station (99)
4032	BST84032	Sonny Red - Out of the Blue (97,99)
4033#	BST84033	Dizzy Reece - Soundin' Off (103)
4034	8-32089-2	Lee Morgan - Leeway (103)
4035#	CP32-9515	Duke Pearson - Tender Feelin's (98)
4036	BST84036	Lou Donaldson - Sunny Side up (99,100)
4037	8-56581-2	Horace Parlan - Us Three (102)
4038#	BST84038	Jackie McLean - Capuchin' Swing (102)
4039	BST84039	Stanley Turrentine - Look Out! (104)
4040	BST84040	Freddie Hubbard - Open Sesame (104)
4041	BST84041	Tina Brooks - True Blue (105)
4042	7-84042-2	Horace Silver - Horace-Scope (106)
4043#	BST84043	Horace Parlan Quintet - Speakin' my Piece (107)
4044	CP32-9518	The Three Sounds - Moods (105)
4045	BST84045	Freddie Redd Quintet - Shades of Redd (109)
4046	BST84046	Duke Jordan - Flight to Jordan (108)
4047	7-84047-2	Art Taylor - A.T.'s Delight (108)
4048	BST84048	Donald Byrd - Byrd in Flight (99,106)
4049	7-46532-2	Art Blakey and The Jazz Messengers - A Night in Tunisia (108,109)
4050	BST84050	The Incredible Jimmy Smith - Home Cookin' (82,92)
4051	BST84051	Jackie McLean - Jackie's Bag (88,110)
4052	8-21737-2	Tina Brooks - Back to the Tracks (110,111)
4053#	BST84053	Lou Donaldson - Light Foot (87)
4054#	BST84054	Art Blakey and The Jazz Messengers - Meet You at the Jazz Corner of the World, Volume 1 (110)
4055#	BST84055	Art Blakey and The Jazz Messengers - Meet You at the Jazz Corner of the World, Volume 2 (110)
4056	8-59380-2	Freddie Hubbard - Goin' Up (111)
4057	7-84057-2	Stanley Turrentine with The Three Sounds - Blue Hour (114)
4058	BST84058	Hank Mobley - Roll Call (113)
4059	7-84059-2	Kenny Drew - Undercurrent (113)
4060	BST84060	Donald Byrd at The Half Note Cafe,Volume 1 (112)
4061	BST84061	Donald Byrd at The Half Note Cafe,Volume 2 (112)
4062#	BST84062	Horace Parlan Trio plus Ray Barretto - Headin' South (113)
4063	8-28978-2	Kenny Dorham - Whistle Stop (115)
4064	5-21959-2	Grant Green - Grant's First Stand (116)
4065	BLJ84065	Stanley Turrentine - Comin' Your Way (116)
4066	BST84066	Lou Donaldson - Here 'Tis (116)
4067	BST84067	Jackie McLean - Bluesnik (115)
4068	BST84068	'Baby Face' Willette - Face to Face (117)
4069	BST84069	Stanley Turrentine - Up at Minton's,Volume 1 (118)
4070	BST84070	Stanley Turrentine - Up at Minton's,Volume 2 (118)
4071	BST84071	Grant Green - Green Street (120)
4072#	BST84072	The Three Sounds - Feelin' Good (105)
4073	BST84073	Freddie Hubbard - Hub Cap (120)
4074	BST84074	Horace Parlan - On the Spur of the Moment (119)
4075#	BST84075	Donald Byrd - The Cat Walk (121)
4076	BST84076	The Horace Silver Quintet at The Village Gate - Doin' the Thing (122,123)
4077	BST84077	Dexter Gordon - Doin' Allright (121)
4078	7-84078-2	Jimmy Smith - Midnight Special (102,103)
4079	BST84079	Lou Donaldson - Gravy Train (121)
4080	CP32-9522	Hank Mobley - Workout (119)
4081#	BST84081	Stanley Turrentine - Dearly Beloved (124)
4082#	BST84082	Horace Parlan - Up and Down (124)
4083	BST84083	Dexter Gordon - Dexter Calling (122)
4084	BST84084	Baby Face Willette - Stop and Listen (123)

TOCJ-

4085	BST84085	Freddie Hubbard - Ready for Freddie (126)
4086	BST84086	Grant Green - Grantstand (125)
4087	BST84087	Leo Parker - Let Me Tell You 'Bout It (126)
4088#	BST84088	The Three Sounds - Here We Come (114)
4089	BST84089	Jackie McLean - A Fickle Sonance (128)
4090	7-46523-2	Art Blakey and The Jazz Messengers - Mosaic (127)
4091	BST84091	Sonny Clark - Leapin' and Lopin' (129)
4092#	BST84092	Kenny Clarke-Francy Boland & Co. - The Golden Eight (455)
4093	BST84093	Ike Quebec - Heavy Soul (129)
4094	BST84094	Fred Jackson - Hootin' 'n Tootin' (134)
4095	7-84095-2	Leo Parker - Rollin' with Leo (128)
4096	BST84096	Stanley Turrentine - That's Where It's At (132)
4097#	BST84097	Art Blakey and The Afro-Drum Ensemble - The African Beat (133)
4098	BST84098	Ike Quebec - Blue and Sentimental (131)
4099	BST84099	Grant Green - Sunday Mornin' (124)
4100#	BST84100	Jimmy Smith Plays Fats Waller (133)
4101	BST84101	Donald Byrd - Royal Flush (127)
4102#	BST84102	The Three Sounds - Hey There! (125)
4103	BST84103	Ike Quebec Sextet - Easy Living (133)
4104	BST84104	Art Blakey and The Jazz Messengers - Buhaina's Delight (130,131)
4105	8-21736-2	Ike Quebec - It Might as Well be Spring (130)
4106	7-46527-2	Jackie McLean - Let Freedom Ring (136)
4107#	BST84107	Don Wilkerson - Preach Brother! (140)
4108	BST84108	Lou Donaldson - The Natural Soul (138)
4109	7-46506-2	Herbie Hancock - Takin' Off (139)
4110	8-53355-2	The Horace Silver Quintet - The Tokyo Blues (141)
4111	BST84111	Grant Green - The Latin Bit (137)
4112	4-98794-2	Dexter Gordon - Go! (142)
4113#	BST84113	Freddie Roach - Down To Earth (141)
4114	BST84114	Ike Quebec - Soul Samba (Bossa Nova) (143)
4115	BST84115	Freddie Hubbard - Hub-Tones (144)
4116#	LNJ80118	Jackie McLean Quintet (139)
4117	BST84117	Jimmy Smith - Back at The Chicken Shack (102,103)
4118	BST84118	Donald Byrd - Free Form (131)
4119#	BST84119	Charlie Rouse - Bossa Nova Bacchanal (145)
4120#	BST84120	The Three Sounds - It Just Got To Be (114)
4121#	BST84121	Don Wilkerson - Elder Don (137)
4122	7-84122-2	Stanley Turrentine - Jubilee Shout!!! (145)
4123	BST84123	Kenny Burrell - Midnight Blue (147)
4124	7-84124-2	Donald Byrd - A New Perspective (147)
4125	8-54325-2	Lou Donaldson - Good Gracious! (148)
4126	7-84126-2	Herbie Hancock - My Point of View (151)
4127	BST84127	Kenny Dorham - Una Mas (One More Time) (152)
4128#	BST84128	Freddie Roach - Mo' Greens Please (148,151)
4129	BST84129	Stanley Turrentine - Never Let Me Go (150)
4130	BST84130	John Patton - Along Came John (152)
4131	8-21288-2	The Horace Silver Quintet - Silver's Serenade (153)
4132	BST84132	Grant Green - Feelin' The Spirit (146)
4133	7-84133-2	Dexter Gordon - A Swingin' Affair (142)
4134	7-84134-2	Horace Parlan - Happy Frame of Mind (150)
4135	7-84135-2	Freddie Hubbard - Here to Stay (146)
4136#	BST84136	Solomon Ilori and His Afro-Drum Ensemble - African High Life (153)
4137	BST84137	Jackie McLean - One Step Beyond (153)
4138	8-52433-2	Harold Vick - Steppin' Out (154)
4139#	BST84139	Grant Green - Am I Blue (154)
4140	7-84140-2	Joe Henderson - Page One (155)
4141#	BST84141	Jimmy Smith - Rockin' the Boat (149)
4142#	LT-1082	Blue Mitchell Quintet (157)
4143	7-84143-2	John Patton - Blue John (155,156)
4144	8-32129-2	Johnny Coles - Little Johnny C (156)

 827

TOCJ-
4145# BST84145 Don Wilkerson - Shoutin' (156)
4146 BST84146 Dexter Gordon - Our Man in Paris (154)
4147 7-84147-2 Herbie Hancock - Inventions and Dimensions (157)
4148# BST84148 George Braith - Two Souls in One (157)
4149 BST84149 Hank Mobley - No Room for Squares (151,158)
4150# BST84150 Stanley Turrentine - A Chip Off the Old Block (158)
4151 BST84151 Andrew Hill - Black Fire (159)
4152 BST84152 Joe Henderson - Our Thing (157)
4153 7-84153-2 Grachan Moncur III - Evolution (160)
4154 BST84154 Grant Green - Idle Moments (159)
4155 BST84155 The Three Sounds - Black Orchid (135,136)
4156 BST84156 Art Blakey and The Jazz Messengers - The Freedom Rider (117,123)
4157 7-46137-2 Lee Morgan - The Sidewinder (161)
4158# BST84158 Freddie Roach - Good Move (160)
4159 BST84159 Andrew Hill - Judgment! (162)
4160 BST84160 Andrew Hill - Smoke Stack (160)
4161# BST84161 George Braith - Soul Stream (161)
4162# BST84162 Stanley Turrentine - Hustlin' (162)
4163 7-46524-2 Eric Dolphy - Out to Lunch! (163)
4164 BST84164 Jimmy Smith - Prayer Meetin' (149)
4165 8-32087-2 Jackie McLean - Destination...Out! (158)
4166 7-46510-2 Joe Henderson - In 'n Out (165)
4167 BST84167 Andrew Hill - Point of Departure (164)
4168# BST84168 Freddie Roach - Brown Sugar (164)
4169 7-84169-2 Lee Morgan - Search for The New Land (163)
4170 7-84170-2 Art Blakey and The Jazz Messengers - Free For All (162)
4171# BST84171 George Braith - Extension (164)
4172 BST84172 Freddie Hubbard - Breaking Point! (166)
4173 BST84173 Wayne Shorter - Night Dreamer (165)
4174# BST84174 'Big' John Patton - The Way I Feel (168)
4175 BST84175 Herbie Hancock - Empyrean Isles (168)
4176 BST84176 Dexter Gordon - One Flight Up (167)
4177 8-32092-2 Grachan Moncur III - Some Other Stuff (169)
4178 7-84178-2 Blue Mitchell - The Things to Do (169)
4179# BST84179 Jackie McLean - It's Time! (169)
4180 7-84180-2 Anthony Williams - Life Time (171)
4181 7-84181-2 Kenny Dorham - Trompeta Toccata (172)
4182 7-46514-2 Wayne Shorter - Ju Ju (169)
4183# 5-21958-2 Grant Green - Talkin' About! ((172)
4184# BST84184 Sam Rivers - Fuchsia Swing Song (175)
4185 BST84185 The Horace Silver Quintet - Song for My Father (159,173)
4186 BST84186 Hank Mobley - The Turnaround! (151,177)
4187 BST84187 Larry Young - Into Somethin' (174)
4188 7-84188-2 Donald Byrd - I'm Tryin' to Get Home (175,176)
4189 7-84189-2 Joe Henderson - Inner Urge (175)
4190# BST84190 Frederick Roach - All That's Good (172)
4191 7-84191-2 Duke Pearson - Wahoo! (175)
4192# BST84192 Big John Patton - Oh Baby! (178)
4193 BST84193 Art Blakey and The Jazz Messengers - Indestructible (165,166)
4194 7-46509-2 Wayne Shorter - Speak No Evil (176)
4195 7-46339-2 Herbie Hancock - Maiden Voyage (179)
4196 BST84196 Freddie Hubbard - Blue Spirits (177)
4197# BST84197 The Three Sounds - Out of This World (134,135)
4198 BST84198 Bobby Hutcherson - Dialogue (179)
4199 BST84199 Lee Morgan - The Rumproller (181)
4200 BST84200 Jimmy Smith - Softly as A Summer Breeze (78)
4201 BST84201 Stanley Turrentine - Joyride (181)
4202 8-59962-2 Grant Green - I Want To Hold Your Hand (179)
4204 BST84204 Dexter Gordon - Gettin'Around (182)
4205 8-32091-2 Pete La Roca - Basra (181)

TOCJ-		
4207	BST84207	The Night of the Cookers - Live at Club La Marchal with Freddie Hubbard,Vol. 1 (180)
4208	BST84208	The Night of the Cookers - Live at Club La Marchal with Freddie Hubbard,Vol. 2 (180)
4209	7-46511-2	Hank Mobley - Dippin' (183)
4212	BST84212	Lee Morgan - The Gigolo (183,184)
4214	8-54327-2	The Blue Mitchell Quintet - Down With It! (184)
4215	BST84215	Jackie McLean - Right Now! (176)
4216	7-46135-2	Anthony Williams - Spring (184)
4218#	BST84218	Jackie McLean - Action (172)
4220	7-84220-2	The Horace Silver Quintet - The Cape Verdean Blues (185,186)
4221	7-84221-2	Larry Young - Unity (186)
4222	7-84222-2	Lee Morgan - Cornbread (185)
4224	7-84224-2	The Ornette Coleman Trio at The "Golden Circle",Stockholm,Volume 1 (187,188)
4225	7-84225-2	The Ornette Coleman Trio at The "Golden Circle",Stockholm,Volume 2 (187,188)
4227	BST84227	Joe Henderson - Mode For Joe (189)
4229#	BST84229	Big John Patton - Got a Good Thing Goin' (192)
4230	7-84230-2	Hank Mobley - A Caddy for Daddy (188)
4231	7-46530-2	Bobby Hutcherson - Happenings (190)
4232	BST84232	Wayne Shorter - Adam's Apple (190)
4237	BST84237	Cecil Taylor - Unit Structures (192)
4238	BST84238	Donald Byrd - Mustang (193)
4239	7-89795-2	Big John Patton - Let 'em Roll (188)
4243	BST84243	DelightfuLee Morgan (191,192)
4244	8-59378-2	Bobby Hutcherson - Stick Up! (194)
4250	7-84250-2	Horace Silver Quintet/Sextet - The Jody Grind (196,197)
4251	BST84251	Jack Wilson - Something Personal (194)
4252	7-89792-2	Duke Pearson - Sweet Honey Bee (198)
4253	8-21290-2	Grant Green - Street of Dreams (174)
4259	BST84259	Donald Byrd - Blackjack (198)
4260	7-46535-2	Cecil Taylor - Conquistador (196)
4262	8-53356-2	Jackie McLean - New and Old Gospel (201)
4263	7-84263-2	Lou Donaldson - Alligator Bogaloo (201)
4264	7-46512-2	McCoy Tyner - The Real McCoy (201)
4270#	BST84270	Jack Wilson - Easterly Winds (206)
4271	7-84271-2	Lou Donaldson - Mr. Shing-A-Ling (206)
4273	7-84273-2	Hank Mobley - Hi Voltage (206)
4274#	BST84274	Tyrone Washington - Natural Essence (208)
4275	7-84275-2	McCoy Tyner - Tender Moments (207)
4276	BST84276	Introducing Duke Pearson's Big Band (208)
4277	7-84277-2	Horace Silver Quintet - Serenade to a Soul Sister (210,211)
4279	7-46136-2	Herbie Hancock - Speak Like A Child (210)
4280#	BST84280	Lou Donaldson - Midnight Creeper (211)
4282	7-84282-2	Elvin Jones Trio - Puttin' it Together (212)
4283	8-59379-2	Booker Ervin - The In Between (208)
4284	BST84284	Jackie McLean - 'Bout Soul (205)
4288	8-59964-2	Hank Mobley - Reach Out! (209)
4292#	BST84292	Donald Byrd - Slow Drag (202)
4306	8-31223-2	John Patton - Understanding (220)
4312	8-59961-2	Lee Morgan - Charisma (195)
4313#	BST84313	Lonnie Smith - Turning Point (222)
4318	8-28267-2	Lou Donaldson - Hot Dog (226)
4319	7-89796-2	Donald Byrd - Fancy Free (227,228)
4321	BST84321	Herbie Hancock - The Prisoner (225)
4334#	BST84334	Jack McDuff - Moon Rappin' (234)
4342	8-28265-2	Grant Green - Green is Beautiful (237)
4344#	BST84344	Duke Pearson - How Insensitive (224,225)
4351	8-28266-2	Lonnie Smith - Drives (236)
4353	BST84353	Chick Corea - The Song of Singing (240)
4357#	BST84357	Candido - Beautiful (249)

TOCJ-
4372# BST84372 Richard Groove Holmes - Comin' on Home (252)
4373# BST84373 Grant Green - Visions (252)
4422# BST84422 Marlena Shaw - Marlena (262)

TOCJ-
5187/88 (2 CD Set) Jazz Piano - Best Record Collection

Nat King Cole (468) | Thelonious Monk (20)
Lennie Tristano (472) | Bud Powell (27)
Art Tatum (474) | Wynton Kelly (29)
Duke Ellington (477) | Kenny Drew (34)
Claude Williamson (488) | Elmo Hope (36)
Hank Jones (484) | Horace Silver (39)
George Shearing (487) | Herbie Nichols (48)
Earl Hines (520) | Sonny Clark (72)
Russ Freeman (547) | Duke Pearson (98)
Hampton Hawes (549) | Horace Parlan (102)
John Lewis (550) | The Three Sounds (105)
Bobby Timmons (550) | Duke Jordan (108)
Jimmy Rowles (551) | Andrew Hill (159)
Les McCann (556) | Herbie Hancock (210)
Chick Corea (585) | McCoy Tyner (214)
Ralph Peterson (589) | Michel Petrucciani (322)
Bill Evans (627) | Don Pullen (326)
Cecil Taylor (453)

5189 (Capitol) I Wish You A Merry Christmas:
Duke Pearson (230) (& further titles not from BN)
5190 7-92563-2 Michel Petrucciani - Music (331)
5191/92 (Capitol) The Duel (2 CD Set):

Art Blakey (41) | Cannonball Adderley (79)
Sonny Rollins (71) | Michel Petrucciani (322)
Bud Powell (27) | Horace Parlan (102)
Miles Davis (31) | Kenny Dorham (46)
Jackie McLean (208) | Don Pullen & George Adams (313)
Johnny Coles (156) | Don Pullen (326)
Hank Mobley (99) | (& further titles not from BN)

5193 7-91650-2 Charnett Moffett - Beauty Within (326)
5194 7-92051-2 Andrew Hill - Eternal Spirit (328)
5195 (Capitol) My Funny Valentine:

Kenny Burrell (53) | Sonny Clark (86)
Duke Pearson (96) | (& further titles not from BN)

5197 7-92356-2 Stanley Jordan - Cornucopia (315,325,329,330)
5198 7-91915-2 Bobby Watson - The Inventor (330)
5199 7-93170-2 Tony Williams - Angel Heart (331)
5200 7-92894-2 John Scofield - Time On My Hands (332)
5201 (Capitol) Jazz Beatles Hits:

Lee Morgan (191) | Grant Green (179)
Stanley Jordan (304) | Stanley Turrentine (214)
Bobby McFerrin (540) | (& further titles not from BN)

5202 (Capitol) Jazz Classic Hits:

Lou Donaldson (96) | Ike Quebec (143)
(& further titles not from BN)

5203 Jazz CM Hits:

Nat King Cole (481) | Art Farmer (624)
Glen Gray (486) | Bud Powell (88)
Cannonball Adderley (488) | Art Blakey (85)
Nancy Wilson (493) | Herbie Hancock (139)
Artie Shaw (499) | Lee Morgan (161)
Bud Shank (563) | Hank Mobley (183)
George Adams (588)

TOCJ-

5204 (Capitol) Jazz Screen Hits:
Art Blakey (130) Lee Morgan (191)
Dexter Gordon (182) Duke Jordan (108)
Grant Green (124) (& further titles not from BN)

5212 7-93598-2 McCoy Tyner - Things Ain't What They Used To Be (332)

5215 7-93670-2 Benny Green - Lineage (335)

5217 Take Me To The Festival '90 (Mt. Fuji):
Tania Maria (540) Terumasa Hino (592)
George Adams (588) Ellis Marsalis (591)
Rachelle Ferrell (593) Rick Margitza (329)
Eliane Ellias (592) John Scofield (332)

5219 7-94204-2 The Manhattan Project (334)

5229 (Capitol) Starlight Special:
Kenny Drew (549) Wynton Kelly (29)
Sonny Clark (87) Grant Green (179)
At Blakey (130) (& further titles not from BN)

5230 7-94347-2 Don Pullen - Random Thoughts (335)

5231/38 (8 CD Set) Blue Note - The SP Days (1939-1952):
Meade Lux Lewis (1) Art Hodes (8,11,13,15)
Albert Ammons (1) Sidney De Paris (9)
A. Ammons & M.L. Lewis (2) Ike Quebec (10,14,15,18)
Port Of Harlem (2,3) Jimmy Shirley (12)
Earl Hines (3) Benny Morton (13)
Pete Johnson (4) Sammy Benskin (15)
Josh White (4) Pigmeat Markham (15)
Sidney Bechet (4) Jimmy Hamilton (16)
Teddy Bunn (4) Baby Dodds (16)
Meade Lux Lewis (5) Bechet-Nicholas (17)
Edmond Hall (5,6,7,8) John Hardee (17)
James P. Johnson (6,7,11) Babs Gonzales (18)
Clyde Bernhardt (25) Vic Dickenson (32)

5239 Soul Fingers...And Funky Feet:
Lou Donaldson (116) Lonnie Smith (216)
Baby Face Willette (123) Reuben Wilson (219)
Stanley Turrentine (150) John Patton (220)
Freddie Roach (148) Richard Groove Holmes (252)
Jimmy Smith (149) Jimmy McGriff (583)
Larry Young (186)

5253 7-93841-2 +1 Lou Rawls - It's Supposed To Be Fun (334,335,337,595)

5254 (EMI-USA) Stanley Jordan (304,316,329,330) (& further titles not from BN)

5255 7-94857-2 Yule Struttin' (A Blue Note Christmas) (see page 780)

5257 7-94591-2 Don Grolnick - Weaver Of Dreams (328)

5258 7-94335-2 Tommy Smith - Peeping Tom (335)

5259 (Capitol) Yasukuni Terashima Presents Jazz:
Kenny Drew (34) Don Pullen (335)
Tony Williams (309) (& further titles not from BN)

5260 Blue Note At The Hibiki:
Dexter Gordon (182) Lee Morgan (77)
Bud Powell (88) Lou Donaldson (87)
Duke Pearson (98) Jackie McLean (115)
Jimmy Smith (60) Horace Silver (173)
McCoy Tyner (325) Art Blakey (131)
Sonny Rollins (71) Ike Quebec (130)

5269 Art Blakey Memorial (85,101,109,127)

5274/76 (3 CD Set) The History Of Art Blakey & The Jazz Messengers -The Legend (21,39,40,41,44, 49,62,85,86,90,101,109,110,117,119,123,127,130,133,162,165,166)

5278/80 7-94848/49/50-2 Dexter Gordon - Nights At The Keystone (3 CD set) (457)

5281 7-95263-2 Bireli Lagrene - Acoustic Moments (337,338)

5285 7-94858-2 Rick Margitza - Hope (336,337)

5286 7-95148-2 Bobby Watson & Horizon - Post-Motown Bop (340)

 831

TOCJ-			
5287	7-95138-2	Joey Calderazzo - In The Door (339)	
5290	7-95479-2	John Scofield - Meant To Be (341)	
5291	7-90264-2	Dianne Reeves - I Remember (322,323,339)	
5292	7-94971-2	Andrew Hill - But Not Farewell (338,339)	
5293	7-94861-2	Blue Beat (see page 780)	
5294	7-96098-2	Blue Ballads (see page 781)	
5295	7-95591-2	Blue Porter (see page 781)	
5296		Weekend Jazz For Lovers:	
		Frank Rosolino (477)	Hank Mobley (46)
		Nat King Cole (482)	Jackie McLean (208)
		Peggy Lee (485)	Jimmy Smith (70)
		Vic Damone (490)	Donald Byrd (95)
		Sonny Criss (531)	Duke Pearson (96)
		Joe Pass (559)	Stanley Turrentine (171)
		Horace Silver (173)	The Three Sounds (125)
5298		Jazz Blues For A Love Affair:	
		Cannonball Adderley (488)	Kenny Burrell (147)
		Supersax (504)	Jimmy Smith (103)
		Sonny Criss (531)	Horace Parlan (100)
		Chris Connor (581)	Horace Silver/Bill Henderson (82)
		Art Farmer (624)	Herbie Hancock (168)
		Lou Donaldson (83)	The Three Sounds (125)
5299		Jazz Memories On The Street Of Love:	
		Sonny Criss (532)	Hank Mobley (66)
		Chet Baker (547)	Duke Pearson (96)
		Annie Ross (553)	Dexter Gordon (122)
		Ray Bryant (575)	Sonny Clark (86)
		Milt Jackson (621)	Grant Green (116)
		Cannonball Adderley (79)	Lee Morgan (191)
5300		Jazz Ballads For The Midnight Hour:	
		Art Pepper (464)	Kenny Drew (34)
		Nat King Cole (484)	Jimmy Smith (77)
		Dinah Shore (487)	Louis Smith (454)
		John Lewis (550)	Dexter Gordon (142)
		Chet Baker (550)	Miles Davis (31)
		Sarah Vaughan (580)	Ike Quebec (133)
		The Three Sounds (83)	
5351	7-46848-2	The Complete Art Pepper Aladdin Recordings,Vol.1 - The Return Of Art Pepper (464,465)	
5352	7-46853-2	The Complete Art Pepper Aladdin Recordings,Vol.2 - Modern Art (465)	
5353	7-46863-2	The Complete Art Pepper Aladdin Recordings,Vol.3 (464,465)	
5354	7-90583-2	Bill Evans/Jim Hall - Undercurrent (626,627)	
5419		Thad Jones/Mel Lewis Orchestra - Central Park North (587)	
5520*	8-27820-2	Rachelle Ferrell (333) (*:Somethin' Else label) (& further titles from Somethin' Else label)	
5601	7-95414-2	Greg Osby - Man Talks For Moderns Vol.X (340)	
5602		It's A Guitar:	
		Earl Klugh (508)	Stanley Jordan (304,596)
		Al Di Meola (539)	Bireli Lagrene (321,337)
		John Hart (589)	John Scofield (332,341)
5603		It's A Piano:	
		Tania Maria (541)	Michel Petrucciani (331)
		Renee Rosnes (590)	Don Pullen (335)
		Gil Goldstein (591)	Benny Green (335)
		Eliane Elias (592)	Joey Calderazzo (339)
		Geri Allen (593)	Andrew Hill (338)
		Gonzalo Rubalcaba (594)	
5604	7-96485-2	Benny Green - Greens (342)	

TOCJ-

5608 Take Me To The Festival '91 (Mt. Fuji '91):
George Adams (588) Dianne Reeves (323,339)
Gonzalo Rubalcaba (594) Tony Williams (331)
Stanley Jordan (598) Benny Green (335)

5609 7-95480-2 Michel Petrucciani - Playground (342)
5617 7-96452-2 Tommy Smith - Standards (341)
5618/19 (2 CD Set)(Capitol) Impressions Of Paris:
Duke Jordan (108) Thad Jones (55)
Herbie Hancock (313) McCoy Tyner (325)
(& further titles not from BN)

5629 7-95137-2 Bob Belden - Straight To My Heart (The Music Of Sting) (343)
5630 The Modern Jazz Giants - John Coltrane (71,577,620)
5631 The Modern Jazz Giants - Art Pepper (464,465)
5632 The Modern Jazz Giants - Miles Davis (31,34,41,472,473)
5633 The Modern Jazz Giants - Chick Corea (240,585)
5634 The Modern Jazz Giants - Thelonious Monk (20,21,22,28,32)
5637 The Modern Jazz Giants - Herbie Hancock (139,168,179,210,313)
5638 The Modern Jazz Giants - Cannonball Adderley (79,488,490,492,493,496)
5639 The Modern Jazz Giants - Sonny Rollins (59,63,71,73)
5640 The Modern Jazz Giants - Bud Powell (25,27,37,88,570)
5644 Funktified...And Groovin' Hard:
Baby Face Willette (117) John Patton (178)
Fred Jackson (134) Reuben Wilson (224)
Jimmy Smith (148) Lou Donaldson (226)
Freddie Roach (160) Lonnie Smith (230)
Grant Green (172)

5645/46 (2 CD Set) Jimmy Smith - The King Of Jazz Organ (50,51,54,70,78,98,101,103)
5648 BST84323 Duke Pearson - Merry Old Soul (= 28WD-1001) (223,230)
5656 7-97796-2 Rick Margitza - This Is New (343)
5657 Miles Davis Memorial Album (31,34,79,472)
5658 Miles Davis Plays Blues & Ballads (31,34,79,475)
5659/60 (2 CD Set) The Complete Miles Davis On Blue Note - Tempus Fugit (31,34,41)
5663 TOCJ-1588 Sonny Clark - Cool Struttin' (76)
5664 Intro LP606 Art Pepper - Modern Art (464,465)
5665 TOCJ-4009 Bud Powell - The Scene Changes (88)
5666 TOCJ-4003 Art Blakey - Moanin' (85)
5667 7-46095-2 John Coltrane - Blue Train (71)
5668 7-46339-2 Herbie Hancock - Maiden Voyage (179)
5669 7-46137-2 Lee Morgan - The Sidewinder (161)
5671 TOCJ-1595 Cannonball Adderley - Somethin' Else (79)
5674/75 (2 CD Set) (Capitol) Memories Of New York:
Kenny Drew (34) The Three Sounds (91)
Art Blakey (130) (& further titles not from BN)

5676 7-46314-2 Don Pullen/George Adams - Breakthrough (313)
5677 7-46294-2 Freddie Hubbard & Woody Shaw - Double Take (312)
5678 7-46993-2 Charnett Moffett - Net Man (318)
5679 7-46289-2 Tony Williams - Foreign Intrigue (309)
5680 7-46397-2 Dexter Gordon - The Other Side Of Round Midnight (310,313)
5681 7-46290-2 OTB - Out Of The Blue (309)
5682 7-46291-2 McCoy Tyner & Jackie McLean - It's About Time (308)
5683 7-46093-2 Kenny Burrell & Grover Washington - Togethering (304)
5684 7-46427-2 Michel Petrucciani - Power Of Three (314)
5685 7-46757-2 Tony Williams - Civilization (316)
5686 7-46147-2 One Night With Blue Note,Volume 1 (306)
5687 7-46148-2 One Night With Blue Note,Volume 2 (306,307)
5688 7-46149-2 One Night With Blue Note,Volume 3 306,307)
5689 7-46150-2 One Night With Blue Note,Volume 4 (306)
5690 7-95477-2 Bobby McFerrin & Chick Corea - Play (337)
5702 7-96429-2 McCoy Tyner - Soliloquy (341,342)
5705 7-98167-2 John Scofield - Grace Under Pressure (347)

TOCJ-
5708 7-98165-2 Joey Calderazzo - To Know One (345)
5709 7-98166-2 Don Pullen - Kele Mou Bana (344)
5710 A Helluva Jazz:
Sonny Criss (531) Warne Marsh (532)
Art Pepper/Joe Morello (465) Beverly Kenney (571)
Lawrence Marable (463) Doug Watkins (454)
Bob Gordon (547) Howard McGhee (637)
Jimmy Rowles (534) Elmo Hope (42)
5711 7-98171-2 Benny Green - Testifyin' (346)
5712 Take Me To The Festival '92:
Gonzalo Rubalcaba (598) Bob Belden (343)
Terumasa Hino (592) Don Pullen (344)
Lawrence Marable (463) Dianne Reeves (339)
Albert Collins (533) Joey Calderazzo (339)
5713 (Capitol) Standards For You - My Funny Valentine:
Cannonball Adderley (79) Dexter Gordon (457)
Herbie Hancock (313) McCoy Tyner (325)
(& further titles not from BN)
5714 (Capitol) Standards For You - Summertime:
Sonny Clark (72) The Three Sounds (91)
(& further titles not from BN)
5715 7-98169-2 Tony Williams - The Story Of Neptune (347)
5716/17 (2 CD Set) The Essential Blue Note Classics:
Albert Ammons (1) Art Hodes (8)
Sidney Bechet (3,4,12) Sidney De Paris (9)
Port Of Harlem (3) Ike Quebec (10)
Earl Hines (3) Benny Morton (13)
Teddy Bunn (4) Bunk Johnson/Sidney Bechet (13)
Edmond Hall (5,6,7,8) Bechet/Nicholas (17)
James P. Johnson (6,7) Vic Dickenson (32)
5720 7-98636-2 Joe Lovano - From The Soul (348)
5721 7-98959-2 New York Stories (348)
5723 7-96580-2 Blue Piano Volume One (see page 782)
5724 7-96904-2 Blue Piano Volume Two (see page 782)
5725 7-96581-2 Blue Guitar (see page 782)
5726 7-96582-2 Blue Vocals Volume One (see page 782)
5727 7-96583-2 Blue Vocals Volume Two (see page 782)
5728 7-99614-2 T.S. Monk - Take One (345)
5730 8-15892-2 Us3 - Cantaloop (CD single) (350,351)
5731 7-99829-2 Bob Belden - Turandot (352)
5732 7-99659-2 Pyrotechnics - New British Music From Blue Note (349,350)
5733 Make It Phunky:
Art Blakey (86) Bobby Hutcherson (211)
Larry Young (174) Donald Byrd (202)
Grant Green (166,233,246)
Stanley Turrentine (162)
5734 8-54326-2 Donald Byrd - Places And Spaces (283)
5735 8-28268-2 Bobby Hutcherson - San Francisco (245)
5736 BST-84335 Lee Morgan - The Sixth Sense (207)
5737 8-28269-2 Duke Pearson - The Right Touch (205)
5738 BST-84293 Duke Pearson - The Phantom (215,217)
5739 7-98581-2 Orphy Robinson - When Tomorrow Comes (345)
5740 Roswell Presents: Introducing BN 4000:
Horace Silver (106) Herbie Hancock (139)
Lou Doinaldson (96) Grant Green (172)
Jackie McLean (91) Pete La Roca (181)
Wayne Shorter (200) Richard Groove Holmes (252)
Reuben Wilson (254) Stanley Turrentine (104)
Horace Parlan (102) Duke Pearson (224)
5742 7-98170-2 Kevin Eubank - Turning Point (347)

834

TOCJ-

5745 7-80590-2 Michel Petrucciani - Promenade With Duke (355)

5746 7-80251-2 Bireli Lagrene - Standards (353)

5749 7-99886-2 John Scofield - What We Do (352)

5750 Kuma - Chang (Original Soundtrack):
- Chet Baker (549)
- Clifford Brown (38)
- Benny Goodman (481)
- Sonny Clark (87)
- George Adams (588)
- Horace Silver (173)
- Art Blakey (40)
- Stanley Turrentine (116)
- Cannonball Adderley (79)

5751 7-99786-2 Thelonious Monk - Live At The Five Spot (454)

5752 7-99830-2 Joe Lovano - Universal Language (353,354)

5753 7-80883-2 Us3 - Hand On The Torch (350,351)

5755/56 (2 CD Set) No Room For Squares:
- Art Blakey (85)
- Donald Byrd (106)
- Sonny Rollins (71)
- Baby Face Willette (117)
- Horace Silver (89)
- Jimmy Smith (103)
- The Three Sounds (89)
- Fred Jackson (134)
- Walter Davis (93)
- Stanley Turerntine (132)
- Freddie Redd (100)
- Ike Quebec (131)
- Duke Pearson (98)
- Grant Green (124)
- Lou Donaldson (100)
- Kenny Burrell (147)
- Horace Parlan (102)
- Freddie Roach (151)
- Freddie Hubbard (104)
- Jackie McLean (153)
- Tina Brooks (105)
- Joe Henderson (155)
- Art Taylor (108)
- Hank Mobley (158)

5757 7-98635-2 Greg Osby - 3-D Lifestyles (354,355)

5758 BNJ-71106 Soho Blue:
- Wayne Shorter (190)
- Don Wilkerson (140)
- Kenny Dorham (46)
- Jimmy Smith (103)
- Art Blakey (40)
- Donald Byrd (202)
- Jackie McLean (115)
- Horace Silver (141)
- Stanley Turrentine (181)

5759 7-99106-2 Blue Break Beats (see page 784)

5760 7-96563-2 So Blue,So Funky (see page 782)

5762 7-46511-2 Hank Mobley - Dippin' (183)

5763 TOCJ-1579 Sonny Clark Trio (72)

5764 7-46136-2 Herbie Hancock - Speak Like A Child (210)

5765 TOCJ-4185 Horace Silver - Song For My Father (159,173)

5767 TOCJ-4204 Dexter Gordon - Gettin' Around (182)

5773-4 7-99031-2 Tony Williams - Tokyo Live (348,349)

5778 (E)BNSLP-1 Blue Bossa:
- Horace Parlan (113)
- Kenny Dorham (46)
- Charlie Rouse (145)
- Grant Green (137)
- Big John Patton (188)
- Horace Silver (185)
- Duke Pearson (226)
- Carmen McRae (289)

5779 (E)BNSLP-2 Blue Bop:
- Don Wilkerson (140,156)
- Art Blakey (109)
- Tina Brooks (105)
- Horace Silver (106)
- Donald Byrd (112)

5780 (E)BNSLP-3 The Baptist Beat:
- Lou Donaldson (148,201)
- Hank Mobley (113)
- Horace Silver (196)
- Stanley Turrentine (150)
- Big John Patton (188)
- Freddie Roach (148)
- Jimmy Smith (312)

5781/86 (6 CD set) J-Ladies Collection - Special Box I (slip case of individual CDs)

5783 TOCJ-1588 Sonny Clark - Cool Struttin' (76)

5785 TOCJ-4009 Bud Powell - The Scene Changes (88)

5786 TOCJ-4003 Art Blakey - Moanin' (= CP35-3090) (85)

5787-92 (6 CD Set) J-Ladies Collection - Special Box II (slip case of individual CDs)

5787 7-46095-2 John Coltrane - Blue Train (71)

TOCJ-
5788 7-46339-2 Herbie Hancock - Maiden Voyage (179)
5789 7-46137-2 Lee Morgan - The Sidewinder (161)
5791 TOCJ-1595 Cannonball Adderley - Somethin' Else (= CP35-3070) (79)
5793 Take Me To The Festival '93:
George Adams (588) Benny Green (342)
Junko Onishi (601) John Scofield (352)
Horace Silver (106,173)
5795 7-80902-2 Joey Calderazzo - The Traveller (354)
5796 7-84467-2 Benny Green - That's Right (355,356)
5797 (CD single) Us3 - Tukka Yoot's Riddim (350,351)
5821 The Best Of Miles Davis - New Edition (31,34,41,79)
5822 The Best Of Bud Powell - New Edition (25,27,37,68,82,88)
5823 The Best Of Art Blakey - New Edition (40,49,85,90,109,127)
5824 The Best Of Thelonious Monk - New Edition (19,20,21,22,28,32)
5825 The Best Of Jimmy Smith - New Edition (50,51,55,60,70,98,102,149)
5826 The Best Of Sonny Rollins - New Edition (59,63,71,73)
5827 The Best Of Horace Silver - New Edition (39,44,45,58,64,89,94,106,173,185)
5828 The Best Of Lee Morgan - New Edition (62,72,77,161,181,185,207)
5829 The Best Of Sonny Clark - New Edition (67,70,72,75,76,129)
5830 The Best Of Herbie Hancock - New Edition (139,151,168,179,210,225)
5832 7-80698-2 Irakere - Live At Ronnie Scott's (344)
5833 7-80597-2 Chucho Valdes - Solo Piano (344)
5834 7-89233-2 Don Pullen - Ode To Life (356)
5836 7-89282-2 The Best of Chick Corea (197,240,585)
5838 7-80701-2 Afro Blue (see page 774)
5839 7-80707-2 California Cool (see page 774)
5840 7-89907-2 Blue Break Beats Volume Two (see page 778)
5841 7-80679-2 Blue 'N Groovy (see page 773)
5844 New Directions Of Blue Note: Blue Mellow Groove:
Gene Harris (273) Bobby Hutcherson (276)
Maxi (297) Gene Harris (280)
Donald Byrd (267) Lou Donaldson (266)
Bobbi Humphrey (281) Donald Byrd (264)
Marlena Shaw (274y) Bobby Humphrey (281)
Donald Byrd (274) Gene Harris (273)
Moacir Santos (270) Marlena Shaw (274)
5845 New Directions of Blue Note: Blue Saudade Groove:
Moacir Santos (270) Ronnie Foster (272)
Donald Byrd (267) Moacir Santos (263)
Ronnie Foster (278) Donald Byrd (265)
Moacir Santos (270) Moacir Santos (277)
Bobbi Humphrey (272) Horace Silver (263)
Duke Pearson (241) Bobbi Humphrey (267)
Noel Pointer (295) Marlena Shaw (275)
5846 New Directions Of Blue Note: Blue Bitter Groove:
Horace Silver (263) Duke Pearson (241)
Eddie Henderson (287) Bobbi Humphrey (282)
Moacir Santos (270) Marlena Shaw (268)
Horace Silver (276) Rico (647)
5847 7-89050-2 T.S. Monk - The Changing Of The Guard (356)
5848 (Capitol) Phat Jazz - Cool Spinnin' An' Hot Movin':
Us3 (350) Orphy Robinson (345)
Greg Osby (340,354) (& further titles not from BN)
5849 TOJJ-5849 +3* Mo' Deep Mo' Phunky:
Geri Allen (600) Wayne Shorter (183)
Charlie Rouse (145) Bobby Hutcherson (183)
Horace Parlan (113) Dianne Reeves (322)*
The Three Sounds (196) Dexter Gordon (142)*
Grant Green (172) Reuben Wilson (235)*
Greg Osby (354)

TOCJ-
5851 Elle Jazz - Joy Spring:
Sonny Clark (72,76)
Lou Donaldson (155)
Joey Calderazzo (339)
Art Tatum (474)
Mel Torme (475)
Metronome All Stars (475)
Nat King Cole (479)
George Shearing (487)
Cannonball Adderley (492)
Richard Elliot (541)
Hoagy Carmichael (551)
Joe Pass (561)
Sonny Stitt (572)
Zoot Sims (625)

5852 Elle Jazz - Something Cool:
Charlie Rouse (145)
Ike Quebec (143)
Hank Mobley (183)
June Christy (477)
Art Pepper (465)
Hank Jones (486)
Mark Murphy (489)
George Shearing (493)
Cannonball Adderley (493)
Blossom Dearie (494)
Dave Koz (509)
Joao Gilberto (521)
Chet Baker (547)
Bud Shank (549)
Sarah Vaughan (580)

5853 Elle Jazz - Shades Of Autumn:
Art Blakey (85)
Michel Petrucciani (342)
Mose Allison (319)
Jo Stafford (469)
Woody Herman (471)
Art Tatum (476)
Nat King Cole (480)
Stan Kenton (484)
George Shearing (484)
Dinah Shore (487)
Peggy Lee (490)
Julie London (534)
Gerry Mulligan (545)
Joe Pass (561)
Stan Getz (570)
Johnny Smith (571)

5854 Elle Jazz - Winter Blue:
Ike Quebec (111)
Duke Jordan (108)
Mel Torme (536)
Charles Brown (464)
June Christy (483)
Glen Gray (484)
Les Brown (486)
Nancy Wilson (488)
George Shearing (487)
Julie London (534)
Chet Baker (548)
Hoagy Carmichael (551)
Modern Jazz Quartet (624)
Sauter-Finnegan (625)
Lena Horne (630)

5855 Elle Jazz - Daydreams:
Elmo Hope (36)
Lou Donaldson (87)
Ronnie Laws (296)
Dianne Reeves (322)
Bob Cooper (479)
George Shearing (482)
June Christy (483)
Peggy Lee (490)
Julie London (535)
Richard Elliot (541)
Chet Baker (549)
Bob Brookmeyer (552)
Joe Pass (561)
Ray Bryant (575)
Sarah Vaughan (581)
Sauter-Finnegan (625)

5856 Elle Jazz - Takin' A Chance On Love:
Lee Morgan (75)
Jimmy Smith (77)
Stanley Turrentine (127)
Ronnie Laws (296)
Bob Cooper (480)
George Shearing (492)
Nancy Wilson (502)
Nat King Cole (494)
Julie London (534)
Richard Elliot (541)
Chico Hamilton (550)
Johnny Hartman (572)
Eddie Lockjaw Davis (574)
Rachelle Ferrell (593)
Chick Corea (585)

TOCJ-
5857 Elle Jazz - Jazz After Dark:
Elmo Hope (42) | George Shearing (481)
Lou Donaldson (32) | Keely Smith (485)
Cannonball Adderley (79) | Supersax (504)
Art Blakey (85) | Richard Elliot (541)
Jimmy Smith (98) | Annie Ross (553)
The Three Sounds (125) | Count Basie (573,577)
Dexter Gordon (142) | Art Farmer (624)

5858 Elle Jazz - Crazy Moon:
Bud Powell (27) | Dianne Reeves (339)
Jimmy Smith (64) | Miles Davis (475)
Freddie Hubbard (146) | The Four Freshmen (480)
Dexter Gordon (167) | Benny Goodman (481)
Art Blakey (130) | Nat King Cole (482)
Grant Green (132) | George Shearing (487)
Lou Donaldson (199) | Supersax (504)
The Three Sounds (125)

5860 Us3 - Cantaloop/Tukka Yoot's Riddim/I got it goin' on (350,351)

5861 (Capitol) J-Wave Romantic Selection:
Lou Donaldson (83) (& further titles not from BN)

5862 7-81357-2 Cassandra Wilson - Blue Light 'Til Dawn (356,359,361)

5864 Lou Donaldson - Alligator Boogaloo & Funky Hits (201,206,211,220,226,231,243)

5865 7-89622-2 The Best Of Grant Green - Street Funk & Jazz Grooves (125,172,174,233,237,246,257,260)

5866 7-89606-2 Donald Byrd - Early Byrd - The Best of the Jazz Soul Years (193,198,202,227,242)

5867 8-27533-2 Giant Steps (see page 786)

5868 7-89286-2 Kevin Eubanks - Spirit Talk (774)

5873 Jazz Piano Greats:
Hank Jones (486) | The Three Sounds (105)
George Shearing (487) | Kenny Drew (34)
John Lewis (550) | DukeJordan (108)
Bud Powell (570) | Sonny Clark (72)
Ray Bryant (575) | Wynton Kelly (29)
Chick Corea (585) | Horace Silver (39)
Bill Evans (627) | Thelonious Monk (20)
McCoy Tyner (214)

5874 Jazz On Lennon And McCartney:
Peggy Lee (494) | Gil Goldstein (591)
Nancy Wilson (495) | Lee Morgan (191)
Jackie and Roy (499) | Stanley Jordan (304)
Mel Torme (501) | Bobby McFerrin (540)
Bud Shank (566) | Grant Green (179,237)
Buddy Rich (564) | Stanley Turrentine (214)
Jazz Crusaders (566)

5875 Jazz Screen Hits:
Nat King Cole (469,478,482) | Duke Jordan (108)
Laurindo Almeida (492) | Freddie Roach (151)
Mel Torme (501) | McCoy Tyner (325)
Julie London (536) | Lee Morgan (191)
Holly Cole (542) | Grant Green (124)
Tommy Flanagan (622) | Herbie Hancock (313)

5876 8-32749-2 Marlena Shaw - Live At Montreux (268)

5877 7-89542-2 Marlena Shaw - Who Is This Bitch,Anyway? (274,275)

5878 BNLA-606-G Marlena Shaw - Just A Matter Of Time (286)

5879 7-89540-2 Carmen McRae - Can't Hide Love (288,289)

5880/81 BNLA -709-H2 Carmen McRae - At The Great American Music Hall (2 CD Set) (290)

838

TOCJ-

5882 Real Blue - No Room For Squares II:

- Don Wilkerson (140)
- Dexter Gordon (142)
- Ike Quebec (143)
- Stanley Turrentine (150)
- Freddie Hubbard (146)
- Harold Vick (154)
- Herbie Hancock (157)
- Freddie Roach (160)
- George Braith (161)
- Wayne Shorter (165)
- Duke Pearson (175)
- John Patton (178)

5883 8-27765-2 John Scofield & Pat Metheny - I Can See Your House From Here (365)

5884 8-28014-2 Joe Lovano - Tenor Legacy (360)

5894 7-89662-2 Fareed Haque - Sacred Addiction (360)

5897 7-80883-2 +4 Us3 - Hand On The Torch (350,351)

5922 8-28974-2 Lena Horne - We'll Be Together Again (362)

5924 7-89678-2 Javon Jackson - When The Time Is Right (361,362)

5925 Funky! Blue Note Super Hits:

- Lou Donaldson (201)
- Horace Silver (173)
- Herbie Hancock (168)
- Art Blakey (85)
- Jimmy Smith (50)
- Sonny Clark (76)
- Lee Morgan (161)
- Hank Mobley (183)
- Grant Green (146)

5926 8-27327-2 John Scofield - Hand Jive (362)

5929 8-29268-2 Benny Green - The Place To Be (366,367)

5930 8-28432-2 McCoy Tyner & Bobby Hutcherson - Manhattan Moods (364)

5931 8-29351-2 Jacky Terrasson (369,370)

5932 7-80587-2 Michel Petrucciani - Live (346)

5933 Blue Note Presents Blue Note Big Hits:

- Sonny Clark (76)
- John Coltrane (71)
- Bud Powell (88)
- Art Blakey (85)
- Lee Morgan (161)
- Horace Silver (173)
- Hank Mobley (183)
- Herbie Hancock (179)
- Lou Donaldson (201)

5934 Blue Note Presents Blue Note Standards:

- Cannonball Adderley (79)
- Thelonious Monk (21)
- Dexter Gordon (182)
- Sonny Clark (72)
- Jackie McLean (96)
- Art Blakey (85)
- McCoy Tyner (214)
- Donald Byrd (87)
- Clarke-Boland (455)
- Sonny Rollins (71)

5935 Blue Note Presents Blue Note Ballads For Lovers:

- Jimmy Smith (64)
- Stanley Turrentine (116)
- Miles Davis (34)
- Dexter Gordon (142)
- Duke Pearson (98)
- Hank Mobley (130)
- Clifford Brown (38)
- Lou Donaldson (121)
- Grant Green (125)
- Freddie Hubbard (104)
- Ike Quebec (131)

5936 Blue Note Presents Blue Note Hip & Funk:

- Herbie Hancock (168)
- Kenny Dorham (46)
- John Patton (220)
- Don Wilkerson (140)
- Bobby Hutcherson (245)
- Horace Silver (185)
- Lou Donaldson (116)
- Grant Green (246)
- Lonnie Smith (216)
- Stanley Turrentine (150)

5937 Blue Note Presents Blue Note Blues In The Night:

- Lou Donaldson (83)
- Horace Parlan (102)
- Kenny Burrell (147)
- Horace Silver (58)
- Tina Brooks (105)
- The Three Sounds (105)
- Milt Jackson (30)
- Grant Green (124)
- Kenny Drew (113)
- Sonny Clark (87)

5938 8-29269-2 Joe Lovano - Rush Hour (368,369)

TOCJ-

5941/44 (4 CD Box) Rare Tracks - The Other Side Of Blue Note 4000 Series:

Jimmy Smith (70) Jimmy Smith (92)
Art Blakey (85) Lou Donaldson (87)
Dizzy Reece (83) Stanley Turrentine (114)
Bud Powell (88) Baby Face Willette (117)
Jackie McLean (91) Grant Green (120)
Horace Silver (94) Horace Parlan (119)
The Three Sounds (91) Horace Silver (122)
Kenny Burrell (93) Dexter Gordon (121,122)
Art Blakey (101) Jimmy Smith (103)
Sonny Red (99) Lou Donaldson (121)
Lou Donaldson (99) Hank Mobley (119)
Stanley Turrentine (104) Baby Face Willette (123)
Freddie Hubbard (104) Freddie Hubbard (126)
Tina Brooks (105) Leo Parker (120)
Horace Parlan (107) Sonny Clark (129)
Freddie Redd (109) Ike Quebec (129,131)
Duke Jordan (108) Stanley Turrentine (132)
Art Blakey (108) Grant Green (124,125)

5945 8-31677-2 Bobby McFerrin - Bang! Zoom (378)
5946 Best Of One Night With Blue Note (306,307)
5947 8-29511-2 Dianne Reeves - Quiet After The Storm (374,375)
5949 8-31877-2 An Evening With Lena Horne (373)
5950 8-30491-2 Gonzalo Rubalcaba In The USA - Imagine (357,370)
5955 7-46853-2 The Complete Art Pepper Aladdin Recordings,Vol.2 - Modern Art (465)
5963 Mt. Fuji Festival - 10th Anniversary Album:

Art Blakey (85) Terumasa Hino (592)
Horace Silver (173) Rachelle Ferrell (593)
Herbie Hancock (313) Gonzalo Rubalcaba (598)
Don Pullen/George Adams (313) Junko Onishi (606)
Dianne Reeves (318)

5964 Lexington Avenue - No Room For Squares III:

Kenny Dorham (46) Jimmy Smith (55)
Jutta Hipp (52) Johnny Griffin (52)
Gil Melle (51) J.R. Monterose (57)
Horace Silver (45) Lou Donaldson (43)
Herbie Nichols (48) Lee Morgan (58)
Kenny Burrell (53) Clifford Jordan & John Gilmore (61)

5965 8-30244-2 Javon Jackson - For One Who Knows (376)
5966 Herbie Hancock - We Love Herbie (139,151,168,179,210)
5967 CJ32-5020 +4 Dianne Reeves - The Nearness Of You (322,323,339,650)
5968 8-30271-2 Don Pullen - Live...Again (361)
5969 8-30645-2 Kurt Elling - Close Your Eyes (366,370,374)
5991 8-32073-2 Eliane Elias - Solos And Duets (375)
5992 8-32127-2 Jazz To The World (see page 790)
5993 (Capitol) I Wish You A Merry Christmas (= TOCJ-5189):
Duke Pearson (230) (& further titles not from BN)
5994 8-32801-2 John Scofield - Groove Elation (382)
5996 8-32861-2 +1 Cassandra Wilson - New Moon Daughter (380,381)
5997 8-37570-2 Jacky Terrasson - Reach (382)
5999 8-32800-2 Don Pullen - Sacred Common Ground (379)
6031 part of 8-29125-2 Joe Lovano - Live At The Village Venguard (377)
6032 8-33390-2 Denise Jannah - I Was Born In Love With You (379,380)
6033 8-36909-2 The Doky Brothers (383)

TOCJ-6035		Hard Bop! - No Room For Squares IV: Sonny Rollins (63) Curtis Fuller (75) Clifford Jordan (65) Horace Silver (76) Hank Mobley (66) Lee Morgan (77) Sonny Clark (67) Lou Donaldson (83) Bud Powell (68) Louis Smith (80) John Coltrane (71) Kenny Burrell (50)
6036	8-34813-2	Max Roach With The New Orchestra Of Boston (364,383)
6039		Lee Morgan - Live At The Lighthouse (244,245)
6041	(J)CJ28-5021	Sunday Afternoon Jazz (see page 814)
6042	(J)CJ28-5022	Midnight Jazz Piano (see page 814)
6043	(J)CJ28-5023	Lullabies For Lovers (see page 814)
6044	(J)CJ28-5024	Twilight Time Jazz (see page 815)
6046	(J)CJ28-5176	Jazz Cruise At The Seaside (see page 817)
6047	(J)CJ28-5177	Jazz On A Sunny Afternoon (see page 817)
6048	(J)CJ28-5178	Jazz Piano For Swingin' Lovers (see page 818)
6049	(J)CJ28-5179	Jazz Ballads In A Midnight Mood (see page 818)
6051	TOCJ-5296	Weekend Jazz For Lovers (see page 831)
6053	TOCJ-5298	Jazz Blues For A Love Affair (see page 831)
6054	TOCJ-5299	Jazz Memories On The Street Of Love (see page 831)
6055	TOCJ-5300	Jazz Ballads For The Midnight Hour (see page 831)
6056	8-36545-2	Dianne Reeves - The Palo Alto Sessions (457-458,506)
6057	8-37101-2	Charlie Hunter - Ready...Set...Shango! (386,387)
6058	8-37731-2	The Blue Note All-Stars - Blue Spirit (387)
6059	8-36728-2	Carnegie Hall Jazz Band (384)
6060	(Capitol)	Jazzy Fish - Shonan Beach FM Jazz Selection: Earl Klugh (293) Herbie Hancock (139) Doky Brothers (383) Caecilie Norby (373) (& further titles not from BN)
6061	8-37319-2	Greg Osby - Art Forum (389)
6062	8-36490-2	Javon Jackson - A Look Within (389)
6063	8-34634-2	Renee Rosnes - Ancestors (383)
6064	8-38268-2	Dianne Reeves - The Grand Encounter (391)
6067		Have Guitar ... Will Travel,Feat. Grant Green: Ike Quebec (132) Lattu Young (174) Baby Face Willette (117) John Patton (188,192) Don Wilkerson (137) Reuben Wilson (233) Herbie Hancock (151) Grant Green (246) George Braith (161)
6068	8-52037-2	Benny Green - Kaleidoscope (396)
6069	8-37718-2	Joe Lovano - Celebrating Sinatra (395)
6084	8-52727-2	Kurt Elling - The Messenger (388,391,397,399)
6085	8-52420-2	Charlie Hunter - Natty Dread (392)
6086	8-52419-2	Fareed Haque - Deja Vu (397)
6087	8-53068-2	Everette Harp - What's Goin' On (394)
6088		The Best Of Dianne Reeves (318,319,322,343,391,541,607,611,612,650)
6094	8-56254-2	Thierry Lang (655)
6095	8-53428-2	John Coltrane -The Ultimate Blue Train (71)
6096	8-55484-2 +2	Jacky Terrasson with Cassandra Wilson - Rendezvous (402,406)
6098/99 (2 CD Set)	(Toshiba-EMI)	Swing Journal GD Presents The Modern Jazz Story: Art Blakey (40) The Three Sounds (83) Cannonball Adderley (79) Herbie Hancock (179) Dexter Gordon (154) Tony Williams (184) Jimmy Smith (70) (& further titles not from BN)

841

TOCJ-		
6100		Speedball - No Room For Squares V: Lee Morgan (184) / Jack Wilson (206) Donald Byrd (193) / Horace Silver (210) John Patton (188) / Lee Morgan (195) Bobby Hutcherson (194) / Lonnie Smith (222) Horace Silver (196) / Lou Donaldson (226) Duke Pearson (198) / Grant Green (237)
6102		The Best Of Miles Davis (31,34,41,472,473)
6103		The Best Of Sonny Rollins (59,63,71,73)
6104		The Best Of John Coltrane (71,577,620)
6105		The Best Of Bud Powell (27,37,68,82,88,570,573,574,581)
6106		The Best Of Thelonious Monk (20,21,22,28,32)
6107		The Best Of Art Pepper (464,465)
6110		The Best Of Herbie Hancock (139,151,157,168,179,210)
6127		Sonny Criss - Jazz U.S.A. (531)
6131		Jazz Sax On Blue Note: Hank Mobley (99) / Tina Brooks (105) Dexter Gordon (142) / Ike Quebec (143) Sonny Rollins (63) / Stanley Turrentine (150) Cannonball Adderley (79) / Joe Henderson (165) Lou Donaldson (116) / Jackie McLean (110) John Coltrane (71) / Wayne Shorter (165)
6132		Jazz Piano On Blue Note: Thelonious Monk (20) / Duke Pearson (98) Herbie Nichols (48) / Horace Parlan (102) Horace Silver (58) / Duke Jordan (108) Sonny Clark (76) / Kenny Drew (113) Bud Powell (88) / Herbie Hancock (168) The Three Sounds (91) / McCoy Tyner (201)
6133		Jazz Trumpet On Blue Note: Miles Davis (31) / Thad Jones (55) Donald Byrd (95) / Clifford Brown (38) Freddie Hubbard (104) / Dizzy Reece (97) Lee Morgan (62) / Louis Smith (454) Kenny Dorham (46) / Blue Mitchell (169)
6134		Jazz Guitar On Blue Note: John Scofield (347) / Charlie Hunter (392) Grant Green (179) / Earl Klugh (293) Kenny Burrell (94) / Kevin Eubanks (348) Bireli Lagrene (353) / Michel Petrucciani with Jim Hall (314) Stanley Jordan (304) / John Scofield & Pat Metheny (365) Fareed Haque (360)
6135		Jazz Vocal On Blue Note: Dianne Reeves (322) / Kurt Elling (366) Cassandra Wilson (356) / Cassandra Wilson (380) Carmen McRae (288) / Carmen McRae (290) Bobby McFerrin (337) / Marlena Shaw (274) Caecilie ?orby (373) / Holly Cole (542) Sheila Jordan (142) / Rachelle Ferrell (593)
6136	8-37627-2	Pat Martino - All Sides Now (396,397,400)
6137	8-53328-2	Eliane Elias - The Three Americas (398,399)
6138	8-54876-2	Pete 'LaRoca' Sims - Swing Time (403)
6139	8-56543-2	Greg Osby - Further Ado (404)
6140	8-56810-2	Renee Rosnes - As We Are Now (404)
6141		Dear...Tribute To Tony Williams: Herbie Hancock (151,168,179) / BN All Stars (306) Kenny Dorham (152) / Tony Williams (309,322,347,349) Wayne Shorter (178)
6143	8-57302-2	Dexter Gordon - The Squirrel (456)
6144	8-56973-2	Dianne Reeves - That Day... (409,410)

842

TOCJ-			
6145/46	8-56399-2	Blue Note - A Story In Modern Jazz (2 CD Set) (see page 799)	
6147		1947...When Jazz Got Rhythm:	
		Benny Goodman (468)	Dexter Gordon/Wardell Gray (638)
		Stan Kenton (469)	Dodo Marmarosa (638)
		Red Norvo (469)	Howard McGhee (638)
		Stan Hasselgard (470)	Dexter Gordon/Teddy Edwards (638)
		Metronome All Stars (470)	Babs Gonzales (18)
		Bud Powell (570)	Tadd Dameron (19)
		Charlie Parker (637,638)	Thelonious Monk (19,20)
		Dexter Gordon (638)	Art Blakey (21)
		Erroll Garner (638)	
6148		Grant Green - Airegin: The Complete Quartets With Sonny Clark,Vol.1 (132)	
6149		Grant Green - Oleo: The Complete Quartets With Sonny Clark,Vol.2 (132,134)	
6150	8-56680-2	Javon Jackson - Good People (411)	
6151	8-57729-2	Bob Dorough - Right On My Way Home (407,408)	
6152		Jazz On TV:	
		Bud Powell (88)	Bobby McFerrin (540)
		Judy Garland (480)	Bill Perkins/Richie Kamuca (551)
		Cannonball Adderley (488)	Bud Shank (563)
		Nancy Wilson (493)	Sarah Vaughan (578)
		George Shearing (489)	George Adams (588)
		Nat King Cole (494)	Hugh Lawson (591)
		Julie London (536)	Art Farmer (624)
6153		Jazz On The Street:	
		XXL (651)	Everette Harp (394)
		Dave Koz (510)	Caecilie Norby (390)
		Holly Cole (542)	Jacky Terrasson (402)
		Najee (544)	Lou Donaldson (201)
		Bob Belden (611)	Lee Morgan (161)
		Us3 (350)	
6154	8-57150-2	Lee Konitz - Alone Together (401)	
6160	8-54052-2	Pieces Of A Dream - Pieces (405,406,407,408,410)	
6161	8-56991-2	Yule Be Boppin' (see page 800)	
6162	8-36736-2	The Last Time I Committed Suicide (soundtrack) (see page 793)	
6167	8-59509-2	Tim Hagans & Marcus Printup - Hubsongs (412)	
6168	8-37628-2	Mark Shim - Mind Over Matter (402,403)	
6169	8-57891-2	Bob Belden - Tapestry (407,408,411,412)	
6170	8-57875-2	Ronnie Laws - Harvest For The World (410)	
6181	8-56092-2	Joe Lovano & Gonzalo Rubalcaba - Flying Colors (402)	
6182	(Capitol)	Bye Bye Blackbird - Jazz CM Hits:	
		Jimmy Smith (98)	Bud Powell (88)
		(& further titles not from BN)	
6184	8-23213-2	Lee Morgan - Standards (198)	
6185	8-21281-2	The Three Sounds - Standards (95,134,140,141)	
6186	8-21282-2	Jimmy Smith - Standards (70,82,92)	
6187		Jazz Ballad At One In The Morning:	
		Cannonball Adderley (490)	Miles Davis (34)
		Holly Cole (542)	Cassandra Wilson (356)
		Sonny Stitt (571)	McCoy Tyner (325)
		Jackie McLean (611)	Dianne Reeves (391)
		Milt Jackson (621)	Dexter Gordon (182)
		Earl Klugh (509)	Freddie Hubbard (104)
6188		Morning For Couples Is Jazz Time:	
		Art Pepper (465)	Herbie Hancock (179)
		Richard Elliot (542)	Grant Green (179)
		Eliane Elias (592)	Doxy Brothers (383)
		Art Farmer (620)	Bireli Lagrene (353)
		Earl Klugh (293)	Marlena Shaw (274)
		Caecilie Norby (373)	

TOCJ-

6189 Jazz Vocal Is A Sign Of Love:
Ernestine Anderson (617) Holly Cole (542)
Nat King Cole (482) Chet Baker (549)
Dinah Shore (487) Rachelle Ferrell (593)
Peggy Lee (490) Carmen McRae (288)
Vic Damone (490) Caecilie Norby (390)
Nancy Wilson (502) Cassandra Wilson/Jacky Terrasson (402)
Julie London (534) Dianne Reeves (322)
Tania Maria (541)

6190 Jazz Piano For A Lonesome Night:
Al Haig (646) Bill Evans/Jim Hall (627)
Paul Smith (483) Duke Pearson (96)
George Shearing (492) McCoy Tyner (325)
Clare Fisher (561) Benny Green (342)
Ray Bryant (575) Michel Petrucciani (331)
Junko Onishi (603) Jacky Terrasson (370)
Ron Carter (609)

6191 Rendezvous At Jazzclub With You Tonight:
Don Wilkerson (140) Herbie Hancock (151)
Grant Green (246) Horace Silver (122)
Lou Donaldson (201) Reuben Wilson (224)
Kenny Dorham (46) Us3 (350)
Tina Brooks (105)

6192 8-59417-2 Brian Blade - Fellowship (413)
6194 7-46513-2 Sonny Clark - The Complete Cool Struttin' Session (76)
6197 8-23108-2 Charlie Hunter - Return Of The Candyman (413)
6198 8-59651-2 Jacky Terrasson - Alive (411)
6199 4-93155-2 Tommy Flanagan - Sunset And The Mockingbird (405)
6227 8-21431-2 George Howard - There's A Riot Goin' On (417,418,419)
6228 (Toshiba-EMI) Jazz Love Songs - Romantic Or Sentimental?:
Dexter Gordon (182) Dianne Reeves (374)
Tal Farlow (41) Herbie Hancock (139)
Miles Davis (31) (& further titles not from BN)

6229 4-93011-2 +2 Medeski,Martin & Wood - Combustication (415)
6243 UAJ14014+1 Billie Holiday - Lady Love (619)
6247 UAJ14017 Duke Ellington - Money Jungle (628)
6248 7-84458-2 Milt Jackson - Bags' Opus (621)
6257 4-93711-2 Don Byron - Nu Blaxploitation (417,418,419)
6258 4-93760-2 Greg Osby - Zero (418,419)
6259 8-33114-2 Joe Lovano - Trio Fascination (413)
6261 8-53082-2 Pat Martino - Stone Blue (420)
6266 8-23487-2 Stefon Harris - A Cloud Of Red Dust (414)
6267 7-99106-2 Blue Break Beats (see page 784)
6268 7-89907-2 Blue Break Beats Volume Two (see page 778)
6269 8-54360-2 Blue Break Beats Volume Three (see page 797)
6270 4-94027-2 Blue Break Beats Volume Four (see page 757)

TOCJ-
6271/74 (4 CD Box) Swing Journal Presents The Blue Note:

Thelonious Monk (22)
Bud Powell (25)
Fats Navarro/McGhee (23)
James Moody (23)
Miles Davis (31)
J.J. Johnson (36)
Clifford Brown (38)
Wynton Kelly (29)
Kenny Drew (34)
Herbie Nichols (48)
Jutta Hipp (52)
Tal Farlow (41)
Gil Melle (51)
Thad Jones (55)
Horace Silver (44)
Kenny Dorham (46)
Hank Mobley (46)
Johnny Griffin (52)
Sonny Clark (75)
John Coltrane (71)
Paul Chambers (67)
Lee Morgan (77)
J.R. Monterose (57)
Louis Smith (80)
Sonny Rollins (71)
Curtis Fuller (75)
Freddie Redd (100)
Freddie Hubbard (104)
Dexter Gordon (142)
Art Blakey (101)
Duke Jordan (108)
Donald Byrd (95)
Duke Pearson (175)
Horace Pazrlan (102)
Jimmy Smith (50)
Lou Donaldson (116)
Baby Face Willette (117)
The Three Sounds (91)
Grant Green (124)
Ike Quebec (143)
Kenny Burrell (147)
Stanley Turrentine (150)
Jackie McLean (153)
Joe Henderson (155)
Andrew Hill (159)
Eric Dolphy (163)
Herbie Hancock (168)
Wayne Shorter (169)
Larry Young (186)
Ornette Coleman (187)
Bobby Hutcherson (190)
McCoy Tyner (201)
Chick Corea (240)

6284 8-33588-2 Everette Harp - Better Days (421,422)
6285 Funk Is A Four-Letter Word:

Ronnie Foster (265)
Bobby Hutcherson (245)
Bobbi Humphrey (267,269)
Alphonse Mouzon (265)
Grant Green (260)
Donald Byrd (255)
Eddie Henderson (287)

6286 BN-LA059-F Alphonse Mouzon - The Essence Of Mystery (265)
6287 7-84466-2 Donald Byrd - Blackbyrd (264)
6288 4-98542-2 Bobbi Humphrey - Blacks And Blues (267)
6289 BN-LA 260-G Moacir Santos - Saudade (270)
6290 BN-LA 313-G Gene Harris - Astral Sign (273)
6291 BN-LA 368-G Donald Byrd - Stepping Into Tomorrow (274)
6292 BN-LA 425-G Ronnie Foster - Cheshire Cat (278)
6293 BN-LA 551-G Bobby Hutcherson - Montara (282)
6294 BN-LA 636-G Eddie Henderson - Heritage (287)
6295 BN-LA 738-H Maxi Anderson - Maxi (297)
6302 Howard McGhee - Nobody Knows You When You're Down And Out (629)
6307 Blue Note Nonstop 60 Trax (various artists)
(Note:This CD is made of short excerpts from 60 BN titles - 0'57" to 1'39" - not mentioned in session listings)
6308 7-46295-2 Michel Petrucciani - Pianism (312)
6309 7-46427-2 Michel Petrucciani - Power Of Three (314)
6310 7-48679-2 Michel Petrucciani - Michel Plays Petrucciani (322)
6311 7-92563-2 Michel Petrucciani - Music (331)
6312 7-95480-2 Michel Petrucciani - Playground (342)
6313 7-80590-2 Michel Petrucciani - Promenade With Duke (355)
6314 7-80589-2 Michel Petrucciani - Live (346)

"24 Bit By RVG" Series

Note: In following series,all issues are equivalent to previous CD or LP issues shown in second cilumn.

TOCJ-		
9001	TOCJ-1595	Cannonball Adderley - Somethin' Else (79)
9002	TOCJ-1588	Sonny Clark - Cool Struttin' (76)
9003	TOCJ-4003	Art Blakey - Moanin' (85)
9004	TOCJ-4009	Bud Powell,Vol.5 - The Scene Changes (88)
9005	TOCJ-1577	John Coltrane - Blue Train (71)
9006	TOCJ-4195	Herbie Hancock - Maiden Voyage (179)
9007	TOCJ-1579	Sonny Clark Trio (72)
9008	TOCJ-4157	Lee Morgan - The Sidewinder (161)
9009	TOCJ-1521	Art Blakey - A Night At Birdland,Vol.1 (40,41)
9010	TOCJ-1522	Art Blakey - A Night At Birdland,Vol.2 (40,41)
9011	TOCJ-1581	Sonny Rollins - A Night At The Village Vanguard,Vol.1 (73)
9012	TOCJ-1590	Lee Morgan - Candy (75,77)
9013	TOCJ-4024	Jackie McLean - Swing,Swang,Swingin' (96)
9014	TOCJ-1569	Paul Chambers - Bass On Top (67)
9015	TOCJ-4017	Horace Silver - Blowin' The Blues Away (94,95)
9016	TOCJ-4031	Hank Mobley - Soul Station (99)
9017	TOCJ-4123	Kenny Burrell - Midnight Blue (147)
9018	TOCJ-4041	Tina Brooks - True Blue (105)
9019	TOCJ-4040	Freddie Hubbard - Open Ssame (104)
9020	8-56581-2	Horace Parlan - Us Three (= BLP4037) (102)
9021	TOCJ-1557	Lee Morgan,Vol.3 (62)
9022	TOCJ-1501	Miles Davis,Vol.1 (31,34)
9023	TOCJ-1502	Miles Davis,Vol.2 (31,34,41)
9024	TOCJ-1526	Clifford Brown Memorial Album (35,38)
9025	TOCJ-1524	Kenny Dorham - 'Round Midnight At The Cafe Bohemia (54)
9026	TOCJ-1503	The Amazing Bud Powell,Vol.1 (25,27)
9027	TOCJ-1504	The Amazing Bud Powell,Vol.2 (25,27,37)
9028	TOCJ-4002	Jimmy Smith - House Party (70,77,78)
9029	TOCJ-1527	The Magnificent Thad Jones (55)
9030	TOCJ-1539	Horace Silver - 6 Pieces Of Silver (58)
9031	TOCJ-4114	Ike Quebec - Soul Samba (143)
9032	TOCJ-4052	Tina Brooks - Back To The Tracks (110,111)
9033	TOCJ-4046	Duke Jordan - Flight To Jordan (108)
9034	TOCJ-4094	Fred Jackson - Hootin' N' Tootin' (134)
9035	TOCJ-4179	Jackie McLean - It's Time (169)
9036	TOCJ-4026	Donald Byrd - Fuego (95)
9037	TOCJ-4035	Duke Pearson - Tender Feelin's (98)
9038	TOCJ-4132	Grant Green - Feelin' The Spirit (146)
9039	TOCJ-4018	Walter Davis Jr. - Davis Cup (93)
9040	TOCJ-4057	Stanley Turrentine With The Three Sounds - Blue Hour (114)
9041	TOCJ-1510	Thelonious Monk - Giant Of Modern Music,Vol.1 (20,21,22)
9042	TOCJ-1511	Thelonious Monk - Giant Of Modern Music,Vol.2 (20,21,28,32)
9043	TOCJ-1530	Jutta Hipp With Zoot Sims (56)
9044	TOCJ-1536	J.R. Monterose (57)
9045	TOCJ-4146	Dexter Gordon - Our Man In Paris (154)
9046	TOCJ-1519	Herbie Nichols Trio (48,49,53)
9047	TOCJ-1576	Sonny Clark - Sonny's Crib (70)
9048	TOCJ-1593	Lou Donaldson - Blues Walk (83)
9049	TOCJ-4059	Kenny Drew - Undercurrent (113)
9050	TOCJ-4007	Donald Byrd - Off To The Races (87)
9051	TOCJ-4058	Hank Mobley - Roll Call (113)
9052	TOCJ-4076	Horace Silver - Doin' The Thing (122,123)
9053	TOCJ-4109	Herbie Hancock - Takin' Off (139)
9054	7-84078-2	Jimmy Smith - Midnight Special (102,103)
9055	BLP4068	Baby Face Willette - Face To Face (117)
9056	BLP4130	John Patton - Along Came John (152)

846

TOCJ-

9057	8-21736-2	Ike Quebec - It Might As Well Be Spring (= BLP4105) (130)
9058	CP32-9518	The Three Sounds - Moods (= BLP4044) (105)
9059	TOCJ-4173	Wayne Shorter - Night Dreamer (165)
9060	7-46514-2	Wayne Shorter - Juju (= BLP4182) (169)
9061	TOCJ-1535	Kenny Dorham - Afro-Cuban (45,46)
9062	TOCJ-4175	Herbie Hancock - Empyrean Isles (168)
9063	CJ28-5147	Sonny Clark - Dial S For Sonny (= BLP1570) (67)
9064	CJ28-5146	Hank Mobley (= BLP1568) (66)
9065	8-32089-2	Lee Morgan - Lee Way (= BLP4034) (103)
9066	TOCJ-1507	Art Blakey & The Jazz Messengers - A The Cafe Bohemia,Vol.1 (49,50)
9067	TOCJ-1508	Art Blakey & The Jazz Messengers - A The Cafe Bohemia,Vol.2 (49,50)
9068	8-53355-2	Horace Silver - The Tokyo Blues (= BLP4110) (141)
9069	7-84140-2	Joe Henderson - Page One (155)
9070	TOCJ-1583	Curtis Fuller,Vol.3 (75)
9071	CJ28-5077	The Three Sounds - Bottoms Up (= BLP4014) (83,84,89)
9072	CJ28-5092	Duke Pearson - Profile (= BLP4022) (96)
9073	TOCJ-4071	Grant Green - Green Street (120)
9074	TOCJ-4111	Grant Green - The Latin Bit (137)
9075	7-89392-2	Freddie Redd - The Connection (= BLP4027) (100)
9076	TOCJ-4039	Stanley Turrentine - Look Out (104)
9077	4-98794-2	Dexter Gordon - Go! (= BLP4112) (142)
9078	TOCJ-4012	Lou Donaldson With The Three Sounds (89)
9079	7-46524-2	Eric Dolphy - Out To Lunch (= BLP4163) (163)
9080	TOCJ-4199	Lee Morgan - The Rumproller (181)
9081	CP32-9522	Hank Mobley - Workout (= BLP4080) (119)
9082	7-46532-2	Art Blakey - A Night In Tunisia (= BLP4049) (108,109)
9083	TOCJ-4127	Kenny Dorham - Una Mas (152)
9084	TOCJ-1578	Lee Morgan - The Cooker (72)
9085	TOCJ-1575	Lee Morgan - City Lights (69)
9086	TOCJ-1574	Hank Mobley - Peckin' Time (77)
9087	5-21959-2	Grant Green - Grant First Stand (= BLP4064) (116)
9088	TOCJ-1545	Lou Donaldson - Wailing With Lou (59)
9089	TOCJ-4036	Lou Donaldson - Sunny Side Up (99,100)
9090	TOCJ-4185	Horace Silver - Song For My Father (159,173)
9091	7-84008-2	Horace Silver - Finger Poppin' (89)
9092	TOCJ-4023	Dizzy Reece - Star Bright (97)
9093	TOCJ-4032	Sonny Redd - Out Of The Blue (97,99)
9094	TOCJ-4045	Freddie Redd - Shades Of Redd (109)
9095	TOCJ-1533	Intoducing Johnny Griffin (52)
9096	7-84047-2	Art Taylor - A.T.'s Delight (108)
9097	TOCJ-4119	Charlie Rouse - Bossa Nova Bacchanal (145)
9098	TOCJ-4082	Horace Parlan - Up & Down (124)
9099	7-84019-2	Donald Byrd - Byrd In Hand (92)
9100	TOCJ-4011	Jimmy Smith - The Sermon (70,78)
9101	7-46511-2	Hank Mobley - Dippin' (= BLP4209) (183)
9102	7-46136-2	Herbie Hancock - Speak Like A Child (= BLP4279) (210)
9103	7-84263-2	Lou Donaldson - Alligator Boogaloo (201)
9104	8-32091-2	Pete La Roca - Basra (= BLP4205) (181)
9105	TOCJ-1515	Jutta Hipp At The Hickory House,Vol.1 (52)
9106	TOCJ-1516	Jutta Hipp At The Hickory House,Vol.2 (52)
9107	TOCJ-1523	Introducing Kenny Burrell (53)
9108	CJ28-5145	Lee Morgan,Vol.2 (= BLP1541) (58)
9109	8-37647-2	Paul Chambers - Whims of Chambers (= BLP1534) (57)
9110	7-81558-2	Sonny Rollins,Vol.2 (63)
9111	TOCJ-4154	Grant Green - Idle Moments (159)
9112	BST84345	Jackie McLean - Demon's Dance (208)
9113	TOCJ-1562	Horace Silver - The Stylings Of Silver (64)
9114	CJ28-5068	Horace Parlan - Movin' & Groovin' (= BLP4028) (100)
9115	TOCJ-4204	Dexter Gordon - Gettin' Around (182)
9116	TOCJ-1600	Introducing The Three Sounds (83,84)

 847

TOCJ-		
9117	TOCJ-4097	Art Blakey - The African Beat (133)
9118	TOCJ-4091	Sonny Clark - Leapin' And Lopin' (129)
9119	7-81559-2	Johnny Griffin - A Blowing Session (63)
9120	TOCJ-1567	Curtis Fuller - The Opener (66)
9121	7-81542-2	Sonny Rollins (59)
9122	TOCJ-1571	Bud Powell,Vol.3 (68)
9123	TOCJ-1598	Bud Powell,Vol.4 (82)
9124	TOCJ-1509	Milt Jackson (22,28,30)
9125	TOCJ-4051	Jackie McLean - Jackie's Bag (88,110)
9126	CJ28-5149	Lou Donaldson - Lou Takes Off (= BLP1591) (76)
9127	TOCJ-1513	Thad Jones - Detroit-New York Junction (51)
9128	TOCJ-4004	Art Blakey - Holiday For Skins,Vol.1 (86)
9129	TOCJ-4005	Art Blakey - Holiday For Skins,Vol.2 (86)
9130	7-84042-2	Horace Silver - Horace-Scope (106)
9131	TOCJ-4149	Hank Mobley - No Room For Squares (151,158)
9132	8-59962-2	Grant Green - I Want To Hold Your Hand (= BLP4202) (179)
9133	7-46512-2	McCoy Tyner - The Real McCoy (= BLP4264) (201)
9134	TOCJ-1538	Introducing Lee Morgan (57)
9135	TOCJ-1531	The Fabulous Fats Navarro,Vol.1 (19,23,25)
9136	TOCJ-1532	The Fabulous Fats Navarro,Vol.2 (22,23,25)
9137	8-52438-2	Here Comes Louis Smith (= BLP1584) (454)
9138	TOCJ-1580	Johnny Griffin - The Congregation (73)
9139	TOCJ-4021	Kenny Burrell At The Five Spot Cafe (93,94)
9140	TOCJ-4107	Don Wilkerson - Preach Brother (140)
9141	7-46140-2	Horace Silver & The Jazz Messengers (= BLP1518) (44,45)
9142	TOCJ-1520	Horace Silver Trio/Art Blakey-Sabu (33,39)
9143	TOCJ-4084	Baby Face Willette - Stop And Listen (123)
9144	TOCJ-1537	Lou Donaldson Quartet/Quintet/Sextet (32,33,43)
9145	TOCJ-1543	Kenny Burrell,Vol.2 (50,53,54)
9146	TOCJ-4099	Grant Green - Sunday Mornin' (124)
9147	7-84126-2	Herbie Hancock - My Point Of View (151)
9148	8-59380-2	Freddie Hubbard - Goin' Up (= BLP4056) (111)
9149	TOCJ-4048	Donald Byrd - Byrd In Flight (98,99,106)
9150	TOCJ-1573	John Jenkins With Kenny Burrell (69)
9151	TOCJ-4270	Jack Wilson - Easterly Winds (206)
9152	TOCJ-1528	Jimmy Smith At Club Baby Grant,Vol.1 (56)
9153	TOCJ-1529	Jimmy Smith At Club Baby Grant,Vol.2 (56)
9154	TOCJ-1540	Hank Mobley Sextet (58)
9155	8-37668-2	Hank Mobley And His All Stars (= BLP1544) (59)
9156	TOCJ-4038	Jackie McLean - Capuchin' Swing (102)
9157	TOCJ-4101	Donald Byrd - Royal Flush (127)
9158	TOCJ-1582	Cliff Jordan - Cliff Craft (74)
9159	TOCJ-4062	Horace Parlan - Headin' South (113)
9160	7-46509-2	Wayne Shorter - Speak No Evil (= BLP4194) (176)
9161	7-84224-2	Ornette Coleman At The Golden Circle,Vol.1 (187,188)
9162	7-84225-2	Ornette Coleman At The Golden Circle,Vol.2 (187,188)
9163	TOCJ-4025	Lou Donaldson - The Time Is Right (96,97)
9164	TOCJ-4073	Freddie Hubbard - Hub Cap (120)
9165	7-46530-2	Bobby Hutcherson - Happenings (= BLP4231) (190)
9166	TOCJ-4093	Ike Quebec - Heavy Soul (129)
9167	TOCJ-4020	The Three Sounds - Good Deal (91)
9168	TOCJ-4243	Lee Morgan - Delightfulee (191,192)
9169	TOCJ-4013	Jackie McLean - New Soil (91)
9170	7-84147-2	Herbie Hancock - Inventions And Dimensions (157)
9171	8-28978-2	Kenny Dorham - Whistle Stop (= BLP4063) (115)
9172	TOCJ-1550	Hank Mobley (62)
9173	TOCJ-1564	Paul Chambers Quintet (65)
9174	TOCJ-4043	Horace Parlan - Speakin' My Piece (107)
9175	8-56583-2	Further Explorations By The Horace Silver Quintet (= BLP1589) (76)
9176	7-46523-2	Art Blakey - Mosaic (= BLP4090) (127)

848

TOCJ-
9177 TOCJ-1565 Cliff Jordan (stereo version) (65)
9178 TOCJ-4069 Stanley Turrentine - Up At Minton's,Vol.1 (118)
9179 TOCJ-4070 Stanley Turrentine - Up At Minton's,Vol.2 (118)
9180 TOCJ-1512 Jimmy Smith - A New Star-A New Sound (50)
9181 TOCJ-4006 Dizzy Reece - Blues In Trinity (83)
9182 7-84221-2 Larry Young - Unity (186)
9183 TOCJ-1596 Kenny Burrell - Blue Lights,Vol.1 (81)
9184 TOCJ-1597 Kenny Burrell - Blue Lights,Vol.2 (81)
9185 TOCJ-1560 Hank Mobley (63)
9186 7-84134-2 Horace Parlan - Happy Frame Of Mind (150)
9187 TOCJ-4088 The Three Sounds - Here We Come (114)
9188 TOCJ-4098 Ike Quebec - Blue And Sentimental (131)
9189 7-84181-2 Kenny Dorham - Trumpeta Toccata (172)
9190 TOCJ-1551 Jimmy Smith At The Organ,Vol.1 (61)
9191 TOCJ-1552 Jimmy Smith At The Organ,Vol.2 (60,61)
9192 TOCJ-1566 Lou Donaldson - Swing And Soul (65)
9193 TOCJ-1554 Art Blakey - Orgy In Rhythm,Vol.1 (62)
9194 TOCJ-1555 Art Blakey - Orgy In Rhythm,Vol.2 (62)
9195 TOCJ-4089 Jackie McLean - A Fickle Sonance (128)
9196 TOCJ-4187 Larry Young - Into Somethin' (174)
9197 7-84222-2 Lee Morgan - Cornbread (185)
9198 TOCJ-4066 Lou Donaldson - Here 'Tis (116)
9199 TOCJ-1546 The Magnificent Thad Jones (55,59)
9200 TOCJ-1594 Louis Smith - Smithville (80)
9201 BLP5066 Hank Mobley Quartet (46)
9202 TOCJ-1505 The Eminent J.J Johnson Vol.1 (36,43)
9203 TOCJ-1506 The Eminent J.J Johnson Vol.2 (36,43,48)
9204 TOCJ-1514 Jimmy Smith At The Organ,Vol.2 - The Champ (51)
9205 TOCJ-1549 Clifford Jordan/John Gilmore - Blowing In From Chicago (61)
9206 TOCJ-1592 Sonny Clark Quintets (75,76)
9207 TOCJ-4015 Art Blakey & The Jazz Messengers At The Jazz Corner Of The World,Vol.1 (90)
9208 TOCJ-4016 Art Blakey & The Jazz Messengers At The Jazz Corner Of The World,Vol.2 (90)
9209 TOCJ-4029 Art Blakey & The Jazz Messengers - The Big Beat (101)
9210 TOCJ-4054 Art Blakey & The Jazz Messengers - Meet You At The Jazz Corner Of The Word, Vol.1 (110)
9211 TOCJ-4055 Art Blakey & The Jazz Messengers - Meet You At The Jazz Corner Of The Word, Vol.2 (110)
9212 TOCJ-4067 Jackie McLean - Bluesnik (115)
9213 TOCJ-4074 Horace Parlan - On The Spur Of The Moment (119)
9214 TOCJ-4075 Donald Byrd - The Cat Walk (121)
9215 TOCJ-4116 Jackie McLean Quintet (139)
9216 7-84133-2 Dexter Gordon - A Swingin' Affair (142)
9217 TOCJ-4156 Art Blakey & The Jazz Messengers - The Freedom Rider (117,123)
9218 7-84169-2 Lee Morgan - Search For The New Land (163)
9219 TOCJ-4212 Lee Morgan - The Gigolo (183,184)
9220 8-59961-2 Lee Morgan - Charisma (195)
9221 BLP5023 Kenny Drew Trio (34)
9222 BLP5025 Piano Interpretations By Wynton Kelly (29)
9223 BLP5029 Elmo Hope Trio (36)
9224 BLP5035 Sal Salvador Quintet (39)
9225 BLP5042 Tal Farlow Quartet (41)
9226 BLP5044 Elmo Hope Quintet,Vol.2 (42)
9227 BLP5056 Jutta Hipp Quintet (451)
9228 BLP5067 Lou Mecca Quartet (46)
9229 BLP5068 The Prophetic Herbie Nichols,Vol.1 (47)
9230 BLP5069 The Prophetic Herbie Nichols,Vol.2 (48)
9231 TOCJ-4137 Jackie McLean - One Step Beyond (153)
9232 TOCJ-4184 Sam Rivers - Fuschia Swing Song (175)
9233 7-46135-2 Tony Williams - Spring (184)
9234 TOCJ-4232 Wayne Shorter - Adam's Apple (190)

TOCJ-
9235 TOCJ-4237 Cecil Taylor - Unit Structures (192)
9236 8-28982-2 Ornette Coleman - The Empty Foxhole (195)
9237 8-53356-2 Jackie McLean - New And Old Gospel (201)
9238 7-84282-2 Elvin Jones - Puttin' It Together (212)
9239 7-84332-2 Wayne Shorter - Super Nova (231)
9240/41 BN-LA015-G2 Elvin Jones - Live At The Lighthouse (2 CD Set) (262)
9242 TOCJ-4030 Jimmy Smith - Crazy Baby (98)
9243 TOCJ-4053 Lou Donaldson - Light Foot (87)
9244 TOCJ-4086 Grant Green - Grantstand (125)
9245 TOCJ-4108 Lou Donaldson - The Natural Soul (138)
9246 TOCJ-4117 Jimmy Smith - Back At The Chicken Shack (102,103)
9247 7-84124-2 Donald Byrd - A New Perspective (147)
9248 8-52433-2 Harold Vick - Steppin' Out (154)
9249 TOCJ-4139 Grant Green - Am I Blue (154)
9250 TOCJ-4192 Big John Patton - Oh Baby (178)
9251 BST84267 Duke Pearson - The Right Touch (205)

TOCJ-
65250 4-99503-2 Medeski,Martin & Wood - Combustication Remix EP (415)

66003 4-94211-2 Blue Note Salutes Motown (see page 758)
66005 (Capitol) Jazz CN Hits Special:
Art Blakey (85) Cannonball Adderley (79)
(& further titles not from BN)
66006 Boogie Woogie And Piano Classics - Melancholy:
A. Ammons & M.L. Lewis (1,2) Pete Johnson (4)
Earl Hines (3) James P. Johnson (6)
66007 Sidney Bechet & The Port Of Harlem Jazzmen - Summertime (2,3,4)
66008 Sidney Bechet & The Blue Note Jazzmen,Vol.1 - St. Louis Blues (12,17)
66009 Sidney Bechet & The Blue Note Jazzmen,Vol.2 - I Found A New Baby (24,26)
66010 8-21260-2 Edmond Hall - Profoundly Blue (5,7,8)
66011 Jamming In Jazz With The Blue Note Jazzmen - High Society :
Edmond Hall (6) James P. Johnson (11)
Sidney de Paris (9)
66012 Art Hodes' Back Room Boys - Low Down Blues (8,11,13,15,16)
66013 Art Holdes' Hot Five & Seven - Shine (14,16)
66014 Swing Sessions - Victory Stride:
James P. Johnson (7) Jimmy Hamilton (16)
Benny Morton (13) Sammy Benskin (15)
66015 Ike Quebec Quintets & Swingtet - Blue Harlem (10,14)
66016 Ike Quebec Swing Seven - Topsy (15,18)
66017 John Hardee Swingtets - Tired (17,18)
66018 4-98240-2 John Coltrane - Trane's Blues (see page 763)
66019 4-96685-2 Joe Chambers - Mirrors (424,425)
66020 8-54123-2 +1 Cassandra Wilson - Traveling Miles (416,423,424)
66021 Herbie Hancock - Riot (151,157,210,225)
66022 4-97945-2 Stefano Di Battista - A Prima Vista (425)
66027 8-33060-2 Dianne Reeves - Bridges (426)
66029 4-99351-2 Us3 - Flip Fantasia : Hits & Remixes (350,351,393)
66031 Art Blakey - The Blue Note Years (40,49,85,90,101,109,127,130)
66032 Thelonious Monk - The Blue Note Years (19,20,21,22,28,32,63)
66033 Bud Powell - The Blue Note Years (25,27,37,68,82,88,154)
66034 Horace Silver - The Blue Note Years (39,45,58,76,89,94,106,122,141,173,185)
66035 Miles Davis - The Blue Note Years (31,34,41,79)
66036 Sonny Rollins - The Blue Note Years (59,63,71,73)
66037 Jimmy Smith - The Blue Note Years (50,54,55,60,61,64,70,74,98,103,133)
66038 Sonny Clark - The Blue Note Years (67,70,72,75,76,86,87,129)
66039 Lee Morgan - The Blue Note Years (58,62,77,161,181,184,185,191,195,207)
66040 Sidney Bechet - The Blue Note Years (3,4,12,13,16,17,24,26,30,37)
66041 John Coltrane - The Blue Note Years (57,63,70,71)

TOCJ-
66042 Kenny Burrell - The Blue Note Years (50,53,81,93,94,147,151)
66043 Hank Mobley - The Blue Note Years (46,63,66,77,99,113,119,158,183,209)
66044 Lou Donaldson - The Blue Note Years
(59,76,83,89,96,100,116,121,201,206,211,226)
66045 Grant Green - The Blue Note Years (116,120,124,137,146,159,172,179,246)
66046 Jackie McLean - The Blue Note Years (96,102,110,115,136,153,169,172,187,208)
66047 Dexter Gordon - The Blue Note Years (121,122,142,154,167,182)
66048 The Three Sounds - The Blue Note Years (83,89,91,105,114,125,134,135)
66049 Wayne Shorter - The Blue Note Years (165,169,176,178,183,186,190,200,231)
66050 Herbie Hancock - The Blue Note Years (139,151,157,168,179,210,225)
66051 Big Hits - Moanin':
Art Blakey (85) Horace Silver (94)
John Coltrane (71) Freddie Hubbard (104)
Sonny Clark (76) Joe Henderson (155)
Bud Powell (27) Herbie Hancock (179)
Jackie McLean (208)
66052 Standards - Autumn Leaves:
Cannonball Adderley (79) Jimmy Smith (133)
Hank Mobley (183) Dexter Gordon (122)
Thad Jones (55) Grant Green (116)
Jackie McLean 596) Bl:ue Mitchell (157)
The Three Sounds (105) Stanley Turrentine (150)
66053 Piano Moods - Cleopatra's Dream:
Bud Powell (88) Horace Parlan (102)
Sonny Clark (72) Duke Jordan (108)
Horace Silver (58) Duke Pearson (198)
The Three Sounds (91) McCoy Tyner (201)
Thelonious Monk (21) Herbie Hancock (210)
Jutta Hipp (52)
66054 Ballads - I Remember Clifford:
Lee Morgan (62) Donald Byrd (127)
Jutta Hipp (56) Dexter Gordon (121)
Jimmy Smith (64) Grant Green (125)
Miles Davis (34) Lou Donaldson (59)
Duke Pearson (96) Clifford Brown (38)
Ike Quebec (133)
66055 Breakbeats - The Sidewinder:
Lou Donaldson (201) Grant Green (246)
Kenny Dorham (46) Don Wilkerson (140)
Lee Morgan (161) Lonnie Smith (216)
Herbie Hancock (168) Donald Byrd (264)
Blue Mitchell (184)
66056 4-98756-2 Jacky Terrasson - What It Is (427,429)
66057 4-99527-2 Benny Green - These Are Soulful Days (430,431)
66058 4-99241-2 Gonzalo Rubalcaba - Inner Voyage (428)
66059 4-98917-2 Chucho Valdes - Briyumba Palo Congo (428)
66060 The RVG Album:
John Coltrane (71) Ike Quebec (129)
Lee Morgan/R. Van Gelder (85) Dexter Gordon (142)
Art Blakey (85) Kenny Burrell (147)
Hank Mobley (99) Lee Morgan (161)
Donald Byrd (127) New Directions (615)
66061 4-99187-2 Charlie Hunter & Leon Parker - Duo (430)
66062 4-99997-2 +1 Renee Rosnes - Art & Soul (433)
66063 Blue Note - Heart Of Modern Jazz:
Art Blakey & The JM (127) Lee Morgan (161)
John Coltrane (71) Herbie Hancock (306)
H.McGhee-Fats Navarro (23) Us3 (350)
Miles Davis (41)
66065 4-99545-2 Don Byron - Romance With The Unseen (432)

851

TOCJ-		
66066	4-99826-2	Eric Dolphy - The Illinois Concert (456)
66067	5-22342-2 +2	Caecilie Norby - Queen Of Bad Excuses (434,435)
66068	4-97431-2	Jason Moran - Soundtrack To Human Motion (425)
66069	8-23392-2	Mark Shim - Turbulent Flow (432)
66070	4-99546-2	Stefon Harris - Black Action Figure (433)
66071		BFC Jazz: Cannonball Adderley (79) Peggy Lee (490) Art Blakey (85) Chet Baker (547) Caecilie Norby (373) Sarah Vaughan (576) Nat King Cole (482) Mel Torme (644) Dinah Shore (487)
66072	5-21484-2	The Lost Sessions (see page 767)
66073	5-21455-2	Art Blakey - Drums Around The Corner (85,90)
66074	5-21436-2	Lou Donaldson - Man With A Horn (127,155)
66075		Tina Brooks - The Waiting Game (118)
66076		Freddie Redd - Redd's Blues (115)
66077	5-21811-2	Patricia Barber - Modern Cool (658)
66078	5-20827-2	Eliane Elias - Everything I Love (437,438,440)
66079	GXF-3056	Sonny Clark - My Conception (90)
66080	GXF-3067	Jackie McLean-Tina Brooks - Street Singer (110)
66081	GP-3186	Tommy Flanagan - Lonely Town (622)
66082		Stanley Turrentine & The Three Sounds - Blue Hour,Vol.2 (106,114)
66083		Ike Quebec - From Hackensack To Englewood (92,93)
66084	5-21688-2	Latino Blue (various artists - see page 768)
66085	5-20730-2	Chucho Valdes - Live At The Village Vanguard (435)

852

TOCP-
3401 7-80883-2 Us3 - Hand On The Torch (350,351)
3402 7-81357-2 Cassandra Wilson - Blue Light 'Til Dawn (356,359,361)
3406 7-95137-2 Bob Belden - Straight To My Heart (The Music Of Sting) (333,338,343)
3407 7-95477-2 Bobby McFerrin & Chick Corea - Play (337)
3408 8-27765-2 John Scofield & Pat Metheny - I Can See Your House From Here (365)
3409 8-32222-2 Caecilie Norby - Caecilie (373)
6681 7-46906-2 Dianne Reeves (318,319)
6685 7-46092-2 Stanley Jordan - Magic Touch (304)
6687 7-48385-2 Earl Klugh - Living Inside Your Love (293)
6688 7-48386-2 Earl Klugh - Finger Paintings (296,297)
6689 7-48389-2 Earl Klugh - Magic In Your Eyes (633,634)
6690 BN-LA462-G Carmen McRae - I Am Music (279,280)

TOCP-
7455/56 (2 CD Set) Twin Best Bow:
Cannonball Adderley (79) Herbie Hancock (179)
Bud Powell (88) Jackie McLean (96)
Hank Mobley (183) Miles Davis (31)
Clifford Brown (38) Horace Silver (94)
John Coltrane (71) Thad Jones (55)
Thelonious Monk (21) Sonny Rollins (71)
Jimmy Smith (98) Paul Chambers (67)
Art Blakey (85) Sonny Clark (76)
Lee Morgan (161)
7662 (Capitol) Missing You Jazz:
Dianne Reeves (339) (& further titles not from BN)
7871 CP32-5448 The Blue Note Jazz Story (see page 820)
7872 CJ28-5171 Blue Note For You - Originals (see page 817)
7873 CJ28-5172 Blue Note For You -Standards (see page 817)
8581 Toshiba-EMI Now Jazz:
Art Blakey (85) Miles Davis (31)
Bud Powell (88) Herbie Hancock (179)
(& further titles not from BN)
8639 8-32222-2 Caecilie Norby - Caecilie Norby (373)
8642 8-31809-2 Charlie Hunter - Bing,Bing,Bing (376)
8657 8-29266-2 Greg Osby - Black Book (367)
8751 Toshiba-EMI Now Jazz 2:
Sonny Clark (76) Herbie Hancock (68)
Cannonball Adderley (79) (& further titles not from BN)
8893 8-36594-2 The New Groove - The Blue Note Remix Album (385,386)
8901 7-48389-2 Earl Klugh - Magic In Your Eyes (633,634)
8902 7-48385-2 Earl Klugh - Living Inside Your Love (293)
8903 7-48386-2 Earl Klugh - Finger Paintings (296,297)
8904 7-48387-2 Earl Klugh - Crazy For You (293,538)
8915 8-35283-2 Blue Note Plays Jobim (see page 792)
8963 Blue Note Hits!:
Sonny Clark (76) Cannonball Adderley (79)
Art Blakey (85) Lou Donaldson (201)
Bud Powell (88) John Coltrane (71)
Lee Morgan (161) Thelonious Monk (21)
Herbie Hancock (179)
8966 Hip Hop Jazz:
XXL (651) Digable Planets (569)
Spearhead (510) Bob Belden/Greg Osby (608)
The Pharcyde (510) Us3 (350)
Guru's Jazzamatazz (511) Greg Osby (367)
The Solsonics (511) Easy Mo' Bee/Horace Silver (386)
8968 8-53422-2 Caecilie Norby - My Corner Of The Sky (390 391)
9055 (EMI-USA) Earl Klugh - Best Now (285,293,296,297) (& further titles not from BN)

TOCP-

50040 8-30027-2 Us3 - Broadway & 52nd (393)

50060 Bud Powell - Cleopatra's Dream (27,37,68,82,88,154,570,571,581)

50085 8-53325-2 +3 Helen Eriksen - Standards (395)

50230 Now Jazz 3:

Lee Morgan (161)	Sonny Clark (72)
John Colrane (71)	Dexter Gordon (182)
Lou Donaldson (201)	Joe Henderson (155)
Horace Silver (173)	Sonny Rollins (71)
Hank Mobley (183)	Thelonious Monk (21)

50370 Toshiba-EMI Now Jazz 4:

Herbie Hancock (139)	Kenny Dorham (46)
Horace Silver (58)	Art Blakey (85)
Lee Morgan (62)	(& further titles not from BN)

50403 8-21220-2 +2 Viktoria Tolstoy - White Russian (409)

65031 Toshiba-EMI Now Jazz Vocal:

Carmen McRae (288)	(& further titles not from BN)

65099 DeeJay Cool Cuts Blue (617,618)

65100 Blue Jams:

Us3 (351)	Dream Warriors & Gang Starr (515)
The Roots Remix (386)	Gang Starr (511)
Diamond D remix (386)	Guru & Chaka Khan (511)
Channel Live (510)	Guru & MC Solaar (511)
Mellow Man Ice (509)	AZ (513)
Aceyalone (510)	The Jaz (513)
DreamWarriors (515)	Boogie Monsters (569)

65158 4-96968-2 Helen Eriksen - Love Virgin (445)

65250 4-99503-2 Medeski,Martin & Wood - Combustication Remix EP (415)

65352 Toshiba-EMI Now Jazz Ballad:

Lee Morgan (62)	Cannonball Adderley (79)
Dexter Gordon (182)	(& further titles not from BN)

65367 5-23220-2 +1 Dr. John - Duke Elegant (517)

65391 5-20208-2 +2 Ronny Jordan - A Brighter Day (438,439)

65445 5-25271-2 Medeski,Martin & Wood - Tonic (433)

65446 5-25251-2 The Jazz Mandolin Project - Xenoblast (441)

<u>VICTOR label</u>

VICJ-5154 The Modern Jazz:

Sonny Clark (76)	Bud Powell (88)
Cannonball Adderley (79)	(& further titles not from BN)

THE NETHERLANDS

DISKY label

Note: Following issues are reissues of Japanese compilations.

DC

85981-2	CJ28-5178	Jazz Piano For Lovers (see page 818)
85982-2	CJ28-5022	Jazz Piano Delight (see page 814)
85985-2	TOCJ-5298	Sweet And Dangerous Jazz Blues (see page 831)
85987-2	CJ28-5021	Brunch Time Jazz (see paeg 814)

TURKEY

BLUE NOTE label

100301-2 Onder Focan - Beneath The Stars (414)

Index of Artists

ALTSCHUL,Mike (reeds) (273 280)
ALVAREZ,Chico (tp) (468 469 470 474 475)
ALVAREZ,Ruben P. (perc) (661)
ALVES,Donald (vo) (270)
ALVES,Louis (perc) (277)
ALVES,Luis (b) (523 525)
ALVIN,Danny (dm) (7 8 9 11 14 17)
AMEDEO (ss,as,ts) 657
AMENDOLA,Scott (dm) (386 387 392 400 413)
AMES SINGERS,The Morgan (280)
AMLOTTE,Jim (tb) (484 486 488 489 491 498 562)
AMMONS,Albert (p) 1 2 (2)
AMMONS,Gene (ts) (81 473) 558
AMOPOL,Michael (b) (652)
AMSALLEM,Franck (p) (348 608)
AMSTER,Rob (b,el b) (366 388 392 397 399 405 416 418 440 441)
AMUEDO,Leonardo (g) (394)
AMY,Curtis (ss,ts) (492) 557 560
ANASTASIO,Troy (g) (441)
ANDERSEN,Jacob (perc) (373 390)
ANDERSON,Cat (tp) (477 478 631)
ANDERSON,Dale (vb,marimba) (500)
ANDERSON,Ernestine (vo) 617
ANDERSON,Frank (p,org) (249 587)
ANDERSON,Herbert (tp) (567)
ANDERSON,Hugh (dm,perc) (489 566 567)
ANDERSON,Jay (b) (320 332 338 339 343 352 353 354 608)
ANDERSON,Jim (frh) (611)
ANDERSON,John (tp) (464 467 468 575)
ANDERSON,Maxi (vo) 297 (539)
ANDERSON,Ray (tb) (308 320 650)
ANDERSON,Vanessa (vo) (512)
ANDRADE,Hector (timbales,cga,perc) (506)
ANDRADE,Leny 522
ANDRE,Wayne (tb) (543 635)
ANDRESS,Tuck (g) (396)
ANDREWS,Jeff (el b) (323 608)
ANDREWS,Reggie (keyb,arr) (258 263 295)
ANDREWS,Russ (ts) (584)
ANDREWS SISTERS,The (vo) 637
ANDRIKA (vo) (512)
ANGEL,The (remix,arr) (385 386)
ANGELO,Nelson (perc) (523 524)
ANTHONY,Al (as) (467 468)
ANTHONY,Mike (g) (566 567 568)
ANTOINE,Marc (g) (422)
ANTON,Artie (dm) (479)
ANTONACCI,Ana Caterina (vo) (515)
ANTONION,Larry (b) (400)
APELLANIZ,Norberto (cga) (216)
APLANALP,Richard (bs) (566 567)
APPEL,Toby (viola) (368)
ARCHEY,Jimmy (tb) (26 27 30 37)
ARCHIBALD (vo) 530
ARGUDIN,Maria del Carmen (vo) (610)
ARGUELLES,Julian (ts,bs) (350 351 360)
ARMANDO,Ray (cga,perc) (252 254 256 268 269)
ARMIN,Richard (cello) (660)
ARMOUR,Ed (tp) (628)
ARMSTRONG,Jackie (tb) (516)
ARMSTRONG,Joseph (cga) (246 247 385)
ARMSTRONG,Louis (tp,vo) 482 516 577 578
ARMSTRONG,Trevor (dm) (239 240)
ARNETT,Jan (b) (215 584)
ARNO,Victor (v) (485 487 491 497)
ARNOLD,Buddy (ts) (491)
ARNOLD,Horace (dm,perc) (587)
ARNOLD,Jay(ts) (228)
ARNONE,Don (g) (41)
ARNOPOL,Michael (b) (658 661)
ARONOV,Benny (p) (483)
ART ENSEMBLE OF CHICAGO 520
ASCHER,Ken (el p) (537)
ASHBY,Dorothy (harp) (281 282 297 298)
ASHBY,Harold (ts,cl) (631 632)
ASHBY,Irving (g) (460 464)
ASHBY,Jay (tb) (541)
ASHFORDJack (perc,tamb) (297 538)
ASHFORD,Marilyn (vo) (649)
ASHTON,Bob (cl,ts,bs) (180 181 495 586)
ASPIRINA (perc) (655)
ASPLUND,Peter (tp) (409)
ASSIS BRASIL,Victor 524
ASSUMPAO,Nico (el b) (606)
ATKINS,Chet (g) (633)
ATKINSON,Lisle (b) (581)
ATKINSON,Wayman (ts) (553)
ATTIG,Jurgen (el b) (323)
AUD,Francis (vo,perc) (379)
AUDINO,John (tp) (496 497 503 559 562)
AULD,George (ts) (500)
AUSTER,Paul (sound effects) (658)
AUSTIN,Patti (vo) (293 633)
AVELAR,Carlos Ortega (p) (534)
AVERHOFF,Carlos (ts) (344)
AXELROD,David (arr,cond) 500 (501) 502
AYERS,Roy (vb) (194 439)
AZ (rapper) 513
AZARELLO,Joe (p) (566)
AZEN,Harry (strings) (466)
AZEVEDO,Mike "Baiano" (cga,perc) (506)
AZZI,Christian (p) (639 640)

BA,Oumar (vo) (445)
BABASIN,Harry (b,cello) (545 547 638)
BABATUNDE (cga) (506)
BABBITT,Bob (b) (286)
BACCUS Jr.,Eddie (ss) (405 410 436 437)
BACKENROTH,Hans (b) (526)
BACKO,Jacko (kalimba,vo) (662)
BACON,Kenny (vo) (655)
BAD NEWS (rapper) (354 355)
BADRENA,Manolo (perc,vo) (305 398 539 541)
BAGLEY,Don (b) (474 475 476 478 482 498 535)
BAHAMADIA (rapper) (569)
BAILEY,Benny (tp) (115)
BAILEY,Buster (cl) (467)
BAILEY,Colin (dm) (290 536 560 561 562)
BAILEY,Dave (dm) (65 83 96 116 120 121 552 553 620 629)

BAILEY,Don (b) (73 82)
BAILEY,Donald (dm) (51 54 55 56 60 61 64 66 67 70 74 75 77 78 80 82 84 92 98 101 10 103 125 133 148 149 157 203 212 225 228 229 243 244)
BAILEY,Donald (hca) (568)
BAILEY,John "Buddy" (vo) (625)
BAILEY,Pearl (vo) 575
BAILEY,Philip (perc,vo) (288 634)
BAILEY,Victor (b,el b) (321 513 653)
BAILLY Jr.,Octavio (b) (492 493)
BAIN,Bob (g) (489 490 494 503)
BAIRD,Taswell (tb) (570)
BAIZ,Jimmy (b) (534)
BAKER,Anita (vo) (652)
BAKER,Chet (tp,flh) (476 545 546) 546 547 548 549 550 551 553 (553 563 566)
BAKER,George (223)
BAKER,Israel (v) (229 485 487 493)
BAKER,Michael (dm) (324 325 650)
BAKER,Shorty (tp) (460 534)
BALBOA,Buddy (sax) (576)
BALDWIN,Charles (b,dm programming) (371 372 381 437)
BALES,Kevin (p) (420)
BALKE,Jon (el p) (395)
BALL,Ronnie (p) (532)
BALL,Tommy (tp) (452 454)
BALLARD,Butch (dm) (477 574)
BALLARD,Fred (tp) (249 250)
BALLOU,Dave (tp) (387 388)
BALTAZAR,Gabe (as) (489 491 562)
BALTAZAR,Norman (tp) (491)
BANANA,Milton (dm) 521 522 524
BANBARA 505
BANCROFT,Tom (dm) (350)
BANK,Danny (bs,fl) (42 180 181 191 495 584 628 645)
BANKS,Buddy (b) (638)
BANKS,Clarence (tb) (373)
BANKS,Martin (tp) (107 566)
BANNEVILLE,Annette (vo) 520
BAPTIST,Rick (tp) (656)
BAPTISTA,Cyro (perc) (359 376 380 381 389 410 411 444 517 544 610 653)
BARAB,Seymour (cello) (257 258 260 261 262 264 271 300 301)
BARAK,Ann (v) (293)
BARAKAAT,Nasir (g) (461)
BARARD,David (el b) (517)
BARBARO,Clifford (dm) (421)
BARBER,Bill (tu) (473 475 555 556 645)
BARBER,John (tu) (472)
BARBER,Julian (v,viola) (224 257 258 260 261 262 293 610 633)
BARBER,Patricia (p,org,vo) 652 658 661
BARBIERI,Leandro "Gato" (ts) (189 195)
BARBOUR,Dave (g,orch) (459 466 467 468 469)
BARBOUR,Don (vo) (480)
BARBOUR,Ross (vo) (480 489)
BARCELO,Lincoln (ts,fl) (528)
BARCELONA,Danny (dm) (577 578)
BARENA,Manolo (perc,bgo) (426)
BARFIELD,Tinker (el b) (327 328 334 335)
BARHART,Scotty (tp,flh) (373)
BARKER,Guy (tp) (349 351 652)
BARKER,Laverne (b) (21)
BARKSDALE,Everett (g) (8209 476)
BARLOW,Varney (dm) (194 219)
BARNARD,Cecil (p) (268)
BARNES,Allan (ts,fl) (268 270)
BARNES,Bob (vo) (299 300)
BARNES,George (g) (534 646)
BARNES,Gerry (vo) (513)
BARNES,Katresse (vo) (513)
BARNET,Charlie (ss,ts) 474
BARNEY,Tom (b) (541)
BARNUM,H.B.(arr,cond) (496 497 498 499 500 502 595)
BARON,Art (tb) (379 380)
BARON,Bernard (b) (291)
BARON,Joey (dm,perc) (290 299 347)
BARONE,Gary (tp) (291 292 566 567)
BARRATT,Glenn (keyb,programming) (371 372 381)
BARRETO,Julio (dm) (357 370 601 602 603 610)
BARRETTO,Ray (cga,vo) (65 83 85 86 87 96 107 113 147 150 171 173) 382 406 422
BARRON,Bill (ts) (623)
BARRON,Kenny (p) (199 208 215 232 378 391 566 602 604 614)
BARROWS,John (frh) (625)
BARRY,Bob (dm) (453)
BARRY,David (g) (363)
BARTEE,Claude (ts) (233 237 243 246 247 260 385)
BARTH,Benny (dm) (554)
BARTH,Bruce (keyb) (303)
BARTHELMY,Paul (tb) (456)
BARTHOLOMEW,Dave (vo,tp,cond) (463 529 530) 531
BARTO,Lin (bs,fl) (528)
BARTON,Dee (dm) (498)
BARTON,Dee (tb) (491)
BARTZ,Gary (fl,as) (217 238 246 274 289 294) 506
BAS,Vlady (as,cl) (528)
BASCOMB (Jr.),Wilbur (el b) (261 265 266 271)
BASHORUN,Joe (p,keyb,perc) (345 349 358)
BASIE,Count (p) 573 (573) 574 575 576 577 578 630
BASIE ORCHESTRA,Count (373 573 574)
BASO,Evaristo (b) (64)
BASS,Fintella (vo) (520)
BASS,Herb (tp) (518)
BASS,Mickey (b) (218 246 646)
BASS,Sid (arr) (533)
BASSEY,Shirley (vo) 516 632
BASSO,Guido (flh) (660 661)
BASTOS PINHEIRO,Roberto (vo) (540)
BATEMAN,Edgar (dm) (630)
BATES,Django (p,keyb,g,vo) 349
BATES,Tyler (g) (655 656)
BATISTA Jr.,Pablo (perc) (436)

BATTAGELLO,Walter (tp) (563)
BAUER,Billy (g) (470 472 473 475)
BAUTISTA,Roland (g) (279 296 506 507 538 634)
BAUZA,Mario (dir) (573)
BAVO,Sarah (vo) (64)
BAY,Victor (v) (480 484 488)
BAYETE: see COCHRAN,Todd
BAYLOR,Marcus (dm) (423 424)
BAZLEY,Tony (dm) (554)
BAZZLE,Germaine (vo) (391)
BEACH,Frank (tp) (478 488 489 490)
BEACH,Thelma (strings) (285)
BEACHILL,Pete (tb) (652)
BEARD,Jim (el p,org,synth,synth programming, perc) (329 330 421 424 653 659)
BEARDON,Michael (keyb,synth,b) (363 421)
BEASLEY,John (p) (375)
BEASTIE BOYS (vo) 509
BEAU,Heinie (as) (466 468)
BEAUJOJAN,Marcel (v) (639)
BEAUJOLAIS,Roger (vb) (350)
BECHET,Sidney (ss,cl) (3) 3 (4) 12 13 (16) 17 24 26 30 37 639 640 644
BECK,Donald (Donnie) (b,el b) (291 296 385 506)
BECK,Gordon (p) (649)
BECK,Joe (g) (250 278 281 508 509)
BECKHAM,Steve (keyb) (371)
BECKMAN,Dawn (vo) (386)
BEECHAM,Ralph (vo) (298)
BEECHER,Francis (g) (472)
BEENER,Elaine (vo) (219)
BEHRENDT,Bob (tp) (491)
BEIRACH,Richie (p) 594 599
BELAIR,Mark (vb,perc) (368)
BELDEN,Bob (ts,ss,arr,synth) 332 (334 335) 338 343 352 353 (367 376 379 380 398) 407 408 411 412 (423 440) 603 606 607 611
BELGRAVE,Marcus (tp,flh) (593 599 609)
BELL,Aaron (tu) (512)
BELL,Khalil (shaker) (439)
BELL,Poogie (dm) (438)
BELL,Vincent (g) (262)
BELLER,Alex (v) (480 484 488)
BELLICOURT,Henri (cl) (639)
BELLOW,Myer (viola) (229 285)
BELLSON,Louis (dm) 476
BELNICK,Arnold (strings) (296)
BELNICK,Blanche (v) (298)
BEMKO,Gregory (cello) (474 475)
BEMKO,Harold (cello) (568)
BEN,Tony (cga) (286)
BENDITSKY,Naoum (cello) (488)
BENEDETTI,Vince (p) (229)
BENEKE,Tex (ts) (637)
BENFORD,Tommy (dm) (517)
BENJAMIN,Joe (b) (534 552 573 578 622 632 640)
BENNETT,Benny (dm) (643)
BENNETT,Brian 516
BENNETT,Edward (Ed) (b,dm) (290 291)
BENNETT,Erroll "Crusher" (perc) (312)
BENNETT,Joe (tb) (554 555 645)
BENNETT,John (tb) (239 240)
BENNETT,Max (b) (479 480 490 492 493 534 567)
BENNETT,Sherron (vo) (394)
BENNETT,Tony (vo) 574 646
BENOIT,Dave (p,el p) (284 286)
BENSKIN,Sammy (p) (13) 15 (17 449)
BENSON,George (g,vo) (201 209 211 242 278 305 317 327 393)
BENSON,Walter (Walt) (tb) (471 484)
BENTLEY,Lord (p): see THOMPSON,Sir Ch.
BENTYNE,Cheryl (vo,arr) (649)
BERG,Bob (ts) (275 276 283 284 294 386)
BERG,Dick (frh) (219 220 236)
BERG,George (ts) (628)
BERGCRANTZ,Anders (tp) (434)
BERGER,Karl (p,vb) (195)
BERGERON,Chuck (b) (589)
BERGHOFER,Chuck (b) (289 496 498)
BERGLUND,Dan (b) (409)
BERGMAN,Edward (v) (497)
BERGONZI,Jerry (ts) (339 345) 592
BERGSTROM,Paul (cello) (296)
BERK,Dick (dm) (568 569)
BERKHOUT,Bernard (cl) (337)
BERLINER,Jay (g) (153 262 264)
BERMAN,Marty (reeds,bs,bass cl) (485 550 551)
BERMAN,Seymour (viola,v) (260 261 262 264 271 300 301)
BERNARD,Cy (cello) (484)
BERNARD,Henri (ts) (642)
BERNHARDT,Clyde (tb,vo) 25
BERNHARDT,Ernie (tp) (489)
BERNHART,Milt (tb) (212 468 469 470 472 474 475 477 480 481 482 483 484 485 486 488 490 551)
BERRIOS,Steve (perc) (269 378 390)
BERROA,Ignacio (dm) (428)
BERRY,Bill (tp) (577 582 583 585)
BERRY,Emmett (tp) (467 534)
BERT,Eddie (tb) (33 51 236 237 242 450 469 470 472 475 573 587 628)
BERTAUX,Marc (el b) (445)
BERTEAUX,Bob (b) (486)
BERTHOUMIEUX,Marc (acc) (432)
BERTONCINI,Gene (g) (247 256 259 260 266 386 502)
BESIAKOW,Ben (p,el p,org) (373 434)
BESSON,Herb (tu) (367)
BESSY,Jimmy (tp) (221)
BEST,Clifton "Skeeter" (g) (92 93)
BEST,Denzil (dm) (142 144 467 473)
BEST,Donald (vb) (147)
BEST,John (tp) (481 483 490 491 503)
BETHEL,Bill (dm) (518)
BETTIS,Nat (perc) (221 227 228)
BETTS,Harry (tb,arr) (470 474 475 476 480 488 564)
BEUKES,Lionel (b) (525)
BEUTLER,Allan (bs) (491 567)
BEVERLY,Frankie 506
BEY,Andy "Chief" (vo,perc) (133 153 173 221 224

BOWLAND,Randall (Randy) (g) (436 540)
BOWLER,Phil (b) (588 590 600 612)
BOWMAN,Dave (p) (449)
BOWMAN,Dean (vo) (417 662)
BOWNE,Dougie (dm,perc) (380 38 525 544)
BOYD,Emanuel (Manny) (fl,ts) (271 272 286 287 292 297 298 299)
BOYD,Jacquelyn (vo) (394)
BOYD,Nelson (b) (19 23 3 473)
BOYER,Ed (b) (268)
BOYS CHOIR OF HARLEM (vo) 598
BOZE,Calvin (vo) 461
BRADER III,Ken (tp,flh) (435 436)
BRADLEY,Joe (p) (553)
BRADLEY,Oscar (dm) (447 466)
BRADLEY,Oscar Lee (dm) (470 529 530)
BRADLEY,Will (tb) (479 481)
BRADLEY Jr.,James (dm) (536 537)
BRAFF,Malcolm (p) 661
BRAFF,Ruby (tp,c) (479 481 646)
BRAGA,Paulo (dm,bongos,vo) (606 613)
BRAITH,George (ss,strich) (155 156) 157 161 164
BRAITHWAITE,Wayne (el b) (304 317 512 540)
BRANDON,Kevin (el b) (325)
BRANNON,Teddy (p) (466)
BRANSON,Regis (keyb b,vo) (512)
BRASHEAR,Oscar (tp,flh) (253 263 273 275 276 277 278 281 282 285 289 352 386 400 409 410 506 653)
BRAUD,Wellman (b) (16 637)
BRAUN,Rick (flh) (422 429)
BRAXTON,Anthony (fl,cl,as) (246 247)
BREACH,Thelma (v) (493)
BREAUX,Zachary (sampled rh g) (439)
BRECHTLEIN,Tom (Tommy) (dm) (360 540)
BRECKER,Amanda (Elias) (vo) (600 602 613)
BRECKER,Matthew (programming,mixer) (423 446)
BRECKER,Michael (Mike) (ts) (263 294 317 328 329 339 383 391 427 428 586 587 613) 653 (659)
BRECKER,Randy (tp,flh) (208 221 222 241 243 250 263 269 270 294 328 329 347 361 373 382 383 391 399) 586 587 653 (660)
BREEN,Larry (b) (468 471)
BREGMAN,Buddy (arr) (555)
BREHM,Simon (b) (640)
BREIT,Gary (org) (381)
BREIT,Kevin (g,el g,guit-organ) (380 381 423 424 444 544 611 660 661)
BRETTON,Elise (vo) (224 225)
BREWSTER,Roy (vtb) (557)
BRICE,Percy (dm) (467 482 484 576)
BRIDGEWATER,Cecil (tp) (250 251 259 383 456 648)
BRIGGS,Bernie (b) (450)
BRIGGS,Bunny (b)
BRIGGS,David (p) (536)
BRIGGS,Jimmy (vocal arr) (254)
BRIGHT,Ronnell (p) (256 495 496 504 576)
BRILE,Richard (viola) (610)
BRILHART,Verlye (harp) (489)
BRINKLEY,Kent (b) (278)
BRISBOIS,Bud (tp) (486 487 489 492 497 567)
BRISCOE,Ted (b) (461)
BRITT,Johnny (vo) (363)
BRITT,Tina (vo) 630
BROCK,William (keyb) (372)
BROMBERG,Brian (b) (613)
BROOKMEYER,Bob (tb,vtb,p) (548 552) 552 (582 583 586 622) 623 645
BROOKS,Hadda (p,vo) 635
BROOKS,Harold "Tina" (ts) (78) 79 (80 81 93 94 104) 105 (109 110) 111 (115) 118
BROOKS,Kenny (ts) (392)
BROOKS,Ron (b) (221 234 456)
BROOKS,Roy (dm) (97 106 122 123 152 153 157 159 162 458)
BROOKS Jr.,Roy (dm) (124)
BROOKS III,Cecil (dm) (338)
BROOKSHIRE,Nell (vo) (632)
BROOM (BROOME),Bobby (g) (316 517)
BROWN,Al (viola) (229)
BROWN,Alex (vo) (231 363)
BROWN,Alexandra (vo) (296 417)
BROWN,Anthony (maracas) (309)
BROWN,Benjamin (b) (362 373 384 393 412 421 425)
BROWN,Cameron (b) (313 318 430)
BROWN,Charles (p,vo) 461 464
BROWN,Cleo (vo) 474
BROWN,Clifford (tp) 35 (36) 38 (40 41) 548 (642) 642 (643) 643
BROWN,Clyde (bass tb) (475)
BROWN,Deborah (vo) (383)
BROWN,Delmar (keyb) (420)
BROWN,Donald (p) (322)
BROWN,Eddie (reeds) (475)
BROWN,Eddie "Bongo" (perc) (635)
BROWN,Garnett (tb,arr) (199 204 205 206 208 209 211 221 225 265 266 271 283 285 384 582 583 584 585 586)
BROWN,Gary (b) (337)
BROWN,George Edward (dm) (216)
BROWN,Gerry (dm) 281 (291) 294 (653)
BROWN,Harold (dm) (647)
BROWN,Henry "Pucho" (timbales) (216)
BROWN,John (as) (459 570)
BROWN,Johnny (g) (461)
BROWN,Josh (tb) (660 661)
BROWN,Lawrence (tb) (631)
BROWN,Les (as) 486
BROWN,Maurice (cello) (475)
BROWN,Mel (dm) (561)
BROWN,Mildred (vo) (254)
BROWN,Ollie E. (dm,perc,arr) (656)
BROWN,Peter (el b) (305)
BROWN,Ray (b,cello) (194 219 225 488 500 563 638 644)
BROWN,Raymond (tp) (283)
BROWN,Ron (b,el b) (267 586)
BROWN,Rosalyn (vo) (254)
BROWN,Roy (vo) 532

BROWN,Russell (Russ) (tb) (488 619)
BROWN,Ruth (vo) 585
BROWN,Sam (g) (215 217 238 261 385 587)
BROWN,Sheree (vo) 508
BROWN,Sidney (tu) (447)
BROWN,Stumpy (bass tb) (486)
BROWN,Ted (ts) (532)
BROWN,Tiny (vo) (530)
BROWN,Tyrone (b) (593)
BROWN,Vernon (tb) (449 479)
BROWN,Willard (as,bs) (466 467)
BROWN,William (vo) (503)
BROWN Jr.,Vernon (p,org) (400)
BROWNSEY,Lois (vo) (436)
BRUBECK,Dave (p) 645
BRYAN,Duggy (g) (647)
BRYANT,Bobby (Bob) (tp) (212 227 275 276 386 492 494 567 568)
BRYANT,Lance (ss) (403)
BRYANT,Paul (org) 557
BRYANT,Ray (p) (62 65 69 86) 575 (621)
BRYANT,Rocky (dm) (352)
BRYANT,Tommy (b) (575)
BRYANT,Warren (cga) (253)
BRYANT,William (Willie) (dm) (400 538 539)
BUCK,Carol (cello) (602 610)
BUCKINGHAM,Katisse (fl) (386)
BUCKLEY,Steve (as) (349)
BUCKNER,Teddy (tp) (466)
BUDIMIR,Dennis (g) (274 275 277 279 280 282 288 289 290 295 490 494 557 561 562 563 566 567)
BUDSON,Robert (p) (291)
BUDWIG,Monty (Monte) (b) (44 485 536 551 552 555 556)
BUFFINGTON,Jim (frh) (175 176 191 212 213 214 219 220 236 257)
BUFFINGTON,Ruth (v) (293)
BUFFUM,Denyse (Nadeau) (strings) (298 595)
BUFFUM,Julius (strings) (280)
BUGNON,Alex (keyb) (540)
BUGNON,Cyrille (as,ts) (390)
BULDRINI,Fred (v) (293)
BULLOCK,Hiram (g,el g) (305 539 635 659)
BUNCH,John (p) (563)
BUNDOCK,Rowland (b) (637)
BUNKER,Larry (dm,perc,vb) (44 289 485 487 488 489 490 493 497 532 545 546 548 559 563 619 621)
BUNN,Jimmy (p) (459 637 638)
BUNN,Teddy (g,vo) (2 3) (4) 4
BUNNETT,Jane (ss,fl) 655 662
BURGESS,Bob (tb) (235 476 551)
BURGHER,Russ (tp) (467)
BURK,David (Dav) (v,viola) (218 229 567)
BURKE,Clayton (vo) (379)
BURKE,Clifford (vo) (379)
BURKE,Sonny (keyb,arr,cond) (297 471)
BURKE,Vinnie (b) (46)
BURKS,Edward (tb) (536)
BURKS,Jane (vo) (536)
BURKS,John (tp) (126)
BURNETT,Carl (dm,cga) (218 231 239 254 255 268)
BURNETT,Joe (tp,mell) (486 489)
BURNHAM,Charlie (v) (356 359 381)
BURNO,Dwayne (b) (414 418 607)
BURNS,Dave (tp) (23 42 108 128 140 570)
BURNS,Ralph (arr) (475)
BURRAGE,Ronnie (dm) (315 324 365 378)
BURRELL,Kenny (g) (50) 50 (51) 53 (54 55 57) 60 (61 67 69 70 75 78) 81 (82) 90 (92) 93 94 (103 141 143 145 146) 147 (147 148) 151 152 154 (162) 173(180 181 212 213 214 220) 235 236 (236) 304 (307 312) 316 (319 454 486 604)
BURROUGHS,Alvin (dm) (470)
BURROUGHS,Clark (vo,arr) (655)
BURTIS,Sam (tb) (537 539)
BURTON,Abraham (as) (408)
BURTON,Barbara (vb,perc) (249)
BURTON,Esther (vo) (536)
BURTON,Gary (vb) (645)
BURTON,Willard 505
BUSBY,Laddie (tb) (516)
BUSHNELL,Bob (el b) (586)
BUTCHER,George (p,keyb) (43 286)
BUTERA,Sam (ts) (482 485)
BUTLER,Allen (fl) (567)
BUTLER,Artie (p,arr) (503)
BUTLER,Billy (g) (194 580)
BUTLER,Frank (dm) (553)
BUTLER,George (speech) (291)
BUTLER,Melvin (ts,ss) (413 442)
BUTLER,Ross (tp) (459)
BUTTERFIELD,Billy (tp) (481)
BUTTERFIELD,Don (tu) (45 175 176 191 495 624 628)
BUTTS,Jimmy (b) (18)
BYAM,Roger (ts) (596)
BYARD,Jaki (p) (175 577 627 628)
BYAS,Don (ts) (640 641)
BYERS,Billy (tb,arr) (212 219 222 229 255 472 652)
BYRD,Charlie (g) (450)
BYRD,Donald (tp,flh) (57 58 59 60 63 65 70 76 82 83 86) 87 (88 90 91) 92 (93) 95 98 99 106 112 120 121 127 131 (131) 147 (149 151 167 173 174) 174 (175) 175 176 193 198 (199 200) 202 (202) 206 227 228 229 235 242 250 255 260 264 267 268 270 274 283 289 291 (298 385) 453 (454 617)
BYRD,Jerry (g) (234)
BYRNE,Bobby (tb) (534)
BYRON,Don (cl,arr,comp) (359) 415 417 418 419 432 (593 595 660)

"C",Ced (keyb) (656)
"C",Vic (bass g) (656)
CABELL,Marvin (ss,ts) (228 230 248)
CABLES,George (p,el p) (222 286 287 297 298 299 403 457)
CABRERA,Felipe (el b) (357 370 601 602 610)
CADRECHA,John (g) (295)

CASSIDY,Eva (vo) (371 372)
CASTELLUCCI,Stella (harp) (273 297)
CASTILLO,Emilio (horns) (378)
CASTOR,Jimmy (ts,vo) 505
CASTRO,Joe (p) (486 488)
CASTRO,Lenny (perc) (429)
CASTRO-NEVES,Oscar (g,vo) (398 399 613)
CATALANO,Billy (tp) (484)
CATANZARO,Gherardo (p) (393)
CATENA,Francesco (org) (515)
CATHCART,Jack (cond) (480)
CATHCART,Jim (v) (474 475)
CATHELL,Dick (flh) (647)
CATHERINE,Philip (g) (281)
CATLETT,Sidney (dm) (2 3 4 6 7 9 16 17)
CATUREGLI,Alex (tp) (518)
CAVALIERE,Bernie (ts) (518)
CAVANAUGH,Dave (ts,arr) (469 485)
CAVANAUGH,Mike (el p) (279)
CAVE,John (frh) (485 644)
CAYIMMI,Dori (g,vo,arr) (375 654)
CECCARELLI,André (dm) (353)
CECCHI,Al (dm) (568)
CEDRAS,Tony (acc,g) (359 381 421)
CENTALONZO,Rick (fl,oboe) (427 429)
CENTENO,Francisco (b,el b) (293 295 297 385 633)
CENTOBIE,Leonard "Bujie" (cl) (14)
CESINHO (dm) (525)
CEZAR,Silvio 521
CHACON,Rodolfo (vo) (655)
CHAIKIN,Jules (tp) (559 560)
CHALOFF,Serge (bs) (471 473 475) 479 482
CHAMBERLAIN,Gerald Ray (tb) (272)
CHAMBERLAIN,Rick (tb) (435 436)
CHAMBERLAIN,Trisha (vo) (273)
CHAMBERS,Dennis (dm) (323 343 613)
CHAMBERS,Henderson (tb) (16 630)
CHAMBERS,Jeff (b) (428)
CHAMBERS,Joe (dm,perc) (166 168 174 177 179 182 183 186 189 190 200 204 206 207 208 211 215 221 227 230 232 233 352 353) 424 425 (607)
CHAMBERS,Joe (p) (611)
CHAMBERS,Paul (b) (48 53) 57 (58 62 63) 65 (65 66) 67 (68 69 70 71 72 73 75 76 77 80 86 87 88) 90 (90 91 97 99 101 102 103 108 109 110 111 113 115 119 122 127 130 131 157 177 195 197) 453 463 (554 555 560 573 621 623 624 645)
CHAMBLEE,Eddie (ts) (143 580)
CHANCLER,Leon "Ngudu" (dm) (253 291 298 318 507)
CHANEY,Jack (ts) (468)
CHANNEL LIVE 510
CHAPIN,Earl (frh) (236 556)
CHAPMAN,Peter (b) (240)
CHAPPELL,Gus (tb) (480)
CHAPPELL,Marvin (dm) (268 272)
CHARLES,Dennis (dm) (453 555)
CHARLES,Ray (vo) (327)
CHARLES,Teddy (vb) (474 619)
CHASE,Bill (tp) (574)
CHAUSOW,Robert (v) (610)
CHEATHAM,Doc (tp) (573)
CHEATHAM,Jimmy (bass tb,arr) (584)
CHELINSKY,David (g) (397)
CHEN,Phillip (g) (647)
CHENOLL,José (tb) (528)
CHERICO,Vince (dm) (382 406 422)
CHERRY,Don (c) 189 195 197
CHERRY,Ed (g) (421)
CHERRY,Vivian (vo) (293 633)
CHESTNUT,Cyrus (p) (380)
CHEVALIER,Eric (programmng) (445)
CHIEF CLIFF SINGERS (379)
CHILD'S VIEW (mixing) (618)
CHILDERS,Buddy (tp) (212 288 467 468 469 470 474 475 476 478 486 568)
CHILDS,Billy (p,synth) (318 319 339 343 360 426 457)
CHIRILLO,James (g) (368)
CHISHOLM,George (tb) (516)
CHIVILY,Pet (b) (487 489)
CHOKAN,Kevin (g) (408)
CHORAL THUNDER VOCAL CHOIR (658)
CHRISTENSEN,Tom (ts) (396)
CHRISTIAN,Charlie (g) (5)
CHRISTLIEB,Donald (bassoon) (568)
CHRISTLIEB,Pete (fl,ts) (285 289 568)
CHRISTY,June (vo) (467) 467 (470) 475 477 478 481 483 485 486 (487) 488 493
CICALESE,Angelo (as) (472)
CICCHETTI,Mike (ts) (478)
CINDERELLA,Joe (g) (51)
CINELU,Mino (perc) (318 402 404 406 416 427 429 540 542)
CIPRIANO,Gene (ts,woodwinds,oboe) (295 297 352 483 568)
CIRELLI,Peter (tb) (303)
CISI,Emmanuelle (ts,vo) (445)
CLARK,Arthur (bs) (271 646)
CLARK,Bill (dm) (481 640)
CLARK,Bob (tp) (480)
CLARK,Buddy (b) (480 504 532)
CLARK,Harold (ts) (467)
CLARK,Jackie (g) (536)
CLARK,John (frh) (591)
CLARK,John (frh) (347 352 367 368 396)
CLARK,Lillian (vo) (224 225)
CLARK,Mahlon (as) (478)
CLARK,Sonny (p) (66) 67 (68 69) 70 72 (72 73 74 75) 75 (76) 76 (77 79 80 81) 86 (86) 87 (88) 90 (128) 129 (132 133 134 135 139 140 142 143 145 463 482 531 532 619)
CLARK,Troy (vo) (394)
CLARKE,Kenny (dm) (22 23 30 31 35 36 42 43 48 53 154 450) 455 (471 473) 519 (646)
CLARKE,Mike (dm) (287)
CLARKE,Neil (perc) (439 458 635)
CLARKE,Selwart (viola,dir) (228 229 630)
CLARKE,Stanley (b,el b) (318 326 333 426 649) 653
CLARKSON,Jeff (p) (477)

872

874

HENSON,Nick (reeds) (456)
HEPBURN,Donald (el p) (284 285)
HEPBURN,Michael (el p) (284 285)
HERBERT,Mort (b,v) (488 577 578)
HERBIG,Gary (as,reeds) (291 295 352)
HEREDIA,Joe (dm) (457)
HERFURT,Arthur "Skeets"(as,fl) (471 478 481 482 484 486 493 497)
HERINGTON,Jon (John) (g) (421 424 542)
HERMAN,Sam (g,shaker) (582 583)
HERMAN,Woody (cl) 471 473
HERNANDEZ,Gregorio (vo) (655)
HERNANDEZ,Julio (el b) (657)
HERNANDEZ,Maridalia (vo) (610)
HERNANDEZ,Papito (b) (657)
HERNANDEZ,Raulito (timbales) (655)
HERNANDEZ,Rene (p) (573)
HERRING,Michael (g) (405 406)
HERRING,Vincent (as,ts,ss) (412 424)
HERWIG,Conrad (tb) (443)
HEWITT,Howard (vo) (394 656)
HEY,Jerry (tp) (394 513)
HEYDORFF,Paul (tb) (489)
HIBBLER,Al (vo) 460
HICKS,John (p) (206 209 323 390 443 564)
HICKSON,Dick (bass tb) (257)
HIDALGO,Givanni (cga,perc) (610)
HIGGINBOTHAM,J.C. (tb) 2 (2 3)
HIGGINS,Billy (dm) (127 128 129 131 136 137 139 140 142 146 150 161 163 172 174 176 177 180 181 182 183 184 185 187 188 189 191 192 193 194 195 197 198 199 200 201 202 204 206 207 209 213 215 218 219) 310 (577 595 603 608 615)
HIGGINS,Daniel (as,ts) (513)
HIGGINS,Monk (ts,p,org,perc,arr) (218 227 231 239 254 255 256) 586 632
HILL,Andrew (p) (157 158) 159 160 162 164 (164) 168 177 (179) 186 191 199 202 207 213 216 219 227 228 229 233 234 236 237 238 239 328 338 339 (442)
HILL,Calvin (b) (648)
HILL,Delbert (ts) (253 646)
HILL,Freddy (tp) (212 255 492 496 500 559 560 562 568)
HILL,Jim (bass tb) (486)
HILL,Nicky (ts) (452)
HILLYER,Lonnie (tp) (628)
HINANT,Peppy (dm) (563)
HINDMAN,Stephen: see DJ KINGSIZE
HINDS,Alan (g) (541)
HINES,Earl (p) 3 520
HINES,Gregory (vo) (300)
HINO,Kenji (el b) (605)
HINO,Motohiko (dm) (605 614 617)
HINO,Terumasa (tp,c) 592 596 601 605 609 (617)
HINSHAW,William Alfred (frh) (497)
HINTON,Milt (b) (10 18 35 111 129 130 133 136 151 152 481 484 486 575 578 628)
HINTON,Todd (tp) (438)
HIPP,Jutta (p) 52 56 451
HIRSHFIELD,Jeff (dm) (320 332 338 343 352 354 397)
HITCHCOCK,Jack (vb) (46)
HITE,Les (as,dir) (447)
HITTNER,Frank (bs) (577)
HIUTON,Mick (b) (351)
HIXSON,Dick (tb) (534 645)
HOBGOOD,Laurence (p) (366 370 374 388 392 397 399 405 416 418 440 441 607)
HOBO,Willie 505
HOCHBERG,Eric (b) (366 374 388 607)
HOCHHALTER,Paula (cello) (651)
HODEIR,Andre (arr,cond) (639)
HODES,Art (p) 7 8 9 11 (12) 13 14 15 16 (16 17 24)
HODGES,Johnny (as) (631 637)
HODGKISS,Allan (rh g) (519)
HOENIG,Ari (dm,perc) (432 441)
HOGAN,Wilbert (dm) (128 134 135 136 138 139)
HOGGARD,Jay (vb) (309 314 605)
HOLDEN,Carol (tp) (456)
HOLDGREFE,Gerard (b) (514)
HOLEN,Marc (perc) (430 435 436)
HOLIDAY,Billie (vo) 462 (466) 619
HOLLADAY,Marvin (bs) (487 489)
HOLLAND,Dave (g,b) (240 246 247 328 345 347 348 370 413 423 587 651)
HOLLAND,Milt (dm,perc) (492 494)
HOLLEY,Major (b) (147 150 563)
HOLLIDAY,Jack (p,arr) (450 641)
HOLLINGSWORTH,Mark (bs) (394)
HOLLOWAY,Charlene (vo) (410)
HOLLOWAY,Paula (vo) (410)
HOLMAN,Bill (ts,bs,arr) (299 476 478 486 487 551 552 553 554 564)
HOLMAN,Thomas (dm) (219)
HOLMES,Jim (v) (474 475)
HOLMES,Leroy (arr,cond) 630
HOLMES,Richard "Groove" (org) 252 (492) 557 558 567
HOLMES,Rick (narr) (503)
HOLMES,Rodney (perc) (415)
HOLMES,Wayne (party noise,keyb,vo) (363 422)
HOLT,Scotty (b) (199 201 205 208 215)
HOLZMAN,Adam (synth,el p) (331 342 343 346 352 603)
HOLZMAN-LITTLE,Carrie (viola) (651)
HONDA,Tamaya (dm) (614)
HONDA,Yuka (synth,dm programming) (415)
HOOD,Bill (ts,bs) (551 567)
HOOPER,Nesbert "Stix" (dm) (253 257 258 326 557 558 559 560 561 562 563 564 566 568)
HOPE,Elmo (p) (35) 36 42 (43) 553
HOPPER,Luico (el b) (508 509)
HORN,Jim (fl,as) (218 496 500 586)
HORN,Paul (fl,as,ts,reeds) (485 486 488 493 555) 565
HORNE,Lena (vo) 362 373 384 393 412 421 630
HORNER,Tim (dm) (617)
HORTA,Toninho (perc) (523 524)
HORTON,Steve (g) (512)
HOUSTON,John (p) (532 533)

880

881

882

LIVELY,Bob (as) (467)
LIVING TIME ORCHESTRA,The (303)
LIVINGSTON,Ulysses (g) (4 459 466 468)
LIVOTI,Joseph (v) (488 491)
LIVRAMENTO,Joe (tp) (573)
LLEWELIN,Jack (rh g) (519)
LLOYD,Charles (fl,ts) 303 (306 494)
LLOYD,James (keyb,synth,p) (371 381 405 406 407 408 410 436 437 539 540 541 542 648 649)
LLOYD,Jerry (tp) (56)
LO,Ted (synth) (540)
LO BORGES (g,vo) 524
LO CASCIO,Alex (dm) (655 656)
LOBO,Edu (vo,orch) 523
LOBO,Marco (perc) (525)
LOCKE,Joe (vb) (406 426)
LOCKER,Richard (cello) (293)
LOCKWOOD,Didier (v) (445)
LODDER,Steve (keyb) (358 360)
LOEB,Chuck (g) (305)
LOFTON,Lawrence "Tricky (tb) (557)
LOGAN,Steve (b,el b) (346 352)
LOGGINS,Kenny (vo) (394)
LOMBARDI,Clyde (b) (33 38 41 471 472)
LONDON,Julie (vo) 534 535 536
LONG,Jerry (vo) (240)
LONG,Ron (b) (569)
LONGMIRE,Wilbert (g) 567
LONGNON,Guy (tp) (640)
LONGSTRETH,Kimberley (vo) (391)
LOOKOFSKY,Harry (v) (262 264)
LOPER,Charles (Charlie) (tb) (227 276)
LOPES,Joe (as) (504)
LOPEZ,Caesar (ss,as) (344)
LOPEZ,Ivan (bgo) (468)
LOPEZ,Orlando (perc) (567)
LOPEZ,Perry (g) (43 45)
LORBER,Jeff (g,keyb,synth,arr) (405) 654 (656)
LOS ANGELES PHILHARMONIC ORCH. 298 (299)
LOTT,Carl (dm) (566 567 568)
LOUIS,André (ts) (518)
LOUVEL,Olivie g) (431)
LOVANO,Joe (ss,ts,dm) (331 332 341 347) 348 (352 353) 353 354 360 (361 364) 366 368 369 377 (379 387 388 390) 395 396 402 403 404 (408) 413 415 430 443 (542 543) 595 606 612 (650)
LOVE,Geoff (arr,cond) (516)
LOVELLE,Herbie (dm) (249 266 587)
LOVETT,'Sam Baby'(dm) (469)
LOVITT,Les (tp) (352)
LOWE,John (woodwinds,bs) (295 493 563)
LOWE,Mundell (g) (471 578 625)
LOWTHER,Henry (tp) (652)
LOWTHER,Ken (bs) (518)
LOZEAU,Kenny (vo) (379)
LUBAMBO,Romero (g) (331 426)
LUBE,Dan (v) (480 481 485 488 497)
LUBBOCK,Jeremy (arr) (384)
LUC,Sylvain (g,mand) (445)
LUCARAIN,Norbert (clay pot) (659)
LUCAS,Al (b) (11 15 128 137 461)
LUCAS,Buddy (hca) (266 271 646)
LUCAS,Harold (vo) (625)
LUCAS,Ray (dm) (204 214)
LUCAS,Reggie (g) (294)
LUCIEN,Jon (vo) (458 635)
LUCUMI (cga,bata dm) (662)
LUENING,Warn (tp,flh) (276)
LUGG,George (tb) (12 14)
LULU ON THE BRIDGE (score) 658
LUMIA,Guy (v) (293 300 301)
LUNDY,Benjamin (ts) (473)
LUNDY,Curtis (b,el b) (323 402 403 581)
LUSTGARTEN,Alfred (v) (485 497)
LUSTGARTEN,Edgar (Ed) (cello) (279 280 285 295 296 481 482 485 487 488 493)
LUSTGARTEN,Jackie (cello) (276)
LUSTGARTEN,Kathleen (cello) (276)
LUTCHER,Nellie (p,vo) 468 470
LUTER,Claude (cl) 639 640 644
LYLE,Bobby (el p) (286 291 296 324 325 385 422) 506 507
LYLE,Joy (v) (284)
LYLE,Russell (fl,ts) (219 226)
LYMPERIS,Bob (tp) (467)
LYNCH,Carl (g) (266)
LYON,Jimmy (p) (39)
LYONS,Jimmy (as) (192 196 226)
LYRA,Katherine (vo) (281 282)
LYTLE,Johnny (vb) 563 565 586

M'BOOP,Abdou (perc) (346)
M'TUME (perc): see MTUME
MABERN,Harold (p) (177 180 183 184 187 189 218 231 233 244 245 256 630)
MacDONALD,Kirk (ts) (660 661)
MacDOUGAL,E. Parker (ts) (452)
MACE,Tommy (sax) (466)
MACHITO (maracas,leader) (470) 573
MACHU,Gwenche (vo) (538)
MACK,Clifford (tamb) (242)
MACK,Lynn (vo) (273 280)
MACKAY,Dave (p) (563)
MACKEL,Billy (g) (642)
MACKEY,Richard (frh) (497)
MACKIE,Hank (g) (372)
MacKINNON,Steven (keyb,p) (660)
MACKREL,Dennis (dm) (379 380)
MADDEN,Dave (ts) (467)
MADERA,Jose (ts,perc) (537 573)
MADI,Kalil (dm) (196)
MADISON,Jimmy (dm) (305)
MADREDEUS 526
MAEBE,Arthur (Art) (frh,tu) (231 568)
MAGALHAES,Pedro Ayres (g) (526)
MAGALHAES,Veronica (vo) (525)
MAGALHAES,William (keyb,vo) (525)
MAGNUS,Brian (el b) (276)
MAGRO,Joe (ts) (467)
MAGRUDER,Charles (vo) (224 225)
MAGRUDER,John (bs,fl,cl) (563)

884

890

PIERCE,Tim (g) (612)
PIERSON,John (tb) (250)
PILLOW,Charles (oboe,woodwinds) (336 379 607 611)
PILTCH,David (Dave) (b) (542 544 650)
PILTCH,Rob (g) (544)
PINGITORE,Mike (g) (466)
PINKSTON,Valerie (vo) (422)
PINTAVALLE,John (v) (368 610)
PISANI,Nick (v) (481)
PISANO,John (g) (493 494 503 561 562)
PITMAN,Bill (g) (494)
PITTERSON,Karl (keyb) (647)
PIZZARELLI,Bucky (g) (199)
PIZZI,Ray (ss,as) (263 270 276 277 284 285 286 295)
PLA,Enrique (dm) (344 414)
PLA,Roberto (Latin perc) (350-351)
PLAINFIELD,Kim (dm) (541)
PLATER,Bobby (as) (630)
PLATT,Jack (dir) (518)
PLAXICO,Lonnie (b) (338 340 356 381 389 402 404 416 418 424 425 426 597 604 605)
PLEASURE,Morris (keyb) (512 513 542)
PLUMMER,Bill (b) (494)
POINDEXTER,Pony (as) (556)
POINTER,Louvinia (vo) (633 635)
POINTER,Noel (v) (293) 295 296 (385) 633 635
POLITTE,Charlotte (el p,synth,synth programming) (280 281 288)
POLLACK,Malcolm (vo) (602)
POLLAN,Al (tu) (644)
POLLIKOFF,Max (strings) (633)
POLLO,Lou (rh g) (396)
POMARA,Simon (perc) (337)
POMEROY,Herb (tp) (450) 452 (479)
POMPOSELLO,Tom (slide g) (542 543)
PONDER,Jimmy "Fats" (g) (206 210 212 214 217 220 223 227 228 305)
PONOMAREV,Valery (tp) (581 648)
PONTIEUX,Loic (dm) (337 338)
PONTY,Jean-Luc (v) 568 569
POOLE,Carl (tp) (479 481)
POOLE,George (cello) (493)
POOR,George (tp) (449)
POPE,Odeon (ts) (648)
POPOWYCZ,Roman (tp) (456)
POPWELL,Robert (el b) (298)
PORCARO,Jeff (dm) (295)
PORCARO,Joe (perc) (566 567)
PORCELLI,Bobby (as,fl) (345 356 372)
PORCINO,Al (tp) (235 236 237 242 469 470 473 475 480 486 495 560 566 619)
POREE,Greg (g) (255)
PORRET,Max (fl) (639)
PORT OF HARLEM JAZZMEN 2
PORT OF HARLEM SEVEN 3
PORTER,Bobbye: see HALL,Bobbye Porter
PORTER,Curtis (*aka* HADI,Shafi) (as,ts) (66 645)
PORTER,Darryl (party noises) (394)
PORTER,Gene (ts) (466)
PORTER,Jake (tp) (462 466)
PORTER,Karl (bassoon) (228)
PORTER,Phil (org) (629)
PORTER,Roy (dm) (637 638)
PORTINHO (shaker) (602)
POSK,Tony (v) (293 633)
POTTER,Chris (ts,ss) (383 404)
POTTER,Tommy (b) (25 556 570 577 638 639)
POTTS,Bill (arr) 622 (641)
POTTS,Steve (as) (584)
POUNDS,Raymond (dm) (508 538 634)
POWELL,Benny (tb) (42 59 175 176 208 209 212 213 214 221 235 236 237 242 270 485 566 573 574 575 576 577 578 587 646)
POWELL,Bud (p) 25 27 37 68 82 88 (154) 570 571 573 574 581
POWELL,Doc (g) (394 422 542)
POWELL,Forrest (tb) (447)
POWELL,Gordon "Specs" (dm) (15 254)
POWELL,Herbie (g) (622)
POWELL,Jesse (ts) (474)
POWELL,Jim (tp,flh) (332 338 343 352)
POWELL,Kobie (vo) (350-351)
POWELL,Mel (p) (479 481)
POWELL,Petsye (vo) (270)
POWELL,Ron (perc) (322 650)
POWELL,Seldon (fl,ts,bs) (151 152 265 266 271 335 542 543 571 585 586 627 628 635 646)
POZAR,Bob (dm,perc) (456)
POZO,Chano (bgo,cga) (22 23 570)
PRATT,David (cello) (491)
PRATT,Dean Robert (tp,flh) (272)
PRATT,Jimmy (dm) (554)
PREISS,Reinhold (b) (503)
PRELL,Don (b) (549 551 554)
PRELL,Michelin (dm) (240)
PRESENCER,Gerard (tp) (350-351 652)
PRESKILL,Bill (synth programming) (360)
PRESS,Seymour (reeds) (534)
PRESSMAN,Constance (strings) (295 296)
PRESTON,Billy (org) 495
PRESTON,Don (synth) (272 273)
PRESTON,Eddie (tp) (632)
PREVIN,Andre (p,arr,cond) 487 (535 621)
PREVITE,Bobby (dm) (352)
PRICE,Jesse (dm,vo) (469) 469
PRICE,Lon (arr) (335)
PRICE,Mike (tp) (277)
PRIDDY,James (Jimmy) (tb) (480 484)
PRIEST,Maxi (vo) (410)
PRIESTER,Julian (tb) (120 194 195 197 199 200 203 204 207 208 222 227 228 231 233 234 235 279 281 282 287 453 507)
PRIETO,Dafnis (dm) (662)
PRIMA,Louis (vo) 482
PRINCE,Bill (tp) (566)
PRINCE,Fulumi (vo) (219 226)
PRING,Bob (tb) (500)
PRINTUP,Marcus (tp) 375 (385) 389 390 412 420 (426) 607
PRIORE,Jennifer (vo) (336)

893

REINHARDT,Django (g) 517 (517) 518 519
REINHARDT,Joseph (rh g) (517 518 519)
REINHARDT,Ron (keyb) (367 384 543)
REINS,Gray (tp) (567)
REIS,Nando (el g) (525)
REIS,Tim (ss,ts) (338 343 352 426 427)
REISLER,Jerry (v) (296)
REIT,Peter (frh) (332 338 343 352)
REMI,Salaam (arr,mixer) (510)
REMY,Pierre (tb) (518)
REMY,Tony (g,el g) 350 (350-351 393)
RENARD,Alex (tp) (518)
RENATO,Jose (vo) (540)
RENAUD,Henri (p) (519 625 641 642 643)
RENDELL,Don (ts) (639 644)
RENDON,Joe (bgo) (397)
RENZI,Mike (p,arr) (362 373 384 393 421 425)
RENZI,Paul (ts) (489 491)
REPASS,Morris (bass tb) (270)
RESNICOFF,Richard (Richie) (g) (250 251 259 269 564)
RESTIVO,Dave (p) (661)
REUMONT,Rene (frh) (639)
REUSS,Allan (g) (467 468 478)
REVELL,Graeme (arr,cond,comp) (658)
REVIS,Eric (b) (392 408)
REY,Alvino (cond) (483)
REY,Augie (vo) (281 282)
REYES,Gerardo (vo) (610)
REYES,Senen (backgr. vo) (509)
REYES,Tony (b) (535)
REYES Jr.,Walfredo (dm,perc) (654)
REYNOLDS,Dick (tb,arr) (478 535)
REYNOLDS,Todd (v) (421)
REYS,Rita (vo) 337
RIBEIRO,Francisco (cello) (526)
RIBIERO,Pery (vo) 521
RIBOT,Marc (g,v) (525 635)
RICARD,Kevin (perc) (422)
RICCI,Paul (as) (479)
RICE,Kenneth (dm) (280 507)
RICE,Purnell (dm) (126 128)
RICH,Buddy (dm) 563 564 566
RICH,Cathy (vo) (564)
RICHARDS,Emil (vb,perc) (279 280 284 286 482 484 487 490 491 535)
RICHARDS,Michele (strings) (595)
RICHARDSON,Barney (b) (456)
RICHARDSON,Calvin (vo) (435)
RICHARDSON,Claytoven (vo) (337)
RICHARDSON,Jerome (fl,cl,ts,bs) (219 220 225 235 236 237 242 254 270 275 276 277 283 284 285 289 296 362 386 542 543 582 583 585 586 587) 626 (628 645)
RICHARDSON,Rodney (b) (449 460 461)
RICHARDSON,Soko (dm) (536)
RICHARDSON,Wally (g) (227 229 232 233 234 242 250 583)
RICHARDSON (Jr),Sylvan (keyb,b,el b,vo) 350 (358 360)
RICHMAN,Al (frh) (475)
RICHMAN,Boomie (ts) (479)
RICHMOND,Bill (dm) (484)
RICHMOND,Dannie (dm) (69 313 318 622 628 645)
RICHMOND,Kim (ss,reeds) (360 456)
RICHMOND,Terepai (dm,perc) (658)
RICKERT,Ralf (flh) (654)
RICO: see RODRIGUES,Rico
RIDDELL,Don (vo) (224 225)
RIDDICK,Malcolm (g) (219)
RIDDLE,Nelson (arr,cond) (478 479 480 481 484 488)
RIDGE,Byron (rh g) (536)
RIDGEWAY,Esther (vo) (508)
RIDGEWAY,Gloria (vo) (508)
RIDGEWAY,Gracie (vo) (508)
RIDL,James (p) (403)
RIDLEY,Larry (b) (120 158 177 183 184 185 196 197 629)
RIEBE,Pepito (bgo) (639)
RIEL,Alex (dm) (383 390 399 659)
RIGGINS,Emmanuel (org) (237 243 252 257)
RIGGINS,Karriem (dm) (614)
RIGGS,James (cl,ss) (379 380)
RIGOLO,Carl Vincent (perc) (595)
RILEY,Ben (dm) (237 238 239 328 419 627)
RILEY,Jim (as) (641)
RILEY,Herlin (dm,perc) (320 391 409 606)
RILEY,Herman (reeds) (253 568)
RILEY,John (dm) (589)
RILEY,Stephen (ts) (389 390)
RINEY,Sam (fl,as) (352 611)
RIOS,Carlos (g) (508)
RIPPERTON,Minnie (vo) 507
RISER,Paul (arr) (514)
RITCHIE,Larry (dm) (100 180 534)
RITENOUR,Lee (g) (270 275 280 284 285 286 288 295 297 653)
RIVERA,Dave (p) (14)
RIVERA,Joseph (perc) (195)
RIVERA,Mario (bs) (204)
RIVERA,Ray (dm) (535)
RIVERS,Sam (ts) (131 171 174) 175 (179) 182 (184 191) 196 (199) 200 (207)
RIVERS,Silvester (el p) (538)
RIZZI,Tony (g) (478 485 486)
ROACH,Freddie (org) (129 130 138 139) 141 146 148 151 160 163 164 172 (175) 185
ROACH,Max (dm) (26 27 32 48 49 52 53 55 59) 364 383 (450 466 467 472 474 475 570 620 628 638) 639 648
ROB (synth) (632)
ROBELLO,Jason (p,keyb) (350)
ROBERTS,Bobby (g) (485)
ROBERTS,Chapman (vo,dir) (299 300)
ROBERTS,George (tb,bass tb) (476 477 478 480 481 483 484 488 489 619)
ROBERTS,Howard (g) (44 222 225 255 481 483 484 485 492 496) 498 (500 551 560)
ROBERTS,Li'l John (dm) (394 417 421 422 429)
ROBERTS,Lisa (vo (296)

895

896

898

SMITH,Jimmie (dm) (222 255 604 616)
SMITH,Jimmy (org,vo) 50 51 (51) 54 55 56 60 61 64 66 67 70 74 75 77 78 80 82 (84) 92 98 101 102 103 125 133 148 149 (292 305 307) 312 604
SMITH,Johnny (g) (571) 571
SMITH,Johnny "Hammond" (el p,synth) 646 647
SMITH,Joseph (Joe) (dm) (27)
SMITH,Keely (vo) 484 485
SMITH,Lonnie (org) (201 206 211) 216 222 230 235 236 (236) 242 (277 386) 606 (618)
SMITH,Louis (tp) 80 (81) 454 (620)
SMITH,Lucy (arr) (658)
SMITH,Marvin "Smitty" (dm) (322 323 347 370 590 591 651)
SMITH,Mike (ts) (350-351 393)
SMITH,Nick (keyb b) (385)
SMITH,Nolan (tp) (295)
SMITH,Oscar (b) (12)
SMITH,Paul (p) (478 481) 483 (485 489)
SMITH,Phyllis (vo) (172)
SMITH,Richard (g) (367 384 541)
SMITH,Ron (el g) (417)
SMITH,Ronald (tb) (492)
SMITH,Roy R. (g) (649)
SMITH,Songai Sandra (vo) (247)
SMITH,Stuff (v) (482)
SMITH,Teddy (b) (170 173 626)
SMITH,Terry (g) (239 240)
SMITH,Tommy (ts) 324 334 341 350 351
SMITH,Vivian (p) (15)
SMITH,Warren (Jr.) (dm,marimba,tamb,tympani, vb) (257 258 261 269 627 628 635)
SMITH,Willie (as,ts) (459 460 461 476 480 484 496)
SMITH,Willie (orchestrations) (443)
SMULYAN,Gary (bs) (367 379 380 384 443)
SMYLIE,Dennis (cl) (368)
SNOW,Phoebe (vo) (543)
SOARES,Elza (vo) 522
SOCARRAS,Alberto (fl) (473)
SOCOLOW,Frank (ts) (39)
SOLAL,Martial (p) (519)
SOLDO,Joe (cl,as) (625)
SOLOFF,Lew (tp) (305 384 539 541 653)
SOLOMON,Clifford (ts) (492 641 642 643)
SOLOMON,Daniel (vo) (336)
SOLOMON,Phil (strings) (475)
SOLSONICS,The 511
SOM TRES 523
SOMMER,Ted (perc) (286 571)
SOMMERS,Avery (vo) (294)
SONG,Rahni (p,keyb,vo) (512)
SOONSARI,Klaus (dm) (383)
SONS OF CHAMPLIN,The 501
SOON E MC (vo) 520
SORVINO,Mira (vo) (658)
SOSSON,Marshall (v) (295 296 480 482 485 488 491 493 497 498 567)
SOTO,Federico Aristides (cga) 428
SOTTILE,John (tp) (563 564)
SOUDIEUX,Emmanuel (b) (518 519)
SOUTHERN,Jeri (vo) 487
SOUTHERN,Ronghea (g) (274)
SOUZA,Bebeto Jose (b) (226)
SOYER,Janet (harp) (576)
SPANIER,Calder (as) (386 387)
SPANIER,Eddie (dm) (467)
SPANN,Les (g,fl) (626 628)
SPARKS,Melvin (g) (216 222 226 231 235 236 249 250 254 259)
SPAULDING,James (fl,as) (144 166 167 174 175 177 178 180 183 186 191 193 194 195 197 198 200 204 205 207 208 211)
SPEARHEAD 510
SPEARS,Louis (tb) (253)
SPEARS,Maurice (tb) (273 275 276 289 298 386)
SPECIALTIES UNLIMITED (vo) (231)
SPENCER,Christine (vo) (224 225 232 233)
SPENCER,Danny (dm) (221 234)
SPENCER (Jr.),Leon (org,el p) (243 249 250 254 259 567)
SPICE,Irving (v) (260 261 262 264)
SPIEGELMAN,Stanley (viola) (480)
SPIKER,Dan (tb) (641)
SPINDLEY,Bradley (perc) (625)
SPINOZZA,David (g) (242 249 254 261 265 266 271 537 587)
SPORNY,Dick (tb) (456)
SPROLES,Victor (b) (180 181 207 219 452)
SPRUILL,Stephanie (cga,vo) (264 267 272 273 288 289 296 504 646)
SPYER,Cecilia (vo) (525)
SQUAJELLA,Appio (fl,frh) (554)
ST. CYR,Johnny (bjo) (516)
ST. GERMAIN (mixer,vo) 662
ST. GERY,Yannick (p) (644)
ST. JAMES,Sylvia (vo) (634)
ST. PAUL (g,cymbals,dm) (659)
STACEY,Jeremy (dm) (351)
STACEY,Paul (g,el g) (334)
STACY,Jess (p) (468)
STAFF,Sam (bs) (39)
STAFFORD,Jo (vo) 468 469
STALLINGS,Ron (fl) (337)
STAMM,Marvin (tp) (204 208 209 211 221 235 236 237 257 258 491 583 584)
STAMP,Clarence (dm) (530)
STANGERUP,Frank (keyb) (383)
STARKEY,Clifford (keyb) (371 372)
STARLING,Ray (mell) (491)
STARLING,Ray (p) (564)
STARR,Kay (vo) (467) 488 491
STARR,Ron (ts,fl,cl) (563)
STATEN,Kenneth (vo) (385)
STATHAM,David (frh) (239 240)
STATON,Dakota (vo) 483
STEELE,Larry (el b) (239 240)
STEIG,Jeremy (fl) 235 (236) 238
STEIN,Nancy (cello) (458)
STEINBERG,Albert (strings) (218)
STEINHOLTZ,Gerald (Jerry) (perc) (280 298)
STEPANSKY,Joseph (strings) (285)

901

902

903

280 281 297 298 410)
WATERS,Oren (vo) (273 276 281 298 410)
WATERS,Tony (cga) (646)
WATKINS,Derek (tp) (652)
WATKINS,Doug (b) (44 45 46 49 50 58 59 60 62 71 75 77 79 95 98 99 103 115 120 453) 454
WATKINS,Joe (dm,vo) (47 451 453)
WATKINS,Julius (frh) 43 45 (131 152 236 471 554 555 624 645)
WATKINS,Mitch (g) (320)
WATKISS,Cleveland (vo) (350)
WATROUS,Bill (tb) (352)
WATSON,Bobby (as,ts,arr) 323 (327 328 330 334 335) 336 340 (343 348 391 407 581) 581 (588 590 592) 608 (648)
WATSON,Ken (perc) (212)
WATSON,Pamela (vo,keyb) (581)
WATSON,Wah Wah (g) (281 429 506 514)
WATSON,Willie (frh) (239 240)
WATTS,Ernie (fl,as,ts,reeds) (218 253 273 276 277 282 289 294 295 386 457 503 506 564) 567 (567 568)
WATTS,Jeff "Tain" (dm) (329 343 389 390 399 438)
WATTS,Nathaniel (b) (507)
WAVERLEY,Mike (bass tb) (563)
WAYNE,Chuck (g) (461 554 555 625)
WAYNE,Max (b) (467)
WEBB,Doug (ss) (360)
WEBB,Lance (vo) (539)
WEBB,Spider (dm) (279)
WEBB Jr.,Shelby (arr) (658)
WEBSTER,Ben (ts) (7 491) 514 515 (557 575 644)
WEBSTER,Freddie (tp) (466)
WEBSTER,Rufus (p) (467)
WECHSLER,Walter "Moe"(p) (471)
WECKL,Dave (dm) (321)
WEED,Buddy (p) (37 466 625)
WEEDON,Paul (g) (138)
WEIDLER,George (as) (469 470)
WEIDLER,Warren (ts) (469 470)
WEIR,Michelle (vo) (655)
WEISS,David (tp) (608)
WEISS,Doug (b) (365 377 608)
WEISS,Sammy (dm) (468)
WEISS,Sid (b) (9)
WEISS,William (v) (482)
WELDON,Myron (as) (413)
WELLER,Don (ts) (349 652)
WELLESLEY,Charles "Sonny" (b) (92 93)
WELLINS,Bobby (ts) (645)
WELLMAN,Ricky (dm) (603)
WELLS,Dave (tb) (464 493 563)
WELLS,Junior (hca) (542 543)
WELLS,Tony (vo) (224 225)
WELSH,Chauncey (tb) (625)
WENDHOLT,Scott (tp) (378)
WERNECK,Regina (vo) (270)
WERNER,Kenny (Ken) (p) (354 395 396 404 415 595)
WERTH,George (tp) (503)
WERTICO,Paul (dm,perc) (366 374 388 397 399 416 607)
WESS,Frank (fl,as,ts) (384 485 572 573 574 575 576 577 578)
WESS,Richard (arr,cond) (494 536)
WEST,Alvy (sax) (466)
WEST,Bernie (vo) (462)
WEST,Bob (b,el b) (218 227 500 561 566 567 586)
WEST,Danny Quebec (as) (19)
WEST,Harold "Doc" (dm) (460 637)
WEST,Richard (b) (562)
WEST,Rudy (vo) (462)
WESTBROOK,Chauncey "Lord" (g) (145)
WESTON,Mildred (vo) (219)
WESTON,Paul (arr,cond) (468 469)
WESTON,Randy (p) 512 621 623 624
WESTON,Tim (g,arr) (654)
WETMORE,Dick (v) (454)
WETTLING,George (dm) (448 449)
WETZEL,Ray (tp) (467 468 469 470 474)
WHALEY,Tom (dm) (319)
WHALUM,Kirk (ts (343 394 656)
WHARTON,Gib (pedal steel g) (359 381)
WHEAT,David (g) (553)
WHEATON,Will (vo) (394 422)
WHEELER,Audrey (vo) (513 540)
WHEELER,Brad (ss) (416)
WHEELER,Dave (bass tb,tu) (489 491)
WHETSOL,Arthur (tp) (637)
WHITAKER,Harry (p,el p) (261 269 270)
WHITAKER,Mary (v) (610)
WHITAKER,Rodney (b) (391 603 609 612)
WHITE,Andrew (as,oboe) (246 247)
WHITE,Arthur (as) (581)
WHITE,Booker (cond) (324)
WHITE,Brenda (vo) (635)
WHITE,Chris (b) (512)
WHITE,Fred (vo,dm) (394 634)
WHITE,Hank (flh) (205)
WHITE,Harold (dm) (248)
WHITE,John (vo) (512)
WHITE,Josh (vo,g) 4
WHITE,Lenny (dm,synth programming) (233 234 331 333 539 591 593 649 659)
WHITE,Mark (g) (303)
WHITE,Michael (ambient tp) (660)
WHITE,Michael (dm) (422 513 656)
WHITE,Michael (v) (501 647)
WHITE,Peter (g) (429)
WHITE,Ronald (tp) (253)
WHITE,Scott (vo) (512)
WHITE,Verdine (el b) (288 298)
WHITEMAN,Paul (orch) 466
WHITFORD,Jack (saxes) (239 240)
WHITING,Fred (b) (637)
WHITLEY,Chris (g,slide g) (361 381)
WHITLOCK,Bob (b) (494 545 625)
WHITMAN,Jerry (vo) (503)
WIBE,Joan (vo) (224 225)
WICKMAN,Putte (cl) (640)
WIDLOWSKI,Jim (dm) (388 392 399)

WIDMARK,Anders (p) (526)
WIERINGA,Frans (p) (514)
WIGGINS,Gerald (p) (44 465 466 485 491 496 619 653)
WILD,Kenny (b) (291 292)
WILDER,Joe (tp) (257)
WILFONG,Lonnie (tp) (518)
WILKENSON,Geoff (programmming) (350-351)
WILKERSON,Don (ts) 137 140 156 (461)
WILKINS,Dave (tp) (516)
WILKINS,Ernie (ts,arr) (573 578)
WILKINSON,Geoff (samples,programming) (393)
WILKINSON,Sheila (vo) (263)
WILLARD,Maxine: see WATERS,Maxine
WILLERS,Michael (dm) (279)
WILLETTE,Baby Face (org) (116) 117 123
WILLIAMS,Adrienne (vo) (567)
WILLIAMS,Anthony (Tony) (dm) (149 151 152 153 160 163 164 168) 171 (175 178 179) 184 (306) 309 (310) 316 (318) 322 (326) 331 347 348 349 (352)
WILLIAMS,Buddy (dm) (362 510 540)
WILLIAMS,Charles (dm) (532)
WILLIAMS,Charles "Buster" (b) (194 222 223 225 247 265 279 312 365 495 496 497 564 566 568 599)
WILLIAMS,Cootie (tp,vo) (632)
WILLIAMS,David (b) (601 615)
WILLIAMS,Denise (Deneice) (vo) (288 298)
WILLIAMS,Ed (Eddie) (tp) (226 231 254)
WILLIAMS,Eddie (b) (461 462)
WILLIAMS,Eddy (ts) (86 88)
WILLIAMS,Floyd (dm) (452)
WILLIAMS,Francis (tp) (573)
WILLIAMS,Gareth (el p) (393)
WILLIAMS,George (arr) (630)
WILLIAMS,Greg (dm) (260)
WILLIAMS,Herbie (tp) (451)
WILLIAMS,James (p) (315 320 324 369 389 598 648)
WILLIAMS,Jerry (cga) (586)
WILLIAMS,Joe (vo) 241 (391 543) 573 574 (575) 575 (576) 576 577 578 579 582 583
WILLIAMS,John (b) (211 222 245)
WILLIAMS,John (bs) (373)
WILLIAMS,John (p) (39)
WILLIAMS,Johnny (b) (2 3 7)
WILLIAMS,Johnny (dm) (637)
WILLIAMS,Lawrence (reeds) (296)
WILLIAMS,Leroy (dm) (228 230 246 248)
WILLIAMS,Lillian (vo) (238 239)
WILLIAMS,Mary Lou (arr) (468)
WILLIAMS,Michael (tp,flh) (373)
WILLIAMS,Mike (as) (393)
WILLIAMS,Patrick (arr) (537)
WILLIAMS,Raymond (tp,flh) (612)
WILLIAMS,Richard (tp) (168 208 223 566 582 583 585 586 587 628)
WILLIAMS,Ricky (keyb) (286)
WILLIAMS,Robin (vo) (313)
WILLIAMS,Rudy (as) (18)
WILLIAMS,Sandy (tb) (8 13 15)
WILLIAMS,Tony (dm): see WILLIAMS,Anthony
WILLIAMS,Walter (tp) (447 642 643)
WILLIAMS,Willie (ts,ss) (330 356 372)
WILLIAMS,Woody (dm) (420)
WILLIAMS,Yvette (vo) (394)
WILLIAMS,Yvonne (vo) (612)
WILLIAMS IV,Harold "Ivory" (org,p)
WILLIAMS Jr.,Carl (vo) (271)
WILLIAMSON,Claude (p) (474 475 479) 480 (480 481 549 551)
WILLIAMSON,Steve (ss,as) (350-351 393)
WILLIAMSON,Stu (tp,vtb) (476 478 479 480 548 552 553 619)
WILLIS,Caroline (vo) (284 286)
WILLIS,Dave (saxes) (239 240)
WILLIS,Larry (p) (176 185 187 192 265 317)
WILLOUGHBY,Tanya (vo) (512)
WILSHIRE,Teacho (arr) (627 628)
WILSON,Cassandra (vo) (354) 356 359 361 380 381 (389 397 399 402) 416 423 424 (444 603) 607 (611) 653
WILSON,Chick (fl,cl) (332 338 343 352 353)
WILSON,Denni s (tb) (384)
WILSON,Eileen (vo) (503)
WILSON,Gerald (tp,arr,cond) (289 467 493) 559 560 566 567 (580)
WILSON,Glenn (bs) (332 338 352)
WILSON,Jack (p,arr) 194 206 219 222 225 228 229 243 244 (255 493 559 560 580)
WILSON,Nancy (vo) 488 488 490 493 494 495 496 497 498 499 500 501 502 503 504 507
WILSON,Ollie (tb) (471 473)
WILSON,Perry (dm) (416)
WILSON,Reuben (org) 216 219 223 224 233 243 248 254 608
WILSON,Roland (b,el b,cga) (227 228 229 634)
WILSON,Shadow (dm) (19 22 50 51 461 572)
WILSON,Steve (ss,as,fl) (398 414 415 439 588 589 590 600)
WILSON,Teddy (p) (7)
WIMBERLY,Bill (bass tb) (564)
WIMBERLY,Mike (bass tb) (566 567)
WIND,Martin (b) (401)
WINDING,Kai (tb) (450 468 471 472 475)
WINLEY,Harold (vo) (625)
WINSBERG,Louis (g) (399 432 438 659)
WINSLOW,Ray (tb) (577)
WINSTON,Ella (vo) (646)
WINTER,Paul (v,fl) (261 262 264 271 300 301)
WISE,Fritz (dm) (646)
WISE,Hershel (strings) (324)
WITHERSPOON,Jimmy (vo) 555 646
WITTMAN,Ben (dm) (415 417 418 419)
WOFFORD,Mike (p) (561 566 567)
WOLF,Joe (synth programming) (656)
WONDER,Stevie (hca) (317)
WOOD,Booty (tb) (632)
WOOD,Chris (b,el b) 415 433
WOOD,Gloria (vo) (481) 490
WOODE,Jimmy (b) (450 451 455 480)

Addendum

Page 446 - Paco Sery - Voyages (CD 5-21758-2).Personnels details on the various tracks are the following:

Jean-Philippe Dary(keyb) Jean-Pierre Taïeb(g) Guillaume Farley(rh g) Michel Alibo(b) Paco Sery(dm,rh g, comp,arr).

Donne-moi une chance CD BN 5-21758-2

Pierre Dreuvet,Nicolas Folmer(tp) Nelly Jallerat(bass cl) Philippe Sellam,Stefano di Battista,Daniel Scannapieco(saxes) Guillaume Farley(b,vo) Paco Sery(dm,perc,keyb,bass synth,rh g,comp,arr, programming) Mustafa Assemian,Fredo Piot(perc) Guillaume Farley,Helene Mittret,Mustafa Assemian,Paco Sery(choir).

Partage CD BN 5-21758-2

Guillaume Farley(vo) Jean-Pierre Taïeb(g) Guy N'Sangue(b) Paco Sery(dm,ac g,keyb,sanza,comp,arr) Julien Agazar(talk box) Ali Keïta(balafon).

Lucie CD BN 5-21758-2

Pierre Dreuvet,Nicolas Folmer(trp) Philippe Sellam,Stefano di Battista(saxes) Eric Legnini(clavinet) Berth Gielen(org) Jean-Pierre Taïeb(rh g) Daniel Romeo(rh g,b) Paco Sery(dm,keyb,rh g,slap b,comp,arr) Daara J (voice).

Nasty girl CD BN 5-21758-2

Daara J,Awa Timbo(vo) with Flavio Boltro(tp) Stefano di Battista(sax) Julien Agazar(keyb) Daniel Romeo (b,g) Paco Sery(dm,perc,keyb,comp,arr) Bessy Gordon,Isabel Gonzalez,Nadia N'Guyen(choir).

Pygmee rap CD BN 5-21758-2

Pierre Dreuvet(tp) Nelly Jallerat(bass cl) Philippe Sellam(sax) Julien Agazar,Eric Legnini(keyb) Thierry Eliez (Hammond org) Daniel Romeo(g) Cesar Anot,Thierry Fanfan(b) Paco Sery (keyb,comp,arr,keyb, programming) Isabel Gonzalez,Bessy Gordon,Freddy Meyer,Mike Robinson,Mustafa Asseman,Paco Sery (choir) Angelique Kidjo(vo).

Dialogue CD BN 5-21758-2

Xalat(g,voices,choir) Paco Sery(arr,keyb,snare dm) Abdou Maye(lead vo).

Win CD BN 5-21758-2

Taoufik(keyb) Paolo Pondi(g) Guillaume Farley(b,g) Paco Sery(dm,perc,keyb,g,comp,arr,programming) Bessy Gordon,Nadia N'Guyen,Isabel Gonzalez,Mustafa Assemian,Helene Nach,Zoko,Paco Sery(choir).

Maghreb CD BN 5-21758-2

Manu Dibango(ts) Mustafa Assemian(vo,perc) Etenne M'Bape(b) Paco Sery(dm,perc,keyb,arr,comp, programming) Bessy Gordon,Isabel Gonzalez,Paco Sery,Mustafa Assemian,Cesar Anot(choir).

Bassam CD BN 5-21758-2

Eric Legnini(p) Jean-Pierre Taïeb,Olivier Ajavon(g) Paco Sery(perc,vo,g,comp,arr) Isabel Gonzalez,Bessy Gordon,Nadia N'Guyen,Cha Undra,Mamadou(choir) Oumou Kouyate,Paco Sery(voices).

Guerini blues CD BN 5-21758-2

908

Dimitrus Evans(vo) Julien Agazar,Eric Legnini(keyb) Jean-Marie Ecay(g) Thierry Fanfan(b) Paco Sery (dm,perc,timbales,keyb,comp) Fredo Piot,Mustafa Assemian(timbales) Isabel Gonzalez,Bessy Gordon, Freddy Meyer,Mike Robinson,Mustafa Assemian,Paco Sery,Nadia N'Guyen,Cha Undra(choir).

Thank full — CD BN 5-21758-2

Dianne Reeves(lead vo) Paco Sery(sanza,perc,comp,arr) Nanda Kuma(tablas) Isabel Gonzalez,Bessy Gordon,Cha Undra,Nadia N'Guyen,Mustafa Assemian,Paco Sery(choir).

Senza univers — CD BN 5-21758-2

Eric Legnini(p) Olivier Monteil(dm,perc) Paco Sery(dm,keyb,perc,comp,arr,programming)

Jungle — CD BN 5-21758-2

Paco Sery,Jean-Philippe Dary(keyb,programming).

Break interlude — CD BN 5-21758-2

Mewe(vo) Eric Legnini(p) K Brisca,Guillaume Farley(g) Abib Faye(b) Paco Sery(dm,perc,keyb,g,comp,arr, programming) Isabel Gonzalez,Bessy Gordon,Marie Celine Chrone,Nadia N'Guyen,Dangui,Abou What, Balou Canta,Mustafa Assemian,Paco Sery(choir).

Faut pas nous blaguer — CD BN 5-21758-2

Nelly Jallerat(bass cl) Paco Sery(vo,dm,perc,timbales,comp,arr,programming) Mustafa Assemian,Fredo Piot,Moktar Samba,Anga Miguel Diaz(perc) Paco Sery,Zoko,Mustafa Asemian,Oumar Toure,Daby Toure (choir).

Salt peanuts — CD BN 5-21758-2

ADDITIONAL CD/LP ISSUES

Note: Following recent issues have not been included in session listings.

BLUE NOTE label

5-23445-2	5-23445-1* Blue Juice,Volume 3: (* 2-LP Set)	
	Christo redentor	Ferrante & Teicher
	California dreaming	Bobby Womack
71774	Spinning sheel	Peggy Lee (Capitol - Jan. 31,1969)
71291	Hard to handle	Patti Drew (Capitol - 1968)
	Collision in black	Blue Mitchell (218)
27137	Knock out drop	Joe Frazier (Capitol - Aug. 5,1969)
	Listen here	Richard Groove Holmes
	Afro party	Grant Green (257)
	Shortnin' bread	George Semper
	Pygmy,pt.2	Billy Larkin & The Delegates (Pacific Jazz)
	Ooga mooga	George Nardello
	Funky Broadway	Truman Thomas
59919	Up & at it	Cannonball Adderley (Capitol - June 13,1968)
	Harlem River Drive	Eddie Palmieri
	Swahili suite	Blue Mitchell (218)
	Do the jake	Victor Feldman
71840	Sitting on the dock of the bay	Peggy Lee (Capitol - Feb. 21,1969)
	Theme de yoyo	Art Ensemble of Chicago
	Cuchy fruito man	Ray Terrace
	Funky beat	Claude Giari
	Jaguar	John Gregory
19170	Funky whistler	Bill Doggett (Roulette - 1967)

5-23448-2	5-23448-1* Blue Brazil,Volume 3: (* 2-LP Set)	
	Samba das cinco	Taiguara
	Ponteio	Formula 7
	Upa neguinho	Nelsinho e sua Orquestra
	Deixa eu dizer	Claudia
	O que vem de baizo nao me atinge	Elza Zoares & Roberto Ribeiro
	Tudo de voce	Wilson Simonal
	Bateria e solo de percussao	Monsueto
	Nao adianta	Leny Andrade
	Galope	Luiz Gonzaga Jnr
	Mar azul	Som Imaginario
	Berimbau	Golden Boys
	Alvoroco	Leny Andrade
	Vou deitar e rolar	Milton Banana Trio
	Chove chuva	Nelsinho e sua Orquestra
	A volta do passaro Amerindio	Taiguara
	Antes que a cidade durma	Wanderlea
	Ponta negra	Danilo Caymmi
	Mal de amor	Elza Soares e Miltinho
	Educaçao sentimental	Egberto Gismonte
	Os borges	En Famila
	Os grilos	Marcos Valle
*	The world goes on	Som Tres
*	A fonte secou	Claudia

Note: Last two titles are on LP issue only.

5-23451-2	(Europe) Blue Mambo:	
	Judo mambo	Jimmy Smith (55)
	Mambo inn	Grant Green (137)
	Niger mambo	Stanley Turrentine (167)
	Caravan	Gonzalo Rubalcaba (428)
	Ponle La clave	Chucho Valdes (428)
IM-3835	Mambo da la Pinta	Art Pepper (Aladdin - Aug. 1956) (464)
15043	Peanut Vendor	Stan Kenton (Capitol - Feb. 12,1956)
6579-5	Viva Prado	Stan Kenton (Capitol - Sept. 12,1950)
31812	Always true to you in my fashion	Peggy Lee (Capitol - May 28,1959)
31813	Mambo in Miami	George Shearing (Capitol - May 28,1959)
18532	Mambo N°2	George Shearing (Capitol - March 4,1958)
18529	Mambo Caribe	George Shearing (Capitol - March 4,1958)
32235	On the street where you live	Peggy Lee (Capitol - Aug. 14,1959)
	Peter Gunn mambo	Jack Costanzo (Liberty -c. 1961)
5678-3	Mambo jambo	Dave Barbour (Capitol - March 17,1950)
12752	Hernando's hideaway	Billy May's Rico Mambo Orch. (Cap.-May 26,1954)
	Tito's grove	Tito Puente Jr. (EMI-Latin c.1995-96)[1]
	Dos generaciones	Tito Puente Jr. & Tito Puente (EMI-Latin) [2]

[1]: Tito Puente Jr. (cga,vo).(Miami Sound Studios) Miami,c. 1995-96
[2]: Same as [1] with Tito Puente(timbales) added.

5-23842-2	EMI (Spain) Jazz - Los Veinte Del Siglio Veinte:	
	Tune up	Sonny Rollins (71)
	Straight no chaser	Thelonious Monk (28)
	Ornithology	Charlie Parker (451)
	Smile	Dexter Gordon (122)
	A night in Tunisia	Bud Powell (27)
	Blues march	Art Blakey (85)
	Lou's blues	Lou Donaldson (32)
	Cantaloupe island	Herbie Hancock (168)
5-23843-2	Acid Jazz - Los Veinte Del Siglio Veinte:	
	Cantaloop (Flip fantasia)	Us3 (350)
	Different rhythms,different people	Us3 (351)
	Come on everybody (Get down)	Us3 (393)
	Move your hand (Michael Franti remix)	Lonnie Smith (386)
	God man cometh	Greg Osby (354)
	Sugar craft (Yuka Honda remix)	Medeski,Martin & Wood (415)
5-24415-2	5-24115-1* Scotch & Sofa: (* 2-LP Set) (France only)	
	Out of this world	The Three Sounds (134)
	Dancin' in an easy groove	Lonnie Smith (230
	I heard it through the grapevine	Earl Klugh (293)
	One cylinder	Lou Donaldson (201)
	The phantom	Duke Pearson (217)
	Estavanico	Donald Byrd (242)
	Neophilia	Lee Morgan (245)
	Xibaba	Donald Byrd (242)
	Nostalgia	Eddie Henderson (287)
	Bouquet	Bobby Hutcherson (190)
5-24418-2	5-24418-1* Chips & Cheers: (* 2-LP Set) (France only)	
	Away we go	Buddy Rich (Pacific Jazz) [1]
	Yeh yeh	The Three Sounds (196)
	Bunda amerela	Duke Pearson (215)
	Oblighetto	Jack McDuff (234)
	Wack wack	Buddy Rich (Pacific Jazz) [2]
	Currents/Pollen	Elvin Jones (269)

(continued on next page)

Ain't no sunshine Bobbi Humphrey (269)
In the beginning Jeremy Steig (238)
Listen here Gene Harris (261)
Koko and Lee Moe Gene Harris (280)
94177 Open eyes Eddie Henderson (Capitol - May 1977)
Think twice Donald Byrd (274)
Lonely town,lonely street Bobbi Humphrey (261)
96131 This love I have Minnie Ripperton (Capitol - 1979 - from Epic label)

[1]: Chuck Finlay,Oliver Mitchell,John Sottile,Yoshito Murakami(tp) Jim Trimble,John Boice,Robert Brawn (tb) Ernie Watts,Jimmy Mosher(as) Jay Corre,Robert Keller(ts) Meyer Hirsch(bs) Ray Starling(p) Richie Resnicoff(g) James Gannon(b) Buddy Rich(dm).
(Western Recorders) LA,June 27,1967
[2]: Bobby Shew,John Sottile,Yoshito Murakami,Chuck Findley(tp) Jim Trimble,Ron Meyers(tb) Bill Wimberly (bass tb) Quinn Davis(as) Ernie Watts(as,fl) Jay Corre,Robert Keller(ts,cl, fl) Marty Flax(bs) Ray Starling(p) Richard Resnicoff(g) James Gannon(b) Buddy Rich(dm).
(Chez Club) LA,February 22,1967

5-25984-2 Blue Series Sampler III (Europe only):
24760 I wish I knew how it would feel to be free
Billy Taylor Trio (Capitol - Nov. 16,1963)
Upa neguinho Nelsinho e sua Orquestra (EMI-Brazil)
Sunshine of your love Gerald Wilson (Pacific Jazz - Sept. 2,1968) (566)
Rev. Moses Lou Donaldson (201)
California dreaming Bobby Womack
Think twice Donald Byrd (274)

5-26906-2 BN (Spain) Rhythm 'N Blue Note (2 CD Set):
CD1: Intro Us3 (393)
Bring down the birds Herbie Hancock (645)
For what it's worth Lou Rawls (498)
Cantaloop (Nellee Hooper remix) Us3 (351)
Listen here (remix) Gene Harris/Guru (385)
Always there Ronnie Laws (279)
Midnight creeper Lou Donaldson (211)
Sunflower Alphonse Mouzon (265)
A little warm death Cassandra Wilson (381)
The beat goes on Buddy Rich (564)
The sidewinder Lee Morgan (161)
Street lady Donald Byrd (267)
The worm Jimmy McGriff (586)
Sugarcraft Medeski,Martin & Wood (415)
La fiesta Stanley Turrentine (195)
CD2: Cantaloupe island Herbie Hancock (168)
Listen here Ronnie Laws (400)
Light my fire Shirley Bassey (632)
Sky islands Dianne Reeves (319)
Sookie sookie Grant Green (246)
Dominoes Donald Byrd (291)
I had a little talk Horace Silver/Andy Bey (251)
Pillars Greg Osby (367)
Whatever happened to Gus Medeski,Martin & Wood/Guru Remix (415)
Save the children Marlena Shaw (262)
Twilight Maze (509)
This is soul Paul nero (502)
Sunshine of your love Gerald Wilson (567)
The caterpillar Lou Donaldson (254)

JAPAN

BLUE NOTE/FABULOUS label

TOCP-65247 Diggin' On Blue - Mixed By Biz Markie:
Biz Markie(turnstables,mixer,vo) Big Daddy Kane,DJ Barry B,Physciles,Vace Wright,Rog Nice,DJ D Demo,Greg Nice,Smooth H. Bee,Rass Kass,Mr. Man(vo).
NYC,c. Summer 1999
Remixing and talking over sections of the following selections:

Prelude	Gene Harris (273)
Lansana's priestess	Donald Byrd (267)
Blue mode	Reuben Wilson (235)
Pot Belly	Lou Donaldson (243)
Night flight	Lee Morgan (192)
Ease back	Grant Green (233)
Smiling faces sometimes	Bobbi Humphrey (261)
Little green apples	Monk Higgins (586)
Woman of the ghetto	Marlena Shaw (268)
Three is the magic number	Bob Dorough (504)
Brother soul	Lou Donaldson (220)
You & music	Donald Byrd (283)
Sookie sookie	Grant Green (246)
My little girl	Bobbi Humphrey (272)
Holy Thursday	David Axelrod (500)
The sidewinder	Lee Morgan (161)
One cylinder	Lou Donaldson (201)
Repeat after me	Gene Harris & The Three Sounds (231)
Shack up	Banbara (505)
Whole lotta love	Ike & Tina Turner (632)
Sitting duck	Gene Harris & The Three Sounds (218)
Inside you	Eddie Henderson (287)
Wind parade	Donald Byrd (283)
Harlem River Drive	Bobbi Humphrey (267)
Ain't it funky now	Grant Green (237)
Everyman's your brother	The Fourth Way (501)
Ronnie's Bonnie	Reuben Wilson (219)

TOCP-65248 Diggin' On Blue - Mixed by Lord Finesse:
Lord Finesse(turnstables,mixer,vo) Evel D,DJ Tony Touch,Kool G Rap,Rass Kass,Diamond D,O.C.,A.G., Big L (R.I.P.),DJ Premier,Akibyele,Crazy Legs,X-Men,Guru,Mr. Walt(vo).
(The Crib,Bronx NY,D & D Studios) NYC,c. Summer 1999
Remixing and talking over sections of the following selections:

Intro	
Night whistler	Donald Byrd (283259)
Oblighetto	Jack McDuff (234)
Chicago damn	Bobbi Humphrey (267)
Prelude	Gene Harris (273)
Peace of mind	Gene Harris (298)
We've only just begun	Grant Green (252)
Back on the track	Jimmy McGriff (232)
San Francisco lights	Bobbi Humphrey (273)
Monkin' around	Blue Mitchell (218)
My little girl	Bobbi Humphrey (272)
Living inside your love	Earl Klugh (293)
El mundo de maravillas	Bobbi Humphrey (261)
Montara	Bobby Hutcherson (282)
Procession	Bobby Hutcherson (245)

(continued on next page)

913

Just a love whold	Bobbi Humphrey (267)
Maybe tomorrow	Grant Green (252)
Soul symphony	The Three Sounds (231)
Now	Bobby Hutcherson (232)
At the source	Bobby Hutcherson (253)
Feel like makin' love	Marlena Shaw (274)
You're welcome,stop on by	Lou Donaldson (271)
Sittin' duck	Gene Harris & The Three Sounds (218)
Repeat after me	The Three Sounds (231)
Sugar hill	The Three Sounds (218)
Get out of my life woman	Joe Williams (582)
Hot rod	Reuben Wilson (254)
We're in love	Reuben Wilson (254)
Think twice	Donald Byrd (274)
Dominoes	Donald Byrd (283)
Spinning sheel	Lonnie Smith (236)
Everything I play is funky	Lou Donaldson (236)
Pot Belly	Lou Donaldson (243)
Tennessee waltz	Lou Donaldson (243)
It's your thing	Lou Donaldson (226)
Ode to Billie Joe	Lou Donaldson (206)
Change	Donald Byrd (283)
Who's makin' love	Lou Donaldson (226)
Absolutions	Lee Morgan (245)
Soul symphony	The Three Sounds (231)
Down here on the ground	Grant Green (247)
Raise	Greg Osby (355)

TOCP-65249 Diggin' On Blue - Mixed By Pete Rock:
Pete Rock(turnstables,mixer,vo)Lord Jamar,Talib Kweli,Poppa Wu,Vinia Mojica,DJ Kaori,Akko,Shabaam Sahdeeq,Shawn J. Period,Helen Simmons,Tahir,M-1(vo)

(Greene Street Studios) NYC,c. July 1999

Remixing and talking over sections of the following selections:

Sittin' duck	Gene Harris & The Three Sounds (218)
Summer song	Ronnie Foster (259)
Little green apples	Stanley Turrentine (220)
We're in love	Reuben Wilson (254)
Ollilloquy Valley	Herbie Hancock (168)
Shirl	Bobby Hutcherson (260)
I remember Summer	Gene Harris (273)
In what direction are you headed?	Lee Morgan (256)
Repeat after me	The Three Sounds (231)
Hunk o' funk	Jack McDuff (240)
Summertime	Lou Donaldson (220)
Mystic brew	Ronnie Foster (259)
I don't want nobody	Grant Green (257)
Turning point	Lonnie Smith (Eddie Gale) (222)
Wrong or right	Bobby Hutcherson (272)
Smiling faces sometimes	Bobbi Humphrey (261)

About the Compilers

MICHAEL CUSCUNA is the co-author, with Michel Ruppli, of the first edition of *The Blue Note Label*, and the producer of all Blue Note records released in the United States.

MICHEL RUPPLI is the author of numerous discographies, including *The Decca Labels* (Greenwood, 1996) and *The MGM Labels* (Greenwood, 1998).